COMPARATIVE URBAN STRUCTURE

COMPARATIVE URBAN STRUCTURE
Studies in the Ecology of Cities

KENT P. SCHWIRIAN

Ohio State University

D. C. HEATH AND COMPANY
Lexington, Massachusetts Toronto London

Copyright © 1974 by D. C. Heath and Company.

Published simultaneously in Canada.

Printed in the United States of America.

International Standard Book Number: 0-669-82966-8

Library of Congress Catalog Card Number: 73-746 1

To

Pat

Julie

John

Tom

Preface

Ecological studies of the internal structure of metropolitan areas have increased greatly over the last few years. Contributions by sociologists, geographers, economists, and urban planners have expanded greatly our knowledge of city structure not only in the United States but in other societies as well. The purpose of this book is to bring together a collection of papers that represents recent findings that will be useful for students of comparative urban structure. This book does not attempt to cover all aspects of the current literature but is limited to models of internal metropolitan ecological structure. Those interested in such other topics as the process of urbanization, historical ecology of the city, the ecology of social problems, or urban research methods will find excellent treatment elsewhere.

The papers that I have selected for inclusion have been assigned at one time or another to students in my various courses in ecology and urban sociology that I have taught since 1962. I can, therefore, attest to the pedagogical utility of each paper. Space limitations have precluded me from including other items. The papers are grouped into seven sections:

The first is an overview of general urban models and illustrates the broad interest in ecological data from both substantive and planning perspectives. The second section deals with gross city and fringe patterns of metropolitan differentiation. The discussions range from the utility of the concept of megalopolis to the general patterns of city-suburban differentiation and related consequences. The third section deals with population density models both in terms of general patterns and in terms of the accompanying social consequences. Section four treats some of the general factors in the organization of urban space including sector and zonal patterns. Economic, environmental, and family housing needs are considered as factors effecting urban population patterns. Section five is devoted to factorial ecology. Studies presenting data from the U.S., Canada, Egypt, India, Europe, and Puerto Rico are included. Both the social area analysis and factorial ecological perspectives are represented. The sixth and seventh sections are devoted to studies of residential segregation of status, racial, and ethnic groups. The status segregation papers reveal similar findings in a variety of cultural settings while the ethnic and racial studies indicate both the similarity and differences in the segregation of ethnics and blacks in American cities.

This particular organization fits my own view of the ecological literature; however, there are no reasons why the papers cannot be assigned in other sequences more amenable to other instructors. Undoubtedly the reader will find some overlapping of discussions among the papers of a given section. Even though there is some duplication, each paper makes a unique contribution to the section.

At this time I express my appreciation to the various journals, editors, and authors for their permission to include their work among this collection. Also I would like to express my appreciation to the staff at D. C. Heath and Company for expediting the book's publication. Finally, I express my appreciation to Ellen Sanders for her splendid typing and proofing of large portions of the manuscript.

K. P. S.

Contents

PART I   **Urban Models: An Overview**   1

    1   KENT P. SCHWIRIAN

    Some Recent Trends and Methodological Problems in Urban Ecological
    Research   3

    2   LESLIE J. KING

    Models of Urban Land-Use Development   32

    3   KENNETH J. SCHLAGER

    A Land-Use Plan Design Model   49

PART II   **Metropolitan Differentiation: The City and the Fringe**   61

    4   BEVERLY DUNCAN, GEORGES SABAGH, and MAURICE D. VAN ARSDOL, JR.

    Patterns of City Growth   63

    5   HAL H. WINSBOROUGH

    An Ecological Approach to the Theory of Suburbanization   74

    6   LEO F. SCHNORE

    The Timing of Metropolitan Decentralization: A Contribution to the Debate   80

    7   LEO F. SCHNORE

    Satellites and Suburbs   90

    8   REYNOLDS FARLEY

    Suburban Persistence   98

    9   ROBERT H. WELLER

    An Empirical Examination of Megalopolitan Structure   109

    10   JOHN C. WEICHER

    The Effect of Metropolitan Political Fragmentation on Central City Budgets   118

PART III Urban Density Patterns and Consequences 139

11 BRIAN J. L. BERRY, JAMES W. SIMMONS, and ROBERT J. TENNANT

Urban Population Densities: Structure and Change 141

12 BRUCE E. NEWLING

Urban Growth and Spatial Structure: Mathematical Models and Empirical Evidence 154

13 ROY C. TREADWAY

Social Components of Metropolitan Population Densities 165

14 PETER W. AMATO

A Comparison: Population Densities, Land Values and Socioeconomic Class in Four Latin American Cities 185

15 HAL H. WINSBOROUGH

The Social Consequences of High Population Density 193

16 OMER R. GALLE, WALTER R. GOVE, and J. MILLER McPHERSON

Population Density and Pathology: What are the Relationships for Man? 198

PART IV Factors in the Organization of Urban Space 215

17 CHAUNCY D. HARRIS and EDWARD L. ULLMAN

The Nature of Cities 217

18 BRIAN J. L. BERRY

Internal Structure of the City 227

19 HOMER HOYT

Recent Distortions of the Classical Models of Urban Structure 233

20 PETER W. AMATO

Environmental Quality and Locational Behavior in a Latin American City 245

21 WILLIAM H. FORM

The Place of Social Structure in the Determination of Land Use: Some Implications for a Theory of Urban Ecology 257

22   AVERY M. GUEST

Patterns of Family Location   264

PART V   **The Factorial Ecology of Cities   277**

23   WENDELL BELL

Economic, Family, and Ethnic Status: An Empirical Test   279

24   MAURICE D. VAN ARSDOL, JR., SANTO F. CAMILLERI, and CALVIN F. SCHMID

The Generality of Urban Social Area Indexes   287

25   THEODORE R. ANDERSON and LEE L. BEAN

The Shevky-Bell Social Areas Confirmation of Results and a Reinterpretation   295

26   THEODORE R. ANDERSON and JANICE A. EGELAND

Spatial Aspects of Social Area Analysis   302

27   KENT P. SCHWIRIAN and MARC MATRE

The Ecological Structure of Canadian Cities   309

28   KENT P. SCHWIRIAN and RUTH K. SMITH

Primacy, Modernization, and Urban Structure: The Ecology of Puerto Rican Cities   324

29   A. H. LATIF

Factor Structure and Change Analysis of Alexandria, Egypt, 1947 and 1960   338

30   BRIAN J. L. BERRY and HOWARD SPODEK

Comparative Ecologies of Large Indian Cities   349

31   FRANK L. SWEETSER

Factorial Ecology: Helsinki, 1960   371

PART VI   **Social Status Differentiation and Segregation   385**

32   OTIS DUDLEY DUNCAN and BEVERLY DUNCAN

Residential Distribution and Occupational Stratification   387

33 SURINDER K. MEHTA

Patterns of Residence in Poona (India) by Income, Education, and Occupation (1937–65) 398

34 KENT P. SCHWIRIAN and JESUS RICO-VELASCO

The Residential Distribution of Status Groups in Puerto Rico's Metropolitan Areas 412

35 A. H. LATIF

Residential Segregation and Location of Status and Religious Groups in Alexandria, Egypt 423

36 JOHN FINE, NORVAL D. GLENN, and J. KENNETH MONTS

The Residential Segregation of Occupational Groups in Central Cities and Suburbs 433

37 ELEANOR P. WOLF and CHARLES N. LEBEAUX

On the Destruction of Poor Neighborhoods by Urban Renewal 444

38 HOWARD M. BAHR

The Gradual Disappearance of Skid Row 449

PART VII   Ethnic and Racial Differentiation and Segregation   455

39 DAVID WARD

The Emergence of Central Immigrant Ghettoes in American Cities: 1840–1920 457

40 STANLEY LIEBERSON

The Impact of Residential Segregation on Ethnic Assimilation 475

41 STANLEY LIEBERSON

Suburbs and Ethnic Residential Patterns 483

42 SURINDER K. MEHTA

Patterns of Residence in Poona, India, by Caste and Religion: 1822–1965 493

43 MAURICE D. VAN ARSDOL, JR. and LEO A. SCHUERMAN

Redistribution and Assimilation of Ethnic Populations: The Los Angeles Case 572

44 KARL E. TAEUBER

The Effect of Income Redistribution on Racial Residential Segregation 534

45 REYNOLDS FARLEY and KARL E. TAEUBER

Population Trends and Residential Segregation since 1960 541

46 THEODORE G. CLEMENCE

Residential Segregation in the Mid-Sixties 549

47 HAROLD M. ROSE

The Spatial Development of Black Residential Subsystems 555

48 OZZIE L. EDWARDS

Patterns of Residential Segregation Within a Metropolitan Ghetto 577

49 F. JAMES DAVIS

The Effects of a Freeway Displacement on Racial Housing Segregation in a Northern City 585

50 W. CLARK ROOF

Residential Segregation of Blacks and Racial Inequality in Southern Cities: Toward a Causal Model 590

COMPARATIVE
URBAN
STRUCTURE

Urban Models: An Overview

part i

The three papers in this section acquaint the student with the concerns of urban ecologists with the internal structure of the metropolis. The paper by Schwirian (1) which serves as the introduction to this whole volume, discusses some of the basic substantive trends in the study of the internal structure of the metropolis as well as some of the main methodological problems that plague many of the current lines of analysis. The paper begins by describing the concept "model" and the utility of thinking in terms of ecological models. The paper points out that ecological models may be divided generally in terms of their focus. Some deal with the characteristics of *subareas* in the city while others focus upon the characteristics of urban *subpopulations*. Three main categories of models deal with subareas and are the *classic*, the *factorial*, and the *density* models. Originally, many of these models were viewed as essentially competitive in their explanation of urban structure but more recent empirical findings have indicated that they are more complementary than antagonistic. Two additional major sets of models deal with the characteristics of urban subpopulations. These are the *segregation* models, which focus upon the residential differentiation of class, race, and ethnic groups, and the *locational* models, which deal with the relative spatial position of the groups in the city and the metropolitan fringe.

Investigations of the various basic ecological models in a number of differing cultural settings have suggested that the ecological structure of any given city is to some extent a function of the level of economic development of the society in

1

which the city is located. Indeed, it seems that societal modernization is accompanied by changing urban ecological structures. The link between city structure and societal development is also discussed by Schwirian.

Empirical studies of the various ecological models have encountered a variety of methodological problems. Among those discussed in the first paper are a number common to all ecological models: comparability of data inputs and units of analysis among societies, cross-sectional versus longitudinal analysis, and the expanse of the community investigated—cities versus metropolitan areas. In addition, it is pointed out that each of the models has unique methodological problems associated with it. Schwirian introduces some new data in the course of the discussion of several of the problems.

The two other papers in Part I describe types of ecological models other than those discussed by Schwirian and serve to illustrate the scope of the concerns with urban ecological structure. King's paper (2) covers the general problem of constructing ecological models for the forecasting of urban land use development. The paper surveys several of the basic issues involved in modeling complex urban systems and raises some questions in regard to modeling and social planning. Thus, this paper is concerned with the set of problems that emerge when substantive concerns merge with planning issues.

Schlager's paper (3) describes in considerable detail the requirements, mathematical structure, and application of one land use and transportation model and serves as a good example of applied ecological model building. At the outset, Schlager alludes to very different orientations toward model building, one passive and the other active in terms of social planning. The more passive orientation sees the city as a natural phenomenon whose structure and change is determined by basic scientific laws. The purpose of modeling is thus to uncover these laws and to use them to forecast the future urban configuration. The more active orientation views the city as a subject for design. Accordingly, modeling the city goes hand in hand with the development of a plan for the "conscious synthesis of urban form to meet human needs." With an accurate model of the city we may assess the effects of considered changes upon the whole system. Certainly, the passive and active views are not mutually exclusive. In fact, we see increasingly the merger of the two perspectives.

Students who are having their first exposure to urban ecological concerns would best spend their time upon the first paper and defer until later the other two. Students who have a fairly good grasp of basic substantive issues will probably find quite intriguing the extensions and applications of basic notions into complex applied models as presented by King (2) and by Schlager (3).

KENT P. SCHWIRIAN

Some Recent Trends and Methodological Problems in Urban Ecological Research

This discussion has two major purposes. The first is to introduce some of the most basic models of urban ecological structure and to discuss major trends in their development and application. The second focus is upon some of the more basic methodological problems that plague current ecological investigations. However, before we turn to these major considerations we need to look more closely at two terms that will appear repeatedly throughout the following discussions. The studies collected in the following pages are about urban ecological models. The last two concepts, ecological *and* models, *need some explication.*

Human ecology as a content area of the social sciences generally is concerned with four major variables and their interrelationships: population, social organization, technology, and environment [Duncan 1959]. Urban *ecological* investigations usually are concerned with the distribution of population characteristics, organizations, activities, and behaviors across the urban terrain as mediated by transportation technology. The ecologist is not interested simply in spatial distributions per se. Spatial distributions are taken to reflect the operation of social processes; so the ecologist investigates spatial distributions in relation to various elements of social organization such as the division of labor, the urban land market, racial and ethnic cohesion and viability, and degree of life cycle differentiation. Thus if we were to view the city as a large chessboard with the population as its pieces, we would find the ecologist studying the location and movement of the different pieces with a view to uncovering the shifting rules that govern the action.

Much urban ecological research is organized and oriented in terms of one of several differing but basic ecological models. The term *model* as used by social scientists is both ubiquitous and ambiguous. Basically a model is an isomorphic abstraction of the essential properties of some phenomenon. Or, stated differently, a model is a set of abstract statements about a phenomenon of interest that are used to characterize and/or explain its essential properties. Models take different forms. Some times a model may be a set of declarative sentences that may extend to a short paragraph or to a whole volume. Other times a model may be presented graphically as in a flow chart or a path diagram. Occasionally models may take the form of clusters of axiomitized propositions. With increasing frequency models are being developed in the form of systems of equations—thus the term mathematical models. Regardless of the model's format its basic components are (1) a number of concepts, some of which are dependent variables or variables to be described or explained, and some of which are independent variables or the variables which do the explaining; and (2) specification of the linkages among the variables, or in effect, indications of which variables are related and the nature of their relationship.

Model building as an end in itself has little virtue. Its main utility for the scientist is that it provides a mechanism by which he can organize a portion of reality into a manageable, testable form. To think about his work as model building forces the scientist to confront his basic assumptions, suppositions, and propositions. Model building engenders a drive for clarity, specificity, and explicitness that is necessary for the development of scientific laws.

One becomes quickly overwhelmed by the number of models in the social science literature. In addition, even a casual perusal of the literature makes obvious the wide discrepancies among models in their clarity and explicitness. Indeed, in addition to building new models a major effort today among social scientists is to attempt to introduce more rigor into many of the older and more fruitful models, thereby further illuminating major theoretical arguments and drawing fresh inferences implicit in the discourse [see for example Schwirian and Prehn 1962; Stinchcombe 1968].

One way to look at urban ecological models is in terms of the focus of the model. Some writers emphasize the characteristics of subareas in the city, while others emphasize the characteristics of urban subpopulations. Thus some models attempt to describe or explain differences in the characteristics of urban neighborhoods while others attempt to describe or explain differences in the distributional properties of differing urban groups.

As depicted in Figure 1, three major groups of models deal with the characteristics of urban subareas. They are (1) classic models, (2) factorial models, and (3) density models. The term *classic* is used to describe the concentric zone, the sector, and the multiple nuclei models for two main reasons, the first being that these models were really among the first to receive

major acclaim as contributing to our understanding of urban ecological patterning. The second reason is the rather seminal contribution the models made to the whole development of the study of the internal structure of the city. Indeed, these models are exceedingly important in understanding the direction of much current ecological research.

A second major category of ecological models includes those whose names arise for good or ill from the general statistical technique employed. Thus *factorial models* are those that attempt to identify the major dimensions of differentiation among subareas through application of factor analytic techniques to urban subarea indicators. Factorial studies may be distinguished broadly in terms of their initial orientation. Some start with a *social area analysis* perspective. Studies with this perspective tend to limit their attention to the dimensions of *social rank, familism, ethnicity*, and sometimes *migrant status*. The other factorial models tend to go beyond the social area dimensions and they, as a class, tend to be more inductive and pragmatic in variable selection.

The third set of models dealing with the characteristics of urban subareas consists of those dealing with subarea differences in population density. These models tend to be quite sophisticated mathematically and frequently involve attempts to describe density curves. These models by and large do go beyond simple curve fitting in that they attempt to develop reasonable and testable explanations for observed density patterns. In addition to the concern with density per se, with increasing frequency ecologists are becoming concerned with the impact of density variations upon the life styles and well-being of urbanites.

Two major sets of ecological models deal with the characteristics of urban groups or subpopulations. One of these focuses upon the residential segregation of race, ethnic, and status groups while the other set of models deals with the relative position or location of race, ethnic, and status groups in urban space.

The segregation models generally are

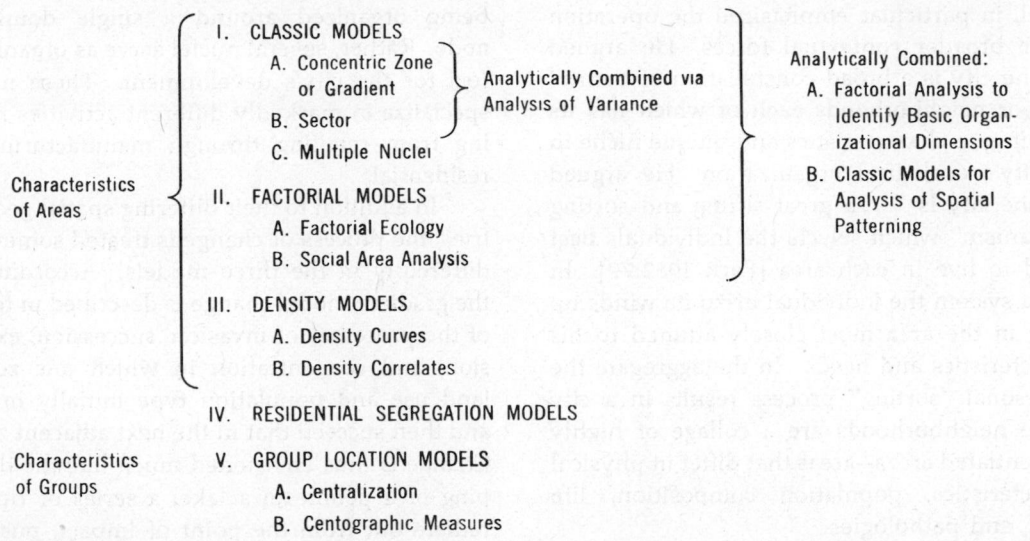

FIGURE 1. Major Ecological Models

based upon comparisons of the distribution of the populations of interest across the residential units of the city—census tracts, blocks, or wards. The residential differentiation among populations is usually a function of the degree of social distance among them. Studies of segregation conclude that three sets of factors account for a particular group's segregation: (1) social status difference between it and the majority population; (2) self-selection in terms of key social characteristics in the residential search process; and (3) enforced patterns of discrimination in the operation of the housing market.

The models which deal with the physical location of populations in urban space generally are concerned with the position of particular groups in relation to the central business district and/or in relation to the physical position of other groups. The term *centralization* is frequently used to describe the extent to which groups cluster around the central urban node or are dispersed toward the periphery. The relative position of groups in relation to the city's center is frequently accounted for by the interplay of group status level, group assimilation, neighborhood physical conditions and the quality and composition of local housing stocks, age of area, and land market machinations.

Increasingly the location of urban groups vis-à-vis each other as well as the city's center is being treated in terms of a set of concepts and a measurement approach known as *centographic analysis*. Through centographic techniques the mean empirical location of a group in urban space may be determined as well as the extent and shape of the group's distribution around the mean location [Lee 1967].

The following sections of this discussion are devoted to a further examination of these models and to a consideration of the methodological problems involved in their use.

CLASSIC MODELS

Three models are included within this category: the concentric zone or gradient model [Burgess 1925], the sector model [Hoyt 1939], and the multiple nuclei model [Harris and Ullman 1945]. All three of these models focus upon the differential distribution of population and housing in urban space. They argue, in effect, that the gross distributional pattern of the city is a result of the interplay of socioeconomic forces of competition in the urban land market. In describing the process of residential site selection, Park, who was associated with Burgess in the development of the concentric zone model, in particular emphasized the operation of the broader contextual forces. He argued that the city is a broad constellation of natural areas or neighborhoods each of which has its own unique characteristics and unique niche in the city's ecological organization. He argued that the city is "... a great sifting and sorting mechanism" which selects the individuals best suited to live in each area [Park 1952:79]. In such a system the individual urbanite winds up living in the area most closely attuned to his characteristics and needs. In the aggregate the impersonal "sorting" process results in a city whose neighborhoods are a collage of highly differentiated areas—areas that differ in physical characteristics, population composition, life styles, and pathologies.

In addition to focusing upon the operation of the urban land market the three classic models share other assumptions. Some of these were first suggested by Quinn [1940] as being implicit in the concentric zone or gradient model, but they seem also to apply to the sector and multiple nuclei models as well. They are (1) the existence of social class gradations within the population; (2) a growing and expanding city; (3) an industrial-commercial urban economic base; (4) private ownership of property; (5) specialization in land use; (6) efficient, cheap, and rapid transportation; (7) freedom of residential choice for the higher socioeconomic strata.

Although the classic models share a preoccupation with the operation of the broader socioeconomic forces within the city, the specific spatial configurations they propose differ quite markedly. The concentric zone model argues that population and housing vary by distance gradient from the city's center. The sector model stresses that population and housing differ more in terms of homogeneous wedges running from the city's center to the periphery than by distance gradient. The multiple nuclei model starts with a notion altogether different from that of the gradient and sector models. Unlike the gradient and sector models the multiple nuclei model does not portray a city as

being organized around a single dominant node. Rather, several nuclei serve as organizing foci for the city's development. These nuclei specialize in markedly different activities ranging from retailing through manufacturing to residential.

In addition to their differing spatial geometries, the process of change is treated somewhat differently in the three models. According to the gradient model change is described in terms of the processes of invasion, succession, extension, and concentration in which one zone's land use and population type initially invade and then succeed that in the next adjacent zone. Change is thus envisioned much like the dropping of a pebble in a lake: a series of ripples radiate out from the point of impact, pushing into each other in their outward flow.

One systematic attempt to investigate change in urban subarea characteristics within the Burgess framework was done by Hagerty [1971]. He applied a Markov chain analysis to census tract education level changes between 1940 and 1960 in Milwaukee, Minneapolis, Rochester, Denver, Houston, Dallas, Hartford, and Portland. Through this process analysis he was able to identify trends in urban spatial development not evident in cross-sectional studies. He reports a definite trend through time toward a direct relationship between subarea social status and distance from the city's center. This trend is manifest even in those cities whose present cross-sectional pattern is that of inverse status gradient! Thus, regardless of initial locational pattern, time seems a key factor for the process of urban change to produce a concentric zonal pattern.

Propositions for predicting change in the concentric zone model are somewhat vague and amorphous. More specific are the propositions of the sector model. Based upon his study of a large number of U.S. cities Hoyt puts forth a series of hypotheses to account for sectorial change. As summarized by Thomlinson [1969: 146–147] they are:

1. High-grade residential growth tends to proceed from the given point of origin ei-

ther along established lines of travel or toward another existing nucleus of buildings or trade areas.

2. The zone of high rent tends toward high ground which is free from risk of floods and to spread along lake, bay, river, and ocean ports, where such waterfronts are not used by industry.

3. High-rent residential districts tend to grow toward the section of the city that has free open country beyond the edges and away from "dead end" sections which are prevented from expanding by natural or artificial barriers.

4. The high-priced residential neighborhood tends to grow toward the homes of community leaders.

5. Sometimes trends of office buildings, banks, and stores pull the high-priced residential neighborhoods in the same general direction.

6. High-grade residential areas tend to develop along the fastest existing transportation lines.

7. Deluxe apartment areas tend to be established near the business centers in old established residential areas.

8. The growth of high-rent neighborhoods continues in the same direction for a long period of time.

9. High-rent neighborhoods do not skip about at random in the process of movement; they follow a definite path in one or more sectors of the city.

10. It is possible, under some conditions, for high-rent areas to "double back," or return toward the center of the city.

11. High-rent areas tend to be adjoined by medium-rent areas, and sharp disjunctions in rental areas are not frequent.

Change is treated by the multiple nuclei model in terms of the factors that account for the emergence of separate nuclei within the city. Harris and Ullman's discussion of the multiple nuclei model lists four factors which account for the rise of differentiated urban districts: (1) certain activities require specialized facilities located in only one or a few sections of the metropolis; (2) certain like activities profit from adjacent congregation; (3) certain unlike activities are antagonistic or detrimental to each other; and (4) certain activities are unable to afford the costs of the most desirable locational sites [Harris and Ullman 1945: 7-17].

The three classic models have had an enormous impact upon urban sociology and urban geography, and the use and development of these models have been thoroughly reviewed by Mayer [1965], Sjoberg [1965], and Berry [1965]. Although the classic models initially appear to be quite antagonistic in their description of urban spatial structure, much recent research has found them to be more complementary than opposing. For example, in comparing the spatial distributions of two variables called "residential prestige" and "urbanization," Anderson and Egeland [1961] concluded that residential prestige is distributed sectorally while urbanization, which is a measure of familial and housing patterns, was distributed by distance gradient. A similar finding is reported by Schwirian and Matre [1969] in a study of eleven principal Canadian cities. Other researchers have found that when concentric zones and sectors are considered jointly, significant variations in demographic and housing variables are explained. Here I refer to such work as that by deVise, who in a study of Chicago found that if subareas were formed by a combination of concentric zone and sector location, the resulting residential areas would have fairly uniform social and economic properties [deVise 1960]. In fact, most serious students of the city suggest that to some extent most cities display some properties of all three of the locational models.

Thus, all three of the classic models have come to be used increasingly to supplement each other in the description of urban spatial differentiation. Furthermore, a third model, factorial ecology, has been added to the classic models in recent studies. The net effect of this analytical combination has been a very comprehensive approach to ecological phenomena.

FACTORIAL MODELS

Among the most frequently used ecological approaches today is that of factorial ecology. Actually the term *factorial ecology* refers to a number of differing approaches to the analysis of urban subarea characteristics that share in common the use of factor analysis as their analytical tool. The two major factorial approaches are *social area analysis* and *factorial ecology per se* [Berry and Rees 1969]. The difference between social area analysis and the more general factorial ecology is in the data inputs of the analysis. Social area analysis limits the input variables to those called for in the theoretical scheme of Shevky, Bell, Greer, and others [Bell 1955; Greer 1962; Clignet and Sween 1969] while factorial ecology includes a much wider range of variables and generally almost all of those at hand. The social area variables deal with social rank as indicated by education and occupation; familism or life style (sometimes called urbanism) as indexed by fertility, female labor force participation, and housing arrangements; ethnicity as measured by relative concentrations of minority groups; and, sometimes, migrant status as treated by population mobility rates. The social area framework maintains that the nature of the relationships among the variables and their corresponding factor clusters are to some extent a function of the degree of society's economic development or "societal scale." Societal scale is taken generally to mean the extent of the division of labor within society and the degree of elaboration of the integrating mechanisms and institutions. Hence as society modernizes or increases in scale the degree of societal differentiation increases, and this becomes reflected in increasing specialization of urban land use and population differentiation.

In small-scale societies, or ones low on the modernization continuum, there is little social differentiation; that is, social rank is highly related to family form, and both in turn are related to ethnicity and migrant status. These correlations mean that differential population distribution in the city does not occur in terms of them. In a large-scale society where social differentiation has occurred, areas of the city specialize in terms of characteristics which themselves are becoming independent. In cities in large-scale societies neighborhoods become specialized in terms of their status composition. Furthermore, among neighborhoods at various status levels there is a wide variety of family forms evident. Likewise within ethnic areas there are status and familism gradients present.

Factorial ecology differs from social area analysis in that factorial ecology is more inductive and includes a wider range of variables than does social area analysis, although the social area analysis variables are usually included. In describing factorial ecology, Berry and Rees have written: "A data matrix is analyzed containing measurements on m variables for each of n units of observation (census tracts, wards . . .), with the intent of (1) identifying and summarizing the common patterns of variability of the m variables in a smaller number of independent dimensions r, that additively reproduce this common variance; and (2) examining the patterns of scores of each of the n observational units on each of the r dimensions. The dimensions isolated are an objective outcome of the analysis" [Berry and Rees 1969: 458–459].

Since the inputs for factorial ecology are larger in number and of a wider variety of social and physical phenomena than are the inputs for social area analysis, the resulting number of factors extracted in factorial ecology usually exceeds that of social area analysis. Thus, factorial ecology usually identifies many more *dimensions* of urban social and physical organization. For example, Murdie [1969] in a longitudinal study of the factorial ecology of metropolitan Toronto identified the following factors in 1951: economic status, family status, ethnic status, recent growth, service-clerical employment, and household characteristics. For 1961 he identified economic status, family status, Italian ethnic status, Jewish ethnic status, recent growth, and household and employment characteristics. The six factors for 1951 explain

72.2 percent of the variance in the correlation matrix, while for 1961 they explain 75.0 percent. Had Murdie limited the analysis to only the social area dimensions he would have explained only 49.9 percent of the variance for 1951 and 55.9 percent for 1961. Murdie employed 86 variables for the 1951 analysis and 78 for 1961 [Murdie 1969]. Another example can be found in a study by Sweetser [1969]. In a factorial analysis of Helsinki data he reports several ethnic factors; in analysis of Boston data Sweetser has identified a nonwhite factor separate from other ethnic factors such as Italian and Irish ethnic status.

The discovery of factors unique to data inputs for specific cities makes factorial ecology studies difficult to compare, and herein lies one of the largest problems of this approach. Different inputs lead to different resulting factor structures. Social area analysis has escaped this problem to a great extent since the input variables are largely determined by the theoretical framework and not simply by what data are at hand. Thus, the tendency in social area analyses is to limit the factor analysis to aggregates of variables comparable among cities. However, unique configurations in the development of any one city are often missed. Although the data inputs for the social area analysis studies are fairly comparable, the resulting factor structures are often quite varied. Berry and Rees have identified seven possible results just using the social area analysis variables and they present empirically discovered examples of each [Berry and Rees 1969: 468].

With increasing frequency the concentric zone, sector, and factor analytic models are being used jointly in current research. There seem to be two major patterns for this analytic convergence. The first of these includes investigations that calculate separate factor analyses of similar variables for different sectors and zones within a single city. One of the current leading exponents of this line of analysis is Frank Sweetser. Sweetser's long-range goal is to develop a typology of cities classified in terms of their similar ecological configurations as measured by their factor structures. However, he argues that before this goal can be achieved a number of procedural problems must be resolved. One of these involves the relative stability of ecological factors. In order to identify the factors that are common to all portions of one city, he advocates separate factor analyses for the different zones and sectors. From the results he identifies the factors common to the metropolis as a whole and sorts out those that are zone or sector unique. Once having identified the basic factors for a city they may then be compared to those from other cities. The cities are then classified as to similarity in basic factors [Sweetser 1969].

The second pattern for this analytical convergence among the models may be seen in the work of Anderson and Egeland [1961], of Schwirian and Matre [1969], and of Berry and Rees [1969]. In each of these studies the major dimensions of ecological organization for a city are identified through factor analysis of a number of variables. Then, the spatial distribution of the factors in terms of gradients and sectors is determined. In a study of four U.S. cities (Akron, Dayton, Indianapolis, and Syracuse), Anderson and Egeland examined the distribution of the social area analysis indexes of social rank and familism (urbanization) by gradient and by sector. Rank and familism were identified as basic community dimensions in past factor analytic studies. As was mentioned previously, analysis of variance of the two indexes showed that social rank or prestige varied by sector in the cities while urbanization or familism varied by concentric zone. Schwirian and Matre present similar findings for a number of large Canadian cities. Likewise, Berry and Rees in their study of Calcutta first determined the major factors and then fit a trend surface analysis to the factor scores. Once the surfaces had been established they were then evaluated in terms of sectors and gradients.

In summary of the analytical convergence in current ecological research the factorial, concentric zone, and sector models are coming to play unique and complementary roles. Factor analysis is generally used to identify basic dimensions of urban organization while the concentric zone and sector models are used to ascertain the spatial differentiation of these dimensions in relation to the city's center and to each other.

Relation of Urban Ecological Differentiation to Societal Development

The comparative interests of social scientists has produced a large number of studies of urban structure in a variety of societies. The growing mass of such materials is reflected in a growing number of summary reviews as found in such sources as Hauser and Schnore [1965] and in Breese [1969]. Rather than being content with simple descriptive comparisons of U.S. and non-U.S. cities, urban ecologists are attempting to explain differences between U.S. and other cities in terms of theories of societal development.

Comparative studies of concentric zone and sector models have noted either reversal in patterns predicted on the basis of findings on U.S. cities (such as in Latin America) or the prevalence of multiple nucleation (as in some African or Asian cities). The difference between U.S. and foreign cities are usually explained by some combination of the following three factors: (1) *Differences in urban function.* Although U.S. cities are commercial-industrial centers, many of the nonwestern cities are primarily, or were at the time of location, primarily administrative centers. Thus, difference in primary function resulted in different land use patterns and differential population distributions within the city. Explanations of this type are most elaborately illustrated in Sjoberg's *Pre-Industrial City* [1960]. (2) *Differences in level of transportation and transportation ownership patterns.* The spread of the population in urban space is a direct function of mode of transportation and access to transportation of large segments of the population. In countries with a more restrictive transportation pattern than that of the United States, different forces work to sort the population, thereby producing a different spatial pattern. (3) *Level of technology at the time of city location.* Implied in this notion are two ideas. First, the ecological pattern for a given city is largely determined by existing modes of transportation. And, second, once such patterns are established there is enormous inertia to their change. Change, when it comes, in most cases, is slow, disjunctive, disrupted, and piecemeal. Credence for this explanation has been given by Schnore's [1965] work on age of city as an ecological variable, and in the interest of other ecologists in so-called "historical residuals."

The vast number of studies of non-U.S. cities, then, leads to the conclusion that in terms of the gradient and sector model the differences between our cities and those abroad are a result of differences in societal modernization—that is, differences in level of industrialization and transportation technology, primary function, and age. Furthermore, many of these studies assert or imply that the non-U.S. cities are becoming more like U.S. cities as they take on greater industrial and commercial functions.

To date no formal attempt has been made to tie the classic ecological models into a developmental theory of society, even though such inferences abound in the literature. Perhaps the closest attempt at developing such a theory is that by Schnore in his review of the spatial structure of North and South American cities. Schnore concludes that "What does emerge from this review is the possibility that (a) the Burgess concentric zone scheme, wrongly regarded as indigenous to the United States, and (b) the preindustrial pattern, erroneously identified as unique to Latin America, are *both special cases more adequately subsumed under a more general theory of residential land use in urban areas*" [Schnore 1965: 374].

In the course of the discussion Schnore speculates that there might well be a sequential pattern of ecological change as societies modernize. In the early pattern of city development the "inverse gradient" characterizes the city in which the affluent population lives near the city's center and the lower-income groups live toward the periphery. With growth, modernization, and aging, the central portions of the city become less attractive residentially and the upper class migrates toward the periphery. The vacated areas in the inner portions of the city become the targets for those urbanites who cannot survive in the stiffer competition for fringe housing. Although this "theory" is intuitively appealing, no test of it has yet been made. Of course, longitudinal data would be required and for most cities of the world good small-area data for past years are simply not available.

Although Schnore's speculation is far from a theory of ecological dynamics, it does provide a foundation for future research endeavors and serves as a call for less descriptive cross-sectional studies and for more explanatory dynamic investigations.

Factorial ecology, specifically social area analysis, has tied explanations of urban ecological structure to a much more specific theory of social change. As has already been mentioned, as the degree of modernization within a society increases so too does the differentiation of the social system and the spatial segregation of population types. In low-scale societies there are sufficiently high correlations among the variables of social rank, familism, and ethnicity to prevent factorial separation of them, while in large-scale societies the correlations among the variables are reduced sufficiently to permit the separation of rank, familism, and ethnicity. Accordingly, it is inferred that as the scale of society changes so too does the degree of factor separation. Most studies, however, have *not* been longitudinal as required for test of the theory but have been cross-sectional comparisons of cities in different societies. If the three factors of rank, familism, and ethnicity fail to separate, it is then argued that the society in which the cities are located is low on the scale of modernization. A recent example of this line of analysis is a study of Cairo by Abu-Lughod [1969]. With data for both 1947 and 1960 Abu-Lughod reports that social rank and familism load on the same factor each year and that this combined factor accounts for approximately half of the total matrix variation. The failure of rank and familism to separate is attributed to the different degree of modernization in Egypt as compared to that of the United States.

Perhaps an even greater contribution of the Abu-Lughod paper than its empirical findings on Cairo is her discussion of the conditions under which social rank and familism factors would appear for a given city and under which conditions the two factors would separate from each other. For a social rank vector to be identified the following conditions must be met: (1) that the effective ranking system in a city be related to the operational definition employed; and (2) that the ranking system be manifested in a pattern of residential segregation of persons of different ranks at a large enough scale to be picked up at the level of analysis (census tract, ward, etc.). For a familism factor to appear there must be (1) variability in family types due to either "natural" causes such as those associated with stages in the life cycle or to other "social" causes such as those associated with other divisions in the society such as social rank or ethnicity; and (2) differentiation among subareas within the city in attractiveness to different types of families. Finally, for familism and social rank factors to separate from each other the following conditions must be met: (1) that there be no strong linkages between social rank and such familism variables as fertility, completed family size, and the propensity to remain within extended households; (2) that stages in the life cycle were clearly distinguished from one another with each stage being associated with a change in residence; (3) that sufficiently large subareas within the city offered at all economic levels, highly specialized housing accommodations suited to families at particular stages in the life cycle; and (4) that cultural values permitting and favoring mobility to maximize housing efficiency are generally unencumbered by restrictive regulations or strong sentiments [Abu-Lughod 1969: 108–109].

Although the social area analysis framework has been widely applied by both sociologists [Abu-Lughod 1969; Anderson and Egeland 1961; Anderson and Bean 1961; Udry 1964; Schwirian and Matre 1969; Schwirian and Smith 1971; Latif 1971a] and geographers [Robson 1969; Timms 1971] its reception by ecologists has been far from uncritical. Early criticisms by Hawley and Duncan [1957] have focused upon its theoretical foundation, the link between the theory and its empirical indexes, the extent to which social areas have spatial meaning, the adequacy of tract data for analysis of urban ecological structure, and the heterogeneity of the units of observation. In another series of papers Van Arsdol, Camilleri, and Schmid [1958, 1961, 1962] have explored empirically the utility of the Shevky-Bell typology. One of their main arguments is that the combined indexes of social rank, urbanization (familism), and segregation have little empirical or logical advantages over and above the more traditional census tract measures upon which the social area indexes are based.

In response to the criticisms of social area analysis by Van Arsdol, Camilleri, and Schmid, Bell and Greer organize their comments around the following: "They are in part right—to the extent to which there is some trust in one of their criticisms; they are part wrong—to the extent that they have been incautious in reaching conclusions which their data do not support, unreasonable in applying standards of evaluation, misleading in explaining what their data mean, and contradictory in concluding that one can't deduce from the Shevky theory and going ahead and doing just that. They are also in basic disagreement with Shevky (and with us) regarding epistemology, which leads them to reach different evaluations than we would, even if we could agree on everything else" [Bell and Greer 1962: 3–4].

And so it goes!

The net effect of the critical reviews of social area analysis has been to clarify the basic issues in the model and its application, although an examination of the recent literature must lead one to conclude that the main thrust of social area analysis has not been greatly deflected by the past controversies [see, for example, Greer, McElrath, Orleans, and Minar 1968].

DENSITY MODELS

Many analyses of the density patterns of the residential population of large cities have shown very consistent findings. Density peaks near the city's center—the point of optimum total access for the residential population—and declines with increasing distance from the center in all directions. Thus, there is a well-defined density gradient such that the highest densities are in the inner portions of the city while the lowest densities are in the fringe areas. In plotting density values for urban subareas on the vertical axis of a graph with distance of the subareas from the city's center on the horizontal axis, a negative exponential curve is approximated. Actually there is a decline in density in those areas immediately adjacent to the city's center because land use there is preempted by nonresidential activities. Many have described the appearance of the density-distance curve as resembling a volcano with the lower density crater at the city's core. It has been suggested that if hotel accommodations were classified as "residential" land use then the true peak of highest density would occur at the city's center [Hoover 1968: 249].

Density's decline with distance is basically a function of two things: (1) the rate at which households are willing to trade residential site space against the time and money cost of transportation to work and other major activities; and (2) the cost in time and money of transportation. Research has shown that while the negative exponential curve does indeed describe the pattern for many cities, there are differences in the slopes of the curves among cities at a given point in time, and among points in time for a given city [Clark 1951]. In summarizing these patterns of urban density Hoover [1968: 250–251] notes that:

1. the larger the city the higher the central density;
2. the larger the city the flatter the density-distance curve;
3. as cities in developed societies grow the density-distance curve becomes flatter;
4. age of the city is an important factor in the determination of density patterns since the level of transportation technology and original social structural patterns determine the initial population distribution, which becomes subject to enormous forces of inertia;
5. central density levels have been declining along with the flattening of the density-distance curve even though the cities have experienced net population increase.

In a comparative study of the density-distance slopes for several cities Muth has concluded that the slopes are steeper in the older cities, in cities that have higher housing qualities in the central city, and in cities where manufacturing employment is relatively more concentrated in the city rather than the suburbs. The slopes are flatter where automobile ownership is greater, where the recent community growth rates are higher, where income level is higher, and where size is comparatively large [Hoover 1968: 251].

The exponential decline of density with increasing distance from the city's center seems to describe the distribution of other urban characteristics as well. For example, studies have shown similar declines for net manufacturing employment density, daytime population, and land values. Much work is currently being done linking the similarity in curves between the density-distance model and the distribution of land values. Much of this work is taking the form of mathematical models and probably more will be similarly phrased in the future [for example, see Casetti 1971].

With increasing frequency, social scientists are becoming concerned not only with density patterns as such, but with the social concomitants of density variations as well. Two papers in this book reflect this interest in the correlates

of density—those by Winsborough [1965] (15) and by Galle, Gove, and McPherson [1972] (16). In another paper an analysis of the ecological correlates of mortality in a large Midwestern city by Schwirian and LaGreca [1971] shows that (1) the environmental conditions under which a population lives have a relationship with its mortality level over and above the effects of the population's social status, which is related to both mortality and environmental conditions; and (2) the environmental conditions seem to be intervening variables between status and mortality—that is, the effect of the status variables upon mortality level seem to be mediated by the physical conditions of the subareas.

Household density or crowding (a ratio of 1.01 or more persons per room) was one of the environmental variables employed in the analysis. The data show that with other such variables controlled as age structure, education and income levels, racial composition, and other housing conditions, that crowding has a partial correlation of 0.33 with subarea mortality level.

The mediating effect of housing crowding between status and mortality is illustrated by the results of the path analysis calculated upon their data. The model is presented in Figure 2. The model suggests that mortality level of urban subareas is a direct result of the concentration of elderly in the area, the density of

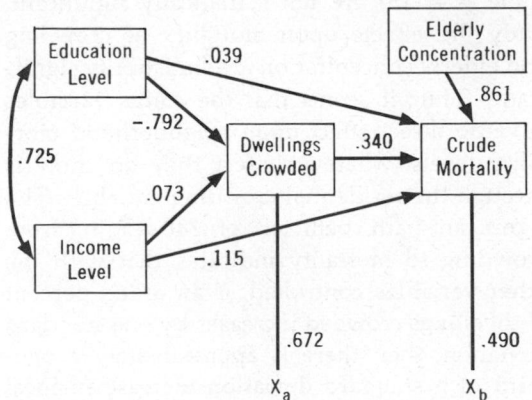

FIGURE 2. Path Model for Mortality, Status, Age, and Crowding

household units, and the two status variables education and income levels. The model also indicates that in addition to the direct effects of education and income the status variables are hypothesized to have indirect effects upon mortality through the crowding variable. Schwirian and LaGreca's data are for 1960 for 73 census tracts in Columbus, Ohio.

To examine the model in Figure 2 the path coefficients are calculated for the relationships indicated by arrows in the diagram. The path coefficients are the standardized partial regression coefficients. To calculate them for the paths leading directly to mortality, for example, a multiple correlation and regression is performed with mortality as the dependent variable and with elderly concentration, housing crowding, education, and income as independent variables. The path coefficients are the standardized partial regression coefficients for the independent variables and indicate the proportion of a change in the dependent variable that accompanies a one "standard" deviation change in the independent variable with the other independent variables controlled. The higher the path coefficient value, the greater the effect of the independent variable.

The path coefficients for the model show that approximately 76 percent of subarea mortality variation is a function of the four independent variables. However, the effects of the two status variables (education = .039 and income = -.115) are not statistically significant. Only the effects upon mortality of crowding and elderly concentration are statistically significant. Thus it seems that the status variables have no direct effect upon neighborhood mortality levels; whatever effect they do show is through the residential crowding variable. The significant path coefficient of .340 leading from crowding to mortality indicates that with the other variables controlled, if an area's percent of dwellings crowded increases by one standard deviation, then there is approximately a one-third of a standard deviation increase in local mortality. These data certainly support the notion that with status and age controlled the den-

sity of household units has an impact upon the risk of death in urban neighborhoods.

Segregation and Location

Ecological investigations of the residential segregation of social status groups have led to the following conclusions: (1) that the residential dissimilarity of social status groups is present in cities in many different cultural settings; (2) that the degree of residential dissimilarity among specific groups is a function of the degree of social distance among them; (3) that the social status groups that are the most segregated residentially are those at the top and at the bottom of the social status hierarchy; (4) that social status groups are not uniformly distributed across the city, rather, some tend to be centralized while others tend to be decentralized; (5) whether it is the upper or the lower status group that is the more centralized is a function of the level of economic development of a society in which the city is located—in developed societies the upper status groups are more decentralized and the lower status groups are the more centralized, while in developing societies the reverse seems to hold; and (6) that the status groups most centralized and the most decentralized are those that are the most residentially segregated. These generalizations have been well documented for U.S. cities [Duncan and Duncan 1955; Uyeki 1964], as well as for cities in Puerto Rico [Schwirian and Rico-Velasco 1971], India [Mehta 1968], Egypt [Latif 1971b], and England [Collison 1960].

The most frequently used measure of residential dissimilarity and segregation in recent studies is the index of dissimilarity. To measure the dissimilarity in residential distribution between pairs of social status groups the formula is employed:

$$\Delta = \Sigma \mid X_i - Y_i \mid / 2.$$

In this formula X_i is the proportion of the total persons in status group X that live in area i and Y_i is the proportion of the total persons in status group Y that also live in area i. The resulting index value indicates the proportion of the one group that would have to shift its area of residence for its group distribution to be exactly like that of the other group. Thus, the higher the index value, the more dissimilar the two groups are in their residential patterning. To measure the segregation of one status group from all others combined we employ the following modified form of the index of dissimilarity:

$$S = \Sigma \mid X_i - Y_i \mid / \, 2 \, (1 - p).$$

In the segregation formula X_i, the proportion of the total persons in the specific status group of interest that live in area i, and Y is the proportion of all groups combined (including members of group X) that live in area i. The p in the formula is the proportion of the total population that group X represents.

The index of dissimilarity has been employed not only in the study of status segregation within cities but has also been used to compare the levels of segregation of specific occupational groups in cities and suburbs. In a study of the Boston, Kansas City, Los Angeles, Miami, Minneapolis-St. Paul, Philadelphia, San Diego, and Syracuse metropolitan areas, Fine, Glenn, and Monts [1971] report generally higher dissimilarity values for pairs of occupational groups in the cities than in the suburban areas. Thus it seems that the suburban areas were no more homogeneous than the city areas. If anything the suburbs were slightly more heterogeneous. In explaining the generally greater segregation in the cities the authors suggest that in cities higher status and lower status workers can be highly segregated without anyone living beyond easy access to work or services and institutions because of the greater density and compactness of the overall settlement patterns and the better public transportation facilities. In the suburbs very high levels of segregation in this comparatively sparsely settled zone would make the access to work and to other services which are typically located near those

of higher status much too costly for the lower income worker.

The study of the residential segregation and location of ethnic groups is usually treated in terms of the process of cultural assimilation. Essentially it is argued that in the case of American cities, newly arriving ethnic groups originally settled in highly segregated areas located in the inner urban core, being vacated in the process of urban expansion. This segregated, centralized location pattern of the incoming ethnics emerged because of the immigrants' generally impoverished financial conditions and lack both of familiarity with the dominant culture and acceptance by the indigenous population. It has been argued that the high degree of segregation had impact upon various aspects of their assimilation to the dominant culture. Lieberson [1961] has shown that highly segregated immigrant groups are less likely to become citizens, to speak English, to intermarry, and to have more of its members deviate from general intergenerational occupational mobility patterns.

Length of tenure of the immigrant groups in the society has been shown by many studies to be related to both degree of segregation and extent of residential centralization [Cressey 1938; Ford 1950; and Duncan and Lieberson 1959]. Presumably the longer the ethnic group is within the society, the more assimilated it becomes, and the less differentiated it is from the indigenous population in social characteristics and residential patterning.

While ethnic segregation largely has been portrayed as an inner city phenomenon, Lieberson [1962] has shown similar patterns of segregation in the cities and fringe areas of 10 metropolitan communities: Boston, Buffalo, Chicago, Cincinnati, Cleveland, Columbus, Philadelphia, Pittsburgh, St. Louis, and Syracuse. Furthermore over the 20-year period covered in the study Lieberson reports that the changes in ethnic distributions in the suburbs are very similar to the patterns of change for the same ethnic groups within the cities. By way of summary Lieberson writes, "These results suggest that differences in the population composition of suburbs and central cities may obscure the existence of similar behavioral patterns for comparable groups in the two parts of a metropolis" [Lieberson 1962: 673].

One problem that has marked the whole analysis of ethnic residential distribution and segregation is the link between ethnicity and social status. Thus the question is raised as to how much of the differentiation among ethnic groups is a function of social class differences and how much is a function of ethnicity alone. Darroch and Marston [1971] address this question directly in a very detailed study of Toronto. Although theirs is basically a one-city study, they do report support for their findings for Montreal and Vancouver as well. Essentially, they use data on the association between ethnicity (as measured by ethnic origin, mother tongue, and birthplace) and educational, income, and occupational aspects of social status to generate expected segregation patterns for the ethnic groups based upon their status level only. These patterns based upon their status level are compared to the actual segregation patterns. Through the comparisons Darroch and Marston are able to estimate the amount of the level of segregation for the various groups attributable to their status level. In all cases, the status differences among the groups account for only relatively small proportions of their segregation levels.

Treated differently from ethnic segregation in American cities is that of the black population. The most comprehensive study to date of black residential segregation in urban areas is that by Taeuber and Taeuber [1965]. Their study presents the indexes of residential segregation for 207 cities. The index is based upon the index of dissimilarity, and the unit of observation is the city block. The highest index recorded is 98.1 for Fort Lauderdale. In effect this means that for the residential distribution of whites and blacks to be the same in Fort Lauderdale, approximately 98 percent of the blacks would have to change their block of residence!

The lowest index reported was 60.4 for San José. The rather high level of black segregation in American cities is indicated by the distribution of the segregation indexes from the Taeubers' study. Only 8 cities have indexes of less than 70. Half of the cities have indexes of over 87.8, and one-fourth have values greater than 91.7.

The Taeubers point out in analysis of the city segregation values that in American cities the high level of racial segregation is true generally for cities in all regions of the country, for large and small cities, for industrial and commercial cities, for metropolitan and suburban communities, for cities with relatively large concentrations of blacks and for cities with comparatively small numbers of blacks, for cities where the whites and blacks are economically well off as well as for cities where the economic conditions are poor.

Is black-white residential segregation increasing or decreasing? In analyzing the data for 109 cities between 1940 and 1960 the Taeubers show that between 1940 and 1950 a majority of cities in both the North and the South had an increase in their segregation indexes. Between 1950 and 1960 more than three-quarters of the Southern cities had increases again in segregation levels, while only 16 percent of the cities in the North and West had increases again.

Although there is a generally high degree of racial segregation in all U.S. cities, Schnore and Evenson [1966] have examined in detail differences among Southern cities in segregation level. Essentially they found that the older Southern cities have generally lower segregation indexes than the younger cities. This pattern holds even with other variables controlled such as percent nonwhite population and subregion location (South Atlantic vs. South Central). The inverse relationship between city age and level of segregation is frequently attributed to the tendency in older Southern cities for the black population to live in side streets or along alleys in back of the whites' residences.

This "back-yard" locational pattern did not develop in the newer cities of the South; thus the initial level of black-white segregation in the new cities was greater than in the older ones.

How much of the residential segregation between blacks and whites is a function of the status differences between the two populations, and how much is a function of race alone? In attempting to sort out the effects of socioeconomic differences upon black-white segregation the Taeubers engage in a rather detailed analysis of variance of the percent of each nonwhite census tract for several cities. They find basically that the net effect of economic status upon black-white segregation is comparatively small and the effect of the economic factors seem to diminish over time. In projecting their findings into the future the Taeubers suggest that even if nonwhite occupational status improves in the future, as it did between 1950 and 1960, the decline in black-white residential segregation will be relatively small.

The tendency for ethnic groups to disperse residentially through time in the city has not been duplicated by the black population. Studies of black residential movement have largely been couched in terms of the invasion-succession process. In analysis of the data on racial change of subareas in several cities Taeuber and Taeuber [1965: 104–105] identify several different types of subareas:

1. Established Negro areas: In both 1940 and 1950 the nonwhites made up over 90 percent of the areas' population.
2. Stable interracial areas: Both the white and the black population were stable in these areas between 1940 and 1950.
3. Consolidation areas: Areas in which the percentage of nonwhites increased. These areas were subdivided into
   a. Succession tracts: The nonwhite population was 250 or more in 1940 and increased between 1950 and 1960, while the white population decreased in the period.
   b. Invasion tracts: The nonwhite population was less than 250 in 1940 and increased to more than 250 while the white population decreased over the period.
   c. Growing tracts: The white population was either stable or increasing over the 10-year period while the nonwhite population increased.
   d. Declining tracts: The nonwhite population was stable or decreased in the 10-year period at a lesser rate than the white population decreased.
4. Displacement areas: The percentage of the population nonwhite decreased by either an increase of the white population coupled with a decrease in the nonwhite population; or the white population grew more rapidly than did the black population; or the black population declined more rapidly than did the white population.

Perhaps one of the most striking aspects of the Taeubers' analysis of the variety of urban subareas is that the process of black-white neighborhood change is portrayed as a very complex phenomenon. They demonstrate that to talk about racial neighborhood transition simply in terms of invasion-succession is grossly inadequate.

In studying the distribution of census tracts across the various categories for a number of cities the Taeubers report a variety of patterns. Differences among cities in subarea types are explained by the Taeubers in terms of differential black-white growth. The Taeubers go on to examine the concomitants of residential succession, the socioeconomic characteristics of areas with a changing racial composition, class segregation within the black residential community, and the degree of similarity in social characteristics between whites and blacks in racially mixed areas.

Although black areas do indeed spread in urban residential space there is a definite tendency for the blacks, unlike the nationality ethnics, to remain residentially centralized. A number of different measures of residential centralization have been employed in recent studies. One such gross measure of the centralization of specific groups is to compare the percent of the group in the metropolitan fringe to the percent of the total population in the fringe. Thus:

Centralization = % of the specific group in the
fringe area/percent of the
total population in the fringe.

Thus if 30 percent of the metropolitan population resides in the fringe areas while 40 percent of the white population is located in the fringe, then the index of centralization for the whites would be:

$$\text{Centralization} = 40/30$$
$$= 1.333.$$

Or if only 25 percent of the black population lived in the fringe of the same metropolitan area, then their index of centralization would be:

$$\text{Centralization} = 25/30$$
$$= .835$$

Index values of greater than 1.000 indicate a decentralized pattern for the group of interest, while values of less than 1.000 indicate a centralized pattern. In this hypothetical example the whites are decentralized while the blacks are centralized.

Another measure of residential centralization may be obtained by calculating the mean distance the population of interest is from the city's center. Thus the formula:

$$\text{Centralization} = (\Sigma\, DP)\,/\,N.$$

In this formula P is the number of persons in a given subarea and D is the subarea's distance from the city's center. The N in the formula is the total population or the sum of the P for the separate areas. The larger this index the greater the average distance each member of the group is from the city's center.

The third measure of centralization is similar to the index of segregation described earlier. First the urban subareas are ordered by increasing distance from the city's center. Then the cumulative percentage of both the group of interest and of the total population is calculated, starting with the areas closest to the city's center and then proceeding to the areas at the greatest distance. The two cumulative percentage distributions are then compared. From the comparison it may be ascertained if the group of interest is more or less centralized than the total population [Duncan and Duncan 1955: 157].

So far the discussion has focused mainly upon some of the principal substantive concerns in ecological analysis. However, there are numerous methodological problems that face the ecological researcher in the examination of these models. Some of the major issues are described in the following section.

SOME METHODOLOGICAL PROBLEMS IN THE ANALYSIS OF URBAN ECOLOGICAL MODELS

Usually ecologists are dependent upon official sources of information for their data. The problems and pitfalls of using international statistical sources have received considerable attention already [see, for example, Carrier and Farrag, 1959]. Of concern here are those special problems faced in the test of ecological models which usually demand high quantities of detailed urban subarea data. And unfortunately for comparative ecological research such data are not collected for many world cities, thereby precluding the possibility that their ecological structure may be identified through application of rigorous statistical procedures. However, with increasing frequency such data are becoming available, and in the next twenty years it is quite likely that some usable data will exist for many of the world's largest urban complexes.

Where the data for cities in other societies do exist there are still four major problems common to all ecological investigations: (1) the comparability of urban subarea units across societies; (2) the variations in quality of urban subarea data between societies; (3) alternatives in cross-sectional and longitudinal analyses; and (4) the appropriateness of various units of analysis—the city versus the metropolitan area.

The comparability of subarea units across societies is best viewed in terms of the theoretical concept of "natural area" or neighborhood that underlies most ecological analyses. Basic ecological theory asserts that the city may be viewed as a collection of differentiated natural areas which are unique to a large extent in population composition, subculture, and emergent behaviors. Ecological models attempt to describe and explain both the pattern of differentiation among the neighborhoods and their particular spatial geometry. In working with subarea data collected by official sources two important questions emerge. The first is to what extent are the official statistical subareas adequate operationalizations of the natural area. The second question is to what extent do the subarea units of cities in one society correspond to those of other cities in the same and in other societies. That is, to what extent are the census tracts of Chicago, San Juan, and Montreal; the shiyakhat of Cairo and Alexandria; and the wards of Tokyo and Calcutta similar operationalizations of the cities' natural areas? Unfortunately ecologists have given little more than passing concern to these questions since such systematic evaluations are usually beyond the resources of the individual investigator, who is faced all too often with making do with the data on hand.

The variations in quality of urban subarea data among societies is one of the most serious problems the comparative ecologist faces. For valid data on a massive scale to be obtained in any nation the whole research process must be characterized by excellence all the way from research design through data collection to analysis. Unfortunately, the research resources are simply inadequate in many nations. This results in the collection of dubious data which invalidate any attempt to analyze the figures systematically. Indeed through the efforts of the United Nations and other organizations research skills and capabilities are being upgraded, but it will be some time before comparative researchers can place complete trust in the official statistics of many nations. More concern needs to be devoted by ecologists to the problems of validity in the official statistics which they so voraciously consume.

Another fundamental problem arises when the ecologist attempts to investigate theories about the operation of longitudinal processes and all that are at hand are cross-sectional data. Especially in the developing nations urban subarea data do not extend back in usable form for more than 5, 10, or 20 years at most. While this problem is not unique to ecology, ecologists have not tended to attempt to construct the type of causal models that may be tested with cross-sectional data that other sociologists have. For example, ecologists have not expressed their theories in the form of sets of recursive equations [Blalock 1964]. Were they to do so, some headway could be made in assessing the reasonableness of some ecological assertions. At any rate ecologists are somewhat fortunate here since many nations are collecting urban subarea data that in 20 to 30 years will form a solid foundation for longitudinal investigations.

In studying the ecological structure of a given community the researcher is faced with the decision as to the extent of the community he includes in the analysis. Should the city or the metropolitan area be the focus? For comparative research the issue becomes to what extent are the metropolitan and city units comparable ecological aggregates across societies. In some nations the officially defined metropolitan areas are almost totally urban with the resident population entirely included in the urban labor force. In other nations the metropolitan areas are "over-bound" in the sense that they include large fringe agricultural populations. Thus when comparing two such communities—a totally urban aggregate with one that mixes urban and agricultural populations and areas—the ecologist has two strictly noncomparable phenomena. Generally there is much more similarity among nations in what they define officially as the "city" unit than there is in what is defined as the "metropolitan area." Unless the ecologist is certain as to the comparability of two metropolitan areas from different nations, it is far safer for the investigation to be limited to the city segments of the metropolises.

SOME PROBLEMS IN THE USE OF FACTORIAL MODELS

In the course of the emergence of factorial ecology and social area analysis a number of methodological problems have become evident in the application of factor analysis techniques to urban subarea data. Factor analysis is a very general and flexible technique for determining underlying common patterns in rather large masses of data. The utility of factor analysis for social research has been extolled at length by a number of social scientists. Rummel, who sees factor analysis as a very basic "calculus of social science" given the types of data and problems we face at one point, writes: "Factor analysis can be—and is being—so generally applied and the factor model is so amenable to structuring our social knowledge and theories I hazard a prediction that courses in factor analysis will eventually be required for undergraduate social scientists" [Rummel 1970: 4–5]. Well, maybe. At any rate there is little doubt that an intelligent reading of the ecological literature is demanding some basic feel for what factor analysis is all about.

In calculating a factor analysis the researcher usually proceeds as follows:

1. For each unit of observation—which in the case of factorial ecology or social area analysis is the census tract—the researcher assembles scores on each variable used to characterize the unit of observation (for example, income level, racial composition).
2. The variables used to characterize the observation unit are standardized. That is, each distribution is converted into the form where the mean value is equal to zero and standard deviation is equal to 1.0.
3. The zero-order correlation matrix is calculated for all of the variables. That is, all the r between each pair of variables across the census tracts are determined.
4. The techniques of either principal component analysis or factor analysis are applied to the correlation matrix. Here the researcher has a very large selection of specific computational models he may employ, and he should select the one most congruent with the assumptions of his analytical model. From the application of these techniques a series of factors or dimensions are extracted from the correlation matrix which identify clusters of highly interrelated variables. Each variable's correlation with each factor is then determined. The correlation of the variable with the factor is commonly referred to as the variable's "loading" on the factor.
5. The extracted factors may or may not be rotated in order to clarify their structure and thus the resulting interpretation. Here again the researcher has alternative choices of computational models that may be applied to the rotation process.

As factor analytic techniques have been employed to urban subarea data a number of problems have emerged. They are (1) comparability of factors across studies given differing data inputs; (2) general methods of computation—factor analysis versus component analysis; (3) type of factor rotation employed—orthogonal versus oblique; and (4) extent of the community studied and its implications for the description of urban structure.

As was discussed earlier, the comparability problem between studies has become particularly nagging. Since the social area studies limit their inputs to variables measuring social rank, familism, and ethnicity their inputs are fairly comparable. But what social area studies gain in comparability among themselves they lose in explaining total variance in ecological structure for the particular city investigated. By limiting the variable inputs to the three social area dimensions other important general and unique local configurations in the development of the city may be missed. The results of factorial ecological studies that have widely discrepant inputs are impossible to compare in more than the most general of terms.

Factorial ecological investigations have used a variety of computational techniques in seeking to identify aggregates of variables differentiated in urban space. Some early studies employed *cluster analysis* [Tyron 1955] and its extension of *linkage analysis* [Sweetser 1962]. In more recent studies cluster and linkage analyses have been supplanted by principal *components analysis* [Gittus 1964–1965] and *factor analysis* [Carey 1966]. Even though either components or factor analysis is employed in ecological investigations there has been little systematic consideration as to which model best fits the substantive problem. An essential and basic difference between the two statistical models is that components analysis takes the data as given and determines the dimensions of the space defining them. Components analysis makes no assumption about the existence of common factors in the problem. It is certainly time for ecologists to consider seriously the efficacy of the two models for identifying major dimensions of urban structure since their alternative application to a given set of data can produce somewhat different results [Harman 1967; Rummel 1970; King 1969].

Additionally, ecologists should pay more attention in intercity comparisons as to the similarity or dissimilarity in statistical models. All too frequently incautious comparisons of factor structures for different cities are made with the structure of one of the cities derived by factor analysis while that of the other city was calculated through components techniques.

Although the choice between the computational models of factor analysis and components analysis is indeed a problem, another serious concern is the particular factor rotation model employed. In almost all of the factorial ecological studies where factor rotation is calculated, the orthogonal model is selected. There has been some controversy in the statistical literature over the relative merits of orthogonal versus oblique factor rotation [Rummel 1970: 386]. Factorial ecologists have ignored this controversy and have seemingly relied upon an uncritical selection of the orthogonal approach. The essential difference between orthogonal and oblique rotation models is that if there is a lack of correlation among obliquely rotated factors it is an *empirical* finding, while the lack of correlation among orthogonally rotated factors is *imposed* by the orthogonal model. That is, the oblique rotation provides for the possibility of correlation among the factors while the orthogonal does not. Of course, it is quite possible that an oblique rotation will yield uncorrelated factors, in which case the orthogonal solution may give a better approximation of simple structure. However, if oblique rotation is bypassed in favor of the orthogonal, which itself may be considered as a special case of oblique rotation, the researcher will never know if there is an underlying relationship among the factors which may be of some substantive interest in itself.

Essentially it is argued here that ecologists should opt more frequently for oblique rotation than they do currently. Basically, it seems that the assumptions of the oblique rotation model are more justifiable in terms of empirical conditions than are those of the orthogonal model.

In urban ecological research there is general consensus that social status, familism, and ethnicity are meaningful dimensions of urban organization. In urban subarea studies whose purpose is to identify these dimensions for a given city it is common practice to rotate the extracted factors orthogonally. The orthogonal model demands that the dimensions be completely uncorrelated with each other. Now we know from numerous studies that the dimensions are not unrelated. For example we know that race *is* related to social status; that race *is* related to fertility; and that fertility *is* related to social status. Since these variables are related indeed it seems that the more appropriate research strategy would be to apply an oblique rotation to extracted factors which provides for these interrelationships. After the data have been rotated in such fashion, then the researcher's concern can be with both the emergent factor structure and the correlations among the factors.

At this point we might ask, does the form of factor rotation greatly affect the emergent factor structure? While we know that theoretically we may ask what might happen empirically to typical urban subarea data, as a partial answer to this question I have selected two cities whose data will be rotated with both orthogonal and oblique (Biquartimin) techniques. The cities are fairly representative of two major types. One is a large city in a highly developed society—Ottawa, Canada. The other is a small city in an emerging society—Mayaguez, Puerto Rico. Current theories about the relationship between urban structure and societal development would lead us to expect the factorial structure of Ottawa to be highly differentiated with factors corresponding to social status, familism, and ethnicity while the factor structure of Mayaguez should be much less differentiated with perhaps one or two factors that represent more generally a social organization dimension. For the census tracts of both cities we have selected six variables which measure level of education; level of occupation; infertility; female participation in the labor force; housing in single-family units; and concentration of foreign born. The operationalizations of these measures have been discussed elsewhere [Schwirian and Smith 1971; Schwirian and Matre 1969].

The data for each city were submitted to the same form of principal components analysis and then the extracted factors were rotated orthogonally. A second analysis was performed and the factors were rotated through an oblique rotation. The results appear in Table 1.

For Mayaguez, which is the city in the developing society, three factors were rotated orthogonally. Factor I seems to tap a fairly gen-

eral social organization dimension since all but the dwelling unit variable load on it. Factor III seems also to be a social organization factor which differs from the first in that foreign born loads high on III, low on I. Also, infertility loads high on I and low on III. The second factor is unique in the sense that only one variable—dwelling—has a high loading on it. In the oblique rotated factor structure Factor I is a "stronger" social organization factor since all but one of the variables now correlates with it. Factor II is still the dwelling unit factor, and Factor III is very weak and no longer potentially meaningful. The factor congruency scores [Harman 1967: 270] show that oblique Factor I correlates very strongly with both orthogonal Factors I and III. Oblique Factor II correlates strongly with orthogonal II, and oblique Factor III is generally uncorrelated with both orthogonal I and III. Thus for Mayaguez, which is a small city in a developing society, the oblique rotation gives a more parsimonious summary of the general undifferentiated nature of its urban subareas. That is, for the residential areas of Mayaguez social status is associated with ethnicity and both, in turn, are associated with infertility and female labor force participation. Only housing type is independent of the more general social organization dimension.

For Ottawa, which is a large city in a highly developed society, we would predict marked factorial differentiation. Both the orthogonal and oblique rotations yield very similar factor structures. For both factors, social status separates from the familism and ethnic indicators. Also the ethnic variable separates from status and familism. Women in the labor force and dwelling units separate from status, ethnicity, and fertility. The similarity in factor structure for the two techniques is well illustrated by the factor congruency scores, all of which are over 0.99. Thus while there is marked factorial differentiation, the orthogonal and oblique factor rotations yield very similar factor structures; but where there is very little differentiation factorially the oblique rotation which does not force factor independence results in a more par-

TABLE 1. Orthogonal and Oblique Rotated Factors and Factor Congruency Scores for Mayaguez, Puerto Rico and Ottawa, Canada

Mayaguez	Orthogonal			Oblique		
	I	II	III	I	II	III
Occupation	.775	.189	(.577)	(.938)	.150	−.169
Education	(.702)	−.053	(.691)	(.988)	−.095	−.025
Infertility	(.923)	−.019	.369	(.883)	−.054	−.410
Women in Labor Force	(.572)	.085	(.783)	(.968)	.042	.126
Multiple Dwelling	.026	(.997)	.062	.024	(.998)	−.028
Foreign Born	.366	.086	(.921)	(.939)	.042	.371

Ottawa	Orthogonal				Oblique			
	I	II	III	IV	I	II	III	IV
Occupation	(.978)	−.107	−.064	.038	(.983)	−.010	−.050	.048
Education	(.925)	−.317	−.029	−.024	(.909)	−.230	−.003	.003
Infertility	.024	.269	.209	(.939)	.056	.204	.147	(.913)
Women in Labor Force	.098	(.905)	.190	.264	−.015	(.895)	.126	.168
Multiple Dwelling	−.408	(.855)	.011	.129	−.336	(.829)	−.050	.031
Foreign Born	.064	.122	(.971)	.191	−.048	.062	(.963)	.115

Mayaguez				Ottawa				
	Congruency				Congruency			
Orthogonal		Oblique		Orthogonal		Oblique		
	I	II	III		I	II	III	IV
I	.957		.348	I	.996			
II		.996		II		.993		
III	.968		.188	III			.995	
				IV				.995

simonious summary of the undifferentiated factor pattern.

Illustrative of the growing concern among ecologists for the problems engendered by the application of various computational models in factor analytic studies is a paper by Hunter [1972], which points out that for any given city the factored results that are obtained may indeed vary according to the factor and rotation algorithms employed. To ensure that the factors extracted are not simply artifacts of the computational procedures, Hunter suggests that the researcher should actually apply several different factor and rotation techniques to the data. If the researcher finds one or more factors regardless of computational methods employed he can then conclude that such factors are not artifacts of a single method. I am sure that most researchers who have engaged in factor analytic studies would agree that such a procedure would be quite cumbersome. Since Hunter does not provide an empirical example of this approach we must wait to see the efficacy of such analytical strategy. Undoubtedly in the near future we shall see several more papers similar to Hunter's in exploring the issues generated in the application of factor analytic techniques to urban data [for example, see Berry and Smith 1972].

Another problem in the factor analysis approach to urban subarea data is that of the extent of the community area studied. The choice is generally between the total metropolitan area or the city segment only. One investigator, Frank Sweetser [1969], argues that the subareas of the metropolis are sufficiently unique in social organization that separate factor analyses should be calculated for the different areas. Accordingly, then, the argument is not whether to factor the data for the city's subareas *or* the metropolitan subareas. Both city and fringe areas should be separately factored and then compared. Although his argument for the factoring of the metropolis' subareas is indeed interesting, current practice in ecological research has been to focus on either the city or the metropolitan area exclusively.

In the case that a given metropolitan area's boundaries are "true bound" in the sense that the statistical area corresponds to the expanse of urban functional integration, then the whole metropolitan area is the appropriate choice. In the case of metropolitan areas that are "overbound" and therefore have included in their official statistics values describing not only the urban population but the surrounding functionally differentiated fringe population as well, the city is the more appropriate choice for the analysis.

If alternative factor analyses were calculated for the metropolitan expanse of a community and then for the city segment, a differing factor structure would result only if (1) the fringe segment of the metropolitan area were so different ecologically from the city portion that the network of relationships among the subarea variables would differ greatly between the city and fringe, i.e., that there would be a significant difference between the correlation matrix for the city and the correlation matrix for the fringe; and (2) the number of subarea units in the fringe were large in comparison to the number for the central city.

Some relevant data on this problem might be of some interest here. I have taken the census tract data for San Juan, Puerto Rico and have alternatively factored the city data and the data for the total metropolitan area. The city analysis is based upon 86 tracts. The metropolitan analysis is based upon 137 tracts, since 51 tracts are located outside the city in the fringe. The fringe segment of the San Juan metropolitan area has a larger concentration of agricultural workers than does the city, and the fringe population has a lower social status as indi-

cated by education, income, and occupation [Schwirian and Rico-Velasco 1971]. The variables for the analysis are the typical social area analysis variables and were factored and rotated through the Oblimin Oblique Technique. The results appear in Table 2. From the table it may be noted that the factors correspond to the following dimensions: social rank (with female labor force participation), housing, fertility, and foreign born. The factor congruency scores between the matching factors of the city and the metropolitan area are all over 0.98. Thus, even though the fringe segment of the San Juan metropolitan area is somewhat differentiated ecologically from the city, the emergent factor structures are very similar. In interpreting these data, though, one caveat does need to be entered. On the basis of my experience in Puerto Rico it seems that the San Juan metropolitan area is fairly "true bound."

DISTANCE GRADIENT AND SECTOR MODELS

Studies of the spatial ecology of cities generally take as a starting point the geometric aspects of the Burgess [Park, Burgess, and McKenzie 1925; Hoyt 1939] theories. According to the Burgess model there is a direct relationship between neighborhood social status and distance from the center of the city. Thus, the concentric zone scheme associated with Burgess envisions a city whose inner core is made up of low status populations and whose outer fringe is populated by those of higher social status.

The main alternative model to that of Burgess is the sector model associated with Hoyt. On the basis of a study of a large number of American cities Hoyt argues that the status differences among subareas are distributed more by sector than by distance gradient. As described previously, a number of studies have provided support for the sector proposition, including those by Anderson and Egeland [1961], by Schwirian and Matre [1969], and by Schwirian and Smith [1971]. These studies have not served to invalidate the concentric zone approach but have led to a picture of the

TABLE 2.   Oblique Rotated Factors for San Juan, Puerto Rico City and SMSA, 1960

| Variables | | Factors | | | | | | |
| | City | | | | SMSA | | | |
	I	II	III	IV	I	II	III	IV
Occupation	.878	.063	.015	.195	.831	.090	.018	.233
Education	.908	−.091	−.008	.142	.904	−.030	.001	.171
Infertility	.254	.100	.830	.123	.398	.162	.719	.101
Women in Labor Force	.822	−.144	.271	−.147	.938	−.068	.121	−.089
Dwellings	−.079	.990	.050	.022	−.026	.993	.044	.022
Foreign Born	.349	.107	−.144	.762	.304	.076	.069	.810

Factor Congruency Scores

| City | | SMSA | | |
	I	II	III	IV
I	.992			
II		.993		
III			.955	
IV				.989

metropolis in which status is distributed by sector while familism, particularly housing, is distributed more by distance gradient.

One major criticism of studies examining either or both the concentric zone and sector models is that of the methodology employed in the delineation of urban sectors and zones. In applying the concentric zone scheme it is fairly common practice for investigators to mark off arbitrary distances from the center of the city that yield a regular spatial pattern of concentric circles usually at a one-mile distance from each other. In applying the sector model it has been usual practice for the investigator to lay off sectors at a set degree of angle from a north-south orientation at the city's core. Usually the sectors are at 30-degree width, but some studies have identified sectors of less while others have identified sectors of wider angle—perhaps even 90 degrees. The essential point here is that in empirical practice ecologists have used fairly arbitrary measures of sectors and concentric zones in the partitioning of urban subareas [see Murdie 1969, for example].

In using these arbitrary delineations ecologists have been all too eager to assume that their arbitrary urban geometrics are adequate operationalizations of the classic schemes.

There is danger in such practice. In a 1940 paper James Quinn pointed out that a crucial test of the basic models can be made only if *ecological* and not just arbitrary spatial delineations are followed. Thus in laying off the distance gradients within a city a time-cost function should be employed rather than a set mileage factor. And in laying off sectors rather than using angles the sectors should follow ecological barriers including main routes of transportation, railroad lines, bodies of water, and major topographical distortions. The main reasons ecologists have opted for the more arbitrary approach is, no doubt, because of limited time and funds. However, it is certainly time that we determine the analytical implications of the arbitrary techniques we so frequently use.

To obtain some relevant data for assessing the effect of arbitrary versus ecological delineation of urban subareas I have taken the census tract data for the Columbus, Ohio, SMSA and have applied two schemes to the delineation of the subareas. The first is arbitrary and is fairly representative of common practice today. First, distance zones were laid off at one-mile distances from each other starting at the center of the city (the intersection of Broad and High

Streets). Three mileage zones were identified. Then eight sectors were laid off at 45-degree angles to each other with the initial orientation being north-south and the orientation node being the main intersection. The census tracts at the 24 intersections of distance and sector demarcation were selected for analysis.

The second scheme is more in keeping with the ecological assumptions of the zone and sector models. To establish travel time zones from the center of the city we ascertained the average travel time in morning traffic between the central intersection and outlying points using the main arteries from the city's center to the periphery. Then zones were marked off at five-minute intervals. As might be expected, the resulting isochronal zones were not geometrically circular. They reflected distortions generated by density variations in housing and shopping and arterial confluence. Eight sectors were laid off which followed the city's rivers, main streets, and rail lines. At the intersection of each of the three isochronal zones and eight sectors a tract was selected for analysis. Thus this scheme yielded 24 tracts, as did the more arbitrary approach.

The question to be answered here is: do we reach the same conclusion about the distribution of subarea characteristics by sector and distance by using the arbitrary scheme and the ecological scheme for subarea delineation? Two variables were selected for investigation that in past studies were found to vary by distance and sector: (1) the median school years of the adult population of the tract, and (2) the percent of the dwellings in the area that contain only one

unit. The data are from the 1960 census of population. To aid in assessing the relative importance of distance and sector effects the two-way analysis of variance was calculated even though the tracts are a population and not a strict random sample. Two ANOVA's are performed, one for the data classified by the ecological scheme. The results are in Table 3.

In terms of the education variable both approaches lead us to reject the null hypothesis regarding the distance effect, and both schemes lead us to fail to reject the null hypothesis about the sector effect. Thus with both schemes we conclude that the distribution of education level in the Columbus SMSA is a function of distance gradient and not sector location. Approximately 41 percent of the total sum of squares of education level is explained by distance in the arbitrary scheme while approximately 30 percent is explained by distance in the ecological classification.

In terms of the housing variable both the arbitrary scheme and the ecological approach lead us to reject the null hypothesis about the distance effect and both lead us to fail to reject the null hypothesis about the sector effect. Thus with both schemes we conclude that the distribution of single unit housing in Columbus is a function of distance gradient and not sector. About 77 percent of the sum of squares of housing is explained by distance by the arbitrary scheme and about 56 percent is explained by the ecological scheme.

These data indicate that both the arbitrary and the ecological approach lead to the same conclusion about the distance and sector effects

TABLE 3. Two-Way ANOVA for Education and Housing Variables for Columbus, Ohio, 1960 SMSA Tracts Classified by Arbitrary and Ecological Sectors and Zones

Source	Education F ratio (% SS)		Housing F ratio (% SS)	
	Arbitrary	Ecological	Arbitrary	Ecological
Distance	8.91*(40.6)	4.67*(30.3)	47.60*(76.8)	17.47*(55.7)
Sector	1.72	1.06	2.12	1.97

* F is statistically significant beyond .05

on the two variables. Thus we tentatively conclude that if the arbitrary schemes are *detailed enough* they probably do little violence to our conclusions about the ecological distribution of phenomena in the city. Still further explorations of additional variables in other cities need to be made before any firm conclusions can be reached.

SEGREGATION MODELS

The measurement of residential segregation in cities has been the subject of several discourses. The issues generally revolve around (1) the criteria a segregation index should satisfy, (2) the appropriateness of alternative units of observation, and (3) the similarity in existing indexes both conceptually and empirically. It is not the purpose of this paper to review the various discussions since they have been so ably treated in other sources [see, for example, Taeuber and Taeuber 1965]. The focus of this discussion is upon the measurement of the clustering aspect of segregation which is generally ignored by most segregation indexes. The essential point here is that for most of the segregation indexes used in ecological research today there is any number of spatial patterns of ghetto distribution that yield the same segregation index value. For example, in Figure 3 are two cities divided into a number of city blocks. The shaded blocks are assumed to be totally black in population while the unshaded areas are assumed to be totally white. If the *index of dissimilarity*, which is one of the most frequently used segregation measures, is applied to the two distributions the resulting value is 100 in both cases. For the city on the left the blacks are highly ghettoized into four adjacent black blocks. However, for the city on the right the black blocks are scattered throughout the city such that each black block is adjacent only to totally white blocks. While the blacks of both cities are totally segregated according to the index of dissimilarity they are much less concentrated in city A than they are in city B. It seems on the basis of these figures that both total degree of segregation and extent of clustering are separate independent variables that would have differing behavioral consequences for both white and black urban populations.

Given that clustering is different from segregation, there should be an increasing concern among ecologists for the measurement of the clustering aspect of ethnic residential distributions. One attempt to handle this problem has been made by Virginia Sharp [1970a, 1970b]. Through discussion of the Sharp Index of Segregation we illustrate one attempt to measure residential segregation by focusing upon the clustering problem. The Sharp Index is:

$$S = 100 - \frac{\sum_{i=1}^{K} \left(\frac{\sum_{i=1}^{m} P_j}{m} \right)}{K}$$

where $K =$ the total number of areas for the city—in most cases census tracts or enumeration districts.

$m =$ the total number of blocks within tract i with the percentage of nonwhite occupied housing units greater than the city average of percent nonwhite occupied households.

$P_j =$ percent of blocks adjacent to block j (where block j contains greater than the city average percent nonwhite occupied housing units) containing less than the city average percent of nonwhite occupied housing units.

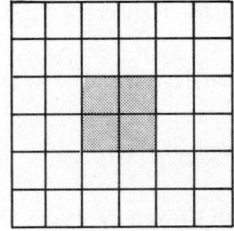 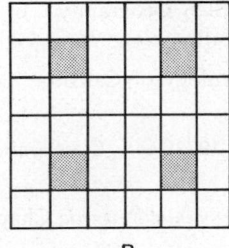

A   B

FIGURE 3. Distribution of Totally White (Unshaded) and Totally Black (Shaded) Blocks in Two Cities.

Applying this index to the examples in the figure we find the *S* for city A to be 38.5 percent, while the *S* for city B is 0.0. Thus for a black block in city A, on the average of 38.5 percent of the surrounding blocks will also be black blocks. For city B, on the average none of the surrounding blocks will be black. The higher the index the greater the percentage of adjacent blocks that will be black.

This index satisfies a number of criteria for "good" segregation indexes: (1) its base is a nonnegative function of the proportions black in the tracts, and the tract population; (2) the index value ranges from 0 to 100 with 0 equaling no concentration and 100 complete concentration; (3) the intermediate index values may cover the possible intermediate score values; (4)

the index is independent of the size of the total population and the percent black of the city; and (5) the index is applicable across cities where block data are available. The only major merit the index does not have is ease of hand computation. But with the use of computers the calculations may be done quickly and easily.

Even though this index is more difficult to calculate than the more standard measures used today it enables us to get a fix on the clustering aspect of residential location and segregation. While there might be some problems with the Sharp Index I hope the discussion of it will stimulate some interest, concern, and future work by ecologists along this line.

BIBLIOGRAPHY

Abu-Lughod, Janet L., 1969. "Testing the Theory of Social Area Analysis: The Ecology of Cairo, Egypt," *American Sociological Review*, 34: 198–211.

Anderson, Theodore R., and Lee L. Bean, 1961. "The Shevky-Bell Social Areas: Confirmation of Results and a Reinterpretation," *Social Forces*, 40: 119–124. [No. 25 in this volume.]

——, and Janice Egeland, 1961. "Spatial Aspects of Social Area Analysis," *American Sociological Review*, 26: 392–399. [No. 26 in this volume.]

Bell, Wendell, 1955. "Economic, Family, and Ethnic Status: An Empirical Test," *American Sociological Review*, 20: 45–52. [No. 23 in this volume.]

——, and Scott Greer, 1962. "Social Area Analysis and Its Critiques," *Pacific Sociological Review*, 5: 3–9.

Berry, Brian J. L., 1965. "Research Frontiers in Urban Geography," in Philip M. Hauser and Leo F. Schnore (eds.), *The Study of Urbanization*. New York: Wiley.

——, and Philip H. Rees, 1969. "The Factorial Ecology of Calcutta," *American Journal of Sociology*, 74: 445–491.

——, with the assistance of Katherine B. Smith, 1972. *City Classification Handbook*. New York: Wiley.

Blalock, Hubert M., 1964. *Causal Inferences in Nonexperimental Research*. Chapel Hill: University of North Carolina Press.

Breese, Gerald (ed.), 1969. *The City in Newly Developing Countries*. Englewood Cliffs, N.J.: Prentice-Hall.

Burgess, E. W., 1925. "The Growth of the City," in Robert E. Park, E. W. Burgess and R. D. McKenzie (eds.), *The City.* Chicago: University of Chicago Press.

Carey, G. W., 1966. "The Regional Interpretation of Manhattan Population and Housing Patterns Through Factor Analysis," *The Geographical Review,* 56: 551–569.

Carrier, N. H., and A. M. Farrag, 1959. "The Reduction of Errors in Census Population for Statistically Under-Developed Countries," *Population Studies* 12: 240–285.

Casetti, Emilio, 1971. "Equilibrium Land Values and Population Densities in an Urban Setting," *Economic Geography,* 47: 16–20.

Clark, Colin, 1951. "Urban Population Densities," *Journal of the Royal Statistical Society,* Series IA, 114: 490–496.

Clignet, Remi, and Joyce Sween, 1969. "Accra and Abidjan: A Comparative Examination of the Theory of Increase in Scale," *Urban Affairs Quarterly,* 4: 297–324.

Collison, Peter, 1960. "Occupation, Education, and Housing in an English City," *American Journal of Sociology,* LXV: 588–597.

Cressey, Paul F., 1938. "Population Succession in Chicago, 1898–1930," *American Journal of Sociology,* 44: 59–68.

Darroch, A. Gordon, and Wilfred G. Marston, 1971. "The Social Class Basis of Ethnic Residential Segregation: The Canadian Case," *American Journal of Sociology,* 77: 491–510.

de Vise, Pierre, 1969. *A Social Geography of Metropolitan Chicago.* Chicago: Northeastern Illinois Metropolitan Area Planning Commission.

Duncan, Otis Dudley, 1959. "Human Ecology and Population Studies," in Philip M. Hauser and Otis Dudley Duncan, *The Study of Population.* Chicago: The University of Chicago Press.

——, and Beverly Duncan, 1955. "Residential Distribution and Occupational Stratification," *American Journal of Sociology,* 60: 493–503. [No. 32 in this volume.]

——, and Stanley Lieberson, 1959. "Ethnic Segregation and Assimilation," *American Journal of Sociology,* 64: 364–374.

Fine, John, Norval D. Glenn, and Kenneth Monts, 1971. "The Residential Segregation of Occupational Groups in Central Cities and Suburbs," *Demography,* 8: 91–101. [No. 36 in this volume.]

Ford, Richard G., 1950. "Population Succession in Chicago," *American Journal of Sociology,* 56: 156–160.

Galle, Omer, Walter R. Gove, and J. Miller McPherson, 1972. "Population Density and Pathology: What are the Relationships for Man?" *Science,* 176: 23–30. [No. 16 in this volume.]

Gittus, Elizabeth, 1964–1965. "An Experiment in the Definition of Urban Subareas," *Transactions of the Bartlett Society,* II: 107–120.

Greer, Scott, 1962. *The Emerging City.* New York: The Free Press.

——, D. C. McElrath, P. W. Orleans, and D. W. Minar (eds.), 1968. *The New Urbanization.* New York: St. Martin's Press.

Hagerty, Lee J., 1971. "Another Look at the Burgess Hypothesis: Time as an Important Variable," *American Journal of Sociology,* 76: 1084–1093.

Harman, Harry H., 1967. *Modern Factor Analysis.* Chicago: University of Chicago Press.

Harris, Chauncy D., and Edward L. Ullman, 1945. "The Nature of Cities," *The Annals of the American Academy of Political and Social Science*, CCXLII: 7–17. [No. 17 in this volume.]

Hauser, Philip, and Leo F. Schnore (eds.) 1965. *The Study of Urbanization*. New York: Wiley.

Hawley, Amos H., and Otis Dudley Duncan, 1957. "Social Area Analysis: A Critical Appraisal," *Land Economics*, 33: 337–345.

Hoover, Edgar M., 1968. "The Evolving Form and Organization of the Metropolis," in Harvey S. Perloff and Lowdon Wingo, Jr., *Issues in Urban Economics*. Baltimore: The Johns Hopkins Press.

Hoyt, Homer, 1939. *The Structure and Growth of Residential Neighborhoods in the United States*. Washington: Federal Housing Administration.

Hunter, Alfred A., 1972. "Factorial Ecology: A Critique and Some Suggestions," *Demography*, 9: 107–118.

King, Leslie J., 1969. *Statistical Analysis in Geography*. Englewood Cliffs, N.J.: Prentice-Hall.

Latif, A. M., 1971a. "Factor Structure and Change of Alexandria, Egypt, 1947 and 1960." Unpublished paper, Department of Sociology, University of Manitoba. [No. 29 in this volume.]

——, 1971b. "Residential Segregation and Location of Status and Religious Groups in Alexandria, Egypt." Unpublished paper, Department of Sociology, University of Manitoba. [No. 35 in this volume.]

Lee, Douglass B., Jr., 1967. *Analysis and Description of Residential Segregation*. Ithaca, New York: Center for Housing and Environmental Studies, Division of Urban Studies, Cornell University.

Lieberson, Stanley, 1961. "The Impact of Residential Segregation on Ethnic Assimilation," *Social Forces*, 40: 52–57. [No. 40 in this volume.]

——, 1962. "Suburbs and Ethnic Residential Patterns," *American Journal of Sociology*, 67: 673–681. [No. 41 in this volume.]

Mayer, Harold, 1965. "A Survey of Urban Geography," In Philip Hauser and Leo F. Schnore (eds.), *The Study of Urbanization*. New York: Wiley.

Mehta, Surinder K., 1968. "Patterns of Residence in Poona (India) by Income, Education, and Occupation (1937–1965)," *American Journal of Sociology*, 60: 493–503. [No. 33 in this volume.]

Murdie, Robert A., 1969. *Factorial Ecology of Metropolitan Toronto, 1951–1961*. Chicago: Department of Geography, University of Chicago Research Paper No. 116.

Park, Robert E., Ernest W. Burgess, and Roderick D. McKenzie, 1925. *The City*. Chicago: University of Chicago Press.

Park, Robert A., 1952. *Human Communities*. New York: The Free Press.

Quinn, James, 1940. "The Burgess Zonal Hypothesis and Its Critiques," *American Sociological Review*, 5: 210–218.

Robson, B. T., 1969. *Urban Analysis*. Cambridge: Cambridge University Press.

Rummel, R. J., 1970. *Applied Factor Analysis*. Evanston, Ill.: Northwestern University Press.

Schnore, Leo F., 1965. "On the Spatial Structure of Cities in the Two Americas," in Philip M. Hauser and Leo F. Schnore (eds.), *The Study of Urbanization*. New York: Wiley.

——, and Philip C. Evenson, 1966. "Segregation in Southern Cities," *American Journal of Sociology*, 72: 58–67.

Schwirian, Kent P., and Anthony J. LaGreca, 1971. "An Ecological Analysis of Urban Mortality Rates," *Social Science Quarterly*, 52: 574–587.

——, and John W. Prehn, 1962. "An Axiomatic Theory of Urbanization," *American Sociological Review*, 27: 812–825.

——, and Marc D. Matre, 1969. "The Ecological Structure of Canadian Cities," research paper, Department of Sociology, The Ohio State University. [No. 27 in this volume.]

——, and Jesus Rico-Velasco, 1971. "The Residential Distribution of Status Groups in Puerto's Metropolitan Areas," *Demography*, 8: 81–90. [No. 34 in this volume.]

——, and Ruth K. Smith, 1971. "Primacy, Modernization, and Urban Structure: The Ecology of Puerto Rican Cities." Paper presented at the 1971 meetings of the American Sociological Association, Denver. [No. 28 in this volume.]

Sharp, Virginia, 1970a. "Changes in Spatial Residential Segregation Through Time: A Case Study." Columbus: Department of Geography, The Ohio State University.

——, 1970b. "Toward a Quantitative Measure of Spatial Segregation." Columbus: Department of Geography, The Ohio State University.

Sjoberg, Gideon, 1960. *The Pre-Industrial City*. Chicago: University of Chicago Press.

——, 1965. "Theory and Research in Urban Sociology," in Philip M. Hauser and Leo F. Schnore (eds.), *The Study of Urbanization*. New York: Wiley.

Stinchcombe, Arthur L., 1968. *Constructing Social Theories*. New York: Harcourt, Brace, and World.

Sweetser, Frank L., 1962. *The Social Ecology of Metropolitan Boston: 1960*. Massachusetts Department of Mental Health.

——, 1969. "Ecological Factors in Metropolitan Zones and Sectors," in Mattei Dogan and Stein Rokkan, *Quantitative Ecological Analysis in the Social Sciences*. Cambridge: M.I.T. Press.

Taeuber, Karl E., and Alma F. Taeuber, 1965. *Negroes in Cities*. Chicago: Aldine.

Thomlinson, Ralph, 1969. *Urban Structure, The Social and Spatial Character of Cities*. New York: Random House.

Timms, D. W. G., 1971. *The Urban Mosaic*. Cambridge: Cambridge University Press.

Tyron, Robert C., 1955. *Identification of Social Areas by Cluster Analysis*. Berkeley: University of California Press.

Udry, J. R., 1964. "Increasing Scale and Spatial Differentiation: New Tests of Two Theories from Shevky and Bell," *Social Forces*, 42: 403–413.

Uyeki, Eugene S., 1964. "Residential Distribution and Stratification, 1950-1960," *American Journal of Sociology*, 69: 491–498.

Van Arsdol, Maurice D., Jr., Santo F. Camilleri, and Calvin F. Schmid, 1958. "The Generality of the Urban Social Area Indexes," *American Sociological Review*, 23: 277–284. [No. 24 in this volume.]

——, Santo F. Camilleri, and Calvin F. Schmid, 1961. "An Investigation of the Utility of Urban Typology," *Pacific Sociological Review*, 4: 26–32.

——, Santo F. Camilleri, and Calvin F. Schmid, 1962. "Further Comments on the Utility of Urban Typology," *Pacific Sociological Review*, 5: 9–13.

Winsborough, Halliman H., 1965. "The Social Consequences of High Population Density," *Law and Contemporary Problems*, 30 (Winter): 120–126. [No. 15 in this volume.]

2

LESLIE J. KING

Models of Urban Land-Use Development

This paper reviews the general problem of constructing models for the forecasting of urban land-use development. In particular, the different analytical approaches adopted in constructing such models are discussed and the extent to which computer facilities were utilized is noted. This general review brings into focus several of the basic issues involved in modeling complex urban systems and prompts some questions as to the overall utility of social planning and engineering.

Particular emphasis is placed on those land-use studies and models that are essentially positive in their approach—that is, those that deal mainly with explanations of what has happened in urban land-use patterns and with the prediction of future developments consistent with these explanations or understandings. But some more challenging and provocative normative analyses—that is, studies of what land-use patterns should or could be consistent with certain objectives, constraints, and standards—have been proposed, for example, in the work on land-use design being pursued by the Southeastern Wisconsin Regional Planning Commission [Southeastern Wisconsin Regional Planning Commission 1968]. Much of this work is still only in the development phase, but again, it prompts an interesting set of questions concerning the philosophy and strategy of social planning. Some of these questions, for example, concerning the nature of the objective functions to be optimized and the value system implied, will be considered at a later point in this paper.

LAND-USE FORECASTING

The past efforts at forecasting urban land-use development appear to have been prompted by at least two major considerations:

1. It has been established analytically in some contexts (for example, trip-generation studies and financial analyses) and suspected for many others (for example, the overall level of social welfare in the city) that the pattern and nature of land uses are significant predictor variables.

2. The recognition that land-use patterns in any urban area are influenced, in turn, by many complex and interacting forces that are dynamic both over time and space. Within the city, for example, particular areas are specialized in certain land-use activities, but these functions may change over time as competing land uses wax and wane in their fortunes.

Given these considerations, it is perhaps not surprising to find that most of the major urban land-use studies have been set within the context of transportation planning programs. It is really only in these types of programs that serious consideration has been given in the past to systems analysis of the urban complex. This emphasis upon land-use and transportation systems will undoubtedly continue, but it is also possible that land-use forecasting will assume additional future importance in the con-

Reprinted by permission from David Sweet, ed. *Models of Urban Structure*, Lexington, Mass.: D. C. Heath, 1972, pp. 3–26.

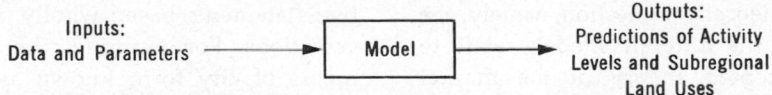

FIGURE 1. Land-Use Modeling Process

text of planning and shaping the form of the city (the relevance to zoning controls is obvious) and in predicting future requirement levels for municipal and other services.

The "typical" approach in land-use modeling is to assume first that certain factors or values are given (these are the so-called exogenous factors in some of the models); the model then generates certain levels of employment, and/or economic activity, and/or population by use of mathematical functions or statistical estimators. These derived levels are then allocated spatially to different areas of the city, again by the use of particular allocation functions; and finally, the future land uses in each area are derived by the use of land-requirement functions for the different allocated variables.

In very crude form then, the problem involves the three components shown in Figure 1. There are the data inputs which involve the exogenously determined values and the data to be used in estimating the different parameters of the model. (This latter phase is often referred to as the calibration of the model.) Then there is the model which performs the generation and allocation of the variables of interest. As discussed later, this model may be of many different forms, perhaps a set of rules and procedures for a game simulation on the one hand, or a set of complex mathematical functions on the other. Finally, there are the outputs which are the predicted levels of development for each land-use activity and each subregion of the city.

Obviously, the above comments grossly oversimplify both the modelling process and the nature of the land-use development models. The published literature, in fact, provides ample evidence of different ways of viewing these components. Britton Harris [1968], for example, on the basis of extensive experience in this field of research, emphasizes the following six major dimensions of land-use modelling:

1. *descriptive* or empirically based statements versus *analytic* or deductive formulations;
2. *holistic* approaches which attempt to deal with the total urban environment versus *partial* analyses focusing on certain selected aspects of the urban complex;
3. *macro* or aggregative models versus *micro* and behavioral models;
4. *static* versus *dynamic* formulations;
5. *deterministic* models which do not allow for chance elements in the land-use process, versus *probabilistic* models which attempt to deal with such elements; and
6. *simultaneous* versus *sequential* solutions.

Harris presents an excellent review of the different models of commercial, residential, and industrial land uses within the framework of his discussion of the dimensions of modeling.

Kilbridge et al. [1969] have also recently examined the dimensions of urban planning models. Their review is more general than that of Harris, and they stress (1) the *subject* of the model, (2) its *function*, (3) the *theory* on which the model is based, and (4) the *method* by which the model uses the theory.

Again, Wilson [1968], in discussing models of urban planning, constructs a "hierarchical relevance tree" setting out the tasks of such models and their interrelationships. He recognizes three broad levels of policy, design, and understanding. Within these categories, the following eight tasks are identified:

Policy:	(1) Action,
	(2) Goals,
	(3) Evaluation
Design:	(4) Plan formulation,
	(5) Design techniques,
	(6) Problem formulation
Understanding:	(7) System models,
	(8) Techniques

Lowry [1968], in discussing seven of the more highly developed land-use models, deals with a broader theoretical question, namely, the extent to which the different models relate to a generally accepted theory of the market mechanism for urban land. Lowry's contention is that "the market processes of transactions between willing buyers and willing sellers determine the spatial organization of urban activities." He defines an investment function by means of which owners appraise the merits of site improvements, and an evaluation function relating to the price a particular establishment will be willing to pay for a certain site.

Lowry's subsequent review of the seven models considers the extent to which these functions are treated—either implicitly or explicitly—in the models. Lee [1969] outlines an excellent discussion of the conceptual frameworks, the techniques, the model constructions, and the particular applications which have characterized urban land-use analyses to date. In the same vein, Lamb [1967] has reviewed some 10 different land use models with emphasis upon the analytical frameworks employed in them.

The reviews by the authors mentioned above are illuminating and provocative. But, with the exception of the ones by Lee and Lamb, they deal essentially with broader issues than those concerning this paper. The concern here is mainly with the methods and forms of land-use modeling, with some related features of computer utilization, and with selected problems associated with these approaches.

The discussion in this paper is strongly influenced by the comments of Geisler et al. [1962] on the continuum of systems-analysis techniques. They note that increasing abstraction in analysis involves moving from left to right along the scale shown in Figure 2.

Most of these levels are apparent in the literature of urban land-use studies. At the lower level, there have been numerous qualitative statements based wholly on empirical observations. For example, the idealized statements of city form known as the concentric zone theory [Burgess 1925], the sector or wedge hypothesis [Hoyt 1939], and the multiple nuclei theory [Harris and Ullman 1945] are all empirically based and together represent fairly low levels of abstraction.

In Figure 2 there are three levels involving some form of *simulation*, and some different applications of these analyses to urban land-use studies are reviewed in the following section. So-called "simulation studies" include a variety of different approaches and levels of abstraction. At one extreme are "hand simulations" such as those performed by the Northeastern Illinois Planning Commission [1968]. In that study, the patterns of Chicago's urban growth from 1965 to 1990 were forecast using five different models—the "dispersed regional city design," the "finger design," the "multi-cluster design," the "satellite cities-greenbelt design," and the "current trends development design." Each model was considered in turn and its implications were noted and evaluated by the researchers. The models were essentially qualitative statements of urban form, and no computer systems analysis was involved. By contrast, the simulation model developed by Crecine [1964] is far toward the other end of the systems-analysis continuum. In this study, "simulation" implies a particular approach using the computer to obtain the solution for a set of mathematical equations.

In this paper, hand simulations are ignored in regard to their content, and only those simulations involving the use of computers, in one way or another, are reviewed.

One-to-one simulations (the second level of abstraction in Figure 2) do not appear very relevant in urban land-use studies. In such simulations, reality is replicated, but at a different

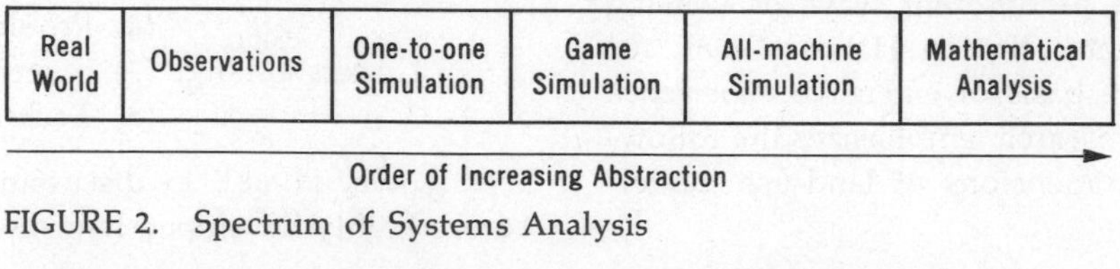

Real World	Observations	One-to-one Simulation	Game Simulation	All-machine Simulation	Mathematical Analysis

Order of Increasing Abstraction →

FIGURE 2. Spectrum of Systems Analysis

scale. The Link trainer used in flight training, or the wind tunnel testing of models, are essentially one-to-one simulations. Obviously, analogous models of the city would be prohibitive in cost even if they were useful in research and training, which is most doubtful. Urban situations are typically competitive ones, often involving conflict and stress, and reflecting a complex range of decisions made by both the private and public sectors. Hence, game simulations appear more appropriate, and three attempts at developing such simulations are reviewed in the following section.

Game simulations involve inputs from teams of players who act out certain decision-making roles within the constraints of a set of rules. By contrast, all-machine simulations involve samplings from probability functions, and the sampled values are the inputs to the models. Some of these probabilistic approaches to land-use modeling are also reviewed in the next section.

At the highest level of abstraction are the mathematical models for which the solutions are derived analytically. In land-use modeling there have been different forms of mathematical models employed. Some have involved sets of simultaneous linear equations, other linear programming formulations, and still others, non-linear differential equations and recursive programming. These efforts are also considered in the following section.

The importance of computer facilities varies from level to level. In game simulations, a computer typically serves as the central banker or information bank and monitors the operation of the game. In the City I game [Washington Center for Metropolitan Studies, 1968], for example, an IBM 1130 is involved. The development of software for these game simulations is costly; therefore, there are high computer expenses involved in the running of the game. All-machine simulations depend even more heavily upon computer facilities, and in the case of models such as that developed at the University of North Carolina, there is considerable expense involved in both program adaptation and machine runs.

The mathematical analyses, on the other hand, involve computers in a less intimate manner than do the simulation models. Problems of statistical estimation of parameters and solution of equations are easily programmed for the computer, and the time and costs involved usually are not as great as with the simulation studies. These comparisons are noted in more detail in the following review of specific models.

MODELS OF URBAN LAND-USE DEVELOPMENT

The major structural features of different land-use models are briefly reviewed below within the framework suggested by Figure 2.

GAME SIMULATIONS

By definition, a simulation is an attempt to replicate or to create a likeness of reality. But, since the effort is directed toward an understanding of the real-world system in question, there is always some simplification of reality involved. Orcutt [1963, 22] has noted that "simulation of a social system involves building and operating a model designed to represent those features of the system which are deemed to be significant in view of the objectives behind the simulation."

With regard to game simulations in particular, Geisler et al. [1962] note that their purpose is "the study of decision rules in the context of a given organization and environment." From the point of view of urban land-use modeling, this means an emphasis on the decision-making processes which determine the city's land-use pattern. The complexity of designing such game simulations for urban problems is obvious; for one thing, urban land-use patterns are in part determined by public sector decisions (for example, in highway planning, education, municipal services, and zoning) and also by private sector decisions (for example, in the location and development of businesses and residences and in travel patterns). Further, the intersectoral relationships—for example, between the public and private sectors, between employers and workers, and between productive activities—are exceedingly complex and hence difficult to untangle and to allow for in the game simulation. Notwithstanding the conceptual problems, the design problems, and the high development and operating costs of game simulations, some notable progress has been made along these lines by at least three groups. These are discussed below. Kibel [1970] has provided a much more detailed and informative review of the topic of urban gaming.

Cornell Land Use Game (CLUG)

The efforts at game simulation by the Cornell planning department have been directed by Dr. Alan G. Feldt [1965]. Essentially, the model allows for the development of an urban community, beginning with an open area in which the land is owned only by the game operator. The players begin with small amounts of capital, and they may use this to bid for land and to develop the properties they purchase. The model allows for residential, commercial, and industrial development, some simple input-output relations concerning payments and purchases among these sectors, and for property assessments to pay for the cost of municipal services. A number of variations on the basic game are possible [Feldt 1966].

Feldt [1965] notes several significant points with respect to this game simulation:

1. It is "fundamentally a communications device, intended for an educational milieu—whether that be in a formal classroom or in actual planning practice." The CLUG model is already widely known in both educational and professional circles in this country.
2. The game generally allows for the development of a city of approximately 250,000 population over 25 or so rounds. This takes about 15 to 20 hours, including instruction time. But, beyond this, the operation of the game becomes too awkward in terms of the amount of information to be processed. As reported to date, this game simulation has not made much use of computers; the City

I game reported on below is in many respects a computerized version of CLUG.
3. An attempt to modify the model to fit a real-world situation, specifically Syracuse, New York, revealed among other things that "the scale utilized in the elementary version of CLUG was too gross to allow for detailed handling of patterns of intraurban land-use development." For example, the basic residential unit in the early model consisted of 1000 employed persons and around 4000 total population.

No recent literature on this model seems available; presumably, work on the project is continuing.

METRO Urban Game Simulation

This game simulation is directed by Dr. Richard Duke and has been developed with support from Michigan State University, the University of Michigan, and the Tri-County Regional Planning Commission [Duke 1964]. The game simulation is a fairly complex one and is based on some earlier efforts in this field by the same group. Their Metropolis I was a hand simulation which was subsequently programmed for a computer as Metropolis II. All three models are tailored to the particulars of the urban community of Lansing, Mich., and data for this city are used to provide many of the parameter estimates.

Some brief comments are made here on three features of the game simulation, namely the player roles, the types of decisions which have to be made, and the specific simulation models which are involved.

The players each have two roles: one as a member of a government team (either central city or suburb or urbanizing township), and the other as a member of a professional association team (politicians, planners, land developers, and educators).

Decisions have to be made by each team concerning budgets, issues, and policies. These decisions are important inputs to the simulation models of voter response, macroeconomic and demographic growth, and population and economic-firm redistribution.

The game simulation, then, involves sequences of activities and interactions both between the players themselves and between the players and the computer.

Duke [1966] stresses that the aims of the METRO project are to

1. simulate growth patterns that would occur naturally, and enable their comparison with planned growth patterns;
2. illustrate the kinds of information which are available to decision makers;
3. similarly inform decision makers about the analytical techniques and models that are available for evaluating and implementing decisions; and
4. to provide information on the implications for urban development of alternative action programs.

Environmentrics

The original City I model developed by this group under the direction of Dr. Peter House [Washington Center for Metropolitan Studies 1968] was a computerized version which incorporated elements of both the CLUG and Metropolis models. The game simulation was programmed for an IBM 1130 computer. Typically, it involved nine teams of four to five players each, and there were two main groups in the game—the public and the private sectors. The former controlled by a "bureaucracy" comprising an elected mayor and two councillors, and the department of zoning, highways, education, public works and safety, and finance. Eight of the teams were thereby represented on this bureaucracy, while the ninth remaining team functioned as the "mass media." The other players on the eight teams and the "mass media" team functioned as the private sector.

The public sector had to work out a budget and plan for different public-sector activities—for example, providing fire and police services and building highways and schools. In addition, they acted on requests from the private sector—concerning zoning changes, etc.

The private sector could purchase and develop properties as they chose. A number of industrial, commercial, and residential developments were possible, and each of these involved certain development costs, service and transportation costs, taxes, and income. A set of intersectoral relations were specified in the model.

As in the METRO project, the computer provided projections of population and employment levels, and subregional allocations of these variables.

There were a number of more subtle possibilities in the model, including provisions for borrowing money from the central computer, for renovating or even demolishing properties, and for variations in pricing policies associated with service establishments.

The successor to the City I game, developed by House and his colleagues, is the City II model, which incorporates further refinements. A regional model has also been developed.

These game simulations are not strictly land-use forecasting techniques. By their very nature, they do not involve a set of mathematical solutions and depending to some extent upon the inclinations of the players, they may or may not emphasize questions concerning the land-use pattern of the city. They are all non-zero-sum games, which means that the gains by any one team do not have to be balanced by the losses of another, and certainly in the case of the City I game, it is possible for the players to emphasize the role-playing activities without any realistic concern for the spatial patterning of the urban complex. But, the pedagogical values of these game simulations for policymakers, planners, and educators cannot be stressed enough. They give a player a "feel" for the complexity of relationships and decision-making processes which dictate the land-use pattern of the city. Also, it would seem quite possible to use these game simulations under fairly well-controlled rules to consider the implications of certain alternative policies and programs. Duke [1966] has noted this possibility with regard to the METRO project.

MACHINE SIMULATIONS

Simulations which focus on what are assumed to be random or chance elements in the determination of urban land-use patterns are considered here. These models involve variables whose behaviors are best described by probability distributions. Random samplings are made by the computer to simulate these probability distributions, and the solutions to the models are inferred from the behavior of these random numbers. It is because these models involve the use of randomly chosen numbers that they have been called "Monte Carlo" methods.

There are three qualifications which should be made at this point. The first is a technical one and need not concern us further. It is that Monte Carlo methods are much more general and powerful than their application in simulating probabilistic processes (which is the role described here) might suggest. Hammersley and Handscomb [1964] make this point very clear. Second, in urban land-use modeling, a number of other machine simulations have been proposed that are not properly classified as Monte Carlo models. In fact, B. Harris [1961] has noted four conditions, any one or combinations of which might justify the use of simulation techniques:

1. a mathematical solution is impossible because too many variables are involved;
2. the relationships between variables may not be simple linear ones;
3. the model is dynamic and the important lags are long ones; and
4. the processes involved are stochastic (probabilistic).

There are studies by Crecine [1964], Ellis [1967], Schlager [1964], the Arthur D. Little Company [1966], Forrester [1969], and the Center for Real Estate and Urban Economics (Berkeley) [1968] that all use machine simulation techniques, especially in solving sets of difference equations to obtain land-use and related forecasts. Some of these models are described in the section below on mathematical analyses.

The third qualification is that Monte Carlo models represent an essentially low-level approach to the study of probabilistic systems, and again there are other land-use studies, notably by Curtis Harris [1968] and the Arthur D. Little Company [1966], that develop more formal stochastic models of land-use processes. These also will be mentioned later.

In the context of systems analysis of urban land-use, Monte Carlo models are associated especially with the University of North Carolina planning group [Donnelly et al. 1964]. Their model simulates the conversion of open space into residential land use. A map of the study area is divided into a large number of square grid cells, and for each cell available for development an "attractiveness measure" is computed. A given number of new residential units have to be located in each prediction period, and these are assigned to the different cells by the use of random numbers and probability functions which reflect the distribution of attractiveness measures.

This North Carolina model is highly aggregative (emphasizing development), and it is restricted to only residential land use. Carlson [1968] has reviewed the operational aspects of the model and reported on the results of a questionnaire survey of 175 planning agencies in the United States concerning its use. Problems loomed large concerning a lack of staff programmers capable of adapting the model and the inability or unwillingness to collect the data required in computing the attractiveness measures. Carlson, however, is optimistic as to the utility of the model, and he provides some useful guidelines for its adaptation.

A Monte Carlo approach to predicting future land-use changes, which is similar in its design to the North Carolina work, has been used by Morrill in studying the expansion of the residential urban fringe [Morrill 1965] and the negro ghetto [Morrill 1965].

MATHEMATICAL ANALYSES

Models employing sets of mathematical equations that are solved to yield forecasts of economic activity and land-use requirements for different subregions of the city are considered below. The types of mathematical equations vary from model to model, and the methods of obtaining solutions to these equations may involve mathematical analysis or some form of simulation.

The classical approach to mathematical prediction, at least in the physical sciences, has been to structure a set of differential equations. Such equations express the rate of change in particular variables as functions of the changes in other variables, and they can be solved to yield values for the system variables for any points in time in the future (or in the past). In the social sciences, differential equations have been used in studying phenomena such as population growth and changes in different economic variables, and it is perhaps not surprising that attempts have been made to structure differential equations for the prediction of urban land-use levels.

The best documented attempt along these lines was the work done on the POLIMETRIC model in Boston. This model, which has since been discarded by the Boston group, has been described by Irwin and Brand [1965]:

"Basically, it is comprised of a series of nonlinear differential equations of the following form:

$$\frac{dR_{i\ell}}{dt} = f\left[R_{i\ell}\left(\sum_{p}^{L} M_{p\ell} \sum_{p=1}^{L} M^t_{\ell p} \right) \right].$$

where

i = number of the located variable
$\quad (i = 1, 2, \ldots, i, \ldots, N)$
ℓ = number of the subregion
$\quad (\ell = 1, 2, \ldots, \ell, p, \ldots, L).$

Stated in words, the rate of change over time t of activity i in subregion ℓ is a function of the present level of the activity in subregion ℓ, $(R_{i\ell})$, plus a function of all movements of the activity i from all other subregions p into subregions ℓ,

$$\left(\sum_{p=1}^{L} M^t_{\ell p} \right)$$

minus all movements of that activity i from the subregion ℓ out to all other subregions

$$\left(\sum_{p=1}^{L} M^t_{p\ell} \right)$$

These in- and out-movements are called in-migrations and out-migrations."

This model appears to have been discarded largely because of problems inherent in the data requirements [Irwin and Brand 1965]. The matrix of in- and out-migrations which is suggested by the model presumably would involve extremely difficult estimation problems. The model subsequently was modified by the Delaware Valley Planning Commission [Seidman 1969] as the basis of their residential and manufacturing location submodels, but in these versions, the differential-equation form was not retained.

Aside from its use of differential equations to predict changes over time, the POLIMETRIC model was somewhat distinctive in its attempts to handle nonlinear relationships. By contrast, most of the other well-known land-use models deal with linear relationships, often in the form of multiple-regression equations. The EMPIRIC model developed for the Boston area illustrates this point. This model distinguishes between certain output or *located variables* (specifically, white-collar and blue-collar population, retail and wholesale employment, manufacturing employment, all other employment, total resident population, total employment) that are to be predicted for each subregion in the city and the predictor or *locator variables* (namely, intensities of land use, automobile and transit accessibilities, quality of water and sewage-disposal systems). The model is based on the notion that "the change in the subregional share of located variable i in subregion ℓ is proportional to (1) the change in the subregional share of all other located variables in subregion ℓ, (2) the change in the subregional share of a number of locator variables in subregion ℓ, and (3) the absolute value of the subregional shares of other locator variables" [Irwin and Brand, 1965].

In equation form, the model is

$$\Delta R_i = \sum_{\substack{j=i \\ j \neq i}}^{M} a_{ij} \, \Delta R_j + \sum_{k=1}^{M} b_{ik} \, (Z_k \text{ or } \Delta Z_k),$$

where

ΔR = change in located variable
     ($i, j = 1, 2, \ldots, N$)
Zk = value of kth locator variable
     at start of forecast period
ΔZ = change in locator variable

and a_{ij} and b_{ik} are coefficients estimated from data for 1950 and 1960.

There is one such equation for each located variable and "the equations are used to estimate future subregional shares of each located variable by substituting into each equation the pertinent values of the locator variables for the subregion and solving the equations simultaneously for the subregional located variable." [Hill, Brand, and Hanson 1965]. These shares are then converted into absolute levels through multiplication by the exogenously determined control levels for each of the located variables.

The EMPIRIC model is operational and is currently used for projection and analysis in Boston; it will likely be applied further in other cities.

Another well-documented model involving sets of equations is the one developed by Lowry [1964]. This model uses an iterative procedure to forecast the spatial distribution of population and employment in a city given an exogenously determined level of basic employment, that is, employment in "export" industries which "are relatively unconstrained in local site selection by problems of access to local markets."

The Lowry model consists of nine structural equations which generate retail employment and number of households in the city, allocate these totals among the subregions of the city by use of functions in which accessibility indices appear, and compute the amount of land required for retail establishments in each subregion.

The Lowry model was developed originally for Pittsburgh, and subsequently it appears to have been adapted to the needs of other groups, particularly the Bay Area Simulation Study [Center for Real Estate and Urban Economics, 1968]. Garin and Rogers [1966] have discussed possible alternative formulations of the model in matrix algebra terms, while Crecine [1964] has developed a time-oriented version of the model. Crecine's work apparently was prompted by dissatisfaction with three of the characteristics of the Lowry model. First, the original model is a static-equilibrium one and assumes that, in any particular forecast period, all retail establishments and households can move. Second, the households in the model are not differentiated by type, and finally, the model relates to a "region" rather than to the particular boundaries of a city. In Crecine's TOMM model, therefore, only a portion of the establishments and households can move in any time period, households are differentiated by income, housing, and social characteristics, and city census tracts are used as the areal units for forecasting. Many of the equations in the model now become difference equations relating the levels at one time period to those of the previous time periods.

There are other models involving sets of equations which might be cited. The Activities Allocation model developed by the Delaware Valley Regional Planning Commission [Seidman 1964], for example, actually involves a set of seven submodels which are run sequentially for five-year recursion periods for the nine-county Philadelphia region.

In all of the above models, whether they are linear or nonlinear in form and whether they are solved iteratively to arrive at an equilibrium situation or recursively to project the amount of change occurring in the future, there is no explicit consideration of an overall objective function and related constraints and the types of normative solutions which these features would suggest. There have been attempts, however, to structure normative models of urban land use by way of mathematical programming techniques.

Perhaps the best known of these attempts is the Herbert-Stevens [1960] model. This involves a linear program in which households are distributed spatially so as to maximize the aggregate "rent-paying ability." The objective function for the model is

$$\max Z = \sum_k \sum_i \sum_h x_{ih}^k (b_{ih} - c_{ih}^k),$$

where

Z = aggregate rent-paying ability
k = subscript for regions
i = subscript for household groups or types
h = subscript for residential bundles or packages of characteristics
x = solution variable for number of households
b = the residential budget (including transportation)
c = annual residential cost, exclusive of site cost.

The solution was subject to three constraints:

$$\sum_i \sum_h s_{ih} x_{ih}^k \leqslant L^k \qquad (1)$$

$$\sum_k \sum_h - x_{ih}^k = N_i \qquad (2)$$

$$\text{all } x_{ih}^k \geqslant 0. \qquad (3)$$

where

s = site area
L = land area available for residential use
N = exogenous number of households to be located.

As in any linear programming solution where the primal problem involves maximization, there is a dual problem of minimization. In this case, it is total aggregate costs which are minimized.

The model, then, provides for the maximization of the sum of the budget residuals available for land rent. But, in fact, this solution proved elusive, and subsequent modifications of the model sought only to maximize the "bid rent," defined as "a budget residual covering the entire residential package of site and structure (but not the cost of transportation)" [Lowry 1968]. Because of the detailed data requirements of this model, few planning agencies have applied it in practice [Hemmens 1968].

Linear programming also has been used in the Southeastern Wisconsin Regional Planning Commission (SEWRPC) Land-Use Simulation Model. [Southeastern Wisconsin Regional Planning Commission 1966]. In the residential and industrial sectors of this model, linear programs are formulated that provide for the minimization of land-development costs. In addition, the residential land-development process over time is handled by way of recursive linear programming, in which the solution of a program for one time period provides the parameters for the succeeding linear program [Schlager 1966]. Housing demand is thus allowed to build up over time.

In its early work on the land-use design model (as distinct from the land-use and economic simulation studies), the SEWRPC group contemplated the use of linear and dynamic programming. However, these efforts have given way to a model based on an alternative form of mathematical analysis, linear graph theory [Southeastern Wisconsin Regional Planning Commission 1968].

For completeness, one approach to the mathematical modeling of urban land-use systems is mentioned briefly. This involves the formulation of stochastic models, that is, models of probabilistic processes operating over time. As part of the San Francisco CRP study, a Markov chain analysis of the deterioration of housing units was undertaken [Wolfe 1967]. The states of the model were different levels of housing quality, and there were transition probabilities for the movements from one state to another. Deterioration was an absorbing state, and the behavior of the system over time with respect to this state could be studied.

Harris [1968] has outlined a more general stochastic model for residential development. A parcel of land may be developed or undeveloped, and given m parcels of land, there are thus 2^m states of development for the whole area. The model is semi-Markovian in the sense that there is a waiting time, in itself a random variate, associated with the move from one state to another. More recently, Bourne [1969] has suggested the use of a transition probability matrix in conjunction with regression equations as a means of allocating land-use development. For each subarea of the city, regression analyses yield estimates of the levels of new construction. Also derived for each subarea is a matrix of transition probabilities describing the change over time from one land-use type to another. The regression estimates are combined with these probabilities to predict the future land-use structure of the subarea.

CHARACTERISTICS OF LAND-USE MODELS

The history of the attempts to forecast urban land development is comparatively short, most of the efforts having been made in the current decade. Most of the models reviewed above, then, are essentially first- or second-generation models and the technical features and shortcomings of the models are not yet documented in much detail. But there are five characteristics which can be noted, starting with computer-system requirements.

Computer-System Requirements

A recent survey by Hemmens [1968] has provided some valuable information on this point, As part of a questionnaire survey of large planning agencies, the extent and level of computer use was probed. Hemmens reports that

> Most of the agencies which reported their computer usage utilize more than one computer system. Typically, they use a small computer which is operated by the agency itself or by another public agency, and they rent time on a large computer from a service bureau or other vendor.

The reliance upon service bureaus is more pronounced in the case of those agencies heavily committed to land-use forecasting by use of the mathematical models discussed above. The Bay Area Transportation Commission models are to operate on a CDC 3800 computer with 65K memory; the Delaware Valley RPC models and the Boston EMPIRIC model require IBM 7094 or equivalent capability; the SEWRPC land-use simulation was originally programmed only for an IBM 1620, but the later models are designed for the IBM 360 system.

Given the complexity of the simulations which may be involved and/or the large number of multiple-regression equations which may have to be solved, it is clear that the use of sophisticated land-use forecasting models will require access to computers of at least the IBM 7090 series level and, increasingly, of the 360 series level. Even allowing for access to such computer facilities, the operating costs of these models are high. The metropolis model, for example, requires more than 15 minutes of IBM 7090 time per time period; while the activities allocation model of the Delaware RPC requires as much as 50 minutes of IBM 7094 time for one run [Lamb 1967].

Aggregation Problems

In most of the urban land-use studies there are at least three forms of aggregation problems which have to be resolved.

The first is the level of spatial aggregation, which has to do with the number of subregions comprising the city for which forecasts are to be made. Lowry in his empirical analysis of the Pittsburgh data used 650 one-square-mile tracts; the EMPIRIC model, on the other hand, was tested originally for 29 subregions representing the Boston region and, later, for 123 and 134 sub-regions. In the context of estimating parameters and analyzing relationships, this decision as to the level of spatial aggregation is not unimportant. It is clear, for example, that parameter estimates for one level of aggregation will not be applicable at another and, consequently, many computations will have to be repeated if forecasts are required for these different levels. Again, relationships which hold at one level may not be as significant at another. This was apparent in some of the sensitivity analyses on the EMPIRIC model [Irwin and Brand 1965]. These kinds of considerations, which in one sense are problems of spatial filtering, are discussed in the spatial-statistics literature [King 1968], and in the statements on ecological fallacies in theory construction [Goodman 1959]. Fleet and Robertson [1968] have at least drawn attention to the issues in the context of trip-generation studies.

A second problem of aggregation has to do with the number of variables employed in the model. Most of the models are highly aggregative in this respect; the EMPIRIC model, for example, deals with only seven located variables, and the Lowry model deals with even fewer. Obviously, the utility of the models would be enhanced by greater detail in the number of forecasted variables, but problems of data availability loom large in this regard. In speaking of the variables used in land-use and urban development studies, there is also another important aspect to the problem of aggregation. This has to do with the macro level on which the studies focus, and the fact that questions of individual behavior are ignored. The need for disaggregation along these lines will be discussed in greater detail in the subsequent section on "underlying theory."

Finally, there is aggregation over time with respect to the length of the forecast periods. Most of the models employ five- or ten-year periods, which appear satisfactory in view of the typical goal for most planning agencies of developing a master plan for some future date near the turn of this century. Again, disaggregation with respect to this feature would pose serious problems in regard to data for parameter estimation and forecasting.

Data Availability

The urban development models, for the most part, are particularly demanding regarding data requirements. Carlson [1968], in his survey related to the potential use of the North Carolina model, reported that only 9 of the 135 agencies responding had already collected all the necessary data for the model, while 23 percent of the respondents felt that the data requirements were excessive. The main difficulty in all the models is that the data have to be available for the areal subregions of the city, and there must also exist some historical data for the city, to obtain estimates of the model's parameters (that is, to calibrate the model). The latter point emphasizes again one of spatial-aggregation problems, namely, that the model parameters typically are estimated from historical data for the city as a whole and are then used in obtaining forecasts for very detailed subregions of the city!

Alonso [1968] has drawn attention to some important problems concerning data quality. He cautions against measurement error and the compounding of such errors in modeling situation, and questions whether, in urban land-use studies, the models might not have outrun the capacity of the data. Alonso suggests that, if this is the case, then the quality of the data might have resulted in a deterioration of the predictions. Alonso offers the following "rules of thumb" for model building:

1. avoid intercorrelated variables;
2. add where possible;
3. if addition is not possible, multiply or divide;
4. avoid, as far as possible, taking differences or raising variables to powers; and
5. avoid as far as possible models which proceed by chains.

Underlying Theory

Some comments on the theoretical bases of urban land-development models are in order, because as Lowry [1968] notes, "in choosing a model for a particular purpose, the planner will do well to understand what is left out as well as what is left in."

For the most part, the models reviewed in this report have dealt with macro-level variables and relationships. Indeed, with but few exceptions, the models have been structured along the lines of macroeconomic models, with the emphasis being placed typically upon problems of estimation and forecasting, rather than upon questions related to the underlying theory. This is true, for example, of the EMPIRIC, the BASS, and the Lowry models. Not surprising, Lowry [1968] can find little explicit consideration of a theory of the urban land market in his review of seven well-known models.

It is becoming clear, however, that these aggregate statements are not enough, and that increased attention must be given to the theory of individual behavior and the nature of the decision-making processes. B. Harris et al. [1968] in summarizing the conclusions of the Dartmouth conference notes that "there is a strong but not unanimous feeling among model-builders that one direction for improving the accuracy with which models reproduce the real world lies in the expansion of studies of the behavior of decision units." Once this possibility is admitted, however, the problems of data availability are increased many times. By the same token, it is well established that the use of aggregate spatial data does not allow for meaningful statements to be made about individual behavior, and that if the new direction in modeling is to be pursued, then individual survey data tabulated by subregions and cross classified must be obtained. It is important to note that considerable progress is being made in the direction of developing behavioral models of urban spatial structure which should have important ramifications for the modeling of urban land use.

Lowry's [1968] criticism of existing land-use models concerning their apparent disregard of any theory of land market mechanisms, can be extended also to other theoretical topics of urban spatial structure. . . . In general, the argument could be made that the urban land-use models developed to date, have not been strongly *spatial* in character. Admittedly, they have sought to allocate land-uses by subregions and they have in different cases employed certain distance-decay relationships in handling accessibility questions and travel patterns, but for the most part, they have ignored the quite extensive and varied literature on urban spatial structure developed especially by the economists, geographers, regional scientists, and sociologists.

The third point with regard to the theoretical bases of the land-use models has to do with the lack of any broader contexts within which the models are set. That is to say, the models are often neatly structured as regards the particular analytical questions they were designed to solve, but there is generally lacking any consideration of the relationships and feedback loops between the analysis and other facets of the social planning task. Clearly, a land-use allocation model must take for granted certain goals and objective functions and in turn, the solutions which it yields may be only some of the alternatives confronting society. These questions of goal formulations, of defining appropriate utility functions, of evaluating and choosing between alternatives, and of deciding upon means and policies whereby implementation takes place are themselves proper subjects of study and topics for theoretical reasoning. It is these considerations which scholars such as Boyce, Day, and McDonald [1969] and B. Harris [1961] are pursuing.

One final point which should be made concerning the theoretical bases of the urban land-development models is that they deal with the city essentially as a *closed system*. The models generally take as given certain exogenous forecasts of regional employment and population. In the cases of most of the models discussed up to this point, this feature imposes no really serious constraint since the models are developed for large metropolitan regions and the possible errors stemming from a lack of closure are probably less serious than those associated with the internal workings of the model. But, for small urban areas, the exogenous factors are certain to be much more important in a relative sense, and the internal urban forecasts may be rendered invalid by only a small variation in these exogenous levels. The notions of spatial linkages and spatial hierarchies are relevant in this context, and the applications of sophisticated urban land-development models certainly should be consistent with these patterns.

Application of Models

In a review of the applications of the above models to specific planning problems, two interesting points emerge. First, it is clear that much of the model development has been accomplished by "in-shop" research but that this work often has not been tied too closely to the immediate problems faced by the planning group in question as regards developing a master plan for its region. This is illustrated by the experiences of SEWRPC. This group has published some of the more intriguing and advanced mathematical statements of urban land-use forecasting, but, in fact, their own regional land-use plan for 1990 was developed by conventional, nonanalytic methods and the land-use simulation model was used merely in testing the consequences of alternative policies [Southeastern Wisconsin Regional Planning Commission, 1968]. The more recent work of this group on the land-use design model is purely an in-shop research project sponsored by HUD.

Second, many planning agencies, in some cases those of large metropolitan areas, are not involved as yet either in model-building or analytical land-use forecasting. The work of the Northeastern Illinois Planning Commission illustrates this point. Their recommended land-use plan for Chicago for 1990 was derived from a hand simulation in which the consequences of five different qualitative models of urban form were evaluated.

The limited extent of the application of the land-use models is borne out in several recent reports. Hemmens [1968] in his survey of some 34 major planning agencies received responses from 26, and of these, only 16 "reported on either current usage or active development of models." Hemmens notes the difficulties these agencies experience in developing the models and making them operational from the point of view of staffing and data facilities. Further, he stresses the lack of communication between agencies and the related absence of any serious cumulative work on the different models. Boyce, Day, and McDonald [1970], in a survey

of the plan-making process and evaluation methodologies associated with the work of the 13 largest planning programs, notes that as of 1969 only four of them—for Baltimore, Boston, Philadelphia, and the Twin Cities—have actually used computer models of urban growth and development to elaborate a set of alternatives.

The work on urban development models, then, has still a long way to go before operational packaged models are available for wide dissemination and use by small planning agencies. The increasing involvement of several commercial consulting firms in this area of land-use planning will possibly facilitate the development of these standard model procedures, although, typically, these privately developed models suffer from a lack of exposure in the published literature. On a national level, HUD could provide a valuable service by promoting the development of a land-use-model package similar to the transportation-network-analysis package provided by the Bureau of Public Roads.

Given the likelihood that these packaged models will be available in the not-too-distant future, and assuming that the numbers of agency personnel better trained in analytical techniques will slowly increase, then it might seem premature for small planning agencies to contemplate seriously the implementation of expensive and "low-reliability" forecasting schemes at this time.

CONCLUSIONS AND RECOMMENDATIONS

This paper was prepared originally as part of a specific report to the planning agency of a city of under 100,000 population. The recommendations included in that report are reproduced here in summary of some of the points made above. In structuring such recommendations for small metropolitan centers it is important to keep in mind certain background considerations:

1. It is unlikely that small planning agencies either will have, or can afford, the necessary resources of hardware and manpower for

the development, implementation, and monitoring of complex, computerized models of urban land use. At present, these models are far too expensive, both in development and operating costs, for small agencies to experiment with.

2. The overall state of the art in land-use modeling is not that advanced, and no agency or consulting firm can provide a readily adaptable, packaged land-use model which small cities might be able to use.

3. The sensitivity of land-use model projections to changes in the exogenous factors has not yet been investigated in detail. Therefore, for urban economies in which the external spatial linkages are strong, the relevance of existing land-use-forecasting techniques is not clearly established.

4. The previous point notwithstanding, small urban centers with specialized economies may be comparatively easy to model as regards the relevant endogenous variables and the important relationships.

The following general recommendations might be emphasized:

1. Interested planning agencies undertake a serious evaluation of the overall goals towards which their efforts in land-use analysis are to be directed. If the aim is simply to derive parameters for input to transportation programs, then one set of procedures will be adequate. If the goal is to design land-use plans for the city consistent with certain objectives and constraints, then other approaches will be necessary. Specification of goals is critical.

2. Agencies might begin simply with the development of regression analyses for the prediction of land uses by census tracts or traffic zones within the city. These models could utilize standard stepwise regression programs, could emphasize the effects on land-use patterns of a few easily obtained variables, and could be calibrated with historical data. These efforts would at least provide a framework for organizing existing land-use data and, depending upon the results, they may offer a convenient approach to forecasting and sensitivity analysis. There are some simple techniques such as shift analysis which also could be incorporated into the regression analyses.

3. Agencies seriously consider the pedagogical value to be derived from the participation of their personnel and selected community leaders and citizens in game-simulation sessions conducted by Environmetrics or the METRO project group.

BIBLIOGRAPHY*

Alonso, W., 1968. "The Quality of Data and the Choice and Design of Predictive Models," Highway Research Board Special Report No. 97. Washington, D.C.: Highway Research Board, pp. 178–192.

Arthur D. Little Corp., 1966. "Model of San Francisco Housing Market," San Francisco CRP C–65400.

---

* Since this paper was prepared a number of other related statements have appeared in journals such as *Land Economics, Environment and Planning,* and *The Journal of the American Institute of Planners.*

Bourne, L. S., 1969. "A Spatial Allocation-Land Use Conversion Model of Urban Growth," *Journal of Regional Science*, 9: 261–272.

Boyce, D. E., N. D. Day, and C. McDonald, 1970. *Metropolitan Plan Making.* Philadelphia: Regional Science Research Institute Monograph Series No. 4.

Burgess, E. W., 1925. "The Growth of the City: An Introduction to a Research Project," in R. E. Park et al., *The City.* Chicago: University of Chicago Press, pp. 47–62.

Carlson, E. D., 1968. "Operational Aspects of a Probabilistic Model for Residential Growth," University of North Carolina, Environmental Policies and Urban Development Thesis Series No. 10. 89 pp.

Center for Real Estate and Urban Economics, 1968. "Jobs, People and Land. Bay Area Simulation Study." Berkeley: Special Report No. 6.

Crecine, J. P., 1964. "TOMM," Pittsburgh CRP Technical Bulletin No. 6. 18 pp.

Donnelly, T. G., et al., 1964. "A Probabilistic Model for Residential Growth." University of North Carolina: Urban Research Monograph.

Duke, R. D., 1964. *Gaming-Simulation in Urban Research.* Institute for Community Development and Services, East Lansing: MSU.

——, 1966. "The METRO Urban Game Simulation: An Experiment in In-Service Training," *Proceedings of the Fourth Annual Conference on Urban Planning and Information Systems*, Berkeley, pp. 142–154.

Ellis, R. H., 1967. "Modeling of Household Location: A Statistical Approach," *Highway Research Record*, No. 207, pp. 42–52.

Feldt, A. G., 1965. "The Cornell Land Use Game." Miscellaneous Paper No. 3, Center for Housing and Environmental Studies, Cornell University.

——, 1966. "Current Developments in Heuristic Gaming at Cornell University," *Proceedings of the Fourth Annual Conference on Urban Planning and Information Systems*, Berkeley, pp. 160–167.

Fleet, C. R., and S. R. Robertson, 1968. "Trip Generation in the Transportation Process," *Highway Research Record*, No. 240, pp. 11–31.

Forrester, J. W., 1969. *Urban Dynamics.* Cambridge, Mass: M.I.T. Press.

Garin, R. A. (comment by A. Rogers), 1966. "A Matrix Formation of the Lowry Model for Intrametropolitan Activity Allocation," *Journal of the American Institute of Planners*, 32: 361–366.

Geisler, M. A., W. W. Haythorn, and W. A. Steger, 1962. "Simulation and the Logistics Systems Laboratory," Rand Corp. Mem. RM–3281–PR.

Goodman, L. A., 1959. "Some Alternatives to Ecological Correlation," *American Journal of Sociology*, 64: 610–625.

Hammersley, J. M., and D. C. Handscomb, 1964. *Monte Carlo Methods.* London: Methuen and Co., Ltd., pp. 1–9.

Harris, B., 1961. "Some Problems in the Theory of Intra-Urban Location," *Operations Research*, 9: 695–721.

——, 1968. "Quantitative Models of Urban Development: Their Role in Metropolitan Policy-Making," in H. S. Perloff and L. Wingo (eds.), *Issues in Urban Economics.* Baltimore: The Johns Hopkins Press, pp. 363–412.

——, et al., 1968. "Construction of Models." Panel discussion, Highway Research Board Special Report No. 97. Washington, D.C.: Highway Research Board, pp. 193–216.

Harris, C. C., 1968. "A Stochastic Process Model of Residential Development," *Journal of Regional Science*, 8: 29–39.

Harris, C. D., and E. L. Ullman, 1945. "The Nature of Cities," *The Annals of Sociology*, 242: 7–17.

Hemmins, G. C. (ed.), 1968. "Urban Development Models," Highway Research Board Special Report No. 97, Appendix A, pp. 253–262.

Herbert, J. D., and B. H. Stevens, 1960. "A Model for the Distribution of Residential Activity in Urban Areas," *Journal of Regional Science*, 2: 21–36.

Hill, D. M., D. Brand, and W. B. Hansen, 1965. "Prototype Development of a Statistical Land Use Prediction Model for the Greater Boston Region," *Highway Research Record*, 114: 51–70.

Hoyt, H., 1939. *The Structure and Growth of Residential Neighborhoods in American Cities.* Washington, D.C.: FHA.

Irwin, N. A., and D. Brand, 1965. "Planning and Forecasting Metropolitan Development," *Traffic Quarterly* (October), pp. 520–540.

Kibel, B. M., 1970. "The Evolution of a Dynamic Planning Model." Unpublished Ph.D. dissertation, Berkeley: University of California.

Kilbridge, M. D., R. P. O'Block, and P. V. Teplitz, 1969. "A Conceptual Framework for Urban Planning Models," *Management Science*, 15 B: 246–266.

King, L. J., 1968. *Statistical Analysis in Geography.* Englewood Cliffs, N.J.: Prentice Hall, pp. 154–162.

Lamb, D. C., 1967. "Research of Existing Land-Use Models," Report No. 00010045, Southwestern Pennsylvania Regional Planning Commission, Pittsburgh.

Lee, D. B., 1969. "Models and Techniques for Urban Planning," CAL Rep. No. VY–2474–G. 1, Cornell Aeronautical Lab., Inc.

Lowry, I. S., 1964. "A Model of Metropolis," Rand Corp. Memorandum RM–4035–RC.

——, 1968. "Seven Models of Urban Development: A Structural Comparison," in G. C. Hemmings (ed.), *Urban Development Models.* Highway Research Board Special Report No. 97, pp. 121–163.

Morrill, R. L., 1965. "Expansion of the Urban Fringe: A Simulation Experiment," *Papers of the Regional Science Association*, 15: 185–202.

——, 1965. "The Negro Ghetto: Problems and Alternatives," *Geographical Review*, 55: 339–361.

N. E. Illinois Planning Commission, 1968. *The Plan Study: Methodology.* Chicago: NIPC.

Orcutt, G. H., 1963. "Views on Simulation and Models of Social Systems," in A. C. Hoggatt and F. E. Balderston, *Symposium on Simulation Models.* Cincinnati: South-Western Publishing Co.

Schlager, K. J., 1964. "Simulation Models in Urban and Regional Planning," *SEQRPC Technical Record*, 2: 36.

——, 1966. "A Recursive Programming Theory of the Residential Land Development Process," *Highway Research Record*, 126: 24–32.

Seidman, D. R., 1964. "Report on the Activities Allocation Model," Penn-Jersey Study Paper No. 22.

——, 1969. "The Construction of an Urban Growth Model," DVRPC Plan Report No. 1, Technical Supplement, Vol. A. Philadelphia: Delaware Valley Regional Planning Commission.

Southeastern Wisconsin Regional Planning Commission, 1966. "A Mathematical Approach to Urban Design," Technical Report No. 3, p. 54.

——, 1968. "A Land Use Plan Design Model," Technical Report No. 8, p. 102.

Washington Center for Metropolitan Studies, 1968. "City 1 Player's Manual." Unpublished draft copy (October 3).

Wilson, A. G., 1968. "Models in Urban Planning: A Synoptic Review of Recent Literature," *Urban Studies*, 5: 249–276.

Wolfe, H. B., 1967. "Models for Condition Aging of Residential Structures," *Journal of the American Institute of Planners*, 33: 192–196.

3

KENNETH J. SCHLAGER

A Land-Use Plan Design Model

Postwar advances in applied mathematics and electronic computation have stimulated great interest in the application of mathematical models and data processing systems to urban and regional planning. Significant progress has been made in the application of these techniques to urban transportation planning, and more recently a number of research projects aimed at the development of land-use models have been initiated. There seems little question that the long-range potential impact of these methods will be revolutionary, but some critics have questioned the relevance of current planning models to the real problems of planners. The obvious question is: What problems are current models able to solve?

Even a brief review of current land-use planning models will reveal a strong emphasis on explaining and predicting human behavior. Quite correctly, many of these models include the word forecasting somewhere in their title description [1]. Such an approach conceives of the urban complex as a phenomenon to be explained scientifically and as a changing configuration that can be predicted in the same way that the solar system can be predicted from the theories of physics. Indeed, such an approach is well designated as applied social physics. The philosophy underlying this approach is the natural result of the direct transfer of the methodology of the physical sciences.

Reprinted with permission from the *Journal of the American Institute of Planners*, Special Issue, Vol. XXXI, No. 2, Urban Development Models: New Tools for Planning (May 1965), pp. 103–111.

PLAN DESIGN: THE CENTRAL PROBLEM

A contrasting viewpoint conceives of the urban complex as a subject for design. In this approach, the plan is a conscious synthesis of urban form to meet human needs. Rather than serving as a negative restraint on undesirable aspects of human behavior, the plan serves as a positive force for the directed development of the community.

This design viewpoint is not new. It has provided the basis for architectural and engineering achievement for centuries. What is new, or at least overlooked in recent years, is the possibility of using recent advances in applied mathematics and electronic computation for plan design. Design, and not explanation and prediction, becomes the primary problem for solution.

The subject of this paper is land-use plan design and a land-use plan design model now under development. Design, however, is but one of a sequence of functions in the planning process. For this reason, the introduction of the design model will be preceded by a discussion of the role of mathematical models in a specific land-use, transportation planning sequence.

A system diagram illustrating the functional relationships in the planning process is shown in Figure 1. Although this diagram specifically represents the planning sequence related to the formulation of a regional land-use, transportation plan, it is typical of other planning sequences.

The first function in the planning sequence is that of forecasting population and employment, as a basis for determining future land-use requirements. In the current Land Use Transportation Study of the Southeastern Wisconsin Regional Planning Commission, new methods of socioeconomic forecasting are being investigated in an attempt to provide more accurate and comprehensive employment and population forecasts. These new techniques, which center around the Regional Economic Simulation Model, are the subject of another paper [2] and will not be discussed in detail here.

Whatever the method used, population and employment forecasts must be provided as the output of the first step of the planning sequence.

In the second function, aggregate land-use demand requirements are determined by applying a conversion coefficient, usually designated as a design standard, to each employment and population category. Such a multiplication and summation will result in a detailed classified set of aggregate demands for residential, industrial, commercial, and other land uses. These aggregate demands provide one of the primary inputs to the third function: plan design.

Plan design lies at the heart of the planning process. The land-use plan design function consists essentially of the allocation of a scarce resource, land, between competing and often conflicting land-use activities. This allocation must be accomplished so as to satisfy the aggregate needs for each land use and comply with all the design standards (derived from the plan objectives) at a reasonable cost.

The plan selected in the design stage of the planning process must be implemented in the real world. Private decisions of land developers, builders, and households may run contrary to the land pattern prescribed in the plan. This problem of plan implementation is the function of the third stage of the planning process illustrated in Figure 1, land-use plan implementation test.

Land-use plan implementation is simulated in the Land Use Simulation Model by detailed representation of the decision processes of households and business firms influential in land development. Public land-use control policies and public works programs are exogenous inputs to the model. In practice, a number of experimental simulation runs must be performed with different land-use control policies and public works programs until a set of policies and programs are determined that result in the implementation of the target land-use plan. The feedback on the diagram between land-use development and land-use plan design

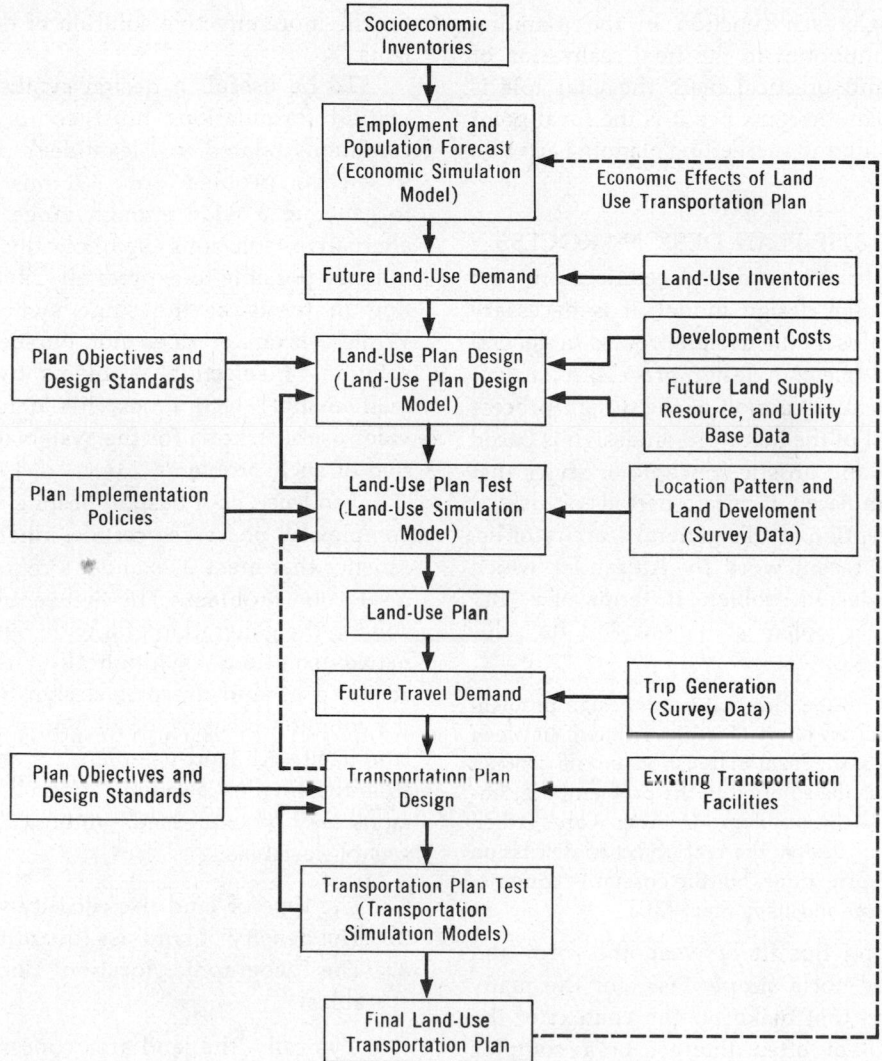

FIGURE 1. Land-Use, Transportation Study Planning System Diagram

accounts for the changes that will probably be needed in the plan design to make it realizable. The output of the third stage of the process is a land-use plan capable of practical implementation.

The remaining stages of the planning sequence depicted in Figure 1 relate to the development of a transportation plan. The primary inputs to a transportation system are the trips generated as a function of land use. For this reason, the land-use plan is shown in the diagram as an input to the transportation plan design. No models are indicated in the transportation plan design function: none exist, to my knowledge. Trip distribution and traffic assignment models may be used to test the plan intuitively designed by the transportation planner. As a result of model simulation, the transportation plan network is revised until a satisfactory system is developed.

Although each function in the planning process is important to the final realization of a creative and practical plan, the vital role is played by plan design since it is the focal point of all preceding and succeeding planning activity.

THE LAND-USE PLAN DESIGN PROCESS

To appreciate the need and requirements for a land-use plan design model, it is necessary to examine closely the design process in general and the land-use plan design process in particular. Analytical discussion of the design process is rare. Most of the literature on design is based on intuitive and artistic concepts or styles that have predominated in certain periods of history.

An exception to this general scarcity of literature is a recent work by Alexander which defines the design problem in terms of a "fit" between the problem statement and its solution:

> It is based on the idea that every design problem begins with an effort to achieve fitness between two entities: the form in question and its context. The form is the solution to the problem; the context defines the problem. In other words, when we speak of design, the real object of discussion is not the form alone, but the ensemble comprising the form and its context [3].

Achieving this fit between the form and its context is not a simple task, for the many requirements that make up the context of the design problem often interact in a complex manner. Attempts to satisfy one design requirement often lead to a violation of another. Faced with such complexity, the designer may be tempted to ignore the real design problem and substitute a traditional design. Although such an approach may be acceptable in a political sense, the original problem remains unsolved.

Difficulties in the design process derive primarily from the inability of the human designer to manipulate simultaneously a large number of interacting design relationships. Mathematics, particularly in its newer forms such as modern algebra, provides a powerful tool for the manipulation of these relationships

for the more effective solution of design problems.

To be useful in design synthesis, mathematical formulations must comply with two conditions related to Alexander's definition of a "selection problem": one, "It must be possible to generate a wide enough range of possible alternative solutions symbolically"; two, "It must be possible to express all criteria for solution in terms of the same symbolism" [4]. While Alexander does not pursue the direct solution of selection problems by means of mathematical techniques, his definition provides useful criteria for the systematic formulation of such problems.

Land-use plan design, despite its admitted complexity, possesses certain inherent characteristics that meet Alexander's requirements of a selection problem. The first requirement, involving the generation of a wide range of alternative solutions symbolically, is naturally achieved in land-use plan design by reason of the common measure of all land-use plans: the land itself. All land-use plans for areas ranging from the smallest subdivision to multi-stage regions may be expressed symbolically by three sets of variables:

1. The type of land use (quality variables)
2. The density of land use (quantity variables)
3. The geographic location (location variables)

Typically, the land area concerned will be subdivided into a grid of "zones" of equal area. The location variable is determined by the geographic coordinates of the zone in question. For each zone, the types and densities of land uses may be expressed as a measure of the activities in that zonal area. The amount of detail provided will depend on the coarseness of the grid. For small areas, a zone may be as small as individual residential lot parcels. In large regions, they may be counties or even states. The key point is that all land-use plans may be expressed by these three classes of variables.

The grid nature of the coordinate system does not limit the results to rectangular plans. On the contrary, the most complex and irregular plan may be expressed with the designated variables if an appropriate grid size is selected.

The second condition, relating to the symbolic relationship between alternative forms and design requirements, is also complied with in the land-use plan design problem. All design requirements or "standards" restrict in some way the set of acceptable land-use plans. For a design model, these requirements may be divided into two primary classes:

1. Requirements that restrict the minimum or maximum numerical value of a land use or a relationship between land uses *within a grid zone* (intrazonal standard). Examples of these requirements are the exclusion of flood plain areas from development in a given grid zone (maximum value standard) or prevention of the simultaneous development of both industrial and residential land in the same grid zone (relationship standard).
2. Requirements that restrict a relationship between land uses *between grid zones* (interzonal standard); for example, the need to provide an elementary school within a specified distance (or time) of all residential units.

In either class, the design requirement can be expressed symbolically as an algebraic equality, or more often an inequality, using the three classes of variables noted above. Again, compliance with this condition, like the first, is possible because land-use planning is concerned with a single measurable resource, land. That these claims of symbolic design alternative generation and requirements-alternatives comparison are authentic will become more apparent as the design model methodology is explained further.

It is useful at this point to provide a specific, succinct statement of the land-use plan design problem indicating the nature of both the design requirements and the design alternatives. To an experienced urban planner the problem will certainly not be new, since it is the same basic problem that he has been concerned with intuitively during his past design experiences. The problem, as stated below, may seem excessively quantitative, and the emphasis on minimal costs may appear unnecessary, but fundamentally it is the same problem of urban form design that has challenged man since cities were found useful. In brief, the problem of the designer of urban form is:

1. Given design requirements expressed as:
   a. A set of design standards in terms of restrictions on land-use relationships that may exist in the plan
   b. A set of needs or demands for each type of land use based on forecasts of future urban activity
2. Synthesize a land-use plan design that satisfies both the land-use demands and design standards considering the current state of both natural and manmade land characteristics, at a minimal combination of public and private costs.

The conceptual basis for minimal costs, it must be emphasized, is not to provide a cheap plan but to avoid unnecessary expenditures of precious resources as long as the design standards and land demands are complied with in the plan design.

Intrazonal design standards may take the form of limitations on density or restrictions of the types of land use that may coexist within a zone. An example of an interzonal design standard would be the provision of a regional shopping center within a certain travel time of every residential area. Land-use demand requirements would restrict the set of acceptable plans to those that provided the aggregate total of each land-use need over the entire design area. The current state of the land, whether developed or in a natural state, is a primary consideration in plan synthesis because of the relationship of the land to both the design standards and the costs associated with new or renewed development.

THE DESIGN MODEL

Two related mathematical techniques will now be discussed as possible frameworks for a land-use plan design model. The first technique, linear programming, has a record of successful accomplishment in other fields and has efficient, highly developed computational procedures. Dynamic programming, the second and newer technique, while not as productive in previous applications or standardized computational procedures, is less restricted in its assumptions and, potentially at least, is a more flexible framework for a land-use plan design model.

Both linear and dynamic programming are sometimes classified as subsidiary fields under the general title of mathematical programming. Such a general classification is desirable, inasmuch as both fields have as their objective the solution of problems involving the optimization (maximization or minimization) of some objective, such as cost, within the restrictions of certain constraints such as design standards. The techniques involved differ considerably, however, with linear programming imposing rather severe restrictions on the nature of both the objective and constraints while dynamic programming is almost unrestricted in its formulations of both the objective and constraint functions. Linear programming models, on the other hand, can usually be solved by the use of standardized computational procedures, while dynamic programming usually provides at least a serious challenge and often insurmountable obstacles to an efficient computational solution. With either technique, the sheer size of many land-use plan design problems bring with them what has been called the "curse of dimensionality," which militates against any simple "brute force" approach to solution.

The linear programming formulation of the land-use plan design model problem is straightforward. The objective function relates to the cost of developing land for a given land use:

$$c_t = c_1 x_1 + c_2 x_2 + \ldots + c_n x_n$$

where the variables x may represent residential, industrial, or other land uses in given areas and the constants c the costs of developing this land. Land-use categories may be subdivided into subsidiary classes such as single family residential, multifamily residential, and the costs may

be related to the topography and soil characteristics of the area. With each subdivision, of course, the number of variables grows larger, and the computation time for a model solution is increased. In practice, a compromise must be made between the desire for detail and reasonable solution times. With the rapid developments in computer technology, however, this problem will be of decreased significance in the coming years.

The equality and inequality constraints in the linear programming formulation of land-use plan design include the following:

1. The total demand requirement for each land-use category (equality constraint):

$$d_1 x_1 + d_2 x_2 + \ldots + d_n x_n = E_k$$

where

E = regional land-use demand requirement for each land use

d = service ratio coefficients which provide for supporting service land requirements, such as streets, which are necessary for primary land-use development

2. Maximal (minimal) limits on land uses within a zone:

$$x_1 + x_2 + \ldots + x_n \leqslant F_m$$

where

F_m = upper limit on land use n in zone m

3. Interzonal or intrazonal land use relationship constraints:

$$x_n \leqslant G x_m$$

where

G = ratio of land-use n allowed relative to land-use m with land-uses m and n in the same or different zones.

The land-use demand equality constraint (1) follows a standardized format with one equation for each primary land-use category.

Since some land uses such as single family residential are usually subdivided further according to lot sizes, the number of demand equations in a typical design model may exceed 20 relationships. It is important to emphasize that only primary land uses such as residential, industrial, agricultural, and recreational land are directly determined. Service ratios incorporated in the *d* parameters account for secondary land uses such as local streets and parks.

The second and third categories of constraints reflect the design standards and may take a wide variety of forms. The maximal constraint will usually reflect a density standard, but it also may provide for the exclusion of an unsuited soil type for a given type of land use. Land-use relationship constraints will result from design standard restrictions on coexistent land uses within a zone or in adjacent zones. Accessibility standards for employment and shopping areas will also be reflected in this type of constraint.

The above constraint relationships reflect the types encountered so far in experimental plan design model runs in test areas. Other constraint forms may be needed when a complete regional plan design is attempted, but they may be easily included as long as they are linear, continuous constraints. Nonlinear discontinuous constraints are not possible with linear programming and account for the primary disadvantages of the method.

For a region subdivided into about 30 zones, the size of a typical linear program for a land-use plan design is about 60 equality and inequality constraints and 400 variables. Computer time on an IBM 1620 computer is about three hours. On larger systems, such as the IBM 7090, it would take less than 30 minutes.

MODEL APPLICATION

Some initial experience with applications of the model will now be detailed in order to provide the reader with an idea of the input data requirements and computational characteristics of the model.

Four primary sets of input data are required for model operation:

1. The costs of unimproved land and land development for each primary land-use activity for each type of soil
2. The aggregate demand for each primary land-use activity
3. Design standards which reflect the plan objectives and restrict the set of acceptable plans by limiting interzonal land-use relationships
4. The current land inventory, which will include both land-use activities by area and soil characteristics.

Land-development cost data may be obtained either by engineering estimates or by statistical analysis of recent land development in the area. The former approach has been used in the initial tests of the model in the Waukesha city pilot area. Collection of land-development cost data is always expensive and in many cases difficult or even impossible to obtain. Land developers are usually extremely reluctant to reveal their costs, and the cost data obtained is of uneven quality since many developers do not maintain complete records. For all these reasons, engineering cost estimates are usually preferable if competent professional experience is available.

In the Waukesha area, separate land-development cost estimates were made for five sizes of residential lots with their associated service land uses, such as streets, neighborhood shopping, schools, and parks. Additional cost estimates were made for industrial, regional shopping, and regional park land uses. These were not gross estimates but detailed analyses of the costs of each improvement related to both the land use and the type of soil involved. All estimates were subdivided into their component parts, each with its individual cost.

Separate cost estimates were prepared for each of three classes of soil. Soil data were obtained from a comprehensive soil survey made in southeastern Wisconsin as part of the Land Use Transportation Study. Unimproved land costs presented a special problem since they could not be obtained from engineering estimates. Assessed and equalized land-value data were obtained from each of the communities and were adjusted on the basis of prices realized in recent land transactions in the area.

Initial tests of the model used historical aggregate land-use demands for 1950–1962 to provide comparisons between actual and "optimal" land development in the area. Typically, however, a design application of the model will require forecasts of future land-use demands, which may be obtained by applying design standards to forecasts of population and employment in the region of interest.

The various forms of design standards usually provided were described in the previous section. In current tests of the model, design standards were limited to the exclusion of development from areas such as flood plains, along with the provision of service ratios for the amounts of secondary land (streets, parks) required to support the primary land uses. Design standards for the regional land-use plan are still in preparation and will be used in model tests as soon as they become available.

An inventory of both current land-use activities and soil characteristics is critical for model application. In current tests, developed areas were eliminated from consideration for future land development. It is possible, however, to consider redevelopment in the form of urban renewal as a set of alternatives in the design. For this approach, redevelopment costs would be required. Through the use of the soil inventory, it was possible to assign a development cost to each subarea in the test area.

Proper presentation of the Land Use Plan Design Model output is an important consideration in achieving acceptance of its design by planners and governmental officials. Initial model outputs were in tabular form and were meaningful only to someone familiar with the operation of the model. Improved presentation was later achieved by tabular designation of the intensity of each land-use activity in each zone. Printed output was supplemented by colored

land-use maps manually prepared from the tabular print-out.

AVAILABLE MATHEMATICAL MODELS

Although linear programming provides a reasonably satisfactory framework for a land-use plan design model, it possesses certain inherent disadvantages that restrict its usefulness in design. The primary limitation is the need for continuous rather than discrete values for the land-use variables. Land-use design choices are by nature usually discrete rather than continuous. The basic element of residential land use is the subdivision rather than the lot. Industrial land-use units tend to be industrial parks rather than individual factory sites, much less land acreage. While it is possible to round off the linear programming solution to satisfy these natural discrete levels, such a solution does not usually correspond with the associated discrete optimal combination. A second limitation of linear programming is the need for both a linear objective function and linear constraints. The linear objective function is not a severe limitation, because the inaccuracies introduced by a linear approximation of costs are usually less than the errors of cost estimation. In the few instances where known nonlinear cost functions occur, such as in the plant capacities of areawide facilities for water supply or sewage treatment, the cost break may usually be satisfactorily approximated by a multivariable series of linear cost variables.

Nonlinear constraint relationships present a more serious problem. Certain design standards are inherently nonlinear, and a linear approximation sometimes provides an unsatisfactory substitute. When a design model is not able to provide satisfactorily for a design standard, it loses most of its usefulness.

Dynamic programming, another member of the mathematical programming family, has the potential for removing the two primary restrictions inherent in linear programming. Although dynamic programming may be used to solve the same land-use plan design problem, it is based on a different class of mathematical procedures, which are capable of handling discrete and nonlinear objective functions and constraint relationships.

Richard Bellman of the Rand Corporation was the originator of dynamic programming and has developed the theory and application of this multistage approach to decision making to a high degree in the last decade. A large number of classes of dynamic programming processes have been formulated for problems in production scheduling, rocket trajectories, and feedback control systems, but the class of process of primary interest in design is the allocation process [5]. In a dynamic programming model, the basic cost and design relationships are similar to those defined for the linear programming model, but the method of computation differs and permits the use of more complex and discrete relationships.

THE DESIGN VIEWPOINT IN
URBAN PLANNING

The ultimate contribution of this paper will depend on its success, or the lack of it, in accomplishing at least a partial reorientation of land-use model development toward design. Although the importance of forecasting land-use development was indicated by the role of the Land Use Simulation Model briefly described earlier in this paper and detailed in another recent paper [6], the dangers and limitations of nondesign-oriented models that are only remotely related to the synthesis of better urban and regional plans should be apparent.

The need for design models in urban planning is fortunately accompanied by greater possibilities for their success. Industrial applications of mathematical models in normative functions such as production scheduling and optimal product design have been conspicuously more successful than attempts to simulate human behavioral patterns in a market. Quite simply, it is much easier to use a model to tell people what they *should do* than to explain *what they are doing*. Given the fantastic complexity of the modern metropolis, would it not be well to emphasize model development in areas that

promise both a significant contribution and a high probability of success?

The image of design in urban planning as a remnant of a bygone age of the "city beautiful" must be replaced by a new design concept based on the creative synthesis of complex plans using all the tools provided by modern technology.

POSTSCRIPT: COMMENTARY ON FIVE
YEARS OF DEVELOPMENT EXPERIENCE

The original concept of a Land Use Plan Design Model was originated in the summer of 1964 at the Southeastern Wisconsin Regional Planning Commission (SEWRPC) by Kenneth J. Schlager and was further developed in detail for the publication of the foregoing original paper in the JAIP in May of 1965. This original paper stirred enough interest to serve as the basis for a research proposal to the Department of Housing and Urban Development. The proposal resulted in a research grant to SEWRPC under the Urban Planning Research and Demonstration program with the project designation of Wisconsin PD-1. This project has proceeded through two phases and is currently at the beginning of a third and concluding phase. This commentary will relate some of the experience gained during this research program and reflect some thoughts on the future potential and limitations of urban design models.

In summary, the purpose of Phase I of Wisconsin PD-1, which began in October of 1966 and ended in January of 1968, was to develop a Land Use Plan Design Model and apply it to a small community as a test vehicle. Two important lessons were learned in Phase I. The first was learned early in Phase I and influenced the course of action. The second became apparent too late to have any effect on Phase I but became a primary determinant of the Phase II Program. These two were:

1. Since the nature of urban design is such that it deals with discrete objects (schools, hospitals, shopping centers, etc.) rather than areas of land, the use of linear pro-

gramming as the model algorithm became undesirable if not infeasible.

2. The computer programs for reducing raw data to meaningful model inputs is as challenging a task as the computer program for the model itself.

The impact of the first lesson was felt early so that little time was spent with linear programming, and the model algorithm was formulated to deal directly with discrete elements designated as "modules" which were placed in geographic areas known as "cells" subject to certain constraints and with the objective of minimizing development and operating costs. The model algorithm, which used a steeper descent search approach, operated fairly satisfactorily in Phase I but its limitations became quite apparent with the larger scale applications of Phase II.

Data-reduction problems, the second lesson, were painfully obvious later in Phase I in which model input data was provided through a series of unrelated data processing programs. This piecemeal approach, with its clumsy inconvenience, served as the incentive for an integrated data-reduction program package in Phase II.

Phase II, which began in July of 1968 and ended in September of 1969, was concerned mainly with the application of the model on a larger scale to the development of a regional land-use plan. Since the SEWRPC is a regional planning agency and had previously developed a regional land-use plan by traditional methods, the plan developed by the model could be subject to some searching comparisons.

Since the Southeastern Wisconsin region is large in size (2,689 square miles), Phase II was dominated by data-reduction activities. With the experience of Phase I in mind, a great deal of effort was directed toward the development of an integrated data-reduction system. Integration was enlarged such that the data-reduction program and the model operating programs blended into one system with raw module, constraint, cost, and topographic data as inputs and a land-use plan as an output.

In Phase II with the data-reduction problem under control, the first opportunity arose to see the results of model operation with realistic input data. Although the results of these initial model runs were encouraging in that they resembled a plausible plan considering the goals of constraint observance and cost minimization, need for future improvement of the model was indicated in two areas:

1. The model algorithm seemed slow in operation and did not provide a true optimal (or even near optimal) solution.

2. The design constraints, which are intended to reflect the objectives of the design other than minimal cost, require a great deal of thought and study.

The original model algorithm assigns modules to areal cells in a series of binary partitions. The whole design area is first partitioned into two subareas, and each module is assigned to one of these two subareas based on constraint observance and cost minimization. Each subarea is in turn divided in half, and modules are assigned to each half again. This process continues until the smallest area is assigned: a single cell. This approach leads to "holistic" errors in that modules are assigned early in the process to a set of cells that later prove to be nonoptimal. Since such errors cannot be corrected, they result in permanent misallocation of modules contrary to an optimal plan. After a great deal of investigation of possible improvements in the present algorithm, a new approach to algorithm formulation seemed desirable.

The other problem concerning constraint formulation was less a mathematical problem than a value problem. Quite simply, the professed goals, objectives, and design criteria do not reflect the real goals, objectives, and design criteria. In the language of social psychology there is a "hidden agenda" of plan requirements. The problem is to uncover this hidden agenda of real design requirements and convert them into constraints for input to the model.

Results to date and the nature of existing problems indicated the need for a two-pronged attack to make the model a useful tool for planners, architects, and engineers:

1. A program to document the existing model and associated data-reduction programs in the form of a User's Manual understandable by the practitioner such as the planner, architect, or engineer.
2. A research program to explore fundamental questions of algorithm operation and constraint formulation.

Fortunately, financial support has been obtained for both programs. A development program to document the present model with some minor improvements will be funded by the United States Department of Housing and Urban Development under the Wisconsin PD-1 Program to the Southeastern Wisconsin Regional Planning Commission. A second research-oriented program is being funded by the National Science Foundation through Marquette University. Together these programs have the potential of reducing the design model research to date to a system useful in the practical world of design.

NOTES

1. *Review of Existing Land Use Forecasting Techniques,* Traffic Research Corporation, presented to the Boston Regional Planning Project, Toronto (1963).

2. Schlager, Kenneth J., "Simulation Models in Urban and Regional Planning," *Technical Record,* Southeastern Wisconsin Regional Planning Commission, Waukesha, Wisconsin, II, No. 1 (1964).

3. Alexander, Christopher, *Notes on the Synthesis of Form,* Harvard University Press, Cambridge, pp. 15–16 (1964).

4. *Ibid.,* pp. 74–75.

5. Bellman, Richard E., and Dreyfus, Stuart E., *Applied Dynamic Programming,* Princeton University Press, Princeton (1962).

6. Schlager, op. cit.

Metropolitan Differentiation: The City and the Fringe

part ii

The papers in this section deal with the general topics of metropolitan expansion and the differentiation of the city and fringe areas within the metropolis. Underlying the papers are several basic questions. Among them are: What are the processes by which metropolitan areas grow, expand, and become internally differentiated? Is urban decentralization a relatively new or old phenomenon? How are the patterns of neighborhood change related to the overall processes of city growth and expansion? To what extent is suburbanization a different process from that of normal city fringe expansion? Are suburban communities an undifferentiated lot? How do suburbs change through time? Does suburban development have an impact upon city government functions and expenses? Is there a tendency for a new "super metropolis" or "megalopolis" to emerge in the densely settled highly urbanized regions?

The first paper, by Duncan, Sabagh, and Van Arsdol [4] puts suburban development into the perspective of metropolitan expansion and population redistribution from mature to undeveloped subareas. Their study of Los Angeles involves an application of cohort analysis to the city's residential areas. They report that the rapidity of population redistribution among areas in the metropolis is a function of both the overall rate of metropolitan population growth and the ratio of new dwellings to incremental population. Residential construction translates city-wide growth into areal redistribution. The "flight to the suburbs" noted after World War II resulted from three general factors: the accelerated rate of population redistribution within the metropolis; the maturity of the central city's neighborhoods; and the rigidity of the city corporate limits.

The paper by Winsborough [5] attempts to explain suburbanization in terms of two basic dimensions of urban population distribution: *concentration* and *congestion*. Starting with basic density-distance models, Winsborough derives the two concepts. Variation in either concentration or congestion may lead to an overall increase in the areal size of the settlement. Although they are related concepts they may act independently of each other to affect metropolitan spread.

Schnore's paper [6] essentially argues that a critical factor in understanding the process of metropolitan decentralization is the timing of the onset of the process. The discussion is oriented toward answering three basic questions: (1) When did decentralization begin in individual U.S. cities? (2) What are some basic characteristics of cities that began decentralizing at different times? and (3) What is the link between the concepts of "decentralization" and "metropolitanism"? Data are from 99 large decentralized metropolitan areas. The discussion ties decentralization into classical ecological theory through such concepts as *interdependency, territorial division of labor,* and *dominance.*

Studies of metropolitan patterning have long noted that the fringe communities are not a generally undifferentiated lot. Clearly functional differences are manifest among suburbs. Most basic is the distinction between "residential" and "employing" specializations or, in effect, "suburbs of production" and "suburbs of consumption." The second paper by Schnore [7] focuses upon the functional specialization of the suburbs and summarizes what is known about the two types of communities. Schnore also deals with the implications of such differentiation for metropolitan research. Farley's study [8] explores the implications of sustained suburban growth for the compositional characteristics of individual suburbs. Farley shows that suburban areas have been growing more rapidly than the central cities; that the status gap between central city and suburban populations persists; and that individual suburban communities maintain their particular socioeconomic characteristics for long periods even though sustaining rapid population growth. These findings strongly suggest the force of ecological momentum attained by individual communities almost at the outset of their settlement. It seems that the specialization of the suburb initially produces an original socioeconomic composition that attracts selective migrants through time mainly of similar characteristics thereby producing a rather stable social composition.

A popular notion is that our metropolitan communities are expanding and growing into each other and reorganizing themselves into supermetropolitan communities or "megalopolises." The concept of megalopolis was applied originally to the highly urbanized densely settled eastern U.S. coast. However, the concept has become fairly popular so it is not uncommon to hear passing reference to southern California's, or Lake Michigan, or the Lake Erie megalopolis. As popular as the term has become, many feel that insufficient empirical evidence has been amassed to designate any urban region as "megalopolitan." Weller [9] attempts carefully and systematically to explore the whole notion of megalopolitan structure and its application. He points out that for a megalopolis truly to emerge it takes more than just the growing together of formerly separate metropolitan centers. The key characteristic of the megalopolitan community is an increasing complementary functional specialization and, therefore, a growing interdependency among the separate metropolises within the complex. To investigate empirically the degree of specialization among the cluster of 39 metropolitan centers on the east coast, Weller deftly employs industrial labor force data. His results strongly suggest that the concept of megalopolis should be used with great care, and the rather easy and arbitrary designation of various urban regions as "megalopolises" should be tempered.

The final paper in this section, by Weicher [10], is concerned with the implications of fringe growth. Weicher attempts to investigate the effects of suburban development and political fragmentation upon the fiscal position of city governments. His analysis involves the development of a sophisticated mathematical model and is applied to actual metropolitan data. Essentially, Weicher reports that cities seem to spend more on providing services to manufacturing establishments than they receive in revenue from them. Also cities seem to gain more in tax income from retail establishments than they spend in providing services to them. Furthermore, Weicher maintains that central cities are able to exploit suburbanites. The fiscal crisis of the city is not a product by itself of the loss of manufacturing to the suburbs, Weicher concludes; nor, he maintains, is the crisis a result of suburbanization and political fragmentation. Weicher also raises a question about the ability of metropolitan forms of government to solve the basic fiscal problem. All-in-all, this is a very provocative paper that will be of interest to many urban specialists.

4

BEVERLY DUNCAN
GEORGES SABAGH
MAURICE D. VAN ARSDOL, JR.

Patterns of City Growth

ABSTRACT

Residential construction is proposed as the mechanism whereby city-wide population growth is translated into population redistribution from mature to relatively undeveloped areas. Cohort analysis of Los Angeles residential areas indicates that the rapidity of redistribution varies directly with both the rate of population growth and the ratio of new dwellings to incremental population. The accelerated redistribution in the immediate postwar period, coupled with the maturity of central cities and the rigidity of their corporate limits, resulted in the so-called flight to the suburbs.

Reprinted by permission from the *American Journal of Sociology*, Vol. LXVIII, No. 4 (January 1962), pp. 418–429. Copyright by the University of Chicago.

As the rich descriptive materials on intra-city differentials in growth have accumulated, a recurring observation is the relatively more rapid growth of outlying than of central parts of cities, that is, the pattern popularly termed in recent years the "flight to the suburbs." Students of population distribution have failed to make it clear whether this suburban movement represents a new pattern of growth or whether the only new element is a widening gap between the limits of the political city and those of the physical city. At the same time, they have neglected to test rigorously the long-standing notions about how an urban center expands and how its expansion is reflected in internal growth differentials.

The economists, Hoover and Vernon, have recently reminded sociologists that as a city grows in population it expands physically, whether upward or outward. Their stages in the development of neighborhoods set forth to help explain the "Spread of the People"[1] represent a variation on Burgess' hypothesis of city growth and "general cycles in the life-history of the neighborhood."[2] Hoover and Vernon describe a sequence of stages through which neighborhoods typically proceed: subdivision and building up; transition into intensive residential use; downgrading; thinning out; and, finally, renewal. The rate of population growth is presumed to decelerate as succession proceeds, with peak rates occurring during the building-up phase. Provocative as their scheme is, it remains a moot point whether the developmental stages can serve as anything more than a sensitizing frame of reference. In fact, the scheme may fall into the undeserved disrepute of the Burgess hypothesis because these "ideal-type" stages cannot be readily discerned in all cities.[3]

Two major implications of Hoover and Vernon's proposal as well as Burgess' hypothesis often are ignored in studies of patterns of city growth, perhaps because they are so obvious to common sense. First, an area in intensive urban use has a more limited growth potential than one which includes large tracts of undeveloped land. The differential potential must be reckoned with in any adequate accounting of interarea differences in growth. Second, the present patterning of intraurban population changes can be understood only in terms of the past development of the city, for the form of the city—the "residue" of its past development—is a major element of the context within which growth occurs. Other relevant elements of the context which typically receive little more than token recognition include the size of the population increment in the city as a whole, the expansion of the city's housing supply and the components thereof, and changes in technology, particularly with respect to means of transportation and techniques of housing production.

Neither Burgess nor Hoover and Vernon have specified the growth contexts within which their schemes have descriptive validity. They seem to assume, however, a relatively stable context whose elements include areal differentiation of land uses, city-wide population growth, in part attributable to net in-migration, and a substantial volume of residential construction. To evaluate the descriptive validity

This study was initiated at the Population Research Laboratory, Department of Sociology, University of Southern California, under National Science Foundation Grant No. G9452 and completed at the Population Research and Training Center, University of Chicago, under a grant from the Ford Foundation. Eileen McDonagh, Harold E. Johnson, Robert Cournoyer, and W. Reynolds Farley provided able clerical assistance.

[1] Edgar M. Hoover and Raymond Vernon, *Anatomy of a Metropolis* (Cambridge, Mass.: Harvard University Press, 1959), Chap. VIII.

[2] Ernest W. Burgess, "The Growth of the City," in Robert E. Park, Ernest W. Burgess, and Roderick D. McKenzie, *The City* (Chicago: University of Chicago Press, 1925), Chap. II; and "The Natural Area as the Unit for Social Work in the Large City," *Proceedings of the National Conference of Social Work* (Chicago, 1926).

[3] Davie, in a critique of Burgess' hypothesis, observed: "There is no universal pattern, not even of an 'ideal' type" (Maurice R. Davie, "The Pattern of Urban Growth," in Paul K. Hatt and Albert J. Reiss, Jr. [eds.], *Reader in Urban Sociology* [Glencoe, Ill.: Free Press, 1951], p. 259).

of the scheme, then, allowance must be made for changes in the growth context, whether these be the result of temporary disruptions such as war, of cyclical fluctuations as in the rate of new construction, or of long-run trends like those produced by shifts in modes of intraurban transportation.

Here we have attempted to look at the growth of Los Angeles, over a quarter century, from Hoover and Vernon's perspective, to observe growth differentials between areas in each of five periods between the six censuses taken during the twenty-five-year period, and to investigate changes in the city-wide growth context coincident with changes in internal growth patterns. We then take a "second look" at some recent findings on intermetropolitan differences in rapidity of suburbanization.

STUDY DESIGN

A design appropriate for the analysis of city-growth patterns must both incorporate controls on the growth potential of city sub-areas, or their respective "positions" in the past development of the city, and allow for changes in the growth context. An analogue of the cohort analysis of fertility offers a possible solution.[4] Cohorts of city sub-areas defined in terms of the year at which they were "built up," or reached some other stage of maturation, are identified. Population change in each cohort is traced over a span of years. Comparisons among cohorts both at a given point in time and at the same stage of maturation can be effected. The alternative bases of comparison permit a more thorough assessment of the impact of changes in the city-wide growth context on patterns of growth within the city.

Although a careful sifting of historical documents probably would permit a reconstruction of the expansion of most major cities and identification of built-up portions at various dates, such a procedure calls for sizable resources and

a wide variety of skills.[5] As an alternative we propose an operationally simple procedure which relies on statistics on year built and gross acreage for census tracts and a dwelling-unit density criterion to identify the built-up areas at past dates.

The spatial configuration of built-up areas in the City of Los Angeles at each of several dates as revealed by application of this latter procedure (Figure 1) both suggests the plausibility of the classification and highlights some

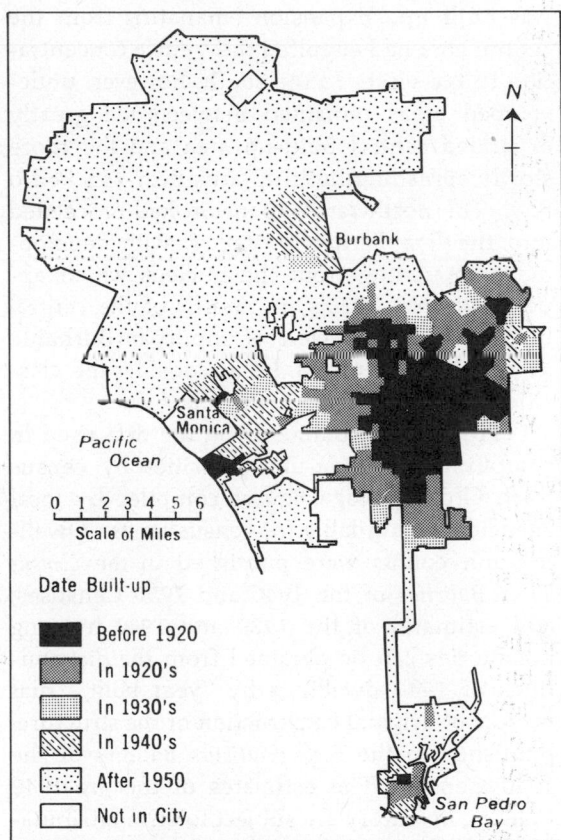

FIGURE 1.   Census Tracts of 1940 Grid Classified by Date Built Up, City of Los Angeles

[4] Pascal K. Whelpton, *Cohort Fertility* (Princeton, N.J.: Princeton University Press, 1954).

[5] For an example, see Marybeth Branaman, *Growth of the San Francisco Bay Area Urban Core* (Real Estate Research Program, Bureau of Business and Economic Research, University of California, Research Report No. 8 [Berkeley: University of California Press, 1956]).

inherent problems. About 10 per cent of the city, as now constituted, was built up by 1920, if only census tracts with a density of at least two dwellings per acre of gross land area are classified as built up. The area built up by 1920 spreads out from the present city center with the development northward truncated, probably by rugged terrain. It includes outlying nuclei in the Venice area (south of Santa Monica on the Pacific Ocean) and in the San Pedro Bay area, west and south, respectively, of the city core. By 1950, about 32 per cent of the city was built up. Expansion emanating from the central core had engulfed the Venice concentration to the west. To the south, however, undeveloped areas remained between the greatly expanded central built-up area and the more slowly spreading built-up area near San Pedro Bay. The northward expansion had proceeded into the San Fernando Valley, with development emanating from the nucleus which appeared in the 1930's just north of the central built-up area and west of suburban Burbank. With this background, let us consider the classification procedure.

First, a few comments on the data used in computing dwelling-unit densities by census tract: Gross acreage figures compiled by local agencies are available for census tracts. Dwelling-unit counts were published in the *Census Tract Bulletins* of the 1940 and 1950 Censuses, and estimates of the 1920 and 1930 housing inventories can be obtained from the distributions of 1940 dwellings by "year built," that is, year of original construction of the structure, published in the *Block Statistics Bulletins* of the 1940 Census. The estimates of the pre-1940 housing inventory are subject to error attributable both to the householder's lack of information about when his dwelling was built and to modification of the housing inventory through time (e.g., loss of units demolished or merged and gain of units through conversion). The city-wide error of estimate appears to be on the order of 10 per cent. (In 1940, some 184,000 units were reported built before 1920 and 424,000 built before 1930. Census counts of "families," roughly equivalent to occupied units, were 159,000 and 369,000 in 1920 and 1930, respectively. The estimate assumes a vacancy rate of 5 per cent.) Errors of estimate probably vary substantially by census tract, however, with a tendency toward larger errors in more mature areas.

A criterion of gross, rather than net, residential density was used both because gross acreage figures are more readily available and because entire census tracts, not segments thereof, are being characterized as built up. The gross-density criterion poses two troublesome problems, however. First, tracts are delineated to equalize tract populations rather than the area of tracts. The average area of the before 1920 tracts was some 200 acres, in contrast to about 4,500 acres for the tracts not yet built up in 1950 (Table 1). Quite possibly, built-up sections of 200 acres exist within the latter group of tracts. Second, intensive urban land-use need not be residential in form. Areas in which residences have given way to industrial or transport use or in which these uses preempted vacant land may appear not yet built up on a gross-density criterion. As a partial compensation, each tract in the present commercial center of Los Angeles was classified as built up before 1920, although three failed to meet the density criterion in 1920 and at subsequent dates.

The fact that nearly 70 per cent of the City of Los Angeles is classified as not yet built up in 1950 may suggest that the density level of two dwellings per acre used here is too high. Although the spillover of the physical city beyond municipal boundaries has received rather more attention, the case of Los Angeles implies that not all of the political city need be in the physical city. A special survey indicated that by 1944 only some 21,000 acres of the 136,000-acre San Fernando Valley, a part of the City of Los Angeles since 1915, were in urban use. The prevalence of open space in the Valley cannot be attributed solely to topography, for

TABLE 1.   Gross Acreage and Housing Inventory of Census Tracts by Date Built Up, City of Los Angeles

Date Built Up	No. of Tracts	Gross Acreage (000's)	Dwelling Units (000's) 1940	1950	Vacant Units (000's) 1940	1950	Units Built (000's) 1930's	1940's
City, Total	302*	288†	529	698	36.2	31.4	102	169
Before 1920	136‡	29	261	268	19.3	11.7	16	13
In 1920's	92	33	163	189	9.8	6.2	34	23
In 1930's	15	11	31	48	1.9	1.5	16	17
In 1940's	17	21	27	63	1.9	3.0	15	35
After 1950	42	194	48	130	3.3	9.0	21	81

* Based on 1940 census tract grid. Tracts 192 and 193 combined to maintain areal comparability.
† Acreage as of 1940. Acreage of Los Angeles reported by City Engineer: 282,700 in 1930; 288,500 in 1940; 289,200 in 1946; 290,200 in 1950; 290,400 in 1953; 291,000 in 1956.
‡ Includes three centrally located tracts with densities less than two dwellings per acre, but over 95 percent of 1940 inventory built before 1920.

only 34,000 acres were considered "unfit" for any use.[6] Moreover, the present level of technology in Los Angeles allows for the building of single-family homes in many sections of mountainous areas at a density of two dwellings per acre, the criterion of classification used here.[7] These considerations lend some plausibility to the classification of 194,000 acres within the city as not yet built up in 1950, although they by no means validate the density level selected.

A number of refinements might be introduced into the classification procedure outlined above, but they are required only if the general utility of this approach to the analysis of patterns of city growth can be demonstrated.

COHORT DIFFERENTIALS

Some analytical possibilities of this approach to the study of city growth patterns can be illustrated with the data on gross population densities shown in Figure 2. The direct association

[6] Charles B. Bennett and Milton Breivogel, "Planning for the San Fernando Valley," *Western City*, April 1945; reprinted by the City Planning Commission, City of Los Angeles, 1945.
[7] City Planning Commission, City of Los Angeles, *1959 Accomplishments* (Los Angeles: City Planning Commission, 1960), pp. 22, 32–33.

between density and maturation of the cohort observed at each census date follows in part from the classification scheme, although it is not a necessary consequence. One might be tempted to draw two inferences from this cross-sectional relationship: first, as an area becomes more mature, its population density increases; and, second, residential settlement patterns have become less dense through time.

The fallacy of the first inference becomes apparent when changes in population density through time are traced for individual cohorts. In the cohort of tracts built up prior to 1920, densities increased for at least twenty-five years after the date built up (until 1946) and declined throughout the last decade of the observation period (1946–56). Densities in the 1920's cohort increased for about fifteen years after the date built up (until 1946), decreased during the following seven years (1946–53), and again increased in the terminal three years of the observation period (1953–56). Densities in the more recently built-up cohorts increased throughout the period of observation. These findings provide another example of the pitfalls inherent in extrapolation from cross-sectional to longitudinal relationships, and vice versa.

Comparisons between cohorts at the same stage of maturation are needed to reveal any

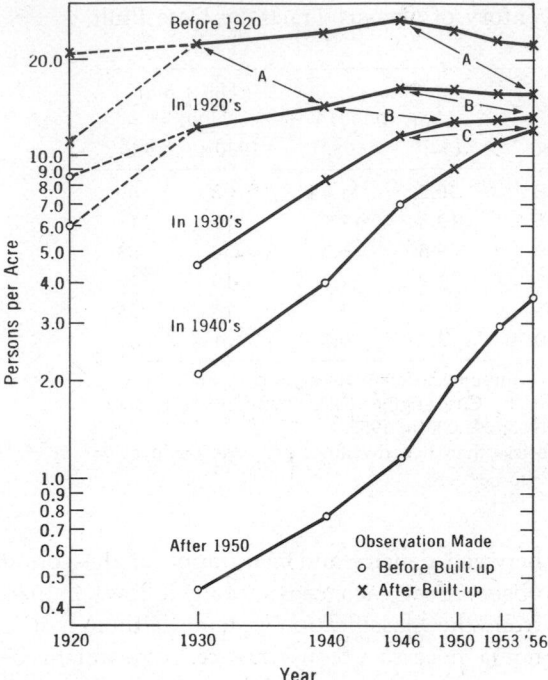

FIGURE 2. Gross Population Density of Census Tracts by Date Built Up, City of Los Angeles 1920–56

trend toward a less dense pattern of settlement. Such comparisons between the before–1920 cohort and the 1920's cohort, as, for example, at A in Figure 2, consistently show higher densities in the older cohort. Similarly, each comparison between the 1920's and 1930's cohorts, as at B, shows a higher density in the older cohort; but the inter-cohort difference in density is less than that between the before–1920 and the 1920's cohorts. Density in the 1930's cohort is slightly lower than it is in the 1940's cohort, however, a decade after each cohort was built up (C, Figure 2). Admittedly, the number of possible comparisons is small, and the time elapsed since date built up is approximate. Nonetheless, these comparisons cast doubt on the proposition that density of settlement has decreased steadily in the last fifty years. These fragmentary findings, however, do suggest that the introduction of a local transport mode which extends the effective limits of a community is conducive to the development of new areas at a relatively low density. The most

striking change in mode of transport within the observation period is, of course, the spread of the automobile, which presumably lessened pressures conducive to high density and permitted so-called urban sprawl. Its effects might have become evident by the 1920's. As residential development reaches the effective community limits, forces leading to denser settlement may again become operative. Quite possibly, without modification of local transport modes, future population increments in Los Angeles will gain housing through upward rather than outward expansion.

The broad outlines of population change by cohort over the quarter-century, 1930 to 1956, are in accord with Hoover and Vernon's formulation. Rapid growth is evident during the building-up phase, that is, in the period shortly before the date built up. Lesser population increases occur as transition into intensive residential use proceeds, and eventually population losses are observed as the "thinning-out" sets in. The cohort built up before 1920 gained population in each period prior to the end of World War II and lost population in each postwar period. The 1920's cohort also grew during the prewar decade and war years and lost population in the immediate postwar periods, but a population increase was again recorded in the mid-1950's. The cohorts built up in the 1930's or more recently gained population throughout the observation period.

Incidentally, these cohort patterns are the modal patterns for individual tracts in the respective cohorts. Although the cohort pattern is the "best" single prediction for its component tracts, the modal pattern is observed in only four-fifths of the tracts built up in the 1940's, half the 1930's tracts, and about three-tenths of the 1920's and before-1920 tracts. Nearly three-fifths of the 1920's and before-1920 tracts did, however, exhibit the cohort characteristic of population increase through World War II followed by loss in the late 1940's. These observations about variability within cohorts should be balanced with a caution about assuming constant change throughout an intercensal period. Were the censuses more closely spaced,

TABLE 2. Population of Census Tracts by Date Built Up, City of Los Angeles, 1930 to 1956

	Date of Census					
Date Built Up	April 1, 1930	April 1, 1940	January 28, 1946	April 1, 1950	September 26, 1953	February 25, 1956
	Total Population (in thousands)					
City, Total	1,238.0	1,504.3	1,805.7	1,970.4	2,104.7	2,243.9
Before 1920	655.8	710.0	766.9	717.4	660.8	645.2
In 1920's	401.5	472.3	536.8	527.1	511.6	517.6
In 1930's	49.2	90.9	124.0	136.9	139.1	143.6
In 1940's	44.3	84.1	147.3	189.8	229.1	248.4
After 1950	87.3	147.0	230.7	399.2	564.0	689.2
	Average Annual Percentage Change over Preceding Date					
City, Total		2.2	3.4	2.2	1.9	2.7
Before 1920		0.8	1.4	−1.5	−2.2	−1.0
In 1920's		1.8	2.3	−0.4	−0.8	0.5
In 1930's		8.5	6.2	2.5	0.4	1.3
In 1940's		9.0	12.9	6.9	5.9	3.5
After 1950		6.8	9.8	17.5	11.8	9.2

Source: 1930 and 1940 population from Earl Hanson and Paul Beckett, *Los Angeles: Its People and Its Homes* (Los Angeles: Haynes Foundation, 1944); 1946 population from Bureau of the Census, Series P-SC, No. 188; 1950, 1953, and 1956 population from Bureau of the Census, Series P-28, Nos. 603 and 927.

additional reversals in the direction of population change for cohorts and their component tracts probably would be found.

One departure from the generalized pattern of population changes accompanying maturation is, then, the mid-1950's reversal of postwar population loss in the 1920's cohort. We also have noted that the onset of population decline coincided with the end of World War II both in the before-1920 and 1920's cohorts, although the latter was presumably less mature at the time. The intercensal growth rates in Table 2 show that in both cohorts the average annual growth rate was more rapid during the war years (1940–46) than during the prewar decade. Another type of discrepancy is the relatively rapid growth rate of the 1930's cohort during the 1940 decade as compared with the growth rate of the 1920's cohort during the 1930 decade, that is, these cohorts evidence a growth differential during the same stage of maturation. Such deviations from, or fluctuations about, the "normal" growth curve may represent responses and compensations to changes in the city-wide growth context.

Temporal covariation between two indicators of the growth context—city-wide population growth and city-wide volume of new construction—and a summary measure of the patterning of city growth, the index of population redistribution among cohorts, might be taken as evidence of internal adjustments to contextual changes. (The redistribution index is half the sum of the absolute values of the differences between the percentage distributions of population by cohort at two dates.) Tabulated below for each of five intercensal periods are the average annual growth rate for Los Angeles, the number of dwellings added by new construction per 100 population increment, and the redistribution index expressed on an average annual basis.

Period	Growth Rate	New Construction Ratio	Redistribution Index
1930–40	2.2	38	0.7
1940–46	3.4	23	1.1
1946–50	2.2	61	2.2
1950–53	1.9	64	2.2
1953–56	2.7	45	1.7

With only five sets of observations, formal analysis of covariation among the series is precluded. It appears, however, that the new construction ratio varies directly with the redistribution index, at least when the rate of population growth is more or less constant. There also is some suggestion that the population growth rate varies directly with the redistribution index, "holding constant" the new construction ratio. Noteworthy, too, is the acceleration in the rate of population redistribution from more to less mature areas in the immediate postwar periods, when comment on the flight to the suburbs became widespread.

Working with the notion that the city-wide increase of population and the way in which the incremental population is housed are key factors shaping the pattern of city growth, we propose to show that the change in the redistribution pattern that occurred around the end of World War II could be explained largely on the basis of the shift in the ratio of population growth to new construction. To highlight the mechanism, population changes by cohort for the periods 1940–46 and 1946–50 are examined (Table 3).

During the war years, only some 69,000 dwellings were built in Los Angeles although the population increased by 301,000. A sizable portion of the incremental population must have found housing in dwellings which had been vacant, for vacancies fell from 36,000 in 1940 to 5,000 at the time of the 1946 special census. Given this pressure of population on the housing supply, any long-term tendency toward less intensive use of housing space was probably arrested. To demonstrate the implications of this population/housing balance for population redistribution among cohorts, we introduce the assumptions that (a) the 69,000 new units were distributed among cohorts proportionally to the distribution of units built between 1930 and 1950; (b) the 5,000 vacancies existing in 1946 were distributed among cohorts proportionally to the distribution of 1940 vacancies; and (c) the persons per room ratio observed in 1940 persisted throughout the six-year period. (The average number of persons per room is estimated to be 0.69 in 1940. The average number of rooms is estimated to be 3.4 for units vacant in 1940 and 4.5 for units built 1940–44. Estimates are derived from size-of-household and size-of-unit distributions published in the 1940 and 1950 Censuses.) Under these assumptions, the "expected" population change in the city as a whole is 304,000, including an increase of 15,000 military personnel at Fort MacArthur, some 214,000 persons housed in new units, and 75,000 persons housed in units vacant in 1940. The expected increase closely approximates the reported increase of 301,000. In each cohort, an increase in population is expected; and a population increase is observed in each cohort between 1940 and 1946. Moreover, the largest discrepancy between expected and actual changes for a co-

TABLE 3. Actual and Expected Population Changes,* for Census Tracts by Date Built Up, City of Los Angeles, 1940–46 and 1946–50 (In Thousands)

Date Built Up	Actual Change, 1940–46	Expected Change, 1940–46			Actual Change, 1946–50	Expected Change, 1946–50		
		Total	New Con-struction	Vacancy Drop		Total	New Con-struction	Vacancy Rise	Decon-gestion
City, Total	301	304	214	90[†]	165	157	290	−77[†]	−56
Before 1920	57	63	23	40	−50	−30	17	−22	−25
In 1920's	64	65	45	20	−10	− 4	25	−12	−17
In 1930's	33	30	26	4	13	18	24	− 2	− 4
In 1940's	63	59	40	19[†]	42	39	64	−21[†]	− 4
After 1950	84	87	80	7	168	134	160	−20	− 6

* See text for explanation of expected changes.
† Includes change of 15,000 military.

hort is only 6,000 persons, 10 per cent of the actual change, in the group of tracts built up prior to 1920.

In contrast, between 1946 and 1950 some 100,000 units were built in Los Angeles although the population increased by only 165,000. Vacancies rose from 5,000 to 31,000. By 1950, housing space was being used less intensively than at the beginning of World War II. We assume that (a) in each cohort, new units equal units reported built in the 1940's minus the units assumed to have been built 1940–46; (b) the change in vacancies in each cohort equals reported 1950 vacancies minus assumed 1946 vacancies; (c) the persons per room ratio fell from its 1940 to its 1950 level during the four-year period. (The average number of persons per room is estimated to be 0.67 in 1950. The average number of rooms is estimated to be 4.4 for units built 1945–50, 4.5 for units built 1940–44, 4.2 for units built before 1940, and 3.4 for units vacant in 1950.) Under these assumptions, the city-wide population change is expected to be 157,000, including a decrease of 15,000 at Fort MacArthur. The volume of new construction was sufficient to house 290,000. About 62,000 persons would have been displaced from their dwellings, however, by the rise in vacancies; and decongestion, or lessening room densities, would have displaced 56,000. By comparison, the reported change is 165,000. In the most mature cohorts, those built up before 1920 and in the 1920's, losses in population are expected as the net balance of increase through new construction and decrease through rising vacancies and decongestion; a loss in population is observed in each cohort between 1940 and 1946. In each more recently built-up cohort, the population increased as expected during the period. Population losses were substantially larger than expected, or gains less than expected, in the cohorts built up prior to World War II, however, while population increases were greater than expected in the cohorts not yet built up. These discrepancies reemphasize the fact that the assumptions are arbitrary and make no allowance for demolition in mature areas or the inverse association between an area's maturation and average household size.

Nonetheless, the comparisons of expected and actual changes make it clear that the onset of population decline in mature areas and the accelerated shift of population from mature to newer areas observed shortly after the end of World War II can be accounted for in large part by the timing of population growth and new construction. When new construction greatly lags behind population increase, as was the case during the war years, a sizable portion of the population increment must be housed in the existing inventory; consequently, the rate of redistribution appears unduly low, given the population growth rate. On an average annual basis, the expected rate of redistribution was 1.0 per cent. Following such a period of piling up, the redistribution rate accelerates sharply as new construction surges in response to pent-up demand and congestion in the existing inventory is reduced. In the immediate postwar period, the rate of redistribution expected was 1.8 per cent. Over the long run or under "normal" circumstances, new construction will keep pace with population increase; the rapidity of population redistribution from mature to building-up areas then varies directly with the city-wide rate of population increase.

SOME IMPLICATIONS

Generalizing from our case study of Los Angeles, risky as that may be, we submit that temporal and areal variation in the rate of "suburbanization" for cities can be accounted for only by a set of factors which includes indicators of the growth context, including the spatial configuration of built-up sub-areas. Although such factors have been assigned an important role in the patterning of city growth by students of an ecological persuasion,[8] attempts to quantify their impact on intraurban growth differentials have been few. Moreover, Bogue and Harris

---

[8] Leo F. Schnore, "Metropolitan Growth and Decentralization" and "The Growth of Metropolitan Suburbs," in William M. Dobriner (ed.), *The Suburban Community* (New York: G. P. Putnam's Sons, 1958).

found a correlation of only .3 between rapidity of suburbanization and the rate of population growth during the 1940's for 125 principal standard metropolitan areas.[9] They point out, however, that a sizable part of the intermetropolitan variation in rate of suburbanization, and presumably an even larger part of the "unexplained" variation, may stem from the vagaries of central-city annexation and disconnection.[10]

We have, therefore, re-examined the relationship between rate of suburbanization, adjusted for central-city annexation and disconnection, and area-wide population growth for the 160 standard metropolitan areas for which the 1950 population of the 1940 central city could be estimated.[11] Rough adjustments of the 1950 central-city and suburban-ring populations to allow for change in the residence allocation of college students and in the size of the armed forces between 1940 and 1950 also were made.[12] The suburbanization measure is the algebraic difference between the 1950 and 1940 percentages of metropolitan population living in the suburban ring, a positive value denoting suburbanization; this also was Bogue and Harris' measure. The latter apparently were correct in attributing their "disappointing" results in large part to uncontrolled differentials in annexation and disconnection among central cities. The correlation between the adjusted rate of suburbanization and the adjusted rate

of population growth is .56, substantially higher than the .3 based on unadjusted data. Incidentally, the rapidity of suburbanization during the 1940's appears to have been underestimated by Bogue and Harris, who were working with unadjusted data. They report a mean of 3.5 percentage points with a standard deviation of 5.0 for the suburbanization variable;[13] the mean of the adjusted measure is 6.1 percentage points with a standard deviation of 4.8.

Pursuing the hunch that not only the growth context but also the spatial configuration of built-up sub-areas shape the pattern of city growth, we added to the growth rate as predictors of suburbanization the population density of the central city and the total population of the standard metropolitan area, in the initial year, 1940. The multiple correlation between rapidity of suburbanization during the 1940's and the three predictors is .62 for the 160 standard metropolitan areas, and the beta coefficients (partial regression coefficients in standard form) indicate that each variable makes a significant, independent contribution to the explanation of variance in the dependent variable. The beta coefficients of rate of suburbanization on growth, density, and size are (a) growth, holding constant density and size, .62; (b) density, holding constant growth and size, .34; and (c) size, holding constant growth and density, −.17. Within this framework, rapid metropolitan growth and a densely populated central city are conducive to rapid suburbanization, while a large metropolitan population inhibits it. This might be taken to mean that growth tends to take the form of outward expansion until the spread of the city begins to present a barrier to internal transport and communication, at which juncture growth takes the form of upward expansion near the metropolitan core.[14]

[9] Donald J. Bogue and Dorothy L. Harris, *Comparative Population and Urban Research Via Multiple Regression and Covariance Analysis* (Oxford, Ohio: Scripps Foundation, Miami University, 1954), p. 75.

[10] Ibid., p. 52.

[11] Eight areas with central cities of less than 50,000 in 1940 were excluded. Estimates of the 1950 population in area annexed during the 1940's were based on block statistics or taken from Donald J. Bogue, *Components of Population Change, 1940–50* (Oxford, Ohio: Scripps Foundation, Miami University, 1957), Appendix, Table II.

[12] The "college" adjustment was the difference between the estimated 1950 college enrolment (half the enrolment of eighteen- and nineteen-year-old persons plus the enrolment of persons twenty or more) and the estimated 1950 college students whose parental home was in the area (2 per cent of the population). It was assumed that no armed forces had been present in any area in 1940, and they are, therefore, excluded from the 1950 population.

[13] Bogue and Harris, op. cit., p. 41.

[14] See also the findings reported by Edward Gross, "The Role of Density as a Factor in Metropolitan Growth in the United States of America," *Population Studies*, VIII (November 1954), 113–20.

The explanation of differences among the metropolitan areas in rapidity of suburbanization during the 1940's lies in large part in their differential rates of population growth. Moreover, the relationship between area-wide population change and population redistribution between central city and suburban ring is closer when allowance is made for population density in the central city and size of the metropolitan population. We again propose activity in residential construction as the mechanism whereby the growth is translated into redistribution. Over the decade, areal differences in new construction paralleled areal differences in population growth, and the ratio of new construction to population increment was more or less constant among the growing areas. The increase in the proportion of the metropolitan housing inventory located in the suburban ring and, hence, the suburbanization of the metropolitan population should vary directly with the rate of new construction under these circumstances, for new construction will be concentrated in subareas of the metropolis not yet built up, subareas located primarily in the suburban ring. Density of central city and size of metropolitan population provide controls on the extent to which the central city is built up and the pressure toward intensive residential use engendered by a large population.

The "flight to the suburbs," therefore, appears to be virtually synonymous with the "growth of the city." Two circumstances presumably account for the popularization of the new phrase in the late 1940's: First, the shifting balance of new construction to population growth during the 1940's resulted in an accelerated redistribution of population from mature to relatively undeveloped areas in the immediate postwar period. Second, the gap between the limits of the physical city and the boundaries of the corporate city widened appreciably in the 1940's. In the oldest metropolitan centers, the proportion of population in the physical city living in the corporate city dropped from 77 to 67 per cent between 1910 and 1940; by 1950, less than 62 per cent resided in the corporate city.[15] During the 1940's, annexations to the central city amounted to less than three square miles in 36 of these 44 metropolitan centers. Given the rigidity of corporate city boundaries, the extension of the physical city produced the flight to the suburbs

---

[15] Figures for 1910 and 1940 from Warren S. Thompson, *The Growth of Metropolitan Districts in the United States: 1900–1940* (Washington: Government Printing Office, 1947), Table IV. The 1950 figure is a maximum estimate derived from statistics published in the 1950 Census of Population on population of 1940 Metropolitan Districts and of urban places.

5

HAL H. WINSBOROUGH

An Ecological Approach to the Theory of Suburbanization

ABSTRACT

Suburbanization is a result of variation in two theoretically elemental aspects of urban population distribution, congestion and concentration, which can be derived from ecological theory about the structure of the city. Measures of these aspects need not vary together; variation in either may lead to increase in the areal size of the population agglomeration. Both are related to the population size of the agglomeration. Variables suggested by the ecological theory of the structure of the city are associated with variation in the aspects of suburbanization.

Few social trends have received as much attention as the suburbanization of American cities. This process is thought to have vast implications for our national life, affecting such diverse phenomena as the mental and moral health of the population, the efficiency of political control, and the vulnerability of cities to atomic attack. Despite the presumed importance of the suburbanization trend, so little is known of the process that Bogue and Harris, at the conclusion of their extensive study, were led to remark, "A fairly complete, theoretically sound and stable explanation of relative suburbanization remains to be developed."[1]

Although suburbanization means many different things,[2] basic to all notions is the phenomenon of the sprawl of urban population agglomerations over the landscape. It is in this narrow sense that the term "suburbanization" is used in this paper. By so doing, it is not our intention to suggest that distinctions between the word "suburb" and such words as "satellite" or "fringe" are not useful. Rather, we hold, with Schnore, that such entities "are themselves merely constituent parts of a larger urban complex—the metropolitan structure as a whole."[3] By using "suburbanization" as noted above, we have defined it as a phenomenon pertaining to the metropolitan structure that is basic to the development of the various

Reprinted by permission from the *American Journal of Sociology*, Vol. LXVIII, No. 5 (March 1963), pp. 565–570. Copyright by the University of Chicago.

This is Paper No. 16 in the series, "Comparative Urban Research," issued by the Population Research and Training Center, University of Chicago, under a grant from the Ford Foundation.

[1] Donald J. Bogue and Dorothy L. Harris, *Comparative Population and Urban Research via Multiple Regression and Covariance Analysis* ("Scripps Foundation Studies in Population Distribution," No. 8 [Oxford, Ohio: Scripps Foundation, Miami University, 1954]), p. 72.

[2] Bogue and Harris use no less than fifteen dependent variables in their analysis of the state and the process of suburbanization (ibid., p. 52).

[3] Leo F. Schnore, "Satellites and Suburbs," *Social Forces*, XXXVI (December 1957), 121–127. [No. 7 in this volume.]

types of peripheral communities, regardless of their functional or organizational characteristics.

The thesis of this paper is that a theory of suburbanization in this limited sense remains to be developed for two reasons:

1. The phenomenon of suburbanization has been thought of as a single process when, in fact, it is a result of changes in two aspects of urban population distribution that are theoretically and empirically distinct.

2. Explanations of the variation in suburbanization have not been based on the considerable body of ecological theory about the structure of the city as a whole.

We will argue that variation in suburbanization is a result of variation in two theoretically elemental parameters of urban population distribution which we will label "congestion" and "concentration." It will be noted that these aspects of suburbanization can be derived from a theory of the structure of the city. We will show empirically that these parameters need not vary in the same direction at the same time, and argue theoretically that variation in either of these parameters may lead to increase in the areal size of the population agglomeration. Further, we will demonstrate that these two aspects of suburbanization are theoretically and empirically related to variation in the population size of urban agglomerations and can, in part, be seen as ways of accommodating variation in population size.

THEORIES OF URBAN STRUCTURE

One body of current theory about the structure of the city focuses on the competition among land-users for accessible land.[4] Because land near the center of the city is thought to be, on the average, the most accessible to all parts of the city, many businesses and services find central location desirable and are willing and able to pay large sums for parcels of the small quantity of land near the center. Households are not, by and large, able to compete for this extremely accessible land, but they too find advantage in locating near the center of the city because of reduced costs of travel to work, to shopping, and to the services offered in the center.

Considering only residential land, location near the center means higher land costs but lower transit cost. Location farther from the center, on the other hand, means increased transportation costs but diminished land costs because of less competition and because the supply of land increases in proportion to the square of distance from the center. Given these conditions, if persons locate their residences to minimize their total "cost," an equilibrium is reached when location at any distance from the center of the city is equally "costly." When such an equilibrium is reached, there is a particular distribution of population by distance from the center of the city. Hence, there is a particular distribution of population density by distance from the center.

Using this line of reasoning, Muth constructed a model that predicts an exponential decline in population density with distance from the center.[5] In this model, Muth assumes the usual economist's conditions of firm equilibrium, the usual function of transportation cost with distance and an exponential decline in cost of housing with distance from the center which he justifies empirically. This exponential decline in density has been reported previously as an empirical finding by Clark[6] and by Stewart and Warntz.[7] The exponential function may be given by

$$d(r) = d(0) \, e^{-r/g}, \qquad (1)$$

---

[4] See, e.g., Amos Hawley, *Human Ecology* (New York: Ronald Press Co., 1950), esp. Chaps. XIII and XIV.

[5] Richard F. Muth, "The Spatial Structure of the Housing Market" (paper presented at a joint session of the Econometric Society and the Regional Science Association in St. Louis, December 2, 1960).

[6] Colin Clark, "Urban Population Densities," *Journal of the Royal Statistical Society*, Ser. A., CXIV (1957), 490–496 (see also his "Urban Population Densities," *Bulletin of the International Statistical Institute*, XXXVI, No. 4 (1957), 60–90.

[7] John Q. Stewart and William Warntz, "Physics of Population Distribution," *Journal of Regional Science*, I, No. 1 (1958), 99–123.

where $d(r)$ is the density at r distance from the center of the city, $d(0)$ is the density extrapolated to the center itself, and g indicates how density declines with distance. A more satisfying interpretation of the parameter g can be gained by noting that, if the foregoing actually describes the decline in density with distance and if the city were circular, then the population $p(r)$ of a zone of width dr at r distance from the city center would be given by

$$p(r) = 2\pi d(0)re^{-r/g}\, dr. \tag{2}$$

The latter is a unimodal function with maximum at $r = g$ as can be shown from its first and second derivatives. Thus, g may be interpreted as a kind of average distance of persons from the city center.[8]

ASPECTS OF SUBURBANIZATION

In the model situation, equation (1) distinguishes between, and provides a measure for, the two elemental aspects of suburbanization. The parameter g indicates concentration because it measures average distance from the city center; similarly, the parameter $d(0)$ is an indicator of congestion because it measures crowding in or near the city center.

If one is interested in the state of suburbanization at a given time, the values of these parameters describe the elemental aspect of population distribution in the urban aggregate. If one is interested in the process of suburbanization over time, changes in these parameters describe basic changes that may occur in population distribution.

Changes in the areal size of the model population agglomeration can result from a change in either of these two parameters. This assertion can be justified as follows: Suppose the "edge of town" is defined, as is approximated in the urbanized area concept used by the Bureau of the Census, as the distance from the

center of the city, a, where the population density falls to a given figure, L. Then, rewriting equation (1),

$$L = d(0)e^{-a/g} \tag{3}$$

and

$$a = g\,[\log_e d(0) - \log_e L]. \tag{4}$$

Thus, with g constant, a is a function of $d(0)$. With $d(0)$ constant, a is a function of g.

It is not empirically necessary that these two aspects of urban population distribution vary together. This can be shown by estimating the parameters g and $d(0)$ for one city over a fairly long period of time. Data can be compiled on the population density of mile zones in Chicago for every decade from 1860 to 1950. The parameters of equation (1) are estimated by fitting to these data the linear equation

$$\log_{10} d(r) = \log_{10} d(0) - \frac{\log_{10} e}{g}\,(r). \tag{5}$$

Table 1 presents these parameters.

TABLE 1.   Parameters for Equation $d(r) = d(0)e^{-r/g}$ Where $d(r)$ is Population Density at r Distance from Center of City, for Chicago, 1860–1950*

Year	g	$d(0)$ (Thousands)	Correlation Coefficient	No.
1860	1.09	30.0	−.98	4
1870	1.14	70.8	−.99	6
1880	1.26	96.6	−.98	7
1890	1.97	86.3	−.98	13
1900	2.41	100.0	−.97	14
1910[†]	2.71	100.0	−.97	15
1920[†]	4.36	51.2	−.97	8
1930	5.60	49.1	−.94	8
1940	5.85	46.2	−.93	8
1950	6.51	46.5	−.95	8

*Data for 1910 and before are taken from *Report of the Chicago Traction and Subway Commission, 1916, on a Unified System of Surface, Elevated and Subway Lines* (Chicago, 1916), p. 73. Data for 1920 and later are compiled by grouping community areas.

†Since data for 1910 and before are taken from one source and data for 1920 and after compiled from other sources, comparison of parameters between 1910 and 1920 is unreliable.

---

[8] Further, Taitel has shown that $2g$ is the mean distance of all persons from the center of the city when the city is circular and the decline in density continues to infinity (Martin Taitel, "On Problems of Measuring the Distribution of Population in an Urban Area," *Proceedings of the Social Statistics Section of the American Statistical Association*, 1960, pp. 160–165).

If by suburbanization one has in mind the concept measured by the parameter g, then Chicago has been deconcentrating since 1860. On the other hand, if one has in mind the concept measured by $d(0)$, then Chicago was growing more congested from 1860 to 1900 or 1910. Since that time congestion has decreased. From these data, then, we may conclude that it is not necessary that these two aspects of suburbanization vary together.

From one point of view, it is not very surprising that g increases through the one hundred year period in Chicago. After all, the population size would seem to imply increase in area and, hence, an increase in average distance from the city center. This view, however, ignores the fact that population increase in the model city can be accommodated by increase in g or by increase in $d(0)$. This last assertion can be justified as follows: if the relationship expressed in equation (2) holds, then the population P of a circular city out to the limits of the city at distance a from the center is given by

$$P(a) = 2\pi \int_0^a d(0)\, ae^{-a/g} da \qquad (6)$$

or evaluating the integral,

$$P(a) = 2\pi g^2 d(0) \times \left[1 - \frac{(a/g) + 1}{e^{a/g}} \right]. \qquad (7)$$

The expression $2\pi g^2\, d(0)$ is the population that would exist within the model city if its limits (and the fit of eq. [1]) extended extremely far from the center of the city.[9] The expression within brackets is a correction factor to adjust the population to compensate for setting the limits of the city at a finite distance from the city.

Once again, if the edge of the city is defined where the density falls to some value L, then equation (7) can be rewritten

$$P = 2\pi g^2 d(0) \times \left\{ 1 - \frac{\log_e[d(0)/L] + 1}{d(0)/L} \right\}. \qquad (8)$$

From equation (8) it is clear that population size is theoretically a function of the parameters g and $d(0)$.

However, it is worthwhile to question whether equation (8) is empirically justified. For Chicago from 1910 to 1940 the population of the metropolitan district is roughly the population within a density of 150 persons per square mile. For 1950 the population of the urbanized area is roughly the population within a density of 2,000 per square mile. If estimates of g and $d(0)$ are taken from Table 1 and if we consider Chicago a half-circle city, then Table 2 presents population estimates of the urban agglomeration from 1910 to 1950. Considering the crude assumptions involved in these calculations, the findings in Table 2 justify empirically an investigation of the implications of equation (8).

Equation (8) suggests that an increase in population size will require a modification of one or both of the parameters g and $d(0)$. In Chicago, up to 1900, it appears that population increase was accommodated by both a decrease in concentration and an increase in congestion. After 1900, apparently, it was no longer necessary to increase congestion to increase population. Deconcentration was satisfactory to accommodate the increase in population and even to permit decongestion to occur.

It is worth noting that population size in equation (8) is proportional to the square of g when $d(0)$ is constant. Thus, cities which already have a large value of g can accommodate more people by a unit increase in that parameter than can cities having a smaller initial value.

TABLE 2. Actual and Estimated Population for Chicago Area, 1910–50

Date	Actual Population (000)	Estimated Population (000)	Error (000)	Per Cent Error
1910	2,446.9	2,279.6	−167.3	−6.8
1920	3,178.9	2,993.5	−185.4	−5.8
1930	4,364.8	4,733.4	+368.6	+8.4
1940	4,499.1	4,855.0	+355.9	+7.9
1950	4,920.8	5,074.0	+153.3	+3.1

[9] This equation, in a slightly different form, can be found in Clark, op. cit.

EXPLANATIONS OF ASPECTS OF SUBURBANIZATION

Muth has demonstrated that synchronic variations in the parameter g in United States cities in 1950 are associated with variations in variables having to do with transportation costs within the city.[10] The variable of transportation costs is, of course, derived from the theory of urban structure that was used in isolating a as an aspect of suburbanization. The following data illustrate the fact that pursuit of this line of reasoning may lead to explanation of changes in suburbanization.

For eight cities it is possible to compute g for 1890 and for 1950 and also to obtain data on the ratio of mass transit passenger rides to population. These data are given in Table 3, along with the correlation between distance and density for each city in each time period. In 1890 the correlation between g and rides per

person was .42. In 1950 the correlation was −.68. Because the degrees of freedom here are certainly small and the sample of cities is not at all random, these results must be taken as only suggestive. These data do suggest, however, that intensive use of mass transit in 1890 implies a city that was relatively deconcentrated while in 1950 it suggests a city that was relatively concentrated. The difference in these two correlations is probably to be explained by the introduction of the automobile. In 1890 mass transit was probably the most efficient way to get to work. In 1950 mass transit is in competition with the auto.

Just as theory may be useful in explaining variation in suburbanization, so may the investigation of suburbanization be useful to theory. The equilibrium type of theory used in the foregoing pages necessarily neglects many aspects of reality. One of the theoretically interesting aspects of reality ignored by this model is the effect of previous growth on present city struc-

[10] Muth, op. cit.

TABLE 3. Comparison of Relationship between Parameter g and Rides per Person on Mass Transit in Eight Cities, 1890 and 1950

City	1890*			1950†		
	Value of g	Value of r[‡]	Transit Ratio	Value of g	Value of r[‡]	Transit Ratio
Boston	3.31	−.74	252	3.33	−.59	164
Cincinnati	.85	−.90	128	1.45	−.82	114
Detroit	1.87	−.80	111	10.00	−.55	102
Kansas City	1.37	−.90	286	3.85	−.57	105
Philadelphia	1.95	−.62	158	2.50	−.71	148
Pittsburgh	1.10	−.76	134	11.11	−.14	85
St. Louis	1.08	−.73	150	3.57	−.53	136
Washington, D.C.	2.02	−.94	153	3.70	−.52	135

  * Data for 1890 were compiled from U.S. Census Office, *Report on Vital and Social Statistics in the United States at the Eleventh Census: 1890*, Part II, "Vital Statistics, Cities of 100,000 Population and Upwards," pp. 143–334. Data for Boston and Philadelphia were taken from U.S. Census Office, *Vital Statistics of Boston and Philadelphia Covering a Period of Six Years Ending May 31, 1890*. Data for Washington, D.C., were taken from U.S. Census Office, *Vital Statistics of the District of Columbia and Baltimore Covering a Period of Six Years Ending May 31, 1890*. In all cases distance from the center of the city was estimated from ward maps included in the various volumes.

  † For 1950 values of g and r are taken from Richard F. Muth, op. cit. The transit ratio is computed from data in *Transit Facts*, a mimeographed publication of the Public Administration Clearing House in co-operation with the American Transit Association.

  ‡ The value of r is the value of the correlation between distance from the center of the city and the logarithm of population density.

ture. This aspect is of theoretical concern because of its importance in one of the early descriptions of city structure—the Burgess zonal hypothesis. In that hypothesis, zonal variation in city structure was thought to be the result of the very growth of the city.

In order to investigate the influence of the timing of growth on density, we have computed, using small area data within the city, correlations among the logarithm of density, distance from the center of the city, and as a measure of the age of the area, the percentage of dwellings built before 1920. These correlations were computed for Chicago and Cleveland in 1940. They are presented in Table 4. Distance and age are negatively correlated and density and age positively correlated in both Chicago and Cleveland. The latter correlation is stronger in Chicago and the former stronger in Cleveland. The first-order partial correlation between the logarithm of density and distance, holding constant age of dwellings, is about —.60 for both Chicago and Cleveland. Thus, the relationship between density and distance, although somewhat augmented by the influence of age of dwellings, cannot be explained by that variable.

The relationship between age and density, on the other hand, is diminished considerably when distance from the center of the city is held constant. In Chicago it drops to .30 while in Cleveland it drops to —.08. Thus the partial correlation of age and density remains significant in one of the cities.

Looking at this finding in a different way, we note that for Chicago the value of g computed from the zero-order regression of density on distance is 5.3, while the value of g computed from the first-order partial regression is 6.0. In Cleveland, on the other hand, g computed from the zero-order regression is 3.0, while g computed from the first-order partial regression coefficient is 2.9. In Chicago the influence of the time of growth seems to have restrained deconcentration, while in Cleveland it has had little influence.

Thus we find that the pattern of settlement over time may make a difference in the degree

TABLE 4. Correlations between Distance from Center, Logarithm of Population Density, and Age of Dwellings, Chicago and Cleveland, 1940*

City	Distance	Density	Age
Chicago[†]			
Distance	—	—.69	—.45
Density	—.60	—	.52
Age	—.15	.30	—
Cleveland[‡]			
Distance	—	—.65	—.62
Density	—.60	—	.35
Age	—.53	—.08	—

* Zero-order correlations are given above the diagonal, first-order partial correlations below.

† Data on density and distance from the center of Chicago for square mile areas within the city and towns outside the city are taken from Richard V. Rockwell, "Metropolitan Lane Values as a Function of Population Growth and Decentralization" (unpublished Master's thesis, University of Chicago, August, 1956). Data on age of dwellings are estimated for mile zones and towns from 1940 census data for census tracts.

‡ Data for Cleveland are drawn from the *Real Property Inventory of the Cleveland and Metropolitan District and Cuyahoga County,* 1941.

of concentration found in the city. We also find that the importance, or even the existence, of these effects may vary from city to city. These results, then, point up the complex theoretical problem of the influence of previous growth on present structure. It suggests that the present theory of urban population distribution should be modified to account for influences of previous growth patterns on current population distribution.[11]

SUMMARY

This paper has argued that the state or process of suburbanization in a city is not a single thing but the result of changes in two elemental aspects of urban population distribution, concentration, and congestion. The parameters of

[11] A sound beginning on this kind of theoretical modification is provided by Beverly Duncan, Georges Sabagh, and Maurice D. Van Arsdol, Jr., "Patterns of City Growth," *American Journal of Sociology,* LXVII (January 1962), 418–429. [No. 4 in this volume.]

the distribution of population over the urban aggregate provide well-defined and empirically productive measures of the state of concentration and congestion of the city. Changes in the population distribution resulting in the phenomenon of urban sprawl can, this paper asserts, be best understood in terms of changes in these two parameters.

6

LEO F. SCHNORE

The Timing of Metropolitan Decentralization: A Contribution to the Debate

Metropolitan Decentralization is one of the most thoroughly explored areas of investigation in the study of population distribution in the United States [1]. However, little explicit attention has been directed toward differences in the timing of the outward shift of residential population in individual areas. Yet it can be argued that variations in the timing of decentralization around individual cities are facts of crucial importance in acquiring an understanding of the whole phenomenon. For one thing, analysis of these differences among cities might provide some clues to the causal factors involved, particularly if it should be found that cities experiencing relatively early decentralization reveal systematic differences in other characteristics from those undergoing decentralization more recently. Perhaps even more fundamental is the fact that "decentralization"—however it may be defined in operational terms—is ordinarily conceived as a *process*, so that temporal considerations are necessary in the very nature of the case.

THE DEBATE OVER TIMING

Unfortunately, the American literature exhibits little agreement upon the simple issue of when the movement got under way. One of the most thorough of the American studies bears the subtitle "Deconcentration Since 1920," suggesting a rather recent phenomenon [2]. Closer examination, however, reveals that this phrase is clearly intended to characterize a whole aggregate of cities and is not to be taken as a description of the experience of individual places. Still, this characterization makes intuitive sense, in view of the presumed importance of the private automobile—which became widely used only after World War I — in permitting wider residential dispersion without loss of contact with the center.

Other portions of the American literature suggest that viewing decentralization as a recent phenomenon can be seriously misleading. After all, the Census Bureau was led to assemble data for large cities and their adjacent areas as early as the thirteenth census of 1910. Rapid peripheral growth must have been clearly evident well before that date; in fact, official discussions in various census sources make this abundantly

Reprinted by permission of the *Journal of the American Institute of Planners*, Vol. 25 (November 1959), pp. 200–206.

clear. In addition, of course, Adna F. Weber had clearly perceived an outward shift of residential population around certain larger cities in the last quarter of the nineteenth century [3]. The view that decentralization is a process of long standing has been most vigorously stated by Robert Schmitt.

> There is nothing new about suburbanization. For at least a century, large American cities have grown chiefly by peripheral accretion. Population has always increased more rapidly on the outskirts than close to the central business district. . . .Suburbanization is old stuff [4].

PROBLEMS OF MEASUREMENT

One major difficulty is immediately encountered in any attempt to approach the question of the timing of decentralization empirically. The data are assembled in terms of politically defined areal units, and we are without any precise standards or criteria for the very definition of decentralization. The resulting lack of conceptual precision can be indicated in the form of a question: at what point does "normal" city growth—which almost inevitably occurs at the periphery of existing settlement—become "decentralization"? This is more than merely a matter of quibbling over definitions. Most of that which has been labelled "decentralization" may simply represent the exhaustion of space for residential development within city boundaries. If a growing city is unable, for whatever reason, to annex surrounding territory, little else can be expected than relatively high rates of growth at the periphery. In fact, sheer availability of space for residential development may be so significant as to make most hypothetical "determinants" of decentralization redundant in any real explanatory sense [5].

At any rate, the data presented here have been assembled in order to throw light upon these fundamental and interlocking questions: (1) When did decentralization, as commonly measured, begin in individual cities of the United States? (2) What are some of the characteristics of cities that have undergone decentralization at different time periods? (3) What is

the theoretical link between "decentralization" and "metropolitanism"?

A review of the literature on decentralization yields a long list of "factors" said to be causally operative; these range from rather gross attributes of cities themselves (e.g., sheer size) to the most subtle psychological motivations of persons. To reconcile these "explanations" in some orderly theoretical fashion would be an imposing task indeed. Our intention here is not to undertake such an exercise in codification, but merely to provide some base-line descriptive data with respect to the timing of decentralization as it is frequently measured, and to discuss some of the implications of our findings for theory and further research.

DATA AND PROCEDURES

The empirical materials presented here are based upon the observed growth of the 99 metropolitan central cities that have had a population of at least 100,000 at some point in their developments. For comparative purposes, official areal definitions of Standard Metropolitan Areas in the 1950 census were retrojected to the earliest possible date; this procedure affords at least a rough control over total area and permits the observation of the relative redistribution of population within these areas for a series of decades. Growth rates for the individual cities and their respective "rings" were then compared.

Especially close attention had to be given to annexations and detachments of area by the central cities. Since annexations far outnumber detachments of territory, the over-all effect of these areal changes has been to understate decentralization as measured by comparison of city-versus-ring growth rates. With respect to timing, the effect has been to delay decentralization as narrowly defined here. Many cities have maintained higher growth rates by almost continuous areal expansion at the expense of the ring. In this study, annexation imparts a bias in the direction of classifying cities as "decentralizing" *later* than they would actually appear to be if city area were truly held constant. However, careful attention was given to the annexation history of each city throughout the entire period under review, so this bias is minimized although not entirely eliminated [6].

At any rate, following a review of city and ring growth and of annexations, each city was classified according to the *earliest* decade in which relative decentralization became evident, that is, the earliest decade in which ring growth began *systematically* to exceed that of the city. At least three consecutive decades of higher ring growth had to be registered before a city was classified as decentralizing [7].

FINDINGS

Peripheral growth in excess of that of the center is clearly not a unique product of the 'twenties—nor of the twentieth century, for that matter. Table 1 contains our basic data with respect to the timing of decentralization. It can be seen that one city (New York) was "decentralizing" as early as the 1850's and that it was joined by nine others before the turn of the century [8]. (See the "total" row at the bottom of the table.) However, it is equally clear that it was not until the 'twenties that the majority of these cities began to exhibit lower growth rates than their own rings. Fully 60 cities began to decentralize within the space of twenty years—between 1920 and 1940. It appears that decentralization occurred with a rush following World War I; thus Hawley's reference to "deconcentration since 1920" is confirmed as a summary description of a majority of large cities in the United States.

Table 1 also contains basic information on the history of urban development in this country (see the "total" column at the extreme right). Although at least one city of 50,000 population (again, New York) could be found as early as 1800, the forty-year interval between 1880 and 1920 appears to have been the most intensive "city-building" period in the history of the United States. Over 60 places achieved a size of 50,000 during this interval.

The five places reaching 50,000 prior to 1850 (New York, Philadelphia, Baltimore, Boston, and New Orleans, in that order) show no clear-cut pattern; the first large cities apparently began to decentralize at widely separated dates, and in no particular sequence. Those reaching 50,000 in 1850 or later, however, show a rather clear pattern. Among these 94 cities, only three (Duluth, Beaumont-Port Arthur, and Baton Rouge) began to decentralize before reaching this minimum size. It is perhaps more important that only one of these cities (Washington, D.C.) failed to begin decentralization within five decades after reaching this minimum size, and most cities began within four decades. As a result, there is a rather clear correlation between the timing of decentralization and sheer age of settlement, as these characteristics are measured here; in general, the older places tended to decentralize earlier. But what other features are associated with early or late decentralization?

Certain selected characteristics of this same universe of American cities are set out in Table 2. It should be noted that these characteristics are among those previously investigated by Thompson, Bogue, and Hawley in their studies of metropolitan decentralization, in which these items were revealed to be important differentiating factors. Table 2 indicates that each of these variables shows a rather clear pattern with respect to the timing of decentralization. To summarize the findings, the *earliest* decentralization was exhibited by cities that are currently largest, and located in the Northeast, at deep water sites, relatively close to other metropolitan centers. However, all these characteristics are themselves related to age of settlement, for this description would also serve to characterize the oldest cities. These facts suggest that a notion of "metropolitan maturity" might be usefully applied. Age certainly appears to be important, but age *per se* can hardly be decisive. As we shall argue in the following section, the organizational concomitants of long-term settlement may be the factors deserving further study.

TABLE 1. The Timing of Urban Growth and Decentralization in the United States: 99 Metropolitan Areas with Central Cities of 100,000 or More Inhabitants

Census Year in Which the Central City First Reached 50,000	Decade In Which "Decentralization" Began										Continued "Centralization"	Total Number of Areas
	1850's	1860's	1870's	1880's	1890's	1900's	1910's	1920's	1930's	1940's		
1800	1	—	—	—	—	—	—	—	—	—	—	1
1810	—	—	—	—	—	1	—	—	—	—	—	1
1820	—	—	—	—	1	—	—	—	—	—	—	1
1830	—	—	—	1	—	—	—	—	—	—	—	1
1840	—	—	—	—	—	—	—	1	—	—	—	1
1850	—	—	1	1	1	—	—	—	—	—	—	3
1860	—	—	1	—	—	4	1	1	1	—	—	8
1870	—	—	1	—	—	2	1	3	—	—	—	7
1880	—	—	—	—	1	2	4	5	3	—	—	15
1890	—	—	—	—	—	—	5	7	3	—	—	15
1900	—	—	—	—	1	1	2	3	12	—	—	19
1910	—	—	—	—	—	—	—	4	11	—	—	15
1920	—	—	—	—	—	—	—	2	2	—	—	4
1930	—	—	—	—	—	—	—	1	—	—	4	5
1940	—	—	—	—	—	—	—	—	—	1	1	2
1950	—	—	—	—	—	—	—	1	—	—	—	1
Total No. of Areas	1	0	3	2	4	10	13	28	32	1	5	99

83

TABLE 2. The Timing of Decentralization and Selected Characteristics of 99 Metropolitan Areas with Central Cities of 100,000 or More Inhabitants

Selected Characteristics	Number of Areas in which Decentralization Began in: 1910's or Earlier	1920's	1930's or 1940's	Number of Areas Showing Continued Centralization	Total Number of Areas
Central City Size, 1950					
1,000,000 or over	5	1	0	0	6
500,000–1,000,000	8	3	1	0	12
250,000–500,000	5	8	6	0	19
100,000–250,000	15	16	26	5	62
Census Region					
Northeast	16	6	5	0	27
North Central	6	11	9	0	26
South	6	8	15	5	34
West	5	3	4	0	12
Distance to Nearest Metropolis[a]					
less than 50 miles	19	12	12	0	43
50 to 100 miles	9	13	11	3	36
Over 100 miles	5	3	10	2	20
Geographic Site Features[a]					
Sea or lake coast	20	6	5	1	32
Navigable river	10	14	7	0	31
Other (land-locked)	3	8	21	4	36
Total	33	28	33	5	99

[a] See Amos Hawley, *The Changing Shape of Metropolitan America* [2]; these classifications are used with the kind permission of the author.

What are we to infer from these findings? Certain conclusions are immediately evident. Just as the designation "metropolitan" loses specificity when applied wholesale to all cities of 50,000 or over, the label "decentralization" appears to be robbed of much of its denotative value when it is applied to all these places in which city growth rates have fallen below those of immediately surrounding areas, without any regard for the precise period in which this shift occurred. To call a city of 50,000 a "metropolis" —thereby implying that it is somehow equivalent to places inhabited by millions—may be highly gratifying to the residents of the smaller city, but it hardly enhances our knowledge of metropolitanism. By the same token, we may do well to devise different labels for the outward shifts of higher growth rates of the 1850's as against the 1950's, for they may be qualitatively different phenomena. However, this raises the whole question of definition to which we have alluded above, and we must return again to the conceptual considerations that gave rise to this study.

THE THEORY OF METROPOLITAN DECENTRALIZATION

We have already commented upon the difficulties stemming from a lack of base-line comparisons between "normal" city growth and decentralization. But there is another major flaw in current approaches to metropolitan development. The bulk of the research literature on decentralization, including the material contained here, exhibits one striking feature. The statistical and other data assembled only rarely include elements that can be viewed as structural, despite the fact that the theoretical literature has treated the rise of metropolitanism as essentially an organizational change, in which whole areas and their constituent units (manufacturing establishments, commercial enterprises, private households, etc.) are brought into a new kind of relationship. Despite this clear theoretical emphasis, the data assembled by researchers have only tangential bearing upon the crucial structural features of metropolitan areas as conceived by the major theorists.

Yet, to point to this wide gap between current research and existing theory is perhaps to point to a way out of the dilemma. What is obviously required at this point is a great deal of exploratory effort aimed at specifying the critical organizational features of both (1) "metropolitanism" and (2) "decentralization." Both concepts have an obvious demographic component of a very simple type. For "metropolitan" areas, a minimum population-size criterion is certainly to be desired—although the limit may turn out to be well above that in current census usage. At the same time, any reasonable definition of "decentralization" will probably *include* the existence of peripheral rates of growth in excess of the rates for the centers themselves.

However, failure to move beyond these minimal definitions is to invite continued confusion. In common usage, a "metropolitan" area is more than merely a large assemblage of people concentrated in a relatively limited space. Large and dense agglomerations have been known throughout history. The added element in any reasonable conception of "metropolitan" is a matter of social and economic organization—some unique structural configuration that is lacking in the densely settled alluvial plains of contemporary agrarian societies and in the large preindustrial cities of the past.

TRADITIONAL THEORY

Judging from the general tenor of the American theoretical literature, the key structural feature of the metropolitan area is an extremely high degree of *interdependence* that is reflected in an intricate *territorial division of labor.* To quote N. S. B. Gras, the economic historian, "We may think of metropolitan economy as an organization of people having a large city as a nucleus. . . . Mere agglomeration of individuals, important as that is, does not constitute a metropolis. . . . What counts most is commercial dominance over a wide area. . . " [9].

Yet Gras went on to qualify the notion of "dominance" as some kind of one-way street. It is true that the outlying area is dependent upon the city, but the center is also dependent upon the hinterland. In Gras' own words, "Interdependence of the parts is really the key to the whole thing"[10]. Working with a highly similar conception, R. D. McKenzie described the modern metropolitan community as a "new type of supercommunity organized around a dominant focal point and comprising a multiple of differentiated centers of activity" [11].

These writers make it abundantly clear that we cannot profitably conceive the metropolitan area as a simple two-part arrangement of center and ring, a large city with its adjacent territory. To the extent that this oversimplified model has found its way into the literature on metropolitan areas, it constitutes a theoretical retrogression from the pioneering work of Gras and McKenzie. The metropolitan community must be viewed—in organizational terms throughout—as a highly specialized mosaic of subareas tied together into a new functional unity. Moreover, it is to be viewed as a multi-nucleated territorial system. Within these broad areas, the large centers are marked by functional diversity, while the smaller places, many of them formerly independent cities in their own right, tend to be narrowly specialized. At the same time, however, the main centers are specialized in the coordinating functions of administration and control. It is a striking fact that the very best empirical work that has been conducted in terms of this conception of metropolitan structure, the research by Bogue, Kish, and Isard and Whitney, has been essentially static in orientation, so very little light is shed upon such "processes" as decentralization [12].

By the same token, "decentralization" requires further specification in structural terms. The existing literature is less helpful here, but something more than rapid peripheral growth is implied in much of the theoretical literature. Aside from attempts to characterize living outside city boundaries as "a way of life," the underlying theme in these accounts, implicit as it may be, is best identified as organizational *complexity*, a functional unity that is achieved over a broader area of interdependence by virtue of movement and exchange.

MOVEMENT AND METROPOLITANISM

One of the key features distinguishing the true metropolis from the large cities of past history (and other high-density assemblages of people) is the ease and rapidity of exchange or movement, whether of persons, commodities, or information. However, even the smaller cities of the Western world, which also enjoy the advanced transportation and communication facilities of the metropolis, share this ease of movement. The *unique* features distinguishing movement in the metropolitan area appear merely to reflect the enhanced complexity associated with a system of interdependent nuclei.

Physical movement in the metropolitan area is much less simple with respect to direction and over-all orientation. In contrast with the simple in-and-out movement between center and periphery of the smaller city, the metropolitan area appears to have a very high proportion of *lateral movements*, in complicated crosscurrents and eddies. Commuting, in particular, is not merely a matter of centripetal and centrifugal flows morning and evening, but a confusing and asymmetrical compound of variously oriented threads of traffic, overlaying the older (and perhaps rudimentary) center-oriented pattern.

This greater complexity of movement, of course, is related to the structural feature that

we have identified as typologically essential to metropolitanism—interdependence reflected in an extreme territorial division of labor. Organizational interdependence between the constituent segments of the whole metropolitan area is only achieved via specialization of land use, and areal specialization requires complex movement systems [13]. It is obvious that the functional fragmentation of space requires movement, and that as the underlying patterns of interdependence become more complex, the manifest patterns of movement will become progressively less simple [14].

In fact, "*decentralization*," defined in terms of organizational complexity and measured by patterns of movement between subareas, *may even serve as a rather readily observed index of "metropolitanism."* Complex movement systems may be assumed to arise out of the decentralization of many of the constituent functional units of the total area, including places of employment as well as households. Such a complex movement system would necessarily represent a high degree of interdependence of parts, the very feature which we have previously identified as the major organizational element in theoretical discussions of metropolitan phenomena [15].

IMPLICATIONS FOR FURTHER STUDY

The problem of availability of data for observation cannot be ignored. Some attention must necessarily be given the construction of indexes to stand for these rather vague and abstract terms—"complexity," "interdependence," etc. As a beginning in this direction, we might suggest the use of direct observations of movement. Ratios of lateral to centripetal-centrifugal trips can be assembled on a comparative basis (e.g., for a range of various-sized cities). Hypothetically, the "true" metropolitan areas would show very high proportions of lateral movement, while smaller areas (non-metropolitan cities) would exhibit high proportions of simple in-and-out movement.

Available traffic data, however, are rather scattered and they refer to different dates. Moreover, they cover a biased sample of cities—

those experiencing particularly severe problems of congestion. It is at this point that the "place of work" question on the 1960 census should be most useful. Present plans call for the identification of work sites on a county basis, with separate identification of cities of 50,000 or more inhabitants. With somewhat more detailed areal codes, reliable ratios of lateral to centripetal-centrifugal movement could be computed for metropolitan areas. Work-trips having their origins *and* destinations within different parts of the ring could be treated as lateral, while exchanges *between* city and ring could be treated (separately) as centripetal and centrifugal.

One of the most significant by-products of this work would be the provision of a standardized and rigorous test of the current delineations of the individual metropolitan areas. Any doubts concerning the inclusion or exclusion of particular outlying counties could be resolved in a systematic fashion with these commuting data. It must be remembered that commuting is one of the criteria that the federal government attempts to use in its current delineation procedures. In the absence of adequate data, however, commuting patterns must be estimated. The result of these suggestions would be a reconceptualization of metropolitan areas as essentially "commuting areas." However, there is nothing to prevent the use of additional criteria, newspaper circulation, telephone traffic, etc. But at least one of the defining criteria would be available on a comparable basis, if only after the census was completed.

In any event, the judicious use of movement data should enhance our understanding of the structure of today's metropolitan area. Decentralization is too often conceived in oversimplified terms. The central city is thought to remain the major work site for a dispersed labor force, while surrounding municipalities are considered to be little more than "dormitories" or "bedroom towns." However, indirect evidence reveals that outlying centers in many areas regularly attract significant numbers of workers who live elsewhere. Many of these "satellites," or employing subcenters, like some residential suburbs, were formerly semi-independent centers that were drawn into the orbit of the larger central city with the development of faster means of transportation and communication, while others appear to have developed as appendages of the metropolis. Whatever their past history, however, they are now involved in the territorial division of labor of the metropolitan area as a whole, and movement data are most appropriate for showing the vital links that have been forged between them and other parts of the metropolitan area.

RESEARCH ALTERNATIVES

Assuming more intensive research along these lines, the prospects are excellent for increased knowledge of the structure and dynamics of contemporary metropolitan areas. We have far fewer opportunities to reconstruct the history of metropolitan decentralization, except for case studies of individual areas [16]. Historical-statistical investigations of any scope are obviously limited to a few pieces of data available for the period under review. Such items are usually very simple, either those "static" attributes that do not change (e.g., location) or those less complex "dynamic" variables that are readily accessible in such sources as the census (e.g., size and rate of growth). However, much remains to be done even within the narrow limits imposed by the available data. To a certain extent, imaginative research design can offset the disadvantages encountered in longitudinal study. One such suggestion has been put forward by Otis Dudley Duncan:

Extensive attempts to measure the [suburban] trend and efforts to isolate its determinants are prominent in the literature. This is a field of research with more than ordinary difficulties of conceptualization and measurement. All too often researchers . . . have somewhat naively accepted findings of differential growth rates between central and peripheral portions of urban communities as evidence of a specific process of "suburbanization" or "decentralization," without attempting an operational distinction between these alleged processes and the normal tendency for expansion to occur on the periphery of the community area. One may hazard a guess as to the approach needed to clarify this problem. Comparative studies in considerable longitudinal depth should match a city of a given size at a recent date with one of the same size at a remote date, and note whether the recent pattern of growth is a more dispersed or "suburban" one than that occurring at the earlier period. An adequate comparison would require detailed examination of patterns and changes of population density [17].

Thus the foregoing suggestions regarding the use of movement data represent only one of many possible approaches toward the fusion of research and theory on metropolitanism and decentralization. Whatever its merits, however, we would underscore the desirability of incorporating *organizational* variables in the study of metropolitan areas and population redistribution, whether the approach is longitudinal or cross-sectional. Perhaps the fact that a very large share of the research on these topics is carried on by sociologists and economists, who have a theoretical heritage of concepts of structure and change, will soon yield happier results. At any rate, we can hopefully expect new insights to emerge soon from the new research which is increasingly oriented to expanding the body of theory.

NOTES

1. For example, Warren S. Thompson, *The Growth of Metropolitan Districts in the United States, 1900–1940* (Washington: Government Printing Office, 1947); Donald J. Bogue, *Population Growth in Standard Metropolitan Areas, 1900–1950* (Washington: Government Printing Office, 1953).

2. Amos H. Hawley, *The Changing Shape of Metropolitan America* (Glencoe: Free Press, 1956).

3. *The Growth of Cities in the Nineteenth Century* (New York: Macmillan Co., 1899), especially pp. 458–475.

4. "Suburbanization: Statistical Fallacy?" *Land Economics*, 32 (Feb., 1956), pp. 85–87. See, however, the comment following Schmitt's by Amos H. Hawley, "A Further Note on Suburbanization," ibid., pp. 87–89.

5. Leo F. Schnore, "Metropolitan Growth and Decentralization," *American Journal of Sociology*, 63 (September 1957), pp. 171–180.

6. These areal changes are ignored or obscured in almost all the available studies of decentralization, including previous work by the writer, with the notable exception of a recent study by Donald J. Bogue, *Components of Population Change, 1940–1950: Estimates of Net Migration and Natural Increase for Each Standard Metropolitan Area and State Economic Area* (Oxford, Ohio and Chicago: Scripps Foundation for Research in Population Problems and Population Research and Training Center, 1957); for a summary, see Donald J. Bogue and Emerson Seim, "Components of Population Change in Suburban and Central City Populations of Standard Metropolitan Areas: 1940–to–1950," *Rural Sociology*, 21 (September–December 1956), pp. 267–275. In the present study, areas (in square miles) of each city at each census date were examined in order to determine whether or not territorial changes had taken place in the intervening decades.

7. Since an element of judgment is necessarily involved—especially in view of the frequency of annexation—a complete list of the cities has been prepared, with all relevant data clearly indicated. This list is available from the author upon request.

8. The other cities that apparently began to decentralize before 1900 are: Cincinnati, San Francisco, New Haven, Boston, Albany, Baltimore, St. Louis, Scranton, and Duluth.

9. *An Introduction to Economic History* (New York: Harper and Brothers, 1922), p.184.

10. Ibid., p. 187.

11. *The Metropolitan Community* (New York: McGraw-Hill Book Co., 1933), pp. 6–7.

12. Donald J. Bogue, *The Structure of the Metropolitan Community* (Ann Arbor: University of Michigan Press, 1949); Leslie Kish, "Differentiation in Metropolitan Areas," *American Sociological Review*, 19 (August 1954), pp. 388–398; Walter Isard and Vincent H. Whitney, "Metropolitan Site Selection," *Social Forces*, 27 (March 1949), pp. 263–269. All these are based upon the 1940 census data.

13. Donald L. Foley, "Urban Day-Time Population: A Field for Demographic-Ecological Analysis," *Social Forces*, 32 (May 1954), pp. 323–330.

14. Still another aspect of this complexity to be noted is the increasingly *indirect* (and decreasingly observable) nature of the relationships between the constituent units of the metropolitan area as a whole. Metropolitan organization appears to ramify into patterns so intricate as to defy description. In this connection, it is interesting to note that the sociological and anthropological literature on community organization is almost entirely confined, in an empirical sense, to much smaller places.

15. Decentralization is too often conceived as involving only the outward shift of residential population. Complete understanding of the phenomenon will come only when all the constituent functional units in the community have been systematically examined with respect to their physical dispersion. The most valuable material that is currently available is to be found in the series of studies in population distribution sponsored by the Scripps Foundation for Research in Population Problems, especially those by Cuzzort, Kitagawa, and Bogue on the suburbanization of services and manufacturing.

16. See Hans Blumenfeld, "The Tidal Wave of Metropolitan Expansion," *Journal of the American Institute of Planners*, 20 (Winter 1954), pp. 3–14.

17. "Human Ecology and Population Studies," in Philip M. Hauser and Otis Dudley Duncan (editors), *The Study of Population* (Chicago: University of Chicago Press, 1959), p. 697.

7

LEO F. SCHNORE

Satellites and Suburbs

The purposes of this paper are threefold: (1) to set forth an explicit distinction between two types of metropolitan subcenter—suburbs and satellites; (2) to summarize presently available information on these two basic types; and (3) to suggest some important and immediate implications for research that seem to follow from these considerations.

SUBURBS VERSUS SATELLITES

The distinction made here cannot be claimed as original. In a book published over forty years ago, Taylor discussed the unique functional position of "satellite cities." Such places were recognized by Taylor as basically subordinate to larger centers, yet retaining a high degree of independence stemming from their importance as production and employment centers [1]. It was Douglass, however, who first made this distinction in clear-cut terms when he discussed two broad types labelled "suburbs of production" and "suburbs of consumption" [2].

By "suburbs of production," Douglass referred to the type of subcenter discussed by Taylor—the satellite offering employment for at least its own residents, and frequently for other commuting workers as well. By "suburbs of consumption," Douglass referred to the suburb as it is described in its popular connotation, i.e., as a "dormitory town" or "bedroom city." The

key functions of such subcenters are not production or employment, but rather the provision of residential amenities. They serve, in a sense, as reservoirs of the manpower required to staff the productive enterprises in the central city, in satellite employing places, and elsewhere.

In one form or another, this distinction has gained some currency. In a 1943 article on "Suburbs," Chauncy Harris claimed that "the commonest types of suburb are housing or dormitory suburbs and manufacturing or industrial suburbs" [3]. More recently, Reiss has noted that "suburbs often are polarized as 'residential' and 'industrial suburbs,' the residential suburb being considered the modal type" [4]. Despite this seeming agreement, a careful and systematic definition has yet to become established among sociologists. As Shryock has indicated, "in the literature, *suburb* is used almost as loosely by the social scientist as by the layman. . . . We badly need some basic concepts here to guide our operational definitions" [5].

The most logically conceived set of definitions appears to be the one recently outlined by Walter T. Martin. To quote Martin at length,

In general, the term "suburb" refers to the relatively small but formally structured community adjacent to and dependent upon a large central city . . . Certain features of suburban communities may be designated as definitive characteristics. These are the characteristics essential to suburban status. In combination they differentiate invariably between suburban and nonsuburban communities. The two definitive char-

Reproduced by permission from *Social Forces*, Vol. 36 (December 1957), pp. 121–127.

acteristics treated first are a unique ecological position in relation to a larger city and a high rate of commuting to that city. . . .

Ecological position—By definition *suburban areas,* however sub-categorized, are *primarily residential areas* having a peculiar location; that is, they are farther away from the center of the major city than urban neighborhoods but closer than rural neighborhoods. They lie outside the limits of the central city but remain dependent upon the city as a source of necessary goods and services. The ecological position thus differs from both urban and rural positions. . . .

Commuting—Commuting to work, the second definitive characteristic of suburbs, is a direct outgrowth of the ecological position. Thus communities located adjacent to larger urban centers but *providing jobs for their own residents as well as others* are classified as *satellite cities* rather than suburbs. . . . [6].

Taking Martin's core definitions as a basis, it seems desirable to make explicit some of the outstanding structural and functional differences between the two types.

Structure

In *spatial* terms, both suburbs and satellites are often physically indistinguishable from adjacent areas, hemmed in on all sides by other municipalities. Many of these sub-centers, of course, were originally independent and self-contained cities in their own right; now engulfed by the expanding metropolis, they have somehow resisted annexation and have retained at least political autonomy. Other suburbs and satellites apparently had their origin in the exhaustion of space in the nearby central city, developing as the metropolis spilled over its former boundaries. Yet they are treated as separate legal entities [7]. Whatever their past history, however, *all* suburbs and satellites have one structural feature in common. Although they are treated as separate units for a limited range of purposes, including the reporting of data, *they are themselves merely constituent parts of a larger urban complex*—the metropolitan structure as a whole.

The structure of suburbs and satellites can also be treated in *temporal* terms [8]. Like other

parts of the entire metropolitan area, they represent *sources* and *destinations* of the internal circulation of commodities and people that make up the daily rhythm of community activity. It is at this point, however, that the two types can be distinguished most clearly. We can say that *goods and services* tend to flow out of the *employing satellites* to other areas (both local and non-local), while *persons* are attracted into these areas for employment. On the other hand, *residential suburbs* send out *workers* and tend to receive an influx of *goods and services* for consumption by their inhabitants. These are the major components of the daily ebb and flow of movement that give the whole metropolitan community its temporal organization.

Functions

The general functions of the two types of subcenter can thus be conceived as polar in nature. Stated in most succinct terms, (1) *residential suburbs are suppliers of labor and consumers of commodities.* Conversely, (2) *employing satellites are consumers of labor and suppliers of commodities.* This conception is in accord with Douglass' original idea that manufacturing subcenters represent the decentralization of production, while residential suburbs manifest the decentralization of consumption.

CHARACTERISTICS OF SUBURBS AND SATELLITES

Assuming the validity of this simple dichotomy, the first question that occurs is the sheer number of subcenters of each type that may be found within metropolitan areas. Here we are able to draw upon two studies using essentially similar methodology. Kneedler presented an "economic base" classification of all of the incorporated places of 10,000 or more inhabitants lying within the Metropolitan Districts defined in the 1940 census [9]. In this study, 160 "dormitory" suburbs were identified, together with 173 satellite subcenters, with the latter classified according to their major economic functions (manufacturing, retail trade, wholesale trade, mining, education, and government).

The same general economic types were recognized in a follow-up study by Jones, who classified 183 suburbs and 180 satellites lying within the Standard Metropolitan Areas identified in the 1950 census [10].

Despite minor differences in the operational definitions used by Kneedler and Jones, the two studies yield the same general picture. First of all, the relative balance between the two types appears to have been similar at both dates, with satellites slightly outnumbering suburbs at the earlier date. However, it must be remembered that these data refer only to incorporated places of 10,000 and over; other data (to be presented below) suggest that satellites tend to be larger in size than suburbs. Thus if the data were available for the full size range of sub-centers, it is probable that residential suburbs would predominate numerically.

Secondly, with respect to the *economic bases* of satellites, both studies reveal that the overwhelming majority (81 percent in 1940 and 77 percent in 1950) are manufacturing subcenters. The next most frequent major activity is retail trade (12 percent in 1940 and 18 percent in 1950). Mining is the major function of only a few metropolitan satellites, while areas in which wholesale trade, education, and government predominate are even more infrequent [11].

In general, then, employing satellites are typically industrial subcenters, so that their characterization as producing places seems most appropriate. Unfortunately, these studies give us no detailed information on the economic activities predominating in residential suburbs. However, it can be generally stated that the bulk of employment that does occur in this type of subcenter lies in the general categories of retail trade and services—particularly in the lines that are relatively inexpensive and frequently needed by a residential population.

The economic characteristics of these subcenters serve to document the basic distinction under discussion. But what of the other characteristics of the two major types? Are there any other general features that serve to distinguish between them? Fortunately, the use of Jones' classification of 1950 metropolitan subcenters

allowed the present writer to make a summary comparison of the two basic types. At the risk of oversimplification, the results of that study can be summarized very briefly [12].

In general, *employing satellites* tend to be concentrated in the heavily industrialized areas of the Northeastern and North Central regions. They appear relatively more frequently in the metropolitan areas with smaller central cities, but they tend themselves to be larger than residential suburbs. Satellites also tend to be older than suburbs. Although satellites appear throughout the metropolitan area, they are more frequently found beyond the limits of the densely settled urban core. As distance from the central city increases, in fact, satellites are found with relatively greater frequency. Finally, these employing satellites are typically characterized by low rent levels.

In contrast, *residential suburbs* are distinctly different, although they are found in the metropolitan areas of all the major regions. They tend to appear with increasing relative frequency near larger central cities, but they are themselves smaller than satellites. Residential suburbs predominate among the more recently incorporated subcenters. Very few of them lie either outside the densely occupied urbanized area or farther than 30 miles from the central city. Finally, rents are higher than average in these residential suburbs.

These data throw further light on the nature of satellites and suburbs, and they also serve to underscore the utility of the distinction. Still further insights can be gained, however, by a closer look at more detailed data on *the characteristics of the populations* occupying these two types of place. At this point we can draw upon a case study of the Chicago Metropolitan District (1940) by Dornbusch [13]. Dornbusch used the basic dichotomy discussed here, further subdividing residential suburbs according to rent level. However, rather than discuss the detailed comparisons between the three resulting types, we will continue to confine our attention to the major differences between satellites and suburbs in general.

Dornbusch's research shows that residents

of Chicago satellites tend to have lower average education, and they contain higher proportions of foreign-born whites. In the matter of housing, these employing satellites exhibit lower average rent levels, they have higher proportions of tenant-occupied dwellings, and they have higher proportions of crowded dwellings. The satellites appear to have slightly higher fertility than residential suburbs. In fact, the satellites contain somewhat younger populations. In terms of occupational make-up, roughly two out of three of the employed residents of satellites are found in the "blue-collar" categories, as contrasted with one out of three in the suburban population. At the same time, a somewhat smaller percentage of persons is found to be employed in satellites.

In general, the images that emerge from Dornbusch's results are those of two rather clearly contrasting types:

(1) *employing satellites containing younger populations of lower than average socioeconomic status*—as measured by educational, ethnic, residential, and occupational variables; and (2) *residential suburbs containing slightly older populations of higher than average socioeconomic status.* Suggestive as these data may be, it must be remembered that they refer to the suburbs and satellites of only one Metropolitan District in 1940. However, the conceptual significance of the results— together with the relative simplicity of the methodology employed—would seem to recommend replication for other areas and more recent periods.

SATELLITE AND SUBURBAN GROWTH

Having reviewed the relative numbers of satellites and suburbs, as well as some of their more distinctive characteristics, we may now turn to the matter of their relative rates of growth in recent years.

A study by Harris provides information for the 1930–1940 decade. On the basis of an examination of growth rates in all places of 10,000 and over in 11 Metropolitan Districts, Harris reported that the growth rates of residential suburbs (average 11.7 percent) were well in excess of the rates found in industrial satellites (average 1.7 percent) [14].

A more recent study by the present writer revealed that the same general tendency persisted in the 1940–1950 decade. Suburban growth (average 31.9 percent) was well in excess of that of satellites (average 17.0 percent). This study covered all of the suburbs and satellites of 10,000 and over in all of the Standard Metropolitan Areas of the United States, and the relatively large number of cases (416) permitted the successive control of a number of relevant variables.

On the average, suburbs grew faster than satellites in all regions, in all central city size classes, in all satellite and suburban size classes, in all concentric distance zones, and in metropolitan areas of every major type of economic activity. One minor exception appeared when rent level was controlled, for the prevailing differential was reversed in the high-rent category. The only major reversal was found when suburbs were classified according to their dates of incorporation; the differential in favor of residential suburbs was found to characterize only the older places, i.e., those incorporated before 1900. Thus the control of six out of seven relevant factors did not alter the over-all pattern of growth differentials in any significant respect. Suburban growth appears to have continued well in excess of that of satellites in the most recent intercensal decade.

These findings may be viewed as reflections of a fundamental alteration of metropolitan organization in the direction of greater functional and territorial complexity. In many respects, it can be argued that these growth differentials simply mirror the changing distribution of housing opportunities emerging as a result of new patterns of building activity in these areas.

Residential suburbs appear to be growing more rapidly because they are becoming even more residential in character, by means of large increments in housing construction. At the same time, employing satellites appear to be growing less rapidly because they—like the central cities themselves—are becoming more *exclu-*

sively devoted to industry and other employ-ment-producing activities. In these employing satellites the process of land-use conversion—from residential to industrial, commercial, and transportation uses—is apparently (1) driving out pre-existent residential uses of land and (2) discouraging new construction of housing [15].

RESEARCH IMPLICATIONS

The first research question that presents itself concerns the *source* of these growth differentials. However, "source" can be taken to mean either of two things. First of all, we can pose the question in broad demographic terms, by asking "what are the relative contributions of natural increase and net migration to these observed differentials?" In addition, we can ask about the areal or geographic sources of the migrants contributing to the growth of suburbs and satel-lites. The question then becomes "what are the relative sizes of migrant streams from (1) the central city, (2) other suburbs, satellites, and nearby fringe areas, and areas outside the met-ropolitan community in question?" Both of these detailed questions are in need of answers. Moreover, the basic distinction between sub-urbs and satellites should be kept in the fore-front of the analysis, for these two types appear to differ with respect to the relative importance of natural increase and net migration, and they may also differ with respect to the geographic sources of persons migrating to them.

Demographic Sources of Growth

The data from Dornbusch's study of Chicago suburbs and satellites might suggest that natu-ral increase contributes more importantly to the growth of satellites than to suburbs. After all, his data indicate that satellites have higher fer-tility ratios. In addition, satellites tend to have lower proportions of persons over 65 years of age, so that they might be expected to have lower death rates.

However, the apparent trends in popula-tion growth and residential construction in met-ropolitan areas suggest that this hypothesis be given more elaboration. On the basis of a pre-liminary analysis of the growth of satellites and suburbs between 1940 and 1950, it appears that natural increase may indeed be especially im-portant to the typical satellite because it offsets net losses of migrants. In other words, satellites may be able to exhibit growth only because of recent high rates of natural increase. Suburbs, on the other hand, appear to be growing more rapidly from *both* demographic sources—natural increase and net in-migration. Thus it appears that employing satellites—which are *functionally* similar to the central city, in that they draw workers from other areas—are also highly simi-lar to the metropolis in their sources of growth [16].

Geographic Sources of Growth

Unfortunately, available census data do not per-mit investigation of the detailed geographic sources of recent migrants to satellites and sub-urbs. The 1950 census data on migrants are coded in categories (based on county units) that are inappropriate to the type of study needed here. For the moment, we will have to be con-tent with inferences drawn from scattered case studies and older census data.

Case studies of outlying areas indicate that the popular notion of "decentralization" as sim-ply a "flight from the city" is a gross oversimpli-fication [17]. In addition, studies by Thompson and Hawley, based upon 1935–1940 migration data, show that a substantial component of met-ropolitan ring growth comes from other areas [18]. Much of this growth—which may be la-belled "accretion at the periphery" in contrast to outward relocation from the city—must have taken place in satellites and suburbs, as well as in the "fringe" and open country.

It seems feasible to use the sample survey technique in studies focussed *specifically* upon the geographic sources of migrants to suburbs and satellites. In view of the lack of appropriate census data on this question, such case studies will probably remain the major source of our information for some time.

The Question of Classification

We need more data on daily commuting (recurrent movements) as well as migration (nonrecurrent movements). In fact, a major research question concerns the very basis of the distinction between these two functional types of area. Up to this time, we have had to depend upon manipulation of census data in order to classify subcenters in these terms. The work of Harris, Kneedler, and Jones has been particularly ingenious, but deficiencies in the basic data reduce the potential value of their contributions.

In *theory*, the types developed by these writers depend essentially upon a comparison of (1) the number of employed people *living* in a given area with (2) the number of people *working* in that area. This is basically a question of "day-time" versus "night-time" population, for suburbs and satellites are dispersing and attracting areas in the daily ebb and flow of movement. Subordinate centers that attract more workers every day than the number of people who sleep there every night are labelled satellites, while those having substantially more residents than jobs are classified as suburbs.

In *practice*, however, many difficulties are encountered in the use of census data in classifying particular areas in these terms. For one thing, the requisite data on employment (the number of jobs in a given area) are not generally available for smaller places—those under 10,000 inhabitants. Moreover, the data for larger places are inadequate in many respects. The employment data have been derived from the Censuses of Business and Manufacturing, while the numbers of employed residents have been drawn from the Population Census. The discrepancy in the very dates of these censuses (e.g., 1947, 1948, and 1950), means that inaccuracies enter the final results. Annexation comprises a major source of difficulties. In addition, any substantial change in employment opportunities or in available housing between these dates can seriously distort the basic "employment-residence ratio." The statistics for the numerator and the denominator of this ratio refer to different time periods, and changes in either element can artificially raise or lower the true value of the ratio. Still another weakness is the fact that all job categories have not been included in the computation of the ratio.

Many of these difficulties may be surmounted in the forthcoming population census. It seems almost a certainty that the 1960 census will contain a question on the individual's place of work. It remains to be seen, however, whether the Census Bureau will be able to present tabulations in sufficient detail to permit the accurate classification of individual suburbs and satellites in these terms. Considerations of cost will undoubtedly prohibit full detail for smaller places, and other priorities will inevitably compete for the funds available. In view of these considerations—and mindful of the additional fact that published census data are at least five years away—we might do better to consider alternative sources of data.

Because the fundamental distinction between satellites and suburbs is essentially a question of commuting flows, our attention is immediately drawn to traffic data as a possible source of information. "Origin-and-destination" data available from sample studies permit the identification of satellites and suburbs in a number of metropolitan areas. Punchcards for individual workers contain information on place of employment and place of residence, together with other characteristics. All work-trips to a given satellite or suburb can simply be tabulated by the place of residence of the workers. The simple balance between residents and job opportunities yields an identification of the two main types of subcenter discussed here. In addition, detailed information can be gained on main streams of commuters, and the direction of these streams throughout the entire area—centripetal, centrifugal, and lateral. Furthermore, the characteristics of the workers in these various commuting streams can be compared.

In summary, these detailed commuting data can be used to identify individual suburbs and satellites according to their basic type in many metropolitan areas. Comparison of such results with those derived from analysis of census data should be particularly interesting. In addition, these commuting data will yield information that is not presently available from census sources.

CONCLUSION

As Woodbury has observed, "dormitory towns are only one species of suburb" [19]. This paper calls attention to the available evidence supporting a fundamental distinction between satellites (employing sub-centers) and suburbs (residential sub-centers). However, it may well be that these two types are too broadly defined for many research purposes. Dornbusch's study indicates that rent level is another variable of real significance, while Martin suggests population size and density as additional criteria. The demographic source of growth may even be an important distinguishing characteristic. On the face of it, it seems that a place growing or maintaining its size by natural increase might be significantly different from one expanding mainly via net migration.

Whetten has argued that "there is need for further identification and classification of suburban populations into meaningful groupings or community types" [20]. The present writer can only agree—hoping that this chapter will help to fill this gap in our knowledge of metropolitan areas. But there are other gaps to be closed. A single example will suffice. One closely related concept that has been ignored in this presentation is that of the "fringe." Although it is used with increasing frequency, there is still little agreement on the fundamental meaning that should be assigned to the term. However, if we are careful to build upon the theoretical and research foundations already established, it should not be too long before we have a much more complete understanding of the structure and functions of the metropolitan area and *all* of its constituent parts.

NOTES

1. Graham R. Taylor, *Satellite Cities* (New York and London: D. Appleton and Co., 1915).

2. Harlan Paul Douglass, *The Suburban Trend* (New York and London: The Century Co., 1925), pp. 74–92. See also his article, "Suburbs," in *The Encyclopaedia of the Social Sciences* (New York: The Macmillan Co., 1934), XIV, pp. 433–435. This distinction can also be found in Louis Wirth, "Urbanism as a Way of Life," *American Journal of Sociology*, 44 (July 1938), pp. 1–24, and in C. D. Harris and E. L. Ullman, "The Nature of Cities," *The Annals*, 242 (November 1945), pp. 7–17. [No. 17 in this volume.]

3. C. D. Harris, "Suburbs," *American Journal of Sociology*, 49 (May 1943), p. 6.

4. Albert J. Reiss, Jr., "Research Problems in Metropolitan Population Redistribution," *American Sociological Review*, 21 (October 1956), p. 575.

5. Henry S. Shryock, Jr., "Population Redistribution within Metropolitan Areas: Evaluation of Research," *Social Forces*, 35 (December 1956), pp. 155–156.

6. Walter T. Martin, "The Structuring of Social Relationships Engendered by Suburban Residence," *American Sociological Review*, 21 (August 1956), pp. 447–448; italics added. A highly similar—though less detailed—distinction was previously outlined by Harris and Ullman, as follows: "Satellites differ from suburbs in that they are separated from the central city by many miles and in general have little daily commuting to or from

the central city, although economic activities of the satellite are closely geared to those of the central city." Chauncy D. Harris and Edward L. Ullman, "The Nature of Cities," *The Annals,* 242 (November 1945), pp. 7–17. [No. 17 in this volume.]

7. These diverse historical origins comprise a key dimension in an interesting typology of suburbs developed by Stuart A. Queen and David B. Carpenter. See *The American City* (New York: McGraw-Hill Book Co., 1953), pp. 116–131.

8. For a complete discussion of the temporal aspect of community structure, see Amos H. Hawley, *Human Ecology* (New York: The Ronald Press, 1950), pp. 288–316.

9. Grace M. Kneedler, "Functional Types of Cities," *Public Management,* 27 (July 1945), pp. 197–203; reprinted in Paul K. Hatt and Albert J. Reiss, Jr. (eds.), *Reader in Urban Sociology* (Glencoe: The Free Press, 1951), pp. 49–57.

10. Victor Jones, "Economic Classification of Cities and Metropolitan Areas," in *The Municipal Year Book 1953* (Chicago: The International City Managers' Association, 1953), pp. 49–57.

11. It is rather interesting to note the specialties in which few satellites are represented— transportation, and resort, retirement, and recreational services. These functions are more likely to be found in independent cities, far from metropolitan centers.

12. Leo F. Schnore, "The Functions of Metropolitan Suburbs," *American Journal of Sociology,* 61 (March 1956), pp. 453–458.

13. Sanford M. Dornbusch, "A Typology of Suburban Communities: Chicago Metropolitan District, 1940," Urban Analysis Report No. 10 (University of Chicago: Chicago Community Inventory, May 1952). Wirth long ago presented the notion that "A one-industry city will present *different sets of social characteristics* from a multi-industry city, as will . . . *a suburb from a satellite, a residential cuburb from an industrial suburb* . . ." See Louis Wirth, "Urbanism as a Way of Life," *American Journal of Sociology,* 44 (July 1938), pp. 1–24; italics added.

14. C. D. Harris, op. cit.

15. See Leo F. Schnore, "The Growth of Metropolitan Suburbs," *American Sociological Review,* 22 (April 1957), pp. 165–173. It might also be noted here that this general process of land-use conversion has yet to run its course. See Dorothy K. Newman, "Metropolitan Area Structure and Growth as Shown by Building-Permit Statistics," *Business Topics,* 4 (November 1956), pp. 1–7.

16. This analysis was confined to the suburbs and satellites of 10,000 and over in the five largest Standard Metropolitan Areas (New York, Chicago, Los Angeles, Philadelphia, and Detroit), and utilized the general method described in detail in Donald J. Bogue and Emerson Seim, "Components of Population Change in Suburban and Central City Populations of Standard Metropolitan Areas: 1940 to 1950," *Rural Sociology,* 21 (September–December 1956), pp. 267–275. In this study, Bogue and Seim present compelling evidence to the effect that recent central city growth was largely a function of natural increase, high enough to offset migration losses. This reverses the long-term situation, in which net in-migration offset extremely low rates of natural increase or even natural decrease. Ideally, of course, suburbs and satellites should be compared with *parts* of the central city, rather than with the central city as a whole. (See Reiss, op. cit.) It should also be noted that *individual* suburbs and satellites exhibit considerable variation within each of these types. Much of this variation may be due to variations in size, age, location, and other characteristics that were not controlled here. One major difficulty that has yet to be surmounted in studies of suburban growth

stems from a lack of appropriate data; there are no reliable statistics on the amount of vacant land available for residential development in sub-centers throughout the nation.

17. See Myles W. Rodehaver, "Fringe Settlement as a Two-Directional Movement," *Rural Sociology,* 12 (March 1947), pp. 49–57; Walter T. Martin, *The Rural-Urban Fringe* (Eugene: University of Oregon Press, 1953), pp. 60–63; Wendell Bell, "Familism and Suburbanization," *Rural Sociology,* 21 (September-December 1956), pp. 276–283.

18. Warren S. Thompson, *Migration Within Ohio, 1935–40* (Oxford, Ohio: Scripps Foundation for Research in Population Problems, 1951); Amos H. Hawley, *Intrastate Migration in Michigan, 1935–40* (Ann Arbor: Institute of Public Administration, University of Michigan, 1953).

19. Coleman Woodbury, "Suburbanization and Suburbia," *American Journal of Public Health,* 45 (January 1955), p. 2.

20. Nathan L. Whetten, "Suburbanization as a Field for Sociological Research," *Rural Sociology,* 16 (December 1951), p. 325.

8

REYNOLDS FARLEY

Suburban Persistence

ABSTRACT

Suburban areas have grown more rapidly in recent decades than have central cities. It has often been suggested that individuals with higher socio-economic status have deserted cities for suburbs, thus increasing city-suburban socio-economic differentials. An analysis of changes in population composition from 1950 to 1960 for certain urbanized areas lends support to this hypothesis. But if suburbs are looked at individually, instead of as aggregates, a different pattern of compositional change emerges. Particular suburbs retain their peculiar socio-economic characteristics for long periods of time and even rapid population growth does not produce substantial changes in a suburb's socio-economic characteristics.

Rapid suburban growth combined with declines in central city population is often assumed to be a post-World War II pattern of urban growth. Theodore White noted:

Reprinted by permission from the *American Sociological Review,* Vol. 29, No. 1 (February 1964), pp. 38–47.

For just as the census of 1890 announced the passing of the frontier, the census of 1960 announced the passing of the great city. For half a century the great urban centers had dominated American culture and politics. Decade by decade, as if by some irrevocable law of history, the great cities had steadily increased in size at every count.

But in 1960 the crest had passed and they were dwindling. . . . two-thirds of the stupendous 28,000,000 (1950 to 1960) growth of the nation had taken place in suburbia.[1]

The recent pattern of suburban growth supposedly has implications for the socio-economic structuring of urban areas. The college-educated white-collar workers, it is thought, have moved to suburbia in large numbers, leaving cities to be populated by non-whites and lower-status whites. Such a process is congruent with the Burgess hypothesis of urban growth. His model suggested that the highest-status residents live on the periphery of the settled area while the central portions contain the newest in-migrants and those whose earning powers condemn them to inexpensive or run down residences.[2]

Schnore attempted to rephrase the Burgess hypotheses and to suggest an evolutionary model for city growth:

With growth and expansion of the center and with radical improvements in transportation and communication technology, the upper strata have shifted from central to peripheral residence, and the lower classes have increasingly taken up occupancy in the central areas abandoned by the elite.[3]

But if this model for city growth is to be validated and if the process of suburbanization is to be understood it will be necessary to describe the dynamics of the growth process. Numerous studies, such as those by McKenzie, Ogburn, Kish, Dornbusch, and Duncan and Reiss have demonstrated that cities and their suburbs differ in composition at one point in time, yet this cross-sectional approach does not reveal how these differences developed nor does it indicate whether cities and suburbs are

becoming more alike or dissimilar in composition.[4]

This paper attempts to analyze change over time in city-suburban status differentials, using census data for 1950 and 1960. Changes in 17 of the 25 largest urbanized areas, all those for which comparisons were feasible, suggest that these cities and the suburban areas are becoming more dissimilar in composition. Generally the suburban areas have shown not only more rapid growth in total numbers but proportionally greater increases in population of higher socio-economic status.

One of the major reasons for increasing city-suburban differentiation is the growth of suburbs. Yet suburbs are not new nor is the flight to suburbia a recent development. As early as the 1760's suburban areas near Boston and Philadelphia were populated and in 1910 one-quarter of the population of the 25 metropolitan districts defined by the Census Bureau lived in suburban zones rather than in central cities.[5] These suburban areas have recently experienced rapid growth, but the Burgess model does not suggest what the relation between the characteristics of suburban areas and population growth might be. Have some types of suburbs experienced more rapid growth than others? Does rapid population growth alter the socio-economic characteristics of a suburb or do suburban places retain their peculiar characteristics even after great population increases?

Two groups of suburbs are analyzed in an attempt to answer questions of this nature. For a group of 137 suburbs of 24 central cities it

[1] T. H. White, *The Making of the President, 1960* (New York: Atheneum Publishers, 1961), p. 217.

[2] R. E. Park, E. W. Burgess and R. D. McKenzie, *The City* (Chicago: University of Chicago Press, 1925), p. 55.

[3] L. F. Schnore, "The Socio-Economic Status of Cities and Suburbs," *American Sociological Review,* 28 (February 1963), p. 84.

[4] R. D. McKenzie, *The Metropolitan Community* (New York: McGraw-Hill, 1934), pp. 180ff.; W. F. Ogburn, *Social Characteristics of Cities* (Chicago: International City Managers' Association, 1937); L. Kish, "Differentiation in Metropolitan Areas," *American Sociological Review,* 19 (August 1954); S. Dornbusch, *A Typology of Suburban Communities* (Chicago: Chicago Community Inventory, 1952); O. D. Duncan and A. J. Reiss, *Social Characteristics of Urban and Rural Communities, 1950* (New York: Wiley and Sons, 1956), Chap. 11.

[5] C. Bridenbaugh, *Cities in Revolt* (New York: Alfred Knopf, 1955), pp. 25 and 231; Bureau of the Census, *Thirteenth Census of the United States, 1910, Population,* Vol. 1, p. 75.

was possible to relate 1920 and 1960 measures of socio-economic composition and growth. Smaller and newer suburbs are included in a description of change for the period 1940 to 1960—the years of post war suburbanization. Although growth was common to almost all of these suburbs, the suburbs that grew most rapidly were those that had the characteristics of highest social status in 1960. Population growth, however, did not greatly change the composition of many suburbs. A sound prediction of the 1960 socio-economic characteristics of a particular suburb could be made merely by knowing that suburb's characteristics in 1920. When the shorter time span—1940 to 1960—is used there is even greater evidence for persistence of suburban characteristics.

As aggregates, central cities and suburban areas have become increasingly dissimilar in socio-economic composition. This finding suggests that the recent growth of suburbs fits the traditional model of city expansion, since the suburban areas have shown the largest gains in higher-status population. Yet as individual entities, suburbs demonstrate a stability of characteristics relatively little affected by population growth. This suggests that the characteristics of a suburb may be fixed relatively early in that suburb's history and subsequent growth reinforces existing socioeconomic residential patterns.

CENTRAL CITY-SUBURBAN AGGREGATE DIFFERENCES

How have cities and suburban areas changed in population size and composition during the recent decade of rapid suburbanization? To answer this question cities were compared with their suburban areas on the basis of census data for 1950 and 1960 urbanized areas. Boundaries for these areas were not restricted to corporation limits but rather were chosen by means of density and land use criteria.[6] The urbanized

area for a city in 1960 may not include exactly the same area as the 1950 urbanized area, since changes in land use or density may have qualified some fringe areas to be included in 1960 which were excluded in 1950. Nevertheless at both dates the urban fringe—that portion of an urbanized area exterior to the city—represents the suburban area since it includes the densely settled land area outside but near a central city.

City-suburban comparisons were made for 17 of the 25 most populous 1960 cities. Eight of the largest cities (Atlanta, Dallas, Houston, Memphis, Milwaukee, San Antonio, San Diego and Seattle) were excluded because, between 1950 and 1960, each city annexed an area containing a large population in 1960, thus complicating any interannual city-suburban comparisons. Although only 17 of the 213 urbanized areas defined in 1960 were used in this analysis, these 17 areas contained 54 per cent of the total population living in urbanized areas in 1960.[7]

The pattern of population loss in the central city and population increase in the suburban ring appeared in 14 of the 17 areas examined. None of the cities grew as rapidly as its suburban area. One of the most striking changes was the central cities' gain of non-white population. In 1950 about 14 per cent of the total population of these cities was non-white but by 1960 the non-white population had increased to 21 per cent. These suburban areas, however, generally had little non-white population at both dates; about 5 per cent of their aggregate population was non-white in both 1950 and 1960.[8]

In the aggregate the suburban population became more sharply differentiated from central city population in socio-economic status during the 1950's. The proportion of adult males who were high school graduates, for example, increased by 6.2 percentage points in the suburbs but only by 1.6 points in the central cities. The proportion of white-collar workers

---

[6] U. S. Bureau of the Census, *Census of Population, 1960,* Vol. 1, Part A, p. xix.

[7] Ibid., Table 22.
[8] Ibid. and PC(1)–B, Table 13.

in the male labor force increased by 3.6 points in the suburbs compared with 0.9 points in central cities.[9]

Because much of the discussion of city-suburban differentiation has been based on the residential patterns of well-educated adults and white-collar workers, city-suburban differences in the distributions of education and occupation are examined in detail for each urbanized area. To determine in a concise manner whether a city and its suburban area became more similar or more dissimilar in composition from 1950 to 1960, indices of occupational dissimilarity

were computed using the Census Bureau's nine non-agricultural occupational categories plus the category unemployed. The numerical value of this index of dissimilarity states the percentage of the labor force in either area that would have to change occupations for the occupational distributions of both areas to be identical.[10]

The index of occupational dissimilarity for a city and its fringe in 1950 may be contrasted to the same index comparing the two areas in 1960. If the index for 1960 has a larger numerical value than the index for 1950, the two areas have become more dissimilar in occupational composition. Educational dissimilarity indices were computed in an analogous manner, using eight educational attainment levels. These indices are presented in Table 1.

[9] The percentage of the male population ages 25 and over with a complete high school education increased from 36.5 in 1950 to 38.1 in 1960 in the cities and from 44.0 to 50.2 in the suburbs. The percentage of the civilian male labor force in white-collar occupations increased from 38.0 in 1950 to 38.9 in 1960 in the cities and from 41.4 to 45.0 in the suburbs. U. S. Bureau of the Census, *Census of Population, 1960*, PC(1)–C, Tables 73 and 74.

[10] O. D. Duncan and B. Duncan, "Residential Distribution and Occupational Stratification," *American Journal of Sociology*, 60 (March 1955): 494. [No. 32 in this volume.]

TABLE 1. Indices of Dissimilarity Comparing Central Cities with the Remainder of the Urbanized Area

Urbanized Area	Indices of Educational Dissimilarity			Indices of Occupational Dissimilarity		
	1950	1960	Difference	1950	1960	Difference
Detroit	7.0	14.2	7.2	7.2	14.9	7.7
St. Louis	11.6	18.4	6.8	13.1	20.6	7.5
Chicago	9.8	16.2	6.4	11.5	17.4	5.9
Washington	17.7	23.7	6.0	21.9	28.5	6.6
Minneapolis-St. Paul	8.1	14.0	5.9	9.3	13.4	4.1
Pittsburgh	4.6	10.2	5.6	9.0	10.5	1.5
New Orleans	5.0	9.7	4.7	9.2	12.4	3.2
Denver	8.3	12.7	4.4	11.6	9.3	−2.3
Buffalo	9.8	14.0	4.2	9.7	14.6	4.9
Cincinnati	6.0	9.7	3.7	8.9	9.6	0.7
Philadelphia	13.8	17.4	3.6	13.0	17.1	4.1
New York	5.3	8.2	2.9	8.4	11.2	2.8
Boston	8.8	11.5	2.7	11.8	15.3	3.5
San Francisco-Oakland	8.6	9.7	1.1	9.4	11.3	1.9
Los Angeles	4.6	5.6	1.0	8.5	8.5	0.0
Baltimore	15.7	16.5	0.8	12.5	16.4	3.9
Cleveland	25.6	26.2	0.6	27.4	27.0	−0.4

Sources: U.S. Bureau of the Census, *Census of Population, 1950*, Vol. II, Tables 34 and 35; U.S. Bureau of the Census, *Census of Population, 1960*, PC(1)–C, Tables 73 and 74.

A general pattern of increasing dissimilarity clearly appears. Considering educational dissimilarity, the 1960 index for each area exceeded the 1950 index. For many of the urbanized areas the increase was sizeable; for instance, the value for the Detroit area doubled. Considering occupational composition, in each urbanized area except Cleveland, Denver, and Los Angeles, the city and urban fringe became more dissimilar in occupational composition.

The distributions of educational attainment and occupational composition are summarized by the per cent of the male population aged 25 and over with a high school education and the per cent of the male labor force holding white-collar jobs. Table 2 presents these figures for each city and its fringe.

In both years the suburban areas generally exceeded the cities in percentage high school graduates. During this decade city-suburban

TABLE 2. Comparison of Educational and Occupational Composition of Central Cities and Their Urban Fringe Areas, 1950 and 1960 (Male Population Only)

Urbanized Area	Per Cent High School Graduate			Per Cent White-Collar Workers*		
	City	Fringe	Difference	City	Fringe	Difference
Baltimore						
1950	26.6	39.7	13.1	34.4	37.8	3.4
1960	27.4	42.3	14.9	34.6	42.8	8.2
Boston						
1950	42.5	50.1	7.6	34.9	42.1	7.2
1960	42.8	54.3	11.5	36.4	46.9	10.5
Buffalo						
1950	29.5	39.0	9.5	30.4	36.8	6.4
1960	29.9	43.6	13.7	29.3	38.5	9.2
Chicago						
1950	35.8	45.5	9.7	36.1	41.4	5.3
1960	35.7	53.9	18.2	34.9	45.3	10.4
Cincinnati						
1950	32.9	32.4	−0.5	37.4	37.6	0.2
1960	33.6	43.3	9.7	37.9	45.1	7.2
Cleveland						
1950	30.2	55.8	25.6	26.5	53.9	27.4
1960	28.9	55.1	26.2	24.5	50.2	25.7
Denver						
1950	50.5	48.1	−2.4	47.3	30.3	−17.0
1960	51.6	62.3	10.7	46.6	48.5	1.9
Detroit						
1950	33.3	39.1	5.8	30.3	30.9	0.6
1960	32.8	45.9	13.1	30.5	39.1	8.6
Los Angeles						
1950	50.4	51.4	1.0	42.2	40.6	−1.6
1960	53.7	53.0	−0.7	45.6	41.7	−3.9
Minneapolis-St. Paul						
1950	43.7	51.7	8.0	42.6	47.5	4.9
1960	46.1	60.1	14.0	42.2	50.9	8.7
New Orleans						
1950	29.9	29.2	−0.7	39.0	36.8	−2.2
1960	33.4	44.8	11.4	39.5	42.9	3.4

TABLE 2.   *(Continued)*

	Per Cent High School Graduate			Per Cent White-Collar Workers*		
Urbanized Area	City	Fringe	Difference	City	Fringe	Difference
New York						
1950	35.7	40.1	4.4	42.4	42.1	−0.3
1960	37.8	45.6	7.8	43.5	46.0	2.5
Philadelphia						
1950	29.8	43.5	13.7	33.6	43.3	9.7
1960	30.7	48.1	17.4	35.0	46.1	11.1
Pittsburgh						
1950	33.0	37.6	4.6	32.8	32.0	−0.8
1960	34.4	53.1	18.7	33.8	37.2	3.4
St. Louis						
1950	25.9	37.5	11.6	34.4	43.4	9.0
1960	26.2	44.1	17.9	31.4	46.7	15.3
San Francisco-Oakland						
1950	45.6	54.2	8.6	39.8	42.5	2.7
1960	47.7	56.6	8.9	41.3	44.9	3.6
Washington						
1950	48.3	66.0	17.7	46.2	60.5	14.3
1960	45.8	67.4	21.6	45.6	63.3	17.7

* The per cent white collar equals the sum of male professional managerial, clerical, and sales workers divided by the total male civilian labor force.
   Sources: U.S. Bureau of the Census, *Census of Population, 1960*, PC(1)-C, Tables 73 and 74; U.S. Bureau of the Census, *Census of Population, 1950* Vol. II, Tables 34 and 35.

differences increased because the suburban areas showed greater increases in high school educated population than did central cities. In fact in the central cities of Chicago, Cleveland, Detroit and Washington the proportion with a high school education declined. A similar pattern of change emerges for occupational composition. In 1950 five of the central cities had a larger percentage of the male labor force in white-collar occupations than their suburban areas. In 1960 only one city—Los Angeles—had a larger percentage of its male labor force in white collar jobs than its suburban area.

The indices of dissimilarity with respect to socio-economic status (Table 1) and the city-suburban differences in the proportion of well educated adult males and white collar workers (Table 2) both point to increasing differentiation between the city and suburban populations in socio-economic status. Inspection of Table 2 suggests that this has come about because suburban areas gained high-status population at a faster rate than central cities. From 1950 to 1960 suburban areas have grown faster than cities and have undergone compositional changes which make these areas increasingly dissimilar to cities.

SUBURBAN PERSISTENCE, 1920 TO 1960
Suburbs have long surrounded central cities. At the turn of this century Adna Weber wrote: "The movement toward the suburbs, which is stronger in America than elsewhere with the exception of Australia, not only necessitates frequent annexations of territory, but even then baffles the statistician."[11] Ample research has shown that population decentralization has been occurring at least since 1920, that there are blue-collar as well as white-collar, industrial as well as dormitory, and heterogeneous as well as homogeneous suburbs. And yet the relations

11 A. F. Weber, *The Growth of Cities in the Nineteenth Century* (New York: Macmillan, 1899), p. 36.

between suburban growth and compositional change have not been explored. The following analysis attempts to elucidate the role of growth in the process of suburbanization.

Measures of a suburb's socio-economic status may be compared at different points in time to analyze changes in the composition of individual suburbs. The Census of 1920 tabulated school enrollment for 16 and 17 year olds in cities of population 10,000 or more. In suburbs such as Cleveland Heights, Ohio and Newton, Massachusetts, typical exclusive residential areas, large percentages of the teen-age population were enrolled in school, while in industrial suburbs such as Hoboken and Hamtramck low percentages were enrolled. The percentage of 16 and 17 year olds attending school in 1920 may be considered a measure of a suburb's socio-economic status, and for 1960 the percentage of the population 25 years of age or older with a high school diploma may be regarded as a roughly comparable measure.

A comparison of these status measures for 1920 and 1960 was possible for 137 suburbs of 24 central cities. To be included a suburb had to be within a 1920 metropolitan district, within a 1960 urbanized area and have retained its corporate identify for this period.

Table 3 presents the regression of the 1960 measure on the 1920 measure. A high degree of persistence in relative position is apparent, the zero order correlation coefficient being .81. Suburbs high or low on the measure for 1920 tended to retain the same position in 1960. This 40-year persistence of socio-economic characteristics contrasts surprisingly with the apparent fact of rapid change in suburbia.

Population growth is one of the distinctive features of suburban areas. Although the 137 suburbs examined are relatively old—the minimum population was 10,000 in 1920—they did experience rapid growth between 1920 and 1960. Their total population increased from 4.2 million in 1920 to 6.8 million in 1960, an increase of 63 per cent which is almost as large as the nation's increase of 68 per cent for this

TABLE 3. Summary of Regression Analysis for 137 Suburbs of 24 Central Cities

Variables

Education, 1960—Per cent of a suburb's 25 and over population with a high school education in 1960. (Mean = 41.46, Standard Deviation = 12.94)

Education, 1920—Per cent of the 16 and 17 year old population of a suburb enrolled in school in 1920. (Mean = 38.24, Standard Deviation = 15.42)

Growth—One minus the proportion of a suburb's 1960 population accounted for by its 1920 population. (Mean = 28.58, Standard Deviation = 37.41)

Zero Order Regressions

	Education, 1960 on Education, 1920	Education, 1960 on Growth
Slope	$.682 \pm .053$	$.174 \pm .071$
Intercept	15.18	36.50
Correlation coefficient	.812	.501

Multiple Regression

Intercept	16.08
Partial regression coefficients	
Free variable: Education, 1920	$.610 \pm .022$
Free variable: Growth	$.072 \pm .018$
Partial correlation coefficients	
Free variable: Education, 1920	.779
Free variable: Growth	.355
Multiple correlation coefficient	.839

Percentage of Variance Explained

Explained by zero order regression of education, 1920 on education, 1960	65.9
Additional with growth	4.4*
Unexplained	29.7
Total	100.0

* Significant by F test at .01 level.

Sources: U.S. Bureau of the Census, *Fourteenth Census of the United States, 1920, Population*, Vol. III, Table 10; U.S. Bureau of the Census, *Census of Population, 1960*, PC(1)–C, Tables 32 and 81.

period.[12] To analyze the relation between growth and the status measures for 1920 and 1960 multiple regression was used and the results are presented in Table 3.

The measure of growth used in this analysis is somewhat unusual. The measure is equivalent to 1.00 minus the proportion of the suburb's 1960 population accounted for by its 1920 population. Thus a suburb whose population tripled during the 40-year period is scored .67 on this measure, that is, 1.00 minus .33. A place losing population during the interim receives a score of less than zero. These growth scores for the 137 suburbs are distributed more or less normally and are, therefore, more appropriate for regression analysis than the conventional measure, percentage change in population.

The association of growth and socio-economic level over the 40-year span was explored with two questions as guides. First, did growth occur indiscriminately throughout the suburban area or was it related to the characteristics of the suburbs? Second, did rapid growth produce substantial compositional change and lessen persistence of socio-economic characteristics?

To answer the first question we note the positive association of socio-economic level in 1960 and growth during the years 1920 to 1960 ($r = .50$). This indicates that growth did not occur indiscriminately among suburbs but that suburbs with high growth rates were those with high-status characteristics in 1960. This relationship is consistent with the notion that the more exclusive suburbs have absorbed the spill-over of higher status residents from the central city as well as attracted higher-status immigrants to the area.

Second, a comparison of the zero-order correlation coefficients indicates that initial

(1920) educational level is a far more powerful predictor of current (1960) educational level than is growth during the intervening years. The educational characteristics of these suburbs have generally persisted from 1920 to 1960. A comparison based on the partial correlation coefficients leads to the same conclusion. Persistence of educational level, irrespective of differential growth, is a powerful factor accounting for current educational level, while differential growth, irrespective of initial educational level, is a much weaker explanatory factor.

The partial regression coefficient relating 1960 educational level to growth during the years 1920 to 1960 is significantly different from zero. When variance among suburbs in current educational level is partitioned, as in Table 3, it can be seen that the use of a growth variable adds a small but significant increase to the variance explained by initial educational level alone. A high initial educational level coupled with rapid growth represents the combination most favorable to a high current educational level, though the influence population growth exerts is relatively small, as illustrated by a hypothetical comparison of two suburbs. Consider two suburbs, each having one-half of the 16 and 17 year old population enrolled in school in 1920. Assume that the population of one suburb triples from 1920 to 1960 while that of the other suburb remains constant. Using the regression equations described in Table 3, we would predict that in the rapidly growing suburb the percentage high school graduate in 1960 would be 51.4, while in the suburb that experienced no growth it would be 46.6.

SUBURBAN PERSISTENCE, 1940 TO 1960

Suburbs described in the analysis of change from 1920 to 1960 had populations exceeding 10,000 in 1920 and might be expected to undergo less change than suburbs that started with smaller populations and grew more rapidly. Little socio-economic information for cities of under 10,000 population in 1920 was given by

---

[12] U. S. Bureau of the Census, *Fourteenth Census of the United States, 1920, Population,* Vol. III, Table 10; U. S. Bureau of the Census, *Census of Population, 1960,* Vol. 1, Part A, Table 3 and PC(1)-A, Table 5.

the Census. As an alternative, suburban persistence and growth will be described for the period 1940 to 1960 for suburbs of Boston, Chicago and Cleveland. [Table 4] Since a shorter time span is involved, greater persistence might be expected, but the rapid post war suburban growth may have introduced new patterns of compositional change.

All suburbs of Chicago and Cleveland within the 1940 metropolitan district and within the 1960 Standard Metropolitan Statistical Area, which had populations in 1940 exceeding 2500, and which retained their identity for this period were included. Towns within the 1940 Boston metropolitan district and 1960 Standard Metropolitan Statistical Area for which 1940 and 1960 figures were tabulated were also used.

Percentage of the population aged 25 and over with a high school education was used as a socio-economic measure at both dates. The growth measure described above was also employed in this analysis. Mean values for these measures are:

	Boston	Chicago	Cleveland
Number of Suburbs	50	61	25
1940% H.S. Graduate	40.0	33.6	39.1
1960% H.S. Graduate	57.6	53.1	55.6
Mean 1940 Population	29,100	15,700	13,200
Mean 1960 Population	36,000	27,100	26,100
Mean Growth Measure	26.8	45.5	51.0

Turning again to the questions posed earlier about the relations of initial and current socio-economic level and growth, we note first the association of growth and high current socio-economic level. Although these correlation coefficients are not extremely high, they indicate that the suburbs that had grown most rapidly were those with higher-status characteristics in 1960. Second, the results indicate

that initial socio-economic level is a far more powerful predictor of current socio-economic level than growth in Chicago and Cleveland and a somewhat more powerful predictor in Boston. These results are consistent with those obtained from the analysis of 1920 to 1960 change.

When the partial correlation coefficients are examined, however, it becomes clear that growth is relatively more important in respect to initial level when smaller suburbs are included and when the time span is shortened. Together initial level and growth account for about 90 per cent of the variance in current educational level among the suburbs of these three cities, and in each case, the growth factor contributes a significant increment to the explained variance. Such a growth pattern indicates that in the last 20 years, population growth has upgraded the relative socio-economic position of a suburb.

This can be illustrated by a comparison of suburbs assumed to have similar percentages of high school graduates in 1940 but different growth rates. Assume that two Cleveland suburbs both had 40 per cent of the adult population high school graduates in 1940 but that the population of one suburb doubled while that of the other neither increased or declined. The regression model predicts that 65 per cent would be high school graduates in 1960 in the growing suburb and 57 per cent in the other suburb. This is consistent with the notion that the higher-status members of the community have increasingly chosen suburban residences in the more exclusive suburbs. But the persistence of suburban characteristics, even among these rapidly growing suburbs, cannot be overlooked. For each set of suburbs the initial educational level served as a powerful predictor of current educational level, indicating that even rapid population growth did not greatly shift the relative socio-economic positions of these suburbs.

CONCLUSIONS AND SUMMARY

The pattern of urban development indicated by the analyses presented in this paper is consis-

TABLE 4. Summary of Regression Analysis for Suburbs of Boston, Cleveland, and Chicago

Variables:
Education, 1940—Per cent of a suburb's 25 and over population with a high school education in 1940
Education, 1960—Per cent of a suburb's 25 and over population with a high school education in 1960
Growth—One minus proportion of a suburb's 1960 population accounted for by its 1940 population

	Boston		Chicago		Cleveland	
	Education, 1960 on Education, 1940	Education, 1960 on Growth	Education, 1960 on Education, 1940	Education, 1960 on Growth	Education, 1960 on Education, 1940	Education, 1960 on Growth
Zero Order Regressions						
Intercept	12.15	41.44	22.55	49.56	26.92	39.06
Slope	.886 ± .105	.352 ± .176	.909 ± .094	.078 ± .145	.733 ± .165	.131 ± .242
Correlation coefficient	.888	.602	.917	.127	.858	.324
Multiple Regressions						
Intercept	16.87		15.75		27.21	
Partial regression coefficients						
Free variable: Education, 1940	.782 ± .016		.930 ± .033		.751 ± .035	
Free variable: Growth	.231 ± .008		.134 ± .021		.151 ± .025	
Partial correlation coefficients						
Free variable: Education, 1940	.944		.941		.926	
Free variable: Growth	.821		.548		.728	
Multiple regression coefficient	.964		.942		.936	
Percentage of Variance Explained						
Explained by zero order regression of education, 1960 on education, 1940	78.8		84.0		73.5	
Additional with growth	14.4*		4.7*		14.1*	
Unexplained	6.8		11.3		12.4	
Total	100.0		100.0		100.0	

* Significant by F test at .01 level.
Sources: U.S. Bureau of the Census, *Sixteenth Census of the United States, Population*, Vol. II, Tables 30 and 31; U.S. Bureau of the Census, *Census of Population. 1960*, PC(1)–C, Tables 32 and 81.

tent with the Burgess model. The central parts of the area are built up first; over time as the housing quality in the center deteriorates the resident population is made up of lower status and in-migrant groups unable to afford the newer, more desirable housing on the periphery. During the 1950's the proportion non-white rose sharply in central cities, but remained constant in suburban areas. The proportions of white-collar workers and high-school graduates, although rising in urbanized areas as aggregates, remained nearly constant in central cities but increased substantially in the suburbs.

Population growth between 1920 and 1960 tended to flow to the higher status suburbs. As suggested earlier the movement from central cities to suburbs may be selective of higher-status population leaving the city in search of more desirable residential areas. It has been shown that occupational groups tend to live near their jobs but that the top white-collar groups depart from this rule to choose low density communities even if these communities are not readily accessible.[13] Thus growth may have occurred in more exclusive suburbs as the higher-status workers who could afford commuting costs sought residence in high-status suburbs while the growth of lower-status suburbs may have been dependent upon the expansion of employment opportunities proximate to these suburbs and the large scale decentralization of manufacturing that has occurred only recently.[14] This type of differential suburban growth would foster increasing city-suburban differences.

Individual suburbs, however, rank in much the same way with respect to status level in 1960 as they did 20 or 40 years earlier. In fact a sound prediction of the current educational level of a suburb's adult population can be made by knowing the school attendance rate of its adolescent population 40 years earlier.

What reasons can be given for suburban persistence? Why shouldn't population growth within a suburb change the compositional characteristics of that suburb? Consider some examples:

Evanston and Hammond are approximately equal in population size, at the same distance from Chicago's Loop, comparable in age, and both have Lake Michigan frontage. Yet the inhabitants of these suburbs have quite different characteristics. A meat packing plant was the first establishment to attract residents to Hammond, and excellent rail facilities fostered later industrial growth, while the history of Evanston was dependent upon Methodist institutions including Northwestern University.

Parma and Shaker Heights, two of Cleveland's largest suburbs, were settled at approximately the same time and are the same distance from Cleveland. Census figures for 1960 show that college graduates and professional workers formed a sizably larger percentage of Shaker Heights' population than of Parma's.[15] When these suburbs were laid out, real estate promoters planned numerous small homes in Parma and large expensive homes in Shaker Heights.[16]

The specialization involved in the origin of a suburb may have implications for its distinctive socio-economic composition, so that once a suburb is established, the population that moves into that suburb tends to resemble the population already living there.

The feasibility of analyzing longitudinally compositional changes within urban areas has been demonstrated. Yet from an analysis based

---

[13] E. M. Hoover and R. Vernon, *Anatomy of a Metropolis* (Cambridge, Mass.: Harvard University Press, 1959), p. 157; O. D. Duncan and B. Duncan, op. cit.

[14] D. J. Bogue and E. M. Kitagawa, *Suburbanization of Manufacturing Activities* (Oxford, O.: Scripps Foundation, 1954), p. 128.

[15] In 1960 the percentage of the male labor force holding professional jobs was 13.6 in Parma and 26.8 in Shaker Heights. The percentage of the population 25 and older having completed four or more years of college was 7.0 in Parma and 31.7 in Shaker Heights. U.S. Bureau of the Census, *Census of Population, 1960*, PC(1)–C, Table 72.

[16] M. Schauffler, "The Suburbs of Cleveland." Unpublished Ph.D. dissertation, University of Chicago, Department of Sociology, 1941, p. 67.

on measurements made at two or three points in time processes can only be inferred. Characteristics of migrants to and from cities and suburban areas and rates of migration flow need to be studies. For example, Goldstein suggests that the growth pattern of many American metropolitan areas may be similar to that of Copenhagen.[17] He discovered that a movement of persons with high incomes to Copenhagen was countered by a movement of persons with low incomes out of suburbs and into the central city. Net figures concealed a much greater gross movement which had the effect of raising the socio-economic characteristics of suburban areas and lowering these characteristics for the central city. Clearly continued research in the dynamics of suburbanization is needed.

---

[17] S. Goldstein, "Some Economic Consequences of Suburbanization in the Copenhagen Metropolitan Area," *American Journal of Sociology*, 68 (March 1963).

9

ROBERT H. WELLER

An Empirical Examination of Megalopolitan Structure

SUMMARY

Recently, the emergence of a new community form has attracted considerable attention. Gottmann has written of the "megalopolis," and others have written of the development of "urban fields" which will replace the traditional concepts of "city" and "metropolis." The belief underlying these efforts is that an increasing intermetropolitan division of labor is bringing about a new type of community. Now, if we are to understand the process of urbanization in an industrialized society which is characterized by constantly shrinking spatio-temporal barriers, it seems necessary to determine if a new community form actually is present.

This study of the metropolitan northeastern portion of the United States utilizes Census data on the industrial composition of the labor force in 1950 and 1960, and compares the variance of location quotients in various industries with that in retail food in an effort to determine whether there has been increasing economic differentiation. The author finds scant evidence of an increasing intermetropolitan division of labor and questions the validity of "megalopolis" as a community form.

Reprinted by permission from *Demography*, Vol. 4, No. 2 (1967), pp. 734–743.
   The author is indebted to Professor Allan Feldt of Cornell University for critically appraising various drafts of this paper. The author alone is responsible for any shortcomings of the present analysis.

Recently, the emergence of a new community form has attracted considerable attention. Gottmann has written of the "megalopolis" in referring to the urbanized Atlantic seaboard from southern New Hampshire to northern Virginia.[1] Megalopolis is conceptualized as a chain of contiguous metropolitan communities bound together by a web of variegated interrelationships. Its major feature is a vast concentration and variety of people, things and functions; and it is viewed as the economic hinge of the nation, linking the North American continent and the foreign markets accessible by the Atlantic Ocean. Thus, Megalopolis is viewed as a functional entity, a super-metropolis, whose parts are interdependent and whose activities dominate the American economy.[2] And this concept is not without adherents. In a discussion of American urbanization, Friedmann and Miller have written: "The older established centers, together with the intermetropolitan peripheries that envelop them, will constitute the new ecological unit of America's post-industrial society that will replace the traditional concepts of the city and metropolis. This basic element of the emerging spatial order we shall call the urban field. . . ."[3]

If we are to understand the nature of urbanization in an industrialized society characterized by constantly shrinking spatio-temporal barriers, it seems necessary to determine empirically whether a new community form actually is emerging. At the outset, it is acknowledged that the areas designated by Gottmann as Megalopolis undoubtedly are the commercial and economic dominants of America. This report focuses, rather, on whether or not there is an increasing intermetropolitan division *within* Megalopolis. If so, this concept does identify a supercommunity; if not, Megalopolis is a mere configuration of metropolises which share a common geographic area.

BACKGROUND

The concept of the metropolitan community is itself a relatively recent development. The classic presentation of this concept occurred when Gras published his *Introduction to Economic History*.[4] His basic theme was that with each stage of technological development, man has simultaneously developed a community organization "suitable to the techniques of wresting a livelihood from the resources of nature."[5] Gras collated information about the technological progress of man through recorded history with comparable information about his economic and social organization and presented a five-stage classification of community organization on a continuum. The metropolis represents the last of these ideal types. Each stage is distinguished by the function that the community performs for the population of an area or for a given group of people. Thus, what distinguishes a metropolis from a city is not size or shape, but the economic function of commercial dominance over a wide area.[6]

The concept of the metropolitan unit—comprised of both the metropolitan city and the surrounding countryside—as the ecological dom-

---

[1] Jean Gottmann, *Megalopolis: The Urbanized Northeastern Seaboard of the United States* (New York: Twentieth Century Fund, 1961).

[2] For instance, Gottmann (ibid., p. 100) writes, "Despite the lively competition between the cities and the efforts at decentralization of various overcrowded activities, a specialization worked itself out, establishing *a new division of labor not only between groups of people but also between sections of the region, between places in "Megalopolis."* Elsewhere ("Megalopolis or the Urbanization of the Northeastern Seaboard," *Economic Geography*, XXXIII [1957]: 189–200), after stating that "megalopolis" is of Greek origin and means a very large city, Gottmann refers to this region as an urban system. See also, Howard J. Nelson, "Megalopolis and the New York Metropolitan Region: New Studies of the Urbanized Eastern Seaboard," *Annals of the Association of American Geographers*, LII (1962), 307–310.

[3] John Friedmann and John Miller, "The Urban Field," *Journal of the American Institute of Planners*, XXXI (1965). See also, Christopher Tunnard, "America's Super-Cities," *Harper's Magazine* (August 1958): 59–65.

[4] Norman S. B. Gras, *An Introduction to Economic History* (New York: Harper and Brothers, 1922). For an excellent summary, see Donald J. Bogue, *The Structure of the Metropolitan Community: A Study of Dominance and Subdominance* (Ann Arbor: University of Michigan Press, 1950), pp. 7–8.

[5] Bogue, ibid.

[6] Gras, op. cit., p. 184.

inant of a technologically advanced society was further advanced by McKenzie through methods quite different than those of Gras. McKenzie concluded that the development of the metropolis had been made possible by greatly improved transportation, which multiplied the avenues of contact within an area and brought formerly independent communities into a single functioning unit. And he asserted that the economic unity of the metropolitan area is based on territorial differentiation and specialization of parts functionally integrated into a balance of spatial and temporal relations.[7] Bogue, influenced by the conceptual structure of both Gras and McKenzie, published *The Structure of the Metropolitan Community*,[8] in which the principal concern is the interrelationships between the metropolitan center and its hinterland.

Thus, considerable attention has been devoted to the assertion that the metropolis is a form of social organization that represents an adaptive response of man to his physical, sociocultural, and technological environment and that this community form is the commercial and economic dominant of American society. It has also been suggested that there is an intermetropolitan division of labor and an interrelationship based on the functional specialization of metropolises in various types of economic activity. This analysis, then, is directed towards answering the question of whether the so-called "megalopolitan structure" is an example of intermetropolitan interdependence or whether it is simply what it most obviously appears to be—a number of contiguous metropolitan areas whose extremities have begun to overlap.[9]

Three major types of economic activity are necessary for the survival of any community: (1) that which is required for the maintenance of the physical community; (2) the services, including trade, necessary to maintain the population at a given level of living; and (3) manufacturing activity for local consumption.[10] Subsumed under these are the various types of occupational and industrial activity.[11] In any community the configuration of the established economic system must be such that any goods and services that cannot be produced locally will be imported from other areas. This can be effected only through local production of surpluses in some commodities to be exchanged for those items not produced locally. The community can export these commodities in two ways—it can ship out the product or service, or it can temporarily attract consumers from other areas. This is called export activity.[12]

Of course, cities are not self-sufficient entities but carry on exchanges both with their hinterland and with other cities through the indirect medium of the market, which serves to relate intercommunity needs among them. A functionally specialized city, then, is one whose export activity is quite different from that of the average city.[13]

The development of functional specialization between cities has been made possible

---

[7] R. D. McKenzie, *The Metropolitan Community* (New York: McGraw-Hill Book Company, 1933).

[8] Bogue, op. cit.

[9] Thus, Jerome Picard writes in "Urban Regions of the United States" (*Urban Land*, XXI, 4 [April 1962]: 3): "A popular misconception has led to calling this a 'city 500 miles long.' It most definitely is *not* a single city, but a region of concentrated urbanism—a continuous zone of metropolises, cities, towns and exurban settlement within which one is never far from a city."

[10] Otis D. Duncan and Albert J. Reiss, Jr., *Social Characteristics of Urban and Rural Communities, 1950* (New York: John Wiley and Sons, Inc., 1956), p. 216.

[11] For a study linking the occupational and industrial composition of a community, see Omer R. Galle, "Occupational Composition and the Metropolitan Hierarchy: The Inter- and Intra-Metropolitan Division of Labor," *American Journal of Sociology*, LXIX (1963): 260–269.

[12] For a sophisticated handling of the dichotomy between maintenance and export activities, see Albert J. Reiss, Jr., "Functional Specialization of Cities," in Paul K. Hatt and Albert J. Reiss, Jr. (eds.), *Cities and Society: The Revised Reader in Urban Sociology* (Glencoe: The Free Press, 1957), pp. 555–576; and Gunnar Alexandersson, *The Industrial Structure of American Cities* (Lincoln: University of Nebraska Press, 1955).

[13] Duncan and Reiss, op. cit., p. 217. For a brief discussion of the European origins of the concept of functional specialization, see Alexandersson, op. cit., p. 20.

largely by the general contraction of space and time produced by improvements in transportation and communication with the resulting fluidity of products and people, combined with the development of extremely large cities, itself made possible by these and other technological advances. Since specialization in an activity by a particular population aggregate is indicative of interdependence with other populations, the patterning of functional specialization may be used to examine the pattern of interdependence which exists among the various components of an urban system.[14]

It should be noted that all cities perform virtually all economic functions (for example, wholesale trade), but that they do so to varying degrees, with some cities becoming specialized in one or more types of activity and exporting the product of this activity to other areas and communities. But, since functional specialization of one area implies interdependence with another, any functional interrelationships existing within a system of metropolitan areas should be evident through an examination of employment statistics by industry. Consequently, if there is an intermetropolitan division of labor within Megalopolis, this should be revealed by a pattern of complementary functional specialization among the various metropolitan units. Further, this pattern should have increased temporally as the resultant of the process of differentiation of economic activity and the continued development of the inter-metropolitan division of labor.

Unless such a pattern exists among the metropolitan areas of Megalopolis and unless the intensity of the pattern has increased through time, it is difficult to conceive of Megalopolis as anything other than a grouping of contiguous metropolises sharing a common geographic area.

METHODS

The units selected for this analysis are the thirty-one metropolises within the area designated by Gottmann as Megalopolis. These were classified as Standard Metropolitan Areas in 1950 and Standard Metropolitan Statistical Areas in 1960.[15] Whether or not a given metropolis is functionally specialized in a particular type of activity has been determined through the use of location quotients, given in the ratio p_i/P_i, where p_i is the proportion of the local labor force engaged in a particular activity, and P_i is the proportion of some base or stan-

---

[14] This notion is stated explicitly by Noel P. Gist and Sylvia Fleis Fava (Urban Society [5th ed.; New York: Thomas Y. Crowell Company, 1964], 248), who write, "To the extent that specialization within a region occurs, to that extent there must be interdependence of the parts one on another." This is also a recurring theme in Amos H. Hawley, Human Ecology: A Theory of Community Structure (New York: The Ronald Press Company, 1950), especially in Chapter 12. Conceptually direct approaches to measuring systematic interdependence, or in testing for interdependence to ascertain whether a system exists, may be found in Walter Isard and Robert Kavesh, "Economic Structural Interrelations of Metropolitan Regions," American Journal of Sociology, LX (1954): 152–62; and in Ralph W. Pfouts, "Patterns of Economic Interaction in the Crescent," in Urban Growth Dynamics in a Regional Cluster of Cities, ed. F. Stuart Chapin, Jr., and Shirley F. Weiss (New York: John Wiley and Sons, Inc., 1962), pp. 31–58.

[15] There were 39 SMSA's in this area in 1960. Under 1950 definitions, however, many of the eight additional SMSA's would not have qualified as SMA's. For a discussion of the differences in definition between SMA's and SMSA's as well as changes in boundary and title occurring to various SMSA's between 1950 and 1960, see Office of Statistical Standards, Standard Metropolitan Statistical Areas (Washington, D.C.: Government Printing Office, 1961). It was felt that analysis should be limited to units for which comparable data are available, at the same time recognizing that the process of economic differentiation implied by Megalopolis and similar concepts should foster the rise of new metropolitan areas specialized in particular types of economic activity. The places included in this study, by their 1950 SMA designations, are: Albany-Schenectady-Troy; Allentown-Bethlehem-Easton; Atlantic City; Baltimore; Boston; Bridgeport; Brockton; Fall River; Harrisburg; Hartford; Lancaster; Lawrence; Lowell; Manchester; New Bedford; New Britain-Bristol; New Haven; Philadelphia; Providence; Reading; Scranton; Springfield-Holyoke; Stamford-Norwalk; Trenton; Washington; Waterbury; Wilkes-Barre-Hazleton; Wilmington, Worcester; and York. The New York-New Jersey Standard Consolidated Area was used in 1960 because of its correspondence to the 1950 New York-Northeastern New Jersey SMA. For an appraisal of the extent to which SMA's correspond to communities, see Allan G. Feldt, "The Metropolitan Area Concept: An Evaluation of the 1950 SMA's," Journal of the American Statistical Association, LX (1965): 617–636.

dard population engaged in that activity. The usual inference drawn is that a ratio equal to unity indicates that local production is sufficient to satisfy local consumption, so that the community neither imports nor exports the products of that activity. Accordingly, a ratio greater than unity indicates export of the particular commodity, and a ratio less than unity implies the community cannot satisfy local consumption demands and must import the product to meet this deficiency.[16]

There are two types of export activity in which a metropolis can engage and which produce two conceptually distinct types of functional specialization—that between metropolitan city and hinterland and that between metropolises. Since our concern is intermetropolitan interdependence, that which exists between city and hinterland should be controlled. While in the present analysis this has been attempted through the selection of the base population, in other analyses, the conventional procedure has been to use the United States labor force as the base. This however, certainly would include the effects of metropolitan hinterland specialization, large numbers of nonmetropolitan workers and consumers, and interregional diversity of consumption and demand patterns. The base population used in this report is the collective labor force of the thirty-one metropolitan units of analysis. If the pattern of metropolis-hinterland interdependence were the same for all metropolises, this procedure would in fact control for that relationship and any differences would represent intermetropolitan exchanges. While this is not strictly the case, it is felt that a general similarity in this respect exists among metropolitan areas, that any errors incurred will not be cumulative from metropolis to metropolis, and that the effect of these errors will be similar in 1950 and 1960.

Two procedures have been followed to assess the existence of increasing differentiation between the various metropolitan areas. Location quotients for each activity have been determined and the variance of these ratios computed at each point of time. If differentiation occurred during the intercensal period, the variances should be larger in 1960 than in 1950. The second procedure has been to form ratios of the standard deviation of the location quotients in each activity to that in retail food, on the assumption that retail food activity basically represents nonexported activity. Therefore, variation in retail food activity between metropolitan areas can be regarded as approximately the amount of variation that can be expected by chance. If these ratios are not greater than unity, little support for interdependence is present. Further, the change in the 1950–60 period can be measured by summing these ratios at each point of time and comparing the two statistics. If, on the one hand, the aggregate 1960 statistic is larger than the 1950 measure, it seems safe to assert that the process of differentiation toward an intermetropolitan division of labor occurred. On the other hand, if the 1960 statistic is not larger than in 1950, little support is present for the notion that a new community form is emerging.

RESULTS AND CONCLUSIONS

The labor force profiles in the broad industrial groups are presented in Table 1. Little change occurred in the overall distribution during this period. The largest increases occurred in the categories "professional services" and "other industries." (The increase in the last was primarily attributable to an increase in the category of "industry not reporting.") The largest

---

[16] Obviously, these arguments rest on a number of assumptions which may or may not be tenable in a given case. For a discussion of this problem, see John M. Matilla and Wilbur Thompson, "The Measurement of the Economic Base of the Metropolitan Area," *Land Economics*, XXXI (1955): 215–228; and George H. Hildebrand and Arthur Mace, Jr., "The Employment Multiplier in an Expanding Industrial Market: Los Angeles County, 1940–1947," *Review of Economics and Statistics*, XXXII (1950): 241–249. An earlier statistic from which the location quotient has been developed may be found in the "coefficient of localization," in A. J. Wensley and P. Sargent Florence, "Recent Industrial Concentration," *Review of Economic Studies*, VII (1940): 139–158.

TABLE 1. Industrial Characteristics of the Metropolitan Labor Force, 1950 and 1960

	Percent of Total Labor Force		1950 1960
Industry	1950	1960	
Construction	5.625	4.985	.886
Manufacturing	32.319	30.899	.956
Utilities, Transportation and Communication	8.349	7.198	.862
Wholesale Trade	4.197	3.867	.921
Retail Food	6.552	. 5.379	.821
All Retail Trade	15.696	13.737	.875
Finance, Insurance and Real Estate	5.358	5.780	1.079
Business and Repair Services	2.746	2.969	1.081
Personal Services	6.248	5.109	.818
Professional Services	10.062	12.832	1.275
Public Administration	6.032	6.221	1.031
Other Industries[a]	3.345	6.403	1.914

[a] Includes nonurban activities, such as agriculture, forestry and fisheries, and mining, and industry not reported.

Source: All data in this report are computed from the United States Census of Population, Table 35, "Economic Characteristics of the Population by Sex, for Standard Metropolitan Areas, Urbanized Areas, and Urban Places of 10,000 or More: 1950," and Table 75, "Industry Group of Employed Persons and Major Occupational Group of Unemployed Persons, by Sex, for Standard Metropolitan Statistical Areas, Urbanized Areas, and Urban Places of 10,000 or More: 1960."

TABLE 2. Location Quotients of General Types of Industrial Activity, 1950 and 1960

	Mean of Location Quotients			Standard Deviation of Location Quotients			Standard Deviation of LQ_j to LQ in retail food		
Industry	1950	1960	1960/1950	1950	1960	1960/1950	1950	1960	1960/1950
Construction	.995	1.042	1.047	.228	.190	.833	1.318	1.080	.819
Manufacturing	1.215	1.213	.998	.377	.337	.894	2.179	1.915	.879
Utilities, Transportation and Communications	.811	.813	1.002	.259	.213	.822	1.497	1.210	.808
Wholesale Trade	.707	.745	1.054	.200	.182	.910	1.156	1.034	.894
Retail Food	.897	.946	1.055	.173	.176	1.017	1.000	1.000	1.000
All Retail Trade	.942	.996	1.057	.115	.109	.948	.665	.619	.931
Finance, Insurance, and Real Estate	.639	.708	1.108	.374	.319	.853	2.162	1.813	.839
Business and Repair Services	.814	.762	.936	.180	.226	1.256	1.040	1.284	1.235
Personal Services	.862	.897	1.041	.456	.398	.872	2.636	2.261	.858
Professional Services	.902	.924	1.024	.178	.171	.961	1.029	.972	.945
Public Administration	.873	.891	1.021	.894	.776	.868	5.167	4.409	.853
Total							19.849	17.597	.887

decreases occurred in the categories "personal services" and "retail food." These industrial categories declined by about 20 per cent over the respective 1950 portions of the labor force.

As a result of this stability, there was little change in the means of the location quotients (Table 2). When the standard deviations of the location quotients are examined, the only large increase in variability occurs in the category "business and repair services." Since decreases in variability occur in most of the other general categories of economic activity, it appears that metropolitan areas have become more alike rather than more differentiated in this respect.[17] When ratios are formed of the standard deviation of the location quotients in each activity to that of retail food, there is a cross-sectional evidence of interdependence at each point of time, but there is *no* evidence of increasing interdependence except in "business and repair services." When a summary statistic is formed by summing these ratios, this figure drops from 19.85 in 1950 to 17.60 in 1960—a decline of 11 percent.

On the basis of these broad categories of economic activity, there is little empirical evidence for the notion of an increasing economic differentiation among the thirty-one metropolitan areas included in this study. Since it is possible that these more general types of activity might conceal more detailed interdependence, the additional step has been taken of performing a similar analysis using more detailed industry groups. (See Table 3.)

When this is done, the labor force profile is not quite as stable as when the more general categories are used. The standard deviations of the location quotients show that substantial increases occurred in four activities during the 1950–60 period: "nondurable fabricating," "trucking," "utilities and sanitary services," and "business services." (See Table 4.) There is also considerable cross-sectional evidence of interdependence, as indicated by the ratio of the various standard deviations to that of retail food. However, there is only evidence of substantial increased differentiation or interdependence in the four types of activity mentioned above, while in twelve of the industry groups there is evidence of *decreased* interdependence. In this case, the aggregate statistic declines from 60.53 in 1950 to 53.13 in 1960—a decrease of 12 percent.

To sum up: there is but limited evidence of increasing economic interdependence among the metropolitan areas of Megalopolis. If anything, their labor forces have become more homogeneous. One must therefore question the validity of concepts like Megalopolis as representing a new community form and ecological unit and consider them as clusters of large, contiguous cities until some evidence is made available to support the Megalopolitan concept.

---

[17] An increase in homogeneity of economic activity should not be entirely surprising. Relatively advantageous locations for a given type of economic activity are dependent upon more favorable accessibility to basic industry inputs from regional and national sources and to regional and national markets. Basic industry inputs would include intermediate factors such as a skilled labor force, economies of scale, industry linkages, and so on, as well as the basic resources. As transportation and communication networks continue to improve within a region, any given point within that region will have better access both to the input factors and to the existing markets. Eventually this would reduce variance in accessibility for different points within the region. Further, the various metropolitan areas within the megalopolitan region have been experiencing population growth, which enlarges existing markets and creates new ones. These two factors, combined with the market orientation of the regional economy, are conducive to ubiquity of production and economic activity, and would lead to homogeneity of labor force profiles for the various metropolitan communities contained within the megalopolitan region. For a treatment of the consequences of variations in access characteristics, see Harvey S. Perloff et al., *Regions, Resources and Economic Growth* (Lincoln: University of Nebraska Press, 1960).

TABLE 3. Detailed Industrial Characteristics[a] of the Metropolitan Labor Force, 1950 and 1960

Industry	Percent of Total Labor Force		
	1950	1960	1960 / 1950
Construction	5.625	4.985	.886
Durable Processing	2.429	2.201	.906
Durable Fabricating	11.411	12.935	1.134
Nondurable Processing	9.412	7.466	.793
Nondurable Fabricating	9.066	8.297	.915
Railroads	1.741	1.009	.580
Trucking	1.219	1.247	1.023
Other Transportation	2.445	2.124	.869
Telecommunications	1.445	1.505	1.042
Utilities and Sanitary Services	1.500	1.312	.875
Wholesale Trade	4.197	3.867	.921
Retail Food	6.552	5.379	.821
Other Retail Sales	9.145	8.359	.914
Finance, Insurance, and Real Estate	5.358	5.780	1.079
Business Services	1.342	1.866	1.390
Repair Services	1.404	1.104	.786
Private Household	2.787	2.249	.807
Other Personal Services	3.460	2.860	.827
Entertainment	1.101	.810	.736
Hospitals, Welfare, and Other Professional Services	5.749	7.445	1.295
Educational Services	3.212	4.576	1.425
Public Administration	6.032	6.221	1.031
Other Industries	3.345	6.403	1.914

a With the exception of manufacturing activity, these categories follow those of the condensed classification of the United States Census, with the following alterations. The 1950 categories, "hotels and lodging places" and "other personal services," have been combined to equal the 1960 category, "other personal services." The 1950 categories, "medical and other health services" and "other professional and related services," have been combined to correspond with the 1960 category, "hospitals, welfare and other professional services," which consists of "hospitals," "welfare, religious and nonprofit membership organizations," and "other professional and related services." "Educational services, government" and "educational services, private" have been collapsed into "educational services." Retail food is the combination of "food and dairy products stores, and milk retailing" and "eating and drinking places." Manufacturing activity has been divided into four types, following the scheme presented in Otis D. Duncan et al., *Metropolis and Region* (Baltimore: The Johns Hopkins Press, 1960), pp. 57–58.
Source: See Table 1.

TABLE 4. Location Quotients of Detailed Industrial Activities, 1950 and 1960

Industry	Mean of Location Quotients			Standard Deviation of Location Quotients			Standard Deviation of LQ_j to LQ in Retail Food		
	1950	1960	1960/1950	1950	1960	1960/1950	1950	1960	1960/1950
Construction	.995	1.042	1.047	.228	.190	.833	1.318	1.080	.819
Durable Processing	1.522	1.353	.889	1.642	1.149	.700	9.491	6.528	.688
Durable Fabricating	1.188	1.237	1.041	.908	.698	.769	5.249	1.966	.756
Nondurable Processing	1.575	1.451	.921	1.207	.924	.766	6.977	5.250	.752
Nondurable Fabricating	.793	.923	1.164	.450	.575	1.278	2.601	3.267	1.256
Railroads	1.070	1.019	.952	.886	.854	.964	5.121	4.852	.947
Trucking	.937	1.016	1.084	.222	.339	1.527	1.283	1.926	1.501
Other Transportation	.515	.454	.882	.290	.292	1.007	1.676	1.659	.990
Telecommunications	.735	.331	1.131	.322	.279	.866	1.861	1.585	.852
Utilities and Sanitary Services	.966	1.026	1.062	.194	.237	1.222	1.121	1.347	1.202
Wholesale Trade	.707	.745	1.054	.200	.182	.910	1.156	1.034	.894
Retail Food	.897	.946	1.055	.173	.176	1.017	1.000	1.000	1.000
Other Retail Sales	.975	1.028	1.054	.009	.008	.889	.052	.045	.865
Finance, Insurance, and Real Estate	.639	.708	1.108	.374	.319	.853	2.162	1.813	.839
Business Services	.560	.596	1.064	.327	.380	1.162	1.890	2.159	1.142
Repair Services	1.057	1.043	.987	.172	.177	1.029	.994	1.006	1.012
Private Household	.785	.839	1.069	.480	.489	1.019	2.775	2.778	1.001
Other Personal Services	.925	.942	1.018	.629	.561	.892	3.636	3.188	.877
Entertainment	.813	.778	.957	.393	.325	.827	2.272	1.847	.813
Hospitals, Welfare, and Other Professional Services	.852	.890	1.045	.223	.167	.749	1.289	.949	.736
Educational Services	1.024	1.004	.980	.249	.253	1.016	1.439	1.438	.999
Public Administration	.873	.891	1.021	.894	.776	.868	5.167	4.409	.853
Total							60.530	53.126	.878

JOHN C. WEICHER

The Effect of Metropolitan Political Fragmentation on Central City Budgets

INTRODUCTION

This study seeks to investigate the effect of suburbanization and metropolitan political fragmentation on the fiscal positions of local governments within the metropolitan area. It is particularly concerned with the effect of suburban population on central city expenditures and revenues, and with the effect of business activity in a city on the city's budget. It is argued that generally accepted notions on these subjects are inconsistent, and that previous scholarly research has been inadequate. A model is developed which does avoid the methodological shortcomings of the previous research, and tests the extents to which city expenditures or revenues are affected by the existence of suburban population and city business activity.

The results have interesting implications about the causes of current fiscal problems in metropolitan areas, particularly central cities, and about the direction of further research into these problems.

Prevailing notions about the relationship between the entities within a municipality and the municipality's fiscal situation, in the absence of any suburbs, run somewhat as follows: A city has two major components, business and population, which it taxes and to which it provides services. Business activities may be subdivided into "industry," meaning primarily manufacturing, and "commerce," usually meaning retailing; the nonmanufacturing and nonretailing activities of the Central Business

District (CBD) may be explicitly mentioned separately, or implicitly included as part of "commerce."

Population may also be subdivided, usually into three groups on the basis of income: the rich, or well-to-do; those of middle-income; and the poor. The city taxes and serves all entities within it; however, on balance the city receives more in taxes from business and the well-to-do than it spends in providing services to them, and spends more in serving poor residents than it receives in taxes from them. Put another way, the city redistributes income to its poor residents, from business and the well-to-do, and perhaps from the middle income group.

This pattern has been fragmented by suburbanization, creating fiscal problems for many municipalities. As suburbs have developed, industry, commerce, and the various population groups have tended to fall under separate political jurisdictions. As a result, municipalities within a metropolitan area have had widely unequal tax bases and expenditure needs. Central cities have lost substantial parts of the groups which are net revenue sources,

Reprinted with permission from David Sweet, ed., *Models of Urban Structure*, Lexington, Mass.: D. C. Heath, 1972, pp. 177–204.

I am grateful to many of the participants at the conference for helpful comments on an earlier draft of this paper. I would also like to thank my colleagues, Ben E. Laden, Richard D. Porter, and Richard T. Stillson for their comments. Remaining errors, of course, are solely my own responsibility.

and have been left with nearly all of the metropolitan area's poor. In particular, middle-income residents and manufacturing have left the central city for its suburbs. Overall, the central city has fewer rich residents, relative to its poor, than it used to, and still fewer middle-income residents. Concurrently, the central city has less business activity; the greatest decline has been in manufacturing, although retailing and CBD activities have also shown some tendency to disperse into the suburbs. The result of this pattern of movement, it is believed, is that central cities face a fiscal crisis: they have been left with the group which demands more in services than it can pay for, and have lost many of the entities which are net revenue sources.

However, the suburbs are not without problems. The groups which have left the central city have gone to the various suburbs in different proportions. Some suburbs consist entirely of well-to-do residents, with no business of any kind within their borders, while others may have a handful of residents together with a very large number of manufacturing plants; a wide variety of intermediate cases also exist.

The fiscal situations of the suburbs also vary. Suburbs consisting largely of businesses, or of well-to-do residents, are generally believed to be exceptionally, and perhaps unfairly, fortunate. On the other hand, "Many suburbs and small towns that have become mainly the abode of the resident-commuter have had their own financial crises, because the local property tax—the main source of local revenue—is an inadequate source of local finances if it has to be levied almost exclusively on residential property. Thus, suburbanization has, at times, added the problems of the 'unbalanced' suburban community to the plight of the metropolitan center. The former, in an attempt to create a sounder property tax base, has often offered special concessions to commerce and industry in an attempt to lure them away from the metropolitan center, thereby adding further to the latter's difficulties" [de Torres 1967].

These prevailing notions are frequently invoked in advocating public policies to deal with municipal problems, such as metropolitan government, or federal aid to local governments on an unconditional basis. Yet these notions about the ways in which city governments redistribute income have been subjected to very little in the way of rigorous analysis. Indeed, it is not difficult to show that they are mutually inconsistent, particularly when used to analyze the fiscal problems of municipalities within a single metropolitan area.

For example, middle-income families are regarded as desirable residents for central cities. They are desirable partly for political reasons, to promote political stability in the central city, but partly also in the belief that they may be taxed to provide services to poorer residents [Fitch 1964: 114]. But, when this group leaves the central city for a homogeneous middle-income suburb, they are believed to be unable to pay for municipal services to themselves alone, unless industry is present to share the tax burden [Fitch 1964: 115]. It is not clear what, if anything, has happened to change them from net sources of revenue in the central city to net recipients of subsidies in the suburbs.[1]

A second example of inconsistency may be seen in the argument by central cities that they are "exploited" by their suburbs, in that the central cities must provide services to nonresidents who do not pay taxes to the central city.[2] This claim conflicts with the notion that business establishments are net sources of revenue for municipal governments. If nonresidents enter the central city, they do so largely to make use of its business establishments, to work, shop, or entertain themselves. Therefore, by implication the central city has retained a larger share of its business establishments than of its population; presumably it can tax these businesses to provide services to its population.

To take an extreme illustration, if the central city has lost *only* population so that it is surrounded by purely "bedroom communities," then it has lost only some entities which do not "pay for themselves." It may still be possible that the city's fiscal situation is worsened, however, if the loss of tax revenue (in this case, through a loss in the residential property tax base) is greater than the decline in expenditures (which would include schools, and services provided to residential property, such as police and fire protection, sanitation, street maintenance, etc.). This is an empirical question, but it is surely possible that the sales tax revenue derived from suburbanites shopping in the city, or the property taxes paid by the businesses at which they shop and the factories at which they work, are greater than the expenditures on services which the city provides to them while they are in the city.

If, on the other hand, business establishments have followed residents to the suburbs, then the city can hardly claim that it is being exploited by the suburbs, which now contain both the residents and the business activity that serves them. If the residents involved were well-to-do or middle-income families which were net sources of revenue to the central city, then the city's financial plight may be worsened, but it is the former residents and businesses who are no longer being exploited by the city, rather than the city now being exploited by the suburbs.[3]

These examples demonstrate that the analysis of income redistribution between business and people is related to the analysis of redistribution between central city residents and suburbanites. The empirical work in this study will present results bearing on both types of redistribution. The question of the extent to which cities redistribute income among resident population groups is not discussed in this paper, but is deferred for future study.

PREVIOUS RESEARCH

The effect of political fragmentation on local government fiscal patterns has been investigated frequently in recent years, in a variety of contexts. The studies may be conveniently classified on the basis of the dependent variable chosen, which has been either local government expenditures or the local government tax base.

The former approach has been more common; there are a large and growing number of "expenditure function" studies, investigating the factors which affect intercity variations in local government expenditures.[4] Many have looked at the relationship between suburbanization of population and central city expenditures, usually finding that an increase in suburbanization (measured as the ratio of suburban population to SMA population) increases expenditures per capita by the central city. In the pioneering analysis of this relationship, Hawley claimed that these results "indicate that the size of the metropolitan population not included in the corporation limits of the metropolitan center represents a cost factor to the residents of the center. The latter are carrying the financial burden of an elaborate and costly service installation, i.e., the central city, which is used daily by a non-contributing population that in some instances is more than twice the size of the contributing population" [Hawley 1956: 781–782].

Brazer, Kee, Bahl, and Campbell and Sacks have also generated the same statistical results, but have not drawn Hawley's conclusion that central cities were being exploited by their suburbs. They have instead pointed out that it is necessary to investigate the revenues which central cities receive from suburbanites, as well as the expenditures the cities incur on account of the suburbanites. None have carried out such an investigation.[5]

Fewer studies have looked at the extent of business activity as a determinant of local government expenditures. The first study to include a variable to represent business activity (in this case, retail trade) is by Scott and Feder [1957]. They used retail sales per capita as a proxy for "the general level of business activity in the city" [Scott and Feder 1957: 10–11] and found a positive and significant correlation, which they took to indicate "the existence of a close relationship between fiscal capacity and per capita government expenditures" [Scott and Feder 1957: 1]. Subsequently Brazer used a broader measure of business activity (the ratio of employment in manufacturing, trade and services to population) finding generally positive relationships which were not consistently significant [Brazer 1959: 30]; Bahl used measures of both central city retail trade and central city total employment, finding positive and generally significant effects on expenditures for both, with the retail trade coefficients more consistently significant [Bahl 1969, Ch. 3].

Unfortunately, the theoretical foundations of these studies are so defective that the results have no implications about either the extent of income redistribution between business and population or the question of exploitation between city and suburb. The reason is that local governments face a budget constraint which greatly affects their fiscal behavior. Generally, they are required to balance their budgets, at least for current operating expenditures; they cannot print money, of course, and have limited borrowing powers, particularly on current account. The budget constraint, which for most local governments is a legal as well as political necessity, requires that revenues approximately equal expenditures on an annual basis. (Local governments are not prohibited from running surpluses, but the recurrent fiscal crises confronting them suggest that they rarely manage to do so.) The budget constraint therefore implies that any factor which affects revenues of municipalities, will also affect expenditures, and vice versa. Indeed, in those studies which have used factors affecting revenues as independent variables in expenditure regressions, the revenue factors have usually been more significant than have been factors affecting expenditures directly, such as demographic characteristics.[6] This result has been noted before, but its significance has been overlooked: it completely vitiates the usefulness of the previous studies for our purposes.

The importance of the budget constraint, and the inadequacy of the previous research, can be demonstrated by means of a simple model of a municipal government. The model describes the process by which the city adjusts its budget in response to changes in population or business activity. It is assumed that the city starts in equilibrium, with expenditures equal to revenues; a change then occurs in either city or suburban population, or city business activity, which affects both the city's tax base and its expenditures. The city adjusts to the impact by altering either its tax rate or its expenditures, or both, so as to reach a new equilibrium with a balanced budget, satisfying the budget constraint.

Algebraically, the model can be written as follows:

$$W_0 = \alpha C_0 + \alpha' S_0 + \beta B_0 \qquad (1)$$

$$X_0 = a C_0 + a' S_0 + b B_0 \qquad (2)$$

$$t_0 = \frac{X_0}{W_0} \qquad (3)$$

$$R_0 = t_0 W_0 = X_0 \qquad (4)$$

where

W = tax base,
X = expenditures,
R = revenues,
t = tax rate,
C = central city population,
S = suburban population,
B = business activity.

(The subscript 0 refers to the initial level of the variables.)

Now let there be an increase in the number of entities to be taxed and served, in each category. The tax base will increase because of the greater number of entities which can be taxed, and the level of expenditures also will increase because of the greater number of entities to be served. However, the level of expenditures will also change for another reason: if expenditures and the tax base change in different proportions, then the city budget is out of balance, and the city must adjust either its expenditures or its tax rate, or both, to restore the balance. The new level of expenditures is thus greater than the old by an amount a for each new city resident, a' for each suburbanite, and b for each unit of business. This component of the new level of expenditures may be referred to as X_N. However, if the change in expenditures by the municipality, measured by $(X_N - X_0)$, differs from the change in its revenue, measured by $t_0(W_1 - W_0)$, the city no longer has a balanced budget. In reacting to the imbalance, the city may alter its expenditures; this change will be referred to as X_w. The sum of these changes represents the net change in the city's expenditures. Algebraically,

$$X_1 = X_{N1} + X_{W1}, \tag{5}$$

where

$$X_{N1} = aC_1 + a'S_1 + bB_1 \tag{6}$$

$$X_{W1} = d[t_0(W_1 - W_0) - (X_{N1} - X_0)]. \tag{7}$$

(The subscript 1 refers to the new levels of the variables.)

In equation (7), the terms in parentheses are the changes in the tax base and expenditures generated by the changes in population and business. The entire term in brackets represents the net change in the city's budget, given the initial tax rate. This term may conveniently be called "surplus" revenue; it may be either positive or negative. If it is positive, the city is "richer" as a result of the increased number of entities within it: it gets more in revenue, at the initial tax rate, than it spends in providing the initial level of services to the new entities. The parameter d is the fraction of the surplus revenue that the city spends on additional services; $(1 - d)$ is the fraction returned to individuals in the form of lower taxes.[7] The parameter d lies between 0 and 1, inclusive; if it is 0, the city chooses to keep the level of services constant, and lower taxes by the full amount of the surplus; if d is 1, the city chooses to keep the initial tax rate and spend all of the surplus on additional municipal services. At intermediate values, of course, the city both lowers taxes and raises expenditures.

In the new equilibrium, equation (1) now becomes:

$$W = \alpha C_1 + \alpha'S_1 + \beta B_1. \tag{8}$$

Equation (7) can be simplified (since, from equation (4), $t_0 W_0 = X_0$) and then rewritten in terms of C, S, and B by substitution from Equations (8) and (6):

$$X_{W1} = d(t_0 \alpha C_1 + t_0 \alpha'S_1 \, t_0 \beta B_1 \\ - aC_1 - a'S_1 - bB_1). \tag{9}$$

Equation (5), the new level of expenditures, now becomes:

$$X_1 = [a + d(t_0 \, \alpha - a)] \, C_1 + [a' + d(t_0/\alpha' \\ - a')] \, S_1 + [b + d(t_0 \beta - b)] \, B_1, \tag{10}$$

after collecting terms. The new tax rate is

$$t_1 = \frac{X_1}{W_1}. \tag{11}$$

The coefficients in equation (10) measure the effect of population or business on municipal expenditures.[8] The meaning of any of the coefficients is somewhat more complicated than the previous literature has suggested. For example, in regard to suburban population, a' is the amount by which expenditures change as the number of suburbanites changes, *ceteris paribus*; it is nonnegative. The term in parentheses is the net effect of an increase in suburban population on the central city budget, given the initial tax rate. This term is positive if the central city receives more in revenue from suburbanites than it spends in serving them, and negative if the opposite is true. The sign of this term, taken by itself, therefore, measures whether the central city exploits, or is exploited by, its suburbs.

Unfortunately, however, the sign of the parenthetical term has no effect on the sign of the coefficient (the bracketed expression). The coefficient is always positive: since $0 \le d \le 1$, $b \ge db$; and dt_0 is positive.

The same analysis applies to the coefficient of business activity. The sign of the parenthetical term measures whether cities receive more in tax revenue than they spend in serving businesses; but whether it is positive or negative, the coefficient is positive.

The previous literature can be analyzed in terms of this model. While none of the studies have contained explicit models, they all appear to have estimated equation (10) or some variant of it cross-sectionally.[9] In the context of this model, it is clear that Hawley is wrong in asserting that his results imply that suburbanites exploit the central city; also, Brazer, Kee, and Bahl have misinterpreted the meaning of their results. They appear to believe that they have estimated a structural relationship between suburbanization and city expenditures; in fact, because of the budget constraint, they have estimated a reduced-form relationship which has no useful interpretation. A regression analysis of revenues, if carried out, would have almost the same results, since revenues and expenditures must be approximately equal; comparison of the results of expenditure and revenue analyses which they suggested, would therefore have no implications about the direction of exploitation.[10]

The same problem exists with regard to business activity. Scott and Feder appear to believe that $b = 0$; they refer to business activity as representing increased "fiscal capacity," with no mention of possible additional demands for expenditures. Brazer and Bahl, however, recognize that their coefficients include both expenditure and revenue effects [Brazer 1959: 21; Bahl 1969: 83]; however, they have not realized the coefficient for business must be positive nor that the coefficients for business and suburban population have the identical form, and are therefore equally useless for analyzing the impact of political fragmentation on local government finance, or for determining the directions of income redistribution generated by municipal budgets.

The alternative approach in previous research has been to use the tax rate as the dependent variable. This approach has the virtue of being methodologically correct; it can be shown, using our model, that the change in the tax rate, given an increase in resident or suburban population or city business activity, depends on whether the entity "pays its own way." In the case of business activity, the change in the tax rate will be positive if the city spends more in serving the businesses than it receives in tax revenue from them at the initial tax rate, and negative if businesses are net sources of revenue.[11] The major problem with this approach is empirical; the data on the tax base (and therefore on the tax rate) are extremely poor. The tax base for most local governments largely consists of real property, the value of which is very difficult to measure. The commodity changes hands infrequently, so that there is no well-established market price for it. Instead, data on "value" are usually assessed values, representing more or less expert opinion as to what the property would sell for, if it were sold.

These assessed values are generally regarded as poor proxies for market value; the standard public finance texts point out that substantial inter-area and intra-area disparities exist [Cf. Due 1968: 431–432]. This can easily be verified by examining data on the ratios of assessed to sales value in the *Census of Governments* [Vol. II, 1967], showing substantial variation within an individual city, within its suburban area, between city and suburb, and between different metropolitan areas. These disparities greatly reduce the usefulness of the tax rate approach; it is very difficult to know whether the response of the tax rate to a change in population or business activity represents what actually happened to the tax base, or what the local assessor(s) thought should have happened.

Given the data problems, it is not surprising that there have been few empirical analyses. There have been five studies of the relationship between business activity and the local tax rate. Two [Isard and Coughlin 1957; Groves and Riew 1963] have been concerned with developing a method of analysis whereby local governments could estimate for themselves the fiscal impact of various kinds of growth, rather than with estimating actual impacts; the data in these studies have been primarily used for illustrative purposes, although all of the examples indicate that businesses (particularly manufacturing) are net sources of revenue for cities.

The empirical analyses have been confined to individual metropolitan areas. Margolis, studying San Francisco-Oakland, concluded that cities with concentrations of business activity (relative to population) had higher tax rates than "dormitory" cities; expenditures per capita were higher in the "business" cities, and real property values per capita were lower. Since the two central cities were "business" cities, with higher concentrations of business than most of their suburbs, Margolis concluded that the central cities were exploited by their suburbs. The results also imply that cities redistribute income from population to business establishments [Margolis 1957].

The other two studies [Brazer 1964; Loewenstein 1963] have challenged Margolis' conclusions. Margolis examined only the total expenditures of the municipal government; Brazer pointed out that this procedure caused school taxes and expenditures to be excluded, since school districts in California are independent units of government, having separate taxing and spending powers. [Brazer 1964: 136]. In a study of Detroit, Brazer found that property tax rates (including school and county taxes) were higher for "dormitory" suburbs than for "business" suburbs. While this result reverses Margolis' conclusions, it is not directly comparable, since Brazer did not present property tax rates for the municipalities alone, and neither he nor Margolis has amended the latter's results to include school systems. It is also true that San Francisco and Detroit are very different areas, and the results may be due to differences in tastes or other omitted factors.

Loewenstein investigated the effect of industry on tax revenues and local government expenditures in three suburban townships around Philadelphia; he concluded that in at least two cases, industrial development had increased revenues more than expenditures, largely because workers at the new plants did

not move into the suburbs when the plants did, but chose to commute from greater distances. His conclusion is somewhat weakened by his choice of particular establishments: the plants chosen were generally large and frequently provided their own "municipal services," such as roads, sewers, and water. Loewenstein also assumed that there was no increase in expenditures on local government services as a result of increased commuting into the suburban areas, and that the presence of industry exerts no influence on the value of other property in the suburb. These assumptions raise the probability that his results would differ from those of Margolis, but they also reduce the usefulness of his analysis for comparative purposes.

With the possible exception of Margolis' work, there have been no direct investigations of the relationship of the central city tax rate to the *extent* of suburbanization. The intrametropolitan studies, of course, are not designed to shed any light on this question. There are only one or two central cities in each SMA, so that statistical analysis is impossible. A number of studies have concluded that central city tax rates are generally higher than suburban rates [Advisory Commission on Intergovernmental Relations, 1967, Vol. II], but they have not indicated how central city rates are affected by differences in the relative importance of suburban population. There have been no nationwide cross-sections using the tax rate approach; such a cross-section could generate a statistical test of the relationship, but would be subject to the data limitations to an even greater extent than the intra-metropolitan studies.

In summary, previous research on the fiscal effects of political fragmentation does not provide any clear or even probable answers. There is little empirical basis for asserting that central cities are exploited by their suburbs, or that businesses are net sources of revenue to local governments, which appear to be the prevailing opinions; nor is there much basis for asserting the opposite.

THE THEORETICAL MODEL

While the analysis of total municipal expenditures does not generate a test of prevailing notions about the fiscal impact of political fragmentation, it is possible to disaggregate expenditures in order to develop a model which does generate such a test.[12]

This model rests on the assumption that, at least to some extent, population and business desire different services from the municipal government. In particular, some services are demanded only by city residents; these would include education, public libraries, and perhaps recreation. Other services are demanded by both city residents, suburbanites, and businesses; these would include police and fire protection, sanitation, streets, and water, for example.

These differences in the demand for particular services affect the amounts spent on the services. If the basic model developed in the preceding section is disaggregated into two sectors, sector Y consisting of services provided only to residents, and sector Z consisting of services provided to all three groups, then the initial situation in the city is as follows:

$$W_0 = \alpha C_0 + \alpha' S_0 + \beta T_0 + \gamma M_0 \quad (12)$$

$$Y_0 = ayC_0 \quad (13)$$

$$Z_0 = a_z C_0 + a'_z S_0 + b_z T_0 + g_z M_0 \quad (14)$$

$$X_0 = Y_0 + Z_0 \quad (15)$$

$$t_0 = \frac{X_0}{W_0} \quad (16)$$

where

T = retail trade,
M = manufacturing,

in addition to the variables previously defined. "Business activity" is thus disaggregated into two components. The subscripts y and z in the expenditure regressions are used to distinguish the amounts spent to provide each kind of service to the particular entity, such as resident population.

Again, an increase in the number of entities to be taxed and served will affect both the tax base and the level of expenditures; and again the new level of expenditures has two components. This is true of each category of services. Algebraically,

$$Y_1 = Y_{N1} + Y_{W1} \quad (17)$$

$$Z_1 = Z_{N1} + Z_{W1} \quad (18)$$

The components may be rewritten in the form of Equations (6) and (7):

$$Y_{N1} = a_y C_1 \quad (19)$$

$$Y_{W1} = d_y[t_0(W_1 - W_0) - (X_{N1} - X_0)] \quad (20)$$

$$Z_{N1} = a_z C_1 + a'_z S_1 + b_z T_1 + g_z M_1 \quad (21)$$

$$Z_{W1} = d_z[t_0(W_1 - W_0) - (X_{N1} - X_0)] \quad (22)$$

where

$$X_{N1} = Y_{N1} + Z_{N1}. \quad (23)$$

The bracketed terms in equations (20) and (22) are identical, and also are identical to the bracketed term in equation (7): the only differences between the right-hand sides are in the parameters d, d_y, and d_z. These parameters represent propensities to spend on public services out of the city's surplus revenue, after it has met the demands for additional services in *both* categories generated by the increased population and business.

As in the total expenditure model, the new tax base is a function of the increased number of entities to be taxed:

$$W_1 = \alpha C_1 + \alpha' S_1 + \beta T_1 + \gamma M_1. \quad (24)$$

By a process of substitution similar to that used to derive Equation (10), Equations (17) and (18) can be written as:

$$Y_1 = [a_y + d_y(t_0\alpha - a)]C_1 + d_y(t_0\alpha' - a')S_1$$
$$+ d_y(t_0\beta - b)T_1 + d_y(t_0\gamma - g)M_1 \quad (25)$$

$$Z_1 = [a_z + d_z(t_0\alpha - a)]C_1 + [a' + d_z(t_0\alpha' - a')]S_1 + [b + d_z(t_0\beta - b)]T_1$$
$$+ [g + d_z(t_0\gamma - g)]M_1 \quad (26)$$

where

$$a = a_y + a_z; \quad (27)$$

for the other coefficients, since $b_y = 0$ by assumption,

$$b = b_z. \quad (28)$$

Equations (25) and (26) imply that, for the purposes of testing the prevailing hypotheses, the analysis of municipal expenditures on services provided to nonresidents and businesses, as well as residents, is no more useful than the analysis of total municipal expenditures; however, the analysis of expenditures on services provided *only* to residents does generate a test.[13]

The effect of an increase in business activity on expenditures for Y, for example, is entirely due to the businesses' effect on surplus revenue; any increased expenditure on Y will come about because the businesses are a net source of revenue to the municipality, given the original tax rate. The sign of the coefficients of T_1 and M_1 will be positive if the prevailing hypotheses are true; while the sign of the coefficient of S_1 will be negative.

In the next section of the paper, equation (25) will be estimated empirically; however, it is useful before doing so to extend the model to take into account the distribution of income within the city, in order to improve the specification of the model. Since the empirical work will analyze expenditures on education, it is also useful to include a measure of school enrollment as an independent variable, to allow for the fact that the service is provided to a specific subset of the city's population.

The central city population is conveniently divided into two groups, the rich and the poor. The city spends different amounts on providing

services to members of the two groups, and raises different amounts of revenue from them, since the tax bases are different. Algebraically, the two-category model becomes:

$$W_0 = \alpha_R C_{R0} + \alpha_p C_{P0} + \alpha'S_0 + \beta T_0 + \gamma M_0 \quad (29)$$

$$Y_0 = a_{Ry}C_{R0} + a_{Py}C_{P0} + eE_0 \quad (30)$$

$$Z_0 = a_{Rz}C_{R0} + a_{Pz}C_{P0} + a'S_0 + bT_0 + gM_0. \quad (31)$$

(The subscripts R and P refer to the rich and poor residents, respectively. The variable E is public school enrollment.)

As population and business increase, the tax base and the level of expenditures change in the same manner already described, and the new equilibrium levels are:

$$W_1 = \alpha_R C_{R1} + \alpha_p C_{P1} + \alpha'S_1 + \beta T_1 + \gamma M_1 \quad (32)$$

$$Y_1 = [a_{Ry} + d_y(t_0\alpha_R - a_R)]C_{R1} + [a_{Py}$$
$$+ d_y(t_0\alpha_P - a_P)]C_{P1}$$
$$+ d_y(t_0\alpha' - a')S_1 + d_y(t_0\beta - b)T_1$$
$$+ d_y(t_0\gamma - g)M_1 + eE_1 \quad (33)$$

$$Z_1 = [a_{Rz} + d_z(t_0\alpha_R - a_R)]C_{R1} + [a_{Pz}$$
$$+ d_z(t_0\alpha_P - a_P)]C_{P1}$$
$$+ [a' + d_z(t_0\alpha' - a')]S_1 + [b$$
$$+ d_z(t_0\beta - b)]T_1$$
$$+ [g + d_z(t_0\gamma - g)]M_1. \quad (34)$$

In order to eliminate multicollinearity between C_{R1} and C_{P1} in the empirical estimation, when all variables are deflated by C_1, it is useful to rewrite Equations (33) and (34), utilizing the fact that $C_{R1} = C_1 - C_{P1}$. These equations then become

$$Y_1 = [a_{Ry} + d_y(t_0\alpha_R - a_R)]C_1 + [a_{Py}$$
$$+ d_y(t_0\alpha_P - a_P)$$
$$- a_{Ry} - d_y(t_0\alpha_R - a_p)]C_{p1} + d_y(t_0\alpha'$$
$$- a')S_1$$
$$+ d_y(t_0\beta - b)T_1 + d_y(t_0\gamma - g)M_1 + eE_1 \quad (35)$$

$$= [a_{Rz} + d_z(t_0\alpha_R - a_R)]C_1$$
$$+ [a_{pz} + d_z(t_0\alpha_p - a_p)$$

$$- a_{Rz} - d_z(t_0\alpha_R - a_R)]C_{p1} + [a'$$
$$+ d_z(t_0\alpha' - a')]S_1$$

$$+ [b + d_z(t_0\beta - b)]T_1 + [g + d_z(t_0\gamma - g)]M_1 \qquad (36)$$

Equations (35) and (36) will be estimated for certain services in the next section of this paper.[14]

It is probably unnecessary to point out that the model developed in this section is very crude. It clearly ignores important factors which affect the expenditures of cities. The independent variables employed are gross measures which obscure important differences between individual members of the same category: people have different incomes and tastes; individual manufacturing plants may have greatly differing demands for a particular service, depending on such factors as size of plant and the relative importance of land and labor in the production function; and so on. Other types of activity, such as central offices and government itself, also generate revenues or demand expenditures by the local government.

These limitations should of course be kept in mind in interpreting the empirical results in the next section.

EMPIRICAL RESULTS

As previously mentioned, empirical estimation of municipal expenditure regression has generally been carried out using cross-sectional data, rather than time series. This applies to studies of both total expenditures and individual service categories. The reason is that data, particularly for independent variables, is much more readily available for cross sections. For dependent variables, some time-series data is available; the *Compendium of City Government Finances* has provided annual municipal expenditure data for large cities in the United States since 1949, and some data on education expenditures are published by several sources.[15] However, there are few independent variables

for which annual estimates for individual cities are available, apart from population. More comprehensive data are available cross-sectionally, particularly from the *Census of Population and Housing,* the *Census of Business,* and the *Census of Manufactures.*

Given the greater availability and reliability of the cross-sectional data, this study will follow previous expenditure analyses in estimating cross-sectional expenditure regressions. If the model of the previous section is applied to a cross section of cities, it implies that the prevailing hypotheses may be tested by investigating whether cities with greater suburban population, retail trade, and manufacturing spend more on the services provided only to residents.

Rather than investigating the broad expenditure categories Y and Z, this study analyses expenditures on individual categories of services. Theoretically this is as acceptable for testing the prevailing hypotheses, while empirically it is far more desirable. Theoretically, it can be shown that disaggregation of Equation (35) into several individual categories of Y does not affect the interpretation of the coefficients of S_1, T_1, or M_1, which are the coefficients of particular interest.[16]

Empirically, it is highly preferable to disaggregate. Statistical analysis of total expenditure functions is rendered difficult by the fact that total expenditures and those for individual categories reported by different local governments depend to a great extent on the division of labor between state governments, counties, municipalities, and special districts; without adjusting for these differences, analysis of municipal expenditures tends to become analysis of local government structure.[17] Recognition of this problem has led more recent studies to focus on either individual categories of expenditures, or those which all cities under study appear to perform—the "common functions," to use Brazer's convenient term. However, as he said, "in its narrowest construction this would probably permit inclusion only of police and fire protection."[18]

The problem is particularly acute for the services included in Y. In accordance with the model developed in the previous section, the analysis is restricted to central cities of Standard Metropolitan Statistical areas. Among these, however, data on library expenditures are available only for the very largest cities, and some of these operate public libraries through special districts which are not coterminous with the central city. For parks and recreation, per capita central city expenditures in 1960 varied from 49 cents in Rockford, Illinois, to $77.27 in Atlantic City, New Jersey.[19]

Education appears likely to be the only service which is both provided only to people and performed by local governments throughout the country. Accordingly, the test of the competing hypotheses will be carried out using education expenditures as the variable γ.[20] To eliminate the effects of city size, Equation (35) is deflated by central city population, converting it to an estimation of school expenditures per capita.

It is then estimated by ordinary least-squares (t-ratios of coefficients appear in parentheses under the coefficients):

$$\frac{Y_1}{C_1} = 14.648 - 1.197 \frac{C_{p1}}{C_1} + .0409 \frac{S_1}{C_1}$$
$$\quad (2.05) \quad (7.41) \quad\quad (5.23)$$

$$+ .00944 \frac{T_1}{C_1} - 0.322 \frac{M_1}{C_1} + 3.443 \frac{E_1}{C_1}$$
$$\quad (2.60) \quad\quad (2.07) \quad\quad (17.66)$$

$$R^2 = .775 \quad\quad\quad F = 113.1 \quad (37)$$

The results in equation (37) are mixed.[21] They support the prevailing hypothesis in the case of retail trade and refute it in the case of manufacturing. In terms of income redistribution, the results imply that cities spend more on serving manufacturing establishments than they receive in taxes from them; and that cities spend less in serving retail stores than they receive in taxes from them.

The positive coefficient for suburban population implies that central cities exploit their suburbs. Since central cities do not provide schooling for the children of suburbanites, the coefficient measures only the surplus revenue that the central city receives from suburbanites. The positive coefficient refutes the prevailing hypothesis about the direction of exploitation.

It has previously been demonstrated in [Note] 16, above, that the analysis of expenditures on individual Z services is of little use in determining the directions of income redistribution within the metropolitan area. However, it is still worthwhile to estimate equation (36), because the results in equation (37) have implications for the signs to be expected in estimations of equation (36). The coefficients of S_1/C_1 and T_1/C_1 should be positive; the coefficient of $M_1 C_1$ may have either sign.

Municipal expenditures on three services provided to both people and business are analyzed in Table 1. The services shown are police protection, fire protection, and highways, services which seem likely to be provided on the most uniform basis by municipal governments in different parts of the country.[22] Expenditures are again deflated by central city population.

Ordinary least-squares analysis of Equation (36) for the three services produces the results shown in Table 1.[23]

TABLE 1. Regression Analysis of Selected Municipal Expenditure Categories

Variable	Police Protection	Fire Protection	Highways
Constant	7.00028	6.14409	3.79130
	(3.31)	(4.31)	(3.14)
C_{p1}/C_1	−0.07986	−0.08747	−0.05411
	(1.49)	(2.41)	(1.77)
S_1/C_1	0.00530	0.00202	−0.01155
	(2.02)	(1.14)	(1.03)
T_1/C_1	0.00253	0.00219	0.00195
	(2.16)	(2.77)	(2.91)
M_1/C_1	0.05631	0.10647	0.07429
	(1.14)	(3.20)	(2.64)
R^2	.115	.195	.125
F	5.31	9.87	5.83

The results in Table 1 are in general consistent with those predicted by the model in light of equation (37), although there are discrepancies. The coefficients of T_1/C_1 are all positive and significant. The results for S_1/C_1 are less clearly consistent with those to be expected; the coefficients for police and fire protection are positive, although only the former is significant, while the coefficient for highways is negative, even though insignificant. It may be that central cities provide no fire protection to suburbanites while the latter are in the central city, which might explain the lack of significance of this coefficient. The coefficient of highways, however, is simply at variance with the predicted coefficient.[24]

The results for M_1/C_1 are interesting primarily because of their different signs from that in equation (37). Education expenditures are negatively related to manufacturing activity in the central city, while expenditures for other services are positively related to it. These results are consistent with those of Margolis and of Williams, et al., but they are not consistent with what has been termed the prevailing hypothesis.

SUMMARY AND CONCLUSIONS

This study has investigated some of the directions of income redistribution generated within metropolitan areas by the taxing and spending policies of local governments. It has shown that, contrary to prevailing notions, cities appear to spend more on providing services to manufacturing plants than the cities receive in tax revenue from them. On the other hand, cities appear to receive more in tax revenue from retail stores than they spend in providing services to them. The results also imply that central cities are able to exploit suburbanites.

The results indicate that current beliefs about the causes of fiscal problems in central cities are at least in part mistaken. The loss of manufacturing to the suburbs has not, by itself, produced the fiscal crisis of our cities; further, the results suggest that suburbanization and political fragmentation have not created these problems. A possible implication of these results is that metropolitan government or some other form of area-wide cooperation will not reduce the fiscal problems of the cities; however, it is entirely possible that concentration of low-income residents within central cities has generated some of the problems,[25] so that bringing well-to-do and middle-income residents under the same government as the poor may relieve the fiscal pressures on cities, although bringing manufacturing activity back under the same government will not do so. Perhaps the fiscal problems of cities are generated simply by changing tastes for local government services, or by changes in the relative prices of these services, along the lines suggested by Baumol [1967].

It may be noticed that the coefficients of determination in Table 1 are rather low, even though the F-ratio is significant at the 1-percent level in each case. The low coefficients of determination are not in themselves particularly disconcerting; it is not the purpose of this study to "maximize R^2", but rather to investigate the effect of certain independent variables upon expenditures. However, it is obvious that variables which do affect municipal expenditures have been omitted from the model. It is possible that the variables actually may be proxies for some of the omitted variables, so that the results are in fact false.[26]

It is always necessary to bear this possibility in mind when interpreting the results of this study, and for that matter of any of the numerous expenditure studies already made. However, it is surely preferable to try to isolate specific variables whose effect on expenditures can be predicted on the basis of theory, rather than to engage in attempts at statistical explanation whose results are subject to any of several interpretations a posteriori.

The implications for future research clearly lie in the direction of further refinement of formal models. The crudeness of the models developed in this paper was discussed at the conclusion of "The Theoretical Model" section; desirable modifications, in addition to those discussed there, can easily be suggested. It would also be useful to try to extend the present analysis to additional services, particularly in the Y category. The wide variability in the assignment of functional responsibility for these services, as noted, makes this difficult, but perhaps more refined models can be developed to overcome this data problem.

The crudeness of the model, however, should not be allowed to obscure the fact that it *is* a model, capable of generating tests of competing hypotheses. In this respect, this study differs fundamentally from the mainstream of expenditure analyses in state and local finance, which have generally lacked any but the most rudimentary theoretical framework. They have tended to serve as a kind of guide for municipal officials and city planners, focussing their attention on the independent variables as affecting various classes of expenditures, rather than on the dependent variables as being affected by different factors. This approach is probably useful for some practical purposes, telling municipal policy makers that if certain things happen in a city (i.e., if the independent variables vary in certain ways), municipal expenditures will be increased, or decreased, in various categories; however, it does not illuminate the underlying structural relationships. One result is that notions such as the prevailing hypotheses are accepted without questioning, and used as guides to policy.

It seems clear that more attention should be directed to the formulation of specific models of urban fiscal structure, and less to the kind of wholly empirical analysis of expenditures that has been generally produced.

NOTES

1. One hypothesis that has been offered is that new suburban municipalities incur heavy capital costs in establishing a municipal government. The validity of this hypothesis rests fundamentally on the existence of economies of scale. If metropolitan area population increases, both current and capital expenditures would be expected to increase, whether or not the new residents live in the central city or in suburbs. However, it is possible that capital facilities can be provided more economically for larger populations, in which case suburbanization could increase the expenditures necessary to achieve a given level of municipal services. Most studies, however, find little if any evidence of economies of scale, at least when measured in expenditure terms.

    A second hypothesis is that the problem is psychological: middle income families move from apartments in central cities to owner-occupied houses in suburbs, and suddenly become aware of the property tax burden. In this case, the "problem" is not very interesting to an economist, if indeed it exists at all [Fitch 1964: 115, 124].

2. For example, see "No Matter the Name, the Game's Still the Same," *The National Observer*, April 1, 1968, p. 1. Mayor Joseph L. Alioto of San Francisco, in proposing a 1% payroll tax on nonresident commuters, is quoted as saying: "The revenues the commuters bring into the city do not begin to match the cost to the city for added traffic policemen, parking complexes, transportation services, all the myriad other daily services . . . "

3. It is frequently argued that political fragmentation generates intra-metropolitan external diseconomies, and a suboptimal allocation of resources; examples include water and air pollution. This study does not touch on these problems; the services analyzed

are not commonly believed to generate such externalities. This study is concerned only with the effect of political fragmentation on the city budget, not on the "social welfare function."

4. Different studies have used different measures of expenditures. The most common have been total municipal expenditures per capita, or total municipal current operating expenditures per capita (excluding capital outlays). All of the studies referred to in this section have used one or both of these measures. Another approach has been to analyze expenditures per capita on individual functions, such as police and fire protection, or groups of services. Studies using this approach will be discussed in Section IV. (Some studies have used both approaches and will be discussed in both sections.) A convenient summary of the more important "expenditure function" studies may be found in Hirsch [1968], pp. 498–501.

5. See Brazer [1959], pp. 57–58; Kee [1965], p. 347; Kee [1967], p. 210; and Bahl [1969], p. 23. The only investigation of both expenditures and revenues of central cities is Feinberg [1965]. He found that the decline of the city reduced its revenues, particularly from the property tax, but also reduced expenditures. His method of analysis, relying only on correlation coefficients, provided no way of measuring the relative changes of expenditures and revenues, although he seems to believe that the decrease in revenues was greater.

6. E.g., Brazer [1959], Campbell and Sacks [1967], and Bahl [1969]. Kee [1965] finds the same phenomenon for categories other than education. Bollens and Schmandt [1965], p. 366, have also commented on the relative importance of the revenue factors.

7. This approach to municipal expenditures is somewhat analogous to the standard theory of consumer demand. For example, Lipsey and Stelner [Economics, 1966, pp. 71–73] list six factors affecting market demand: tastes, the size of the population, the level of income of the average household, the distribution of income, the price of the commodity, and the prices of substitutes and complements. The above formulation of municipal expenditures (best defined as quantity times price) concentrates on two of these factors: the size of the "population" (including suburbanites and businesses) and the average level of wealth, rather than income, since wealth is probably the best measure of the tax base. The distribution of income will be introduced into the model in a subsequent formulation. Tastes, and the prices of substitutes and complements, are ignored in the simple model presented in this paper; a more complete model undoubtedly should attempt to take them into account.

8. The assumption that the coefficients a, a' and b do not change as more entities are served implies constant returns to scale, if expenditures are regarded as a proxy for output. This assumption is made for expository convenience; the model would not be changed in any important way by assuming increasing or decreasing returns to scale. It is also possible that the services may be pure "public goods," so that the marginal cost of providing the services to additional persons or businesses is zero; in this case the only effect on expenditures arises through the increased revenue generated. However, there is little basis for arguing a priori that the more important services, in a financial sense, such as police and fire protection, sanitation, and education, are pure public goods. "General control" (including the mayor and city council) may be a public good, but this is a relatively small part of municipal expenditures, amounting to 5.1 percent in 1960.

9. Given the available data, time-series analyses are far more difficult. If the model is interpreted cross-sectionally, then equation (10) implies that cities with more business activity, *ceteris paribus*, may spend more on public services than "bedroom" cities,

whether or not the additional business activity brings in more revenue to the city treasury than it costs the city to provide services to it.

10. The only study to take explicit account of the budget constraint is Gramlich [1969], who incorporated it into a model of the entire state and local government sector as part of the Federal Reserve Board–MIT macro-economic model. He found that state and local governments did in fact react to the budget constraint, concluding that, "the budget constraint comes through . . . strongly . . . it is quite important statistically, and it profoundly alters the state and local response to external shocks" [Gramlich 1969: 181]. Gramlich's results are especially noteworthy because he was working with quarterly data, while the usual statutory budget constraint is either annual or biennial.

11. Formal proof of this statement is omitted, in the interests of conserving space; the simplest approach is to examine the difference between t_1 and t_0 in response to a change in any independent variable.

12. It will be convenient in the remainder of this paper to refer to the hypotheses that central cities are exploited by suburban residents, and that businesses are net sources of revenue to the cities in which they are located, as the "prevailing hypotheses" about the fiscal impact of suburbanization and business activity, respectively.

13. The previous literature does not shed much light on the hypotheses under study. A number of studies have investigated the determinants of local government expenditures on individual categories of services, including several of the categories that would be included in Y. However, almost none of these have used any measures of business activity among their independent variables. In a study of Philadelphia suburbs, Williams et al. [1965] have come closer to testing the hypothesis than has anyone else. They divided suburbs into "Industrial and Commercial Centers" and "Residential" (the latter again subdivided by density), and found that Industrial and Commercial Centers spend more than the other types of suburbs for each function, with the exception of planning, libraries, and refuse disposal. In the next chapter, school expenditures will also be seen to be lower for the Centers. Thus, for the Industrial and Commercial Centers, services which relate to residential amenities and to home and school environment receive somewhat less emphasis than the industrial and commercial property servicing functions such as servicing of streets, and fire and police protection" [Williams et al., 1965: 112).

However, the analysis in support of this conclusion consists entirely of a simple comparison of mean per capita expenditures of each group of suburbs, with no attempt to determine if the means are significantly different between the groups. Further, no evidence is in fact presented in the next (or any other) chapter about the school expenditures of these groups of suburbs, although there are several more statements to the effect that school expenditures for the industrial suburbs are lower.

There have been three other relevant studies. Brazer [1959] found no significant relationship between "Employment per 100 of Population in Manufacturing, Trade and Services," and noncapital recreation expenditures per capita for any of several sets of cities; he also found no significant relationship between the same independent variable and education expenditures for the 40 largest cities, the only group for which education expenditure data were available to him. Brazer's results, taken at face value, imply that there is no income redistribution, but rather that the city engages in benefit taxation of businesses, which "get what they pay for" from the municipal government.

More recently, Bahl [1969], in amplifying on Brazer's work, has found a positive and generally significant relationship between per capita retail sales and per capita expenditures on parks for 198 central cities in 1960. He also found that the ratio of city employment to city population had no effect on parks expenditures, and that the percentage of city employment engaged in manufacturing had a negative effect. Bahl's work is of interest in that it is the first to separate "business" into retail trade and manufacturing; however, he does not look at the possible implications of his results in regard to the prevailing hypothesis.

Davis [1965] found a positive relationship between per capita industrial property and education expenditures in school districts around Pittsburgh. However, he found no relationship between industrial property and education expenditures for school "jointures," comprising districts which have agreed to make joint expenditure decisions. He regarded industrial property as representing wealth which could be taxed without regard to the preferences of its (absentee) owners. Davis' results in part support the prevailing hypothesis, though, like Bahl, he does not consider his results in that context; indeed, he appears to believe that industrial property constitutes solely a measure of fiscal capacity without generating any expenditure demands, in the manner of Scott and Feder's interpretation of per capita retail sales [Davis 1965: 96].

The previous literature is far from conclusive. Williams et al. provide evidence against the prevailing hypothesis about business activity; Davis provides some evidence for it; Bahl provides evidence both ways.

The impact of suburbanization is also unclear from the literature. Brazer [1959] found that an increase in suburbanization raised education expenditures and lowered those for parks, using the 40 largest cities in 1950; Bahl [1969], found no significant relationship between suburbanization and parks expenditures.

14. The coefficients in equations (35) and (36) are rather unwieldy; it may be helpful to explain their components. For example, in the coefficient of C_1 in either equation a_{Ry} is the amount spent to provide the service to a rich resident, in the initial equilibrium; it is also the amount the city would spend if the tax base and expenditures changed in the same proportion as the result of an increase in rich residents. The term in parentheses measures the surplus revenue generated by an increase in the number of rich residents, it is positive if the rich residents are taxed to provide services to other groups, and negative if these others are taxed to provide services to rich residents. The parameters d_y and d_z represent marginal propensities to spend on the respective services out of this surplus revenue.

In equation (35), the coefficients of S_1, T_1, and M_1 contain only the surplus revenue and the marginal propensity to spend on the service Y; the service is not provided to suburban population or city businesses.

15. Sources of data for school systems include U.S. Department of Health, Education and Welfare, Office of Education, *Current Expenditures Per Pupil in Large Public School Systems* [Washington, Government Printing Office, 1962]; National Education Association, Research Division, *Selected Statistics of Local School Districts* [Washington: National Education Association], entitled *Selected Statistics of Local School Systems* beginning in 1963–64; as well as the *Compendium of City Government Finances*. The usefulness of these sets of data over time is limited. The first two change in cities covered and data reported from year to year, while the last provides expenditure data without enrollment for cities in which the school systems are part of the municipal government, without separate taxing powers.

16. The interpretation of other coefficients, however, is affected. If Z is also disaggregated, then individual coefficients may be negative if surplus revenue is negative. For example, the coefficient of manufacturing activity, for a particular service such as police protection, becomes: $g_{police} + d_z (t_0 \gamma - g)$. This *may* be negative, since g_{police} is less than g. This coefficient, however, does not test the prevailing hypothesis; g_{police} is still nonnegative, and the entire coefficient may be positive even if the surplus revenue (the

term in parentheses) is negative. A negative coefficient, however, is very strong refutation of the prevailing hypothesis, in regard to business.

The prevailing hypothesis in regard to suburbanization implies that surplus revenue is negative; a negative coefficient for suburbanization in a Z service regression would be strong support of the prevailing hypothesis, since the amount spent by the city to provide the service to suburbanites cannot be less than zero. A positive coefficient, in this case also, however, does not test the hypothesis.

Several studies have estimated "non-education" expenditures, which nearly corresponds to the entire Z category, although it is more inclusive [Kee 1965; Kee 1967; Campbell and Sacks 1967]. The results of these studies are useless for our purposes, as the model demonstrates. Other studies have looked at individual Z services [Brazer 1959; Williams et al., 1965; Bahl 1969], usually finding positive or insignificant coefficients for suburbanization or business. These results would be useful as evidence on the prevailing hypotheses only if they were negative; as argued above, it is incorrect to infer from them that the prevailing hypotheses are true or false.

17. "Data in this report relate only to municipal corporations and their dependent agencies, and do not include amounts for other local governments overlying city areas. Therefore, expenditure figures here for 'education' do not include spending by the separate school districts which administer public schools within most municipal areas. Variations in the assignment of governmental responsibility for public assistance, health, hospitals, public housing, and other functions to a lesser degree, also have an important effect upon reported amounts of city expenditure, revenue, and debt." U.S. Bureau of the Census, *Compendium of City Government Finances in 1960* [Washington: 1961], p. 4.

18. Brazer [1959], p. 69. Even for other common functions there are very large differences between individual cities which are likely to be explainable only on the basis of local government structure. For example, Decatur, Illinois, spent nothing whatsoever on sewers and sanitation in 1960, but it is not (and was not then) noticeably filthier than Peoria or Springfield, which spent $3.49 and $5.28 per capita, respectively, in 1960. Data on expenditures is taken from U.S. Bureau of the Census [1961].

19. The disparities in intercity parks and recreation expenditures, apparently reflecting differences in assignment of governmental responsibility, suggest that Brazer's and Bahl's regression results for this service should not be given too great weight as evidence for or against the competing hypotheses. The argument, however, does not apply to Williams et al., since their study was confined to a single metropolitan area, where presumably all municipal governments have the same responsibilities.

20. Data on education expenditures are taken from U.S. Bureau of the Census, *Census of Governments 1962*, Vol. V [Washington: Government Printing Office, 1964]. Data on all independent variables except enrollment are taken from U.S. Bureau of the Census, *County and City Data Book 1962* [Washington: Government Printing Office, 1962]. The measure of T_1 used is retail sales; the measure of M_1 is employment in manufacturing. Enrollment data are taken from U.S. Bureau of the Census [1964] for those cities whose school systems are legally independent governments, and from U.S. Office of Education [*1962–1963 Education Directory*, Washington: Government Printing Office, 1963], for school systems which are financially dependent on their municipal governments.

Central cities in SMA's having only one central city are included if they had at least 50,000 residents in 1960. In the case of SMA's having more than one central city, smaller central cities are included only if they are at least half as large as the largest central city (e.g., Gary and Hammond), or if their Urbanized Areas are geographically separate (Beaumont and Port Arthur). For 38 central cities which meet these qualifications, part or all of the public schools are organized on a county-wide basis. These, which are primarily in the South, are excluded. In addition, three other cities are omitted for lack of data on some of the independent variables, leaving 168 cities in the analysis.

21. Expenditures and retail sales are in units of dollars per capita; all other variables are per cent. Mean values for the variables are: Y_1/C_1, \$77.80; C_{P_1}/C_1, 17.9 (%); S_1/C_1, 131.2 (%); T_1/C_1, \$1,588.70; M_1/C_1, 12.1 (%); E_1/C_1. 19.8 (%).

The high values for the coefficient of determination and the F-ratio occur because equation (37) is deflated by central city population, in order to compare it to other studies and later work in this paper. If expenditures are deflated by enrollment rather than population, the results are

$$\frac{Y_1}{E_1} = 0.120\frac{C_1}{E_1} - 1.129\frac{C_{p1}}{E_1} + 0.332\frac{S_1}{E_1}$$
$$(1.88) \qquad (7.25) \qquad (4.20)$$

$$+ .00770\frac{T_1}{E_1} - 0.122\frac{M_1}{E_1} + 358.99$$
$$(2.31) \qquad (2.69) \qquad (19.21)$$

$$R^2 = .386 \qquad\qquad F = 20.4 \qquad\qquad (37')$$

The only differences of note are that the constant in equation (37) becomes the coefficient of C_1/E_1 in equation (37'), and ceases to be statistically significant in the usual sense; while the coefficient of E_1/C_1 in equation (37) becomes the constant term in equation (37'). The result of these changes is to lower both the coefficient of determination and the F-ratio, but the signs and significance of the other coefficients are unchanged, and the results have exactly the same implications for the test of the prevailing hypotheses.

22. Brazer [1959], p. 3, found that the coefficients of variation for these three functions were lower than for other common functions in 1951, suggesting, but not proving, that there was less variation in the assignment of government responsibility between states for these three functions. In the present study, the same is true: the coefficients of variation are: police, 40.3; fire, 32.6; highways, 39.1. These are higher than for education (20.6), suggesting more variation in assignment of responsibility for the three common functions, but the difference may also reflect greater variability in tastes for the common functions. By contrast, the coefficient of variation for general control, a common function not analyzed in this study, is 48.8.

23. The data for the dependent variables are from U. S. Bureau of the Census [1961].

24. While at variance with the model, the coefficient appears to be consistent with other empirical work. Bahl [1969] finds a positive insignificant coefficient for C_1/S_1 in his highways regression for both 1960 and 1950, the former even with 16 other independent variables included; his results of course have the same interpretation as that in Table 1. Brazer [1959] found an insignificant relationship for a similar variable for 1950 highway expenditures by 40 large cities; the sign was unreported. In contrast, he found negative coefficients in all other "common functions" regressions, including police and fire protection, which are analogous to the positive coefficients for S_1/C_1 in Table 1.

These sets of results are particularly interesting in light of the fact that this service seems to be generally regarded as an obvious example of suburban exploitation of central cities. See for example Mayor Alioto's comment in [note] 2. The same opinion seems to be stated in at least two public finance texts: Eckstein [1967], p. 48, and Herber [1967], p. 491. Additional investigation of this service clearly is called for.

25. Muth [1967: 291–292] has gone so far as to explain part of the observed pattern of population densities in metropolitan areas on the hypothesis that richer families realize that their taxes are used by central cities to finance expenditures for poorer persons, and that the rich therefore choose to move to suburbs rather than to neighborhoods within the city with similar quality housing.

26. The variable which has most commonly been used in expenditure studies is some measure of aid received from other levels of government. The use of the latter variable has been convincingly criticized by Morss [1966], who has shown that studies using it are in fact regressing expenditures against part of revenue, particularly when total expenditures are used as the dependent variable, or when expenditures on an individual category are regressed against aid earmarked for that category. Since this clearly applies to education expenditures, it is appropriate to exclude this variable from the present analysis. In addition, U.S. Bureau of the Census [1964] does not report intergovernmental aid to education for financially dependent school systems, although such information is available for a smaller number of systems in National Education Association [1961].

Even using this variable, however, coefficients of determination are not particularly high. The most similar study of police, fire and highway expenditures is Brazer [1959]; for 462 cities he obtained coefficients of .26, .27, and .16, respectively. However, Bahl [1969], using nine independent variables, reported coefficients of determination of .54, .41, and .19. Several studies have analyzed education expenditures for smaller groups of central cities (usually about 40); coefficients of determination in these studies include .41 by both Brazer [1959] and Kee [1967], and .53 by Campbell and Sacks [1967].

REFERENCES

Bahl, Roy W., 1969. *Metropolitan City Expenditures.* Lexington: University of Kentucky Press.

Baumol, William J., 1967. "Macroeconomics of Unbalanced Growth: The Anatomy of Urban Crisis," *A. E. R.,* LVII (June): 415–426.

Bollens, John C., and Henry J. Schmandt, 1965. *The Metropolis.* New York: Harper and Row.

Brazer, Harvey E., 1959. *City Expenditures in the United States.* New York: National Bureau of Economic Research.

——, 1964. "Some Fiscal Implications of Metropolitanism," in Benjamin Chinitz (ed.), *City and Suburb.* Englewood Cliffs, N. J.: Prentice-Hall.

Campbell, Alan K., and Seymour Sacks, 1967. *Metropolitan America.* New York: The Free Press.

Davis, Otto A., 1965. "Empirical Evidence of Political Influences upon the Expenditure Policies of Public Schools," in Julius Margolis (ed.), *The Public Economy of Urban Communities.* Washington, D. C.: Resources for the Future.

Due, John F., 1968. *Government Finance.* 4th ed., Homewood, Ill.: Richard D. Irwin.

Eckstein, Otto, 1967. *Public Finance.* 2nd ed., Englewood Cliffs, N. J.: Prentice-Hall.

Feinberg, Mordecai S., 1965. "The Implications of Core-City Decline for the Fiscal Structure of the Core-City," *National Tax Journal,* XVI (December): 213–231.

Fitch, Lyle C., 1964. "Metropolitan Fiscal Problems," in Benjamin Chinitz (ed.) *City and Suburb.* Englewood Cliffs, N. J.: Prentice-Hall.

Gramlich, Edward M., 1969. "State and Local Governments and Their Budget Constraint," *International Economic Review,* X (June): 163–182.

Groves, Harold M., and John Riew, 1963. "The Impact of Industry on Local Taxes—A Simple Model," *National Tax Journal,* XVI (June): 137–146.

Hawley, Amos H., 1956. "Metropolitan Population and Municipal Government Expenditures in Central Cities," in Paul K. Hatt and Albert J. Reiss, Jr. (eds.), *Cities and Society.* Glencoe, Ill.: The Free Press.

Herber, Bernard P., 1967. *Modern Public Finance.* Homewood, Ill.: Richard D. Irwin.

Hirsch, Werner Z., 1968. "The Supply of Urban Public Services," in Harvey S. Perloff and Lowdon Wingo, Jr. (eds.), *Issues in Urban Economics.* Baltimore: Johns Hopkins.

Isard, Walter, and Robert Coughlin, 1957. *Municipal Costs and Revenues Resulting from Community Growth.* Wellesley, Mass.: Chandler-Davis.

Kee, Woo Sik, 1965. "Central City Expenditures and Metropolitan Areas," *National Tax Journal,* XVIII (December): 183–189.

——, 1967. "Suburban Population Growth and Its Implications for Core City Finance." *Land Economics,* XLIII (May): 202–211.

Lipsey, Richard G., and Peter O. Steiner, 1966. *Economics.* New York: Harper and Row.

Loewenstein, Louis K., 1963. "The Impact of New Industry on the Fiscal Revenues and Expenditures of Suburban Communities," *National Tax Journal,* XVI (June): 113–136.

Margolis, Julius, 1957. "Municipal Fiscal Structure in a Metropolitan Region," *J. P. E.,* LXV (June): 225–236.

Morss, Elliott R., 1966. "Some Thoughts on the Determinants of State and Local Expenditures," *National Tax Journal,* XIX (March), 95–103.

Muth, Richard F., 1967. "The Distribution of Population Within Urban Areas," in Robert Ferber (ed.), *Determinants of Investment Behavior.* New York: National Bureau of Economic Research.

National Education Association, Research Division, annual. *Selected Statistics of Local School Districts.* National Education Association.

Scott, Stanley, and Edward L. Feder, 1957. *Factors Associated with Variations in Municipal Expenditure Levels.* Berkeley: Bureau of Public Administration, University of California.

de Torres, Juan, 1967. *Financing Local Government.* New York: National Industrial Conference Board.

U. S. Bureau of the Census, 1964. *Census of Governments 1962.* Vol. V, Washington, D. C.: Government Printing Office.

——, 1968. *Census of Governments 1967.* Vol. II, Washington, D. C.: Government Printing Office.

——, 1961. *Compendium of City Government Finances, 1960.* Washington, D. C.: Government Printing Office.

——, 1962. *1962 County and City Data Book.* Washington, D. C.: Government Printing Office.

U. S. Office of Education, 1962. *Current Expenditures Per Pupil in Large Public School Systems.* Washington, D. C.: Government Printing Office.

——, 1963. *1962-1963 Education Directory.* Washinigton, D. C.: Government Printing Office.

Williams, Oliver P., Harold Herman, Charles S. Liebman, and Thomas R. Dye, 1965. *Suburban Differences and Metropolitan Policies.* Philadelphia: University of Pennsylvania.

The National Observer (April 1, 1968).

Urban Density Patterns
and Consequences

part iii

Urban density patterns in terms of both causes and consequences are the topics covered by the papers in this section. The core notion of this body of literature is the density-distance curve—the measurement of the very decided tendency for density to decline with increasing distance from the center of the city. Studies generally have shown a negative exponential (J-shaped) curve to describe the association in many different cities. Longitudinal analyses have shown that the slope of the curve tends to change through time for individual cities. In addition, the slope of the curve has been shown to vary cross-sectionally between cities. The intercity variations are a function of such structural properties of cities as total size.

The first paper in this section, by Berry, Simmons, and Tennant (11), concerns the nature of the density gradient within large cities in both the western and nonwestern world. In the course of the discussion, the density-distance curve is tied into general economic land use theory. Certainly one general finding that emerges from the discussion is the city-size compactness relationship. It seems that smaller cities are more compact than larger ones, and that the slope of the density-distance curve is steeper in smaller cities than in larger ones. This relationship seems to hold cross-sectionally for many cities and longitudinally for individual cities. The longitudinal pattern for nonwestern cities seems to be different from those of the west. While western urban density gradients decline as cities grow, in nonwestern areas the curve remains constant even though population is growing. The explanations for this difference between cities in the west and those in other world areas are couched in terms of the interplay of the differing socioeconomic patterns and levels of transportation.

Newling's paper (12) provides a general discussion of density models and focuses squarely upon the relationships among density, distance, and population growth. From the propositions that density exponentially declines with distance from the city's center, and that the density gradient falls through time, Newling deduces that the rate of growth is a positive exponential function of distance from the city's center. This proposition is evaluated with several sets of data including Kingston, Jamaica and Pittsburgh, Pennsylvania.

Treadway (13) presents a comparative study of density patterns for several U.S. cities—Columbus, Dayton, Hartford, Miami, and Syracuse. The unique contribution to this section of this paper is that the analysis expands the exponential density model to include such components of overall density as housing-unit density, vacant units, household size, and group-quarter population.

The paper by Amato (14) deals with population density patterns in four Latin American cities: Bogotá, Quito, Lima, and Santiago. The paper analyzes the relationship of population density and land values to social status. In each of the four Latin cities with distance controlled there is an inverse relationship between social class and residential density. Also, land rents when standardized by distance show a positive relationship to class. Amato's approach provides an efficient model for sorting out the distance effect in analyzing the relationship of density and rent to social class.

The papers by Winsborough (15) and by Galle, Gove, and McPherson (16) deal with the correlates of density variations. Winsborough analyzes the relationship between density and several indicators of pathology with a number of social variables controlled. Among the indicators of pathology included are such variables as infant death rate, tuberculosis rate, and public assistance rate. His findings are somewhat mixed in that some of the pathology variables are positively related to density while others are negative.

Galle, Gove, and McPherson's analysis, while generally concerned with the same problem as that of Winsborough, goes beyond it in that it focuses upon an expanded set of local pathologies; it deals with several aspects of population density; and it employs a path analytic model and reasoning. In general, their data certainly suggest that overcrowding may indeed have a negative impact upon the human condition and emergent behaviors. The authors point out in some detail how specific pathologies such as excessive mortality and fertility, ineffectual parental care, juvenile delinquency, and psychiatric disorder may be causally related to density.

Together the papers by Winsborough and by Galle, Gove, and McPherson illustrate some of the problems substantive, empirical, statistical, and inferential that mark this whole line of analysis. Clearly, density cannot be ruled out as a negative agent, but the nature of its impact remains to be ascertained.

11

BRIAN J. L. BERRY
JAMES W. SIMMONS
ROBERT J. TENNANT

Urban Population Densities: Structure and Change

More than a decade ago the economist Colin Clark introduced an article on urban population densities [1] with the remark that this branch of geography appeared to be relatively neglected. He then produced evidence in support of his argument that regardless of time or place the spatial distribution of population densities within cities appears to conform to a single empirically derived expression,

$$d_x = d_o e^{-bx}, \qquad (1)$$

where d_x is population density d at distance x from the city center, d_o is central density, as extrapolated, and b is the density gradient, indicating the rate of diminution of density with distance, a negative exponential decline.

However, despite much recent attention, both theoretical and empirical, and despite Clark's clear identification of his topic as lying within the province of urban geography (indeed, the germ of these ideas is to be found in the work of Mark Jefferson in 1909 [2]), both the topic and Clark's stimulating and fundamental contribution remain neglected by geographers. For example, not a single reference to Clark's paper appears in "Readings in Urban Geography" [3]. There is evidently a need for a careful review of Clark's work, especially in the light of the recent related contributions of Muth, Weiss, Stewart and Warntz, Alonso, Winsborough, Beckmann, and others [4]. This

is the first objective of the present paper. A variety of interesting questions emerge from an inspection of the available evidence. For example: How widespread is the regularity? Does it have a theoretical rationale? What factors influence variations in b from place to place? Why should b diminish through time in Western cities yet remain relatively constant in "non-Western" ones? [5]. These and similar questions are examined here.

THE NEGATIVE EXPONENTIAL DISTRIBUTION

Clark argued that equation (1), which says that urban population densities decline in a negative exponential manner with increasing distance from the city center, "appears to be true for all times and all places studied, from 1801 to the present day, and from Los Angeles to Budapest." In fact, he provided thirty-six examples in which the equation

$$ln \ d_x = ln \ d_o - bx \qquad (2)$$

appeared to be a good fit to the sample data at his disposal [6].

One thing he did not do, however, was to provide a theoretical rationale for his formula.

Reproduced by permission from *Geographical Review*, Vol. 53 (July 1963), pp. 389–405.

And thirty-six cases hardly enable one to assert complete universality for equation (1) regardless of time or place, especially when a sound theoretical base is lacking. Other empirical support is necessary, and it is abundantly provided in the references cited here in [note] 4.

In Chicago, the classic laboratory for urban analysis in the United States, Winsborough [7] shows the pattern to hold for every census year from 1860 to 1950, with the *weakest* correlation between density and distance −0.97. Similarly, Kramer shows that the fit is better for *net* residential densities in Chicago than for gross densities, and that the rate of decline varies by radial sector [8]. Muth, and independently Weiss, found that the pattern holds for all large United States cities studied in 1950 [9]. Sherratt fitted a similar model to data for Sydney, Australia; and Newling found that equation (2) provided a satisfactory fit for Kingston, Jamaica [10]. However, the only evidence provided for Asia relates to Calcutta, in which Kar shows that a negative exponential pattern existed in 1881, 1901, 1921, and 1951. Kar's graphs are presented in Figure 9. We can now fill in this gap a little; for Robert J. Tennant [11] has recently found that Clark's model also applies in Colombo, Hyderabad, Manila, Rangoon, Singapore, Djakarta, and Tokyo (and, independently of Kar, in Calcutta). The relationship for Hyderabad is shown in Figure 1.

Almost a hundred cases are now available, with examples drawn from most parts of the world for the past 150 years, and no evidence has yet been advanced to counter Clark's assertion of the universal applicability of equation (1). To be sure, the goodness of fit of the model varies from place to place, but in every place so far studied a statistically significant negative exponential relationship between density and distance appears to exist.

THEORETICAL RATIONALE

The basic theory of urban land use is by now well known. The argument runs as follows. Sites within cities offer two goods—land and lo-

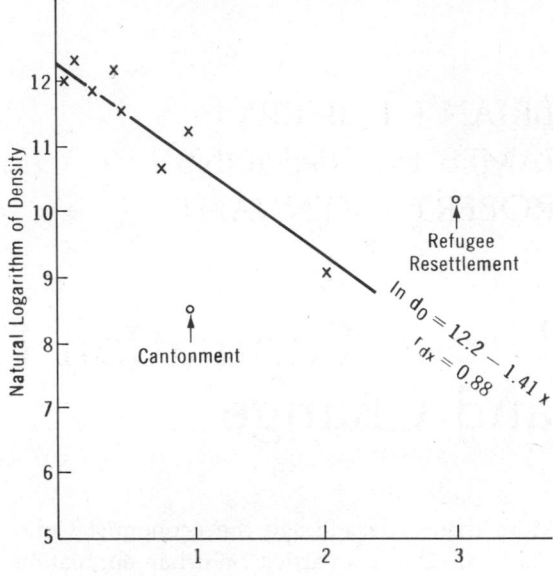

FIGURE 1.   Density-Distance Relationship for Hyderabad

cation [12]. Each urban activity derives utility from a site in accordance with the site's location. Utility may be translated into ability to pay for that site. The most desirable locational property of urban sites is centrality (or maximum accessibility in the urban area, since transport routes converge at the center). For any use, ability to pay is directly related to centrality. The less central the location, the greater are the transport inputs incurred and the lower the net returns. Bid-rent functions thus decline with distance from the city center. However, the intercept (utility derivable from maximum centrality) and the slope (rent-distance trade-off) of this function differ for different activities, and in competitive locational equilibrium, with each site occupied by the use that pays most for the land, the resulting spatial structure of land use is one that is zoned according to relative accessibility. Land prices diminish outward; and as they do, regardless of other changes, land inputs will be substituted for other inputs, and intensity of land use will diminish. Thus declining residential densities should be expected [13].

Most parts of a city are occupied by residential land uses of different kinds. Alonso [14] has shown that bid-rent functions are steeper for the poorer of any pair of households with identical tastes. Hence, in equilibrium, one expects the poor to live near the center on expensive land, consuming little of it, and the rich at the periphery, consuming more of it. Since land consumed by each household increases with distance from the city center, population densities must drop, with due allowance for variation in size of household.

Muth [15] goes further. Making assumptions about relative perfection of competition in the housing market, maximizing or minimizing behavior as appropriate, diminution of price of housing with distance from city center [16], and a demand function for housing linear in the logarithm of price at the center and population, he develops a model in which price per unit of housing, rent per unit of land, and output of housing per unit of land all decline, and per capita consumption of housing increases, with distance from the city center. Net density (output of housing per unit of land divided by per capita consumption of housing) must therefore also decline [17]. Moreover, if the price-distance function is assumed to be negative exponential and the production function for housing logarithmically linear with constant returns to scale, then net population density must decline negative exponentially with distance from the city center.

For the model to hold, a negative exponential price-distance relationship must exist. Also, since Muth's model considers only residential competition, we should expect the negative exponential to be a better fit for net than for gross residential densities, since the gross include all land regardless of use [18].

Evidence can be provided to verify both these points. Figure 2 shows that front-foot values for residential land diminish negative exponentially in all parts of Chicago where undeveloped lots are available for sale. However, the more central parts of the city are largely filled, since the older the development, the less

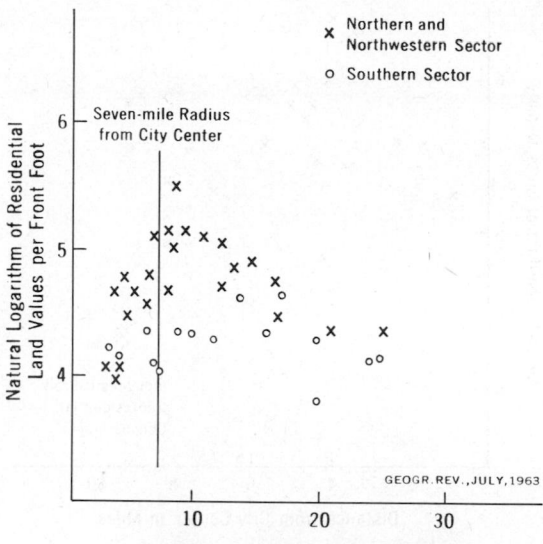

FIGURE 2.   Residential Land Values, Two Sectors of the Chicago Metropolitan Area, 1961. (Source: Olcott's *Blue Book of Land Values* for Chicago, 1961.)

land is available, the less active the land market, and the lower the price. The earliest developments are the most central and are occupied by the lowest socioeconomic groups [19]. Indeed, within a six- or seven-mile radius of the center of Chicago the only market for residential lots is related to renewal activity or intended for conversion to new highways, at condemnation prices, except within the Loop or where private investment is committed to residential renewal. Hence it should be no surprise that the negative exponential price-distance relationship does not begin to take form until newer areas with an active land market for residential use are reached. Notice also in Figure 2 how the rate of decline varies by sector [20].

Since a negative exponential price-distance relationship holds, we should now find a negative exponential decline of densities. Figure 3 shows this to be the case, and the fit for net densities is better than that for gross. Equation (1) is therefore a logical outcome of urban-land-use theory. The theory of urban land use, which originated with Hurd and Haig, and which owes its recent improvements to Rat-

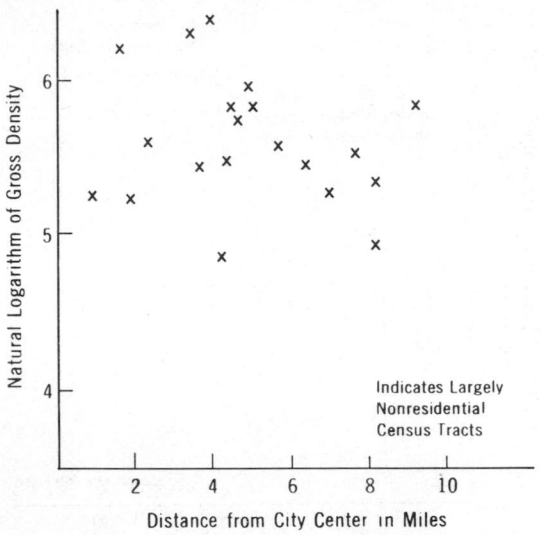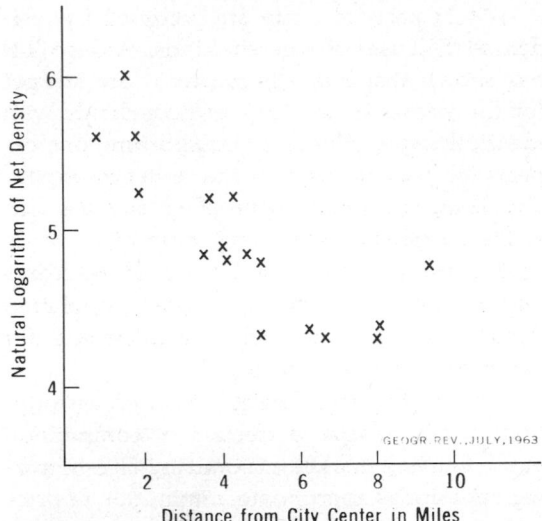

FIGURE 3.   Gross and Net Density Gradients, Chicago, 1960. Note how use of gross densities is complicated by presence of substantial nonresidential areas in certain census tracts.

cliff, Alonso, and Muth, provides the needed rationale for the appearance of Clark's empirical regularity.

IMPLICATIONS OF THE MODEL

From (1) it follows that the population residing within a distance r of the city center is

$$\int_o^r d_o e^{-bz}(2\pi x)\, dx = P_r, \qquad (3)$$

which equals

$$2d_o\pi b^{-2}[1 - e^{-br}(1 + br)] = P_r, \qquad (4)$$

assuming, of course, that a full 360° is concerned [21]. When $r = \infty$, this becomes

$$2d_o\pi b^{-2} = P_\infty. \qquad (5)$$

If population is held constant in (5), we thus expect

$$d_o = (2\pi)^{-1}b^2, \qquad (6)$$

and this indeed appears to be true.

In Figure 4, d_o is graphed against b for United States cities in 1950 [22]. Isolines of city size have been interpolated to hold P constant.

Cities in any size class trend upward with the appropriate slope.

However, another expression exists for central density, d_o. Weiss [23] found that for the United States in 1950 the density-distance gradient b could be calculated for any city by using the expression

$$b = (10^5/P_m)^{1/3} \text{ in } mi^{-1}, \qquad (7)$$

where P_m is the population of the metropolitan area. From this

$$P_m = 10^6 b^{-3}. \qquad (8)$$

Muth's data, for central cities, P_c, indicate the exponent of b to be -2.65, which is of the right relative order of magnitude [24].

Substitution of (8) in (5) results in the expression

$$d_o = (10^5/2\pi)b^{-1,} \qquad (9)$$

which obviously differs from (6), in which population is held constant. Apparently (9) applies to different subsets of cities (for example, the subset starred in Figure 4 which has the correct slope of -1) defined in terms of factors influencing central density, d_o, regardless of city

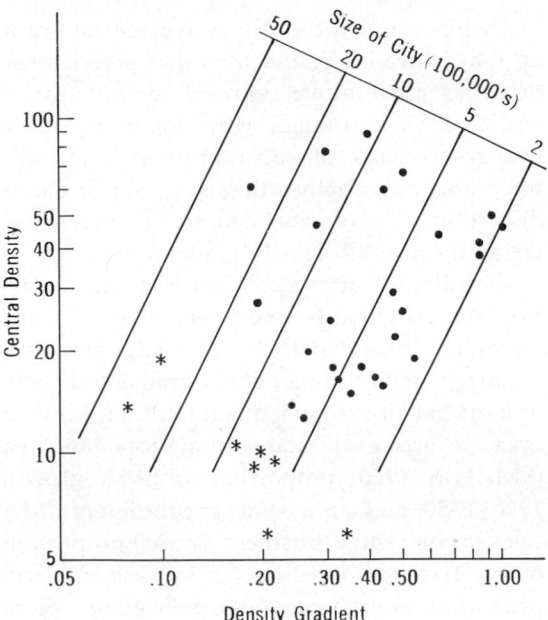

FIGURE 4.   Central Densities and Density Gradients Related to City Size, U.S. Cities 1950

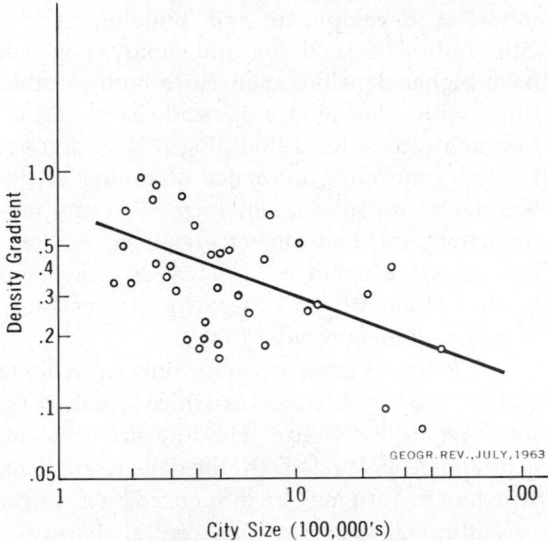

FIGURE 5.   Relationship between City Size and Density Gradient, U.S. Cities, 1950

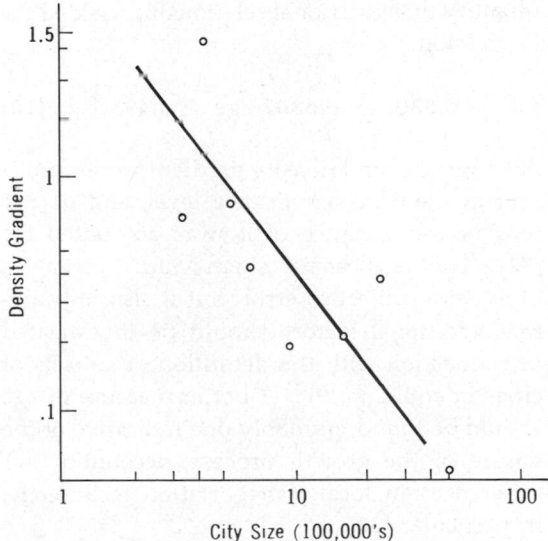

FIGURE 6.   Relationship between City Size and Density Gradient, Selected Asian Cities, Postwar

size [25]. Equation (6) applies to subsets of cities of the same size, and equation (9) to subsets of cities with similar histories of development.

Equation (8) is of further interest. It says that as the population of a city increases, the density gradient diminishes, or that small cities are more "compact" than larger cities by virtue of their steeper density gradients. Figure 5 shows how the relationship holds for thirty-six United States cities in 1950 [26]. Asian cities are graphed in Figure 6 [27]. It is obvious that Asian cities, with a greater intercept and a steeper slope, are far more compact than their United States counterparts of equivalent size, yet the generalization that compactness diminishes with size again holds.

FACTORS INFLUENCING CENTRAL DENSITY AND DENSITY GRADIENT
Enough has been said in connection with equations (6) through (9) to indicate that a more penetrating analysis is required of factors influencing central density and the density gradient in any cross section of cities. For purposes of analysis, Muth's data for United States cities will be used, since he has already provided the parameters d_o and b for each in 1950.

The most obvious influence on population densities near the city center is the age and mode of development and building. Older cities built with small lots and subdivisions will have higher densities than cities built at other times with other modes of subdivision. Winsborough [28] follows Boulding [29] in arguing for the controlling influence of timing of development on subsequent form. "At any moment the form of any object, organism, or organization is the result of its laws of growth up to that moment," and "Growth creates form, but form limits growth" [30].

But age of cities is useful only in defining similar subsets of cities for which equation (9) holds regardless of size. Holding size constant, central density is related to the density gradient, which in its turn may be influenced by a variety of additional factors. Thus central density is a function both of age and, as a composite surrogate for these other factors, of density gradient. A regression equation computed to quantify this functional relationship yielded the expression

$$d_o = 0.5302 + 0.6362 \text{ age} - 3.495 \ b^{-1}. \quad (10)$$

Both age [31] and density gradient were significant at the 0.01 significance level, and 61 per cent of the variance of d_o was accounted for [32]. This is pleasing, since Muth's estimates of d_o were subject to error, but it also indicates that additional factors should be investigated in connection with the definition of subsets of cities in equation (9). A better measure of age should be found, probably one indicative of the nature of the growth process, accounting for differences in local transportation technology, in particular [33].

Equations (3), (4), and (5) assume a circular city, with integration of equation (1) proceeding over the full 360° of the circle and the city center located at the center of the circle. Yet cities that conform to these assumptions are hard to find. Asymmetry and lopsidedness are common, elongations and crenulations many. Theoretically at least, one would expect the density gradient to diminish as shape distortions increase, because areas that would normally be occupied by certain densities are now no longer available, and uses that prefer these densities must move outward to the nearest available sites (though with some inevitable changes because of substitution effects). We must find out whether this is so, and if shape distortion, size of city, and so on interact to create the overall density gradient [34].

Muth [35], after a detailed multiple regression analysis, rejected no fewer than nine different variables hypothesized to have some influence in determining density gradient: density of local transit systems; quantity of local transit trackage; area of the standard metropolitan area (SMA) in 1950; proportion of SMA growth 1920–1950; median income; proportion of SMA sales in the central business district; proportion of central-city dwelling units substandard; proportion of urbanized-area male employment in manufacturing; and average density of central city. Only size of SMA and proportion of manufacturing outside the central city clearly appeared to bear significant relationships to b, though per capita car registrations showed a significant partial correlation, and the signs of other items, such as median income, indicated behavior in the right direction. Muth argued that size of city was significant only because other variables existed which were significant, and which could be approximated in sum by such a surrogate.

This leads us to postulate that density gradient is a function of size of city, shape distortion, and proportion of manufacturing outside the central city. A regression equation of the form

$$\log b = 3.08 - 0.311 \log P - 1.0 \log A \\ + 0.407 \log M \quad (11)$$

resulted for the sample of forty-six United States cities [36]. Only size of city (P) was significant at the 0.05 level, and scarcely 40 per cent of the variance of b was explained. However, there is reason to believe that at such conventionally high significance levels the risk of making errors of the other kind (rejecting true hypotheses) is somewhat too large for comfort, and there is thus reasonable doubt whether shape distortion (*A*) and spatial pattern of employment in manufacturing (*M*) should be rejected, the more so since Muth did find *M* to be significant. A final decision cannot be made at this time, and further work is required. The only positive conclusion is to reiterate the relationship already found by Weiss and Muth, and remarked briefly in passing by Clark, that *b* diminishes as size of city increases, so that smaller cities are more compact than larger.

CHANGES THROUGH TIME

The size-compactness relationship so far derived is cross-sectional. It applies to different cities in a region at the same period of time. One can argue from this cross-sectional pattern that as cities grow they should experience diminishing density gradients and degrees of compactness.

All the evidence indicates this to be true in cities of Europe, North America, and Australia. Clark [37] found diminishing gradients through time for London, Paris, New York, Chicago, Berlin, and Brisbane, for example. The curves for London are reproduced in Figure 7. Table 1 lists central densities for Chicago from 1860 to 1950 by decades [38]. A progressive

TABLE 1. Central Densities and Density Gradients in Chicago,* 1860–1950

Decennial Census	Central Density	Density Gradient
1860	30.0	0.91
1870	70.8	0.87
1880	96.6	0.79
1890	86.3	0.50
1900	100.0	0.40
1910	100.0	0.36
1920	73.0	0.25
1930	72.8	0.21
1940	71.1	0.20
1950	63.7	0.18

* Urbanized area.

decline in density gradient is evident, together with first an increase, and later a decrease, of central density. This phenomenon reappears in Clark's results, and Winsborough associated it with a shift in local transport technology. For example, in 1890, when mass transit was the most rapid and flexible transportation system available, there was a positive correlation between population concentration [39] and intensive use of mass transit in Chicago; but by 1950, when mass transit was competing with automobiles, the direction of the correlation was reversed [40]. Figure 8 shows the relation

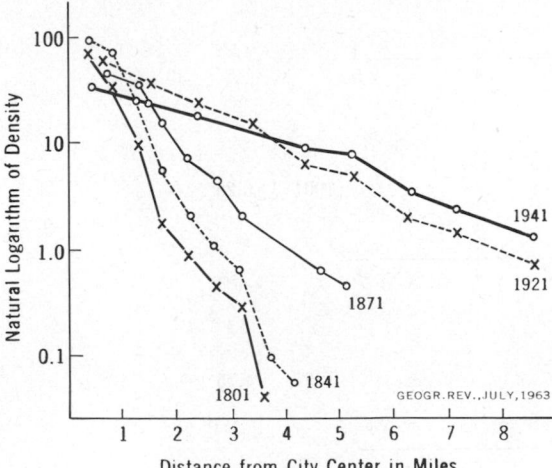

FIGURE 7. Density-Distance Gradients for Lonson, 1801–1941 (after Clark)

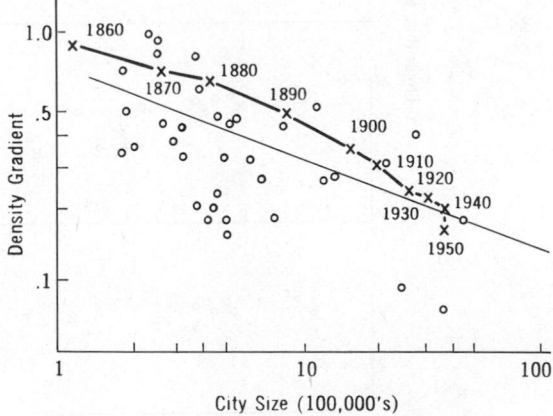

FIGURE 8. Chicago's Diminishing Density Gradient, 1860–1960, Compared with the 1950 United States Cross Section

of Chicago's density-gradient time path to the 1950 cross-sectional picture for the United States.

CONTRASTING CHANGES IN WESTERN AND NON-WESTERN CITIES

As Western cities grow through time they experience steady decreases in density gradient, and therefore in degree of compactness, whereas central densities first increase and later decrease. But the same changes do *not* occur in non-Western cities. Figure 9 shows density gradients and central densities for Calcutta from 1881 to 1951 [41]. Central density increased steadily, but although the urbanized area did expand, the density gradient remained constant. This tendency toward increased overcrowding with maintenance of a constant degree of compactness appears to be characteristic

not only for the rest of the Indian urban scene [42] but also more generally in the non-Western world.

Figure 10 summarizes the cross-sectional and temporal patterns that may therefore be identified. At any point in time the empirical regularities to be observed are the same for both Western and non-Western cities. But through time the patterns differ. In the West central densities rise, then fall; in non-Western cities they register a continual increase. In the West density gradients fall as cities grow; in non-Western cities they remain constant. Hence, whereas both degree of compactness and crowding diminish in Western cities through time, non-Western cities experience increasing overcrowding, constant compactness, and a lower degree of expansion at the periphery than in the West [43].

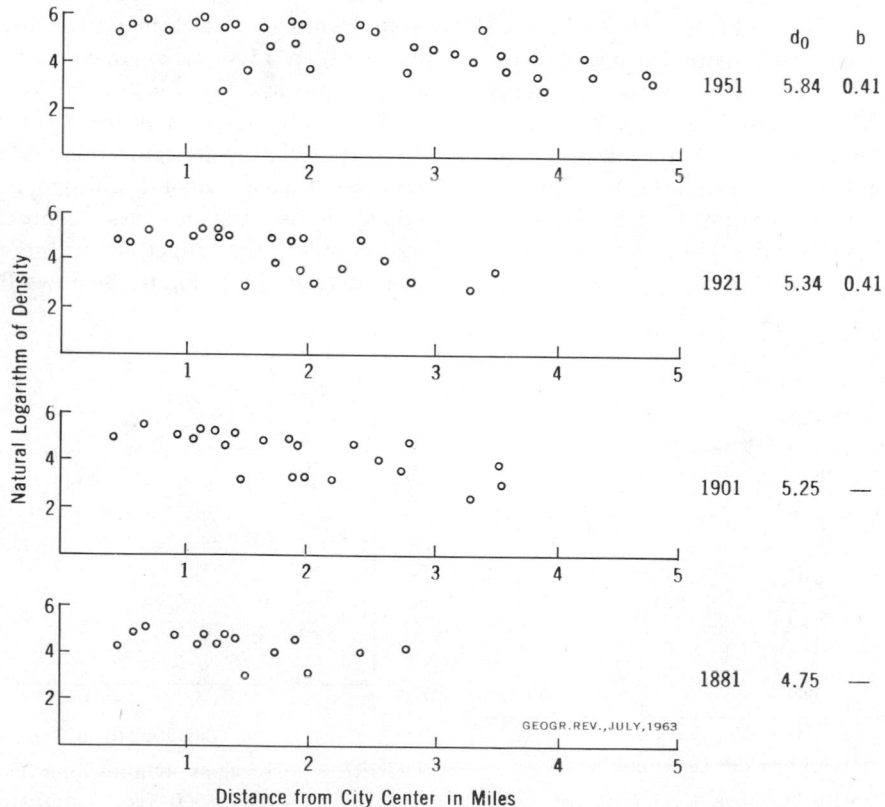

FIGURE 9.   Density Gradients for Calcutta, 1881–1951

URBAN POPULATION DENSITIES

A. CROSS-SECTIONAL, WESTERN AND NONWESTERN

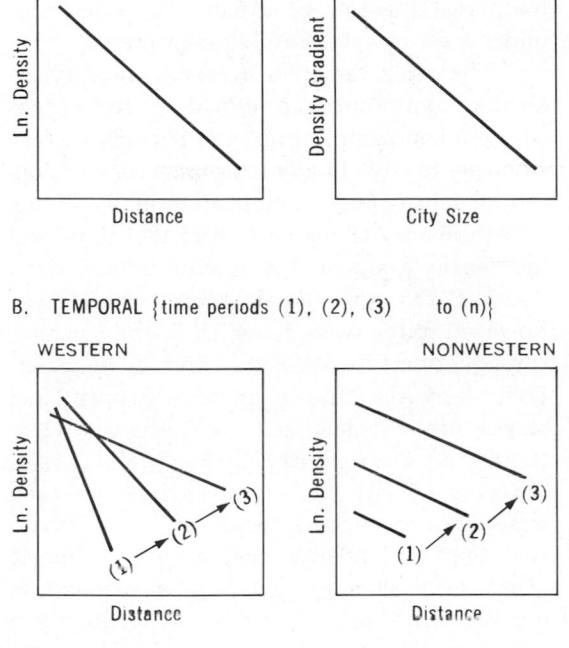

B. TEMPORAL {time periods (1), (2), (3)   to (n)}

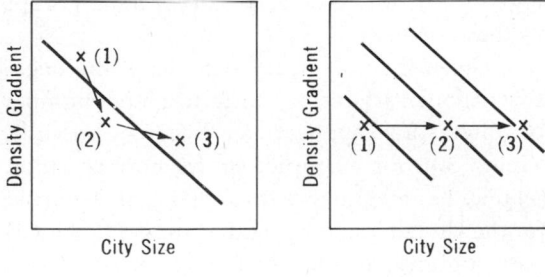

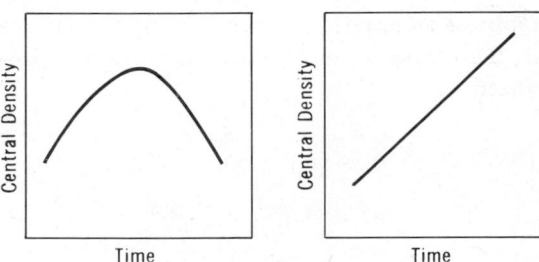

FIGURE 10. Cross-Sectional and Temporal Comparisons, Western and Non-Western Cities

Colin Clark [44] observed that there are "two possibilities for development, if the population is increasing. Either transport costs are reduced, enabling the city to spread out; or they cannot be reduced, in which case density has to increase at all points." In this, however, he identified the permissive factor for the accelerated *sprawl* of Western vis-à-vis non-Western cities (on the supply side) rather than the real reason for accompanying differentials in density gradient (which is on the demand side).

Alonso [45] showed that the rich, in Western cities, live at the periphery on cheap land and consume more land at lower densities than the poor do who live at the center. The Western world has also experienced a revolution in levels of living such that the richer, more mobile groups have increased not only numerically but also proportionally. Hence accelerated sprawl facilitated by improved transportation systems has been stimulated by greater demands for peripheral lower-density land, with attendant reductions of the density gradient. The Western world has experienced significant changes in the nature of *demand* for residential land. Changed transport systems have merely ensured an adequate supply to meet the demands.

However, the socioeconomic pattern of non-Western cities is markedly different. Sjoberg [46] writes:

> . . . the feudal city's land use configuration is in many ways the reverse of that in the highly industrialized communities. The latter's advanced technology fosters, and is in turn furthered by, a high degree of social and spatial mobility that is inimical to any rigid social structure assigning persons, socially and ecologically, to special niches.
> [There are] three patterns of land use wherein the non-industrial city contrasts sharply with the industrial type: (1) the pre-eminence of the "central" area over the periphery, especially as portrayed in the distribution of social classes, (2) certain finer spatial differences according to ethnic, occupational, and family ties, and (3) the low incidence of functional differentiation in other land use patterns [47].

Chatterjee [48] reiterates the regularity:

> The influence of the caste system is reflected in the usual concentration of the higher castes in the central areas of good residential localities, while the lower caste groups usually occupy the fringe.... The people still attach more importance to these centrally-situated residential areas.... Thus, in spite of the modern development of road transport, the residential decentralization or movement towards the fringe outside the old residential areas is not very marked [49].

If in Western cities the poor live at the center and the more mobile rich at the periphery, in non-Western cities the reverse is true. The least mobile groups occupy the periphery. Any income improvements lead to greater demands for central locations, and increased overcrowding. Sprawl reflects projection of the overall surface outward as densities increase throughout, in a periphery of degrading and depressing slums. Degree of compactness of the non-Western city remains, therefore, relatively unchanged, with the least mobile groups located at the periphery. In spite of reductions of transport costs in non-Western cities, the groups located where the possibilities of saving are greatest are the groups least able to take advantage of the possibilities. Changes on the supply side occasioned by transport improvements are of little utility. Differences in movements of central densities and density gradients through time are a function of the inverted locational patterns of socioeconomic groups within Western and non-Western cities, and attendant contrasts in demands for residential land.

Regardless of time or place, the expression

$$d_x = d_o e^{-bx} \qquad (1)$$

provides a statistically significant fit to the distribution of population densities within cities.

Apparently, this negative exponential decline of density with distance represents a condition of competitive locational equilibrium in an active housing market, and it may be derived from traditional theories of urban land economics under a set of very simple assumptions.

The two parameters, d_o (central density, indicating concentration or crowding) and b (density gradient, indicating compactness), vary from city to city. In any temporal cross section, central density appears to be determined by the growth history of the city up to that time, and the density gradient is a function of city size.

Western and non-Western cities differ, however, in the ways in which d_o and b change through time. In Western cities d_o increases, then decreases, and b steadily drops. Later stages are characterized by deconcentration (falling d_o) and suburbanization (falling b, or "decompaction"). Non-Western cities, however, experience continued increases in d_0 (overcrowding) and relative constancy of b (hence urban expansion without suburbanization in the Western sense). The contrast results from differing patterns of location displayed by higher- and lower-level socioeconomic groups in these cities.

Given the universal existence of the negative exponential density pattern, a large number of interesting applications become possible. Weiss [50], for example, shows how equation (7) may be integrated with Zipf's rank-size rule for the United States to create a model that facilitates optimal location of market-oriented servicing units. The effectiveness of urban geography as an applied science is likely to increase in the world as more such findings are produced.

NOTES

[1] Colin Clark, "Urban Population Densities," *Journal of the Royal Statistical Society*, Ser. A, 114 (1951): 490–496. See also his "Urban Population Densities," *Bulletin de l'Institute International de Statistique*, 36, Part 4 (1958), 60–68.

[2] Mark Jefferson, "The Anthropography of Some Great Cities," *Bulletin of the American Geographical Society*, 41 (1909): 537–566. This article also contains interesting discussions of the reasons for the growth of very large cities (p. 539), of the definition of cities (pp. 543–544), and of the dangers of "fictitious accuracy" of measurements, together with the need for recording both point estimates (means) and variances (size of errors) (pp. 555–556).

[3] Harold M. Mayer and Clyde F. Kohn (eds.), *Readings in Urban Geography* (Chicago, 1959).

[4] Richard F. Muth, "The Spatial Structure of the Housing Market," *Papers and Proceedings of the Regional Science Association*, 7 (7th Annual Meeting), 1961 (Philadelphia, 1962): 207–220; Herbert K. Weiss, "The Distribution of Urban Population and an Application to a Servicing Problem," *Operations Research*, 9 (1961): 860–874; John Q. Stewart and William Warntz, "Physics of Population Distribution," *Journal of Regional Science*, 1 (1958): 99–123. William Alonso, "A Theory of the Urban Land Market," *Papers and Proceedings of the Regional Science Association*, 6 (6th Annual Meeting), 1960 (Philadelphia, 1961): 149–158; Halliman H. Winsborough, "A Comparative Study of Urban Population Densities" (unpublished Ph.D. dissertation, Department of Sociology, The University of Chicago, 1961); Martin J. Beckmann, "On the Distribution of Rent and Residential Density in Cities" (paper presented to the Interdepartmental Seminar on Mathematical Applications in the Social Sciences, Yale University, 1957); G. G. Sherratt, "A Model for General Urban Growth," *Management Science—Models and Techniques*, 2 (1960): 147–159; Bruce E. Newling, "Urban Population Densities—A Comment on Colin Clark's Paper with Special Reference to Kingston, Jamaica" (unpublished manuscript, Northwestern University, 1960); Hans Blumenfeld, "Are Land Use Patterns Predictable?" *Journal of the American Institute of Planners*, 25 (1959): 61–66; Carol Kramer, "Population Density Patterns," C[hicago] A[rea] T[ransportation] S[tudy] *Research News*, 2 (1958): 3–10; "Chicago Area Transportation Study (Final Reports)," Vols. 1 and 2, 1959–1960; "Residential Density Model, Seattle Metropolitan Area, 1961" (King County Planning Department; mimeographed); Willard B. Hansen, "An Approach to the Analysis of Metropolitan Residential Expansion," *Journal of Regional Science*, 3 (1961): 37–56; Beverly Duncan, Georges Sabagh, and Maurice D. Van Arsdol, Jr., "Patterns of City Growth," *American Journal of Sociology*, 67 (1961–1962): 418–429 [No. 4 in this volume]; N. R. Kar: "Growth, Distribution and Dynamics of the Population Load in Calcutta" (1962; mimeographed); Lowdon Wingo, Jr., "An Economic Model of the Utilization of Urban Land for Residential Purposes," *Papers and Proceedings of the Regional Science Association*, 7 (7th Annual Meeting), 1961 (Philadelphia, 1962): 191–205; idem: *Transportation and Urban Land* (Resources for the Future, Inc., Washington, D.C., 1961); Wilbur Smith and associates, *Future Highways and Urban Growth* (New Haven, 1961), especially pp. 14–18.

[5] The terms "Western" and "non-Western" are preferred to Sjoberg's "industrial" and "preindustrial" (Gideon Sjoberg: *The Preindustrial City—Past and Present* [Glencoe, Ill., 1960]), though they have the same connotation.

[6] Clark, *Journal of the Royal Statistical Society* [see footnote 1 above]. Most of Clark's historical materials were derived from Adna F. Weber's monumental source, *The Growth of Cities*

in the Nineteenth Century (Columbia University Studies in History, Economics and Public Law, Vol. 11; New York, 1899).

[7] Op. cit. [see footnote 4 above], pp. 13–21.

[8] This information was used as a basis for projecting density distributions in the Chicago Area Transportation Study.

[9] Forty-six in Muth's case.

[10] Newling also shows the use of the model in defining the "real" limits of the city. See also Winsborough's comments on deconcentration, suburbanization, and so on.

[11] Robert J. Tennant: "Population Density Patterns in Eight Asian Cities" (paper read at West Lakes Division meeting of the Association of American Geographers, 1961).

[12] Alonso, op. cit. [see footnote 4 above].

[13] For a review of these ideas, see William L. Garrison and others, *Studies of Highway Development and Geographic Change* (Seattle, 1959), pp. 61–65. Rural analogies via a Von Thünen formulation are collected together in Michael Chisholm, *Rural Settlement and Land Use* (London, 1962). Beverly Duncan, in her paper "Variables in Urban Morphology" (Population Research and Training Center, The University of Chicago, 1962, mimeographed), shows extremely high correlations between a number of variables and measures of accessibility, distance from city center, and so on. Winsborough, op. cit. [see footnote 4 above], provides a systematic integration of views of land economists with those of human ecologists (especially Burgess, Hawley, Quinn, and Duncan).

[14] Op. cit. [see footnote 4 above].

[15] Op. cit. [see footnote 4 above].

[16] This decline is exemplified nicely for many different kinds of housing by W. C. Pendleton in "The Valuation of Accessibility" (The University of Chicago, 1962 [a prospective dissertation in urban land economics]; mimeographed).

[17] Since the model considers only the housing market, Muth is talking about *net* residential densities, though he always says *gross*.

[18] This was pointed out by Winsborough, op. cit. [see footnote 4 above], pp. 23–24.

[19] Alonso, op. cit. [see footnote 4 above], and Duncan, op. cit. [see footnote 13 above].

[20] One can go to Homer Hoyt's classic *One Hundred Years of Land Values in Chicago* (Chicago, 1933) and construct similar graphs for different times from 1836 on, supplementing for the last three decades with George C. Olcott's annual *Blue Book of Land Values for Chicago*, and find a repetition of the negative exponential pattern.

[21] Expressions (3), (4), and (5) are due to Clark, *Journal of the Royal Statistical Society* [see footnote 1 above].

[22] The parameters are to be found in Muth, op. cit. [see footnote 4 above], Table 1.

[23] Op. cit. [see footnote 4 above].

[24] Computed from Muth's Table 1.

[25] Winsborough argues that the most significant of these factors is age of growth of the city.

[26] Muth's Table 1 is again the source.

[27] From Tennant, op. cit. [see footnote 11 above].

[28] Op. cit. [see footnote 4 above], pp. 9–10.

[29] K. E. Boulding: "Toward a General Theory of Growth," in Joseph J. Spengler and Otis Dudley Duncan (eds.), *Population Theory and Policy* (Glencoe, Ill., 1956), pp. 109–124.

[30] This is Boulding's "first principle of structural growth." Winsborough says that "the timing of growth affects the density patterns... different influences on the pattern of development at different times and the resultant structure of the city sets limits on its subsequent growth..."

[31] Years since the city reached a population of 50,000.

[32] See James W. Simmons, "Relationships between the Population Density Pattern and Site of Cities" (unpublished M.A. thesis, The University of Chicago, 1962) for an elaboration of these results.

[33] Winsborough, op. cit. [see footnote 4 above], shows that the implied central density of Chicago increased until 1900 or 1910 and decreased thereafter, apparently as a result of a shift in local transport that superimposed its effects on the established growth processes. Also, the total population density of a city, D, he found to be positively correlated with percentage of old dwellings, size of city, and percentage of population in manufacturing, and negatively correlated with percentage of dwelling units one-unit detached. For any city he showed D to be a function of d_0, regardless of b; thus by implication d_0 is a function of age, population, and employment. In turn, we shall see that b is a function of the last two variables. For an analysis of declining urban densities (D) in the decade 1950–1960 in the United States, see Ronald R. Boyce, "Changing Patterns of Urban Land Consumption," *Professional Geographer*, 15, No. 2 (1963): 19–24.

[34] Note that Weiss uses only population of metropolitan area in equation (7).

[35] Op. cit. [see footnote 4 above], Table 7.

[36] Simmons, op. cit. [see footnote 32 above]. The index of shape distortion, A, was constructed as the ratio of the sum of distances of points arranged in a regular network within the boundaries of the city's urbanized area from the city center to the sum of distances of points in the same regular network from the center of a circle of the same area as the city. A is 1.0 for a perfectly circular city and increases as distortion of shape does. The index is highly sensitive to elongation or lopsidedness, but not to crenulations, and only slightly to a starfish pattern created by radiating transportation routes. It appears to be fairly highly correlated with physically created distortions, especially the presence of water bodies; thus A is also an index of the influences of city sites on population density patterns. The correlation between A and a site index S was 0.584. S was defined as WT where $W = 1 -$ (water area/total area) in a circle of the same area as the city centered on the CBD, and $T = 1 -$ tan (average slope). $S = WT = 1.0$ for a circular city on a level plain. Of the correlation between A and S, the greatest proportion of the covariance was accounted for by the W component, an indication that major shape distortions are largely a function of location alongside water bodies.

[37] *Journal of the Royal Statistical Society* [see footnote 1 above].

[38] Computed from data in Winsborough, op. cit. [see footnote 4 above].

[39] Measured as b^{-1}.

[40] These review comments are drawn from "Comparative Urban Research: Progress Report to The Ford Foundation, May, 1962" (Population Research and Training Center, The University of Chicago), which summarizes Winsborough's findings and those of several related studies.

[41] This figure was provided by Professor N. R. Kar of Presidency College, University of Calcutta. The authors wish to express their gratitude to him.

[42] See Roy Turner, ed., *India's Urban Future* (Berkeley, 1962).

[43] Winsborough, op. cit. [see footnote 4 above], points out the problems of differentiating between "deconcentration" and "suburbanization" in Chicago. Kar, op. cit. [see footnote 4 above], describes the absence of suburbs around Calcutta.

[44] *Journal of the Royal Statistical Society* [see footnote 1 above], p. 495.

[45] Op. cit. [see footnote 4 above].

[46] Op. cit. [see footnote 5 above], especially pp. 95–103. Quotations on pp. 103 and 95–96, respectively.

[47] See also John E. Brush: "The Morphology of Indian Cities," in *India's Urban Future* [see footnote 42 above], pp. 57–70. Contrast this picture with that provided throughout his book by James M. Beshers: *Urban Social Structure* (Glencoe, Ill., 1962). Paul Wheatley has pointed out (conversation) that the larger Southeast Asian cities do not have what we have termed the "non-Western" socioeconomic pattern, though the smaller and medium-sized towns do, and the result is that population redistribution follows the Western pattern in the larger cities.

[48] A. B. Chatterjee, "Howrah: An Urban Study" (unpublished Ph. D. dissertation, University of London, 1960), p. 233.

[49] It might be noted that the same social pattern is being repeated in new Indian towns. Le Corbusier's plan for the new Punjab (India) capital of Chandigarh has the best quality residences at the center, grading outward to the poorest at the periphery.

[50] Op. cit. [see footnote 4 above]. Another interesting outcome of his model is the ability to calculate how many people reside in the most densely settled parts of the United States. For example, the 3000 most densely occupied square miles today contain the homes of 45,000,000 people.

12

BRUCE E. NEWLING

Urban Growth and Spatial Structure: Mathematical Models and Empirical Evidence

It is well known that the growth of any complex structure is associated with changes in form. The phenomenon is familiar to the biologist, who relates the visible changes of form of a living organism to the differential growth of its parts; it is familiar also to the economist, who

Reproduced by permission from *Geographical Review*, Vol. 56, No. 2 (April 1966), pp. 213–225.

The author acknowledges with gratitude the help of Mr. Bruce Godwin, of the Center for Regional Economic Studies, University of Pittsburgh, who wrote the computer program for estimating city size from the density parameters.

recognizes changes in the structure of a growing economy due to the differential growth of its several sectors. If we accept as a point of departure that geography, as both a physical and a social science, is primarily the study of the spatial structure of processes and the resultant spatial structure of phenomena, then the spatial structure of differential growth is an appropriate focus of attention for geographers; for growth and decay are, after all, the measurable expressions of the processes by which the observable spatial structure of any phenomenon at a given point in time is achieved. In this paper the spatial structure of a single spatial process is discussed, namely the differential growth of population density within cities. Certain empirical generalizations about the spatial variation of density in cities and changes in that spatial variation through time are set forth, from which are deduced the rules of intraurban allometric[1] growth and the density—growth rate relationship. In the manipulation of data within the mathematical framework thus constructed, two urban density constants are tentatively identified, one of which may be of significance in urban planning.

MATHEMATICAL MODELS OF INTRAURBAN GROWTH AND STRUCTURE

Let us assume that population density varies with distance from the center of the city according to the equation

$$D_d = D_o e^{-bd} \qquad (1)$$

where D_d is the population density at distance d from the center of the city, D_o is the density at the center of the city, e is the base of the natural logarithms, and b, the density gradient, is a natural logarithm measuring the rate of change of density with distance. The linear transformation of this function is

$$lnD_d = lnD_o - bd. \qquad (2)$$

This rule was originally formulated by Bleicher[2] and was rediscovered some sixty years later by Clark.[3] Tanner[4] and Sherratt[5] have proposed an alternative model, that density declines exponentially as the square of distance; but Clark's rule appears to describe adequately the behavior of empirical data over a wide range of cases and is here adopted as a basic assumption.

It is also known from wide experience of historical series that the density gradient b falls in value through time as the city grows in population and areal extent. Let us assume that b is in fact a negative exponential function of time, such that

$$b_t = b_o e^{-ct} \qquad (3)$$

where b_t is the density gradient at time t, b_o is the initial density gradient, e is the base of the natural logarithms, and the exponent c is a natural logarithm relating the change in the value of the density gradient to the passage of time.

From the two propositions that population density declines exponentially with distance from the center of the city and that the density gradient itself falls through time, we deduce the rule of intraurban allometric growth, namely

---

[1] The adjective "allometric" refers to the systematic differential growth of parts within a complex structure. For a discussion of the concept see, for example, E. C. R. Reeve and Julian S. Huxley, "Some Problems in the Study of Allometric Growth," in W. E. Le Gros Clark and P. B. Medawar (eds.), *Essays on Growth and Form Presented to D'Arcy Wentworth Thompson* (Oxford, 1945), pp. 121–156.

[2] Heinrich Bleicher, *Statistische Beschreibung der Stadt Frankfurt am Main und ihrer Bevölkerung (Frankfurt am Main, 1892).*

[3] Colin Clark, "Urban Population Densities," *Journal of the Royal Statistical Society,* Ser. A, 114, Part 4 (1951): 490–496; idem, "Transport—Maker and Breaker of Cities," *Town Planning Review,* 28 (1957–1958): 237–250; idem, "Urban Population Densities," *Bulletin de l'Institut International de Statistique,* 36, Part 4. (1958): 60–68; idem, "The Location of Industries and Population," *Town Planning Review,* 35 (1964–1965): 195–218.

[4] J. C. Tanner, "Factors Affecting the Amount of Travel," Road Research Technological Paper No. 51, Department of Scientific and Industrial Research, London, 1961.

[5] G. G. Sherratt, "A Model for General Urban Growth," in C. West Churchman and Michel Verhulst (eds.), *Management Sciences, Models and Techniques: Proceedings of the Sixth International Meeting of the Institute* [of Management Sciences] (2 vols.; New York, 1960), vol. 2, pp. 147–159.

that the rate of growth of density is a positive exponential function of distance from the center of the city, expressed by the equation

$$(1 + r_d) = (1 + r_o)e^{gd} \qquad (4)$$

where r_d is the percentage rate of growth at distance d, r_o is the percentage rate of growth at the center of the city, e is the base of the natural logarithms, and g, the intraurban growth gradient, measures the rate of change of the rate of growth with distance from the center of the city.

Since both density and the rate of growth are functions of distance from the center of the city, we can express the rate of growth as a function of density with the following equation

$$(1 + r_D) = AD^{-k} \qquad (5)$$

where r_D is the percentage rate of growth during a given period when the density at the beginning of the period is D, A is a constant, and the exponent k is the ratio of the intraurban growth gradient (g) to the population density gradient (b).

In equation (5), therefore, we have arrived deductively at a formal statement of the relationship between population density and the rate of growth. We should expect, other things being equal, that increasing density would have a depressive effect on the rate of growth, and equation (5) shows that the two variables are indeed inversely related.

Some other observations are appropriate with respect to the density-growth rate rule. First, we would have derived the same relationship if we had assumed that population density, and hence the rate of growth, were exponential functions of the square of distance: in other words, for present purposes it does not matter that we chose Clark's model of the spatial variation of population density instead of the Sherratt-Tanner model. Nor, indeed, does it matter that, for example, we have ignored the possibility of systematic spatial variation in density with distance laterally from the main radial routes: the density-growth rate rule holds re-gardless of location within the urban complex.

In the second place, it is important to note that equation (5) is not only a descriptive statement of the relationship between population density at the beginning of a period and the rate of growth which prevails during that period. If the density gradients are declining exponentially through time, as was assumed in equation (3), then equation (5) describes the variation in the rate of growth with variation in density in successive time periods; that is, it is a predictive statement also. This fact clearly has important ramifications in the field of planning.

If we assume that population density declines exponentially with distance from the center of the city and that the city is circular in shape, then, as Clark has shown, the total population within a given distance d from the center of the city can be conceived as the solid of revolution generated by the density curve about the vertical axis. Hence

$$P_d = \int_o^d D_o e^{-bx}(2\pi x)dx, \qquad (6)$$

which is evaluated as

$$P_d = 2\pi D_o b^{-2}[1 - e^{-bd}(1 + bd)] \qquad (7)$$

where P_d is the population residing within distance d from the center of the city, D_o is the central density, b is the density gradient, and e is the base of the natural logarithms. The term 2π is the radian measure of a complete revolution about a point, and for incompletely circular cities the radian measure will, of course, be less than 2π.

If we solve for d in equation (2) and substitute the solution in equation (7), the equation can be rewritten as

$$P_R = 2\pi D_o b^{-2}[1 - (D_a/D_o) \\ (1 + InD_o - InD_a)] \qquad (8)$$

where P_R is the population residing in the urban region between the center of the city and that distance d at which the density is D_d.

We now demonstrate that equation (7) is useful for estimating the population size of the city of fixed radius (the central city proper), and that equation (8) is useful for estimating the population size of the urbanized region whose radius is changing but whose perimeter density may be assumed to be fixed.

EXPERIMENTS WITH URBAN GROWTH AND DENSITY DATA

A. Urban-Region Population Estimates

Obviously it is difficult to measure the radius of the urban region, since to do so requires access to maps showing the extent of settlement, with adjustments made for irregularities in the perimeter caused by the digital extension of settlement along the major transportation lines. It is simpler to assume some constant perimeter density for all urban regions and to use this, together with the central density and density gradient parameters in equation (8), to make the total population estimates. Stewart[6]

has suggested that the perimeter density of American urban regions is about 2000 persons per square mile, and this figure is accordingly employed with the parameter estimates developed by Muth[7] to calculate the population of each of forty-six urban regions in the United States.

Table 1 presents the estimates so obtained, together with estimates based on an assumed perimeter density of zero, and the actual population of each SMA and urbanized area in 1950 for purposes of comparison. These data, also presented graphically in Figures 1–4, demonstrate the efficiency of Muth's parameter estimates and pari passu the validity of Stewart's perimeter density constant. With respect to both the SMA and the urbanized area, we conclude that an assumed perimeter density of 2000 per square mile provides an estimate superior to the estimate obtained with an assumed perimeter density of zero; and that it provides a better estimate of the population of the SMA than of the urbanized area.

[6] John Q. Stewart, "Urban Population Densities," *Geographical Review*, Vol. 43 (1953), 575–576.

[7] Richard F. Muth, "The Spatial Structure of the Housing Market," *Papers and Proceedings of the Regional Science Association*, 7 (7th Annual Meeting), 1961 (Philadelphia, 1962): 207–220.

TABLE 1.   Density Parameters, Population Estimates, and SMA and Urbanized-Area Populations for Selected United States Urban Regions, 1950 (Population in millions)

Urban Region	Density Parameters[a]		Population Estimates		Actual Population[b]	
	Central[c]	Gradient[d]	I[e]	II[f]	SMA	UA
1 Akron, Ohio	38	.84	0.34	0.27	0.41	0.37
2 Atlanta, Ga.	22	.48	0.60	0.41	0.67	0.51
3 Baltimore, Md.	69	.52	1.6	1.4	1.3	1.2
4 Birmingham, Ala.	9.4	.20	1.5	0.68	0.56	0.45
5 Boston, Mass.[g]	78	.30	2.7	2.4	2.9	2.2
6 Buffalo, N. Y.[g]	29	.19	2.5	1.9	1.1	0.80
7 Chicago, Ill.[h]	60	.18	6.2	5.3	5.5	4.9
8 Cincinnati, Ohio[g]	120	.69	0.79	0.72	0.90	0.81
9 Cleveland, Ohio[g]	22	.13	4.1	2.8	1.5	1.4
10 Columbus, Ohio	10	.19	1.7	0.83	0.50	0.44
11 Dallas, Tex.	26	.48	0.71	0.51	0.61	0.54
12 Dayton, Ohio	18	.32	1.1	0.71	0.46	0.35
13 Denver, Colo.	17	.33	0.98	0.62	0.56	0.50

TABLE 1. (Continued)

Urban Region	Density Parameters[a]		Population Estimates		Actual Population[b]	
	Central[c]	Gradient[d]	I[e]	II[f]	SMA	UA
14 Detroit, Mich.[g]	19	.098	6.2	4.1	3.0	2.7
15 Flint, Mich.	26	.73	0.31	0.22	0.27	0.20
16 Fort Worth, Tex.	17	.42	0.61	0.38	0.36	0.32
17 Houston, Tex.	14	.28	1.1	0.65	0.81	0.70
18 Indianapolis, Ind.	9.2	.18	1.8	0.80	0.55	0.50
19 Kansas City, Mo.	13	.26	1.2	0.67	0.81	0.70
20 Los Angeles, Calif.[g]	14	.078	7.2	4.2	4.4	4.0
21 Louisville, Ky.[g]	29	.47	0.41	0.31	0.58	0.47
22 Memphis, Tenn.	14	.22	1.8	1.1	0.48	0.41
23 Miami, Fla.[g]	14	.24	0.76	0.44	0.50	0.46
24 Milwaukee, Wis.[g]	61	.44	0.99	0.85	0.87	0.83
25 Nashville, Tenn.	9.3	.071	12.0	5.3	0.32	0.26
26 New Haven, Conn.	46	.99	0.29	0.24	0.26	0.24
27 New Orleans, La.	35	.41	1.3	1.0	0.69	0.66
28 Oklahoma City, Okla.	16	.43	0.54	0.33	0.33	0.28
29 Omaha, Nebr.	18	.38	0.78	0.50	0.37	0.31
30 Philadelphia, Pa.	86	.40	3.4	3.0	3.7	2.9
31 Pittsburgh, Pa.	17	.091	13.0	8.1	2.2	1.5
32 Portland, Oreg.	11	.16	2.7	1.4	0.70	0.51
33 Providence, R. I.	14	.41	0.52	0.30	0.68	0.58
34 Richmond, Va.	41	.82	0.38	0.31	0.33	0.26
35 Rochester, N. Y.	43	.64	0.66	0.53	0.49	0.41
36 Sacramento, Calif.	15	.36	0.73	0.43	0.28	0.21
37 St. Louis, Mo.[g]	47	.28	1.9	1.6	1.7	1.4
38 San Diego, Calif.	18	.39	0.74	0.48	0.56	0.43
39 San Jose, Calif.	21	.46	0.62	0.42	0.29	0.18
40 Seattle, Wash.[g]	25	.31	0.82	0.59	0.73	0.62
41 Spokane, Wash.[g]	5.9	.34	0.32	0.094	0.22	0.18
42 Syracuse, N. Y.	48	.92	0.36	0.29	0.34	0.27
43 Toledo, Ohio	6.1	.20	0.46	0.29	0.40	0.36
44 Utica, N. Y.	51	1.2	0.22	0.19	0.28	0.12
45 Washington, D. C.	20	.27	1.7	1.2	1.3	1.3
46 Wichita, Kans.	19	.53	0.42	0.28	0.22	0.19

[a] Muth, op. cit. [see text footnote 7 above], Table 1.

[b] Donald J. Bogue, *Population Growth in Standard Metropolitan Areas, 1900–1950* Washington, D. C.: Scripps Foundation for Research in Population Problems, 1953).

[c] Thousands per square mile.

[d] Rate of change of density per mile, expressed as a natural logarithm.

[e] Estimated from Muth's density parameters, and assuming a perimeter density of zero, with adjustments made for those urban regions which occupy less than a full circle.

[f] Estimated from Muth's density parameters, and assuming a perimeter density of 2000 persons per square mile, with adjustments made for those urban regions which occupy less than a full circle.

[g] The urban region is assumed to occupy 50 percent of a full circle.

[h] The urban region is assumed to occupy 53.5 percent of a full circle.

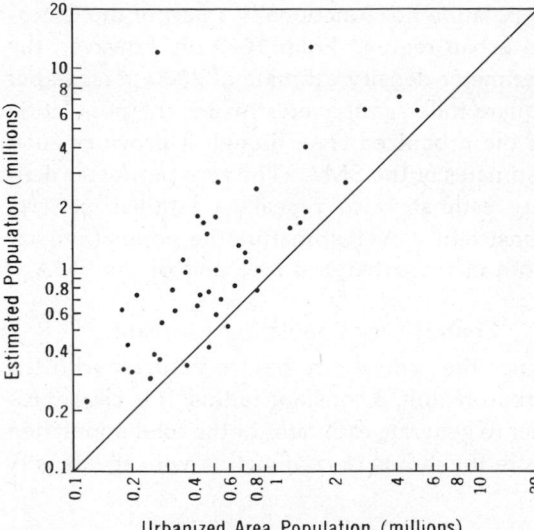

FIGURE 1.   Populations of Forty-Six Urbanized Areas in the United States, 1950, Compared with Population Estimates Based on Muth's Density Parameters and an Assumed Perimeter Density of Zero

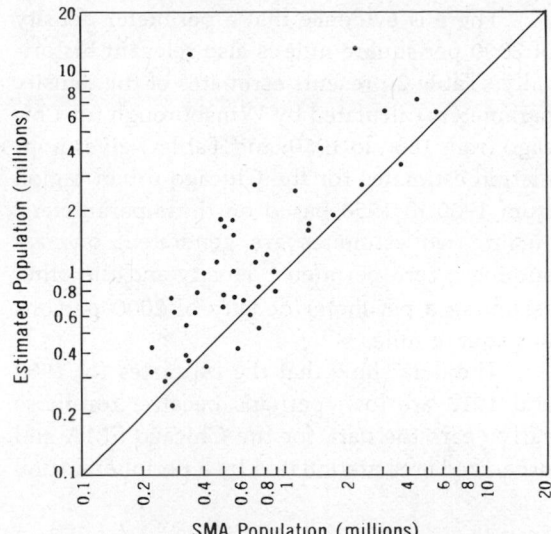

FIGURE 2.   Populations of Forty-Six SMA's in the United States, 1950, Compared with Population Estimates Based on Muth's Density Parameters and an Assumed Perimeter Density of Zero

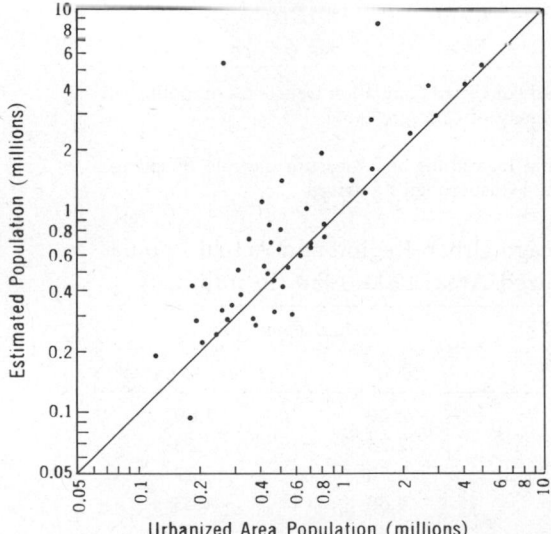

FIGURE 3.   Populations of Forty-Six Urbanized Areas in the United States, 1950, Compared with Population Estimates Based on Muth's Density Parameters and an Assumed Perimeter Density of 2000 per Square Mile

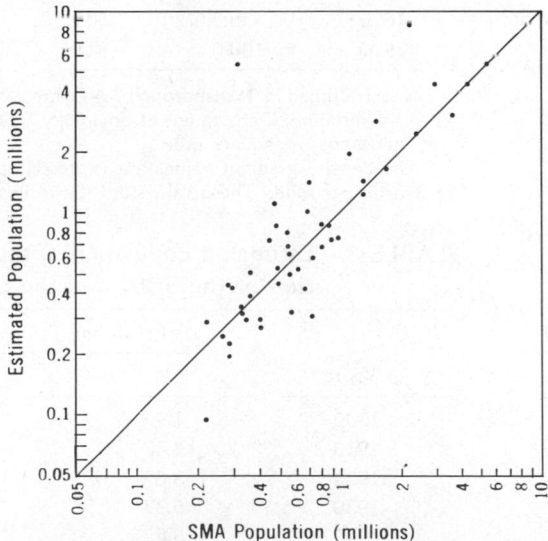

FIGURE 4.   Populations of Forty-Six SMA's in the United States, 1950, Compared with Population Estimates Based on Muth's Density Parameters and an Assumed Perimeter Density of 2000 per Square Mile

There is evidence that a perimeter density of 2000 per square mile is also relevant historically. Table 2 presents estimates of the density parameters calculated by Winsborough for Chicago from 1860 to 1950; and Table 3 gives population estimates for the Chicago urban region from 1900 to 1950 based on these parameters. Again, two estimates are generated, one assuming a zero perimeter density and the other assuming a perimeter density of 2000 persons per square mile.

The data show that the estimates for 1900 and 1910 are low, perhaps because for those early years the data for the Chicago SMA and urbanized area are inflated by a peripheral rural population not functionally a part of the Chicago urban region. From 1920 on, however, the perimeter density estimate of 2000 persons per square mile again overestimates the population of the urbanized area, though it provides good estimates of the SMA. The zero perimeter density estimate also repeats a familiar pattern, consistently overestimating the population size both of the urbanized area and of the SMA.

B. Central-City Population Estimates

Since the central city has, in contrast with the urban region, a constant radius, it is clearly easier to generate estimates of the total population from the radius in conjunction with the density

TABLE 2.   Central Density and Density Gradient Parameters for Chicago, 1860–1950

Year	Central Density[a]	Density Gradient[b]	Year	Central Density[a]	Density Gradient[b]
1860	30.0	.917	1910	100.0	.369
1870	70.8	.877	1920	73.0	.251
1880	96.6	.781	1930	72.8	.215
1890	86.3	.508	1940	71.1	.210
1900	100.0	.415	1950	63.7	.182

Source: Halliman H. Winsborough: "A Comparative Study of Urban Population Densities" (unpublished Ph.D. dissertation, Department of Sociology, The University of Chicago, 1961).

[a] Thousands per square mile.

[b] The density gradient values are expressed as natural logarithms and measure the rate of change of density per mile. These values are the reciprocals of Winsborough's *g* values.

TABLE 3.   Estimated Population of the Chicago Urban Region and Actual Population of the SMA and the Urbanized Area, 1900–1950 (In millions)

Year	Population Estimates		Actual Population	
	I[a]	II[b]	SMA[c]	Urbanized Area[d]
1900	1.95	1.76	2.09	1.89
1910	2.47	2.23	2.75	2.53
1920	3.89	3.40	3.52	3.29
1930	5.31	4.64	4.68	4.43
1940	5.42	4.72	4.83	4.52
1950	6.43	5.53	5.50	5.05

[a] Estimated from Winsborough's density parameters (see Table 2 above), assuming a perimeter density of zero, and assuming that the Chicago urban region occupies 53.5 percent of a full circle.

[b] Estimated from Winsborough's density parameters, assuming a perimeter density of 2000 persons per square mile, and assuming that the Chicago urban region occupies 53.5 percent of a full circle.

[c] Bogue, op. cit. [see footnote *b* in Table 1 above].

[d] Ibid. These figures are the sum of the central-city population and the population of the urban ring.

parameters in equation (7). Table 4 presents such estimates for the city of Chicago, with a constant site factor and a single adjustment made in the radius for the major annexations that occurred between 1880 and 1890. The table reveals how closely the estimates agree with the actual population for the years listed and attest to the reliability of Winsborough's parameter estimates.

C.   Intraurban Growth and the Critical Density

Figure 5 presents a historical series of density curves for Kingston, Jamaica, for which the parameters are listed in Table 5. The striking feature of the diagram is the intersection of the density curves for 1911, 1943, and 1960 at an almost identical radius (one thousand yards) and density (30,000 persons per square mile).

A circle with a radius of one thousand yards covers an area of one square mile and coincides broadly with the area of the present-day central business district (Figure 6). We may surmise, therefore, that in the competition between land uses in twentieth-century Kingston commercial use is displacing residential use on the valuable centrally located land where residential density has historically exceeded 30,000 persons per square mile. Below this critical density, on the other hand, population growth is positive, and presumably residential use is in general more important than commercial use in the competition for available space.

In cities such as Pittsburgh topographic controls and the development of the city through the coalescence of several primary settlement nodes have produced a highly complicated spatial structure that is not adequately described in terms of simple linear distance from the center of the city. This is amply demonstrated when density and growth rate data

TABLE 4.   Actual and Estimated Population of the City of Chicago, 1860–1950 (In millions)

| Year | Population | | Year | Population | |
	Actual[a]	Estimated[b]		Actual[a]	Estimated[b]
1860	0.112	0.113	1910	2.19	2.18
1870	0.209	0.292	1920	2.70	2.78
1880	0.503	0.480	1930	3.38	3.36
1890	1.10	1.08	1940	3.40	3.36
1900	1.70	1.79	1950	3.62	3.50

[a] U.S. Bureau of the Census.

[b] Estimated from Winsborough's density parameters (see Table 2 above), with assumed radii of five miles from 1860 to 1880 and ten miles from 1890 to 1950, and assuming that the site of the city occupies 53.5 percent of a full circle.

TABLE 5.   Central Density and Density Gradient Parameters for Kingston, Jamaica, 1891–1960

Year	Central Density[a]	Density Gradient[b]	Year	Central Density[a]	Density Gradient[b]
1891	49.4	1.635	1943	49.8	0.876
1911	68.4	1.443	1960	40.7	0.526

Source: Bruce E. Newling: "The Growth and Spatial Structure of Kingston, Jamaica" (unpublished Ph.D. dissertation, Department of Geography, Northwestern University, 1962).

[a] Thousands per square mile.

[b] The density gradient values are expressed as natural logarithms and measure the rate of change of density per mile.

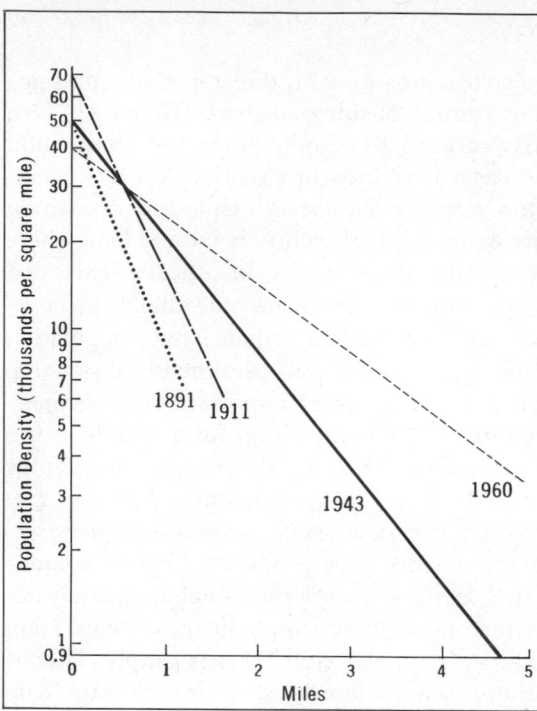

FIGURE 5.   Kingston, Jamaica. Population Density
Curves for Selected Years, 1891–1960

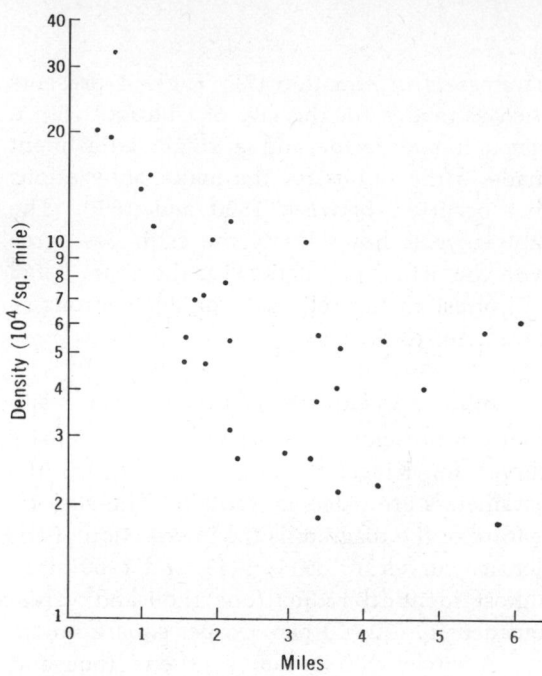

FIGURE 7.   Relationship between Population Density on Residential Land in 1950 and
Distance from the Center of Pittsburgh,
by Wards

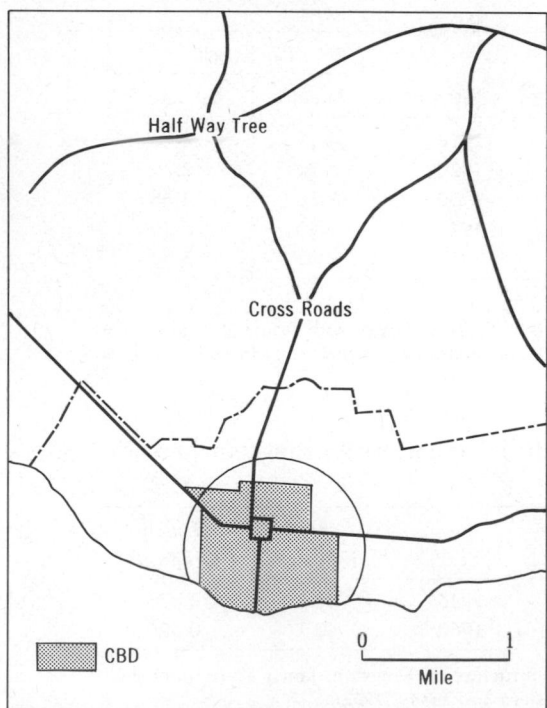

FIGURE 6.   Kingston Metropolitan Area. Post-1911
Central Circular Square Mile of Popu-
lation Loss and Contemporary Central
Business District

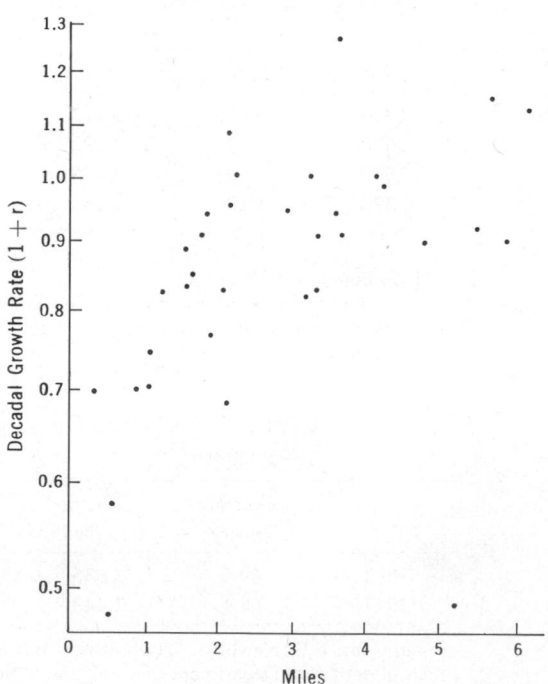

FIGURE 8.   Relationship between the Rate of Population Change 1950–1960 and Distance
from the Center of Pittsburgh, by
Wards

(Table 6) are related to distance from the city center, as in Figures 7 and 8. In both diagrams it is clear that distance has little explanatory power.

Yet the basic logic of the urban spatial system can be identified if we dispense with distance and simply relate the rate of growth to density, as in Figure 9, according to the density-growth rate rule expressed formally in equation (5). We can now identify a relationship so strong that with thirty-one observations[8] the coefficient of determination (r^2) indicates that more than 88 percent of the variation in the growth rate among Pittsburgh's wards is associated with variation in density among the wards. We conclude that the unexplained variation in the data (12 percent) has no special significance in terms of the spatial structure of

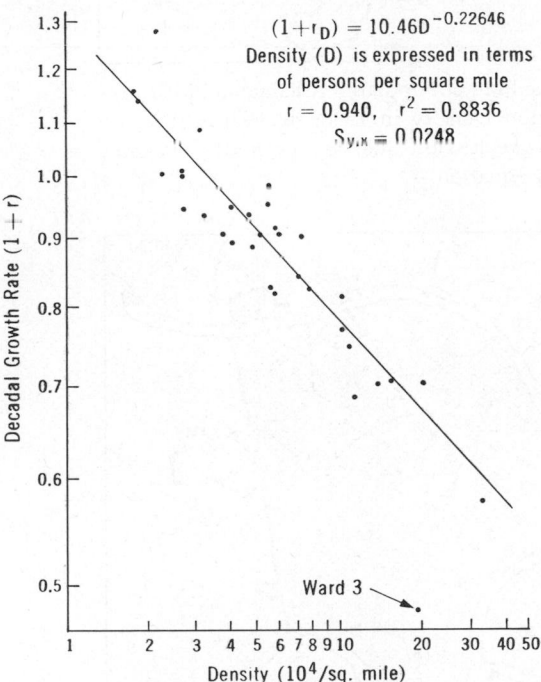

FIGURE 9. Relationship between Population Density on Residential Land in 1950 and the Rate of Population Change 1950–1960 in Pittsburgh, by Wards. Ward 9 is excluded from the calculation of the regression equation.

[8] Ward 3 was excluded because it was cleared in the urban renewal program.

TABLE 6. Distance from the City Center, Net Residential Density in 1950, and Population Growth Rate $(1 + r)$ 1950–1960 for the Wards of the City of Pittsburgh

Ward	Distance (miles)[a]	Density 1950[b]	Growth Rate 1950–1960[c]
1	0.35	199,770	.6962
2	0.60	327,290	.5745
3	0.57	191,686	.4770
4	2.09	78,195	.8243
5	1.77	71,405	.9018
6	2.15	112,512	.6810
7	3.60	40,410	.9428
8	3.34	56,819	.8210
9	3.18	100,429	.8131
10	4.23	54,842	.9794
11	4.77	40,480	.8896
12	5.58	57,798	.9150
13	6.02	60,736	.9045
14	4.15	22,758	.9997
15	3.65	52,314	.9036
16	2.17	54,624	.9495
17	1.12	100,005	.7419
18	1.55	47,437	.8839
19	2.18	31,405	1.0744
20	2.28	26,438	1.0036
21	1.91	100,237	.7617
22	1.09	150,298	.7004
23	0.94	137,325	.6969
24	1.58	55,962	.8242
25	1.66	69,664	.8425
26	2.92	27,437	.9432
27	3.31	37,261	.9030
28	3.35	18,515	1.1261
29	3.26	26,733	.9972
30	1.85	47,277	.9347
31	5.78	17,965	1.1469
32	3.62	21,843	1.2671

[a] Airline distance from Mellon Square to the center of the ward.

[b] Persons per square mile of residential land. These figures are estimates based on the United States census and the net acreage of land in residential use in 1952 according to the land-use survey conducted by the Pittsburgh City Planning Department. The change in residential acreage between 1950 and 1952 is assumed to have been negligible.

[c] The decadal growth rate $(1 + r)$ is formed by the ratio of the 1960 population to the 1950 population.

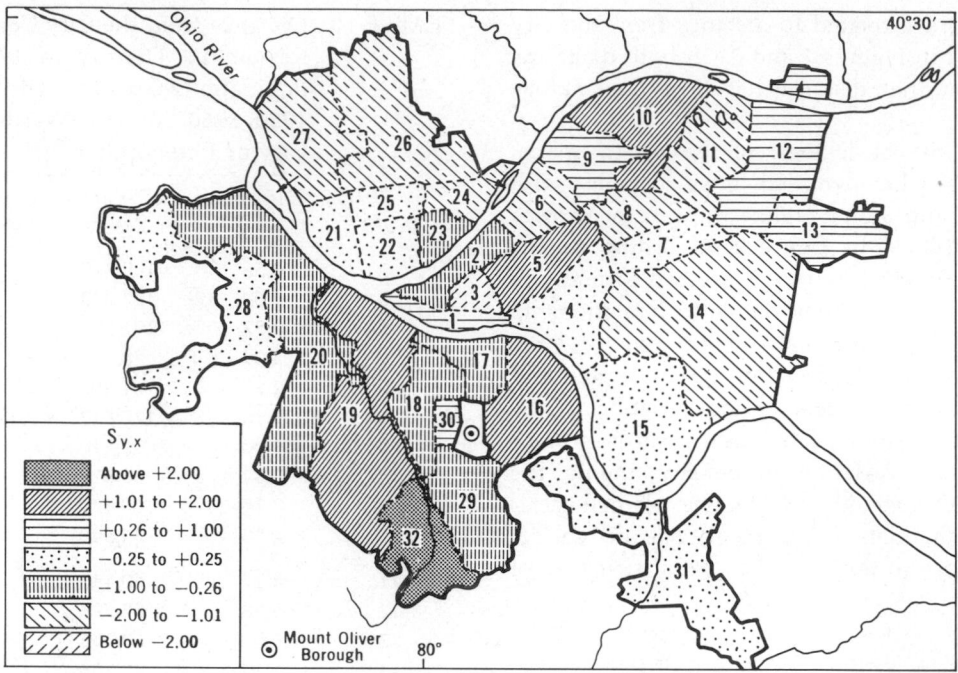

FIGURE 10. Residuals from the Regression of the Rate of Population Change in Pittsburgh, 1950–1960, on Residential Population Density in 1950, by Wards (Ward 3 is expressed as a residual from the regression line, though it was excluded in the calculation of the regression equation.

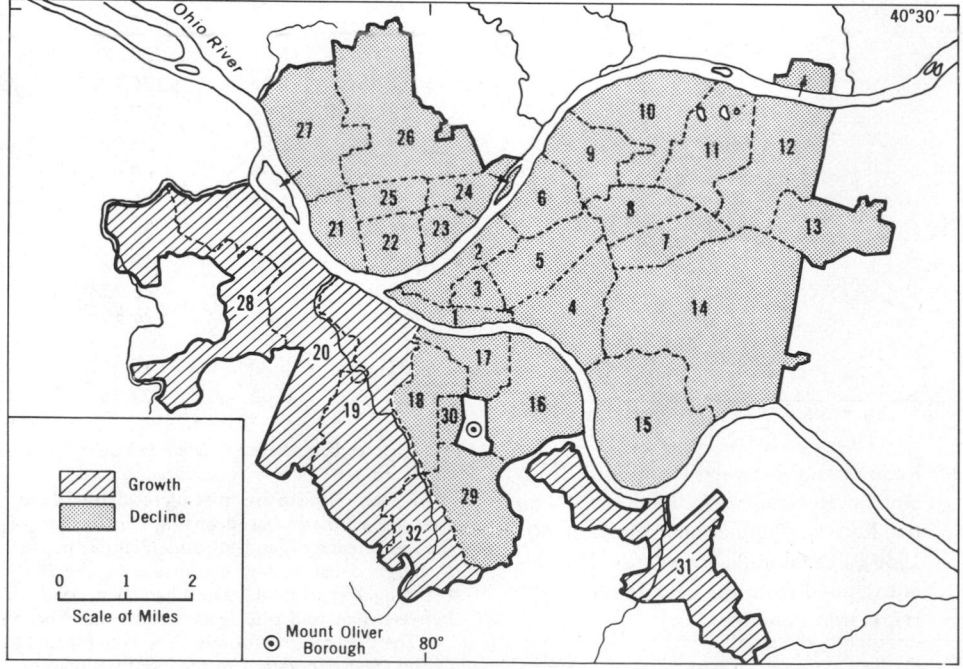

FIGURE 11. Population Growth and Decline in Pittsburgh, 1950–1960, by Wards

the city: the spatial distribution of residuals from the regression line (Figure 10) appears to be entirely random and unrelated to the spatial pattern of any other social or economic variable.

By setting r equal to zero in the regression equation

$$(1 + r_D) = 10.46D^{-.22646} \qquad (9)$$

we solve for density D to obtain 32,000 per square mile as the critical density above which growth is negative and below which growth is positive. The extraordinary correspondence of this value with the critical density obtained for Kingston is noteworthy, though one hesitates to generalize from only two results. One obvious difference between the two situations is that in Kingston the area of negative growth coincides with the central business district, whereas in Pittsburgh (Figure 11) it is widely spread through the city and is associated with urban renewal activities, the decay of old neighborhoods, and racial change, in addition to the expansion of the commercial areas.

The inverse relationship between population density and the rate of growth, the identification of a critical density, and the observation that negative growth, occurring as it does above the critical density, is not solely attributable to competition between commercial and residential use of land all lead one to speculate that perhaps there is indeed some optimum urban population density to exceed which inevitably incurs social costs. We may surmise that certain events in the history of the city will cause this optimum to be exceeded (for example, heavy immigration without a commensurate expansion of housing and the supply of social overhead capital), with deleterious consequences for the affected areas (such as blight, crime and delinquency, and other social pathological conditions), and an eventual decrease in their population. If these speculations have any validity, then it is clear that the identification of such critical densities in cities is important in the field of planning.

13

ROY C. TREADWAY

Social Components of Metropolitan Population Densities

ABSTRACT

The decline of population density from the center of metropolitan areas can be expressed mathematically as $d_r = d_0\, e^{gr}$ where d_r is the population density of a subarea at distance r from the center, d_0 is the hypothetical density at the center, and g is the population-density gradient, empirically always negative. Expanding this exponential model permits examining systematically the relationship between distance from center and various components of population density—housing-unit density, vacant units,

Reprinted by permission from *Demography*, Vol. 6, No. 1 (February 1969), pp. 55–74.

household size, and group-quarters population—and the change over time in these components. For the metropolitan areas of Columbus, Dayton, Hartford, Miami, and Syracuse in 1950 and 1960, housing-unit density decreased from the center more sharply than population density. Vacancies, which increased slightly at the center, were proportionately low in the stable middle zones but somewhat higher in the rapidly growing outer zones. While household size decreased around the center between 1950 and 1960, on the periphery it remained constant or increased slightly because of increased family size. During the same decade, the group-quarters population, relative to total population, shifted outward from the center to the periphery to a small extent.

Population density varies extensively in metropolitan areas, its most characteristic feature being its regular decline from the center of a metropolis to the outer edges. Many factors help account for this consistent decline of density, including the regular variations in a number of population and housing characteristics. Changes over time of some of these characteristics—such as density of housing units and structures, proportion of vacancies, size of household, and proportion of institutional population—have been studied in different contexts and for different purposes, but they have not in general been related to changes in population density, especially by distance from the center of the metropolis. Thus, in this paper I will examine these various characteristics as they influence residential density and change in density over time using an expanded formal model of decreasing density with distance from the center of the city.

POPULATION DENSITY AND ITS COMPONENTS

Almost universally, population density of a metropolitan area is highest around the center and falls off regularly to the periphery. According to current ecological theory, variations in residential density develop in response to the continual and pervasive process of competition between activities for space and location [Hawley 1950: 382–402]. The center of a metropolitan area, located at the intersection of the principal transportation routes, is the most accessible point in the area. Competition is most

intense for the most accessible points with the areas around these points being competed for successively less intensively. All business, manufacturing, financial, and governmental activities, as well as households, have transportation and space requirements; they tend to be located where space and transportation costs are minimized. Although certain activities and certain households can and must make more intensive use of space than others, greater intensity of space use implies the need for greater densities at the most accessible and often most central locations. Successively less intensive use of land with increasing distance from the center to the periphery of a metropolitan area will result. Thus, in general, residential densities will decline regularly from the center of the city to its outskirts. For a more detailed and formal discussion of the competitive process, see Alonso [1960], Wingo [1961], Muth [1961], and Berry, Simmons, and Tennant [1963].

Variations in intensity of land use reflect the differences in a number of housing and population characteristics. Foremost among these is housing-unit density, the number of housing units per area, which according to ecological theory also decreases with distance from the center of the metropolis. An inverse relation between dwelling-unit density and distance from the center has been reported by Winsborough [1962: 42], who analyzed data for community areas in Chicago in 1940. The change over time in the steepness of the decline of housing-unit density with distance from the center varies systematically, but the density-distance relationship holds at all times. This relationship is confounded in part, however, by the time at which various subareas were built up. Areas built earlier in a city's history tend to be denser (as well as closer to the center) than those built later. Winsborough [1962: 43–44] has found that both population and housing density are positively related to the "age" of a subarea, as measured by the percentage of 1940 units built before 1920; Duncan, Sabagh, and Van Arsdol [1962: 418–425] and Hoover and Vernon [1962: 183–199] report similar results. Indeed, the time at which a subarea was developed has a significant and lasting effect on the housing (and population) density of the subarea at a later time.

The number of housing units per area, whether in large apartments or single-family homes, is the principal component of population density, and any change in the number of units per area will be instrumental in population change. Increase in population density depends in large part on new construction of housing units or conversion of large old structures to apartments; conversely, demolition of housing or merger of apartments will likely bring a decrease in density. Thus, the redistribution of population, involving changes in density, is directly sensitive to the amount of housing construction, alteration, and demolition in any area.

The redistribution of population also reflects housing construction indirectly via the number of vacant housing units available. During World War II in the United States, population redistribution apparently took place at a much slower rate than would have been expected from the total population growth rate alone; this was due in part to the failure of housing construction to keep up. Population increased in the existing housing inventory, and the proportion of vacancies decreased. After World War II, as construction of new housing increased, more housing units became vacant and redistribution of population was greater than expected due to population growth.

Duncan, Sabagh, and Van Arsdol [1962: 425–427] report this process occurring in the city of Los Angeles, beginning before World War II in the 1930's and continuing at least through 1956. Similarly, Taeuber and Taeuber [1965: 153–154] found that the increases in vacancies in both the Negro residential areas and the cities they studied in the 1960's were apparently related to expansion of the housing market within the Negro areas. If such changes were coupled with the new construction being primarily on the periphery on less-developed land, housing being torn down at the center to make way for new commercial buildings and roads, and the increased vacancies occurring mainly in the poorer, less suitable housing around the center; population decentralization as well as redistribution would result.

The increased construction of new housing units after World War II also permitted average household size to decline even though average family size increased due to higher fertility. The lessened need for relatives and even nonrelatives to live with another family allowed new, small households of single individuals and couples to be set up, thus reducing the size of the remaining households. (For a description of the trend in household and family size and fertility in the United States between 1950 and 1965, see United States Bureau of the Census [1966b: 1–2; 1966a: 12].) Decreased household size will bring about lower population density, and smaller households tend to live nearer the center in housing units of smaller size while larger families live in suburbs where there is more space. Thus, for community areas of Chicago in 1940, Winsborough [1962: 42] found that total population per unit was positively related to distance from the center. In addition, he noted that "both structures per area and units per structure are negatively related to distance with the latter correlation being somewhat stronger" [Winsborough 1962: 42]. Hoover and Vernon [1962: 168–173, 219–226] report similar findings. Thus, household size per se will increment population density at the periphery more than it will at the center while structure density and units per structure will do the opposite.

THE NEGATIVE EXPONENTIAL MODEL

The decline of population density with distance from the center of a metropolis can be expressed mathematically. This mathematical relationship was noted empirically by Clark [1951: 490–496] and given a theoretical basis by Muth [1961: 207–210] and others [Alonso 1960: 149–158; Wingo 1961: 191–205; Berry, Simmons, and Tennant 1963: 389–405; and Winsborough 1962: 35–49, and 1963: 464–470]. Let d_r be the population density of a small area (such as a census tract) at a distance r in miles from the center of the metropolis, d_o be the hypothetical density at the center, and g be the density gradient which indicates how abruptly density changes with increasing distance from the center. Then,

$$d_r = d_o e^{gr} \qquad (1)$$

According to all empirical evidence, g is negative, indicating a decline in density with distance, consistently with the theoretical formulations. This model fits the variations in population density for many urban areas in different countries and in different periods of time. Muth [1961: 214] concludes that "it would seem that the negative exponential function is the best simple approximation to the pattern of population density decline with distance from the center in urban areas." For reports of research on the negative exponential model in a large number of different types of cities, see Clark [1951: 490–496], Stewart and Warntz [1958: 99–123], Winsborough [1962: 41–48, and 1963: 565–570], Duncan and Davis [1953: 18], and Berry, Simmons, and Tennant [1963: 393–405].

(Clark [1951]; Muth [1961]; Berry, Simmons, and Tennant [1963]; and others use a minus sign before the exponent g [or equivalent notation]. Winsborough [1962 and 1963] uses the reciprocal of the exponent also preceded by a minus sign as his notation. I have not used a minus sign here for later notational convenience. Thus, if density decreases with distance, the value of g will be negative and will be written as negative in value; all the other researchers present the values of g as positive since the negative sign is included in the equation.)

The parameter g, which has been called a measure of concentration [Winsborough 1963: 567], indicates how steeply density declines from the center. The value of the coefficient d_0 is an extrapolation of the relationship between density and distance from the center and does not represent the actual density at the center. Residential population density tends to be less immediately around the center than in surrounding areas since commercial, transportation, wholesaling, and other activities replace population; such activities use the central area more intensively than households and therefore can compete more successfully for central land. In addition, density at a point (the center) has no meaning anyhow. Nevertheless, d_0 does summarize for the entire metropolitan area what the density at the center would be, based on densities over the entire area. In this sense, d_0 may be considered a measure of concentration.

While this model of exponentially declining densities with distance from the center was developed to explain the structure of the city for one point in time, it can also help explain the processes of population growth and decentralization within urban areas over time. The total population growth of an urban area must somehow be accommodated either through increasing densities at the center, that is, building upwards and increasing congestion; or through flatter density gradients, that is, growth primarily at the periphery or expansion of the urban area with resulting decreasing concentration; or through some combination of both [Winsborough 1963: 567]. If transportation costs are reduced, or, in other words, the effect of distance is made less great, the city can spread out at lower densities in the center and at greater distances from the center. Thus the gradient will become flatter, and decentralization will have taken place. The same result will occur if housing costs are reduced or real income is increased since this will have the effect of reducing the monetary components of transportation costs for each household involved.

These changes in densities between two points in time can be made more explicit by considering the mathematical model more closely. If at a second point of time, the density-distance relationship is expressed as:

$$d_r' = d_0' e^{g'r} \tag{2}$$

where the primes represent the respective values of the densities and gradients at the second time, then the rate of population growth for a subarea at distance r from the center over time (I_r) can be computed by:

$$I_r = \frac{P_r'}{P_r} = \frac{d_r'}{d_r} = \frac{d_0' e^{g'r}}{d_0 e^{gr}} = I_o e^{br} \tag{3}$$

where P_r' and P_r represent the population of the area at the second and first points of time respectively, $I_0 = d'_0/d_0$ and $b = g' - g$. The value of I_0 indicates the hypothetical rate of increase at the center, summarizing what might be expected at the center based on rates of growth in all other parts of the urban area according to the model. The gradient of growth, b, is a measure of decentralization; if it is positive, areas farther from the center are growing faster than those closer to the center, and density is increasing faster in areas away from the center. For alternative forms of this "rule of intraurban allometric growth," see Newling [1966: 214] and Olsson [1966: 36].

The effect of various housing and population characteristics on population density by distance from the center can be examined by further expanding the negative exponential model. Population density (P/A) of a subarea has the following components: (1) housing-unit density, the ratio of total housing units to area (U/A); (2) the ratio of occupied to total units (O/U); (3) average household size, the ratio of household population to occupied housing

units (H/O); and (4) the ratio of total to household population (P/H). Housing units refer to both dwelling units in 1950 and housing units in 1960 as defined by the United States Bureau of the Census and reported in their publications. A unit is occupied if it was the usual place of residence for the person or group of persons living in it at the time of enumeration or if its usual residents were only temporarily absent. Vacant units included all units which are not occupied. Household population consists of those persons who occupy a housing unit. Group-quarters population refers to all population which is not household population. For further details, see United States Bureau of the Census [1952: 2–3, and 1962b: 5].

The interrelation of these housing and population characteristics may be given more explicitly by the equation:

$$P/A = (U/A) \cdot (O/U) \cdot (H/O) \cdot (P/H). \tag{4}$$

The ratio of occupied to total units (O/U) reflects the proportion of vacant units, which is the amount that this ratio is less than unity. Similarly, the ratio of total population to household population (P/H) indicates the relative number of persons living in institutions or other group-living arrangements since the difference between total and household population is this group-quarters population; the extent to which this ratio (P/H) exceeds unity is the ratio of group-quarters to household population.

(As we have seen, Winsborough [1962] has decomposed population density in a similar manner, breaking up density into three components: population per housing unit; units per structure; and structures per acre [or structure density]. The product of these components equals population density. I have not been able to use either units per structure or structures per area in my analysis because the necessary data on structures were lacking.)

It follows that the rate of population growth of an area can be decomposed into ratios of change of each of these four components of population density. If symbols with primes are used to indicate the number of people and units in the terminal year and symbols without primes the number in the initial year, the rate of population increase (I) can be given as:

$$I = \frac{P'}{P} = \frac{P'/A}{P/A}$$

$$= \frac{U'/A}{U/A} \cdot \frac{O'/U'}{O/U} \cdot \frac{H'/O'}{H/O} \cdot \frac{P'/H'}{P/H}. \qquad (5)$$

Note that the change in population and housing-unit densities is equivalent to population and unit growth, respectively, since area is constant. Thus, population growth can be analyzed by looking at changes in its various components.

Equations (1), (2), and (3) can be written in linear form by taking naturallogarithmic transformations:

$$\ln d_r = \ln d_0 + gr, \qquad (6)$$

$$\ln d'_r = \ln d_0' + g'r, \qquad (7)$$

and

$$\ln I_r = \ln (d_0'/d_0) + (g'' - g)r$$
$$= \ln I_0 = + br. \qquad (8)$$

The values for the parameters $\ln d_0$ and g, $\ln d'_0$ and g', and $\ln I_0$ and b for each metropolitan area can be computed by taking the regression of the natural logarithms of density and growth rates on distance from the center of each tract. The assumption is made that the logarithms of density and growth are linearly related to distance from the center.

(Used as weights for the computation of the regression of the natural logarithm of population densities in 1950 and in 1960 and of population change between 1950 and 1960 on distance from the center were the 1950 population of each tract. These weights are used to give greater importance in computation of the regression coefficients to those tracts which had larger populations in 1950, exactly in proportion to their 1950 population. The same weights were used in computing all regressions so that all the regression coefficients were consistent with one another.)

The linear regression of the natural logarithm of all the components on distance can also be computed, thus extending the regression analysis of population density and growth. For each component the gradient indicates how much that component differs with distance from the center. The central value of each component is a measure of the change of the component at the center extrapolated from changes over the entire area. The model assumes a linear relation of the natural logarithm of each component with distance. While such an assumption is clearly not true in many cases, the model does provide a first approximation of direction and strength of change of each component with distance and is consistent with the regression analysis of natural logarithm of density and growth with distance.

The gradients and natural logarithms of central values of the components of density sum to the total values of the coefficients for each year and component; similarly, the values of the gradient and natural logarithm of central values of growth sum to the total value of the respective growth components. For a proof, see Treadway [1967: 312–316]. Thus, by examining each coefficient, we can assess the relative contribution of each component to the variations in density and to the process of decentralization.

The typical direction and value of the curves of each component of population density at time 1 and at time 2 (identified as 1950 and 1960, respectively) are shown in Figure 1; those of the components of population change over time (between 1950 and 1960) are presented in Figure 2. They illustrate the general relationships of the components to one another at both time periods and over time and are representative of the curves of each component in the metropolitan areas of the study.

The curves presented in Figures 1 and 2 were derived from data from the Hartford metropolitan area but were adjusted slightly for visual purposes. They are typical, however, of

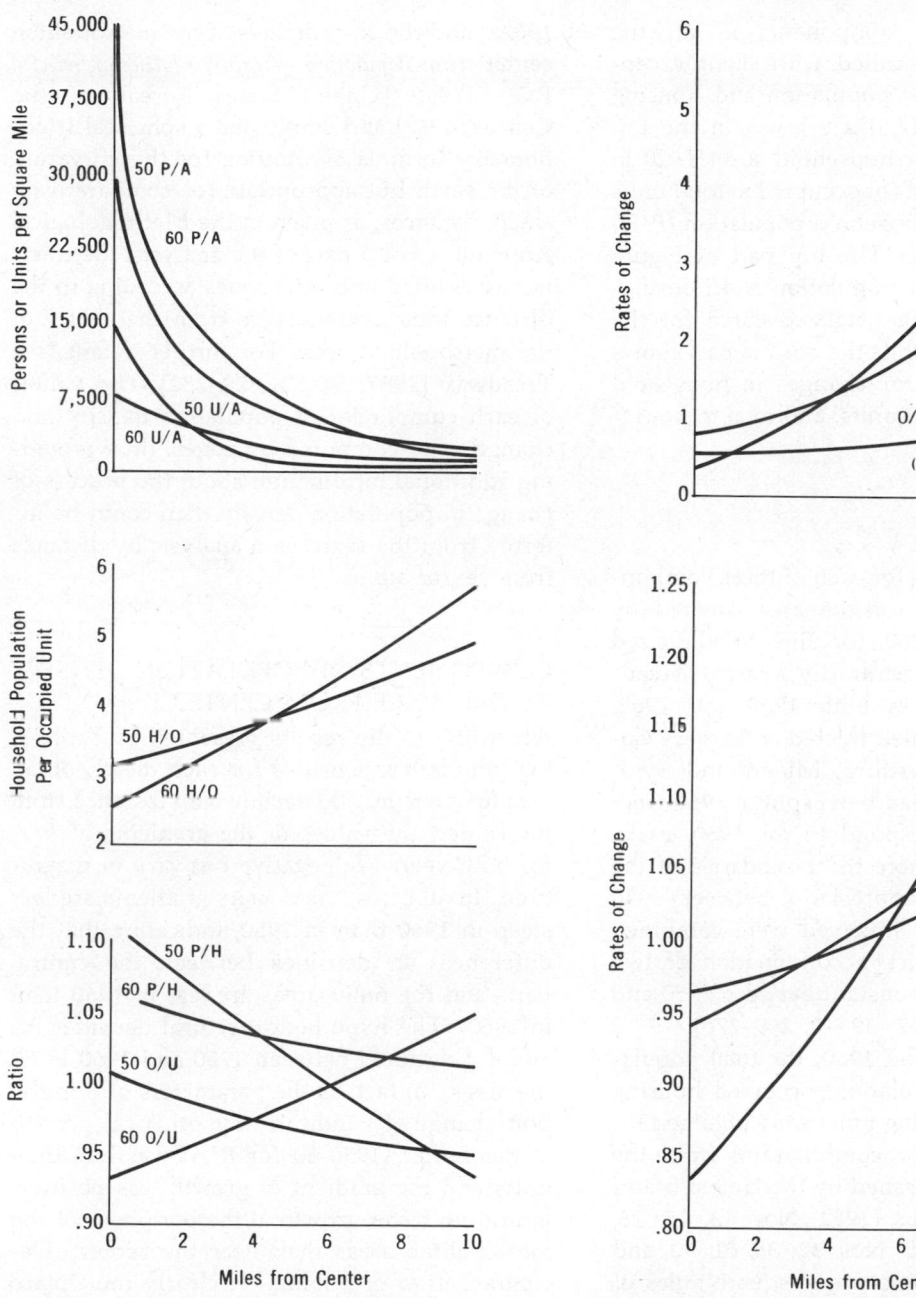

FIGURE 1. Typical Values of Components of Population Density by Distance from Center, 1950 and 1960

FIGURE 2. Typical Values of Components of Population Change by Distance from Center, 1950–1960

the curves of the components in all the metropolitan areas studied with slight exceptions. The curves for population and housing density (P/A and U/A) are given in the top panel of Figure 1, for household size (H/O) in the middle panel, and for occupied to total units (O/U) and total to household population (P/H) in the bottom panel. The top part of Figure 2 presents curves for population and housing-unit change (and a generalized curve for the other components) while the bottom part shows the detailed curves for changes in household size, occupied to total units, and total to household population.

SOURCE OF DATA

Data by census tracts for each of these components were gathered for the area covered by census tracts in 1950 for five middle-sized metropolitan areas, arbitrarily chosen [Treadway 1967: 29–31], in both 1950 and 1960. These areas, also called tracted areas were Columbus, Dayton, Hartford, Miami, and Syracuse. Tracts which had been split in 1960 were recombined to correspond to the 1950 tracts. In the few cases where the boundaries of the tracts had changed appreciably between 1950 and 1960, the tracts involved were combined to form just one tract, a combination of two or three 1950 tracts, constant between 1950 and 1960 [Treadway, 1967, 39–40, 269–278].

For both 1950 and 1960, the total population, household population, occupied housing units, and total housing units were obtained for each census tract (or combination) from the census tract reports issued by the United States Bureau of the Census (1952, Nos. 13, 15, 23, 31, and 54 and 1962b, Nos. 32, 36, 61, 90, and 154). The areal dimensions in square miles of each tract were either supplied by a local agency or determined originally. (See acknowledgments.) Distance from the center of the metropolitan area to the center of each tract was computed using estimates of the longitude and latitude of each tract from the *National Location Code* [United States Bureau of the Census,

1962a] and the co-ordinates of the metropolitan center from *Population Within 50 Miles of Selected Points: 1960* [United States Bureau of the Census, 1963] and employing a spherical-trigonometry formula accounting for the curvature of the earth but appropriate for comparatively small distances, as given in the Methodological Appendix. For a part of the analysis, the tracts were classified into mile zones according to the distance their centers were from the center of the metropolitan area. For further details, see Treadway [1967: 51–52, 279–282]. The values of each component of population density and change were computed by zones, thus providing additional information about the process of change in population density than could be inferred from the regression analysis by distance from center alone.

COMPONENTS OF POPULATION DENSITY BY DISTANCE FROM CENTER

According to the results presented in Table 1, the population densities for each metropolitan area for each year do decline with distance from the center; the values of the gradients of P/A for both years are negative but vary in magnitude. In all cases, the density gradients are less steep in 1960 than in 1950, indicating that the differences in densities between the central parts and the outer areas are less in 1960 than in 1950. The hypothetical central densities (d_0 and d'_0) declined between 1950 and 1960 in all the areas. In fact, as the parameters of population change (I_0) indicate, hypothetical growth at the center (1950-60 for P/A) was less than unity and the gradient of growth was positive, indicating faster growth at the periphery of the metropolitan areas than near the center. Decentralization of population clearly took place between 1950 and 1960. All of this is illustrated distinctly in Figures 1 and 2. The goodness of fit of the model, as measured by the coefficients of determination, which range from .68 to .78 in 1950 and from .42 to .78 in 1960, is fairly strong.

TABLE 1.   Hypothetical Values at Center, Gradients by Distance from Center, and Coefficients of Determination of Population and Housing Ratios, for 1950, 1960, Change 1950 to 1960

Tracted Area, Coefficient, and Year	Component[a]				
	P/A	U/A	O/U	H/O	P/H
Columbus					
Value at Center[b]					
1950	38250	8537	.990	3.036	1.491
1960	29216	8047	.937	2.792	1.382
Change 1950 to 1960	.761	.943	.947	.920	.927
Gradient					
1950	−.5487	−.5044	−.0020	.0177	−.0599
1960	−.4219	−.4047	.0010	.0302	−.0484
Change 1950 to 1960	.1268	.0997	.0030	.0126	.0116
Coefficient of Determination[c]					
1950	.71	.48	.19	.08	.02
1960	.64	.47	.00	.18	.02
Change 1950 to 1960	.39	.21	.04	.08	.01
Dayton					
Value at Center[b]					
1950	22181	6594	.983	3.181	1.076
1960	17814	6136	.947	2.942	1.042
Change 1950 to 1960	.803	.931	.963	.925	.969
Gradient					
1950	−.4677	−.4808	−.0008	.0172	−.0032
1960	−.3546	−.3897	.0011	.0322	.0019
Change 1950 to 1960	.1131	.0911	.0019	.0150	.0051
Coefficient of Determination[c]					
1950	.71	.70	.02	.01	.00
1960	.62	.63	.01	.24	.00
Change 1950 to 1960	.31	.23	.02	.19	.02
Hartford					
Value at Center[b]					
1950	44868	13674	.991	3.001	1.104
1960	29333	12041	.931	2.493	1.050
Change 1950 to 1960	.654	.881	.939	.831	.951
Gradient					
1950	−.8001	−.8215	−.0052	.0430	−.0164
1960	−.5978	−.6825	.0108	.0789	−.0050
Change 1950 to 1960	.2023	.1390	.0160	.0359	.0114
Coefficient of Determination[c]					
1950	.73	.74	.07	.27	.10
1960	.60	.67	.10	.39	.02
Change 1950 to 1960	.54	.39	.15	.39	.09
Miami					
Value at Center[b]					
1950	24233	8265	.915	2.776	1.155
1960	19358	9175	.881	2.285	1.048
Change 1950 to 1960	.799	1.110	.963	.823	.907

TABLE 1. *(Continued)*

Tracted Area, Coefficient, and Year	Component[a]				
	P/A	U/A	O/U	H/O	P/H
Gradient					
1950	−.3368	−.3247	−.0127	.0212	−.0203
1960	−.2007	−.2400	.0030	.0411	−.0049
Change 1950 to 1960	.1358	.0848	.0157	.0199	.0154
Coefficient of Determination[c]					
1950	.68	.66	.10	.15	.20
1960	.42	.50	.01	.23	.04
Change 1950 to 1960	.63	.38	.32	.20	.20
Syracuse					
Value at Center[b]					
1950	24186	6775	1.001	3.249	1.098
1960	22613	7223	.980	2.977	1.073
Change 1950 to 1960	.935	1.066	.979	.916	.977
Gradient					
1950	−.4943	−.4832	−.0118	.0084	−.0077
1960	−.4367	−.4432	−.0086	.0213	−.0062
Change 1950 to 1960	.0577	.0400	.0032	.0129	.0016
Coefficient of Determination[c]					
1950	.78	.75	.46	.10	.02
1960	.78	.76	.36	.29	.01
Change 1950 to 1960	.35	.26	.13	.41	.01

[a] Component: *P/A*: Population per area in square miles (population density).
 U/A: Housing units per area in square miles (housing-unit density).
 O/U: Occupied housing units divided by total housing units.
 H/O: Household population divided by occupied housing units (household size).
 P/H: Total population divided by household population.
[b] Value at center indicates the hypothetical value of the component at the center of each area, transformed from the natural logarithm to the actual value.
[c] Coefficient of determination: the square of the correlation coefficient between the natural logarithm of the component and distance from the center of the city.
 Source: United States Bureau of the Census [1952 and 1962b] and local agencies.

The population densities by zones for both years, as presented in Table 2, also show that density decreases regularly from the center, as generally hypothesized. The few exceptions are: the zero-mile zone of Columbus in 1960 which is less dense than the one-mile zone, probably due to commercial expansion in the downtown area and the strong influence of the Ohio State University in the one- and two-mile zones; and the two-mile zone in Miami which is less dense than the three-mile zone, probably because of the various islands in the two-mile zone, including the resort area of Miami Beach.

Total Housing Units

The decline of housing-unit density from the center of these metropolises in both years was the major component of the negative gradient of population density, and, therefore, change in housing-unit density accounted in large part for the change in population density. For instance, all of the gradients of housing-unit density, given in Table 1, are close to those of population density. Although for three of the areas in 1950 the housing-unit gradients are smaller (and thus less steep) than the population gradients, by 1960 the housing-unit gradients became steeper in all the areas except Columbus, and there the difference between the gradients was much less than in 1950. In fact, for all areas, housing units did not grow as fast as population at the periphery, but neither did they

TABLE 2.   Ratios of Population, Housing Units, and Area by Zones, 1950, 1960, Change 1950 to 1960

Tracted Area, Year, and Zone (in miles)	Component[a]				
	P/A	U/A	O/U	H/O	P/H
Columbus					
1950					
0.0– 0.9	14060	3872	.980	2.955	1.253
1.0– 1.9	14032	4261	.985	3.213	1.040
2.0– 2.9	11506	3294	.988	3.137	1.127
3.0– 3.9	2460	736	.986	3.293	1.029
4.0– 4.9	1502	454	.973	3.332	1.021
5.0–14.9	188	55	.976	3.419	1.017
Total	942	277	.983	3.235	1.068
1960					
0.0– 0.9	9378	3392	.874	2.552	1.236
1.0– 1.9	13193	4433	.927	3.159	1.016
2.0– 2.9	11522	3606	.949	2.986	1.128
3.0– 3.9	3412	1063	.960	3.265	1.024
4.0– 4.9	2839	892	.948	3.332	1.007
5.0–14.9	451	234	.927	3.567	1.021
Total	1278	401	.938	3.256	1.045
1950 to 1960[b]					
0.0– 0.9	.667	.876	.892	.864	.986
1.0– 1.9	.940	1.040	.941	.983	.977
2.0– 2.9	1.001	1.095	.961	.952	1.001
3.0– 3.9	1.387	1.444	.974	.991	.995
4.0– 4.9	1.890	1.965	.974	1.000	.986
5.0–14.9	2.401	2.413	.950	1.043	1.004
Total	1.357	1.444	.954	1.006	.978
Dayton					
1950					
0.0– 0.9	14816	4848	.971	2.888	1.089
1.0– 1.9	10667	3093	.986	3.320	1.054
2.0– 2.9	7152	2138	.984	3.289	1.034
3.0– 3.9	2674	729	.982	3.456	1.080
4.0– 4.9	1024	278	.979	3.661	1.029
5.0–14.9	386	106	.973	3.559	1.050
Total	1964	572	.981	3.332	1.051
1960					
0.0– 0.9	11244	4049	.917	2.841	1.066
1.0– 1.9	9266	3049	.948	3.106	1.032
2.0– 2.9	7812	2515	.972	3.125	1.022
3.0– 3.9	3683	1103	.961	3.333	1.042
4.0– 4.9	2388	668	.938	3.760	1.014
5.0–14.9	818	234	.948	3.635	1.015
Total	2519	775	.952	3.328	1.026

TABLE 2. *(Continued)*

Tracted Area, Year, and Zone (in miles)	Component[a]				
	P/A	U/A	O/U	H/O	P/H
1950 to 1960[b]					
0.0– 0.9	.759	.835	.944	.984	.979
1.0– 1.9	.869	.986	.961	.936	.979
2.0– 2.9	1.092	1.176	.988	.950	.988
3.0– 3.9	1.378	1.514	.978	.964	.964
4.0– 4.9	2.332	2.407	.958	1.027	.985
5.0–14.9	2.119	2.203	.974	1.021	.967
Total	1.283	1.356	.970	.999	.976
Hartford					
1950					
0.0–0.9	22432	6782	.984	2.970	1.132
1.0–1.9	8026	2364	.990	3.177	1.079
2.0–2.9	6364	1859	.973	3.473	1.013
3.0–3.9	999	278	.973	3.535	1.043
4.0–9.9	582	162	.963	3.619	1.039
Total	2072	602	.978	3.329	1.057
1960					
0.0–0.9	17362	7238	.915	2.466	1.063
1.0–1.9	7067	2549	.952	2.779	1.047
2.0–2.9	6652	2100	.973	3.210	1.014
3.0–3.9	1883	551	.972	3.437	1.024
4.0–9.9	1090	305	.975	3.577	1.025
Total	2421	782	.960	3.128	1.031
1950 to 1960[b]					
0.0–0.9	.774	1.067	.930	.830	.939
1.0–1.9	.880	1.078	.962	.875	.970
2.0–2.9	1.045	1.129	1.000	.924	1.001
3.0–3.9	1.885	1.977	.999	.972	.982
4.0–9.9	1.861	1.885	1.012	.988	.987
Total	1.168	1.299	.982	.940	.975
Miami					
1950					
0.0–1.9	12430	4235	.886	2.815	1.176
2.0–2.9	6984	2615	.890	2.928	1.025
3.0–3.9	7303	2849	.857	2.882	1.038
4.0–4.9	5650	2013	.882	3.107	1.023
5.0–5.9	2099	718	.887	3.201	1.029
6.0–7.9	2364	882	.819	3.231	1.014
8.0–9.9	678	263	.772	3.282	1.019
Total	2983	1095	.856	3.030	1.051
1960					
0.0–1.9	13756	6157	.874	2.419	1.057
2.0–2.9	7331	3108	.897	2.587	1.016
3.0–3.9	9226	4184	.864	2.532	1.008
4.0–4.9	7572	2991	.893	2.796	1.014

TABLE 2. (Continued)

Tracted Area, Year, and Zone (in miles)	Component[a]				
	P/A	U/A	O/U	H/O	P/H
5.0–5.9	3191	1121	.910	3.086	1.013
6.0–7.9	4996	1821	.890	3.022	1.020
8.0–9.9	2438	832	.888	3.252	1.014
Total	4801	1881	.885	2.831	1.020
1950 to 1960[b]					
0.0–1.9	1.107	1.454	.986	.859	.899
2.0–2.9	1.050	1.189	1.008	.884	.991
3.0–3.9	1.263	1.469	1.008	.878	.971
4.0–4.9	1.342	1.486	1.012	.900	.991
5.0–5.9	1.520	1.560	1.026	.964	.984
6.0–7.9	2.114	2.066	1.087	.935	1.006
8.0–9.9	3.597	3.169	1.150	.991	.995
Total	1.611	1.719	1.034	.934	.971
Syracuse					
1950					
0.0– 0.9	17385	5330	.975	3.092	1.082
1.0– 1.9	10994	3204	.981	3.238	1.080
2.0– 2.9	5327	1485	.985	3.161	1.052
3.0– 4.9	1433	413	.973	3.508	1.018
5.0–14.9	108	34	.888	3.511	1.026
Total	431	128	.957	3.347	1.054
1960					
0.0– 0.9	14228	5232	.946	2.775	1.036
1.0– 1.9	10355	3303	.964	3.010	1.080
2.0– 2.9	6292	1945	.974	3.270	1.016
3.0– 4.9	2213	640	.972	3.501	1.016
5.0–14.9	190	56	.908	3.682	1.011
Total	534	165	.947	3.309	1.030
1950 to 1960[b]					
0.0– 0.9	.818	.982	.970	.897	.957
1.0– 1.9	.942	1.031	.983	.930	1.000
2.0– 2.9	1.181	1.310	.989	.945	.966
3.0– 4.9	1.544	1.552	.999	.998	.998
5.0–14.9	1.760	1.664	1.023	1.049	.985
Total	1.238	1.294	.990	.989	.977

[a] P/A: Population per area in square miles (population density).
  U/A: Housing units per area in square miles (housing-unit density).
  O/U: Occupied housing units divided by total housing units.
  H/O: Household population divided by occupied housing units (household size).
  P/H: Total population divided by household population.
[b] 1950 to 1960: Ratios in 1960 divided by similar ratios in 1950. Change for P/A and U/A ratios is population and housing-unit growth respectively.
Source: United States Bureau of the Census [1952 and 1962b] and local agencies.

decline as fast at the center, as shown in Figures 1 and 2. Indeed, in Miami and Syracuse housing units would hypothetically have increased at the center if unit growth rates were extrapolated (since the central ratios are 1.110 and 1.066, respectively) even though the hypothetical central value of population growth indicated a decrease. Even according to the zonal rates of growth in Table 2, housing units changed less than population in most zones.

Some of the increase in housing units between 1950 and 1960 may be due to a slight change in definition from dwelling unit in 1950 to housing unit in 1960. In practice, in 1960 a few more housing units were included than dwelling units in 1950. This may be especially true for the central areas of the metropolitan areas since single rooms, rooming houses, and light-housekeeping quarters were most affected by the change in definition. For further details on the distinction, see the "Introduction" to United States Bureau of the Census [1962b: 5].

Vacancies

Although housing-unit change was the major source of change for population in all zones, changes in vacancies played an important role over and above that of housing units in determining the population density of areas at different distances from the center. The fairly rapid construction of new housing units permitted vacancies to increase overall but not uniformly by zones. These differences in vacancies by distance from the center influenced population density by distance appreciably.

For each metropolitan area as a whole except Miami, the proportion of vacant housing units, equal to one minus the O/U ratio in Table 2, is rather small in both years (less than 7 percent) although the vacancy rate increased between 1950 and 1960, reflecting a loosening in the housing market overall. Moreover, the percentage of vacancies does vary by distance from the center, changing over time. In 1950, for instance, vacancies tended to be slightly higher on the periphery than in the center for

all of the areas; the gradients of the O/U ratios in 1950 are all negative, indicating a decline in the number of occupied units to total units with increasing distance from the center. (The interpretation of the change in the O/U ratios between 1950 and 1960, however, is not completely clear because of the change in the definition of dwelling unit to housing unit.) Pressure on central housing was slightly greater in 1950 than on peripheral housing; central housing units were used somewhat more intensively than peripheral ones, and population density was augmented by this more intensive use of housing to a greater extent around the center than on the outskirts.

In Miami the proportion of vacancies was large in both years (between 12 and 15 percent) and decreased between 1950 and 1960. As a resort area, Miami's proportion of vacancies in both years is relatively high since the data were obtained for April 1 during the off season for tourists. The slight decline in vacancies between 1950 and 1960 in Miami comes partially from its rapid population growth, with which new construction has not been able to keep up, and partially from its high number of vacancies in 1950. Nevertheless, the same processes were at work on vacancies by distance from the center in Miami as in the other areas.

By 1960, although pressures on the use of housing had let up somewhat (Miami being an exception), this was less true for the outer areas than the inner ones. Housing vacancies were generally greater at the center than on the periphery; the 1960 gradients of the O/U ratios are positive (except in Syracuse), indicating a slightly greater proportion of units being occupied with increasing distance from the center. (The comparison between the 1950 and 1960 O/U curves can be seen in Figure 1.) Furthermore, for all of the areas, as Table 1 shows, vacancies have increased (hypothetically) at the center, even in Miami. The more rapid overall growth of housing units than population permitted the somewhat less desirable housing at the center to be used less intensively than it was in 1950 and than housing on the periphery. As shown in Figure 2, the greater increases in vacancies at the center than at the periphery added to the general trend of population decentralization since the gradients of change in O/U ratios are all positive.

These regression-analysis results are very general, however, and do not reveal a number of exceptions. Indeed, the coefficients of determination are not very large for either year (ranging from .00 to .19 except in Syracuse where they are .46 and .36). An examination of the zonal O/U ratios in Table 2 reveals a curvilinear pattern of vacancies for most of the areas in both years; vacancies tend to be lowest in the middle zones and somewhat higher near the center and on the periphery. The vacancies of the central-most zone in particular have increased the most, and the zones in which the lowest rate of vacancies is found has moved outward a mile or two between 1950 and 1960. Thus, because of these shifts, the direction of gradients of vacancies changed from negative to positive. In Syracuse, the unusually high proportion of vacancies in the outer, primarily rural, zone has kept the gradient negative in 1960 even though it is smaller than in 1950.

In addition, vacancies seem to play an important role in facilitating population change of an area. At least, those zones, both central-most and outer-most, where the greatest amount of population change is taking place, both increase and decrease, are the ones in which the highest proportion of vacancies are found in both years. Turnover and redistribution of population are greatest in those zones with the most vacancies and lowest in the most-stable middle zones. Under conditions of a continued relaxed housing market, one may guess that in the future the outer vacancies will decline as the newly constructed houses are lived in, that central vacancies will also decline as some of the vacant units are removed from the housing market and as these aging areas are rebuilt, and that in the middle zones vacancies will increase as the housing

there deteriorates and as the zones of stable residences move slowly outward from the center.

Household Size

Since the size of the household constitutes the major difference between housing and population density, the examination of variations in household size over time and by distance from the center is crucial for explaining variations in population density. For the metropolitan areas as a whole household size has remained fairly constant between 1950 and 1960, declining just about two-tenths a person only for Hartford and Miami; as shown in Table 2, household size varies between 3.0 and 3.4 persons per unit among all the metropolitan areas in both years except in Miami in 1960, where the average size of household is slightly larger than 2.8 persons. Nevertheless, household size varies fairly regularly by zone, increasing with distance from the center in both 1950 and 1960. (The changes in household size, however, are probably also affected by the change in definition from dwelling unit to housing unit; the few more households identified in 1960 will tend to be small ones, thus adding to the decline in household size, especially at the center.) The H/O gradients in Table 1 are all positive in both 1950 and 1960, more strongly so than the vacancy gradients. This is consistent with the expectations of larger families on the periphery and smaller households in apartments near the center.

Between 1950 and 1960 the difference between the central and the peripheral household size has become greater. The 1960 gradients of household size (H/O) in Table 1 are larger than the 1950 gradients, and the gradients of change in household size are all positive (see Figures 1 and 2). This is actually due to the decline of household size toward the center rather than to any large increases on the outskirts. Hartford and Miami had small declines in household size in the outer zones while the other areas had very slight increases in the peripheral areas; in the central-most zone average household size dropped between three- and five-tenths of a person in all the tracted areas except Dayton, where there was virtually no change. Thus, changes in household size contributed to population decentralization, the relatively faster growth of population away from the center.

As noted above, these changes reflect both the increasing family size in the United States and decreasing household size. With the shift from the relatively tight housing market of 1950 to a much looser one in 1960, many families did not have to have relatives and nonrelatives living with them, and smaller households could be formed. Housing for such households is most prevalent at the center; thus, central households declined in size. At the outskirts the increase in family size seems to have offset other losses because of fewer relatives and non-relatives living with families; thus, peripheral household size changed only slightly. Because of this general trend in shifts in household size and composition in the United States, influenced indirectly by changes in the housing market, household size has become more sharply differentiated by distance from the center in 1960 than in 1950.

Group-Quarters Population

Although little has been written discussing the location of group-quarters or institutional population, such population also contributes in an uncertain manner to declining densities from the center of the metropolis, sometimes to a greater extent than vacancies. At least, the ratios of total to household population tend to decline with distance from the center slightly for all the areas except Dayton in 1960, as shown in Table 1; in Dayton in 1960, the group-quarters gradient is positive though very small (.0019), indicating a very weakly increasing proportion of group-quarters population with distance from the center. Thus, as represented in Figure 1, the proportion of group-quarters population falls off away from the center though less so in 1960 than in 1950. In fact, according to the positive gradients of change in group-quarters population, group-quarters population

seems to be moving away from the center slightly faster than total population, and the curve of change in total to household population, given in Figure 2, is upwardly increasing with distance from the center. Some aspects of the change in group-quarters population, however, are also likely due to the change in definition of housing unit from dwelling unit. Since a few more households were identified in 1960 than in 1950, group-quarters population would appear to have declined more than actually, affecting central areas more than peripheral areas.

The last part of the analysis is extremely tenuous since the coefficients of determination for group-quarters population are all very small, ranging from .00 to .20. In fact, the ratios of total to household population are hardly monotonically decreasing with distance from the center, much less exponentially decreasing, since according to Table 2, the zonal ratios are somewhat erratic by distance from the center. In most of the tracted areas, however, the one- or two-mile zones have significantly higher ratios than the other zones; in these inner zones are located the one or two major institutions—a hospital, penitentiary, or university—with which the group-quarters population is connected. Thus, group-quarters population declines slightly with distance from the center and moves outward slowly due to the stability of the centrally-located, principal institutions of each metropolitan area.

COMPARATIVE IMPORTANCE OF COMPONENTS

Each component of population density influences the steepness of the population-density gradient to some extent; some make the decline of population density with distance from center more abrupt while others retard its decline. Since the gradients of the components of population density sum to the gradient of population density, the proportion of the gradient of population density that the gradient of each component comprises can be computed by dividing the component gradient by the population-density gradient. In a similar manner the proportion of the population-change gradient that each component-of-change gradient contributes can be computed. According to these proportions, given in Table 3, housing-unit density (U/A) is by far the most important component of the decline of population density with distance from the center. Its gradient accounts for at least ninety percent of the gradient of population density in all areas in both years and at times even slightly exceeds the population-density gradient slightly. Household size always offsets (even though to a slight extent) population-density decline from the center of the city since its proportionate

contribution is always negative. Vacancies (O/U) and group-quarters population (P/H) generally have small effect on the decline in population density with distance, neither enhancing nor retarding it very much.

Each of the components of change in population density reinforces the process of population decentralization, in which population decreases around the center and increases on the periphery; this is shown clearly in Figure 2. From the proportion of each component's change gradient of the population-change gradient reported in Table 3, we can see that changes in housing units contribute more than

TABLE 3. Proportionate Contribution to Gradient of Population Density and Change by Components, 1950, 1960, 1950 and 1960

Tracted Area and Year	Component[a]				
	P/A	U/A	O/U	H/O	P/H
Columbus					
1950	1.000	.919	.004	−.032	.109
1960	1.000	.959	−.002	−.072	.115
Change 1950 to 1960	1.000	.786	.024	.099	.091
Dayton					
1950	1.000	1.028	.002	−.037	.007
1960	1.000	1.099	−.003	−.091	−.005
Change 1950 to 1960	1.000	.805	.017	.133	.045
Hartford					
1950	1.000	1.027	.006	−.054	.020
1960	1.000	1.142	−.018	−.132	.008
Change 1950 to 1960	1.000	.687	.079	.178	.056
Miami					
1950	1.000	.964	.038	−.063	.060
1960	1.000	1.196	−.015	−.205	.024
Change 1950 to 1960	1.000	.624	.116	.147	.113
Syracuse					
1950	1.000	.978	.024	−.017	.016
1960	1.000	1.015	.020	−.049	.014
Change 1950 to 1960	1.000	.693	.055	.224	.028

[a] Component: P/A: Population per area in square miles (population density).
U/A: Housing units per area in square miles (housing-unit density).
O/U: Occupied housing units divided by total housing units.
H/O: Household population divided by occupied housing units (household size).
P/H: Total population divided by household population.
Source: United States Bureau of the Census [1952 and 1962b] and local agencies.

three-fifths to decentralization in all areas and up to four-fifths in Dayton. Shifts in household size are next in magnitude; such shifts added to decentralization between one-tenth and one-fourth of total population decentralization. Relative alterations in vacancies and group-quarters population were less important but still in most areas augmented population decentralization appreciably.

SOCIAL COMPONENTS, POPULATION DENSITY, AND CHANGE

I have argued in this paper that not only is population density related in a systematic fashion to distance from the center of metropolises but so is change over time of population density and of its components. These orderly changes take place, however, within a specific historical context, which includes both the previous and current economic, social, and technological conditions of the metropolises being studied. For instance, for the metropolitan areas in this research, located in the (primarily Northern) United States between 1950 and 1960, the housing market was expanding fairly rapidly, transportation systems were generally improving, and birth rates remained relatively high, among other factors. In addition, basically inflexible layouts and sizes of structures built under previous and different housing and transportation arrangements served to inhibit drastic changes in population and housing configurations.

Thus, for these metropolitan areas, the net effect of all of these factors on the components of population density and change has been to encourage population decentralization. With the loosening of the housing market and increasing family size, population decline at the center was able to take place not only through demolition (or merger) of housing units but also through increased vacancies, smaller household size, and even a smaller proportion of group-quarters population to total population; the poorer housing at the center was demanded less, and more people were able to form their own small household who previously had to live with other households. At the same time, in the outer parts of the metropolises, population increase came about primarily through construction of new housing units while proportions of vacancies and group-quarters population and size of households remained relatively stable despite increased family size. The proportion of vacancies, while changing little (except in Miami), remained higher on the periphery than in the middle zones because of new construction and changing population on the outskirts.

These particular changes in the proportion of vacancies, household size, and group-quarters population differentially by distance from the center may not occur in the same way in other places or at other times. Few studies, however, have been carried out on the various components of population density under other social and economic circumstances than those reported here. As mentioned above, a number of writers [Winsborough 1963; Clark 1951; Muth 1961; and Berry, Simmons, and Tennant 1963] have studied the population density-gradient only in metropolises in different countries and at different times. Winsborough [1962: 42–48] has investigated the effect of size of structure to understand how population density develops by distance from the center under different transportation systems and types of housing. Berry [1964: 150–151], Berry, Simmons, and Tennant [1963: 395–396], Olsson [1966: 35–36], and others have attempted to integrate the population-density gradient with the development of central-place theory and other inter-city relationships in different countries and at different times, thus emphasizing the importance of further studies of the population-density gradient. On a closely related and overlapping problem of explaining where socioeconomic-status groups live by distance from the center of cities in Northern and Latin America, Schnore [1965: 347–398] has outlined the major concepts which could serve as the basis for further study of the population-density gradient.

These few studies, however, do point the way to further research on metropolitan population density, including its social components. Thus, in order to develop a more general theory explaining population distribution within metropolitan areas than I have presented here, both the current and past economic and social conditions must be taken into consideration as they affect the components of population density, for it is through the processes of change in these components that the negative gradient of population density with distance from the center results. A wider examination of these various processes of change in all the components needs to be carried out on a much broader range of cities, such as Western and Southwestern cities in the United States, non-American cities elsewhere in the world, both smaller and larger cities in size, and cities at other times in history. Such studies over a longer historical period and in other economic and cultural contexts will help make more explicit the process of changes in residential densities resulting from systematic, differential changes in the social components of population density.

METHODOLOGICAL APPENDIX

Professor Waldo R. Tobler of the Department of Geography, The University of Michigan, supplied the formula for computing distance between the tract center and the center of the tracted area.

Where

X_i = longitude of census tract in radians,

Y_i = latitude of census tract in radians,

X_o = longitude of center of tracted area in radians,

Y_o = latitude of center of tracted area in radians,

R = 3960.407 miles per radian approximately at 45° latitude, and

DC = distance from census tract to center of tracted area in miles, then

$$DC = 2R \text{ Arcsin } \{ \cos(Y_o) \cos(Y_i) [\sin^2 ((X_i - X_o) /2) + \sin^2 ((Y_i - Y_o)/2)]\}^{1/2}.$$

The latitude and longitude coordinates in degrees, minutes and seconds were converted to radians by the following formula:

where Deg = degrees,

Min = minutes,

Sec = seconds, and

Rad = 0.0174539925 radians per degree, then X or Y = Rad (Deg + Min/60 + Sec/3600).

ACKNOWLEDGMENTS

This is a revised version of a paper entitled "Residential Densities of Metropolitan Population" discussed at the annual meetings of the Population Association of America, April 18–20, 1968 in Boston, Massachusetts. The research reported was carried out as part of the author's doctoral dissertation at the University of Michigan [Treadway: 1967]. The research was supported in part by the Metropolitan Community Research Project of The University of Michigan and by the Population Council. I am indebted to Otis Dudley Duncan, Amos H. Hawley, Ronald Freedman, David Goldberg, and Waldo Tobler for advice and criticism, and to Leroy Gould and Zvi Namenwirth, who read an earlier version of this paper.

For the areal dimensions of census tracts in square miles in each metropolitan area, I am grateful to the following organizations: Bureau of Business Research, The Ohio State University [1964] for Columbus; City Plan Board of Dayton for a map of Dayton used by the Census Map Area Computer; Capitol Regional Planning Agency for Hartford; and Reinhold P. Wolff Economic Research for Miami. The areal dimensions for Syracuse were obtained by hand computations from tracing graph paper. For details, see Treadway [1967: 50].

REFERENCES

Alonso, William, 1960. "A Theory of the Urban Land Market. *Papers and Proceedings of the Regional Science Association,* 4: 149–158.

Berry, Brian J. L., 1964. Cities as Systems within Systems of Cities. *Papers and Proceedings of the Regional Science Association,* 13: 147–163.

——, James W. Simmons, and Robert J. Tennant, 1963. "Urban Population Densities: Structure and Change." *Geographical Review,* 53: 389–405. [No. 11 in this volume.]

Bureau of Business Research, The Ohio State University, 1964. "Population Density of Census Tracts, Columbus and Franklin County, Ohio, 1960, Supplement to 1960 Census Tract Street Directory, Columbus and Franklin County, Ohio." Monograph Number 104. Columbus, Ohio: The Ohio State University.

Clark, Colin, 1951. "Urban Population Densities." *Journal of the Royal Statistical Society,* Ser. A., 114: 490–496.

Duncan, Beverly, Georges Sabagh, and Maurice Van Arsdol, Jr., 1962. "Patterns of City Growth." *American Journal of Sociology,* 67: 418–429. [No. 4 in this volume.]

Duncan, Otis Dudley, and Beverly Davis, 1953. "Measures of Population Distribution in an Urban Area." Unpublished manuscript, Chicago Community Inventory, University of Chicago.

Hawley, Amos H., 1950. *Human Ecology: A Theory of Community Structure.* New York: Ronald Press.

Hoover, Edgar M., and Raymond Vernon, 1962. *Anatomy of a Metropolis.* Garden City, N. Y.: Doubleday and Co.

Muth, Richard F., 1961. "The Spatial Structure of the Housing Market." *Papers and Proceedings of the Regional Science Association,* 7: 207–220.

Newling, Bruce E., 1966. "Urban Growth and Spacial Structure: Mathematical Models and Empirical Evidence." *Geographical Review,* 56: 213–225. [No. 12 in this volume.]

Olsson, Gunnar, 1966. "Central Place Systems, Spatial Interaction, and Stochastic Processes." *Papers and Proceedings of the Regional Science Association,* 18: 13–45.

Schnore, Leo F., 1965. "On the Spatial Structure of Cities in the Two Americas," in Philip M. Hauser and Leo F. Schnore (eds.), *The Study of Urbanization.* New York: Wiley.

Stewart, John Q., and William Warntz, 1958. "Physics of Population Distribution." *Journal of Regional Science,* 1: 99–123.

Taeuber, Karl E., and Alma F. Taeuber, 1965. *Negroes in Cities.* Chicago: Aldine.

Treadway, Roy C., 1967. "Metropolitan Population Decentralization." Unpublished Ph.D. dissertation. Department of Sociology, The University of Michigan.

United States Bureau of the Census, 1952. *U. S. Census of Population: 1950.* Vol. 3, *Census Tract Statistics.* Washington, D. C.: Government Printing Office.

——, 1962a. *National Location Code.* Washington, D. C.: Government Printing Office.

——, 1962b. *U. S. Censuses of Population and Housing: 1960.* Final Report, PHC (1), Census Tracts. Washington, D. C.: Government Printing Office.

———, 1963. *Population Within 50 Miles of Selected Points: 1960*. Geographic Reports, GE-10, No. 1. Washington, D. C.: Government Printing Office.

———, 1966a. "Fertility of the Population: June, 1964 and March, 1962." *Current Population Reports*, Series P–20, No. 147. Washington, D. C.: Government Printing Office.

———, 1966b. "Household and Family Characteristics: March, 1965." *Current Population Reports*, Series P–20, No. 153. Washington: Government Printing Office.

Wingo, Lowdon, Jr., 1961. "An Economic Model of the Utilization of Urban Land for Residential Purposes." *Papers and Proceedings of the Regional Science Association*, 7: 191–205.

Winsborough, Hal H., 1962. "City Growth and City Structure." *Journal of Regional Science*, 4: 32–49.

———, 1963. "An Ecological Approach to the Theory of Suburbanization." *American Journal of Sociology*, 68: 565–570.

14

PETER W. AMATO

A Comparison: Population Densities, Land Values and Socioeconomic Class In Four Latin American Cities

This study extends and compares earlier findings on the relationship of population densities and land values to socioeconomic class in Bogotá, Colombia, with those in three other Latin American capital cities: Quito, Ecuador; Lima, Peru; and Santiago, Chile.[1]

The cities chosen for a comparison with Bogotá share many similarities but also exhibit

a number of differences. All were founded by the Spanish in the 16th century, planned and laid out upon principles later embodied in the Laws of the Indies. All developed for several centuries around a central plaza, the focus of the city's governmental, ecclesiastical and intellectual life. And all have experienced a breakdown of these traditional land uses and a sharp segregation of residential uses along socioeconomic lines. These changes generally occurred with the advent of industrialization and the growth of commerce around the turn of the twentieth century. The cities differ most dramatically in population size and, to a somewhat lesser extent, in economic base and industrial mix. However, they all share to a large degree various characteristics common to cities ex-

---

From *Land Economics*, Vol. 41, No. 4 (November 1970) (© 1970 by the Regents of the University of Wisconsin), pp. 447–455.

The research on which this article is based was performed under a grant from the Ford Foundation, 1968. It was additionally supported by the University of Wisconsin Graduate School 1968–69.

[1] Peter W. Amato, "Population Densities, Land Values, and Socioeconomic Class in Bogotá, Colombia," *Land Economics* (February 1969), pp. 66–73.

periencing high rates of urbanization. Bogotá (1964 population estimate of 1,697,311) has been growing at the phenomenal rate of 6.7% per year over a ten-year period, while Lima (1967 population estimate of 2,390,300) has averaged a 6% increase per year. Quito, the smallest city studied, with a 1967 population estimate of 412,000, had a yearly growth rate of approximately 4% between 1964 and 1967.[2] Santiago, the largest city, with 2,670,442 inhabitants in 1967, has shown the most limited growth rate—slightly under 4% per year for the period 1965–67 and a decline for the years, 1963–65.[3]

In addition to the generally rapid rate at which population has been increasing, all of the cities have simultaneously experienced significant additions to their urbanized land areas. Bogotá has added land area to its municipal boundaries at an even greater rate than the rate at which its population has been increasing. Between the years 1950–61, the population of Bogotá doubled, whereas the urbanized area quadrupled. Within the short three-year period 1961–64, the city's population registered an increase of less than 25 per cent, yet the land area almost doubled.[4] Quito has also experienced rapid increases in its land area very similar to the rates achieved by Bogotá. Over the ten-year period 1958–67, population increased less than 25 per cent while the populat-

ed land area of the city increased threefold.[5] Lima had an urbanized land area of 8,441 hectares in 1959, which increased to 14,381 by 1967. This growth in land area, although not as dramatic as that of either Bogotá or Quito, was nevertheless significantly greater than the city's population increase.[6] Santiago also experienced land area increases at a faster rate than its population was growing, but its percentage growth was not as spectacular as that of any of the other cities.

Several reasons may be advanced as causes for the great increase in the urbanized area in the cities in question. Calculations are based upon gross land areas. Increases in commercial and industrial land, normal in the course of city development, tend to increase the ratio of overall urbanized land to population increase. Also, improved transportation facilities and increases in the number of roads, together with wider automobile ownership by upper and upper-middle income classes, permit various groups to live at lower densities and greater distances from the city center.

POPULATION DENSITIES AND SOCIOECONOMIC CLASS

Population densities for Bogotá indicate a distribution from a high of over 675 inhabitants per hectare (one hectare equals approximately 2.47 acres) to a low of only nine inhabitants per hectare. Areas inhabited by the middle-income groups tend to have the highest density ratings in the city, whereas the lower socioeconomic groups have ratings which cluster in the middle ranges of the population density scale. The upper socioeconomic groups have scores which range from the middle to the lower indices of population density.[7]

---

[2] City growth rate figures for Bogotá, Quito, and Lima based upon calculations from *Aunario del Distrito Especial de Bogotá*, vol. 25 (Bogotá: Departamento Administrativo Nacional de Estadística, 1964); "Cifras Provisionales," *DINEC*, Lima, Peru, 1966; and "Encuesta de Ingresos y Gastos Familiares, Ciudad de Quito," unpublished document, *Pontíficia Universidad Católica Del Ecuador, Instituto De Investigaciones Económicas*, 1967.

[3] "Población por Provincias, Departamentos y Comunas, Estimado Al 30 de Junio y 31 de Diciembre de 1967," *Departamento de Estadística*, Santiago, Chile.

[4] *Anuario Municipal de Estadística*, Vol. 15, 1954; *Anuario Estadístico de Bogotá*, D. E., Vol. 18 (1954), and Vol. 22 (1961); and *Anuario Estadístico del Distrito Especial de Bogotá*, Vol. 25, 1964 (Bogotá, Departamento Administrativo Nacional de Estadística). It should be noted that the great land increase in the city of Bogotá from 1961–64 was due in part to the annexation during this period of six smaller townships to the city's municipal boundaries.

[5] "Encuesta de Ingresos y Gastos Familiares, Cuidad de Quito," op. cit., and General Luis T. Paz Y Mino, *Cartografia Quiteña* (Quito: Imprenta Municipal, 1961).

[6] *Plan de Desarrolo Metropolitano Lima-Callao, Esquema Director 1967–80* (Lima: Oficina Nacional De Planeamiento y Urbanismo, 1967), p. 67. During this period the gross population density in the city dropped from 194.5 persons per hectare to 171.0.

[7] Amato, op. cit., pp. 67–68.

If a comparison is made with Quito, we find a distribution ranging from a high of 792 inhabitants per hectare to a low of only two. Close examination reveals that although the lower-income groups in Quito occupy areas of both maximum and minimum densities, their scores tend to cluster more in the middle ranges. The lower middle-income group cluster towards the higher ranges, and the upper-income groups have scores which range from middle to low density ratings. Lima, on the other hand, shows fewer extremes in its population density scores than either Bogotá or Quito. Lima's scores range from a high of 369 inhabitants per hectare to a low of nine. Lima has several residential sections populated at even higher densities but these areas are small. The figure of 369 inhabitants per hectare is the average computed for several center city sections. The lower middle-income sectors, together with the upper stratum of the low-income groups, occupy areas of highest population density in the city. The upper socioeconomic classes tend to live in areas of least density, as do some sectors of the population at the lowest end of the socioeconomic scale.

Santiago has a distribution of population densities which range from a high of 175 inhabitants per hectare in areas populated by a large middle-income group living within or near the city center, to a low of six inhabitants per hectare in areas primarily inhabited by middle-income groups further out from the city center which are generally suburban in character, composed of single family detached or semi-detached homes. The case of Santiago is somewhat similar to that of Lima. Although population densities in Santiago tend to be the least among all of the cities in question, some small areas have even higher density ratings than 175 inhabitants per hectare. The low income groups generally live within the upper ranges of population densities, and the upper socioeconomic groups occupy the middle ranges.

Nevertheless, as in the case of Bogotá, the extent to which population density relates to socioeconomic class is generally obscure if all sectors or zones are simply ranked by class and by density.[8] A clearer indication of these relationships may be obtained if all areas upon which data are collected are averaged accordingly to socioeconomic class and weighted by the amount of population residing within the area. This results in a distribution of population density scores for the cities of Quito, Lima, and Santiago which resembles conditions found in Bogotá (See Table 1.)

TABLE 1.   Density Ratings by Socioeconomic Class: Four Latin American Cities (inhabitants per hectare)

Class	Bogotá	Quito	Lima	Santiago
U. 1	44	55	66	60
M. 2	142	164	224	130
M. 3	158	478	225	100
L. 4	167	295	278	—
L. 5	133	217	128	82
L. 6	140	166	177	—

Sources of data: (Bogotá) Planning Department of the Special District of Bogotá. (Quito) "Encuesta de Ingresos y Gastos Familiares, Ciudad de Quito," op. cit. (Lima) Plan de Desarrollo Metropolitano Lima-Callao, op. cit., and Oficina Nacional de Planeamiento y Urbanismo, Lima. (Santiago) Armand Mattelart, *Atlas Social De Las Comunas De Chile,* Editorial del Pacifico, S.A., Santiago, Chile, 1965. Also, Ministerio de la Vivienda y Urbanismo, Oficina de Planificación y Dessarrallo.

Socioeconomic class ratings for each city were developed on a six point scale; upper class U. 1; middle class M. 2 and M. 3; and lower class L. 4, L. 5, and L. 6. A few minor adjustments were made for the city of Bogotá. Santiago has only four ratings: One upper, two middle and one lower class rating which range from L. 4 to L. 6.

In each city the upper socioeconomic class is found residing in the lower ranges of population densities. Moreover, an interesting phenomenon becomes apparent. The upper classes live in areas of similar population densities regardless of city size. On the other hand, the middle-, and upper- lower-income groups in each city, as found in Bogotá, live in areas of highest density. The scores for such areas

---

[8] A complete listing of population densities for all four cities may be obtained from the author.

range from a high of 478 persons per hectare in Quito, to 130 persons per hectare in Santiago. The lowest-income groups are shown to live in areas of middle range scores varying from a high of 177 in Lima to a low of 82 in Santiago.

These findings become clearer if they are graphically displayed using only three socioeconomic class distinctions. (See Figure 1). None of the curves coincide exactly with that of Bogotá. This of course would not be expected. Their general shapes, however, are all close approximations rising from low density ratings for the upper class to high points for the mid-

dle-income groups and dropping again to lower values for the lowest socioeconomic classes. The only exception to this rule is the City of Lima, in which density values for the lower-income class are somewhat higher than those found in the middle-income ranges.

As in the case of Bogotá, these questions may now be raised: Does an inverse relationship exist between density and distance from the city center? How do these variables relate to socioeconomic class? Population densities, when standardized by a factor of distance from the city center, show more meaningful socioeconomic class-density groupings in Bogotá than in the other three cities. It has been demonstrated in Bogotá that the lowest socioeconomic population groups occupy the middle ranges and the upper-income classes live at the lowest end of the density-distance scale.[9]

If population densities for the cities of Quito, Lima, and Santiago are standardized by distances from the center city, a drop is noted from high density middle-income ratings to a more even progression from the lower to upper

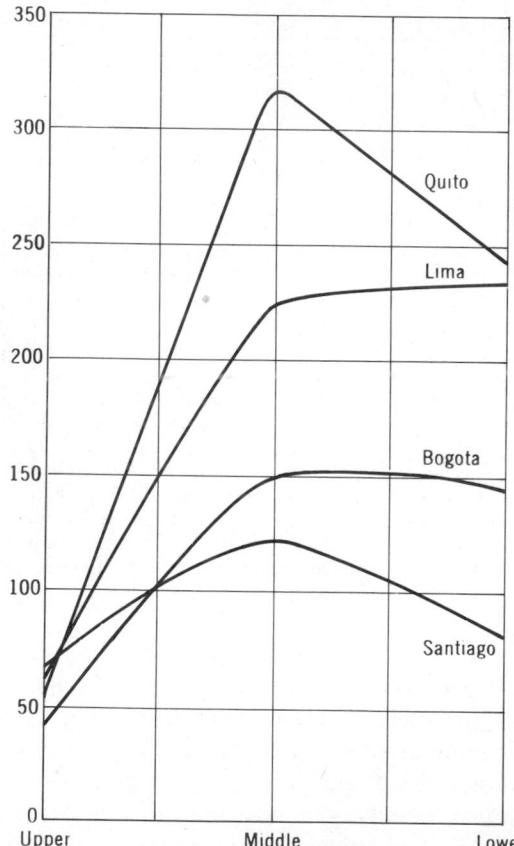

FIGURE 1. Density Rating Curves by Socioeconomic Class (inhabitants/hectare). (Source: Data based upon information supplied in Table 1 averaged by socioeconomic class.)

TABLE 2. Density-Distance Ratings by Socioeconomic Class

Class	Bogotá	Quito	Lima	Santiago
U. 1	375	164	381	363
M. 2	710	224	1048	211
M. 3	738	238	1020	613
L. 4	824	332	1056	—
L. 5	874	220	1533	838
L. 6	890	350	1137	—

In order to obtain a density distance rating (De Di), the densities (de) of all city subdivisions grouped by socioeconomic class were multiplied by the distance in kilometers (di) separating the approximate geographic center of each area from the center city. This product in turn was multiplied by the population (p) residing in each subdivision. The sum of the products was then divided by the total population for each socioeconomic class (P). The resulting quotient is a density factor standardized by distance from the center city and may be expressed by the formula:

$$De\ Di = \left[\sum \frac{p\ (de \cdot di)}{P}\right]$$

---

[9] Amato, op. cit., Table 2.

score ranges according to socioeconomic class standings. (See Table 2).

This is very clearly discerned in the case of Quito, which shows an almost systematic progression along the socioeconomic spectrum. The density distance score of the upper class (U.1) is the lowest in the city. The lowest income class (L.6) has the highest rating. Significantly, Quito is much smaller than Bogotá. Thus, although Quito has higher density ratings throughout the socioeconomic scale, its density-distance curve lies below that of Bogotá at every point of classification.

Lima's density ratings are higher than those of Bogotá and remain higher when rated on the basis of density-distance factors. The areas of highest density-distance are in the lower ranges of the socioeconomic scale. The city of Santiago closely follows the above rule. Its only difference is in the middle-income groups (M.2) that live predominantly in and around the city center and score lowest of all groups in density-distance rankings.

These density-distance relationships may be better understood when graphed. (See Figure 2). The model developed previously for Bogotá appears to be consistent for the three other Latin American capital cities, which vary greatly in size. In all cases, using a density-distance factor, the upper socioeconomic classes live in the areas of least density. Among cities, particularly Bogotá, Lima, and Santiago, the differences are surprisingly small. The upper classes not only live at approximately the same low densities in these cities but they also live at approximately the same relative distances from the city center. The middle-income groups, on the other hand, live in the areas of highest density in all the cities studied, although these high ratings are compensated by close center city locations. The middle-income groups have clearly traded off additional space and lower densities for higher accessibility to the downtown areas. Their density-distance curves thus lie below the low-income groups who live at relatively high densities and at more distant locations.

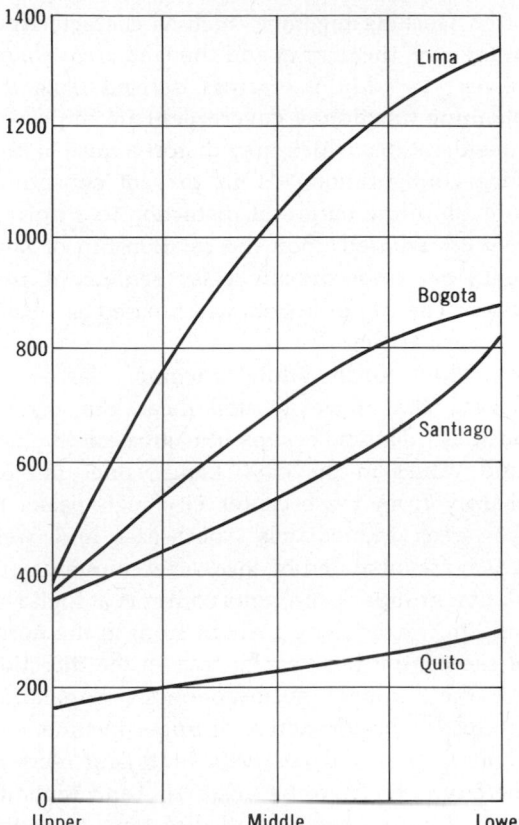

FIGURE 2.   Density-Distance Rating Curves by Socioeconomic Class (inhabitants/hectare × kilometers). (Source: Data based upon information supplied in Table 2 averaged by socioeconomic class.)

LAND VALUES AND SOCIOECONOMIC CLASS

Highest land values in a city should, to a great extent, reflect population densities or occur about a central place nearest areas of highest interchange and interaction among individuals. Land values would then decrease in steps or gradients to the most distant and generally most sparsely populated areas of the city. Cities which follow this basic pattern are typified as having "normal" rent cone configurations. Nevertheless, exceptions to this rule are common. The sum total of factors affecting land values, particularly residential land values, are complex and involve a number of different variables often working together, such as characteristics of the city, the district and the land areas themselves. In addition, factors derived from the planning function of government are important considerations which may distort a normal rent cone configuration.[10] Our present concern is to explore the nature of distortion to a normal rent cone based upon the relationship of land rents to socioeconomic class settlement patterns. The city of Bogotá will be used as a basis for comparison.

The upper-middle income classes in Bogotá that have located near the central business district, occupy the areas of highest land values in the city. Land values fall off sharply from these center city high peaks to the areas immediately south-east and west which are inhabited by low socioeconomic population groups. Land rents continue at high ratings, however, along a broad front to the north of the central business district in the direction of the upper socioeconomic population groups.[11] The correlation of upper-income, residential areas and relatively high land rents in the city is found to be positive. Land rents do not fall away evenly in all directions from the areas of highest rental but follow very closely the locations of socioeconomic population groupings.

Quito displays a land rent configuration similar to that of Bogotá. Areas of highest value are found within the center city near and surrounding the major plaza in sectors predominately inhabited by the middle income groups. From this area of peak values, land rents rapidly decrease in the directions to the south, east, and west and, as in the case of Bogotá, continue at high values along a broad front to the north of the central city in the direction of the upper-income, residential area. Areas of low-income population groupings tend to have scores which cluster in or near the lower ranges of land rents for the city.

The municipality of Lima indicates fewer variations in land values than do either Bogotá or Quito. Nevertheless, the areas of highest land value conform to the same model as those of Bogotá and Quito, occurring where population densities and interaction are highest—in the center business district occupied by the middle-income groups. Land rents remain relatively high throughout the center city but appear to be almost equally as high in the more distant upper income areas as they are in the middle-income areas. Land rents decrease rapidly, however, in the direction of low income population groups.

Santiago shows a land rent distribution which places a large segment of the middle-income class in areas of the highest land rents in the city—in or near the central business district. Values then decrease at further distances

TABLE 3. Land Values by Socioeconomic Class (dollars per square meter for 1966 & 1967)

Class	Bogotá	Quito	Lima	Santiago
U. 1	14.77	16.36	21.93	10.52
M. 2	26.15	8.36	22.44	26.31
M. 3	18.46	28.64	22.00	1.87
L. 4	15.54	8.27	11.85	—
L. 5	16.46	5.55	6.41	1.00
L. 6	8.38	3.73	7.04	—

Sources of data: (Bogotá) Compiled and computed from Archives of Lonja de la Propiadad Raiz, Bogotá, and from the files of Catastro in Bogotá. (Quito) Compiled and computed from base map, "Municipio De Quito," Departamento Technico, Valores del Suelo (Sucres por meter) January 1966. (Lima) Office of Catastro, Lima, Peru. All figures based on commercial land values. (Santiago) "Land Prices in Greater Santiago, Plan No. 7," Metropolitan Planning Department of Santiago, Archive No. 29, February 1965; and from the offices of Corporación Mejoramiento Urbano de Santiago (CORMU).

All land values have been converted to U.S. dollars based upon a base year of 1967 for Quito, Lima, and Santiago, and 1966 for Bogotá. It should be remembered, however, that these figures are approximate and comparisons between cities are not as valid as within cities. Also, large portions of the central business districts of Lima and Santiago are commercial and have been eliminated from consideration. Thus, their highest land values have not been taken into consideration, and their overall scores appear generally low if compared to Bogotá or Quito.

[10] E. G. Sibert, "Town Planning and Land Values," *Journal of Town Planning Institute* (January 1952); and Amato, op. cit., pp. 69–70.

[11] Amato, op. cit.

from the center city but not entirely equally in all directions. High land rent contours follow the areas occupied by the upper-income classes, though they are not as pronounced as in the cities of Bogotá, Quito, or Lima. On the other hand, the low income areas, located towards the periphery of the city, score in or near the lowest ranges of land rents. The land rent configuration in Santiago—more than in any of the other cities—approaches that of a normal rent cone. This information, if averaged by socio-economic class will give us a clearer indication of the relationship of income, class and land rents within each city and among all the four cities. (See Table 3.)

It is evident that among all four cities the low-income populations live in areas of lowest land rents. The middle-income classes live in areas of highest land rents, generally in or near the center city within areas of highest population densities and the upper-income groups tend to live in relatively high land rent areas. If we now assume a normal rent cone for the cities in question, land values should vary as a function of distance from the center city.[12] The method of standardization used is, in principle, similar to that which was previously applied to population densities.[13]

On the basis of this method, several upper-income areas in the City of Quito place near the top of the rating scale, scoring five places in the first ten ranks. The middle-income areas also place high with scores clustering near the upper and middle ranges of the rating scale. The lower-income groups score in the lowest ranges of the land value-distance scale. An examination of Lima and Santiago indicates similarities to land value-distance trends displayed in Bogotá and Quito. Land rents, when standardized by distance from the center city, relate to socioeconomic class in such a manner that the upper-income classes consistently score in the highest ranges of the scale; the scores of the middle-income groups range from upper to middle value ratings; and values in the low income areas cluster at the lowest ranges of the scale.

If all areas upon which data is collected are now averaged according to socioeconomic class and weighted by the amount of population residing within the area (see Table 4) a distribution of land rent-distance factors results which very accurately resembles the general distribution found in Bogotá. In every case, land rents, when standardized by distance from the center city, follow socioeconomic class very closely. Land rents drop off in value with distance from the center city but decrease relatively much more rapidly toward areas occupied by the lower-income groups than toward areas occupied by upper- and upper-middle income groups. Moreover, within the middle- and low-income categories, the higher-income groups generally occupy more expensive land rated in terms of distance from the center city. This

TABLE 4. Land Value-Distance Ratings by Socio-economic Class

Class	Bogotá	Quito	Lima	Santiago
U. 1	132.92	50.00	146.70	68.42
M. 2	150.62	29.55	130.70	45.26
M. 3	99.23	18.77	84.11	6.31
L. 4	71.15	9.00	95.07	—
L. 5	59.62	7.64	88.96	4.91
L. 6	55.85	10.45	53.04	—

The distances from the center city (di) in kilometers to the approximate geographic center of each of a city's subdivisions grouped by socioeconomic class were multiplied by the average value of land (lv) assumed to be acting at the center of each area in question. This product in turn was multiplied by the amount of land area (h) in hectares in each subdivision, and the sum of the products was then divided by the total amount of hectares (H) contained within each socioeconomic class. This may be expressed by the formula:

$$Lv\, Di = \left[\sum \frac{h\,(lv \cdot di)}{H} \right]$$

---

[12] The points of highest land value in Bogotá, Lima, and Santiago do not coincide precisely with the major plaza but lie within the central business district, from a few to several blocks away. Nevertheless, all differences are slight and do not appreciably affect the resulting analysis or conclusions.

[13] A complete listing of land rent-distance factors for all four cities may be obtained from the author.

holds true for all groups with the only exception being the lowest income class in Quito, which occupies higher land rent-distance ratings within its own groups. All other classes follow the same pattern as that of Bogotá.

CONCLUSIONS

Our analysis of residential density patterns for Quito, Lima, and Santiago indicates that all follow the model developed earlier for Bogotá. The upper-income groups occupy areas of least density; the middle-income groups occupy areas of highest density; and the low-income groups occupy areas between these other two groups. If density scores are standardized in terms of distance from the center city, the socioeconomic groups arrange themselves on a scale from upper to lower according to class rank. As in the case of Bogotá, this indicates the relative economic advantage to each class of obtaining low density living at varying distances from the center city. There are few exceptions to this general rule despite city size.

Land rents for the cities in question also follow the general model developed for Bogotá. They reflect accessibility and, to a degree, population densities and socioeconomic class. The highest values are found in the downtown commercial and business centers of all the cities, at the points of highest interchange and interaction of individuals in areas occupied predominantly by middle income populations. From this point, land rents decrease in gradients or steps to the most distant areas of the city. They tend, however, to follow the contours of socioeconomic class more closely than distance alone. This phenomenon becomes clearer when land rents are standardized in terms of distance from the center city. A high degree

of correlation is found between the price of land and the socioeconomic class residing on it.

Thus, we conclude that, despite the quantitative and qualitative differences among the four Latin American capital cities regarding various demographic features, inhabited land area, size of the urban area and economic base, all display regularities in several urban phenomena. These phenomena appear to be based on the general spatial behavioral patterns of various socioeconomic classes in the rapidly developing city. Obviously, several questions arise: How stable will the present density and land rent gradients remain over time? What relations will they bear to socioeconomic class, particularly as significant subnodes of employment are dispersed throughout the urban areas? Will not new gradients of density and land value tend to form as new sub-centers for commercial, social, cultural and/or recreational activities develop outside of the center city? Evidences of the development of new sub-centers have already occurred in the larger cities of Santiago and Lima and to a certain degree in Bogotá as well. The effect that the continuation of this trend may have on the present density, land value and class relationships is difficult to foretell. Nevertheless, it may be expected that, as improvements in transportation take place and as middle-income groups gain wider automobile ownership, they will increasingly trade off high density city locations for lower density suburban living. This trend would most probably accentuate the dispersal of the center city and succeed the urban cores to the lowest income groups. The results in the long run may be density-land value and class relationships very similar to those presently existing in many major North American cities.

15

HAL H. WINSBOROUGH

The Social Consequences of High Population Density

The man who participates in decisions about urban affairs today seems a most unreasonably imposed-upon fellow. Not only is he called upon to be comfortable in both of C. P. Snow's two cultures (on the one hand considering engineering problems and on the other choosing among competing notions of urban esthetics), but he is frequently asked to show some familiarity with a third minor but lustily growing culture: that of the social sciences. To walk in the elegant and orderly garden of natural science and to trace subtle paths in search of taste no doubt offer some pleasure. To hack one's way through the tangled thicket of the social sciences, however, must frequently seem an imposition—especially so if one's major business lies elsewhere.

The motive of this paper is to offer some aid and comfort to the person who looks in the social sciences for assistance in making choices in urban planning.

Let us begin by arguing that most work in the social sciences can be divided into two kinds. The distinction between the two depends on taste and judgment as to how things in the social world are to be explained. One group of social scientists, who may be designated behavioralists, explain things in terms of the actions which individuals take. From the point of view of the behavioralists, if we know enough about the causes, motives for, and constraints upon individual action we can account for the behavior of groups of people, or even of whole cities, by a process of aggregation.

The second group, whom we will call the structuralists, argue that the very collection of persons into groups provides possibilities and produces characteristics which are not to be derived from a summation of the characteristics of individuals. For example, the law of a country is not easily explained in terms of the motives and actions of the persons presently resident there.

Each of these points of view can be made persuasively by their adherents. Each has been productive of exciting research and discovery. When each is on its home ground all is well. However, when both points of view seem to apply at the same time, or when one tries to take both factors into account at once, the problem becomes complex and the dogmatic statements issuing from both camps become vociferous. It is at this juncture that one must keep one's head and, recognizing the limits as well as the extent of knowledge, try to assess the balance of effects in exercising decision.

Since all of the foregoing no doubt seems fairly abstracted from the everyday decision in

Reprinted, with permission, from a symposium Urban Problems and Prospects, appearing in *Law and Contemporary Problems* (Vol. 30, No. 1, Winter 1965), published by the Duke University School of Law, Durham, North Carolina. Copyright, 1965, by Duke University.

This paper is based on research supported by a grant from the Duke University Council on Research. Some of the computations involved were carried out in the Duke University Computing Laboratory, which is supported, in part, by the National Science Foundation.

urban affairs, let us consider an extended example. A not uncommon problem in urban planning concerns the proper level of population density for which to plan. Certainly various levels of density have various costs and various advantages. Supposing that an intrepid man began to search the literature in sociology in hopes of finding some guidance about the nature of these costs and advantages: what might he find?

He would discover that two somewhat separate traditions in sociology argue that the level of population density in a human society has important social consequences. Each tradition is based on the writings of one of the founding fathers of modern sociology and each has fairly vigorous present-day adherents. The consequences presumed by these two traditions are, however, rather different. On the one hand, the structuralists, following a Durkheimian point of view, see high population density, along with high population size, as a prerequisite for the development of division of labor.[1] On the other hand, behaviorally-oriented followers of Simmel stress the psychological—and even physiological—strain involved in the frequent stimulation and interaction concomitant with dense living.[2]

The Durkheimian position is succinctly summarized by Halbwachs as follows:[3]

> In reality, the division of labor results from the expansion of human groups and from the increase in their density. These are necessary conditions, (1) for the appearance and development . . . of a great variety of aptitudes and also of needs; (2) for bringing aptitudes and needs together in reciprocal stimulation . . . and (3) for establishing increasingly precise adaptation between the techniques of the more and more specialized producers and the needs of the more and more diversified consumers.

This point of view has received theoretical and empirical elaboration in the development of central place theory. This theory argues that a certain number of consumers are necessary within a given radius of a center for the support of a specific good or service.[4] Whether a specific good or service becomes a central one, then, depends upon the population density of the area in question, that is, upon whether it will find a sufficient number of consumers within its range. Some recent developments in this theory suggest it may apply to the distribution of services in the city as well as the distribution of cities in space.[5]

The Simmelian point of view has also received recent empirical support—a good deal of it from studies of animal behavior. In an attempt to investigate the relationship between animal behavior and population characteristics in a species living in the wild, Calhoun confined a group of wild rats to a quarter-acre enclosure.[6] He provided an abundance of food and relative freedom from predators. Population did not rise as expected because of an increase in infant mortality. This increase, Calhoun held, came about because stress from social interaction led to disruption of maternal behavior. Pursuing this hypothesis under laboratory conditions, Calhoun permitted caged populations of experimental rats to develop about twice the density which seemed to provide only moderate stress.[7]

[1] Emile Durkheim, *The Division of Labor in Society*, pp. 256–282 (George Simpson transl. 1960).

[2] Simmel, *The Metropolis and Mental Life*, in Paul K. Hatt and Albert J. Reiss (eds.), *Cities and Society*, pp. 635–647 (1957).

[3] Maurice Halbwachs, *Population and Society*, p. 173 (Otis Dudley Duncan and Harold W. Pfauts transl., 1960).

[4] A concise presentation of central place theory is given in Ullman, "A Theory of Location for Cities," in Hatt and Reiss, op. cit. supra note 2, at pp. 227–236. For a more lengthy treatment, see August Losch, *The Economics of Location* (William H. Woglam and Wolfgang F. Stolper transl., 1954). Additional citations can be found in Brian J. L. Berry and Allen Pred, *Central Place Studies: A Bibliography of Theory and Applications* (1961).

[5] Carol, "The Hierarchy of Central Functions Within the City," *Annals of the Association of American Geographers*, 50: 419 (1960). Some additional pertinent discussion is found in Ludlow, "Urban Densities and Their Costs: An Exploration Into the Economics of Population Densities and Urban Patterns," in Coleman Woodbury (ed.), *Urban Redevelopment: Problems and Practices*, pp. 102–120 (1953).

[6] Calhoun, "A Method for Self-Control of Population Growth Among Mammals Living in the Wild," 109: *Science*, 92 (1949).

[7] Calhoun, "Population Density and Social Pathology," *Scientific American*, (February 1962), pp. 139–148.

His results were dramatic. Many females became unable to carry pregnancy to full term. Many of those who did were unable to survive the delivery. Of those who survived, many subsequently fell so short in their maternal functions that infant mortality ran as high as 96 per cent in some experimental groups.

Males, too, exhibited strange behavior, ranging from sexual deviation to cannibalism, and from frenetic overactivity to pathological withdrawal.

Calhoun holds that these disturbances in behavior are the result of the stress from social interaction. Other investigators have found a direct relationship between density and adult animal mortality. Deevey cites some literature in support of this relationship and offers a physiological explanation of the relationship between the stimulation due to increased interaction and mortality.[8]

In summary, then, there is considerable evidence supporting both consequences of high levels of population density. Given the weight of the evidence it would seem unwise to simply disregard one or another of these effects. The problem becomes one of assessing the outcome of their joint influence. In a paper in which he speculates on the combination of these effects on human populations, Calhoun conceptualizes the problem as follows.[9] He associates the level of density which maximizes the division of labor with what he calls the economic climax state of the society. That level of density which minimizes psychological and physiological stress from interaction he associates with the social climax state. Of these he says:[10]

> It is logical to assume that the social climax can be achieved at a lower density than the economic climax. Thus the population characteristic of the economic climax community may serve as a yardstick of value judgment at what level the population should stabilize. Since this level is

likely to be attained in the United States within the next 50 or 100 years, any individuals or groups who encourage population growth at a rate likely to make this level to be exceeded, draw upon themselves the onus of contributing to the difficulties of achieving the climax social community.

Although Calhoun's statement may well be correct, it seems an oversimplification of a complex problem. First, it seems likely that, as with the problem of optimum city size, the optimum level of density, taking into account both stress and the division of labor, may vary with the characteristic to be optimized.[11] Further, there remains the question of the relative magnitude of the effects of stress and the division of labor upon a characteristic to be optimized. Given that the human animal is subject to the psychological and physiological stress due to interaction documented for other animals, it remains a question, for instance, whether easier access to medical facilities in a dense population may not significantly ameliorate effects of stress on adult human mortality.

By the time our urban decision-maker had reached this point in his search of the sociological literature, he would no doubt feel that his patience as well as the accumulated knowledge was exhausted. Not a great deal of specific information about the problem of the effects of various density levels within the urban community has been provided. In fact, about all that has been accomplished is to suggest that the decision about the level of population density is an important one.

Given all the foregoing information, how should a man try to influence the decision process with respect to population density levels? Certainly the behavioralists' findings are impressive. But in many circumstances the pressure of costs will argue for higher density. Since the latter argument has a kind of life of its own, perhaps one should use his influence to argue for lower density presuming that the

---

[8] Deevey, "The Hare and the Haruspex: A Cautionary Tale," *Yale Review* 40: 161 (1959).

[9] Calhoun, "Social Welfare As a Variable in Population Dynamics," *Cold Spring Harbor Symposia on Quantitative Biology* 22: 339–356 (1957).

[10] Ibid. at p. 355.

[11] Duncan, "Optimum Size of Cities," in Hatt and Reiss, op. cit. supra note 2, at pp. 759–772.

net result will approximate Calhoun's social climax state.

Would such a decision be justified? Would further research on the problem make this decision strategy wrong? I was curious enough about these questions to try to carry the research process along another step in the hope of being able to make some pertinent assessment.

To begin this investigation, I returned to the original Simmelian topic of people living in the city. I investigated the relationships between population density and a series of variables similar to or suggested by Calhoun's work as they occurred in the seventy-five Community Areas in the city of Chicago. These Community Areas are a partitioning of the land area of the city which was accomplished some years ago and are convenient for this analysis because they demonstrate a considerable variability in population density.

Five variables suggested by Calhoun's writings were readily available.[12] They are the infant death rate, an over-all death rate which has been adjusted for differences between areas in age composition, a tuberculosis rate, an overall public assistance rate adjusted for differences in age composition, and a measure of the rate of public assistance to persons under eighteen years old. Pearsonian correlation was used as a measure of the association between each of these variables and the level of population density over the community areas. These correlations are given in the first column of Table 1. All but one of the variables showed a positive correlation with population density. That is, the higher the density the higher the rates. The exception to this rule was the overall death rate, which showed no appreciable association with density.

These findings certainly suggest that increased density has a deleterious effect on the population. To assume that this effect is caused by increased stress is, however, a long logical leap. In fact, only a moderate acquaintance with cities would suggest an alternative explanation. People of lower socioeconomic status—people more likely, irrespective of density, to score higher on all of the rates investigated—tend to live closer to the center of the city than do persons of higher socioeconomic status. Further, population density declines in a regular way as one moves outward from the city center. These facts suggest that socioeconomic status may be confounding the relationships which we wish to investigate. Another variable which may confound the relationships is quality of housing, which also has association with density and with each of the rates. Finally, any effects of stress which may be present are confounded because the number of in-migrants to each area is likely to be different.

In order to avoid these confounding variables, then, one would like to investigate the associations between population density and each of the five rates "controlling" for socioeconomic status, quality of housing, and migration.[13] We have chosen to accomplish this by partial correlation, a fairly satisfactory technique which allows one to approach the "control" of the classical experiment. A list of the variables "partialed out" can be found in note a-2 of Table 1. The values of the partial correlations are given in column two of that table.

Removing the effects of socioeconomic status, quality of housing, and migration changes the pattern of the findings considerably. The overall death rate, which had originally shown no relationship with density, changed to a strong negative association: the higher the density, the lower the rate. The infant mortality rate, however, which had originally been posi-

---

[12] Data are taken from Philip M. Hauser and Evelyn M. Kitagawa (eds.), *Local Community Fact Book for Chicago, 1950* (1953).

[13] It may be noted that one of the variables held constant, per cent of dwelling units having more than 1.51 persons per room, is related to the number of persons per room, a component of total density. This aspect of density was treated separately because of some thought that its effects might be different from those of total density. The finding was, however, that the pattern of partial correlations was similar to that for total density except that all correlations except for those for assistance to juveniles were smaller and that public assistance was signed positively and assistance to juveniles was signed negatively.

TABLE 1.   Zero-Order and Partial Correlation of Gross Population Density and Stated Dependent Variable; Community Areas, City of Chicago, 1950

Dependent Variable	Variable Set Held Constant[a]	
	1	2
Infant Deaths per 100 Live Births	.32†	.33†
Age Standardized Deaths per 1000 Persons	.14	−.62†
Tuberculosis Cases per 10,000 Persons 15 Years and Older	.20*	−.67†
Age Standardized Public Assistance per 1000 Persons	.37†	−.39†
Quintile Ranking of Public Assistance to Persons under 18 per 1000 Persons under 18	.45†	.14

[a] 1. Zero-order correlations
2. Percent of workers in professional, technical, and kindred occupations
   Median income of families
   Median years of school completed by persons 25 years and older
   Percent of population foreign born white
   Percent of population Negro
   Median age
   Percent of dwelling units owner occupied
   Median rent of renter occupied dwelling units
   Percent of dwelling units with no water, no bath, or dilapidated
   Percent of dwellings built before 1920
   Percent of dwellings with 1.5 or more persons per room
   Percent of persons one year and older living in same household, 1949 and 1950
* Significantly different from zero at the .05 level.
† Significantly different from zero at the .01 level.

tively associated with density, continued virtually unchanged in its association with density. Thus, after control, one mortality rate is in the direction predicted by the behavioralists and another in the direction predicted by the structuralist argument. The tuberculosis rate, which originally had a positive association with density, becomes, under control, strong and negative. This is a very odd finding, suggesting that, *ceteris paribus*, high density leads to low tuberculosis rates. Both public assistance measures were originally positively associated with density. After control, each has changed but in a somewhat different way. Overall public assistance becomes negatively associated with density while assistance to persons under eighteen years of age demonstrates no appreciable association.

After control for the three confounding factors, then, we have a fairly mixed bag. One rate shows the positive association with density predicted by the behavioralists' argument.[14] Three show the negative association predicted by the structuralist argument. The final rate shows no association.

Perhaps the only order that we can bring to these heterogeneous findings is to suggest

[14] An interesting methodological point arises in using the data in this fashion. At first blush, it appears that we are committing the "fallacy of ecological correlation" in investigating a phenomenon which occurs at the individual level using aggregated data for census tracts. It seems to us, however, that our problem is rather different from that usually discussed in terms of the classical fallacy. Our problem is not to assess the existence of an individual effect of density on stress. Such an assessment can be performed with considerably greater elegance and precision in an experiment. In the main we find Calhoun's demonstration fairly compelling as to the existence of the effect. Rather, it is our aim to investigate the balance of effects, individual and aggregative, which derive from the variation in density. Thus we argue that, rather than being fallacious, an ecological correlation is a convenient device to investigate the balance of effects in the aggregate.

that the effects of density on the young seem to be different from the effects on the adult population. The findings certainly add weight to the previously stated guess that the optimum level of density varies with the thing to be optimized.

Before proceeding further let me insert the scholar's usual note of caution. Clearly the foregoing findings are rather tentative. Inferences from high order partial correlations is a notoriously tricky game. I have investigated the effects of density as it varies within only one city. Clearly there might be different outcomes in other cities, and variation between cities might produce still other outcomes. Despite these demurs, the results of the analysis are strong and curious enough to warrant further investigation.

Where does all this leave the man who must arrive at some policy with respect to urban planning? Not very far along, I expect. The original strategy proposed before the statistical analysis seems to fare reasonably well. It might be modified only by suggesting that lower density should be accompanied with a diminution of the catchment area for medical facilities.

If all the foregoing is taken as a cautionary tale, I suppose its moral is to take with a grain of salt dogmatic claims by either behavioralists or structuralists when good sense or the pressure of realistic constraints suggests that variables from the opposite camp should be taken into consideration. No doubt some day the social sciences will offer a larger fund of demonstrated principles to aid the decision-maker. But it will certainly be a long time before solutions to problems in urban affairs can be spewed forth from a computer without the inclusion of a factor of good judgment.

16

OMER R. GALLE
WALTER R. GOVE
J. MILLER McPHERSON

Population Density and Pathology: What Are the Relations for Man?

Studies of various animal populations suggest that high levels of population density frequently produce "pathological" behavior. The results of these studies, coupled with an increased concern about high rates of growth in the human population, have led to speculations about the implications of high levels of density for human populations. We begin this article with a review of some of these studies, noting the implications of possible animal-human similarities, and then take the animal studies as a serious model for human populations and devise a test case.

In 1962, Calhoun published an article detailing the ways in which overcrowding affects the behavior of rats. In his experiment, he gave

Reprinted by permission from *Science*, Vol. 176, pp. 23–30, 7 April 1972. Copyright 1972 by the American Association for the Advancement of Science.

the rats sufficient food and water, but the density of the population was substantially higher than it is in the rats' natural habitat. Calhoun observed the following "pathological behaviors" under these conditions: increased mortality, especially among the very young; lowered fertility rates; neglect of the young by their mothers; overly aggressive and conflict-oriented behavior; almost total withdrawal from the community (the "somnambulists"); and sexual aberrations and other "psychotic" behavior [1]. It should be noted that these aberrations were much more common in the central pens, where the rats *voluntarily* congregated.

In recent years it has become clear that rats are not alone in being adversely affected by high density [2, 3]. A study by Susiyama [4] of wild monkeys indicated that high density led to a general breakdown in the monkeys' social order and resulted in extremely aggressive behavior, hypersexuality, the killing of young, and so on. High density appears to cause death in hares [5] and shrews [6]. Morris [7] has found that high density causes homosexuality in fish. Probably the most frequently demonstrated effect of density is in the area of natality. For example, under conditions of high density the clutch size of the great tit decreases [8], as does the number of young carried by shrews [6]. It appears likely that high density reduces the fertility of elephants [9]. Female house mice abort if they smell a strange male mouse [10], as do shrews [11].

In sum, high population density appears to have a serious inhibiting effect on many animals. It must be noted, however, that the effect of density is not uniform among different species; different species react to density in different ways. It is probably inevitable that increasing knowledge of the effect of density on animal behavior leads to concern about the effect density may have on human behavior. By now, the idea that density has, or at least may have, serious consequences for man appears to have fairly wide acceptance. Such acceptance is obvious in much popular writing [12] as well as in work specifically aimed at behavioral scientists [13].

DENSITY AND PATHOLOGY IN HUMAN POPULATIONS

Although many people have written about the effect overcrowding has on human behavior, there is a paucity of good research. A detailed and careful review of the existing literature by Schorr led him to believe that the effect of poor housing (overcrowding) has been understated. Schorr concluded that poor housing (overcrowding) had the following effects [14, pp. 31–32]:

> A perception of one's self that leads to pessimism and passivity, stress to which the individual cannot adapt, poor health, and a state of dissatisfaction; pleasure in company but not in solitude, cynicism about people and organizations, a high degree of sexual stimulation without legitimate outlet, and difficulty in household management and child rearing . . .

Other authors interpret the existing data differently and feel that such relations have not, in general, been clearly established [15].

The evidence on the relations of pathological behavior and high population density is ambiguous; before the issue is decided, a number of studies of different populations in different settings will have to be undertaken. If, as Hall [3] has suggested, different cultures and different ethnic groups have different spatial requirements, the issue becomes quite complex. A recent and important interview study in Hong Kong suggested that within that culture and in that setting, where virtually everyone lives in an overcrowded environment, variations in crowding are not related to severe emotional strain, but are related to a lack of control over children [16].

We will look at the relation between population density and a variety of pathological behaviors as they vary over the community areas of Chicago [17]. Even if we use the animal studies as a guide, it is not obvious what effects we should look for in humans because, as noted before, density appears to affect different species in different ways. Our analysis will thus, of necessity, be exploratory. Since Calhoun's study has received more attention than others, we use his results as a starting point. There are several practical reasons for doing so. First, he covers a wider range of "pathologies" than do most other researchers. Second, there are a number of indices in the Chicago data that will serve as surrogate measures of Calhoun's "pathologies." In particular, there are indices of (i) fertility, (ii) mortality, (iii) ineffectual care of the young, (iv) asocial, aggressive behavior, and (v) psychiatric disorder. [In Table 1] are operational definitions of the measures that we use in the statistical analysis.

For each of the 75 community areas of Chicago, the *Local Community Fact Book for Chicago* [18] provides information on the number of persons residing in that area. This, combined with the size of the land area included in each community area [19], gives a measure of population density—the number of persons per acre.

The first two measures we use for indices of "social" pathology are distinctly biological in nature—mortality and fertility. The immediate cause of mortality will generally be specific diseases, although mortality rates will also be affected by such variables as malnutrition, accidents, and suicide. Variations in fertility are due to differences in conception, gestation, parturition, and the factors involved in these processes. However, as Calhoun noted, the factors involved in determining variations in mortality and fertility are largely social in nature. Thus, although mortality is largely the consequence of disease, we are interested in variations in mortality as social phenomena because such variations appear to be indirectly caused by, and certainly are associated with, such variables as social class, ethnicity, and, possibly, population density. The same may be said for the factors involved in the determination of variations in fertility. Let us define, then, the first measure of social pathology as the "standard-

TABLE 1. Zero-Order, Multiple, and Partial Correlation Coefficients for Social Pathology, Population Density, Ethnicity, and Social Class (Chicago, 1960)

	Social Pathologies				
Parameter	Standard Mortality Ratio	General Fertility Rate	Public Assistance Rate	Juvenile Delinquency Rate	Admissions to Mental Hospitals
Population Density and Social Pathology					
Zero-order Correlation Coefficient of each pathology with population density*	0.283	0.373	0.337	0.492	0.349
Partial Correlation Coefficient of each pathology with population density, controlling for social class and ethnicity	−0.177[†]	−0.023[†]	−0.118[†]	0.227[†]	0.142[†]
Social Class, Ethnicity, and Social Pathology					
Multiple Correlation Coefficient of each pathology with social class and ethnicity	0.828	0.853	0.885	0.927	0.546
Multiple-Partial Correlation Coefficient of each pathology with ethnicity and social class, controlling for population density	0.817	0.827	0.871	0.907	0.466

* The measure of density, persons per acre is transformed into natural logarithms.
[†] Not significantly different from zero at $P = .05$.

ized mortality ratio." This measure is the age-adjusted death rate of a given community area, expressed as a ratio to the death rate for the total population of Chicago in 1960. Our second measure of social pathology will be the "general fertility rate," which is simply the number of births in a community area per 1000 women ages 15 to 44 in the same area.

As a measure of ineffectual parental care of the young, we will use the number of recipients of public assistance under 18 years old in May 1962 per 100 persons under 18 years old in April 1960. Although this is not an ideal measure of ineffectual parental care, families receiving such assistance are typically disrupted, having only one parent in residence, and the family is not providing for the children in the normal societal manner. We shall call this the "public assistance rate," but it should be remembered that the rate refers only to the *young* persons of the community area. Our measure of asocial, aggressive behavior will be the "number of male individuals brought before the Family Court of Cook County on delinquency petitions during the years 1958–61 per 100 male population 12–16 years of age in 1960" [18]. We refer to the measure simply as the "juvenile delinquency rate." Finally, as an indication of withdrawal and other psychotic behavior, the fact book reports age-adjusted rates of admissions to mental hospitals for 1960–1961 per 100,000 persons in the community area in 1960. This we shall call the rate of "admission to mental hospitals" [20].

Variations in the five social pathologies we have just defined are normally explained by social structure factors, such as social class and ethnic (or racial) status. For example, it is assumed that variations in the mortality rate arise from such factors as exposure to disease, access to medical assistance, and knowledge about effective preventive measures and that such factors are mediated by one's social class and ethnic status. Similar arguments are made regarding the other pathologies. The precise explanations of the way in which class and ethnicity relate to each pathology would probably differ—in fact, there may be more than one explanation of how class and ethnicity relate to a particular pathology. Nevertheless, most sociologists see these social structure variables as the primary factors determining the variations in the rates of these pathologies. The case for the population density argument will be substantially strengthened if we can demonstrate not only that variations in population density make a significant contribution to the amount of variance explained in selected social pathologies, but that this contribution remains significant even after taking into account (or controlling for) the traditional sociological variables, social class and ethnic status.

We have chosen three measures as indicators of social class: the percentage of employed males in the community area who have white-collar occupations; the median number of years of school completed by all persons 25 years of age and older in a community area; and the median family income for all families residing in that community area. We have combined these measures into an index of social class [21]. This index was developed in a blatantly post hoc fashion in which we maximized the degree to which class is associated with variations in the different pathologies. Our index of ethnicity is also based on three measures: the percentage of Negroes in the community area, the percentage of Puerto Ricans in the community area, and the percentage of foreign-born in the community area. Again, this index was developed in a post hoc fashion, in which we maximized the degree to which ethnicity is associated with variations in the different pathologies [22].

PRELIMINARY RESULTS

Table 1 exhibits, for each of the measures of social pathology, four different correlation coefficients. The relation between population density and social pathology is given, as is the more traditional problem of the relation between social structure and social pathology.

The causal model implicit in an argument like Calhoun's is simply

$$u$$
$$\downarrow$$
$$\text{Density} \longrightarrow \text{Pathology}$$

(The u in this model indicates unmeasured variables not taken into account that impinge on pathological behavior.) For this model, a relevant measure is the set of zero-order correlations between density and each of the five pathologies [23]. These are presented in Table 1. For each social pathology, the relation with density is significantly different from zero, but it is relatively small. Furthermore, one of the five coefficients, though significant, is in the wrong direction. That is, the animal studies consistently indicate that the higher the population density, the lower the level of fertility. Here, the relationship is positive: the higher the density, the higher the fertility. However, some investigators might argue that high rates of fertility are pathological for urban populations [24]. Thus, one might conclude that population density has a small but significant effect on social pathology: the higher the density, the higher the pathology.

We know, however, that the lower one's social class and ethnic status, the more likely one is to live in areas with a high population density. Thus, it may be that class and ethnicity account for the variations both in population density and in pathology, and that there is no *causal* relation between density and pathology. Alternatively, class and ethnicity may affect density, and density may, in turn, affect the pathologies. In this case, density partially "interprets" the way in which class and ethnicity relate to the pathologies. We assume that, in this latter instance, class and ethnicity also affect the pathologies in ways unrelated to density. These two possibilities are presented in Figure 1.

If the relation between density and pathology is spurious, then when we control for class and ethnicity, the partial correlation between density and pathology should approach zero. In contrast, if density is an intervening variable that only partially mediates the effects of class

DENSITY AS A SPURIOUS RELATION

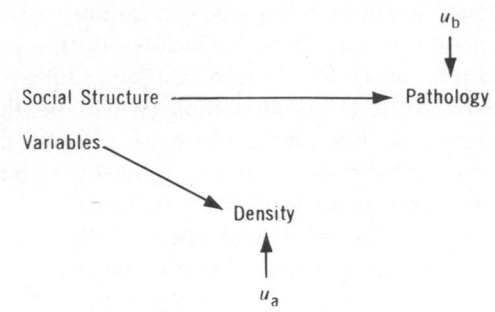

DENSITY AS AN INTERVENING VARIABLE

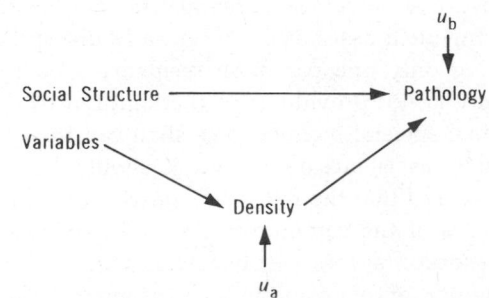

FIGURE 1.   Models of Density as a Spurious Relation and as an Intervening Variable; u_a and u_b represent all the unmeasured variables impinging on density and pathology that are not taken into account in the models.

and ethnicity, the partial correlation between density and pathology will not go to zero when class and ethnicity are used as controls, although it may be reduced. Furthermore, if density is a major intervening variable, the partial correlation between the social structure variables and the pathologies would be noticeably reduced when density is used as a control.

As is apparent from Table 1, when class and ethnicity are used as controls, the correlations between density and the pathologies are not significantly different from zero. Furthermore, Table 1 shows that controlling for density has virtually no effect on the correlation between the social structure variables and the pathologies. One may assert that these data indicate that the relation between density and the pathologies is spurious [25]. These results are similar to those of Winsborough, who used 1950 data for Chicago [26].

DIMENSIONS OF POPULATION DENSITY

However, before we accept such a conclusion, a reappraisal of our measure of density (persons per acre) may be in order. When the animal ecologists refer to overpopulation of a particular species, they generally indicate the number of animals per some unit of area, such as an acre. However, in the case of human populations, the situation is substantially more complex, especially in an urban setting. On the one hand, there is what might be called overcrowding at the personal, or individual, level. That is, it is possible for an individual to have privacy in the particular housing unit in which he resides, or is he constantly in contact with others? We refer to this type of overcrowding as "interpersonal press." As we have developed the concept, interpersonal press is composed of two distinct factors: the number of persons per room and the number of rooms per housing unit [27].

Population density may also be affected by more "structural" factors. In the urban setting there is considerable variation in the kinds of

structures persons live in and in the spacing of these structures. If each individual housing unit is a single, detached structure, then there must be many individual structures per acre to achieve a high level of population density. Alternatively, if there are many high-rise apartment buildings in the area, then the number of housing units per structure will increase dramatically, while another measure, the number of residential structures per acre, may stay relatively low.

A given level of population density in a community area can be achieved by different combinations of four components of density: (i) the number of persons per room; (ii) the number of rooms per housing unit; (iii) the number of housing units per structure; and (iv) the number of residential structures per acre.

Table 2 shows the interrelations of the various components of population density for Chicago [28]. The first row shows the zero-order correlations between the overall measure of population density (persons per acre) and each of the four components of this overall level. The next row shows the results of a multiple regression analysis of each of the four components of population density on the gen-

TABLE 2. The Interrelations among the Components of Population Density (Chicago, 1960). (All measures of density are transformed into natural logarithms. For this reason, the multiple regression analysis of the four components of density on persons per acre yields a multiple r of 1.00, and the unstandardized regression coefficients are also 1.00.)

| Measures of the Interrelations | Components of Population Density | | | |
	Persons per Room	Rooms per Housing Unit	Housing Units per Structure	Structures per Acre
Zero-Order Correlations with persons per acre	0.146	−0.560	0.741	0.717
Standardized Regression Coefficients from a multiple regression analysis of the four components of population density on persons per acre	0.226	0.242	0.811	0.699

eral measure of population density (persons per acre). Both rows indicate that it is the structural measures of density (housing units per structure and structures per acre) which account for most of the variance in persons per acre, while the measures of interpersonal press (persons per room and rooms per housing unit) have only a modest relation to persons per acre.

These data thus suggest that the preceding analysis of the relation between density and pathology may have yielded misleading conclusions. This is particularly obvious if the effect of density on pathology is primarily a consequence of interpersonal press. Therefore, we reanalyzed the relation between density and pathology by breaking down population density into its four component parts.

We are still essentially testing the two models outlined in Figure 1, with the one difference that, as density has been broken down into four components, our measure of density is now represented by multiple components; the relation between density and each pathology will therefore be represented by a multiple correlation coefficient. As before, if the relation between the components of density and the pathologies is spurious, the multiple-partial correlation between density and the pathologies should approach zero when we control for class and ethnicity; if density is an intervening variable, the multiple-partial correlation should not go to zero, although it may be reduced [29]. The importance of density as an intervening variable should be directly related to the reduction of the multiple-partial correlation between the social structure variables and the pathologies when density is used as a control.

As is shown in Table 3, the results of the analysis when population density is broken down into its four components are strikingly

TABLE 3.   Social Pathology, Density, Ethnicity, and Social Class Reexamined

	Social Pathologies				
Parameter	Standard Mortality Ratio	General Fertility Rate	Public Assistance Rate	Juvenile Delinquency Rate	Admissions to Mental Hospitals
Population Densities and Social Pathology					
Multiple Correlation Coefficients of the four components of density* on each of the social pathologies	0.867	0.856	0.887	0.917	0.689
Multiple-Partial Correlation Coefficient of each pathology with the four components of density, controlling for ethnicity and social class	0.476	0.371	0.584	0.498	0.508
Social Class, Ethnicity, and Social Pathology					
Multiple Correlation Coefficient of each pathology with social class and ethnicity	0.828	0.853	0.885	0.927	0.546
Multiple-Partial Correlation Coefficient of each pathology with ethnicity and social class, controlling for the four components of population density*	0.143[†]	0.351	0.574	0.574	0.086[†]

* All measures of density are transformed into natural logarithms.
[†] Not significantly different from zero at $P = .05$.

different from the results of the original analysis shown in Table 1. Density is now related to each of the pathologies, and in each case a significant relation between the components of density and the pathologies remains when class and ethnicity are used as controls. Furthermore, the relation between the social structure variables and the pathologies is markedly reduced when the components of density are used as a control. From this revised analysis it appears that at least some of the components intervene between class and ethnicity and the various pathologies, thereby partially interpreting that relationship. We will assume that this is correct, although we emphasize that we have not proved it. For example, we are simply assuming that class and ethnicity "cause" density and thereby ignore the possibility that density (through selective migration) "causes" class and ethnicity.

With the posited model in mind, let us attempt to evaluate the contributions made by class, ethnicity, and the four components of density. Following Duncan [30], we can do this in two different ways. First, we can work back from effect to cause. In this case, the multiple correlation between the components of density and pathology represents the total "effect" of density, including both its "unique" contribution to the variance of the pathology in question and the contribution it "transmits" from the social structure variables (class and ethnicity). The increment added by class and ethnicity that is not "routed" through density can be calculated by subtracting the variance explained by density from the variance explained by density, ethnicity, and class. Alternatively, we can go from earliest cause to effect. In this case, the multiple correlation of ethnicity and class with the pathologies represents the total effect of these social structure variables, including the effect routed through density. We can then calculate the independent effect of density (the effect that is unrelated to ethnicity and class) by subtracting the variance explained by ethnicity and class from the variance explained by density, ethnicity, and class.

The results of these analyses are presented in Table 4. If we work back from effect to cause, density appears to "account" for most of the variance, with the social structure variables having relatively little effect on the pathologies except through their effect on the components of density. On the other hand, if we go from earliest cause to effect, we see that class and ethnicity do, at least indirectly, account for

TABLE 4.   The Proportion of Variance Explained by the Four Components of Density and by Class and Ethnicity

Manner of Partitioning the Explained Variance between the Major Variables	Social Pathologies				
	Standard Mortality Ratio	General Fertility Rate	Public Assistance Rate	Juvenile Delinquency Rate	Admissions to Mental Hospitals
Working Backward from Effect to Cause					
Total "Effect" of the Four Components of Density	75.2	73.3	78.7	84.1	47.5
Increment Added by Class and Ethnicity	0.4	3.2	7.0	5.3	0.4
Total Variance Explained	75.6	76.5	85.7	89.4	47.9
Working Forward from Prior Cause to Effect					
Total "Effect" of Class and Ethnicity	68.5	72.8	78.3	85.9	29.8
Increment Added by the Components of Density	7.1	3.7	7.4	3.5	18.1
Total Variance Explained	75.6	76.5	85.7	89.4	47.9

most of the variance of the pathologies. It is noteworthy that in most cases the independent increment of explained variance added by either the social structure variables or by the components of density is fairly small. These findings are consistent with the second model proposed in Figure 1; that is, the results are compatible with the assumption that the components of density interpret the relation between the social structure variables and the pathologies.

As a step toward identifying the relative importance of each of the four components of population density, a multiple regression analysis was run for each of the five social pathologies. In four of the five cases, the standardized regression coefficients indicated that the number of persons per room is the most important determinant of the effect of density on pathology. The exception is admissions to mental hospitals, in which case the most important component of density is the other measure of interpersonal press—rooms per housing unit. Next, we found that in four of the five cases the second most important component is hous-

ing units per structure. When an analysis such as that outlined in Table 4 is performed on a comparison between the effect of persons per room and rooms per housing unit when class and ethnicity are taken into account, the results are strikingly similar. That is, the values differ only slightly from those in Table 4, in which all four components of density are considered.

Table 5 presents a similar analysis, but with only one component of density considered —persons per room. Because we already suspected that persons per room is not strongly related to admission to mental hospitals, we first focused our attention on the other four pathologies. For these pathologies, the total amount of explained variance dropped relatively slightly. As we move from effect to cause, we find that persons per room accounts for most of the explained variance, although the relation is not as strong as when we used all four components of density. However, compared to our earlier analysis, there is a noticeable increase in the independent increment added by class and ethnicity. Most of this increase can be attributed to the fact that housing

TABLE 5.   The Proportion of Variance Explained by Persons per Room and by Class and Ethnicity

	Social Pathologies				
Manner of Partitioning the Explained Variance between the Major Variables	Standard Mortality Ratio	General Fertility Rate	Public Assistance Rate	Juvenile Delinquency Rate	Admissions to Mental Hospitals*
Working Forward from Prior Cause to Effect					
Total "Effect" of Persons Per Room	60.5	65.4	73.3	61.5	15.8(46.8)
Increment Added by Class and Ethnicity	9.8	9.5	10.1	24.4	15.6(0.2)
Total Variance Explained	70.3	74.9	83.4	85.9	31.4(47.0)
Working Forward from Prior Cause to Effect					
Total "Effect" of Class and Ethnicity	68.5	72.8	78.3	85.9	29.8(29.8)
Increment Added by Persons Per Room	1.8	2.1	5.1	0.0	1.6(17.2)
Total Variance Explained	70.3	74.9	83.4	85.9	31.4(47.0)

* The numbers in parentheses indicate the values that occur when rooms per housing unit are used instead of persons per room.

units per structure are no longer treated as part of density.

This analysis suggests that, for mortality, fertility, public assistance, and juvenile delinquency, the most important component of density is persons per room. Next, but considerably less important, is the number of housing units per structure. For these four pathologies, the other two components of density—rooms per housing unit and structures per acre—appear to be relatively unimportant.

The pattern is quite different for admissions to mental hospitals. When Table 5 is compared with Table 4, one can easily see the marked decline in the total amount of variance explained, when the only component of density considered is persons per room. This is not surprising, since the standardized regression coefficients indicate that rooms per housing unit is the most important component of density as a predictor of admissions to mental hospitals. In Table 5 we have put in parentheses the variance associated with rooms per housing unit. In comparing these with those obtained when the four components of density are used, it is apparent that rooms per housing unit can account for virtually all of the variance in hospital admissions associated with density.

If our assumptions are correct, these data indicate that density—particularly persons per room (except in the case of admissions to mental hospitals)—may be an important factor in the development of various pathologies.

HOW DENSITY MAY RELATE TO PATHOLOGY

Before considering each pathology separately, let us make some general observations. First, as the number of persons in a dwelling increases, so will the number of social obligations, as well as the need to inhibit individual desires. This escalation of both social demands and the need to inhibit desires would become particularly problematic when people are crowded together in a dwelling with a high ratio of persons per room. Second, crowding will bring with it a marked increase in stimuli that are difficult to ignore. Third, if human beings, like many animals, have a need for territory or privacy, then overcrowding may, in fact, conflict with a basic (biological?) characteristic of man [31].

It would seem reasonable to expect that people would react to the incessant demands, stimulation, and lack of privacy resulting from overcrowding with irritability, weariness, and withdrawal. Furthermore, people are likely to be so completely involved in reacting to their environment that it becomes extremely difficult for them to step back, look at themselves, and plan ahead [32]. It would certainly seem that in an overcrowded situation it would be difficult for them to follow through on their plans. Thus, we might expect the behavior of human beings in an overcrowded environment to be primarily a response to their immediate situation and to reflect relatively little regard for the long-range consequences of their acts.

It seems from the above discussion that the most important component of density, as far as the pathologies are concerned, would be persons per room. This, of course, is the component that our analysis has indicated to be most important. Furthermore, it would seem that, to the degree persons in different dwelling units are involved with each other because of spatial arrangements (that is, could hear arguments, television, and so on), many of the reactions that occur on the interpersonal level (such as irritation and withdrawal) might also occur at this interunit level of interaction. Probably the most significant indicator of overcrowding at the interunit level of interaction is housing units per structure—and this, in our analysis, was the second most important component of density.

We now turn to a brief discussion of the possible effect of density (overcrowding) on each of the five pathologies under consideration.

Mortality

There are at least four possible ways in which overcrowding may be related to mortality. First, increased contact with others increases one's chances of contracting various infectious diseases. Such contact would presumably be related to both the number of persons per room and the number of housing units per structure. Second, if persons do become tired and run-down because of overcrowding [33], overcrowding would increase their susceptibility to disease. Third, sick persons in an overcrowded situation are likely to be constantly disturbed by the activity of others and thus will often not get the rest and relaxation that is important to treatment. And fourth, if overcrowding is associated with irritability, withdrawal, and ineffectual behavior, the treatment the sick person receives (from family members) will not be as effective in an overcrowded situation. Regarding the above points, we would note that investigations of overcrowding do indicate that it is related to poor health [34] and that controlled studies confirm that improved housing reduces the incidence of illness and death [35].

Fertility

Animal studies indicate that overcrowding leads to a drop in natality. However, we found the exact opposite—namely, the greater the density, the greater the fertility. If we are to consider the animal studies as being relevant to human beings, we must reconcile this difference. We reiterate that, although density has a significant impact on many animals, both the effects of density and the mechanisms involved differ widely from species to species. Second, we note that a frequent effect of overcrowding among animals is the development of hypersexuality [1, 4]. Among human beings, an increase in sexual intercourse is likely to lead to increased natality, for women are receptive and able to conceive for 12 months of the year. In contrast, most female animals are receptive and able to conceive during a very specific and limited period of time, and at this time they typically have sexual intercourse. Therefore there is no reason to believe that increased rates of sexual intercourse among animals would typically lead to increased natality, whereas it would among human beings. Third, we note

that many factors that would appear to limit natality in animals, such as lack of territory [36] or intense social competition [37], do not appear to be major factors in human populations. Fourth, because overcrowding appears to make it difficult to step back, look at one's situation, and plan ahead, it may be that persons in overcrowded situations are less likely to perceive the long-range consequences of having more children and are thus less likely to want to use birth-control techniques. And finally, because overcrowding makes it difficult to follow through on plans, birth control, even if desired, may be ineffectually practiced.

Ineffectual Parental Care (Public Assistance)

Overcrowding may lead to tensions and irritations in the home. Potentially, this could cause the breakup of the family, which might also mean the loss of financial support. Even if the family does not break up, children may receive less effective care in the home because overcrowding leads to ineffectual performance and withdrawal on the part of the parents. Furthermore, in overcrowded situations parents may be less likely to support their children in the usual manner, through gainful employment, because of weariness, poor health, and ineffectual ways of behaving that affect their performance in the larger community.

Juvenile Delinquency

As noted above, in an overcrowded environment parents are likely to be irritable, weary, harassed, inefficient. Children, in turn, are apt to find the home a relatively unattractive place, full of constant noise and irritation, with no privacy, no place to study, and so on. They are thus inclined to seek relief by getting out of the home. In fact, their disappearance may be partially welcomed by the parents, for it removes, temporarily, a source of irritation. Studies of low-income (overcrowded) families indicate, as our analysis would suggest, a strikingly early cutoff point in parental will and ability to contain children [38].

An important factor in the development of delinquent gangs appears to be a high degree of autonomy. We have suggested that such autonomy is probably greater in dwellings with a high persons-per-room ratio. It may also be that autonomy is greater where there are a large number of housing units per structure, which, as we have already argued, may lead to a decrease in communication between persons in different dwelling units. At any rate, the Chicago data indicate that housing units per structure has more "impact" on delinquency than it does on the other pathologies.

Psychiatric Disorder

From the above discussion, it would seem reasonable to anticipate a fairly strong relation between persons per room and admissions to mental hospitals. However, persons per room has a much weaker relation to admissions to mental hospitals than it does upon the other pathologies. In fact, the density component with by far the strongest relation to admissions to mental hospitals is rooms per housing unit, a finding that does not fit readily into our framework.

Admissions to mental hospitals is highly correlated with the percentage of persons living alone ($r = .72$) [39]. It may be that isolation is a contributing factor in the development of mental illness (that is, too little interaction instead of too much). Furthermore, disturbed persons living by themselves are more likely to require hospitalization when they can no longer care for themselves than are persons living with and assisted by others. We suspect, however, that the correlation between rooms per housing unit (or persons living alone) involves primarily a self-selection factor. That is, people who have a history of difficulty in getting along with others are likely to move to small apartments where they live by themselves, and these are the persons who are most likely to be admitted to mental hospitals. If this is the case, then it is the kind of housing that has drawn disturbed persons into particular community areas. This would involve a process that falls completely outside the posited model. It may, of course, be that overcrowding played a role in the creation of the person's initial disorders, which in turn led to his living alone, but these data, while not denying that possibility, do not support it.

CONCLUSION

Our study suggests that overcrowding may have a serious impact on human behavior and that social scientists should consider overcrowding when attempting to explain a wide range of pathological behaviors. Having made this point, we end on a note of caution. We have been using cross-sectional ecological data. Thus, not only have we not proved that there is a causal relation between density and the various pathologies, but the relations that appear at the ecological level may not appear at the individual level. We would also note that, although social structure variables and density are analytically very distinct, they are so highly intercorrelated, at least for these data, that it is difficult to accurately identify their independent effects. Even assuming that the data on Chicago do reflect the importance of density, more research is needed. At the moment, we may speculate about how overcrowding relates to various pathologies, but specific knowledge about causal links, if there are any, is lacking.

REFERENCES AND NOTES

1. J. Calhoun, *Scientific American* 206: 139 (February 1962).

2. For a more extensive review of the literature see R. Snyder, in E. Stellar and J. Sprague (eds.), *Progress in Physiological Psychology*, (New York: Academic Press, 1968), pp. 119–160; V. Wynne-Edwards, *Animal Dispersion in Relation to Social Behavior* (London: Oliver & Boyd, 1962).

3. E. Hall, *The Hidden Dimension* (New York: Doubleday, 1966).

4. Y. Susiyama, in S. Altmann (ed.), *Social Communication among Primates*, (Chicago: University of Chicago Press, 1967); pp. 221–236.

5. J. Christian, *Journal of Mammalogy* 31: 247 (1950).

6. ——and D. Davis, *Science* 146: 1550 (1964).

7. D. Morris, *Behavior* 4: 233 (1952).

8. D. Perrins, *Journal of Animal Ecology*, 34: 601 (1965).

9. R. Laws and I. Parker, in *Symposium of the Zoological Society* (London: Academic Press, 1968) vol. 21, pp. 319–359.

10. R. Chipman, J. A. Holt, K. A. Fox, *Nature* 210: 653 (1966).

11. F. Clulow and J. Clarke, ibid. 219: 511 (1968).

12. R. Ardrey, *African Genesis* (New York: Dell, 1961); *The Territorial Imperative* (New York: Dell, 1966); *The Social Contract* (New York: Atheneum, 1970); D. Morris, *The Naked Ape* (New York: Dell, 1967).

13. J. Calhoun, *Journal of Social Issues* 22: 46 (1966); R. Sommer, ibid., p. 59; L. Duhl (ed.), *The Union Condition* (New York: Basic Books, 1963); D. Heer (ed.), *Readings on Population* (Englewood Cliffs, N.J.: Prentice-Hall, 1968).

14. A. Schorr, *Slums and Social Insecurity* (Washington, D. C.: Government Printing Office, 1963). See also S. Riemer, *American Sociological Review* 8: 272 (1943).

15. D. Wilner and W. Baer, "Sociocultural Factors in Residential Space," mimeographed, prepared for the Environmental Control Administration of the Department of Health, Education, and Welfare and the American Public Health Association (1970); I. de Groot, R. L. Carroll, R. M. Whitman, "Human Health and the Spatial Environment," mimeographed, prepared for the Environmental Control Administration of the Department of Health, Education, and Welfare and the American Public Health Association (1970); R. Mitchell, "Personal, Family and Social Consequences Arising from High Density Housing in Hong Kong and Other Major Cities in Southeast Asia," mimeographed, prepared for the Environmental Control Administration of the Department of Health, Education, and Welfare and the American Public Health Association (1970).

16. R. Mitchell, *American Sociological Review*, 36: 18 (1971). As Mitchell notes, 170 square feet (1 square foot = 0.09 square meter) of floor space per person is held to be the lower limit in Europe, and in 1950 the American Public Health Service set the desirable standard at twice this figure. In Mitchell's study the highest category for floor space per person was 67 or more square feet (shown in two tables) and 100 or more square feet (shown in one table).

17. These are ecological data, and relationships that occur at this level of analysis do not necessarily occur at the individual level. However, it seems to us that ecological measures are appropriate and meaningful when dealing with phenomena such as density. That is, characteristics of areal units may have a significant effect on rates of human behavior.

18. E. Kitagawa and K. Taeuber (eds.), *Local Community Fact Book for Chicago Metropolitan Area, 1960* (Chicago: Chicago Community Inventory, 1963).

19. P. Hauser and E. Kitagawa, *Local Community Fact Book for Chicago, 1950* (Chicago: Chicago Community Inventory, 1953).

20. As noted, there are 75 community areas in Chicago. However, the central business district (community area 32—known as the Loop) is a unique area with regard to various social, economic, and other kinds of indicators. In our case, the measures of pathology are dramatically changed if the central business district is included. Perhaps the most marked case is the rate of admissions to mental hospitals The citywide rate is 297.6; the rate for the Loop is 3757.2, and the next highest rate is 851.1. While the elimination of the Loop does not transform the distribution of admissions to mental hospitals into a normal distribution, it does substantially reduce its deviation from this ideal: skewness is reduced from 7.56 to 2.88, and kurtosis is reduced from 62.32 to 15.14 [for a discussion of skewness and kurtosis, see J. Freund, *Modern Elementary Statistics* (Englewood Cliffs, N.J.: Prentice-Hall, 1960), pp. 99–105]. Other measures, especially the standardized mortality ratio, are affected in similar, although somewhat less drastic, fashion. For this reason our analysis is based on 74 rather than 75 community areas in Chicago around 1960.

21. A regression analysis of income, education, and occupation was run on each of the pathologies. These five regression equations were then used as a basis for constructing the weighted sum of the three measures as a general index. The equation for the index of social class is as follows: index of social class = 0.1 × (median family income) + 10.0 × (median years of school completed) + (percentage of employed males in white-collar occupations)—550.0. Median family income is by far the most important component of the social class index.

22. A regression analysis of percentage of Negroes, percentage of Puerto Ricans, and percentage of foreign-born was run on each of the pathologies. As with social class, these five regression equations were then used as a basis for constructing the weighted sum of the three measures as a general index. The equation for the index of ethnicity is as follows: index of ethnicity = 25.0 × (percentage of Negroes) + 10 × (percentage of Puerto Ricans) + 0.1 × (percentage of foreign-born). The percentage of Negroes is by far the most important component of the ethnicity index.

23. As Blalock notes, grouping by proximity may partially control for independent variables associated with "error" in the dependent variable. Thus to some extent, the size of the correlation between density and the pathologies, and between the social structure variables and the pathologies may be determined by the fact that the community areas, like all ecological variables, involved data grouped by proximity [H. Blalock, *Causal Inferences in Nonexperimental Research* (Chapel Hill: University of North Carolina Press, 1964), pp. 102–114.]

24. In a subsequent section of this article we will discuss the possibility that in human populations high rates of fertility might be a consequence of population density.

25. The same conclusion is reached if one uses regression coefficients. We would note that there are advantages and disadvantages to using either regression coefficients or

partial correlations. Although multiple partial correlations are not strict estimates of the parameters of the causal model, we consider them to be sufficient for our purpose, and using them simplifies the analysis in the second part of the article.

26. H. Winsborough, in T. Ford and G. De Jong (eds.), *Social Demography* (Englewood Cliffs, N.J.: Prentice-Hall, 1970), pp. 84–90.

27. Holding the number of persons per room constant, it is probable that an increase in the number of rooms will increase the likelihood that a person will be able, at least occasionally, to be alone in a room.

28. The number of persons in each community area is reported directly in the *Local Community Fact Book*, as is the number of housing units. The number of rooms per community area and the number of residential structures per community area are, however, based on estimates from open-ended interval data. The fact book reports the number of housing units with 1, 2, 3, 4, 5, 6, 7, and 8 or more rooms in them. To get an estimate of the number of rooms per community area, we multiplied the number of housing units at each level by the appropriate number of rooms. The highest interval was multiplied by 8, even though it was an open-ended interval. The fact book reports the number of housing units in 1-unit structures, 2-unit structures, 3- and 4-unit structures, 5- to 9-unit structures, and 10- or more unit structures. Data from the 1940 fact book suggest that, for that year, slightly over half of the housing units located in the over 10 category were in the over 20 category. To estimate the number of residential structures in the area, we set the midinterval points for these data at 1, 2, 3, 5, 7, and 20. We divided the number of housing units in each category by these midinterval points and added the resulting figures to get the estimate of the number of residential structures for the community area. The four measures of density were then calculated by division: number of persons divided by the number of rooms, the number of rooms divided by the number of housing units, and so on.

29. The cogency of the multiple-partial correlation coefficient as an estimate of the relation is based upon the assumption that all indicators are related to the pathologies in the predicted direction. This assumption is, in general, supported by an examination of a table of the partial regression coefficients relating the four dimensions of density to each of the pathologies, although the general fertility rate increases with density. This table is available from the authors upon request.

30. O. Duncan, in E. Borgatta and G. Bohrnstedt (eds.), *Sociological Methodology* (San Francisco: Jussey-Bass, 1970), pp. 38–47.

31. R. Sommer, *Personal Space: The Behavioral Basis of Design* (Englewood Cliffs, N.J.: Prentice-Hall, 1969).

32. J. Plant, *American Journal of Psychiatry*, 9: 849 (1930); in N. Bell and E. Vogel (eds.), *Modern Introduction to the Family* (New York: Free Press, 1960), pp. 510–520.

33. A. Davis, in W. F. Whyte (ed.), *Industry and Society* (New York: McGraw-Hill, 1946), pp. 84–106.

34. A. Pond, *Marriage and Family Living*, 19: 154 (1957); D. Wilner, R. P. Walkley, M. Tayback, *American Journal of Public Health* 46: 736 (1956).

35. D. Wilner, R. P. Walkey, T. Pinkerton, M. Tayback, *The Housing Environment and Family Life: A Longitudinal Study of the Effects of Housing on Morbidity and Mental Health* (Baltimore: Johns Hopkins University Press, 1962).

36. A. Watson, *Nature*, 215: 1274 (1967).

37. L. Mech, *The Wolf: The Ecology and Behavior of an Endangered Species* (Garden City, N.J.: Natural History Press, 1970).

38. H. Lewis, "Child Rearing Practices among Low Income Families in the District of Columbia," mimeographed, presented at the National Conference on Social Welfare, Minneapolis (1961); S. Riemer, *American Sociological Review*, 8: 272 (1943); R. Mitchell, ibid., 36: 18 (1971).

39. The relation between the percentage of persons living alone and admissions to mental hospitals remains fairly strong, even after class and ethnicity are used as controls ($r = .59$). The percentage of persons living alone also has a high negative correlation with rooms per housing unit ($r = -.91$).

Factors in the Organization of Urban Space

part iv

The papers in this section are concerned mainly with the geometry of urban space and with the factors accounting for ecological patterning within the city. The basic models for describing urban patterning are the concentric zone, sector, and multiple nuclei models. While the three models share several assumptions about the operation of the broader social processes and the urban land market, they forecast radically different geometries of urban space. The paper by Harris and Ullman (17) presents a general discussion of the three basic models. In addition, they present the structure of the city within a fairly broad context of the general economic functions that cities perform. As Harris and Ullman point out, cities serve as central places in trade networks, as nodes in interregional and intraregional transportation systems, and as points for the development of specialized functions.

Berry's paper (18) presents an excellent overview of basic ecological models and describes how some of the basic models might be more closely integrated. The discussion begins by linking the internal structure of the city to the specialized functions that the city performs in extracommunity systems. Subsequent sections of Berry's paper cover density models, social class patterns, and retail business patterns. The paper well illustrates the complementary nature of many basic ecological models and suggests directions for their convergence.

Hoyt's paper (19) updates many of the basic notions associated with the classical ecological models and looks at changes in cities both within and without the United States. Hoyt points out that the principles of city growth and patterning as embodied in the classic models must be subject to modification because of the dynamic changes in the overall society since 1930. Also, in applying the basic models to cities outside the United States, one must recognize critical differences between the United States and the other societies in the underlying factors that produce the urban spatial arrangement.

The influence of locational decisions of the urban upper class upon urban residential patterning in a Latin American city is the topic of Amato's paper (20). The distribution and movement of the upper class in Bogotá certainly seems to correspond to the sector model. Furthermore, it is reported that the upper class sectors are the best in the city. The upper class areas are less humid, cloudy, and damp than those of the other classes. Located away from low land subject to flooding, these areas are generally at higher elevations than the remainder of the city. The areas inhabited by the lower class are the worst in the city, while those of the middle class fall intermediate in quality to those of the upper and lower classes.

The paper by Form (21) presents a stern warning to ecologists to study land use changes in terms of social forces operating through the urban land market rather than in terms of the operation of rather vague ecological processes. Form asserts that the urban land market is highly organized in a sociological sense and is dominated by a number of interacting organizations which are highly self-conscious and purposeful in their action. Therefore, a sociological analysis of the land market's economic behavior is called for.

The final paper in this section, by Guest (22), deals with the effect of a number of ecological variables upon the location of families within the metropolis. The ecological variables include neighborhood age, distance from the city's center, industrial land use, recreational land use, density, and internal space. Among the findings presented is that there is a marked tendency for young and old families to be decentralized and for primary individuals to be centralized. A model is presented and empirically supported which shows the effect of the various ecological variables upon the locational patterning of various family types.

17

CHAUNCY D. HARRIS
EDWARD L. ULLMAN

The Nature of Cities

Cities are the focal points in the occupation and utilization of the earth by man. Both a product of and an influence on surrounding regions, they develop in definite patterns in response to economic and social needs.

Cities are also paradoxes. Their rapid growth and large size testify to their superiority as a technique for the exploitation of the earth; yet by their very success and consequent large size they often provide a poor local environment for man. The problem is to build the future city in such a manner that the advantages of urban concentration can be preserved for the benefit of man and the disadvantages minimized.

Each city is unique in detail but resembles others in function and pattern. What is learned about one helps in studying another. Location types and internal structure are repeated so often that broad and suggestive generalizations are valid, especially if limited to cities of similar size, function, and regional setting. This paper will be limited to a discussion of two basic aspects of the nature of cities—their support and their internal structure. Such important topics as the rise and extent of urbanism, urban sites, culture of cities, social and economic characteristics of the urban population, and critical problems will receive only passing mention.

THE SUPPORT OF CITIES

As one approaches a city and notices its tall buildings rising above the surrounding land and as one continues into the city and observes the crowds of people hurrying to and fro past stores, theaters, banks, and other establishments, one naturally is struck by the contrast with the rural countryside. What supports this phenomenon? What do the people of a city do for a living?

The support of a city depends on the services it performs not for itself but for a tributary area. Many activities serve merely the population of the city itself. Barbers, dry cleaners, shoe repairers, grocerymen, bakers, and movie operators serve others who are engaged in the principal activity of the city, which may be mining, manufacturing, trade or some other activity.

The service by which the city earns its livelihood depends on the nature of the economy and of the hinterland. Cities are small or rare in areas either of primitive, self-sufficient economy or of meager resources. As Adam Smith stated, the land must produce a surplus in order to support cities. This does not mean that all cities must be surrounded by productive land, since strategic location with reference to cheap ocean highways may enable a city to support itself on the specialized surplus of distant lands. Nor does it mean that cities are parasites living off the land. Modern mechanization, transport, and a complex interdependent economy enable much of the economic activity of mankind to be centered in cities. Many of the people en-

Reprinted with permission from *Annals of the American Academy of Political and Social Science*, Vol. CCXLII (November 1945) pp. 7–17.

gaged even in food production are actually in cities in the manufacture of agricultural machinery.

The support of cities as suppliers of urban services for the earth can be summarized in three categories, each of which presents a factor of urban causation:[1]

1. Cities as central places performing comprehensive services for a surrounding area. Such cities tend to be evenly spaced throughout productive territory (Figure 1). For the moment this may be considered the "norm" subject to variation primarily in response to the ensuing factors.

2. Transport cities performing break-of-bulk and allied services along transport routes, supported by areas which may be remote in distance but close in connection because of the city's strategic location on transport channels. Such cities tend to be arranged in linear patterns along rail lines or at coasts (Figure 2).

3. Specialized-function cities performing one service such as mining, manufacturing, or recreation for large areas, including the general tributary areas of hosts of other cities. Since the principal localizing factor is often a particular resource such as coal, water power, or a beach, such cities may occur singly or in clusters (Figure 3).

Most cities represent a combination of the three factors, the relative importance of each varying from city to city (Figure 4).

Cities as Central Places

Cities as central places serve as trade and social centers for a tributary area. If the land base is homogeneous these centers are uniformly spaced, as in many parts of the agricultural Middle West (Figure 1). In areas of uneven resource distribution, the distribution of cities is uneven. The centers are of varying sizes, ranging from small hamlets closely spaced with one

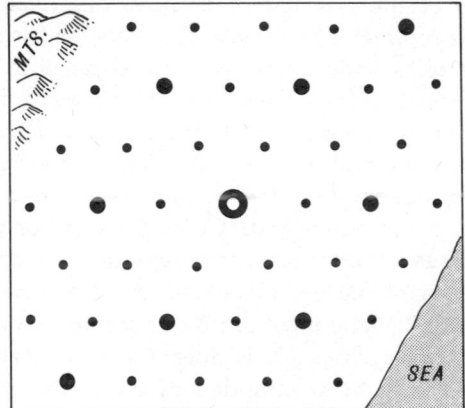

FIGURE 1. Theoretical Distribution of Central Places. In a homogeneous land, settlements are evenly spaced; largest city in center surrounded by 6 medium-sized centers which in turn are surrounded by 6 small centers. Tributary areas are hexagons, the closest geometrical shapes to circles which completely fill area with no unserved spaces.

FIGURE 2. Transport Centers, Aligned along Railroads or at Coast. Large center is port; next largest is railroad junction and engine-changing point where mountain and plain meet. Small centers perform break of bulk principally between rails and roads.

[1] For references see Edward Ullman, "A Theory of Location for Cities," American Journal of Sociology, XLVI (May 1941): 853–64.

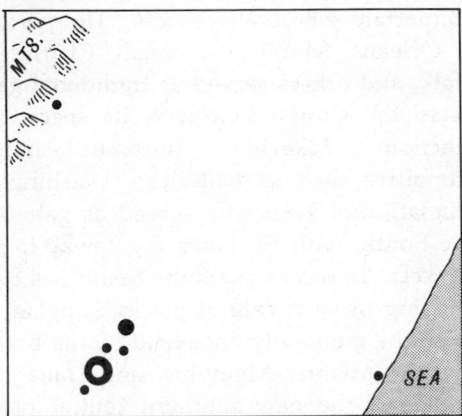

FIGURE 3. Specialized-Function Settlements. Large city is manufacturing and mining center surrounded by a cluster of smaller settlements located on a mineral deposit. Small centers on ocean and at edge of mountains are resorts.

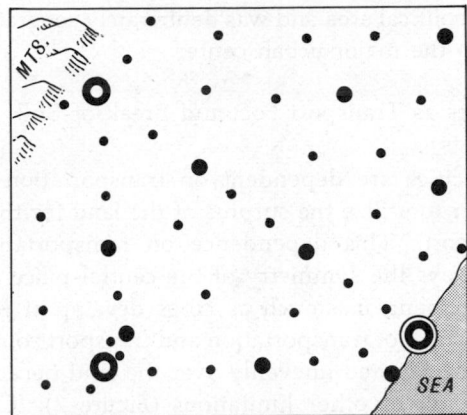

FIGURE 4. Theoretical Composite Grouping. Port becomes the metropolis and, although off center, serves as central place for whole area. Manufacturing-mining and junction centers are next largest. Railroad alignment of many towns evident. Railroad route in upper left of Figure 2 has been diverted to pass through manufacturing and mining cluster. Distribution of settlements in upper right follows central-place arrangement.

or two stores serving a local tributary area, through larger villages, towns, and cities more widely spaced with more special services for larger tributary areas, up to the great metropolis such as New York or Chicago offering many specialized services for a large tributary area composed of a whole hierarchy of tributary areas of smaller places. Such a net of tributary areas and centers forms a pattern somewhat like a fish net spread over a beach, the network regular and symmetrical where the sand is smooth but warped and distorted where the net is caught in rocks.

The central-place type of city or town is widespread throughout the world, particularly in non-industrial regions. In the United States it is best represented by the numerous retail and wholesale trade centers of the agricultural Middle West, Southwest, and West. Such cities have imposing shopping centers or wholesale districts in proportion to their size; the stores are supported by the trade of the surrounding area. This contrasts with many cities of the industrial East, where the centers are so close together that each has little trade support beyond its own population.

Not only trade but social and religious functions may support central places. In some instances these other functions may be the main support of the town. In parts of Latin America, for example, where there is little trade, settlements are scattered at relatively uniform intervals through the land as social and religious centers. In contrast to most cities, their busiest day is Sunday, when the surrounding populace attend church and engage in holiday recreation, thus giving rise to the name "Sunday town."

Most large central cities and towns are also political centers. The county seat is an example. London and Paris are the political as well as trade centers of their countries. In the United States, however, Washington and many state capitals are specialized political centers. In many of these cases the political capital was initially chosen as a centrally located point in the political area and was deliberately separated from the major urban center.

Cities as Transport Foci and Break-of-Bulk Points

All cities are dependent on transportation in order to utilize the surplus of the land for their support. This dependence on transportation destroys the symmetry of the central-place arrangement, inasmuch as cities develop at foci or breaks of transportation and transport routes are distributed unevenly over the land because of relief or other limitations (Figure 2). City organizations recognize the importance of efficient transportation, as witness their constant concern with freight-rate regulation and with the construction of new highways, port facilities, airfields, and the like.

Mere focusing of transport routes does not produce a city, but according to Cooley, if break of bulk occurs, the focus becomes a good place to process goods. Where the form of transport changes, as transferring from water to rail, break of bulk is inevitable. Ports originating merely to transship cargo tend to develop auxiliary services such as repackaging, storing, and sorting. An example of simple break-of-bulk and storage ports is Port Arthur-Fort William, the twin port and wheat-storage cities at the head of Lake Superior; surrounded by unproductive land, they have arisen at the break-of-bulk points on the cheapest route from the wheat-producing Prairie Provinces to the markets of the East. Some ports develop as entrepôts, such as Hong Kong and Copenhagen, supported by transshipment of goods from small to large boats or vice versa. Servicing points or minor changes in transport tend to encourage growth of cities as establishment of division points for changing locomotives on American railroads.

Transport centers can be centrally located places or can serve as gateways between contrasting regions with contrasting needs. Kansas City, Omaha, and Minneapolis-St. Paul serve as gateways to the West, as well as central places for productive agricultural regions, and

are important wholesale centers. The ports of New Orleans, Mobile, Savannah, Charleston, Norfolk, and others served as traditional gateways to the Cotton Belt with its specialized production. Likewise, northern border metropolises such as Baltimore, Washington, Cincinnati, and Louisville served as gateways to the South, with St. Louis a gateway to the Southwest. In recent years the South has been developing its own central places, supplanting some of the monopoly once held by the border gateways. Atlanta, Memphis, and Dallas are examples of the new southern central places and transport foci.

Changes in transportation are reflected in the pattern of city distribution. Thus the development of railroads resulted in a railroad alignment of cities which still persists. The rapid growth of automobiles and widespread development of highways in recent decades, however, has changed the trend toward a more even distribution of towns. Studies in such diverse localities as New York and Louisiana have shown a shift in centers away from exclusive alignment along rail routes. Airways may reinforce this trend or stimulate still different patterns of distribution for the future city.

Cities as Concentration Points for Specialized Services

A specialized city or cluster of cities performing a specialized function for a large area may develop at a highly localized resource (Figure 3). The resort city of Miami, for example, developed in response to a favorable climate and beach. Scranton, Wilkes-Barre, and dozens of nearby towns are specialized coal-mining centers developed on anthracite coal deposits to serve a large segment of the northeastern United States. Pittsburgh and its suburbs and satellites form a nationally significant iron-and-steel manufacturing cluster favored by good location for the assembly of coal and iron ore and for the sale of steel to industries on the coal fields.

Equally important with physical resources in many cities are the advantages of mass production and ancillary services. Once started, a specialized city acts as a nucleus for similar or related activities, and functions tend to pyramid, whether the city is a seaside resort such as Miami or Atlantic City or, more important, a manufacturing center such as Pittsburgh or Detroit. Concentration of industry in a city means that there will be a concentration of satellite services and industries—supply houses, machine shops, expert consultants, other industries using local industrial by-products or waste, still other industries making specialized parts for other plants in the city, marketing channels, specialized transport facilities, skilled labor, and a host of other facilities; either directly or indirectly, these benefit industry and cause it to expand in size and numbers in a concentrated place or district. Local personnel with the know-how in a given industry also may decide to start a new plant producing similar or like products in the same city. Furthermore, the advantages of mass production itself often tend to concentrate production in a few large factories and cities. Examples of localization of specific manufacturing industries are clothing in New York City, furniture in Grand Rapids, automobiles in the Detroit area, pottery in Stoke-on-Trent in England, and even such a specialty as tennis rackets in Pawtucket, Rhode Island.

Such concentration continues until opposing forces of high labor costs and congestion balance the concentrating forces. Labor costs may be lower in small towns and in industrially new districts; thus some factories are moving from the great metropolises to small towns; much of the cotton textile industry has moved from the old industrial areas of New England to the newer areas of the Carolinas in the South. The tremendous concentration of population and structures in large cities exacts a high cost in the form of congestion, high land costs, high taxes, and restrictive legislation.

Not all industries tend to concentrate in specialized industrial cities; many types of manufacturing partake more of central-place characteristics. These types are those that are tied to the market because the manufacturing process results in an increase in bulk or perishability. Bakeries, ice cream establishments, icehouses, breweries, softdrink plants, and various types of assembly plants are examples. Even such industries, however, tend to be more developed in the manufacturing belt because the density of population and hence the market is greater there.

The greatest concentration of industrial cities in America is in the manufacturing belt of northeastern United States and contiguous Canada, north of the Ohio and east of the Mississippi. Some factors in this concentration are large reserves of fuel and power (particularly coal), raw materials such as iron ore via the Great Lakes, cheap ocean transportation on the eastern seaboard, productive agriculture (particularly in the West), early settlement, later immigration concentrated in its cities, and an early start with consequent development of skilled labor, industrial know-how, transportation facilities, and prestige.

The interdependent nature of most of the industries acts as a powerful force to maintain this area as the primary home of industrial cities in the United States. Before the war, the typical industrial city outside the main manufacturing belt had only a single industry of the raw-material type, such as lumber mills, food canneries, or smelters (Longview, Washington; San Jose, California; Anaconda, Montana). Because of the need for producing huge quantities of ships and airplanes for a two-ocean war, however, many cities along the Gulf and Pacific coasts have grown rapidly during recent years as centers of industry.

Application of the Three Types of Urban Support

Although examples can be cited illustrating each of the three types of urban support, most American cities partake in varying proportions of all three types. New York City, for example, as the greatest American port is a break-of-bulk point; as the principal center of wholesaling and retailing it is a central-place type; and as the major American center of manufacturing it is a specialized type. The actual distribution and functional classification of cities in the United States, more complex than the simple sum of the three types (Figure 4), has been mapped and described elsewhere in different terms.[2]

The three basic types therefore should not be considered as a rigid framework excluding all accidental establishment, although even fortuitous development of a city becomes part of the general urban-supporting environment. Nor should the urban setting be regarded as static; cities are constantly changing, and they exhibit characteristic lag in adjusting to new conditions.

Ample opportunity exists for use of initiative in strengthening the supporting base of the future city, particularly if account is taken of the basic factors of urban support. Thus a city should examine: (1) its surrounding area to take advantage of changes such as newly discovered resources or crops, (2) its transport in order to adjust properly to new or changed facilities, and (3) its industries in order to benefit from technological advances.

INTERNAL STRUCTURE OF CITIES

Any effective plans for the improvement or rearrangement of the future city must take account of the present pattern of land use within the city, of the factors which have produced this pattern, and of the facilities required by activities localized within particular districts.

Although the internal pattern of each city is unique in its particular combination of details, most American cities have business, industrial, and residential districts. The forces underlying the pattern of land use can be appreciated if attention is focused on three generalizations of arrangement—by concentric zones, sectors, and multiple nuclei.

Concentric Zones

According to the concentric-zone theory, the pattern of growth of the city can best be under-

stood in terms of five concentric zones [3] (Fig. 5).

1. *The central business district.* This is the focus of commercial, social, and civic life, and of transportation. In it is the downtown retail district with its department stores, smart shops, office buildings, clubs, banks, hotels, theaters, museums, and organization headquarters. Encircling the downtown retail district is the wholesale business district.

2. *The zone in transition.* Encircling the downtown area is a zone of residential deterioration. Business and light manufacturing encroach on residential areas characterized particularly by rooming houses. In this zone are the principal slums, with their submerged regions of poverty, degradation, and disease, and their underworlds of vice. In many American cities it has been inhabited largely by colonies of recent immigrants.

3. *Zone of independent workingmen's homes.* This is inhabited by industrial workers who have escaped from the zone in transition but who desire to live within easy access of their work. In many American cities second-generation immigrants are important segments of the population in this area.

4. *The zone of better residences.* This is made up of single-family dwellings, of exclusive "restricted districts," and of highclass apartment buildings.

5. *The commuters' zone.* Often beyond the city limits in suburban areas or in satellite cities, this is a zone of spotty development of high-class residences along lines of rapid travel.

Sectors

The theory of axial development, according to which growth takes place along main transportation routes or along lines of least resistance

---

[2] Chauncy D. Harris, "A Functional Classification of Cities in the United States," *Geographical Review*, XXXIII (January 1943): 85–99.

[3] Ernest W. Burgess, "The Growth of the City," in Robert E. Park, Ernest W. Burgess, and Roderick D. McKenzie (eds.), *The City* (Chicago: University of Chicago Press, 1925), pp. 47–62; and Ernest W. Burgess, "Urban Areas," in T. V. Smith and Leonard D. White, (eds.), *Chicago: An Experiment in Social Science Research*, (Chicago: University of Chicago Press, 1929), pp. 113–38

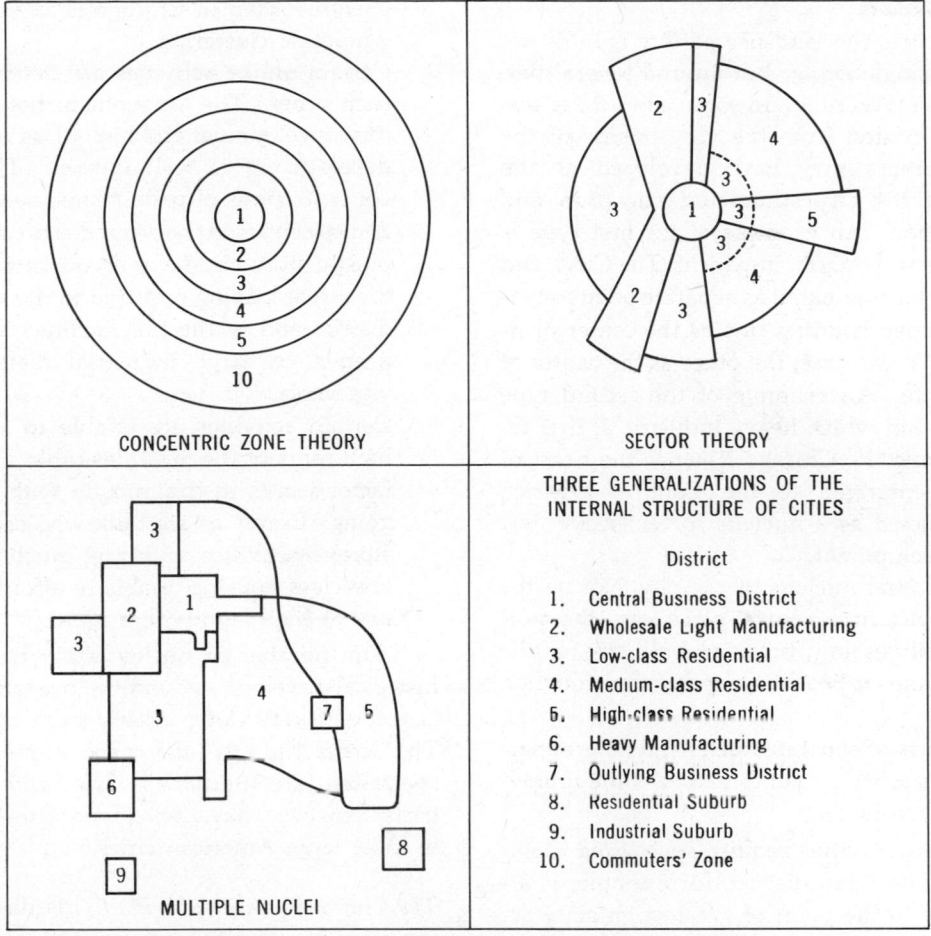

FIGURE 5. Generalizations of Internal Structure of Cities. The concentric-zone theory is a generalization for all cities. The arrangement of the sectors in the sector theory varies from city to city. The diagram for multiple nuclei represents one possible pattern among innumerable variations.

to form a star-shaped city, is refined by Homer Hoyt in his sector theory, which states that growth along a particular axis of transportation usually consists of similar types of land use [4] (Figure 5). The entire city is considered as a circle and the various areas as sectors radiating out from the center of that circle; similar types of land use originate near the center of the circle

and migrate outward toward the periphery. Thus a high-rent residential area in the eastern quadrant of the city would tend to migrate outward, keeping always in the eastern quadrant. A low-quality housing area, if located in the southern quadrant, would tend to extend outward to the very margin of the city in that sector. The migration of high-class residential areas outward along established lines of travel is particularly pronounced on high ground, toward open country, to homes of community leaders, along lines of fastest transportation, and to existing nuclei of buildings or trading centers.

[4] Homer Hoyt, "City Growth and Mortgage Risk," *Insured Mortgage Portfolio*, Vol. I, Nos. 6–10 (December 1936–April 1937), passim; and idem (U. S. Federal Housing Administration), *The Structure and Growth of Residential Neighborhoods in American Cities* (Washington, D. C.: Government Printing Office, 1939), passim.

Multiple Nuclei

In many cities the land-use pattern is built not around a single center but around several discrete nuclei (Figure 5). In some cities these nuclei have existed from the very origins of the city; in others they have developed as the growth of the city stimulated migration and specialization. An example of the first type is Metropolitan London, in which "The City" and Westminster originated as separate points separated by open country, one as the center of finance and commerce, the other as the center of political life. An example of the second type is Chicago, in which heavy industry, at first localized along the Chicago River in the heart of the city, migrated to the Calumet District, where it acted as a nucleus for extensive new urban development.

The initial nucleus of the city may be the retail district in a central-place city, the port or rail facilities in a break-of-bulk city, or the factory, mine, or beach in a specialized-function city.

The rise of separate nuclei and differentiated districts reflects a combination of the following four factors:

1. Certain activities require specialized facilities. The retail district, for example, is attached to the point of greatest intracity accessibility, the port district to suitable water front, manufacturing districts to large blocks of land and water or rail connection, and so on.

2. Certain like activities group together because they profit from cohesion. [5] The clustering of industrial cities has already been noted above under "Cities as concentration points for specialized services." Retail districts benefit from grouping which increases the concentration of potential customers and makes possible comparison shopping. Financial and office-building districts depend upon facility of communications among offices within the district. The Mer-

chandise Mart of Chicago is an example of wholesale clustering.

3. Certain unlike activities are detrimental to each other. The antagonism between factory development and high-class residential development is well known. The heavy concentrations of pedestrians, automobiles, and streetcars in the retail district are antagonistic both to the railroad facilities and the street loading required in the wholesale district and to the rail facilities and space needed by large industrial districts, and vice versa.

4. Certain activities are unable to afford the high rents of the most desirable sites. This factor works in conjunction with the foregoing. Examples are bulk wholesaling and storage activities requiring much room, or low-class housing unable to afford the luxury of high land with a view.

The number of nuclei which result from historical development and the operation of localization forces varies greatly from city to city. The larger the city, the more numerous and specialized are the nuclei. The following districts, however, have developed around nuclei in most large American cities.

The Central Business District. This district is at the focus of intracity transportation facilities by sidewalk, private car, bus, streetcar, subway, and elevated. Because of asymmetrical growth of most large cities, it is generally not now in the areal center of the city but actually near one edge, as in the case of lake-front, riverside, or even inland cities; examples are Chicago, St. Louis, and Salt Lake City. Because established internal transportation lines converge on it, however, it is the point of most convenient access from all parts of the city, and the point of highest land values. The retail district, at the point of maximum accessibility, is attached to the sidewalk; only pedestrian or mass-transportation movement can concentrate the large numbers of customers necessary to support department stores, variety stores, and clothing shops, which are characteristic of the district.

---

[5] Exceptions are service-type establishments such as some grocery stores, dry cleaners, and gasoline stations.

In small cities financial institutions and office buildings are intermingled with retail shops, but in large cities the financial district is separate, near but not at the point of greatest intracity facility. Its point of attachment is the elevator, which permits three-dimensional access among offices, whose most important locational factor is accessibility to other offices rather than to the city as a whole. Government buildings also are commonly near but not in the center of the retail district. In most cities a separate "automobile row" has arisen on the edge of the central business district, in cheaper rent areas along one or more major highways; its attachment is to the highway itself.

The Wholesale and Light-Manufacturing District. This district is conveniently within the city but near the focus of extracity transportation facilities. Wholesale houses, while deriving some support from the city itself, serve principally a tributary region reached by railroad and motor truck. They are, therefore, concentrated along railroad lines, usually adjacent to (but not surrounding) the central business district. Many types of light manufacturing which do not require specialized buildings are attracted by the facilities of this district or similar districts: good rail and road transportation, available loft buildings, and proximity to the markets and labor of the city itself.

The Heavy Industrial District. This is near the present or former outer edge of the city. Heavy industries require large tracts of space, often beyond any available in sections already subdivided into blocks and streets. They also require good transportation, either rail or water. With the development of belt lines and switching yards, sites on the edge of the city may have better transportation service than those near the center. In Chicago about a hundred industries are in a belt three miles long, adjacent to the clearing freight yards on the southwestern edge of the city. Furthermore, the noise of boiler works, the odors of stockyards, the waste disposal problems of smelters and iron and steel

mills, the fire hazards of petroleum refineries, and the space and transportation needs which interrupt streets and accessibility—all these favor the growth of heavy industry away from the main center of the large city. The Calumet District of Chicago, the New Jersey marshes near New York City, the Lea marshes near London, and the St. Denis district of Paris are examples of such districts. The stockyards of Chicago, in spite of their odors and size, have been engulfed by urban growth and are now far from the edge of the city. They form a nucleus of heavy industry within the city but not near the center, which has blighted the adjacent residential area, the "Back-of-the-Yards" district.

The Residential District. In general, high-class districts are likely to be on well-drained, high land and away from nuisances such as noise, odors, smoke, and railroad lines. Low-class districts are likely to arise near factories and railroad districts, wherever located in the city. Because of the obsolescence of structures, the older inner margins of residential districts are fertile fields for invasion by groups unable to pay high rents. Residential neighborhoods have some measure of cohesiveness. Extreme cases are the ethnically segregated groups, which cluster together although including members in many economic groups; Harlem is an example.

Minor Nuclei. These include cultural centers, parks, outlying business districts, and small industrial centers. A university may form a nucleus for a quasi-independent community; examples are the University of Chicago, the University of California, and Harvard University. Parks and recreation areas occupying former wasteland too rugged or wet for housing may form nuclei for high-class residential areas; examples are Rock Creek Park in Washington and Hyde Park in London. Outlying business districts may in time become major centers. Many small institutions and individual light manufacturing plants, such as bakeries, dispersed throughout the city may never become nuclei of differentiated districts.

Suburbs and Satellite. Suburbs, either residential or industrial, are characteristic of most of the larger American cities.[6] The rise of the automobile and the improvement of certain suburban commuter rail lines in a few of the largest cities have stimulated suburbanization. Satellites differ from suburbs in that they are separated from the central city by many miles and in general have little daily commuting to or from the central city, although economic activities of the satellite are closely geared to those of the central city. Thus Gary may be considered a suburb but Elgin and Joliet are satellites of Chicago.

Appraisal of Land-Use Patterns

Most cities exhibit not only a combination of the three types of urban support, but also aspects of the three generalizations of the land-use pattern. An understanding of both is useful in appraising the future prospects of the whole city and the arrangement of its parts.

As a general picture subject to modification because of topography, transportation, and previous land use, the concentric-zone aspect has merit. It is not a rigid pattern, inasmuch as growth or arrangement often reflects expansion within sectors or development around separate nuclei.

The sector aspect has been applied particularly to the outward movement of residential districts. Both the concentric-theory and the sector theory emphasize the general tendency of central residential areas to decline in value as new construction takes place on the outer edges; the sector theory is, however, more discriminating in its analysis of that movement.

---

[6] Chauncy D. Harris, "Suburbs," *American Journal of Sociology*, XLIX (July 1943): 6.

Both the concentric zone, as a general pattern, and the sector aspect, as applied primarily to residential patterns, assume (although not explicitly) that there is but a single urban core around which land use is arranged symmetrically in either concentric or radial patterns. In broad theoretical terms such an assumption may be valid, inasmuch as the handicap of distance alone would favor as much concentration as possible in a small central core. Because of the actual physical impossibility of such concentration and the existence of separating factors, however, separate nuclei arise. The specific separating factors are not only high rent in the core, which can be afforded by few activities, but also the natural attachment of certain activities to extraurban transport, space, or other facilities, and the advantages of the separation of unlike activities and the concentration of like functions.

The constantly changing pattern of land use poses many problems. Near the core, land is kept vacant or retained in antisocial slum structures in anticipation of expansion of higher-rent activities. The hidden costs of slums to the city in poor environment for future citizens and excessive police, fire, and sanitary protection underlie the argument for a subsidy to remove the blight. The transition zone is not everywhere a zone of deterioration with slums, however, as witness the rise of high-class apartment development near the urban core in the Gold Coast of Chicago or Park Avenue in New York City. On the fringe of the city, overambitious subdividing results in unused land to be crossed by urban services such as sewers and transportation. Separate political status of many suburbs results in a lack of civic responsibility for the problems and expenses of the city in which the suburbanites work.

18

BRIAN J. L. BERRY

Internal Structure of the City

I. INTRODUCTION: EXTERNAL DETERMINANTS OF INTERNAL STRUCTURE

Cities are the central elements in spatial organization of regional, national, and supranational socioeconomies by virtue of the interregional organization in a total "ecological field" of the functions they perform.[1] In a specialized society economic activities are undertaken by design, or survive in the market place, at those locations which afford the greatest competitive advantage. Among these activities, those most efficiently performed in limited local concentrations provide the basic support for cities. The location theorist commonly classifies locally concentrated economic activities into those which are raw material oriented, those located at points which are intermediate between raw materials and markets, and those which are market oriented.[2] Raw material orientation includes direct exploitation of resources and the processing of raw materials, and its character is that of the developed resource endowment of different places. Activities in intermediate locations are usually of a processing kind, involved in intermediate and final processing and transformation of raw materials, and most frequently locate at some favorable spot on the transport network, such as an assembly point, a gateway, a break-of-bulk point, or a port. Market-oriented activities may be secondary

(for example, where there is a weight gain involved in the final processing of raw materials on intermediates prior to delivery), but are dominantly tertiary, concerned with the direct service of the consuming population through wholesale, retail, and service functions. The consuming population comprises the workers in the other specialized activities, of course, plus the local population supported by the tertiary trades. Thus, market orientation implies a location best suited to serve demands created by prior stages of the productive process. The three classic principles of urban location derive from the three types of locational orientation of economic activities: cities as the sites of specialized functions; cities as the expressions of the layout and character of transport networks; and cities as central places.[3] All three principles, or some combination of them, may operate in the case of any particular city. However, whereas all cities will have a central business district providing retail and service functions to the city and surrounding populations, the role of the other two principles will vary greatly from one city to another.

In the internal structure of cities these specialized functions have priority. The central business district is a point of focus about which land uses and densities, the spatial patterning

---

[1] J. R. P. Friedmann and W. Alonso, *Regional Development and Planning* (1964); Pappenfort, "The Ecological Field and the Metropolitan Community," *American Journal of Sociology,* 64: 380–385 (1959).

[2] W. Isard, *Location and Space Economy* (1956).

Reprinted, with permission, from a symposium, Urban Problems and Prospects appearing in *Law and Contemporary Problems* (Vol. 30, No. 1, Winter 1965) published by the Duke University School of Law, Durham, North Carolina. Copyright, 1965, by Duke University.

[3] Harris and Ullman, "The Nature of Cities," *Annals* 242: 7–17 (1945). [No. 17 in this volume.]

of the urban population, subsidiary retail and service locations, transportation and commuting patterns, and the like, have evolved. When other specialized activities are performed, they create supplementary or additional nodes. Thus, cities are supported by "basic" activities ("staples") whose locations are determined exogenously to the city by comparative advantage in larger regional, national, and international economic systems. These always include the central business district, the focus not only of the city itself but also of its tributary region, and may include other specialized activities. The skeleton of the city comprises the locations of these basic activities, plus the urban transport network. Flesh is provided by residential site selection of workers with respect to the skeleton, and blood comes from the daily ebb and flow of commuters. Further patterning is provided by the orientation of subsidiaries and business services to the basic activities, and by local shopping facilities to the workers. Shopping trips create another ebb and flow. Further "second-" and "third-round" effects can be described, but these follow logically from the first. The question to be answered here is that of the nature and bases of residential, socioeconomic, and retail patterns within cities. Because the discussion is concerned with the internal structure of the city it thus perforce takes as given the exogenously determined skeleton. Further, it will focus upon the flesh rather than the blood, although the latter is implicit in the discussion of the former.

II. THE RESIDENTIAL PATTERN: URBAN DENSITIES

A simple expression summarizes the population density pattern of cities:

$$d_x = d_0 c^{-bx}, \qquad (1)$$

where d_x is the population density d at distance x from the city center, d_0 is density at the city center, e is the natural logarithmic base, and b is the density gradient. The "city center" is, of course, the central business district, so that when the natural logarithm of population density of small areas within the city is calculated, along with their distance from the central

business district, and a scatter diagram is constructed with distance along the abscissa, the points in the diagram lie around a straight line with downward slope b, or

$$ln \cdot d_x = ln \cdot d_0 - bx. \qquad (2)$$

The gradient b may be considered an index of the "compactness" of the city, just as differences in central density d_0 index the overall level of "crowding." Equation (2) has been shown to be universally applicable to cities regardless of time or place.[4] Why should this be so? Muth has shown how this negative exponential decline of population densities with increasing distance from the city center is a condition of locational equilibrium which stems logically from the operation of a competitive housing market.[5] Seidman has shown it to be a natural consequence of Alonso's locational theory of land use.[6] The theoretical bases of the empirical regularity are thus readily available.

The density gradient b, like the densities it indexes, also shows consistent behavior. For example, in any country at a particular point in time, it falls consistently with city size as follows:

$$ln \cdot b_j = ln \cdot P_0 - c \cdot (ln \cdot P_j), \qquad (3)$$

so that cities have experienced progressive "decompaction" with increasing size. Further, since in the United States, recent expected growth of metropolitan areas between two time periods t and $t + 1$ is a constant proportion of size[7] such that

---

[4] Clark, "Urban Population Densities," *Journal of the Royal Statistical Society*, 114: 490–496 (1951).

[5] R. Muth, *The Spatial Pattern of Residential Land Use in Cities* (in preparation).

[6] D. E. Seidman, *An Operational Model of the Residential Land Market* (1964).

[7] This "law of proportionate effect" may be seen by plotting populations of U.S. cities in 1950 against their populations in 1960. The scatter of points is linear and homoscedastic with a slope of +1.0 on double logarithmic paper. Satisfaction of this assumption means that in steady-state the distribution of towns by size will be lognormal so that Zipf's rank size rule for city sizes holds: $P_r = P_1/r^q$ or $Log \cdot P_r = Log \cdot P_1 - q \cdot Log \cdot r$. In these equations P_r is the population of the city of rank, r, P_1 is thus the largest city, and q is an exponent.

$$ln \cdot P_{t+1} = k + ln \cdot P_t, \qquad (4)$$

which further implies exponential growth of population with time

$$P_t = P_0 e^{kt}, \qquad (5)$$

then

$$b_t = b_0 e^{-ckt}, \qquad (6)$$

which states that the density gradient diminishes through time in a negative exponential manner, which is the case.[8]

Newling has shown, additionally, that the two generalizations that population density declines exponentially with increasing distance from the city center and that the density gradient itself falls through time in a negative exponential manner, together lead to a third regularity, which he calls the "rule of intra-urban allometric growth." [9] This is that the rate of growth of density is a positive exponential function of distance from the city center:

$$(l + r_x) = (l + r_0)e^{gx} \qquad (7)$$

where r_x is the percentage rate of growth of density at distance x, r_0 is percentage growth at the center, and g is the growth gradient, measuring the rate of change of the rate of growth as distance from the center of the city increases. He goes on to show that since both density and the rate of growth are functions of distance from the city center, the rate of growth may be expressed as a direct function of density:

$$(l + r_x) = mD^{-q}$$

where r_x is as above, m is a constant, D is initial density and q relates the rate of change of the rate of growth to the rate of change of density. As density increases, the rate of growth drops.

Moreover, Newling argues for the existence of a "critical density" above which growth becomes negative, i.e., population declines. In several cases he shows a convergence upon 30,000 persons per square mile as this critical density, and in one study he concludes:[10]

> The inverse relationship between population density and the rate of growth, the identification of a critical density, and the observation that negative growth, occurring as it does above the critical density, is not solely attributable to competition between commercial and residential use of land, all lead one to speculate that perhaps there is indeed some optimum urban population density to exceed which inevitably incurs social costs. We may speculate that certain events in the history of the city will cause this optimum to be exceeded (for example, heavy immigration without a commensurate expansion of the housing stock and supply of social overhead capital), with deleterious consequences for the areas concerned (such as blight, crime and delinquency, and other social pathological conditions) and leading to an eventual decline in the population of the affected areas. . . .

If this is so, then consistent relationships are available between size of city and the pattern of population densities within cities, between growth of the urban population and change of densities within. Further, there is the strong suggestion that this chain provides direct links between an overall urbanization process and the occurrence of pathological social conditions in particular parts of particular cities.

III. SOCIAL AND ECONOMIC PATTERNING OF THE RESIDENTS

The generalizations in the preceding section are strong. Equally strong generalizations are now possible concerning the social patterning of the urban residents who live at the density patterns in the changing ways already described.

There has been a long tradition of research by sociologists, geographers, and economists dealing with the social and economic characteristics of urban neighborhoods. Among the

---

[8] Berry, Simmons & Tennant, "Urban Population Densities: Structure and Change," *Geographical Review*, 53: 389–405 (1963). [No. 11 in this volume.]

[9] Newling, "Urban Growth and Spatial Structure: Mathematical Models and Empirical Evidence" (processed, Cornell University, 1965). [No. 12 in this volume.]

[10] Ibid.

earliest descriptive generalizations were those of Hurd, who related neighborhood characteristics, especially income and rentals, to two simultaneous patterns of growth which he called *central* and *axial* growth.[11] Later, Burgess emphasized the importance of outward growth from the center which caused concentric zonations of neighborhoods.[12] Change occurred by the outward movement of the wealthier to the periphery, and the continued expansion of inner zones upon the outer in a process of invasion and succession by the lower status groups living closer to the city center. Hoyt, on the other hand, emphasized the significance of axial growth when he developed his sector concept.[13] According to this notion, status differences established around the city center are projected outwards along the same sector as the city grows, thus creating a wedge-shaped distribution of neighborhoods by type with the higher status groups following scenic amenities and higher ground. In addition, the literature of sociology has been replete with studies of the segregation of ethnic groups in particular localities conforming neither to the concentric nor to the axial schemes.

Considerable debate has taken place about the relative merits of each of these models. A succession of large-scale factor analytic studies conducted since the end of the Second World War now make it possible to state definitively that the three models are independent, additive contributors to the total socioeconomic structuring of city neighborhoods. Factor analysis is a multivariate procedure which permits a mass of data (an example would be the 100+ census characteristics of each of the 800+ census tracts of Chicago) to be examined to determine exactly how many dimensions of variation are expressed by it. In each of the studies the answer is the same: there are just three dimensions of variation. These are (a) the axial variation of neighborhoods by socioeconomic rank; (b) the concentric variation of neighborhoods according to family structure; and (c) the localized segregation of particular ethnic groups.

Neighborhood characteristics involving educational levels, type of occupation, income, value of housing, and the like, are all highly correlated, as they should be, for undoubtedly they are also functionally related. Each varies across the city in the same way: according to sectors. High status sectors search and follow particular amenities desired for housing, such as view, higher ground, and so on. Lower status sectors follow lower lying, industrial-transportation arteries that radiate from the central business district and which, together with that district, form the exogenously determined skeleton of the city. This is consistent with the idea, also, that the lower the income the closer is home to work in the contemporary American city.

Conversely, the age structure of neighborhoods changes concentrically with increasing distance from the city center, along with age of housing, densities, existence of multiple unit structures, incidence of ownership by residents, participation of women in the labor force, and the like. Thus, at the edge of the city are newer, owned, single-family homes, in which reside larger families with younger children than nearer the city center, and where the wife stays at home. Conversely, the apartment complexes nearer the city center have smaller, older families, fewer children, and are more likely to be rentals; in addition, larger proportions of the women will be found to work. This "family structure" pattern is consistent with the ideas of Burgess, and has been called by sociologists the "urbanism-familism" scale.

Thirdly, particular ethnic groups will be found to reside in segregated parts of the city. The most obvious case of segregation today in the American city is that of the Negro, although every new migrant group has also experienced this pattern of living. Along with segregation

---

[11] Richard M. Hurd, *Principles of City Land Values* (1903).
[12] Burgess, "The Growth of the City," in Robert E. Park, *The City* (1925).
[13] Homer Hoyt, *The Structure and Growth of Residential Neighborhoods in American Cities* (1939).

go such other variables as lack of household amenities, deterioration of housing, overcrowding, and the like.

If the concentric and axial schemes are overlaid on any city, the resulting cells will contain neighborhoods remarkably uniform in their social and economic characteristics. Around any concentric band communities will vary in their income and other characteristics, but will have much the same density, ownership, and family patterns. Along each axis communities will have relatively uniform economic characteristics, and each axis will vary outwards in the same way according to family structure. Thus, a system of polar coordinates originating at the central business district is adequate to describe most of the socioeconomic characteristics of city neighborhoods. The exception is in patterns of segregation, which are geographically similar to the particular city, although segregation is a phenomenon which is found in them all. The three classic principles of internal structure of cities are thus independent, additive descriptions of the social and economic character of neighborhoods in relation to each other and to the whole. Although it has yet to be done, it should not be difficult to write the transformation equations from d_x in equation (1), to place the Burgess scheme consistently in the framework of the previous discussions of population density. Addition of an angular specification would then permit use of polar coordinates to specify more fully social and economic conditions. One then speculates whether Newling's constraint leading to negative growth rates is the constraint which is imposed by segregation of new migrant groups into limited areas at high densities ultimately crossing the critical "density threshold." If this is so, then it is possible to package much of the literature concerning social pathology into the same whole, with at least the first contacts made with processes of change in the city and the relationship of these processes to change in the system of cities, and with the particular form in the particular city prescribed by the exogenously determined skeleton of central business district, basic industry, and transport system.

IV.   SERVICES FOR THE RESIDENTS: LOCAL BUSINESS

The central business district provides a range of goods and services for the entire urban population and for the larger tributary region served by the city. In addition, a system of smaller business centers exists within the city to serve the city population with the commodities they require on a weekly or monthly basis. Such purely internal or endogenous business appears even in small towns of less than 1,000 population. It does not begin to assume any identifiable structure until the level of county seats, however, and a variety of internal forms is only clearly distinguishable in the cities which serve as centers for multi-county "functional economic areas." At this stage the structural differentiation of centers and ribbons is clear. Ribbons follow the major section and half-section streets and the radial highways, performing a variety of service functions (building materials and supplies, household requirements), automobile oriented activities (gas, repair, parts), and with many large single-standing, space-consuming stores (discounters, furniture, appliances), in addition to being interspersed with convenience shops (food, drugs, cleaners) for adjacent neighborhoods. Certain stretches of ribbon are devoted to the activities of "specialized functional areas" such as automobile row. At the major and minor intersections of the street system are business centers, differentiated from the adjacent ribbons by the functions they perform, the ways consumers shop in them, and by land values. The centers provide both convenience and such shopping goods as food, drugs, clothing, shoes, and luxuries. Consumers generally shop on foot from store to store, in contrast to their single-purpose trips to ribbon establishments. Land values within the city fall with increasing distance from the city center, but commercial values add extra texture. The ribbons create ridges that rise above the adjacent residential areas. Steeply-rising cones at the intersections of ridges clearly indicate the location and extent of centers. Four levels of outlying centers have been identified beneath the central business district: neighborhood and community shopping centers at the convenience level, and shoppers' and regional centers of a larger kind. The differentiation between these levels is made in terms of the number and variety of functions performed, in the size of trade area served, and the like.[14]

It is axiomatic that retail and service activities are consumer-oriented, since internal business has developed entirely to serve the population residing within the city. Consistent with the earlier sections of this paper, it is also possible to place internal business provision within the same frame. Consider a city divided by the concentric-axial scheme described above, and let R indicate the total retail and service provision of any of the cells defined, with P representing total population of the cell, D the population density, F an index of its family structure, and S an index of its social rank,[15] then

$$R = sP^uD^vF^wS^z \qquad (8)$$

which yields an extremely close fit in every city studied. Moreover, the provision of local business, and local business change, may clearly be related back to the socioeconomic pattern of the city. Similar expressions may be developed for ribbons and centers separately, although in the case of centers certain problems emerge concerning the use of arbitrary cells instead of the market areas of the centers as the units of observation,[16] even though a properly drawn set of circles and radii will, by their inter-

sections, locate the outlying business centers of many cities.

As in the case of socioeconomic structure, however, segregation creates problems for generalization. In Chicago, for example, retail systems assume not one, but two equilibrium positions.[17] In segregated non-white residential areas there is a two-level hierarchy of business centers comprising the neighborhood convenience type and the smaller shoppers' goods type, whereas in the rest of the city a four-level hierarchy of outlying centers exists. All retailing is experiencing changes due to increased scale of retailing, increasing consumer mobility, and rising real incomes. Yet as the non-white residential area expands outwards, still another element of retail change is added. Simply, neighborhood transition means loss of markets, since real income among the non-white population is approximately one-third lower than that of the population displaced. The effects are felt in several stages:

(a) Anticipation of neighborhood transition. In this phase the normal replacement of businesses which fail, or which close because the businessman retires or dies, ceases. Vacancy rates begin to rise. Also, a "maintenance gap" appears because property owners, increasingly uncertain about prospective revenues, reduce normal maintenance expenditures. Dilapidation grows.

(b) During turnover. Demands drop precipitously, especially for higher quality goods, and the specialty shops in the larger business centers fail. Vacancies in centers rise to levels as high as one-third to one-half of the stores.

(c) Stabilization phase. The neighborhood settles down into its lower income character. Because incomes and revenues are lower, it is almost impossible to eliminate the effects of the earlier maintenance gap, and so a general run-down appearance persists. Rents in the business centers drop and activities from the ribbons and new businesses directed at the changed market move in and fill up the centers

---

[14] Brian J. L. Berry, *Commercial Structure and Commercial Blight* (1963).

[15] The social rank and family structure indexes will generally be factor scores produced in a factor analytic study of social and economic differentiation of the city. Brian J. L. Berry, *The Changing Retail Structure of Northeastern Illinois* (1965).

[16] Berry, "The Retail Component of the Urban Model," *Journal of the American Institute of Planners*, 31 (1965).

[17] Berry, op. cit. supra note 14.

once again. Vacancies mount in the abandoned ribbons, settling down in excess of twenty per cent of the stores, but concentrated in the older buildings which, through lack of use, deteriorate more. Zones of segregated housing are thus criss-crossed with ribbons of unwanted, blighted, commercial property. Much that is critical to an understanding of business within the city thus depends less upon the structuring implicit in use of a model such as equation (8) than upon the existence and nature of segregation in the housing market.

CONCLUSION

Although the skeleton of the city is determined by broader regional and supraregional forces, the flesh shows certain simple systematic regularities which are tightly knit into a locational system of simultaneous concentric and axial dimensions. Segregated housing patterns are responsible for the current inability to develop a single model of the whole covering both spatial structure and change.

19

HOMER HOYT

Recent Distortions of the Classical Models of Urban Structure

Since the general patterns of city structure were described by Burgess in 1925[1] and 1929[2] and by myself in 1939[3] there has been a tremendous growth of urban population, not only in the United States, but throughout the world. To what extent has this factor of growth changed the form or shape of urban communities?

While the Burgess concentric circle theory was based on a study of Chicago—a city on a flat prairie, cut off on the east by Lake Michigan

From *Land Economics*, Vol. XL, No. 2 (May 1964) (© 1964 by the Regents of the University of Wisconsin), pp. 199–212.

[1] R. E. Park and E. W. Burgess, *The City* (Chicago: University of Chicago Press, 1925), pp. 47–62.

[2] E. W. Burgess, "Urban Areas," in T. V. Smith and L. D. White (eds.), *Chicago: An Experiment in Social Science Research* (Chicago: University of Chicago Press, 1929), pp. 114–123.

[3] Homer Hoyt, *The Structure and Growth of Residential Neighborhoods in American Cities* (Washington, D.C.: Federal Housing Administration, 1939).

—and patterns of growth in other cities would be influenced by their unique topography, his formulation had a widespread application to American cities of 1929. Burgess made a brilliant and vivid contribution to urban sociology and urban geography which inspired the present writer as well as the sociologists and geographers who made subsequent studies of city patterns.

In the era of the Greek cities in the fifth century B.C. a city was considered an artistic creation which should maintain its static form without change. To take care of population growth, the Greeks sent out colonies, like swarms of bees, to found new cities on the ideal model. Plato said that the ideal city should not contain over 5,000 inhabitants although he himself was the product of an Athens with a 250,-000 population. In the Middle Ages most continental European cities were surrounded by walls and many, like Milan, Italy preserved an unaltered form for hundreds of years.

In the United States, however, there has been a tremendous growth of metropolitan areas since 1930. The number of large urban concentrations with a population of a million or more has increased from 10 to 22. The population in the 140 metropolitan districts was 57,602,865 in 1930, of which 40,343,442 were in central cities and 17,259,423 were outside these cities. In 1940 in these 140 metropolitan districts the population was 62,965,773 of which 42,796,170 were in central cities and 20,169,603 were outside these cities.[4] After World War II, in the rapidly growing decade from 1950 to 1960, the population of 216 Standard Metropolitan Areas grew from 91,568,113 to 115,796,- 265. Most of the growth in the past census decade was in the suburbs, but central city population grew from 52,648,185 to 58,441,995, a gain of only 11 percent, while the population outside central cities increased from 38,919,928 to 57,354,270, a rise of 47.4 percent.[5] The population in the central areas of 12 of the largest American metropolitan regions actually declined in this decade from 22,694,799 to 21,843,214, a loss of 3.8 percent.[6] The population loss in the central cores of these cities was much greater, since some central cities still had room for new growth within the other edges of their boundaries. There was also a displacement of white population by non-white population. From 1930 to 1950 the non-white population in 168 SMA's increased from 4,913,703 to 8,250,210.[7] The chief gain was in the central cities where the non-white population rose

from 3,624,504 in 1930 to 6,411,158 in 1950. From 1950 to 1960 the non-white population in central cities increased to 10,030,314. The non-white population in SMA's outside central cities was only 2,720,513 in 1960. On the other hand while 43,142,399 white persons lived in central cities of SMA's in 1960, 49,081,533 white persons lived in SMA's outside the central cities. While the central city population in these 12 SMA's was declining, population outside these central cities rose from 13,076,711 in 1950 to 20,534,833 in 1960, a gain of 57 percent.

In 1960 the population of the areas outside the central cities in these 12 great metropolitan areas almost equalled the population in the central areas and by 1964 the population in the areas outside the central cities has certainly surpassed the number in the central city.

While the cities of 50,000 population and over have been growing at a rapid rate in the past decade, the smaller cities with less than 50,000 population have been increasing in numbers at a slower pace, or from 27.4 million in 1950 to 29.4 million in 1960.[8] The smaller cities thus would be enabled to maintain their static form with the growth element chiefly affecting the larger metropolitan areas as a result of the shift in population growth from the center to the suburbs and a change in the racial composition of many central cities.

Not merely population growth, but a rise in per capita national income from $757 in 1940 to $2,500 in 1963, with a greater proportionate increase in the middle class incomes, an increase in the number of private passenger automobiles from 22,793,000 in 1933 to 70 million in 1963, and the building of expressways connecting cities and belt highways around cities, were all dynamic factors changing the shape and form of cities since the description of city patterns in 1925 and 1939. Let us examine the different concentric circles or zones or sectors described in the books over a quarter of a century ago and see how the principles then enunciated have been changed by the growth factors.

---

[4] United States Census of Population 1940, Vol. I, Table 18, p. 61.

[5] United States Department of Commerce, Bureau of the Census, *Standard Metropolitan Areas in the United States as Defined October 18, 1963*, Series P–23, No. 10, December 5, 1963. (Newark, New Jersey is included in New York Metropolitan Area).

[6] Baltimore, Boston, Chicago, Cincinnati, Cleveland, Detroit, Minneapolis-St. Paul, New York, Philadelphia, St. Louis, San Francisco-Oakland and Washington, D.C.

[7] United States Census of Population, 1930, 1940, 1950.

THE CENTRAL BUSINESS DISTRICT: FINANCIAL AND OFFICE ZONE AND THE RETAIL SHOPPING ZONE

In 1929 Burgess wrote: "Zone I: The Central Business District. At the center of the city as the focus of its commercial, social and civic life is situated the Central Business District. The heart of this district is the downtown retail district with its department stores, its smart shops, its office buildings, its clubs, its banks, its hotels, its theatres, its museums, and its headquarters of economic, social, civic and political life." [9] Burgess thus accurately described the central business district of Chicago and most large American cities as of the date he was writing (1929), a description which would hold true in the main to the end of World War II. Since 1946, extraordinary changes in the American economy have occurred which have had a pronounced effect on the structure of the downtown business districts of American cities.

Burgess had noted in 1929 the existence of local business centers, or satellite "loops" in the zone of better residences: "The typical constellation of business and recreation areas includes a bank, one or more United Cigar Stores, a drug store, a high class restaurant, an automobile display row, and a so-called 'wonder' motion picture theatre." [10] I also had noted, in 1939, the extensions of stringlike commercial developments beyond the central business districts, and the rise of satellite business centers: "Again, satellite business centers have developed independently beyond the central business district, or on the city's periphery. These are usually located at or near suburban railway stations, elevated or subway stations, intersecting points between radical and crosstown street car lines, or intersecting points of main automobile highways." [11]

In 1964, the central retail district, with its large department stores still remains the largest shopping district in its metropolitan area, and all the outlying business districts at street car intersections, subway or suburban railway stations are still operating, but their dominating position has been greatly weakened by the construction, since 1946, of an estimated 8,300 planned shopping districts, with free automobile parking, in the suburbs or on the periphery of the central city mass. The tremendous growth of the suburban population, which moved to areas beyond mass transit lines, facilitated by the universal ownership of the automobile, and decline in the numbers and relative incomes of the central city population, invited and made possible this new development in retail shopping.

The regional shopping center—with major department stores, variety, apparel and local convenience stores, practically duplicating the stores in the downtown retail area and built on large tracts of land entirely away from street cars, subways, elevated or railroad stations— was virtually unknown prior to World War II. The first of these centers, Country Club Plaza in Kansas City, had been established in 1925 and there were a few others with department stores and a number of neighborhood centers on commercial streets, with parking areas in front of the stores, but the wave of the future was not discerned by planners or land economists before 1946.

There are many types of these new planned centers; the regional center on 50 to 100 acres of land with at least one major department store; the community center on 20 to 30 acres of land with a junior department store as the leading tenant; and the neighborhood center with a supermarket, drug store and local convenience shops on five to 10 acres of land. But the type having the greatest impact on the downtown stores is the regional center which directly competes with downtown in the sale of general merchandise.

General merchandise stores, that is, department and variety stores, had long been the dominating magnets and attractions of the

---

[8] Harold M. Mayer, "Economic Prospects for the Smaller City," *Public Management* (August 1963).

[9] Ernest W. Burgess, "Urban Areas," op. cit.

[10] Ibid.

[11] Hoyt, op. cit. p. 20.

central retail areas. In this field the CBD stores had almost a monopoly in most cities prior to 1920 and even held a dominating position after the establishment of some outlying department stores at street car intersections or subway stations in Chicago and New York. There had been for years neighborhood grocery stores, drug stores and even small apparel and dry goods stores and some variety stores outside the central business district but the department store sales of the CBD's were probably 90 percent or more of the total department store volume of the entire metropolitan area.

In 1958 the central general merchandise stores, chiefly department stores, in the largest cities of a million population and over, had a lower sales volume than the aggregate of the sales of department stores in all the shopping centers outside of the CBD, or $3.6 billion compared to $5.65 billion, as Table 1 shows. There were 125 regional shopping centers in 1958 but many more have been completed since that date and the 1963 United States Retail Census of Shopping Districts will undoubtedly show a still greater increase in the department store sales outside of the CBD.

In 94 metropolitan areas with a population of 100,000 and over and total population of 91,937,103 in 1960, dollar sales outside the CBD's had increased by 53.8 percent, but in the CBD's only 3.4 percent. There was an actual decline in general merchandise sales from 1954 to 1958 in the CBD's of Los Angeles, Chicago, Philadelphia, Detroit, Boston, St. Louis, Washington, D.C., Cleveland, Baltimore, Milwaukee and Kansas City.

These new planned shopping districts, with their ample parking areas, cover more ground than the combined areas of the CBD's in all American cities. I have calculated that there were 30,460 acres or 47.5 square miles in the central business districts of the standard metropolitan areas in the United States in 1960, compared with 33,600 acres or 52.5 square miles in all types of new planned centers.[12] Since 1960, however, many new planned centers have been built and there are now probably 150 regional shopping centers. In 1964 the ground space occupied by these centers, as well as that of the many new discount houses with large parking areas, has considerably increased the space occupied by shopping centers as compared with 1960.

In contrast to the tremendous growth of the planned shopping districts, there has been very limited building of new retail stores in downtown areas; the notable exceptions being Midtown Plaza in Rochester, New York; the redevelopment of the business center of New Haven, Connecticut with new department stores, offices and garages, connected by a new highway to the existing expressway; the location of new Sears Roebuck and Dayton depart-

[12] Homer Hoyt, "Changing Patterns of Land Values," *Land Economics* (May 1960), p. 115.

TABLE 1.   General Merchandise Sales in CBD's by Metropolitan Area Size Groups

| Metropolitan Area Size | Population | (Thousands of Dollars) | | | | Percent Increase 1954–1958 | |
| | | 1958 | | 1954 | | | |
		In CBD	Outside CBD	In CBD	Outside CBD	In CBD	Outside CBD
1,000,000 and Over	61,582,070	$3,577,169	$5,652,995	$3,522,089	$3,837,350	1.6	47.3
500,000–999,000	17,021,848	1,422,369	1,151,601	1,387,056	618,203	4.0	86.3
250,000–499,000	10,491,540	928,358	513,668	849,474	311,573	9.3	64.9
100,000–249,000	2,841,645	279,452	111,774	263,530	62,817	6.0	77.9
Total	91,937,103	$6,227,348	$7,430,038	$6,022,149	$4,829,943	3.4	53.8

Homer Hoyt, "Sales in Leading Shopping Centers and Shopping Districts in the United States," *Urban Land* (Sept. 1961).

ment stores in central St. Paul; and the erection of garages for department stores in other cities.

Office Buildings

Office building expansion, unlike retail stores, bears no direct relation to population growth but depends entirely on the extent to which a city becomes an international or regional office management or financial center. Generalization therefore cannot be made about office buildings which would apply to all cities since the number of square feet of office space per capita in the metropolitan area varies from 2.2 square feet in San Diego to 7.5 square feet in Chicago, 16 square feet in New York and 25 square feet in Midland, Texas.

New York City has become the outstanding headquarters center of the United States, with an estimated 171,300,000 square feet of office space. It has had a tremendous growth since 1946, with 55 million square feet added since World War II. The trend has been uptown, away from downtown Wall Street to Park Avenue, 42nd Street and Third Avenue near Grand Central Station. The world's greatest concentration of office buildings is in the Grand Central and Plaza districts of New York City. From 1947 to 1962 inclusive, there was a total increase of 50,632,000 square feet of rentable office area in Manhattan, of which 33,839,000 square feet, or 66.8 percent, was in the Grand Central and Plaza areas. In the same period, in the lower Manhattan area, or the combined financial, city hall and insurance districts, 10,935,000 square feet or 21.6 percent of the total were constructed. A partial reversal of the uptown trend in Manhattan will result from the proposed building of the World Trade Center with 10 million square feet of office space, in twin towers 1350 feet high, on the Lower West Side. This development, by the Port of New York Authority, will be started in 1965 and is scheduled for completion by 1970.[13]

In Washington, D.C. there is approximately 16 million square feet of office space. An estimated 11 million square feet have been built since 1946, of which 9 million square feet are in the area west of 15th Street, in the direction of the high grade residential growth.

The location of new office buildings in central city areas has been determined in part by the slum or blighted areas, with old buildings which could be cleared away, such as in the Golden Triangle of Pittsburgh or Penn Center in Philadelphia, or location in air rights over railroad tracks as the Merchandise Mart and Prudential buildings in Chicago, the Pan Am Building and other buildings on Park Avenue in New York and the Prudential Building in Boston. The ability to secure land at a relatively low cost on West Wacker Drive in Chicago caused insurance companies to build there.

Sometimes these new office districts are not at the center of transportation. In Los Angeles new office building has moved away from the central business districts toward the high grade residential areas. From 1948 to 1960 15,500,000 square feet of office floor space was constructed in Los Angeles, of which only 1,500,000 square feet was built in the 400-acre area of the central business district, although 1,000,000 square feet were erected in the southwesterly and western fringe areas of the central business district.[14] This decentralization is in marked contrast to the concentration of offices in New York City.

There has also been a tendency for large office buildings of insurance companies, which conduct a self-sufficient operation not dependent on contact with other agencies, to locate on large tracts of land several miles from the center of the city as the Prudential regional office buildings in Houston and Minneapolis in 1951, and the Connecticut General Insurance Company in Hartford. Office centers are also developing around some of the regional shopping centers, as at Northland in Detroit, Ward

---

[13] *The New York Times* (January 19, 1964).

[14] *Los Angeles Centropolis 1980, Economic Survey*, Los Angeles Central City Committee and Los Angeles City Planning Department (December 12, 1960), p. 19.

Parkway in Kansas City and Lenox Square in Atlanta.

In Houston more than 6 million square feet of new office space has been added to downtown areas in the past three years, the growth proceeding westerly in the direction of the high income areas. While the main office building district of most cities is still within the confines of the central area, the office center is not fixed but is moving in the direction of high income areas, as in New York City, Washington, D.C., Los Angeles and Houston. This conforms to the statement I made in 1939.[15]

A tall office building that looms in the sky as a beacon or landmark has been built in many cities of moderate size by banks, oil companies or insurance companies for the sake of prestige, regardless of cost or rental demand. In many cities of growing population few new office buildings have been erected. Thus, generalizations can no longer be made about office building locations which will apply to all cities in the United States.

Hotels and Motels

There is a concentration of hotels near each other in large cities so that they can accommodate conventions but central hotels have declined in importance because of the new motels and motor hotels (with parking) on the periphery of the central business district or on the outskirts of the city. This rapid growth in both intown motels and those on the periphery is a use not anticipated in 1939.

Apartments in Central Areas

There is a trend to the building of new apartments in or near central business districts, such as the Marina Towers in Chicago, the apartments in redeveloped areas in Southwest Washington, D.C. and as proposed for the Bunker Hill redevelopment in downtown Los Angeles. Hence the statement by Burgess that: "Beyond the workingmen's homes lies the resi-

dential district, a zone in which the better grade of apartments and single family residences predominate" must be qualified now, as it was in 1939, when I pointed to the Gold Coast of Chicago and Park Avenue in New York City.[16]

Thus, in view of the shifting of uses in the central business districts, the overall decline in the predominance of central retail areas, the rapid growth of office centers in a few cities compared to a static situation in others, the emergence of redeveloped areas, and intown motels, the former descriptions of patterns in American cities must be revised to conform to the realities of 1964.

THE WHOLESALE AND LIGHT MANUFACTURING ZONE

Burgess described the zone next to the central business district as: "Clinging close to the skirts of the retail district lies the wholesale and light manufacturing zone. Scattered through this zone and surrounding it, old dilapidated buildings form the homes of the lower working classes, hoboes and disreputable characters. Here the slums are harbored. Cheap second hand stores are numerous, and low prices 'men only' moving picture and burlesque shows flourish."[17] This is a vivid description of West Madison Street and South State Street in Chicago in the 1920's. Since that time the wholesale function has greatly declined and with the direct sale by manufacturers to merchants the 4-million-square-foot Merchandise Mart, across the Chicago River north of the Loop, absorbed most of the functions formerly performed by wholesalers. The intermixture of slums and old dilapidated buildings with light industry is being cleared away in redevelopment projects and the West Side Industrial District in Chicago has been created immediately west of the Loop on cleared land.

Light manufacturing, in the garment industry particularly, still clings close to the retail

---

[15] Hoyt, *Structure and Growth*, op. cit., p. 108.

[16] Ibid., p. 23.

[17] Ernest M. Fisher, *Advanced Principles of Real Estate Practice* (New York: The Macmillan Co., 1930), p. 126, citing R. E. Park and E. W. Burgess, *The City*, op. cit., Ch. 11.

and financial center in New York City because the garment industry depends on fashion and the entertainment of out-of-town buyers.

Other light manufacturing industries have tended to move away from the center of the city to the suburbs where they can secure ample land areas for one-story plants, storage, and parking for their employees cars. These new modern plants, in park-like surroundings, which emit no loud noise or offensive odors, are not objectionable even in middle-class residential areas, and workers can avoid city traffic in driving to their place of employment, or they can live nearby.

THE FACTORY OR HEAVY INDUSTRIAL DISTRICT

In 1929 Burgess placed the wholesale district in Zone I, the central business district, and described Zone II as the zone in transition, which included the factory district in its inner belt as follows:

> Zone II: The Zone in transition. Surrounding the Central Business District are areas of residential deterioration caused by the encroaching of business and industry from Zone I. This may therefore be called the Zone in Transition, with a factory district for its inner belt and an outer ring of retrogressing neighborhoods, of first-settlement immigrant colonies, of rooming-house districts, of homeless-men areas, of resorts of gambling, bootlegging, sexual vice, and of breeding-places of crime. In this area of physical deterioration and social disorganization our studies show the greatest concentration of cases of poverty, bad housing, juvenile delinquency, family disintegration, physical and mental disease. As families and individuals prosper, they escape from this area in Zone III beyond, leaving behind as marooned a residuum of the defeated, leaderless, and helpless.[18]

In 1939 I pointed out tendencies of heavy industries to move away from close-in locations in the "transition zone."[19] Since that time heavy manufacturing has tended more and more to seek suburban locations or rural areas, as nearly all workers now come in their own automobiles and for the most part live in the suburban areas themselves. Factory location in slum areas is not now desired for the clerks and factory workers no longer live there. All of the reasons I cited in 1939 for industries moving to suburban areas apply with greater force in 1964.

In regard to residential uses, this zone in transition was defined as the slum and blighted area of Chicago in 1943[20] and under the slum clearance and redevelopment laws which enabled federal authorities to acquire by condemnation, properties in blighted areas, it has been extensively cleared and rebuilt with modern apartments, both private and public. The remnants of this area which have not been cleared away still retain the characteristics Burgess described in 1929, and the problems of juvenile delinquency and overcrowding have been accentuated in the last 35 years by the in-migration of low income Negro families to Chicago as well as to other northern cities.

ZONE OF WORKINGMEN'S HOMES

Encircling the zone of transition, now the slum and blighted area, is Zone III, described by Burgess as follows:

> Zone III: The Zone of Independent Workingmen's Homes. This third broad urban ring is in Chicago, as well as in other northern industrial cities, largely constituted by neighborhoods of second immigrant settlement. Its residents are those who desire to live near but not too close to their work. In Chicago, it is a housing area neither of tenements, apartments, nor of single dwellings; its boundaries have been roughly determined by the plotting of the two-flat dwelling, generally of frame construction, with the owner living on the lower floor with a tenant on the other.[21]

[18] Burgess, "Urban Areas," op. cit.
[19] Hoyt, op. cit. p. 20.

[20] Chicago Plan Commission, *Master Plan of Residential Land Use of Chicago,* Homer Hoyt, Director of Research (1943), Fig. 89, p. 68.
[21] Burgess, "Urban Areas," op. cit.

The buildings in this zone, now 35 years older than when Burgess wrote in 1929, were in general classified in The Master Plan of Residential Land Use of Chicago as "conservation."[22] This area is not yet a slum but next in order of priority to be cleared away. In some blocks older structures can be razed and the newer ones rehabilitated. A large proportion of its former occupants, white families with children of school age, have moved to the suburbs and it is now occupied mainly by single white persons, older white families or by Negro families in all age groups.

In some cases these older close-in residential sections may be rehabilitated and become fashionable, as in the Georgetown area of Washington, D.C., Rittenhouse Square in Philadelphia and the Near North Side of Chicago; and this is an exception to be noted to Burgess' theory.

BETTER RESIDENTIAL AREA

Zone IV: The Zone of Better Residences. Extending beyond the neighborhoods of second immigrant settlements, we come to the Zone of Better Residences in which the great middle-class of native-born Americans live, small business men, professional people, clerks, and salesmen. Once communities of single homes, they are becoming, in Chicago, apartment-house and residential-hotel areas.[23]

This zone was classified in the Master Plan of Residential Land Use of Chicago in 1943 as "stable," indicating that the residences were still of sound construction and had many remaining years of useful life. As the second immigrant settlers, now indistinguishable from the native born population, once moved from Zone III into this area, so now many of the former residents of this area have moved mainly from this area into the new areas near the periphery of the city, or into the suburbs. Some of the areas vacated by them are now occupied by the non-white population.

THE COMMUTERS ZONE

Burgess described the commuters zone as follows:

Zone V. The Commuters Zone. Out beyond the areas of better residence is a ring of encircling small cities, towns, and hamlets, which, taken together, constitute the Commuters Zone. These are also, in the main, dormitory suburbs, because the majority of men residing there spend the day at work in the Loop (Central Business District), returning only for the night.[24]

Burgess thus took into account in his fifth zone the existence of suburban towns. However, he refers to them as a "ring" implying that they formed a circular belt around Chicago. However, at the time Burgess wrote in 1929, there was no circle of towns around Chicago but a pattern of settlement along the railroads with six great bands of suburban settlement radiating out from the central mass of Chicago like spokes of a wheel and with large vacant areas in between.[25] Chicago's early growth had taken the form first of starfish extensions of settlement along the principal highways and street car line.[26] By 1929 the vacant areas in the city between these prongs had been filled in with homes so that there were then in fact belts or concentric circles of settled areas within the City of Chicago. At that time, however, the suburban area of Chicago conformed to the axial pattern of growth with the highest income sector located on one of the six radial bands—the North Shore, along Lake Michigan. There were other high income areas in the other bands of growth but no continuous belt of high income areas around Chicago. Since 1929 the vacant areas between these radial extensions of settlement along suburban railroads have been filled in largely with homes of middle income residents. Many of the new planned shopping districts are now located in between these bands of original settlement along railroads, where large vacant tracts could be secured.

---

[22] Chicago Plan Commission, op. cit.
[23] Burgess, "Urban Areas," op cit.

---

[24] Ibid.
[25] Chicago Plan Commission, op. cit., frontispiece, p. 2.
[26] Ibid., Fig. 3, p. 22.

Beyond his five zones, Burgess later identified two additional zones lying beyond the built-up area of the city: "The sixth zone is constituted by the agricultural districts lying within the circle of commutation . . . The seventh zone is the hinterland of the metropolis."[27]

Richard M. Hurd, in his classic *Principles of City Land Values*[28] had, as early as 1903 developed the central and axial principles of city growth; yet to many persons, before Burgess formulated his theory many years later, cities appeared to be a chaotic mixture of structures with no law governing their growth. Burgess, with acute powers of observation and without all of the great body of census and planning data that has been made available since he wrote, made a remarkable formulation of principles that were governing American city growth in 1929 and he related these principles to the basic facts of human society. Since 1929, however, not only have the vast detailed city data of the United States censuses been made available for study and analysis, but dynamic changes have occurred in our economy which have had a profound influence on the structure of our cities. Since 1929 over 10 million new houses have been constructed on the suburban fringes of American cities, beyond the old central mass, in areas made available for residential occupancy by the increase in the number of private passenger automobiles in the United States from 8 million in 1920 to 66 million in 1964, and the highways subsequently built to accommodate them.

Apartment buildings, once confined to locations along subways, elevated lines or near suburban railroad stations, are now springing up in the suburbs, far from mass transit. Many families without children of school age desire the convenience of an apartment, involving no work of mowing lawns, painting and repairing,

and with the comforts of air conditioning and often a community swimming pool. Complete communities are now being developed in the suburbs, with a mixture of single family homes, town houses and apartments, and with their own churches, schools, shopping centers and light industries, some even with a golf course and bridle paths, of which the 7,000-acre Reston development near the Dulles Airport in the Washington, D. C. area is an outstanding example. Thus the dynamic changes of the past quarter century make it necessary to review concepts developed from studies of American cities in 1925 and 1939.

THE SECTOR THEORY

One concept needs to be examined again—the sector theory of residential development. In 1939 I formulated the sector theory, which was to the effect that the high income areas of cities were in one or more sectors of the city, and not, as Burgess seemed to imply when he said: "beyond the workingmen's homes lies the residential district, a zone in which the better grade of apartment houses and single family residences predominate."

In a study of 64 American cities, block by block, based on the federal government's Work Project Administration's basic surveys of 1934, and studies of a number of large metropolitan areas, I prepared maps showing that high rent areas were located in one or more sectors of the city, and did not form a circle completely around it. Has this changed since 1939? In a survey of the entire Washington, D. C. metropolitan area in 1954 it was found that the main concentration of high-income families was in the District area west of Rock Creek Park, continuing into the Bethesda area of Montgomery County, Maryland. There were other scattered high income clusters in the Washington area. In surveys of other metropolitan areas it was discovered that the main concentration of high income families is on the north side of Dallas, west and southwest sides of Houston, northward along the Lake Shore of Chicago, the south side of Kansas City, in the Beverly Hills

[27] E. W. Burgess, "The New Community and Its Future," *Annals of the American Academy of Political and Social Science,* 149 (May 1930): 161, 162.

[28] Richard M. Hurd, *Principles of City Land Values* (1st edition 1903, republished by *The Record and Guide,* New York, 1924).

area of Los Angeles, on the south side of Tulsa, the north side of Oklahoma City, the west side of Philadelphia, and the southwest side of Minneapolis. In the New York metropolitan area there are a number of nodules of high income in Westchester County, Nassau County, Bergen and Essex Counties in New Jersey, but the predominant movement was northward and eastward.

In a trip to Latin American cities in the summer of 1963 I found that the finest single family homes and apartments in Guatemala City, Bogota, Lima, La Paz, Quito, Santiago, Buenos Aires, Montevideo, Rio de Janeiro, Sao Paulo and Caracas were located on one side of the city only.[29]

The automobile and the resultant belt highways encircling American cities have opened up large regions beyond existing settled areas, and future high grade residential growth will probably not be confined entirely to rigidly defined sectors. As a result of the greater flexibility in urban growth patterns resulting from these radial expressways and belt highways, some higher income communities are being developed beyond low income sectors but these communities usually do not enjoy as high a social rating as new neighborhoods located in the high income sector.

CHANGES IN POPULATION GROWTH IN METROPOLITAN AREAS OUTSIDE THE UNITED STATES

Since the rate of population growth, particularly of the great cities of one million population and over, is a most important element in changing city structure, let us examine these differential rates of growth.[30] There has in fact, been a wide variation in the rate of population growth in the great metropolitan areas throughout the

world since 1940. In England, in London and the other large metropolitan areas, the population has remained stationary; on the Continent of Europe outside Russia, the growth rate of the great metropolitan areas has slowed down to 20 percent in the decade from 1950 to 1960. In Russia, eight of the largest older metropolitan areas increased in population only 15 percent from 1939 to 1962 but in this period many entirely new cities were built and other smaller cities grew in size until Russia now has 176 metropolitan areas with a population of 100,000 or more. China has had a great urban surge since 1945 to 1950 and reports a gain of 91 percent in the population of 18 great metropolitan areas as a result of its enforced industrialization process. This was reportedly carried too far and city dwellers had to be ordered back to the farms to raise food. Japan's five largest metropolitan area concentrations increased in numbers by 41 percent from 1951 to 1961. Fast suburban trains carry workers to and from downtown places of employment. In India, Delhi and New Delhi have more than doubled in population from 1951 to 1961 as a result of greatly expanded government and manufacturing activity. Other great Indian cities have grown rapidly, with 300,000 or more sleeping in the streets of Calcutta. In Australia, Sydney and Melbourne increased by 32 percent from 1951 to 1961. In Egypt, Cairo has gained 155 percent in numbers since 1940 as a result of being the chief headquarters of the Arab world. African cities like Nairobi and Leopoldville have gained rapidly. In Latin America, the urban population has exploded, with eight of its largest metropolitan areas gaining 166 percent from 1940 to 1962. The Sao Paulo metropolitan area, jumping from 1,380,000 to 4,374,000, gained 217 percent. Mexico City shot up from 1,754,000 to 4,666,000, a rise of 166 percent, in the same period of time.

CHANGES IN STRUCTURE OF CITIES OUTSIDE THE UNITED STATES

While there are some similarities in the patterns of urban growth in the United States and

---

[29] "The Residential and Retail Patterns of Leading Latin American Cities," *Land Economics* (November 1963).

[30] Homer Hoyt, *World Urbanization—Expanding Population in a Shrinking World,* Washington, D.C.: Urban Land Institute Technical Bulletin 43 (April 1962). See also "The Growth of Cities from 1800 to 1960 and Forecasts to Year 2000," *Land Economics* (May 1963), pp. 167–173.

foreign cities, as for example, in the sector theory, there are also some marked differences, as a result of the following five factors:

(1) Ownership of Automobiles

The chief factor in enabling city populations to spread out, to develop vast areas of single family homes on wide lots far from main transit facilities, to develop so many new shopping centers and so many dispersed factories, has been the almost universal ownership of the private automobile. Only in the United States, New Zealand, Australia and Canada, which have developed city patterns similar to ours, had a high rate of auto ownership to population in 1955, or from 181 per 1,000 in Canada and 183 in Australia to 339 per 1,000 in the United States.[31] Northern European nations had from 58 to 111 cars per thousand of population but most Asiatic and African nations and most of the South American countries had less than 15 cars per 1,000 population. Argentina and Uruguay had 32 cars per 1,000 population in 1955.

The number of automobiles in northwestern Europe has shown marked gains recently: in West Germany from 1955 to 1963 the rate increased from 58 to 122 per 1,000 persons; in the United Kingdom for the same period the rate increased from 92 to 120 per 1,000 persons; and for the same period in Belgium the rate increased from 60 to 106 per 1,000 persons.

Obviously, in most of the world the urban population must depend upon busses or bicycles and live in apartments which can be economically served by subways, street cars or busses. Hence the great expansion into rural areas can take place only when there are suburban railroads as in Buenos Aires, Rio de Janeiro, Delhi and Tokyo, or subways as in London, Moscow, Tokyo, Madrid, Barcelona and Paris. Poor families live in central areas on steep mountainsides in Rio de Janeiro and Caracas, in shacks built by themselves; they live in blocks of tenements in central Hong Kong;

---

[31] Morton Ginsburg, *Atlas of Economic Development* (Chicago: University of Chicago Press, 1961), p. 74.

sleep on the streets in downtown Calcutta, and build mud huts in central Nairobi.

(2) Private Ownership of Property

The pattern of American cities is the result of private ownership of property, which cannot be taken by condemnation except for a public use or in a blighted area and for which compensation must be paid when appropriated. There is now almost universal zoning control which regulates types of use, density of use and height of buildings; but these controls, first adopted in New York in 1916, had no effect upon early city growth and they have been modified or changed thousands of times. Otherwise it would not have been possible to develop the 8,300 new shopping centers nearly all of which required zoning in depth rather than strip zoning, nor could thousands of apartment buildings have been constructed in suburban areas.

Consequently, it is impossible to preserve green areas and open spaces without paying for the right. While the public cannot prevent the private owner from building on his land, zoning ordinances in some communities requiring one to five acres of land for each house have practically limited the utilization to occupancy by wealthy families because the high cost of sewer and water lines and street pavements in such low density areas virtually prevents building of houses for middle- or low-income family occupancy. Urban sprawl, or the filling in of all vacant areas, has been the bane of planners who would like to restore the early star-shaped pattern. Where the State owns all of the land, as in Russia, or controls it rigidly, as in Finland, dense apartment clusters can be built along subway lines and the areas in between kept vacant.

(3) Central Area Attractions

The central retail areas of foreign cities have not deteriorated as a result of outlying shopping center competition for there are few such centers because very few people own cars. Crowds throng the shops on Florida Street in Buenos Aires and Union Street in Lima, which are closed to automobile traffic in shopping hours. Galerias, an elaborate expansion of the arcade, often extending up to five or six levels, have recently been built in downtown Santiago, Sao Paulo and Rio de Janeiro. Rotterdam has its new central retail area; Cologne its shopping street, a pedestrian thoroughfare. In these foreign cities, residents find the downtown area the chief attraction. The parks of Tokyo, London, Paris, Buenos Aires and Rio de Janeiro are downtown; so are the palaces and government offices, the great cathedrals, the museums, theatres, restaurants and night life of many foreign cities. The Forum and Colosseum in Rome, the Acropolis in Athens, Notre Dame in Paris, Westminster Abbey and the Tower of London are all in or near central areas.[32]

One change is occurring which is altering the skyline of many foreign cities—the advent of the tall office building. Formerly, cities outside the United States prized their uniform skyline broken only by the spire of a great cathedral or an Eiffel Tower. But now tall office buildings loom above London and Milan; they are planned for Paris. Caracas has its 30-story Twin Towers; Rio de Janeiro a new 35-story office building, El Centro; Mexico City its 32-story office building; and Sao Paulo has a great concentration of tall buildings in its downtown area.

(4) Stability of the Currency

The great building boom in the United States has been financed on money borrowed from banks and insurance companies. Despite gradual inflation, most people have confidence in the American dollar. The volume of mortgage credit for building in 1 to 4 family units increased from $17.4 billion in 1940 to $182.4 billion in December 1963. Shopping centers are financed on the basis of guaranteed leases by national chain store tenants which afford sufficient funds to construct the center. In nations like Brazil, however, where the interest rates are 3 to 5 percent a month and the cruzeiro has dropped from 384 to 1300 to the dollar in a year's time, it is impossible to secure long term loans. New buildings can be effected only by paying all cash as the work proceeds. An inflation of any marked extent in the United States would drastically curtail the supply of mortgage funds available for new building.

(5) Redevelopment Laws

The federal government in 1952 was authorized by Congress to pay two-thirds of the difference between the cost of acquiring sites in blighted areas and the re-sale price for new development. This has made possible the clearing and rebuilding of central areas which could not be done without both the power of condemnation and the write-down of the difference between the acquisition cost and the re-use value.

The principles of city growth and structure, formulated on the basis of experience in cities in the United States prior to 1930, are thus subject to modification not only as a result of dynamic changes in the United States in the last few decades but these principles, originating here, are subject to further revisions when it is sought to apply them to foreign cities.

---

[32] Homer Hoyt, "The Structure and Growth of American Cities Contrasted With the Structure of European and Asiatic Cities," *Urban Land*, (Washington, D.C.: Urban Land Institute, September 1959).

20

PETER W. AMATO

Environmental Quality and Locational Behavior in a Latin American City

A significant number of studies concerning residential land use patterns, and changes to these over time, have accumulated in the United States over the past several decades [1]. Although many are descriptive, or take the market place as the final arbiter of location decisions, more recent work is attempting to examine what Chapin calls the "behavioral antecedents of location decisions" [2]. Specifically, efforts are being directed at analyzing activity systems of individuals or households, as well as preferences or felt needs, concerning environmental qualities as variables affecting location behavior. This work in location behavior, although at its infancy in the United States, may well add important additional inputs to the development of land use models in explaining more about the "chemistry of location choices" [Chapin 1967]. Needless, to say, comparable cross-cultural studies do not exist on the changing patterns of land use for any of the major Latin American cities [3]. This does not mean to imply that normative studies concerning land use planning are not underway for many of these cities—some cities are even developing land use and transportation models [4].

Nevertheless, this paper argues that studies concerned with land use planning for the Latin American city must have, as their base, some behavioral understanding of the changes that have occurred in land uses in the past. At this point, many new questions enter the horizon of the planner concerned with cross-cultural studies. We may readily agree with Norton

Ginsburg, that we know very little, for example, concerning the relationship between "value systems and social organization, on the one hand, and the development of city systems and various types of urban morphological patterns, on the other" [Ginsburg 1966]. Perhaps it is too early, given the state of the arts, to determine to what extent culture as an independent variable may be significant in explaining the differences among cities. Or on the other hand, we may, after extensive cross-cultural studies, agree with Schnore in his tentative position that there may be "... some highly general 'functional prerequisite' affecting cities in all cultures, or some 'universal functions' of cities that give rise to cross-cultural regularities in the use of space" [Schnore 1966: 393]. However, it is not the purpose of this paper to attempt anything as grandiose as a relationship between culture and city-form or function. Rather, this paper may be considered a more modest beginning to an examination of the relationship of environmental qualities and the locational behavior of elite residential areas in Bogotá, Colombia.

"Environmental Quality and Locational Behavior in a Latin American City" by Peter W. Amato is reprinted from *Urban Affairs Quarterly*, Volume 5, Number 1 (September 1969), pp. 83–101, by permission of the Publisher, Sage Publications, Inc.
This paper is part of the research findings of the author's doctoral dissertation presented to the Department of City and Regional Planning at Cornell University in 1968 under the title, "An Analysis of the Changing Patterns of Elite Residential Areas in Bogotá, Colombia."

A strong emphasis is placed on the locational decisions of the elite class, since this class has acted as both leaders and major participants in the growth of residential land uses in the city. Moreover, their attitudes and activities have largely controlled the timing and the direction of urban land use growth. Furthermore, there is sufficient evidence to believe that other socioeconomic classes, particularly the middle-income groups, have aspired, and have been partially successful in following the upper classes in their residential locations. Consequently, by studying the spatial behavior of the elite class we gain significant insights over much of the urbanization process.

RESIDENTIAL AREAS OF BOGOTA

The residential areas in the city of Bogotá were originally laid out surrounding a major plaza in a grid pattern. Great prestige was attached to living in areas near the major plaza, and we logically find the most prominent and wealthy families occupying the most central location in the city, from its early founding in 1538 well into the eighteenth century [5] (see Figures 1 and 2). Major migrations from the center of the city began during the early decades of the twentieth century. By the nineteen thirties and forties, only a small percentage of the original elite Bogotáno families remained in the colonial neighborhoods [6]. The first move of the upper classes was to areas immediately north of the then built-up city (see Figure 3). This was followed in the short span of a decade by a second major move to areas farther north within the same sector of development (see Figure 4).

In order to understand these dramatic changes in the locational patterns of the elite class, a number of general assumptions on the generation of land use patterns are set forth [7]:

1. Limits on the possible kinds of spatial patterns will be found in a feudal society, due to its limited technology and means of transportation and communication.

2. A number of spatial patterns will be found in an industrializing society, due to greater technological advances made in transportation and communication. This will great-

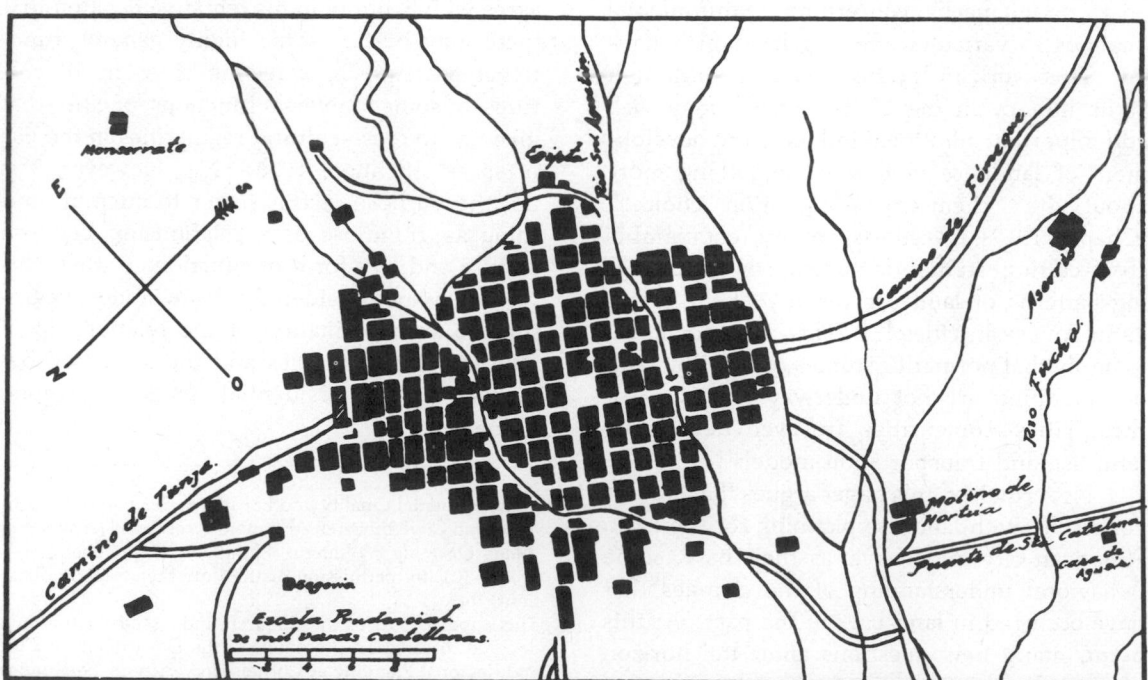

FIGURE 1. Plan of Bogotá, Colombia, 1797

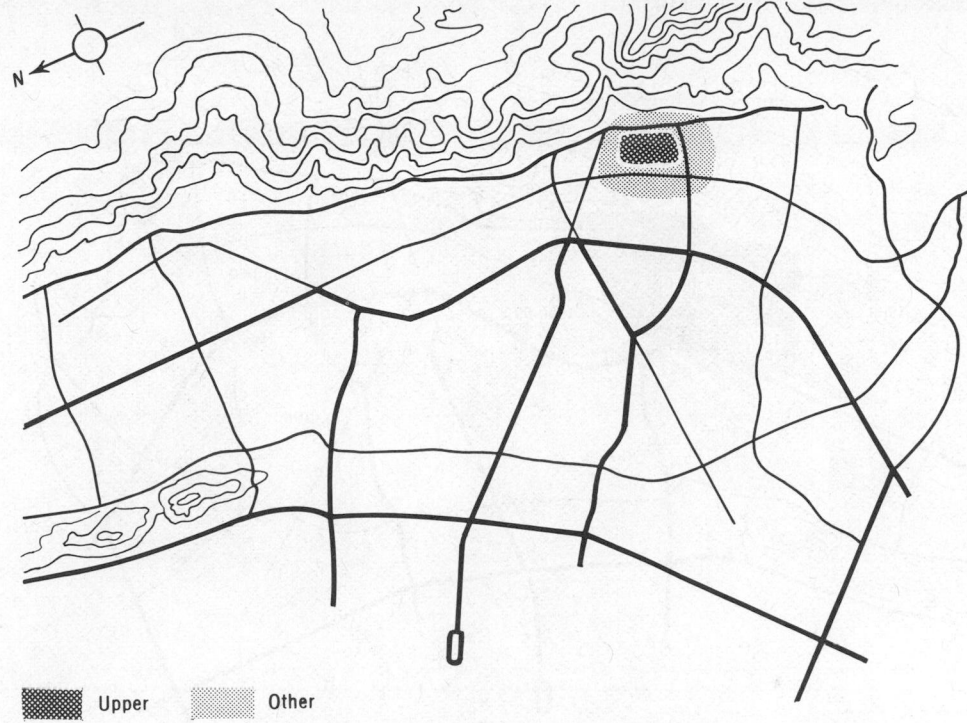

Upper   Other

FIGURE 2.   Socioeconomic Class Locations, Bogotá, Colombia, 1900

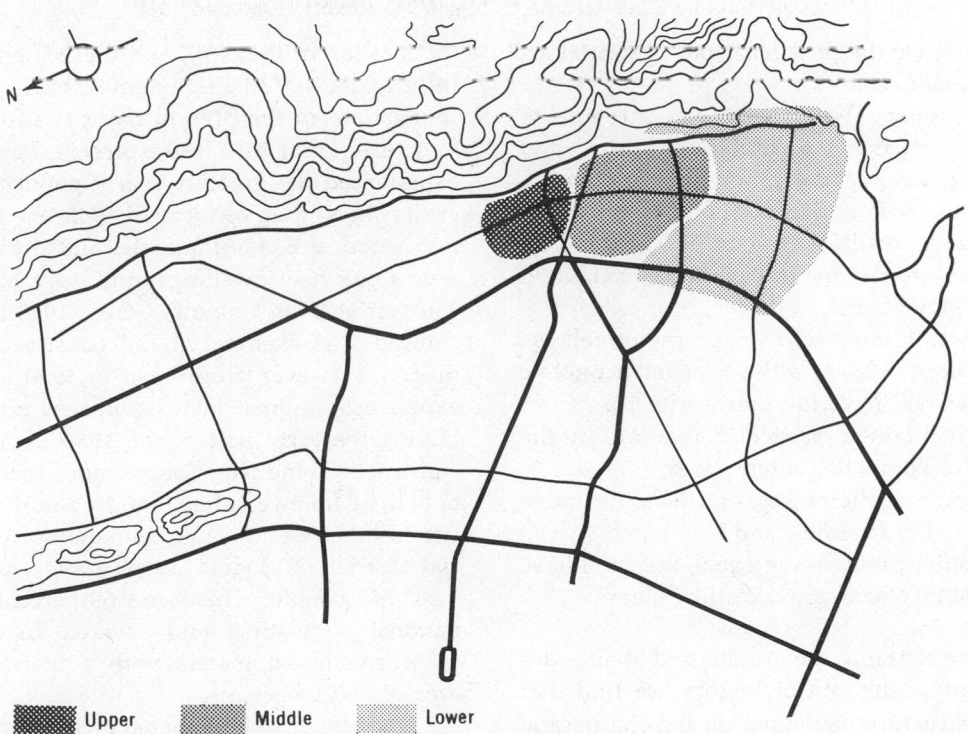

Upper   Middle   Lower

FIGURE 3.   Socioeconomic Class Locations, Bogotá, Colombia, 1935

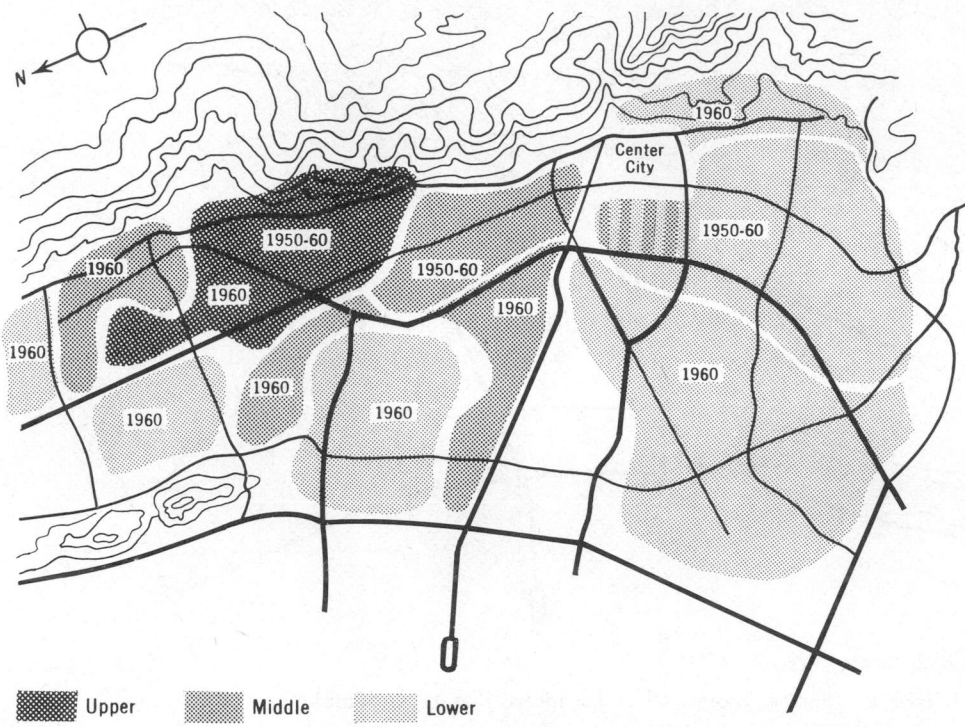

Upper   Middle   Lower

FIGURE 4.   Socioeconomic Class Locations, Bogotá, Colombia, 1950 and 1960

ly increase the possible types of spatial arrangements.

3. The upper-class groups will attempt to maintain their favorable position and prerogatives in the community and in the society. In order to do this they must:
    a. have ready access to the sources of power—governmental, ecclesiastical, and educational, and
    b. isolate themselves from the nonelites.

4. The upper classes with social and economic power will have the prerogative to:
    a. maintain a particular location in the face of competing alternatives,
    b. capture the newest and most desirable residential facilities, and
    c. other things being equal, they will have the ability to live where they please.

If we now examine the growth and spatial development of the city of Bogotá, we find that the city structure of Bogotá during the decade of the 1930s (its major transportation arteries,

the location of industry, and the beginnings of the groupings of socioeconomic classes) laid the foundation for the present day city's form and structure. From 1938 to the present, Bogotá has experienced the greatest yearly population increases in its long history. In 1948, the population stood at 513,681 people, and during this year 1,695 new dwelling units were built [8]. The war years in Colombia, from 1940 to 1947, showed a slackening in the construction industry. However, from 1948 to 1950, the city experienced a great increase in new buildings. During the early part of the 1950 decade, the construction industry once more decreased, only to be followed after 1956 by a fairly steady rise to the present. The population of the special district of Bogotá as of July, 1964, was 1,683,753 people. This was 9.69 percent of the national population, and covered an area of 1,754 square kilometers with a metropolitan area of 8,441 hectares.

Despite this phenomenal increase in population and urban growth, Bogotá today is a city principally oriented along a north-south axis. The city's major plaza has lost its importance as the true focal point of the city, and its residential areas are segregated, with the upper socioeconomic groups occupying the more favorable lands, well served by transportation facilities and away from nuisance land uses. The lower socioeconomic groups have been confined to areas not immediately proximate to the better transportation lines and to areas closer to nuisance land uses. The middle socioeconomic groups occupy lands between these two polar extremes, and in lands jumped over by the upper groups in their move out from the center city (see figure 4).

ENVIRONMENT AS A DETERMINANT OF ELITE LOCATION

We may now ask, to what extent has environment, that complex of climatic, edaphic, and biotic factors, had upon the locations of socioeconomic population groups or ecological patterning in the city during the period of rapid city expansion of the 1930s and 1940s, and subsequently. A tentative hypothesis of this study is that the upper socioeconomic groups have tended to usurp and to occupy the more desirable sections of the city in terms of environmental advantages. These groups have settled in areas of generally more favorable environmental conditions—at higher elevations, in areas experiencing better climate, higher soil fertility, greener areas, and areas best served by transportation and other service facilities. The lower socioeconomic groups, on the other hand, have been relegated to less desirable residential areas of the city, and the middle-income groups have tended to occupy transitional zones between the two polar groups.

The outward move of the elites from the center city during the decade of the 1930s was found not to be haphazard and scattered, but wilful and purposeful in certain specific directions. Factors causative to elite locations were observed to be influenced by a number of interrelated factors, and the final result was the consequence of a mix of factors rather than a single

variable. Nevertheless, a few "key" factors stand out. The first consists of those forces exerted by the external environment, such as climate, topography, and edaphic conditions. The second concerns the availability of communication, transportation, and other municipal services.

THE "PULL" FORCE OF SUPERIOR PHYSICAL CONDITIONS

Given areas of generally equal accessibility to the north, west, and south of the existing city, the elites chose to live to the north. An examination of equally available areas in the city of Bogotá indicates that superior physical conditions are present in the preferred elite locations north of the city, and generally poorer physical conditions are found in areas occupied by lower socioeconomic groups in other locations [9].

Bogotá, located at an elevation of 8,630 feet above sea level, has generally cloudy skies and is subject to considerable rains [10]. During the period 1925-50, the city averaged 190.7 days of rain per year [11], or 52 percent of the days during any year were rainy. This same period registered 915.5 millimeters of rain. The period 1951–64 averaged 191.6 days of rain per year or slightly more than 52 percent of the days during any year. This timespan recorded a total of 936.9 millimeters of rain [12]. The abundance of rain in Bogotá is coupled with generally cloudy skies. During the period 1951–54, Bogotá registered only 1,474.5 hours of sunshine per year, or 37.4 percent of total possible hours of sun for the year [13].

The temperature in Bogotá averages 57° Fahrenheit yearly and will vary during the day from 68° Fahrenheit at noon on a sunny day, to 47° Fahrenheit at night. The average relative humidity stands between 65 percent to 70 percent [14]. Given the above climatic conditions of abundant rains, little sunshine and relatively cool days, prize commodities are, therefore, sunny and warm days [15].

Climatic conditions are not constant on the Sabana of Bogotá, but vary considerably from place to place. To determine what "pull effect" different climatic conditions may have had on the movement of the elites out of the center city during the decades of the 1930s and 1940s, and their eventual spatial configuration, twelve key weather station points to the north, west, and south of the city, as well as within the city, were chosen for analysis (see Figure 5 for location of station points). Readings on several of these locations were gathered for two time periods. Period one includes the years 1950–55, (Table 1.) period two the years 1958–61–62 and 1963 (Table 2.). Readings on the average days of rain per year, the amounts of rainfall, the relative humidity, the temperature, and the hours of sunshine per year, were recorded for these station points as far as data was available (Table 3.).

From the above tables for two time periods, we observe that areas in the higher zones, near the mountains of Guadelupe and Monserrate, experience, on the whole, greater amounts of rainy days and amounts of rainfall than do areas west of the mountains.

El Delirio, which is located southeast of

Barrio Vitelma, registered the greatest amount of rainy days for the 1950–55 period, with 57.2 percent days registering precipitation. This station point also had the greatest amount of rainfall, registering 1319.6 millimeters of rain per year. Other areas near the mountains, such as San Luis and Vitelma, also indicated high percentages of rainy days and experienced some of the highest amounts of rain during this time period. The lowest amount of rainfall and days of rain for both the 1950–55 and 1958–63 period were recorded in Techo to the far west and Chapinero to the north, and Usaquen to the far north also recorded relatively small amounts of rain for at least one of these periods.

Areas more centrally located, such as Instituto Geográfico to the north, and Ciudad Universitaria to the west, recorded the lowest humidity of five station points in which data were collected for this period. It also registered some of the highest temperatures. Techo, on the other hand, had the lowest temperature and the highest humidity levels.

The period 1958–61–62–63 indicates that

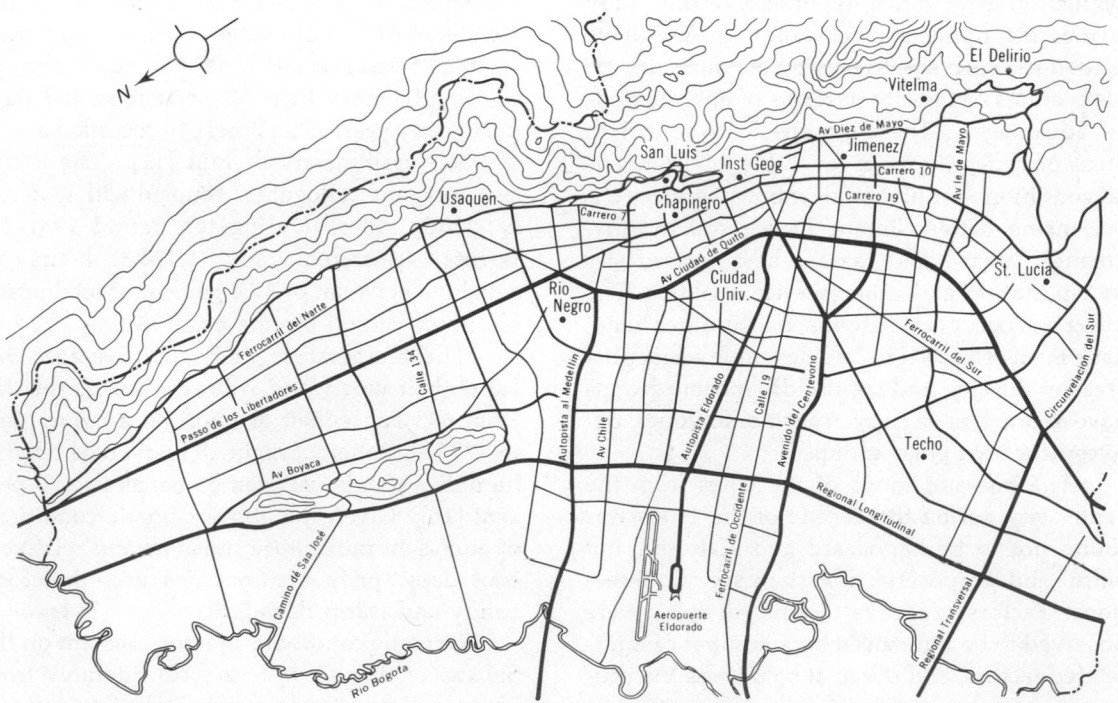

FIGURE 5.   Weather Station Points, Bogotá, Colombia, 1950–63

TABLE 1.   Rankings for Eight Station Points, Days of Rain, Percentages and Amounts, Bogotá, 1950–55[a]

| Station Point | Days of Rain | | Amount of Rain | |
	Average for 1950–55	Percentage of Total Days	Station Point	Amount of Millimeters
(1) El Delirio	203.3	57.2	(1) El Delirio	1319.6
(2) Ciudad Universitaria	204.3	55.6	(2) San Luis	1276.5
(3) San Luis	202.8	55.5	(3) Vitelma	1205.4
(4) Instituto Geográfico[b]	195.4	53.5	(4) Instituto Geográfico	1184.7
(5) Vitelma	173.1	47.5	(5) Ciudad Universitaria	108.9
(6) Techo[c]	171.0	47.0	(6) Chapinero	892.8
(7) Chapinero[d]	121.5	45.8	(7) Usaquen	604.7
(8) Usaquen	120.0	45.5	(8) Techo	558.2

[a] Computed from *Anuario Meteorológico 1950–51*, Ministerio de Agricultura, División de Investigación, (Bogotá, Colombia: May 1955), pp. 17–22 and pp. 31–33. Ibid., Anuario Meteorológico 1949, (March 1955), pp. 15–19 and pp. 26–28. Ibid., Anuario Meteorológico 1952, 1953, 1954 (October 1955); (1952), pp. 26–31 and pp. 38–41; (1953), pp. 26–31 and pp. 37–40; (1954), pp. 24–30 and pp. 36–39. Instituto Geográfico, Departmento de Investigaciónes, *Anuario Meteorológico 1955*, (Bogotá, Colombia I.G.A.C. 1961), pp. 52–54 and p. 65, Multilith.
[b] Computed on four year average.
[c] Computed on three year average.
[d] Computed on two year average.

TABLE 2.   Rankings for Eight Station Points, Days of Rain, Percentages, and Amounts, Bogotá, 1958–61–62–63[a]

| Station Point | Days of Rain | | Amount of Rainfall | |
	Average for 1958–61–62–63	Percentage of Days	Station Point	Amount in Millimeters
(1) Ciudad Universitaria	181.0	49.9	(1) Avenida Jimenez	1034.5
(2) Instituto Geográfico	167.0[b]	45.6	(2) Rio Negro	953.8
(3) Techo	166.0	45.5	(3) Instituto Geográfico	906.5
(4) Rio Negro	164.0	45.0	(4) Usaquen	904.6
(5) La Candeleria	150.0	41.2	(5) Ciudad Universitaria	885.3
(6) Avenida Jimenez	137.5	37.8	(6) La Cendeleria	532.2
(7) Usaquen	126.5	34.7	(7) St. Lucia	511.5
(8) St. Lucia	100.0	27.4	(8) Techo	483.5

[a] Computed from "Boletin Informativo," *Empresa de Acueducto y Alcantarillado de Bogotá, D.E.*, Dirección de Plancamiento, Bogotá, Colombia, years 1958–61–62 and 1963. It should be noted that this period serves as a good contrast since it recorded comparatively fewer days and amounts of rainfall than the earlier 1950–55 period.
[b] Computed on three year average.

TABLE 3. Humidity, Temperature, and Hours of Sunlight for Station Points in the City of Bogotá, 1950–55 and 1958–63[a]

Station Point	Humidity 1950–55	Humidity 1958–63	Temperature[b] 1950–55	Temperature[b] 1958–63	Hours of Sunlight[c] 1950–55	Hours of Sunlight[c] 1958–63
Instituto Geográfico	68.4[d]	60.8	14.4[d]	13.9	1344.0[f]	1411.3
Techo	73.6[e]		13.2[f]			
Ciudad Universitaria	64.3	75.5	13.9	13.5	1472.5[d]	1713.9
Usaquen	72.0		13.4			
Chapinero	70.0[f]		13.6[f]			
Cindinamarca- Bogotá average	63.0	75.2	14.3	13.5		

[a] Computed from *Ministerio de Agricultura,* . . . op. cit., years 1950–51–1952–53–54. *Instituto Geográfico,* . . . op. cit., year 1955. *Boletin Informativo,* op. cit., years 1958–61–62–63.
[b] Computed in degrees centigrade.
[c] Data on hours of sunlight per year are lacking for all station points recording days and amounts of rainfall. Only those listed were available.
[d] Computed on five year average.
[e] Computed on four year average.
[f] Computed on three year average.

the greatest amounts of days of precipitation were registered by station points in Ciudad Universitaria, Instituto Geográfico and Techo. Nevertheless, Techo recorded the lowest amounts of rainfall. The station points of Usaquen to the north, and St. Lucia to the south, recorded the least amounts of rainy days and averaged less amounts of precipitation than more centrally located points—Avenida Jimenez, Instituto Geográfico, and Rio Negro. Areas near the mountains registered high amounts of rainfall for this time period, as they did in the earlier 1950–55 period.

This information indicates that areas to the north of the city have, on the whole, better climatic conditions than other areas, particularly better than areas within the central city or to the west. Areas such as St. Lucia to the far south are also drier than central city locations, but another environmental consideration, soil type, is much poorer.

SOIL CONDITIONS
Soils to the north were also found to be superior to soils in other parts of the city. Their productive capacity, lack of inundations and erosions,

and natural vegetations present favorable conditions for farming. Northern areas also show good soils for the raising of fruit and other types of trees, and may be considered greener than areas to the west and south because of their greater natural vegetation [16].

The above factors, in total, gave areas to the north, in Chapinero and Usaquen, lush images of greenery and plenty. Areas to the south and west were considered barren and bare, and were not prized as areas for homesites or for recreational purposes [see Figure 6]. It may thus be argued that the combination of more favorable climatic and soil conditions to the north of the existing city during the early 1930s determined, to a large degree, the initial movement of the wealthy towards these lands, and largely inhibited their movement to the south and west. Subsequently, lands to the west, and areas jumped over in the north by the wealthy, were occupied by the middle socioeconomic groups. The lower socioeconomic groups were relegated to areas in and around the city center, to the south and west, and to the eastern mountain slopes south of the city— areas of poorer soil and climatic conditions.

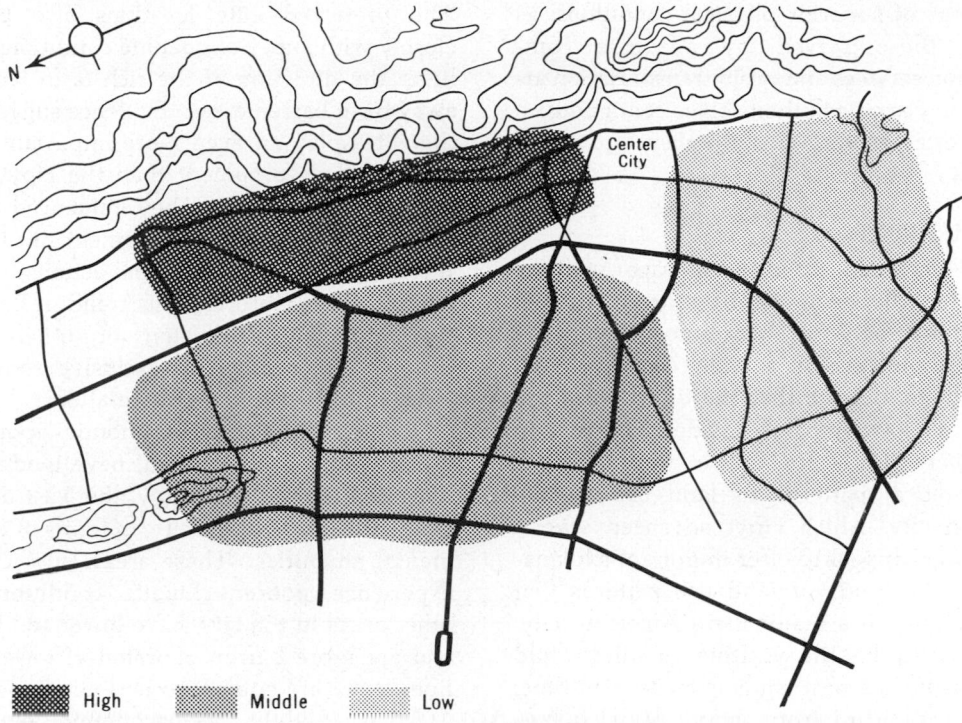

High   Middle   Low

FIGURE 6.   Quality of Climate and Topography, Bogotá, Colombia

TRANSPORTATION AND SERVICE FACILITIES AS DETERMINATES OF ELITE LOCATIONS

We now may ask to what extent has the growth of transportation facilities, particularly the construction and building of roads, as a normative function of government, had on the location of population groups in the city and on the eventual structure and form of city development. A tracing of the development of transportation facilities for the city of Bogotá shows that the growth of the elite population groups, to the north of the old city, followed closely upon the development of means of transportation in this area. Similar developments, however, did not take place to the west or south of the city, although transportation lines also existed in these directions.

The provision of other municipal services such as water, sewerage, and electricity, have not dramatically acted as determinants in the form and structure of the city, as they have

acted as limited factors to its growth and development. The early growth of the city did not depend exclusively on the availability of central water and sewer systems. During the beginning of this century a small amount of growth took place to the north of the city under conditions of limited public services. However, during the 1920s and early 1930s, prior to the elite's large migration out of the central city, most public services were available in the areas north of the old city [17]. On the other hand, the more recent history of the growth of the city of Bogotá, over the past five- to ten-year period, reveals a development mainly confined to areas served by water and sewer systems.

It may thus be reasoned that the availability of communication, transportation, and the municipal services of water, electricity, and sewer facilities in specific areas has correlated to the movement of elites into these areas to the extent to which these facilities were available. The elites may be seen to have moved to those areas of superior physical conditions, as well as those served by adequate communication services and rapid transportation arteries. They arranged themselves contiguous to these arteries or very close to them—generally in a sector pattern.

CONCLUSIONS

We have been concerned in this paper with the relationship between environmental quality and locational behavior, over time, of the upper socioeconomic class in a Latin American city. Our findings indicate that the direction of the growth of upper-income residential areas in Bogotá were of a sector nature. In this regard, the theoretical patterns of land use for the American city, which Hoyt advanced several decades ago, appear to offer important explanations for the kinds of land use patterns that have emerged in a major Latin American city. Hoyt believed that the wealthier families would tend to usurp the best lands in a city over time, and move outward from their original homes in a sector pattern. Moreover, other income groups would accordingly arrange themselves, also in a sector pattern, around or near the elite groups. These concepts bear positive confirmation in this study.

The direction of the growth of upper-income residential areas in Bogotá was observed to be of a sector nature. This pattern roughly placed the elites in the northern sector, the lower-income groups to the south and west, and the middle-income groups to the west, and to areas immediately north of the city. An examination of the environmental conditions of various sectors of the city indicates that significant differences in terms of climate, edaphic, and topographic conditions existed both within and on the peripheries of the city.

The elite residential areas are comparably less humid, cloudy, and damp. Moreover, the areas of elite residences are away from low lands and areas subject to flooding. They are located at generally higher elevations near the eastern mountain ranges bordering the city.

The preferred elite locations also correlate closely with superior edaphic conditions. They lie in the direction of the rich farm lands and away from barren areas. Evidence suggests that the elites play an even more important role in residential development than the Hoyt theory allows. Not only have they influenced the patterns of land use development in the city through their own residential actions, but they have further reinforced this trend in Bogotá by the systematic exclusion of other groups through the passage of exclusive zoning and housing ordinances and regulations.

The lower socioeconomic population groups, on the other hand, have tended to be relegated to, and to occupy, the least desirable residential areas in the city, in terms of environmental amenities. These areas, on the whole, experience poorer climatic conditions than other areas in the city, have lower soil fertility, and are more barren. Located at lower elevations, they are subject to periodic floodings.

The middle socioeconomic population groups are to be found in areas that lie between the upper and lower groups both physically and in terms of environmental conditions. In many cases, they may be considered transitional zones between the two polar groups.

The above factors associate a particular socioeconomic residential pattern with a given set of "pull" forces. Specifically, they associate superior physical conditions with elite neighborhoods. However, we face the difficulty of ascribing to these factors a set of behavioral responses on the part of the elite groups. It can be reasoned that areas to the north of the city were more desirable, and upper-income groups had the power to usurp these lands. Nevertheless, it is not possible to attribute direction and spatial arrangement to any one factor in the environment. Many factors appear to have been involved, and the relative importance of each appears to be less than a cumulative weight of the total factors involved.

Obviously, more research is needed in the area of analysis and evaluation of Latin American city land use patterns. We need to know more concerning the extent to which environmental qualities influence elite residential location behavior, particularly if we seek to understand and evaluate the impact of this group of key decision-makers on the total array of a city's land uses.

NOTES

1. See F. Stuart Chapin [1956:7–99]. In this section Chapin reviews various theories that have a direct bearing on land use determination. These cut across the disciplines of sociology, economics, and political science. They have particular significance as guides for land use planning since they are concerned with human activity in a broad sense. It is not the purpose of this paper to evaluate these concepts critically but simply to state that they exist.

2. See preliminary paper by F. Stuart Chapin [1967]. In this paper Chapin argues that research effort will increasingly be focusing on what he terms "behavioral antecedents" of location decisions. Specifically, Chapin calls for "more sensitive inputs for land use models," which will take into consideration "individual or household preferences which govern location behavior."

3. See, for example, Leo F. Schnore [1966]. See also Peter W. Amato [1968]. These works include description, analysis, and evaluation of empirical studies by Asael T. Hansen, on Merida in Yucatan; Norman S. Hayner's studies of Oaxaca City and Mexico City; H. B. and A. E. Hawthorn's study of Sucre, Bolivia; Caplow's study of Guatemala City; and F. and L. Dotson's study of Guadalajara, Mexico. The Schnore study also includes Leonard's study of La Paz.

4. Examples of this are numerous in Latin American countries. An examination of what exists in the planning literature in Colombia, Ecuador, and Peru indicates that great efforts are being made to provide necessary municipal services and infrastructure, but no substantial studies are underway concerning location change. At present, a team of French scientists are engaged in developing a land use model for the city of Santiago, Chile. Although this study has not been published to date, it does not appear to involve itself to any significant degree with the antecedents of location decisions.

5. The impact of the Laws of the Indies on the early development of Spanish American cities is well documented. See for example: Robert C. Smith [1955], Dan Stanislowski [1950, 1947, and 1946], Leo F. Schnore [1966: 393].

6. A survey of the five principal colonial residential barrios in the city of Bogota reveals that only 7.5 percent of thirty-one, upper socioeconomic families remained within these areas after the 1938–40 period.

7. This author wishes to acknowledge indebtedness for the major content of this list of assumptions to Gideon Sjoberg [1966], and to Leo F. Schnore [1966].

8. Carlos Martinez, "Santa Fe de Bogotá," *PROA*, Volume 10, p. 17. Grafico del Volume de la Construcción Dado en Pesos. See also *Estadistica Municipales*, for the years 1950–1964, "Polbación Calculada en Construcciónes" for the years 1930–1964.

9. Homer Hoyt [1939:117–119] held that preferential environmental qualities will largely determine the direction of the growth of high grade land areas in cities in the United States.

10. According to data collected from the astronomical observatory of Bogotá during a six-year period, from 1934 to 1939, there were only 60 days registered in which the skies were absolutely clear. These were recorded as follows: eleven days in 1934, nine days in 1935, eighteen days in 1936, thirteen days in 1938, and nine days in 1939. See Departamento Agrologico [1962:20].

11. Anuario Municipal de Estadistica, 1950, p. 18.

12. Anuario Estadistico del Distrito Especial de Bogotá, 1964, p. 31.

13. Departamento de Investigaciones [1961:210]. These figures are based upon eleven hours of possible sunlight per day.

14. Anuario Estadistico, 1950, p. 16; Anuario Estadistico 1964, pp. 16 and 34.

15. It should be noted that the desire for sunshine and warmth drives a substantial number of Bogotá's population off the Sabana into the "hot land" towns of Girardot, Melgar, and surrounding pueblos on weekends and holidays.

16. See Peter W. Amato [1968:181–185]. In this study, an intensive investigation is made on soil types on the Sabana of Bogotá. Five types of soils are located and analyzed as to their productivity and natural vegetations.

17. See J. G. White Engineering Corporation [1929].

REFERENCES

Amato, Peter W., 1968. "An Analysis of the Changing Patterns of Elite Residential Locations in Bogotá, Colombia." Ph.D. dissertation, Cornell University.

Chapin, F. Stuart, Jr., 1967. "Activity Systems as a Source of Inputs for Land Use Models." Paper presented at the Highway Research Board Conference on Urban Development Models, June 26–30, Dartmouth College, New Hampshire.

———, 1956. *Urban Land Use Planning* (part 1). Urbana: University of Illinois Press.

Departamento Agrologico, 1962. Levantamiento Agrológico de la Cuenca Alta del Rio Bogotá. Edición Restringida Sugeta O Correciones. Bogotá, D.E. Colombia: Ciudad Universitaria, Instituto Geográfico "Agustin Codazzi."

Departamento de Investigaciones, 1961. Anales de Observatorio Meteorologico Nacional 1960. Bogotá, D.E. Colombia: Ciudad Universitaria, Instituto Geográfico "Agustin Codazzi."

Ginsburg, Norton S., 1966. "Urban Geography and 'Non-Western Areas,'" in Philip M. Hauser and Leo F. Schnore (eds.), *The Study of Urbanization*. New York: John Wiley, pp. 311–346.

Hoyt, Homer, 1939. *The Structure and Growth of Residential Neighborhoods in American Cities.* Washington, D. C.: Federal Housing Administration.

Schnore, Leo F., 1966. "On the Spatial Structure of Cities in the Two Americas," in Philip M. Hauser and Leo F. Schnore (eds.), *The Study of Urbanization.* New York: John Wiley, pp. 347–398.

Sjoberg, Gideon, 1966. "Cities in Developing and in Industrial Societies: A Cross-Cultural Analysis," in Philip M. Hauser and Leo F. Schnore (eds.), *The Study of Urbanization.* New York: John Wiley, pp. 213–263.

Smith, Robert C., 1955. "Colonial Towns of Spanish and Portuguese America," *Journal of the American Society of Architectural Historians* 14 (December):3–12.

Stanislowski, Dan, 1950. The Anatomy of Eleven Towns in Michoacan. Austin: University of Texas Press.

——, 1947. "Early Spanish Town Planning the New World." *Geographical Review,* 37: 94–115.

——, 1946. "The origin and spread of the grid-pattern town." *Geographical Review,* 36:105–120.

White, J. G., Engineering Corporation, 1929. Projecto de alcantarillado para la ciudad de Bogotá. May 1, New York City.

21

WILLIAM H. FORM

The Place of Social Structure in the Determination of Land Use: Some Implications for a Theory of Urban Ecology

Deriving a satisfactory theory of land use change is a pressing problem for both ecologists and urban sociologists.[1] Most of the current thinking on this subject revolves around the so-called ecological processes. A brief inspection of the literature reveals, however, a lamentable lack of agreement on the definition, number, and importance of the ecological processes.[2] It is apparent that the economic model of classical

Reproduced by permission from *Social Forces,* Vol. 32, No. 4 (May 1954), pp. 317–323.

[1] For purposes of simplification this paper will limit itself to a consideration of land use change in middle-size, growing, industrial cities of the United States. Historical analysis of land use change is not within the province of this paper because of the methodological difficulties in reconstructing the ecological processes.

[2] One reason for this confusion centers on the controversy whether human ecology should be related to or divorced from biological ecology. Amos H. Hawley claims that the difficulties of human ecology arise from its isolation from the mainstream of ecological thought in biology; see his "Ecology and Human Ecology," *Social Forces,* 22 (May 1944); 399–405. Warner E. Gettys is of the opinion that human ecology should free itself from its primary dependence on organic ecology; see his "Human Ecology and Social Theory," *Social Forces,* 18 (May 1940); 469–476.

economists from which these processes are derived must be discarded in favor of models which consider social realities.

In studying land use change, this paper proposes that ecology abandon its sub-social non-organization orientations and use the frame of reference of general sociology. Even though the focus of attention of ecology may remain in the economic realm, a sociological analysis of economic behavior is called for. This means that most of the current ecological premises must be converted into research questions capable of sociological verification.

The first step is to analyze the social forces operating in the land market. Obviously the image of a free and unorganized market in which individuals compete impersonally for land must be abandoned. The reason for this is that the land market is highly organized and dominated by a number of interacting organizations. Most of the latter are formally organized, highly self-conscious, and purposeful in character. Although at times their values and interests are conflicting, they are often overlapping and harmonious. That is, their relationships tend to become structured over a period of time. From a study of this emerging structure one obtains a picture of the parameters of ecological behavior, the patterns of land use change, and the institutional pressures which maintain the ecological order.

FOUR ORGANIZATIONAL CONGERIES IN THE LAND MARKET

The interacting groups, associations, and relationships which comprise this emerging structure may be identified by asking such questions as: (a) Who are the largest consumers of land? (b) Which organizations specialize in dealing with land? and (c) Which associations mediate the conflicts of land use? Preliminary research suggests that, among the many associations and interests in American society, four types of social congeries or organizational complexes dominate the land market and determine indirectly the use to which land is put.

The first and most important of these congeries is the real estate and building business.[3] Since they know more about the land market of the city than comparable groups, it is suggested that the study of the real estate-building groups (along the lines of occupational-industrial sociology) would provide more insight into the dynamics of land use change then present studies which are based on the sub-social ecological processes. The analysis of real estate organizations is an especially good starting point to build a sociological ecology because these organizations interact with all of the other urban interests which are concerned with land use.[4]

The second social congeries which functions in the land market are the larger industries, businesses, and utilities. While they may not consume the greatest quantities of land, they do purchase the largest and most strategic parcels. Unknowingly their locational decisions tend to set the pattern of land use for other economic and non-economic organizations. Most of the land use decisions of these central industries and businesses are a response to peculiar historic circumstances in the community. Therefore it would seem fruitless to describe a priori the geometric shape of the city as a series of rings, sectors, or diamonds.

The third social constellation in the land market is composed of individual home owners and other small consumers of land. In a sense their position is tangential to the structure or important only under rather unusual circumstances. Most of their decisions on where to buy, when to buy, and what land to buy are fitted into an administered land market and are

---

[3] It appears that an interpenetration of organization and interests of these two groups is increasing so rapidly in American cities that for many purposes they may be conceived as one interest group.

[4] This is strongly suggested by strikingly parallel studies in two different types of cities. Cf. Everett C. Hughes, "A Study of a Secular Institution: The Chicago Real Estate Board" (unpublished Ph.D. dissertation, University of Chicago, 1928); Donald H. Bouma, "An Analysis of the Social Power Position of the Real Estate Board in Grand Rapids, Michigan" (unpublished Ph.D. dissertation, Michigan State College, 1952).

not, as many would assume, individual, discrete, free, and unrelated. The social characteristics of the consumers, their economic power, degree of organization, and relations to other segments of the community help explain the role they play in the market of land decisions.

The fourth organizational complex is comprised of the many local governmental agencies which deal with land, such as the zoning boards, planning commissions, school boards, traffic commissions, and other agencies. This organizational complex is loosely knit internally, for its segments often function at cross purposes. Their relations to other groups in the community vary with political currents. Unlike other organizations, these governmental agencies are both consumers of land and mediators of conflicting land use interests. Thus political agencies not only acquire land to placate private and public pressures, they are also called upon to resolve conflicts between different types of land consumers. Moreover, some of these governmental agencies try to fulfill a city plan which sets the expected pattern of the ecological development of the city.

These four organizational complexes [5]— real estate, big business, residents, and government—do not comprise all of the organizational entities which participate in land use decisions. However, they are the main ones. Once identified, the problem is to find the nature of the social relationships among these organizational complexes. Is a stable pattern discernable? How does the pattern manifest itself in physical space? In what direction is the pattern emerging as a response to inter-institutional trends in the broader society? To answer these questions, an analytical model is needed to appraise the social relations among the four organizational congeries identified above.

ELEMENTS IN THE ANALYTICAL MODEL

Sociologists have not yet derived completely satisfactory schema to analyze inter-organizational relations, either in their structural or dynamic dimensions. However, ecologists are dependent on such general schema as have already been worked out. Some of the basic elements in the analytical scheme to appraise the relations among the four land consuming groups are described below.

1. The first element in the model is the amount and types of economic resources which each "grouping" has to buttress its land use decisions. Obviously the resources of the four "groupings" differ considerably. Thus, industry has property and capital which are somewhat greater and more mobile than those of the real estate industry. In addition to their tax resources, governmental agencies have the power to expropriate land in their own name or in the name of any interest which can control them. The individual home owner and small businessman, on the other hand, not only have the smallest but the least organized economic resources. The economic resources of each group must be carefully gauged in each community where there is a contest to control particular parcels of land. However, economic resources comprise only one cell in the paradigm needed to analyze the structural setting of land use changes.

2. The second factors which merit consideration are the manifest and latent functions of each "grouping" in the land market. Thus, the functions of the real estate industry include, in addition to maximizing its earnings, bringing knowledge of available land to different segments of the community. Moreover it tries to organize the land market and control land values to assure itself stability and continuity of income. [6] In the process of so doing, the realtors come into contact with political, citizen,

---

[5] Each organizational complex is comprised of groups, associations, aggregations, social categories, and other types of social nucleations. To facilitate communication, the term "grouping" will be used to refer to this organizational complex. I am indebted to Professor Read Bain for pointing to the need for terminological clarification in matters dealing with interaction of different types of social nucleations.

[6] See Everett C. Hughes, "Personality Types and the Division of Labor," in Ernest W. Burgess (ed.), *Personality and the Social Group* (Chicago: University of Chicago Press, 1929), especially pp. 91–94.

and business agencies. [7] The land interests of big business, on the other hand, are much more specific and spasmodic than those of the real estate business. The desire of businessmen to have large stretches of land under one title, to obtain land additions close to present plant operations, and to dominate the landscape of the community, often leads them to make diseconomic decisions which are in conflict with those of other groups.

Government agencies have quite different and sometimes conflicting functions to perform. Among these are: protecting present tax values, acquiring parcels of land for specific public or quasi-public uses, altering certain land use patterns to conform to the plan of the "city beautiful," acting as a clearing house and communication channel for those who need land use data. Most important, they mediate conflicts in land use and exercise their legitimate authority for groups which curry their favor.

Individual residents and small businessmen are mostly concerned with preventing changes in land use. They tend to be defensive-minded and sentimentally attached to their neighborhoods and to fight to prevent the encroachment of usages which would threaten present economic and social investments. In general, resident groupings do not play dynamic roles in changing urban land usages.

3. The internal organization of these four groupings differ considerably. Knowledge of this factor is important to assess the degree to which they may be mobilized to fight for control over desired lands. Often small, unified, and organized groups with meagre economic resources can dominate larger, richer, and more loosely knit groups in a land struggle. These four "groupings" differ in their internal structure and external relations. There is an urgent need for research to study the cleavages, cliques, alliances, and arrangements found within and among these groupings. However, certain trends may now be noted.

The real estate industry is slowly emerging from a haphazard aggregation of local agents to a tightly organized professional or fraternal society which seeks to establish control over the land market. [8] Big business and industry, on the other hand, have typically bureaucratic structures capable of marshalling tremendous resources in the community for or against other land-interested groups. Municipal agencies, though individually powerful, are often unaware of each other's activities. Therefore they tend to comprise a loosely knit set of bureaus which often function at cross purposes. Since many governmental agencies are tied into the fabric of private associations, they are united to common action only under unusual external pressures. Individual residents and small businesses are the most loosely organized. [9] In fact, they tend to remain unorganized except under "crisis" conditions.

4. Each grouping has an accountability pattern differing in its consequences for action. Each has different kinds of pressures and influences to which it must respond. For example, the real estate organizations are primarily accountable to themselves and sometimes to their largest customers, the building industry and the utilities. On the other hand, the local managers of larger corporations tend to be accountable to other managers, stockholders, and board members who may not reside in the community. Thus, local managers may have to respond in their land decisions to pressures generated outside of the community. Municipal agencies are formally accountable to the local citizens who are, *according to the issues*, realtors, individual landlords, businessmen, educational, political, or any other organized interest.

---

[7] Ibid., Hughes indicates that the real estate industry is a loose federation of different types of businessmen. Each type plays a different role to correspond to its clientele and market.

[8] Ibid.

[9] Higher status areas of the city are usually more formally organized to protect land uses than are lower status areas. The formation of neighborhood "improvement and betterment" associations stabilizes land use and resists the invasion of other land uses.

Each of the four social congeries being considered is organized differently as a pressure group interested in land use policies. Each, in a sense, lives in a power situation which consists of its relation to the other three. Different kinds of alliances are made among them and among their segments, depending on the issues. The types of collective bargaining situations which arise among them must be studied in a larger context in order to understand the sociology of land use decisions. For example, businessmen who are sometimes appointed as members of city planning commissions may be constrained to play roles incongruous with their business roles. As members of residential and recreational organizations they may be forced to make decisions which may seem contradictory to their economic interests.

5. In land decisions involving the whole city, the image which each grouping has of the city must be appraised. The realtors are usually the most enthusiastic boosters of the city. They envision an expanding city with an ever-growing land market, for this assures them income and security. Consequently, they exert pressure on the municipal agencies to join them in their plans for the "expansive city."

However, municipal officials do not conceive of the city primarily as a market. They see it as the downtown civic center, the city beautiful, and the planned community. Although desiring an expanding city, they are equally concerned with the politics and aesthetics of locating parks, avenues, schools, and other services. At times their aesthetic-political plans conflict with the boom ideology of the realtors and the industry-oriented plans of businessmen. Indeed this is almost inevitable in some situations, for politicians must secure votes to remain in office. Plans for different areas of the city must be weighed in terms of how they affect votes. [10]

The industrialists' conception of the community tends to be more partial than that of any other group. Since industries often have allegiances to non-community enterprises, they are not necessarily enamoured by the vision of the expansive city or the city beautiful. They are inclined to view the city primarily as their work plant and residence. They usually regard the existence of their enterprises as economic "contributions" to the city. Therefore they feel that any land decisions they desire as businessmen, golfers, or residents are "reasonable and proper" in view of their "contribution" to the locality. When their demands are not met, they can threaten to remove the industry to more favorable communities.

The citizen's view of the city is also segmental. He tends to envision it as his neighborhood, his work plant, and "downtown." These are the areas he wants to see protected, beautified, and serviced. Since residents do not comprise a homogeneous group, obviously their community images differ. The nature of the intersection of the segmentalized city images of these four social congeries provides one of the parameters for studying their interaction. Needless to say, other non-ecological images that these groups have of themselves and of each other have a bearing on their relations. However, since the problems of this paper are more structural than social psychological, this area will not be expanded.

6. Other factors in the analytical scheme may be derived which point to the different orientations and relations existing among these groups. For example, their primary value orientations differ. For government, community "service" is ostensibly the chief value; for real estate, it is an assured land market; for business, it is profitable operations; for the resident, it is protection. Another distinction may be in terms of the amount and type of land interests of the groups. Whereas real estate is interested in all of the city's land, municipal agencies are more interested in communal lands, and industry is concerned with its private land use. The future task of sociologists will

[10] For an illuminating case history of this, see William Foote Whyte, *Street Corner Society* (Chicago: University of Chicago Press, 1947), pp. 245-252.

be to select the most important interactional areas of these groups to locate the forces responsible for land use patterns and changes.

LAND USE CHANGES IN A ZONING CONTEXT

Following the selection of some of the important dimensions in the paradigm, the task is to characterize briefly the pattern of the relationships among the four "groupings." In the broadest sense, the model to be followed is that used in analyzing the collective bargaining structure and process. [11] An excellent place to begin observing the "collective bargaining" relations among these groupings is in the zoning process of cities. Zoning is recommended because the methodological problems of studying it are minimal, and yet the kinds of intergroup relations found there are not unlike those in non-zoning relations.

Since almost every city of any consequence in the United States is zoned, any significant deviation in a pattern of land use necessarily involves a change in zoning. It would appear then that sociologists and ecologists should study the relations of land-interested agencies to municipal agencies. [12] Most zoning commissions tend to freeze an already existing pattern of land use. If they formulate plans for city growth, these plans tend to correspond to a sector image of expanding areas of ongoing land use. This results in a rather rigid ecological structure which inevitably generates pressure for changes. Since such changes involve obtaining the consent of municipal agencies, a political dimension insists itself into the study of ecological processes.

Traditional ecologists may object to this social structural and political approach to problems of land use change. They may suggest that the ecological concept of "dominance" provides the answer to the question of which group will determine land use or land use change. An examination of this concept in the ecological literature reveals a basic shortcoming. Ecological dominance refers to economic control in the symbiotic sense; it provides no analytical cues to appraise the relations among organizations which comprise the structure dealing with land use changes.[13]

Traditional ecologists may object that the proposal to study the relations of the four land "groupings" in a political context is merely a methodological innovation, in that the *results* of such a study would point to the same pattern of land use change available by recourse to the traditional ecological processes. They may reason that determination of land use after all is an economic struggle or process, in which the most powerful economic interests determine to what use land will be put. While it is true, they may agree, that this process is not as simple and as impersonal as hitherto believed, the end result is very much the same. [14]

The writer has recently been gathering cases of zoning changes that have occurred in Lansing, its fringe, and in the outlying areas. In addition, cases have been observed where attempts to institute zoning changes have failed. In both types of changes the questions were asked: (a) Did naked economic power dictate the decision to change or not to change the zoning? (b) Could the outcome of these cases be predicted by using a cultural ecology frame of reference? A brief analysis of the cases revealed

[11] Herbert Blumer, "Sociological Theory in Industrial Relations," *American Sociological Review,* 12 (June 1947): 271–278. See also the articles in Richard A. Lester and Joseph Shister (eds.), *Insights into Labor Issues* (New York: The Macmillan Company, 1948); William Foote Whyte, *Pattern for Industrial Peace* (New York: Harper and Brothers, 1951); H. D. Lasswell, *Politics* (New York: McGraw-Hill, 1936).

[12] Richard Dewey, "The Neighborhood, Urban Ecology, and City Planners," *American Sociological Review,* 15 (August 1950): 502–507.

[13] See R. D. McKenzie, *The Metropolitan Community* (New York: McGraw-Hill, 1933), pp. 81–313; Don J. Bogue, *The Structure of the Metropolitan Community* (Horace J. Rackham School of Graduate Studies, University of Michigan, 1949), pp. 10–13.

[14] In this respect the position of the ecologists is not significantly different from the Marxist analysis of land use changes. This may explain the appeal of the ecological approach to some otherwise sophisticated sociologists. I am indebted to G. P. Stone for the elaboration of this idea.

that no simple economic or cultural analysis could account for success or failure of zoning changes. The actual outcome could be better analyzed on the basis of the paradigm suggested above. Four cases will be briefly summarized to suggest typical kinds of alliances found in attempts to change land use.

In Lansing, the zoning commission may recommend changes in zoning but the City Council must approve of them. This means that all changes in land use must occur in a political context. In 1951, a local metal fabricating plant asked the Council to rezone some of its property from a residential to a commercial classification so that an office building could be erected on it. The residents of the area, who are mostly Negroes, appeared before the Council urging it to refuse the request on the ground that the company had not lived up to legal responsibilities to control obnoxious smoke, fly-ash, traffic, and so on. In addition, they contended that space for Negro housing was limited and rezoning would deprive them of needed space. Moreover, they hinted that the company's request came indirectly from a large corporation which would eventually obtain the property. In short, they urged rejection of the request not on its own merits but on the basis that the company had not lived up to its community responsibilities. Company spokesmen denied any deals, promised to control air pollution, and got labor union spokesmen to urge rezoning. The Council complied. Four months later all of the properties of the company, including the rezoned area, were sold to the large corporation in question.

Here is a clear case of economically powerful interests consciously manipulating land uses for their purposes. The question arises: why did not the large corporation itself ask for rezoning? Apparently, it realized that greater resistance would have been met. The local company is a medium-sized, old, home-owned enterprise which has had rather warm relations with its employees. The large corporation, on the other hand, is a large, impersonal, absentee-owned corporation that has at times alienated local people. [15] Therefore, its chances of getting this property without fanfare were increased by the use of an intermediary.

Yet business does not always win. In another case, a respectable undertaker established a funeral parlor in a low income residential area. The local residents objected strenuously to the presence of the business. The legal aspects of the case remained obscure for a time because the undertaker insisted he did not embalm bodies in the establishment. In a preliminary hearing he appeared to have won a victory. The aroused residents called upon the Republican ward leader who promised to talk to the "authorities." Just before a rehearing of the case, the undertaker decided to leave the area for he was reliably informed that the decision would go against him.

Struggles between businessmen and government do not always work out in favor of the former. Currently, the organized businessmen of East Lansing are fighting an order of the State Highway Commission which has passed a no parking ordinance to apply to the town's main thoroughfare. The retailers are fearful that they will lose business if the order holds. Since business will not be able to expand in the same direction if the order holds, pressure to rezone residential areas in the community for commercial and parking purposes will be forthcoming. In a community where residents are a strong, vocal, upper middle status group majority, such pressure may be resisted strongly. Clearly a power struggle involving the State, local businessmen, local government, and the residents will determine the ecological pattern of the city. [16] A knowledge of their relationships is needed to predict the outcome of the struggle and the future ecological changes in the community.

---

[15] For example, workers insist that during the depression the company recruited Southerners rather than local labor.

[16] My colleague, G. P. Stone, suggests that it begins to appear that the State's position will force a very unusual ecological phenomenon: a business district turning its back to the main highway and reorienting itself to the "backyards," as it were.

S. T. Kimball has documented a case where the failure to inaugurate zoning involved the same kind of social structural analysis of group relations as suggested above. Kimball studied a suburban rural township where the upper middle status groups failed in a referendum to obtain zoning in the face of an industrial invasion of the area. An analysis of the case showed that the issue would be misunderstood if studied as a struggle of economic interests. In fact, the industrial interests were not an important variable in the case. The failure of the referendum was accounted for by analysis of five types of relationships: (a) those among the suburbanites, (b) those within the township board, (c) those between the supervisor and his constituents, (d) those between the farmers and suburbanites, and (e) those between the supervisor and the informal "leaders" in the community. [17]

CONCLUSIONS

This paper has proposed the need to consider social structure in addition to ecological and cultural factors in the study of changes in land use. The traditional ecological processes are no longer adequate tools to analyze changes in land use. These processes, like most ecological concepts, are based on models of eighteenth century free enterprise economics. Yet fundamental changes in the structure of the economy call for new economic models which in turn call for a recasting of general ecological theory. The new vital trend of cultural ecology does not do this adequately, for it considers the structural realities of urban society only indirectly.

This paper proposes that ecological change be studied by first isolating the important and powerful land-interested groupings in the city. Certain elements in an analytical scheme have been proposed to study the collective bargaining relationships among these groupings. The *forces* that operate in land-use change may well be studied in the socio-political struggles that are presently occurring in the area of zoning. A brief survey of some changes in urban zoning points to the greater adequacy of the sociological over the traditional ecological analysis for understanding and predicting land use changes.

[17] Solon T. Kimball, "A Case Study of Township Zoning," *Michigan Agricultural Experiment Station Quarterly Bulletin*, 28 (May 1946): 4.

22

AVERY M. GUEST

Patterns of Family Location

ABSTRACT

Theoretical propositions from human ecology are used to develop a model that explains the centralization or decentralization of various types of families, such as married couples with children, in the Cleveland, Ohio, Metropolitan Area. The model shows how proximity to the Central Business District affects neighborhoods in terms of three

Reprinted by permission from *Demography*, Vol. 9, No. 1 (February 1972), pp. 159–172.

characteristics: Age or period of development, both internal and external housing Space, and Site features such as industrial and recreational activity. These structural characteristics are seen, in turn, as the causes of the location of families in relationship to the center of Cleveland. Of the three characteristics, Space generally plays the most important and Site the least important role in determining the location of types of families. However, the location of most types of families is affected by a variety of interrelationships among neighborhood characteristics.

Human ecologists have been primarily interested in how metropolitan population growth and size affect the distribution of land uses in relationship to the Central Business District (CBD), and how these in turn affect the distribution of types of population, such as higher status persons, in relationship to the CBD. There has been some confusion, however, on the issue of whether the spatial organization of the city is determined by short-run competitive pressures for central land or by the past growth of the city.

The importance of short-run competition is emphasized in the work of Hawley [1950]. He argues that large metropolitan areas have vigorous competition for central land, which is highly valued for its centrality to transportation points and all parts of the city. Central land prices are driven up by the bidding, and only those activities willing and able to pay the central rents locate near the CBD. According to Hawley [p. 280], businesses and industries, particularly, outbid other activities for the central land. Recreational and residential activities, with little economic power, are apt to be driven out of the CBD. Furthermore, the residential land which is found near the CBD must be developed intensively, since most residents of the city could not afford large tracts of central land. Thus, residential areas around the CBD in large cities would be expected to have a large number of dwellings-per-acre of residential land, and each residential unit would have little internal space, or few rooms-per-dwelling. Using this basic theory about the segregation of land uses in large cities, Hawley has argued that the congestion or high intensity of land use around the CBD drives higher status persons to the outskirts.

Other human ecologists, while not seriously disagreeing with the above analysis, have placed more emphasis on past growth of the city as a determinant of land use patterns. In short, the age of a neighborhood may affect other neighborhood characteristics independently of short-run competition. In fact, the relationship between distance from the CBD and the characteristics of neighborhoods may be partially due to the fact that old neighborhoods are located close to the CBD. Thus, Winsborough [1963] has shown how age affected neighborhood density in Chicago independently of distance from the CBD. This finding can be interpreted within the context of improved transportation technology (primarily the automobile), which has permitted persons to live at low density far from their work place. Beverly Duncan [1964] has shown how old Chicago neighborhoods are particularly apt to be located near manufacturing employment. Much of the tendency for manufacturing activity to be centrally located may be due to a former dependence on water transport facilities which were located near the CBD. The development of rail and motor transport has allegedly permitted the decentralization of manufacturing.

Human ecologists, on the whole, have been more interested in applying their theory of the segregation of land uses to the location of higher status persons and racial and ethnic groups than to types of families. Nevertheless, Burgess [1963], perhaps the best known human ecologist, argued that homeless men and unmarried young adults would be found disproportionately near the center of cities whereas married couples with children would be found disproportionately toward the outskirts of cities. Burgess' predictions appeared related to the availability of large, single family dwellings on the outskirts for families in the childbearing stage and to the availability of small, multiple unit housing in the area around the CBD for homeless men and unrelated one- or two-person households.

Burgess' [1963: 64] observation that "The larger the city, the more differentiated its areas and its family types" was fully consistent with ecological theory. However, it was often difficult to determine from Burgess' work whether he subscribed to views emphasizing short-run competition or previous growth as important in determining the spatial organization of the city.

The validity of the Burgess viewpoint about the importance of space for family location has been clearly demonstrated. For instance, Rossi [1955] showed for a sample of Philadelphia families that intraurban mobility was most characteristic of two types of families, those in the childbearing period in search of housing space and those who had completed childbearing and were seeking less space.

There is also ample evidence to suggest that age and site features of neighborhoods, integral to human ecology theories, affect the distributions of types of families. In regard to site, David Riesman [1957] has suggested that one of the prime causes of suburbanization, pri-

marily among families in the childbearing period, has been flight from the "industrialism" of the central city and the drawing power of the green spaces on the outskirts. In his study of Toronto suburbs, Clark [1966] found that both housing space and age were important in predicting the location of types of families. Younger families with children were primarily found in newly developed, single unit areas, whereas older families, often through the childbearing stage, were found in older suburbs. Clark's analysis would suggest that neighborhoods pass through life cycles in which newly built housing is inhabited by newly formed families whereas older housing tends to have families who have "aged" with the neighborhood. This pattern is also suggested by Hoover and Vernon [1962: 219–226] in their study of the New York Metropolitan Region.

Using ideas of the human ecologists, we have thus suggested theoretical justification for a model of family distribution in old, large metropolitan areas. As indicated in Figure 1, this model shows distance from the CBD affecting Site (recreational and industrial land uses) and the distribution of housing by Age or period of development and Space (dwellings-per-area and rooms-per-dwelling). In turn, these variables affect the distributions of types of families. If past growth of the city is impor-

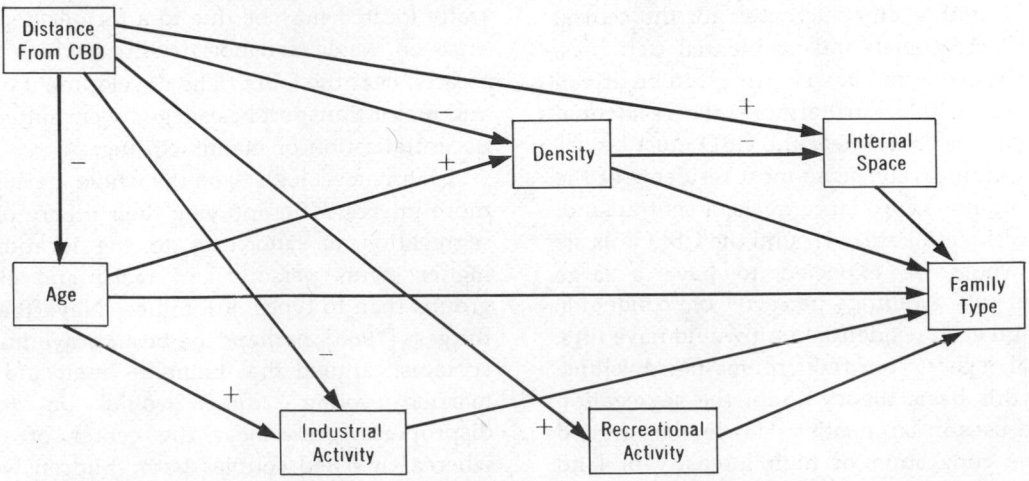

FIGURE 1. Hypothesized Model of Family Location

tant for present structure, Age may also have an effect on the distributions of types of families through its effect on density and location of industrial activity, independent of distance. Finally, we have included a path from dwellings-per-acre to rooms-per-dwelling, since most low density, single unit housing seems to be larger in size than multi-dwelling apartment housing.

This model will be evaluated with the statistical technique of path analysis, using census tract data drawn from the 1960 and 1963 statistical reports for the Cleveland, Ohio, Metropolitan Area. Cleveland, old and large in population, represents the type of place where the arguments of the human ecologists could be validly tested. Families will be characterized by their stage in the married-life cycle and by the presence of a married couple in the household.

Our model is admittedly limited in the sense that we have not included all variables which might affect the location of family types. The effects of some of these variables, such as tract racial composition, owner occupancy status, and rent and housing evaluation levels, has been discussed elsewhere [Guest 1970: 57–81]. In general, except for race, these other variables had little partial relationship with the proportions of various family types once the effects of the Age, Space, and Site variables had been controlled. When the model was run separately for black tracts, the results were similar though less clear.

In the next section, we shall operationalize the six types of families to be used in the empirical analysis. Following this, we shall test our model and discuss the results.

FAMILY TYPES

We defined six types of families or pseudo-families on the basis of available 1960 data. Four types represent idealized stages in the life cycle of married couples: Young Couples, husband under 45 with no children under 18 at home; Young Families, husband under 45 with children under 18 at home; Old Families, husband over 45 with children under 18 at home;

Old Couples, husband over 45 with no children under 18 at home. The other two types of families, Single Heads and Primary Individuals, do not contain married couples as heads of the household. In Single Head families, there are relatives (perhaps some children) living together, while Primary Individual living units generally consist of one to three unrelated individuals.

The number of each of the four types of married couples is based on data reported for a 25 percent sample of all married couples [U. S. Bureau of the Census 1962, Table P-1]. For Cleveland, the same table also shows that 98 percent of all married couples have their own households.

While a typical married couple will move through these four stages of Young Couple, Young Family, Old Family, and Old Couple, it appears that many married couples (as defined by the U. S. Census Bureau) would not follow such an idealized pattern. Most of the problems with the data are discussed elsewhere by Edwards [1970].

The other two types of families, Single Heads and Primary Individuals, are based on a census household or living unit definition. Most of these two types of households are headed by persons from broken marriages, single adults, and widowed persons, particularly the latter. Census data for the U.S. population in 1960 showed that 46.9 percent of Single Heads and 47.2 percent of Primary Individuals households were headed by widowed persons, presumably elderly in age [U. S. Bureau of the Census 1964, Table 2].

To control for variation in population size of census tracts, we have operationalized each family type as a percentage of the total of the six family types in the tract. This poses some problems in interpreting the results of the statistical analysis, since the six types are logically interrelated—knowledge of the proportions of five types in a census tract automatically indicates the proportion of the sixth type. However, without this standardization procedure, the results of the regression analysis or path analysis would have become confounded with population size.

As Table 1 shows, it is indeed true that these family types vary with distance from the Cleveland CBD. Young Families and Old Families in the mature childbearing stage are found disproportionately on the outskirts of Cleveland, while Single Heads and Primary Individuals are found more often near the center. Old Couples, presumably just through the childbearing period, are somewhat decentralized, although the relationship with distance is slightly curvilinear. The peak concentrations occur near the outskirts, but there is a clear drop in concentration in the last two mile-distance zones. The sixth family type, Young Couples, presumably about to begin childbearing, shows little relationship with distance from the CBD.

However, it should be emphasized that most of the variance in each family type is left unexplained by linear distance from the CBD. We were unable to find significant other spatial patterns, such as sectoral or location in relationship to Lake Erie, that might account for much more of the variance in the family types.

These relationships between distance and the proportion of each family type are generally consistent with our expectations. Given that families with children, Young Families and Old Families, should be attracted to the outskirts by the presence of recreational activity and spacious housing, we would expect them to be particularly decentralized. Young Families might also be decentralized through the use of new housing. Single Heads and Primary Individuals should be particularly centralized by their use of the small space of central housing. Furthermore, since these families are often headed by elderly widowed persons, they might be found particularly in old housing near the city center. There may be some propensity for widows to live in the neighborhood where they lived as spouses in families with children. The relatively strong propensity for Old Couples to be decentralized is somewhat surprising, given the fact that they should have fewer space needs than families in the childbearing stage and that they might be found in the old housing near the city center. On the other hand, the weak relationship between the proportion of Young

TABLE 1. Mean Proportion of Family Types by One Mile Distance Zones from Cleveland CBD[a]

Zone	Family Type					
	Young Couples	Young Families	Old Families	Old Couples	Single Heads	Primary Indiv.
0–1 (13)	5.7	16.7	5.2	12.0	10.5	50.8
1–2 (35)	7.5	25.3	8.0	16.4	17.0	25.6
2–3 (46)	8.1	27.6	8.7	20.3	14.6	20.5
3–4 (47)	8.3	27.6	9.6	23.7	12.8	17.8
4–5 (46)	7.3	25.2	11.2	27.6	11.6	16.9
5–6 (44)	6.3	28.8	13.0	28.9	9.6	13.3
6–7 (35)	6.0	32.3	13.9	29.1	8.3	10.4
7–8 (28)	8.0	41.1	13.4	23.3	6.7	7.4
8 plus (59)	6.5	39.6	14.8	25.4	6.1	7.5
Grand Mean (353)	7.2	30.4	11.4	24.1	10.8	16.1
Standard Deviation	3.0	10.7	4.8	7.1	4.9	12.7
Zero-Order r with linear Distance from CBD	−.10	.52	.54	.43	−.65	−.60

[a] Number of tracts in parentheses.

Couples and distance from the CBD is generally expected. Location in areas of new housing might lead to their decentralization. But this family type should have little tendency to locate in reference to Site or Space. Some of these families might seek large amounts of space in preparation for childbearing, whereas others would seek small amounts for their current minimal needs.

THE MODEL

In this section, we shall test the model outlined in Figure 1 by first determining whether the model of the relationships among the distance, Age, Space, and Site variables has empirical support. We shall then determine whether the model can account for the relationships among the distance and family type variables. And finally, we shall show how various paths explain the centralization or decentralization of various family types.

In interpreting the results, it should be remembered that the analysis is based on cross sectional data. Since some of the human ecologists' arguments are based on propositions about change over time, it would be valuable to have a longitudinal analysis. However, data on family composition of tracts for decades before 1960 are not in readily analyzable form.

In testing our original model, we drew data on Age and Space characteristics from Table H–1 of the census tract report [U. S. Bureau of the Census 1962]. Distance from the census-defined CBD was estimated in terms of one mile concentric zones. Site characteristics were drawn from a special 1963 survey (Cleveland-Seven County Transportation Land Use Study, 1968).

The sample will consist of 353 census tracts found in the Cleveland Standard Metropolitan Statistical Area (SMSA), consisting of Cuyahoga and Lake Counties. Fourteen census tracts were eliminated from the analysis because they had fewer than 100 persons, had significant institutionalized populations, or lacked data on Site characteristics.

Our tool of analysis, path analysis, can help in handling two principal tasks: (a) determining whether the structural variables account for the relationships between distance from the CBD and the proportions of family types, and (b) showing the relative importance of various paths in accounting for these relationships. Thus, as an example, we can try to reproduce the correlation between linear distance from the CBD and the proportion of Young Families, and then we can show whether the decentralization of new areas or the decentralization of low density housing is more important in accounting for the location of Young Families. These two tasks can be accomplished by using the fundamental theorem of path analysis, $r_{ij} = \Sigma p_{iq} r_{jq}$, where i and j denote two variables in the system and the index q runs over all variables from which paths lead directly to variable X_i. Some of the basics of path analysis are explained by O. D. Duncan [1966]. The basic inputs into the model, the zero order correlations among variables, are shown in Table 2. Since some of the correlations among variables are quite high, there are clearly problems in distinguishing the effects of one variable from the effects of another. The distance and Age and the distance and density (dwellings-per-area) variables are particularly associated. The same problem was found when alternate measures of Age were used, such as period of housing build-up.

Since the dependent variables in the analysis are the variances of the family type proportions, the reader should be aware that we are not showing how a specific level of density, for instance, affects the proportion of a certain family type. Our concern is explaining the variance that exists, not the amount of the variance. As Table 1 shows, some of the family types tend to have much more variance then others, particularly Young Families and Primary Individuals. However, this issue is not the concern of the present study.

In testing our original model, paths were generally kept if the path coefficients equalled at least .10 and the correlations between most pairs of variables could be closely reproduced. As we shall shortly note, paths had to be added

TABLE 2.   Zero Order Correlations of Structural Characteristics and Family Types

Selected Characteristics	Age[a]	Internal Space[b]	Density[c]	Industrial[d]	Recreational[e]
Age	—				
Internal Space	−.31	—			
Density	.66	−.65	—		
Industrial	.22	−.36	.30	—	
Recreational	−.25	.17	−.31	−.15	—
Distance	−.74	.55	−.82	−.30	.29
Young Couples	.07	−.29	.20	.20	−.08
Young Families	−.65	.36	−.53	−.01	.11
Old Families	−.44	.67	−.66	−.24	.16
Old Couples	−.12	.65	−.44	−.35	.12
Single Heads	.61	−.27	.59	.15	−.30
Primary Individuals	.53	−.74	.67	.19	−.08
Mean Value	.70	5.1	2.2	−4.8	−5.7
Standard Deviation	.34	.9	1.3	2.0	1.8

[a] Age—proportion of household units built before 1940.

[b] Internal space (rooms-per-dwelling)—mean number of rooms per household unit.

[c] Density (dwellings-per-acre)—natural logarithm of number of household units per acre of residential land.

[d] Industrial—natural logarithm of proportion of total land area in industrial uses.

[e] Recreational—natural logarithm of proportion of total land area in recreational open spaces such as parks and golf courses.

where their absence would mean large differences between implied and actual correlations.

As predicted, Age and distance both made independent contributions to residential density (see Figure 2), although the effect of Age was quite small. In other words, there is little evidence that neighborhood Age had much effect on areal density independent of distance from the CBD. It is also noteworthy that our model could almost perfectly reproduce the correlations among Age, industrial, and recreational variables by the paths from distance to each of these variables. Therefore, we dropped the hypothesized path from Age to the industrial variable.

Our original model also had to be revised by adding paths from the Age and industrial variables to internal space, rooms-per-dwelling. Without these paths, there were serious differences between the implied and actual correlations for several pairs of variables in the model. Our additional paths suggest that older areas tend to have more internally spacious

housing than newer areas, and that industrial areas have smaller living units than nonindustrial areas. The reasons for these clear relationships are not readily explainable. As a result of these multiple paths to rooms-per-dwelling, distance from the CBD has both negative and positive impact on the internal space of housing.

Given this basic empirical model, we can undertake our two most important tasks: (a) explaining the correlations between distance from the CBD and the proportions of family types, and (b) indicating the strengths of various paths in explaining these correlations. We shall discuss each of these in turn.

As Table 3 shows, our model does an excellent job of reproducing correlations between distance from the CBD and the proportions of various family types, particularly in regard to Young Families, Old Families, and Primary Individuals. Of the other three types, only Old Couples and Single Heads had clear relationships with distance from the CBD. The failure of the model in predicting completely the spa-

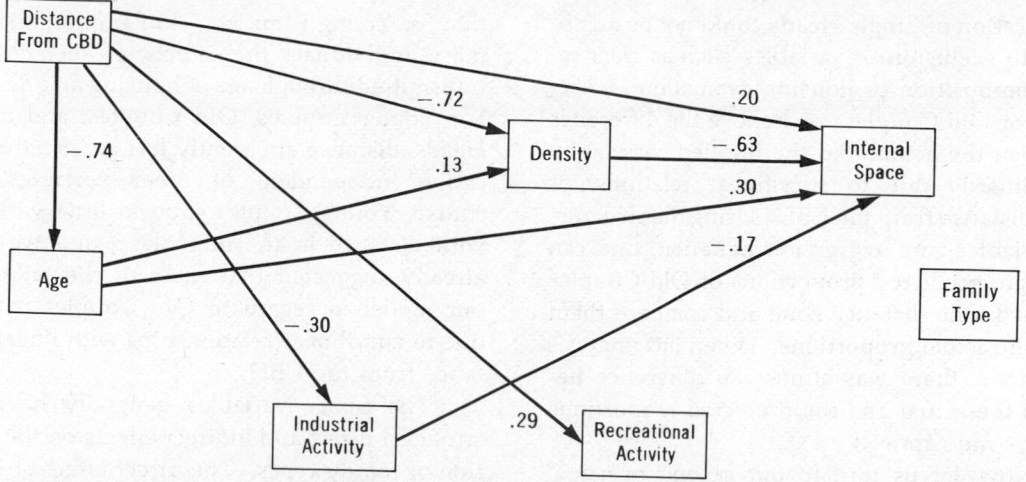

FIGURE 2. Actual Model of Family Location

All path coefficients were at least three times as large as their standard errors. Lines or paths to family types are not shown.

Relationship	Actual ®	Implied ®	Coefficients of Determination (R²) for Dependent Variables	
a. Age–Industrial	.22	.22	a. Age	.55
b. Age–Recreational	−.23	−.21	b. Density	.68
c. Recreational–Internal Space	.09	.14	c. Internal Space	.50
d. Industrial–Recreational	−.12	−.08	d. Industrial	.09
e. Density–Industrial	.30	.22	e. Recreational	.08
f. Density–Recreational	−.31	−.21		

TABLE 3. Standardized Partial Regression Coefficients (Path Coefficients) for Effects of Structural Variables on Location of Family Types[a]

Variable	Family Type					
	Young Couples	Young Families	Old Families	Old Couples	Single Heads	Primary Indiv.
Age	−.06	−.60	−.11	.19	.37	.31
	(.07)	(.05)	(.05)	(.05)	(.05)	(.04)
Internal Space	−.24	.21	.46	.53	.09	−.63
	(.07)	(.05)	(.05)	(.05)	(.05)	(.04)
Density	.04	−.08	−.30	−.18	.37	.13
	(.08)	(.07)	(.06)	(0.7)	(.07)	(.05)
Industry	.11	.21	.04	−.15	−.02	−.12
	(.06)	(.04)	(.04)	(.04)	(.04)	(.03)
Recreation	−.03	−.07	−.03	.00	−.12	.12
	(.06)	(.04)	(.04)	(.06)	(.04)	(.03)
R^2	.09	.50	.55	.46	.46	.67
Implied r with Distance	−.16	.53	.56	.35	−.55	−.60
Actual r with Distance (353 tracts)	−.10	.52	.54	.43	−.65	−.60

[a] Standard Errors in parentheses.

tial location of Single Heads could not be attributed to exclusion of variables such as tract racial composition or housing evaluation levels.

For Old Couples, we believe the difference between the actual and the implied correlation is primarily due to curvilinear relationships with distance from the CBD. Using the structural variables in a regression equation, one can generate predicted proportions of Old Couples for each mile distance zone and compare them with the actual proportions. When this analysis was done, there was almost no difference between the actual and the predicted proportions for any mile zone.

Now, let us turn to our second principal task, showing how different paths lead to the centralization or decentralization of various family types. The direct effects of each predicting variable are shown in Table 3, and the effects of various paths from distance to family types are shown in Table 4.

In general, the most important variables for predicting the proportions of family types are those relating to Age and Space. Site features play very little role. The model demonstrated that for Young Families, Old Families, and Primary Individuals the effects of distance are transmitted through age of housing and density. For Young Couples, Old Couples, and Single Heads, distance apparently has an effect on location independent of other variables. Of course, Young Couples showed little variation with distance in the first place, and we have already suggested that most of the failure of our model in regard to Old Couples may be due to curvilinear relationships with linear distance from the CBD.

The Space variables generally have the strongest direct and indirect effects on the location of family types. The direct effect of internal space or rooms-per-dwelling is particularly impressive. Young Families, Old Families, and Old Couples show fairly clear tendencies to be located in areas of internally spacious housing, while Young Couples and Primary Individuals are located disproportionately in the opposite types of areas. Most of the effect of the internal space variable is transmitted through the distance-density relationship. In short, much of the tendency for Young Families, Old Families,

TABLE 4. Values for Paths from Distance to Family Types

Selected Variables	Family Type					
	Young Couples	Young Families	Old Families	Old Couples	Single Heads	Primary Indiv.
Di–Ag	.04	.44	.08	−.14	−.27	−.23
Di–De–Ro	−.11	.09	.21	.24	.04	−.28
Di–Ag–Ro	.05	−.05	−.10	−.12	−.02	.14
Di–Ro	−.05	.04	.09	.11	.02	−.13
Di–Ag–De–Ro	−.01	.01	.03	.03	.01	−.04
Di–In–Ro	−.01	.01	.02	.03	.00	−.03
Di–De	−.03	.06	.22	.13	−.27	−.09
Di–Ag–De	.00	.01	.03	.02	−.04	−.01
Di–In	−.03	−.06	−.01	.05	.01	.04
Di–Re	−.01	−.02	−.01	.00	−.03	.03
Sum	−.16	.53	.56	.35	−.55	−.60

Symbols: Di–Distance from CBD
Ag–Age
Ro–Internal space or rooms per dwelling
De–Density or units per acre
In–Industrial activity
Re–Recreational activity

and Old Couples to be found on the outskirts may be attributed to the existence there of low density, spacious housing. Young Couples and Primary Individuals are centralized for the opposite reasons. Density or dwellings-per-area also has a strong direct effect on location for Old Families, Old Couples, and Single Heads, independent of the number of rooms-per-dwelling. The first two family types are partially decentralized due to their use of low density housing on the outskirts, regardless of the number of rooms-per-dwelling, whereas Single Heads are particularly centralized due to their use of high density housing, regardless of its other characteristics. These results, then, suggest that much of the distribution of families is simply a function of differential intensity of residential land use.

Age of area has strong direct effects on the location of three types of families. Young Families are found particularly in new areas, while Primary Individuals and Single Heads, often widowed persons, are found particularly in old areas. Thus, much of the tendency for these families to be centralized or decentralized may be explained by the location of old housing near the city center and new housing on the outskirts, regardless of the other characteristics of housing. Since Age has little effect on density, very little centralization or decentralization of family types may be attributed to indirect effects of Age. There is some tendency for Age to operate indirectly through the rooms-per-dwelling variable, but we have little understanding of why this should occur.

Although the effects are small, Site features actually operate opposite to expectations for some family types. For instance, Young Families and Old Families are found particularly in areas of industry and little recreation when other ecological variables are controlled. It should be emphasized, however, that the effects are very weak.

Given this model, we may now summarize the reasons for centralization or decentralization of types of families.

Young Families and Old Families are de-centralized, but apparently for somewhat different reasons. Young Families are on the outskirts primarily due to the presence of relatively new housing, while Old Families are there because of low density housing.

Both Primary Individuals and Single Heads are found toward the CBD because they live in old areas. Primary Individuals are also particularly centralized because of residence in high density areas; density is less important for Single Heads.

Of the other two types, only Old Couples had much relationship to distance from the CBD. In this case, paths have noticeably opposite effects. Thus, Old Couples are decentralized due to residence in low density areas but centralized due to residence in older areas; that is, there are forces pulling them toward both the center and outskirts of Cleveland. There is also some tendency for location in new neighborhoods to decentralize Young Couples, whereas location in high density neighborhoods tends to centralize them.

A composite model of the distribution of families in relationship to the CBD would indicate whether the tendency of various types of families to live in the same or different neighborhoods could be due to attraction or repulsion by the same ecological features. To determine whether this is true, we can compare the actual correlations between the proportions of each family type over the census tracts with the correlations implied by our model. As Table 5 shows, the implied correlations are generally similar in size to the actual, although the levels of relationship often differ substantially. For instance, while the tendency of Young Families and Primary Individuals to locate in different areas can be explained partially by neighborhood characteristics (basically Age and Space variables), there is also a very large unexplained difference between them. At this point, we cannot say why this difference occurs.

SUMMARY AND DISCUSSION

It is clear that the arguments of the human ecologists are valuable for understanding the

TABLE 5. Implied and Actual Correlations Among Family Types[a]

Family Type	Family Type					
	Young Couples	Young Families	Old Families	Old Couples	Single Heads	Primary Indiv.
Young Couples		.06	−.40	−.38	.11	.03
Young Families	−.07		.28	−.14	−.39	−.73
Old Families	−.19	.40		.47	−.41	−.63
Old Couples	−.21	.16	.43		−.25	−.43
Single Heads	.08	−.42	−.35	−.16		.21
Primary Individuals	.20	−.48	−.59	−.44	.38	

[a] Actual above diagonal; implied below.

location of types of families in the metropolis. Much of the tendency for family types to be located close to or distant from the CBD may be explained through the distance-density and distance-Age relationships. In fact, the tendency for Young Families and Old Families to be decentralized and for Primary Individuals to be centralized can be almost completely explained by the model.

Given the massive evidence [Muth, 1969] that population densities decline in a fairly regular manner with distance from the CBD, one would expect generally similar patterns of family distribution in most American metropolitan areas. Indeed, we [Guest 1970] have shown that patterns of family distribution in sixteen other metropolitan areas are generally similar to those found in Cleveland.

The direct effect of areal Age on patterns of family location may indicate the importance of the neighborhood life cycle in understanding the distribution of population. Neighborhoods, regardless of their housing and Site characteristics, may indeed pass through life cycles in their family composition, from Young Families to Old Couples, Primary Individuals, and Single Heads. This, of course, has been only suggested, not demonstrated by the model. While areal Age may exert a direct effect on family location, there is little evidence that it has much indirect effect through other variables.

The ecologists' model would suggest that patterns of family distribution in relationship

to the CBD should be most distinct in the largest metropolitan areas, whether for reasons stemming from the greater competition for central land or from the generally old age of the area around the CBD. However, we have elsewhere [Guest 1970: 162] correlated (for Cleveland and the sixteen other metropolitan areas) population size with the predicted change in the proportion of each family type for each mile distance zone from the CBD. This analysis showed that the proportions of Young Families and Old Families increased most rapidly with distance from the CBD in the smallest places, while the proportions of Single Heads and Primary Individuals decreased most rapidly with distance from the CBD in the smallest places. This result was consistent with Muth's [1969: 152] finding that the density gradient changed most rapidly in the smallest places. While these results seem to be contradictory to current ecological theory, we have no present explanations. Obviously, more research is needed into the process of neighborhood change as cities age and grow in population.

While this paper has been directed toward an analysis of family location in terms of human ecology theory, it is perhaps appropriate to note the relationship of our results to the other major tradition of urban spatial research, factorial ecology. For a full analysis of factorial ecology, see Rees [1970]. The factorial ecologists, in numerous studies of the organization of U. S. cities, have produced at least two principal dimensions of urban differentiation, socioeconomic status and family status. These dimensions have resulted from the application of factor analytic techniques to matrices of correlations among population and housing characteristics for census tracts. The factorial ecologists have generally produced a family status dimension that indicates the joint presence (or absence) in tracts of low female labor force participation, high fertility, a young age structure, and single unit housing.

In regard to our analysis, the family status dimension probably corresponds most closely to the disproportionate presence in certain tracts of Young and Old Families and the absence of Single Heads and Primary Individuals. As Table 5 shows, there is some tendency for Young and Old Families to be found together in tracts not inhabited by Single Heads and Primary Individuals. And, of course, the presence or absence of single unit, or low density, housing on the family dimension is consistent with our finding that the residential density pattern has a strong effect on the location of families. Furthermore, the factorial ecologists have found that the family dimension varies concentrically with distance from the CBD, in a manner consistent with the variation of Young and Old Families and Single Heads and Primary Individuals.

Beyond this clear similarity, our results diverge. Most importantly, our results suggest that patterns of family location cannot be completely, or even primarily, summarized by one dimension, family status. The generally low intercorrelations among the types of families would suggest that most neighborhoods are apt to have a relatively wide range of family types.

Furthermore, there are multiple interrelations of Age, Site, and Space variables which produce the locations of various types of families. It would also seem that the factorial ecologists have been particularly neglectful of the role of past urban growth or areal age in determining the location of families.

To us, exciting research questions center around the effects of historical, technological, and population processes in determining the structure of the city. Human ecology has a long tradition of theory and analysis from which this search may be continued. The factorial ecologists have barely begun.

An important recent series of articles on factorial ecology [Berry 1971] indicates an awareness of some of my criticisms. For instance, various authors recognize the possibility that family locational patterns cannot be summarized neatly in one dimension, that housing age or period of construction affects the types of families in a neighborhood, and that general location patterns of types of families must be understood as products of the city's past growth. This suggests the probability that there is convergence in the work of factorial ecology and human ecologists.

ACKNOWLEDGMENTS

This research was supported by grants from the National Institutes of Health to the Center for Demography and Ecology, University of Wisconsin; from the University of Wisconsin Institute for Research in Poverty; and from the University of Wisconsin Graduate Research Committee. An earlier draft of this paper was improved immeasurably by the comments of James A. Davis.

REFERENCES

Berry, Brian J. L. (ed.), 1971. "Comparative Factorial Ecology." Special Issue, *Economic Geography*, 47, No. 2.

Burgess, Ernest, 1967. "The growth of the City," in Robert E. Park, Ernest W. Burgess, and Roderick D. McKenzie (eds.), *The City*. Chicago: University of Chicago Press.

——, Harvey J. Locke, and Mary Margaret Thomas, 1963. *The Family*. New York: American Book Co.

Clark, S. D., 1966. *The Suburban Society*. Toronto: University of Toronto Press.

Cleveland-Seven County Transportation-Land Use Study, 1968. Supported by the commission of that name. Cleveland, Ohio.

Duncan, Beverly, 1964. "Variables in Urban Morphology," in Ernest W. Burgess and Donald J. Bogue (eds.), *Contributions to Urban Sociology*. Chicago: University of Chicago Press.

Duncan, Otis Dudley, 1966. "Path Analysis: Sociological Examples," *American Journal of Sociology*, 72:1–16.

Edwards, Ozzie L., 1970. "Patterns of Residential Segregation within a Metropolitan Ghetto." *Demography*, 7:185–193. [No. 48 in this volume.]

Guest, Avery M., 1970. "Families and Housing in Cities." Unpublished Ph.D. dissertation, University of Wisconsin, Madison.

Hawley, Amos H., 1950. *Human Ecology: A Theory of Community Structure*. New York: Ronald Press.

Hoover, Edgar M., and Raymond Vernon, 1962. *Anatomy of a Metropolis*. New York: Anchor Books.

Muth, Richard F., 1969. *Cities and Housing*. Chicago: University of Chicago Press.

Rees, Richard, 1970. "Concepts of Social Space: Toward an Urban Social Geography," in Brian J. L. Berry and Frank E. Horton (eds.), *Geographical Perspectives on Urban Systems*, Englewood Cliffs, N.J.: Prentice-Hall, Inc.

Riesman, David, 1957. "The Suburban Dislocation." *Annals of the American Academy of Political and Social Science* 314:123–146.

Rossi, Peter, 1955. *Why Families Move*. Glencoe, Ill.: The Free Press.

United States Bureau of the Census, 1962. *U. S. Censuses of Population and Housing: 1960. Census Tracts*. Final Report PHC(1)–28. Washington: Government Printing Office.

——, 1964. *U. S. Census of Population: 1960. Subject Reports. Persons by Family Characteristics*. Final Report PC(2)–4B. Washington: Government Printing Office.

Winsborough, Hal H., 1963. An Ecological Approach to the Theory of Suburbanization. *American Journal of Sociology*, 68:565–570. [No. 5 in this volume.]

The Factorial Ecology of Cities

part v

In recent years there has been a very rapidly growing literature dealing with the factorial ecology of cities. Factorial ecology involves the application of factor analysis techniques to urban subarea data in order to identify the basic demographic dimensions along which subareas become differentiated. Two major emphases are found in factorial ecology: social area analysis and factorial ecology per se. The two approaches differ in the initial selection of inputs. Social area analysis elects variables which basically reflect social rank, family form, and ethnicity. Of major concern to the social area analyst is the extent to which the three dimensions are independent of each other. Their degree of independence is discussed usually in terms of an underlying model of social change espoused by social area analysts.

Factorial ecology per se is also concerned with the basic dimensions of city patterning but in selecting input variables factorial ecologists are not restricted to only those dealing with the rank, familism, and ethnicity dimensions. The theoretical discussions of factorial ecology results frequently involve the same theoretical model as that employed by the social area analysts.

There are nine papers in this section that deal with social area analysis and factorial ecology. Their focus is mainly upon the substantive findings for a number of world cities. While factorial ecology is fraught with a number of methodological issues, their discussion is taken up in the paper by Schwirian (1) in Part I.

analysis and presents an empirical test of the model for Los Angeles and San Francisco. The paper concludes that the factors of economic rank, family status, and ethnic status are necessary to account for variations among subareas in a number of specific variables. Furthermore, Bell reports that for both cities the index measuring familism is unidimensional, as is that for social rank.

The generality of the social area indexes is the topic of the paper by Van Arsdol, Camilleri, and Schmid (24). In a study of 10 regionally diverse U.S. cities they note some support for the social area hypotheses, but also show some interesting deviations from predicted patterns. In the course of their discussion they suggest some alternative models to those of social area analysis. They also point out that their study focuses upon the general empirical validity of the indexes and is not really a test of the theory itself. Neither is it an examination of the degree of integration between the theory and its indexes nor of the relative utility of the social area model as opposed to alternative models.

The Anderson and Bean (25) paper presents a thoughtful discussion of the social rank and urbanism dimensions of social area analysis. On the basis of data from Toledo they conclude that the concept of *residential prestige* is better suited to describe the status dimension of urban area differentiation, given the areal nature of the data, than is the more usual concept of *social rank*. In addition to finding an important residential prestige factor in Toledo, they also find that the housing characteristics of the urbanism dimension tend to form a separate factor from those variables describing family characteristics.

The spatial patterning in terms of concentric zones and sectors of the social area analysis indexes is the topic of the Anderson and Egeland (26) paper. In a cross-sectional analysis of several U. S. cities they find the residential prestige (social rank) index distributed primarily by sector and the urbanism dimension distributed primarily by distance gradient. They also report differences among cities in which sector contains the high prestige residential area. Thus, the high prestige areas of one city tend to be oriented differently in terms of the compass from those of other cities.

Several papers in this section focus upon the factorial ecology of cities outside of the U. S. and are attempts to verify U. S. findings in other cultural settings. The generality of the social area model for Canadian cities is discussed by Schwirian and Matre (27) as well as the spatial patterning of the indexes in terms of sectors and concentric zones. The data, from the 11 largest Canadian cities, show generally a factorial separation of social rank from the other variables and of ethnicity. The indicators of familism tend to separate from each other in many of the cities. Spatially, it seems that for most of the cities the social rank index is distributed more by sector than distance gradient while the familism index, particularly the housing variable, is distributed more by distance than sector. There seems to be no systematic pattern among the cities as to the spatial distribution of ethnicity.

Urban ecological patternings are argued by Schwirian and Smith (28) to be largely a function of city size and level of economic development of the society in which the city is located. Data from similarly sized cities in Puerto Rico and Canada show that in a highly developed society there is marked factorial differentiation in cities regardless of their population size, while in a newly developing society the larger the city the more ecologically differentiated it is. Differences in ecological differentiation among the various size cities in Puerto Rico is explained in terms of a diffusion model of social change.

The paper by Latif (29) presents a longitudinal analysis of the factorial ecology of Alexandria, Egypt in comparison to that of Cairo. Latif reports both similarities and differences between the ecological structure of the two Egyptian cities and discusses them in terms of societal development. Also of a comparative nature is Berry and Spodek's (30) study of the factorial ecology of India's large cities. Their paper is largely concerned with the effect of change and increasing diversity of Indian society upon the urban ecology of its cities. It seems that social status is the key factor in the urban geography of the Indian cities. The caste status and class status systems are reinforcing each other in the spatial patterning of the urban areas. Recent changes have also promoted the increasing importance of familism as a dimension of urban organization.

The last paper in this section, which deals with a large European city, is Sweetser's discussion of Helsinki (31). Sweetser reports six fundamental dimensions in the city's residential patterning. They are socioeconomic status, progeniture, feminine careerism, residentialism, established familism, and postgeniture.

23

WENDELL BELL

Economic, Family, and Ethnic Status: An Empirical Test

In *The Social Areas of Los Angeles* Shevky and Williams construct an urban typology based on three dimensions: economic status, family status, and ethnic status. [1] They have demonstrated the use of their typology as an analytic method for the study of certain aspects of the social structure of large cities by applying it to the 1940 census data for Los Angeles County. The unit of analysis is the census tract, and each tract population is typed with respect to its con-

[1] Eshref Shevky and Marilyn Williams, *The Social Areas of Los Angeles, Analysis and Typology* (Berkeley and Los Angeles: University of California Press, 1949). Shevky and Williams name the three dimensions social rank, urbanization and segregation respectively. For reasons stated elsewhere, the writer prefers the alternative terms *economic status* to social rank, *family status* to urbanization, and *ethnic status* to segregation. These latter designations will be used throughout this paper. The term "status" is used to indicate that a sub-population's *position* with respect to each dimension is determined. No prestige connotation is implied here by the use of the term "status."

Reprinted by permission from the *American Sociological Review*, Vol. 20, No. 1 (February 1955), pp. 45–52.

The writer gratefully acknowledges the grant of a Predoctoral Research Training Fellowship by the Social Science Research Council in 1951–52 under which this and related studies were executed. Special acknowledgement is also made to Professors Leonard Broom, William S. Robinson, and Eshref Shevky of the University of California, Los Angeles, for their advice and counsel.

figuration of scores on the indexes of economic status, family status, and ethnic status. Since the original formulation of the method by Shevky and Williams, several minor methodological revisions have been made which permit the use of the typology in the study of different cities at the same time and the study of the same city at two different times. [2] While later modifications may be introduced to refine the technique still further, the typology, as presently constructed, constitutes a usable framework for the systematic comparative study of the broad outlines of the social structure of contemporary American cities. It is the purpose of this paper to test the extent to which the three dimensions are necessary to account for social differentiation between urban sub-populations in two metropolitan areas, and to determine whether the indexes selected to measure the three dimensions are unidimensional measuring instruments.

THE HYPOTHESES

Shevky and Williams do not devise any test to determine if their specification of economic status, family status, and ethnic status, as three factors of modern social differentiation, is empirically supported by the social relations in the Los Angeles Area. Yet, the adequacy of their urban typology rests upon the extent to which these three factors do, in fact, account for the observed social differentiation between census tract populations in the region under study.

To provide such a test, the following hypothesis was formulated:

H₁—Economic status, family status, and ethnic status, each represent a discrete social factor which is necessary to account for the differences between urban sub-populations with respect to social characteristics.

[2] For example, see Wendell Bell, "The Social Areas of the San Francisco Bay Region," *American Sociological Review,* 18 (February 1953): 39–47; and Eshref Shevky and Wendell Bell, *Social Area Analysis: Theory, Illustrative Application, and Computational Procedures* (Stanford: Stanford University Press, 1955).

Shevky and Williams, in addition to specifying the three social dimensions, select a set of measurements for each of them, from which indexes are constructed. A second hypothesis, formulated here, concerns the unidimensionality of these indexes of the three social factors. That is, even if economic status, family status, and ethnic status are three social dimensions necessary to account for the social differentiation of sub-populations in Los Angeles in 1940, these indexes might not be adequate measures of them. By unidimensionality is meant that each of the three indexes should order the census tracts along a single continuum, and a continuum discrete from the other two continua. The index of economic status, composed of measures of occupation, education, and rent, for example, should measure only one thing, and should, when applied, order the census tracts along a single scale. Unambiguous interpretation of index scores for census tracts requires that every index score should represent a point on a single scale commensurate with the value or size of the score. That is, a specific census tract's score on the index of economic status should reflect only one configuration of scores on the three measures, occupation, education, and rent. If these three measures vary independently, the confusion in interpreting an economic status score can readily be seen. Similarly, the implicit assumption made by Shevky and Williams is that the three measures composing the index of family status represent a single continuum and a different continuum from that measured by the index of economic status. Finally, it is assumed that the index of ethnic status measures still another discrete continuum. The unidimensionality of the index of ethnic status, however, is not tested here since it was used as a composite index from the beginning of the analysis.

The elements of the second composite hypothesis are as follows:

H₂ₐ—Measures of occupation, education, and rent compose a unidimensional index of the economic status of urban sub-populations.

H_{2b}—Measures of fertility, women in the labor force and single-family detached dwelling units compose a unidimensional index of the family status of urban sub-populations. [3]

The definitions of the seven variables are as follows:

Economic Status

1. Occupation—the number of craftsmen, operatives and laborers per one thousand employed persons.
2. Education—the number of persons twenty-five years old or over who have completed grade school or less per one thousand persons twenty-five years old or over.
3. Rent—average rent per capita.

Family Status

1. Fertility—the number of children under age five per one thousand women in the fifteen to forty-four age group.
2. Women in the labor force—the number of women in the labor force per one thousand women of fourteen years of age and over.
3. Single-family dwelling units—the percentage of all dwelling units which are single family detached.

---

[3] Stated in relation to high family status the variables are fertility, single-family detached dwelling units, but women *not* in the labor force. Thus a high score on the index of family status indicates that the tract population contains many intact families with many children, with the women in the home as wives and mothers, and with the typical mode of residence being the single-family detached house.

Ethnic Status

1. Subordinate ethnic groups—the number of Orientals, Negroes, Mexicans, plus the number of foreign-born white from Italy and Russia per one thousand persons.

THE CENTROID SOLUTION

The first step in testing these two interrelated hypotheses was to compute the intercorrelations between the seven measures: occupation, education, rent, fertility, women in the labor force, single-family dwelling units, and subordinate ethnic groups. Twenty-one correlation tables were constructed, and Pearsonian coefficients were computed summarizing the covariation among these measures over the 570 census tracts in the Los Angeles Area as of 1940. That is, the interrelationships between these seven measures were determined for the tracts used by Shevky and Williams in the analysis of the Los Angeles Area. Table 1 contains these intercorrelations. Variables three and five—rent, and women in the labor force—were reflected, making their definitions consistent with the other measures in their respective indexes. As now defined, occupation, education and rent show low economic status; fertility, *women not in the labor force*, and single family dwellings show high family status, and ethnic status shows high ethnic status. That is, all the signs of the correlation coefficients in columns three and five and in rows three and five were reversed.

TABLE 1.   Correlation Matrix for the Seven Measures, Los Angeles, 1940

Measures	1 Occ.	2 Educ.	−3 Rent	4 Fert.	−5 WLF	6 SFDU	7 SEG
1 Occupation		.730	.710	.810	.560	.373	.319
2 Education	.730		.696	.650	.277	.047	.649
−3 Rent	.710	.696		.538	.311	.049	.356
4 Fertility	.810	.650	.538		.690	.560	.383
−5 WLF	.560	.277	.311	.690		.680	−.063
6 SFDU	.373	.047	.049	.560	.680		−.030
7 SEG	.319	.649	.356	.383	−.063	−.030	

The centroid matrix resulting from factoring the correlation matrix by Thurstone's method is shown in Table 2.[4]

TABLE 2.   The Centroid Matrix, Los Angeles, 1940

Measures	I	II	III	h^2
1 Occupation	.886	.075	−.233	.845
2 Education	.777	.511	.088	.873
−3 Rent	.693	.390	−.361	.763
4 Fertility	.913	−.189	.089	.877
−5 WLF	.646	−.560	−.185	.765
6 SFDU	.485	−.635	.065	.643
7 SEG	.465	.447	.444	.613

THE HYPOTHESIZED MATRIX

There are many ways to express the results of this factorial analysis, but just one of these has relevance here. The purpose is to test two specific hypotheses. Consequently, it is possible to set up the hypotheses in the form of expected factor loadings or item-factor correlations in the rotated matrix. The two interrelated hypotheses both imply, if they are true, a specific structure in the rotated matrix. If these hypotheses are true, the rotated matrix should contain three factors; first, economic status, with heavy factor loadings on occupation, education, and rent, and with small factor loadings on the other measures; second, family status, with heavy factor loadings on fertility, women in the labor force, and single-family dwelling units, and with small factor loadings on the other measures; and third, a factor of ethnic status with a heavy factor loading on just one measure, the measure of subordinate ethnic groups. The predicted item-factor correlations, that is, the

expected pattern of the rotated matrix if the hypotheses were true, are given on the left side of Table 3.[5]

TABLE 3.   The Hypothesized Matrix and the Observed Matrix, Los Angeles, 1940

Measures	Predicted			Observed		
	I	II	III	I	II	III
1 Occupation	+	0	0	+	0	0
2 Education	+	0	0	+	0	+
−3 Rent	+	0	0	+	0	0
4 Fertility	0	+	0	0	+	0
−5 WLF	0	+	0	0	+	0
6 SFDU	0	+	0	0	+	0
7 SEG	0	0	+	0	0	+

I Economic Status
II Family Status
III Ethnic Status
0 Small Factor Loadings
+ Large Factor Loadings

ROTATION TO TEST THE HYPOTHESIS

The method of averages was used to rotate the centroid matrix.[6] This method gives an easy approximation to the method of oblique axes, and rotates the centroid matrix in such a way that the hypothesized matrix will be reproduced, if possible. That is, if the intercorrelations in the original correlation matrix are such that it is possible to reproduce the hypothesized matrix, the method of averages will approximate that reproduction. The rotated matrix and the transformation matrix resulting from the application of this method to the centroid matrix are shown in Table 4.

For a comparison of the general pattern of the item-factor correlations of the rotated matrix with the hypothesized matrix, the loadings in the rotated matrix were dichotomized either as high or low and placed in another matrix.[7]

---

[4] L. L. Thurstone, *The Vectors of the Mind* (Chicago: The University of Chicago Press, 1935). Ordinarily more than seven variables are used in factor analysis, but in this case the number of measures is limited to those actually used by Shevky and Williams. Using the criterion for the number of factors given in Quinn McNemar, "On the Number of Factors," *Psychometrika*, 7 (March 1942): 9–18, it was determined that there still is left a small amount of common variation in the variables after the three factors are removed.

[5] For another example of rotation to test a hypothesis see William S. Robinson, "The Motivational Structure of Political Participation," *American Sociological Review*, 17 (April 1952): 151–156.

[6] Thurstone, op. cit.

[7] Item-factor correlations above .200 in absolute value were considered high, and values below .200 were considered low.

TABLE 4.   The Rotated Matrix, Los Angeles, 1940

Measures	I	II	III
1 Occupation	.482	.193	−.094
2 Education	.319	−.044	.282
−3 Rent	.653	−.192	−.189
4 Fertility	.109	.562	.176
−5 WLF	.148	.617	−.193
6 SFDU	−.147	.727	.015
7 SEG	−.109	.044	.576
Transformation	.279	.407	.135
Matrix=	.353	−.786	.179
	−.892	.465	.975

I Economic Status
II Family Status
III Ethnic Status

This observed matrix, summarizing the results of the rotated matrix, is given on the right side of Table 3. Comparing the predicted item-factor correlations, on the left side of Table 3, with the observed item-factor correlations, it can be seen that twenty of the twenty-one observed loadings are as predicted. Thus the general pattern of the observed factor loadings verifies the original hypotheses.

As is shown in Table 4, Factor I, economic status, is most highly correlated with occupation (.482), education (.319), and rent (.653); while the correlations with fertility (.109), women in the labor force (.148), single-family dwelling units (−.147), and the item of subordinate ethnic groups (−.109) are all small enough to be considered negligible. In other words, Factor I is a basic continuum composed of the three items: occupation, education, and rent.

Examination of the item-factor correlations for Factor II reveals that the largest factor loadings are again occurring with the hypothesized items. Family status has large factor loadings with the items of fertility (.562), women in the labor force (.617), and single-family dwelling units (.727). (In terms of its relation to high family status, of course, "women in the labor force" should read "women not in the labor force.") Occupation (.193), education (−.044), rent (−.192), and subordinate ethnic groups

(.044) have loadings on Factor II low enough to warrant the conclusion that the measures of fertility, women in the labor force, and single-family dwelling units make up another basic continuum, discrete from the first, and that this continuum is the dimension of family status.

From the last column in Table 4 it can be seen that the item of subordinate ethnic groups has the largest factor loading (.576) on the third factor, the factor of ethnic status. Although the measure of low education (.282) slightly exceeds the expected item-factor correlation with ethnic status, the correlations with the other five measures support the hypothesis that the index of ethnic status is another discrete dimension composed of just one item, a measure of subordinate ethnic groups. The factor loadings on occupation (−.094), rent (−.189), fertility (.176), women in the labor force (−.193), and single-family dwelling units (.015) are small enough to support this conclusion.

The results of the factorial analysis show that three factors, economic status, family status, and ethnic status, are necessary to account for the social differentiation of urban subpopulations in the Los Angeles Area as of 1940.[8] The factor analysis also demonstrates that the indexes of economic status and family status are unidimensional measuring instruments in the sense that the measures composing each index have high patterns of intercorrelation with one another.

THE CORRELATIONS BETWEEN THE FACTORS

Although the three hypothesized factors have been shown to be discrete social dimensions in the differentiation of the Los Angeles population, the problem of determining the relation-

---

[8] Daniel O. Price, in his "Factor Analysis in the Study of Metropolitan Centers," *Social Forces*, 20 (May 1942): 449–455, completed one of the first multiple factor analyses using population data. However, he was concerned with the problem of *inter*-city differentiation rather than *intra*-city differentiation which is the concern of this paper. He identified four basic factors: degree of maturity, the extent to which a city is a service center, the level of living, and the per capita trade volume of a city.

ships between these discrete factors remains. Each index has been shown to measure a different thing, but are the things they measure in any way related? The correlations between the three underlying continua are shown in Table 5. These correlations represent the relations between the factors after the uniqueness and error have been removed. Each factor has been here defined so that a high score equals a high value with respect to the factor.

TABLE 5. Correlations Between the Factors, Los Angeles, 1940

Factors	Economic Status	Family Status	Ethnic Status
Economic Status	1.00	−.50	−.73
Family Status	−.50	1.00	.15
Ethnic Status	−.73	.15	1.00

When interpreting these correlations it is well to remember that they reflect the association of census tract *averages* on the three factors. The correlation (−.73) between economic status and ethnic status, for example, indicates that census tracts with large concentrations of Negroes, Orientals, Mexicans, Italians and Russians in Los Angeles tended to be those census tracts also characterized by low scores on the index of economic status. This does not indicate that members of these groups were necessarily of low economic status as individuals, but rather it shows that many members of these groups, *whatever their individual economic status*, lived in areas characterized by a predominant number of low economic status people.[9]

The low correlation between the factor of family status and the factor of ethnic status (.15) shows that census tracts characterized by large concentrations of these five ethnic groups tended to have scores along the entire continuum of family status. In other words, there was little relationship between census tract scores on the

family status factor and the census tract scores on the factor of ethnic status.[10]

The relationship between economic status and family status (−.50) indicates that in 1940 Los Angeles census tracts characterized by high economic status were more likely to be characterized by low family status—that is relatively few children under age 5, many women in the labor force, and many multiple-family dwellings—than they were to be characterized by high family status—that is, many children under age 5, many women *not* in the labor force, and many single-family dwellings. This relationship especially reflects the high negative relationship between fertility and the factor of economic status.

THE SAN FRANCISCO BAY REGION FACTORIAL ANALYSIS

The two hypotheses implicit in the Shevky-Williams typology verified for the Los Angeles Area were also tested by the use of a factor analysis of the 1940 census data for the San Francisco Bay Region, where the typology also has been applied. Again, twenty-one correlation tables were constructed; and the interrelations between the seven measures were computed for the 243 census tracts of the Bay Region. The Pearsonian correlation coefficients are shown in Table 6.[11]

Factoring the correlation matrix by the centroid method resulted in the centroid factor matrix reproduced in Table 7.[12]

---

[9] For a statement of the relation between ecological correlations and individual correlations see William S. Robinson, "Ecological Correlations and the Behavior of Individuals," *American Sociological Review*, 15 (June 1950): 351–357.

[10] Shevky and Williams, op. cit., found that there was a slight tendency for ethnic status to vary indirectly with family status when economic status was low, and to vary directly when economic status was high in Los Angeles, 1940. In the San Francisco Bay Region in 1940 there is a small negative correlation between ethnic status and family status at all levels of economic status, but this relationship is more marked at high levels of economic status.

[11] The measure for subordinate ethnic groups includes only four groups for the San Francisco Bay Region, namely, Orientals, Negroes, Mexicans and foreign-born whites from Italy.

[12] Using the criterion for the number of factors given in McNemar, op. cit., it was determined that there still is left a small amount of common variation in the variables after the three factors are removed.

TABLE 6. Correlation Matrix for the Seven Measures, San Francisco Bay Region, 1940

Measures	1 Occ.	2 Educ.	−3 Rent	4 Fert.	−5 WLF	6 SFDU	7 SEG
1 Occupation		.780	.775	.678	.482	.190	.135
2 Education	.780		.796	.490	.126	−.255	.488
−3 Rent	.775	.796		.555	.260	−.051	.360
4 Fertility	.678	.490	.555		.759	.476	.205
−5 WLF	.482	.126	.260	.759		.753	−.066
6 SFDU	.190	−.255	−.051	.476	.753		−.248
7 SEG	.135	.488	.360	.205	−.066	−.248	

TABLE 7. The Centroid Matrix, San Francisco Bay Region, 1940

Measures	I	II	III	h²
1 Occupation	.844	.185	−.319	.848
2 Education	.711	.659	.053	.943
−3 Rent	.771	.457	−.179	.835
4 Fertility	.866	−.256	.114	.828
−5 WLF	.679	−.650	−.073	.889
6 SFDU	.357	−.744	−.175	.712
7 SEG	.301	.394	.426	.427

The hypothesized or predicted matrix was constructed, and the method of averages was used to rotate the centroid factor matrix in such a way as to reproduce the hypothesized matrix, if possible. The hypothesized matrix is shown at the left side of Table 8.

TABLE 8. The Hypothesized Matrix and the Observed Matrix, San Francisco Bay Region, 1940

Measures	Predicted			Observed		
	I	II	III	I	II	III
1 Occupation	+	0	0	+	0	0
2 Education	+	0	0	+	0	+
−3 Rent	+	0	0	+	0	0
4 Fertility	0	+	0	0	+	+
−5 WLF	0	+	0	0	+	0
6 SFDU	0	+	0	0	+	0
7 SEG	0	0	+	0	0	+

I Economic Status
II Family Status
III Ethnic Status
0 Small Factor Loadings
+ Large Factor Loadings

Again, the large factor loadings and small factor loadings are predicted from the hypotheses.

The rotated matrix is given in Table 9. The general pattern of the item-factor correlations was found as before by dichotomizing the rotated factor loadings into high and low item-factor correlations. The right half of Table 8 contains the summarized results of the rotated matrix. Comparing the predicted matrix, based on the hypotheses, to the observed matrix, it can be seen that nineteen of the twenty-one observed item-factor correlations are as predicted. The measures of education and fertility according to the hypotheses should have low item-factor correlations with the factor of ethnic status, but their factor loadings on this factor actually ex-

TABLE 9. The Rotated Matrix, San Francisco Bay Region, 1940

Measures	I	II	III
1 Occupation	.635	.070	−.178
2 Education	.467	−.105	.209
−3 Rent	.602	−.071	−.028
4 Fertility	.097	.630	.215
−5 WLF	.031	.711	−.029
6 SFDU	−.031	.573	−.183
7 SEG	−.098	.106	.496
Transformation	.343	.449	.143
Matrix =	.406	−.689	.083
	−.847	.569	.986

I Economic Status
II Family Status
III Ethnic Status

ceed the .200 level. As may be observed in Table 9 however, the factor loadings on the factor of ethnic status for the measure of education (.209), and the measure of fertility (.215) barely exceed the .200 limit for small loadings, and the general pattern of factor loadings, even for these two items, supports the original hypotheses.

Reviewing the item-factor correlations given in Table 9, the first factor, economic status, is loaded heavily on occupation (.635), education (.467), and rent (.602). It has small loadings on fertility (.097), women in the labor force (.031), single-family dwelling units (−.031), and subordinate ethnic groups (−.098). The factor of family status has small loadings on the measures of occupation (.070), education (−.105), rent (−.071), and subordinate ethnic groups (.106), but has large loadings on fertility (.630), women in the labor force (.711), and single-family dwelling units (.573). The factor of ethnic status has its largest loading on the measure of subordinate ethnic groups (.496). The factor loadings other than those of the measures of education and fertility on the factor of ethnic status are all below the .200 level; they are occupation (−.178), rent (−.028), women in the labor force (−.029), and single-family dwelling units (−.183).

It has been tested empirically that the social dimensions of economic status, family status, and ethnic status are necessary to account for the social differentiation found between census tract populations in the Bay Region.[13] Also, the indexes constructed to measure economic status and family status are found to be unidimensional measuring instruments.

THE CORRELATIONS BETWEEN THE FACTORS

Table 10 contains the correlations between the rotated factors of economic status, family status, and ethnic status for the San Francisco Bay Region. While there are no striking differences between these relations and those shown for the Los Angeles Area in Table 5, it is worth mentioning that the correlation between family status and ethnic status is slightly negative in the Bay Region, but is positive in the Los Angeles Area. Also the negative relationship between economic status and family status is less marked in the Bay Region than in Los Angeles. The general pattern of relationships, however, is the same in both regions: middle range negative correlations between economic status and family status, high negative correlations between ethnic status and economic status, and relatively low correlations between ethnic status and family status.

TABLE 10. Correlations Between the Factors, San Francisco Bay Region, 1940

Factors	Economic Status	Family Status	Ethnic Status
Economic Status	1.00	−.33	−.62
Family Status	−.33	1.00	−.21
Ethnic Status	−.62	−.21	1.00

SUMMARY

Two hypotheses which are implicit in the Shevky-Williams approach to urban differentiation and which underlie the validity of their social types of urban sub-populations were tested for the 1940 populations of the Los Angeles Area and the San Francisco Bay Region. The method of factor analysis was used in a hypothesis-testing framework, which permitted a comparison of the structure of the rotated matrix predicted from the hypotheses with the structure of the rotated matrix computed from the

[13] From the factor analysis described here we can only conclude that the three factors are *necessary* to account for the observed social variation between census tract populations. However, there is some evidence to conclude that the Shevky-Williams factors are *adequate* as well as necessary to account for most of the observed social variation between tract populations which can be extracted from the population and housing data given in the census tract bulletins for the Bay Region as of 1940. Using a much larger universe of variables Professor Robert C. Tryon, University of California, Berkeley, has located three principal clusters which are comparable to economic status, family status, and ethnic status. These three clusters almost completely account for the covariation—thus variation, since the communalities are so large—between tract populations with respect to census variables.

empirical relations in each of the urban areas. From the comparison of the predicted with the observed values in each of the two regions, it was concluded that the two hypotheses were supported.

The verification of the first hypothesis leads to the conclusion that economic status, family status, and ethnic status are three social factors which are necessary to account for variation between census tract populations with respect to certain variables contained in available census data for each urban area. To the extent to which the variables used represent significant aspects of the social differentiation of modern urban society, we can conclude also that these three factors are necessary to account for the observed social differentiation between sub-populations in Los Angeles and in the San Francisco Bay Region. Since these three dimensions are used as the basic elements in the Shevky-Williams typology, these findings represent a partial validation of the urban social area types constructed by Shevky and Williams.

Further validity can be attributed to the typology because the second hypothesis was verified for both urban areas. The indexes selected to measure economic status and family status were shown to be unidimensional measuring instruments.

24

MAURICE D. VAN ARSDOL, JR.
SANTO F. CAMILLERI
CALVIN F. SCHMID

The Generality of Urban Social Area Indexes

Eshref Shevky and his associates Marilyn Williams and Wendell Bell have advanced a system for analyzing census tract populations within a framework of a small number of measures which they regard as having high theoretical significance. The Shevky system, which has become known as "social area analysis," was first applied to Los Angeles[1] and later was used in a study of the San Francisco Bay Region.[2] More recently, Shevky and Bell presented a detailed theoretical discussion which includes the rationale for selection of the measures and mode of analysis.[3]

The Shevky group has differentiated the areal structure of the urban community in terms of an attribute space, delimited by dimensions de-

Reprinted by permission from the *American Sociological Review*, Vol. 23, No. 3 (June 1958), pp. 277–284.

This research was financed by grants from the Research Committee and Agnes Anderson Committee of the Graduate School of the University of Washington. Grateful acknowledgment is made to Wendell Bell for a critical reading of the initial draft of this paper.

[1] Eshref Shevky and Marilyn Williams, *The Social Areas of Los Angeles: Analysis and Typology* (Berkeley and Los Angeles: University of California Press, 1949).

[2] Wendell Bell, "The Social Areas of the San Francisco Bay Region," *American Sociological Review*, 18 (February 1953): 39–47.

[3] Eshref Shevky and Wendell Bell, *Social Area Analysis: Theory, Illustrative Application, and Computational Procedures* (Stanford: Stanford University Press, 1955).

fined by Shevky as "social rank," "urbanization," and "segregation."[4] The index of "social rank" is derived from census tract measures of occupation and education; the "urbanization" index from measures of fertility, women in the labor force, and single family dwelling units; and the "segregation" index from measures of ethnic groups in spatial isolation.[5] Urban typologies are constructed by establishing arbitrary cutting points for the index scores which delimit social area types having the same patterns of census tract scores on the indexes.[6] Social area analysis has been advanced by its proponents as providing a framework for comparative and successional studies and for other forms of research.[7]

Shevky's system has been criticized at both theoretical and empirical levels. Amos Hawley and Otis Dudley Duncan have expressed doubt that the rationale for social area analysis provides a satisfactory theoretical basis for describing social differentiation in geographically delimited areas.[8] In addition, Duncan has questioned the empirical validity and generality of the key indexes—social rank, urbanization, and segregation.[9] While both questions ultimately must be answered, this paper is concerned primarily with the generality of the Shevky indexes. For social area analysis to have the broad comparative utility for which it was intended, the areal units compared must be describable within a common set of measures, which can be observed in the same areas and in other areas at different points in time. While the census measures from which the social

rank, urbanization, and segregation indexes are derived can be observed for many kinds of areal units, ranging from census tracts through regions, these observations in themselves are not sufficient to establish the general applicability of the indexes. The specific claim and distinguishing feature of the Shevky system is that the census measures should be combined in a *particular* way to provide a frame of reference of comparative value. The problem then, in any specific application, centers upon whether or not the six census measures are related in the manner specified by Shevky. By means of factor analysis of 1940 census tract data for Los Angeles and the San Francisco Bay Region, Bell has shown that the census measures form a structure consistent with Shevky's formulations.[10] In the present paper more evidence of a similar nature is presented in order to describe the structure of the measures and dimensions for a larger series of American cities.

FACTOR INTERPRETATION OF SHEVKY INDEXES

The Shevky dimensions of social rank, urbanization, and segregation are abstract variables which cannot be observed directly. Shevky has indicated, however, that the dimensions are reflected in census tract measures, and that indexes of the dimensions can be derived from weighted combinations of census measures. Shevky's description of urban structure can be understood to imply a specific pattern of correlations between observable census measures and abstract dimensions or factors, as shown in Table 1.[11] In Table 1 a plus sign (+) indicates a high positive correlation between a measure listed in a row and a factor listed in a column; a zero sign (0) indicates a low correlation. The mode of combination of the census tract measures shown in Table 1 implies the following set of factor hypotheses:

[4] Ibid., pp. 17–27, 68. Bell has substituted the terms "economic status," "family status," and "ethnic status" for the dimensions referred to by Shevky as social rank, urbanization, and segregation.

[5] Ibid., pp. 54–57.

[6] Ibid., pp. 57–58, Shevky and Williams, op. cit., pp. 63–68.

[7] Shevky and Bell, op. cit., pp. 20–22.

[8] Amos Hawley and Otis Dudley Duncan, "Social Area Analysis: A Critical Appraisal," *Land Economics*, 33 (November 1957): 337–345.

[9] Otis Dudley Duncan, review of Shevky and Bell, *Social Area Analysis*, in *American Journal of Sociology*, 61 (July 1955): 84–85.

[10] Wendell Bell, "Economic, Family, and Ethnic Status: An Empirical Test," *American Sociological Review*, 20 (February 1955): 45–52. [No. 23 in this volume.]

[11] Ibid., p. 47.

Hypothesis 1: At least three factors are necessary to account for the correlations between urban census tract populations with reference to measures of occupation, education, fertility, women in the labor force, single family dwelling units, and a measure of spatially isolated ethnic groups. Hypothesis 2a: Measures of occupation and education are highly correlated with a single factor defined as "social rank" for urban census tract populations.

Hypothesis 2b: Measures of fertility, women in the labor force, and single family dwelling units are highly correlated with a single factor defined as "urbanization" for urban census tract populations.

Hypothesis 2c: A measure of spatially isolated ethnic groups is highly correlated with a single factor defined as "segregation" for urban census tract populations.

TABLE 1. Hypothesized Shevky Matrix

Measure[†]	Factor[*]		
	SR	U	Seg.
Occ.	+	0	0
Educ.	+	0	0
Fert.	0	+	0
WLF	0	+	0
SFDU	0	+	0
Negro	0	0	+

[*] + denotes high positive correlation
0 denotes low correlation
[†] The following abbreviations are used in the table: Occ. = occupation; Educ. = education; Fert. = fertility; WLF = women in the labor force; SFDU = single family dwelling units; Negro = Negro population (spatially isolated ethnic group); SR = social rank factor; U = urbanization factor; Seg. = segregation factor.

Hypothesis 1 specifies the number of expected factors or columns necessary to account for the major portion of the intercorrelations of the census measures. McNemar's criterion for the number of factors can be used to evaluate the number of factors extracted from the intercorrelations.[12] Hypotheses 2a, 2b, and 2c

specify the correlations expected between the measures and factors shown in Table 1. The pattern of correlations can be tested by rotating the axes of an observed factor matrix to the position where they become the best possible least squares *approximations* of the correlations in the hypothesized matrix. The approximations of the observed correlations to the predicted correlations can be evaluated by the following criteria: for any row or column, the observed correlations corresponding to plus (+) entries must be greater than the observed correlations corresponding to zero (0) entries. That is, a *complete pattern* of correlations must be obtained in order to accept hypotheses 2a, 2b, and 2c.[13] The Shevky description of the measures and indexes is acceptable if hypotheses 1, 2a, 2b, and 2c are accepted for relevant applications of the census tract measures.

AVAILABLE INFORMATION

Ten large American cities—Akron, Ohio; Atlanta, Georgia; Birmingham, Alabama; Kansas City, Missouri; Louisville, Kentucky; Minneapolis, Minnesota; Portland, Oregon; Providence, Rhode Island; Rochester, New York; and Seattle, Washington—were chosen for analysis.[14] In selecting the cities, consideration was given to their representatives in terms of size, geographic distribution by census regions

[12] Quinn McNemar, "On the Number of Factors," *Psychometrika,* 7 (March 1942): 9–18.

[13] Typical criteria for significant correlations in rotated factor matrices regard correlations between measures and factors greater than +.20 as significantly positive, correlations between +.20 and −.20 as equal to zero, and correlations less than −.20 as significantly negative. These criteria emphasize individual correlations, however, rather than the pattern they show. There are no satisfactory criteria known to the authors for evaluating within a system of probability logic the departures of an obtained pattern of correlations from a hypothetical pattern in a rotated factor matrix. This problem may be resolved by establishing criteria which are not evaluated within a probability frame of reference.

[14] The ten cities were selected from a list of twenty cities with between 200,000 and 500,000 population in 1940, as used in Calvin F. Schmid's correlational and scale analyses of the ecological structure of American cities. See Calvin F. Schmid, "Generalizations Concerning the Ecology of the American City," *American Sociological Review,* 15 (February 1950): 264–281.

and areal, demographic, economic, and social characteristics.[15]

The basic data for the census tract measures are incorporated in the series of census tract bulletins prepared in conjunction with the Seventeenth Decennial Census, taken as of April 1, 1950.[16] Census tracts with less than 100 total population or more than ten per cent military or other institutional population were excluded from analysis.[17] The measures and the expected dimensions, according to Shevky's formulations, are as follows:

Social rank dimension[18]

Occupation: 1,000 minus the number of craftsmen, operatives, and laborers per 1,000 employed persons minus persons with occupations not reported.

Education: 1,000 minus the number of persons twenty-five years old and older who have completed no more than grade school per 1,000 persons twenty-five years old and older minus persons with school years not reported.

Urbanization dimension

Fertility: 1,000 minus the number of children under five per 1,000 females fourteen years old and older.

Women in the labor force: the number of females in the labor force per 1,000 females fourteen years old and older.

Single family dwelling units: 1,000 minus the number of single family dwelling units per 1,000 dwelling units.

Segregation dimension

Negro population: the number of Negroes per 1,000 total population.

To make the measures consistent with the expected dimensions, values of the measures of occupation, education, fertility, and single family dwelling units were subtracted from 1,000. With the exception of the segregation measure, these measures parallel those used in Shevky's and Bell's study of the San Francisco Bay Region for 1950.[19]

TESTS OF SHEVKY INDEXES

The census tract measures were computed for the 1950 census tract populations of the ten cities. Ten matrices of product-moment correlation coefficients were computed between the measures for the separate cities.[20]

Hypothesis 1 specifies that at least three factors are necessary to account for census tract variation with respect to the six measures. Fac-

---

[15] For a more extended discussion of these criteria, see Victor Jones, "Economic Classification of Cities and Metropolitan Areas," *The Municipal Yearbook* (1953), pp. 49–54, 69; Howard J. Nelson, "A Service Classification of American Cities," *Economic Geography*, 31 (July 1955): 189–201; and U.S. Bureau of the Census, *U.S. Census of Population, 1950*, Vol. 1, *Number of Inhabitants*, U.S. Government Printing Office, Washington, D.C., 1954, pp. iv–xix.

[16] U.S. Bureau of the Census, *U.S. Census of Population, 1950*, Vol. III, *Census Tract Statistics*, U.S. Government Printing Office, Washington, D.C., 1952.

[17] In 1950, there was a total of 781 census tracts in the ten cities. Fourteen of these tracts were eliminated from the study, leaving 767 tracts. Census tract designations of the eliminated tracts are as follows: Atlanta–F35, F54; Birmingham–54, 58; Kansas City–1; Minneapolis–46; Portland–54; Rochester–38, 89; and Seattle–D8, F1A, F1C, F2, and L5. The number of tracts included for each of the cities is as follows: Akron, 57; Atlanta, 73; Birmingham, 56; Kansas City, 98; Louisville, 90; Minneapolis, 120; Portland, 60; Providence, 37; Rochester, 87; and Seattle, 89.

[18] The variable, "average rent per capita," used by Bell ("Economic, Family, and Ethnic Status: An Empirical Test," op. cit.) was eliminated from this study because of the wide divergences in the percentage of rented dwelling units by census tracts, as well as the continuation of rent controls in many American cities until 1950, the time when these data were compiled.

[19] The Shevky-Bell indexes of segregation (op. cit., pp. 24–25, 56–57) are based on series of subordinate ethnic groups empirically determined to be spatially isolated. In general, these groups were drawn from non-whites and from foreign-born populations of eastern and southern European extraction. This measure was not used in the present study, since it could not be assumed that all of the groups comprising the Shevky-Bell measure of segregation were uniformly subordinate and isolated throughout the ten cities. The Negro population was accordingly selected as an indicator of segregation for the ten cities.

[20] All of the correlations reported in this study represent association of census tract measures and *not* of the characteristics of the individuals upon which the census tract measures are based. See W. S. Robinson, "Ecological Correlations and the Behavior of Individuals," *American Sociological Review*, 15 (June 1950), pp. 351–357.

tor matrices of correlations between the measures and factors were derived from the correlation matrices by the multiple-group method of factor analysis;[21] three factors were extracted by this procedure. Applications of McNemar's criterion[22] indicated that there may be more than three factors which may be derived from the correlation matrices of the measures in all of the cities except Rochester; however, the size of the residual correlations was negligible. The hypothesis was accepted that at least three factors are necessary to contain the six census tract measures in each of the separate cities.

Hypotheses 2a, 2b, and 2c express expected correlations of census tract measures, with the three factors verified by tests of the first hypothesis. As shown in Table 2 the multiple-group factor matrices for the cities were rotated to least-squares approximations of the hypothesized matrix of Table 1.[23] The parentheses in Table 2 indicate those measure-factor correlations specified by the hypotheses as having the highest positive values. The rotated matrices reproduce all eighteen of the hypothesized measure-factor correlations for Akron, Birmingham, Louisville, Minneapolis, Portland, Providence, Rochester, and Seattle; therefore hypotheses 2a, 2b, and 2c were accepted for these cities. The rotated matrices for Atlanta and Kansas City reproduce sixteen of the eighteen hypothesized measure-factor correlations. For each of these two cities, the correlation of fertility with the social rank factor was higher than with the urbanization factor requiring rejection of hypotheses 2a and 2b.

In summary, at least three factors were necessary to account for census tract variation in each of the ten cities studied, and the six census tract measures were related to the dimensions in the manner specified by Shevky in eight of the cities. While the factor analysis techniques did not produce exactly the structure of the dimensions specified by Shevky in two of the cities, 176 of 180 total correlations in the rotated matrices were established as hypothesized. The Shevky indexes appear to have high generality for the cities of this study.

ALTERNATIVE ANALYSES

It is possible that the rejection of the Shevky hypotheses in two cities was due to chance factors alone. On the other hand, a systematic reinterpretation of the Shevky dimensions may contribute to further understanding of the nature of the measures used in this study.

Atlanta and Kansas City are the two cities for which hypotheses were not confirmed. Atlanta, together with Birmingham and Louisville, is in the U.S. Bureau of the Census Southern Census Division, while Kansas City is a border city in the North Central Census Division. Table 2 indicates that Atlanta, Birmingham, Louisville, and Kansas City are characterized by higher positive correlations of fertility with social rank than are the remaining six cities. The populations of these four cities include relatively large proportions of Negroes. This fact, combined especially with the unfavorable economic position of the Negroes, may indicate that the range of family forms in these cities, as described by the fertility measure, has not become disassociated from social rank.[24] These considerations suggest a modified factor analysis model for Atlanta and Kansas City, and an alternative model for Birmingham and Louisville, with fertility designated as a component of so-

[21] See L. L. Thurstone, *Multiple Factor Analysis*, Chicago: The University of Chicago Press, 1947, pp. 149–170; and Paul Horst, "Simplified Computations for the Multiple Group Method of Factor Analysis," *Educational and Psychological Measurement*, 16 (1956), pp. 101–109. The multiple-group and product-moment correlation matrices are available upon request from the authors.

[22] McNemar, "On the Number of Factors," op. cit., pp. 9–18.

[23] See Paul Horst and K. W. Schaie, "The Multiple Group Method of Factor Analysis and Rotation to a Simple Structure Hypothesis," *Journal of Experimental Education*, 24 (March 1956): 231–237.

[24] See Shevky and Bell, op. cit., p. 13. Among the ten cities, Birmingham, Atlanta, Louisville, and Kansas City rank from one to four respectively in the proportions of their populations classified as Negro in the 1950 census.

TABLE 2.   Rotated Factor Matrices, Ten Cities: 1950*

City and Measure	Factor SR	U	Seg.	City and Measure	Factor SR	U	Seg.
Akron				**Minneapolis**			
Occ.	(.933)	.086	.256	Occ.	(.762)	.112	.121
Educ.	(.590)	−.125	−.323	Educ.	(.670)	−.094	−.026
Fert.	.240	(.686)	−.235	Fert.	.152	(.698)	−.205
WLF	−.155	(.827)	−.030	WLF	−.050	(.913)	−.061
SFDU	−.131	(.624)	.144	SFDU	−.084	(.757)	.224
Negro	−.056	−.087	(.636)	Negro	.103	−.050	(.423)
Atlanta				**Portland**			
Occ.	(.917)	.121	.044	Occ.	(.691)	.238	−.037
Educ.	(.856)	.020	−.402	Educ.	(.709)	−.225	−.046
Fert.	.528	(.457)	.065	Fert.	.011	(.846)	−.333
WLF	.143	(.654)	.196	WLF	−.049	(.940)	−.111
SFDU	−.392	(.696)	−.204	SFDU	.048	(.866)	.442
Negro	−.431	.034	(.662)	Negro	−.051	−.001	(.460)
Birmingham				**Providence**			
Occ.	(.806)	.209	−.017	Occ.	(.792)	.052	.223
Educ.	(.661)	−.063	−.351	Educ.	(.706)	−.128	.098
Fert.	.492	(.583)	−.126	Fert.	.155	(.444)	−.380
WLF	.164	(.699)	.273	WLF	.002	(.703)	.147
SFDU	−.426	(.852)	−.167	SFDU	−.276	(.288)	.182
Negro	−.438	−.015	(.553)	Negro	.274	−.028	(.516)
Kansas City				**Rochester**			
Occ.	(.925)	.174	.067	Occ.	(.910)	.126	−.143
Educ.	(.883)	.032	−.211	Educ.	(.822)	−.124	−.179
Fert.	.613	(.523)	.139	Fert.	.292	(.662)	−.014
WLF	.016	(.901)	−.070	WLF	−.185	(.794)	−.220
SFDU	−.316	(.805)	−.003	SFDU	−.105	(.522)	.332
Negro	−.268	.080	(.503)	Negro	−.036	.074	(.524)
Louisville				**Seattle**			
Occ.	(.833)	.043	.142	Occ.	(.848)	.110	.213
Educ.	(.712)	−.013	−.195	Educ.	(.631)	−.181	−.257
Fert.	.360	(.483)	−.086	Fert.	.030	(.859)	−.159
WLF	.028	(.516)	.155	WLF	.040	(.907)	−.085
SFDU	−.334	(.563)	−.091	SFDU	−.132	(.743)	.162
Negro	−.075	−.017	(.444)	Negro	−.039	−.080	(.592)

* See Table 1 for explanation of abbreviations.

cial rank rather than a component of the urbanization dimension.

An alternative model also may be described for Providence. Table 2 shows that the single family dwelling units measure has a fairly high negative correlation with social rank for most cities. The absolute value of this correlation for Providence (−.276), however, approximates the absolute value of the correlation of single family dwelling units with urbanization (.288). The small proportion of single family dwelling units and the high population density

TABLE 3.   Alternative Factor Models: 1950*†

Measure	Atlanta, Birmingham, Kansas City, Louisville			Measure	Providence		
	SR	U	Seg.		SR	U	Seg.
Occ.	+	0	0	Occ.	+	0	0
Educ.	+	0	0	Educ.	+	0	0
Fert.	+	0	0	Fert.	0	+	0
WLF	0	+	0	WLF	0	+	0
SFDU	0	+	0	SFDU	−	0	0
Negro	0	0	+	Negro	0	0	+

* + denotes high positive correlation.
   0 denotes low correlation.
   − denotes high negative correlation.
† See Table 1 for explanation of abbreviations.

in Providence suggest that considerable value may be attached to single family dwelling units and that possession of such dwellings is associated in some degree with occupational and educational attainments. If this is the case, the proportion of single family dwelling units in a census tract may then be associated with social rank rather than with urbanization.

The expected factorial structure of the alternative models is shown in Table 3. These models were tested by the same procedures used in the original factor analyses. The axes of the initial multiple-group measure-factor matrices for the five cities were rotated to their respective models. Table 4 indicates the measure-factor correlations in the rotated matrices for the social rank and urbanization factors.[25] Measure-factor correlations with the highest expected values are indicated in parentheses.

When pattern criteria for the rotated matrices for Atlanta, Birmingham, Kansas City, and Louisville were applied, all of the factor loadings specified in the alternative model for these cities were reproduced. The measure-factor correlations of fertility with social rank were greater than with urbanization for each city. The correlations of fertility with urbanization

in Table 4 may be compared with the same correlations for the tests of the Shevky hypotheses in Table 2. For each city, the correlations were less than in the rotated matrices obtained in the tests of the Shevky hypotheses. An examination of Table 4 shows that all of the factor loadings specified in the alternative model for Providence were reproduced. The measure-factor correlation of single family dwelling units with urbanization was less than in the rotated matrix obtained in the test of the Shevky hypotheses.

Due to possible chance fluctuations in the original factor analyses and the *ex post facto* nature of the analyses for the alternative models, no priority can be claimed for the latter. Furthermore, it is possible to satisfy the conditions for other models within the framework of factor analysis. The utility of the alternative models, as based on the census tract measures used in this study, remains to be demonstrated.

INTERCORRELATIONS OF DIMENSIONS

Shevky has not specified the form of the interrelations of the social rank, urbanization, and segregation dimensions. Presumably the dimensions become differentiated in a process of urban development and would not be found in folk society. Shevky has not described the point, however, at which such differentiation takes place. Knowledge of the association of

[25] As no further rotations were made of the segregation axes, the correlations of the measures with the segregation factor are identical with Table 2.

TABLE 4.   Rotated Factor Matrices for Alternative Models: 1950*

City and Measure	Factor†	
	SR	U
Atlanta		
Occ.	(.966)	−.071
Educ.	(.768)	−.070
Fert.	(.695)	.293
WLF	.406	(.515)
SFDU	−.206	(.721)
Negro	−.266	−.006
Birmingham		
Occ.	(.902)	.010
Educ.	(.673)	−.219
Fert.	(.700)	.427
WLF	.386	(.621)
SFDU	−.165	(.887)
Negro	−.473	.100
Kansas City		
Occ.	(.857)	−.098
Educ.	(.678)	−.083
Fert.	(.682)	(.201)
WLF	.148	(.696)
SFDU	−.127	(.670)
Negro	−.006	−.083
Louisville		
Occ.	(.949)	−.078
Educ.	(.848)	−.174
Fert.	(.678)	.416
WLF	.264	(.551)
SFDU	−.076	(.619)
Negro	−.185	.074
Providence		
Occ.	(.859)	.131
Educ.	(.863)	−.013
Fert.	.227	).583)
WLF	−.274	(.615)
SFDU	(−.507)	.155
Negro	.116	−.150

* See Table 1 for explanation of abbreviations.

† Factors for segregation index same as in Table 2.

the dimensions becomes important as a basis for further evaluations of the Shevky theory.

In the reported factor analysis tests, the social rank, urbanization, and segregation factors were allowed to assume whatever relationships

were necessary to best fit the predicted models. Factor correlations were computed from the original rotated matrices for all cities.[26] As Table 5 indicates, these correlations show a rather consistent pattern. The low correlations, ranging from −.143 in Akron to .224 in Atlanta, between social rank and urbanization factors, indicate that they are almost independent of each other. The segregation factor, however, is related to both social rank and to urbanization. Correlations of segregation with social rank are consistently negative for the separate cities and range from −.015 in Atlanta to −.752 in Providence. Segregation is positively correlated with urbanization, with values varying from effectively zero in Portland to .344 in Akron.

TABLE 5.   Correlations Between Primary Factors, Ten Cities: 1950*

City	Factor		
	SR–U	SR–Seg.	U–Seg.
Akron	−.143	−.462	.344
Atlanta	.224	−.015	.243
Birmingham	.097	−.379	.300
Kansas City	.003	−.149	.317
Louisville	.174	−.305	.572
Minneapolis	.002	−.675	.047
Portland	.055	−.573	−.048
Providence	.026	−.752	.099
Rochester	.117	−.217	.259
Seattle	.122	−.454	.237

* SR denotes social rank; U, urbanization; and Seg, segregation.

SUMMARY AND COMMENT

This research is concerned with the empirical generality of the Shevky system of social area analysis. The factor analysis tests of hypotheses show that the present form of the Shevky system has high generality for the cities included in this study. Although the Shevky measures do appear to differentiate social rank, urbanization, and segregation factors in the spatial patterning of cities, minor variation is

[26] These correlations were computed according to procedures reported by Thurstone, op. cit., pp. 137–138.

observed in the internal structure of these factors. It is not known whether the variation from the Shevky system has occurred by chance. Alternative models of the measures and dimensions were described for some of the cities, but due to the ex post facto nature of this portion of the analysis, no priority can be claimed for the alternative models over the Shevky model. It remains to be demonstrated whether the alternative models are an artifact of the particular set of measures used in this study or provide a useful device for the reinterpretation of the Shevky theory.

This study focusses upon the general empirical validity of the Shevky indexes. The tests of hypotheses concerning the construction of indexes and measures are not at the level of the theoretical constructs defined by the Shevky theory. No tests have been made of the Shevky theory, the adequacy of the integration of the indexes with that theory, or of the utility of the Shevky model or the alternative models for testing significant hypotheses concerning population differentiation. These matters should be investigated further. Such investigation may be facilitated by the results of this research.

25

THEODORE R. ANDERSON AND LEE L. BEAN

The Shevky-Bell Social Areas: Confirmation of Results and a Reinterpretation

ABSTRACT

A factor analysis of census tract data in Toledo, Ohio confirms the general structure found by Shevky and Bell, except that urbanization and family status appear as separate factors. The factors are interpreted in more strictly spatial terms. For example, urbanization becomes type of dwelling or population density.

The research to be reported in this paper was designed to extend our knowledge of the Shevky-Bell typology of urban social areas. Shevky and Bell utilize census data classified by census tracts and suggest that these tracts be classified according to three basic variables:

social rank, urbanization (or family status) and segregation.[1] In an important study, Van Arsdol, Camilleri, and Schmid confirmed the factorial existence of these three indices through factor analyses of six variables derived

Reproduced by permission from *Social Forces*, Vol. 40, No. 2 (December 1961), pp. 119–124.

Paper read at the annual meeting of the Eastern Sociological Society, April 1960.

[1] A substantial amount of research has already been reported involving this typology, most of which is noted in a recent article by Wendell Bell. See Wendell Bell, "Social Areas: Typology of Urban Neighborhoods," in Marvin B. Sussman (ed.), *Community Structure and Analysis* (New York: Thomas Y. Crowell, 1959), pp. 61–92.

from census tracts in 10 cities.[2] They found that these six tract characteristics (including measures of occupation, education, fertility, women in the labor force, single-family dwellings, and Negroes) separated into essentially the same three factors in each of the 10 cities. In particular, occupation and education always appeared in the same factor (social rank); fertility, percent women in the labor force, and percent single-family dwelling units in another (urbanization or family status); and percent Negro always appeared by itself (segregation). The only slight exception occurred with respect to fertility which was, in three southern cities, about equally represented in both the social rank and urbanization factors. On the whole, however, the evidence presented by these authors represents a strong confirmation of the stable existence of the dimensions suggested by Shevky and Bell. That is, these six variables regularly factor in a way consistent with the Shevky-Bell hypothesis.

The question remains, however, as to whether this structure would appear if variables other than those suggested in the above study were included in the analysis. Would the same three factors appear, would they be the only factors, and would it continue to be reasonable to interpret them as social rank, urbanization, and segregation? It is important eventually to develop a definitive answer to these questions because this typology is increasingly being used for other research purposes.[3] It was the objec-

tive of the research reported in this paper to increase our understanding of this approach to the classification of urban areas. In particular, this research involved the determination and interpretation of the factorial structure underlying several variables in a single city. Since attention was focused on the Shevky-Bell typology each variable included in the study was chosen because, on a priori grounds, it appeared to measure one or another of the Shevky-Bell dimensions. Toledo was selected as the city to be analyzed partly on the grounds that it was a city in the North, and hence not likely to be subject to the fertility problem uncovered in the earlier factor analysis. It was selected also because it was on roughly the same size as those cities studied earlier. One of Toledo's 55 census tracts was eliminated from the analysis because its population was largely institutional. Thirteen census tract characteristics (listed in Table 1) were contained in the analysis including the six used by Van Arsdol, Camilleri, and Schmid. The results suggest various ways in which the typology and its interpretation might be profitably modified.

[2] Maurice D. Van Arsdol, Jr., Santo F. Camilleri, and Calvin F. Schmid, "The Generality of Urban Social Area Indexes," *American Sociological Review*, 23 (June 1958): 277–284 [No. 24 in this volume]; and Maurice D. Van Arsdol, Jr., Santo F. Camilleri, and Calvin F. Schmid, "An Application of the Shevky Social Area Indexes to a Model of Urban Society," *Social Forces*, 37 (October 1958): 26–32.

[3] For example, see Walter C. Kaufman and Scott Greer, "Voting in a Metropolitan Community: An Application of Social Area Analysis," *Social Forces*, 38 (March 1960): 196–204; Scott Greer, "Urbanism Reconsidered: A Comparative Study of Local Areas in a Metropolis," *American Sociological Review*, 21 (February 1956): 19–25; and Wendell Bell and Maryanne T. Force, "Urban Neighborhood Types and Participation in Formal Association," *American Sociological Review*, 21 (February 1956): 25–34.

TABLE 1. A Listing of the 13 Variables Included in the Factor Analysis*

Variable	Short Identification	Detailed Identification
1	Occupation	Percent of all employed persons classified as craftsmen, operatives, and laborers.
2	Education	Percent of all persons 25 years old and over reporting 8 or fewer years of schooling.
3	Fertility ratio	Ratio of children under 5 to women 15 to 45 years of age.
4	Females in the labor force	Percent of all females 14 years of age and over who are in the labor force.
5	Multifamily dwelling units	Percent of all dwelling units in structures containing 2 or more dwelling units.
6	Negro	Percent of all persons who are Negro.

TABLE 1. *(Continued)*

Vari-able	Short Identi-fication	Detailed Identification
7	Residential stability	Percent of all persons residing in the same dwelling in 1950 and 1949.
8	Percent married	Percent of all persons 15 years old and over who are married.
9	Income	Median family income.
10	Families	Ratio of families to unrelated individuals.
11	Owner occupancy	Percent of all dwelling units which are owner occupied.
12	Double occupancy	Percent of all married couples living without their own household.
13	Crowding	Percent of all dwelling units with 1.01 or more persons per room.

* All observations were drawn from U. S. Bureau of the Census, *U. S. Census of Population: 1950,* Vol. III, *Census Tract Statistics,* Chapter 56, (Washington, D. C.: U. S. Government Printing Office, 1952).

MAJOR EMPIRICAL FINDINGS

Tables 2 and 3 present the basic empirical findings to be discussed in the next section. Four factors were extracted from the original correlation matrix (Table 2) using Thurstone's complete centroid method.[4] All residual elements remaining after the extraction of these factors are very small (the largest being −.069), indicating that no other factors of any importance are contained in the original correlations (see Table 2). The four factors were rotated orthogonally to a simple structure. Graphs of these rotated factors indicated that no appreciable improvement would result from oblique rotations. Therefore, none were attempted. The rotated factors and the factor structure are presented in Table 3.

An examination of this table shows that the basic pattern found in earlier studies was reproduced here, with one important exception. Factor *A* loads on all the variables represented in the urbanization or family status variables (variables 3, 4, and 5.) Its highest loadings are on owner-occupancy (11) and multifamily dwelling units (5). Factor *B* also loads on 2 of the 3 original family status variables (3 and 4) as well as a few others, particularly families (10) and double occupancy (12). From these results it would appear that the urbanization or family status variable identified by Shevky and Bell has broken into two orthogonal components, one more closely identified with the term "urbanization," the other with the term "family status." In particular, the loadings on Factor *A* suggest that it can be considered as a measure of urbanization while the loadings on Factor *B* suggest it as a measure of family status.

Occupation and education are most highly loaded on Factor *C*, which is clearly the social rank factor. Factor *D* is, equally clearly, the segregation factor since its high loadings are on Negroes (6), double-occupancy (12), and crowding (13). These two factors are almost exact duplications of the original indices.

DISCUSSION AND INTERPRETATION

In interpreting any classification scheme it is desirable first to consider what it is that is being classified. In the analysis presented above, as in the earlier researches, the unit being classified is a census tract which is a territorial subdivision of a city. The fact that census tracts are the units under analysis presents immediate problems, primarily because most sociologists and ecologists are not interested in tracts as such. Census tracts are essentially arbitrary subdivisions of the city's space and are not sociologically unitary. Their boundaries are not politically or socially defined in most instances nor do the residents as a whole constitute a group or social structure in any meaningful sense. For this reason it is not immediately clear why sociologists should attempt to classify and analyze these units. Indeed, many sociologists have resolved the problem by simply rejecting the usefulness of census tract information.

---

[4] L. S. Thurstone, *Multiple-Factor Analysis* (Chicago: The University of Chicago Press, 1947), pp. 161–170.

TABLE 2. Original Correlation Matrix (Above Diagonal) and Residual Elements (Below Diagonal)*

	1	2	3	4	5	6	7	8	9	10	11	12	13
1		903	112	−048	−138	139	398	132	−418	126	069	424	455
2	000		−117	154	153	333	169	−095	−642	−055	−224	641	696
3	035	−001		−691	−445	−542	292	515	380	230	407	−597	−363
4	017	009	−054		742	234	−477	−656	−555	−436	−689	384	255
5	−026	000	004	005		241	−671	−706	−708	−709	−977	329	472
6	−009	007	−069	018	006		−129	−063	−535	−297	−279	730	702
7	015	−026	032	−026	044	044		471	423	630	699	−072	−283
8	022	−011	028	045	014	038	005		478	451	652	−253	−253
9	−018	021	−004	−048	012	003	003	−024		650	777	−651	−796
10	−005	009	−002	−011	011	−019	−005	007	044		749	−170	−403
11	029	−008	014	−015	−024	020	−003	−014	−013	−030		−381	−579
12	013	028	000	−007	030	011	−008	−019	−005	046	−041		770
13	−012	015	003	−024	025	013	−041	045	−037	054	−022	015	

* Decimal signs omitted.

TABLE 3. Original Centroids, Orthogonally Rotated Factors, and the Rotated Factor Pattern; Toledo Census Tracts, 1950*

Variable	Original Centroids				h^2	Rotated Factors				Rotated Factor Patterns			
	I	II	III	IV		A	B	C	D	A	B	C	D
1	−260	781	220	399	885	−073	093	−932	−015			—	
2	−558	729	207	358	1014[a]	207	017	−979	−100			—	
3	603	141	614	−027	761	−458	735	025	105	—	+		
4	−698	−398	−247	299	796	732	−444	−037	246	+	—		
5	−818	−494	187	049	951	971	−017	041	073	+			
6	−580	320	−311	−464	751	297	−366	−206	−698		—		—
7	501	513	−189	267	621	−703	−105	−316	124	—			
8	605	452	083	−261	645	−710	259	−031	−270	—			
9	914	−158	−235	032	917	−776	−019	482	286	—		+	
10	632	338	−310	248	671	−765	−188	−101	200	—			
11	859	398	−293	040	984	−986	−089	026	046	—			
12	−722	411	−370	−095	836	369	−510	−489	−449	+	—	—	—
13	−799	435	111	−264	910	526	−040	−535	−587	+		—	—
% Var. Expl.	46.0	21.5	8.4	6.7	82.6	41.5	9.7	21.1	10.3				

* Decimal signs omitted throughout. Each number has three digits after the decimal, except the percentages.
[a] These h^2 figures are only estimates of the true communalities which cannot exceed 1.00.

298

THEODORE R. ANDERSON 299

Shevky and Bell have proposed another very simple solution. They disavow any direct interest in the territorial unit as such and focus attention instead upon the individuals residing within the territory. In particular, they claim to be able to place people in *social* categories (or in *social* areas) in their terminology on the basis of the characteristics of the tract within which they live. Hawley and Duncan have discussed the implications of this transposition in their general criticism of the theoretical structure of social area analysis. [5] It is not necessary here to elaborate this discussion except to note that the validity of the Shevky-Bell solution to the problem has not been firmly established, and that it may well involve an oversimplification of the basic problem. In any event, in this paper the factors will be interpreted entirely as descriptions of the local territorial areas (that is, the census tracts) from which the original data were drawn. In contrast to the Shevky-Bell solution, the approach adopted here involves examining the tracts as such in order to develop spatial concepts which will have considerable explanatory significance with respect to social behavior and structure.

Three major properties of the census tract become apparent once attention is focused upon its territorial nature. First, the tract is located somewhere with respect to the basic facilities of the city. Since location is not contained in any census tabulation, however, no variables measuring characteristics of location directly are included in the factor analysis. This fact is somewhat unfortunate since *it is primarily with respect to location that the census tract is a homogeneous mass.* But, despite the fact that the tract's specific spatial is unknown, it is critical to recognize that it is a location. Second, the territory contains various types of physical facilities. In particular, as a residential area it contains houses or dwelling units. These dwelling units

themselves possess a variety of relatively permanent characteristics which could become a basis for classifying the area. Third, the territory also contains a population of people which possesses many characteristics. The predominant types of housing found within the tracts and the major compositional characteristics of the residential population form the bases upon which the classification of these areas is erected. The position taken in this paper is that the dimensions originally hypothesized by Shevky and Bell can better be interpreted by keeping these three aspects of the census tract firmly in mind rather than by proceeding in the manner of Shevky and Bell. In particular, as the following discussion will show, the relationship between space and its contents on the one hand and social behaviors and interactions on the other will thereby become much clearer.

In the light of these considerations the Shevky-Bell variables or dimensions will be reinterpreted in this and the following paragraphs. Shevky and Bell identified three important ways of classifying census tracts which they call urbanization or family status, social rank, and segregation. Four factors appeared in the Toledo study reported here, but the overall empirical pattern was quite similar to that hypothesized by Shevky and Bell. These authors, however, display their interest in social rather than territorial areas in the very names which they have assigned to their dimensions. The term "urbanization" has usually referred either to human values, or to patterns of social interaction, or to the structure of an entire community, rather than to individual areas within a city. The term "family status" obviously refers to a family in the sense that only a family possesses family status in any direct way. Furthermore, the term social rank is normally used to refer to the socioeconomic or class position of individual people or families within a community. Not one of these terms, as used in the past, measures characteristics of local residential areas within a large city. The term segregation is the only exception. It is customary

---

[5] Amos H. Hawley and Otis Dudley Duncan, "Social Area Analysis: A Critical Appraisal," *Land Economics,* 33 (November 1957): 337–345.

to refer to a neighborhood as relatively segregated or unsegregated. If the other terms are to be applied to neighborhoods, then great care must be exercised to avoid confusion with their other denotations.[6]

The problem of interpreting these factors is perhaps most pronounced with respect to the factor which has been labelled *social rank*. All of the studies of this typology including this one have found or used a factor whose highest loadings are on variables measuring the occupational and educational composition of the population residing in the neighborhood. In the Toledo analysis, for example, education loads −.979 on Factor C while occupation loads −.932 on it. [7] Clearly, this factor measures something in the domain of socioeconomic status. Equally clearly, since most tracts are quite heterogeneous with respect to the socioeconomic composition of their populations, the index does *not* measure the socioeconomic status of the individual residents with any appreciable precision. The problem of interpretation is further complicated by the fact that certain variables which, on an individual or family level, are usually highly correlated with socioeconomic status have relatively low loadings on this factor. Thus, median income loads only .482 on Factor C as opposed to a loading of −.776 on Factor A which has been identified with urbanization. Furthermore, percent owner-occupied loads only .026 on Factor C, and −.986 on Factor A. It seems clear that people with higher income are drawn only in part to areas where the average occupational-educational level is high. These people appear to be drawn much more strongly to areas where urbanization is low (that is, where single-family dwelling units predominate). For these reasons the direct

labelling of this factor as social rank seems inappropriate. As an alternative it is here suggested that this factor be classed a measure of the *prestige value* of the neighborhood. Urban neighborhoods are evaluated by the residents, and these evaluations tend to be relatively permanent. This prestige is reflected in the residential choices of individuals and hence might well be measured by occupational and educational differentials. The evaluation of a neighborhood may well persist despite considerable change in the structure of the dwelling units. For instance, an area which has possessed large single family units and enjoyed high prestige will tend to remain attractive to young professionals and managers even though its houses are subdivided into apartments, and garden apartments are built in the area. The important point is that by identifying this factor as a measure of the prestige of the neighborhood the independence of Factors A (urbanization) and C (prestige value) is interpretable.

A problem of interpretation also exists in connection with the factor which Shevky and Bell have labelled urbanization or family status. At the empirical level in this study, two factors, rather than one, were found in this domain. The existence of these two factors suggests a means of interpreting them which should prove quite powerful in further work. Factor A is almost equivalent to the percent of dwellings in multi-unit structures (loading .971). As might be expected home ownership also loads very highly on this factor (−.986). It is clear that this factor separates apartment house areas from single family dwelling unit areas. The term urbanization appears to be satisfactory as a description of this factor, provided that its specific meaning is kept in mind. An area with a high proportion of apartments can reasonably be called a highly urbanized area. The important point is that this factor measures a property of the dwelling units within the area rather than the people there. It is a useful variable in explaining human behavior to the extent that the structure of dwelling units imposes certain constraints upon the nature of social relationships and human in-

---

[6] It is clear, of course, that words are largely arbitrary symbols for underlying conceptualizations. It is not the purpose of the above comments to quibble over these words, which may well be used in the way Shevky and Bell do, but rather to illustrate their social orientation.

[7] Remember that both variables are measured inversely. That is, education is measured by the percent of persons with little or no education and occupation by the percent in blue collar occupations.

teractions. By identifying it in this manner the possibility of investigating the nature of these constraints is clear. But other loadings on this factor suggest that it is a very important variable in explaining at least the residential behavior of people within a city. All of the variables except occupation and education clearly have nonzero loadings on Factor A (urbanization). Of particular interest is the high negative loading of income (−.776), suggesting that those people in a position to realize their housing values tend to seek out areas of relatively low urbanization. Further, the loading on fertility (−.458) suggests that family size influences the choice of residential areas by urbanization. Both of these facts are relatively well known and have been demonstrated before, but they do serve to illustrate ways in which housing constrains social behavior.

That the structure of housing is not entirely selective of family-related population characteristics is demonstrated by the very existence of Factor B. This factor, which is orthogonal to Factor A (urbanization), loads most highly on fertility (.735), double occupancy (−.510), and females in the labor force (−.444). Thus, the single concept of urbanization is not sufficient to account for variations in these and similar population characteristics. All of these variables describe characteristics of the population rather than of the dwelling units. It is difficult to name Factor B mainly because no one variable has a very high loading on it. Average family status is a loose designation which could be justified if it could be demonstrated that these variables also cluster on an individual family basis: that is, if these variables characterize families unidimensionally as well as neighborhoods. Only further research can provide a definitive answer, but tentatively the term family status will be retained.

In conclusion, this paper has essentially relocated the results of Van Arsdol, Camilleri, and Schmid in demonstrating the factorial existence of the Shevky-Bell dimensions. The characteristics which were combined in the single index of urbanization in the earlier studies were found to possess two common dimensions in Toledo. In particular the housing characteristics formed one factor while family characteristics formed another. The importance of identifying these factors as measures of residential neighborhoods as such was stressed. Only when they are interpreted in this way do the factors provide a clear conceptual base upon which to build a theory relating space to social behavior.

26

THEODORE R. ANDERSON
JANICE A. EGELAND

Spatial Aspects of Social Area Analysis

ABSTRACT

This paper reports a test of Burgess' concentric zone and Hoyt's sector hypotheses of urban residential structure using the structural dimensions suggested by Shevky and Bell. Residential areas in four cities were studied. Each city was selected because it possessed a roughly circular total shape and because its population was between 200,000 and 500,000. The results indicate clearly that Burgess' concentric zone hypothesis is essentially supported with respect to urbanization but not with respect to social rank (or prestige value as this dimension is termed in this paper), while Hoyt's sector hypothesis is supported with respect to social rank (prestige value) but not with respect to urbanization.

INTRODUCTION

A classic problem in urban ecology has been the succinct description of the location of residential areas by type. Hurd,[1] as early as 1903, developed the conception that urban growth proceeded according to two patterns: central growth and axial growth. By these terms he meant to convey the idea that growth tends to occur in all directions outward from the center of the city, and that it occurs most rapidly along major transportation routes. In consequence, at any one time the total structure of the city forms a roughly star-shaped pattern. While Hurd discussed the location of residential areas by type (especially by income or rental value),

he did not systematically use the principles of central and axial growth to generate over-all, concise descriptive generalizations.

Burgess,[2] during the 1920's, emphasized the importance of central (or concentric) growth and used this pattern to generate the now-famous concentric zone hypothesis of the distribution of residential areas, by type. Residential areas were classified both according to the density characteristics of dwelling units and according to the typical socio-economic status of the residents. According to his hypothesis, these two classifications were inversely related to

Reprinted by permission from the *American Sociological Review,* Vol. 26, No. 3 (June 1961), pp. 392–399.

Revision of a paper presented at the annual meeting of the Eastern Sociological Society, April 23–24, 1960.

[1] Richard M. Hurd, *Principles of City Land Values* (New York: The Record and Guide, 1903.) "A continual contest

exists between axial growth pushing out from the centre along transportation lines and central growth, constantly following and obliterating it, while new projections are being made further out the various axes" (p. 59).

[2] Ernest W. Burgess, "The Growth of the City," in Robert E. Park (ed.), *The City* (Chicago: University of Chicago Press, 1925).

each other (i.e. high status persons lived in low dwelling unit density areas and vice versa). Residential areas were then classed into four types, each forming a concentric band about the center of the city—which was, itself, called Zone 1. Zone 2, immediately adjacent to the center, was characterized by rooming houses, tenements, and other forms of structures in which dwelling unit densities are very high and also by a population of low socio-economic status and usually of recent immigrant stock. Moving outward, the zones became progressively less dense in dwelling unit patterns (out of the single-family, large-lawn suburban or commuters zone) and characterized by residents of increasingly high socio-economic status.

Burgess' hypothesis formed the basis for a vast amount of research during the ensuing years. In these researches the concept of four distinct zones (or five counting the central business district) was dropped rather early and replaced by an indefinite number of concentric zones arbitrarily located at half-mile or mile intervals around the central business district. The typical method used to "test" the hypothesis was to aggregate relevant information within each zone, express the aggregated information in the form of an average for the zone, and note the variation in this average from zone to zone. If the average or aggregate measure declined regularly (or increased regularly) with increasing distance from the center, then the Burgess zonal hypothesis was held to be confirmed, but if the measure went down and then up, or varied in some other irregular manner, then the hypothesis was held suspect for that characteristic.[3] This methodology is important for two reasons. First, it in effect transforms the Burgess hypothesis into the hypothesis that regular gradients will be found by distance from the center of the city in characteristics

such as average dwelling unit density and average socio-economic status. Second, it tests this hypothesis by examining the regression line and its regularity alone, without considering the variation of local areas within a zone about the zonal average or regression. By ignoring the variation of individual tracts about the regression line it is (a) impossible to bring the relatively powerful, modern statistical procedures to bear upon the tests, since unexplained, or residual, or random variation is not estimated, except very indirectly through variation in the zonal means about the regression line. It is also (b) essentially impossible to compare the effectiveness of the Burgess hypothesis with that of any competing hypothesis, since one cannot estimate the proportion of the total variance that is accounted for by the hypothesis in question.

Hoyt,[4] in 1939, emphasized the axial pattern of growth and proposed the sector hypothesis as a description of the location of residential areas classified according to average rental value of dwelling unit (or socioeconomic status of residents). For 19 selected cities, Hoyt observes, "the highest rental area is in every case located in one or more sectors on the side of the city. Except for Oklahoma City, Oklahoma, and Charleston, South Carolina, these high rent sections are on the periphery of one or more sectors of the city."[5] He also finds that "low rent areas extending from the center to the edge of the city are found in practically every city."[6] Hoyt thus sees the city as basically divided into sectors (with respect to the residential rental values) within which a concentric pattern may or may not be found. If a concentric pattern is found within the sector, Hoyt observes that average rental value increases with increasing distance from the center of the city. Hoyt's analysis is similar to that of Burgess' followers

---

[3] See, for example, Ralph C. Fletcher, Harry L. Hornback, and Stuart A. Queen, *Social Statistics of St. Louis by Census Tracts, 1935*, for the use of this general method in connection with many characteristics of residents and dwelling units.

[4] Homer Hoyt, *The Structure and Growth of Residential Neighborhoods in American Cities* (Washington, D.C.: United States Government Printing Office, 1939).

[5] Ibid., p. 75.

[6] Ibid., p. 76.

in that it also fails to permit the estimation of error variances, hence making it difficult to tell how decisive his findings are.

In the twenty years following the publication of Hoyt's work relatively little has been done to advance (directly) the solution to the problem of succinctly describing the pattern of residential areas classified by type within cities. Urban ecologists have tended to shift their attention to problems existing at the metropolitan level of organization, or to problems involved in relating spatial structure to other aspects of urban social organization. In a very general sense, the state of knowledge about the location of residential areas (by type) within the city is the same today as it was in 1939. No important new hypothetical structure has been proposed—multiple nucleation is primarily a metropolitan rather than a city phenomenon—and no systematic, statistical comparison of the hypotheses of Burgess (as modified) and Hoyt has been published. It is the purpose of this paper to correct this latter deficiency.

In one important related area, however, a major advance has occurred. Obviously, before the concentric zone and sector hypotheses can be meaningfully compared, a characteristic of local areas must be selected for analysis. Should the rental value of dwelling units be used? Or the proportion of dwelling units which are in single-family structures? Or the proportion of dwelling units occupied by non-whites? Or what? The census alone reports on a very large number of characteristics both of dwellings and of residents for local areas (census tracts) within many large cities. Earlier research on the concentric zone hypothesis suggests that some of these characteristics will manifest a zonal pattern and that others will not. To compare the hypotheses on all of the characteristics for which data are available would be tedious to say the least. Furthermore, the results would almost certainly be ambiguous.

Fortunately, such a laborious procedure is no longer necessary. Shevky and Bell[7] have de-

veloped three indices of urban neighborhoods which have considerable promise and which they call urbanization (or family status), social rank, and segregation. A recent study by Van Arsdol, Camilleri, and Schmid[8] has shown that these indices possess a rather stable structure from one city to another within the United States. There is also some reason to believe (though it is a more speculative point at the present) that these indices effectively summarize the bulk of the common information contained in the characteristics reported for census tracts by the census. As more evidence accumulates, it will probably be shown that these indices should be modified somewhat, but in their present form they appear to be sound first approximations. Thus, it is possible today to compare the zonal and sector hypotheses in terms of the Shevky-Bell indices with considerable confidence that the results will have general significance.

One conceptual modification of the Shevky-Bell system will, however, be incorporated in this paper. Anderson and Bean,[9] in a factor analysis of Toledo data, have shown that the social rank index might better be considered as a measure of the prestige value of a neighborhood. These two concepts (i.e. social rank and prestige value) are superficially very similar. However, recent studies of socio-economic status have indicated that socio-economic status is not simply a unidimensional phenomenon.[10] In particular, measures based on occupation and education are not closely correlated to measures based on income. The term, prestige, has come to be identified with the invid-

[7] For a recent discussion of these indices, and an extensive bibliography of work already done using them, see Wendell Bell, "Social Areas: Typology of Urban Neighborhoods,"

in Marvin B. Sussman (ed.), *Community Structure and Analysis* (New York: Thomas Y. Crowell Company, 1959), pp. 61–92.

[8] Maurice D. Van Arsdol, Jr., Santo F. Camilleri, and Calvin F. Schmid, "The Generality of Urban Social Area Indexes," *American Sociological Review*, 23 (June 1958): 277–284. [No. 24 in this volume.]

[9] Theodore R. Anderson and Lee L. Bean, "The Shevky-Bell Social Areas: Confirmation of Results and a Reinterpretation," paper presented at the annual meeting of the Eastern Sociological Society, April 23–24, 1960. [No. 25 in this volume.]

[10] See, for instance, Joseph A. Kahl and James A. Davis, "A Comparison of Indexes of Socio-Economic Status," *American Sociological Review*, 20 (June 1955): 317–325.

ious ranking of occupations and of educational categories. Since the Shevky-Bell social rank index is based almost entirely upon the occupational and educational composition of the tract's population, the term prestige value seems more appropriate than social rank. This index will be called a measure of the prestige value of a neighborhood (rather than its social rank) throughout the remainder of this paper.

PROBLEM

This paper reports a statistical comparison of the concentric zone and sector hypotheses of urban residential structure, where residential structure is measured by the prestige value (social rank) and the urbanization indices proposed and developed by Shevky and Bell. The third index (segregation) was not included primarily because the distribution of Negroes within the large U.S. city is known not to fit either of these patterns well. The index components used in this study are the same as those used by Van Arsdol, Camilleri, and Schmid. Equal weight was assigned to each component when it was expressed in standard score form. Thus, the prestige value index consisted of the percentage of employed persons *not* classified as craftsmen, operatives, and laborers, added to the percentage of persons twenty-five years old and over who have completed at least one to three years of high school. The urbanization index consisted of the fertility ratio (reflected), plus the percentage of all females fourteen years of age and over who are in the labor force, plus the percentage of all dwelling units that are multi-family. In each case the unit of observation was a census tract.

The basic statistical tool used in the study was the analysis of variance, since sectors are qualitative, and distances from the center of the city were only ranked in this study. Four cities (Akron and Dayton, Ohio, Indianapolis, Indiana, and Syracuse, New York) were selected for study on the basis of their having populations between 200,000 and 500,000 in 1950 (thus rendering them roughly comparable as to size), because their outlying territory was also

tracted, and on the basis of their having roughly circular over-all shapes. This last criterion was invoked as a means of eliminating the dominant impact of major geographical disturbances that might destroy the possibility of filling each cell in the variance analysis data matrix. Thus, a city located on a large body of water (and hence not circular) will not extend as far in some sectors as in others, tending to confound sectors and distances. To achieve independent estimates of the main effects, it was necessary to consider only reasonably circular cities.

Within each city, sectors were identified in the following manner. First, the center of the city was located, using a detailed map showing the location of major buildings (and transportation routes). Then the direction, due east, was labelled direction O, and sectors were marked off at successive thirty-degree angles from this direction. Thus, each city was divided into 12 sectors, each 30 degrees wide. One of these sectors was selected randomly, and each third sector from this one was included in the

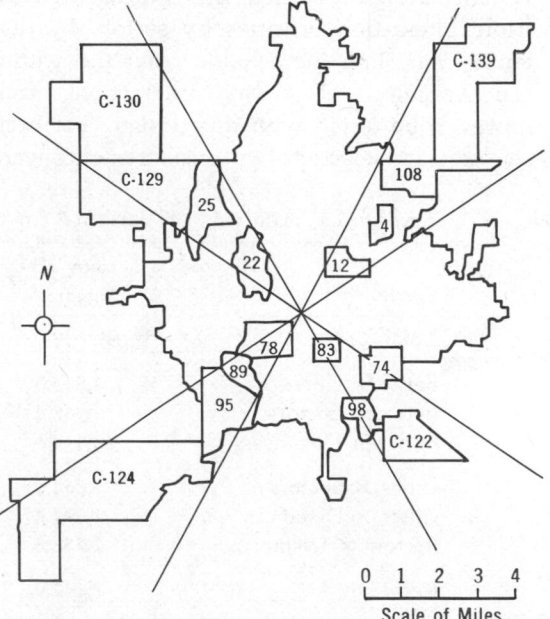

FIGURE 1. Map of Indianapolis and Suburbs Showing Sectors and Tracts Used in the Analysis

sample. Hence, in each city, four sectors were studied. The sectors studied in each city had the same orientation as those in each other city. In particular, the Northeast, Northwest, Southwest, and Southeast sectors were used in each city. This structure permitted a three-way analysis of variance designed to be used, including cities, distances, and oriented sectors. Within each selected sector, four census tracts were selected in such a way as to secure one as near as possible to the center, one as far from the center as possible, and two located one-third and two-thirds of the way between these. Essentially no random selection of individual tracts was involved since rarely did more than four tracts effectively meet the selection criteria. Indeed, the usual problem was to find four appropriate tracts, not to select from among some larger number.

In this manner, 64 census tracts were selected, one each from the 64 cells formed by all possible combinations of four cities, four oriented sectors, and four ranked distances. Thus, a "one observation per cell" analysis of variance design was used, which means that the triple interaction of cities by sectors by distances was indistinguishable from the within cell variance. Two-way interactions can, however, be tested with this design. For each census tract selected, two measurements were computed: the urbanization index and the prestige value index. The results of the analyses of these two measures will be presented separately.

RESULTS: URBANIZATION

The urbanization index contrasts areas characterized by many apartments, families with few young children, and families in which the wife works (high urbanization) with areas characterized by many single-family dwellings, families with many young children, and families in which the wife does not work (low urbanization). Where are such areas located within the city? Table 1 provides at least a partial answer. None of the interactions is significant. Cities differ somewhat in urbanization, sectors within cities do not differ, and distances differ a great deal. An examination of the Variance Estimates column of Table 1 shows clearly that the variation between distances is by far the largest in the entire table. Clearly, urbanization within a city is a concentric phenomenon and not a sectorial phenomenon.

Locating the high and low average scores for cities and distances reveals, first, that Syracuse has the highest average score on urbanization (113.7) while the other cities are about equal. (The norm for the entire sample is 100.) This finding suggests that eastern cities may be

TABLE 1. Analysis of Variance for the Urbanization Index

Source	Sum of Squares	df	Variance Estimates	F	Decision on H_0
Total	49,639.0	63	—	—	—
Between Cities	4,816.3	3	1,605.4	5.68*	Reject
Between Sectors	948.4	3	316.1	1.12*	Accept
Between Distances	28,418.6	3	9,472.8	33.49*	Reject
Cities × Sectors	3,864.0	9	429.3	1.62	Accept
Cities × Distances	1,692.2	9	188.0	.71	Accept
Sectors × Distances	2,756.6	9	306.3	1.16	Accept
Residual	7,142.9	27	264.6	—	—
Pooled Error	15,275.8	54	282.9	—	—

* Since the interactions were not significant, the main effects were tested from the pooled error estimate (residual plus the interactions).

more urbanized than are midwestern cities, a fact which has long been recognized at least with respect to multi-family dwelling units. Second, these comparisons reveal that, as expected, tracts located nearest the city center are most highly urbanized (129.6) while tracts furthest from the center are least urbanized (73.4). This finding suggests that the principal impact of the urbanization index is to differentiate between near-center and far-from-center areas, between central and peripheral areas.

RESULTS: PRESTIGE VALUE

The prestige value (or social rank) index contrasts areas characterized by a resident population with a high proportion of persons with at least a high school education and a high proportion of persons with non-manual occupations (high prestige) with areas characterized by many laborer residents and many persons with relatively little education (low prestige). Where are areas of high prestige found within the city? Table 2 presents the analysis of variance results for prestige value using the same design as in the case of urbanization. Only the interaction F values have been presented in this table for a reason that will become clear in a moment.

An examination of the interaction F values indicates that only the cities by sectors interaction is significant and that its significance is essentially beyond doubt. Cities and sectors do interact. What this interaction means, in partic-

ular, is that the sector that manifests a high prestige in one city is not oriented in the same direction from the center as the high prestige sector in another city. For example, the sector with the highest prestige (among those studied) was the southeast sector in Akron, the northwest sector in Dayton, the southeast one in Indianapolis, and the northeast one in Syracuse. Thus the interaction here indicates that cities are not uniformly structured with respect to prestige value. This should surprise no one. The interaction between cities and sectors is so great, however, with about 60 per cent of the total sum of squares contained in it, as to completely dominate the main effects. The implication to be drawn from the size of this interaction is that cities should not be combined in comparing sectors and distances on prestige variations. Therefore, main effects were not tested from this table, but rather were tested separately for each city, producing four separate two-way analyses of variance.

The results as shown in Table 3 are clear. In each city tested, the null hypothesis must be rejected with respect to sectors. In three of the four cities, the null hypothesis is accepted with respect to distances. Prestige is primarily distributed within sectors rather than within distance bands. Only in Indianapolis was a significant secondary pattern found with respect to distance. Hoyt's sector hypothesis may be considered confirmed with respect to prestige value.

TABLE 2.   Analysis of Variance for the Prestige Value Index

Source	Sum of Squares	df	Variance Estimates	F	Decision on H_0
Total	32,154.24	63	—	—	—
Between Cities	1,810.77	3	603.59	—	—
Between Sectors	1,835.76	3	611.92	—	—
Between Distances	1,907.26	3	635.75	—	—
Cities × Sectors	19,224.79	9	2,136.09	12.16	Reject
Cities × Distances	1,775.02	9	197.22	1.12	Accept
Sectors × Distances	858.92	9	95.44	.54	Accept
Residual	4,741.73	27	175.62	—	—

TABLE 3. Analysis of Variance of Prestige Value by Distance and Sectors within Each City

Source	Sum of Squares	df	Variance Estimates	F	Decision on H_o
Akron					
Total	7,698.8	15	—	—	—
Between Distances	897.9	3	299.3	1.93	Accept
Between Sectors	5,407.6	3	1,802.5	11.64	Reject
Remainder	1,393.4	9	154.8	—	—
Dayton					
Total	4,816.4	15	—	—	—
Between Distances	607.8	3	202.6	2.88	Accept
Between Sectors	3,576.4	3	1,192.1	16.97	Reject
Remainder	632.1	9	70.2	—	—
Indianapolis					
Total	5.011.3	15	—	—	—
Between Distances	1,694.9	3	565.0	5.77	Reject
Between Sectors	2,435.0	3	811.7	8.29	Reject
Remainder	881.4	9	97.9	—	—
Syracuse					
Total	12,817.0	15	—	—	—
Between Distances	481.7	3	160.6	.54	Accept
Between Sectors	9,641.6	3	3,213.9	10.74	Reject
Remainder	2,693.8	9	299.3	—	—

DISCUSSION

In sum, the principal findings of this study are that urbanization (at the tract level) varies primarily concentrically or by distance from the center of the city, while prestige value (or social rank) varies primarily sectorially, with very little distance variation. These conclusions, of course, are restricted to American cities whose total spatial aspect is roughly circular and which have between 200,000 and 500,000 population. The impact of major geographic disturbances and larger city size on these conclusions remains as a problem for future research. In this connection, it should be noted that it is somewhat surprising to find that prestige value does not vary concentrically. It is common to visualize the suburban sections of a city as having residents of higher average socio-economic status than are found in the central sections of the city. The findings reported here apparently do not support this contention. However, recent evidence indicates that the Shevky-Bell social rank index is not a general measure of the average socio-economic status of local residents. In particular, an article by Anderson and Bean [11] indicates that in Toledo, average family income is more highly loaded on urbanization than on social rank. The apparently higher average socio-economic status of suburban families may be manifest largely in higher average incomes. If so, then this effect is incorporated primarily in the urbanization index in the Shevky-Bell system rather than in the social rank index. This fact further suggests the desirability of substituting the phrase prestige value for social rank. It is also possible that the absence of any marked concentric pattern with

---

[11] Anderson and Bean, op. cit.

respect to prestige value (or social rank) is limited to smaller and medium-sized metropolitan areas. Some very slight evidence in favor of this hypothesis is indicated in this study by the fact that Indianapolis, the largest of the four cities studied here, did show a significant variation in prestige by distance from the center of the city. Despite these qualifications, however, the major impact of the findings reported here is that Burgess' concentric zone hypothesis (as modified) is supported with respect to urbanization but not prestige value, while Hoyt's sector hypothesis is supported with respect to prestige value but not urbanization.

27

KENT P. SCHWIRIAN
MARC MATRE

The Ecological Structure of Canadian Cities

ABSTRACT

This paper examines the ecological structure of 11 principal Canadian cities by testing four propositions based on findings for U.S. cities. First, the factorial ecology of the cities is explored, and the findings show that the Canadian city structure is described generally by vectors corresponding to social rank, familism, and ethnicity. Second, the spatial patterning of the three dimensions is investigated, and the findings indicate that social rank largely is distributed by sector while familism is distributed mainly by distance gradient from the city center. The distribution of ethnicity varies considerably among cities. While the Canadian city findings generally correspond to those for the United States, some differences are reported among which is the instability of the familism vector. Also, it was found that there is some regional variation in Canada in the extent of the correlation of the ethnicity measure with the social rank vector.

INTRODUCTION

With increasing frequency ecological models of urban structure developed on United States cities are being tested in other societies. Two trends mark this current line of analysis. The first is a concern with the relationship between societal structure and the ecological patterning of individual cities. Accordingly, differences among the ecological structures of cities in dif-

Research paper, Department of Sociology, The Ohio State University, 1969.

ferent societies are explained in terms of aggregate differences among the parent societies in "economic development," "societal scale," or, more simply, "modernization." Illustrative of this approach are studies within the "social area analysis" framework (see, for example, Abu-Lughod [1969] and Clignet and Sween [1969]). The second trend is for an analytical combination of several ecological models previously considered more competitive than complementary in the study of a single city. Usually factorial ecology or social area analysis models are used to identify relevant inputs for the more traditional spatial analysis which employs distance gradient and/or sector models (see, for example, Anderson and Egeland [1961], Berry and Rees [1969], and Sweetser [1969].) The net result of these recent efforts has been far more detailed, comprehensive analyses of city structure than past single model efforts have produced.

In this paper we extend this line of research by testing four propositions about urban ecological structure with data from Canada's 11 principal cities.[1] These propositions, based largely upon findings from U.S. cities, focus upon both the factor structure of the cities in terms of the social area analysis variables and the distance gradient and sectoral spatial patterning of the variables.

Our selection of Canada for investigation was prompted by four considerations. First, Canada's level of modernization or "societal scale" is roughly comparable to that of the United States. Thus, according to current theories, the ecological structure of the Canadian cities generally should be similar to those of the United States even though the two societies have many specific cultural differences. Canada, then provides a test of the ecological models developed on U.S. cities that supposedly are generalizable to other similar societies. A second reason in our selection of Canada is that while there are some studies of individual cities (see, for example, Murdie [1969]) and some general discussions of the urbanization process [Stone 1967] a comprehensive picture of Canada's urban ecological structure has yet to be developed. The third factor in the selection of Canada is the availability for a large number of cities of good small-area (census tract) data collected and tabulated by the Dominion Bureau of Statistics. The lack of such data has hindered comparative studies of urbanization in many nations, especially the newly developing ones. Finally, the data collected for the Canadian census tracts permit the development of indexes of subarea population characteristics consistent with those of studies of U.S. cities, thereby maximizing the comparability of findings.

This study deals with 11 major Canadian cities which differ markedly in size and regional location. They are: Calgary, Edmonton, Hamilton, London, Montreal, Ottawa, Quebec, Toronto, Vancouver, Windsor, and Winnipeg. Most other studies of non-U.S. cities have been limited to only one, or at the most, a few from their society. While the findings from such efforts are valuable, all too often the results from a single city are taken as *the* pattern or urban structure for the total society, and possible within-societal variations in urban ecological patterning are ignored. However, it is as imprudent to generalize about urban structure in such societies on the basis of single city studies as it would be to generalize about U.S. city structure with data from only New York or Chicago. In fact, in a comparative study of 10 U.S. cities, marked regional variation in city structure was discovered [Van Arsdol, Camilleri, and Schmid 1958]. Likewise, even in a society with a primate city pattern of urban concentration it is dangerous to generalize about the urban structure of secondary cities with data from only the large or primate city [Schwirian 1969; Schwirian and Smith 1969]. Through analysis of a variety of Canadian cities we include a greater possible range of variation in urban structure, thereby permitting fairly general conclusions to be drawn about Canadian urban patterns.

[1] By "principal" Canadian cities we mean the largest cities with more than 20 census tracts.

HYPOTHESES AND THEORY

The four hypotheses tested here deal with the expected factor structure of ecological variables for the Canadian cities and with the spatial distribution of the clusters identified by the factor analysis.

The first hypothesis is drawn from the theory of societal scale associated with the social area analysis framework. It is: *that the correlations among the ecological variables will be explained by at least three factors which generally correspond to "social rank," "familism," and "ethnicity."* The theory of scale, in effect, asserts that urban residential differentiation is a function of the degree of modernization of the society in which the city is located. The theory maintains that as a society modernizes or increases in "scale" the degree of differentiation increases and is reflected in increasing specialization of urban land use and residential segregation of subpopulations. The dimensions of life viewed as most sensitive to such change and most basic in the urbanites' life parameters are social rank, life style or familism (sometimes called urbanism), and ethnicity [2] [Shevky and Bell 1955; Greer 1962].

Thus in small-scale societies or in societies that are less modern there is little social differentiation; that is, social rank is highly related to family form, and both, in turn are highly related to ethnicity. These high correlations mean that spatial differentiation of the population in terms of the three dimensions does not occur. In large-scale societies where differentiation has occurred, the correlations among the variables are sufficiently reduced that areal specialization of population distribution takes place along the three dimensions.

Abu-Lughod [1969: 208-209] discusses in some detail the conditions required for the emergence and separation of the rank and familism dimensions. For a social rank vector to be identified she argues that the following conditions must be met: (1) that the effective status ranking system in the city be related to the operational definition used; and (2) that the ranking system be reflected in a pattern of residential segregation by rank at sufficient scale to be detected at the level of analysis (census tract, ward, etc.). For a familism factor to appear there must be in the city: (1) variability of family forms associated with stages in the life cycle or with other "social" causes such as those associated with other divisions in society, such as rank or ethnicity; and (2) that the urban subareas be differentiated in their attractiveness to different types of families. For familism and social rank to separate factorially from each other the following conditions must be met: (1) that no strong linkages exist between the rank and familism variables; (2) that stages in the life cycle are distinct from each other with each stage being associated with a change in residence; (3) that all levels of social rank sufficiently large subareas within the city offer highly specialized housing accommodations suited to families at particular life cycle stages; and (4) that cultural values encouraging geographic mobility to maximize housing efficiency generally are unencumbered by restrictive regulations or negative sanctions.

We may add the societal conditions necessary for the emergence of an ethnicity factor and its separation from the rank and familism dimensions. For an ethnic factor to appear in a society there must be differential definitions, values, and behaviors characteristic of subpopulations differing in heritage, physical appearance, and/or philosophical or religious orientation. For ethnicity to separate from social rank and familism, there must be considerable variation in the residential location of ethnic groups at each level of social rank and stage in the life cycle.

In a highly differentiated society the search for housing becomes a complex process. The calculus of the individual urbanite must combine rank, life cycle, and ethnic factors. Different areas of the metropolis offer distinct accommodations in terms of varying mixes of

---

[2] In a recent paper Clignet and Sween [1969] have added a fourth dimension called "migrant status" which they argue is sufficiently different from ethnicity to warrant separate consideration.

rank, life cycle, and ethnic requirements. Individual choice is usually limited greatly by the constraints of availability. As Park noted: "... The city grows by expansion, but it gets its character by the selection and segregation of its population, so that every individual finds, eventually, either the place where he can, or the place where he must live" [Park 1952: 79].

Tests of the theory of scale and urban differentiation generally have employed principal components or factor analysis techniques. In terms of factor structures, the theory leads to the prediction that in a highly differentiated or modern society at least three factors are needed to explain the interrelationships and the resulting factors correspond to social rank, familism, and ethnicity. In a small-scale society, or one in which social differentiation is at a minimum, a fewer number of factors are required—perhaps only one.

Empirical investigations of several cities in differing societies generally have supported the theory. Factorial separation is greatest in U.S. cities [Van Arsdol, Camilleri, and Schmid 1958] and least in African cities [Abu-Lughod 1969; Clignet and Sween 1969]. Intermediate differentiation seems to characterize Rome [McElrath 1962].[3] Since Canada is a fairly large-scale society with a high degree of social differentiation, we expect the factor structure of Canadian cities to be similar to those of the United States. Thus for Canadian cities we expect at least three factors corresponding to social rank, familism, and ethnicity to characterize the network of relationships among the ecological variables for each city.

The remaining three hypotheses deal with the spatial patterning of the social area variables. These hypotheses are based mainly on the work of Anderson and Egeland [1961] and are (2) *that the spatial patterning of "social rank" will correspond to a sectoral distribution;* (3) *that the spatial patterning of "familism" will correspond to a distance gradient or concentric zone distribution;* and

(4) *that the spatial patterning of ethnicity will not correspond consistently to either a gradient or sector pattern.*

Anderson and Egeland's study deals with the spatial distribution of two of the social area indexes which they labeled "urbanization" and "prestige value." Urbanization was measured by a combination of (1) the reflected values of the fertility ratio; (2) the percentage of women 14 years of age and over in the labor force; and (3) the percentage of all dwellings that are multi-family units. Anderson and Egeland modified the social area scheme conceptually by using the term *prestige value* rather than the usual social area term *social rank* to refer to the sum of (1) the percentage of employed persons *not* classified as craftsmen, operatives, or laborers; and (2) the percentage of persons 25 years old and over who have completed at least one year to three years of high school. They justify this modification by arguing that many studies have shown that socioeconomic status is not a unidimensional phenomenon. Measures of occupation and education, while being highly correlated with each other, have low correlations with income. They argue that education and occupation have become to be identified with the prestige dimension of status. While their argument seems sound, few subsequent studies using the education and occupation indicators have adopted the "prestige" terminology. Most have persisted in using the "social rank" denotation for the measures. In this paper we follow current practice and retain the original term "social rank."

For each of four U.S. cities (Akron, Dayton, Indianapolis, and Syracuse) Anderson and Egeland selected 16 census tracts for investigation. After the tracts were classified by sector and distance gradient from the city's center, an analysis of variance was performed to test the significance of the rank and familism distributions. Basically, they found for the cities that the prestige or rank indicators were distributed primarily by sector, while the urbanization of familism variables were distributed principally by distance from the city's center.

---

[3] For an extensive bibliography of studies using the social area framework see Abu-Lughod [1969].

Anderson and Egeland omitted an examination of the ethnicity or segregation dimension because "... the distribution of Negroes within the large U.S. city is known not to fit either of these patterns well" [Anderson and Egeland 1961: 394]. Thus in the study of Canadian cities we have no grounds for predicting either a sectoral or gradient distribution for ethnicity on the basis of U.S. findings. Also, even if Anderson and Egeland had demonstrated either a sectoral or gradient pattern of ethnic distribution for the U.S. cities we could not necessarily hypothesize a similar pattern for Canada since ethnicity itself is quite different in the two societies. For the United States the major component of the ethnic dimension today is race, while in Canada it is national and cultural heritage.

While the study by Anderson and Egeland is the basis for hypotheses two, three, and four it should be pointed out that our study differs from theirs in three major ways, all of which have to do with the selection of cities for investigation. Three characteristics of Anderson and Egeland's cities are (1) at the time of the study the cities were all of similar size (between 200,-000 and 500,000); (2) the cities are restricted to the American Midwest (Akron, Dayton, and Indianapolis) and up-state New York (Syracuse); and (3) geometrically they all have roughly circular overall shapes. The Canadian cities selected for investigation vary greatly in size (114,367–1,191,062). They are located in all regions of Canada—east, midwest, and far west. And they reflect a variety of geometric shapes. The greater variability of the Canadian cities in size, regional location, and shape permit both a greater generality of the findings for Canada than are permitted for American cities in Anderson and Egeland's work, and a more general test of the propositions under consideration.

METHODOLOGY
The variables investigated are based on those used in past studies within the social area framework. Our operationalizations of them

are similar to those used by Van Arsdol, Camilleri, and Schmid [1958], although some modifications have been made to accommodate to differences between U.S. and Canadian census categories. The data for the indexes are from the 1961 Canadian census [Dominion Bureau of Statistics 1961].

The variables are occupation, education, infertility, women in the labor force, multiple dwelling units, and language. They are measured as follows:

1. Occupation: the number of middle and upper status occupations per 1,000 workers in the labor force.
$$= 1,000 - \frac{\text{number of primary, craftsmen, production process and related, and laborers}}{\text{total labor force}} \times 1,000$$

Education: the number per 1,000 adults with a high school or greater education
$$= 1,000 - \frac{\text{number of adults with less than a high school education}}{\text{total number of adults out of school}} \times 1,000$$

Infertility:[4] 1,000-fertility ratio (1,000)
$$= 1,000 - \frac{\text{number of children 0–4 years of age}}{\text{number of women 15 years of age and older}} \times 1,000$$

Women in the Labor Force (Women L-F): number of women per 1,000 women 15 years of age and older in the labor force
$$= \frac{\text{number of women 15 years of age and older in the labor force}}{\text{number of women 15 years of age and older}} \times 1,000$$

[4] Infertility rather than fertility is measured so that a high score on it is consistent with high scores on women in the labor force and multiple dwelling units as indicating high "urbanism" or low "familism."

Multiple Dwelling Units: the number of multiple dwelling units per 1,000 occupied dwelling units

$$= 1,000 - \frac{\text{number of single detached dwelling units}}{\text{total number of dwelling units}} \times 1,000$$

Language: the number of persons per 1,000 who are conversant in a language or languages in addition or in place of English

$$= 1,000 - \frac{\text{number of persons who speak English only}}{\text{total number of persons}} \times 1,000$$

These indexes, with the exception of the language indicator, are very similar to those used in other social area analysis studies. The ethnic population of Canada may be considered in two categories. First, there is the native-born French-speaking peoples, and second there is the variety of foreign-born ethnic groups a considerable percentage of whom immigrated to Canada since 1946. One thing both categories of ethnic groups have in common is linguistic diversity from most native-born Canadians. Language reflects the ability to participate in different culture systems, and our measure is, in effect, the reflected value of those who are bound by their language to the English culture system.

The ethnic constellation for the 11 cities varies considerably among them. Table 1 shows the relative concentration of foreign born in the cities as well as the distribution of the cities' population by ethnic heritage. The percentage of foreign born is smallest in Quebec (2.1%) and greatest in Toronto (41.9%). Ethnic heritage varies considerably by region. The French are most represented in the eastern cities (Quebec, Montreal, and Ottawa); the Germans in the prairies (Edmonton, Winnipeg, and Calgary); the Italians in the Great Lakes cities (Hamilton, Toronto, and Windsor); the Scandinavians in the western prairies and the far west (Edmonton, Calgary, and Vancouver); the

Ukrainians in the western prairies (Edmonton and Winnipeg); and the Asiatics on the west coast (Vancouver). [5]

The six indexes were calculated for all of the census tracts for which complete data were available for the 11 cities. In this study we selected the central city tracts for investigation rather than those for the total metropolitan community since we felt that the type of socio-ecological systems contained within the central city definitions are more comparable across the communities than are those included with the remaining 11 fringe areas. In Table 2 are presented the summary characteristics of the cities. In the table is the total number of tracts in the city and the number used in this analysis. From the table it may be seen that in no city is there a large percentage of the city unanalyzed. The missing tracts reflect incomplete data.

To test the first proposition we calculated a factor analysis on the tract data for each of the 11 cities. We employed a principal factor solution with an orthogonal rotation which used Kaiser's varimax method. Five factors were extracted from the correlation matrixes for each city. The number of factors extracted was determined by our desire to (1) extract the same number of factors in each city; (2) maximize the variable variance explained as indexed by the communality score; and (3) minimize the size of the residual correlations. Analyses with fewer than five factors were performed, and while the conclusions were largely similar to those presented here the size of the residual correlations in some instances were quite high while the variable communalities were low.

Examination of propositions two through four, which deal with the spatial distribution

---

[5] Alternative ethnic indicators were used and comparable findings were discovered. Copies of the results with the additional ethnic indicators are available from the authors. The decision to limit the input to only one ethnic measure reflects our goal (1) simply to discover whether "ethnicity" in a broad sense is a separate dimension of urban organization in Canada; (2) to use a measure that would tap both the foreign-born and native-born French dimensions; and (3) to use one indicator to make the results more comparable to those for U.S. cities which tend to measure ethnicity only in terms of Negro population.

TABLE 1.   Percentage Distribution of Canadian City Population by Heritage, Birth-place, and Recent Immigration Status

City	Heritage							
	British Isles	French	German	Italian	Netherlands	Polish	Russian	Scandinavian
Calgary	58.9	3.8	10.8	1.9	3.5	2.0	1.4	5.6
Edmonton	46.2	6.1	12.2	1.6	3.5	4.0	0.8	5.2
Hamilton	58.9	4.2	5.2	8.5	2.5	4.2	0.5	0.8
London	72.8	3.3	5.8	2.0	3.6	1.9	0.5	1.1
Montreal	12.4	66.6	1.2	6.7	0.2	1.4	0.6	0.2
Ottawa	55.2	25.5	3.5	3.1	1.4	1.3	0.4	0.9
Quebec	3.9	94.3	0.3	0.4	0.0	0.0	0.0	0.1
Toronto	51.8	4.1	4.6	11.6	1.0	4.0	0.6	0.7
Vancouver	59.9	3.2	6.9	3.4	2.4	1.9	1.3	4.9
Windsor	46.5	18.0	4.7	7.5	1.1	3.3	0.8	0.7
Winnipeg	42.8	5.2	11.4	1.6	2.6	6.2	1.0	3.8

City	Heritage				% Foreign Born	% Immigrated Since 1946
	Ukrainian	Other Europe	Asiatic	Other and Not Given	Total[1]	
Calgary	2.8	6.2	1.3	1.7	100.	25.1	13.5
Edmonton	11.6	5.9	0.9	1.8	100.	24.5	13.3
Hamilton	3.1	8.7	0.8	2.7	100.	31.3	18.4
London	1.0	4.6	0.6	2.9	100.	21.5	13.0
Montreal	0.8	8.6	0.7	0.6	100.	17.2	11.8
Ottawa	0.9	3.7	1.1	2.9	100.	15.6	9.9
Quebec	0.0	0.5	0.2	0.1	100.	2.1	1.2
Toronto	3.9	12.9	1.9	3.0	100.	41.9	29.1
Vancouver	4.9	7.0	5.2	1.7	100.	34.5	15.3
Windsor	3.0	10.3	1.4	2.6	100.	27.2	12.6
Winnipeg	13.6	9.4	0.9	1.6	100.	28.5	12.9

[1] In some instances the percentages do not add to 100 percent because of rounding errors. For the total number of persons per city see Table 2.

of the variables, involves a two-way analysis of variance for each city's tract data. For each city 16 census tracts were selected for investigation. Each city was subdivided into 12 sectors of 30 degrees width each with initial orientation being north-south. From these, only sectors that contained census tracts extending from the city's center to the periphery were retained for analysis. Thus, those sectors containing natural features such as rivers or lakes that halt the progression of the tract were excluded. Four sectors were randomly selected from those eligible. Within each of the randomly selected sectors four tracts were chosen for investiga-tion: one which is next to the central business district; one which is one-third of the way out; one which is two-thirds of the way out; and one at the city's periphery. In each city the 16 tracts were classified by sector and by distance from the city center, and a two-way analysis of variance was calculated for each of the social area analysis indexes. The findings from the factor analyses and the two-way analyses of variance are presented in Table 3.

FINDINGS

The first hypothesis tested is that for each city at least three factors are required to account

TABLE 2. Summary Characteristics of 11 Canadian Cities for 1961

City	City Population	Metropolitan Population	Total City Tracts	Tracts Used	Occupation	Education	Infertility	Women in L.F.	Mult. Dwel.	Language
Calgary	249,641	279,062	23	23	723	697	632	361	365	75
Edmonton	281,027	337,568	45	45	702	655	594	380	252	60
Hamilton	273,991	395,189	65	63	553	531	673	333	268	80
London	169,569	181,283	41	40	697	665	647	373	219	45
Montreal	1,191,062	2,109,509	238	237	601	463	731	349	955	824
Ottawa	268,206	429,750	50	47	801	678	701	404	501	318
Quebec	171,979	357,568	38	38	678	449	756	356	933	990
Toronto	672,407	1,824,481	135	120	639	516	764	452	528	107
Vancouver	384,522	790,165	57	56	667	672	775	361	292	59
Windsor	114,367	193,365	25	25	613	521	722	315	272	124
Winnipeg	265,429	475,089	48	48	660	636	746	408	361	70

for the variance in the correlation matrix and that these factors correspond to "social rank," "familism," and "ethnicity." The findings from the separate factor analyses are in Table 3. For each city the five extracted factors account for over 95 percent of the matrix variance. The factors in the table are ordered under the general headings corresponding to the social area analysis dimensions—social rank, familism, and ethnicity. The parentheses indicate which variables are predicted to be highly correlated with the factor. The starred values indicate the highest loading for each variable.

The data in Table 3 show that for all cities a separate social rank factor emerges. Three cities, Edmonton, Toronto, and Vancouver, show two social rank factors. In Edmonton there is a slight tendency for education and occupation to become disassociated. However, Edmonton's factor I and factor II are very similar. The main difference between them is that education dominates factor I while occupation dominates factor II. In Toronto there are two rank factors. However, factor I includes fertility as well as the social rank variables. Factor II tends to be a unique occupation factor. In Vancouver the two-factor social rank pattern is similar to that of Edmonton in that one of the social rank factors is dominated by education while the other is largely an occupation vector. Furthermore, the data in Table 3 show that with the exception of Toronto, social rank generally is separate from the familism indicators. And in the case of Toronto occupation does pull away into a separate factor from the combined rank-fertility dimension (factor I). Also it should be noted that for these eight cities having a single social rank factor, the rank factor accounts for the highest percentage of the explained variance.

Inspection of the familism factors in Table 3 indicates that only in Calgary and Hamilton is there a single familism vector with which all three familism indicators correlate in excess of .300. In the other cities the familism factors tend to be one variable, unique vectors, or various combinations of pairs of variables. The

TABLE 3.   Results of the Factor Analyses of 11 Principal Canadian Cities

Variables	Factors					
	Social Rank		Familism			Ethnicity
City	I	II	I	II	III	
Calgary						
Occupation	(988)*		−026	016	008	015
Education	(950)*		−157	−170	−132	014
Infertility	−066		(432)	(889)*	128	051
Women in L.F.	−064		(945)*	(310)	072	033
Mult. Dwell.	−243		(642)*	(435)	(580)	−021
Language	023		028	012	−002	(999)*
Variance Explained	32%		25%	18%	6%	16%
Edmonton						
Occupation	(415)	(867)*	169	−169		−042
Education	(916)*	(341)	032	036		−137
Infertility	058	155	(904)*	(218)		328
Women in L.F.	036	−128	(207)	(920)*		276
Mult. Dwell.	−264	043	(248)	(364)		793*
Language	−007	−122	190	118		(942)*
Variance Explained	18%	15%	16%	18%		29%
Hamilton						
Occupation	(950)*		174	183	056	−082
Education	(978)*		−096	−077	024	−072
Infertility	068		(301)	(944)*	107	−029
Women in L.F.	182		(697)*	(315)	(608)	−112
Mult. Dwell.	−024		(969)*	(236)	053	029
Language	−107		−006	−012	−026	(994)*
Variance Explained	32%		26%	18%	6%	17%
London						
Occupation	(873)*		155	−029	244	356
Education	(943)*		−148	−208	126	−113
Infertility	017		(951)*	(230)	(−162)	123
Women in L.F.	−323		(212)	(379)	(−826)*	143
Mult. Dwell.	−217		(327)	(834)*	(−360)	138
Language	081		111	090	−087	(980)*
Variance Explained	30%		19%	16%	15%	19%
Montreal						
Occupation	(804)*		−184	−120	372	−249
Education	(930)*		−107	−120	128	−202
Infertility	344		(−336)	(148)	(853)*	−087
Women in L.F.	170		(−903)*	(151)	(286)	−228
Mult. Dwell.	−174		(−125)	(971)*	(096)	026
Language	−286		200	052	(083)	(931)*
Variance Explained	30%		17%	17%	16%	17%

TABLE 3. *(Continued)*

| | Variables | | | Factors | | | |
City	Social Rank I	II	Familism I	II	III	Ethnicity
Ottawa						
Occupation	(959)*		062	192	−026	−151
Education	(898)*		−026	165	234	−304
Infertility	042		(967)*	(−085)	(−234)	010
Women in L.F.	−128		(359)	(−317)	(−853)*	152
Mult. Dwell.	−338		(137)*	(−806)*	(−379)*	217
Language	−317		001	−200	−141	(916)*
Variance Explained	54%		25%	7%	3%	10%
Quebec						
Occupation	(863)*		−346	−033	253	−204
Education	(853)*		145	051	218	−402
Infertility	085		(−912)*	(271)	(217)	−156
Women in L.F.	295		(−198)	(064)	(962)*	−130
Mult. Dwell.	011		(−202)	(978)*	(010)	−000
Language	−407		178	008	−106	(887)*
Variance Explained	29%		18%	17%	17%	17%
Toronto						
Occupation	(639)	(715)*	149	130		−214
Education	(906)*	(161)	013	073		−263
Infertility	916*	169	(071)	(206)		−010
Women in L.F.	198	090	(257)	(939)*		059
Mult. Dwell.	036	075	(960)*	(240)		116
Language	−273	−107	133	061		(943)*
Variance Explained	36%	9%	17%	16%		17%
Vancouver						
Occupation	(958)*	(238)	−006	158		004
Education	(350)	(840)*	029	−260		−295
Infertility	224	280	(195)	(−891)*		077
Women in L.F.	020	077	(979)*	(−122)		−005
Mult. Dwell.	−984	−226	(646)*	(−519)		457
Language	003	−168	054	−086		(977)*
Variance Explained	18%	15%	23%	20%		21%
Windsor						
Occupation	(888)*		322	272	086	114
Education	(900)*		063	090	−188	−359
Infertility	224		(910)*	(230)	(233)	−118
Women in L.F.	237		(230)	(907)*	(251)	−073
Mult. Dwell.	−114		(304)	(320)	(840)*	296
Language	−303		−119	−061	213	(919)*
Variance Explained	30%		18%	17%	15%	18%

TABLE 3.   *(Continued)*

| Variables | Social Rank | | Factors | | | Ethnicity |
| | | | Familism | | | |
City	I	II	I	II	III	
Winnipeg						
Occupation	(907)*		−061	293	022	−104
Education	(916)*		−004	103	−148	−249
Infertility	352		(250)	(882)*	(173)	046
Women in L.F.	−042		(911)*	(223)	(281)	188
Mult. Dwell.	−080		(403)	(133)	(826)*	337
Language	−301		219	053	275	(884)*
Variance Explained	31%		18%	16%	15%	17%

The ( ) indicate the variables predicted to load on the factor and the * indicate the highest loading for a given variable. Decimal points have been omitted.

instability of the familism factors for these cities differs from the findings of Van Arsdol, Camilleri, and Schmid [1958], who found for several U.S. cities fairly strong familism factors. However, some other studies of U.S. cities have failed to find a single familism factor [for example, see Ekstrom 1968]. Within the social area framework the familism dimension has proved to be somewhat troublesome from both empirical and logical standpoints [see Hawley and Duncan 1957].

In all 11 cities language separates from the other two factors thereby supporting the notion that ethnicity is an independent dimension of urban organization. Only in Edmonton and Vancouver do we find a familism variable (multiple dwelling units) correlating with language. A supplementary investigation indicated that in both cities the comparatively high correlation of multiple dwelling units with language is to a large extent a function of the co-occurrence of *comparatively* large concentrations of ethnic group members and multiple dwelling units near the cities' center. In Vancouver the ethnic group is Asiatic while in Edmonton it is Ukrainian.

It also should be pointed out in regard to ethnicity that while the language variable generally disassociates in factor space from the status variables, for a number of eastern Canadian cities many of which have high concentrations of French-speaking peoples, there is a ten-

dency for a low, negative correlation to exist between language and the status vector. The correlation of language with social rank for these cities is Montreal, −.286; Ottawa, −.317; Quebec, −.407; Toronto, −.273; Windsor, −.303; and Winnipeg, −.301.

In summary of the factor analyses for the Canadian cities it may be stated that the social area analysis hypothesis is generally supported since social rank and ethnicity are fairly independent of each other, and that each is fairly independent of the familism indicators. However, contrary to the social area scheme, the familism variable is multidimensional and in most cities we find a factorial separation of infertility, women in the labor force, and multiple dwelling units. Each seems to represent a different "aspect" of familism and gross statements about combined "familism" in these cities would be inappropriate.

The next three hypotheses tested with Canadian city data involve the spatial distribution of the variables and are (1) that social rank is distributed by sector, (2) that familism is distributed by distance gradient, and (3) that the distribution of ethnicity is by neither distance nor sector consistently. Since the social rank factor seems to be general across the cities a single measure of rank is investigated. This single index is a simple sum of the education and occupation indexes. Since familism proved to be multidimensional, two analyses of it are made. First, a combined index of familism is investigated which is a simple sum of the three separate indicators; this is followed by a separate analysis for each of the individual indicators of infertility, women in the labor force, and multiple dwelling units. The investigation of ethnicity is in terms of the distribution of the language variable.

The data for the spatial distributions are presented in Tables 4 and 5. Inspection of Table 4 indicates that, as hypothesized, in most cases social rank is distributed more by sector

than by distance gradient. The percent distribution by sector is larger than that by distance in eight cities, six of which are statistically significant at .05. Three exceptions to this sectorial pattern are Ottawa, Edmonton, and Windsor. In Ottawa almost equal amounts of the sum of squares are explained by sector and by distance, but neither amount is statistically significant. In Edmonton and Winnipeg we find a reversal of the predicted pattern in that a larger percent is explained by distance than by sector. In Edmonton approximately 51 percent of the

TABLE 4.   Percent of the Total Sum of Squares of Social Area Analysis Variables Explained by Sectors and by Distance for 11 Canadian Cities

City	Social Rank Sector	Distance	Familism Sector	Distance	Ethnicity Sector	Distance
Calgary	44.7	17.1	35.7*	41.8*	17.5	22.7
Edmonton	31.7*	50.8*	2.7	93.6*	13.0	62.0*
Hamilton	64.8*	0.8	11.7*	82.1*	71.6*	15.0
London	62.0*	5.0	5.9	75.0*	36.3	23.2
Montreal	52.8*	19.5	11.5*	79.6*	50.0	9.9
Ottawa	22.6	29.3	21.0*	64.6*	81.5*	8.4
Quebec	67.4*	0.5	19.5	50.0*	93.2*	0.6
Toronto	62.8*	11.2	11.7	41.6	16.2	72.9*
Vancouver	35.1	15.6	15.6	57.6*	17.2	39.4
Windsor	18.0	34.8	31.7*	56.0*	28.4	18.2
Winnipeg	68.6*	5.6	6.5	78.5*	17.6	49.1*

* The percentage of the sum of squares is statistically significant beyond the .05 level. The test of significance is the two-way analysis of variance.

TABLE 5.   Percent of the Total Sum of Squares of the Components of the Familism Index Explained by Sectors and by Distance for 11 Canadian Cities

City	Infertility Sector	Distance	Women in Labor Force Sector	Distance	Multiple Dwelling Units Sector	Distance
Calgary	24.0*	61.0*	39.7	26.2	37.8	25.9
Edmonton	3.4	85.3*	4.5	86.4*	1.6	80.9*
Hamilton	27.0	38.7	25.1*	61.7*	8.9	83.0*
London	46.9*	24.5	2.0	71.2*	3.1	82.2*
Montreal	16.0	60.7*	13.8*	78.5*	21.7	49.5*
Ottawa	35.1	24.9	9.6	74.2*	19.8	50.3*
Quebec	26.2*	60.9*	28.7	14.2	4.4	64.8*
Toronto	69.2*	12.7	39.9*	14.8	6.1	71.8*
Vancouver	61.0*	4.7	22.6	24.1	5.2	76.5*
Windsor	3.6	6.3	32.6	30.4	31.5*	61.1*
Winnipeg	24.6	54.3*	6.5	76.3*	7.9	84.6*

* The percentage of the sum of squares is statistically significant at the .05 level. The test of significance is the two-way analysis of variance.

sum of squares is explained by distance gradient and about 32 percent by sector. It should be noted here that in the factor analysis of the Edmonton data education and occupation tended to separate into different vectors. A separate analysis by sector and distance was performed for these two aspects of social rank in Edmonton, and it was found that occupation was distributed by sector (49.6 percent of the sum of squares explained by sector and only 26.2 percent by distance gradient), but that education was distributed by gradient (61.3 percent of the sum of squares explained by distance gradient and only 18.9 percent by sector). Thus, our expectation for the distribution of social rank in Edmonton is supported for one of the rank variables.

The failure of sectors to be important in the distribution of rank in Windsor is largely a function of the shape of the city. Windsor is bound on the north and west by the Detroit River. The incorporation limits of the city roughly parallel the river at a distance of only two to five census tracts in width. The result is a ribbon-shaped city with development largely limited to only a few sectors. Thus major variations can exist only by distance gradient.

Table 4 also contains the distribution of the summed index of familism for the cities. In all cities a larger percentage of the sum of squares of the familism index is accounted for by distance than by sector. The percentage for distance gradient is statistically significant at the .05 level in all but one city. Thus it appears that the distribution of familism corresponds to that predicted by the hypothesis. Since the familism variables generally separated in the factor analyses, a separate examination of the spatial patterning of each was made for each city. Considerable variation is evident in their distribution. In Table 5 it may be noted that it is only the multiple dwelling units variable that consistently corresponds to the distance distribution with the largest concentration near the city's center. In all but one city the percentage of the sum of squares accounted for by distance gradient is greater than that by sector, and that percentage is statistically significant.

In the remaining city the percentage is greater by distance than by sector but the percentage is not significant. The variable infertility is distributed more by distance in seven cities but significant in only five. [6] Women in the labor force is distributed significantly by gradient in only six cities. Thus, it seems that the gradient pattern holds with consistency for only the housing element of familism.

The last proposition examined deals with the distribution of the ethnic variable. In Table 4 it may be noted that the distribution of the language variable in the 11 cities shows considerable variation. The sector pattern is significant for Hamilton, Ottawa, and Quebec while the distance gradient is significant for Edmonton, Toronto, and Winnipeg. For the remaining cities neither the gradient nor the sector model describes a statistically significant percentage of the variation in language distribution. This lack of consistency supports the proposition which states, in effect, that there is considerable difference among cities in the distribution of their ethnic populations.

SUMMARY AND DISCUSSION

The data for the 11 Canadian cities generally are consistent with the hypothesized pattern for a "large-scale" or modernized society. The propositions supported by the data are (1) that the correlations among the variables will be explained by at least three factors which generally correspond to "social rank," "familism," and "ethnicity"; (2) that the spatial patterning of "social rank" will correspond to a sectoral distribution; (3) that the spatial patterning of "familism" will correspond to a gradient pattern; and (4) that the spatial patterning of ethnicity will fit neither a distance gradient nor a sector pattern consistently.

Comparison of the Canadian city findings

---

[6] It should be noted that in Toronto infertility is largely distributed by sector, as is the social rank index. In Toronto's factor analysis infertility correlated strongly with the social rank variables and this is reflected in their similar spatial distribution by sector.

with those for the United States shows the greatest discrepancy to involve the familism dimension. In studies of U.S. cities it has been reported that infertility, women in the labor force, and multiple dwelling units go together into a single familism vector. In the Canadian cities the ecological correlations among the variables are sufficiently lower than those for the United States that there is a marked factorial separation of the three variables. In only two Canadian cities is there a factor with which all of the familism variables correlate in excess of .300.

Among the possibilities for the separation of the familism variables in Canadian city factor space are the following. First, the Shevky-Bell operationalization of familism is actually multidimensional, as some have claimed and as some have demonstrated empirically. The Canadian city data are another demonstration of this multidimensionality. Second, in Canada as compared to the United States there is a greater range of choice in "life styles" that becomes reflected in more heterogeneous residential areas in terms of the familism variables. Thus, in Canada at given levels of fertility there is great variation in female employment and types of dwellings occupied. Likewise, at given levels of multiple dwelling unit concentration there is considerable variation in fertility and female employment. And, at given levels of female labor force participation there is marked variation in fertility and type of dwellings. If, then, there is greater variations in familism combinations in Canada as compared to the United States it might reflect Canada's more recent economic development and differing opportunities for women in it, and/or Canada's more recent immigration experience that may have resulted in a greater variety of family forms and life style than currently characterizes the United States.

A second discrepancy between the Canadian city data and those for the United States is in the spatial distribution of the familism index. While the total familism index for the Canadian cities conforms to the distance gradient pattern, as did that for the U.S. cities studied by Anderson and Egeland, only one of the index components—multiple dwelling units—is distributed uniformly by distance in the cities. Infertility and women in the labor force vary among cities in their spatial patterning. One cannot but help wonder if the components of the familism index for the U.S. cities behave similarly. Since Anderson and Egeland report the distribution for only the total familism measure, the question must remain unanswered currently. If the separate familism variables vary spatially in the U.S. cities as they do in Canada, then support would be lent to the contention that "familism" is indeed multidimensional.

A third discrepancy between the city data for Canada and the United States is the somewhat higher correlations between ethnicity and social rank in the cities of eastern Canada as compared to the United States. It would seem that there is some regional variation in city factor structure between eastern and western Canada. While ethnicity and social rank are clearly separate in the west there is some negative correlation between ethnicity and social rank in the east.

Finally, it has been the purpose of this paper to examine a series of hypotheses about urban ecological structure largely formulated on the basis of U.S. data in another modern, industrial society. With few exceptions the propositions are generally supported. Further extension of this line of analysis need to be made before final confirmation may be attributed to the underlying theories—social area analysis, Burgess concentric zone, and Hoyt sector theory. Of greatest need are studies in the newly emerging nations where good subarea data are being gathered. Also needed are longitudinal studies that will permit the development and test of propositions dealing with urban ecological dynamics. Data collected currently will furnish benchmark information for future longitudinal endeavors. It is only through such efforts that the explanatory value of most ecological theories can be established.

REFERENCES

Abu-Lughod, Janet L. 1969. "Testing the Theory of Social Area Analysis: The Ecology of Cairo, Egypt, *American Sociological Review*, 34: 198–211.

Anderson, Theodore R., and Janice Egeland, 1961. "Spatial Aspects of Social Area Analysis," *American Sociological Review*, 26: 392–399. [No. 26 in this volume.]

Berry, Brian, and Philip H. Rees, 1969. "The Factorial Ecology of Calcutta," *American Journal of Sociology*, 74: 445–491.

Clignet, Remi, and Joyce Sween, 1969. "Accra and Abidjan: A Comparative Examination of the Theory of Increasing Scale," *Urban Affairs Quarterly*, 4: 297–324.

Dominion Bureau of Statistics, 1961. *Census of Canada, Series CT, Population and Housing Characteristics by Census Tracts.* Ottawa.

Ekstrom, Charles, 1968. "Community Social Structure and Issue Differentiation: A Study in the Political Sociology of Welfare," *Sociological Focus*, 1 (no. 3): 1–16.

Greer, Scott, 1962. *The Emerging City*, New York: The Free Press.

Hawley, Amos, and Otis Dudley Duncan, 1957. "Social Area Analysis: A Critical Appraisal," *Land Economics*, 33: 337–345.

McElrath, Dennis C. 1962. *"The Social Areas of Rome: A Comparative Analysis,"* *American Sociological Review,* 27: 376–391.

Murdie, Robert A., 1969. "Factorial Ecology of Metropolitan Toronto 1951–1961." Chicago: Department of Geography, The University of Chicago Research Paper No. 116.

Park, Robert E., 1952. *Human Communities.* Glencoe, Ill.: The Free Press.

Schwirian, Kent P., 1969. "Analytical Convergence in Ecological Research: Factorial Analysis, Gradient and Sector Models." Presented at Conference on Models of Urban Structure, Ohio State University and Battelle Memorial Institute, June 1969.

——, and Ruth K. Smith, 1969. "Primacy, Modernization, and Urban Structure: The Ecology of Puerto Rican Cities." Research paper, Department of Sociology, Ohio State University, Columbus. [No. 28 in this volume.]

Shevky, Eshref, and Wendell Bell, 1955. *Social Area Analysis: Theory, Illustrative Application and Computational Procedures.* Stanford University Series in Sociology No. 1. Stanford: Stanford University Press.

Stone, Leroy O., 1967. *Urban Development in Canada.* Ottawa: Dominion Bureau of Statistics.

Sweetser, Frank, 1969. "Ecological Factors in Metropolitan Zones and Sectors," in Mattei Dogan and Stein Rokkan, *Quantitative Ecological Analysis in the Social Sciences.* Cambridge: M.I.T. Press.

Van Arsdol, Maurice, Jr., Santo Camilleri, and Calvin Schmid, 1958. "The Generality of Urban Social Area Analysis Indexes," *American Sociological Review* 23: 277–284. [No. 24 in this volume.]

28

KENT P. SCHWIRIAN
RUTH K. SMITH

Primacy, Modernization, and Urban Structure: The Ecology of Puerto Rican Cities

ABSTRACT

The central thesis of this paper is that urban ecological structure is a function of both city size and level of economic development of the society in which the city is located. It is also argued that the effect of city size is greatest in societies in the midst of the economic development process. The primary data are for Puerto Rico's three major cities: San Juan, Ponce, and Mayaguez. The analysis reveals both factorial differentiation and spatial patterning consistent with the model. Finally, data from three Canadian cities matched by size with the Puerto Rican cities are introduced into the analysis. The Canadian city findings also support the major thesis of the paper.

A dominant theme in current comparative community research is that the ecological structure of individual cities is to a large extent a function of the level of development of the society in which the city is located. Thus, the causal chain is postulated that societal structure determines urban organization, which in turn determines ecological patterning. With the increasingly comparative interests of ecologists and the increasingly available urban subarea data for world cities the relationship between societal structure and ecological organization is receiving much more attention than ever before. Most studies to date have focused upon cities whose society is at one end or the other of the development scale; either the United States [Shevky and Bell 1955], Canada [Murdie 1966], or Europe [Sweetser 1965; Robson 1969] at the high scale end and either India [Berry and Rees 1969] or South Africa [Clignet and Sween 1969] at the low scale end of the development continuum. Differences in ecological structure between cities at the two ends are usually attributed to differences in societal development.

Frequently it is also argued that as societies at the low end of the development scale modernize, the ecological structure of their cities will become like those of cities in highly developed societies. Unfortunately, insufficient longitudinal data are available for most cities to permit

Paper presented at the 1971 meetings of the American Sociological Association, Denver, 1971. Reprinted by permission of the authors.

the study of the relationship between societal modernization and changing ecological structure. However, the future prospects for such dynamic studies are fairly bright as more nations collect and publish the required urban subarea data [see Schnore 1965].

Relatively neglected in current research are studies of city structure in societies in the midst of development. The few studies of such cities that have been completed do suggest that an evolutionary process of change in ecological structure indeed accompanies societal modernization. While few in number these studies are highly suggestive and contribute substantially to the emergence of sound ecological theory [McElrath 1962]. The purpose of this paper is to contribute to the literature on cities in developing societies by examining the ecological structure of Puerto Rico's three principal cities: San Juan, Ponce, and Mayaguez.

THEORY

Other studies of cities in developing societies have focused only on one city in the society, assuming either that the primate or largest city is the prototype of all other cities in the society such that the ecological patterns which characterize it are evident in the secondary cities, or that in such societies the primate or largest city is the only real urban form worth investigating. Some argue that this exclusive focus on the primate city indeed may be a very poor strategy since the primate city is likely the most atypical city in the whole society, and generalizations about the ecological structure of cities in that society based solely upon it are unwarranted. The unrepresentativeness of the primate city stems from its unique functions and populations, which shape ecological patterns into a form differentiated from those of the other cities. These unique city-shaping elements include main ports, extensive governmental complexes, principal religious and educational institutions, comparatively large concentrations of foreigners and native migrants from the hinterland, centrality in national transportation net-

works, atypical social class compositions, and more extensive communication networks.

In this study of Puerto Rico's urban ecology our selection of the three cities rather than only San Juan is prompted by two concerns. One indeed is the question of the typicality of the primate city's ecological pattern but second and more important is our view of how modernization and urban ecological change occur in a developing nation.

Essentially we suggest that the ecological patterning of cities to a large extent is a function of two independent variables: city size and level of economic development of the society in which the city is located. Thus:

ecological differentiation =
f (city size, level of societal development)

The effects of the independent variables are not additive, however. In societies low on the economic development continuum there is little ecological differentiation regardless of city size. In large-scale societies just the reverse is true. That is, in those societies with marked societal differentiation, community residential patterns are highly differentiated regardless of city size. Thus in both the developed and the very underdeveloped societies city size is not a factor in urban ecological differentiation.

In societies in the midst of the economic development process the rates of social change are not uniform across the whole society. Change proceeds at a much faster pace in the region of the primate city. The primate city is the portal for economic development. Change comes first to the primate city and then diffuses throughout the rest of the society. Since there are differentials in the rate of change there is a bifurcation in life style and social organization between the primate's region and the other more isolated sections of the country. The primate city is the first to take on a changing ecological patterning. In effect, in the midst of the development process the primate city becomes ecologically very much like cities in highly developed societies. The smaller more isolated cities maintain their traditional ecological patterns for a much longer time period. Thus, a cross-sectional investigation of urban ecological patterns in a developing society should show considerable difference in structure between the largest or primate city and the secondary or smaller cities. Thus, city size is a factor in urban ecological differentiation in the developing society, although it is not in either the highly developed society or the generally underdeveloped society. In the developing society, city size is a rough surrogate of the city's niche in the urban system through which changes diffuse.

Puerto Rico is a society midway in the development process. San Juan historically has played the role of primate city. It is Puerto Rico's gateway to the world. It is the filter through which the bulk of the development activities work. Ponce and Mayaguez are clearly secondary to San Juan. They are located in the more isolated sections of the island, and their development has lagged markedly behind that of San Juan. Thus, in terms of the discussion here our general hypothesis is *that the ecological structure of San Juan is that of a city in a high-scale society while the patterns of Ponce and Mayaguez are more like those of the city in a low-scale society.*

By ecological structure we mean both (1) the main dimensions of population patterning within a city, and (2) the spatial geometry of the population dimensions. Thus, by urban ecological structure, we mean both the factorial ecology and the spatial ecology of cities.

Studies of the factorial ecology of the city are of two basic types. They share in common factor analysis as their analytical technique. The two factorial approaches are *social area analysis* and *factorial ecology per se*. The main difference between the social area analysis approach and that of factorial ecology is the nature of the data inputs of the analysis. Social area analysis limits the variable inputs to those associated with the theoretical framework of Shevky and Bell, and Greer [Shevky and Bell 1955; Greer 1962]. Factorial ecology includes a wider range of variables, usually almost all

of those at hand. The social area analysis inputs are subarea measures of social class, familism (fertility, female labor force participation, and housing), and ethnicity. The social area analysis perspective maintains that the pattern of relationship among the variables is a function of the society's scale. Social scale refers to, on the one hand, the extent of the division of labor within the society and, on the other, the degree of elaboration of the integrative mechanisms and institutions.

It is generally argued that in a low-scale society, or one at the lower end of the modernization continuum, the characteristics of status, family form, and ethnicity are highly intercorrelated while in a high-scale society these formerly related variables separate into independent dimensions of life organization. In factor analysis terms this means that there is little factorial separation of the variables in a low-scale society, while in a high-scale society there is considerable separation of the variables in factor space with separate vectors corresponding to social class, familism, and ethnicity.

Factorial ecology also maintains that dimensional separation increases among the variables as the degree of societal development increases. Factorial ecology, however, does not limit itself to class, familism, and ethnicity as the only principal and separate dimensions. Depending upon initial data inputs other factors are likely to emerge including land use, age, and numerous specific ethnic vectors.

In this study we limit the data inputs to those associated with the social area framework, thereby maximizing the comparability of our findings to the large number of other cities using similar inputs. Comparisons among social area studies are more possible than among factorial ecology studies. Since the inputs vary among factorial ecological studies, each resulting factor matrix is therefore unique. It should be noted that by this discussion we do not mean to imply that if two studies were performed on one city, with one using the social area inputs and one using a wider factorial ecology approach, the results of the two analyses would be widely discrepant. On the contrary, there would be great similarity between the overall views of factor structure yielded by the two studies. However, the factorial ecology approach would probably yield more significant factors than the social area analysis, and the correlations of individual variables shared by the two approaches on similar factors would probably vary somewhat between the two studies.

Studies of the spatial ecology of cities generally take as a starting point the geometric aspects of the Burgess [Park, Burgess, and McKenzie 1925] and Hoyt [1939] theories. From Burgess it is deduced that there is a direct correlation between neighborhood social status and distance from the ecological nexus of the city. Thus, the famous concentric zone scheme associated with Burgess envisions a city whose inner core is low in status, whose outer fringe is high in status, and whose middle expanse is midway in the status hierarchy. The two most prominent challenges to the concentric zone scheme come from the Hoyt sector theory and from studies of status residential distributions in cities in low-scale societies.

Hoyt, on the basis of a study of a large number of American cities, argues that status differences are distributed more by sector than by distance gradient. His well-known theory provides an explanation of the sector pattern as well as changes in it. Support for the Hoyt contention is contributed by Anderson and Egeland [1961], who show status to be distributed by sector and other characteristics by distance. Another confirmation of this pattern is provided by Schwirian and Matre [1969]. In a study of the principal Canadian cities they show that measures of status were distributed much more by sector rather than gradient. They also showed that the distribution of housing was by distance rather than sector. Ethnicity in the Canadian cities did not vary systematically by either distance or sector.

The second type of challenge to the concentric zone-distance gradient proposition

comes from general studies of city-fringe status differences in less developed nations, primarily Latin America. These studies have shown that the class level of the urban core as compared to that of the fringe is the reverse of the pattern described for North American cities; that is, the area nearest the central plaza is of higher status than that at the fringe. The difference in status patterns between the Latin American cities and those of North America is usually explained in terms of original colonial settlement patterns in Latin America [Schwirian and Rico 1971]. Some take the status reversal in the Latin cities to represent the typical pattern of cities in less developed societies [Mehta 1969]. The argument is frequently made that in the period before modernization the high-status urbanites congregate at the hub of colonial life while those of lesser status fill in at the periphery. As development proceeds with improvements in transportation and communication, there is a gradual migration of the higher status residents to attractive fringe areas. Their place in the declining central city is taken up by those unable to pay the price of settlement in the new and expensive fringe developments. Thus during the course of modernization the ecological distribution of status groups becomes that currently found in cities in developed nations.

To summarize the debate on the geometry of urban population characteristics we may state (1) that there is some disagreement as to the extent to which status varies by sector and by distance gradient; (2) that there is evidence that housing characteristics tend to show distance gradient distributional patterns; and (3) that the distributional patterns are to some extent a function of the level of societal development.

By way of relating both the factorial and spatial characteristics of cities to a level of modernization or social scale it seems that in low-scale societies there is little factorial differentiation of status, family characteristics, and ethnicity, and there tends to be an inverse status gradient in spatial patterning. In highly developed societies the ecological structure of cities has been described as showing extensive factorial differentiation and a spatial patterning of social status characterized by both sector and positive distance gradient effects. Other characteristics such as housing also show a gradient distribution. According to the theoretical argument of this paper we suggest that cities at the moderate level of development are not uniform in their ecological structure. Rather we argue that the primate city will be similar ecologically to the city in a developed society while the smaller secondary centers will be more like those in societies at the lower end of the social continuum.

METHODS

In selecting San Juan, Ponce, and Mayaguez for investigation we limited our analysis to the three city segments of the metropolitan areas since for the most part the fringe areas are largely agricultural or mixed urban-agricultural, especially in Ponce and Mayaguez. The population size of the cities in 1960 was San Juan, 432,377; Ponce, 114,286; and Mayaguez, 50,147. All of the noninstitutional census tracts for which complete data could be obtained were used in the analysis. The numbers of tracts in the analysis are San Juan, 86; Ponce, 20; and Mayaguez, 11.

For each tract in the three cities the following social area analysis indexes were calculated:

Social Rank

1. Occupation =

$$1,000 - \frac{\text{number of craftsmen, operatives, and laborers}}{\text{number of employed persons} - \text{occupations of employed not reported}} \ (1,000)$$

2. Education =

number of persons 25 years of age and older who have completed no more than grade school

$$1,000 - \frac{}{\substack{\text{number of persons 25} \\ \text{years of age and older} \\ - \text{number of school} \\ \text{years not reported}}} \ (1,000)$$

Familism (Urbanism)

1. Infertility =

$$1,000 - \frac{\substack{\text{number of children} \\ \text{under five years}}}{\substack{\text{females 14 years of age} \\ \text{and older}}} \ (1,000)$$

2. Women in Labor Force =

$$\frac{\substack{\text{number of females 14} \\ \text{years of age and older} \\ \text{in labor force}}}{\substack{\text{number of females 14} \\ \text{years of age and older}}} \ (1,000)$$

3. Multiple Dwellings =

$$1,000 - \frac{\substack{\text{number of single family} \\ \text{dwelling units}}}{\substack{\text{total number of} \\ \text{dwelling units}}} \ (1,000)$$

Ethnicity (Segregation)

1. Foreign Born =

$$\frac{\substack{\text{number of foreign-born} \\ \text{persons}}}{\text{total number of persons}} \ (1,000)$$

To examine the factorial ecology of the cities a separate analysis was conducted for each. The matrix of correlations among the six variables for each city was factored and subjected to an oblique rotation [Schwirian 1971]. Factors retained for rotation were those that explained at least five percent of the matrix variance.

To examine the spatial patterning of the variables an analysis of covariance was performed with the factor scores as dependent variables in each of the three cities. The ANCOVA had distance and sector location as independent variables. Distance was measured in terms of the number of miles between the center of each tract and the central plaza or main intersection of the city. The main plaza for Ponce and Mayaguez were easily identifiable. For San Juan there is much more ambiguity as to the city's focal point. Today's greater San Juan is a complex formed by the conjoining of initially separate settlements. The basic subareas are Old San Juan, which is offshore of the mainland and connected to it by bridges; Santurce, which is the newer section of the city adjacent to the Atlantic beach front; and the Rio Piedras and Hato Rey sections, which are quite a bit inland. We selected as the ecological center a principal intersection in the Santurce area since Santurce has become a major development hub for the whole metropolis.

To designate the sector location of each tract in the three cities we passed perpendicular axes through the central plazas of each city. The initial orientation of the axes were north-south and east-west. Tracts between the axes were designated as separate sectors. Thus, for each city there are four sectors: northwest, northeast, southwest, and southeast.

FINDINGS

The results of the three factor analyses for the Puerto Rican cities appear in Table 1. For the three cities factorial differentiation seems related to city size. The factorial structure for San Juan is much like that of cities in the developed society since status, familism, and ethnicity separate in factor space. Factor I corresponds to the social rank dimension while factor II is dominated by the housing variable. Factor III appears to measure fertility, while factor IV is the ethnic dimension. For San Juan female labor force participation does correlate much more strongly (.823) with social rank than it does in large cities in developed societies. This is not surprising because of the traditional definition of the female role in Latin society. If the upper strata of society are the first to modernize then we would expect the definition of the female role to change first there. Thus, we would expect to find higher rates of female labor force

participation among the more educated segments of the developing society and lower rates among the lower classes. This ecological correlation of .823 of female labor force participation with status is consistent with the model of the diffusion of social change down through the status hierarchy.

TABLE 1.   Oblique Rotated Factors for Puerto Rico's Cities, 1960

Variables	Factors			
City	I	II	III	IV
San Juan				
Occupation	.878	.062	.015	.195
Education	.908	−.091	−.008	.142
Infertility	.254	.100	.830	.123
Women in L.F.	.823	−.144	.271	−.147
Dwellings	−.079	.990	.050	.022
Foreign Born	.349	.107	.144	.762
Ponce				
Occupation	.930	−.020	.048	.086
Education	.883	−.035	.099	.126
Infertility	.335	−.037	.805	.046
Women in L.F.	.968	.037	.079	−.060
Dwellings	−.045	.990	−.012	−.003
Foreign Born	.497	−.034	.121	.663
Mayaguez				
Occupation	.938	.150	−.169	
Education	.988	−.095	−.025	
Infertility	.883	−.054	−.410	
Women in L.F.	.968	−.042	.126	
Dwellings	.024	.998	−.028	
Foreign Born	.939	.042	.371	

The factorial structure of Ponce is generally differentiated. Factor I seems to be the social rank dimension while II is housing, III is infertility, and IV is ethnicity. While Ponce's factor structure is very similar to San Juan's, there is a striking difference. For Ponce, infertility, female labor force participation, and foreign born all correlate more highly with the status dimension than they do in San Juan. Thus, Ponce seems to be slightly less differentiated than is San Juan.

The factorial structure of Mayaguez is highly undifferentiated. Factor I has high correlations of all variables except housing which separates into a unique factor by itself (factor II). The third factor is fairly weak with only moderate correlations of infertility (−.410) and foreign born (.371) with it. Thus, Mayaguez, which is the most isolated of the three cities and the smallest, shows a generally high degree of relationship among the status, familism, and ethnic dimensions.

By way of summary of the three factor structures, it should be noted that the findings generally correspond to those hypothesized. The greatest factorial separation is for San Juan while the least is for Mayaguez. Ponce's degree of separation falls between the two but closer to the San Juan pattern. Also, in each city, regardless of overall factorial differentiation the housing variable was separate from all of the others.

To examine the spatial patterning of the factors, analyses of covariance are performed on the tracts factor scores for each city. The results of the ANCOVA for San Juan are in Table 2. For San Juan the distributions of the factors are fairly comparable to those for cities in large-scale societies. The social status factor differs significantly by sector but not, overall, by distance. The northeast and southwest sectors have the highest status levels. The lack of a distance effect is indicated by the low overall r between distance and status of .0031. There is, however, considerable variation between sectors in the magnitude and direction of the r between status score and distance. The ANCOVA test for interaction is statistically significant beyond the .05 level. For the two northern sectors—those along the beachfront—there is a negative relationship between status and distance while in the southwest, where many new housing developments have appeared at the city's fringe, there is a positive relation between distance and status.

The distribution of multiple dwelling units (factor II) in the city shows significant variation with both sector and distance. The sectors to the north that are located along the Atlantic beach front have greater concentrations of mul-

tiple dwelling units than do the inland sectors. Furthermore, with sector controlled there is a negative relationship between distance from the city's center and concentration of multiple dwelling units. The average within-class r between distance and multiple dwelling units is −.3469.

The distribution of infertility (factor III) shows significant differences neither by sector nor by distance. The distribution of foreign born (factor IV) in San Juan corresponds to a sectoral patterning with the greatest concentration in the northeastern beach front sector. The significant interaction indicates that while the overall r between distance and ethnicity is not significant with sector controlled, there is significant variation between sectors in distance's effect upon foreign born concentrations. In the northwest and southeast there is a negative relationship between distance and foreign-born concentration while there is a low positive relation in the northeast and no relationship in the southwest.

The ANCOVA for Ponce (Table 3) fail to show any significant differences by either sector or distance for the four factors. While within particular sectors the correlations between distance and factor scores are significant the overall r's are not. There is a significant interaction, however, and it involves the foreign-born variable. The r's between distance and foreign-born concentration are positive in three of Ponce's sectors and negative in the fourth. Thus, generally it seems that neither the sector nor distance gradient models provide adequate models for describing the distribution of status, familism, and ethnicity in Ponce.

The ANCOVA for Mayaguez's three factors are in Table 4. Factor I, which is the fairly general social organizational dimension, shows both a significant total correlation with distance ($r = -.7384$) and a significant average within class r of −.6642. Thus, in Mayaguez there is a decided tendency for the classic Latin distributional pattern to hold. The further a tract is from the city's center, the lower the occupational and educational levels of the population,

TABLE 2. Analysis of Covariance of San Juan's Factor Scores by Sector and Distance

Factor Score Means and Correlations with Distance

Factor

Sector	N	I		II		III		IV	
		$\bar{x}$	r	$\bar{x}$	r	$\bar{x}$	r	$\bar{x}$	r
Northwest	9	.1547	−.8271*	1.6056	.2601	.3466	−.4903	.7818	−.4763
Southwest	20	.4050	.6526*	.5145	−.0964	−.3933	.0751	−.2381	.0162
Southeast	50	.2983	.0826	.1633	−.4881*	.0062	−.1510	−.2246	−.1420
Northeast	7	.7751	−.3522	.5724	−.7211*	.6340	−.7400*	1.2790	.2483
Total			.0031		−.4424*		−.2377*		−.3159*
Average within class			.0795		−.3469*		−.1384		−.1443

Analysis of Covariance
F Ratios

Source of Variation	Factor			
	I	II	III	IV
Sector	4.7030*	12.6820*	1.2993	5.7677*
Distance	.5161	11.0800*	1.5834	1.7245
Interaction	3.9259*	2.3264	.7132	3.7440*

* Statistically significant at .05.

331

TABLE 3. Analysis of Covariance of Ponce's Factor Scores by Sector and Distance

Factor Score Means and Correlations with Distance

Sector	N	I		II		III		IV	
		$\bar{x}$	r	$\bar{x}$	r	$\bar{x}$	r	$\bar{x}$	r
Northwest	6	−.3712	−.8541*	−.2702	−.4238	.2514	−.7746*	−.4272	.7660*
Southwest	6	.5415	−.1707	−.0559	−.6361	.0727	−.4411	.4918	−.5274
Southeast	4	−.1894	−.5300	.1502	−.3052	−.0951	−.2222	−.4737	.7577
Northeast	4	−.0659	.8780*	.2889	−.0941	−.3909	−.2299	.3767	.8911*
Total		−.0960		−.3381		−.3733		.2166	
Average within class		−.2617		−.3788		−.4151		.6525	

Analysis of Covariance
F Ratios

Source of Variation	I	II	III	IV
Factor				
Sector	1.2184	.4201	.5058	1.1460
Distance	1.1023	2.5124	3.1233	.2603
Interaction	1.5086	.0644	.6328	3.8244*

* Statistically significant at .05.

TABLE 4. Analysis of Covariance of Mayaguez's Factor Scores by Sector and Distance

Factor Score Means and Correlations with Distance

Sector	N	Factor					
		I		II		III	
		$\bar{x}$	r	$\bar{x}$	r	$\bar{x}$	r
Northwest	3	−.3022	−.9885*	−.8725	−.7074	−.0790	.9995*
Southwest	3	−.3634	−.8662	.4363	.8525	−.1824	.4836
Southeast	2	−.1924	−1.0000*	−.7988	.9992	.0486	.9995*
Northeast	3	.7939	−.6766	.9688	.7992	.2291	−.7021
Total		−.7384*		−.4349		.2349	
Average within class		−.6642*		−.0080		.4414	

Analysis of Covariance
F Ratios

Source of Variation	I	II	III
Sector	.2091	3.3118	.4144
Distance	4.7374	.0004	1.4518
Interaction	.5649	3.3090	3.5590

* Statistically significant at 0.5.

the higher the fertility, the less the propensity for females to be in the labor force, and the less the concentration of the foreign born. Neither the second nor third factors show significant differences in Mayaguez by distance or sector.

DISCUSSION

The central thesis of this paper is that to a large extent urban ecological patterning is a function of both city size and level of economic development of the society in which the city is located. We have suggested that in low-scale societies size makes little difference in urban differentiation, as it does in large-scale societies. But in developing societies size makes considerable difference in ecological differentiation because social change which becomes reflected in ecological patterning proceeds initially in the primate city and then later diffuses to the secondary urban center.

Our empirical focus has been upon the cities of Puerto Rico and our data have generally supported our predictions for the developing society. The ecological patterning of San Juan—the primate city—is very similar to that of cities in highly developed societies. Factorially, social rank, familism, and ethnicity are highly differentiated from each other. Spatially the distribution of social class is more by sector than by distance gradient, while the distribution of housing is both by distance and by sector. Mayaguez, which is the smallest of Puerto Rico's metropolitan centers and the most isolated in the island's transportation network, shows an ecological patterning characteristic of the traditional city. Factorially, social status, familism, and ethnicity are highly interconnected. Spatially Mayaguez shows the classic inverse status gradient with those of upper status and their associated family and ethnic characteristics being concentrated in the inner portion of the city near the *plaza mayor*. Ponce, which is the second city of Puerto Rico, shows a degree of factor differentiation similar to San Juan with the exception of slightly higher correlations of fertility, female labor force participation, and

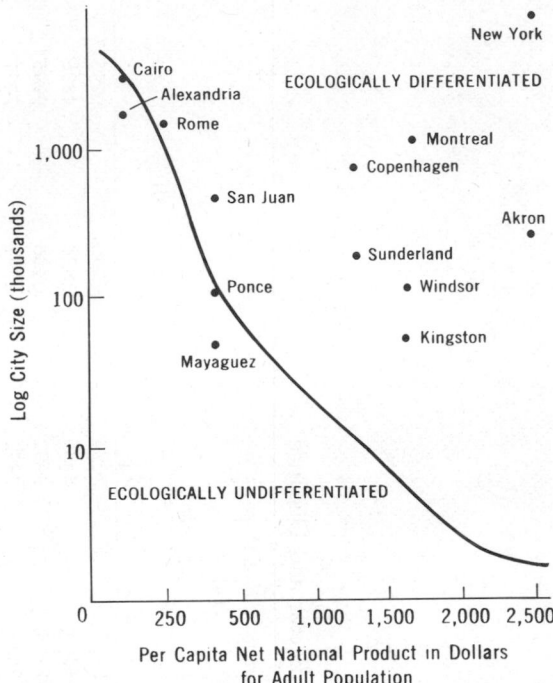

FIGURE 1.   World Cities by Population Size and Scale of Parent Society

foreign born with the status dimension. Spatially, neither the sector nor the distance gradient models describe the distribution of the status, familism, and ethnic factors. The reason for this could be that Ponce is in the midst of a spatial shift in population distribution from that characteristic of Mayaguez to that of San Juan. At its current position the traditional spatial pattern is disrupted while the more modern has yet to emerge. With the 1970 census we will be able to generate the data necessary to evaluate this possibility.

The central argument of this paper is expressed graphically in Figure 1. On the vertical axis are plotted the city size values and on the horizontal axis the values of societal scale, in this example per capita net national product [Heer 1966]. The cities plotted have been selected from those that have been studied through factor analytical techniques. We have selected cities whose societies are spread across the social scale continuum. The cities are plotted by their size at the time of study and by the scale of their parent society. The curve dividing the graph into two sections is meant to be illustrative of our argument and is meant to be neither theoretically derived nor rigorously empirically established. We have drawn the curve on the basis of inspection of the factor matrixes from our own research and those of other studies. The area of the graph above the curve contains those cities with marked ecological differentiation. The area below the curve contains those cities with generally undifferentiated ecological structures. Proximity of a city's point to the curve is a rough indicator of its degree of ecological differentiation.

If the model is generally correct, then empirical studies should show cities plotted below the curve to be ecologically undifferentiated while those above are differentiated. Most studies to date have been of large cities and their findings seem to fit the model, as do the data presented here for San Juan. Studies of smaller cities are fairly rare but are essential to establishing the reasonableness of our argument. Certainly the data for Mayaguez support the model, as do the Ponce findings. But crucial to the model is evidence on the ecological structure of smaller cities in developed societies. Without such data the differences between the two smaller Puerto Rican cities and San Juan could be attributed simply to city size, and it might be anticipated that regardless of social scale smaller cities are just less differentiated than larger ones.

To bring some data on cities in developed societies to bear on this discussion we have matched the three Puerto Rican cities with three Canadian cities of similar size. The population for the Canadian cities is for 1961. The matches are San Juan (432,377)—Ottawa (268,206); Ponce (114,296)—Windsor (114,376); and Mayaguez (50,147)—Kingston (53,526). The size matches for the middle and smallest cities are very good. The only real difference is between Ottawa and San Juan. We permitted this difference since in function both are societal capitals and administrative centers and perform similar control functions within their societies.

For the three Canadian cities we performed the same factor analysis with oblique rotation as we did for the Puerto Rican cities. The similarity between the Canadian and U.S. censuses is sufficient that the indexes for the six variables are just about identical. Thus the resulting factor matrixes are very comparable among the six cities. The indexes for the tracts of Ottawa (47), Windsor (25) and Kingston (13) are

1. Occupation =
$$1,000 - \frac{\text{primary} + \text{craftsmen} + \text{production process and related} + \text{laborers}}{\text{total labor force}} (1,000)$$

2. Education =
$$1,000 - \frac{\text{number of persons with less than a high school education}}{\text{number of persons out of school}} (1,000)$$

3. Infertility =
$$1,000 - \frac{\text{children 0–4 years}}{\text{women 15 years of age and older}} (1,000)$$

4. Women in Labor Force =
$$\frac{\text{women in labor force}}{\text{women 15 years of age and older}} (1,000)$$

5. Multiple Dwelling Units =
$$1,000 - \frac{\text{single detached dwellings}}{\text{multiple dwelling units}} (1,000)$$

6. Foreign Born =
$$\frac{\text{number of persons born outside of Canada}}{\text{total number of persons}} (1,000)$$

TABLE 5.   Oblique Rotated Factors for Canadian Cities, 1961

Variables City	I	II	III	IV
Ottawa				
Occupation	.024	−.087	.080	.977
Education	.225	.042	−.038	.913
Infertility	−.199	−.918	−.126	.067
Women in L.F.	−.840	−.311	−.058	−.027
Dwellings	−.842	.029	.042	−.327
Foreign Born	−.006	−.092	−.984	−.041
Windsor				
Occupation	.117	−.930	.070	.131
Education	−.300	−.910	.125	.047
Infertility	.173	−.593	−.690	.062
Women in L.F.	.207	−.187	−.036	.864
Dwellings	.908	.110	−.077	.204
Foreign Born	.009	.277	−.928	.012
Kingston				
Occupation	.183	−.674	−.556	−.120
Education	−.154	−.948	−.002	−.072
Infertility	−.069	−.041	−.982	.025
Women in L.F.	−.943	−.220	.008	.005
Dwellings	−.925	.142	−.054	−.215
Foreign Born	−.319	−.165	−.015	−.840

The results of the factor analysis for the Canadian cities are in Table 5. In the table it may be noted that all three of the Canadian cities are highly differentiated regardless of city size. All three cities show social status separating from ethnicity and familism. Likewise, ethnicity generally separates from social rank and familism (with the exception of the moderate correlation of fertility with the foreign born dimension in Windsor). Also in both the largest and the smallest Canadian cities female labor force participation and housing separate from infertility while in Windsor all three familism variables separate from each other. Thus, in accord with the theoretical model presented here the Canadian cities fail to show ecological differentiation by city size.

Another way of looking at the effect of city size and societal development upon ecological differentiation is in terms of the r between education level and infertility. In Table 6 the r's

TABLE 6.   Correlations Between Education and Infertility for Canadian and Puerto Rican Cities Classified by City Size and Level of Societal Development.

City Size	Level of Societal Development	
	Moderate	High
Large	San Juan, $r = .591$	Ottawa, $r = .060$
Moderate	Ponce, $r = .716$	Windsor, $r = .280$
Small	Mayaguez, $r = .899$	Kingston, $r = .247$

between education and infertility are classified for the six cities by city size and level of societal development. The lowest r between the two variables is for the large city in the developed society: $r = .060$ for Ottawa. The highest r is for the small city in the developing society: $r = .899$ for Mayaguez. At each level of city size the r for the city in the developing society is larger than the corresponding r for the city in the developed society. Also, as city size increases among the Puerto Rican cities there is more of a rise in the r than there is as size increases among the Canadian cities. Thus the patterns of differences among the r values support the general contention of this paper.

In closing, there are three matters that need to be commented upon. First, the underlying model is essentially dynamic and deals with the transition of urban structure from a traditional to a modern pattern. Our data are cross-sectional by necessity. While they are consistent with predictions from the model, they need to be supplemented with longitudinal analyses. With the 1970 census we will be able to obtain needed temporal data for change analysis in the three Puerto Rican cities. Second, on the basis of the model we predict that the ecological structure of both Ponce and Mayaguez in 1970 will become more factorially differentiated and spatially similar to San Juan. Since the pace of social change is accelerating in Puerto Rico we expect considerably more ecological differentiation of its cities in 1970 than there was in 1960. Third and finally, the model asserts that a city's ecological structure is a function of two dimensions: sheer population size and level of parent society's development. We have used a rough indicator of social scale for the data in Figure 1. No doubt several better ones should be examined before the model is pursued in a quantified form. Another line that needs to be followed in the development of the model is the population size dimension. Population size is an indication of a city's position in society's urban hierarchy. If this is so, then this underlying dimension needs to be identified, clarified, and operationalized so that it may be treated more accurately.

Hopefully when these two dimensions have been quantified more satisfactorily they may serve as two of several independent variables in a multivariate framework which attempts to explain precisely the variations in the ecological structure of cities.

BIBLIOGRAPHY

Anderson, Theodore R., and Janice A. Egeland, 1961. "Spatial Aspects of Social Area Analysis," *American Sociological Review*, 26: 392–399. [No. 26 in this volume.]

Berry, Brian, and Philip H. Rees, 1969. "The Factorial Ecology of Calcutta," *American Journal of Sociology*, 74: 445–491.

Clignet, Remi, and Joyce Sween, 1969. "Accra and Abidjan: A Comparative Examination of the Theory of Increase in Scale," *Urban Affairs Quarterly*, 4: 297–324.

Greer, Scott, 1962. *The Emerging City*. New York: The Free Press.

Heer, David M., 1966. "Economic Development and Fertility," *Demography*, 3: 423–444.

Hoyt, Homer, 1939. *The Structure and Growth of Residential Neighborhoods in American Cities*. Washington: Federal Housing Administration.

Matre, Marc D., and Kent P. Schwirian, 1970. "Highway Development and Community Population Growth in Puerto Rico, 1898–1960." 1970 Annual Meeting of the Population Association of America, Atlanta.

McElrath, Dennis C., 1962. "The Social Areas of Rome: A Comparative Analysis," *American Sociological Review*, 27: 376–391.

Mehta, Surinder K., 1969. "Patterns of Residence in Poona, India by Caste and Religion, 1822–1965," *Demography*, 6: 473–491. [No. 42 in this volume.]

Murdie, Robert A., 1969. *Factorial Ecology of Metropolitan Toronto, 1951–1961*. Chicago: Department of Geography, The University of Chicago Research Paper No. 116.

Park, Robert, E. W. Burgess, and R. D. McKenzie, 1925. *The City*. Chicago: University of Chicago Press.

Robson, B. T., 1969. *Urban Analysis: A Study of a City Structure with Special Reference to Sunderland*. Cambridge: Cambridge University Press.

Schnore, Leo F., 1965. "On the Spatial Structure of Cities in the Two Americas," in Philip Hauser and Leo F. Schnore (eds.), *The Study of Urbanization*. New York: John Wiley, pp. 347–398.

Schwirian, Kent P., 1971. "Some Analytical Problems in the Comparative Test of Ecological Theories." Paper presented at the Institute of Comparative Sociology Conference on Methodological Problems in Comparative Sociological Research, Bloomington, Indiana.

——, and Jesus Rico-Velasco, 1971. "The Residential Distribution of Status Groups in Puerto Rico's Metropolitan Areas," *Demography*, 8: 81–90. [No. 34 in this volume.]

——, and Marc D. Matre, 1969. "The Ecological Structure of Canadian Cities." Research Paper, Department of Sociology, The Ohio State University. [No. 27 in this volume.]

Shevky, Eshref, and Wendell Bell, 1955. *Social Area Analysis, Illustrative Application and Computational Procedures.* Stanford University Series in Sociology, No. 1. Stanford University Press.

Sweetser, Frank L., 1965. "Factorial Ecology, Helsinki, 1960," *Demography*, 2: 372–385. [No. 31 in this volume.]

29

A. H. LATIF

Factor Structure and Change Analysis of Alexandria, Egypt, 1947 and 1960

INTRODUCTION

A current trend in ecological research calls for more detailed analysis of various cities from different parts of the world analysis which would place them on a scale of societal differentiation, or urban development [1]. Such effort, in fact, is aimed at developing a more comprehensive theory of comparative urban ecology. Accordingly, the relationship between urban ecological structure and societal differentiation has to be investigated. Most studies, however, have focused on only one city in a given society without giving much attention to the existing variability in patterns of urban structure [2].

The selection of the city of Alexandria is promoted by the following considerations. First, the study of Cairo by Abu-Lughod [1969] has been cited in the literature as an example to

indicate that the degree of social differentiation in the United Arab Republic's society is less than that of the United States [3]. It is true that if a city does not reflect the ecological pattern of the industrial city then it is not likely that the lesser cities do [4]. This conclusion however, raises an empirical question: To what extent would the same findings derived from one primate city be generalized to the second largest city in the same society? The present

Research Paper, Department of Sociology, University of Manitoba, 1971.

This paper is based upon "The Ecological and Social Structure of Alexandria, Egypt: An Examination of Urban Sub-area Data, 1947 and 1960," unpublished doctoral dissertation, The Ohio State University, 1970. The author would like to acknowledge the kind encouragement and critical comments of Kent P. Schwirian of The Ohio State University.

analysis partially addresses itself to answer this question. Second, while both Cairo and Alexandria are cosmopolitan centers as well as nuclei of nation-wide coordination and service, Alexandria differs from Cairo in terms of age, functional types, size of hinterlands [5], and ethnic composition [6]. In addition, Alexandria as a city is associated with the port function, by which larger overseas hinterlands have been tied in with it for several decades. Such functions may stimulate a pattern of urban growth which may be quite different to that of Cairo. Third, data for the city census tracts are available for 1947 and 1960 and comparable variables similar to those employed by Abu-Lughod [1969] could be devised.

METHOD AND HYPOTHESES

The theoretical foundations underlying our hypotheses are in social area analysis. Two hypotheses were tested on the Alexandria data and they are based on past studies of ecological structure in other countries as well as the data on Cairo presented in Abu-Lughod's paper.

The first hypothesis deals with the expected factor structure of the city. Since the level of modernization in Egypt is not equal to that of the United States, we would not expect as great a factorial separation of social area variables for Alexandria as found for U. S. and Canadian cities [7]. If this hypothesis proves to be true, we will confirm Abu-Lughod's major findings in Cairo, that is, "no factorial separation between the indicators of social rank and the indicators of family cycle stage could be obtained" [8]. If this hypothesis is rejected, we will attempt to find out in what way Alexandria does differ from Cairo.

The second hypothesis deals with the expected ecological variations over the period under investigation. As a modernizing city, Alexandria is expected to experience some variation in its ecological structure which the cross-sectional examination may have failed to predict.

The data reported in this study describe the demographic and ecological structure of eighty-five census tracts in Alexandria for the years 1947 and 1960. The thirteen indexes suggested by Abu-Lughod in her study on Cairo were calculated using data from the 1947 [9] and 1960 [10] Egyptian census figures. Two reasons determined our use of the same variables for Alexandria: (1) these variables are available in the census tract bulletins for 1947 and 1960, and (2) we will attempt to compare our results with those of Cairo. The variables are sex ratio, fertility ratio, males never married, females never married, females divorced, persons per room, male literacy, female literacy, females in school or employed, handicapped rate, male unemployment, Muslims in tract, and demographic density.

Although the indices specified by the social area analysis model could not be formed easily from the Egyptian census, Abu-Lughod successfully made an attempt to find substitute variables devised to reflect the ecological structure of Egyptian cities. Economic status or social rank was represented by male literacy, female literacy, females in school or employed, and male employment status. Familism was measured by the following indicators: fertility ratio, sex ratio, males never married, females never married, females divorced, and persons per room. Percent Muslims in each census tract was selected to measure what has been termed as ethnicity or segregation.

The theoretical and empirical relevance of these indicators has been demonstrated by Abu-Lughod in her study on Cairo. Thus, it was felt that using these variables would be quite legitimate since we are attempting to test the same proposition on another large Egyptian city.

Two analyses were performed to describe the ecological structure of the city and to investigate its variation over time. For the purpose of the first analysis, a matrix consisting of the thirteen indicators was subjected to factor analysis for both 1947 and 1960 data. The second analysis involves the same thirteen indicators using a matrix of proportional change among the indicators between 1947 and 1960.

In each of the analyses, the factor model used was the principal component solution. In each case, the squared multiple correlation coefficient was used as the initial estimate of each communality. Only factors with associated eigenvalues greater than unity were retained for purpose of rotation. Rotation was performed using the varimax rotation.

FINDINGS

The basic findings in this study are reported in Tables 1–6. Table 1 contains the rotated factor matrix for Alexandria in 1947 and 1960. Three factors which have associated eigenvalues greater than unity are presented for both years according to the order in which they were extracted from the matrix of intercorrelations among the variables. As it appears from Table 1, the 1947 factors account for 67.8% of the explained variance, while the three factors in 1960 account for 69.6% of the total variance in the matrix.

Before making any effort to identify the factors, an attempt was made to determine the degree of factor congruence in the two census years using Harman's [11] method for computing the coefficients of congruence. Table 2 shows that the coefficients of congruence are .98, .62, and .82 for Factors I, II, and III respectively. The general pattern that emerges in Table 2 suggests that the factors, in general, are not congruent or similar.

TABLE 2.   Factor Congruence, 1947 and 1960

			1960	
	Factor	I	II	III
1947	I	.98	.35	.48
	II		.62	.59
	III			.82

FACTOR STRUCTURE, ALEXANDRIA: 1947 AND 1960

Table 1 contains the rotated factor matrix for the thirteen variables in 1947 and 1960. The first factor extracted for both years seems to have exactly the same factor loadings on each

TABLE 1.   Rotated Factor Matrix, Alexandria, 1947 and 1960 (Orthogonal Rotation)

Variables	Factor I 1947	Factor I 1960	Factor II 1947	Factor II 1960	Factor III 1947	Factor III 1960	h^2 1947	h^2 1960
1. Sex Ratio	.03	−.16	−.19	.16	.75	.89	.60	.85
2. Fertility Ratio	−.82	−.82	.30	−.24	−.07	.19	.76	.76
3. % Males Never Married	.31	.37	.35	.78	.71	.33	.74	.86
4. % Females Never Married	.68	.71	.17	.49	.47	−.40	.72	.91
5. % Females Divorced	.01	.26	.47	.45	.11	−.53	.24	.55
6. Persons per Room	−.91	−.87	.17	−.05	−.13	.12	.87	.79
7. % Males Literate	.91	.88	−.02	.05	.02	−.12	.82	.79
8. % Females Literate	.91	.92	−.08	.22	.01	−.16	.83	.93
9. % Females in Schools or Employed	.78	.82	.11	.07	.21	−.39	.66	.84
10. % Handicapped	−.76	−.58	−.32	−.01	−.21	.11	.72	.35
11. % Male Unemployed	−.26	−.42	.64	−.30	.05	.15	.49	.29
12. % Muslims in Tracts	−.81	−.82	.42	.23	.02	.17	.84	.76
13. Density (in square kilometers)	.05	−.17	.62	.55	−.28	−.03	.47	.33
Eigenvalue	5.91	6.39	1.75	1.40	1.13	1.25		
% Variance Explained	45.5	49.2	13.5	10.8	8.7	9.7		

of the variables, with high and appropriately signed factor coefficients on variables 2 (fertility ratio), 4 (% females never married), 6 (persons per room), 7 (% males literate), 8 (% females literate), 9 (females in school or employed), 10 (% handicapped), and 12 (% Muslims in tracts), and low coefficients on the remaining variables. Factor I seems, then, to reflect *a general social organization* vector for the city in both years. It should be pointed out, however, that Abu-Lughod [12] has identified the same factor as a "socioeconomic status" or "style of life" factor. Such identification may be justified by knowing the determinants of social class position in the Egyptian society. For Alexandria, as for Cairo, class position could be, as Abu-Lughod suggests, a major determinant of family variations [13]. Thus, higher socioeconomic status seems to be associated with low fertility, literacy (particularly for females), and with delayed age at marriage. This general conclusion has partially been confirmed in a recent study designed to investigate the relationship between educational level of the Egyptian female and the emergence of differential fertility in urban areas [14].

The spatial distribution of factor scores for both years revealed that census tracts with the highest factor score coefficients on Factor I are, in fact, located in what could be termed as the "better areas" in the city. Areas which have the highest factor scores are characterized by low fertility ratio, balanced sex ratio, delayed age at marriage for both sexes, and high literacy rate. There would appear to be a relatively well-defined factor which bears some resemblance to the classical social rank factor.

Table 1 also contains the defining variables for Factor II for 1947 reflecting relatively high factor loadings on variables 11 (% males unemployed) and 13 (demographic density), and insignificant loadings on variable 5 (% females divorced). If we had to identify Factor II for 1947 only, it would have been possible to consider it as a social disorganization factor. This identification reflects the facts of social life in Alexandria as it did for Cairo. Abu-Lughod, for example, has identified the high loading on density and handicapped rate as reflecting some aspects of social disorganization [15]. But for Alexandria in 1947, male unemployment proved to be a sensitive indicator for social disorganization since it carries the highest factor loadings among the defining variables.

The identification of Factor II for 1960 raises a major problem. The fundamental, or the defining variables which explain all the correlations observed for this year are not quite comparable to those identified by Factor II for 1947. For 1947, never-married males appears to be highly loaded only on Factor II. Demographic density proved to be a fundamental variable which accounts for the ecological differentiation in 1960, as it is in 1947. Also, never-married females and females divorced have factor loadings which might aid in identifying Factor II, yet their loadings seem to be insignificant. The reader might observe from Table 1 that variables 3 and 4 in 1947 lack significant factor loadings, as is the case in 1960. If we try to interpret the factor loadings for Factor II for 1960 as we have for 1947, we run into an ambiguous interpretation. The two factors, however, are loaded high on demographic density and relatively high on females divorced. One thing which contributed to such an ambiguous interpretation is the fact that the male unemployment variable does show considerable incomparability. Although male unemployment loads high on Factor II in 1947, the same factor loads considerably lower on the same factor in 1960. Such low loadings for male unemployment in 1960 could give a dubious result, due to suspicious reporting of male unemployment in the 1960 census.

If we look at each factor loading for Factor II for 1960, separately, our identification would be similar to that for 1947. That is, the high loadings on never-married males and females, the high proportion of divorced females, and high demographic density could be defining variables for social disorganization of the urban life in Alexandria. This identification, however, should remain tentative until we look at the spatial distribution of factor scores according to Factor II.

Almost all of the census tracts which rank low on Factor II show some consistency in their relatively low ranking on Factor I, with the exceptions of some inner city tracts in the old districts of the city. The tracts which rank low on Factor II are characterized with a low divorce rate among females, a low handicapped rate, and a high density rate, which are common characteristics of almost all of the social areas in the city. Although a high literacy rate has proved also to be associated with "urbanism" in Egypt [16], Factor II fails to predict it. The tracts which rank high on Factor II are located mostly in the areas which are characterized with a high degree of attraction to rural migrants in the southeast section of the city. Some of these tracts seem to have a high proportion of seasonal workers and construction workers who had migrated to the city from Upper Egypt, soon after the Second World War. Demographic data for Alexandria indicate that more than 40 percent of the population were from outside of the Governorate. Rural migration, in general, has been viewed as the most contributing factor in the rapid increase of the population of Egyptian cities. This process has a considerable effect upon what has been identified as the ruralization process of cities [17].

The variables defining Factor III appear to be similar to those variables defining Factor II. Table 1 shows that in 1947 there are high factor coefficients on variables 1 (sex ratio) and 3 (% males never married), and a moderate factor coefficient on variable 4 (% females never married). For 1960, Factor III loads highly on variables 1 (sex ratio), 5 (% divorced females), and a moderate loading on variable 4 (% never-married females). In general, Factor III appears not to correspond to what has been labeled the "familism" factor. It would appear as if this factor reflects the position of some males in the working classes of Egypt who are likely to delay their marriage due to some family responsibilities. This may be the case since the extended family pattern seems to be very dominant

among these groups. Almost identical factor loadings were found for Cairo in 1947 and 1960; however, Abu-Lughod identified this factor as "male dominance."

Some other general observations must be added. The cross-sectional analysis of the data has confirmed that there is no factorial disassociation between familism and social rank. Both family and social rank variables are reflected in the ecological pattern of Alexandria. This general finding has proved to be consistent with Abu-Lughod's major findings in Cairo, and in contrast with the normal separation of these two sets of indicators in factor analyses of American city data matrixes [18].

What we have identified as a socioeconomic factor is not, however, reflected in clearly separable indicators. It is, for example, highly associated with family characteristics, female status, literacy, and occupational positions for both males and females. In the case of Cairo and Alexandria, as the two largest metropolitan areas in Egypt, the first factor accounts for almost 50% of the explained variance.

In an attempt to investigate the spatial distribution of the extracted factors, a two-way analysis of variance was carried out on the factor scores for a random sample of 36 census tracts. The data for the spatial distribution is presented in Table 3.

Table 3 shows that in 1947, Factor I, or the "style of life" factor, does not show any spatial patterning either in terms of distance

TABLE 3. Percent of the Total Sum of Squares Explained by Zone and Sector for the Three Extracted Factors, Alexandria, 1947 and 1960

		I	II	III
1947	Zone	30.20	43.74*	43.80*
	Sector	1.90	1.93	18.34*
1960	Zone	50.89*	38.65	9.11
	Sector	10.82	6.84	8.09

* The percentage of the sum of the squares is statistically significant beyond the .05 level. The test of significance is the two-way analysis of variance.

TABLE 4. Ecological Factors in Cairo* and Alexandria, 1947 and 1960, Loadings on Three Factors (Orthogonal Rotation)[†]

| Variables[‡] | 1947 | | | | | |
	Cairo	Alexandria	Cairo	Alexandria	Cairo	Alexandria
1. Sex Ratio	−.00	.03	−.05	−.19	(+.96)	(+.75)
2. Fertility Ratio	(−.81)	(−.82)	+.20	+.30	−.20	−.07
3. % Males Never Married	(+.67)	+.31	.01	+.35	.12	(+.71)
4. % Females Never Married	(+.91)	(+.68)	−.07	.17	(+.62)	(+.47)
5. % Females Divorced	(+.42)	.01	+.31	(+.47)	.19	.11
6. Persons per Room	(−.80)	(−.91)	.10	.17	.15	−.13
7. % Males Literate	(+.90)	(+.91)	.12	−.02	.06	.01
8. % Females Literate	(+.95)	(+.91)	−.03	−.08	.17	.01
9. % Females in School or Employed	(+.72)	(−.78)	−.07	.11	.13	+.21
10. % Handicapped	−.08	(−.76)	(+.68)	−.32	−.04	−.21
11. % Males Unemployed	(−.68)	−.26	−.38	(+.64)	−.28	.05
12. % Muslims in Tracts	(−.65)	(−.81)	.16	(+.42)	.02	.01
13. Density (in square kilometers)	−.18	.05	(+.62)	(+.62)	−.16	−.28
	1960					
1. Sex Ratio	−.01	.16	−.03	.16	(+.97)	(.89)
2. Fertility Ratio	(−.89)	(−.82)	−.00	−.24	−.01	−.19
3. % Males Never Married	(+.76)	−.37	−.03	(+.78)	.04	−.33
4. % Females Never Married	(+.95)	(.71)	.11	(+.49)	(+.49)	−.40
5. % Females Divorced	(+.52)	.26	(+.41)	(+.45)	.03	(−.53)
6. Persons per Room	(−.81)	(−.87)	+.32	−.05	.01	−.12
7. % Males Literate	(+.81)	(.88)	−.20	.05	−.07	.12
8. % Females Literate	(+.92)	(.93)	−.19	+.22	.10	.16
9. % Females in School or Employed	(+.85)	(.82)	−.14	.07	.06	−.39
10. % Handicapped	(−.40)	(−.58)	+.32	−.01	.13	.11
11. % Males Unemployed	−.31	(−.42)	.18	−.30	−.03	.15
12. % Muslims in Tracts	(−.56)	(−.82)	(+.55)	+.23	−.06	.17
13. Density (in square kilometers)	−.03	−.17	(+.72)	(+.55)	−.10	−.03

* J. Abu-Lughod, "Testing the Theory of Social Area Analysis" [1], Table 2, p. 207.

† This comparison is based upon our findings in Alexandria and Abu-Lughod's in Cairo. We have placed Factor III for Cairo with Factor II for Alexandria since Factor II for Alexandria reflects the "social disorganization" vector.

‡ The ordering of variables presented in Abu-Lughod's study are replaced here for presentation to fit the ordering of our variables for Alexandria.

gradient or sectorially. This might indicate that the highest socioeconomic groups used to live very close to the center of the city in 1947. The same factor, however, does show significant variations in 1960 which may reflect the suburbanization process and the emergence of new residential areas especially in the northeast section of the city. In general, the spatial distribution of the three factors does show that the underlying dimension of the social areas of Alexandria are most likely to be explained by distance gradient rather than by sector. This spatial patterning, in fact, is a function of the peculiar topographic pattern of the city.

Our findings, therefore, generally support the first hypothesis in this paper—that is, we have not found as great a factorial separation of the social area variables for Alexandria, using data for 1947 and 1960. In addition, the extracted factors have confirmed that the ecological structure of the city did not change drastically over the period under investigation, and this structure does not yet resemble the spatial pattern of the industrial city.

DIFFERENCES AND SIMILARITIES IN THE ECOLOGICAL STRUCTURE OF CAIRO AND ALEXANDRIA

Table 4 shows a comparison between the factor loadings on the same set of indicators for both Cairo and Alexandria in 1947 and 1960. It can be generally observed that the factor coefficients reveal a consistent pattern for the two communities. The only question which might be raised at this point deals primarily with the proper identification of the extracted factors. In order to determine the degree of similarity among the factor of the two cities, we have calculated the coefficient of congruence as suggested by Harman.

The coefficients of congruence presented in Table 5 indicate close congruence on Factor I in 1947 for both Cairo and Alexandria, and extremely close similarity on the same factor in 1960. The same can also be pointed out with

TABLE 5. Coefficients of Congruence Between the Extracted Factors for Cairo and Alexandria, 1947 and 1960

	Factors	I	II	III
1947	I	.91	.48	.34
	II		.84	.59
	III			.90
1960	I	.96	.64	.28
	II		.63	.45
	III			.79

regard to Factor III in 1960. Inconsistencies, however, could be observed with regard to Factor II in 1960. By looking at the factor coefficients on Factor II in 1960, it could be observed that the loadings on the defining variables show some inconsistencies. It would seem reasonable to argue that the determinants of ecological differentia of the two communities do, in fact, show some variations.

Differences between the ecological structure of the two cities can be outlined by looking at Table 4. Loadings on Factor I in 1947 indicate that the coefficients on variable 12 (% Muslims in tracts) are high. To compare this with Cairo, we find the same variable has relatively low factor loadings. This might explain the unique case of Alexandria in regard to its ethnic composition. Alexandria has had a high percentage of foreigners, who have enjoyed a higher standard of living than the Egyptians for many years.

The second marked contrast in the ecology of social class between Cairo and Alexandria appears in the loadings shown by Variable 5 (% Females Divorced) on Factor I. While this variable has shown a positive loading with a socioeconomic rank in Cairo and a very insignificant loading with socioeconomic rank in Alexandria, such negligible loadings of this variable on the socioeconomic status shows a total lack of association, and indicates that divorced females are dispersed among residential areas of both high and low status.

Factor II in 1947 shows some contrasts between the two cities. While Factor II is highly defined by variable 10 (% handicapped) and 13 (demographic density) for Cairo, the same factor shows relatively high loadings on Variable II (% males unemployed), 5 (% females divorced) and 12 (% Muslims in tracts). Ethnicity, as it pertains to the Muslim population in Alexandria, enters into the ecological structure of Cairo quite differently. It seems obvious that the Muslim population in Cairo is dispersed among residential areas which rank either low or high on Factor II. The negligible loadings of male and female literacy for both Cairo and

Alexandria would indicate that the highly disorganized slums tend to have a unique spatial character. These are spatially located in an area of transition as well as in the outskirts, which function as accommodation for rural migrants.

Variables defining Factor III indicate that the factor loadings for both cities in 1947 are quite similar (the coefficient of congruence is .90). However, variable 3 (males never married) shows high positive loadings on this factor for Alexandria, but not for Cairo. Thus, we begin to question Abu-Lughod's identification of this factor as "male dominance." The factor loadings on Factor III for Cairo do not support such identification. The special character of this factor in Alexandria emerges when we observe the high positive loadings on variable 3 (males never married). This, in fact, is consistent with variable 4 (females never married) in spite of its moderate loadings.

Another contrast between the two communities is the fact that Cairo enjoys a higher proportion of never-married males and females than Alexandria. This can be attributed to the fact that an emerging group of young educated persons from rural Egypt prefer to move to Cairo for better educational facilities and job opportunities.

Loadings on Factor II for 1960 show quite a few contrasts between the two communities. Disorganized social areas are identified by three defining variables for Cairo: demographic density, Muslim population, and females divorced. For Alexandria, loadings on the same factor are defined by a surplus of never-married males and females, demographic density, and relatively low loadings on female divorced. Thus, the identification of Factor II for Alexandria in 1960 as a "social disorganization" factor has to be revised. The factor loadings on Factor II for Alexandria indicate the high loadings of single males and demographic density, which describe the physical characteristics of the inner city slums. We say this because "social disorganization" is a very broad generalization and must be supported by more social and economic variables.

Loadings on Factor III in 1960 also show some ecological contrasts between the two cities. This is supported by Table 5, where the coefficient of congruence for Factor III for the two communities is only .79. This factor shows little similarity between the two cities in contrast to Factor I, which yields a coefficient of congruence of .96. This factor has been tentatively designated as a "male dominance" factor. While such identification might be true for Cairo, it does not seem to be the case for Alexandria. The loadings on this factor indicate that Cairo has a surplus of males over females, but for Alexandria, it is clear that the high factor loadings on females divorced and the negatively significant loadings of the sex ratio indicate that this factor is a "female dominance" factor. This might also reveal a change in the position of females in Alexandria from total dependence on male support to a relative economic dependency.

In summary, the cross-comparisons between the factor loadings on the three factors over the decade under investigation indicate the differences and similarities in the ecological structure of the two cities. We do not claim to have covered all of the possible differences and similarities by the cross-comparisons, but the factorial typologies derived from the factor structure have enabled us, to some extent, to classify the residential areas in terms of their ecological factors. In addition, we do not claim that the defining variables underlying the factors are the best to explain the temporal and spatial patterning of the ecological structure of Alexandria, due in part to a lack of census information.

CHANGE ANALYSIS OF ALEXANDRIA 1947 TO 1960

The foregoing discussions have dealt with a cross-sectional analysis based upon factor analysis of the thirteen indicators for 1947 and 1960, respectively. This technique has provided us with a static description of the underlying ecological structure at two points of time. Our findings have indicated that the city did not ex-

TABLE 6.   Loadings on Thirteen Variables Reflecting the Underlying Change Dimensions for Alexandria Between 1947 and 1960 (Orthogonal Rotation)

Variables	Factor I	Factor II	Factor III	h^2
1. Sex Ratio	.09	−.02	−.09	.71
2. Fertility Ratio	.28	.17	.67	.60
3. % Males Never Married	.95	−.03	.10	.92
4. % Females Never Married	.96	−.05	.07	.94
5. % Females Divorced	−.03	.03	−.03	.98
6. Persons per Room	−.53	−.13	.50	.55
7. % Males Literate	.01	.68	−.42	.72
8. % Females Literate	−.10	.47	.10	.57
9. % Females in Schools or Employed	−.06	.80	.09	.69
10. % Handicapped	−.04	−.75	−.15	.65
11. % Males Unemployed	.01	.27	.39	.50
12. % Muslims in Tracts	−.05	−.03	.86	.74
13. Density (in square kilometers)	−.02	.19	.09	.80
Eigenvalue	2.2	1.9	1.8	
% Variance Explained	17.3	14.8	14.1	

perience any drastic change over the intervening period of time. The comparison between Cairo and Alexandria, however, has indicated that Alexandria might have experienced some minor change between 1947 and 1960. The following discussions will be confined to analysis of the underlying dimensions of change between 1947 and 1960.

The analysis has been made within the limitation of the data used for factor analysis. The standardized data for both years were combined into one matrix with 13 variables. Each census tract is represented by two values on each variable: one for 1947 and the other for 1960. We have calculated the ratio of change by employing the formula suggested by Brown and Horton [19]. The ratio of change is used to remove the effects of census tract size.

A principal component analysis coupled with varimax rotation was then performed on a matrix of change ratios. As usual, only factors with associated eigenvalues greater than unity were retained for purpose of rotation.

Table 6 contains the three extracted factors and the amount of variance explained by each factor. The first factor extracted from the matrix of intercorrelations accounts for 17.3% of the variance explained. The loadings on Factor I indicate that the defining variables are within the circle of family characteristics. With high factor coefficients on variables 3 (males never married), 4 (females never-married), and variable 6 (persons per room), it would seem reasonable to suggest that this factor relates to "familistic coptic" factor. Such identification is facilitated by the insignificant factor loading on variable 12 (% Muslims in tracts). It has been generally acknowledged among Egyptians that the Copts represent a large proportion of the adult population who tend to delay their marriages. We cannot claim, however, that family status in Alexandria is a major factor in residential choice, as is the case in the ecological pattern of American cities. But we can still argue that in Alexandria it would appear as if there is a tendency for the family status factor to become disassociated from other underlying ecological dimensions over time. This argument is consistent with current empirical generalizations in regard to the "necessary conditions" under which the familism vector tends to become either independent of, or coalesced with, a socioeconomic vector.

The second factor extracted from the matrix of intercorrelations accounts for only 14.8% of the explained variance. With high coefficients on variables 9 (% females in schools or employed), 10 (% handicapped), 7 (% males literate), and 8 (% females literate), noting the sign in each case, it would seem that this factor corresponds to what might be termed here as an emerging "social rank" vector. Three of the four defining variables on this factor (% females in schools or employed; % males literate; and % females literate) are considered to be legitimate bases for the Egyptian social class structure.

Factor III is identified as a "Muslim concentration" vector, which seems to be the Egyptian counterpart of ethnic dimension reported in the studies of social area tradition. It is the third factor in terms of its relative importance in the factor matrix. With high coefficients on variables 12 (% Muslims in tracts), 2 (fertility ratio), 6 (person per room), and 7 (% males literate), it would appear as if such identification is legitimate. The loadings, however, do not completely support clear disassociation between "ethnicity" and other ecological dimensions.

Since the amount of total variance explained by the three change-dimension factors account only for 46.2 percent, and since the amount of the variance yielded by each factor appears to be similar, it would seem reasonable to conclude that these findings should be viewed as tentative. We suggest that further investigation should deal with data which cover a longer period. While the results of the two analyses for the years 1947 and 1960 do not generally support that there is a clear disassociation between the socioeconomic status factor and the familism factor, the change analysis reveals that the ecological structure of the city might have experienced some change which the cross-sectional analysis of the data has failed to predict.

To assure against the possibility that these findings could be an artifact of the method employed here, we suggest that the intercorrelations among the factors should be examined using an oblique rotation. Since we have employed orthogonal rotation criteria, the data are not now available to use this procedure.

SUMMARY AND CONCLUSION

In this research, two general hypotheses concerning the social differentiation of urban areas were first generated from the current literature in social area studies and then tested using data on Alexandria for the years 1947 and 1960. To test these hypotheses, we have employed a strategy to deal with cross-sectional as well as longitudinal analysis of the data.

Cross-sectional analysis of the data has confirmed that there is no factorial separation between the social rank and familism vectors, as is the case with the ecological factors of cities in high-scale societies. Both familism and social rank variables appear to be coalesced with each other. This finding is consistent with Abu-Lughod's major findings in Cairo, and in contrast with the normal separation of these two sets of indicators in factor analysis of American and Canadian cities.

Comparisons between the factor loadings on the same list of variables for both Cairo and Alexandria in both years supports the fact that the computational model used has produced, to some extent, consistent loading patterns over the period under investigation. However, many points of ecological differences were observed for the two cities. Both the factor loadings on the extracted factors for both cities and the calculated coefficients of congruence support such a conclusion. The cross-comparison between the factor loadings of the two communities support our claim that there is a difference in the factorial structure of the two cities. This has theoretical significance; it implies the variability in the ecological dimensions, especially in those societies which are characterized by a moderate degree of societal development. The analysis of the ecological structures of the two cities, however, show little factorial differentiation.

The cross-sectional analysis of the data has provided us with a static description of the underlying ecological dimensions of the city. To investigate the underlying dimensions of change between 1947 and 1960, a change analysis model was employed. The extracted change dimensions clearly indicate some increasing variability in the ecological structure of the city which the cross-sectional examination failed to predict. Two kinds of change were outlined: variability in family type, and variability in the social status factor. Such a conclusion should not be taken for granted, however, until an extensive analysis is made of the "necessary conditions" needed for the factorial separation among the basic ecological dimensions of the city. It should also be noted that percentage variance explained by the extracted change dimensions does not clearly show significant variations.

To conclude, the descriptions of ecological structures of cities in developing nations should pay some attention to the existing ecological differentiation among cities of different size. It is true that in a society which is undergoing economic development, social change proceeds at a much faster pace in the region of the primate city [20], which is the first to take on a changing ecological patterning. The case of Alexandria, however, has questioned such generalization by pointing out that there might be some differences between the ecological structure of the two largest cities in a developing country such as Egypt. Accordingly, city size as a factor in urban ecological differentiation in the developing society must be clarified.

NOTES

1. See, for example, Janet Abu-Lughod, "Testing the Theory of Social Area Analysis: The Ecology of Cairo," *American Sociological Review*, 34, No. 2 (April, 1969): 198–212; Brian J. L. Berry and P. H. Rees, "The Factorial Ecology of Calcutta," *American Journal of Sociology*, 74, No. 5 (March, 1969): 445–491; Kent P. Schwirian, "Analytical Convergence in Ecological Research," in David Sweet (ed.), *Models of Urban Structure*, New York: D. C. Heath, 1971.

2. Schwirian, "Analytical Convergence," p. 30.

3. Berry and Rees, "Factorial Ecology of Calcutta," p. 467; Schwirian, "Analytical Convergence," p. 26.

4. Schwirian, "Analytical Convergence," p. 27.

5. Janet Abu-Lughod, "Urbanization in Egypt: Present State and Future Prospects," *Economic Development and Cultural Change*, XIII (1965): 136.

6. Mona Sedky, "Groups in Alexandria," *Social Research*, 22 (1955): 441–450.

7. Kent P. Schwirian and Marc Matre, "The Ecological Structure of Canadian Cities," research paper, Department of Sociology, The Ohio State University, 1970. [No. 27 in this volume.]

8. Abu-Lughod, "Testing the Theory of Social Area Analysis," p. 208.

9. Egypt, Ministry of Finance, *Census of Egypt, 1947*, Volume on Alexandria (Cairo: Government Printing Office, 1952.)

10. United Arab Republic, al-Jihaz al-Markazi Lil-Ta'Bi'ah al-'Ammah' Wa-al-Ihsa', Population Census of 1960, Volume on the Governorate of Alexandria (Cairo: Government Printing Office, 1962, in Arabic).

11. Harry H. Harman, *Modern Factor Analysis* (Chicago: The University of Chicago Press, 1967), pp. 270–271.

12. Abu-Lughod, "Testing the Theory of Social Area Analysis," Table 2, p. 207.

13. Ibid, p. 205.

14. Abu-Lughod, "The Emergence of Differential Fertility in Egypt," *The Milbank Memorial Fund Quarterly*, XLIII, No. 2 (April, 1965): 236.

15. Janet Abu-Lughod, "Testing the Theory of Social Area Analysis," Table 2, p. 207.

16. Janet Abu-Lughod, "Migrant Adjustment to City Life: The Egyptian Case," *American Journal of Sociology*, LXVII (July, 1961): 25.

17. Ibid., pp. 22–32.

18. Berry and Rees, "Factorial Ecology of Calcutta," p. 467.

19. L. A. Brown and F. E. Horton, "Social Area Change: An Empirical Analysis," Research Paper, Department of Geography, The Ohio State University, 1970.

20. Kent P. Schwirian, "Some Analytical Problems in the Comparative Test of Ecological Theories," Paper presented at the Institute of Comparative Sociology, Conference on Methodological Problems in Comparative Sociological Research at Bloomington, Indiana, 1971.

30

BRIAN J. L. BERRY
HOWARD SPODEK

Comparative Ecologies of Large Indian Cities

Factorial interpretations of the ecology of Indian cities cannot be cast into the narrow conceptual mould of studies of American cities, for they must contend with a differing form of social differentiation, complex intermixture of occupation and ethnic background, substantially less family-type specialization, differing prevailing modes of urban technology, differing historical attitudes to the city, and contrasting perceptions of the amenities of sites within it. An initial attempt to come to terms with the complexities of these differences has been provided by Berry and Rees [3]. This paper seeks

Reprinted by permission from *Economic Geography*, Vol. 47, No. 2 (Supplement, June 1971), pp. 266–285.

to extend the exploration by examining a group of cities (Ahmedabad, Bombay, Kanpur, Madras, Poona, Sholapur) at a point in time (1961), one of these cities (Poona) over a considerable time-span (1822–1954), and one (Bombay) at a range of observational scales. A primary concern is to penetrate more deeply into traditional styles of Indian culture as they affect residence patterns.

The caveats are predictable. Data are very uneven. The materials on Poona and Sholapur were produced in social surveys under the direction of D. R. Gadgil at the Gokhale Institute of Politics and Economics in Poona and are quite good [9, 10]. Data for the other cities are derived from the Census of India, 1961, which has a somewhat higher degree of error. The Census operation was largely in the hands of state government bureaus responsible to the Central Government Census Office, and these state governments collected different varieties of data. Thus the data for Ahmedabad are richer than those for Madras, which are in turn somewhat richer than the materials available for Bombay and Kanpur. In addition, the census tracts within and among cities differ widely in size, from a few hundred residents to tens of thousands, and very obviously, also in internal homogeneity.[1]

Data over time for all cities except Poona are unavailable since the Indian census only began reporting data for cities by wards in 1961. Also, the number of cities covered is severely limited. The 1961 census promised sections from each state census office treating the large cities of the state. For reasons of noncompliance with this directive, or more simply of delay, most of these city volumes have yet to appear. Some data on a ward basis are available in the census volumes on the districts of India,

but even where such data were available, as for Poona in 1961, there were no accompanying maps to indicate which ward was which. Finally, much data on occupation is gathered on a vertical industrial basis, i.e., the classification of workers by industry included everyone from owners of large factories to machine operators, to factory scavengers, to apprentices in three-man workshops. All these obstacles contribute to making this study still a preliminary one. But it was felt that it would be worthwhile to proceed, despite the difficulties, since these were all the systematic data on Indian cities likely to be available for some years to come.

TRADITIONAL INDIAN RESIDENCE PATTERNS

The empirical part of this study uses factorial methods, results of which have no ready interpretations without an adequate contextual base. Fortunately, there are at least two sources that give a picture of normative patterns of residence in India. The first is ancient religious and policy-making texts, the second is residence patterns in village India.

The Ancient Texts

The texts, dating from perhaps 300 A.D. back to 500 B.C. and covering both the northern Aryan and southern Dravidian areas of India, represent both texts on political management like the *Arthasastra* and texts on architecture and design such as the *Agni Purana*, the *Manasara*, and the *Sukranitisara*. These texts indicate the antiquity of urbanization of India and the types of towns which characterized the subcontinent in ancient times. They included princely cities, temple centers, market places and trading posts, university towns, industrial centers, and nucleated towns formed by the union of two or more villages. But the essential features of all these types of cities included a fortress, religious institutions, and socioeconomic separation of the people into distinct neighborhoods or "natural areas" [11, pp. 9–10]. In the Vedic literature the word *pura*, the modern Sanskrit

---

[1] In the case of Ahmedabad, we undertook tests, using analysis of variance, to assay the relative variability between and within the census tracts. Lacking variance estimates for individuals, internal variability was measured by block-to-block variations within wards, with an average of 20 blocks per ward. As a case in point, female literacy produced an F of 26.7 (28 and 454 d.f.); the greatest source of variability remained that *between* the observational units.

synonym of town, was used in the sense of a fort or stronghold [6, pp. 70–71]. The major towns were associated with capitals of local rulers. "Because India was not brought under the suzerainty of one single emperor, but on the contrary, was a medley of small principalities fighting with one another for overlordship, the military camps were turned into royal capitals. Indeed, each prince had to build a new city in order to demonstrate his grandeur and not to be ensnared in the many byways in the former capital which were better known to the former rulers than to himself" [6, pp. 38–39]. In the Dravidian south, the Tamil word *nakar* carried at least five different meanings: house, temple, palace, castle, city [2, pp. 18–19].

The physical structure of the ancient town reflected its fortress qualities in walls and moats, its royal and administrative buildings either in the center of the town or in the northern quadrant, and temples of the city's tutelary deities, again either in the city center or near the corners of the walls. Most striking was the division of people into distinctly separate quadrants and neighborhoods on the basis of caste or occupational status. For example, the *Artha-sastra* describes the kind of frontier town which the ruler should build; the varna-castes are clearly divided into separate parts of town. Brahmins, the priests and teachers, are grouped in the northern section, around the royal palace; Kshatriyas, the military, are in the east along with some traders; the trading and landholding castes of Vaishyas are in the south; and the Sudras or working classes are in the west. Outcastes are totally outside the city walls, near the cremation grounds.

The *Agni Purana* presents a very similar picture of the division of peoples, although there are significant differences. The temples are not at the center of the town, but at the corners of the walls serving to protect the town spiritually. The shops do not flank the central shrines, but are located near, but not at, the four corners of the town. The main four caste-varna groupings are still divided in the four directions as above, though the agricultural

traders are now to be grouped with Brahmins; many professionals are grouped with the Sudras; and dancers, musicians, and prostitutes have been joined with the trading castes in the south. This last combination is not so unusual since each of these occupations involves contact with diverse peoples and occupations and the provision of services which the dominant culture often regards with mixed emotions.

Ayyar's representation of the form of Madura in South India indicates that this town had similar features in ancient times, but the bulk of the population is left unrepresented. Thus the palace and court retinue are located in the northeast; the religious and educational establishment has its own quarter, though it is now to the east; and the marginal people such as musicians, artists, and dancers are grouped with the prostitutes at the other side of the city to the west. The bazaar area and its craftsmen and merchants are to the south just inside the main gate to the fortified city. No mention is made of the other inhabitants of the city, nor of the outcaste areas, though presumably the latter, as in other ancient cities, are outside the gates.

Was such a rigid form of residential patterns ever employed? Probably not. The projected plans actually indicate not what actual city planning as a socioeconomic phenomenon was like in contemporary times, but more a kind of abstraction following the mechanical setup of different occupational groups, castes, and classes in the city with gods, kings, and priests as the center of the whole scheme. And the plans for different cities, or by different authors, indicate differential groupings, thereby revealing the extent to which values and perceptions can and did vary. The most pronounced characteristic, however, the separation of the court, the Brahmins, and the outcastes into distinct areas, separate from each other and from other elements of the population, seems common throughout. The *Sukranitisara*, one of the architectural treatises, thus specifically groups only the royal palace, court, council buildings, museum, officials, and clerks at the center of the city and the untouchables along-side the cremation grounds on the outskirts.

Caste: Classical and Modern

Clearly, a fundamental determinant of the locational prescriptions in the texts is caste. The classical textual division of people was that of *varna-ashrama-dharma*, the India-wide separation of people into four groupings: Brahmin or teacher-priest, Kshatriya or warrior-prince, Vaishya or wealthy landholder and trader, Sudras or workers, plus outcastes. It is quite unclear that such a four-fold division of society ever existed in social fact; indeed, in modern functional terms, caste is very different from the system presented in the classical texts. The modern view of the Indian caste system which has been developed largely by anthropological work in India over the past twenty years, sees caste groups—*jatis*—as limited in territory and membership, so that far from there being only four all-India castes, there are instead thousands of castes, of which anywhere from two or three to forty or fifty may be represented in any one area. Membership in a caste comes with birth, but does not necessarily determine occupation. It will most likely determine the limit of eligible people for marriage, and it will significantly affect the scope of social and commensal activities. Caste is hierarchical, but not rigidly so. Thus in any one area it is likely that the top and bottom castes will be distinguishable with relatively little difficulty, but the ranking of intermediate castes may be debatable.

Caste and class are antithetical in that the latter system is said to have a rather high degree of potential socioeconomic mobility while the former has relatively little. Caste also is more a village phenomenon than an urban one since in village societies the essential base of wealth and power is in only one sphere, possession of land, while in cities there are many areas in which a man can achieve wealth and power. Polymorphous urban society shakes loose the rigidities of the caste system. One of the most significant variables which the urban ecologist studies everywhere in the world, the social basis

for residential patterns, therefore takes on special interest in India for it relates closely to the power of the caste system in determining residential patterns.

Residence Patterns in Village India

Since India is an urbanizing society in which the early socialization of many urban dwellers still takes place in villages, the role of caste in residence patterns in these village settings is of some importance. Mayer's perceptive study of one village [14, p. 56] is a useful starting place:

> The village does not have streets whose entry is restricted, even in the wards occupied by the Harijans [outcasts]. In general there is a tendency for castes of roughly equal status to inhabit the same locality of the village. All over there is a certain amount of intermingling though it is [not] clear which caste provides the nucleus in any ward. But in the Harijan wards there is clear separation both from other castes and between the Harijan castes themselves. The sweepers are to one side of the village and the tanners to the other. The weavers form a more dispersed pattern, ranging behind the houses of the Rajputs who were, and still to some extent are, their masters.

From further south, in the State of Mysore, Epstein [7] presents maps of two villages. In both villages, the groups who are considered outsiders are clearly located on the fringe in their own groupings: untouchables, Muslims, washermen, and even public works department personnel not native to the village. The other castes and lineages are somewhat more mingled, but the leading lineages including that of the headman tend to have a central location on the most solid and respectable street. Still, among the Hindu castes there is somewhat more mingling in the residence patterns, so that while richer peasants dominate the central area, the artisan groups for the most part live mingled among the other peasant lineages.

Another village of Mysore State, Aminbhavi, is described by Spate and Learmonth [19, p. 201]: "caste and community largely govern the layout. . . . Each caste tends to occupy a solid block of contiguous houses in a lane named from the caste. Low castes and outcastes live on the fringes of the village and even beyond the old moat." The authors add a note about the high correlation between caste status and occupational status. "Occupations likewise are still mainly on a caste basis: the Lingayats provide the bulk of the tenant-farmers, Talwars and Harijans landless agricultural labor; carpenters, smiths, cobblers, washermen, barbers are all separate castes."

From these examples, a few general patterns are observable. The center of the village is usually preempted by the wealthiest and most prestigious caste groupings, as denoted by the lineage of the headman. Outcastes, untouchables, non-Hindus, and nonnatives of the village are located on the periphery of the village, or even outside of it. Other castes often form separate neighborhoods of greater or lesser exclusivity and physical separation from one another, but castes which have only one or two representative families usually locate among more numerous castes of approximately equal ritual, social, and economic status. Both caste membership and class status are thus ingredients in residence patterns, particularly at the extreme ends of the hierarchy.

Residence Patterns in a Small Town

An intermediate case between the large cities analyzed below and the village studies is provided by Fox's monograph on Tezibazar, a town of some 7,000 inhabitants in eastern U. P. He found that "no necessary caste or communal patterning to residential areas exists except for untouchables. Muslim and Hindu, Brahmin and Baniya castes all live intermixed or interspersed" [8, p. 35]. In the past, however, neighborhoods may have been built along a caste basis. What has caused the change? Fox argues that it is the development of business and a political change which has led to the passing of control from the hands of the hereditary Zamindar or landed proprietor to freer and more open competition for economic power in the commercial sphere. Now, especially in the

newer residential quarters, economic class characteristics predominate. "Even in those relatively noncommercial and peripheral sections of the town where some caste-neighborhood congruence exists, it is a residue of the past rather than a presently significant social patterning of town society. This situation is true for all castes and communities other than untouchables" [8, p. 38]. In this town, then, the expected passing of caste-based neighborhoods to those based on economic class is taking place as commerce becomes more lively. Families of various castes come together to live in neighborhoods of a common economic status. Again, however, as in village India, the untouchables remain unintegrated at least in terms of residue into this new class structure.

ECOLOGY OF THE LARGE INDIAN CITIES

Armed with the results of the earlier Berry-Rees study [3], which showed interpenetration of classical and modern elements in the social geography of Calcutta, and a broader contextual base, our analysis of six major cities was designed to explore further the intricacies of India's urban ecology.

Five major categories were chosen as spanning the variables most likely to provide answers relating to these questions concerning the social and physical patterns of India's urban residents. Data were gathered from available sources on: density-distance from center of town; demographic variables; caste, religion, and ethnicity (i.e., ascriptive status); socioeconomic status including education, occupation, and income; and housing data. All cities had at least some data in each category, though the types of data and the amounts varied from city to city.

Since, as in the Berry-Rees study, the primary purpose of the data analysis was an exploratory one of pattern recognition, no elaborate examination of alternative factoring procedures was undertaken. Instead, all the results are based upon principal axis factor analyses with normal varimax rotation and pseudo-inverse orthonormal factor scores. Data were transformed where necessary to satisfy linearity assumptions. A cascading sequence of rotations was undertaken in each case from initial principal axes, beginning with the first pair and then by steps for the first three axes, the first four, etc., until the final rotated solution included all principal axes with eigenvalues exceeding unity.

Tables 1A, 1B, and 1C summarize patterns common to several of the cities and to the earlier Calcutta study: a socioeconomic status factor, a particular index of family-type differentiation, and a communal factor or factors. To the extent that there are repetitive ingredients in the residential systems of the cities under consideration, they may be thought to be general properties of India's urban ecology. Tables 2 through 11 present the factor matrices for the final rotated solutions for each case.

Status Differentiation

The cluster of variables defining high socioeconomic status (SES) in the analyses comprised high rates of male and female literacy, a high percentage of males engaged in occupations of trade and commerce, and, conversely, low percentages of scheduled caste members, and of males in manufacturing. Of these variables, nine cities had available data (Poona in 1822 did not), and eight of them showed this factor as significant in their residential patterns.

The additional variables which correlate with high socioeconomic status in the cities where the variables are available, for the most part, are quite expectable: high proportions of white collar workers, high proportions of nonworkers and of women who do not work, high incomes per capita, and low proportions of huts.

Other parts of the output point to the strong link between caste status and economic status. Wards which had high SES were the same wards which had high proportions of high caste people, Brahmins, and relatively low proportions of Muslims and migrants (non-Marathi in Poona). This may or may not indi-

cate an identity between high caste status and high economic status, but it does indicate that many wards which are high on one index are high on the other. Other loadings link SES with land-use patterns. High status areas are located in the center of town rather than in the suburbs, substantiating the ideas of Sjoberg in *The Preindustrial City* [17].

Maps of the factor scores (not reproduced here because of space limitations) show spatial distributions of SES readily explainable by the historical and economic development of the cities. Poona, for example, developed early around a fort center on the Mutha River. To the east and south of the fort was the commercial center of town, and this area became the chief location for Muslims, non-Marathas, and the commercial life of Poona. To the west of the fort, filling the area between the Mutha River and a vanished river which followed the course of today's north-south Katraj Aqueduct, lived the Brahmins of the town. Poona has had for centuries a most distinguished and large group of Brahmins, running to twenty-five percent of the city's population. During the days of the Maratha Empire, the rulers of the region instituted policies of great liberality towards Brahmins both as religious leaders and as members of government. Even after the fall of the Maratha Empire to the British, the city continued as a center of Brahmin strength and a major educational center with a number of all-India institutions. The map of Poona in 1822 shows the east-west split largely in communal terms, but by 1937 the split between the two sides of town was definitely one of socioeconomic status. Rosenthal [16] reports a scheduled caste member of Congress as saying, "There are two parts to Poona: East and West. The West is highly developed. People there are educated, rich, and have high posts. . . . The East is very undeveloped. Most of the people are laborers and there are many poor persons."

The pattern of Madras is similar, though it was a city built from a mere cluster of villages by the British into a major metropolis of some two million inhabitants. The area around Fort

TABLE 1A. Cities with a Socioeconomic Status Factor

	General factor pattern:		
	Male Literacy		+
	Female Literacy		+
	Males in Trade (%)		+
	Sched Caste (%)		—
	Males in Manufacturing		—

City	Presence as Factor	Additional Variables	
Poona, 1822	See discussion of communal factor		
Poona, 1937	Factor I	Density Factors	+
		Brahmins	+
		Working Females (%)	—
		Non-Working (%)	+
		White-Collar (%)	+
		Industry	+
		Shops	+
Poona, 1954	Factor I (no data on percentage males in manufacturing)	Working Males (%)	—
		Working Females (%)	—
		Income Per Capita	+
		Muslim (%)	—
		Non-Maratha (%)	—
		Brahmin (%)	+
Bombay (15 observations)	Factor III	Houseless (%)	+
Bombay (88 observations)	Factor I	Density	+
Bombay (437 observations)	Factor I	Working Females (%)	—
Kanpur	Factor I		
Sholapur, 1938	See discussion of communal factor		
Ahmedabad	Factor I (no data on percentage of males in trade; manufacturing does not correlate + or —)	Density	+
		Females/Males	+
		Working Males (%)	—
		Working Females (%)	—
		Females in Household Industry (%)	+
		Huts (%)	—
Madras	Factor I (except percentage of males in manufacturing)		
Calcutta	Yes: Berry and Rees (1968)		

TABLE 1B.   Cities with a Familism Index

| | General factor pattern: | Sex ratio | + |
| | | Working males (%) | − |

City	Presence as Factor	Additional Variables	
Poona, 1822	No data		
Poona, 1937	Family survey (data not applicable)		
Poona, 1954	Family survey (data not applicable)		
Bombay (15 observations)	Factor I	Institutional population	−
		Houseless (%)	−
		Literate males (%)	−
		Literate females (%)	+
		Working females (%)	−
		Males in manufacturing (%)	+
		Males in transportation (%)	−
Bombay (88 observations)	Factor III	Literate females (%)	+
		Houseless (%)	−
		Density	−
Bombay (437 observations)	Factor II	Males in manufacturing (%)	−
		Literate females (%)	+
Kanpur	Factor II	Literate males (%)	+
Sholapur	Family survey (data not applicable)		
Ahmedabad	Factor VI	Males in manufacturing (%)	−
		Residential (%)	−
		Factory (%)	−
		Business offices (%)	+
		Shops	+
	Factor I	Correlates with S.E.S.	
	Factor VII	Males in household (%)	+
		Males in construction (%)	+
		Females in household (%)	+
		Factory (%)	+
		Shops (%)	+
Madras	Factor III	Houseless (%)	−
		Males in manufacturing (%)	+
		Males in trade (%)	−

TABLE 1C.   Cities with a Communal Factor or Factors

	General factor pattern:	Brahmin (%)	+
		Muslim (%)	−
		Sched caste (%)	−
		Maratha (%)	+
		Non-Maratha (%)	−
		Lingayat (%)	−

(No factor includes all of these communal variables. The relevant ones are noted below.)

City	Presence as Factor	Additional Variables	
Poona, 1822	Factor I	Brahmin (%)	+
		Muslim (%)	−
		Persons per house (%)	+
		1-story houses (%)	−
		Huts (%)	−
	Factor II	Brahmin (%)	+
		Sched caste (%)	−
		Total population	+
		Persons per house	+
Poona, 1937	Factor I (correlates with S.E.S.)	Brahmin (%)	+
		Sched caste (%)	−
	Factor IV	Brahmin (%)	+
		Muslim (%)	−
		Persons per house	−
		Non-Maratha (%)	−
		Non-working (%)	+
		Owner resident (%)	+
		Area	+
Poona, 1954	Factor I (correlates with S.E.S.)	Brahmin (%)	+
		Muslim (%)	−
		Sched caste (%)	−
		Non-Maratha (%)	−
Bombay (15 observations)	No data		
Bombay (88 observations)	No data		
Bombay (437 observations)	No data		
Kanpur	No data		
Sholapur	Factor I	Brahmin (%)	+
		Maratha (%)	+
		Rooms per family	+
		Square feet per person	+
		1-story houses (%)	−
		Families below poverty line (%)	−
		Families below destitution line (%)	−

TABLE 1C.   (Continued)

City	Presence as Factor	Additional Variables	
		Income per capita	+
		Literate males (%)	+
		Literate females (%)	+
		Working males (%)	−
		Doctors and lawyers (%)	+
		White-collar (%)	+
		Groceries	+
		Hardware	+
		Single males (%)	+
		Single females (%)	+
	Factor II	Lingayat (%)	−
		Non-Maratha (%)	−
		1-story houses (%)	+
		Square feet per person	−
		Literate males (%)	−
		Working females (%)	+
		White-collar (%)	−
		Unskilled (%)	−
		Families below poverty line (%)	+
		Incomes per capita	−
		Groceries	−
		Hardware	−
	Factor III (weak correlation)		
Ahmedabad	No data		
Madras	No data		

St. George, the center of British trade and administration from the seventeenth century onward, has become the hub around which are found the high SES wards. Another center built centuries ago is Santhome and Mylapore, the areas where the Portuguese founded their fort in the late sixteenth century, and it, to this day, remains a high SES area. Finally, a high status zone in the "new residential" area indicates the beginning of suburbanization in Madras city [5, p. 437]. In Madras, the areas of low SES correspond largely to the factory areas in the north, which abut the railroad track, and in the harbor area. The correlation of factory area and low SES residences is obvious and indeed forms a later factor in the analysis.

Ahmedabad, Kanpur, and Bombay also show higher socioeconomic status toward the center of the city, with lower status areas farther out, usually associated with the presence of large industrial areas. In Ahmedabad, the high status areas are all, except one, located in the old city which was surrounded by a wall until the 1920s. The low status areas were, it seems, always outside the old city and indeed, the wealthier citizens wanted it that way. "In a list of municipal wants put forward in the annual report of the Municipal Commission for 1887 to 1888 there was included: The removal of low caste and other such people for the reduction of overcrowdedness" [12, p. 124]. The banishment of low caste people from the downtown was a norm for urban India well before large-scale industrialization. Yet suburbanization has also come to Ahmedabad. The statistics in the fourteenth ward, the large sprawling ward

TABLE 2.   Factor Structure: Ahmedabad*

| Variable | Communality | Factor | | | | | | |
		I	II	III	IV	V	VI	VII
Density	0.818	−0.669	0.482					
Persons per family	0.782	−0.317	0.736					
Total population	0.620				0.631			
Females/males	0.829	−0.343		0.430			−0.561	−0.430
Sched caste (%)	0.828	0.854						
Literate males (%)	0.927	−0.703		0.452	−0.438			
Literate females (%)	0.887	−0.733		0.357	−0.432			
Working males (%)	0.808	0.389					0.644	0.304
Working females (%)	0.888	0.728		−0.501				
Males in farming (%)	0.938			−0.948				
Males in transportation (%)	0.777			−0.830				
Males in manufacturing (%)	0.774				0.735		−0.361	
Males in household (%)	0.761		0.319					−0.773
Males in construction (%)	0.760							−0.768
Females in farming (%)	0.893		−0.363	−0.820				
Females in transportation (%)	0.961				0.950			
Females in manufacturing (%)	0.767				0.801			
Females in household (%)	0.836	−0.545	0.519		0.350			−0.360
Females in construction (%)	0.969					0.920		
Huts (%)	0.782	0.859						
Vacant (%)	0.833		−0.795					
Residential (%)	0.780				0.350		−0.772	
Restaurants (%)	0.741	0.347	−0.399		0.643			
Factories (%)	0.756		0.404				−0.651	0.327
Business offices (%)	0.644		0.419	−0.316			0.596	
Shops (%)	0.469						0.470	0.336
Males in trade (%)	0.807	−0.623	0.436					
Females in trade (%)	0.928					0.900		
Distance	0.731		−0.750					
Eigenvalue	29 Factors	17.4	29.7	41.3	52.4	62.4	72.1	80.3
	7 Factors	21.6	36.9	51.4	65.3	77.7	89.7	100.0

Source: *Census of India 1961*, Vol. V (*Gujarat*), Part X–A(i) (*Special Report on Ahmedabad City*).
    * 34 observations

across the Sabarmati River from the old city, do not reflect the coming of increasing numbers of upper middle-class, white collar workers, or the establishment of the Gujarat University and of the state governmental secretariat in this area; this is because the ward is so large that it includes diverse elements of population in addition to the upper middle-class suburbanites, averaging them out in the census reports.

Kanpur, similarly, has its high SES areas toward the center of the old city. In addition,

the residential section of the cantonment where the British established their homes apart from the Indians, and which has been taken over since Independence as a suburban development of the wealthy Indians, is a second, high status community. Some outlying areas (in ward 84) are also being developed as a suburban, upper middle-class settlement. The low-status neighborhoods tend, again, to be located around the great industrial complexes which are the lifeblood of Kanpur's economy.

TABLE 3.   Factor Structure: Bombay*

| Variable | Communality | Factor | | | |
		I	II	III	IV
Total households	0.971		0.978		
Density	0.935		0.366		−0.838
Total population	0.980		0.984		
Institutional population	0.867	0.687	0.603		
Males/females	0.960	−0.855	−0.399		
Sched caste (%)	0.430			0.400	0.451
Houseless (%)	0.942	0.871		−0.401	
Literate males (%)	0.953	0.381		−0.818	
Literate females (%)	0.990	−0.316		−0.937	
Working males (%)	0.896	0.910			
Working females (%)	0.912	0.505			0.772
Males in manufacturing (%)	0.930	−0.379	0.375	0.782	
Males in trade (%)	0.914			−0.496	−0.796
Males in transportation (%)	0.676	0.786			
Eigenvalue	14 Factors	29.8	51.1	71.4	88.3
	4 Factors	33.8	57.9	81.0	100.0

Source: *Census of India 1961*, Vol. X (*Maharashtra*), Part X(1–B) (*Greater Bombay Census Table*).
 * 15 observations

TABLE 4.   Factor Structure: Bombay*

| Variable | Communality | Factor | | | | |
		I	II	III	IV	V
Total households	0.935		0.956			
Density	0.583	−0.544		−0.415		−0.310
Total population	0.945		0.953			
Institutional population	0.768	−0.327	0.571		0.402	0.324
Males/females	0.892			0.878		
Sched caste (%)	0.580	0.678			0.311	
Houseless (%)	0.814			−0.566	0.631	
Literate males (%)	0.784	−0.797				
Literate females (%)	0.856	−0.770		0.479		
Working males (%)	0.872			−0.922		
Working females (%)	0.819					0.851
Males in manufacturing (%)	0.775	0.478	0.568			0.471
Males in trade (%)	0.801	−0.737				−0.442
Males in transportation (%)	0.800				0.882	
Eigenvalue	14 Factors	21.4	41.0	58.7	69.9	80.2
	5 Factors	26.7	51.1	73.3	87.1	100.0

Source: *Census of India 1961*, Vol. X (*Maharashtra*), Part X(1–B) (*Greater Bombay Census Tables*).
 * 88 observations

TABLE 5. Factor Structure: Bombay*

| Variable | Communality | Factor | | | | |
		I	II	III	IV	V
Total households	0.876			−0.925		
Total population	0.852			−0.907		
Institutional population	0.763					0.844
Males/females	0.895		−0.908			
Sched caste (%)	0.551	−0.721				
Houseless (%)	0.763				−0.818	
Literate males (%)	0.797	0.828				
Literate females (%)	0.846	0.684	−0.551			
Working males (%)	0.873		0.919			
Working females (%)	0.657	−0.564		0.304		0.497
Males in manufacturing (%)	0.671	−0.315	0.369	−0.445	0.369	−0.317
Males in trade (%)	0.637	0.751				
Males in transportation (%)	0.854			−0.901		
Eigenvalue	14 Factors	19.3	35.7	50.5	62.8	71.7
	5 Factors	27.0	49.8	70.5	87.7	100.0

Source: *Census of India 1961,* Vol. X (*Maharashtra*), Part X(1–B) (*Greater Bombay Census Tables*).
* 437 observations

Bombay, too, has its areas of highest SES near the center of town, adjacent to the commercial hub of the city. Conversely, low SES areas are near the ports, the industrial complex, and in outlying areas. For Bombay, we have data on increasingly fine-grained geographic units of observation. The largest units, 15 wards, have populations from 58,000 (Ward T) to 660,000 (Ward G), and are as large as whole cities. It was with these units that the first generalization was made. The next scale of analysis, 88 *sections*, reveals additional patterns; for example, a suburbanized area of high status appears along Mahim Bay and Matunga. The most detailed study, of 437 units called *circles*, indicates that the high status areas downtown are commercial. A few high SES areas are shown scattered even further towards the edge of the city as small suburbanized colonies, but the very lowest status areas dominate the outermost fringes of the city. The industrial and port areas, established for a long time, do not have such low status ratings as the more distant areas, revealing that long-time industrial urbanization has its socioeconomic advantages.

Familism: Male Migrant Areas

Data relating to family structure were available for only four cities (Bombay at each scale of analysis), but on each a "familism" index appeared. However, the factor structure reveals that this element of India's urban ecology is not a measurement of degree of family specialization according to stage in life cycle, as in the United States, but one which picks out areas in which vast numbers of men who are working in the industries of the city come to live. They live without women, though they may be married to women they have left in the village, at least temporarily. A similar factor was noted for Cairo, Egypt by Abu-Lughod [1]. Statistically independent of SES, some of these neighborhoods of factory workers may approach middle-class status, or else the factorial output indicates that many of the migrants live in neighborhoods which are predominantly middle class rather than lower class.

The maps of the factor scores indicate distinct land use associations. In Bombay, the fifteen-ward study shows houseless male workers living without their families to be concentrated

TABLE 6.   Factor Structure: Kanpur*

Variable	Communality	Factor		
		I	II	III
Density	0.671			−0.770
Females/males	0.782		−0.833	
Sched caste (%)	0.617	−0.645		0.448
Literate males (%)	0.795	0.816	−0.356	
Literate females (%)	0.847	0.890		
Working males (%)	0.896		0.895	
Working females (%)	0.538			0.692
Males in manufacturing (%)	0.702	−0.803		
Males in trade (%)	0.845	0.690		−0.598
Eigenvalue	9 Factors	35.0	54.8	74.4
	3 Factors	47.0	73.6	100.0

Source: *Census of India 1961*, Vol. XV (*Uttar Pradesh*), Part X (*Special Report on Kanpur City*).
  * 136 observations

TABLE 7.   Factor Structure: Madras*

Variable	Communality	Factor				
		I	II	III	IV	V
Persons in family	0.834		−0.642			0.570
Households in house	0.854		−0.606			0.645
Total population	0.697		0.825			
Females/males	0.694			0.807		
Sched caste (%)	0.704	0.773				
Houseless (%)	0.744			−0.840		
Literate males (%)	0.847	−0.852			−0.341	
Literate females (%)	0.887	−0.849			−0.358	
Working males (%)	0.692			−0.713	0.321	
Working females (%)	0.712					−0.786
Males in manufacturing (%)	0.718			0.457		0.595
Males in trade (%)	0.813	−0.530	−0.512	−0.507		
Males in household (%)	0.863				0.915	
Females in household (%)	0.865				0.909	
Area	0.679		0.816			
Eigenvalue	15 Factors	17.6	34.1	49.9	64.9	77.4
	5 Factors	22.8	44.1	64.5	83.9	100.0

Source: *Census of India 1961*, Vol. IX (*Madras*), Part X(III) (*Census Table and Primary Census Abstract Madras City*).
  * 100 observations

in the dock areas, the industrial areas, and downtown. Much as one would expect, the houseless workers gravitate to the areas where jobs for unskilled workers are available. Conversely, the most marked positive area of family life is on the fringe of the region where, one presumes, land is available for home building, and indeed, the area may not yet be seen as fully urbanized.

The 88-ward study picks up the same areas

TABLE 8.   Factor Structure: Poona, 1822*

| Variable | Communality | Factor | | | |
		I	II	III	IV
Persons per house	0.687	0.636	−0.515		
1-story houses (%)	0.538	−0.678			
Total population	0.761		−0.715	0.497	
Female/male	0.834			0.902	
Sched caste (%)	0.558		0.688		
Brahmin (%)	0.545	0.607	−0.369		
Muslim (%)	0.670	−0.799			
Huts (%)	0.724	−0.354	0.683		0.306
Distance	0.878				0.937
Eigenvalue	9 Factors	22.3	43.5	56.7	68.8
	4 Factors	32.3	63.2	82.3	100.0

Source: Gadgil, D. R., *Poona: A Socio-Economic Survey, Part II* (Poona: Gokhale Institute of Politics and Economics, 1952), pp. 42–58.

* 22 observations

again in finer detail, revealing additional areas of family dwelling without houseless street-sleepers. Unlike the downtown areas, these areas do not attract transient laborers for, despite their affluence, they do not have many jobs to offer. The fine grained 437-circle analysis comes closer to pinpointing the areas of job availability for transient male labor, separating them from areas of stable residence without commercial land use. Thus, harbor and textile mill areas are strongly marked as low on the familism index; suburban family areas rank high.

Kanpur exhibits a similar separation of industrial areas from residential areas on this index. Interestingly, Kanpur is a city surrounded to the northwest and the southwest by industry. The northwestern quadrant, however, was pioneered more by the British and adjoined the cantonment; no exaggerated familism index, high or low, is in evidence. This may result from British policies in "their" areas of the city, or from an overlap within the same census ward of residential and factory areas so that one balances out the other. The area to the south of the city includes a number of new industries, as well as older ones, and the main railway depot for industry. It has a decidedly low familism index (a factor score of −5.92). The areas

especially high on familism seem to be agricultural areas on the fringe of Kanpur, areas quite removed from industrialization.

The familism index in Ahmedabad appears in two sets of factor loadings. As Factor VI it picks out the railway depot ("Railwaypura" ward; factor score −4.53) and the job-rich, highly transient area around it. The workers here are not in industry, but rather in the commercial and transport occupations connected with the depot. As Factor VII, it distinctly picks out areas of males in household industry and in construction, particularly the new area developing across the Sabarmati River. Similarly, it picks out zones of household industry for men, where hand weaving and some handicrafts are still practiced in the southern areas of the city both within and without the walls. The areas highest on the familism index are: Ranip, a rural area recently annexed to Ahmedabad and so far distant that is not yet mapped; the military cantonment which houses an elite; and ward 22, Gomptipur, which was for some time a separate town, suburban to Ahmedabad.

Finally, the Madras familism map picks out most clearly the harbor area, the natural destination of men travelling alone and seeking work.

Communal Factors

The most significant aspect of the communal element of India's urban ecology may well be the fact that the Government of India refuses to collect data on caste and communal factors in the official census. The only data available on communal affiliation, therefore, are in the surveys of Poona and Sholapur conducted independently by the staff of the Gokhale Institute of Politics and Economics in Poona.

In the study of Poona a clear pattern of communal residence appears. Muslims are not prevalent in neighborhoods where Brahmins predominate, and vice versa. Similarly, Brahmins and untouchables, or scheduled caste members do not in general share the same localities. Indeed, in Poona, the Brahmins are composed of several groups, most prominently of Konkani Brahmins originally from the Konkan coast of western India, in the Ratnagiri District of modern Maharashtra State, and of Deshasta Brahmins who come from the *Desh* or the "country," the internal plateau regions of Maharashtra [13, p. 5]. In 1937 the Konkani Brahmins were heavily over-represented in Sadashiv ward while the Deshastas were more prominent in Budhwar, Shukrawar, and Shanwar. Konkanis are also more highly represented in the highest income brackets and in the highest levels of occupational types. Within an already elite group, the Konkanis (or Chitpavans as they are often called) are the most elite.[2] A similar separation between the two principal Brahmin groups appears for 1954 [18].

The Sholapur survey shows that wards with high proportions of Brahmins are also high in Marathas, the dominant indigenous caste of the region in terms of numbers. While the Maratha caste is not high in socioeconomic status, working essentially in farming in the rural areas and in craft and industrial jobs in the cities, it is quite respectable in ritual status. The Marathas are the traditional rulers who employed the Brahmins as the administrators of the empire. Conversely, Lingayats and non-Marathas tend to be disproportionately high in the same wards, again no surprise on ritual lines since neither has a niche in the local Hindu caste structure, non-Marathas since they are immigrants and Lingayats because they follow a deviant form of Hinduism. Occupationally, however, they bridge a wide spectrum of activities from large scale trade to factory workers and private artisans.

The Sholapur study is unique in that it shows communal status rather than socioeconomic status as the most significant variable in residence patterns. Sholapur did not show the clear presence of a socioeconomic status variable. And though Factor I, the communal status factor, here is linked with socioeconomic status, this factor is recessive while the caste factor is dominant. The analysis of Sholapur broke into nine factors, highest of any city, and it had 33 variables for consideration. This finer-grained information base may well be responsible for the greater weighting of the communal factors as compared with the SES variables, and clearly the two are interrelated. Sholapur remains as testimony of the power of caste and communal factors in the formation of neighborhood in a modern Indian industrial city.

Clustering of communal residential areas is, of course, predictable, and in Poona reveals remarkable long-term stability. Over a period of 150 years, from the ruler's social survey of 1822 to the surveys of the Gokhale Institute in 1937 and 1954, the center of the old city retained its social pattern quite apart from an almost tenfold gain in population. The Brahmin high-caste high SES group dominated the western region of the city between the Mutha River and the present-day Katraj Aqueduct. The center of the town, along a north-south axis, was and is dominated by the market functions of the town and houses the traders, the

---

[2] Simply in terms of residence choices, this division in the Brahmin community reinforces the model of different groups sorting themselves out residentially according to SES. Dynamically, the preeminence of the Chitpavans may well owe to the fact that the rulers of Poona in its first heyday, the second half of the eighteenth century to 1818, were Chitpavan Brahmins. Doubtless they gave special encouragement to fellow caste members.

TABLE 9.   Factor Structure: Poona, 1937*

Variable	Communality	I	II	III	IV	V	VI	VII	VIII	IX
					Factor					
Density	0.790	0.382		0.621				0.351		
Persons per house	0.818					0.832				
1-story houses (%)	0.684	−0.752								
Total population	0.855			0.840						
Females/males	0.874							0.897		
Sched caste (%)	0.758	−0.682							0.429	
Brahmin (%)	0.808	0.612	0.373		−0.469					
Muslim (%)	0.767		−0.358		0.647			−0.323		
Maratha (%)	0.786						−0.686	0.306		
Non-Maratha (%)	0.715				0.750					
Square feet per capita	0.891		0.893							
Huts (%)	0.641	−0.343				0.503				
Literate females (%)	0.874	0.349	0.701							−0.305
Literate males (%)	0.857	0.562	0.697							
Working males (%)	0.855		−0.437			−0.570				
Working females (%)	0.751	−0.429	−0.512			0.340		−0.312		
Nonworking (%)	0.748	0.668	0.344		−0.335					
Professionals and owners (%)	0.692		0.668							0.400
White-collar (%)	0.681	0.771								
Unskilled (%)	0.763	−0.829								
Artisan (%)	0.834								−0.863	
Numbers of doctors and lawyers	0.879	0.424	0.364	0.675						
Owner residences (%)	0.787	0.337			−0.374	−0.638				
Income per capita	0.861		0.879							
Industry	0.862	0.356		0.810						
Shops	0.789	0.382		0.695						
Males 15+ (%)	0.877						−0.819			
Distance	0.753									0.790
Area	0.808			0.703	−0.457					
Persons per family	0.902					−0.613	0.436			−0.492
Eigenvalue 30 Factors		16.5	30.9	41.7	50.3	57.7	64.9	70.2	75.0	79.9
9 Factors		20.7	38.7	52.2	63.0	72.3	81.3	87.8	94.0	100.0

Source: Gadgil, D. R., *Poona: A Socio-Economic Survey* 2V. (Poona: Gokhale Institute of Politics and Economics, Vol. 1, 1945, Vol. 2, 1952).
  * 22 observations

Muslims, and the nonlocal groups of the society. The eastern and northeastern quadrants of the city house the untouchables and scheduled caste members for the most part. Thus the old central city retained a clear caste-class correlation over time, and residential patterns clearly separate out along this line. However, Poona has recently experienced suburbanization, and for the first time large numbers of people are moving away from the center of town. In the suburbs, class and occupation are bringing together groups from diverse castes. In addition, newer migrants have tended to cloud the older outlines. Rosenthal [16] quotes a Brahmin leader as saying, "Formerly there was a communal aspect to the controversy between East and West, . . . but now there is little because scheduled caste people have settled in large numbers in the West. Very few differences remain."

VARIATIONS IN TIME AND AREA

The Poona and Bombay materials permit us to add further insights into variations of the results in time and area.

Data on Poona are unusually rich both in quantity and time, thanks to the work of Gadgil and Gokhale Institute of Politics and Economics in Poona. Materials are available from the records of the Maratha administrators which date back to 1822, and from Gadgil's social surveys of 1937 and 1954. Therefore, we can examine materials on the size of the city, its density, the external connections with other cities, the economic functions of Poona, and the social

areas of the city over time. This provides strong indication of the effects of various processes over time, and thus brings us back to the original idea of ecology as expressed by the early Chicago school, a concern with process over time.

Poona began as a temple and fort complex, located slightly away from the river bank, and it had in the early seventeenth century many of the features of the classical Indian city. The priests and the administrators grouped themselves around the temple and fort-administrative area. Off to the east, on marshy land undesired by other groups, the servants and untouchables resided.

Rivers and streams flowing from south to north divided the city into three major sectors. In the west between the Mutha River and a now-dry stream which followed the course of the contemporary Katraj Aqueduct was the Brahmin sector of the city. In the central city,

TABLE 10. Factor Structure: Poona, 1954*

Variable	Communality	I	II	III	IV	V	VI
				Factor			
Density	0.678			0.772			
Total population	0.632	0.419				0.588	
Females/males	0.914						0.906
Sched caste (%)	0.855	−0.655			0.558		
Brahmin (%)	0.940	0.923					
Maratha (%)	0.680					−0.806	
Non-Maratha (%)	0.805	−0.317		0.611	−0.361	0.331	
Artisan (%)	0.827			0.310	−0.837		
Muslim (%)	0.820	−0.830					
Literate males (%)	0.871	0.799			−0.369		
Literate females (%)	0.870	0.899					
Working males (%)	0.927	−0.493	−0.790				
Working females (%)	0.795	−0.520		−0.563			0.377
Owner residences (%)	0.819		0.360		−0.470		0.609
Income per capita	0.702	0.778					
Males 15+ (%)	0.857		−0.842				
Distance	0.801				0.636	0.548	
Areas	0.748			−0.669		0.425	
Persons in family	0.780		0.683	0.441			
Eigenvalue	19 Factors	27.4	39.1	50.7	62.2	72.0	80.6
	6 Factors	34.0	48.5	62.9	77.2	89.3	100.0

Source: Sovani, N. V., *Poona: A Re-Survey* (Poona: Gokhale Institute of Politics and Economics, 1956).
* 22 observations

between the old river and the Nagzari stream was the bazaar and shop area of the city inhabited by commercial and artisan castes and by non-indigenous people. Initially the untouchables lived in the eastern sector.

Poona took on great importance in the eighteenth century as the location of the court of the local ruler and also of the *Peshwa* or prime minister and de facto ruler of the spreading Maratha Confederacy. The city expanded during this time, essentially in a north-south direction, following the earlier three divisions and natural topographical features. Successive areas were added to the city by the Peshwa, who turned each new ward over to a nobleman for management and ordered him to bring a full population to it. Sometimes people were already living there, sometimes they came later; the dates given to wards indicate the year of assignment to the nobleman. However, as wards were added, their residents took on the same character as earlier ones in their section, and so the 1822 analysis revealed clear communal distinctions as the prevailing element in the town's social geography.

Expansion of the town beyond the triangular area bounded by the hilly ridges to the south, the river to the west, and the marshy land to the east took place only in the nineteenth century, and more prominently in the twentieth. The British after conquering Poona in 1818, built their cantonments to the east and the north, Poona Cantonment (the civilian area) and Kirkee Cantonment (the military area), respectively. Later in the nineteenth century, Indian settlement spread west of the river, establishing there an outpost of the old Brahmin sector in a highly intellectual area of colleges and schools. Finally, the twentieth century, especially after independence, has seen the development of Poona as an industrial area with the spread of factories along the railway lines, especially to the west, toward Bombay. Both the 1937 and 1954 analyses reveal the additional British and industrial ingredients in the town's social map.

The physical expansion of the city, espe-cially in recent years, has not quite led to suburbanization. The population has continued to pour into the old core city, boosting the population densities there. Maps from Gadgil's study [9] indicate the increasing density of the central area. A later compilation by Brush [4] indicates that densities are still increasing in the central areas, and the relative sparseness of population in the surrounding area. Brush notes "in 1881 Poona's population was recorded as 99,421; fifty years later it had increased to 213,680, with little change of area. By 1961 the old city had been enlarged more than ten times, from 2390 acres to 27,190 acres, and the population had grown to 597,419, but without any large shift of people into areas incorporated into Greater Poona" [4, p. 379]. Brush correctly suggests that if Poona follows patterns of western cities, with the spread of cheap and rapid public transportation in the city, the suburban exodus will soon come. At present workers travel by bike from the central city to jobs on the periphery. The city now seems ready for the jump to a reverse situation.

The size and density changes have come about largely by a change in the economic, political, and social functions which Poona has played throughout the historical period covered. It changed from a governmental center under the Marathas to a British governmental and military center, the headquarters of the southern command of the Indian army, to an industrialized metropolis to some extent before Independence and much more rapidly since then.

What ecological change has been associated with these functional and demographic changes? At least until the last decade, they did not upset the basic structure of the core city. But the creation of the cantonment areas by the British did lend to these new areas quite different characteristics from the older parts. There was greater diversity, with more foreigners and fewer Hindus. Further change was introduced by industrialization and by the consequences of partition. Each factory attracted its cluster of migrant workers, and the gen-

TABLE 11.   Factor Structure: Sholapur*

Variable	Commu-nality	Factor								
		I	II	III	IV	V	VI	VII	VIII	IX
1-story houses (%)	0.830	−0.371	0.607	−0.303				0.373		
Females/males	0.870				−0.350	0.795				
Sched caste (%)	0.827			−0.396					0.740	
Brahmin (%)	0.934	0.897								
Lingayat (%)	0.904		−0.913							
Christian (%)	0.864				0.875					
Muslim (%)	0.714									0.734
Maratha (%)	0.916	0.335					−0.863			
Non-Maratha (%)	0.793		−0.597	−0.324		0.335				
Rooms per family	0.827	0.717								
Square feet per family	0.970			0.896						
Square feet per person	0.948	0.364	−0.421	0.711						
Huts (%)									0.859	
Literate males (%)	0.823	0.558	−0.362	0.315						
Literate females (%)	0.940	0.888								
Working males (%)	0.860	−0.559		−0.319			−0.608			
Working females (%)	0.776		0.344	−0.338			0.324			
Numbers of doctors and lawyers	0.901	0.880								
White-collar (%)	0.894	0.467	−0.524	0.467						
Professionals and owners (%)	0.587						−0.606			
Unskilled (%)	0.795		−0.317	−0.425	0.391				0.497	
Artisan (%)	0.843									0.901
Families below poverty line (%)	0.921	−0.814	0.381							
Families below destitution line (%)	0.893	−0.643				−0.303	0.481	−0.359		
Income per capita	0.858	0.514	−0.300		0.306		−0.453			−0.334
Groceries	0.890	0.633	−0.574							
Hardware	0.906	0.343	−0.858							
Industry	0.896				−0.357	−0.628		0.389		
Males 15–45 (%)	0.767							0.821		
Females 15–45 (%)	0.827			−0.510		−0.664				
Single males (%)	0.900	0.805								
Single females (%)	0.909	0.547		0.748						
Persons per family	0.900			0.597		0.364	0.339	−0.457		
Eigenvalue	33 Factors	22.3	34.6	44.4	51.8	59.3	66.4	73.3	79.7	86.0
	9 Factors	25.9	40.2	51.6	60.2	68.9	77.2	85.2	92.7	100.0

Source: Gadgil, D. R., *Sholapur City: Socio-Economic Studies* (Poona: Gokhale Institute of Politics and Economics, 1965), *passim.*
* 27 observations (family survey)

eral acceleration of rural-to-urban migration impelled many lower caste Indians to the cities, where they filled most of the empty spaces, clouding the earlier social differentiation. When more data from the 1961 census become available, they will therefore show substantial smoothing of the social lines that remained essentially stable in the three analyses, 1822–1954.

Bombay's three-level analyses provided the opportunity for exploring the effects of differing geographical units of observation on the results of factorial ecologies of Indian cities. By and large, the factorial results were remarkably stable, which is pleasing. However, as the finer-grained analyses were undertaken, much greater insight was provided into the city's social map. With 437 units of observation, for example, docks were clearly separated from wealthier higher socioeconomic areas behind them, a feature clouded by the 88 sections and 15 wards. What the results therefore indicate is a clear need in factorial ecologies for some notion of the size and character of neighborhood groupings in Indian cities; hopefully this will serve as a guide to appropriate observational units that will provide a proper degree of geographic detail to general ecological themes repeating themselves through a variety of scales of analysis.

CONCLUSIONS

To the extent that the evidence analyzed reveals, socioeconomic status appears to be the dominant of these overarching themes in the residential geography of the Indian city today. The communal and caste status of the classical texts and of village India, and of Poona in 1822, is being transformed into class status as an outgrowth of city life [15]. While this is taking place, residual caste status and class status reinforce each other, so that the dominant spatial pattern remains that of high-status neighborhoods in central areas and low-status neighborhoods at the periphery.

If ecology is to be understood as process in time, much more historical study of urban ecology is needed in India, where traditional patterns have great longevity and where social areas display great resistance to change. Among the active forces which have introduced new elements into the social geography of the Indian city are: the British cantonments, built on different social bases than old Indian areas, often creating a dual city structure and a second set of higher socioeconomic status central and lower socioeconomic status peripheral neighborhoods; newer institutional areas devoted to government or education, although the latter tend to be Brahmin and the former (even in Chandigarh) tend to repeat the traditional core-to-periphery distribution by SES; and industry. It is this latter element that created a second factor in India's urban ecology by 1961: the family-type distinction between familial areas and zones housing new male migrants, clustered around the commercial core of the city, docks, mills, and new factory estates. Outlying industry, rather than improved transportation, has also promoted limited "suburbanization" and is one of the contributing causes of increasingly specialized neighborhoods in all cities.

What seems clear is that the increasingly diverse bases of social and economic power, which city life in modern India is generating, are transforming the urban structure. No longer are land or rulership or priesthood the bases of status or neighborhood and community, although their effects are still marked in India's urban landscapes. The issue is whether the emerging forms are converging on the model of the industrial metropolis, as suggested by Berry and Rees in Calcutta [3], or whether some new synthesis of traditional and modern will emerge.

NOTES

1. Abu-Lughod, J., 1968. "A Critical Test for the Theory of Social Area Analysis: The Factorial Ecology of Cairo, Egypt." Unpublished paper, Department of Sociology, Northwestern University.

2. Ayyar, C. P., 1916. *Venkatrama: Town Planning in Ancient Dekkan*. Madras: Law Publishing House.

3. Berry, B. J. L., and P. H. Rees, 1969. "The Factorial Ecology of Calcutta," *American Journal of Sociology*, 74: 445–491.

4. Brush, J. E., 1968. "Spatial Patterns of Population in Indian Cities," *Geographical Review*, 58 (July): 362–391.

5. Dupuis, J., 1960. *Madras et Le Nord du Coromandel*. Paris: Librarie d'Amerique et d'Orient.

6. Dutt, B. B., 1925. *Town Planning in Ancient India*. Calcutta: Thacker, Pink and Co.

7. Epstein, T. S., 1962. *Economic Development and Social Change in South India*. Manchester: Manchester University Press.

8. Fox, R. G. *Tezibazar*.

9. Gadgil, D. R., 1945, 1952. *Poona: A Socioeconomic Survey*. 2 Vols. Poona: Gokhale Institute of Politics and Economics.

10. Ibid., 1965. *Sholapur City: Socioeconomic Studies*. Poona: Gokhale Institute of Politics and Economics.

11. Ghurye, G. S., 1961. *Caste, Class, and Occupation*. Bombay: Popular Book Depot.

12. Gillion, K. L., 1969. *Ahmedabad*. Berkeley: University of California Press.

13. Karve, D. D., 1963. *The New Brahmans: Five Maharashtrian Families*. Berkeley: University of California Press.

14. Mayer, A. C., 1960. *Caste and Kinship in Central India: A Village and Its Region*. Berkeley: University of California Press.

15. Rosen, G., 1965. *Democracy and Industrial Change in Modern India*. Berkeley: University of California Press.

16. Rosenthal, D. B., "The Politics and Government of Two Indian Cities." Unpublished monograph, State University of New York at Buffalo, Department of Political Science.

17. Sjoberg, G., 1960. *The Preindustrial City*. Glencoe: Free Press.

18. Sovani, N. V., D. P. Apte, and R. G. Pendse, 1956. *Poona: A Re-Survey*. Poona: Gokhale Institute of Politics and Economics.

19. Spate, O. H. K., and A. T. A. Learmonth, 1967. *India and Pakistan*. Methuen and Co., Ltd.

31

FRANK L. SWEETSER

Factorial Ecology: Helsinki, 1960

In a previous paper, by conceiving of ecological structure as factor structure, the ecological structures of Helsinki and Boston were compared. Since exact cross-national replication of variables was not possible, a crucial step in the method was the demonstration that ecological factors were invariant under substitution of variables. This conclusion was established by factoring two 20 × 20 correlation matrices, based on seventy statistical areas, for the same city at the same time (Helsinki, 1960), with fourteen substitute variables in one of the matrices, and noting that the factorial structure remained the same in both (orthogonally rotated) matrices.[1]

The present paper takes its departure from this finding. Looking toward a comprehensive description of the underlying factorial structure of Helsinki social ecology, the original twenty-variable matrix was modified by elimination of three variables to reduce redundancy and by the addition of twenty-five variables to add relevant detail. The resulting variables (see Table 1) were intercorrelated, factored, and rotated to produce a forty-two-variable, six-factor orthogonal factor matrix (see Table 2). This matrix is the basis for the testing of several hypotheses and for a summary interpretation of Helsinki ecological structure.

The methodological Hypothesis (1) to be tested is that *ecological factors are invariant under addition of variables.* Four substantive hypotheses, set forth in the original statement of the

research design [2] and refined by insights gained from the analysis of the twenty-variable-factor matrix, may be specified: Hypothesis (2): three fundamental dimensions of the ecological differentiation of Helsinki's residential areas are *socio-economic status, progeniture* (young familism), and *"Urbanism"* (these are the three factors identified in the analysis of the twenty-variable

Reprinted by permission from *Demography*, Vol. 2 (1965), pp. 372–385.

This paper is based on unpublished 1960 Finnish census tabulations processed for the Helsinki Ecology Project, which was initiated by the writer during his tenure as a Fulbright Lecturer in Urban Sociology at the University of Helsinki. The project is sponsored by the Institute of Sociology of the University of Helsinki, the Helsinki City Statistical Office, the Alcohol Policy Research Institute, the Population Policy Research Institute, and the United States Educational Foundation in Finland. Financial support was provided mainly by the City of Helsinki and by the Educational Foundation. This enterprise was made possible by the active cooperation and assistance of many individuals, whose help is gratefully acknowledged. Those most directly involved are thanked by name in Frank L. Sweetser, "Factor Structure as Ecological Structure in Helsinki and Boston," *Acta Sociologica* (in press).

[2] As stated before computer processing of the data: "... techniques of factor analysis will be applied, and it is expected that a strong social rank factor will emerge, with a weaker familism factor and an urbanization factor separating from familism. It is also expected that ethnicity will fail to emerge as a clearly defined factor, or will show as a minor factor only. Since a wider variety of variables is included ... than in [the twenty-variable matrix], the appearance of several minor factors is likely. ... The purpose of [the "Design"] is to obtain a comprehensive picture of the underlying factorial structure of Helsinki social ecology, [and] to examine effects of including additional variables on factor loadings of the more important factors. These major factors, it is expected, will be closely similar to corresponding factors of [the twenty-variable matrix]." Sweetser, "Design for Correlation and Factor Analysis" (Helsinki: Sosiologian laitos, Helsingin yliopisto, 23 June, 1963).

---

[1] Sweetser, "Factor Structure as Ecological Structure in Helsinki and Boston," *Acta Sociologica* (in press).

TABLE 1. Forty-Two Ecological Variables, Helsinki, 1960

Variable Numbers*	Name	Variable definition
		Age Variables[a]
* 1.	Elementary school age	% of Finnish- and Swedish-speaking population age 6–13 years
* 2.	Retirement age	% of Finnish- and Swedish-speaking population age 65 years and over
3.	Middle age ratio	% of Finnish- and Swedish-speaking population age 20–64 who are age 20–39 years
4.	Pre-adolescent age ratio	% of Finnish- and Swedish-speaking population age 0–14 who are 0–6 years
		Sex Variables
* 5.	Proportion male	% of total population male
6.	Unattached males	% of subtenents living alone who are male
		Ethnic Variables (Swedish Language)
* 7.	Swedish-speaking Finns	% of total population speaking Swedish as principal language
8.	Swedish-speaking pupils	% of Swedish-speaking population age 7–15 years
9.	Swedish middle age ratio	% of Swedish-speaking population age 20–64 who are age 20–39 years
10.	Swedish adult males	% of Swedish-speaking population age 20–64 who are male
11.	Swedish fertility	Ratio of Swedish-speaking children under 5 years to Swedish-speaking males age 20–49 years[b]
		Variables of Family and Youth
12.	Males married, wife present	% of males age 20 and over married, with wife present
13.	Husband-wife families	% of all families with husband and wife both present
14.	Large families	% of all families with three or more children under age 18 years
15.	Children per couple	Mean number of children under 18 years of age per couple with children under 18
16.	Preschoolers per couple	Mean number of children under 7 years of age per couple with children under 7
* 17.	Fertility	Number under 5 years per 1000 males 20–49 years (Finnish- and Swedish-speaking population)[a][b]
* 18.	Non-family population	% of total population living alone as subtenants or in institutions
* 19.	Male delinquency rate	Number of boys age 15–17 years old referred for serious offences per 100 males age 15–17 years
		Locational Variables (Birth and Work)
* 20.	Born in Helsinki	% of total population born in Helsinki (1960 boundaries)
21.	Work near home	% of economically active population who work in the statistical area ("census tract") of residence
22.	Work downtown	% of economically active population who work in the central business district (*Keskusta*)

TABLE 1. *(Continued)*

23.	Commutation	% of economically active population who (a) have no fixed work-place; (b) work outside Helsinki city; (c) either live in the suburbs (*Esikaupunki*) and work in the urban core (*Kantakaupunki*); or vice versa
24.	Day population working	% of day population employed

Household and Housing Variables

25.	Female-"child" families	% of all families consisting of a female head and her "child" of any age
* 26.	Home ownership	% of occupied dwellings occupied by owners (including share-holders)
27.	1- & 2-room dwellings	% of dwellings with 1 or 2 rooms (including kitchen)
* 28.	Room-crowding	Number of persons per 100 rooms
* 29.	Housing defects	Mean of percent dwellings lacking central heat and percent dwellings lacking water closet
* 30.	Detached dwellings	% of dwellings in 1- or 2-family detached structures
* 31.	New housing	% of dwellings built 1951–1960
32.	Floor area in dwellings	% of total enclosed floor area in dwellings
33.	Floor area per dwelling	Mean floor area of dwellings (square meters)

Employment and Occupational Variables[c]

* 34.	Working women	% of females age 15 and over economically active
* 35.	Male prof.-mgr. occs.	% employed males in professional and managerial occupations
36.	Female prof.-mgr. occs.	% employed females in professional and managerial occupations
* 37.	Male cler.-serv. occs.	% employed males in clerical, sales and service occupations
38.	Female cler.-serv. occs.	% employed females in clerical, sales and service occupations
39.	Blue collar occupations	% of economically active persons (male and female) employed in blue collar occupations

Educational Variables

* 40.	Low educational status	% adults (age 25 and over) who have passed neither middle school nor student examinations
* 41.	Adult college status	% adults (age 25 and over) who have passed the student examination to qualify for admission to the university
42.	Academic youth	% of youth (age 15–24 years) who have passed the middle school or the student examination

---

* Variables were also included in the Helsinki matrix of 20 variables. See Table 3, below.

[a] Age data are for the combined Finnish-speaking and Swedish-speaking population for whom detailed age tabulations were available by statistical areas; these two language groups, in effect, constitute the total population, since they include 99.3 percent of it.

[b] A ratio of children to males was used to measure fertility in Helsinki's statistical areas because the conventional ratio of children to women was found to be seriously distorted there by the very large excess female populations in some areas. The ratio used here relates the number of children under 5 years to an estimate of the number of pairs of potential parents, the number of males age 20–49 years. It appears to be a suitable measure for Helsinki, where most married couples live together, and nearly all statistical areas have excess females in the adult population.

[c] Occupational classification is based on a special tabulation of Finnish two-digit occupational codes, sorted into the appropriate U.S. Census categories. This classification was made with the very helpful assistance of Dr. Kettil Bruun, Dr. Kalevi Heinila, Dr. Paavo Piepponen and Maisteri Marjotta Marin.

TABLE 2. Ecological Factors in Helsinki, 1960—Loadings of Forty-Two Variables on Six Factors (Orthogonal Rotation)[a] (Decimal Points Omitted)

		Factor Loadings[b] and Communalities						
		Factor I	Factor II	Factor III "Urbanism"	Factor IV	Factor V	Factor VI	
*Variable**		Socioeconomic Status	Progeniture	(career women)	Residentialism	Established Familism	Postgeniture	h^2
No.	Name							
* 1	Elementary school age	−14	24	16	05	(82)	(−35)	.90
* 2	Retirement age	23	(−55)	−13	−17	−23	(56)	.77
3	Middle age ratio	−13	(73)	06	23	19	(−40)	.80
4	Pre-adolescent age ratio	−27	(85)	−10	18	−07	−17	.87
* 5	Proportion male	(−53)	(37)	−26	03	18	(−55)	.82
6	Unattached males	(−65)	22	−22	−04	06	−21	.57
* 7	Swedish-speaking Finns	(75)	−20	−30	−21	−04	16	.76
8	Swedish-speaking pupils	14	11	−17	28	(44)	−29	.42
9	Swedish middle age ratio	05	(69)	12	26	20	−23	.65
10	Swedish adult males	−30	14	−02	04	03	(−68)	.57
11	Swedish fertility	34	(51)	−05	13	19	−10	.44
12	Males married, wife present	09	(48)	15	(50)	(35)	−26	.70
13	Husband-wife families	−11	(40)	−20	23	22	(−79)	.94
14	Large families	03	20	−10	01	(91)	−16	.90
15	Children per couple	10	01	−16	−19	(92)	00	.92
16	Preschoolers per couple	−14	32	−29	−29	(62)	07	.68
* 17	Fertility	−19	(73)	−06	25	(41)	−12	.82
* 18	Non-family population	17	(−53)	08	(−36)	−30	17	.56
19	Male delinquency rate	−32	−18	26	−09	−17	10	.25
* 20	Born in Helsinki	32	26	−05	(35)	(47)	01	.52
21	Work near home	16	−17	00	(−84)	20	−04	.80
22	Work downtown	(76)	−19	04	−12	−21	14	.69
23	Commutation	−13	(56)	−23	(52)	15	−32	.78
24	Day population working	14	−29	13	(−85)	−15	09	.87
25	Female, "child" families	12	(−39)	24	−20	−23	(79)	.94

TABLE 2. (Continued)

No.	Variable* Name	Factor I Socioeconomic Status	Factor II Progeniture	Factor III "Urbanism" (career women)	Factor IV Residentialism	Factor V Established Familism	Factor VI Postgeniture	h²
*26	Home ownership	15	17	05	(73)	−17	−26	.68
27	1- and 2-room dwellings	(−53)	−15	30	(−36)	−25	(48)	.82
*28	Room crowding	−86	−01	31	−12	−08	07	.86
29	Housing defects	−78	12	(−39)	02	29	04	.86
*30	Detached dwellings	−51	06	(−50)	39	17	−31	.79
*31	New housing	16	(52)	21	(45)	01	(−51)	.80
32	Floor area in dwelling	10	21	−16	(84)	02	−10	.80
33	Floor area per dwelling	(76)	−19	(−42)	02	10	−19	.84
*34	Working women	17	05	(73)	−22	−33	15	.74
35	Male professional-mgr. occs.	(96)	07	04	10	12	03	.95
36	Female professional-mgr. occs.	(72)	−09	(39)	06	18	21	.76
*37	Male clerical-service occs.	(76)	−05	31	−13	−12	17	.74
38	Female clerical-service occs.	(71)	00	−27	−15	−10	−20	.65
39	Blue collar occupations	(−96)	04	−19	02	−04	−13	.98
40	Low educational status	(−97)	−09	−09	−07	−09	−11	.98
*41	Adult college status	(95)	11	08	06	11	08	.94
42	Academic youth	(91)	−14	06	03	−01	26	.92
	Variance	11.299	5.150	2.446	4.676	4.418	4.084	32.073ᶜ
	% of variance	35.2	16.1	7.6	14.6	13.8	12.7	100.0

*Variables marked with an asterisk (*) were also included in the Helsinki matrix of 20 variables (see Table 3). Variables are concisely defined in Table 1.
ᵃ Principal components factorization with highest r's in diagonals; verimax orthogonal rotation of 7 factors. The seventh factor was dropped as too ambiguous to interpret. (This factor had a latent root below unit [.96]. Latent roots for Factors I–VI ranged from 13.28 to 1.05).
ᵇ Loadings at ± .35 or higher (significant at .02 > p > .01) are enclosed in parentheses.
ᶜ Column sum of h² is 32.05. The difference is due to rounding error.

375

matrix); Hypothesis (3): a fourth factor, relating in some way to home ownership and new housing, will attain clear definition in the forty-two-variable matrix (this factor loaded, respectively, at 0.76 and 0.65 on the two variables in the smaller matrix but was insufficiently defined for interpretation); Hypothesis (4): additional factors in the larger matrix will relate to specialized phases of urbanism or familism; Hypothesis (5): ethnicity will fail to emerge as a separate dimension of Helsinki's ecological structure.

INVARIANCE OF ECOLOGICAL FACTORS UNDER ADDITION OF VARIABLES

To facilitate discussion of the methodological hypothesis, variables included in both the large and the small analyses are indicated in Tables 1 and 2 by asterisks. Table 3 presents these seventeen duplicated variables in order of loadings on the three principal factors, placing the loadings for the factors in the twenty-variable and the forty-two variable matrix in adjacent columns, factor by factor. Both matrices were factored by the principal components method with the highest column r's placed in the diagonals of the correlation matrices as communality estimates. Varimax orthogonal rotations were performed on four and seven factors, respectively, to produce the data of Tables 2 and 3.[3] Significant loadings of $\pm .35$ or above are enclosed in parentheses in both tables.[4]

Inspection of the loading profiles in Table 3 reveals immediately the close similarity of each of the factors in the two matrices. The relative invariance of the factors was tested by

means of the coefficient of congruence suggested in Harmon,[5] producing values of 0.998 for Factor I, 0.932 for Factor II, 0.931 for Factor III, and 0.826 for Factor IV. Applying the criteria for evaluating this measure suggested by the writer elsewhere,[6] it appears that congruence is established for the first three factors and that Factor IV is "closely similar" in the two matrices. Since four ecological factors derived from a twenty-variable analysis for Helsinki remain invariant when a further analysis including more than twice as many variables is carried out, it is concluded that Hypothesis (1) has been confirmed for these data: ecological factors are invariant under the addition of the specified variables in Helsinki, 1960.

The logic of the evidence, of course, does not require that the argument run from the smaller matrix to the larger; it could as well move from the larger to the smaller, so that we might also conclude from Table 3 that ecological factors are invariant under the subtraction of the specified variables. Interestingly enough this is one of the conclusions of the only comparable study of ecological differentiation known to the writer, which used large and small factor matrices for a single city at one point in time. Schmidt and Tagashira find for Seattle " . . . that a reduced set of 10 variables represent sufficiently three basic factor dimensions existing in the original set of 42 variables."[7] Obviously, the findings from Seattle and from Helsinki mutually confirm the validity of the method. We are encouraged, therefore, in generalizing that *ecological factors are invariant under substitution, addition, and subtraction of variables.*

---

[3] In both the large and the small matrix, rotation included one factor with a latent root slightly below unity (0.96 and 0.94, respectively). As explained below, the addition of variables produced an interesting specification of Factor IV in the large matrix.

[4] The mean of the coefficients of correlation in the smaller matrix is slightly larger than that in the larger matrix. As a consequence, the estimated level of probability is $p = 0.01$ for the twenty-variable matrix, and $0.02 > p > 0.01$ for the forty-two-variable matrix, when the method of estimation suggested by Harry H. Harmon in *Modern Factor Analysis* on pp. 439, 441 (Chicago: University of Chicago Press, 1960), is applied.

---

[5] Ibid., p. 257, formula 12.31.

[6] Sweetser, "Ecological Factors in Suburb and Metropolitan Core: Boston, 1950 and 1960" (paper presented at Eastern Sociological Society Annual Meeting, April 11, 1964).

[7] Calvin F. Schmidt and Kiyoshi Tagashira, "Ecological and Demographic Indices: A Methodological Analysis," *Demography*, I (1964), pp. 194–211. The fact that Schmidt and Tagashira also included 42 variables in their larger matrix is purely fortuitous. The quotation is from a summary published in *Population Index*, XXIX (July 1963): 232.

TABLE 3.   Comparisons of Four Ecological Factors in a Twenty-Variable and a Forty-Two Variable Matrix,[a] Seventeen Identical Variables: Helsinki, 1960

| | | Factor loadings[b] and Coefficients of Congruence | | | | | | | |
| | | Factor I Socio-Economic Status | | Factor II Progeniture | | Factor III "Urbanism" | | Factor IV Residentialism | |
No.	Name	20-var	42-var	20-var	42-var	20-var	42-var	20-var	42-var
40	Low educational status	(−99)	(−97)	−02	−09	−07	−09	−05	−07
35	Male professional-mgr. occs.	(98)	(96)	06	07	−02	04	09	10
41	Adult college status	(97)	(95)	05	11	05	08	06	06
7	Swedish-speaking Finns	(73)	(75)	−28	−20	−16	−30	−25	−21
28	Room crowding	(−85)	(−86)	04	−01	(36)	31	−13	−12
37	Male clerical service occs.	(73)	(76)	−22	−05	(41)	31	−01	−13
29	Housing defects	(−72)	(−78)	30	12	(−42)	(−39)	−22	02
30	Detached dwellings	(−50)	(−51)	22	06	(−67)	(−50)	28	(39)
5	Proportion male	(−55)	(−53)	(44)	(37)	(−35)	−26	25	03
20	Born in Helsinki	(39)	32	(58)	26	−11	−05	−02	(35)
17	Fertility	−12	−19	(83)	(73)	−08	−06	14	25
1	Elementary school age	−07	−14	(75)	24	−14	16	−05	05
18	Non-family population	12	17	(−73)	(−53)	11	08	−25	(−36)
2	Retirement age	24	23	(−67)	(−55)	03	−13	(−47)	−17
31	New housing	14	16	(52)	(52)	06	21	(65)	(45)
34	Working women	12	17	−16	05	(82)	(73)	08	−22
26	Home ownership	14	15	12	17	−10	05	(76)	(73)
	Coefficients of congruence	.998		.932		.931		.826	

[a] Principal components factorization with highest r's in diagonals; varimax orthogonal rotations of four factors and seven factors for 20- and 42-variables matrices, respectively.

[b] Loadings at ± .35 or higher are statistically significant at p = .01 in the 20-variable matrix; and at .02 > p > .01 in the 42-variable matrix. These significant loadings are enclosed in parentheses.

FACTORIAL STRUCTURE OF HELSINKI'S SOCIAL ECOLOGY

The four substantive hypotheses may be considered in relation to the forty-two-variable, six-factor matrix of Table 2. The data are reorganized in Table 4 to list significant loadings, factor by factor, in order of magnitude. In examining these data, the bi-polarity of the ecological variables used should be kept in mind; interpretation may sometimes be facilitated by reflecting the sign. Negative loadings for, say, proportion male (variable 5) or new housing (variable 31) could be interpreted with complete propriety as *positive* loadings for proportion female or older housing.

Hypothesis (2)

This hypothesis is confirmed. Three of the fundamental dimensions of Helsinki's ecological structure as revealed in the larger matrix are indeed *socio-economic status* (Factor I), *progeniture* (Factor II), and *feminine careerism*, a specific aspect of "urbanism" (Factor III). Moreover, Factor I is, by far, the strongest of the ecological dimensions in Helsinki, as shown by the fact that it accounts for no less than 35.2 per cent of the common factor variance of the six factors (Table 2). Factor II, with 16.1 per cent of the common factor variance, is less than half as potent but is still the second strongest factor among the six. Factor III, however, although

TABLE 4. Significant Loadings of Forty-Two Variables on Six Factors, Helsinki, 1960[a]

Variable Name	No.	Positive	Negative
Socio-Economic Status (Factor I)			
* Low educational status	40		−.97
Blue collar occupations	39		−.96
* Male prof.-mgr. occs.	35	.96	
* Adult college status	41	.95	
Academic youth	42	.91	
* Room crowding	28		−.86
* Housing defects	29		−.78
Work downtown	22	.76	
Floor area per dwelling	33	.76	
* Male cler.-serv. occs.	37	.76	
* Swedish-speaking Finns	7	.75	
Female prof.-mgr. occs.	36	.72	
Female cler.-Serv. occs.	38	.71	
Unattached male	6		−.65
1- & 2-room dwellings	27		−.53
* Proportion male	5		−.53
* Detached dwellings	30		−.51

Variable Name	No.	Positive	Negative
Progeniture (Factor II)			
Pre-adolescent age ratio	4	.85	
* Fertility	17	.73	
Middle age ratio	3	.73	
Swedish middle age ratio	9	.69	
Commutation	23	.56	
* Retirement age	2		−.55
* Non-family population	18		−.53
* New dwellings	31	.52	
Swedish fertility	11	.51	
Males married, wife pres.	12	.48	
Husband-wife families	13	.40	
Female-"Child" families	25		−.39
* Proportion male	5	.37	

TABLE 4. (Continued)

| Variable | | Factor Loadings | |
Name	No.	Positive	Negative
Career women (Factor III)			
*Working women	34	.73	
*Detached dwellings	30		−.50
Floor area per dwelling	33		−.42
*Female prof.-mgr. occs.	36	.39	
*Housing defects	29		−.39
Established familism (Factor V)			
Children per couple	15	.92	
Large families	14	.91	
*Elementary school age	1	.82	
Preschoolers per couple	16	.62	
*Born in Helsinki	20	.47	
*New housing	8	.44	
*Fertility	17	.41	
Males married, wife present	12	.35	

| Variable | | Factor Loadings | |
Name	No.	Positive	Negative
Residentialism (Factor IV)			
Day population	24		−.85
Floor area in dwelling	32	.84	
Work near home	21		−.84
*Home ownership	26	.73	
Commutation	23	.52	
Males married, wife present	12	.50	
*New housing	31	.45	
*Detached dwellings	30	.39	
*1- and 2-room dwellings	27		−.36
*Non-family population	18		−.36
*Born in Helsinki	20	.35	
Postgeniture (Factor VI)			
Husband-wife families	13		−.79
Female-"child" families	25	.79	
Swedish adult males	10		−.68
*Retirement age	2	.56	
*Proportion male	5		−.55
*New housing	31		−.51
1- and 2-room dwellings	27	.48	
*Middle age ratio	3		−.40
*Elementary school age	1		−.35

* Variables also in 20-variable matrix marked with asterisk (*). See Table 3
a Level of significance: .02 > p > .01.

clearly manifest, is the weakest of the six factors, with only 7.6 per cent of the variance. Each of these factors deserves a brief comment.

Factor I, *socio-economic status*, retains in the large matrix exactly the same character it presented in the smaller one. A close scrutiny of the loadings of additional variables on this factor (seen most conveniently in Table 4) brings out the substantive invariance of the factor neatly. Variable 27 (one- and two-room dwellings), which loads negatively, and variable 33 (floor area per dwelling), which loads positively, amplify our understanding of the negative loading of variable 28 (room-crowding) on the dimension of socio-economic status. Similarly, the addition of three variables measuring the occupational status of women (variable 39, combining male and female blue collar occupations, and variables 36 and 38, female professional-managerial and clerical-service occupations) shows that the relation of both sexes, occupationally, to Factor I is similar. In a city like Helsinki, with the male and female labor force almost exactly equal in size, this is an important confirmation.

Again, the relative femininity of higher status areas in Helsinki, shown first by a significant negative loading of variable 5 (proportion of total population male), is reinforced by the negative loading of variable 6 (unattached males); and the high positive loading of variable 42 (academic youth) on Factor I confirms the importance of high educational status of youth as well as of adults in this ecological dimension.

Finally, the substantial positive loading (0.76) of variable 22 (work downtown) adds one new bit of information: the white collar workers, who are more numerous in the higher status residential areas than elsewhere in Helsinki, are especially likely to be employed in the central business district. For Factor I, then, what is gained from the expanded matrix is confirmation and specification of the characteristics of this fundamental dimension of socio-economic status.

Factor II, *progeniture*, is similarly confirmed. The positive loading of the preadolescent age

ratio (variable 4) on this factor is especially indicative. Since the variable is defined as the per cent of population age 0–14 who are 0–6 years old, this might be called a "pre-school" variable. Its strength (0.85) accentuates the young familism we sought to suggest in naming the factor. Equally interesting is the failure of such new variables as large families (14) and children per couple (15) to attain significant loadings of *progeniture* (loadings are 0.20 and 0.01, respectively; see Table 2). Space does not permit further elaboration, but scrutiny of the data will show that for this factor the additional variables serve to confirm and broaden inferences derived from the smaller matrix.

Factor III, *feminine careerism*, although it gained only two new significant loadings in the large matrix, became more specifically subject to interpretation. In the analysis of the twenty-variable matrix, Factor III had been seen as "somewhat ambiguous," and it was identified as "urbanism" partly on the ground that this was a somewhat ambiguous term.[8] It is the significant positive loading of female professional-managerial occupations (variable 36) on Factor III, coupled with the negative (though non-significant) loading of variable 38 (female clerical-service occupations) at –0.27 which suggests the special character of this factor. Not only working women but working women in the higher rather than the lower status white collar occupations mark the factor; hence *feminine careerism* seems to describe the particular aspect of urbanism it represents.

Hypothesis (3)
This hypothesis is also confirmed. This fourth factor of the twenty-variable matrix is clarified

---

[8] In Sweetser, "Factor Structure as Ecological Structure in Helsinki and Boston," the conclusion was stated as follows: "Factor III is somewhat ambiguous. However, the occurrence . . . of high or fairly high positive loadings for working women, and negative loadings for high school [in three comparable twenty-variable matrices—two for Helsinki and one for one Metropolitan Boston] suggests that aspects of an urban type of social structure are involved in this factor, and the label "urbanism" (itself somewhat ambiguous) is therefore applied to it."

by additional variables and changed loadings and emerges as the third strongest factor in the rotated matrix, accounting for 14.6 per cent of the (six factor) common factor variance (see Table 2). Not only did Factor IV add significant loadings for six new variables, but the vector reorientation in the larger matrix increased the loadings for three variables to the level of significance: variable 18, non-family population loading negatively; and variables 30 (detached dwellings) and 20 (born in Helsinki) loading positively. At the same time the new vector reduced the negative loading of variable 2 (retirement age) below the level of significance (see Table 3). Substantial positive loadings of home ownership (variable 26) and new housing (variable 31) are retained in the large matrix.

But the three highest loadings on Factor IV are for new variables, and among them, they provide the necessary additional clues for its interpretation. Variable 24 (proportion of the *daytime* population economically active) and variable 21 (proportion of the *resident* population working near home) both load negatively at –0.85 and –0.84, respectively. Variable 32 (percent of total enclosed floor area in dwellings) loads positively at 0.84 on Factor IV.

Putting these and other attributes shown in Table 4 together, it is evident that areas strong in this factor are characterized by an emphasis on the residential use of land, tending to the exclusion of other uses; that the daytime population is residential rather than economically active, with work tending to be relegated to other areas; that home ownership, and, to a lesser extent, new, detached, non-small dwellings occupied by husband and wife families are typical. In the United States, this might describe a factor of "suburbanism," and, to some extent, this label would be appropriate for Factor IV in Helsinki, too. However, the greater frequency of apartment ownership in Finland, coupled with the construction of much new in-town housing during the last decade and a half, means that the factor also operates in the urban core. *Residentialism* therefore, seems an appropriate identification for Factor IV, which clus-

ters certain attributes more frequently, perhaps, in the suburbs but may also mark in-town residential areas.

Hypothesis (4)

The hypothesis "that additional factors in the larger matrix will relate to specialized phases of urbanism or familism" is also confirmed by the data, but not in exactly the manner expected. In fact, the new factors are both best interpreted as factors of familism, although by reflection they should be contorted to a semblance of "urbanism" factors.[9] Factor V is clearly the aspect of familism missing from *progeniture* and is readily interpreted as *established familism*. Accounting for 13.8 percent of the six-factor common variance (see Table 2), it is a reasonably strong factor, with eight significant loadings, all positive, and ranging from 0.92 to 0.35 for variables 15, 14, 16, 17, 20, 8, 17, and 12, in that order. A mere listing of the variables establishes the identification of the factor; children per couple, large families, elementary school age, pre-schoolers per couple, born in Helsinki, Swedish-speaking pupils, fertility, males married with wife present.

Factor VI is not so obvious, but its nature seems established by the nine significantly loaded variables of Tables 2 and 4. Variables 13 and 25 loading negatively and positively, respectively, on the factor at 0.79 define the family type involved as *lacking* husband-wife families and marked by females-"child" (any age) families.[10] Variables 10 and 5 establish the femininity of the factor by their negative loadings on proportions male at –0.68 for the adult

---

[9] Like the ecological variables, the six rotated factors are bi-polar. Interpretation, therefore, requires considering meanings of the factors as they might appear with signs of loadings reversed. Although we were seeking a factor which could justly be labeled "urbanism," it was our conclusion that interpretation of Factors V and VI as familism factors is the only appropriate one for the Helsinki data.

[10] These families lack male heads but might include, for example, an elderly widow and her middle-aged spinster daughter, as well as a divorced young mother and her child. The variable cannot, therefore, be equated with "families lacking male head" in the ordinary sense which implies also the presence of young children.

Swedish-speaking population and at –0.55 for the total population. The elderliness marking that factor and the relative scarcity of children are manifest in a positive loading of 0.56 for variable 2 (retirement age) and the negative loadings of –0.40 and –0.35 for variables 3 and 1 (the middle age ratio-per cent of those 20–64 who are under 40 years old and the elementary school age population).

Finally, the relative scarcity of new housing (variable 31 loads at –0.51) and the prevalence of one- and two-room dwellings (variable 27 loads positively at 0.48) associate older, small dwellings with the factor. In combination, these characteristics may be interpreted as indicating a late stage of familism overlapping the "stage of the empty nest" and a later stage of retirement and senescence. We designate this factor "progeniture" and see it as the final aspect of ecological familism.

Hypothesis (5)

Although negative, this hypothesis has special significance for the development of ecological theory, since it asserts that "ethnicity"—which Tryon,[11] Shevky, Williams, and Bell,[12] and Schmidt and Tagashira,[13] among others, have correctly identified as a fundamental dimension of ecological differentiation in American cities—is *not* a meaningful factor in Helsinki. The evidence is clear. There is only one ethnic minority group of any size in Helsinki, the 14.5 per cent of the city's population who speak Swedish as their principal language. Together with the Finnish-speaking majority, this group constitutes 99.3 per cent of Helsinki's population. Yet, although five variables specific to the Swedish-speaking population were included in

a forty-two-variable analysis (variables 7–11, Table 1), not even a suggestion of a meaningful Swedish-speaking ethnic factor emerged. Each of these five "ethnic" variables loads significantly on one factor, and on one factor only. And four of the five significant loadings serve merely to confirm the character of the factor as encompassing the Swedish-speaking along with the majority population. Swedish fertility and Swedish youthful middle age load positively on *progeniture* (variables 9 and 11, Factor II in Table 2); Swedish-speaking pupils (variable 8) loads positively on *established familism*, Factor V; Swedish adult masculinity (variable 10) loads negatively on *postgeniture*, Factor VI.

In short, the one comment that can be made on the position of the Swedish-speaking ethnic minority in the ecological differentiation of Helsinki's residential areas is to note their tendency to be more numerous in higher status areas (variable 7; Swedish-speaking Finns, loads positively at 0.75 on Factor I, *socio-economic status*). These findings confirm, from a wide spectrum of variables, the conclusion drawn by the writer from a study of "Educational Status in the Statistical Areas of Helsinki":

> As between language groupings, the Swedish-speaking minority has a higher average [educational] status in all city areas, a fact which arises from the cultural history of this group, which in the past was the dominant managerial and governing elite. Today, however . . . higher educational status for both Swedish- and Finnish-speaking groups is found in the same areas. Ecologically the pattern is dominated by status differences, with little or no segregation by language groups apparent. . . .[14]

For ecological theory, the lesson is plain: variables which are of paramount importance in one urban sociocultural setting may be of no consequence in another. Clearly, a universal

[11] Robert C. Tryon, *Identification of Social Area by Cluster Analysis* (Berkeley: University of California Press, 1955).

[12] Cf. Eshref Shevky and Wendell Bell, *Social Area Analysis: Theory, Illustrative Applications and Computational Procedures* (Stanford: Stanford University Press, 1955), and Eshref Shevky and Marilyn Williams, *The Social Area of Los Angeles* (Berkeley: University of California Press, 1949).

[13] Schmidt and Tagashira, op. cit.

[14] Sweetser, "Koulutustaso Paakaupungin Eri Alueilla" ("Educational Status in the Statistical Areas of Helsinki"), *Helsinki City Statistical Monthly Review* (October 1963), p. 334. (English summary.)

theory of urban ecological structure must consider such basic differences in elucidating the fundamental dimensions of urban ecological differentiation as it manifests itself under varying conditions in various parts of the urban-industrial world.

SUMMARY AND CONCLUSIONS

Methodologically, we conclude that the general invariance of ecological factors under substitution, addition, and subtraction of variables is established by our Helsinki data. Substantively, we have found that Helsinki's social ecology is well described by a factor model which identifies six fundamental dimensions in the differentiation of the city's residential areas: *socioeconomic status, progeniture, feminine careerism, residentialism, established familism,* and *postgeniture.* "Ethnicity" is conspicuously absent from this list. Both the methodological and the substantive conclusions are based on the empirical evidence derived from comparison and analysis of a twenty-variable and an expanded, forty-two-variable orthogonally rotated factor matrix for the seventy statistical areas of the city of Helsinki as of 1960.

The differences (such as the lack of an ethnic factor) and the similarities between Helsinki's ecological structure and that of American cities are striking, as has been brought out in another paper.[15] Indeed, the very interesting discovery that there are no less than three factors of familism in Helsinki, each related to a different stage of the family life cycle, suggests that the variables of aging and the passage of time ought to be more self-consciously considered in the theoretical deliberations of social ecologists. Patterns of family formation and levels of fertility may change relatively quickly, as has happened in both the United States and Finland during the past two decades.

Some of the features of familism in Helsinki social ecology evidently relate to the subsidence of the Finnish birth rate during the 1950's, followed by a much shorter post-war baby-boom than the United States experienced.[16] It is perhaps for this reason that the Helsinki familism factors so clearly distinguish stages in the family life cycle. But the general importance of the finding is that it emphasizes the relative instability of family demographic characteristics and reminds us that, while we may expect to find familism in some form as an important ecological dimension in any city, the form may be expected to vary from place to place and from time to time.

Just as striking is the substantive stability of socio-economic status as an ecological dimension. It is dominant and identical in the large and the small Helsinki matrices. As shown elsewhere, it is dominant and virtually identical in Boston and Helsinki;[17] in the suburbs and the metropolitan core of Boston itself; and in Boston in 1960 compared to 1950.[18] Unlike familism, then, this factor appears to be related to relatively permanent and very slowly changing characteristics of people and the areas they occupy.

These observations raise many questions about comparative ecological structure and about the changing conditions which may bring about changes in patterns of ecological differentiation. Fortunately, our methodological conclusion offers a hopeful approach to further studies of ecological differentiation on a new plane of objectivity. For the demonstrated invariance of ecological factors means that the techniques of modern factor analysis may be

---

[15] Sweetser, "Factor Structure as Ecological Structure in Helsinki and Boston."

[16] Differences between United States and Finnish postwar fertility are discussed in Sweetser and Paavo Piepponen, "Nuoret ikäluokat Suomessa ja Yhdysvalloissa" ("The Youthful Population of Finland and the United States"), *Yearbook of Population Research in Finland 1963–1964* (Helsinki: Population Research Institute, 1964), pp. 7–21.

[17] Sweetser, "Factor Structure as Ecological Structure in Helsinki and Boston."

[18] Sweetser, "Ecological Factors in Suburb and Metropolitan Core: Boston 1950 and 1960."

applied with confidence to the domain of ecological variables to produce a consistent, objective description of the fundamental dimensions underlying ecological structure.[19] This in turn means that (1) systematic cross-national and intra-national comparisons of residential area differentiation are now possible on a non-ethnocentric basis; (2) the relationship of numerous variables to fundamental ecological dimensions can be determined by adding the variables to the factorization and interpreting the new variables in terms of the fundamental dimensions; and (3) fundamental dimensions derived as ecological factors from large matrices can be expressed adequately by fewer variables, thus achieving a simplicity desirable for some kinds of analysis.

The broad applicability, objectivity, and flexibility attained by using factor structure as a model for ecological structure should usher in a new era of ecological research, leading ultimately to a broadening and deepening of theories of social ecology and urban sociology and to a clearer understanding of the relationships between the characteristics of residential areas and the behavior of their residents.

---

[19] Throughout this paper, we use the term "modern factor analysis" as does Harmon (op. cit.), to indicate the objective analytic procedures made available during the past few years of mathematical development and the increased accessibility of high-speed computers.

Social Status Differentiation and Segregation

The last two sections of this book are concerned with urban residential segregation patterns. The papers in this part focus upon the segregation and residential locational patterns of social status groups, while the papers in the last section are devoted to racial and ethnic segregation patterns. Perhaps the most central notion of the segregation literature is that the social distance separating various groups is reflected in the degree of physical distance among them in their residential separation. The first paper in this section, by Duncan and Duncan (32), is an analysis of the residential distribution of various occupational groups in Chicago. The data deal with four aspects of the residential patterning of the occupational groups: (1) the degree of residential segregation of each group in relation to all others; (2) the degree of dissimilarity in residential distribution between all pairs of occupational groups; (3) the relative concentration of each occupational group in low rent areas, and (4) the degree of centralization of each group. The data clearly support the social distance proposition and also show the direct status gradient characteristic of industrial cities.

The next three papers examine the relationship between social and spatial distance in other societies. Mehta's paper (33) focuses upon income, education, and occupation in the residential patterning of a large Indian city. His findings are very consistent with those for other cities. For all three status indicators, as the social distance increases between pairs of groups so too does their degree of residential dissimilarity. Also, the most segregated groups are those whose status is least ambiguous—

part vi

those at the top and at the bottom of the status pyramid. The location of the various groups is typical of that found for nonindustrial cities in that the upper status groups are centralized while the lower status groups are decentralized.

Schwirian and Rico (34) investigate status segregation and centralization in Puerto Rico's metropolitan areas. Essentially, they point out that for all three indexes of social status—occupation, education, and income—the typical patterns of dissimilarity between pairs of groups and the segregation of specific groups appear in each of the three metropolitan areas. However, the centralization patterns differ among the three communities and these differences are explained in terms of a diffusion model of social change. Latif's (35) analysis of status segregation in Alexandria, Egypt, also includes a consideration of the residential differentiation of major religious groups as well. Once again in another very different cultural setting the findings corroborate the basic notion that social and physical distance are highly related.

The comparative segregation of status groups in the cities and the suburbs is the topic of the paper by Fine, Glenn, and Monts (36). Their study focuses upon the cities and suburbs of eight U.S. metropolitan areas at two points in time. Essentially, they report that the differences in the occupational distribution between cities and suburbs are small and that the indexes of residential dissimilarity between pairs of specific occupational groups were higher in the cities than in the suburbs thereby indicating that the suburbs are not much more homogeneous status-wise than are the cities.

The last two papers in this section focus upon patterns of change in highly segregated areas of large cities. Wolf and Lebeaux (37) discuss the effect of urban renewal upon poor residential areas. They conclude that major differences among slum areas exist in the vitality of social relations, the satisfactions gained from the neighborhood, and the likely impact of change upon local residents. Bahr (38) examines the disappearance of skid rows in American cities in the final selection of this section. It seems that the decline of skid row reflects more of a dispersement of its population to other areas than a diminution of the number of homeless individuals.

32

OTIS DUDLEY DUNCAN
BEVERLY DUNCAN

Residential Distribution and Occupational Stratification

The idea behind this paper was forcibly stated—in fact, somewhat overstated—by Robert E. Park: "It is because social relations are so frequently and so inevitably correlated with spatial relations; because physical distances so frequently are, or seem to be, the indexes of social distances, that statistics have any significance whatever for sociology. And this is true, finally, because it is only as social and psychical facts can be reduced to, or correlated with, spatial facts that they can be measured at all."[1]

This study finds a close relationship between spatial and social distances in a metropolitan community. It suggests that a systematic consideration of the spatial aspect of stratification phenomena, though relatively neglected by students of the subject,[2] should be a primary focus of urban stratification studies. Aside from demonstrating the relevance of human ecology to the theory of social organization, the study offers further evidence for the suitability of a particular set of methodological techniques for research in comparative urban ecology. These techniques are adaptable to a wide variety of problems in urban ecological structure, permit economical and objective comparisons among communities, and thus overcome some of the indeterminacy of a strictly cartographic approach. The techniques are here applied to only one metropolitan community, Chicago; however, comparative studies, conducted on an exploratory basis, indicate their ability to produce significant results.

DATA AND METHOD

The sources of data for this study, except as noted otherwise, were the published volume of 1950 census-tract statistics for Chicago and adjacent areas[3] (coextensive with the Chicago Metropolitan District, as delineated in 1940), and the census-tract summary punch cards for this area obtained from the Bureau of the Census. The ecological analysis pertains to employed males fourteen years old and over, classified into the eight major occupation groups listed in the tables below. The occupation groups disregarded in this analysis (farmers and farm managers, farm laborers, private household workers, and occupation not reported) include only twenty-one thousand of the one and a half million employed males in the Metropolitan District.

Reprinted from *The American Journal of Sociology*, LX (March 1955): 493–503, by permission of the authors and The University of Chicago Press.

The authors wish to acknowledge the financial support of the Social Science Research Committee and the Population Research and Training Center of the University of Chicago.

[1] "The Urban Community as a Spatial Pattern and a Moral Order," in *The Urban Community*, ed. Ernest W. Burgess (Chicago: University of Chicago Press, 1926), p. 18.

[2] See, however, the discussion of "dwelling area" by W. Lloyd Warner et al., *Social Class in America* (Chicago: Science Research Associates, 1949), pp. 151–154.

[3] *1950 United States Census of Population*, Bulletin P–D10.

A portion of the analysis is carried through with the census tract as the area unit. There are 1,178 census tracts in the Metropolitan District, of which 935 are in the city of Chicago and 243 in the adjacent area. The remainder of the analysis rests on a scheme of zones and sectors, delineated rather arbitrarily. Tracts were assigned to circular zones, concentric to the center of the city at State and Madison streets, with one-mile intervals up to fourteen miles, two-mile intervals up to twenty-eight miles, and with residual categories of tracts more than twenty-eight miles from the city center and tracts in the adjacent area too large to be classified by zones. The latter category contains only 1.4 per cent of the employed males. Five sectors were established, with boundaries approximating radial lines drawn from the city center. The North Shore sector runs along Lake Michigan through such suburbs as Skokie, Evanston, Lake Forest, and Waukegan; the Northwest sector extends through Park Ridge and Des Plaines to Arlington Heights; the West sector includes the suburbs of Cicero, Oak Park, and Berwyn, running out as far as Wheaton and Naperville; the Southwest sector is approximately bisected by a line running through Blue Island, Harvey, and Chicago Heights to Park Forest; and the South Shore sector runs along Lake Michigan through the Indiana suburbs of East Chicago, Hammond, Gary and East Gary. Combining the zone and sector schemes yielded a set of 104 zone-sector segments; that is, area units averaging about ten times the size of a census tract, though with considerable variation in area and population.

The spatial "distance" between occupation groups, or more precisely the difference between their areal distributions, is measured by the *index of dissimilarity*. To compute this index, one calculates for each occupation group the percentage of all workers in that group residing in each area unit (tract or zone-sector segment). The index of dissimilarity between two occupation groups is then one-half the sum of the ab-solute values of the differences between the respective distributions, taken area by area. In the accompanying hypothetical example the index of dissimilarity between occupations A and B is 20 per cent (i.e., 40/2). This may be interpreted as a measure of displacement: 20 percent of the workers in occupation A would have to move to a different area in order to make their distribution identical with that of occupation B.

When the index of dissimilarity is computed between one occupation group and all other occupations combined (i.e., total employed males except those in the given occupation group), it is referred to as an *index of segregation*. [4] An equivalent and more convenient means of computing the segregation index is to compute the index of dissimilarity between the given occupation group and total employed males (i.e., all occupations), "adjusting" the result by dividing by one minus the proportion of the total male employed labor force included in that occupation group.

Area		A	B	Diff.
1		10%	15%	5%
2		20	15	5
3		40	25	15
4		30	45	15
	Total	100%	100%	40%

The indexes of segregation and dissimilarity were computed on both a tract basis and a zone sector segment basis to determine the effect of the size of the area unit on the results. While the indexes for tracts are uniformly higher than for zone-sector segments, this effect can be disregarded for purposes of determining the relative positions of the occupation groups. The product-moment correlation between the two sets of segregation indexes in Table 2 is

---

[4] For discussion of the index of dissimilarity as a segregation index see Otis Dudley Duncan and Beverly Duncan, "A Methodological Analysis of Segregation Indexes," *American Sociological Review*, XX (April 1955): 210–217.

.96. The correlation between the two sets of dissimilarity indexes in Table 3 is .98, with the segment-based index (s) related to the tract-based index (t) by the regression equation, $s = .8t - 1.3$. These results indicate that for the kind of problem dealt with here the larger, and hence less homogeneous, unit is as serviceable as the smaller one. This suggests that some of the recent concern about census-tract homogeneity may be misplaced. [5]

The *index of low-rent concentration* is obtained by (1) classifying tracts into intervals according to the median monthly rental of tenant-occupied dwelling units; (2) computing the percentage distribution by rent intervals for each occupation group and for all occupations combined; (3) cumulating the distributions, from low to high rent; (4) calculating the quantity $\Sigma X_{i-1}Y_4 - \Sigma X_iY_{i-1}$, where X_i is the cumulated percentage of the given occupation through the ith rent interval, Y_i is the cumulated percentage of all occupations combined, and the summation is over all rent intervals; and, finally, (5) "adjusting" the result (as for the segregation index) to obtain an index equivalent to the one obtained by comparing the given occupation group with all other occupations combined. This index varies between 100 and − 100, with positive values indicating a tendency for residences of the given occupation group to be in areas of relatively low rent and with negative values indicating relative concentration in high-rent areas.

The *index of centralization* is computed in the same fashion, except that tracts are ordered by distance from the center of the city, that is, are classified according to the zonal scheme. A negative index of centralization signifies that the given occupation group tends to be "decentralized," or on the average located farther away from the city center than all other occupations, while a positive index is obtained for a relatively "centralized" occupation.[6]

OCCUPATION AND SOCIOECONOMIC STATUS

Selected nonecological indicators of the relative socioeconomic status of the major occupation groups are shown in Table 1. The professional and managerial groups clearly have the highest socioeconomic rank, while operatives, service workers, and laborers are clearly lowest in socioeconomic status. The ranking by socioeconomic level would probably be agreed on by most social scientists. The major occupation groups correspond roughly with the Alba Edwards scheme of "social-economic groups." Edwards does not separate sales workers and clerical workers by "social-economic group," and the group of service workers, except private household, contains individual occupations variously classified by Edwards as skilled, semi-skilled, and unskilled, predominantly the latter two.

A ranking in terms of median income results in two reversals in rank. The 1949 median income of male managerial workers in the Chicago Standard Metropolitan Area was about $500 greater than that of professional workers, although both were substantially above that for sales workers. The median income for the craftsmen-foremen group was about $500 higher than that for clerical workers. In fact, the median income for the craftsmen-foremen group was only slightly below that for sales workers, whereas the median income for clerical workers was only slightly above that for operatives.

[5] Jerome K. Myers, "Note on the Homogeneity of Census Tracts: A Methodological Problem in Urban Ecological Research," *Social Forces*, XXXII (May 1954): 364–66; Joel Smith, "A Method for the Classification of Areas on the Basis of Demographically Homogeneous Populations," *American Sociological Review*, XIX (April 1954): 201–207.

[6] The indexes of low-rent concentration and of centralization are formally identical with the index of urbanization proposed in Otis Dudley Duncan, "Urbanization and Retail Specialization," *Social Forces*, XXX (March 1952): 267–271. The formula given here is a simplification of the one presented there; and the area units and principle of ordering are, of course, different.

TABLE 1. Selected Indicators of Socioeconomic Status of the Major Occupation
Groups

Major Occupation Group*	Median Income in 1949[†]	Median School Years Completed[‡]	Edwards' Socioeconomic Group[§]	Per Cent Nonwhite[‖]
Professional, Technical, and Kindred Workers	$4,387	16+	1	2.7
Managers, Officials, and Proprietors, except farm	4,831	12.2	2	2.2
Sales Workers	3,698	12.4 ⎫	3	⎰ 2.8
Clerical and Kindred Workers	3,132	12.2 ⎭		⎱ 7.4
Craftsmen, Foremen, and Kindred Workers	3,648	9.5	4	4.9
Operatives and Kindred Workers	3,115	8.9	5	12.4
Service Workers, except private household	2,635	8.8	5–6	23.0
Laborers, except farm and mine	2,580	8.4	6	27.4

* Does not include farmers and farm managers, private household workers, farm laborers, and occupation not reported.

[†] For males in the experienced labor force of the Chicago Standard Metropolitan Area, 1950. Source: *1950 U.S. Census of Population,* Bulletin P–C13, Table 78.

[‡] For employed males twenty-five years old and over, in the North and West, 1950. Source: *1950 U.S. Census of Population,* Special Report P–E No. 5B, Table 11.

[§] Approximate equivalents. Source: Alba M. Edwards, *Comparative Occupation Statistics for the United States, 1870 to 1940* (Washington, D.C.: Government Printing Office, 1943).

[‖] For employed males in the Chicago Metropolitan District, 1950. Based on nonwhites residing in census tracts containing 250 or more nonwhite population in 1950. These tracts include 95.8 per cent of all nonwhite males in the Metropolitan District.

However, in median school years completed, professional workers clearly rank first, while there is little difference in the medians for the managerial, sales, and clerical groups. The median drops sharply, over 2.5 years, for the craftsmen-foremen group and declines further for each group in the order of the initial listing.

In the Chicago Metropolitan District the proportion of nonwhites in an occupation group appears to be closely related to its socioeconomic status. The proportion is very low in the professional, managerial, and sales groups, but it is somewhat higher for clerical workers than for the craftsmen-foremen group. Increasing proportions are observed for operatives, service workers, and laborers, in order.

The suggested ranking is in general conformity with the National Opinion Research Center's data on popular attitudes toward occupations, except that sales occupations appear to rank below clerical and craft occupations in the NORC results.[7] An inadequate sampling of occupational titles within the sales group may account in part for the low prestige rating of sales workers obtained by the NORC. Furthermore, their data do not differentiate prestige ratings by sex. Particularly in a metropolitan area, the male sales worker group is more heavily weighted with such occupations as advertising, insurance, and real estate agents and sales representatives of wholesale and manufacturing concerns than is the case for female sales workers, among whom retail sales clerks are the large majority.

The failure of different bases of ranking to give identical results has been discussed by

[7] National Opinion Research Center, "Jobs and Occupations: A Popular Evaluation," *Opinion News,* IX (September 1, 1947): 3–13.

writers on stratification in terms of "disaffinity of strata" and "status disequilibrium."[8] The reversals in rank between the professional and managerial groups and the clerical and crafts workers are most frequent. The upshot seems to be that no one ranking can be accepted as sufficient for all purposes. The examination of residential patterns discloses other instances of disequilibrium, which are of interest both in themselves and as clues to the interpretation of those already noted.

RESIDENTIAL PATTERNS

Four aspects of the residential patterning of occupation groups are considered. The first is the degree of residential segregation of each major occupation group with respect to all others, that is, the extent to which an occupation group is separated residentially from the remainder of the employed labor force. The second is the degree of dissimilarity in residential distribution among major occupation groups, that is, the extent to which pairs of occupation groups isolate themselves from one another. The third aspect is the degree of residential concentration of each occupation group in areas characterized by relatively low rents. Finally, the degree of centralization of each major occupation group (i.e., the extent to which an occupation group is concentrated toward the center of the metropolitan community) is examined. In each case the spatial patterning of the residences is considered in relation to socioeconomic level.

A clear relationship of the ranking of major occupation groups by socioeconomic status and by degree of residential segregation is shown in Table 2. Listed in the order given there, the indexes of residential segregation form a U-shaped pattern. The highest values are ob-

served for the professionals and laborers and the lowest value for the clerical workers. The degree of residential segregation varies only slightly among the professional, managerial, and sales groups; however, it declines markedly for the clerical workers and then increases regularly for each successive group.

TABLE 2. Index of Residential Segregation of Each Major Occupation Group, for Employed Males in the Chicago Metropolitan District, 1950

Major Occupation Group*	By Census Tracts	By Zone-Sector Segments
Professional, Technical, and Kindred Workers	30	21
Managers, Officials, and Proprietors, except farm	29	20
Sales Workers	29	20
Clerical and Kindred Workers	13	9
Craftsmen, Foremen, and Kindred Workers	19	14
Operatives and Kindred Workers	22	16
Service Workers, except private household	24	20
Laborers, except farm and mine	35	29

* Does not include farmers and farm managers, private household workers, farm laborers, and occupation not reported.

This finding suggests that residential segregation is greater for those occupation groups with clearly defined status than for those groups whose status is ambiguous. The latter groups are necessarily subject to cross-pressures from the determinants of residential selection; for example, the clerical group has an income equivalent to that of operatives but the educational level of managerial workers.

To check the hypothesis that spatial distances among occupation groups parallel their social distances, the indexes of dissimilarity in residential distribution among major occupation groups are shown in Table 3. As previously indicated, a listing of major occupation

[8] Cf. Pitirim A. Sorokin, *Society, Culture, and Personality* (New York: Harper & Bros., 1947), pp. 289–294, on disaffinity of strata. On status disequilibrium cf. Emile Benoit-Smullyan, "Status, Status Types, and Status Interrelations," *American Sociological Review*, IX (April 1944): 154–161; Harold F. Kaufman, *Defining Prestige in a Rural Community* ("Sociometry Monograph," No. 10 [New York: Beacon House, 1946]).

TABLE 3.   Indexes of Dissimilarity in Residential Distribution among Major Occupation Groups, for Employed Males in the Chicago Metropolitan District, 1950

(Above diagonal, by census tracts; below diagonal, by zone-sector segments)

Major Occupation Group*	Major Occupation Group*							
	Prof., Tech., Kindred	Mgrs., Offs., Props.	Sales Wkrs.	Clerical, Kindred	Crafts-men, Foremen	Oper-atives, Kindred	Service, exc. Priv. Hshld.	Laborers, exc. Farm and Mine
Professional, Technical Kindred Workers		18	15	28	35	44	41	54
Managers, Officials, and Proprietors, except farm	8		13	28	33	41	40	52
Sales Workers	11	7		27	35	42	38	54
Clerical and Kindred Workers	20	18	17		16	21	24	38
Craftsmen, Foremen, Kindred Workers	26	23	25	12		17	35	35
Operatives, Kindred Workers	31	29	30	16	14		26	25
Service Workers, except private household	31	31	30	19	25	19		28
Laborers, except farm and mine	42	41	42	32	30	21	24	

* Does not include farmers and farm managers, private household workers, farm laborers, and occupation not reported.

groups by socioeconomic level can at best only roughly approximate a social distance scale. Similarly, a measure of dissimilarity in residential distribution can only approximate the spatial distance between groups—the index measures only the dissimilarity of the residential distributions with respect to a particular set of areas and is insensitive to other important aspects of the spatial pattern such as proximity of areas of concentration.

Nonetheless, the data in Table 3 indicate the essential correspondence of social and spatial distance among occupation groups. If it is assumed that the ordering of major occupation groups corresponds with increasing social distance (e.g., the social distance between professional and sales workers is greater than that between professional and managerial workers), and if it is assumed that the index of residential

dissimilarity approximates the spatial distance between the two groups, the expected pattern would be the following: Starting at any point on the diagonal, the indexes would increase reading up or to the right (down or to the left, in the case of the indexes below the diagonal, based on zone-sector segments). It is clear that the expected pattern, though not perfectly reproduced, essentially describes the observed pattern. The exceptions are few and for the most part can be explained hypothetically; such hypotheses provide clues for additional research.

The least dissimilarity is observed between professional and managerial workers, managerial and sales workers, and professional and sales workers. Furthermore, the dissimilarity of each of these groups with each other occupation group is of approximately the same degree. In fact, three of the inversions of the expected pattern concern the comparison between the managerial group and sales workers; that is, the residential dissimilarity of sales workers with craftsmen-foremen, operatives, and laborers is slightly greater than that of the managerial group, although their difference in terms of socioeconomic level is presumably less.

The residential distribution of clerical workers is more dissimilar to the distribution of sales workers, professional, and managerial workers than to that of the craftsmen or the operatives. Hence, although clerical workers are often grouped with professional, managerial, and sales workers as "white-collar," in terms of residential distribution they are more similar to the craftsmen and operatives than to the other white-collar groups.

The remaining inversions of the expected pattern involve service workers, except private household. One-fifth of these are "janitors and sextons." Presumably a substantial proportion of the janitors live at their place of work in apartment buildings housing workers in the higher status occupation groups.[9] It is hypothesized that this special circumstance accounts for the tendency of service workers to be less dissimilar to the higher status groups than expected on the basis of socioeconomic status.[10] At the same time the color composition of the service group presumably acts in the opposite direction. In so far as residential segregation on basis of color, cutting across occupational lines, exists within the metropolitan community, occupational status is rendered at least partially ineffective as a determinant of residential location. These factors, however, probably do not wholly explain the largest single deviation from the expected pattern, the much larger index of dissimilarity between craftsmen-foremen and

service workers than between clerical and service workers.

The first column of Table 4 shows the indexes of low-rent concentration of the occupation groups. Some caution must be exercised in interpreting them, since the tabulation on which they are based did not distinguish between male and female workers, and the indexes had to be computed for total employed persons rather than males. It is clear, nonetheless, that the degree of low-rent concentration is inversely related to the socioeconomic status of the occupation groups. All four of the white-collar occupation groups have negative indexes, signifying relative concentration in high-rent areas, whereas all four of the blue-collar groups have positive indexes. Again, there is a relatively sharp break between the clerical and the other three white-collar groups. The managerial group has a slightly greater index of low-rent concentration than the professional group, despite the higher income level of the former. It is even more striking that the low-rent concentration of craftsmen-foremen is substantially higher than for clerical workers, again the reverse of the relative positions on income. It can be shown that in 1940 the combined clerical and sales group tended to spend a larger proportion of its income for rent than did the group of craftsmen, foremen, and kindred workers. For example, for tenant families with wage and salary incomes between $2,000 and $3,000 in 1939, and without other income, 63 per cent of the families headed by a clerical or sales worker paid $40 per month or more rent, as compared with only 38 per cent of families whose heads were craftsmen, foremen, or kindred workers.[11]

The index of low-rent concentration for service workers, although positive, is low compared to the other blue-collar groups. This exception to the expected pattern no doubt has the same explanation as advanced above; that

---

[9] Cf. Ray Gold, "Janitors versus Tenants: A Status-Income Dilemma," *American Journal of Sociology*, LVII (March 1952): 486–493.

[10] This effect has been definitely noted in data, not shown here, for female private household workers, about one-fourth of whom "live in."

[11] Data for the Chicago Metropolitan District, 1940, from Table 11, *Families: Income and Rent, Population and Housing, 16th Census of the United States: 1940.*

TABLE 4.   Indexes of Low-Rent Concentration and of Centralization for Major Occupation Groups, Chicago Metropolitan District, 1950

Major Occupation Group*	Index of Low-Rent Concentration (Total Employed Persons)	Index of Centralization (Employed Males)					
		Metropolitan District	Sector				
			North Shore	North-west	West	South-west	South Shore
Professional, Technical and Kindred Workers	−32	−14	−15	−20	−29	−20	5
Managers, Officials, and Proprietors, except farm	−30	−12	−20	−16	−19	−15	1
Sales Workers	−25	− 5	−15	−12	−12	− 9	8
Clerical and Kindred Workers	− 9	5	7	2	1	5	9
Craftsmen, Foremen, and Kindred Workers	11	− 8	6	− 6	− 7	− 5	−26
Operatives, Kindred Workers	29	10	21	16	18	8	− 4
Service Workers, except private household	7	21	16	18	20	16	36
Laborers, except farm and mine	32	7	9	21	30	16	− 1

* Does not include farmers and farm managers, private household workers, farm laborers, and occupation not reported.

is, that a substantial proportion of service workers live in comparatively high status areas in connection with their place of employment.

The indexes of centralization of the occupation groups are given in Table 4, both for the Metropolitan District as a whole and within each of the five sectors. According to the Burgess zonal hypothesis, there is an upward gradient in the socioeconomic status of the population as one proceeds from the center to the periphery of the city. Hence one would expect the degree of residential centralization of an occupation group to be inversely related to its socioeconomic status. The data provide general support for this hypothesis, although there are some significant exceptions. Thus, for the Metropolitan District as a whole, three of the four white-collar indexes are negative (indicating relative decentralization), and three of the four blue-collar indexes are positive (indicating relative centralization). The exceptional

cases are again the clerical and craftsmen-foremen groups.

In three of the five sectors (Northwest, West, and Southwest), the hypothesized pattern of centralization indexes is perfectly reproduced, except for the inversion between clerical workers and the craftsmen-foremen group, which appears in all sectors. For the North Shore sector the principal deviation from the pattern is the comparatively low degree of centralization of service workers and laborers. In this sector the managerial group is somewhat more decentralized than the professional group, as is also true in the South Shore sector. The latter sector exhibits a quite marked departure from the expected pattern, in that the only decentralized occupations are those in the blue-collar category. There is a small measure of confirmation for the hypothesized pattern, in that within the white-collar category the least centralized groups are the professional and managerial, and within the blue-collar category the most decentralized is the craftsmen-foremen group. The high index for service workers is doubtless due to the relatively high proportion of nonwhites in this occupation, and the relatively central location of the South Side "Black Belt," a large portion of which falls in the South Shore sector. The decentralization of the other blue-collar groups is attributable to the presence of the Indiana industrial suburbs on the periphery of the South Shore sector. A similar effect of some industrial suburbs at the northern end of the North Shore sector is observable in the low centralization index for laborers in that sector. It is apparent that expectations based on the zonal hypothesis must be qualified by recognizing distortions of the zonal pattern produced by peripheral industrial concentrations. Such concentrations appear only in certain sectors, and, where they are absent, the zonal hypothesis leads to a realistic expectation concerning the pattern of residential centralization by socioeconomic status.

RESIDENTIAL SEPARATION AND DISSIMILARITY OF OCCUPATIONAL ORIGINS

There are good reasons for supposing that residential patterns are related to occupational mobility. For example, ecologists have noted a tendency for advances in socioeconomic status to be accompanied by migration toward the city's periphery. Residential segregation is doubtless one of the barriers to upward mobility, in so far as such mobility is affected by the opportunity to observe and imitate the way of life of higher social strata. Among the findings reported above, at least one may have an explanation that involves mobility. It is surprising that the residential patterns of sales workers do not differ more than they do from those of professional and managerial workers; since the income of sales workers is well below that of either, they rank lower in prestige, and their educational attainment is substantially less than that of professional workers. But there are data which suggest that a sizable proportion of sales

workers are moving to a higher occupational level, or aspire to such a move, anticipating it by following the residential pattern of the higher group. The Occupational Mobility Survey found that for males employed in both 1940 and 1950 there was a movement of 23 percent of the men employed as sales workers in 1940 into the group of managers, proprietors, and officials by 1950. This is the largest single interoccupational movement in the mobility table, except that 23 per cent of laborers moved into the group of operatives and kindred workers.

Another aspect of occupational mobility is illuminated by the data in Table 5, which shows indexes of dissimilarity among the major occupation groups with respect to the distribution of each group by major occupation group of the employed male's father. These indexes, therefore, pertain to differences among the major occupation groups in background, origin, or recruitment. The hypothesis to be tested is that, the greater the dissimilarity between a pair of occupation groups in occupational origins, the greater is their dissimilarity in residential distribution.

The pattern of Table 5 is clearly like that of Table 3. The indexes of dissimilarity with respect to residence, computed on the zone-sector segment basis, correlate .91 with the indexes for occupational origin. The correlation is .94 for the residential indexes based on census tracts, with the regression of the tract-based index (t) on the index of dissimilarity in occupational origin (u) being $t = 1.2u - 1.8$. The hypothesis is thereby definitely substantiated.

In Table 5 all but one of the inversions of the pattern expected on the assumption of an unequivocal ranking of the occupation groups involved the sales and service workers. Sales workers are closer to professional workers with respect to occupational background than are the managerial workers and farther from each of the blue-collar groups. Actually, a more consistent pattern would be produced by ranking sales workers second in place of the managerial group. In this respect the data on occupa-

TABLE 5. Indexes of Dissimilarity in Distribution by Father's Occupation among Major Occupation Groups, for Employed Males in Six Cities in the United States, 1950

Major Occupation Group[†]	Major Occupation Group*						
	Mgrs., Offs., Props.	Sales Wkrs.	Clerical, Kindred	Crafts-men, Foremen	Opera-tives, Kindred	Services, Incl. Priv. Hshld.	Laborers, exc. Mine
Professional, Technical, and Kindred Workers	20	16	27	38	39	34	46
Managers, Officials, and Proprietors, except farm		11	28	31	34	30	42
Sales Workers			26	35	37	35	47
Clerical and Kindred Workers				18	20	28	39
Craftsmen, Foremen, Kindred Workers					14	25	31
Operatives, Kindred Workers						22	23
Service Workers, including private household							20

Source: Unpublished data from Occupational Mobility Survey, Table W–9. For description of sampling and enumeration procedures see Gladys L. Palmer, *Labor Mobility in Six Cities* (New York: Social Science Research Council, 1951).

[†] Does not include farmers and farm managers and occupation not reported. A small number of private household workers are included with service workers, and a small number of farm laborers with laborers, except mine.

tional origins are more consistent with the ecological data than are the data on socioeconomic status in Table 1. In terms of the indexes of dissimilarity in occupational origins, service workers are closer to the first three white-collar groups than are any of the other blue-collar groups. However, in comparisons among the clerical and blue-collar groups, service workers clearly rank next to last, or between operatives and laborers. Again, the factor of occupational origins is more closely related to residential separation than are the indicators of socioeconomic status.

The last point deserves emphasis. Not only do the indexes of dissimilarity on an area basis have the same general pattern as those on an occupational origin basis but also the deviations from that pattern occur at the same points and in the same direction. This cannot

be said regarding the several indicators of socioeconomic status. If income determined residential separation, managers would outrank professionals, and clerical workers would be virtually identical with operatives in the separation from other groups. If education determined residential separation, there would be substantial differences between the indexes for professional workers and managerial workers. Neither of these hypotheses is borne out by the data, whereas differences in occupational background lead to accurate, specific predictions of the pattern of differences in residential distribution.

The ecological analysis has provided strong support for the proposition that spatial distances between occupation groups are closely related to their social distances, measured either in terms of conventional indicators of socioeconomic status or in terms of differences in occupational origins; that the most segregated occupation groups are those at the extremes of the socioeconomic scale; that concentration of residence in low-rent areas is inversely related to socioeconomic status; and that centralization of residence is likewise inversely related to socioeconomic status. These results are in accord with accepted ecological theory, provide support for it, and demonstrate the relevance of ecological research to the theory of social stratification.

These generalizations, however, are perhaps no more significant to the advancement of knowledge than are the instances in which they do not hold and the additional hypotheses advanced to account for the exceptions. Conventional measures of socioeconomic status do not agree perfectly as to the rank order of the major occupation groups, nor do the several ecological indexes. The prime case in point occurs at the middle of the socioeconomic scale, at the conventional juncture of white-collar and blue-collar occupations. Clerical and kindred workers have substantially more education than craftsmen, foremen, and kindred workers, and the clerical occupations are usually considered of greater prestige than the craft and related occupations. However, craftsmen-foremen have considerably higher incomes on the average, and, among males, their nonwhite proportion is smaller. The pattern of the indexes of dissimilarity in residential distribution clearly places the clerical group closer to the other white-collar groups than the craftsmen-foremen are, and the clerical workers' index of low-rent concentration is less than that of the craftsmen and foremen. But in terms of residential centralization the clerical group tends to fall with the lower blue-collar groups, and the craftsmen-foremen group with the other white-collar groups. In general, it would appear that "social status" or prestige is more important in determining the residential association of clerical with other white-collar groups than is income, although the latter sets up a powerful cross-pressure, as evidenced by the compara-

tively high rent-income ratio of clerical families. To account fully for the failure of clerical workers to be residentially decentralized like the other white-collar groups, one would have to consider work-residence relationships. Data on work-residence separation for a 1951 Chicago sample show that clerical workers resemble craftsmen, foremen, and kindred workers in the degree of separation much more than they do sales, managerial, or professional workers.[12]

Perhaps the most suggestive finding of the study is that dissimilarity in occupational origins is more closely associated with dissimilarity in residential distribution than is any of the usual indicators of socioeconomic status. This result can only be interpreted speculatively. But one may suppose that preferences and aspirations concerning housing and residential patterns are largely formed by childhood and adolescent experiences in a milieu of which the father's occupation is an important aspect.

The discovery that "status disequilibria" are reflected in inconsistencies in the ordering of occupation groups according to their residential patterns provides a further reason for distinguishing "class" from "social status" elements[13] within the complex conventionally designated as "socioeconomic status." Apparently, attempts to compound these two can at best produce a partially ordered scale; at worst, they may obscure significant differences in life-style, consumption patterns, and social mobility.

There is one important qualification of the results reported. Like census tracts, broad occupation groups are not perfectly homogeneous. The managerial group includes proprietors of peanut stands as well as corporation executives, and night-club singers are classified

[12] Beverly Duncan, "Factors in Work-Residence Separation: Wage and Salary Workers, Chicago, 1951" (paper presented at the annual institute of the Society for Social Research, Chicago, June 5, 1953).

[13] See "Class, Status, Party," in H. H. Gerth and C. W. Mills (eds.), *From Max Weber: Essays in Sociology*, (New York: Oxford University Press, 1946).

as professional workers along with surgeons. One would therefore expect to find a much sharper differentiation of residential patterns if more detailed occupational classifications were available. In particular, the points at which cross-pressures on residential location develop should be more clearly identified.

Further research should seek other forces producing residential segregation. Ethnic categorizations other than race are doubtless relevant though difficult to study directly for lack of data. In general, the patterns described here would be expected to hold for females, but significant deviations might also occur, in part because the residence of married females is probably determined more by their husbands'

occupation than by their own, and in part because the occupations that compose each of the major occupation groups are different for females from those for males (as mentioned above in regard to sales workers). Both race and sex would bear upon residential patterns of private household workers, who are predominantly female and nonwhite. A final class of especially important factors is the effect of the location of workplaces on residence. There is evidence that residences are not distributed randomly with respect to places of work. If location of work is controlled, an even sharper differentiation of residential patterns than that described here may be revealed.

33

SURINDER K. MEHTA

Patterns of Residence in Poona (India) by Income, Education, and Occupation (1937-65)

An analysis of the residential distribution of socioeconomic groups in Poona (India) shows distinct patterns that appear to have largely maintained themselves over a thirty-year span. There is a graded hierarchy in the extent of residential dissimilarity as one moves up the socioeconomic ladder, and segregation in residence is greatest for the highest and the lowest status groups. Unlike the situation in cities in the United States, the rich, the better educated, and those pursuing the higher-level occupations generally tend to be centralized, while those belonging to the low socioeconomic status groups are decentralized. However, the extent of concentration in low-rent areas is negatively associated with status.

Reprinted by permission from the *American Journal of Sociology*, Vol. 73, No. 4 (January 1968), pp. 496–508. Copyright by the University of Chicago.

This study was carried out in India while the author was a 1965–66 Faculty Research Fellow of the American Institute of Indian Studies. The author also wishes to acknowledge his deep gratitude to the Gokhale Institute of Politics and Economics, Poona, which provided facilities without which this research could not have been carried out and where the staff fully accepted him as one of its own. Special thanks are due to Mrs. Kumudini Dandekar, who had new runs made of the data from the *Family Planning Evaluation Scheme Survey, Poona City, 1964–65* (Gokhale Institute) and made these data available for this study.

This study is essentially a replication of the Duncans' study of patterns of residence in Chicago,[1] which has also inspired other studies of various cities in the United States[2] and in England.[3] These studies follow in the tradition of the well-known urban ecological studies of the Chicago School but utilize a methodology peculiarly suited to comparative urban analysis. It is essentially Park's insight that "social relations are so frequently and so inevitably correlated with spatial relations"[4] which has guided or, rather, provided a viewpoint for these studies.

The present study's scene shifts to an altogether different socioeconomic and cultural milieu, and it is in its comparative aspect that the real value of this study lies. Our effort here is to add to the literature one more study showing city residential patterns that are in some respects variant from the U. S. pattern and in other respects similar to it.

POONA—A BRIEF DESCRIPTION

Poona is situated in the western part of Maharashtra State, about 120 miles east-southeast of Bombay. The city "lies on an extensive plain, surrounded by singularly scraped hills from 1,900 to 2,300 feet high." From the north the Mula River comes to join the Mutha River, which flows from the southeast, and together they form the river which bounds the city proper on the north.

While mention is made of the Poona region in a copperplate inscription dated A.D. 758, "available historical records do not furnish a separate history of Poona City until well into the seventeenth century," although the city is probably hundreds of years older. The city has had a violent history. It has been sacked and much of it razed, only to rise and be sacked and razed again. In 1817 the English forces occupied Poona and soon thereafter established Poona Cantonment adjoining the eastern boundary, and Kirkee Cantonment to the north.[5] Under the British, Poona City, besides remaining the headquarters of Poona District, became the summer capital of the Bombay Presidency.

Poona experienced a period of rapid prosperous development and drew migrants from all over India in the latter half of the eighteenth century, which facts are reflections of its political position under the Peshwa rulers. With the fall of the Peshwas in the first quarter of the nineteenth century, Poona entered a period of political decline as well as of economic and demographic stagnation, which lasted until 1920 or so. Thereafter, with the growing importance of Poona as a military and political center under the British, and during the post-independence period, Poona's economic situation improved, and considerable growth in population occurred.[6]

In the last two decades, many new industries have located in Poona on the outer fringes of the city, and industrial estates have been established along highways radiating from it. Poona also serves as an administrative and transportation center and, to some extent, as

[1] Otis Dudley Duncan and Beverly Duncan, "Residential Distribution and Occupational Stratification," *American Journal of Sociology*, LX, No. 5 (March 1955): 493–503. [No. 32 in this volume.] Also see their *The Negro Population of Chicago* (Chicago: University of Chicago Press, 1957).

[2] Arthur H. Wilkins, "The Residential Distribution of Occupation Groups in Eight Middle-Sized Cities in the United States in 1950" (unpublished Ph.D. dissertation, University of Chicago, 1956); Richard W. Redick, "Population Growth and Distribution in Central Cities, 1940–50," *American Sociological Review*, XXI, No. 1 (February 1956): 38–43; Otis Dudley Duncan and Stanley Lieberson, "Ethnic Segregation and Assimilation," *American Journal of Sociology*, LXIV, No. 4 (January 1959): 364–374; Stanley Lieberson, *Ethnic Patterns in American Cities* (Glencoe, Ill.: Free Press, 1963); Eugene S. Uyeki, "Residential Distribution and Stratification, 1950–60," *American Journal of Sociology*, LXIX, No. 5 (March 1964): 491–498.

[3] Peter Collison and John Mogey, "Residence and Social Class in Oxford," *American Journal of Sociology*, LXIV, No. 6 (May 1959): 599–605.

[4] Robert Ezra Park, "The Urban Community as a Spatial Pattern and a Moral Order," *Human Communities* (Glencoe, Ill.: Free Press, 1952), p. 177

[5] D. R. Gadgil, *Poona: A Socio-Economic Survey*, Part I: *Economic* (Gokhale Institute of Politics and Economics Publication No. 12 [Poona, 1945], pp. 1–12.

[6] D.R. Gadgil, *Poona: A Socio-Economic Survey*, Part II (Gokhale Institute of Politics and Economics Publication No. 25 [Poona, 1952]), pp. 319–324.

a retail trade center. But pre-eminently, it is an educational center of national renown, and some of its research institutes have an international reputation.

Poona is thus an ancient Indian city that has in recent decades experienced European influence and some industrialization and modernization. It should, therefore, provide an especially interesting case study of changing patterns of residence.[7]

DATA AND METHODS

The Poona Municipal Corporation, comprising Poona City (eighteen wards), the suburban municipalities (two wards), and a number of outlying villages and communities (eight wards), but excluding the Poona and Kirkee cantonments, had roughly an area of forty-six square miles and a population of 278,000 in 1941. By 1961 the corresponding area had grown to about sixty-eight square miles comprised of some thirty-seven wards with a total population of 598,000.[8] In this study, what we call "Poona City" comprises the eighteen old wards of the city proper along with the two suburban municipality wards. In 1937 Poona City had a total area of fourteen square miles and a population of roughly 225,000. For purposes of comparison, we took the same wards to constitute Poona City in 1964–65 and added one adjoining ward with an area of one and one-half square miles and a population of about 8,900 in 1961. We added this ward because, unlike the wards comprising the surrounding villages and industrial estates, it is well integrated in the residential community of the city and is eminently urban in character. In 1961 Poona

City had a population of 531,000. What we call "Greater Poona" was somewhat larger but more or less coterminous with the aforementioned Poona Municipal Corporation area of 1961. The Poona and Kirkee cantonments, with a combined population of about 60,000 in 1937 and 124,000 in 1961, are altogether excluded from this study, as the requisite data were unavailable for 1937 and 1964–65.[9]

The 1937 survey, from which data for the present study are taken, was a random sample which took every fifteenth house, beginning with the first one on a listing of houses that was made for each of the eighteen wards for the city proper and adjoining suburban wards. All families[10] residing in a particular house were deemed to be part of the sample.

The 1964–65 data for this study are taken from the *Family Planning Evaluation Scheme Survey of Poona*, which was essentially a 1 per cent cluster-type random sample. Thus, compared to the 6–7 per cent random sample of 1937, the 1964–65 sample is subject to a greater statistical variance,[11] but at the same time it would tend to give a greater homogeneity to the characteristics of the population of each ward,[12] inasmuch as it was a cluster sample.

The methods employed for studying the patterns of residential distribution in Poona are the same as those employed by the Duncans in their study (see n.2 above) of residential patterns in Chicago. The interested reader may refer to it for details; they are briefly recapitulated here, with some additional comments.

---

[7] As the title of this paper indicates, we have not been able to study residential patterns by occupation, etc., prior to 1937. However, in another paper, on residential patterns by caste, we will present an analysis covering the years 1822, 1937, 1954, and 1965.

[8] N. V. Sovani, D. P. Apte, and R. G. Pendse, *Poona: A Resurvey* (Gokhale Institute of Politics and Economics Publication No. 34 [Poona, 1956]), Table 1.1, p. 2; Census of India, *1961 Census, Final Population Totals* (Paper No. 1 of 1962), Table V, p. 258; the area data were supplied by Dr. A. Bopegamage of the Gokhale Institute.

[9] This omission of the two cantonment areas, considering their unique characteristics and their European populations, is most unfortunate.

[10] The family was defined as "any group of persons living together as a separate economic unit" (Gadgil, *Poona:* Part I, p. 40).

[11] In 1937 a total of 4,529 families were interviewed; in 1964–65 a total of 1,176 households were in the sample, and a total of 1,444 couples in these households were interviewed. Wherever the tables in this article show the corresponding sample numbers to be lower than these figures, this is due to the lack of relevant data for part of the sample.

[12] Throughout this study the residential patterns of the population are studied on the ward basis.

Index of Dissimilarity

This index measures the extent of non-overlap in the patterns of residence of any two groups, and ranges from zero to one hundred.

Index of Segregation

This index is similar to the index of dissimilarity, except that now the residential distribution of a given group is compared to the residential distribution of all the other groups taken together.

The problem of choosing the appropriate areal units for research on patterns or degrees of segregation has been dealt with by a number of writers,[13] and it is a vexing one indeed. Theoretically, it can be seen that, for a given city, if the number of areal units is increased by choosing very small units (for instance, dwelling units or, more strictly still, the spaces occupied by individual persons) for research, then complete segregation or dissimilarity will be found, and the value of the indexes will be one hundred; if, on the other hand, the areal unit chosen is so large as to encompass the city as a whole, then no segregation or dissimilarity will be found, and the index values will be zero.[14] This also points to the fact that the index measures only the degree of interareal-unit segregation and does not measure the extent of intra-areal-unit segregation.

We may also point out that the more natural the areal units (natural in the ecological or sociocultural sense as opposed to units that are arbitrary, such as those resulting from imposing a grid on a map of a city) chosen for research on segregation, the greater the tendency for the index values to be large. And the more refined or smaller the population groups (for instance, detailed occupation groups versus major occupational ones) under study, the greater the tendency for the index values to be large.

Index of Centralization

This index measures the extent to which a given group is centralized with respect to the rest of the population. The areal units are classified and ordered by distance zones, from closest to farthest and beginning from the center. Let X_i be the cumulated percentage distribution of group A with the ordering of the areal units as specified, and let Y_i be the corresponding cumulated percentage distribution for the total population. Then the "unadjusted" index of centralization for group A will be

$$\Sigma(X_{i-1}Y_i) - \Sigma(Y_{i-1}X_i),$$

and the "adjusted" index would be this quantity divided by one, minus the proportion of the total population that group A comprises.[15] The index value ranges from one hundred to minus one hundred, with the positive sign indicating centralization and the negative sign showing decentralization of the given group with respect to all other groups in the population. It should be mentioned that the value of the index has a tendency to increase slightly as the number of concentric zones is increased by narrowing their widths.

Index of Low-Rent-Area Concentration

This index is computed in the same manner as the index of centralization, except that now

---

[13] An excellent discussion of this topic and a review of the pertinent literature is to be found in Karl E. Taeuber and Alma F. Taeuber, *Negroes in Cities: Residential Segregation and Neighborhood Change* (Chicago: Aldine Publishing Co., 1965), Appendix A.

[14] The shape of the areal units, even if the areal size of the units is kept constant, will affect the index value. For further discussion of this general problem, see John K. Wright, "Some Measures of Distributions," *Annals of the Association of American Geographers*, XXVII, No. 4 (December 1937): 177–211. Also see Otis Dudley Duncan and Beverly Duncan, "A Methodological Analysis of Segregation Indexes," *American Sociological Review*, XX, No. 2 (April 1955): 210–217; and the communications to the editor entitled "In Defense of a Segregation Index" (by Donald O. Cogwill)

[15] This adjustment increases the unadjusted index value to one that would be obtained if Y_i, instead of representing the cumulated percentage distribution of the total population, represented the cumulated percentage distribution of the total population, less the population of group A. This procedure of computing the "unadjusted" index first and then adjusting it saves a great deal of computational work. This also applies to the index of segregation.

the ordering of the areal units is from those with the lowest rent to those with the highest. A negative index value indicates that the given group is relatively less concentrated in low-rental areas with respect to the remainder of the city's population, while a positive index value indicates the contrary.

RESIDENTIAL PATTERNS BY INCOME

Studies of cities in the United States, Latin America, and Europe have shown that the patterns of residential distribution differ among socioeconomic groups.[16] The patterns of residential distribution differ among the various groups, presumably because of differences in ability to afford housing amenities and surroundings, prestige-maintenance pressures, cultural preferences, and discrimination. As a guiding hypothesis we maintain that social, economic, and cultural forces operate in *all* urban environments, irrespective of the milieu,

and that these forces sift and sort population groups in such a manner that characteristic residential patterns emerge. The specific patterns that emerge in different socioeconomic and cultural milieus within various cities may, however, differ.

For Poona City we note that in 1937 (see Table 1) a clear pattern of dissimilarity in residential distribution exists among income groups, and a clear pattern of segregation is also apparent.[17] If income is one factor that differentiates families in their patterns of residence in a consistent and predictable manner,

---

[16] Some of these studies will be cited for comparative purposes at relevant points in the text of this paper.

[17] As mentioned previously, throughout this study the areal unit employed in the analysis is the ward. In fact, this is the only type of intracity unit for which any data are available. Historically, most of the eighteen wards of the old city of Poona and some of the newly created wards were more or less natural ecological and/or cultural areas, although the delimitation was to some extent based on considerations of administrative convenience. Many of the newly delimited wards of Greater Poona, however, are delimited mostly for administrative purposes, on an ad hoc basis, when they are incorporated into the Poona Municipal Corporation area; on the other hand, some of the newly added wards consist of clearly recognizable communities.

TABLE 1.   Indexes of Dissimilarity and Segregation in Residential Distribution for Sample Families Grouped by Annual Income, Poona City, 1937

Income Groups (in Rupees)	Index of Dissimilarity among Income Groups									Index of Segregation from All Other Families	Number of Families in Group
	II	III	IV	V	VI	VII	VIII	IX	X		
I. < Rs. 100	21	27	27	32	33	39	43	41	46	28	280
II. 100– 150		16	13	16	17	26	30	32	38	12	379
III. 150– 200			12	21	18	27	30	36	43	15	544
IV. 200– 300				16	17	27	32	34	40	14	932
V. 300– 400					12	21	26	31	41	13	757
VI. 400– 500						19	28	29	39	11	387
VII. 500– 750							18	14	30	20	494
VIII. 750–1,000								23	36	25	192
IX. 1,000–2,000									21	27	321
X. 2,000 +										37	190
Total Number of Families in Sample											4,529*

* Includes fifty-three families for whom income data were unavailable.
Source of basic data: D. R. Gadgil, *Poona: A Socio-economic Survey*, Part II (Poona, 1952). Henceforth, this source will be identified as *Poona*, Part II, and the companion volume to this will be identified as *Poona*, Part I.

then moving from left to right and from bottom to top from the diagonal in the table, and taking successive pairs of index-of-dissimilarity values, one should find that the second value in each pair tends to be the larger one.[18] Our findings, with a few exceptions, are highly consistent with our expectations.

The indexes of segregation in Table 1 depict a U-shaped pattern, moving from the lowest to the highest income group. When the Duncans ordered occupational groups by socioeconomic status in their Chicago study, they noted a similar U shaped segregation pattern; Uyeki found the same phenomenon in his Cleveland study.[19]

The patterns of residential dissimilarity and segregation found for Poona City in 1937 are also found for the city and for Greater Poona in 1964–65, over a quarter of a century later (see Table 2).

Indexes of centralization and of low-rent-area concentration for income groups are presented in Table 3.[20] The sets of indexes of centralization for Poona City (1937 and 1964–65) and for Greater Poona (1964–65) clearly show that the pattern of centralization by income is in the exact opposite of that found in cities in the United States today. However, in their earlier stages, most U. S. cities had their high-rent

---

[18] It should be pointed out that mathematically the successive pairs of index-of-dissimilarity values are not independent (see Lieberson, op. cit., pp. 38–40 et passim).

[19] Duncan and Duncan, "Residential Distribution and Occupational Stratification," op. cit., and Uyeki, op. cit. The only income group which is different from the regularity of the U-shaped pattern is group II, which also deviates from the expected pattern of indexes of dissimilarity in our study. The reason for the deviancy of this income group may be that it contains most of the domestic servants' families, who are often given residential quarters within the compound of the employing family's residence or who reside close by.

[20] For purposes of computing the indexes of centralization, we chose as the center of the city a point in one of the oldest wards of Poona. This ward, called Budhwar Peth, forms the city's core and is the heart of its business district. From the point chosen as the center, we drew concentric distance zones on a map of the city and thus ordered the wards by distance from the center. Whenever a given ward fell in two or more distance zones, which was often the case, it was deemed to fall wholly in that zone which contained the major portion of its area. If the major portion of the ward's area did not clearly fall within any one zone, then it was deemed to belong to that zone which contained the central swath of the swaths cut by the various zonal lines.

TABLE 2.   Indexes of Dissimilarity and Segregation in Residential Distribution for Sample Couples Grouped by Monthly Income, Poona City and Greater Poona, 1964–65*

Income Groups (in Rupees)	Index of Dissimilarity among Income Groups							Index of Segregation from All Other Couples	Number of Couples in Sample
	I	II	III	IV	V	VI	VII		
I. Up to Rs. 50		28	33	46	49	47	59	32	94
II. 51–100	29		19	32	35	41	54	19	424
III. 101–150	38	23		30	29	33	59	18	232
IV. 151–200	49	34	32		20	26	39	27	112
V. 201–250	52	37	35	21		21	45	29	57
VI. 251–350	50	43	37	28	25		43	33	51
VII. 350+	64	61	65	46	49	47		51	46
Index of segregation from all other couples	33	22	22	30	33	35	58		1,016[†]
Number of couples in sample	124	508	278	120	59	54	55	1,198[†]	

* Poona City figures are above the diagonal; Greater Poona figures are below the diagonal.
[†] Excluding 246 couples whose income or ward of residence was not ascertained or recorded.
Source of basic data: Gokhale Institute's *Family Planning Evaluation Scheme Survey* for Poona.

residential areas much closer to the city center than they do today.[21] In Oxford, England, Collison and Mogey found that people of the highest social class live closest to the center of the town.[22] Many Continental European cities also show the same phenomenon.[23] Studies of Latin-American cities have also shown the desirability of residing near the plaza or at other locations (on high ground perhaps) near the center of the city.[24]

---

[21] Cf. Homer Hoyt, *The Structure and Growth of Residential Neighborhoods in American Cities* (Washington, D.C.: Federal Housing Administration, 1933); and the series of land-use maps of Detroit presented by L. S. Wilson, "Functional Areas in Detroit, 1890–1933," *Papers of the Michigan Academy of Science, Arts, and Letters,* XXII (1947): 399–408, and reprinted in Amos H. Hawley, *Human Ecology: A Theory of Community Structure* (New York: Ronald Press, 1950), pp. 386–390.

[22] Op. cit. However, though this was in a general way the case for the town as a whole, in at least two out of five sectors of the town the most centralized people were those belonging to the lowest class.

[23] Some of these studies are reprinted in George A. Theodorson (ed.), *Studies in Human Ecology,* Part III: "Cross-Cultural Studies" (New York: Row, Peterson, 1961). Also see Dennis C. McElrath, "The Social Areas of Rome: A Comparative Analysis," *American Sociological Review,* XXVII, No. 3 (June 1962): 376–391.

[24] Some examples of these studies are: Theodore Caplow, "The Social Ecology of Guatemala City," *Social Forces,* XXVIII (December 1949): 113–135; Asael T. Hansen, "The Ecology of a Latin American City," in E. B. Reuter (ed.), *Race and Culture Contacts* (New York: McGraw-Hill Book Co., 1934), pp. 124–142; Harry B. Hawthorn and Audrey E. Hawthorn, "The Shape of a City; Some Observations on Sucre, Bolivia," *Sociology and Social Research,* XXXIII (November–December 1948): 87–91; and Norman S. Hayner, "Mexico City: Its Growth and Configuration," *American Journal of Sociology,* L, No. 4 (January 1945): 295–304. For a comparative analysis of residential patterns of North American and Latin-American cities, see Leo F. Schnore, "On the Spatial Structure of Cities in the Two Americas," in Philip M. Hauser and Leo F. Schnore (eds.), *The Study of Urbanization* (New York: John Wiley & Sons, 1965), pp. 347–398. The tendency for the elite to be centralized in their residential locations has been noted in other Indian cities. See the study of Bangalore, a city somewhat larger than Poona, by Noel P. Gist, "The Ecological Structure of an Asian City: An East-West Comparison," *Population Review,* II, No. 1 (January 1958): 17–25, and the study of Howrah by A. B. Chatterjee, "Ecological Structure of Calcutta's Twin," *National Geographical Journal of India,* XI, Part II (June 1965): 59–62. Also see John E. Brush's article entitled "The Morphology of Indian Cities," in Roy Turner (ed.), *India's Urban Future* (Berkeley: University of California Press, 1962), pp. 57–70. However, the authors of a recent study of Gorakhpur, a city which experienced rapid growth

Thus, it is clear that universally the most pervasive ecological pattern of cities is one where the elite tend to reside near the center of a city rather than in the periphery. However, nearly all of the studies of European and Latin-American cities have shown that there is a tendency, to a lesser or greater degree, for the traditional pattern of the desirability of city-center residential location to change toward the current U. S. pattern. This also seems to be the case in Poona as far as the highest income group is concerned.[25]

Within Poona City, while the relatively high income groups have continued to remain centralized from 1937 to 1964–65, the highest income people have definitely become decentralized in their residential location pattern, although in 1964–65 the extent of their decentralization was less in the Greater Poona area as compared with the Poona City area. What has happened is that some of the heavily built-up central wards which were medium-to-high rental areas in 1937 have become low-rental areas by now, while many of the peripheral wards which had large empty spaces have experienced a boom in the building of spacious modern houses for the elite. Many houses for the elite are also going up in the most distant peripheral sections (beyond Poona City) of Greater Poona, but these areas also contain slumlike communities, in which, by tradition,

---

between 1951 and 1961, noted that "in the farthest circle of residential zone lie the habitations of the elite groups" (see Radhakamal Mukerjee and Baljit Singh, *A District Town in Transition: Social and Economic Survey of Gorakhpur* [Bombay: Asia Publishing House, 1965]).

[25] Of course, in Table 3, neither the data nor the income classes for 1937 are directly comparable with those for 1964–65. But there is other evidence available to support this conclusion. For instance, in Poona City in 1937, of the three highest rent-area wards, one had a peripheral location, one was close to the center, and one had a median location, whereas the three wards with the lowest rent areas were all peripherally located. Comparable data for 1954 (data for 1964–65 are lacking) show that, of the three highest rent-area wards, two were peripherally located and one had a median location; whereas, of the five wards with the lowest rent areas (three wards were tied for the third lowest rent rank), two were peripherally located, two had median locations, and one was Budhwar Peth, in the center of the city.

TABLE 3. Indexes of Centralization and Low-Rent-Area Concentration for Family Income Groups with Respect to Total Sample Populations, Poona City, 1937 and 1964-65, and Greater Poona, 1964-65.

Families Grouped by Annual Income (in Rupees)	Index of Low-Rent-Area Concentration, Poona City, 1937	Index of Centralization, Poona City, 1937	Couples Grouped by Monthly Income	Index of Centralization	
				Poona City 1964-65	Greater Poona 1964-65
I. <Rs. 100	12.9	−14.6	I. Up to Rs. 50	− 9.2	−14.6
II. 100– 150	5.0	− 4.6	II. 51–100	− 9.7	−10.1
III. 150– 200	1.0	− 8.2	III. 101–150	8.3	3.6
IV. 200– 300	7.9	− 9.8	IV. 151–200	5.7	12.1
V. 300– 400	0.4	0.8	V. 201–250	16.8	24.2
VI. 400– 500	− 2.9	1.9	VI. 251–350	21.4	26.9
VII. 500– 750	− 7.2	16.9	VII. 351 +	−14.6	− 6.9
VIII. 750–1,000	− 1.2	19.2			
IX. 1,000–2,000	−12.6	17.0			
X. 2,000 +	−26.4	− 0.1			

Source of basic data: *Poona*, Part II, and *Family Planning Evaluation Scheme Survey*.

members of the depressed castes live.[26] Also in these areas are the *bastis* of the newly-arrived unskilled laborers and peons employed by the industries that have lately sprung up along the highways and railroad lines to the city. The new and fashionable residences of the upper-income group house some of the old elite who have moved from their old central ward locations; but these residences also house the managerial and technical elite who have recently come to Poona.

---

[26] The peripheral residential location of depressed castes has been noted in Bangalore by Gist, op. cit. In a study under way, we have found a similar phenomenon to have existed in Sholapur in 1938. In Greater Bombay today, it is quite evident to any observer who has taken the trains running from Bombay Island to the suburban areas toward the north that the poor, members of the depressed castes, and members of the Scheduled Tribes are to be found in great numbers living in unbelievably tiny, dirty, ramshackle houses made out of bits of wood, gunnysacks, or mud, and squeezed together on narrow strips of filthy, empty land along one or both sides of the railway tracks. In the identification of the population groups squatting here (who sometimes pay high rents to landowners for the privilege of being allowed to stay there), some familiarity with information in the 1961 census is very helpful (see *Census of India, 1961*, Vol. X: *Maharashtra, Part X [1-B], Greater Bombay Census Tables* [Bombay: Government Central Press, 1964]).

RESIDENTIAL PATTERNS BY EDUCATION

We have no adequate data on the educational characteristics of the population by residence for Poona in 1937. The data for 1964-65, however, show that the observed patterns of residence by levels of educational attainment (see Tables 4 and 5) are in confirmation of the patterns of residential distribution by income groups.

RESIDENTIAL PATTERNS BY OCCUPATION

Table 6 shows the major occupational groups for which residential location data were available for 1937, in the order of their rank by socioeconomic status. No relevant 1964-65 data comparable to those for 1937 are available for ranking the occupational groups by socioeconomic status. It may be presumed, however, that the major occupational groups have in general maintained their relative rankings.[27]

---

[27] From comparable data available from a 1953-54 survey of Poona, we ranked the occupational groups by socioeconomic status and found only one change in the relative rankings of groups: group IV, the lowest professional and administrative posts, had moved from an unweighted mean rank of 4.5–5.3 higher than for group V, which tied it with the mean rank for group VI. These data are taken from Sovani, et al., op. cit., pp. 164–213, 411, and 416–417.

TABLE 4.   Indexes of Dissimilarity and Segregation in Residential Distribution for Couples Grouped by Education of Husbands, Poona City and Greater Poona, 1964–65*

Educational Level Groups	Index of Dissimilarity among Educational Level Groups					Index of Segregation from All Other Couples	Number of Couples in Sample
	I	II	III	IV	V		
I. Illiterate		27	45	55	59	36	156
II. Literate up to 7th Standard	27		28	40	54	26	513
III. Above 7th Standard but below S.S.C.†	45	29		28	51	25	98
IV. S.S.C. but below Graduate	59	43	29		27	34	232
V. Graduate or above, Technical Degree, Diploma, etc.	63	55	51	29		45	110
Index of Segregation from All Other Couples	36	25	25	37	48		1,109‡
Number of Couples in Sample	217	624	108	252	123	1,324‡	

* Poona City figures are above the diagonal; Greater Poona figures are below the diagonal.
† S.S.C. = secondary school certificate.
‡ Excluding 120 couples for whom ward of residence or education of husband was not known.
Source of basic data: Same as Table 2.

TABLE 5.   Indexes of Centralization for Couples Grouped by Education of Husbands with Respect to All Couples in Sample, Poona City and Greater Poona, 1964–65

Educational Level Groups	Index of Centralization	
	Poona City	Greater Poona
I. Illiterate	−23.1	−29.3
II. Literate up to 7th Standard	− 3.0	− 5.0
III. Above 7th Standard but below S.S.C.*	15.9	19.1
IV. S.S.C. but below Graduate	14.7	21.3
V. Graduate or Above, Technical Degree, Diploma, etc.	− 3.3	6.2

* S.S.C. = secondary school certificate.
Source of basic data: Same as Table 2.

Table 7 gives the indexes of dissimilarity and segregation for the eleven major occupational groups, listed in the order of their rank on our socioeconomic status scale. Concerning the indexes of dissimilarity, it is clearly evident that the occupational groups were distinctly differentiated in an expected manner in their residential patterns in this city in 1937 and continue to remain differentiated in a similar fashion.[28] Regarding the three sets of indexes of segregation, each set is, more or less, in accordance with our specifications.

Table 8 gives the indexes of low-rent-area concentration and indexes of centralization for the occupational groups. The patterns of resi-

[28] Differential residential patterns by occupation in some of the Indian cities have been briefly referred to by Gist, op. cit.; Mukerjee and Singh, op. cit.; Meera Guha, "The Morphology of Calcutta," *Geographical Review of India*, XV, No. 3 (September 1953): 20–28; and Howard F. Hirt, "Spatial Aspects of the Housing Problem in Aligarh, U.P., India." *Population Review*, II, No. 1 (January 1958): 37–45.

TABLE 6.   Selected Indicators of Socioeconomic Status for Families Grouped by Major Occupation Group of Head of Household, Poona City, 1937

Major Occupation Groups	Annual Income in Rupees		Proportion Belonging to High Castes*		Proportion Belonging to All Depressed Castes		Proportion of Earners Who Are Literate		Un-weighted Mean of Four Rankings
	Median	Rank	%	Rank	%	Rank	%	Rank	
I. Beggars and Prostitutes	158	1	4.4	1	22.1	1	18.5	1	1.0
II. Unskilled Manual Workers	182	2	4.8	2	20.4	2	25.4	2	2.0
III. Skilled Manual Workers	281	4	5.4	3	12.4	3	39.9	3	3.3
IV. Lowest Professions and Administrative Posts	277	3	32.6	6	9.1	4	84.2	5	4.5
V. Small Business	282	5	8.6	4	4.8	6	48.3	4	4.8
VI. Highly Skilled and Supervisory Manual	393	6	20.4	5	5.1	5	85.4	6	5.5
VII. Medium Business	776	8	47.1	7	0.9	9	92.2	7	7.8
VIII. Clerks and Shop Assistants	546	7	57.0	8	1.4	8	98.0	10	8.3
IX. Pensioners	1,052	9	57.8	9	2.5	7	94.7	8	8.3
X. Intermediate Professions and Administrative Posts	1,406	10	62.9	10	0.0	10.5	98.0	10	10.1
XI. Highest Professions, Owners of Factories and Large Shops	2,000+	11	77.0	11	0.0	10.5	98.0	10	10.6
All Occupations	314		22.2		9.5		57.1		

* Of the groupings by caste made in the Poona study, the highest caste was, of course, the Brahmins, and we judged the next highest group to be the one which consisted of Gujaratis, Marwadis, and Jains. We have combined these groups for our indicator of socioeconomic status.

† Whereas the other three indicators are based on characteristics of the family, this indicator refers to all earners.

Source of basic data: *Poona,* Part I, and *Poona,* Part II.

dential location observed here for the occupational groups are similar to those observed for income and educational groups and need no further comment. Mention should be made of group XI, the highest status occupational category. For the Poona City area, this group showed a slight degree of decentralization in 1937 as well as in 1964–65. However, whereas in 1937 this group was in fact somewhat concentrated in wards lying close to the city center, by 1964–65 this group was underrepresented in the central and nearby wards, with a large proportion of its members in the outer, but not in the most peripheral, wards of Poona City and Greater Poona.

CONCLUDING REMARKS

Our study of Poona shows findings that are remarkably consistent with ecological theory. Patterns of residential distribution by income, edu-

TABLE 7. Indexes of Dissimilarity and Segregation in Residential Distribution for Sample Populations Grouped by Occupation, Poona City, 1937 and 1964–65, and Greater Poona, 1964–65*

Major Occupation Groups	Index of Dissimilarity among Major Occupation Groups											Index of Segregation from All Other Families or Couples	Numbers of Families or Couples
	I	II	III	IV	V	VI	VII	VIII	IX	X	XI		
I. Beggars and Prostitutes		49	56	57	48	61	53	58	64	63	63	54	68
	x†	*x*	*x*	*x*	*x*	*x*	*x*	*x*	*x*	*x*	*x*	*x*	*x*
II. Unskilled Manual Workers			14	19	20	29	27	33	43	45	44	19	943
	x†		*35*	*42*	*45*	*22*	*45*	*47*	*x*	*50*	*63*	*35*	*234*
III. Skilled Manual Workers				23	22	29	29	37	46	48	45	22	914
	x	*36*		*40*	*38*	*21*	*39*	*38*	*x*	*41*	*62*	*22*	*114*
IV. Lowest Professions, etc.					26	19	24	22	28	29	33	13	350
	x	*45*	*41*		*63*	*46*	*52*	*61*	*x*	*54*	*70*	*46*	*67*
V. Small Business						22	15	29	41	41	48	17	560
	x	*52*	*44*	*64*		*31*	*40*	*44*	*x*	*42*	*52*	*35*	*27*
VI. Highly skilled, etc.							18	23	33	31	39	19	333
	x	*30*	*23*	*45*	*35*		*35*	*37*	*x*	*38*	*59*	*16*	*133*
VII. Medium Business								22	39	36	43	17	342
	x	*47*	*38*	*51*	*46*	*37*		*36*	*x*	*45*	*56*	*32*	*131*
VIII. Clerks and Shop Assistants									19	17	36	22	421
	x	*53*	*42*	*61*	*47*	*39*	*38*		*x*	*29*	*42*	*32*	*89*
IX. Pensioners										15	36	35	121
	x	*x*	*x*	*x*	*x*	*x*	*x*	*x*		*x*	*x*	*x*	*x*

? >

TABLE 7. *(Continued)*

| Major Occupation Groups | Index of Dissimilarity among Major Occupation Groups | | | | | | | | | | | Index of Segregation from All Other Families or Couples | Numbers of Families or Couples |
	I	II	III	IV	V	VI	VII	VIII	IX	X	XI		
X. Intermediate Professions, etc.											38	34	143
	x	59	44	57	48	40	47	33	x		39	37	91
XI. Highest Professions, Owners, etc.												37	76
	x	67	64	70	56	62	57	42	x	45		52	25
Index of Segregation from All Other Couples	x	38	23	43	41	19	34	35	x	42	55		4,529‡
Number of Couples in Samples	x	326	132	75	30	148	148	91	x	101	26	1,077	911§

[∆] Poona City 1937 figures are above diagonal (upper rows), Poona City 1964–65 figures are above diagonal (italicized lower rows); Greater Poona 1964–65 figures are below diagonal.

† Requisite data for computing the index were not available.

‡ Including 255 families with no earners and three families where occupation of head of household was unclassified.

§ Excludes 367 couples whose ward of residence was not known or where the husband was following an agricultural occupation, was a student, unemployed, retired, or his occupation was not known.

Sources of data: *Poona*, Part II, and *Family Planning Evaluation Scheme Survey*.

cation, and occupation groups show that residential dissimilarity increases between groups in correspondence with increasing disparity between any two groups in terms of these indicators of socioeconomic status.[29] Regarding segregation, the index values describe a characteristic U-shaped pattern as one moves from lower to higher socioeconomic status groups. As might have been expected, the higher-status groups, compared with the lower-status groups, are less concentrated in the low-

rental areas of Poona.[30] In general, this summarization of the findings applies to Poona City for 1937 and 1964–65 and to Greater Poona for 1964–65.[31] We would now like to present a

[29] These indicators are not, of course, independent of each other. In fact, it would have been revealing also to study the patterns of residence by each of these indicators of socioeconomic status while at the same time controlling for one or both of the other two indicators, but we were unable to do this for lack of suitable data.

[30] For the Indian scene, one of the most important factors that affect the ecological patterns of residence is caste. We are now in the process of analyzing caste patterns of residence in Poona and Sholapur cities and shall report our findings in the near future. For lack of space we could not incorporate the analysis by caste in the present paper.

[31] The reader may have noted that index values for dissimilarity, segregation, and centralization are generally higher in 1964–65 compared with 1937. It is quite possible that Poona has undergone increased residential differentiation of socioeconomic groups as the city experienced much new physical expansion, rapid population growth, rising incomes, and the development of a fairly efficient intracity transportation system. On the other hand, the increase in the index values may be a reflection of the 1964–65 cluster-type random sample.

TABLE 8.   Indexes of Centralization and Low-Rent-Area Concentration for Major Occupation Groups with Respect to Total Sample Populations, Poona City, 1937 and 1964–65, and Greater Poona, 1964–65

Major Occupation Groups*	Index of Low-Rent-Area Concentration Poona City, 1937	Index of Centralization		
		Poona City, 1937	Poona City, 1964–65	Greater Poona, 1964–65
I. Beggars and Prostitutes	13.1	−22.1	x†	x
II. Unskilled Manual Workers	5.0	−20.2	−21.2	−32.4
III. Skilled Manual Workers	2.8	−18.4	− 3.2	− 0.8
IV. Lowest Professions, etc.	3.7	3.3	−22.1	−14.9
V. Small Business	4.7	8.5	16.4	18.4
VI. Highly Skilled, etc.	− 5.8	20.7	− 2.1	4.2
VII. Medium Business	−10.2	16.4	27.4	21.9
VIII. Clerks and Shop Assistants	−10.9	17.1	16.8	27.0
IX. Pensioners	− 2.8	16.3	x	x
X. Intermediate Professions, etc.	− 5.2	12.3	11.5	17.2
XI. Highest Professions, Owners, etc.	−15.1	− 5.3	− 6.3	6.8

* Families grouped by occupation of head of family for 1937, and couples grouped by occupation of husband for 1964–65.
† Requisite data unavailable.
Sources of basic data: *Poona*, Part II, and *Family Planning Evaluation Scheme Survey*.

few remarks for discussion concerning centralization of population groups.

In the cities of the United States, the upper, and even the middle, classes started to decentralize their residential locations from forty to fifty years ago—earlier than elsewhere in the world. This occurred because of the rapid growth of the cities and the consequent congestion, dilapidation, and encroachment of business on erstwhile desirable residential areas near the center of cities. At times when incomes in the cities were rapidly increasing, the big cities in the United States experienced a large influx of immigrants from Europe and migrants from those parts of the country that lagged behind in economic development. Later, the Negro population, as well as some Puerto Ricans, started coming to the cities. Successive waves of these in-migrants settled, to greater

or lesser extent, in the deteriorating areas near city centers. The in-migrants were unable to find housing elsewhere in the cities because of their low incomes and because of discrimination; furthermore, many of them wished to live side by side with people of their own ethnic or racial backgrounds. The influx of these in-migrants in turn led to an increased exodus of the middle and upper classes to outlying residential areas. These classes were given greater incentive to sell their property and move because of the increases in land prices resulting from the expansion of the central business district, the ready market that the in-migrants constituted for their houses, and because of their ability to purchase expensive new housing elsewhere in, or just outside of, the city. Of course, one of the most important factors operating in the suburbanization of the population was the early development of fast and efficient means of communication (for example, the telephone), public transportation and private transportation (namely, the automobile). Whereas commuter trains and trolleys enabled communities to grow up along these lines of transportation, the automobile allowed communities to flourish in the interstices.

In the last ten years, there has appeared in some U. S. cities a tendency for some of the higher socioeconomic status people to return to residential localities near city centers. This incipient reversal of the prevailing patterns of residential location by class is due to the fact that as more and more of the population—including members of the lower-middle class—has encroached upon the outlying residential districts and suburbs, the previous residents of these areas have been pressed to move farther and farther out. This has in turn led to impractical increases in commuting distances, transportation costs and commuting time. These people are having to face a growing dilemma: either they can continue to move out farther and preserve their suburban way of life or they can return to the inner redeveloping areas of the city and readopt urbanism as a way of life. People in many cities (Philadelphia, for example) have begun to choose the latter and are "returning home."

In a number of European cities, the process of suburbanization of the upper and middle classes can also be seen, but it is of recent origin. Western European cities experienced much of their growth earlier than U. S. cities at a time when means of communication and transportation were rudimentary and expensive. Furthermore, the rates of city growth were generally lower then than they were when the United States started on the path of rapid industrialization and urbanization. The consequence was that deterioration and dilapidation of residential areas in western European cities did not occur, or occurred only very gradually, and the upper classes continued to remain in the city. Only in recent years, because of in-creased affluence and the ubiquitous automobile, has the suburbanization of the upper classes started. In some of the Latin-American cities, suburbanization of the upper and middle classes has also begun to take place, as essentially the same set of factors that led to suburban growth in the United States has begun to operate in these cities. The same process may well have begun in the eastern European cities; it has certainly made its appearance in southern Europe.

In Indian cities, decentralization of the upper classes, not to mention the middle classes, has hardly made an appearance. The reason for this is that urban growth rates have in general not been high, means of communication and transportation are rudimentary at best, and the in-migrants to the cities have such low purchasing power that they cannot buy houses in or near a city center, or anywhere else for that matter; they are forced to settle on outlying tracts of vacant land, to build their shacks on patches of land within the city (but away from the city center), or to become pavement dwellers. In almost all large Indian cities, these three patterns of residential location (if pavement dwelling can be described as "residential") coexist among the poor in-migrants. Furthermore, since economic mobility is so low, the middle classes, and even the upper classes, have not been able to "trade up" in their "consumption" of houses, and either the slow or the expensive means of intracity transportation, or both, have contributed to the desirability of residential location remaining close to the city center. Finally, the traditional caste structure, tied up as it has been with economic and social power, favors residential centralization for the upper castes and relegation of outlying areas to the lower castes and the untouchables. City-center location makes the separation of residence from place of work minimal for those who can afford the high land prices; provides security in times of unrest and violence in the countryside; and enables residents to enjoy what the city has to offer. The poor have to live outside the city and must therefore spend a larger share of their time and money to bring their wares and produce to the city market or to work at menial tasks in the city.[32]

In a city such as Poona, however, which has, in recent years, grown rapidly, found new industrial wealth, developed a fairly efficient bus transportation system, and acquired a fleet of motorized rickshaws, some taxis, and a number of private automobiles, the elite have started to decentralize in their choice of residential location.

[32] In the United States, the lower classes may someday be pushed out of their city homes as real estate prices shoot up as a consequence of the renovation of entire city neighborhoods, the building of new town houses, and the erection of expensive high-rise apartment buildings. At such a time, U. S. poor will also have to spend a larger share of their time and money getting to the city from the suburban homes to which they will have been relegated.

34

KENT P. SCHWIRIAN
JESUS RICO-VELASCO

The Residential Distribution of Status Groups in Puerto Rico's Metropolitan Areas

The purpose of this paper is to investigate the pattern of residential segregation of status groups in Puerto Rico's three metropolitan areas. The findings showed that in all three areas: (1) as the social status distance between groups increases so too does the degree of dissimilarity of their residential distributions; (2) the status groups most residentially segregated are those at the top and at the bottom of the status pyramid; (3) the pattern of residential centralization of status groups for Ponce and Mayaguez are such that the highest status groups are the most centralized while the lowest status groups are the most decentralized, but in San Juan it is the highest status groups that are the most decentralized and the lowest status groups that are the most centralized. The data are from the 1960 census. Indicators of status employed are education, occupation, and income. Differences in findings about centralization between San Juan and the other cities are explained in terms of differential economic development.

Reprinted by permission from *Demography*, Vol. 8, No. 1 (February 1971), pp. 81–90.

Among the most prominent features of urban ecological structure are (1) the residential segregation of socioeconomic status groups from each other, and (2) the differential distribution of status groups in urban residential space. Most studies to date have focused upon United States cities but as high quality urban subarea data become available there is an increasing number of studies of city structure in other societies. Through utilization of these new data comparative ecological analysis is attaining a degree of rigor previously impossible. In this paper we extend this comparative line of analysis by investigating the residential distribution of social status groups in Puerto Rico's three metropolitan areas: San Juan, Ponce, and Mayaguez. Our aims are to (1) provide data about the structure of these metropolitan areas in a largely Latin context that are directly comparable to data on cities in the United States; and (2) provide benchmark data against which later Puerto Rican data may be compared, thereby contributing to the longitudinal investigation of ecological structure and change. Thus we provide both cross-sectional data for the comparative analysis of North American and Latin American cities and a quantitative foundation for a study of the changing ecology of three Latin cities. The data analyzed here are from the 1960 census of United States population.

THEORY

In recent years there have been several studies of the residential segregation and location of urban social status groups. The similarity of findings among such societies as the United States, Canada, England, and India have led one investigator [Mehta 1969] to conclude (1) that the residential dissimilarity between status groups is a universally pervasive phenomenon; (2) that as the social status distance between groups increases so too does the degree of dissimilarity in residential distribution; (3) that the overall pattern of urban residential segregation is such that the most highly segregated groups

are those at the top and at the bottom of the social status hierarchy; (4) that differential centralization of status groups is a uniform urban characteristic although whether it is the higher or lower status groups that are highly centralized is a function of the level of industrial development of the city; and (5) that the groups most centralized and the most decentralized are those that are the most segregated.

Discussions of the residential centralization of social status groups in large cities suggest that two somewhat opposite patterns characterize the cities of the Western Hemisphere. One pattern supposedly describes the structure of North American cities while another characterizes a Latin American pattern.

The North American model is derived mainly from the writings of Burgess [1925] and it is argued that there is a direct relationship between social status and distance of residence from the center of the city. Thus, the low status residents are concentrated in the inner parts of the city while the higher status are concentrated at the periphery. Support for the model for U.S. cities is reported by many investigators including Schnore [1965a], Uyeki [1964] and others. Also, there is some support for the notion for Canadian cities as reported by Guest [1969]. However, it should be noted that while gross city-fringe status differences correspond to the Burgess model, studies by Anderson and Egeland [1961] for the U.S. and by Schwirian and Matre [1969] for Canada have demonstrated that a larger percent of the variance in the residential distribution of social status within the cities is accounted for by sectoral patterning rather than by distance gradient.

The Latin American model has been described in a number of investigations including those by Hayner [1945], the Dotsons [1956], and others. Essentially, this model states that the distribution of social class aggregates in the Latin cities is opposite from that for cities in industrial North America. Accordingly, clustered near the city's center or *plaza mayor* are the upper status groups while the periphery contains those of low socioeconomic status.

The middle status aggregates supposedly fall between the two.

The difference between the North American and Latin American patterns is usually attributed to the historical differences in location factors or disparate levels of societal industrialization, or both. In general, the Latin American cities were structural extensions of the great cities of colonial Iberia but the Latin American city was not the result of commerce and mercantile activities. The Latin American cities were political and administrative contact points between the conquerors' homeland and the natural and human resources of the new continent. The ecological patterning of these cities was not the cressive result of the interplay of social and economic values in a free-wheeling urban land market. Rather, the ecological patterns reflect specific instructions given by the Spanish ruler to the conquistadors for the founding of the towns. By 1681 the collection of royal orders, ordinances, and instructions issued for the establishment of the colonial cities became a significant segment of the famous Laws of the Indies.

According to the regal location decisions the main focus of the Latin city in the colonial period was the central plaza (*plaza mayor*). It was the starting point for land use allocation. After the main streets were laid out the land around the plaza was subdivided for specific uses. The main church or cathedral usually occupied an entire block adjacent to the plaza (although in a few cities the church was located in the middle of the square). On the other side of the plaza the government or town council houses as well as other administrative buildings were located. The remaining land was made available to the higher status families who elected to locate near the hub of Spanish colonial life. The rest of the urban land at some distance from the central plaza was occupied by colonists of lesser status, "criollos" (Spanish born in America), Indians, and later on by mixed bloods such as "mestizos" (Spanish and Indian), "mulattoes" (Spanish and Negroes), and "zambos" (Indians and Negroes). Thus an inverse status

gradient pattern initially developed that became one of the basic ecological features of the Latin American city.

The apparent differences between the North American and Latin American models in their ecological patterning of status seem to reflect more basic differences between cities in industrial and nonindustrial societies. In commenting upon such differences Mehta has written:

> Differential residential centralization (or decentralization) of groups is universal. In preindustrial cities, in cities that had become relatively large before modern developments in transportation, particularly the automobile, and in communication had taken place, higher-status groups tend to be centralized, and the lower-status groups tend to be decentralized. In those cities which grew recently and along with improvements in transportation and communication, the situation is reversed; the privileged groups are decentralized, and the poor are centralized. [Mehta 1969: 490].

Currently a number of urbanists are suggesting that an evolutionary sequence may be underway in urban development in which the status distribution pattern characteristic of the city in nonindustrial society gives way to that of the industrial as the society modernizes. In a recent essay Schnore asks the question: "Does the residential structure of the city evolve in a predictable direction?" [Schnore 1965b: 374]. That is, are both the North American pattern and the Latin American pattern special cases of a more general land use process? Some support for this notion comes from both historical studies of U.S. cities which show that in much earlier periods the higher status groups were residentially located near the city's center and some recent descriptions of the emergence of high and middle status housing developments at the fringe of some Latin metropolitan areas.

While the development of a dynamic model linking together these different patterns is a laudable goal for ecological analysis there are two major problems which must be overcome. The first is the current lack of good historical data on the ecological structure of cities in both North and Latin America. The second is the lack of comparable ecological analyses of the current structure of cities in the different cultures. The first problem reflects not only the comparatively late entry of historians into the urban field but also the general ineptitude of social scientists in historical research particularly in non-English languages. The second problem dealing with comparative studies reflects two matters. The first is the basic nature of many of the first studies of the Latin city. More than a few of these were "by-product" studies. In these the researcher did not focus primarily upon propositions dealing with urbanization per se, but, rather used data collected for other purposes to draw some inferences about city patterning. Since these studies had differing foci, the available data for urban exploration varied between studies making systematic comparisons difficult if not impossible in most cases. The second matter leading to the lack of comparable studies is the general unavailability of current small area data for many of the Latin cities.

Our aim in this paper is to aid in the solution of the second problem in this area—the lack of comparable ecological analyses. In our investigation we are able to employ concepts and measures used in previous studies of North American cities since the 1960 U.S. census includes data for Puerto Rico comparable to those for the rest of the U.S. Also, the data presented here will provide a foundation for future longitudinal analysis as subsequent small area census data become available.

The study hypotheses are based in part on studies of status segregation in other world cities and on general discussion of gross city-fringe status differentials in Latin American cities [Dotson and Dotson 1956; Guest 1969; Hayner 1945; Mehta 1968, 1969; Schnore 1965; Schwirian and Rico 1970; Collison 1960; Collison and Mogey 1959; Uyeki 1964]. We hypothesize that in the three Puerto Rican Metropolitan Areas:

1. status groups have dissimilar residential distributions;

2. the degree of residential dissimilarity between status groups is a function of the degree of status differences between them;

3. the most residentially segregated groups are those at the top and at the bottom of the status pyramid;

4. the pattern of centralization is that typical of Latin American cities with the highest status groups most centralized and the low status groups the most decentralized.

Even though Puerto Rico is politically tied to the United States the basic hypothesis of this paper is that the ecological patterning of status groups in the three Puerto Rican cities corresponds to that predicted by the general model for Latin American cities. That is, that the higher status groups are residentially congregated in the city while the low status groups are in the fringe. We base this proposition on the following: (1) the ecological patterning of the Puerto Rican cities was established basically under Spanish rule before the American occupation of the island in 1898, and once such fundamental patterns are established they are highly resistant to change; and (2) while Puerto Rico's affiliation with the United States has existed for approximately 70 years Puerto Rico has maintained its own culture and its own pattern of development, and while it is influenced by the U.S. it has not become a microcosm of general Yankee American culture. For example, factors leading to the flight to suburbia of the U.S.'s middle and upper status groups in the post-1945 period have not had their counterparts in Puerto Rico.

METHODS

To measure the differential distribution between pairs of social status groups we employ the index of dissimilarity (Δ) which is $\Sigma |X_i - Y_i|/2$ where X_i is the percentage of one group living in area i and Y_i is the percentage of the second group living in that area. To measure the total segregation of specific groups we employ the index of segregation which is, in effect, the degree of dissimilarity between the residential distribution of the one group and that of all other groups. The formula is $\Sigma |X_i - Y_i|/2(1 - P)$ where X_i is the percentage of the specific group in area i, Y_i is the percentage of all groups in the area, and P is the percentage group X is of the total of all groups.

Residential centralization is measured by computing the mean distance each status group is from the center of the city. The formula $\Sigma DP/N$, where the summation is over all areas of the city, D is the distance of the area from the city center, P is the size of the particular group in the area at that distance, and N is the total number of the particular group in the city [Gibbs 1961: 244]. The higher the index value the greater the mean distance of the group from the city's center. To compute the index of centralization we established zones in each of the three cities by starting at the central point of the city and drawing concentric circles at progressive distances from the center. Once the zones were established, usual procedures for calculating the mean for grouped data were employed.

For San Juan, the largest of the three cities, the concentric zones have a radius of one mile which together yield five distance zones. In Ponce and Mayaguez the radius of each zone is one-half mile. In each of the two smaller cities three distance zones were identified. In Ponce and Mayaguez it was easy to establish the city's central point or *plaza mayor*. San Juan presents somewhat of a problem in the identification of this point. The current city of San Juan consists of several initially separate settlement nuclei that have grown together over the years. Three of the most basic settlement segments are Old San Juan which is offshore the main island connected to it through bridges; Santurce which consists of that part of the city on the mainland adjoining the Atlantic; and the Rio Piedras and Hato Rey areas which are inland of Old San Juan and Santurce. In selecting the central point of San Juan we took a principal intersection in the business and financial section of Santurce since it is a development hub for the metropolitan area as a whole.

In delineating the residential areas for the study we confined our efforts to the city seg-

ments of the Standard Metropolitan Statistical Areas (SMSA's) and excluded the fringes. There are two reasons for this. First, in another paper we have already demonstrated that the fringe areas of the SMSA's are of a decidedly lower status than the cities (Schwirian and Rico, 1970). Second, the fringe areas of the three SMSA's have very large concentrations of agricultural and mixed urban and agricultural populations. Thus, the inclusion of these largely agricultural, lower status populations would greatly distort the pattern of urban status segregation actually characteristic of the city areas (see Table 1).

In investigating social status distributions we employ three indicators: Occupation, Education, and Income. Our categories of the three variables are those in the census tabulations—nine categories of occupation, eight of education, and fourteen of income. The data are from the 1960 census tract reports for each of the cities.

FINDINGS

The first two propositions are that the status groups have dissimilar residential patterns in each of the three cities and that the degree of segregation between any two groups is a function of the status distance between them. The data for each of the three status variables in each of the three cities support these two propositions.

In Table 2 are the indexes of dissimilarity for San Juan's occupational groups. Each group is much more residentially similar to those near it in the status hierarchy than it is to those further away. For example the index for the categories of professionals and of managers is 16 while it is 66 for the categories of professionals and laborers. Likewise the occupational data for Ponce show the same overall pattern. In Ponce the index of dissimilarity (Δ) for professional and managers is 24 while it is 61 for professional and laborers. The corresponding values for Mayaguez are similar; the Δ for professional and managers is 18 and that for professional and laborers is 51 (see Table 3).

TABLE 1.   City and Fringe Social Status Characteristics for Puerto Rico's Three Standard Metropolitan Statistical Areas, 1960

	San Juan SMSA			Ponce SMSA			Mayaguez SMSA		
Characteristic	Total	City	Fringe	Total	City	Fringe	Total	City	Fringe
Population Size									
Number, 000's	588.8	432.4	156.4	145.6	114.3	31.3	83.8	50.1	33.7
Percent	100	73	27	100	78	22	100	60	40
Median School									
Yrs. Completed	7.4	8.0	4.6	4.9	5.7	3.0	4.9	5.9	3.8
Median Family									
Income, $	2,346	2,471	1,997	1,409	1,552	942	1,341	1,348	1,202
Pct. Employed									
in Agriculture	2.3	0.9	7.0	10.7	3.5	41.8	11.9	2.5	27.8

Note: These data and those in Tables 2–7 are based on tabulations in census tract reports, U.S. Census of Population and Housing: 1960, *Final Reports* PHC (1)–178, 179, and 180.

TABLE 2.   Indexes of Dissimilarity, Segregation, and Centralization for Major Occupation Groups of Employed Males, San Juan, 1960

Major Occupation Group	Dissimilarity with Group									% Total	Segre- gation	Central- ization
	1	2	3	4	5	6	7	8	9			
1. Laborers		24	60	21	25	41	52	57	66	8.8	36	2.32
2. Serv. Wkrs.			57	17	19	28	36	44	55	10.4	23	2.28
3. Pvt. Hshld.				58	61	60	66	56	61	0.4	57	1.67
4. Operatives					11	27	38	44	54	14.8	22	2.36
5. Craftsmen						24	35	43	51	19.7	21	2.45
6. Sales							23	29	37	10.6	14	2.52
7. Clerical								28	31	10.6	25	2.58
8. Managers									16	13.2	32	2.47
9. Professional										11.5	42	2.67

Note: Number of employed males (base of percentage distribution) = 83,316.

TABLE 3.   Indexes of Dissimilarity, Segregation and Centralization for Major Occupation Groups of Employed Males, Ponce and Mayaguez, 1960

Major Occ. Group	Dissimilarity: Above Diagonal, Ponce; Below Diagonal, Mayaguez									% Total		Segre- gation		Central- ization	
	1	2	3	4	5	6	7	8	9	P	M	P	M	P	M
1. Labor		31	54	32	31	39	46	46	61	15.6	11.5	34	27	1.04	.78
2. Serv.	28		42	18	16	20	33	35	46	7.4	7.9	20	16	.86	.60
3. P. H.	57	47		50	47	48	47	46	41	0.5	1.0	43	42	.94	.56
4. Oper.	15	19	49		9	17	28	35	51	19.9	19.3	17	12	.91	.70
5. Craft	23	19	49	12		12	23	28	46	20.9	19.5	11	14	.90	.66
6. Sales	28	13	41	19	21		20	22	38	10.1	12.2	14	13	.85	.63
7. Cler.	39	28	39	26	23	25		17	29	6.4	7.3	21	19	.85	.64
8. Mgrs.	41	28	32	27	28	20	18		24	12.1	13.4	25	22	.86	.58
9. Prof.	51	34	36	36	37	29	25	18		7.1	7.9	42	32	.80	.55

Note: Number of employed males = 19,556 for Ponce, 9,104 for Mayaguez.

The pattern of the indexes for education in the three cities are very similar to those for occupation in that the categories of school years completed that are the most similar are those adjacent to each other and those most dissimilar are those furthest away. In San Juan the Δ for those with no school and those with 1–4 years of elementary school is 7 while the index for those with no school and those with 4 or more years of college is 69 (see Table 4). Likewise in Ponce the Δ for the no-school-completed category and the 1–4 years of elementary school is 7 while it is 67 between those with no school and those with 4 or more years of college. The same pattern as in San Juan and Ponce holds for the distribution of the educational groups

in Mayaguez. For the no-school-completed group and 1–4 years of elementary the Δ is 11 while it is 54 between no school completed and 4 or more years of college (see Table 5).

As with the other two status variables in the cities the income categories are residentially most similar to those near them in the income distribution and most dissimilar to those further away. For San Juan those who earn $15,000 per year and over have a Δ of 29 with the next highest income category but have a Δ of 76 with those who earn less than $500. In Ponce the index of dissimilarity between the top and bottom income groups is 81 while it is 33 between the top two groups and 12 between the bottom two income groups. In Mayaguez

TABLE 4.   Indexes of Dissimilarity, Segregation, and Centralization for Educational Groups of Persons 25 Years of Age and Over, San Juan, 1960

Number of School Years Completed	Dissimilarity with Group								% Total	Segregation	Centralization
	1	2	3	4	5	6	7	8			
1. None Completed		7	19	33	37	52	64	69	12.5	32	2.30
2. Elem. 1–4 yrs.			16	30	33	50	62	68	21.1	32	2.31
3. Elem. 5–7 yrs.				16	20	37	50	58	16.0	16	2.39
4. Elem. 8 yrs.					12	25	39	49	9.4	13	2.41
5. H.s. 1–3 yrs.						20	34	47	11.0	14	2.53
6. H.s. 4 yrs.							21	32	13.3	29	2.58
7. Coll. 1–3 yrs.								21	8.0	41	2.74
8. Coll. 4 yrs. +									8.6	50	2.61

Note: Number (base of percentage distribution) = 194,792.

TABLE 5.   Indexes of Dissimilarity, Segregation, and Centralization for Educational Groups of Persons 25 Years of Age and Over, Ponce and Mayaguez, 1960

Number School Years completed	Dissimilarity: Above Diagonal, Ponce; Below Diagonal, Mayaguez								% Total		Segregation		Centralization	
	1	2	3	4	5	6	7	8	P	M	P	M	P	M
1. None		7	15	29	28	43	52	67	17.7	16.4	21	20	.92	.68
2. E 1–4	11		11	26	22	40	50	66	27.9	27.6	19	14	.90	.68
3. E 5–7	12	12		16	15	34	44	61	18.1	20.3	10	8	.88	.65
4. E 8	22	14	14		10	20	28	47	8.3	8.0	16	9	.82	.64
5. Hs 1–3	25	18	16	8		24	32	51	8.9	9.6	14	11	.84	.60
6. Hs 4	35	28	24	14	12		13	30	9.9	9.4	30	21	.82	.61
7. C 1–3	46	39	35	26	25	19		25	4.8	4.1	38	31	.83	.54
8. C 4+	54	51	46	37	36	28	13		4.3	4.5	56	43	.82	.52

Note: Number = 48,064 for Ponce, 23,488 for Mayaguez.

TABLE 6. Indexes of Dissimilarity, Segregation, and Centralization for Family Income Groups, San Juan, 1960

Annual Family Income, $	Dissimilarity with Group														% Total	Seg.	Cent.
	1	2	3	4	5	6	7	8	9	10	11	12	13	14			
1. Under 500		20	17	17	19	25	33	40	47	52	57	63	72	76	10.6	32	2.05
2. 500–699			17	20	21	27	34	41	48	52	57	64	74	78	2.8	31	2.17
3. 700–999				14	16	23	30	39	47	52	58	66	75	79	4.6	30	2.21
4. 1,000–1,499					14	21	30	39	46	52	59	65	75	79	11.7	33	2.24
5. 1,500–1,999						16	24	32	40	46	52	60	71	77	10.7	26	2.21
6. 2,000–2,499							15	22	29	34	41	50	66	73	10.2	16	2.33
7. 2,500–2,999								18	25	29	38	49	65	74	6.8	19	2.44
8. 3,000–3,499									21	22	30	43	61	72	6.2	21	2.61
9. 3,500–3,999										15	21	32	55	68	5.2	25	2.66
10. 4,000–4,999											15	29	52	64	8.3	29	2.79
11. 5,000–5,999												21	45	61	5.8	33	2.81
12. 6,000–9,999													31	47	11.5	44	2.77
13. 10,000–14,999														29	3.7	57	2.38
14. 15,000 & over															1.8	66	2.11

Note: Number (base of percentage distribution) = 87,612.

TABLE 7. Indexes of Dissimilarity, Segregation, and Centralization for Family Income Groups, Ponce and Mayaguez, 1960

Income, 000's of $	Dissimilarity: Above Diagonal, Ponce; Below Diagonal, Mayaguez														% Total		Seg.		Cent.	
	1	2	3	4	5	6	7	8	9	10	11	12	13	14	P	M	P	M	P	M
<1. 0.5		12	8	11	15	21	35	30	40	48	53	67	77	81	19.6	21.5	23	16	.92	.67
2. 0.5–	13		11	20	23	28	42	37	50	55	62	71	80	82	6.1	4.9	28	19	.98	.72
3. 0.7–	10	16		13	16	20	34	29	40	47	53	65	74	80	8.3	9.9	18	16	.94	.70
4. 1.0–	8	15	5		12	18	29	25	36	44	49	62	74	80	14.8	15.9	16	15	.91	.70
5. 1.5–	14	19	15	14		15	22	18	29	39	45	60	72	81	11.2	12.4	14	11	.90	.66
6. 2.0–	27	29	24	25	18		17	12	22	31	38	52	66	75	9.3	8.5	10	19	.87	.67
7. 2.5–	19	26	20	20	18	13		10	17	26	34	48	64	75	5.8	4.8	22	13	.86	.65
8. 3.0–	30	38	31	31	26	16	19		15	25	32	46	61	73	5.1	4.9	15	22	.87	.60
9. 3.5–	32	35	30	32	22	18	22	12		19	23	38	57	70	3.5	3.3	24	21	.83	.60
10. 4.0–	37	42	42	40	32	27	24	19	28		19	31	51	71	4.9	4.3	33	30	.85	.60
11. 5.0–	45	47	44	45	40	30	32	26	28	33		25	45	71	2.7	2.2	40	38	.84	.57
12. 6.0–	43	49	44	46	41	38	34	27	32	26	31		24	49	5.9	4.7	54	36	.90	.58
13. 10.0–	57	58	60	59	52	51	52	45	46	45	44	23		33	1.8	1.6	65	51	.92	.54
14. 15.0+	78	85	78	79	74	73	75	65	67	62	68	45	44		0.8	1.1	73	73	.81	.65

Note: Number = 22,384 for Ponce, 10,916 for Mayaguez.

the Δ's for the lowest income categories increase from 13 to 78 up the income hierarchy while the Δ's for the top income category increase from 44 to 78 going down the status hierarchy (see Tables 6 and 7).

The third proposition examined here is that the most residentially segregated groups are those at the top and at the bottom of the status pyramid. Thus when the segregation indexes are plotted against the status levels of the categories we would expect a U-shaped curve to result. The data for each index of status in each city support the proposition.

For occupation in each city the top three

status groups and the bottom three groups are more segregated than the middle three categories. Thus, the high status categories of professional, managers, and clerical as well as the lower status categories of private household workers, service, and laborers are more segregated than the more middle ranked categories of sales, craftsmen and operatives. The similarity in ranking for the three cities of the occupational categories on the segregation index is very great as measured by the Kendall measure of concordance for the three which is .97.

For the education variable the most segregated groups are those with either one to three years of college or four or more years of college and those with either no years of school or with less than three years of elementary school. The similarity in the pattern of segregation between the groups is great as indicated by the W of .92.

The income data generally correspond to those for occupation and education in the three cities. As with the other two status variables the patterns of segregation for income are fairly similar across the three cities. The W for them is .82. It should be noted, though, that the distribution of segregation indexes for the income categories in the cities is more J-shaped than U-shaped. This reflects to some extent the set of categories for the distribution. Far greater distinction is made among the range of low income categories than is made among the higher range of income.

The fourth and final hypothesis investigated here is that the classic Latin American pattern holds with the highest groups being the most centralized and the lowest status groups being the least centralized. The centralization scores on all three of the status variables for Ponce and Mayaguez support the proposition since in those two cities it is the highest status groups that are the most centralized and the lowest status groups the most decentralized. However, the data for San Juan do not support the proposition. In fact, the pattern for San Juan is just the opposite of that predicted by the Latin American model; that is, in San Juan

the most centralized groups are generally those of lowest status while the least centralized groups are those of highest status.

The rank order correlations between occupational status and mean distance from the center of the city are: San Juan .88, Ponce −.80 and Mayaguez −.50. The r's between distance and education are: San Juan .98, Ponce −.88 and Mayaguez −.98. For income and centralization the r's are: San Juan .54, Ponce −.68 and Mayaguez −.87. Thus with the exception of only two out of the nine r's there seems to be a strong relationship between status level and mean distance from the city's center. The two comparatively smaller r's still indicate a moderate relationship between centralization and social status.

One of the weaker relations is between occupation and centralization for Mayaguez. It seems that in Mayaguez the private household workers are somewhat more centralized in a Latin city than would be expected given the status elevation of the occupation. It could be argued that the private household workers are centralized so as to live closer to their upper status employers who are residentially centralized. While this might be so, the private household workers still have large indexes of dissimilarity with the higher status groups. Furthermore, the segregation index of the private household workers is the highest of all occupational groups. The picture that emerges is that while both upper status occupations and private household workers are centralized, they are still quite segregated from each other residentially.

The second somewhat weaker association is for San Juan's income and centralization distributions. This reflects the fact that while generally in San Juan the lower income groups are centralized and the middle and upper middle income groups are decentralized, the highest income category is much more centralized than would be expected. This results because of the rather large concentration of high income people along the beach front which is not far distant from the center of Santurce.

SUMMARY AND DISCUSSION

The data presented here for the three principal urban centers of Puerto Rico generally support the hypotheses based on studies in other societies. For the three indexes of social status in each city it was found that (1) the social status groups have dissimilar residential patterns such that the groups that are most similar to each other are those closest in the status hierarchy while those most dissimilar are those furthest away; (2) the most segregated groups are those at the top and the bottom of the status rankings; (3) the pattern of residential centralization for the status groups is such that the classic Latin pattern seems to hold for Ponce and Mayaguez. In those cities it is the highest status groups that are the most centralized and the lowest status groups that are the most decentralized. The pattern more typical of an industrial nation holds for San Juan. In San Juan the centralization pattern is the opposite of that for the other two cities since San Juan's high status groups are generally decentralized while the low status groups are the most centralized.

The most unique finding of the study is the difference between the centralization pattern for San Juan and the other two cities. On the basis of our experience in Puerto Rico we argue that the difference in the centralization pattern of the status groups between San Juan and the other two cities generally reflects the present point at which Puerto Rico is in the economic development process. San Juan is Puerto Rico's gateway to development. Modernization in the San Juan area is proceeding at a faster pace and is further ahead than in the other parts of the island. Ponce and Mayaguez are in the more isolated regions in which the traditional Latin cultural patterns are more prominent than they are in greater San Juan.

The difference between San Juan and the other two cities in ecological patterning has been noted in other studies. Schwirian and Smith [1969] in a factorial study of census tract data report a pattern of ecological differentiation of social status, familism, and ethnicity for San Juan fairly characteristic of cities in industrial North America. The factorial patterning of Mayaguez and Ponce shows much less differentiation and is more typical of cities in traditional societies.

Finally, we anticipate that the difference in the residential centralization between San Juan and Mayaguez and Ponce will diminish as development accelerates throughout the island. Thus, when the 1970 census tracts data are available, we expect an even greater ecological similarity among the three cities than there was in 1960.

ACKNOWLEDGMENTS

This is a revised version of a paper presented at the 1970 annual meeting of the American Sociological Association, Washington, D. C.

The authors express their appreciation to the Mershon Center of Ohio State University for the financial support of the project *Modernization and Ecological Change in Puerto Rico* from which the data presented here are drawn.

REFERENCES

Anderson, Theodore, and Janice Egeland, 1961. "Spatial Aspects of Social Area Analysis." *American Sociological Review*, 26: 392–399. [No. 26 in this volume.]

Collison, Peter, 1960. "Occupation, Education, and Housing in an English City." *American Journal of Sociology*, 65: 588–597.

—— and John Mogey, 1959. "Residence and Social Class in Oxford." *American Journal of Sociology*, 64: 599–605.

Dotson, Floyd, and Lillian O. Dotson, 1956. "Urban Centralization and Decentralization in Mexico. *Rural Sociology*, 21: 41–49.

Gibbs, Jack P., ed., 1961. *Urban Research Methods.* Princeton, N. J.: D. Van Nostrand.

Guest, Avery M., 1969. "The Applicability of the Burgess Hypothesis to Urban Canada." *Demography*, 6: 271–277, 493.

Hayner, Norman, 1945. "Mexico City: Its Growth and Configuration." *American Journal of Sociology*, 50: 294–304.

Mehta, Surinder K., 1968. Patterns of Residence in Poona (India) by Income, Education, and Occupation (1937–1965). *American Journal of Sociology*, 73: 496–508. [No. 33 in this volume.]

——, 1969. "Patterns of Residence in Poona, India, by Caste and Religion: 1822–1965." Demography, 6: 473–491. [No. 42 in this volume.]

Schnore, Leo F., 1965a. *The Urban Scene.* New York: The Free Press.

——, 1965b. "On the Spatial Structure of Cities in the Two Americas," in Philip M. Hauser and Leo F. Schnore (eds.), *The Study of Urbanization.* New York: John Wiley.

Schwirian, Kent P., and Marc D. Matre, 1969. "The Ecological Structure of Canadian Cities." Research paper, Department of Sociology, The Ohio State University. [No. 27 in this volume.]

——, and Jesus Rico-Velasco. 1970. City-Fringe Status Differences in Puerto Rico's Metropolitan Areas. Working paper, Mershon Caribbean Project, The Ohio State University.

——, and Ruth K. Smith, 1969. "Primacy, Modernization, and Urban Structure: The Ecology of Puerto Rican Cities." Working paper, Mershon Caribbean Project, The Ohio State University. [No. 28 in this volume.]

Uyeki, Eugene, 1964. "Residential Distribution and Stratification, 1950–1960." *American Journal of Sociology*, 69: 491–498.

35

A. H. LATIF

Residential Segregation and Location of Status and Religious Groups in Alexandria, Egypt

In the present paper we shall confine our attention to the problem of residential distribution of major religious and status groups in Alexandria. The main focus of this paper is to determine to what extent these groups are residentially segregated from each other. The answer to this question, in fact, will serve as a useful reflection of Alexandria's social structure, which in turn is a function of the level of industrial development of the city.

So far, urban ecologists have taken account of the tendency of people to select residential sites in cities on the basis of racial, cultural, religious, or ethnic preferences to choose residential locations that are symbolic of wealth, power, or social prestige.[1] Current research has revealed the fact that differences of social class, religion, and ethnic origin are among the major factors that have the greatest impact on the city's spatial structure. The ecological analysis in this regard is aimed at determining the pattern of residential segregation of status groups from each other and their differential distribution in urban residential space.

THEORY

Research on U.S. cities has indicated that the spatial location among status groups parallel their social distance. The generalizations in this respect have achieved their empirical validity. An initial and important study by Duncan and Duncan reveals that "spatial differences between occupation groups are closely related to their social distances, measured either in terms of conventional indicators of socio-economic status or in terms of differences in occupational origins; that the most segregated occupational groups are those at the extremes of the socio-economic scale; that concentration of residence in low-rent areas is inversely related to socio-economic status; and the centralization of residence is likewise inversely related to socioeconomic status".[2]

There has, of course, been a long tradition of research by human ecologists in the United States dealing with the segregation of urban status groups. Empirical investigations have confirmed that groups of similar socioeconomic status will have similar residential patterns; and, as the status level widens, location of residence will become increasingly dissimilar.[3]

Research paper, Department of Sociology, University of Manitoba.

[1] Noel P. Gist, "The Ecology of Bangalore, India: An East-West Comparison," *Social Forces*, Vol. 35, No. 4 (May, 1957), p. 361.

[2] O. D. Duncan and B. Duncan, "Residential Distribution and Occupational Stratification," *The American Journal of Sociology*, 64 (1960): 502. [No. 32 in this volume.]

[3] See, for example, Theodore R. Anderson, "Social and Economic Factors Affecting the Location of Residential

With relation to the spatial location of social status groups, human ecologists have indicated that poorly educated and low-income groups frequently have been found to be over-represented among the residents of the central city in metropolitan areas, and higher status groups tend to reside in the suburbs.[4]

Working primarily on data for American cities, human ecologists have studied the relationships between social correlations such as income, occupation, race and ethnic background, and residential segregation. For example, Duncan and Duncan in their study on "Residential Distribution and Occupational Stratification," have demonstrated that occupational groups in Chicago vary in the degree of residential segregation from one another. Wilkins[5] has reached the same conclusions in a study on the residential distribution of occupation groups in some middle-sized cities in the United States. Lieberson has studied the assimilation rates for a number of cities. He found a consistent association through time between residential desegregation of an ethnic group and increasing socioeconomic similarity to native whites.[6] Karl and Alma Taeuber, and Clemence have concluded, by observing census information for large American cities, that Negro areas are becoming more racially distinct and the general trend, in relation to Negro residen-

tial patterns, is toward polarization rather than dispersion of the nonwhite population.[7]

Generally, speaking, research on dissimilarity and segregation in residential distribution in U.S. cities has shown that the degree of residential segregation among status groups is inversely related to appropriate indicators of their socioeconomic status and their social distance from each other.

Comparative studies on the subject have shown that the spatial segregation of population types is a function of the degree of modernization and differentiation within a society. Recently, Mehta has made some tentative, general observations in relation to such types of spatial segregation:

1. The phenomenon of residential dissimilarity among groups, whether religious, ethnic, racial, caste, occupation, or other, is universal and tends to increase with increasing disparity among the group's socioeconomic status or prestige ranking.

2. The phenomenon of residential segregation of groups is universal, and the segregation curve which emerges when groups are ranked high to low on the same socioeconomic scale is characteristically U-shaped.

3. Processes of modernization and industrialization have little or no impact on the above two phenomenon.

4. Differential residential centralization (or decentralization) of groups is *universal*. In preindustrial cities, in cities that had become relatively large before modern developments in transportation, particularly the automobile, and in communication had taken place, higher status groups tend to be centralized, and the lower-status groups tend to be decentralized. In those cities which grew recently and along with improvements in transportation and communication, the situation is reversed; the

Neighborhoods," *Papers and Proceedings of the Regional Science Association,* 9 (1962): 161–170; Alba M. Edwards. "Socioeconomic Groups of the United States," *Journal of the American Statistical Association,* 15 (June 1917): pp. 643–61; Leo F. Schnore, "The Socioeconomic Status of Cities and Suburbs," *American Sociological Review,* Vol. 28 (February 1963): pp. 76–85; Eugene S. Uyeki, "Residential Distribution and Stratification, 1950–1960," *American Journal of Sociology,* LXIX, no. 5 (March 1964): 491–498; and James O. Wheeler, "Residential Location by Occupational Status," *Urban Studies,* 5, no. 1 (February 1968): 24–32.

[4] Leo F. Schnore, *The Urban Scene* (New York: The Free Press, 1965).

[5] Wilkins, *The Residential Distribution of Occupation Groups in Eight Middle-Sized Cities of the United States in 1950.* Unpublished Ph.D. dissertation, Dept. of Sociology, Univ. of Chicago, 1956.

[6] Stanley Lieberson, *Ethnic Patterns in American Cities* (New York: The Free Press of Glencoe, 1963), p. 105. See Table 30.

[7] Theodore G. Clemence, "Residential Segregation in the Mid-Sixties," *Demography,* 4, No. 2 (1967): 568 [No. 46 in this volume]; Karl Taeuber and Alma Taeuber, "The Negro as an Immigrant Group," *American Journal of Sociology,* 69 (January 1964): 374–382.

privileged groups are decentralized, and the poor are centralized.

5. Those who are highly centralized are highly segregated, in each case because of either poverty or riches; those who are highly decentralized are also highly segregated, and again they are so because of either poverty or riches.

6. Those who are neither centralized nor decentralized are not highly segregated, in each case because of lack of poverty or riches.[8]

To deal with the residential distribution of status groups in Alexandria, a number of propositions are drawn upon:

1. There is a difference in the residential distribution of social groups in Alexandria.

2. The residential dissimilarity between status groups reflect the social distance among them.

3. Religion is one of the factors which underlie the residential patterning among social groups in Alexandria.

4. The pattern of centralization among status groups is typical to that of modernizing cities, with the highest-status groups most centralized and the low-status groups the most decentralized.

METHOD

1. Techniques Employed

The analysis is carried out using indexes of dissimilarity, segregation, and centralization. The index of dissimilarity is computed using the percentage of all persons in a given category residing in each area unit. The formula used for calculation purposes is

$$\frac{\Sigma |x_i - y_i|}{2}$$

where x_i is the percentage of one group living in area i and y_i is the percentage of the second

group living in that area. The index of segregation is similar to the index of dissimilarity, except that now the residential distribution of a given group is compared to the residential distribution of all the other groups taken together. Duncan and Duncan suggested an "adjustment" for this technique by dividing the results by one minus the proportion of the total persons within a given category.[9] The formula used is

$$\frac{\Sigma |x_i - y_i|}{2(1 - p)}$$

where x_i is the proportion of the specific group in area i and y_i is the proportion of all groups in the area. p is the proportion group x is of the total of *all* groups.

The index of centralization is computed using the formula suggested by Gibbs.[10] The formula is

$$\frac{\Sigma DP}{N}$$

where D is the distance of the area from the center of the city. P is the size of the particular group at that distance, and N is the total number of the particular group.[11] The higher the index value the greater the mean distance of the city's center.[12]

In addition to these three techniques, we have selected a random sample of 36 census tracts by Zones and Sectors and employed a two-way analysis of variance to determine the spatial distribution of variables.

---

[8] Surinder K. Mehta, "Patterns of Residence in Poona, India, by Caste and Religion: 1822–1965," *Demography*, 6, no. 4 (November 1969): 490. [No. 42 in this volume.]

[9] Duncan and Duncan, "Residential Distribution and Occupational Stratification," p. 498.

[10] Jack P. Gibbs (ed.). *Urban Research Methods*, Princeton, N.J.: D. Van Nostrand, 1961, p. 244.

[11] See the advantages of using this formula instead of Duncan and Duncan's, that is, $\dfrac{|\Sigma x_i - \Sigma y_j|}{2(1 - p)}$ in Kent P. Schwirian and Jesus Rico-Velasco, "The Residential Distribution of Status Groups in Puerto Rico's Metropolitan Areas," *Demography*. [No. 34 in this volume.]

[12] Schwirian and Rico-Velasco, "Residential Distribution of Status Groups in Puerto Rico's Metropolitan Areas," p. 8.

2. Data Preparation

Data for the present analysis are from the published census of population of Alexandria, 1960. Three variables were chosen for the final analysis: occupation,[13] education,[14] and religion.[15] In connection with the first variable, agriculture, hunting, and mining and quarrying are eliminated from the analysis.

The analysis is carried through two stages suggested by the Duncans[16]: (a) we have delineated the 116 census tracts into which the city was administered in 1960; and (b) we have drawn scheme of zones and sectors of the city. Then we have assigned census tracts to four sectors: Northeast, Southeast, Northwest, and Southwest. Nine zones are suggested by the geographical pecularity of the city. Tracts are assigned to nine zones concentric to the city's center with one-kilometer intervals up to the fifth kilometer, then with three intervals up to the ninth zone. Combining the zones and sectors yielded a set of 36 zone-sector segments. Since Alexandria's growth has spread out toward the East, with little growth toward the West,[17] nine zones are located eastward with only seven zones westward.

Unfortunately, the distribution of population by income is unavailable in the Egyptian census. However, occupation and education seem to be sensitive indicators of the social status distribution of groups in Egyptian society.[18]

FINDINGS

The theoretical assumptions underlying the use of indexes of dissimilarity in residential distribution imply that as socioeconomic differences increase, so too, does the degree of residential dissimilarity. As far as residential dissimilarity among occupational groups goes, the dissimilarity values tend to increase as we move from the top professions to those at the bottom. The values should increase from left to right.

In regard to patterns of segregation, the values follow a U-shaped curve, that is, the highly segregated groups would be the people at the two extremes. The index of centralization values indicate that the occupational groups have relatively different locations as measured by their mean distance from the city's center. These trends are shown in Table 1.

We have used the ranking of occupational categories as reported in the census which reflects, in a general way, the hierarchy of occupational status in Egyptian society. We do not claim, however, that such hierarchy is supported by empirical investigation. Unfortunately, Service and Entertainment workers are grouped together in the census. Personal Service includes such occupations as maids, domestic servants, housekeepers, waiters, and barmen. Thus, Category 7 includes entertainment workers such as night club singers, dancers, etc., along with service workers. Accordingly, any statistical values in relation to this occupational category may produce dubious results.

The index of dissimilarity values support the first proposition stated above, that the occupational groups in Alexandria have dissimilar

---

[13] Occupations by census tracts are classified into 11 categories: Technical Professional; Executive-Managerial; Clerical Office; Sales and Commerce, Agricultural; Hunting-Fishing; Mining and Quarrying; Transport and Communication; Artisans and Craftsmen; Service and Entertainment; Unclassified Occupation; and Unemployed.

[14] Education by census tracts are classified into 8 categories: Illiterate; Barely Reads; Reads and Writes; Elementary School; Completed Intermediate; Went Beyond Intermediate; College or Higher; and not indicated.

[15] Religious affiliations by census tracts are classified into four categories; Muslems; Coptics; Jews; and other (Christians).

[16] Duncan and Duncan, "Residential Distribution and Occupational Stratification," p. 494.

[17] M. Subhi Abdal-Hakim, 1968. *Madinat al-Iskandariyah* (The City of Alexandria), (Cairo, Misr Bookshop, 1958, in Arabic), pp. 166–172.

[18] See, for example, Janet Abu-Lughod, "The Emergence of Differential Fertility in Egypt," The Milbank Memorial Fund Quarterly, XLIII, no. 2 (April 1965); "Urbanization in Egypt: Present State and Future Prospects," *Economic Development and Cultural Change*, XIII (1965); and "Testing the Theory of Social Area Analysis: The Ecology of Cairo, Egypt," *American Sociological Review*, 34, no. 2 (April 1969).

TABLE 1. Indexes of Dissimilarity, Segregation, and Centralization for Major Occupational Groups of Total Employed 15 Years and Above, Alexandria, Egypt, 1960

Major Occupation Groups[a]	Index of Dissimilarity								% Total	Segregation	Centralization
	1	2	3	4	5	6	7	8			
1. Technical-Professional	10	19	42	41	48	29	45		5.55	53	4.58
2. Executive-Managerial		19	41	41	48	28	46		2.82	52	4.77
3. Clerical Office			25	25	32	18	29		10.06	47	4.11
4. Sales, Commerce				16	14	18	18		14.15	40	3.97
5. Transportation, Communication					14	20	16		5.66	39	3.99
6. Artisans, Craftsmen						25	14		38.44	52	4.00
7. Service, Entertainment[b]							26		17.50	48	4.89
8. Unskilled Occupations									5.82	41	4.25
N = 348,396									100.00		

Source: Census of the United Arab Republic, 1960, Vol. I, *The Governorate of Alexandria* (In Arabic: *Muhafazat al-Iskandriyah*), Cairo: Government Printing Office, 1962, Table XVI, pp. 86–101.

[a] Does not include Agriculture, Fishing and Mining Occupations. Statistical analysis based only on data for 98 census tracts.

[b] Service and entertainment workers are grouped together in the census.

residential distributions. The values indicate that the index value is 48 between Technical-Professionals and laborers (Artisans and Craftsmen), and it is the same value (48) between Executive-Managerials and laborers. The index value for Professionals and Managers is only 10.

If increasing social distance is paralleled by increasing dissimilarity in residential location, we can argue, then, that the findings support this argument. However, service and entertainment occupations provide striking exceptions. We believe that this might be due to the error in combining these two different occupational categories together.

From the indexes of segregation for major occupational groups, is it apparent that Technical-Professional, Executive-Managerial, and Artisan and Craftsmen are the most segregated

groups in Alexandria. Transportation and Communication occupations yield the least degree of residential segregation. While the values of segregation are relatively close in their magnitudes, the findings still support the idea that the groups who are at the top and the bottom of the occupational hierarchy are the most segregated groups.

The centralization values indicate that professional and managerial occupations tend to be decentralized in relation to the city center. These findings are not, however, surprising for two reasons. First, the city's expansion has recently been toward the east, especially along the shore of the Mediterranean Sea. The upper and middle classes are mostly located in el Raml. Second, the University of Alexandria is located in the East at al Shatbi, which is located only a short distance from the center of the city.

The highly centralized groups in Alexandria are among sales and commerce workers, transportation workers, and artisans and craftsmen. The index of centralization for service and entertainment workers yields a value of 4.89, which indicates that this group is highly decentralized. This result, however, seems to be a dubious one, as indicated before, and should be disregarded in the analysis.

Our findings do not, however, support the fourth proposition and indicate that the highest occupational groups are decentralized and the middle and lower occupational groups are centralized. This might reveal the stage of development of Alexandria, which has experienced rapid growth and development in recent years. These findings do support the fact that "an evolutionary sequence may be underway in urban development in which the status distribution pattern characteristic of the city in nonindustrial society gives way to that of the industrial as the society modernizes."[19]

In the distribution of residential areas according to educational attainment of the population, the dissimilarity values seem to indicate different patterns. It can be seen in Table 2

[19] Schwirian and Rico-Velasco, "Residential Distribution of Status Groups in Puerto Rico's Metropolitan Areas," p. 83.

that the various educational groups have a dissimilar residential pattern. The first three categories, Illiterate, Barely Reads, and Reads and Writes, are for those who have not attended formal schools. Those who can read and write are most likely to have learned through informal education, or, at least have spent some time in schools and then dropped out later. Formal schooling is compulsory for children six years of age. After spending six years in Elementary School, the person has to be enrolled in the Preparatory Schools, where he spends three more years. After passing a national contest, the student is then admitted either to general high schools or vocational training schools. To get a college degree requires at least four academic years.

The index of dissimilarity values indicate that there is a distinct place, educationally, in the system of Egyptian urban areas. The most segregated groups are those with a college education and those with no years of formal schooling. The index of segregation values also support this previous finding. However, inconsistencies are reported in Table 2 for those who have no formal years of schooling (Illiterates) and for those who have completed high school. The index values for both groups is 30. The index values suggest that the patterns of

TABLE 2.   Indexes of Dissimilarity, Segregation, and Centralization for Major Educational Groups 6 Years and Above, Alexandria, Egypt, 1960

Major Educational Groups[a]	Index of Dissimilarity							% Total	Segregation	Centralization
	1	2	3	4	5	6	7			
1. Illiterate		28	16	32	37	41	59	48.22	30	5.12
2. Barely Reads			30	37	39	42	57	1.26	29	4.59
3. Reads and Writes				20	23	27	45	35.92	15	5.04
4. Elementary Education					11	18	32	3.52	25	5.06
5. Completed Intermediate						12	26	8.90	30	4.88
6. Went Beyond Intermediate							31	0.24	31	4.90
7. College or Higher								1.94	46	5.20
		N = 1,025,953						100.00		

Source: Census of the United Arab Republic, 1960, Vol. 1, Table XV, pp. 70–85.
[a] Some categories are combined because of small numbers, and the statistical analysis is based on data for 98 census tracts.

residential distribution for those who have a college degree are distinct and clear. The segregation index for educational groups follows a J-shaped curve instead of the usual U-shaped curve supported in other investigations.

The index of centralization values indicate that those who have completed their college education are among the most decentralized groups in Alexandria. This is also supported by the index of centralization for professionals and managers as shown in Table 1. The index values for illiterates is 5.12, which also indicates the decentralization of this group. This might be best explained by the fact that the percentage of illiterates is 48.2, and thus, the illiterates are most likely to be residentially dispersed all over the city.

The differences in residential distributions for the major religious groups in Alexandria is presented in Table 3. The index values indicate both Jews and foreign Christians have a distinct residential location. The Muslims and the Coptics seem to be comparatively the same in their residential patterns. The values for Muslims and Jews, and Muslims and other Christian groups are 75 and 79, respectively.

The index of segregation values also indicates that the degree of residential segregation for both Muslims and Coptics is relatively close in comparison to other religious groups.

However, the Coptics and the Jews are most likely to be linked in their places of residence. This is supported by looking at the index of centralization values for both Coptics and Jews, which suggests that these two religious groups live close to the city center. The degree of segregation for all religious groups indicates that the most segregated religious groups are both the Jews and the foreign Christians. These Christians, though, are decentralized in their residential location. The segregation values follow a J-shaped curve.

As far as residential distribution for the major religious groups in Alexandria goes, certain aspects of segregation by ethnic groups of preindustrial cities are characterized in present-day Alexandria. Sjoberg has described this segregation thus: "Segregation by ethnic groups . . . occurs widely in preindustrial cities. The Jews in Europe have had their well-defined ghettos, persisting in some locales well into the twentieth century, and Jewish quarters have long been part of the urban scene throughout the Middle East. Ethnic quarters tend to be self-sufficient entities to the extent that urban living allows, physically and socially, the separation from the rest of the community.[20]

---

[20] Geodon Sjoberg, *The Preindustrial City: Past and Present* (New York: The Free Press, 1960), p. 100.

TABLE 3.   Indexes of Dissimilarity, Segregation, and Centralization for Major Religious Groups, Alexandria, Egypt, 1960

Major Religious Groups[a]	Index of Dissimilarity				% Total	Segregation	Centralization
	1	2	3	4			
1. Muslims		46	57	79	89.26	50	5.44
2. Coptics[b]			49	56	10.52	45	4.64
3. Jews				38	0.19	72	4.04
4. Others[c]					0.03	76	4.06
	N = 1,439,288				100.00		

Source: Census of the United Arab Republic, 1960, Vol. 1, Table XII, pp. 34–38.

[a] Statistical analysis is based on data for 98 census tracts.

[b] Coptics are Egyptian Christians and are classified in the Census into three Categories: Orthodox, Protestants, and Catholics.

[c] Mostly are Christians foreign-born or first generation, and are classified in the Census into three categories: Orthodox, Protestants, and Catholics.

TABLE 4. Indexes of Segregation and Centralization for Major Occupational Groups for the Whole Metropolitan Area by Zone-Sector Segments, Alexandria, 1960

Major Occupational Groups	Metropolitan Area		Northeast		Southeast		Northwest		Southwest	
	Seg.	Cent.	Seg.	Cent.	Seg.	Cent.	Seg.	Cent.	Seg.	Cent.
Tech.-Professional	53	4.58	40	5.61	38	5.31	50	5.60	43	8.44
Exec.-Managerial	52	4.77	49	6.15	52	5.02	56	3.47	39	8.71
Clerical Office	47	4.11	53	4.97	45	4.18	51	4.85	45	8.19
Sales, Com.	40	3.97	27	4.68	47	4.77	43	5.14	45	7.64
Trans., Comm.	39	3.99	35	5.92	37	4.15	38	6.05	55	8.30
Artisans, Craft.	52	4.00	36	4.76	46	4.43	48	6.47	50	4.18
Service, Enter.	48	4.89	35	6.47	40	5.00	46	4.27	46	7.79
Unskilled	41	4.25	33	4.94	41	4.27	42	5.90	59	5.90

Our findings, then, support the third proposition that religion is expected to be one of the factors which underlie the residential distribution in Alexandria.

The material we have presented may be more meaningful if we look at some of the features of the geographical distribution of the occupational groups. This is done because we want to know to what extent occupational status is effective as a determinant of residential location. We have followed the method suggested by Collison[21] in dividing the city into sector-zone segments. The division of the city into four major sectors and nine zones is suggested by its geographical and typographical pattern.

The data presented in Table 4 requires detailed comments. While professionals and managers are highly segregated and decentralized in the whole metropolitan area, some variations do occur when checking their distribution by zones and sectors. In the Northeastern section of the city, both groups hold a high degree of residential segregation. However, the degree of residential centralization differs. As shown in this table, Technical-Professionals are most likely to be centralized in this area, while the Executive-Managerial group is decentralized. The same variation carried by the index of centralization values is apparent. In the southeast-

ern section of the city both groups are decentralized and Executive-Managerial groups are highly segregated in this area. Data for service and entertainment workers' residential patterns indicate that they are decentralized in the Northeast, Southeast, and Southwest sections of the city, except in the Northwest section. The central city is located in the Northwestern section. Thus, many of the service and entertainment workers seem to like to reside near the center of the city. Some members of this category, such as hotel servants, live at their place of work.

The data in Table 4 suggest, therefore, that the Technical-Professional and Executive-Managerial groups, who are considered to be at the top of the occupational hierarchy, are dissimilar or differentiated from the other groups in their residential patterns. However, differences in skills do not seem to produce very much differentiation. In fact, to determine just how effective the occupational status is as a determinant in residential location, an analysis of housing characteristics, rental values, and income must be incorporated. At this time, data are unavailable for these variables.

THE SPATIAL DISTRIBUTION OF SOCIAL STATUS CHARACTERISTICS

At this point in our analysis, it is necessary to examine the spatial distribution of the social status characteristics in Alexandria. Such a de-

[21] Collison, "Occupation, Education, and Housing in an English City," pp. 595–596.

termination must be made if we are to find the clues to the aggregate social structure of the city. Residential location reveals the effects of social structure.[22]

To examine the spatial distribution of the social status characteristics, we have employed the same categories: Occupation, Education, and Religion. Such spatial distribution involves a two-way analysis of variance for a selected 36 census tracts. We divided the city into four major sectors and nine zones as mentioned earlier. Then we randomly selected 36 census tracts extending from the city's center to the periphery. However, those sectors in the fringes with a high proportion of agricultural activities are excluded from the analysis. Nine zones are selected from each sector: one which is next to the city's, then, one for each kilometer up to the third zone, then another census tract for every three kilometers up to the ninth zone. In the westward sections, only seven zones could be retained for final analysis.

Table 5 shows the spatial distribution of the occupational variables which reflect the "style of life," or the socioeconomic characteristics.

The data suggest that the higher socioeconomic groups, as reflected in the occupational hierarchy of the city, are neither primarily distributed by sector or zone. This finding may highlight the data presented in Table 1 in relation to the residential location of the higher status groups. There is no indication that there is a spatial gradient for the higher status groups

from the city center to the periphery. Thus, the higher status groups and the middle status groups live within the city. The data also suggest that service workers are spatially distributed by the distance gradient. Probably service workers in Alexandria come from satellite agricultural communities in the periphery to work in the city but live outside.

Data presented in Table 6 suggest that middle and higher educational groups are sectorially distributed and live within the city. Table 7 indicates that both Jews and other Christians are spatially distributed in sectors rather than in zones. The percentage of the total sum of squares for Muslims suggest a gradient pattern, yet it lacks statistical significance. However, it does indicate that Muslims are most likely to be residentially dispersed within the city and toward the periphery.

CONCLUSION

The overall results from the present analysis permit some statements to be made concerning the spatial patterning of residential location for the major status and religious groups in a developing city. The findings support the fact that there is a difference in the residential distribution of social groups in the city. If increasing social distance is paralleled by increasing dissimilarity in residential location we can argue, then, that the findings support this argument.

Our findings, however, do not completely support the pattern of centralization among status groups, which is typical to that of modernizing cities, with the highest status groups most centralized and the lowest status groups the most decentralized. The findings indicate,

---

[22] James M. Beshers, *Urban Social Structure* (New York: The Free Press, 1962), p. 88.

TABLE 5.   Percentage of the Total Sum of Squares Explained by Sector and Zone for Major Occupational Groups, Alexandria, 1960

	Technical-Profess.	Executive-Managerial	Clerical-Office	Sales-Commerce	Trans.-Comm.	Artisans-Crafts.	Service-Enter.	Unskilled
Sector	23.77*	25.10*	18.02	12.54	11.2	14.7	15.66	13.90
Zone	35.22	29.00	28.05	30.56	26.8	26.01	36.73*	25.74

* This symbol indicates that the percentage of the sum of the squares is statistically significant beyond the .05 level. The test of significance is the two-way analysis of variance.

for example, that the highest occupational groups are decentralized and the middle and lower occupational groups are centralized. This might reveal the stage of development of Alexandria, which has experienced rapid growth and development in recent years. Thus, the foregoing observations indicate that the ecological structure of the city is undergoing a significant change. It is expected that residential configuration of the city will evolve a pattern similar to the Western configuration. This could be achieved along with developments in industrialization, transportation, and communication.

TABLE 6. Percentage of the Total Sum of Squares Explained by Sector and Zone for Major Educational Groups, Alexandria, 1960

	Illiterate	Barely Reads	Reads Writes	Elem. Ed. 4 Years	Comp. Int. 9 years	Beyond Inter.	College or 13 years*
Sector	8.68	8.68	21.41	30.90*	33.67	21.40	47.54
Zone	23.70	24.30	18.32	16.41	19.62	22.61	18.40

* The percentage of the sum of the squares is statistically significant beyond the .05 level. The test of significance is the two-way analysis of variance.

TABLE 7. Percentage of the Total Sum of Squares Explained by Sector and Zones for Major Religious Groups, Alexandria, 1960

	Muslims	Coptics	Jews	Others
Sector	8.73	37.85	32.85*	44.35*
Zone	20.32	15.95	17.21	18.08

* The percentage of the sum of the squares is statistically significant beyond the .05 level. The test of significance is the two-way analysis of variance.

36

JOHN FINE
NORVAL D. GLENN
J. KENNETH MONTS

The Residential Segregation of Occupational Groups in Central Cities and Suburbs

The impression of journalists and social critics in the 1950's that post-war suburbia was uniformly middle-class has been generally rejected by social scientists, but there is a persisting belief in a high degree of residential segregation by social level in suburbia and in a high degree of socio-economic homogeneity within suburban neighborhoods. A comparison of eight central cities with their suburban zones in 1950 and in 1960 revealed, for both dates, (a) small differences in occupational distributions between the central cities and the suburban zones and (b) generally higher Index of Residential Dissimilarity values for pairs of occupational groups in the central cities. These findings indicate that suburban neighborhoods, at least in the eight suburban zones studied, were little, if any, more occupationally homogeneous than the central city neighborhoods. This suggests that the belief in homogeneous suburban neighborhoods should be added to the growing list of discredited "myths of suburbia."

The early literature on the post-World-War-II suburbs in the United States was concerned especially with what the authors perceived to be the homogeneity of the populations of specific suburbs or of suburbia as a whole [e.g., Whyte 1956]. By the late 1950's and early 1960's, social scientists had come to recognize that suburbia as a whole is quite heterogeneous occupationally and economically rather than being populated very largely by middle-class "organization men" and prosperous manual workers who have adopted middle-class life styles and values [e.g., Berger 1960, 1961; Dobriner 1963]. However, most of the social scientific as well as journalistic observers of subur-

bia have persisted in assuming that people at the various social levels are highly segregated from one another in suburbia and that most suburbs or suburban neighborhoods contain primarily people within a rather narrow range of income, education, and occupational prestige [Wrong 1967; Wood 1959; Dobriner 1963; Lee 1963; Boskoff 1970; Broom and Selznick 1968; Coleman 1966; Beshers 1962; Fava 1956; Packard 1959; Bernard 1962; Martin 1956]. If the contention is simply that each suburb tends to contain a more homogeneous population than

Reprinted by permission from *Demography*, Vol. 8, No. 1 (February 1971), pp. 91–101.

the central city, then its validity is hardly in doubt. However, most of the authors imply, and some explicitly state, that suburban neighborhoods are typically more homogeneous than central city neighborhoods. References to "one-class" suburbs and suburban neighborhoods are legion, and usually it is implied that one-class neighborhoods are more characteristic of the suburbs than of the central cities. Some authors believe that suburban neighborhoods had become less homogeneous, less "monolithic," by the early 1960's [Dobriner 1963; Wrong 1967], but they do not challenge the impression that most of the mass produced post-war suburbs initially contained inhabitants highly uniform in their status characteristics.

Since a number of consequences (mainly detrimental) have been attributed to living and growing up in homogeneous suburban neighborhoods [e.g., Whyte 1956; Lee 1963; Riesman 1957], it is important to know whether or not there is, or has been, as much segregation by social level in the suburbs as alleged and whether or not suburban neighborhoods have really become more heterogeneous. So far, there has been no adequate empirical investigation of these questions. The existing evidence pertains to specific suburbs; there is not even an adequate treatment of all of the suburbs around a single central city.

In this paper we report a study designed to provide some of the needed evidence pertaining to these and related questions. Our concern with the alleged homogeneity of suburban neighborhoods leads us to consider each of the two determinants of degree of homogeneity, namely, (1) degree of residential segregation by social level and (2) degree of representation of all social levels in suburbia. Our primary focus is on the former factor, but the latter cannot be neglected. Even if suburban residents in the higher and the lower social levels are not highly segregated from one another, the neighborhoods will tend to be homogeneous if few lower-stratum people live in the suburbs.

METHODS

The study covers two dates, 1950, when the mass produced post-war suburbs were new and were just beginning to attract the attention of social commentators, and 1960, when, according to some social scientists, the trend toward greater heterogeneity of the mass produced suburbs was well under way. Data were analyzed for each date for eight Urbanized Areas of considerably varying population size and economic base and in several regions of the country. Two, Boston and Philadelphia, are old, large eastern cities which tend to conform roughly to the Burgess concentric scheme [Schnore 1963], at least in that people in the suburbs tend to be of higher status than people in the central cities (Table 2). Others (especially Los Angeles and San Diego) are newer and have no apparent tendency to conform to the Burgess scheme.

In spite of their diversity, the eight Urbanized Areas are not a random sample of all Urbanized Areas and are not necessarily representative of the universe. Rather, for a study broader in scope than this one, we drew a random sample of 15 from all Urbanized Areas for which the central cities were census tracted in 1950. When we moved from that study to this one, we could use only eight of the original 15 Urbanized Areas, because large portions of the suburbs of the other seven were not tracted in 1950. Therefore, generalization from this study to all Urbanized Areas must be very tentative.

For each Urbanized Area, we compared measures of segregation for the central city (or central cities) with measures for the suburban zone. We used the Index of Residential Dissimilarity, with census tracts the areal units, to measure the segregation between each pair of occupational groups [Duncan and Duncan 1955]. The central city values were computed from data on the census tracts predominantly (in terms of area) in the central city (or cities), and the suburban values were computed from data on census tracts predominantly in the Urbanized Area but outside the central city or cities. Location of the census tracts was determined by comparing census tract maps with maps of the Urbanized Areas. We used only eight occupational groups (28 pairs), because separate data for the two agricultural groups are not given in the census tract reports, and there were too few private household workers to use as a separate group. The mean of the index values for the 28 pairs of occupational groups is termed the Summary Segregation Index (SSI).

For Minneapolis-St. Paul, we pooled the census tracts in the two central cities to arrive at the central city index values. The Bureau of the Census also designates two central cities for the Los Angeles-Long Beach Urbanized Area, but the cities are not contiguous and one is much larger than the other. Therefore, we used only the census tracts primarily in Los Angeles for the central city data and included the Long Beach tracts with the suburban tracts.

We used census tracts as approximations of neighborhoods only because there is no practical alternative; we do not claim that the tracts are, in any sociologically meaningful sense, usually coincident with neighborhoods. However, people within a census tract do often share such neighborhood facilities and institutions as schools, churches, retail outlets, service establishments, and the like. Census tracts are more or less "neighborhood sized" units in terms of number of inhabitants; therefore, a high degree of segregation by occupational group among neighborhoods would almost always entail a high degree of segregation among census tracts, and vice versa.

Nor is segregation by occupational group a totally adequate measure of segregation by social level. The people in an occupational group do not constitute a social stratum, because the groups overlap considerably in the status characteristics of the detailed occupations they contain, and the people in each detailed occupation vary a great deal on the various dimensions of stratification aside from occupational prestige. However, the use of occupational groups to gauge segregation by social level is preferable to the available alternatives, namely, use of amount of formal education or income. In the adult population, amount of education is related in a negative and approximately linear fashion to age, and there is considerable residential segregation of persons at different stages of the life cycle. Therefore, segregation by amount of education is in part a reflection of segregation by age and thus is not an adequate indicator of segregation by social level. The incomes of adult males are also related to age, although in a nonlinear fashion, so that segregation by income also reflects in part segregation by age and stage of the life cycle.

In order to relate the data on segregation to the issue of the homogeneity of neighborhoods, we compared the occupational distribution of employed central city males with that of suburban males, for both 1950 and 1960. We made this comparison for each Urbanized Area and with the pooled data from all eight Urbanized Areas.

FINDINGS

In Table 1 we present the pooled occupational distributions of employed males in the central cities and in the suburban zones of the eight Urbanized Areas in 1950 and 1960. Obviously, all of the occupational groups well represented in the central cities were also well represented in their suburbs. Overall, the differences between the central city and the suburban distributions were very small at both dates; there was especially little difference in the proportions in the nonmanual, or "middle-class," occupations. Lower-manual workers were less well represented in the suburbs than in the central cities, but the difference was not great.

Although these eight Urbanized Areas are not necessarily representative of all cities and their suburbs, other authors have observed similar small differences in occupational distributions between central cities and suburbs [Lazerwitz 1960; Schnore 1963; Farley 1964]. Undoubtedly, suburbia in the United States was

TABLE 1. Percentage Distribution of Employed Males in Central Cities and suburbs of Eight Urbanized Areas, 1950 and 1960

Occupational Group	1950			1960		
	Central Cities	Sub-urbs	Diff. CC-S	Central Cities	Sub-urbs	Diff. CC-S
Total	100.0	100.0		100.0	100.0	
1) Professional, Technical, and Kindred Workers	10.0	11.7	−1.7	13.6	12.8	0.8
2) Farmers and Farm Managers	0.2	0.4	−0.2	0.4	0.4	0.0
3) Managers, Officials, and Proprietors, exc. farm	12.8	14.7	−1.9	10.9	13.8	−2.9
4) Clerical and Kindred Workers	9.5	8.0	1.5	10.3	8.5	1.8
5) Sales Workers	9.2	9.2	0.0	8.6	9.5	−0.9
6) Craftsmen, Foremen, and Kindred Workers	21.0	23.9	−2.9	19.8	23.8	−4.0
7) Operatives and Kindred Workers	19.7	19.1	0.6	19.9	19.2	0.7
8) Private Household Workers	0.2	0.2	0.0	0.2	0.1	0.1
9) Service Workers, exc. private household	9.3	5.9	3.4	9.3	5.9	3.4
10) Farm Laborers and Foremen	0.3	0.5	−0.2	0.2	0.5	−0.3
11) Laborers, exc. farm and mine	7.8	6.3	1.5	6.8	5.2	1.6
Nonmanual [Sum of (1) and (3) − (5)]	41.5	43.6	−2.1	43.4	44.6	−1.2
Lower Manual [Sum of (7) − (11)]	37.3	32.0	5.3	36.4	30.9	5.5

Note: Persons for whom no occupation was reported are excluded.

TABLE 2. Percentage of Employed Males in Nonmanual Occupations and Percentage in Lower Manual Occupations in the Central City and the Suburbs of Each of Eight Urbanized Areas, 1950 and 1960

Urbanized area	Nonmanual						Lower Manual					
	1950			1960			1950			1960		
	CC	S	Diff.	CC	S	Diff.	CC	S	Diff.	CC	S	Diff.
Boston	38.2	44.4	−6.2	38.7	48.6	− 9.9	41.6	33.2	8.4	41.7	29.3	12.4
Kansas City	44.3	38.2	6.1	43.6	46.4	− 2.8	36.6	39.3	−2.7	37.8	30.8	7.0
Los Angeles	45.7	42.5	3.2	48.4	43.3	5.1	33.7	32.1	1.6	32.0	32.7	−0.7
Miami	42.9	48.3	−5.4	38.7	50.6	−11.9	36.5	27.2	9.3	41.9	25.7	16.2
Minneapolis- St. Paul	44.6	47.7	−3.1	44.4	53.0	− 8.6	34.0	29.0	5.0	35.1	25.5	9.6
Phila.	36.1	45.8	−9.7	37.5	47.5	−10.0	41.6	29.8	11.8	41.9	29.4	12.5
San Diego	42.6	38.8	3.8	46.6	41.2	5.4	32.8	30.8	2.0	29.7	28.8	0.9
Syracuse	42.3	36.7	5.6	44.6	51.1	− 6.5	36.1	35.3	0.8	35.3	24.5	10.8
Mean diff.			−0.7			−4.9			4.5			8.6

Note: Persons for whom no occupation was reported are excluded.

never so uniformly "middle-class" as the journalists portrayed it to be in the early 1950's.

As we point out above, some authors have asserted that suburbia has become less uniform, meaning in most instances, less uniformly middle-class [Dobriner 1963; Wrong 1967; Goldstein and Mayer 1964]. If such a change were to occur, it would lead to a narrowing of occupational differences between the central cities and the suburbs. However, no such decline was evident in the eight Urbanized Areas we studied. The Index of Occupational Dissimilarity between the central cities and the suburbs computed from the pooled data in Table 1 is 7.0 for 1950 and 8.3 for 1960. The data for individual Urbanized Areas in Table 2 indicate even more distinctly a general increase in the central city-suburban differences. Furthermore, a study by Farley [1964] of 17 Urbanized Areas shows a general trend toward greater central city-suburban occupational differences from 1950 to 1960.

A trend away from "middle-classness" may have occurred in some of the mass produced tract developments, but no such trend occurred in the total suburban zone in any of the Urbanized Areas we studied (Table 2). In each of them, the percentage of suburban workers in nonmanual occupations increased from 1950 to 1960, and the percentage in lower-manual occupations decreased in all except Los Angeles, where it remained virtually the same. It seems that the alleged movement of suburbs away from "middle-classness" may be as illusory as the myth that a high degree of middle-class homogeneity ever existed.

The most important revelation of the data in Tables 1 and 2 for our purposes is that people at all broad occupational levels were well enough represented in the suburbs so that the occupational homogeneity of the suburbs we studied depended, in both 1950 and 1960, primarily upon degree of residential segregation by occupational level. To be sure, the very poor may not have been well represented in the suburbs, but employed male workers in lower-

status occupations were. Therefore, we turn now to the data on residential segregation.

The literature would lead one to expect greater segregation by occupational level in the suburban zones than in the central cities, but our data bear out this expectation only in the case of Miami (Tables 3 and 4). For 1960, the Summary Segregation Index is greater for the central city (or cities) except for the Miami Urbanized Area. For 1950, the SSI is identical for the central city and the suburban zone of Philadelphia and is greater for the central city (or cities) for all other Urbanized Areas except Miami. There was apparently no appreciable change in the central city-suburban difference in degree of segregation from 1950 to 1960; at both dates, the mean SSI was three points greater for the central cities than for the suburbs.

One might guess that the central city-suburban difference in SSI values results from a systematic difference in the size of census tracts in the two zones. The Index of Residential Dissimilarity is sensitive to the number and kind of areal units used in its computation, and its values can be lowered by combining units so that each contains a larger and more heterogeneous population. Therefore, if the suburban zones were typically divided into fewer census tracts, relative to population size, than the central cities, then this difference alone might account for the lower SSI values for the suburbs. In fact, the mean number of employed males was greater in the suburban than in the central city tracts in both 1950 and 1960. In 1960, the mean was 1,179 for the suburban tracts and 996 for the central city tracts; in 1950, the means were 1,411 and 1,240 (see Table 5). However, when we consider only those Urbanized Areas in which the mean number of male workers in the central city tracts was greater than or about the same as the mean in the suburban tracts, the mean SSI values are still greater for the central cities, by three points for 1950 and by two points for 1960. Therefore, it seems unlikely that the suburban SSI values would ex-

TABLE 3. Index of Residential Dissimilarity for Paired Occupational Groups, for Central Cities and for Suburban Zones, Eight Urbanized Areas, 1950

Paired occupational groups	Boston CC	S	D	Kansas City CC	S	D	Los Angeles CC	S	D	Miami CC	S	D	Minneapolis-St. Paul CC	S	D	Philadelphia CC	S	D	San Diego CC	S	D	Syracuse CC	S	D	Mean Score CC	S	D
Prof.-Mgr.	17	13	4	10	9	1	15	13	2	10	23	-13	12	10	2	17	12	5	14	10	4	15	10	5	14	13	1
Prof.-Sales	19	14	5	10	7	3	15	13	2	12	17	-5	13	7	6	16	11	5	16	11	5	14	8	6	14	11	3
Prof.-Cler.	25	27	-2	23	30	-7	27	22	5	16	24	-8	23	24	-1	26	23	3	20	14	6	30	18	12	24	23	1
Prof.-Craft.	29	34	-5	33	44	-11	35	32	3	24	44	-20	33	26	7	32	34	-2	28	20	8	34	22	12	31	32	-1
Prof.-Oper.	36	43	-7	43	59	-16	42	40	2	34	44	-10	40	38	2	40	44	-4	35	28	7	43	32	11	39	41	-2
Prof.-Serv.	36	36	0	49	46	3	44	31	13	42	35	7	38	37	1	39	40	-1	35	25	10	36	23	13	40	34	6
Prof.-Lbr.	48	40	8	57	63	-6	56	44	12	68	60	8	46	42	4	55	53	2	43	33	10	49	43	6	53	47	6
Mgr.-Sales	10	10	0	14	12	2	11	11	0	8	16	-8	11	11	0	11	10	1	12	12	0	12	9	3	11	12	-1
Mgr.-Cler.	26	24	2	25	28	-3	24	18	6	13	28	-15	22	20	2	25	23	2	18	15	3	23	12	11	22	21	1
Mgr.-Craft.	28	29	-1	34	41	-7	30	26	4	22	48	-26	30	24	6	29	32	-3	25	20	5	27	14	13	28	29	-1
Mgr.-Oper.	35	38	-3	43	55	-12	37	33	4	32	46	-14	38	33	5	36	41	-5	32	27	5	35	23	12	36	37	-1
Mgr.-Serv.	37	33	4	49	43	6	40	27	13	43	29	14	38	34	4	36	36	0	34	23	11	32	19	13	39	30	9
Mgr.-Lbr.	47	37	10	57	59	-2	51	38	13	68	61	7	44	37	7	50	50	0	42	28	14	43	34	9	50	43	7
Sales-Cler.	26	20	6	18	25	-7	19	15	4	9	17	-8	19	24	-5	25	18	7	11	10	1	18	14	4	18	18	0
Sales-Craft.	28	25	3	30	39	-9	29	24	5	20	37	-17	29	25	4	30	30	0	19	13	6	23	20	3	26	27	-1
Sales-Oper.	34	35	-1	40	54	-14	35	32	3	30	38	-8	34	37	-3	37	40	-3	27	22	5	33	29	4	34	36	-2
Sales-Serv.	36	30	6	46	42	4	37	24	13	41	26	15	33	37	-4	38	35	3	30	21	9	29	20	9	36	29	7
Sales-Lbr.	47	34	13	54	58	-4	51	38	13	68	56	12	41	41	0	52	51	1	41	29	12	42	40	2	50	43	7
Cler.-Craft.	10	13	-3	15	15	0	19	15	4	15	24	-9	13	14	-1	11	15	-4	12	13	-1	10	9	1	13	15	-2
Cler.-Oper.	19	23	-4	26	30	-4	23	23	0	24	26	-2	20	18	2	19	27	-8	20	18	2	18	17	1	21	23	-2
Cler.-Serv.	22	16	6	37	20	17	25	18	7	38	24	14	24	17	7	22	26	-4	25	20	5	20	14	6	27	19	8
Cler.-Lbr.	30	23	7	44	34	10	42	32	10	68	50	18	29	23	6	40	44	-4	37	30	7	31	28	3	40	33	7
Craft.-Oper.	13	17	-4	16	15	1	16	12	4	20	13	7	13	15	-2	14	15	-1	11	13	-2	13	10	3	15	14	1
Craft.-Serv.	13	16	-3	34	11	23	29	19	10	38	31	7	22	20	2	24	23	1	23	18	5	19	14	5	27	19	8
Craft.-Lbr.	27	19	8	38	20	18	37	25	12	64	34	30	24	22	2	40	37	3	34	22	12	28	24	5	36	25	11
Oper.-Serv.	22	16	6	24	13	11	22	22	0	21	24	-3	18	10	8	21	17	4	19	20	-1	16	14	2	20	17	3
Oper.-Lbr.	17	16	1	26	8	19	28	21	7	48	27	21	14	10	4	32	30	2	27	21	6	17	16	1	26	19	7
Serv.-Lbr.	24	17	7	17	17	0	29	23	6	38	38	0	17	13	4	23	24	-1	24	27	-3	18	20	-2	24	22	2
SSI[a]	28	25	3	33	32	1	31	25	6	33	34	-1	26	24	2	30	30	0	26	20	6	26	20	6	29	26	3

[a] Summary segregation index: mean of index values for 28 pairs of occupational groups.

TABLE 4. Index of Residential Dissimilarity for Paired Occupational Groups, for Central Cities and for Suburban Zones, Eight Urbanized Areas, 1960

Paired occupational groups	Boston			Kansas City			Los Angeles			Miami			Minneapolis-St. Paul			Philadelphia			San Diego			Syracuse			Mean score			White workers only[b]		
	CC	S	D	CC	S	D	CC	S	D	CC	S	D	CC	S	D	CC	S	D	CC	S	D	CC	S	D	CC	S	D	CC	S	D
Prof.-Mgr.	18	14	4	15	14	1	17	15	2	14	16	-2	17	15	2	17	14	3	19	12	7	20	8	12	17	14	3	17	13	4
Prof.-Sales	21	15	6	15	14	1	19	15	4	17	21	-4	17	15	2	20	13	7	18	16	2	19	12	7	18	15	3	18	15	3
Prof.-Cler.	26	28	-2	27	31	-4	33	25	8	21	29	-8	25	23	2	27	27	0	24	23	1	29	16	13	27	25	2	26	25	1
Prof.-Craft.	31	31	0	33	37	-4	33	31	2	28	41	-13	33	24	9	32	34	-2	29	27	2	36	22	14	32	31	1	32	31	1
Prof.-Oper.	38	39	-1	43	46	-3	44	40	4	40	47	-7	41	32	9	41	43	-2	38	31	7	45	29	16	41	38	3	39	37	2
Prof.-Serv.	32	32	0	46	46	0	44	31	13	43	40	3	33	28	5	39	37	2	38	28	10	36	28	8	39	34	5	34	32	2
Prof.-Lbr.	42	37	5	54	53	1	55	44	11	60	58	2	43	31	12	55	44	11	43	35	8	51	31	20	50	42	8	45	39	6
Mgr.-Sales	16	13	3	15	13	2	16	14	2	12	12	0	15	12	3	13	15	-2	14	17	-3	14	11	3	14	13	1	14	13	1
Mgr.-Cler.	27	30	-3	32	33	-1	33	25	8	16	29	-13	28	29	-1	31	31	0	22	21	1	25	15	10	27	27	0	26	26	0
Mgr.-Craft.	30	33	-3	36	38	-2	34	31	3	26	42	-16	33	30	3	34	37	-3	26	26	0	29	19	10	31	32	-1	31	32	-1
Mgr.-Oper.	37	41	-4	46	47	-1	43	38	5	38	47	-9	41	37	4	43	45	-2	34	30	4	40	28	12	40	39	1	38	38	0
Mgr.-Serv.	33	35	-2	48	47	1	43	31	12	41	35	6	38	33	5	41	39	2	33	27	6	36	26	10	39	33	6	35	33	2
Mgr.-Lbr.	44	38	6	56	53	3	53	41	12	59	59	0	44	34	10	56	45	11	38	34	4	48	30	18	50	42	8	44	39	5
Sales-Cler.	26	24	2	25	31	-6	30	21	9	14	26	-12	23	26	-3	28	24	4	18	18	0	20	17	3	23	23	0	22	23	-1
Sales-Craft.	28	26	2	33	37	-4	33	26	7	27	41	-14	30	27	3	32	32	0	23	20	3	26	22	4	29	29	0	29	29	0
Sales-Oper.	34	35	-1	41	45	-4	42	35	7	38	45	-7	37	35	2	40	41	-1	31	26	5	36	29	7	37	36	1	35	35	0
Sales-Serv.	33	29	4	44	45	-1	42	27	15	40	33	7	33	31	2	40	36	4	31	23	8	34	26	8	37	31	6	32	30	2
Sales-Lbr.	41	32	9	52	51	1	53	39	14	61	56	3	40	33	7	55	43	12	38	30	8	47	30	17	48	40	8	42	37	5
Cler.-Craft.	15	14	1	19	14	5	23	16	7	18	20	-2	15	13	2	13	16	-3	15	18	-3	13	11	2	16	15	1	16	15	1
Cler.-Oper.	21	18	3	23	19	4	25	22	3	32	28	4	21	18	3	20	24	-4	22	22	0	22	16	6	23	21	2	16	15	1
Cler.-Serv.	21	15	6	30	25	5	23	19	4	34	26	8	20	20	0	22	24	-2	22	20	2	25	16	9	25	21	4	22	20	2
Cler.-Lbr.	26	19	7	36	31	5	38	31	7	57	50	7	26	21	5	38	34	4	32	26	6	35	19	16	36	29	7	21	19	2
Craft.-Oper.	16	15	1	16	16	0	20	14	6	25	21	4	15	12	3	16	15	1	15	13	2	16	10	6	17	16	1	15	14	1
Craft.-Serv.	21	17	4	32	27	5	29	19	10	34	31	3	22	20	2	25	24	1	20	17	3	23	15	8	26	21	5	21	20	1
Craft.-Lbr.	22	17	5	35	29	6	36	27	9	53	47	6	23	18	5	40	31	9	30	20	10	29	19	10	33	26	7	26	22	4
Oper.-Serv.	22	17	5	24	22	2	22	22	0	16	20	-4	21	21	0	18	21	-3	18	20	-2	21	10	11	20	19	1	20	19	1
Oper.-Lbr.	15	14	1	23	20	3	23	22	1	33	34	-1	16	17	-1	29	26	3	23	19	4	18	14	4	23	21	2	19	19	0
Serv.-Lbr.	24	16	8	19	19	0	28	26	2	31	36	-5	22	22	0	23	24	-1	21	23	-2	23	12	11	24	22	2	24	21	3
SSI[a]	27	25	2	33	32	1	33	27	6	33	36	-3	28	24	4	32	30	2	26	23	3	29	19	10	30	27	3	28	26	2
White Workers Only[b]	27	25	2	30	31	-1	31	26	5	23	30	-7	28	24	4	29	29	0	25	23	2	28	19	9	—	—	—	—	—	—

[a] Summary segregation index: mean of index values for 28 pairs of occupational groups.
[b] Mean of indexes calculated over tracts in which more than 50 percent of residents were white.

TABLE 5. Number of Census Tracts and Mean Number of Employed Males per Census Tract in the Central City and the Suburbs of Each of Eight Urbanized Areas, 1950 and 1960

Urbanized Area	Number of Census Tracts				Mean Emp. /Ct, 00's			
	1950		1960		1950		1960	
	CC	S	CC	S	CC	S	CC	S
Boston	158	248	164	276	13	15	9	16
KC	100	10	122	102	13	15	9	10
LA	364	340	636	874	14	15	9	11
Miami	46	40	58	124	16	15	13	10
Minneap.- St. Paul	198	16	204	120	12	24	9	12
Phila.	408	180	378	360	14	13	13	12
San Diego	92	32	138	86	8	8	9	6
Syracuse	62	12	62	14	10	16	9	19

ceed the central city values if the suburban and central city tracts had averaged the same number of people.

One might also guess that the small number of census tracts in some of the suburban zones depresses their SSI values. Beyond a certain number, the number of census tracts should have no effect on the SSI, but below a certain number it may. In order for the SSI to reach its theoretical upper limit of 100, which would mean no intermixture of occupational groups in any census tract, there must be at least eight census tracts (one for each occupational group). All of the central cities and suburban zones contained more than eight tracts, but two of the suburban zones in 1950 (Kansas City and Syracuse) and one in 1960 (Syracuse) contained so few tracts in excess of eight that the number of tracts may have tended to keep the SSI relatively low (Table 5). To the extent that there is any such effect on the SSI, the index may be regarded as unreliable, although it seems more realistic to consider a small number of census tracts a limitation on the kind of segregation measured by the index. In any event, it is important to know whether or not the small number of suburban tracts in some of the Urbanized Areas accounts for the generally lower suburban SSI values.

In excluding the Urbanized Areas in which the suburban tracts had a considerably larger mean number of employed males, we have already excluded Syracuse for both 1950 and 1960, and for 1960 the mean SSI is two points greater for the central cities than for the suburbs for the remaining Urbanized Areas. When we exclude Kansas City, in addition to those we have already excluded, from the 1950 data, the mean SSI is four points greater for the central cities than for the suburbs. Clearly, the overall central city-suburban difference in the SSI is not totally an artifact of differences in the size and number of census tracts.

Although we cannot generalize with confidence from our data to all Urbanized Areas, it seems rather likely that greater residential segregation by occupational level in the central city is, or recently was, typical of Urbanized Areas in the United States. Miami's residential pattern is probably unusual and may be unique. Miami has a large and essentially nonindigenous wealthy population that is highly concentrated in a few of its several suburbs. Therefore, its suburban census tracts are highly varied in their socio-economic characteristics. The tentative conclusion that segregation is greater in the central cities than in the suburbs of most Urbanized Areas is further supported by the data from three other Urbanized Areas from our original sample of 15 for which the suburbs were completely or almost completely tracted in 1960. In each of these, the SSI for 1960 is greater for the central city than for the suburbs, by eleven points for Trenton, by nine points for Denver, and by one point for Rochester.

The sample of eleven formed by adding these three Urbanized Areas still is not a random sample and does not meet the strict requirements for use of tests of significance and generalization to the universe. However, there is little reason to believe that the sample is highly unrepresentative, and therefore we applied a Wilcoxon Matched-Pairs Signed-Ranks Test to the eleven pairs of central cities and suburbs in 1960. The results of a one-tailed test are significant at less than the .005 level. This reinforces our belief that probably segregation was generally greater in central cities than in suburbs throughout the country in 1960.

Although our sample is varied and contains large and smaller and old and newer cities, it does not contain enough of any type to serve as a basis for distinguishing among types of Urbanized Areas in terms of the central city-suburban difference in the residential segregation of occupational groups. The difference is not as great in the two old, eastern Urbanized Areas (Boston and Philadelphia) as in the two newer, western cities (Los Angeles and San Diego), but only the study of additional Urbanized Areas could determine whether or not this reflects a general difference between the older and the newer Urbanized Areas.

We point out above that the belief, expressed by Dobriner [1963] and others that suburbs have become more heterogeneous through a loss of "middle-classness" is not supported by the data on central city and suburban occupational distributions in 1950 and 1960. However, in spite of those data, individual suburbs and suburban neighborhoods could have generally become more heterogeneous if segregation by social level had decreased. If this had occurred, Dobriner [1963: 27] could have been correct when he wrote in the early 1960's that "the 'middle class' suburb a decade ago is fast disappearing from the metropolitan scene. . . ." But again the data fail to support Dobriner's impression. In the eight suburban zones we studied, segregation apparently remained about the same or increased slightly; the mean suburban SSI is 26 for 1950 and 27 for 1960.

To explain completely why the suburban segregation index values are generally smaller than the central city values is beyond the scope of this paper. Indeed, most of the differences are so small that they hardly need explaining; we might merely conclude that there are no important differences between central cities and suburbs in residential segregation by social level. We might agree with Dobriner [1963: 27] that the suburban zone is not now sociologically distinctive, at least insofar as residential patterns are concerned, and we might add that it probably never was.

However, redirecting attention from the SSI to the Index of Residential Dissimilarity values for pairs of occupational groups (Tables 3 and 4) leads to discovery of a greater amount of suburban distinctiveness than the SSI alone reveals. In the case of high-level groups paired with intermediate-level groups, there are no consistent and considerable differences between the central cities and the suburban zones. However, when the two lowest-ranking groups, laborers and service workers, are paired with any of the other groups, the index values are rather consistently, and sometimes very considerably, higher for the central cities. This is true even for Miami, for which most of the other index values and the SSI are higher for the suburbs.

One might suspect that the major reason for this, as well as for the higher SSI values for the central cities, is that the very high degree of Negro-white residential segregation in all Urbanized Areas contributed to segregation by social level (since Negroes are greatly overrepresented as laborers and service workers and whites are overrepresented in the higher levels), and this contribution was mainly in the central cities, where most Negroes lived. In order to determine whether or not Negro-white segregation largely accounts for the higher central city segregation index values, we recomputed all of the index values for 1960 using only those census tracts in which more than 50 percent of the residents were white. There were very few nonwhites in most of these tracts and very few whites in most of the excluded tracts, so the data for the predominantly white tracts are essentially data on the segregation by occupational group of white workers. These data are summarized in the last row and in the last columns of Table 4.

Virtually eliminating the effects of Negro-white residential segregation does reduce the central city-suburban difference, but the difference in the mean SSI declines only from three points to two. The difference in index values with pairs of occupational groups including service workers is reduced considerably, in many cases by about two-thirds. However, the difference with pairs including laborers are generally not reduced more than about a fourth to a third; these remain the greatest differences, generally speaking, and many of them are rather substantial. Therefore, the contribution of Negro-white segregation cannot largely account for the overall greater segregation by occupational group in the central cities nor for the greater segregation there of laborers from higher-status workers.

What then does largely account for the generally greater segregation in central cities? We can offer only a tentative explanation. Because of the greater population density and compactness and the better public transportation facilities of the typical central city, higher-status and lower-status workers can be highly segregated there without anyone living beyond easy commuting range of his place of work. In contrast, it is likely that a very high degree of segregation in the suburban zone would make the journey to work too expensive for many lower-income workers. Many retail and service establishments, schools, and other facilities are in or convenient to high-status

neighborhoods, and a good many laborers, as well as service workers, are employed by these facilities. These workers, in turn, need to live as near as possible, because they, unlike upper-middle-class workers, cannot afford to commute long distances by automobile, and economical public transportation from one segment of the suburban zone to another is often not available. For instance, the janitor at a high-status suburban school may not be likely to live several census tracts away; rather, he may typically live in a lower-income enclave in the same or an adjacent tract.

Of more importance than the reasons for the relatively low level of segregation by social level in suburbia are its probable consequences. The alleged detrimental consequences of living in homogeneous "one-class" neighborhoods (such as the inhibition of development of empathy for and understanding of people in other social strata) that the critics of suburbia have so loudly decried are probably not so great as the critics have believed. To the extent that they are real, they are not likely to be uniquely suburban nor much, if any, more characteristic of suburbs than of central cities. To be sure, people at the different social levels are typically separated by fewer miles and feet in the central cities, which may make some difference in the degree of contact and interaction among them. However, it seems unlikely that this greater physical proximity leads, in itself, to much primary and intimate interaction among the social levels or that it leads to greater sharing of neighborhood institutions and facilities than occurs in the suburbs.

We must stress, however, that we are concerned only with the alleged socio-economic homogeneity of suburban neighborhoods, and we have dealt only with occupational homogeneity. Many students of suburbia have been more concerned with homogeneity in terms of race, ethnicity, stage of the family life cycle, degree of family centeredness, and the like. Many suburban neighborhoods are highly homogeneous in terms of race and probably in terms of some of the other variables. The alleged consequences of these kinds of homogeneity may well be prevalent in suburbia.

One may wonder why the impression that suburban neighborhoods are unusually homogeneous in their socio-economic characteristics has become so prevalent in the absence of empirical support. This apparently incorrect impression may have grown out of the fact that the suburban population is usually less dense, and therefore each cluster of relatively homogeneous residents covers more territory and may be more conspicuous. One large high-rise apartment building with rents within a narrow range may house as many people as a medium-sized tract development, but if it is near housing that is conspicuously more or less expensive, or just architecturally different, it may not give the same impression of a homogenized mass of people as a sprawling sea of tract houses. Central city slums often have considerable architectural variety and cover little territory, but the typical slum may contain a larger number of socio-economically similar people than the typical tract development.

REFERENCES

Berger, B. M., 1960. *Working Class Suburb.* Berkeley: University of California Press.

——, 1961. "The Myth of Suburbia," *Journal of Social Issues,* 27: 38–49.

Bernard, J. 1962. *American Community Behavior.* 2nd ed. New York: Holt, Rinehart, and Winston.

Beshers, J. M., 1962. *Urban Social Structure.* New York: Free Press.

Boskoff, A., 1970. *The Sociology of Urban Regions.* 2nd ed. New York: Appleton-Century-Crofts.

Broom, L., and P. Selznick, 1968. *Sociology.* 4th ed. New York: Harper and Row.

Coleman, J. S., 1966. "Community Disorganization," in R. K. Merton and R. A. Nisbet (eds.), *Contemporary Social Problems.* 2nd ed. New York: Harcourt, Brace, and World.

Dobriner, W. M., 1963. *Class in Suburbia.* Englewood Cliffs: Prentice-Hall.

Duncan, O. D., and B. Duncan, 1955. Residential Distribution and Occupational Stratification. *American Journal of Sociology,* 60: 493–503. [No. 32 in this volume.]

Farley, R., 1964. "Suburban Persistence." *American Sociological Review,* 29: 38–47.

Fava, S. F., 1956. "Suburbanism as a Way of Life." *American Sociological Review,* 21: 34–37.

Goldstein, S. and K. Mayer, 1964. "Population Decline and the Social and Economic Structure of the American City." *American Sociological Review,* 29: 48–54.

Lazerwitz, B., 1960. "Metropolitan Residential Belts, 1950 and 1956." *American Sociological Review,* 25: 245–252.

Lee, D., 1963. "Suburbia Reconsidered: Diversity and the Creative Life," in E. Green (ed.), *Man and the Modern City.* Pittsburgh: University of Pittsburgh Press.

Martin, W., 1956. The Structuring of Social Relationships Engendered by Suburban Residence." *American Sociological Review,* 21: 446–453.

Packard, V., 1959. *The Status Seekers.* New York: McKay.

Riesman, D., 1957. "The Suburban Dislocation," *Annals of the American Academy of Political and Social Science*, 314: 123–143.

Schnore, L., 1963. "The Socio-Economic Status of Cities and Suburbs." *American Sociological Review*, 28: 76–85.

Whyte, W. H., 1956. *The Organization Man.* New York: Simon and Schuster.

Wood, R. C., 1959. *Suburbia: Its People and Their Politics.* Boston: Houghton Mifflin.

Wrong, D. H., 1967. "Suburbs and Myths of Suburbia," in D. H. Wrong and H. L. Gracey (eds.), *Readings in Introductory Sociology.* New York: Macmillan.

37

ELEANOR P. WOLF
CHARLES N. LEBEAUX

On the Destruction of Poor Neighborhoods by Urban Renewal

"Slum clearance" for urban renewal is criticized as destroying social life in "slum" neighborhoods, e.g., residents in Boston's West End showed strong attachment to homes and neighborhood. But most such studies have been in "old-style ethnic" areas; most "slum clearance" now occurs in low-income Negro neighborhoods. A Detroit study of a poor Negro area like those renewed finds fundamental differences between it and West End, including substantially less sentimental attachment to homes, neighborhood, and "external space." Social policy in urban renewal, however, must consider more than social ties and sentiments of attachment to neighborhood. Basic to any program of clearance and relocation of low-income households must be a means of rehousing those who are dislodged. To date, adequate national programs for the rehousing of poor people have not been enacted.

There has been severe criticism of urban renewal projects where land is made available in the central city through what is described as "slum clearance." Some of this criticism challenges the designation "slum" when it is applied to some neighborhoods in which poor people live (many of them in substandard housing), but which these critics assert are not "physically, socially or emotionally harmful to their residents or to the larger community."[1] There

Reprinted from *Social Problems*, Vol. 15, No. 1 (Summer 1967), pp. 3–8, by permission of the Society for the Study of Social Problems.

This is a slightly revised version of a paper read at the annual meeting of the American Sociological Society, September, 1966 at Miami Beach, Florida. We have benefited from comments made by Herbert Gans.

[1] Herbert Gans, *The Urban Villagers* (New York: Free Press, 1962), p. 309.

are also those who, although they do not challenge the "slum" label nor the prevalence of some kinds of deviant behavior, see in such areas a setting for a rewarding and satisfying life. For example, Seeley declares:

> . . . no society in which I have lived before or since seemed to me to present so many of its members . . . so many possibilities and actualities of fulfillment . . . an outlet for aggressiveness, for adventure, for a sense of effectiveness, for deep feelings of belonging without undue sacrifice of uniqueness or identity, for sex satisfaction, for strong if not fierce loyalties, for a sense of independence from the pervasive, omnicompetent, omniscient authority-in-general.[2]

To what extent does the slum clearance phase of urban renewal uproot and destroy a neighborhood matrix of social life which provides profound and irreplaceable satisfactions for its residents? This question, the central concern of this paper, has been the focus of a series of important studies conducted by social scientists in Boston's West End. Their general finding of the strong attachment of residents to their homes and neighborhood, and the deep resentment of these residents at its demolition are well-known and substantially documented.[3]

However, most of the areas slated for clearance in connection with urban renewal programs are neither predominantly Italian (as in the West End) nor Polish (locale of the Seeley quotation), but are occupied by low-income Negro households. Investigation of the extent to which the West End findings apply to such areas becomes, therefore, important both for

social policy and sociological theory. One of the chief research aims of one section of a study conducted at Wayne State University in 1964–65 was to make some such comparisons.[4] The site selected (Detroit Census Tract #515) was chosen because it was an old core-city area, as yet not designated for clearance, and occupied by an almost all-Negro, predominantly low-income population, living in housing of which about 65% was defined by the Census as substandard.[5] Data were obtained by home interviews from a probability sample of 216 households, which constituted approximately one-fourth of the total in the tract.

A most striking contrast exists between #515 and the West End in the extent of positive sentiments about the neighborhood. In the West End three-fourths of the sample expressed predominantly positive feelings, while only about one-fourth of #515 respondents could be so classified. According to Hartman it was clear that most West End residents lived there by choice, rather than as a result of the absence of other alternatives.[6] In #515 almost two-thirds of respondents were either planning to move, "thinking about moving," or said that they would like to move away if they could. Surprisingly, home ownership was not related to residential satisfaction in #515. Owners were as likely as renters to answer Yes to the question: Would you like to move away from here if you could? And a smaller percentage (26% v. 36%) of owners held the area in high

[2] John Seeley, "The Slum: Its Nature, Use and Users," JAIP, XXV (February 1959): 10.

[3] In addition to Gans, op. cit., see Marc Fried and P. Gleicher, "Some Sources of Residential Satisfaction in an Urban Slum," JAIP, XXVII, No. 4 (November 1961; Chester Hartman, "Social Values and Housing Orientations," Journal of Social Issues (April 1963); Marc Fried, "Grieving for a Lost Home," in Leonard J. Duhl, editor, The Urban Condition, New York: Basic Books, 1963. Marc Fried is the Director of the West End Project, "Relocation and Mental Health: Adaptation Under Stress," conducted by the Center for Community Studies in the Department of Psychiatry of the Massachusetts General Hospital and the Harvard Medical School and supported by a grant from the NIMH.

[4] Eleanor P. Wolf and Charles N. Lebeaux, Studies in Change and Renewal in an Urban Community, Vols. I and II, Detroit: Wayne State University, 1965. A series of studies dealing with problems of neighborhood change and urban renewal, including redevelopment and relocation of households and businesses, conducted at Wayne State University with the aid of funds from Detroit's Community Renewal Program and U. S. Housing and Home Finance Agency, (now H.U.D.). The present authors were co-directors of the project.

[5] This is a rough estimate based on 1960 U. S. Census Figures of 54% "deteriorating" and 3% "dilapidated." To this, approximately 10% has been added, based on the consensus of expert local evaluation of the increased deterioration between 1959 and 1964.

[6] Chester Hartman, op. cit., pp. 114–115.

enough esteem to be willing to recommend it to a friend. These responses may perhaps be a consequence of the more genteel social status of these poor elderly owners, most of whom came to live in #515 many years ago. No doubt some of the desire to move was related to the impact of slum-clearance programs already completed in areas nearby, and the judgments of some that #515 would also eventually be cleared. But in this respect the areas were not dissimilar; plans to clear and redevelop the West End had been officially announced five years before the first series of household interviews was conducted.[7]

A number of factors suggest themselves as possibly involved in accounting for this marked difference in general area sentiment.

SOCIAL CLASS DIFFERENCES

The West End was an area mainly of skilled and semi-skilled workers, with only 25% of the earners in the low-status unskilled categories. By contrast, two-thirds of all of the Detroit area workers were classified as "unskilled." Only 45% of the households in #515 derived income solely from employment, and this was often of an irregular type. Most of the remaining households depended wholly or in part on transfer payments. Median household income in the Detroit neighborhood was, in 1963, $3750, and is estimated to have been approximately $4000 in the West End, in 1958.[8]

HOUSING AND RESIDENTIAL FACTORS

Tangible evidence of the West Enders' attachment to the area may be seen in the fact that 55% had lived there 20 years or more. Only 16% of the residents in #515 had lived there for a similar period. However, it was not an area of transiency.[9] Dwelling-units in the two areas were so different that comparisons are dif-

ficult. The West End was made up of multistory rental units, with only 27% of households living at a density ratio (persons per room) as low as .5 or less. Like so much of Detroit, 44% of the units in #515 were owner-occupied, often by elderly persons, an important factor in creating the lesser amount of overcrowding. Sixty-two percent of all #515 households were living at the low density ratio of .5 or less. It may be noted that this finding raises some questions about the great importance attributed to crowding in much of the literature on "slum pathology." It is much stressed, for example, in Alvin Schorr's *Slums and Social Insecurity*, which notes that crowding is usually considered "the key housing factor."[10] Yet Gans describes the more crowded West End as lacking "the social criteria that would have made it a slum."[11] It would seem that crowding has no invariable consequences. More detailed studies of the way in which this factor operates are evidently needed.

Chester Hartman judged, from a study of interviewers' evaluations, that about one-fourth of all dwelling-units in the West End were "poor," or "very bad."[12] Using a similar scale, our interviewers placed 27% of the dwellings they visited in #515 in comparable categories.

Thus, the less-liked poor Negro neighborhood emerges as less crowded, more often owner-occupied, and of about the same physical quality as the much-loved West End.

SOCIAL TIES

Approximately 60% of West End respondents had relatives in the area, as compared with 37% of #515 respondents, who reported kin "in this neighborhood." In part this is the result of the greater size of the Boston area. However, of the Detroit respondents who did have relatives in the neighborhood, only about half reported that they "felt close" to any one of them. In both areas there were numerous and important

---

[7] Herbert Gans, op. cit., p. 282.

[8] From data supplied by Dr. Fried, Director of West End Project.

[9] About two-thirds had lived in their dwellings approximately four years or more. About half had lived in the same house for eight or more years.

[10] U. S. Department of Health, Education, and Welfare, 1964, pp. 16 and 17–22.

[11] Herbert Gans, op. cit., p. 316.

[12] Reported by Gans, op. cit., p. 314.

ties of friendship and mutual aid, a subject which was a central focus of research in both studies.[13] Yet in answer to the question, "For keeping in touch with the people you like to keep in contact with, would you say you're better off living here—or would it be better if you were living someplace else?," only 56% of the Detroit respondents said *Here*. This question was not used in the West End research, but from a number of similar questions it appears that the figure would be much higher. Again, this may be due to the much larger population of West End (about twice as great) but some doubt is cast upon this explanation by our finding that three-fourths of all social ties in #515 existed within the *same block*.

ATTITUDES TOWARD EXTERNAL SPACE

Researchers in the West End noted the importance of the space outside the dwelling as a "meaningful locus for interpersonal contact, leisure-time activities, shopping and services."[14] This appeared to be an important element in the "attachment to place" found by the investigators. Although many #515 residents depended on local stores, an emotional "attachment to place" was not discernible. Many residents were, in varying degrees, afraid of the neighborhood. One-third characterized the area as "not safe," and an additional third (in the course of explaining why they judged it "safe") mentioned conditions (e.g., their protection by constant police surveillance) which suggest considerable uneasiness. Our two participant observers (one single man and one married woman with her husband and child, who took up residence in the area for about a year) reported a large amount of rowdy, violent, and delinquent behavior on streets and playgrounds. There is scant mention of any problem of this nature in West End accounts.[15]

At the risk of obscuring fine distinctions we may characterize Detroit Tract #515 as a low-income residual core-city Negro area with a large proportion of dependent households, an area where, in most cases, people remained for reasons other than preference. A substantial proportion of families might be described as "unstable" or "irregular" in composition.[16] Despite numerous and very important social ties, and many factors of convenience, most residents held the area in low esteem and many considered it dangerous. On most blocks the life-style might be described as *lower-class*.

The West End emerges as a vital working-class area, characterized by stable family life, an area to which residents were attached by ties of sentiment and ethnic identification, as well as convenience and low rent.[17] Seventy-one percent of its residents named the West End as their "real home," the place where they felt they "really belonged." If the life-style was not that of the dominant middle-class variety, it suggested not so much *deprivation* (as in #515) but *difference*, worthy of respect in the eyes of those who lived there. #515 does not reveal this kind of self-esteem; to paraphrase a sentence from William Petersen, it measures itself in the coin of the overall society and finds much less to value.[18] Although many feared eventual urban renewal because of their meager resources for resettlement, there were few comments which suggested that residents thought the area was "too good to tear down." Their negative sentiments did not appear to be based primarily on the physical condition of their

---

[13] See Fried and Gleicher, op. cit., especially pp. 310–311.

[14] Ibid., pp. 311–312. The quotation is from Hartman, op. cit., pp. 129–130.

[15] See Gans, op. cit., pp. 312–313.

[16] Approximately 40% of children under 18 were living with but one, or neither of their parents, in contrast to 11% in the Detroit metropolitan area as a whole. This figure is perhaps a low estimate of the proportion of such children, since in households containing both a husband and wife these persons were assumed to be the parents of any children living with them. There were also a considerable number of temporary unions.

[17] See Gans, op. cit., pp. 244–246, for an excellent summary of working-class vs. lower-class life styles.

[18] From William Petersen, "Success Story, Japanese-American Style," *The New York Times Magazine* (January 9, 1966), p. 43.

dwellings, but rather on the general social characteristics of the neighborhood, i.e., the substantial proportions of persons displaying the kinds of behavior associated with slum life.

SOME IMPLICATIONS OF THE FINDINGS

There are ever fewer old-style ethnic neighborhoods like the West End in the United States, but there are many poor Negro areas like #515, close to valuable downtown lands. *If* it should be established that most of their inhabitants tend to view them as most of our respondents did, does this mean that there need be no hesitation in proceeding with the kinds of slum clearance and redevelopment programs which have been conducted in the past several years? Such a conclusion is unjustified. Positive satisfactions in #515 and similar areas may be few in number but who can calculate their contribution to the lives of those who have so little and whose resources for improving their situation are in no way enhanced by relocation, at least as conducted in the past? Indeed, it is misleading even to describe these programs as "slumclearance." In our experience this term is popularly interpreted to mean that (1) better housing awaits those displaced, and (2) the demolition of the old ("slum") housing has some kind of desirable impact upon the behavior which has become incorporated into the meaning of the term, slum. This is in line with the observation made by the present authors,[4] by Wilson,[19] and others that as a solution to the fundamental problems of American cities, urban renewal as presently conducted (i.e., up to 1966) is largely irrelevant.

The nature and intensity of sentiments felt by residents of areas being cleared for other land uses is but one factor in a complex problem and cannot be considered in a vacuum. In cities with few vacancies in low-income housing it might well be that this alone ought to halt clearance. Herbert Gans has suggested that social scientists should study such neighborhoods to determine whether the "existing social system satisfies more positive than negative functions for the residents" so that planners can decide "whether the destruction of this social system is justified by the benefits to be derived from renewal."[20] Although ultimately such decisions must be made, it is obvious that they require value judgments in addition to scientific knowledge in the assignment of the pluses and minuses. For example: Social ties may be strong and meaningful in a high-crime area, where people aid each other in such activities and in avoiding the police. Or: Relocation of an ethnic community may tend to disperse it if it is Italian (a negative or positive consequence?), but maintain it if it is Negro. Or: Redevelopment of civic centers and central business districts not only may improve the city's financial resources, but may provide intangible gains to city morale, including that of poor people.[21] Or: Because most remaining housing is not likely to be as substandard as that demolished, relocated people *are* often found to be living in better housing which is more costly, and leaves them less to spend on education, medical care, clothes or a new television. There are even instances when important social institutions may be justified in displacing poor residents to modify the character of the immediate environment, e.g., universities and hospitals menaced by nearby populations with high crime rates.[22]

---

[19] James Q. Wilson, "Urban Renewal Does Not Always Renew," *Harvard Today* (January 1965), especially p. 3.

[20] See Gans, op. cit., p. 329; also "Planning for Urban Renewal," *Transaction*, I, No. 1 (November 1963), especially pp. 6–7.

[21] Residents of #515 generally approved of urban renewal when questioned about various aspects of the program in general terms. However, our studies of relocation (Study Directors were Shirley Terreberry for households and Harriet Saperstein for businesses) showed that many of those directly involved in past clearance in Detroit had varying degrees of negative appraisals of this experience. See James Q. Wilson for some discussion of the "symbolic and intangible" benefits of renewal, in Wilson, op. cit., p. 5.

[22] Detroit hospitals long complained of problems with both staff and patients as a consequence of the fear of both these groups apparently resulting from street crime in the area. Wayne State University is now under attack by local citizen's groups for a program of clearance and land acquisition for expansion. This program contains no provision for new subsidized housing at a cost which poor people could pay because, as yet, no Federal legislation exists which makes this possible.

How does one reckon up these "gains and losses?" This dismal arithmetic could perhaps be avoided if Congressional action provided attractive enough housing alternatives for poor people so that relocation would only rarely be "involuntary." But until this is achieved, city governments, hardpressed for funds, try desperately to improve their financial situations and (unlike sociologists) feel compelled to choose the lesser among many evils.

38

HOWARD M. BAHR

The Gradual Disappearance of Skid Row

Annual enumerations of the Bowery, Manhattan's skid-row area, have shown a consistent decline in population. Inquiries were sent to commissioners of welfare in forty United States cities to determine if the declining skid-row population is a local or a national phenomenon. Results indicate that in most cities the skid-row population is declining. Apparently, this decline is not due to a decrease in the absolute size of the homeless population, but rather to several factors which have operated to disperse homeless men from the traditional skid row to other parts of the city.

A recent study of skid-row life observes that skid row seems to be fading from the American scene. A St. Louis newspaper reports that "Old Skid Row is on the Skids." [1] In New York the owner of a Bowery lodging house replies to a query about the future of the Bowery with the phrase "ripe to be torn down and going out of business." These judgments, if accurate, have far-reaching implications both for urban public policy and for future research on homelessness, drinking, and related problems. In this paper we use two types of data—annual population enumerations from one major skid row, and results from a survey of commissioners of welfare in cities throughout the nation—in evaluating these generalizations about the gradual disappearance of skid row.

Reprinted from *Social Problems*, Vol. 15, No. 1 (Summer 1967), pp. 41–45, by permission of the Society for the Study of Social Problems.

This article may be identified as publication No. A-480 of the Bureau of Applied Social Research, Columbia University. It is part of a research program currently financed by a grant (MH–10861) from the National Institutes of Health, U.S. Public Health Service. I am greatly indebted to Theodore Caplow for general guidance and editorial assistance. The research assistance of Richard Riday and Barbara Luise Margolies is gratefully acknowledged. Also, Nan Markel Sigal and Stanley K. Henshaw read an earlier draft of this report and made helpful suggestions.
[1] Samuel E. Wallace, *Skid Row as a Way of Life* (Totowa, N.J.: The Bedminster Press, 1965), p. 202; Dickson Terry, "Old Skid Row is on the Skids," *St. Louis Post-Dispatch* (March 14, 1965), p. 1F.

BOWERY TRENDS

For several years expert observers of Manhattan's Bowery have noted a continuing decline in the number of homeless men there,[2] but until recently, "hard" data applicable to the entire Bowery have not been available to test these observations. In 1964, however, a series of annual enumerations of the area was begun by Columbia University's Bowery Project under the supervision of Professor Theodore Caplow. Three of these enumerations have been completed.[3] In addition, estimates of the population of the Bowery in 1949 and 1963 have been made.[4] These data support the view that the Bowery's population is shrinking.

Over the past 15 years there has been a substantial decrease in the number of homeless men living on the Bowery (see Table 1). Between 1949 and 1966 the population dropped from 13,675 to 5,406, a decline of more than 50 percent. In the year following the 1963 enumeration the population of the Bowery dropped 7 percent, the following year it declined 6 percent, and between 1965 and 1966 censuses it fell 11 percent. If the trend continues, by 1971

the homeless population of the area will be about 3,000.

NATIONAL TRENDS

In an attempt to determine whether the declining Bowery population represented part of a national trend or was limited to New York City, inquiries were sent to commissioners of welfare in forty United States cities having sizable skid-row areas.[5] The letter requested information about recent population trends in each city's skid row(s), and asked if the city sponsored redevelopment or rehabilitation programs that impinged on skid row and its men.

In all, correspondents in twenty-eight cities[6] provided information about population trends affecting their skid rows. Sometimes the commissioners themselves replied, and sometimes the inquiries were referred to local experts on the staffs of agencies dealing more directly with skid row.

Data from the twenty-eight cities are summarized in Table 2. They demonstrate a consistent national trend: the old skid rows seem to be disappearing. However, the trend apparent in Table 2 should be interpreted in the light of some qualifications about the data.

First, the quality of the data varies from city to city. In some cases census statistics or administrative caseloads provided an empirical basis for judgment, but in others we have only the opinion of local experts.

A second qualification concerns the extent of population decline. Some of the reported declines are very large, involving 50 percent or more of the total skid-row population. Declines in other cities may be relatively small.

Despite these qualifications, the data support the position that the population of Ameri-

---

[2] The Bowery reached its peak population during the Depression, when the number of homeless men there on any given day varied from about 15,000 in April, 1930 to over 20,000 in March, 1935. Changes in the capacity of lodging facilities for homeless men also indicate a long-term decline in the population. Lodging houses in Manhattan, most of which were on the Bowery, had a capacity of about 16,000 beds in 1933. Our annual enumerations show the capacity of Bowery facilities in 1964, 1965, and 1966 to be, respectively, 9,219, 8,652, and 8,541 beds. See Nels Anderson, *The Homeless in New York City* (New York: Welfare Council of New York City, 1934), pp. 46–47 and 412–413; and Welfare Council of New York City, *Homeless Men in New York City* (New York: Welfare Council, 1949), pp. 1 and 23.

[3] The methods and findings of these enumerations are reported in George Nash and Patricia Nash, *A Preliminary Estimate of the Population and Housing of the Bowery in New York City* (New York: Bureau of Applied Social Research, Columbia University, 1964); and Michael A. Baker, *An Estimate of the Population of Homeless Men in the Bowery Area, New York City, February 26, 1965* (New York: Bureau of Applied Social Research, Columbia University, 1965). The 1966 census was taken in the same manner as the earlier censuses, and readers are referred to these reports for details of procedure.

[4] Nash and Nash, op. cit., p. 15; and George Nash, *Habitats of Homeless Men* (New York: Bureau of Applied Social Research, Columbia University, 1964), p. C–5. See also a discussion of past enumerations of the Bowery in Baker, op. cit., pp. 23–28.

---

[5] Donald J. Bogue, *Skid Row in American Cities* (Chicago: Community and Family Study Center, University of Chicago, 1963), p. 6.

[6] After three mailings, we had replies from 36 cities. However, correspondents in eight cities were unable to give us any information about recent changes in the population of their skid rows. The "No Information" column of Table 2 includes those eight.

TABLE 1.   Winter[a] Population of the Bowery, 1949 to 1966, and Projections for 1967 to 1971

1949	1963	1964	1965	1966	1967[d]	1969	1971
13,675[b]	6,938	6,477[c]	6,093	5,406	5,000	4,000	3,000

[a] The 1963 estimate is for a day in January. The other figures are for February. Date of enumeration was the last Friday in February.

[b] Presumably a slight over-estimate; it includes homeless men in an adjacent area that in 1963 had a population of 784.

[c] Markel estimates that there were approximately 800 more homeless men in jail on February 28, 1964 than is usually the case. Accordingly, census figures for the Bowery and an adjacent area were adjusted to include these men. The actual enumerated population of the Bowery was 5,773 men. See Nan Markel, *A Preliminary Study of New York's Legal Agencies and Their Effect on Homeless Men and the Bowery*, New York: Bureau of Applied Social Research, 1964, pp. 25–34.

[d] A 1967 enumeration, conducted after this paper was prepared, set the population of the Bowery at 4,851 men.

TABLE 2.   Current Population Trends in Skid Rows in Selected American Cities, 1966

Skid-Row Population				
Increasing	Stable	Decreasing		No Information
Tacoma	Birmingham	Chattanooga	Omaha	Akron
	Boston	Chicago	Philadelphia	Baltimore
	Richmond	Cincinnati	Pittsburgh	Buffalo
		Cleveland	Portland	Columbus
		Detroit	Providence	Denver
		Fort Worth	Rochester	Indianapolis
		Houston	Sacramento	Kansas City
		Milwaukee	St. Louis	Los Angeles
		Minneapolis	St. Paul	Oakland
		Nashville	Toledo	Norfolk
		New Orleans	Seattle	San Jose
		Oklahoma City	San Francisco	Syracuse

can skid-row areas is declining; skid row is indeed "on the skids." Furthermore, the decline can be expected to continue and perhaps accelerate as urban renewal programs now in planning stages are carried out.

REASONS FOR THE DECLINE

To what extent can the decline be attributed? Does it represent a real decrease in the number of homeless people or is it due merely to their dispersion from the skid rows to other areas of the city?

Observers on New York's Bowery attribute the decline there to three factors: (1) national economic prosperity, (2) changes in the composition of the skid-row population which make the area less attractive to working men and pensioners, and (3) changing policies of the Department of Welfare which induce men to live elsewhere. According to the "national prosperity" view skid rows are barometers of the level of the economy. When unemployment is down and business booming, skid rows are almost empty; when business falters and jobs are hard to get, skid rows fill up. As one hotel manager put it, "the lodging houses are barometers of business; business down, you're up."

Changes in the composition of skid-row

populations also are partly due to the state of the economy. When jobs are easy to find, most of the men who want to work are employed. Then only the "hard core" derelicts and unemployables are left on skid row, and they are easy prey for muggers and jack-rollers. It is widely believed on the Bowery that there has been a recent influx of Negro hoodlums, and consequently many older men are afraid to come to the Bowery and walk the streets. According to one informant:

> The backbone of the Bowery, the old pensioner, is going the way of all flesh (death or a home) and this leaves the worst element which tends to chase others. Hence a vicious circle. Medicare should hasten this decline and thus we have left only the rotten core—the wino-derelict.

To some extent the changing character of the Bowery man may be attributed to a Department of Welfare policy of placing unattached men in off-Bowery rooming houses rather than skid-row lodging houses. Naturally the lodging-house owners are unhappy about this policy. In the words of one of them:

> ... the whole city instead of the Bowery then gets ruined.... They [homeless men] belong down here. We're not losing them, they're taking them out. It's not that the men want off the Bowery—they're forced; they [Department of Welfare] won't give them tickets if they stay here; they'd rather be here.

Also, part of the recent population decline may be due to Operation Bowery, a Department of Welfare agency that works to rehabilitate and relocate skid-row men.

It is probable that the factors mentioned above, or similar ones, have influenced population changes on skid rows outside New York City. One important factor operating in many cities which has yet to exert much direct effect on the Bowery is urban renewal. In many cities, urban redevelopment programs have dispersed skid-row populations, replacing skid-row institutions with more respectable facilities such as concert halls and civic centers. Urban renewal for the Bowery area is still in the planning stages.

Neither in New York nor the other cities is it possible to assert that the homeless population is disappearing. In fact, several of the officials who corresponded with us stressed that the population decline on skid row was due to dispersion and did not represent a disappearance of the homeless men. Note, for example, the following comments by informants in Houston, Rochester, St. Louis and San Francisco:

> Many buildings previously housing homeless men have been demolished ... resulting in some rather undefined spread of our skid row area in numerous directions.
>
> ... our traditional Skid Row, has been recently removed by an urban redevelopment project ... making regrouping in other parts of the downtown area a strong possibility, if not an absolute necessity.
>
> The situation hasn't been alleviated, it's merely been displaced. Instead of one big Skid Row we now have a lot of little ones around the city.[7]
>
> It is our impression that ... smaller "skid rows" are proliferating in various areas of the city.... It is also our impression that the number of "unattached" men of low economic status residing outside of institutions has in nowise diminished over the past 15 years in San Francisco.

These remarks may not reflect conditions in other cities, i.e., in some places declines of skid-row populations may represent real attrition of the homeless population. In general, however, there is little evidence that the absolute number of homeless persons is declining.

SUMMARY AND SPECULATIONS

The following conclusions seem warranted by the data: (1) Skid-row populations in most major cities are declining. (2) The declining population need not imply a decrease in the absolute size of the homeless population, but rather seems a result of a number of factors operating to disperse the homeless population from skid row.

To some extent, dispersion of skid-row men will "hide" the problem of homelessness.

---

[7] Terry, op. cit.

If they no longer have an ecological base, homeless men may receive less attention from the general public. On the other hand, an increase in the number of homeless men in a particular neighborhood makes them more visible in that area and may provoke hostile reactions among other residents.[8]

As dispersion of the men and redevelopment of the area eliminate the relatively integrated complex of businesses and institutions that have serviced the homeless population, it may become more difficult for homeless men to meet their needs, and for city agencies to care for them. In particular, the homeless man probably will have to pay more for his food, drink, and lodging, and welfare agencies will find it more expensive to provide services for a widely dispersed population than for a concentration of homeless men.

---

[8] See, for example, Joan H. Shapiro, "Single-Room Occupancy; Community of the Alone," *Social Work*, 11 (October 1966): 25; Martin Arnold, "West Side Asks Aid With Misfits," *New York Times* (March 16, 1965), p. 41; and Jon Lowell, "City Faces Skid Row Cluster, Council Told," *The Detroit News* (February 24, 1967), p. 4–B.

With the dispersion of skid-row men and the transformation of the skid-row area to other patterns of land use, homeless men will no longer have to bear the stigma of skid-row residence. The absence of residential stigma should facilitate their rehabilitation. For example, it would seem that the homeless man living off skid row is less likely to consider himself a "failure," and to be perceived as a failure by others, than if he were on skid row.

In the last two decades the character of the skid-row population has changed. The rate of change may increase as homeless men adapt to life in neighborhoods outside of skid row. In order for welfare agencies and other action groups to cope with the problems of homelessness, they must keep abreast of changes in the composition and size of the homeless population. Changes in public policy and research procedures may be necessary as the centrally-located community of alcoholics, drifters, and other homeless men disappears. In any case, the passing of skid row does not obviate the need for continued attention to homelessness in other social settings.

Ethnic and Racial Differentiation and Segregation

part vii

The papers in this section are concerned with the patterns of ethnic and racial segregation in large cities. The first paper, by David Ward (39), is a historical analysis of the emergence of im migrant ghettoes in America's urban core. The locational patterning of the newly arriving peoples is tied to the rate and scope of expansion of the inner city's business district. The general discussion is illustrated by a longitudinal analysis of urban change in Boston. Lieberson's first paper in this section (40) focuses upon the impact of ethnic residential segregation on rates of cultural assimilation. A study of 10 cities shows relationships between residential segregation and a number of indicators of assimilation. Lieberson's second paper (41) deals with the residential segregation of foreign-born and second generation ethnics in cities and their suburbs. Change in segregation patterns is also a topic of the paper. Similar patterns are reported for ethnics in the cities and suburbs both cross-sectionally and longitudinally.

Comparative data on ethnic segregation is provided by Mehta's study (42). The analysis of the residential distribution of caste and religious groups in Poona, India shows rather constant patterns over 150 years in segregation levels and centralization. The process of ethnic and racial redistribution and assimilation is the topic of Van Arsdol and Schuerman (43). In a study of Los Angeles neighborhoods between 1940 and 1960 the authors show that ethnic increments and redistribution were confined largely to expanding older areas; that Negro segregation is greater than that of other ethnic populations in both older and newer subareas; and that ethnic populations come to have unique patterns of neighborhood structure, which change over long periods of time, as does ethnic composition.

The effect of Negro poverty on Negro housing patterns is the focus of Taeuber's analysis (44). To examine the problem, he worked with Cleveland data to consider the effects of a hypothetical income redistribution program. He concludes that there is little support for the argument that racial segregation simply reflects differences in black-white social status. Aggregate patterns of racial residential segregation in several U.S. cities is analyzed by Farley and Taeuber (45). They show sustained trends of net outmigration of whites from the central cities. Also, they show continued black population growth, mainly from natural increase. Within the cities studied, the residential segregation of blacks and whites has continued. Further support for these trends is found in the paper by Clemence (46). The spatial development of black residential areas is described by Rose (47), who shows in a study of several cities that there is a basic set of forces which operate in all cities to produce black residential communities. Differences between communities seem only to be in terms of the amount of time required for a community to move from white to black.

Segregation within the ghetto is described by Edwards (48). In a study of residential segregation of families by income and by stage in the life cycle, he shows similar patterns in the black and white areas. Evidence is presented which also shows that for a number of reasons the areas of the inner city undergoing white to black residential change seem to function for the black community much in the same way as do the suburbs for the white community—families with higher incomes and couples with children are overrepresented in the areas undergoing racial change as they are in the white suburbs.

In recent years, our large cities have been undergoing massive land use changes through urban renewal and highway building activities. Such activities frequently displace large numbers of primarily the poor and the black. Clearly such activities create a crisis for the city's housing market. What happens to the displaced white and black families and their problems and experiences in the housing market is the topic of the paper by Davis (49).

The final paper in this volume is by Roof (50) and attempts to tie black residential segregation in southern cities to a broader theory of race relations. The data suggest that residential segregation can be viewed as an intervening variable between the antecedents of city age and percent of the population nonwhite, and the consequent variables of inequalities between blacks and whites in education, occupation, and income.

39

DAVID WARD

The Emergence of Central Immigrant Ghettoes in American Cities: 1840–1920

The emergence of concentrations of foreign immigrants on the edge of the expanding central business district was one of the most characteristic manifestations of American urban growth between 1840 and 1920. The settlement of newly arrived immigrants in central urban locations has been closely related to the blighting effects of commercial encroachment into adjacent residential quarters. The concept of blight, however, obscures both the diverse social and physical attributes of central residential districts and the different effects of particular types and periods of business expansion upon central immigrant settlement. The selective adoption, subsequent longevity, and diverse characteristics of immigrant residential locations were primarily determined by the timing and dimensions of the expansion of different segments of the central business district during the second half of the nineteenth century.

During the three generations of sustained and heavy European immigration into the United States, which preceded the immigration restriction legislation of the early 1920's, congested ghettoes of foreign immigrants assumed substantial dimensions within the residential structures of American cities. Most immigrants settled near the sources of unskilled employment and, although suburban industrial districts attracted considerable numbers of immigrant laborers, the majority of newcomers concentrated on the margins of the emerging central business districts. The central business district provided the largest source of unskilled employment opportunities, and many of the adjacent residential quarters had been abandoned by their original residents because of the threatened encroachment of commercial activities. Although some districts retained their middle and high-income occupants, most residential areas

adjacent to the central business district were abandoned to immigrants. Vacated houses were converted into tenements and rooming houses, while vacant lots and rear yards were filled with cheap new structures. On some margins of the central business district newly established immigrant concentrations were rapidly displaced by expanding commercial activities; but because the specialized functional areas of the central business district expanded at different rates in different directions, many adjacent residential districts survived and exhibited striking variations in their relative longevity, physical quality, and social composition. Indeed, the selective adoption and subsequent characteristics of immigrant residential loca-

Reproduced by permission from the *Annals* of the Association of American Geographers, Volume 58 (1968), pp. 343–359.

tions were primarily determined by the timing, dimensions, and direction of the expansion of the adjacent specialized business activity. This paper proposes first, to examine in general the competing and at times complementary claims of immigrants and commerce for central urban locations between 1840 and 1920, and second, to illustrate the relationship of immigrant residential locations to different adjacent business activities in the particular instance of Boston, Massachusetts, during the same period.

IMMIGRANT RESIDENTIAL LOCATIONS AND THE URBAN RESIDENTIAL STRUCTURE

The settlement of newly arrived immigrants on the margins of the central business district has for long been closely associated with the blighting effects of commercial encroachment into adjacent residential districts. The uncertain timing and quality of future commercial developments encouraged the neglect of existing property and the departure of the more prosperous members of the resident population. Once abandoned by their original populations, central residential districts were most frequently adopted by low-income immigrants, and the deterioration of the physical quality of the dwellings was assumed to encourage the social disorganization of the new residents. Blighted conditions thus implied not only bad housing but also pathological social repercussions. Even today, however, blighted conditions do not prevail on all margins of the central business district, and many observers have documented the considerable variations in the social and physical characteristics of the central residential districts. Although a zone of blight adjacent to the central business district formed an integral part of Burgess's concentric scheme of the urban residential structure, he was impressed by the apparently anomalous location of central high-income apartment districts and by the belt-like distribution of Negroes across the otherwise concentric arrangement of urban

social groups.[1] Zorbaugh examined the development and survival of the "Gold Coast" apartment district of Chicago alongside the central business district and the slums of the Near North Side, and Hoyt recognized similar high-rent areas near to the business districts of other American cities. [2] Zorbaugh suggested that the "Gold Coast" was artificially protected by lease conditions and would eventually yield to the competitive demands of commerce. In contrast, Hoyt proposed a sector hypothesis of the residential structure of the city which was in part an effort to recognize the variations in the quality of residential districts on the margin of the central business district.

Since surviving middle and high-income residential districts occupy only a small segment of the residential fringe of the central business district, they are often regarded as local exceptions to the widespread blighted conditions created by the threat of commercial expansion. Re-evaluations of the social organization of low-income neighborhoods have, however, also enlarged our conceptions of the physical and social conditions of central residential districts. It was for long assumed that all low-income neighborhoods were afflicted by pathological social conditions which were directly related to the unhealthy and congested living conditions of tenement housing and to the break-down of the traditional social organization of rural people in the impersonal and anonymous world of the city.[3] Relatively few immigrants escaped the material and social discomforts of congested urban living conditions,

[1] E. W. Burgess, "The Growth of the City," in R. E. Park, E. W. Burgess, and R. D. MacKenzie (eds.), *The City* (Chicago: University of Chicago Press, 1925), pp. 47–62.

[2] H. W. Zorbaugh, *The Gold Coast and the Slum* (Chicago: University of Chicago Press, 1929), pp. 1–16; H. Hoyt, *The Structure and Growth of Residential Neighbourhoods in American Cities* (Washington, D.C.: Government Printing Office, 1939).

[3] R. E. Park and H. A. Miller, *Old World Traits Transplanted* (New York: Harper Bros., 1921), pp. 60–80; O. Handlin, *The Uprooted* (Boston: Little, Brown and Co., 1951), pp. 259–285.

but some immigrant groups were able to re-establish parts of their ancestral social organization in the New World and thereby facilitate their adjustment to the unfamiliar scale of American urban life. For example, Ware demonstrated that the institutions and values of the native American society seemed remote and confusing to most immigrant groups and, therefore, it was the survival of the extended family, along with local political and religious allegiances, that facilitated the adjustment of immigrants and their descendants to American urban life. Similarly, Whyte identified the distinctive internal structure of the street corner society and suggested that earlier observers had failed to recognize the presence of social organization among low income people largely because their customs and values were different from those of the more familiar society of suburban America.[4]

The suburban movement has severely depleted the populations of the original ghettoes of European immigrants; but quite recently Glazer and Moynihan have suggested that ethnic origin has also partly influenced the suburban residential choices and social life of the descendants of immigrants,[5] while immigrants from Puerto Rico and from the American South have partly compensated for the population losses created by the suburban movement. Since, however, the central business district has lost its former pre-eminence as a source of unskilled employment and since low-rent housing is no longer confined to central residential districts, the more recent immigration has had more modest effects upon the central residential pattern than that of the nineteenth century. Although urban renewal schemes have diminished the extent and capacity of many tenement districts, some authorities have suggested that

the material and fiscal priorities of most public improvement schemes have obscured the social attractions of many low rent districts to their resident populations.[6] A preoccupation with the vitality of local neighborhood life has at times degenerated into an uncritical admiration of the culture of poverty; but nevertheless there is a need to identify variations in the social and living conditions of low income residential areas.[7] Some original ghettoes have survived for several generations on the margins of the central business district and, in spite of considerable depopulation, remain attractive to the resident population. Other districts have housed either a rapid succession of diverse immigrant groups or the most impoverished and discriminated social groups in the city and, under these circumstances, pathological social conditions tend to compound the material inadequacies of the housing and neighborhood.

Firey and Jones, in their respective studies of central parts of Boston and Belfast, have related the survival of middle- and high-income districts and the development of different types of low income areas to the sentiments and values of the occupying social groups.[8] Although this perspective provided many new insights into the attachment to a given district of a particular social group, the effect of changes in the central business district upon the original adoption and subsequent survival of the adjacent residential districts remained obscure. Indeed, most recent contributions to our understanding of the residential structure of American cities have acknowledged the locational implications of cultural preferences in their developments of an explanatory focus pioneered some fifty years ago and based upon measures of site costs

[4] C. F. Ware, *Greenwich Village: 1920–1930* (Boston: Houghton Mifflin, 1935), pp. 3–8, 81–126; W. F. Whyte, *The Street Corner Society* (Chicago: University of Chicago Press, 1943), pp. 94–104, 255–278.

[5] N. Glazer and D. P. Moynihan, *Beyond the Melting Pot* (Cambridge: MIT Press, 1964).

[6] H. J. Gans, *The Urban Villagers* (New York: The Free Press of Glencoe, 1962), pp. 3–41; B. J. Frieden, *The Future of Old Neighborhoods* (Cambridge: MIT Press, 1964), pp. 1–5.

[7] G. C. Homans, *The Human Group* (New York: Harcourt, Brace and Co., 1950), pp. 334–68; W. I. Firey, *Land Use in Central Boston* (Cambridge: Harvard University Press, 1947), pp. 170–197, 290–313.

[8] W. I. Firey, op. cit., footnote 7; E. Jones, *A Social Geography of Belfast* (London: Oxford University Press, 1962).

and of accessibility of home to employment.[9] These considerations have provided the most satisfactory principles for an interpretation of the extensive suburban residential additions to American cities since the turn of the century. The emergence and diversification of central residential districts, however, occurred during the course of the second half of the nineteenth century when the suburban alternative to central tenement residence was available only to limited numbers of immigrants and their descendants and when the growth and differentiation of the central business district most profoundly affected the adjacent residential quarters.

IMMIGRANT CONCENTRATION IN CENTRAL URBAN LOCATION

The dense central concentrations of immigrants were thus established at a time when the distributional implications of accessibility were determined not only by the extent and density of the streetcar network, but also by the long working hours, low wages, and unpredictable tenure of unskilled employment.[10] Most newly arrived immigrants sought cheap accommodation partly because of their poverty and partly because of their desire to accumulate savings to finance the passages of relatives. The central tenement districts provided by far the largest supply of cheap living quarters, but because most tenements were overcrowded, badly designed, and poorly—if at all—endowed with sanitary facilities, even low rents were exorbitant. Tenement accommodation, however, could be obtained by the room at fractional rates, whereas self-contained dwelling units which possessed only the minimum requirements for the comfort and health of their

occupants rented at rates far beyond the means of new immigrants.[11] Towards the end of the nineteenth century, legislation was introduced in many cities to improve the living conditions in newly constructed tenements, but even modest structural refinements increased minimum rents and failed to enlarge the supply of low-rent housing.[12] The housing choices of most immigrants were thus largely restricted to central residential districts until either a rise in real incomes made possible suburban residence or public funds were provided to subsidize rent payments.[13]

The central tenement districts also possessed the advantage of convenient accessibility to the growing employment opportunities of the emerging central business district. Although the facilities for local transportation were improved and enlarged during the second half of the nineteenth century, many immigrants were employed in occupations with long and awkward hours and, therefore, preferred a short pedestrian journey to work. The tenure of unskilled employment was also characteristically uncertain, and daily hiring was the common procedure in general laboring and portering. Consequently, immigrants not only faced the problems of numerous changes in the location of their work, but also suffered from frequent spells of unemployment. Under these circumstances, employment in the central business district had the advantage of a wide range of alternative opportunities when regular work was abruptly terminated. Suburban industrial districts also attracted considerable numbers of immigrants, and cheap housing was built in adjacent locations; but the variety of both industrial and commercial employment within and near to the central business district supported far larger numbers of immigrants in central residential locations. The central business district

[9] W. Alonso, *Location and Land Use* (Cambridge: Harvard University Press, 1964); L. Wingo, Jr., *Transportation and Urban Land* (Washington: Resources for the Future, 1961); R. M. Hurd, *Principles of City Land Values* (New York: The Record and Guide, 1903).

[10] D. Ward, "A Comparative Historical Geography of Streetcar Suburbs in Boston, Massachusetts and Leeds, England: 1850–1920," *Annals*, Association of American Geographers, 54 (1964): 477–489.

[11] E.R.L. Gould, "The Housing of the Working People," *8th Special Report of the Commissioner of Labor* (Washington: Government Printing Office, 1895), p. 419.

[12] E.E. Wood, *The Housing of the Unskilled Wage Earner* (New York: Macmillan, 1919), p. 21.

[13] E. Abbott, *The Tenements of Chicago: 1908–1936* (Chicago: University of Chicago Press, 1936), pp. 481–483.

offered the largest and most diverse source of unskilled employment opportunities, and the adjacent tenement districts provided uncomfortable but conveniently located residential quarters which were within the limited financial means of new immigrants.

The first generation of immigrant groups who arrived in American cities in large numbers often provided almost the entire labor force of some activities conducted within the central business district. Irish immigrants first helped to build, and later found employment in, the warehouses and terminal facilities of the business district, whereas German immigrants found employment in the sewing machine and port supply trades which were housed in the upper stories of warehouses.[14] Italian immigrants in part replaced the Irish as general laborers, but the distribution of fresh food also attracted Italians in large numbers.[15] Jewish immigrants, equipped with long experience in the handicraft industries and local commercial life of their East European homelands, rapidly developed many branches of merchandising at a time when retail and wholesale segments of marketing were first firmly separated and established as distinct specialized areas within the central business district.[16] Jewish immigrants also adopted the ready-made clothing industry and, in order to achieve economies of rent and labor, reorganized production within their own residential districts. The clothing industry needed close and immediate contact with the credit and informational facilities of the central business district, and the central tenement districts possessed the advantage of adjacency to the commercial facilities of the city.[17] This ethnic division of labor was neither rigid nor exclusive but, nevertheless, encouraged the concentration of immigrants in those residential districts where they could most effectively obtain employment from their compatriots. Many immigrant business enterprises, which later served the entire city or national market were, moreover, originally founded upon the provision of the distinctive material and dietary needs of the immigrant community.

Group consciousness, as well as economic necessity or advantage, stimulated the concentration of immigrants in the central tenement districts; for once established, the ghetto provided institutions and neighborhood life familiar to the immigrant. Indeed most immigrants preferred to spend their early years in a new country and unfamiliar city in a district which housed their fellow countrymen or coreligionists if not their immediate family and friends. Many contemporary observers were inclined to ignore the positive social attractions of the tenement districts to the newly arrived immigrants, for it was assumed that the congested living conditions resulted in the social disorganization of the resident population and that the concentration of immigrants delayed and discouraged their assimilation into the native American society. In spite of the adverse living conditions, however, some immigrant groups established stable local communities and attracted deservedly laudatory reports upon the stability and moral orthodoxy of their family and neighborhood life.[18] Moreover, in the absence of effective public welfare, residential concentration provided immigrant communities with their share of the patronage of local politics, for the heavily populated ethnic wards provided a major source of voting strength in civic elections.[19] The development of local communities within the tenement districts attracted the ma-

[14]R. Ernst, *Immigrant Life in New York City: 1825–1863* (New York: King's Crown Press, 1949), pp. 17, 61-77; O. Handlin, *Boston's Immigrants: A Study in Acculturation* (Cambridge: Harvard University Press, 1959), pp. 54–87.

[15]R. F. Foerster, *The Italian Emigration of Our Times* (Cambridge: Harvard University Press, 1919), pp. 332–344.

[16]S. Joseph, *Jewish Immigration to the United States from 1881 to 1910* (New York: Columbia University 1914), pp. 42–46.

[17]J. R. Commons, "Immigration and its Economic Effects," *Report of the Industrial Commission XV* (Washington: 1901), pp. 316–326.

[18]W. T. Elsing, "Life in New York Tenement Houses," in *The Poor in Great Cities* (New York: Scribners, 1895), pp. 42–85.

[19]T. J. Lowi, *At the Pleasure of the Mayor: Power and Patronage in New York City, 1898–1958* (New York: The Free Press of Glencoe, 1964).

jority of newly arrived immigrants of similar ancestry and assisted their adjustment to the unfamiliar scale and conditions of American urban life.

The social attractions and political advantages of residential concentration were not, however, characteristic of all tenement districts, nor were they shared by all immigrant groups. The adjustment of different immigrant groups to the changing conditions of residence and employment in American cities was rarely repetitive. Although southern Italian immigrants had lived in large unsanitary villages, and Jewish immigrants had lived in the congested towns of Eastern Europe, many immigrants had no previous experience of crowded living conditions. Certainly relatively few immigrants had faced the problems of residence in cities as large and as complex as those of industrial America, and some groups lacked the numbers to support their own institutions or to lay claim to their proportionate share of political patronage. Moreover most small immigrant groups were composed of young single men who eventually hoped to return to their homelands with the assumed profits of their American employment and, consequently, with neither a family structure nor a permanent commitment to residence in the United States, some degree of social disorganization did compound the material discomfort of their residential quarters.[20] Although the marginal economies and social advantages of scale insulated most large and well established immigrant groups from the problems faced by small groups, all central concentrations of immigrants faced the disturbing effects of displacement by the expansion of the adjacent commercial activities. Even the largest and most organized immigrant groups were unable to establish enduring communities in those tenement districts which suffered from the continuous invasion of business premises. The specialized functional areas of the central business district, however, emerged and expanded at different rates at different times and, accord-

ingly, the effect of the central business district upon the adjacent residential areas was neither continuous nor uniform.[21]

THE EFFECT OF BUSINESS EXPANSION ON IMMIGRANT CONCENTRATION

Thus, although the residential choices of immigrants were largely restricted to central locations, and although the tenement districts fulfilled many of their more immediate social and economic needs, the development and survival of central concentrations of immigrants was primarily dependent upon the rate and dimensions of expansion of the adjacent segment of the emerging central business district. The invasion of business activities into adjacent residential districts occasionally followed so closely upon the departure of the original population that the immigrant newcomers had neither the time nor the incentive to develop a stable neighborhood life. The warehouse quarter, for example, housed both expanding small scale workshop industries and a large proportion of the growing commercial activities of the city and, during the middle decades of the nineteenth century, made greater claims upon the adjacent residential quarters than all the other segments of the central business district combined.[22] (Figure 1). Towards the turn of the century, the demands of regional distribution

[20]Zorbaugh, op. cit., footnote 2, 142–151.

[21]Information on the timing and scale of the expansion of the component specialized areas of the central business district during the nineteenth century is widely scattered and rarely related to the fortunes of adjacent residential districts. J. E. Vance, "Emerging Patterns of Commercial Structure in American Cities," in K. Norburg (ed.), *Proceedings of the I.G.U. Symposium in Urban Geography* (Lund: Gleerups, 1962), pp. 473–483, and D. Ward, "The Industrial Revolution and Emergence of Boston's Central Business District," *Economic Geography*, 42 (1966): 152–171, give some indication of the developmental aspects of the problem, whereas R. E. Murphy and J. E. Vance, "Delimiting the CBD," *Economic Geography*, 30 (1954): 189–222, and D. W. Griffin and R. E. Preston, "A Restatement of the Transition Zone Concept," *Annals*, Association of American Geographers, 56 (1966): 339–350, from an essentially contemporary perspective indicate the diverse characteristics of different edges of the CBD.

[22] N. S. B. Gras, "The Development of the Metropolitan Economy in Europe and America," *American Historical Review*, Vol. 27 (1922), pp. 695–708.

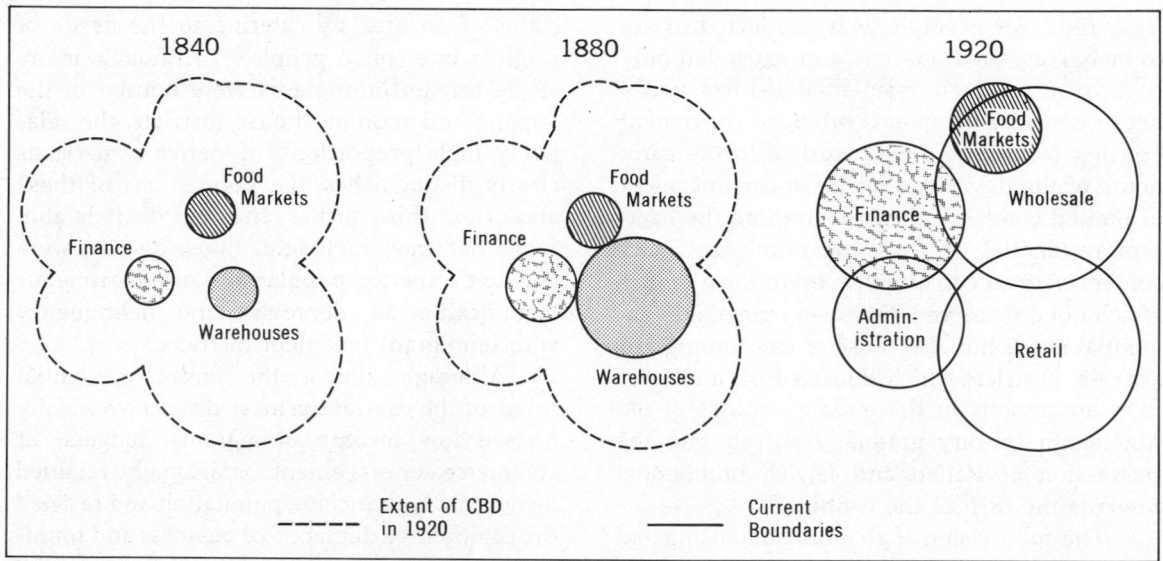

FIGURE 1. Generalized Stages in the Development of the CBD

had displaced most of the workshop industries and stimulated a separation of the retail and wholesale segments of marketing within the central business district (Figure 1). The emergence of a retail quarter and the continued expansion of the warehouse district as the seat of wholesale distribution increased even further the rate and scale of expansion of business premises into a broader segment of the residential fringe of the central business district. Central residential districts adjacent to these rapidly expanding segments of the central business district were most frequently occupied by the smallest or poorest immigrant groups along with remnants from older groups which had moved on to securer residential locations.[23] The residents of these districts did suffer from the social disorganization created by the problems of eviction and residential relocation.

There were, however, central residential districts which failed to attract anticipated commercial developments once they had been abandoned by their original populations. Because of the improvement in the facilities for local movement and the increase in the scale of business organization, the location of the

greatest constructional activity and commercial expansion within the central business district tended to shift during the course of the nineteenth century.[24] Consequently, residential districts adjacent to older centers of growth lost their attractiveness for commercial development. Moreover, the most attractive locations for business had often been preempted early by commercial activities which were unable to maintain their original choices in the face of the expanding needs of more competitive activities. Financial and administrative functions for long occupied separate and diminutive quarters, and only late in the nineteenth century coalesced and expanded their accommodations into premium locations within the existing limits of the central business district rather than at the expense of peripheral residential locations (Figure 1). Other business activities retained their small quarters throughout the nineteenth century and eventually reorganized their facilities by decentralization rather than by central expansion. The distribution of

[23] Zorbaugh, op. cit., footnote 2, p. 127.

[24] L. Grebler, *Housing Market Behavior in a Declining Area* (New York: Columbia University Press, 1952), p. 113 on the up-town shift of retailing on Manhattan Island and the effects on the residential districts near to the original center of growth.

fresh food, for example, was conducted in extremely congested quarters and expanded only slightly into adjacent residential districts, partly because nearby tenements provided convenient housing for laborers who worked in the early hours of the day.[25] Under these circumstances of limited commercial expansion into the adjacent residential districts, the immigrant newcomers were able to establish enduring ghettoes which not only served their own immediate residential needs but also those of later immigrant arrivals. Districts which housed Irish and German immigrants in the middle decades of the nineteenth century gradually passed into the possession of Italian and Jewish immigrants towards the turn of the century.[26]

The subdivision of abandoned housing and the construction of cheap new tenements in their vacant grounds were designed to extract a marginal rental income from buildings and land during the period of uncertain property values which preceded their adoption by commercial activities. Thus, the housing of immigrants was at first regarded as a temporary expedient, but it soon became clear that as long as immigrants arrived in large numbers, the provision of their housing needs would be a source of substantial profit. Once established under favorable conditions on the edge of the central business district, immigrant ghettoes resisted or at least retarded the rate of any subsequent commercial claims upon their quarters.[27] Not all central districts were converted into tenement areas, for it was also possible to obtain a substantial income from lodging or rooming house accommodation. Conversion into rooms was, moreover, less costly than the modifications required for tenement residence, whereas lodging houses tended to maintain the

status of an area by catering to the needs of single white-collar people.[28] Although many single foreign immigrants were housed in the lodging and rooming house districts, the relatively high proportions of native Americans clearly distinguished the populations of these areas from those of the tenement districts and, for a brief time, the lodging house districts were able to escape the popular and often erroneous identification of depravity and delinquency with immigrant tenement districts.

Although almost the entire residential fringe of the central business district eventually housed low income immigrants, lodgers, or commerce, one segment occasionally retained its original high income population and resisted the competitive demands of business and immigrants. The survival of high income residential districts in part depended upon favorable site conditions and long established status. Many central locations which were at one time endowed with advantages of site and status failed to retain their original population, for the quality and needs of the adjacent business activity in part influenced the status of central residential quarters. Financial institutions and the seats of public authority attracted rather than discouraged adjacent residence by people of wealth and status. Throughout the nineteenth century many established families valued their proximity to the sources of political and economic power and the historic status of the adjacent residential quarters. Financial and administrative activities offered only limited unskilled employment opportunities and, consequently, the demand for low rent housing was more limited than on those margins of the business district adjacent to abundant sources of unskilled employment. The different directions and characteristics of the expansion of the central business district directly affected the selective adoption of central residential districts by immigrants and also in part influenced the abandonment of these dis-

---

[25] Zorbaugh, op. cit., footnote 2, p. 166; F. E. Bushee, "Italian Immigrants in Boston," *Arena*, 17 (1896–1897): pp. 722–734.

[26] W. L. Warner and L. Srole, *The Social Systems of American Ethnic Groups* (New Haven: Yale University Press, 1945), pp. 33–52; K. H. Claghorn, "The Foreign Immigrant in New York City," *Report of the Industrial Commission XV* (Washington: 1901), pp. 471–472.

[27] Grebler, op. cit., footnote 24, pp. 106–16.

[28] R. A. Woods (ed.), *The City Wilderness* (Boston: Houghton Mifflin, 1898), pp. 35–39; Zorbaugh, op. cit., footnote 2, pp. 69–86.

tricts by their original populations. Thus, during the course of the nineteenth century, not only tenement districts of varying quality but also lodging houses and substantial town houses developed on different margins of the central business districts of large American cities.

THE RESIDENTIAL STRUCTURE OF CENTRAL BOSTON

As both the first receiving stations of foreign immigrants and the earliest beneficiaries of American industrial and commercial growth, the major seaports of the northeastern coast most clearly exhibited the effects of sustained immigration and of the expansion of the central business district upon the emergence of the central residential districts of large American cities. In Boston, for example, an enduring and diversified residential pattern developed on the edge of the central business district between 1840 and 1920. By 1920, Italian and Russian Jewish immigrants occupied tenements in the North End and in adjacent sections of the West End; smaller and poorer immigrant groups were housed in rather more sordid tenements in the South Cove district, and single men of both immigrant and native American parentage lived in lodging and rooming houses in the South End (Figure 2). Although immigrant settlement and business expansion affected almost the entire fringe of Boston's central business district, Beacon Hill and the adjacent Back Bay continued to house wealthy and socially prominent people in town houses (Figure 2).

Over the past fifty years depopulation and redevelopment have only partly altered the residential pattern established on the edge of the central business district during the nineteenth century. Although many of the tenements in the West End and the South Cove have been demolished and their populations relocated, the North End continues to house a flourishing but much diminished population of Italian-Americans. Beacon Hill and the Back Bay no longer house the élite of Boston's society, and some sections are now devoted to professional offices or specialty retail activities; nevertheless, many of the original town houses maintain their residential function as apartments or rooms. The South End has in part retained its rooming house function, but large sections are now occupied by a substantial Negro community. In spite of these changes in the extent and social composition of the residential fringe of Boston's central business district, substantial remnants of the residential pattern established during the nineteenth century remain to this day.

At one time, with the possible exception of the West End, all the residential districts near to the central business district housed the wealthiest and most socially prominent members of the contemporary urban society. Throughout the colonial period, the North End housed the royal court and its administrative officers,[29] but after the Revolution lost its former status to new developments on the southern and western margins of the town. During the early nineteenth century, the North End housed Yankee craftsmen who gradually occupied the nearby West End[30] (Figure 3). Men of wealth and social prestige established new homes on Beacon Hill near to the new State House and overlooking the Common, and also on the southern edge of the town between Fort Hill and the Common[31] (Figure 3). In 1840 the North End, Beacon Hill, and the inner sections of the South End formed residential appendages onto the still undifferentiated nucleus of the town, whereas the South Cove and Back Bay had yet to be filled (Figure 3). Between 1840 and the outbreak of World War I, the expansion of the central business district and the arrival of large numbers of foreign immigrants changed the appearance and social composition of these central residential districts.

---

[29] T. Pemberton, "A Topographical and Historical Description of Boston in 1797," *Massachusetts Historical Society, Collections*, 3 (1810): 241–304.

[30] E. C. Wines, *Trip to Boston, in a Series of Letters to the Editor of the United States Gazette* (Boston: Little & Brown, 1838), p. 123.

[31] W. M. Whitehill, *A Topographical History of Boston* (Cambridge: Harvard University Press, 1959), pp. 59–65.

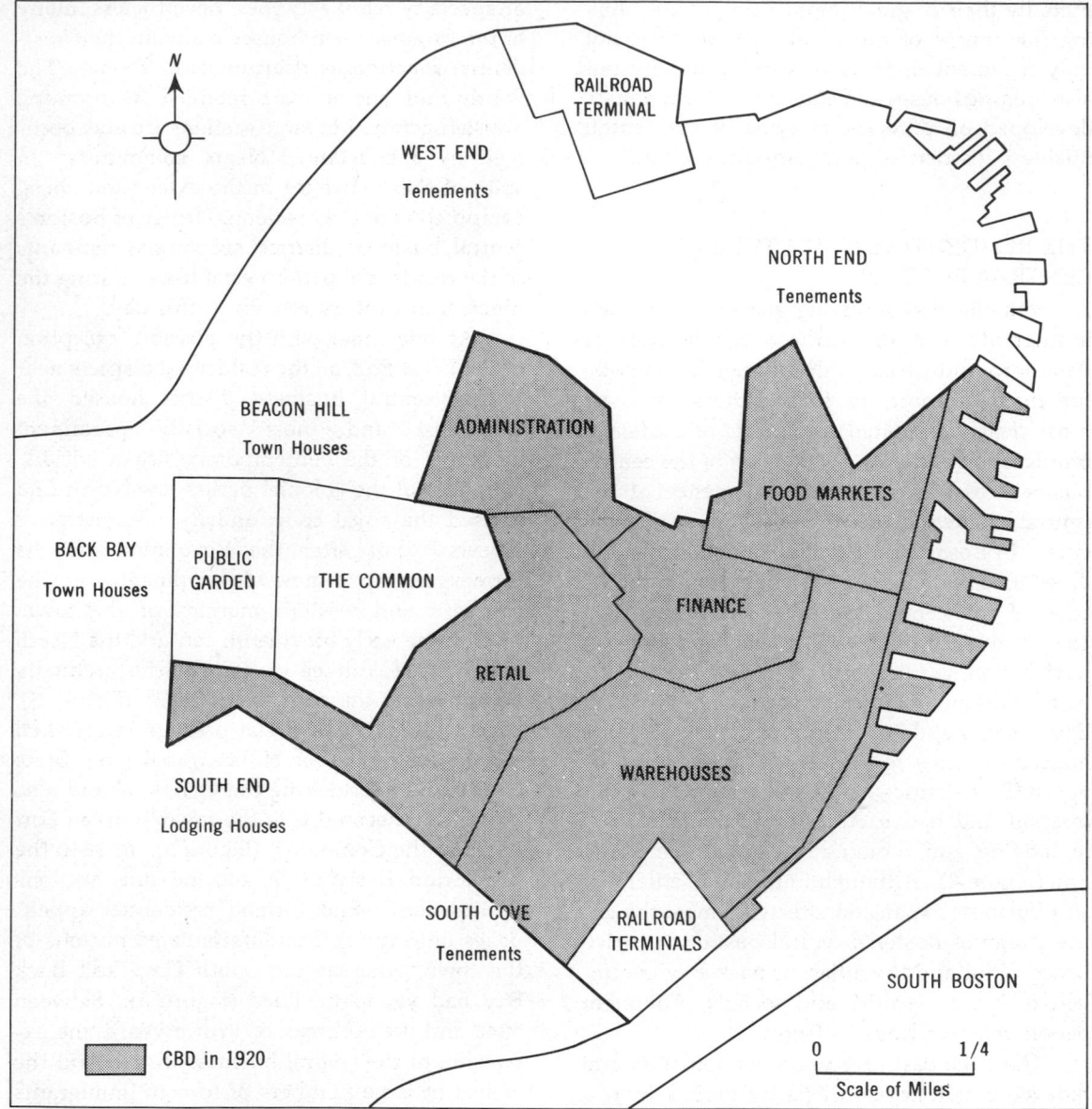

FIGURE 2. Central Boston in 1920

IMMIGRANT SETTLEMENT NEAR TO THE CENTRAL BUSINESS DISTRICT: 1840–1875

Before 1840 Boston's foreign immigrants were small in number and confined to congested housing on the Town Cove waterfront both to the north and south of the emerging commer-

cial focus on State Street[32] (Figure 3). In the two decades before 1840 barely 30,000 immigrants landed in Boston, but in the two decades before the outbreak of the Civil War over

[32] R. H. Lord, et al., *A History of the Archdiocese of Boston*, Vol. 2 (New York: Sheed and Ward, 1944), pp. 35–36; O. Handlin, op. cit., footnote 3, pp. 93–94.

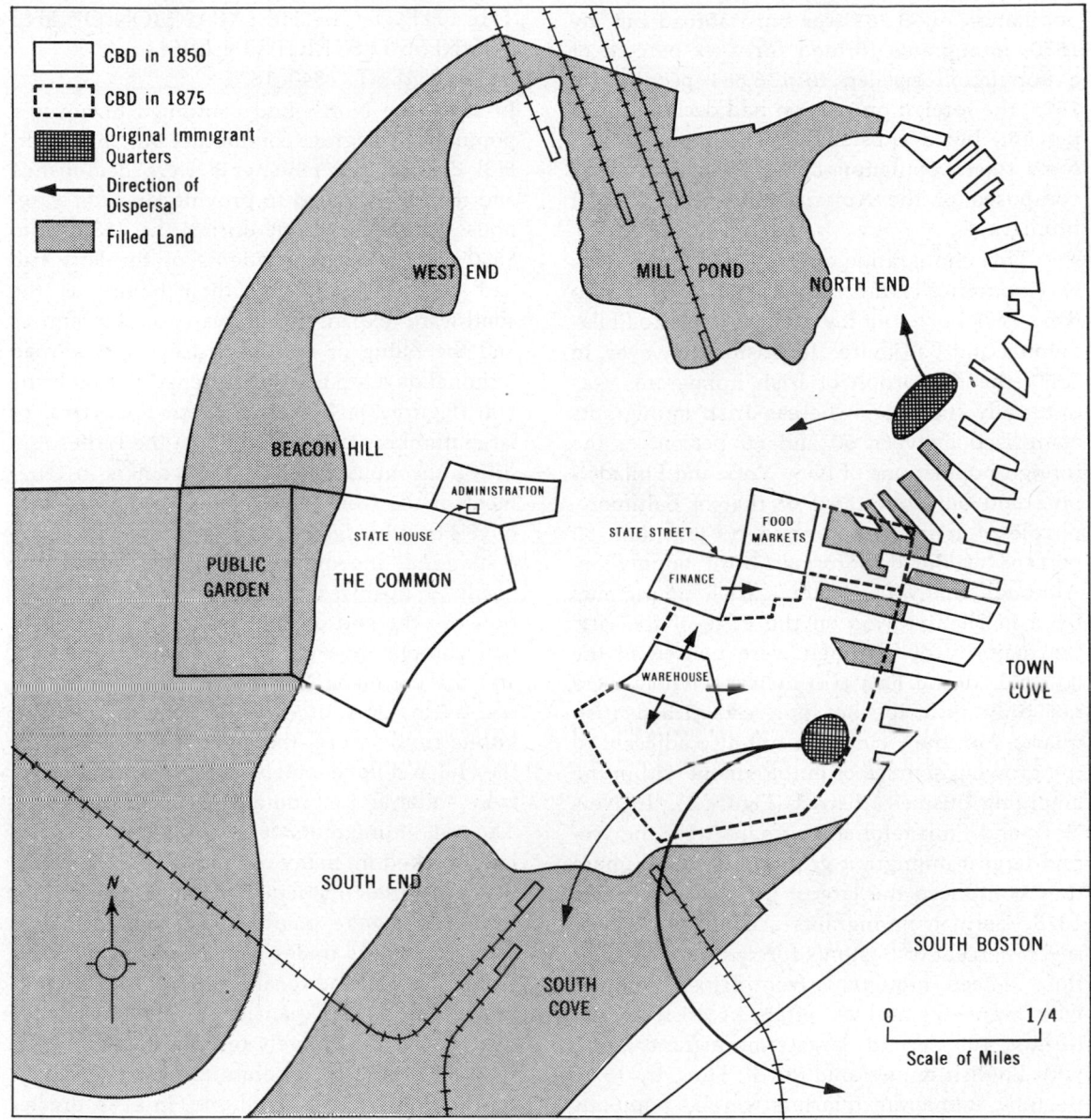

FIGURE 3. Immigrant Settlement and Business Expansion in Boston, 1840–1875

300,000 immigrants arrived in the port; and though the flow of immigration diminished during the Civil War, a further 200,000 immigrants disembarked between 1865 and 1874.[33]

Clearly not all the more than half million immigrants who landed in Boston remained in the city, but many made Boston their temporary home before moving on to New York or the Middle West, and considerable numbers lacked either the financial means or preference to leave the city. In 1840, only fifteen percent of Boston's

[33] Massachusetts Public Document, No. 17, *19th Annual Report of the State Board of Lunacy and Charity* (Boston: 1889), pp. 98–99.

population of 93,383 was born abroad but, by 1850, immigrants formed forty-six percent of a population swelled to 136,881 people. By 1875, the foreign proportion had declined to 34 percent, but a substantial proportion of Boston's total population of 341,919 people was composed of the American born children of immigrants.

This immigration of foreigners into Boston was numerically much smaller than that into New York but about the same as that into Philadelphia and Baltimore. In Boston, however, in 1850, the proportion of Irish immigrants was unusually high for, whereas Irish immigrants comprised between 50 and 60 percent of the foreign populations of New York and Philadelphia and only one-third of that of Baltimore, people of Irish birth formed no less than 83 percent of Boston's foreign-born population. Although many of Boston's Irish immigrants lived in shantytowns on the edge of the city, the majority of Irishmen were housed in the North End and Fort Hill districts, which were not only near to the long established Irish quarters on the waterfront but also adjacent to the growing sources of employment within the emerging business district (Figure 3). In New York and Philadelphia, Germans were the second largest immigrant group, and in Baltimore they comprised the largest group; but even in 1875, German immigrants accounted for only seven percent of Boston's foreign-born population. Indeed immigrants from British America, who were themselves often of Irish origin, formed the second largest immigrant group with English immigrants third. Thus, by 1875, Boston's immigrant quarters were as populous and as extensive as those of Philadelphia and Baltimore, but because the proportion of Irish immigrants was much greater in Boston than in the other Atlantic ports and because many of the British American immigrants were of Irish origin, Boston's ghettoes housed an almost exclusively Irish population.

THE EFFECT OF THE EXPANSION OF THE BUSINESS DISTRICT ON IRISH SETTLEMENT: 1840–1875

In 1875, the North End continued to house a populous immigrant community but, in the Fort Hill district, the tenements were demolished and the Hill levelled to provide land for warehouse premises. Even during the 1830's and 1840's the wealthy residents of the Fort Hill had begun to abandon their homes as the southward expansion of warehouse premises and the filling of the South Cove for railroad terminal developments threatened to engulf the Hill (Figure 3). Moreover, with the arrival of large numbers of immigrants in the forties and fifties, the housing of the newcomers in tenements made from the mansions and in wooden hovels hastily erected in their grounds provided a marginal income in the period before the needs of business preempted the entire location. By the end of the Civil War, warehouses had completely encircled the Hill (Figure 3), and the surviving tenements had been identified as major sources of contagious diseases. Public funds were, therefore, used to remove the Hill and its tenements and to establish level land suitable for commercial development.[34] The Irish immigrants of Fort Hill had built, and later worked in, many of the warehouses which displaced their inadequate homes, while their womenfolk were employed in the expanding sewing machine trades which had further stimulated the demand for more warehouse accommodation. This expansion of the warehouse quarter was thus largely responsible for the relocation of the Irish community further south on the South Cove lands and, in even greater numbers, in South Boston, where new factories and terminal facilities provided growing employment opportunities (Figure 3). By 1875 only a small immigrant community was left in Fort Hill, and even the foreign-born population

---

[34] E. Stanwood, "Topography and Landmarks of the Last Hundred Years," in J. Winsor (ed.), *The Memorial History of Boston* (Boston: James Osgood, 1881), pp. 25–65.

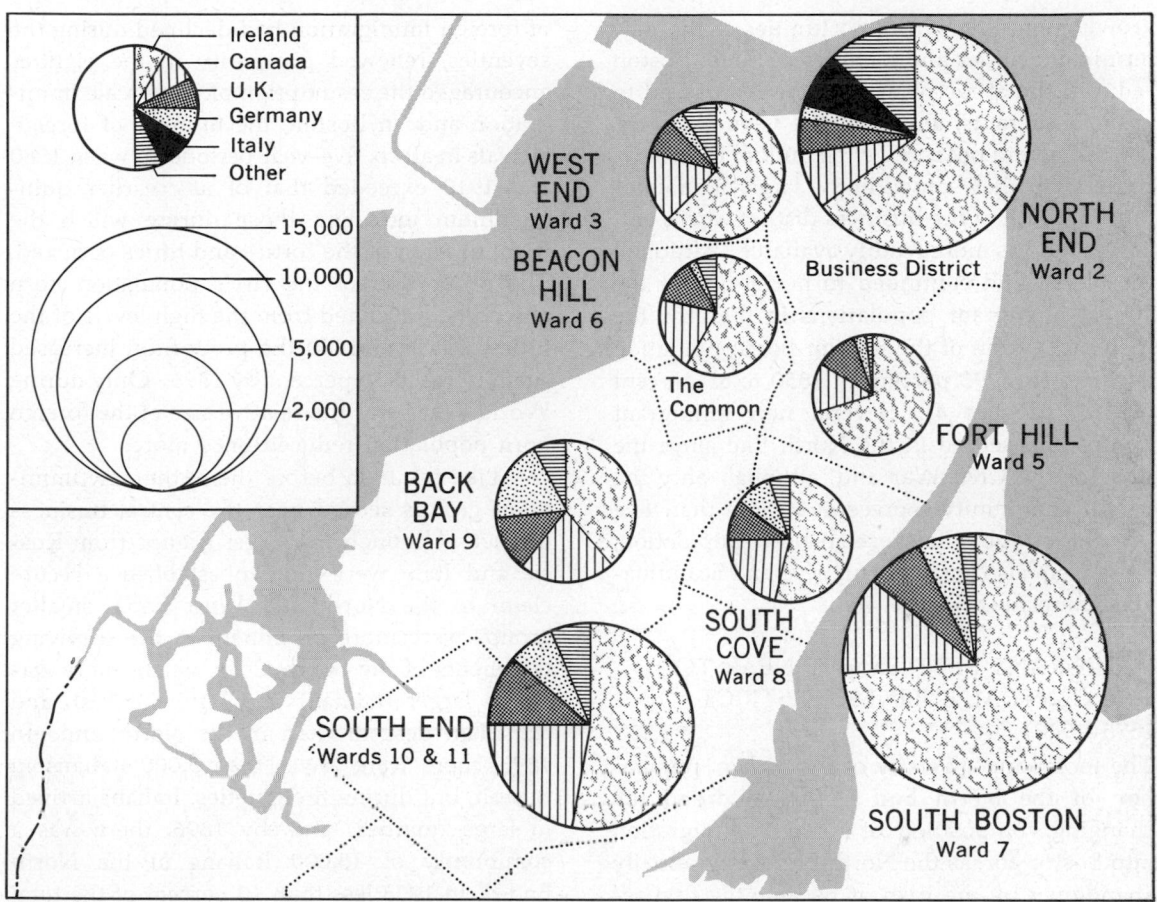

FIGURE 4. Place of Birth of Boston's Immigrants in 1875

of the South Cove amounted to one-half that of South Boston (Figure 4). Within one generation of the heavy Irish influx of the late forties and fifties South Boston had replaced Fort Hill as the most populous Irish district in the city.

In the North End, too, old houses had been converted into tenements and their vacant yards filled with sheds; but the existing houses were smaller and their grounds less extensive than on Fort Hill, for the inhabitants immediately before the Irish were craftsmen. The denser pattern of streets attracted the occasional, if indifferent, attention of the civic authorities, whereas many of the streets of Fort Hill were within the former grounds of mansion houses and, therefore, not only entirely devoid of utili-

ties but also outside of the limited jurisdiction of the city.[35] Living conditions in the North End were, nevertheless, among the worst in the city but, largely because the district was not threatened by the expansion of the adjacent business activity, demolition was relatively rare. Although the warehouse quarter had experienced a vigorous growth between 1840 and 1875, the food markets, which bordered the southern margin of the North End, did not expand to any great extent (Figure 3). The southward shift in the location of laboring employment within the business district, and the

---

[35] Boston City Document, No. 4, *The North End: A Survey and Comprehensive Plan* (Boston, 1919), p.6.

growing employment opportunities of the new terminal facilities and factories of South Boston reduced the attractiveness of the North End to Irish immigrants; and after the Civil War, the North End did not receive the bulk of Irish newcomers, for they settled in the larger Irish community south of the business district where employment was more readily available. Although the North End continued to house one of the largest immigrant populations in the city, the Irish proportion of the foreign-born population declined from 93 percent in 1850 to 65 percent in 1875 (Figure 4). Several new immigrant groups had settled in the North End since the close of the Civil War and, although only the Italian community represented more than five percent of the total foreign-born population, there were also small Portuguese and Scandinavian minorities (Figure 4).

IMMIGRANT SETTLEMENT NEAR TO THE CENTRAL BUSINESS DISTRICT: 1875–1920

The increasing diversity of the foreign population of the North End closely recorded the changing composition of foreign immigration into Boston for, as the North End was gradually abandoned by the Irish, it became the first receiving station of new immigrant groups. In 1875, Irish and Canadian immigrants had represented over three-quarters of foreign-born population in the city, but by 1920 they formed rather less than half the immigrant population. Irish and Canadian immigrants remained the two largest groups, but immigrants from Italy accounted for 16 percent of the foreign-born population, and Jewish immigrants from the Russian Empire accounted for 17 percent. The Polish, Greek, Syrian, and Portuguese communities were not large individually, but together they formed a sizeable segment of the foreign population, whereas the Oriental and Negro minorities greatly increased their representation within the city.[36] Although the size

of foreign immigration had declined during the seventies, renewed prosperity in the eighties encouraged the resumption of large scale immigration and, in Boston, the number of foreign arrivals in all six five-year periods between 1880 and 1910 exceeded that of any earlier quinquennium including those during which the Irish invasion of the forties and fifties occurred. The proportion of the city's population born abroad had declined from the high levels of the fifties, but after 1880 the proportion increased again to reach 36 percent by 1895. Only during World War I was the relative size of the foreign born population reduced once more.

Like the Irish before them, the new immigrant groups settled near the central business district. Although the larger groups from Russia and Italy were able to establish a secure claim to the North and West Ends, smaller groups were more prominent in the surviving tenements of the South Cove, where there was also a larger remnant population of Irish and Canadian descent than in the North End. In 1890, there were fewer than 5,000 Italians in Boston, but during the nineties, Italians arrived in large numbers and, by 1896, there was a community of 18,000 Italians in the North End.[37] In 1905 less than 10 percent of the total population of the North End was of Irish parentage and birth, whereas no less than 60 percent was of Italian extraction and a further 15 percent of Russian-Jewish origin (Figure 5). Until 1875, most foreign immigrants had settled within the confines of the North End and had not spread into the neighboring West End to any great degree. During the eighties, however, the northern margin of the West End was converted into a tenement quarter to absorb the increasing numbers of immigrants and, although many early Jewish immigrants into Boston settled in the North End, most eventually congregated in the West End. In the West End people of Russian-Jewish parentage and birth formed over one half of the total popula-

[36] Massachusetts Public Document, No. 15. 42nd Annual Report of the Bureau of Statistics of Labour (Boston: 1910), p. 230.

[37] Bushee, op. cit., footnote 25, pp. 722–34.

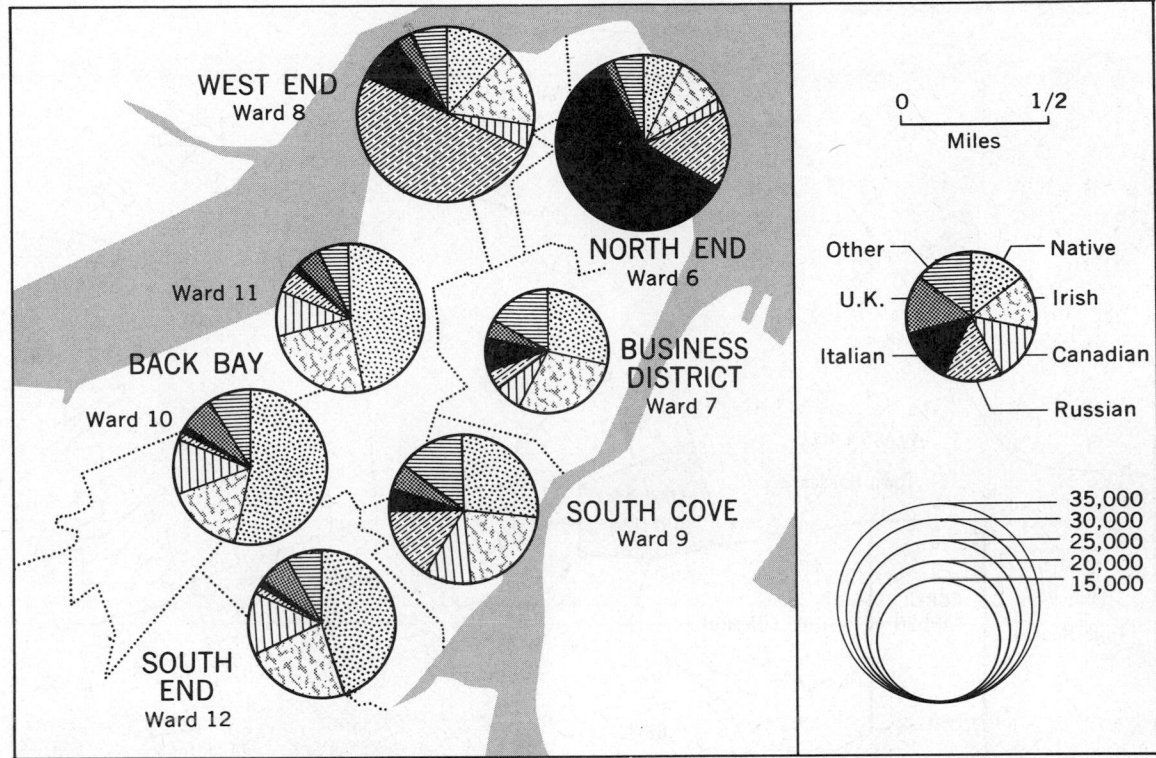

FIGURE 5.   Parentage of the Population of Central Boston in 1905

tion, whereas Italians accounted for only 8 percent of the total (Figure 6). Although Italian and Russian-Jewish immigrants also settled to the south of the central business district, almost two-thirds of the population in the South Cove area was of native, Irish, or Canadian parentage, although Greek, Syrian, and Oriental immigrants were also well represented (Figure 5). Of the smaller groups, only the Portuguese and Poles managed to establish themselves in the North End.

THE EFFECT OF THE EXPANSION OF THE BUSINESS DISTRICT ON IMMIGRANT SETTLEMENT: 1875–1920

With the southward and suburban shift of heavy laboring employment and with the gradual entrance of the older immigrant groups into the ranks of middle income employment, most Irish immigrants abandoned the North End and to a lesser degree the West End. Un-

like the Irish settlement to the south of the business district, business expansion had not reduced the residential capacity of these districts which were therefore rapidly adopted by later immigrant groups. Indeed the North End and the West End provided residential quarters located near to the occupational choices of both Italian and Russian-Jewish immigrants. Some Italian immigrants succeeded the Irish as general laborers under the *padrone* system, but in Boston many also found employment in the service trades and workshop industries of the central business district. In particular, Italians developed the trade in fresh fruit and produce and provided much of labor, and later the management, of the fresh food markets of the central business district.[38] This trade, conducted in the early hours of the day, frequently involved unpredictable working hours and, con-

---

[38] Bushee, op. cit., footnote 25.

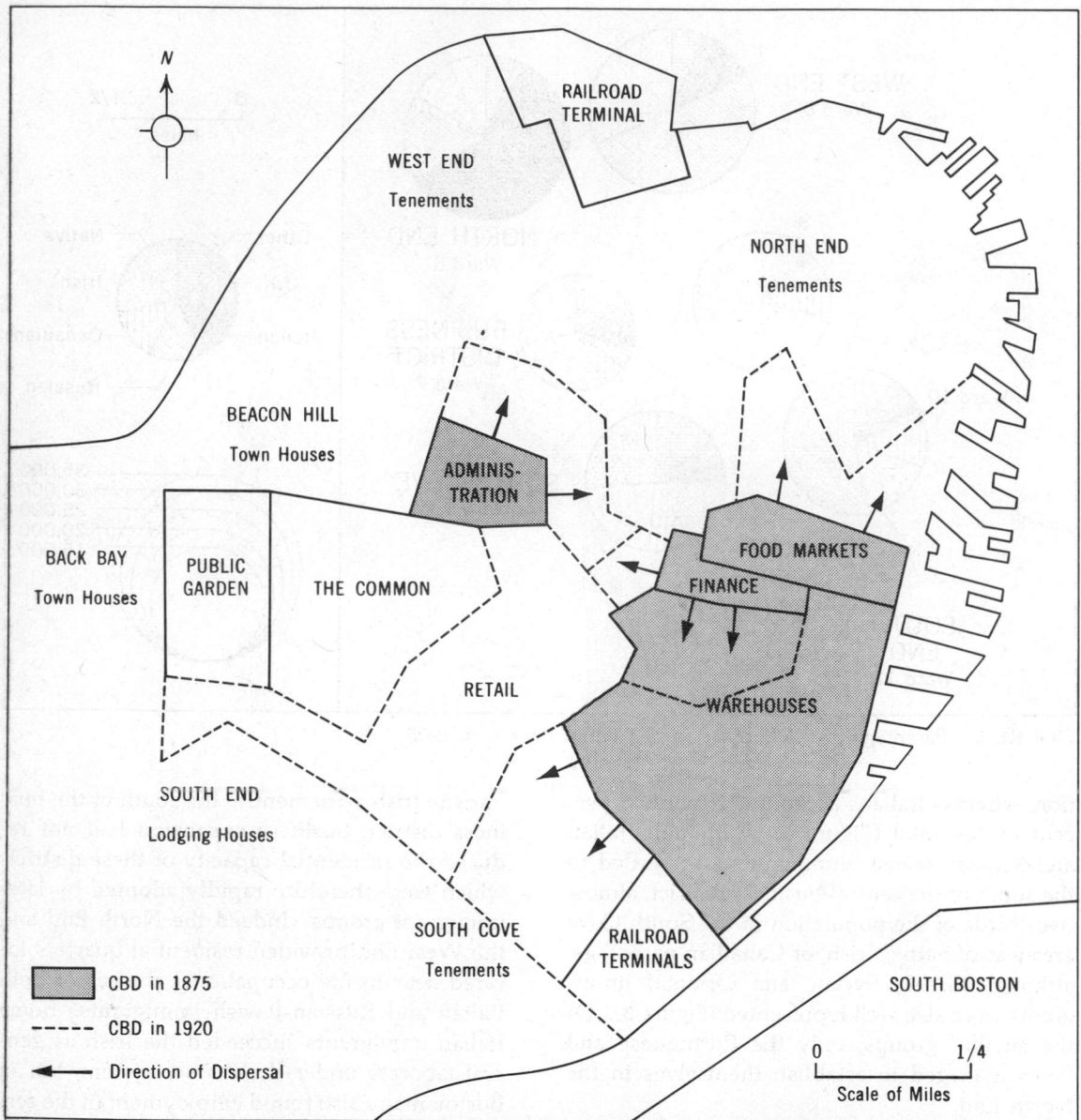

FIGURE 6.   Immigrant Residence and Business Expansion in Boston, 1875–1920

sequently, the laborers in the markets valued residence in the adjacent North End[39] (Figure 6). Jewish immigrants, to an even greater extent than the Italian, avoided employment in general laboring and, in Boston, as in other large cities, they adopted the clothing industry.[40]   During

the eighties, the clothing industry in the workshops of the warehouse quarter was affected by the increasing rents of warehouse locations, and most of the production was contracted out from the central workshop. Jewish immigrants became the main contractors for the merchants and established their trade in the tenements of the West End and the North End, where they used Italian female labor for finishing (Figure

[39] R. A. Woods (ed.), *Americans in Process* (Boston: Houghton Mifflin, 1902), p. 107.

[40] Woods, op. cit., footnote 39, pp. 113–116.

6). The needs of contract clothing necessitated ready access to the business district for the purposes of market information and credit facilities and, consequently, Jewish clothing workers no less than Italian market laborers valued residence adjacency to the business district.

The concentration of the Italians in the North End and of Russian Jews in the West End was also stimulated by group conciousness for, like the Irish before them, they preferred to spend their early years in an unfamiliar city among their compatriots. Living conditions in the North End and the West End were still poor and, during the last two decades of the nineteenth century, the density of people per dwelling and the density of housing per acre, greatly increased. Although living conditions were more congested, the control of contagious diseases had improved and both Jewish and Italian immigrants proved to be more resilient than the Irish in their adjustment to the problems of urban life. Many contemporary observers were disturbed by the social repercussions of congested living, but in the North End and the West End there is abundant evidence to indicate that immigrants reestablished a stable social organization.[41] The success of the Jewish and Italian residence in these districts was, however, assisted by the limited expansion of the central business district into their quarters, for without the threat of displacement both the North End and the West End became premium low-rent housing areas (Figure 6). Some residential buildings gave way to business premises, but many tenements survived well into the twentieth century; some, indeed, remain today. The North End and the West End thus were immigrant ghettoes in which the housing was congested and in which the people were stricken by poverty but, to the newly arrived immigrant, they provided low rent accommodation among friends and, above all, access to employment.

In both the North End and the West End, Italian and Russian-Jewish immigrants were numerous enough to establish their own communities and to control major sources of local employment. In the South Cove tenements, however, a more impoverished and less organized society emerged. This area was largely composed of filled land and had always been one of the most unhealthy areas in the town. The southward expansion of warehouses and the enlargements of the railroad terminals had resulted in the demolition of many tenements and discouraged the improvement of the surviving structures (Figure 6). Many of the less successful Irish and Canadian immigrants continued to reside here along with Boston's smallest and poorest immigrant groups who were unable to establish themselves in either the North End or the West End.[42] The small size, heterogeneity, and poverty of the resident population discouraged the development of local institutions, and employment opportunities were restricted to general laboring on the coal slips and timber yards of the Fort Point Channel. Thus, by the outbreak of World War I, the immigrant residential pattern initiated by the Irish was inherited by their Italian and Jewish successors but whereas the southern margin of the business district was blighted during the middle decades of the nineteenth century, the North End and the West End proved to possess enduring advantages for later immigrant groups.

By the turn of the century the continued southward expansion of the central business district had affected the status and population of the South End. The South End was developed during the fifties and sixties to serve the residential needs of middle income people displaced from the North End by Irish immigrants. In 1850, the new suburb was well removed from the advancing margin of the central business district and was served by the first horse-car services in the city. The South End, however, never fulfilled its early promise, partly because improvements in local transportation opened up more distant areas for suburban de-

[41] Woods, op. cit., footnote 39, pp. 54–55; Bushee, op. cit., footnote 26.

[42] Woods, op. cit., footnote 28, pp. 37–53; R. Murphy, "Boston's Chinatown," *Economic Geography*, 28 (1952): 244–255.

velopments and partly because the residential tastes of the middle-class changed from terraces to single dwellings set in their own grounds. Within one generation cheaper dwellings were built in the district and, towards the turn of the century, the new and growing segment of the business district devoted to retail trade invaded sections of the South End[43] (Figure 6). Because of new regulations the conversion of the terraces into tenements would have been a costly proposition, and many owners sought to salvage their investment by modifications for lodging and rooming house developments. Consequently, the South End housed single white collar workers and relatively few immigrant families. In 1905, almost 50 percent of the population was of American parentage and an additional 30 percent was of Irish and Canadian parentage (Figure 5). Although the South End was rarely marked by the problems of congestion so characteristic of either the North End or the West End, the absence of family structure led to the development of pathological social conditions which many contemporary observers were inclined to identify with tenement residents.

Although the South End never housed large numbers of immigrant families, adjacent commercial expansion had encouraged the departure of the original middle income population and single immigrant men formed a substantial minority of the lodging and rooming house population. Immigrant settlement and commercial expansion thus transformed and diversified almost the entire residential fringe of Boston's central business district. Beacon Hill alone maintained its original status and resisted the potential claims of business and immigrants. Unlike the Fort Hill or, later, the South End, Beacon Hill was not situated alongside an expanding business activity. The financial and public administrative centers, wherein most of the Hill's residents had their major interest, expanded into premium sites within business dis-

trict rather than into adjacent residential quarters (Figure 6). Moreover, two generations had passed since the first Federalist merchants had established their new homes near to the State House and overlooking the Common and, by the mid-sixties, the Hill was associated with ancestral status and wealth and symbolized an older Boston unravaged by immigration or warehouses.[44] Advantages of cultural association and of convenient access to the financial district reinforced the desirable topographic attributes which had attracted its original residents.

The need for high class residences rapidly outgrew the capacity of Beacon Hill and, to fulfill the growing demand for town houses, an expanse of the Back Bay was filled and developed as an exclusive residential district (Figures 3 and 6). To a much greater degree than in most American cities the changes in the desirability of various sections of Boston had left families of great wealth with relatively limited choices for residence and, although filled land had previously been associated with slums and railroads, the Back Bay provided new land both near to Beacon Hill itself and alongside an extension of the Common known as the Public Garden. At about the time when the South End lost its middle-income population, the Back Bay gained a reputation as the home of families of great wealth, and while retail premises invaded the inner precincts of the South End, the Back Bay retained its exclusive status until after the turn of the century.[45] Thus, during a period of heavy immigration and substantial business expansion residential quarters for people of wealth and status were successfully enlarged on one margin of Boston's central business district. The selective abandonment of middle and high-income districts no less than the selective adoption of abandoned locations by incoming immigrant groups recorded the timing, dimen-

[43] A. B. Wolfe, *The Lodging House Problem in Boston* (Cambridge: Harvard University Press, 1912), pp. 9–15.

[44] Whitehill, op. cit., footnote 31, pp. 141–173.

[45] A. Chamberlain, *Beacon Hill: Its Ancient Pastures and Early Mansions* (Boston: Houghton Mifflin, 1925), pp. 44–47.

sions, and characteristics of the expansion of the adjacent specialized business activity.

CONCLUSION

Although the survival of high class residential districts and the distinction between disorganized and stable low-income residential quarters have been recognized in many large American cities, the distributional implications of these findings have rarely been identified. Ecological theories have recognized the influence of the central business district upon the adjacent residential districts and have acknowledged the diversity of their social and material attributes, but the relationship between the type and dimensions of business expansion, and the quality and occupance of the adjacent residential district, has remained obscure. More recent examinations of the urban residential structure have established the impact of transportation and site costs upon the emergence of a suburban residential pattern, but the differentiation of central residential districts occurred before the revolution in local transport was extensive enough to affect the daily movements of the majority of the urban population. This study of Boston clearly illustrates the proposition that timing and dimensions of the expansion of the different specialized functional areas of the central business district affected not only the location and longevity of immigrant ghettoes, but also the disposition of the distinctive residential quarters which developed beyond the expanding fringe of the central business district. Since immigration and business expansion were universal influences upon the course of American metropolitan growth, these findings documented in Boston should have wide applicability to other large American cities.

40

STANLEY LIEBERSON

The Impact of Residential Segregation on Ethnic Assimilation

The residential segregation of immigrants in American cities, long a classical ecological problem, is reexamined for specific immigrant groups in each of 10 cities in an effort to ascertain the impact of segregation on other aspects of ethnic assimilation. Ability to speak English, citizenship, intermarriage, and occupational composition of 10 immigrant groups in each city are viewed as a function of their residential patterns and other ecological factors. The dynamic significance of spatial distribution for other dimensions of social behavior is stressed.

Reproduced by permission from *Social Forces*, Vol. 40, No. 1 (October 1961), pp. 52–57.
   This study was supported by a grant from the Ford Foundation to the Population Research and Training Center, University of Chicago. This is paper number 8 in the series "Comparative Urban Research."

The importance human ecologists attribute to the spatial distributions of human populations and social institutions is not only widely known but, if anything, misunderstood by many of their fellow social scientists. The ecologist's interest in space is often taken as evidence either of a preoccupation with the "subsocial" or of an esthetic satisfaction derived from locating social events in terms of gradients, "natural areas," multicolored maps, and the like. That this monolithic pursuit is to be found in the works of human ecologists—both present and past—ignores the far less constricted rationale which may be offered for this concern.

For example, during the heyday of European immigration to the United States, the propensity of immigrants to first locate in ghettoes and their later movements out of these areas of first settlement were frequently utilized as a measure or index of an ethnic group's assimilation. Studies of such diverse urban centers as Chicago,[1] Durban,[2] Montreal,[3] Paris,[4] and the major cities of Australia[5] attest to the widespread existence of residential segregation and its usefulness as an indicator of ethnic assimilation. Indeed, during the twenties and thirties, ethnic residential patterns were a major research interest of sociologists and others.

However, another dimension to the residential segregation of ethnic and racial groups is frequently overlooked. That is, not only can the residential patterns of ethnic groups be viewed as a significant element in the study of their assimilation and as an indicator of other elements of assimilation but, further, residential segregation has an affect on other aspects of ethnic assimilation. Hawley has hypothesized that physical isolation is a necessary condition for the maintenance of subordinate ethnic group status and, further, that "Redistribution of a minority group in the same territorial pattern as that of the majority group results in a dissipation of subordinate status and an assimilation of the subjugated group into the social structure."[6] Hawley's reasoning is based on the dual effect of residential segregation, that is, both as a factor accenting the differences between groups by heightening their visibility and, secondly, as a factor enabling the population to keep its peculiar traits and group structure. Evidence exists to support both of Hawley's contentions. For example, after finding that the greater the number of Negroes arrested in a district in Philadelphia, the greater the overestimation by policemen of the Negro rate in the district, Kephart has concluded that visibility increases at a more rapid rate than sheer number.[7] And Lieberson has shown close associations exist between the spatial distributions of ethnic populations in Chicago and the location of ethnic physicians' offices.[8]

This paper examines the impact of ethnic residential patterns on other aspects of their assimilation. Roughly 10 ethnic groups in each of 10 United States cities in 1930 were studied in terms of the relationships between their spatial distribution and citizenship, intermarriage, and ability to speak English. In addition, for a more limited number of groups and cities, the impact of residential segregation on occupational composition of ethnic groups was considered for 1950.

---

[1] Otis Dudley Duncan and Stanley Lieberson, "Ethnic Segregation and Assimilation," *American Journal of Sociology,* 64 (January 1959): 364–374.

[2] Leo Kuper, Hilstan Watts, and Ronald Davies, *Durban: A Study in Racial Ecology* (London: Jonathan Cape, 1958).

[3] Eva R. Younge, "Population Movements and the Assimilation of Alien Groups in Canada," *Canadian Journal of Economics and Political Science,* 10 (August 1944): 372–380.

[4] Robert Gessain and Madeleine Doré, "Facteurs comparés d'assimilation chez des Russes et des Arméniens," *Population,* 1 (January-March 1946): 99–116.

[5] Jerzy Zubrzycki, "Ethnic Segregation in Australian Cities," paper read at Internàtional Population Conference, Vienna, 1959.

[6] Amos H. Hawley, "Dispersion Versus Segregation: Apropos of a Solution of Race Problems," *Papers of the Michigan Academy of Science, Arts, and Letters,* 30 (1944): 674. See also Royal Institute of International Affairs, *Nationalism* (London: Oxford University Press, 1939), pp. 281–283.

[7] William M. Kephart, "Negro Visibility," *American Sociological Review,* 19 (August 1954): 462–467.

[8] Stanley Lieberson, "Ethnic Groups and the Practice of Medicine," *American Sociological Review,* 23 (October 1958): 542–549.

DATA AND METHODS

With one exception, published and unpublished United States census reports for 1930 and 1950 were the sources for all analyses made below. Because census tract data were available for only a limited number of cities in 1930, the 10 cities under investigation were not selected randomly.[9] Since the 1930 census gives an unusually extensive array of data on various aspects of immigrant and second generation behavior, it was all the more necessary to include cities for which segregation indexes could be computed. The larger immigrant and second generation groups were studied in each city.

Residential segregation was computed by using indexes of dissimilarity in a manner similar to that utilized in several recent studies.[10] With the exception of Chicago where Community Areas were used, segregation of immigrant groups from the native white population of each city was determined on the basis of their degree of similarity in their intracity census tract distributions. Indexes of dissimilarity were also used to compare the degree of similarity in occupational composition between groups. These indexes range from 0 (complete similarity) to 100 (complete dissimilarity).

Kendall's rank order correlation, *tau*, is the only measure of association used in this study. This type of nonparametric correlation is of particular value in this study since it permits the use of partial correlations.

FINDINGS

Citizenship Status

Naturalization is by no means a perfect indicator of an individual's assimilation. Thus some naturalized immigrants later return to their country of origin whereas not all immigrants remaining in the United States for 20 or more years adopt American citizenship. Nevertheless, it seems reasonable to use citizenship status "as an indication that the assimilative process has proceeded to a moderate extent at least. The fact of naturalization is indicative of an attitude towards the country very different from that of the immigrant who shows no desire to take out naturalization papers."[11]

In 1930, there was a persistent association in all 10 cities between the variations between immigrant groups in their segregation from native whites and their propensity to remain aliens, that is, groups highly segregated from native whites also have proportionately large numbers of adult males who are aliens (Table 1, column 1). These high rank order correlations between segregation and percent alien indicate nothing more than that the spatial distributions of immigrant groups may be used as an indicator of at least one additional dimension of assimilation. In order to infer that the residential segregation of immigrant groups affects the propensities of immigrants to change their citizenship, it is necessary to consider whether this association would exist independently of other major factors influencing the acquisition of American citizenship such as length of residence in the United States and ability to read and write in the English language.

Since literacy in English was not a prerequisite to obtaining first papers,[12] we have at least partially eliminated this factor by considering only the proportions of immigrants who have remained aliens, that is, who had obtained neither first nor second papers. However, if we view acquisition of American citizenship as largely a unilateral and irreversible process, then it is reasonable to assume that length of

[9] For a list of cities for which such data were gathered in 1930, see Howard Whipple Green and Leon E. Truesdell, *Census Tracts in American Cities (Census Tract Manual)*, (revised edition, Washington: United States Department of Commerce, Bureau of the Census, 1937).

[10] Otis Dudley Duncan and Beverly Duncan, "Residential Distribution and Occupational Stratification," *American Journal of Sociology*, 60 (March 1955): pp. 493–503 [No. 32 in this volume]; Duncan and Lieberson, loc. cit.; Kuper, Watts, and Davies, loc. cit.

[11] W. Burton Hurd, "Racial Origins and Nativity of the Canadian People," in Dominion Bureau of Statistics, *Seventh Census of Canada, 1931*, Vol. 13, *Monographs* (Ottawa: Edmond Cloutier, 1942), p. 662.

[12] Bureau of the Census, *Fifteenth Census of the United States: 1930, Population*, Vol. 2 (Washington: Government Printing Office, 1933), p. 401.

TABLE 1. Rank Order Correlations (TAU) Between Naturalization Status, Year of Arrival, and Segregation of Selected Immigrant Groups from Native Whites, 1930

	Percent of Foreign Born Who are Aliens and:		Segregation Foreign Born from Native Whites and:	
City	Segregation Foreign Born from Native Whites (1)	Median Year of Arrival (2)	Median Year of Arrival (3)	Percent of Foreign Born Who are Aliens (Holding Median Year of Arrival Constant) (4)
Boston	.47	.62	.18	.46
Buffalo	.29	.64	.29	.14
Chicago	.42	.73	.24	.37
Cincinnati	.44	.76	.42	.17
Cleveland	.64	.78	.69	.22
Columbus	.24	.71	.31	.03
Philadelphia	.42	.58	.47	.20
Pittsburgh	.56	.44	.47	.45
St. Louis	.56	.49	.56	.40
Syracuse	.50	.86	.50	.16

Note: Citizenship data for foreign born groups in Columbus, Cincinnati, and Syracuse based on all immigrants 21 years of age and older in 1930. Citizenship data for other cities based on immigrants of all ages except those not reporting their status.

residence in the United States would be a major influence, that is, immigrants living in the country for a longer period would be less likely to be aliens than more recent migrants. Consequently, the positive associations between immigrant group differences in length of residence and their proportions alien (Table 1, column 2) are not surprising. Since length of residence is also associated with the degree of immigrant segregation (column 3), the fact that the partial *tau* between segregation and citizenship status remains positive (although lower) in all 10 cities (column 4) indicates that immigrant residential

segregation decreases the proportion of a group taking at least minimal steps towards obtaining United States citizenship. Thus, the magnitude of an immigrant group's isolation from the native white population appears to play a role in influencing the extent to which members of the group are prone to give up ties with their country of birth.

Intermarriage

In terms of theories with probability types of analysis, the examination of simply the number of exogamous and endogamous marriages for members of different ethnic groups is an inadequate indicator of group differentials in the propensity to intermarry. That is, the larger a group is in a given city, the greater the proportion of intragroup marriages we would expect for the group even if members of all groups chose their mates randomly.[13] Due to the limited data available, a rather crude indicator of intermarriage must be used; namely, the percent of the second generation whose parents are of mixed nativity, that is, one parent foreign born and one parent native. The second generation of a given nationality was categorized by the Census Bureau into those who had both parents born in a foreign country and those who had one foreign parent and one native parent. As was noted in an earlier study using similar data, "It should not be overlooked that in many cases the native parent is a second-generation member of the same stock as the foreign parent, but the census data do not permit us to distinguish such cases from those involving intermarriage in a stricter sense."[14] It should also be added that we have no information about the number of cases in which there was intermarriage between persons who were born in different foreign countries and that all of the intermarriage material is based on the nativity classifications of offspring, that is, the second

[13] Franco Savorgnan, "Matrimonial Selection and the Amalgamation of Heterogenous Groups," *Population Studies*, supplement (March 1950), pp. 59–67.

[14] Duncan and Lieberson, loc. cit., p. 370.

generation. Differential fertility and migration, to name but two factors, tend to reduce the usefulness of such data.

Nevertheless, the relationship between segregation from native whites and intermarriage (as measured by the crude indicator discussed above) is a very strong one. In each city, the proportion of the second generation having "mixed" parents is inversely related to the magnitude of the foreign born group's segregation from the native white population (Table 2). And, regardless of methodological shortcomings, these results are consistent with the assumption that residential propinquity is a factor in choice of mate.[15] Thus the more segregated a foreign born group, the more likely marriages are to occur between members of the same group.

Ability to Speak English

Turning to the problem of language spoken by immigrants, one would expect to find an interaction between ability to speak English and segregation from native whites. Assuming that

TABLE 2. Rank Order Correlations (TAU) Between Residential Segregation and Intermarriage, 1930

City	Foreign Born Segregation From Native Whites and Percent of Second Generation with Both Parents Foreign Born
Boston	.60
Buffalo	.69
Chicago	.73
Cincinnati	.53
Cleveland	.78
Columbus	.71
Philadelphia	.67
Pittsburgh	.78
St. Louis	.64
Syracuse	.83

[15] See, for example, Marvin R. Koller, "Residential and Occupational Propinquity," in Robert F. Winch and Robert McGinnis (eds.), *Marriage and the Family* (New York: Henry Holt, 1953), pp. 429–434.

all native whites are able to speak English but no other language, then the larger the proportion of a given immigrant group able to speak English, the smaller the proportion of the immigrant group who would be hampered or handicapped by language differences in their location near native whites. Such would also be the case for native whites if we continue our somewhat arbitrary assumption that they all speak English but no other additional language. From this point of view, ability to speak English can be used as an independent variable in considering the fluctuations between immigrant groups in their segregation from native whites in a city. On the other hand, one could easily enough reverse the line of reasoning and assume that isolated foreign born groups would have less reason and opportunity to learn English than a group widely dispersed among the native white population. Thus, in the latter case, ability to speak English would be the dependent variable and immigrant segregation from native whites the independent variable. At any rate, not only would we expect an interaction between the magnitude of an immigrant group's segregation from native whites and their ability to speak English but, further, it would be necessary to take into account the effect of length of residence in the United States on the ability of immigrants to speak English. That is, length of residence would presumably affect the ability of immigrants to speak English.

The *tau* correlations presented in Table 3 indicate that ability to speak English and segregation are correlated in the direction expected, that is, the more highly segregated an immigrant group is from native whites, the larger the proportion unable to speak English (column 1). Similarly, median length of residence for the immigrant groups in each city is positively related to their ability to speak English (column 2). There is but one exception, Buffalo, where the correlation is nil. Column 3 indicates the correlations considered earlier which show some relationship between length of residence and degree of segregation. Taking into account the findings that both segregation and ability to speak English are in part functions of length of residence in the United States, the partial *tau* correlations between segregation and ability to speak English are computed (column 4). Although these partial correlations are generally lower than the correlations found without taking into account length of residence (compare columns 1 and 4), they are nevertheless all positive and indicate an association between ability to speak English and segregation from native whites even after length of residence is taken into account.

Occupational Composition

Although the use of ethnic occupational composition as an indicator of assimilation is a moot procedure, there is little doubt that the nature of an ethnic group's participation in the economy of a city is an extremely significant

dimension of its adaptation to the new society. Hawley has suggested that residential segregation—regardless of its causes—"is a restriction of opportunity; it hampers the flow of knowledge and experience and thus impedes diversification of interests and occupations."[16] One would therefore expect the occupational composition of highly segregated ethnic groups to be more sharply differentiated from native whites than the occupational composition of those groups less spatially isolated from the native white population. This association is found in four of the five cities for which both occupational and residential data were computed. That is, with the exception of Boston, immigrant occupational segregation from native whites varies with the magnitude of their residential segregation from the native whites in their city (Table 4, column 2).

Not withstanding the importance of these descriptive associations, the critical problem in-

TABLE 3. Rank Order Correlations (TAU) Between Ability to Speak English, Year of Arrival, and Segregation of Selected Immigrant Groups from Native Whites, 1930

| | Percent of Foreign Born Able to Speak English and | | Segregation Foreign Born from Native Whites and | |
| | Segregation Foreign Born from Native Whites (1) | Median Year of Arrival (2) | Median Year of Arrival (3) | Ability to Speak English (Holding Median Year of Arrival Constant) (4) |
City				
Boston	.71	.42	.18	.71
Buffalo	.53	.00	.29	.55
Chicago	.44	.44	.24	.38
Cincinnati	.29	.47	.42	.11
Cleveland	.40	.49	.69	.10
Columbus	.40	.40	.31	.32
Philadelphia	.84	.49	.47	.79
Pittsburgh	.49	.44	.47	.35
St. Louis	.51	.47	.56	.34
Syracuse	.64	.75	.50	.47

TABLE 4. Rank Order Correlations (TAU) Between Residential Segregation of Selected Foreign Born Groups from Native Whites and Foreign Born Occupational Segregation from Native Whites; Deviation of Second Generation Males, Ages 25–44, from "Expected" Occupational Composition, 1950

City*	Number of Groups (1)	Occupational and Residential Segregation (2)	Deviation from Expected Occupational Composition and Residential Segregation (3)
Boston	7	−.05	.14
Chicago	9	.50	.50
Cleveland	8	.29	.36
Philadelphia	7	.52	.24
Pittsburgh	8	.64	.29

* Occupational data based on Standard Metropolitan Areas; residential data based on central cities.

[16] Loc. cit., p. 672.

volves determining whether the magnitude of residential segregation influences the occupational composition of ethnic groups. Clearly, there are a number of general social forces operating to influence an individual's choice of occupation, for example, sex, educational attainment, father's occupation, age, and the like. If ethnic groups differ in these attributes, then we would expect the groups to vary in their degree of occupational similarity to that of the native white population. The influence of segregation on one such general societal pattern is considered below.

Intergenerational Occupational Mobility

It is fairly evident that father's occupation influences the occupations his sons select. For example, one would hardly expect the sons of laborers to have the same occupational distribution as the sons of professionals in a community. Using unpublished data gathered by Gladys L. Palmer for 1950,[17] male intergenerational occupational mobility rates were determined on the basis of data for four combined cities: Chicago, Los Angeles, Philadelphia, and San Francisco. This intergenerational mobility table yielded rates that were largely in the direction one would expect. For example, 29 percent of the sons of professional workers were professionals themselves, whereas only 4 percent of the sons of laborers were professionals. By contrast, 3 percent of the sons of professionals were laborers, whereas 10 percent of the sons of laborers were themselves laborers.[18]

By applying these rates to the occupational composition of each group of older foreign born males in a city, the "expected" occupational distribution of each second generation group of younger males was obtained. Assuming that second generation males between the ages of

25 and 44 in 1950 were the sons of immigrant males of the same nationality who were at least 45 years old in 1950 in a given city and, further, barring questions of differential fertility, mortality, and migration, it is possible to compare the actual occupational composition of second generation males with the composition expected on the basis of the society's intergenerational occupational mobility rates.

Despite the admittedly arbitrary nature of the assumptions, the results in Table 5 indicate that for a number of groups a fairly good prediction of the occupational composition of second generation males could have been made simply on the basis of the general social pattern of intergenerational mobility. That is, knowledge of the occupations of the fathers of second generation males combined with the general intergenerational occupational mobility patterns yields predictions of the occupational composition of second generation members that is fairly close to their actual occupational distributions. But, further, the magnitudes of the deviations in Table 5 are related to the degree of residential segregation of the foreign born groups from native whites in 1950. The correlations shown in Column 3 of Table 4 indicate a persistent pattern in which the more segregated an immigrant group, the greater its deviation from the general intergenerational occupational mobility patterns that exist in our society.

SUMMARY AND CONCLUSION

The magnitude of an immigrant group's residential isolation from the native white population in a city influences other dimensions of the group's assimilation. Highly segregated groups are less apt to become citizens or speak English; and these associations hold after differences between groups in their length of residence are taken into account. In addition, the degree of intermarriage is influenced by an immigrant group's residential segregation. That is, keeping in mind that an admittedly crude indicator was used, groups highly segregated residentially tend to have low rates of intermarriage. Finally, applying intergenerational

---

[17] For a description of the study, see Gladys L. Palmer, *Labor Mobility in Six Cities* (New York: Social Science Research Council, 1954).

[18] For the complete table, see Stanley Lieberson, "Comparative Ethnic Segregation and Assimilation," Ph.D. dissertation, University of Chicago, 1960, p. 255.

TABLE 5.   Indexes of Dissimilarity between the Actual Occupational Distribution of Selected Groups of Second Generation Males (25 to 44 Years of Age) and the Occupational Distribution Expected on the Basis of Intergenerational Mobility Patterns in Several Large United States Cities, 1950

Groups	Boston	Chicago*	Cleveland	Philadelphia*	Pittsburgh
England and Wales	5.04	5.78	11.76	11.68	12.68
Ireland	13.64	12.26	8.28	8.98	11.63
Norway	—	10.01	—	—	—
Sweden	15.42	13.72	—	—	—
Germany	9.70	8.66	10.34	12.54	14.45
Poland	8.82	13.71	15.54	16.14	20.35
Czechoslovakia	—	9.30	13.42	—	20.51
Austria	—	8.51	11.98	7.28	19.69
Russia	25.22	23.79	19.04	22.61	14.66
Italy	7.68	8.99	5.75	9.07	10.43

* Indexes of dissimilarity adjusted for the group's estimated proportion of the total male population in the four cities for which generational mobility patterns were obtained. These adjustments led to minor changes and did not affect the groups' rank order in either Chicago or Philadelphia.

mobility tables to the occupational patterns of second generation groups in five metropolises for which such data were available, it was found that highly segregated first generation groups were more apt to have second generation members deviate from the general pattern of intergenerational occupational choice.

These results may be viewed in two closely related contexts. First, the differential residential segregation of ethnic groups in American cities is an important factor in the assimilation of ethnic groups. Segregation is not only a significant dimension to assimilation but, further, the magnitude of a group's segregation appears to influence other aspects of the group's assimilation. In this respect, support is offered for Hawley's hypothesis that residential dispersion is a basic prerequisite for ethnic assimilation.

Secondly, the results of this inquiry may be used in calling to the reader's attention the fact that examination of the spatial distributions of human populations or social institutions is not merely a convenient tool or indicator for research purposes—as important as this may be—but is, additionally, a potentially significant factor in interpreting and predicting differences in social behavior.

41

STANLEY LIEBERSON

Suburbs and Ethnic Residential Patterns

Residential distributions of foreign-born and second-generation groups in the suburbs of several large metropolitan areas are compared with their compatriots' segregation patterns within the central cities of these metropolises. Differences between specific first- and second-generation groups in the magnitude of their dispersion in suburbs are associated with variations in segregation between the same nationalities residing in the central cities. The changes in ethnic distributions between suburbs during a twenty-year period are similar to those occurring within the central cities for comparable populations. These results suggest that differences in the population composition of suburbs and central cities may obscure the existence of similar behavioral patterns for comparable groups in the two parts of a metropolis.

Suburbs have grown very rapidly in recent decades and are viewed with increasing interest by sociologists and others. At least two major perspectives can be found in the mounting literature on suburbs. First, suburbs are considered as locales in which distinctive and new styles of life occur. Thus, for example, studies of neighboring, political behavior, and leisure activities in suburbs frequently invoke explicit or implicit comparisons with the behavior patterns found in central cities of the metropolis.[1]

A second approach to the study of suburbs, by contrast, stresses the fact that these outlying areas are tied to the central cities—at least to the extent that they are subject to processes encompassing the entire metropolis.[2] From this perspective, the centrifugal processes which lead to differential distributions of human populations and social institutions in the various parts of the metropolis are investigated.

It is clear that these two approaches are complementary rather than contradictory. Interpretations of central city-suburb differences in behavioral patterns must take into account differences in the areas' population composition before attributing causal significance to resi-

Reprinted by permission from the *American Journal of Sociology*, Vol. LXVII, No. 6 (May 1962), pp. 673–681. Copyright by the University of Chicago.

This study was initiated at the Population Research and Training Center of the University of Chicago under a grant by the Ford Foundation and completed at the State University of Iowa as Computer Center Project 178–0004.

[1] Consider, e.g., the following papers in William M. Dobriner (ed.), *The Suburban Community* (New York: G. P. Putnam's Sons, 1958); Sylvia Fleis Fava, "Contrasts in Neighboring: New York City and a Suburban County," pp. 122–31; Robert C. Wood, "The Governing of Suburbia," pp. 165–80; Philip H. Ennis, "Leisure in the Suburbs: Research Prolegomenon," pp. 248–70.

[2] Human ecologists, in particular, have emphasized this approach. See, e.g., R. D. McKenzie, *The Metropolitan Community* (New York: McGraw-Hill Book Co., 1933); Amos H. Hawley, *Human Ecology* (New York: Ronald Press Co., 1950); Leslie Kish, "Differentiation in Metropolitan Areas," *American Sociological Review*, XIX (August, 1954): 388–398; Leo F. Schnore, "Metropolitan Growth and Decentralization," in Dobriner (ed.), op. cit., pp. 3–20.

dence in suburbs per se. That is, differences between behavior in suburbs and central cities may largely reflect the gross differences between populations living in the inner and outer rings of a metropolis. If, for example, a larger percentage of a metropolis' high-income families reside in suburbs than do low-income families, then we would find gross differences between the areas' social life even if the inner ring's high-income families act in a fashion identical to the segment residing in the suburbs. On the other hand, the existence of gradients and other indicators of systematic variations encompassing both the central city and its suburbs precludes neither high selectivity within population segments in their propensities to move to suburbs nor changes in migrants' behavior after the establishment of residence in suburbs.

For example, although data on religious participation in suburbs are themselves of descriptive value, interpretations of differences from central cities must take into account socioeconomic, denominational, and other population attributes associated with church attendance before determining the extent to which such differences are to be attributed to suburban styles of life. Further, since temporal trends may occur within the central city as well as within suburbs, it is necessary to consider whether changes in the population residing in the latter areas are at all different from shifts observed for populations in the central city of comparable social positions.[3]

By examining the positions of various immigrant populations in suburbs, an effort is made in this paper to determine whether the well-documented ethnic colonies and segregation patterns found in the central cities of metropolitan areas[4] are maintained by ethnic

populations residing in suburbs. Since the current interest in suburbs occurs at a period long after the decline of European immigration to the United States, the relative absence of large-scale first-generation ghettoes in suburbs may merely reflect the small numbers present rather than being a result of styles of life peculiar to suburban living. Consequently, both the static and the dynamic aspects of ethnic residential patterns in suburbs are compared with comparable populations in the central city. In addition, attention is given to specific suburbs in an effort to both underscore and interpret variations between suburbs in the retention of their central city's pattern of residential segregation.

DATA AND METHODS

The central-city and suburban residential patterns of both the native white populations and the ten or so largest foreign-born groups are examined in each of the ten Standard Metropolitan Areas in 1950. By "suburbs" is meant here that part of the metropolitan area outside the central city, that is, the residual parts of the county or counties comprise a given Standard Metropolitan Area. For 1930, data are available for specific second-generation groups in addition to the populations studied for 1950. Retrojected Standard Metropolitan Areas, constructed for all but one metropolis in 1930, provide a basis for examining changes during a twenty-year period that are based on identical areal units—although the SMA's for 1930 are particularly arbitrary in delineation. The ten metropolitan areas, indicated below in Table 1, are not selected randomly but are those examined in an earlier study of central-city residential segregation.[5] Use of these cities, however, permits comparison of central-city residential segregation patterns with suburban patterns in the same metropolises. Unless otherwise indicated, the data are derived from published and unpublished United States Census sources.

---

[3] Application of a number of demographic controls in a comparison of church attendance in a central city and its suburbs is found in Basil G. Zimmer and Amos H. Hawley, "Suburbanization and Church Participation," *Social Forces,* XXXVII (May 1959): 348–354.

[4] See, e.g., Otis Dudley Duncan and Stanley Lieberson, "Ethnic Segregation and Assimilation," *American Journal of Sociology,* LXIV (January 1959): 364–374.

---

[5] Stanley Lieberson, *Ethnic Patterns in American Cities* (New York: Free Press of Glencoe, 1962).

In four of the metropolitan areas, residential segregation of specific foreign-born and second-generation groups from the native white population within central cities is measured on the basis of intercensus-tract differences in the proportional distributions of the groups. Indexes of dissimilarity, ranging from 0 (identical proportions) to 100 (complete segregation), are used to measure the degree of residential segregation between populations in the central city.[6] Residential distributions in suburbs are examined in two different contexts. First, the overall degree of residential dissimilarity of ethnic populations residing in suburbs is considered through the application of indexes of dissimilarity to the intersuburb distributions of specific foreign white stock groups in those suburbs with 10,000 or more population in both 1930 and 1950. Additionally, for a limited number of suburbs that are tracted in 1950 and have at least six census tracts, indexes of dissimilarity are used to measure the intertract residential segregation of foreign-born groups within specific suburbs.

Because the index of dissimilarity is affected by the spatial units used, comparisons can not be made between metropolitan areas or between the central city and the suburban ring of a given metropolitan area in the absolute values of the indexes obtained. It is possible, however, to examine the extent to which the groups maintain their relative degree of segregation from native whites in the two rings of a metropolis through the use of such measures of association as Kendall's τ and product-moment correlations. Further, the absolute values of indexes of dissimilarity are utilized in comparing the segregation of the same groups at two different decades in either the central city or suburbs of a metropolis.

FINDINGS

Ethnic Distributions Between Central Cities and Suburbs

Duncan and Reiss report that in 1950 the foreign-born whites comprise a somewhat larger proportion of the population of central cities than of suburbs in urbanized areas (11.1 and 9.1 per cent, respectively).[7] These differences, to be sure, are mild when compared with the Negro population, which at that time comprised 12.6 and 4.5 per cent of the populations of central cities and suburbs, respectively.[8] More detailed examination of the distributions of immigrants and second-generation groups between central cities and suburbs of ten metropolitan areas during a twenty-year span discloses both a net centrifugal shift of the foreign-born and systematic variations between ethnic groups in their propensities to reside in suburbs.

Within each of the ten metropolitan areas investigated, the ten or so largest foreign-born groups have a larger proportion of their members residing in the central cities than do the native white populations of these metropolitan areas. Table 1 indicates the metropolitan areas studied as well as the percentages for each group. Thus, for example, nearly 70 per cent of the Cleveland Standard Metropolitan Area's foreign-born resided within the central city of Cleveland in 1950 whereas only 56.4 per cent of the native white population of the metropolitan area resided in the central city. These differences are found in all ten metropolitan areas investigated. Similarly, in 1930 the leading foreign-born groups had larger percentages of their members residing in the central cities than did the native whites. It is also possible to examine the position of the second-generation segment of each metropolitan area's white population in 1930. In each case, the second generation occupies a position intermediate to that of the first generation and the total native white popu-

---

[6] This index is described in Otis Dudley Duncan and Beverly Duncan, "Residential Distribution and Occupational Stratification," *American Journal of Sociology,* LX (March 1955): 493–503.

[7] Otis Dudley Duncan and Albert J. Reiss, Jr., "Suburbs and Urban Fringe," in Dobriner (ed.), op. cit., p. 51.

[8] *Ibid.* See also Davis McEntire, *Residence and Race* (Berkeley: University of California Press, 1960), pp. 21–24.

lation. That is, the foreign-born are less suburbanized than the second generation, who are, in turn, less suburbanized than the total native white population. Since the ten or so second-generation groups studied in each metropolitan area comprise a major segment of the total second-generation population, we can infer that native whites of native parentage, that is persons of at least third-generation residence in the United States, are even less apt to reside in the central cities.

TABLE 1. Unweighted Mean Per Cent of Selected White Populations Residing in Central Cities of Standard Metropolitan Areas*

Metropolitan Area and Group	1930	1950
Boston (10):[†]		
Foreign-born	N.a.	40.4
Second generation	N.a.	N.a.
Native white	N.a.	31.8
Buffalo (10):		
Foreign-born	69.1	60.4
Second generation	67.7	N.a.
Native white	62.3	51.5
Chicago (10):		
Foreign-born	80.0	75.8
Second generation	76.7	N.a.
Native white	69.2	61.8
Cincinnati (11):		
Foreign-born	77.2	73.4
Second generation	72.6	N.a.
Native white	56.7	51.9
Cleveland (10):		
Foreign-born	82.0	69.9
Second generation	78.4	N.a.
Native white	67.7	56.4
Columbus (11):		
Foreign-born	89.6	81.7
Second generation	87.6	N.a.
Native white	78.8	72.6
Philadelphia (11):		
Foreign-born	75.2	69.8
Second generation	72.4	N.a.
Native white	58.1	51.2
Pittsburgh (11):		
Foreign-born	36.4	34.6
Second generation	35.7	N.a.
Native white	31.9	28.3

TABLE 1. (Continued)

Metropolitan Area and Group	1930	1950
St. Louis (11):		
Foreign-born	68.2	59.2
Second generation	65.0	N.a.
Native white	57.9	47.4
Syracuse (9):		
Foreign-born	77.8	72.2
Second generation	76.3	N.a.
Native white	70.6	63.2

* Unweighted means for foreign-born and second-generation groups based on Germany, Irish Free State, Italy, Poland, and Russia in all ten Standard Metropolitan Areas; England and Wales in all SMA's except Syracuse where Great Britain and Northern Ireland were used; Austria in all except Boston; Hungary (Buffalo, Cincinnati, Columbus, Philadelphia, Pittsburgh); Czechoslovakia (Chicago, Cleveland, Pittsburgh, St. Louis, Syracuse); Lithuania (Boston, Chicago, Philadelphia, Pittsburgh); France (Buffalo, Cincinnati, St. Louis); Rumania (Cincinnati, Columbus, Philadelphia); Sweden (Boston, Chicago, Syracuse); Yugoslavia (Cleveland, Pittsburgh, St. Louis); Greece (Boston, Columbus).

[†] Numbers in parentheses are numbers of foreign-born or second-generation groups.

The decentralization of the metropolitan population, marked by the growth of suburbs, is found for both the foreign-born and native segments of the white population. Comparisons between 1930 and 1950 indicate a decline in the proportions of these populations residing in the central city. For example, in 1930, 82 per cent of Cleveland's major foreign-born groups resided in the central city, whereas this had declined to about 70 per cent in 1950. Similarly, during this period, the percentage of native whites living in the central city declined from 67.7 to 56.4 per cent.

Foreign-born and second-generation groups not only have larger percentages of their metropolitan populations residing in central cities (compared with other white populations), but there is also a fairly persistent tendency among immigrant and second-generation groups for those more highly segregated in the central cities of metropolitan areas to also have lower proportions residing in suburbs (Table 2). Consideration of suburban population composition is therefore magnified in importance by finding that the more highly segregated first- and second-generation groups in the central city tend to have smaller proportions of their total metropolitan population residing in suburbs than do the foreign white groups who are less segregated within the central city.

TABLE 2. Rank-Order Correlations (Kendall) between Segregation of Selected Foreign White Groups and Per Cent of Their Metropolitan Population Residing in Central City*

Metropolitan Area and Group	1930	1950
Boston (10):†		
Foreign-born	N.a.	.42
Second generation	N.a.	N.a.
Buffalo (10):		
Foreign-born	.04	.20
Second generation	.24	N.a.
Chicago (10):		
Foreign-born	.16	.20
Second generation	.29	N.a.
Cincinnati (11):		
Foreign-born	.64	.64
Second generation	.71	N.a.
Cleveland (10):		
Foreign-born	.78	.56
Second generation	.91	N.a.
Columbus (11):		
Foreign-born	.53	.20
Second generation	.20	N.a.
Philadelphia (11):		
Foreign-born	.27	.53
Second generation	.38	N.a.
Pittsburgh (11):		
Foreign-born	−.02	.13
Second generation	−.16	N.a.
St. Louis (11):		
Foreign-born	.20	.09
Second generation	.27	N.a.
Syracuse (9):		
Foreign-born	.17	.22
Second generation	−.06	N.a.

* Foreign-born and second-generation segregation computed on basis of native white and native white of native parentage population distributions, respectively. See Table 1 for list of specific groups included in each standard metropolitan area.

† Numbers in parentheses are numbers of foreign-born or second-generation groups.

Examination of Table 2 indicates the existence of this positive association between central-city segregation and the proportion of a group's metropolitan area population residing in the central city. In 1950, positive correlations are found for approximately ten large immigrant groups in each of the ten metropolitan areas studied. Pittsburgh's foreign-born are the only exception for 1930 to these positive associations and the second-generation groups in Pittsburgh and Syracuse are the only exceptions among the second-generation groups in 1930.[9]

In short, it is clear that we would expect less visible forms of ethnic ghettoes in suburbs because both immigrant and second-generation groups, on the average, are less apt to reside in suburbs, that is, they comprise larger proportions of the central cities' total population than that of the population in suburbs. Further, there is a mild tendency for the more highly segregated immigrant groups in the central city to also have somewhat lower proportions of their total metropolitan population residing in suburbs.

Intersuburb Distributions and Central-City Segregation

The general demographic pattern discussed above has important consequences for the examination of ethnic residential settlements in suburbs. On the average, suburbs differ from central cities in the extent to which they are populated by immigrant and second-generation groups. The gross differences observed between inner and outer rings are in a direction that would lead one to expect less visible first- and second-generation clusters in suburbs than in their central cities. However, it is appropriate to consider here the distinction raised earlier between community differences based on dissimilarities in population composition and differences between communities that can

[9] More exceptions are found when the proportions of immigrants residing in central cities are compared with their centralization within these cities (see Lieberson, op. cit., Chap. IV).

best be attributed to a "community effect" of some sort. That is, we shall apply this distinction by examining the spatial distributions of those immigrant and second-generation members actually residing in suburbs.

The patterns of residential segregation by census tracts within the central cities of four metropolitan areas were compared with the patterns of residential distribution between the suburbs of each of the metropolitan areas considered. The over-all results indicate a close association between the two patterns, that is, immigrant groups most highly segregated from native whites within the central cities of Cleveland, Philadelphia, Pittsburgh, and St. Louis are also the immigrant groups least dispersed among the suburbs surrounding the central city. These correlations between intertract segregation within the central city and intersuburb segregation within the ring are fairly high (Table 3). Thus for the foreign-born groups in both 1930 and 1950 (cols. 1 and 3), we observe that those groups most highly segregated within the central city are also the groups whose outer-ring members are most highly concentrated in a limited number of suburbs. For example, the Yugoslavs, one of the more highly segregated foreign-born populations in the political city of Pittsburgh in 1950, are also highly concentrated in the metropolitan area's suburbs. Nearly 40 per cent of the Yugoslav population living in suburbs of 10,000 or more reside in one city (Aliquippa).

Data are available for determining the residential segregation patterns of second-generation groups within the central cities in 1930 as well as their intersuburb patterns in the same year. The correlations (col. 2, Table 3) again indicate that high residential segregation with the central city is associated with groups whose suburban members are concentrated into a limited number of suburbs, that is, that have high indexes of intersuburb segregation from native whites of native parentage.

Variations between immigrant groups in their segregation from one another in the central cities are also associated with the inter-ethnic patterns found in their suburban distributions, although the correlations are somewhat lower in magnitude. For both 1930 and 1950 (Table 3, cols. 6 and 8), we observe that the patterns of segregation between foreign-born groups in the central cities are similar to their distributions between suburbs. Thus foreign-born groups tend to vary in their suburban distributions from one another in the same fashion as do their compatriots in the central city. A similar set of correlations is found for the segregation pattern between second generation groups in 1930 (col. 7).

In brief, these results suggest that the over-all patterns of foreign-born segregation from

TABLE 3. Product-Moment Correlations between Interact Central-City Segregation and Intersuburban Distribution* of Selected Groups of Foreign White Stock

Metropolitan Area	Foreign-born vs. Native White, 1930 (1)	Second Generation vs. Native White of Native Parentage 1930 (2)	Foreign-born vs. Native White, 1950 (3)	No. of Groups (4)	No. of Pairs of Groups (5)	Foreign-born vs. Foreign-born, 1930 (6)	Second Generation vs. Second Generation, 1930 (7)	Foreign-born vs. Foreign-born, 1950 (8)
Cleveland	.84	.84	.81	10	45	.71	.72	.65
Philadelphia	.53	.70	.60	11	55	.22	.20	.21
Pittsburgh	.76	.91	.74	11	55	.41	.58	.49
St. Louis	.77	.81	.83	11	55	.43	.54	.52

* Intersuburban distributions based on cities of 10,000 or more population in 1930 and 1950.

native whites and from each other found in the central cities of our large metropolises are also found in the groups' intersuburban distributions. Further, the findings hold for 1930 as well as for 1950 and, additionally, for the second-generation groups in the earlier year also. To be sure, immigrants do not comprise a numerically important part of the total suburban population and are thus less visible than the present-day or past European immigrants in our central cities. However, immigrants located in suburbs do follow residential patterns similar to their compatriots in the central city.

Trends in Intersuburb and Central-City Segregation

Changes between 1930 and 1950 in the residential segregation of foreign-born groups in central cities are largely similar in direction to the trends for immigrants in suburbs. The average residential segregation of immigrant groups in central cities declined between the years investigated, both in their segregation from native whites (Table 4, cols. 1 and 2) and from each other (cols. 5 and 6). Cross-sectional declines in the central cities are also observed in comparing the average segregation indexes of the foreign-born and second-generation groups from the native whites of native parentage in 1930 (cols. 9 and 10).

Similarly, the immigrant and second-generation groups' average indexes of segregation between large suburbs show small declines through time—although there are several exceptions. For three of the four metropolitan areas, in 1950 the foreign-born groups are less dissimilar from the intersuburb distributions of native whites (Table 4, cols. 3 and 4) and other foreign-born groups (cols. 7 and 8) than they

TABLE 4. Unweighted Mean Indexes of Intracity Segregation and Intersuburb Distributions of Selected Foreign White Groups

Metropolitan Area	FB vs. NW				FB vs. FB			
	Central City		Suburbs		Central City		Suburbs	
	1930 (1)	1950 (2)	1930 (3)	1950 (4)	1930 (5)	1950 (6)	1930 (7)	1950 (8)
Cleveland	44.9	40.1	28.5	26.8	60.8	54.3	40.4	37.6
Philadelphia	44.3	40.8	25.7	25.3	57.2	53.0	30.5	29.6
Pittsburgh	42.6	38.4	34.0	33.9	57.4	51.6	41.6	42.4
St. Louis	41.4	37.6	32.9	33.5	55.4	49.9	43.5	42.9

Metropolitan Area	Central City 1930		Suburbs 1950	
	FB vs. NWNP (9)	NWFMP vs. NWNP (10)	FB vs. NWNP (11)	NWFMP vs. NWNP (12)
Cleveland	48.4	46.5	29.9	29.4
Philadelphia	47.3	43.4	28.1	27.6
Pittsburgh	45.2	42.5	40.8	37.3
St. Louis	42.0	38.0	33.4	30.3

FB, foreign-born white; NW, native white; NWNP, native white of native parentage; NWFMP, native white of foreign or mixed parentage.

were in 1930. The second-generation groups are also less segregated from native whites of native parentage than are the foreign-born groups in the other rings of all four metropolitan areas (cols. 12 and 11.).

Although not shown here, variations between foreign-born groups in the magnitude of their intertract central-city segregation from native whites and other immigrants in 1950 are closely associated with the residential patterns found within the central city in 1930. In the same fashion, the intersuburb distributions of the immigrant groups are closely correlated between 1930 and 1950. Thus both the 1950 intersuburb and intracentral-city segregation patterns of foreign-born groups tend to be closely correlated with the positions of the same groups twenty years earlier in the suburbs and central cities, respectively.

In summary the findings reported in Table 4 indicate that both central cities and their suburban rings experienced declining segregation of their foreign white populations during the period investigated. Because of limitations in the segregation index which were described earlier, it is impossible to compare absolute values between the two parts of a metropolis. However, the trends through time appear to be fairly similar and, if anything, the declines in central-city segregation are more persistent in the four metropolitan areas examined. Finally, despite the centrifugal population movements and general decline in segregation between 1930 and 1950, correlations indicate that central cities and suburban rings are very similar with respect to the high stability of their foreign-born groups' relative segregation during the period.

Residential Segregation Within Suburbs

Given these generally close relationships between segregation patterns in the central cities and the over-all distributions of the foreign-born between the suburbs, attention is turned to immigrant residential patterns *within* specific suburbs. In four metropolitan areas, segrega-

tion within those suburbs that were subdivided into at least six census tracts in 1950 is compared with the residential segregation of the same foreign-born groups in the central cities.[10] The inclusion of suburbs from four metropolitan areas, combined with the fact that the sampling of suburbs is far from random, calls for cautious interpretation of the variations between suburbs in approximating their central city's segregation pattern.

Non-parametric τ correlations shown in Table 5 indicate positive associations between the segregation ranks of roughly ten foreign-born groups in each suburb and that of their central-city members, that is, immigrant groups in a given suburb tend to vary in their segregation from the suburb's native whites in a manner similar to that of their members in the central city of the metropolis. However, as inspection of Table 5 indicates, the strength of these associations between suburb and central-city patterns of segregation varies considerably. Although no negative association is found in any of the seventeen suburbs compared with their central city, the correlations are significantly different from zero in only about half of these suburbs.

Application of the Kruskal-Wallis one-way analysis of variance to the τ's in Table 5 indicates no statistically significant difference between dormitory, employing, and balanced suburbs in their immigrant groups' approximation of the central city's segregation pattern.[11] A fairly sizable difference is ob-

---

[10] With the exceptions indicated below, the groups included are those listed in n. * to Table 1. However, in several instances there were too few members of a specific foreign-born group in a suburb to justify computation of their segregation. These groups were eliminated by the arbitrary procedure of excluding groups whose total numbers in a suburb were less than twice the number of tracts in the suburb. These exclusions are Clairton, Lithuania; Carnegie, Yugoslavia and Lithuania; Wilkinsburg, Yugoslavia and Lithuania; Granite City, Eire; Chester, Rumania.

[11] Based on classification in *The Municipal Year Book, 1953* (Chicago: International City Managers' Association, 1953), pp. 70–96.

TABLE 5. Rank-Order Correlations (Kendall) between Intertract Central-City and Intertract Suburb Segregation of Selected Foreign-Born Groups from Native Whites, 1950

Metropolitan Area and Suburb	Rank-Order Correlation
Cleveland:	
Cleveland Heights	.51
East Cleveland	.60
Euclid	.16
Garfield Heights	.33
Lakewood	.47
Parma	.07
Shaker Heights	.42
Philadelphia:	
Camden	.55
Chester	.62
Pittsburgh:	
Braddock	.44
Carnegie	.00
Clairton	.47
Duquesne	.33
Wilkinsburg	.56
St. Louis	
East St. Louis	.27
Granite City	.07
University City	.45

served, however, between the metropolitan areas in the ranks of their suburbs' correlations. These findings, of course, can be interpreted only speculatively. However, it should be noted that a fairly strong inverse relationship is found between the extent to which immigrants in suburbs approximate the central-city segregation pattern and the degree to which the suburbs have single-family dwelling units. This suggests that housing characteristics may play an important role in maintaining or changing central-city residential patterns in suburbs. Thus not only do suburbs appear to approximate ethnic segregation patterns in the central city, but it may well be that suburban differences can be considered in terms of continuous variables rather than viewing suburbs and central cities as completely different entities.

CONCLUSIONS

This paper is written with two purposes in mind: first, to examine residential segregation of foreign-born and second-generation groups in suburbs; second, to caution against a tendency to use "suburbanization" as an all-too-easy interpretation of both variations and changes in social life.

With respect to the first goal, the segregation patterns of immigrant and second-generation populations in suburbs are found to be rather similar to those of their countrymen residing in the central cities. If there is something distinctive about suburban living for these ethnic groups, it is not found in terms of sharp deviations from the propensities of their central-city compatriots to segregate residentially. To be sure, because of limitations of data and methodological difficulties, many of the comparisons are based on the intertract segregation of foreign white populations in the central city and only upon their intersuburb distributions in the outer ring (and then solely of suburbs of 10,000 or more population). Nevertheless, the evidence does support the contention that first- and second-generation groups have patterns of segregation from each other and from native white populations that are frequently similar to those of their central-city members. Of course, this does not mean that ethnic segregation is static in metropolitan areas. Indeed, ethnic segregation appears to be declining in both rings of the metropolis.

These results serve to support the second purpose of this paper, that is, they emphasize the analyses required in interpretations of behavioral differences between central-city and suburb residents before attributing causal significance to location in suburbs per se. With respect to foreign-born groups in particular, it is clear that one must consider their numerical importance in suburbs. The fact that smaller proportions of these groups reside in suburbs compared with native white populations—coupled with findings that more highly segregated immigrant populations within the central city are also the least likely of the immigrant groups to reside in suburbs—suggests that visibility of immigrant residential segregation in the outer ring should be considerably less than in the central city. However, as the data indicate, this does not mean that the segregation patterns of immigrants actually residing in suburbs are necessarily different from those in central cities.

Further, it should be recognized that discussions of "suburbs" involve a rather heterogeneous entity, that is, suburbs differ considerably from one another in a wide array of attributes such as the socioeconomic positions of their inhabitants, the extent and nature of their economic activities, distance from the central city, patterns of growth, and, as we have seen earlier, the ethnic composition of their residents. Kish, for example, has shown that suburbs are characterized by increasing differentiation with proximity to the central city.[12] Although there are suburbs occupied primarily by white-collar and professional families of the

white race, several potential pitfalls exist when discussions of "suburban styles" are restricted to these areas. For one, there is the simple fact that many areas lying outside of the central city do not possess these attributes but are nevertheless suburbs.[13] Another, the existence of over-all differences between the suburban ring and the central city may merely reflect the uneven distributions of populations within the metropolitan area, but do not *necessarily* reflect differences in the behavior of populations of comparable social characteristics.

This writer does not question the existence of different and unique styles of life in suburbs. Comparison and control for many population attributes are necessary in endeavoring to account for these phenomena and attributing weights to the relevant variables. In the same fashion in which gross differences between a city's Negro slum area and a high-income white neighborhood are not attributed simply to neighborhood styles of life, the suburban effect is to be analyzed, not merely described.

---

[12] Kish, op. cit.

[13] See, e.g., Bennett M. Berger, *Working-Class Suburb* (Berkeley: University of California Press, 1960).

42

SURINDER K. MEHTA

Patterns of Residence in Poona, India, by Caste and Religion: 1822–1965

An analysis of the residential distribution of caste and religious groups in Poona (India) over the past century and a half shows distinctive patterns of segregation and centralization that have largely remained unchanged despite the city's growth

Reprinted by permission from *Demography*, Vol. 6, No. 4 (November 1969), pp. 473–491.

and development. The upper castes are residentially centralized and the lower castes are decentralized in Poona. Such a centralization of the elite has been observed in most other past and present cities of the world, although the pattern is less common in the contemporary United States. The Jews and Parsees, and the Christians, tend to be highly segregated and decentralized in Poona. However, Negroes in large American cities are generally more highly segregated residentially than the Jews, Parsees, Christians, and even the depressed and untouchable castes in Poona. The American cities show an average degree of segregation of the foreign-born white ethnic groups, and of the native whites of foreign or mixed parentage, from the native whites that is as great, if not greater, than the mean extent of segregation of caste groups in this Indian city.

This paper is a continuation of an analysis of patterns of residence in Poona, India. The first part of the analysis dealt with patterns of residence by income, education, and occupation at two points in time—1937 and 1964–65 [Mehta 1968]. For the present analysis we are more fortunate in having residential data available for caste and religious groups for 1822, 1937, 1954, and 1964–65.

We have then an unusually long time series of residential data for this city. We will be able to examine what changes if any occurred in this city's caste and religious groups' patterns of residence and segregation as the indigenous city came and remained under colonial rule for a century and a quarter. Furthermore, we will also be able to examine whether or not recently emergent forces of modernization and industrialization have brought about any significant changes in these residential patterns. Lastly, and very briefly, we wish to compare the distinctiveness of the extent and nature of segregation of caste and religious groups in contemporary Poona with the residential patterns of ethnic and racial groups in American cities which are relatively new and wholly western.

Poona is the capital of Poona District. It is situated in the western part of Maharashtra State, about 120 miles east-southeast of Bombay. It lies on an extensive plain surrounded by rather barren steep hills. While "available historical records do not furnish a separate history of Poona City until well into the seventeenth century," the city is probably hundreds of years older. The city had had a violent history before the British occupied it in 1817, and soon afterward established Poona Cantonment adjoining the eastern boundary, and Kirkee Cantonment to the north [Gadgil 1945:1–12].

> Poona seems, in the beginning, to have been the headquarters town of a region which, however, was neither densely populated nor rich in agricultural resources. The location of the town seems to have been determined chiefly by the site of the ford on the river Mutha. . . . Poona under the Muslims, before the beginning of the 17th Century, was eminently a fortified place around which the town was established [Gadgil 1952: 1].

* * *

Although in its periods of prosperous growth and development, during the latter half of the eighteenth century, during the 1920's, and since the beginning of World War II, Poona drew migrants from all over India, much of its population is indigenous or is indigenous to the surrounding areas and other parts of Maharashtra State.

Poona has a good-sized Muslim minority which dates from centuries back when Muslim rulers held sway over the city. The Christians are of local origin to some extent but many are from Bombay and other parts of India. Its small Jewish population is of ancient origin in India although the group is not indigenous to Poona. The Parsees originate from Bombay; they are

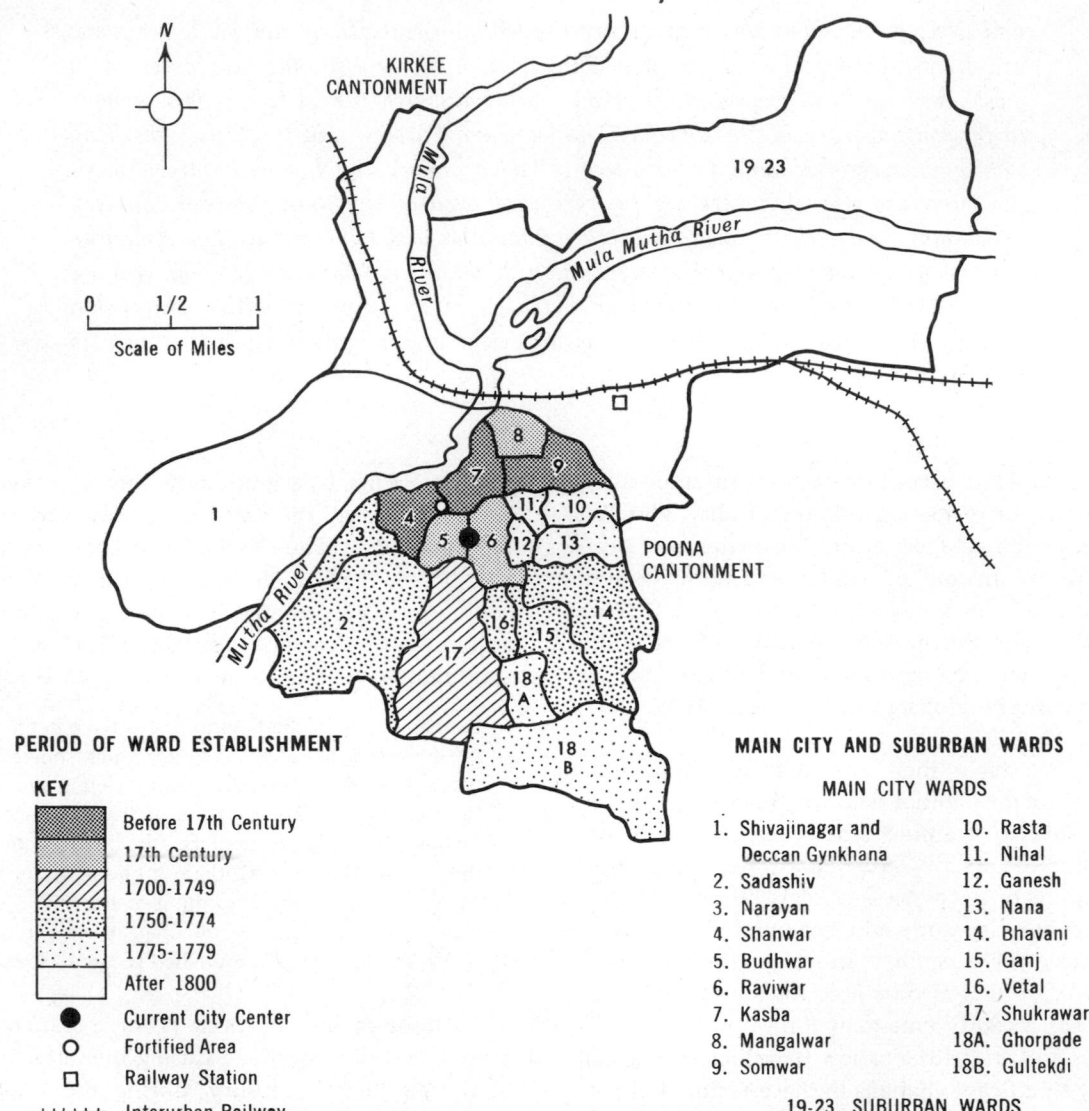

FIGURE 1.   Poona City Wards and Their Period of Establishment. Source: After the map in Sovani, Apte, and Pendse [1956, appearing opposite p. xx]. The period of establishment of wards is taken from the historical account given by Gadgil [1952, pp. 3–24].

a small, but wealthy trading and merchant community largely associated with the cantonment areas. The group "Other Hindus" consists of many different caste groups with their main characteristic being that they are from North and South India and are considered and treated to some extent as foreigners by the local caste groups of Poona.

The Gujarati, Marwadi, and Jains are relatively wealthy traders and merchants mostly, but are integrated in the economic life of both the city and the cantonment areas. The Artisan group consists largely of indigenous elements although a number of the artisan caste groups originate from North and South India. The Marathas and Malis are the largest group. They are indigenous to the area and constitute a complex which includes within it descendents of highest nobility and military leaders of the period of the Maratha regimes. Mainly, however, this group contains the bulk of peasants and laborers, both unskilled and skilled, and some who are small and medium-scale traders. Next to the Marathas in numerical importance are the Brahmins, who are in the main indigenous, but a small number of them had come from outside of Maharashtra. The Brahmins hold a predominant position in Poona; they are well-educated, well-to-do, and are found mainly in professional, administrative, and clerical positions. The Dhangar and Gawli are few in number and are engaged in tending cows, buffaloes, and goats; selling milk; and in unskilled manual work. Persons categorized as members of the Depressed Classes belong to the lowest caste groups such as scavengers, sweepers, leather tanners, and various unskilled laboring groups.

Poona, as we said, is an ancient city with a heterogeneous population composed of various caste and religious groups. In recent decades it has experienced much growth and industrialization and modernization. It has developed a relatively efficient public bus system, acquired a fleet of motorized rickshaws, taxis, and a number of private automobiles; and it has experienced European influence for well over a century. The city should provide, therefore, an interesting case study of long standing patterns of residence of caste and religious groups under the impact of colonialism, and emerging modern urban-industrial forces of change. What changes in patterns of residence and segregation of caste and religious groups have been effected by these forces of change will be examined in this paper.

DATA AND METHODS

The data and methods of analysis of this study have been described elsewhere [Mehta 1968], and a discussion of them need not be repeated here. However, a brief discussion of the 1822 and 1954 data is necessary as they could not be incorporated in the earlier study, because the requisite residential data by income, education, and occupation, were not available. Also, for comparative purposes mention should be made about the nature of the 1937 and 1964–65 data. (Throughout this paper the 1964–65 data will be treated as if they pertain to 1965.)

It should be indicated at the very beginning that the areal unit of analysis throughout this study is the ward. The wards are of varying geographical size, and highly disparate population densities [Brush 1968]. The ward boundaries between 1822 and 1965 have remained in the main unchanged.

The 1822 data are from a census of houses and population. The residential population data by caste and religion are available for only thirteen of the city's then seventeen wards. For four wards the population data by community group had to be estimated from data concerning the number of houses in 1818 occupied by members of different caste and religious groups and the total 1822 population of each of the wards. In the case of one ward, we had to resort to 1764–65 data on the number of houses occupied by members of different caste and religious groups and the 1822 total population for our estimate of its population by caste and religion. (The source for all the 1822 data is Gadgil [1952], pp. 42–58.) In 1822 the city consisted of wards numbered 2 through 18B as shown in Figure 1. The total population of the city at that time was about 79,000.

(Just before the British occupied Poona in 1818 and banished the last of the Peshwa rulers to North India, Poona's population had been estimated by a couple of Englishmen to have been 100,000 and 110,000. It is suspected that the decline in numbers of persons of different castes from 1818 to 1822 was highly selective by caste, and therefore, the estimates of the population by caste for the aforementioned five wards are subject to considerable error.)

The 1937 data are from a 6–7 per cent random sample of families consisting of the families found in every fifteenth house, beginning with the first, taken from a listing of houses. The wards of Poona City at this time were those of 1822, plus ward number 1, and two suburban wards and three other very sparsely populated areas. The number of families in the sample which lived in wards numbered 1 and 19 through 23 constituted fourteen per cent of the total number of families in the sample. Thus, the data for 1822 and 1937 are only fairly comparable. The total population of the city in 1937 is estimated at about 225,000.

The 1954 data are from a four per cent random sample drawn from a rather complete list of all families in Greater Poona made up by the city's Rationing Authorities for purposes of food distribution. [For a detailed description of the 1954 sampling procedure and problems of data collection encountered in the survey, see Sovani, Apte, and Pendse, 1956, Ch. I, especially pp. 3–9.] By 1954 the population of the city had grown to over 400,000 and Greater Poona's population is estimated to have been somewhat over 500,000. (By 1954 the Poona Municipal Corporation area was much enlarged over the area which we have till now called Poona City. This larger area has continued to grow and may be thought of as the metropolitan area of Poona. This enlarged area we have designated as Greater Poona in this study. In 1954, the Greater Poona area includes the two cantonment areas in our study; the 1965 Greater Poona area excludes the cantonment area as no data for them were collected.)

The 1965 data are from a one per cent cluster-type random sample. Thus compared to the 1937 and 1954 data, the 1965 sample is likely to show relatively greater homogeneity for the populations of the various wards. In 1961 Poona City had a population of about 530,000, and Greater Poona's population, exclusive of the 124,000 population of Poona and Kirkee cantonments, was close to 600,000.

PATTERNS OF RESIDENCE: DISSIMILARITY AND SEGREGATION

Some data pertaining to the social and economic characteristics of persons and families belonging to various caste and religious groups are available. We have ranked the caste groups and the religious groups separately for 1822, 1937, and 1954 (Table 1) and 1965 (Table 2) by certain indicators of social and economic status.

We have placed "Other Hindus" alongside of religious groups rather than allocating them to the various caste groups. The reason for this is that we simply did not have the information about which castes these persons or families belonged to available to us. All we know is that all those designated as *pardeshi* (literally foreigners, in the present context migrants from North India), South Indians, and "Other Hindus" in our sources of data are Hindus. However, although they are Hindus, in some ways all of these persons are treated somewhat as foreigners by the caste Hindus indigenous to Maharashtra State. In a sense, the *pardeshi*, South Indians, and "Other Hindus" are outside of the indigenous caste structure. (*Pardeshi* refers to a migrant from North India as well as to members of his family. In fact families continue to be identified as such even when the family migration may have occurred generations ago. Some of Poona's "most respected and ancient families" are *pardeshi* to the local caste Hindus. See Gadgil [1952: 71.] For our analysis, therefore, we decided to consider the *pardeshi*, South Indians, and "Other Hindus" to be extraneous to the local caste system, and decided to treat them all as "Other Hindus," a residual group of Hindus to be differentiated from the indigenous caste Hindus. They are treated in our analysis lumped together, rather than separately, because they all share the characteristic of being "foreign" and because individually their numbers are small and tend to lend instability to the analysis.

On the other hand, we have placed the Gujarati, Marwadi, and Jains among the caste groups despite the fact that the first two are

TABLE 1. Ranking of Caste and Religious Groups by Income and Occupation, High to Low, Poona City 1822, 1937 and 1954

| | 1822, Persons | | | 1937, Families | | | | 1954, Families | | | |
| | Per Cent | | | | Per Cent in occ. | | | | Per Cent in occ. | | |
Group	Well-to-do	Occ.	Mean Rank	Median Annual Income	High	Low	Mean Rank	Median Annual Income	High	Low	Mean Rank
Total	31	46	—	314	18	22	—	1,124	24	21	—
CASTE											
Brahmins	85	7	1.5	583	55	4	1.3	1,767	57	4	1.0
Gujarati, Marwadi, Jains	12	6	2.0	610	28	6	1.7	1,657	37	6	1.0
Artisans	5	68	4.5	308	8	13	3.0	934	12	20	3.0
Marathas, Malis	25	64	3.0	258	7	35	4.3	881	10	31	4.0
Dhangar, Gawlis	0	27	4.3	231	6	34	4.7	760	5	36	5.3
Depressed Classes	0	94	5.8	222	2	47	6.0	849	4	52	5.7
RELIGIOUS GROUP											
Total Hindus	31	47	4.0	389	18	24	3.3	1,137	24	22	4.0
Other Hindus	27	36	3.8	308	13	17	4.3	1,292	27	15	2.7
Muslims	37	36	2.8	319	10	14	4.0	952	14	14	4.3
Christians	100	0	1.3	366	27	7	2.3	1,382	20	16	3.3
Jews, Parsees	0	0	3.3	1,400	59	0	1.0	2,000	67	8	1.0

Note: Low occupations, 1822, include artisans, laborers, and beggars; high occupations, 1937 and 1954, include clerks and shop assistants, pensioners, intermediate and highest professions and administrative posts, owners of large shops and factories; low occupations, 1937 and 1954, include unskilled manual workers. Income figures are in rupees.

Mean rank is unweighted average of ranks with respect to specified income and occupation measures. Mean ranks on the same three variables in 1954 for Greater Poona differ from those for Poona City in only two instances: 4.3 for Muslims, and 3.0 for Christians.

Sources: Derived from Gadgil [1952], Peshwa *Daftur*, Table 1, pp. 46–49, Table 10, p. 77, Table 11, p. 80; Sovani, Apte, and Pendse [1956], Table 1.11, pp. 38–45, Table 1.20, p. 87, and Table 6.3, pp. 420–421.

TABLE 2. Ranking of Caste and Religious Groups by Income and Occupation, High to Low, Greater Poona, 1965

| | Educational Level of Husbands[a] | | Monthly House-hold Income | | Unweighted Mean Rank |
Group	Median	Rank	Median	Rank	
Total	1.7	—	111	—	—
Brahmins	3.5	1.0	176	1.0	1.0
Advanced Hindus	1.8	2.0	155	2.0	2.0
Marathas	1.5	3.5	95	3.0	3.2
Muslims	1.5	3.5	93	4.0	3.8
Intermediate Others	1.4	5.5	89	5.5	5.5
Intermediate Artisans	1.4	5.5	89	5.5	5.5
Depressed Classes	1.2	7.0	85	7.0	7.0

[a] Educational data were available according to the following levels of educational attainment: 1—illiterate; 2—literate up to 7th standard; 3—above 7th standard but below secondary school certificate; 4—S.S.C. but below graduate; 5—graduate or above, technical degree, diploma, etc.

Source: Derived from Family Planning Evaluation Scheme, Poona City, 1964–65 Random Survey, Table 6 x 17 (unpublished data made available to the author by Mrs. Kumudini Dandekar).

regional designations and the Jains are a religious group. In the data available to us the Jains were often not separately identified. When they were, their numbers in the samples were very small; and they tended to have patterns of residence similar to those of the Gujaratis and the Marwadis. In Poona and in the Indian society in general, the Gujarati and Marwadi migrants and their descendents are engaged mostly in retail and wholesale trade and are treated as a caste group. In many ways the position of the Jains tends to be the same.

The reason we are grouping Hindu caste groups on the one hand, and religious groups in a separate group on the other, is an obvious one. In Indian society both caste and religion have an important but differential influence on occupational affiliation, income, education and, we presume, on patterns of residence. We expect that differentiation in residential location would be distinctively different when caste groups are examined vis-a-vis one another than when caste groups are examined in relation to religious groups.

Our earlier analysis for Poona as of 1937 and more recent dates showed that the index of dissimilarity values for the within occupation, income, and education group comparisons tended to increase as the difference between the groups in socio-economic status increased [Mehta, 1968]. This relation between residential dissimilarity and socio-economic difference resembled that reported for American cities in studies of patterns of residence by occupational groups [for example, see Duncan and Duncan 1955; Wilkins 1956; Uyeki 1964]. It has also been observed to apply to Oxford, England [Collison and Mogey 1959]. We expect to find much the same kind of phenomenon again in Poona for within caste group and within religious group comparisons as the difference between the groups in socio-economic status increases.

(The term "higher status" when applied to caste groups here poses no special problem. The ranking of the caste groups as determined by the indicators of socio-economic status utilized in our study is more or less in correspon-

dence with the prevailing caste hierarchy in Indian society in general, and in Poona in particular. However, it cannot be said that in India there is a hierarchy of religious groups wherein the status of Jews and Parsees is higher than of Christians who in turn have a higher status than Muslims, and so on. The religious groups as ranked in our study are ranked strictly empirically with no connotation of differential prestige attachment.)

Indexes of dissimilarity in residential distribution between pairs of castes, pairs of religious groups, and a caste and a religious group are reported in Table 3. The castes are ordered in terms of decreasing socio-economic status as of 1937 (the ordering for 1822 differs slightly as shown in Table 1). The religious groups are ordered roughly in terms of increasing socio-economic status as of 1937 (again, the 1822 ordering is somewhat different).

If residential dissimilarity increased with increasing socio-economic difference between castes, the dissimilarity values for the caste groups should tend to increase left to right from the diagonal for the 1822 data and top to bottom for the 1937 data. The values also should tend to increase from the diagonal, bottom to top for the 1822 data, and right to left for the 1937 data. (It should be pointed out that as noted by Lieberson [1963: 38–40], the dissimilarity values are mathematically not independent in all cases. Thus in Table 3, given that in 1937 the dissimilarity values between caste groups 1 and 2, and 1 and 3, were found to be 67 and 57 respectively, then the dissimilarity value between 2 and 3 is mathematically constrained between 10 and 100. Such a mathematical constraint on the dissimilarity values, however, poses no serious problem for the present study.) Major departures from this expected pattern are observed in the 1822 data, but in general our expectation was clearly borne out for 1937.

In 1937, then, but not in 1822, given any caste group's dissimilarity in its pattern of residence compared with another caste group that was next to it in rank in social and economic

TABLE 3.   Indexes of Dissimilarity in Residential Distribution for Caste and Religious Groups, Poona City, 1822 and 1937
[above diagonal, 1822; below diagonal, 1937]

Group	(1)	(2)	(3)	(4)	(5)	(6)	(7)	(8)	(9)	(10)	(11)
1 Brahmins		54	39	26	54	53	35	61	53	79	78
2 Gujarati, Marwadi, Jains	67		35	59	56	53	47	53	40	83	46
3 Artisans	57	44		38	43	39	25	32	34	64	64
4 Marathas, Malis	53	45	28		47	40	27	48	39	70	74
5 Dhangar, Gawlis	71	56	44	34		52	42	33	49	56	57
6 Depressed Classes	75	63	56	40	34		36	36	31	67	68
7 Total Hindusa	58	44	29	22	39	49		43	35	68	67
8 Other Hindus	65	41	31	30	37	43	30		37	53	71
9 Muslims	72	42	40	40	41	43	37	31		68	60
10 Christians	78	53	60	51	56	46	53	52	47		79
11 Jews, Parsees	89	81	77	70	75	56	73	71	63	35	

a Includes "Other Hindus," group 8; but for each index for Total Hindus and a given caste group or Other Hindus, the given group is excluded from the Total Hindus.

Source: Derived from Gadgil [1952], Table 9, p. 68, Table 3, pp. 53–56, and Table 4, pp. 57–58. 1822 data are from the Peshwa *Daftar, Jamav* Section, and in the case of five wards population data had to be estimated from number of houses occupied by persons belonging to various groups. These housing data referred to years from 1818–22 and in the case of one ward, *Kasba*, the data were for 1764–65. It was necessary to resort to such estimation, admittedly very rough, so that some analysis for 1822 could be incorporated in this study.

position, the extent of dissimilarity in its pattern of residence compared to other caste groups tended to increase as these other caste groups' ranking in social and economic position became more disparate from it.

Again, not in 1822 but in 1937, the within religious groups set of dissimilarity values followed our expectation without exception. Also, not in 1822 but in 1937, the between caste groups and religious groups dissimilarity values tended to increase for higher-status religious groups (top to bottom) and higher-status caste groups (left to right).

It is apparent that in 1937 the patterns of residential dissimilarity for caste and religious groups were clearcut and remarkably in accordance with our expectations based on 20th-century American patterns and our earlier study of Poona, but such was not the case for 1822. We suspect that in the case of the caste groups the findings for 1822 would have been in accordance with our expectations had we had resi-

dential data available for smaller areal units than wards. We have reason to believe that in 1822 there were a number of wards where two or more geographically distinct colonies of caste groups that were quite disparate in their positions in the social hierarchy were to be found side by side within the same ward.

On the other hand, it is likely that the residential patterns of dissimilarity among religious groups and between caste groups and religious groups have to some extent become crystallized over time as a function of the imposition of the British rule in India. In Poona, in 1822, only a few years after the fall and exile of the Peshwa rulers, the patterns of residence by caste and religion were probably still much like those that obtained when the Peshwas ruled; and under the Peshwas the various non-Hindu religious groups had no specially favored social or economic positions. (In fact, members of the higher-caste Hindu groups were the ones that held most of the positions of power and prestige. This, of course, is not to say that Hindus as a group were economically better off than were members of the other religious groups.) By 1937, after British rule and British presence had been in existence for well over a century, and cantonments with their unique social, economic, and political structures had been established, the segregation patterns of non-Hindu religious groups had crystallized. The Parsees and the Christians, for example, were drawn in their choice of residential location to the cantonments or to areas of the city adjoining the cantonments or in proximity to them.

It appears to be the case then that during Poona's precolonial period, socio-economic ranking of groups was not a good indicator of the extent of residential dissimilarity between caste or religious groups. This is the case no matter if we rank the caste and religious groups by their socio-economic standing according to the 1937 or the 1822 data. Nevertheless, as in 1937 so in 1822, the Christians and the Jews

TABLE 4. Index of Segregation in Residential Distribution Between Each Caste or Religious Group and All Others, Poona City, 1822 and 1937

| | Segregation Index | | Number of | |
| | | | Persons, | Families, |
Group	1822	1937	1822	1937
Total			78,289	4,529
Caste				
Brahmins	37	59	18,577	806
G, M, J	46	43	3,947	244
Artisans	23	26	14,028	429
M, M	28	21	21,619	1,427
D, G	41	38	1,405	55
Dep. Classes	33	46	4,763	417
Religious Group				
Total Hindus	35	37	71,422	3,843
Other	40	27	7,083	465
Muslims	35	36	6,767	534
Christians	68	52	55	116
Jews/Parsees	67	71	45	36

Note: See Table 3 for full identification of groups, and for sources.

and Parsees were generally more dissimilar in their patterns of residence vis-a-vis the caste and other religious groups than were the latter groups in relation to one another.

In regard to patterns of segregation for the caste groups, a distinct "U" shaped curve is followed by the index of segregation values in 1937 when the castes are ordered by decreasing socio-economic status. In the case of the religious groups, however, the higher the religious group's economic standing, the more segregated it tended to be. Even in 1822 the data suggest that the case was somewhat similar. (See Table 4.)

The distinctive appearance of the "U" shaped segregation curve when socio-economic groups are ordered high to low has also been noted in other studies [Duncan and Duncan 1955, of Chicago; Uyeki 1964, of Cleveland; Collison and Mogey 1959, of Oxford; Mehta 1968, of Poona], and such a phenomenon by now merits the mantle of a "sociological law." It was many years ago that Park [1925: 14] had insightfully observed:

... A person is simply an individual who has somewhere, in some society, social status; but status turns out finally to be a matter of distance—social distance.

It is because geography, occupation, and all the other factors which determine the distribution of population determine so irresistably and fatally the place, the group, and the associates with whom each one of us is bound to live that spatial relations come to have, for the study of society and human nature, the importance which they do.

It is because social relations are so frequently and so inevitably correlated with spatial relations; because physical distances so frequently are, or seem to be, the indexes of social distances. ...

To examine the extent of stability in the degree of segregation over time, we ranked the caste and religious groups (excluding "Total Hindus," to avoid redundancy) by their segregation indexes in 1822 and in 1937. The r_s, Spearman's rank correlation coefficient, for the 1822 and 1937 rankings turned out to be .60, which is statistically significant at the .05 level (one-tail test), but nevertheless shows considerable change in the relative degree of segregation of the caste and religious groups. Between 1822 and 1937, the largest relative increases in the degree of segregation occurred among the Brahmins and the Depressed Classes. It may be that the increases in segregation of these two groups were, as noted by Gadgil [1952: 29], "part of the general effects on Hindu society of the establishment of British Rule which are noticed in particular by" Ghurye [1932].

Table 5 suggests that the patterns of residential dissimilarity and segregation of groups observed for 1937 are affected to some extent by differential income and to a somewhat greater extent by the differential occupational composition of the caste and religious groups. The expected residential distribution of each caste and religious group was derived in the following manner, with the Brahmins used as an illustration. The Brahmin heads-of-households were categorized by their major occupational group. Each of the major occupational group members (Brahmins) were then distributed to the various wards in proportion to the percentages of all persons, irrespective of caste or religion, of that occupational group residing in these wards. The summation of the expected cases over all eleven major occupational groups then gave us the expected residential distribution of Brahmins by wards. Once this expected distribution of the number of Brahmins, and the expected distribution of the number of each of the other caste and religious groups, by wards was derived, we then computed the sets of indexes of dissimilarity and segregation as shown in Table 5 (above the diagonal). Similarly, the indexes below the diagonal of this table were computed on the basis of the income composition of each of the caste and religious groups. Table 5 may be read then in the same manner as Tables 3 and 4, except that the indexes in the present instance are hypothetical. What the indexes of Table 5 show are the patterns of residence and segregation of the caste and religious groups that would obtain if their group members' residential distribution in 1937

TABLE 5. Indexes of Dissimilarity and Segregation in Residential Distribution for Caste and Religious Groups Resulting from Expected Distributions Based on Their Occupational and Income Characteristics, Poona City, 1937

Group	Dissimilarity Expected: Above Diagonal, on Basis of Occupation; Below Diagonal, on Income											Segregation Expected on	
	(1)	(2)	(3)	(4)	(5)	(6)	(7)	(8)	(9)	(10)	(11)	Occ.	Inc.
1 Brahmins		9	18	19	19	23	18	15	15	13	6	17	11
2 G, M, J	1		15	16	15	20	12	12	10	11	12	11	10
3 Artisans	11	12		5	7	9	6	7	6	6	23	6	2
4 M, M	13	14	3		3	4	8	6	6	7	25	8	6
5 D, G	14	15	4	2		5	5	4	6	9	24	5	5
6 Dep. Classes	15	16	5	2	2		10	9	10	11	28	10	7
7 Total Hindus	11	10	3	7	5	7		5	3	4	19	3	1
8 Other Hindus	9	10	3	4	5	6	1		2	8	20	4	1
9 Muslims	9	10	2	4	5	6	1	1		7	19	3	1
10 Christians	8	9	3	6	7	8	2	2	2		18	5	2
11 Jews/Parsees	10	9	19	21	22	22	17	18	18	17		19	17

Source: Derived from Gadgil, 1952, Table 6, p. 61, Table 7, p. 63, Table 9, p. 68, Table 10, p. 77, and Table 11, p. 80.

Note: See Table 3 for full identification of groups.

was in accordance with their occupation on the one hand, or in accordance with their income on the other.

Thus, hypothetically, in terms of differences in income, the extent of residential dissimilarity between Brahmins and the Depressed Classes turns out to have an index value of 15 (Table 5), whereas the actual dissimilarity index value, without regard to differences in the income of the members of the two caste groups, is 75 (Table 3). In other words, only one-fifth of the actual residential dissimilarity between Brahmins and the Depressed Classes can be attributed to the effect of differences in income of the two groups' members.

In regard to the data of Table 5 in comparison with those of Tables 3 and 4 then, we may make the following observations: Had the residential distributions of the members of each caste and religious group been determined by either their income or their occupational composition, the extent of residential dissimilarity and segregation would have been much less than was in fact the case. However, the fact that the expected indexes of dissimilarity and segregation of the caste and religious groups

based on their occupational composition are almost always higher than those based on the incomes of their group members suggests a closer linkage between residential distribution by caste-religion and occupation, than between caste-religion and income. Stated otherwise, this means that the differential occupational composition of caste and religious groups probably has a greater influence on their patterns of residence and segregation than does the differential income composition of these groups.

Table 6 presents for 1937 the actual indexes of dissimilarity and segregation for income groups (below the diagonal), and the hypothetical, or expected, indexes (above the diagonal), that would have obtained had the families, by caste and religion, of each income group been residentially distributed in accordance with the residential distribution of all families of that caste or religion. Table 7 presents similar data, expected indexes above and actual indexes below the diagonal, with respect to occupational groups.

It is evident from these two tables that in Poona City the indexes of residential dissimilarity and segregation of income and occupa-

TABLE 6.   Indexes of Dissimilarity in Residential Distribution Between Income Groups and Index of Segregation Between Each Group and All Other Families, Actual and Expected Distributions Based on Caste and Religious Composition of Income Groups, Poona City, 1937

Income Group (in rupees)	Dissimilarity: Above Diagonal, Expected on Basis of Caste and Religious Composition; Below Diagonal, Actual										Segregation		Families, No.
	(1)	(2)	(3)	(4)	(5)	(6)	(7)	(8)	(9)	(10)	Exp.	Actual	No.
1 Under 100		1	3	5	7	9	16	20	24	29	8	28	280
2 100–150	21		2	4	6	9	15	19	23	29	8	12	379
3 150–200	27	16		3	6	9	16	20	24	29	9	15	544
4 200–300	27	13	12		4	7	13	17	21	27	7	14	932
5 300–400	32	16	21	16		4	10	14	18	24	3	13	757
6 400–500	33	17	18	17	12		6	11	14	20	2	11	387
7 500–750	39	26	27	27	21	19		6	8	15	8	20	494
8 750–1000	43	30	30	32	26	28	18		4	11	13	25	192
9 1000–2000	41	32	36	34	31	29	14	23		8	17	27	321
10 2000 or more	46	38	43	40	41	39	30	36	21		23	37	190

Note: Total of 4529 families includes 53 with income data unavailable.
Source: Derived from Gadgil [1952], Table 9, p. 68, and Table 11, p. 80.

TABLE 7. Indexes of Dissimilarity in Residential Distribution Between Occupational Groups and Index of Segregation Between Each Group and All Other Families, Actual and Expected Distributions Based on Caste and Religious Composition of Occupational Groups, Poona City, 1937

Occupational group	(1)	(2)	(3)	(4)	(5)	(6)	(7)	(8)	(9)	(10)	(11)	Segregation Exp.	Ac- tual	Families No.
1 Beggars, Prostitutes		10	10	20	9	17	22	31	34	32	40	15	54	68
2 Unskilled Manual	49		5	18	8	14	21	28	31	30	37	14	19	943
3 Skilled Manual	56	14		15	7	9	18	26	30	28	35	11	22	914
4 Low Professions, Adm.	56	19	23		15	9	13	13	17	15	21	8	13	350
5 Small Business	48	20	22	26		10	16	26	31	27	36	10	17	560
6 High Skill, Supvr. Man.	61	29	29	19	22		12	19	24	20	29	6	19	333
7 Medium Business	53	27	29	24	15	18		19	25	20	30	12	17	342
8 Clerks, Shop Assistants	58	33	37	22	29	23	22		7	4	13	19	22	421
9 Pensioners	64	43	46	28	41	33	39	19		6	9	24	35	121
10 Intermediate Prof., Adm.	63	45	48	29	41	31	36	17	15		10	21	34	143
11 High Prof., Big Bus.[a]	63	44	45	33	48	39	43	36	36	38		27	37	76

Dissimilarity: Above Diagonal, Expected on Basis of Caste and Religious Composition; Below Diagonal, Actual

[a] Owners of factories and large shops.
Note: Total of 4529 families includes 255 with no earners and 3 where occupation of household head was not known.
Source: Derived from Gadgil [1952], Table 9, p. 68, and Table 10, p. 77.

tional groups were considerably affected by their differential caste and religious composition, and substantially more so than were the indexes of dissimilarity and segregation of caste and religious groups affected by the differential income and occupational composition of caste and religious groups (compare these tables with Tables 3, 4, and 5). We take this to be support of the notion that the influence of caste and religion is greater than is the influence of income or occupation on Poona City's patterns of residence in 1937. (Incidentally, such analy-

ses are not carried out for the other years due to lack of suitable data. Some such analysis could have been done for 1965, but it would not have been comparable with the analysis for 1937.)

It may also be noted that the indexes of residential dissimilarity and segregation, actual as well as expected, of Tables 5, 6, and 7, are in each case in conformance with our expectations that, with increasing socio-economic status difference between groups, the dissimilarity values for the groups should tend to increase, and that the indexes of segregation should tend to assume a "U" shaped pattern when the groups are arranged from high to low status. These findings also mean that income, occupation, and caste and religion have a mutually reinforcing impact on patterns of dissimilarity and segregation.

In Tables 8 and 10 indexes of segregation are given for Poona City and Greater Poona (including the two cantonment areas in 1954, but excluding them in 1965 due to lack of data) in 1954 and 1965. Again the characteristic "U" shaped pattern of segregation emerges for caste groups for the city as well as the metropolitan area for both years, and the extent of segregation tends to increase for the higher-status religious groups in 1954 as it did in 1822 and 1937.

The indexes of dissimilarity for Poona City and Greater Poona are given in Tables 9 and 10 for 1954 and 1965 respectively. These show that the patterns of dissimilarity noted in 1937 continue to obtain both in the city and in the metropolitan area.

Previously we had noted that there had occurred a good deal of change in the relative extent of segregation of the various caste and religious groups between 1822 and 1937. (Excluding "Total Hindus" to avoid redundancy with its sub-categories of caste groups, the r_s between the rankings of groups on the extent of their segregation in 1822 and 1937 was .60.) Between 1822 and 1954, the r_s for the two sets of rankings for the city dropped to .48. However, as we said, the impact of colonialism on Hindu society was possibly one of crystalizing patterns of segregation. By 1937, the expected "U" shaped segregation curve had very distinctively emerged for the caste groups. Not only that, but the pattern and extent of segregation stabilized for caste and religious groups. Thus, again excluding "Total Hindus," r_s between the 1937 and 1954 segregation rankings of the caste and religious groups was .90 for the city, and .91 for the 1937 city and 1954 Greater Poona data (both correlation coefficients are significant at well beyond the .01 level). For 1954, the segregation ranking of the caste and religious groups was virtually the same for the city and the metropolitan area, the r_s being .97.

PATTERNS OF RESIDENCE: OLD-AREA CONCENTRATION AND CENTRALIZATION

Table 11 presents indexes of old-area concentration for the various caste and religious groups. It may be seen that the higher caste groups tend to be concentrated in the older areas of the city, whereas the lower castes, and especially the Depressed Classes, and all non-Hindu religious communities and the "Other Hindus" are found to be concentrated in the newer areas of the city and of Greater Poona. The rank correlation coefficients given at the bottom of the table indicate the long-lasting and persistently consistent nature of this phenomenon.

TABLE 8. Index of Segregation in Residential Distribution Between Each Caste or Religious Group and All Others, Poona City and Greater Poona, 1954

	Segregation Index		Number of Families	
Group	City	Greater Poona	City	Greater Poona
Total			4,347	5,601
CASTE				
Brahmins	48	56	1,052	1,102
G, M, J	35	34	195	242
Artisans	27	28	414	482
M, M	16	20	1,144	1,387
D, G	25	28	53	69
Dep. Classes	42	39	449	729
RELIGIOUS GROUP				
Total Hindus	43	40	3,869	4,842
Other	20	19	562	831
Muslims	40	37	372	490
Christians	50	53	91	226
Jews/Parsees	76	71	15	43

Note: See Table 3 for full identification of groups.
Source: Derived from Sovani, Apte, and Pendse [1956], Table 1.8, pp. 17–22.

TABLE 9.   Indexes of Dissimilarity in Residential Distribution for Caste and Religious Groups, Poona City and Greater Poona, 1954
(above diagonal, City; below diagonal, Greater Poona)

Group	Group (1)	(2)	(3)	(4)	(5)	(6)	(7)	(8)	(9)	(10)	(11)
1 Brahmins		61	50	38	54	65	45	51	72	75	92
2 Gujarati, Marwadi, Jains	64		31	34	37	48	37	28	38	55	80
3 Artisans	51	31		33	33	44	30	27	37	55	77
4 Marathas, Malis	41	39	34		23	43	17	20	43	53	79
5 Dhangar, Gawlis	56	35	34	28		37	26	23	30	49	72
6 Depressed Classes	74	46	47	45	41		46	35	26	34	63
7 Total Hindus	52	38	30	19	29	46		24	41	53	78
8 Other Hindus	57	32	31	27	30	28	24		32	40	67
9 Muslims	75	33	37	46	28	31	39	34		33	61
10 Christians	84	58	64	62	52	32	55	43	42		43
11 Jews, Parsees	92	71	76	79	65	64	74	67	58	42	

Source: See Table 8.

TABLE 10.   Indexes of Dissimilarity and Segregation in Residential Distribution for Households Grouped by Caste and Religion, Poona City and Greater Poona, 1965

Group	Dissimilarity: Above Diagonal, City; Below Diagonal, Greater Poona (1)	(2)	(3)	(4)	(5)	(6)	(7)	Segregation City	Segregation Greater Poona	Hshlds., No. City	Hshlds., No. Greater Poona
1 Brahmins		50	39	39	69	78	71	51	55	282	298
2 Advanced Hindus	50		32	30	48	64	48	31	31	133	149
3 Marathas	43	33		21	44	53	47	22	22	224	284
4 Intermed. Others	53	37	31		50	50	53	24	32	52	86
5 Intermed. Artisans	69	45	40	51		60	34	46	42	68	77
6 Depressed Classes	78	62	50	56	59		58	59	58	104	133
7 Muslims	71	49	51	64	37	61		45	50	120	124

Note: Households total 983 for City and 1,151 for Greater Poona area, which excludes Poona and Kirkee Cantonments.
Source: Derived from Family Planning Evaluation Scheme Survey, Table 9 x 6.

Table 12 presents indexes of centralization, actual values for 1822, 1937, 1954, and 1965, and expected values based on income and occupational composition of the caste and religious groups in 1937. It may be noted from this and the previous table that there is a high degree of correspondence between the extent of old-area concentration and the extent of centralization of the various caste and religious groups. (The older and more central wards of Poona are, of course, the most densely populated areas of the city. See Brush [1968].) Thus, ranking the caste and religious groups, excluding "Total Hindus," by the extent of their concentration in the older areas of the city and by the extent of their centralization, we find that the r_s for 1822 is .48, .90 for 1937, .98 for 1954, and 1.0 for 1965. (For Greater Poona, the corresponding correlation coefficients are .96 and .88, for 1954 and 1965 respectively.)   Excluding the

TABLE 11. Indexes of Old-Area Concentration for Caste and Religious Groups with Respect to Total Sample Populations, Poona City, 1822, 1937, 1954, 1965, and Greater Poona, 1954 and 1965

Group	City 1822	City 1937	City 1954	Gtr. Poona 1954	Group	City 1965	Gtr. Poona 1965
	(1)	(2)	(3)	(4)		(5)	(6)
Brahmins	24.4	21.6	23.0	38.1	Brahmins	23.8	30.8
G, M, J	19.2	17.0	7.2	7.6	Advanced Hindus	7.2	9.8
Artisans	3.8	13.3	15.2	19.1	Marathas	− 7.3	−13.7
M,M	−12.6	− 0.2	− 2.0	5.5	Intermediate Others	− 6.2	−30.0
D, G	−24.1	− 1.2	− 2.4	− 2.0	Intermediate Artisans	−16.3	− 9.3
Dep. Classes	−18.5	−21.8	−20.7	−28.3	Depressed Classes	−22.8	−26.6
					Muslims	− 7.7	6.5
Total Hindus	4.8	21.7	26.0	29.0			
Other	−11.8	− 6.9	−10.5	−17.3			
Muslims	− 4.7	− 7.5	−17.5	−12.2			
Christians	−19.5	−46.5	−41.9	−52.5			
Jews/Parsees	−26.5	−61.2	−45.7	−55.6			

Note: See Table 9 for full identification of groups. The ordering of wards by age is necessarily a rough one and is based on an historical account given in Gadgil, 1952, pp. 3–24.

Spearman's Rank Correlation Coefficient over groups, excluding Total Hindus, between specified columns is 1/2 = .81; 1/3 = .79; 1/4 = .81; 2/3 = .99; 2/4 = .98; 3/4 = .99; and 5/6 = .54. A value of .75 is significant at the .01 level (one-tail test).

Source: See Tables 3, 5, 8, and 10.

Jews and Parsees, whose numbers were rather small in 1822, the r_s for 1822 turns out to be .76. The high degree of correspondence between the phenomenon of centralization and residential concentration in the older areas of the city (and of Greater Poona) for the caste and religious groups is to be expected in that the older areas of the city are the inner lying wards, and the newer wards are in the out-lying areas of the community.

As Noel P. Gist noted for Bangalore, Chatterjee for Howrah, India, the Hawthorns, Hayner, Hansen, and others for Latin American cities, McElrath for Rome, and Collison and Mogey for Oxford, England, the elite tend to be centralized in their residential locations so that they may be near their place of work and worship, and centers of cultural and political life; the untouchables, members of depressed castes, the mestizos, and members of the lower classes are relegated to the out-lying areas of the city that do not have ready access to that which the city has to offer. (For the relevant literature see Mehta [1968], notes 4, 24, and 25; for some other studies not referred to in these notes, see: Redick [1961]; Cressey [1956]; Ginsburg [1965].) Indeed, this pattern of centralization or decentralization of social and economic groups is the typical one in most parts of the world, and was characteristic of U. S. cities in their earlier historical period. (According to Sjoberg [1960], esp. pp. 95–100, and [1965], such a pattern of residence is typical of the preindustrial cities. The case for European cities prior to the industrial revolution was the same: see Comhaire and Cahnman [1959]. On American cities, see Heberle [1948], and sources cited by Mehta [1968], note 22.)

It is true that during the last two decades or so the decentralization of the upper classes has begun in a number of European and Latin American cities, and signs of the same can be noted even for Poona [Mehta 1968, esp. pp. 500–503]. However, whereas this is the case

TABLE 12. Indexes of Centralization for Caste and Religious Groups with Respect to Total Sample Populations, Poona City, 1822, 1937, 1954, 1965, and Greater Poona, 1954 and 1965

Group	City 1822	City 1937	1937, Expected on Occ.	1937, Expected on Inc.	City 1954	Gtr. Poona 1954	Group	City 1965	Gtr. Poona 1965
	(1)	(2)	(3)	(4)	(5)	(6)		(7)	(8)
Brahmins	26.3	36.7	10.5	6.8	30.5	42.6	Brahmins	28.4	35.4
G, M, J	22.0	31.3	10.5	6.4	16.6	16.6	Adv. Hindus	13.4	14.2
Artisans	1.8	8.8	− 2.1	0.0	9.8	16.5	Marathas	− 4.5	− 1.4
M, M	− 6.9	− 4.2	− 8.2	−4.3	2.4	6.0	In. Others	− 0.5	−24.3
D, G	−21.9	−21.2	− 4.2	−3.3	− 8.0	− 2.4	In. Artisans	−20.3	−11.5
Dep. Classes	−31.7	−41.5	−11.5	−4.6	−35.1	−37.5	Dep. Classes	−38.3	−36.2
							Muslims	−16.2	− 2.4
Total Hindus	− 2.0	12.3	− 7.6	0.5	28.2	26.9			
Other	−32.6	−15.2	− 0.5	0.3	−14.0	−19.0			
Muslims	1.9	0.3	2.1	0.2	−20.5	−12.4			
Christians	−24.2	−40.2	− 1.3	1.4	−47.5	−47.9			
Jews/Parsees	18.0	−53.4	10.9	3.6	−46.3	−67.7			

Note: See Tables 9 and 11 for full identification of groups.

Spearman's Rank Correlation Coefficient over groups, excluding Total Hindus, between specified columns is: 1/2 = .58; 1/5 = .47; 1/6 = .54; 2/3 = .26; 2/4 = .37; 2/5 = .90; 2/6 = .93; 3/4 = .91; 5/6 = .99; 7/8 = .79. Values of .56 and .75 are significant at .05 and .01 levels respectively (one-tail test).

Spearman Coefficient over groups, excluding Total Hindus and Jews/Parsees, between specified columns is: 1/2 = .88; 1/5 = .73; 1/6 = .83; 2/3 = .73; 2/4 = .60; 2/5 = .87; 2/6 = .90; 3/4 = .93; 5/6 = .98. Values of .60 and .78 are significant at .05 and .01 levels respectively (one-tail test).

Source: See Table 11.

for the highest income group as noted in our previous study of Poona, no sign of residential decentralization over time is to be seen among the upper-caste Hindus. In fact, the centralized pattern of residence of upper-caste Hindus and the decentralized pattern of residence of the lower castes are clear-cut and tenacious, having lasted over the nearly 150–year period covered by this study. The rank correlation coefficients for the 1822, 1937, and 1954 rankings of the six caste groups on the extent of their centralization are 1.0 for each pair of dates. Furthermore, for the 1937 data, the ranking on the actual extent of centralization of the caste groups corresponds nearly perfectly with their ranking on the extent of centralization based on their residential distributions expected on the basis of the caste groups' occupational and income composition. This tends to confirm our previous contention that caste, occupation, and in-come tend to complement and reinforce each other's influence on patterns of residential distribution in Poona. This is not very surprising in that these three variables are closely linked, and the influence of each of them on residential distribution should be in the same direction.

As noted by Gist [1958] for Bangalore, our studies of Poona also indicate that at least among the highly educated, those engaged in the highest status occupations, and the very rich, choice of residential location may become highly independent of caste. (This observation is indirectly supported by the data for the highest income and occupation groups in Table 13. For additional comments on the role of caste and mitigation of its importance in Indian cities by virtue of the rising importance of social class, education, income, and westernization among the urbanites, see Clinard [1966, pp. 142–145]; also see, Davis, 1951, pp. 170–176.) For the main body of caste-group members, however, caste interests and loyalties may strongly influence choice of residential sites. (See Table 13; also see Tables 6, 7, and columns (2), (3), and (4) of Table 12.)

TABLE 13. Indexes of Centralization for Income and Occupational Groups, Actual and Expected, Based on Caste and Religious Composition of Groups, Poona City, 1937

Group	Actual	Expected
INCOME		
Under 100	−14.6	− 8.1
100–150	− 4.6	− 7.7
150–200	− 8.2	− 7.1
200–300	− 9.8	− 4.6
300–400	0.8	− 1.0
400–500	1.9	1.4
500–750	16.9	7.4
750–1000	19.2	11.3
1000–2000	17.0	13.8
2000 or more	− 0.1	14.6
OCCUPATIONAL		
Beggars, Prostitutes	−22.1	−12.9
Unskilled Manual	−20.2	−11.7
Skilled Manual	−18.4	− 7.6
Low Professions, Adm.	3.3	3.9
Small Business	8.5	− 3.8
High Skill, Supvr. Man.	20.7	2.4
Medium Business	16.4	11.2
Clerks, Shop Assistants	17.1	14.9
Pensioners	16.3	12.2
Intermediate Prof., Adm.	12.3	15.1
High Prof., Big Business	− 5.3	15.7

Source: Same as Tables 5 and 6.

Regarding the religious groups, the Hindus are the only ones who are centralized in their residential pattern. The Christians, and the Jews and Parsees, are not only highly decentralized within the area of the city proper, but their residential location is greatly affected by the presence of the cantonment areas. Thus, whereas about 13 per cent of the 1954 survey families were found living in the cantonment areas, 65 per cent of the Jews and Parsees and 48 per cent of the Christians and only 10 per cent of all Hindu families belonged to Poona and Kirkee Cantonments. The Christians and the Parsees are often linked in their places of residence, employment, places of business, education, and worship to the cantonments of Indian cities, when the cantonments happen to be there as they are in Poona.

With the exception of the Gujarati, Marwadi, and Jains who are residentially drawn to the cantonment areas for business purposes, the upper-caste Hindus tend to avoid the cantonment areas and the lower castes are drawn to them. For example, in 1954 only 1 per cent of the Brahmin families were found to be living in the two cantonments; whereas 24 per cent of the families belonging to the Depressed Classes lived in them.

CONCLUDING REMARKS

It may be seen from the rank correlation coefficients shown at the bottom of Tables 11 and 12 and from the indexes of segregation given in earlier tables that caste and religious patterns of residence have maintained a high degree of stability over a period of nearly a century and a half despite the fact that during this period Poona has grown greatly in population, developed a fairly efficient transportation and communication system, and has experienced much industrial growth and modernization. (On the importance of these factors in bringing about a change in patterns of residence by social class in an urban community see, Schnore [1965: 372–386].) On the other hand, as noted in another study of this Indian city, these forces of change have led to the beginning of decentralization of the elite [Mehta 1968].

In Poona there is a high degree of correspondence between the phenomenon of the extent of concentration in the older areas of the city and the extent of centralization of the various caste and religious groups. These residential patterns, and the patterns of segregation of caste groups, were found to be, for 1937, in correspondence with the expected residential distributions of groups based on their occupational and income compositions. However, in 1937 the Christians, and the Jews and Parsees, were highly decentralized, whereas the former would have been neither centralized nor decentralized, and the latter would have been somewhat centralized, on the bases of their expected residential distributions (expected on the bases of their income and occupational characteristics).

Much has been said by numerous writers about the high degree of residential segregation of caste and religious groups in Indian cities. This is no doubt true, and the extent of the segregation noted for Poona would have been found to have been somewhat greater had we available requisite residential data for smaller areal units than wards—the areal units for the present study [Mehta 1968: 498–499]. However, recourse to relatively comparable studies employing similar methodology as ours clearly indicates the following:

(a) In general, large American cities show an average degree of segregation of the foreign-born white ethnic groups, or of the native whites of foreign or mixed parentage, from native whites to be as great, if not greater, than the mean extent of segregation of caste groups in Poona. (We computed the unweighted mean of the mean index of segregation of the ethnic groups in each of ten American cities, and the unweighted mean index of segregation of the six caste groups in Poona. The data for the American cities are from Lieberson [1963], Table 4, p. 46.)

(b) The average extent of dissimilarity in residential distribution, or segregation, between ethnic groups and between religious groups is as great, and often greater, in large Canadian and American cities than the mean extent of segregation between caste groups or segregation between religious groups. (For the comparative data see Lieberson [1963], Table 9, p. 57; Duncan [1957], p. 361; and Duncan [1959], Table 2, p. 573, and Table 3, p. 574. In the case of religious groups the comparison is of Poona with only one Canadian City, namely Montreal, Quebec.)

(c) The average extent of segregation of Puerto Ricans in Chicago and New York City [Taeuber and Taeuber 1965: 65–66], of persons with Spanish surnames in large American cities of California and the Southwest [Moore and Mittelbach 1966, Tables 2 and 3], and of Negroes in all of the large American cities [Taeuber and Taeuber 1965: 31–45], is much greater than is the extent of segregation of any of the caste and religious groups, with the possible exception of the small group of Jews and Parsees, in Poona. Negroes in American cities are, however, even more segregated than are the Jews and Parsees in Poona; and the caste-like residential segregation of Negroes in America is much greater than is the segregation of the depressed and the untouchable castes in Poona. (The residential segregation of the depressed and untouchable castes is also much lower in Sholapur, another Indian city for which we have analyzed patterns of residence by caste.)

(d) Whereas in American cities most of the recently arrived foreign-born tend to be somewhat centralized [Lieberson 1963, Table 30; Duncan and Lieberson, 1959, p. 369], and the Negroes tend to be very highly centralized [Redick 1956, Table 4], in Poona the low-status caste groups and the "foreign born" religious groups, such as the Jews and Parsees and the Christians, tend to be highly decentralized.

We would like to conclude this paper with these tentative observations concerning large cities all over the world. We hypothesize that these observations will be applicable to these cities, no matter if they are preindustrial, industrial, or postindustrial, no matter if they are "orthogenetic" or "heterogenetic" [Redfield and Singer 1954].

1. The phenomenon of residential dissimilarity between groups, whether religious, ethnic, racial, caste, occupation, or other, is universal, and tends to increase with increasing disparity between the groups' socio-economic status or prestige ranking.

2. The phenomenon of residential segregation of groups is universal, and the segregation

curve which emerges when groups are ranked high to low on some socio-economic scale is characteristically "U" shaped.

3. Processes of modernization and industrialization have little or no impact on the above two phenomena.

4. Differential residential centralization (or decentralization) of groups is universal. In preindustrial cities, in cities that had become relatively large before modern developments in transportation, particularly the automobile, and in communication had taken place, higher-status groups tend to be centralized, and the lower-status groups tend to be decentralized. In those cities which grew recently and along with improvements in transportation and communication, the situation is reversed; the privileged groups are decentralized, and the poor are centralized.

5. Those who are highly centralized are highly segregated, in each case because of either poverty or riches; those who are highly decentralized are also highly segregated, and again they are so because of either poverty or riches.

6. Those who are neither centralized nor decentralized are not highly segregated, in each case because of lack of poverty or riches.

ACKNOWLEDGEMENTS

This paper is a part of a larger study which was carried out in India where the author was a 1965–66 Faculty Research Fellow of the American Institute of Indian Studies. Some of the expenses for analysis and writing over 1967–68 have been provided by the National Science Foundation (Institutional Grant-67-#10). This paper is a considerably revised version of a paper read at the Population Association of America Meeting April 18–20, 1968, Boston, Massachusetts.

REFERENCES

Brush, John E., 1968. "Spatial Patterns of Population in Indian Cities," *The Geographical Review*, 68: 362–391.

Clinard, Marshall B., 1966. *Slums and Community Development Experiments in Self-Help.* New York: The Free Press.

Collison, Peter, and John Mogey. 1959. "Residence and Social Class in Oxford," *American Journal of Sociology*, 64: 599–605.

Comhaire, Jean, and Werner J. Cahnman, 1959. *How Cities Grew: The Historical Sociology of Cities.* Madison, N.J.: Florham Park Press.

Cressey, Paul, 1956. "The Ecological Organization of Rangoon, Burma," *Sociology and Social Research*, 40: 166–169.

Davis, Kingsley. 1951. *The Population of India and Pakistan.* Princeton, N.J.: Princeton University Press.

Duncan, Otis Dudley, 1957. "Population Distribution and Community Structure," *Cold Spring Harbor Symposia on Quantitative Biology*, 32: 351–371.

———, 1959. "Residential Segregation and Social Differentiation," in *International Population Conference, Wien, 1959.* Wien: International Union for the Scientific Study of Population.

——, and Beverly Duncan, 1955. "Residential Distribution and Occupational Stratification," *American Journal of Sociology*, 60: 493–503. [No. 32 in this volume.]

——, and Stanley Lieberson, 1959. "Ethnic Segregation and Assimilation," *American Journal of Sociology*, 64: 364–374.

Gadgil, D. R., 1945. *Poona: A Socio-Economic Survey. Part I: Economic.* Publication No. 12. Poona: Gokhale Institute of Politics and Economics.

——, 1952. *Poona: A Socio-Economic Survey. Part II.* Publication No. 25. Poona: Gokhale Institute of Politics and Economics.

Ghurye, Govind S., 1932. *Caste and Race in India.* London: Kegan Paul, Trench, Trubner and Co.

Ginsburg, Norton S., 1965. "Urban Geography and 'Non-Western Areas,'" in Philip M. Hauser and Leo F. Schnore (eds.), *The Study of Urbanization.* New York: John Wiley and Sons.

Gist, Noel P., 1958. "The Ecological Structure of an Asian City: An East-West Comparison." *Population Review*, 2: 17–25.

Heberle, Rudolf, 1948. "Social Consequences of the Industrialization of Southern Cities," *Social Forces*, 27: 29–37.

Lieberson, Stanley, 1963. *Ethnic Patterns in American Cities.* New York: The Free Press of Glencoe.

Mehta, Surinder K., 1968. "Patterns of Residence in Poona (India) by Income, Education, and Occupation (1937–1965)," *American Journal of Sociology*, 73: 496–508. [No. 33 in this volume.]

Moore, Joan W., and Frank G. Mittlebach, 1966. *Residential Segregation in the Urban Southwest: A Comparative Study.* Mexican-American Study Project, Advance Report 4. Los Angeles: Division of Research, Graduate School of Business Administration, University of California at Los Angeles.

Park, Robert E., 1925. "The Concept of Position in Sociology." *Publications of the American Sociological Society*, 20: 1–14. Reprinted in Ernest W. Burgess (ed.), *The Urban Community.* Chicago: University of Chicago Press, 1926.

Redfield, Robert, and Milton B. Singer, 1954. "The Cultural Role of Cities." *Economic Development and Cultural Change*, 3: 53–73.

Redick, Richard W., 1956. "Population Growth and Distribution in Central Cities, 1940–50." *American Sociological Review*, 21: 38–43.

——, 1961. "A Demographic and Ecological Study of Rangoon, Burma, 1953." Unpublished Ph.D. dissertation, Department of Sociology, University of Chicago.

Schnore, Leo F., 1965. "On the Spatial Structure of Cities in the Two Americas," in Philip M. Hauser and Leo F. Schnore (eds.), *The Study of Urbanization.* New York: John Wiley and Sons.

Sjoberg, Gideon, 1960. *The Preindustrial City: Past and Present.* Glencoe, Ill.: The Free Press.

——, 1965. "Cities in Developing and in Industrial Societies: A Cross Cultural Analysis," in Philip M. Hauser and Leo F. Schnore (eds.), *The Study of Urbanization.* New York: John Wiley and Sons.

Sovani, N. V., D. P. Apte, and R. G. Pendse, 1956. *Poona: A Resurvey. The Changing Pattern of Employment and Earnings.* Publication No. 34. Poona: Gokhale Institute of Politics and Economics.

Taeuber, Karl E., and Alma F. Taeuber, 1965. *Negroes in Cities: Residential Segregation and Neighborhood Change.* Chicago: Aldine Publishing Co.

Uyeki, Eugene S., 1964. "Residential Distribution and Stratification, 1950–60," *American Journal of Sociology,* 69: 491–498.

Wilkins, Arthur H., 1956. "The Residential Distribution of Occupation Groups in Eight Middle-sized Cities in the United States in 1950." Unpublished Ph.D. dissertation, Department of Sociology, University of Chicago.

43

MAURICE D. VAN ARSDOL, JR.
LEO A. SCHUERMAN

Redistribution and Assimilation of Ethnic Populations: The Los Angeles Case

Redistribution relative to metropolitan growth of Negro, other nonwhite and Spanish name populations is examined in Los Angeles County from 1940 to 1960 for a comparable grid of subareas. The subareas are defined relative to their maturity at different time points in order to partially control for population redistribution effects of neighborhood life histories, the spread of older subareas, and the persistence of neighborhood patterns. Shifts in ethnic concentration are shown for both older and newer subareas. Concurrent changes in neighborhood social structures and ethnic populations are described. Findings are categorized under three themes: First, ethnic population increments and redistribution were generally restricted to expanding older subareas. Ethnic populations did not spatially expand at a rate equal to the spread of the metropolis or of older subareas. Second, segregation is greater in both older and newer neighborhoods for Negroes than for other ethnic populations. Negroes experienced the largest proportional increments in both older and newer subareas, as well as the greatest stability in subarea occupancy. Finally, the spatial separation of ethnic populations impedes assimilation in that unique patterns of neighborhood structure come to characterize different ethnic populations, and changes in ethnic composition are reflected in changes in neighborhood social structures.

Reprinted by permission from *Demography,* Vol. 8, No. 4 (November 1971), pp. 459–480.

Ethnic assimilation within American metropolitan centers has long concerned demographers and human ecologists, as well as social psychologists and specialists in ethnic relations [Crowell 1898; Gordon 1964; Allport 1954; Duncan and Duncan 1957; Grodzins 1958; Taeuber and Taeuber 1965]. Following Hawley [1944], Lieberson proposed [1963: 6] that spatial redistribution of segregated ethnic minorities tends to foster vertical mobility and thus accelerate assimilation. Retardation of such redistribution may inhibit assimilation [Gordon 1964: 108–114 and 235–241], as may the suburban flows of higher status populations which are offset by in-migration of lower status populations to central cities [Goldstein 1963; Schnore 1962, 1963, 1964]. Particularly wanting in such hypotheses and data is illumination of how aggregation and expansion influence intrametropolitan ethnic changes.

We examine redistribution of the majority population and three ethnic minorities within mainland Los Angeles County (the Los Angeles-Long Beach metropolitan area) from 1940 to 1960. This county—the nucleus of one of the three largest population aggregates in the United States—is also one of the few metropolitan areas for which there are data descriptive of the distribution of minorities for three census dates. The minorities referred to are the Mexican-American, Negro, and "other nonwhite" (principally Japanese, plus Chinese, Filipino, American Indian, etc.) populations. In California each of these categories has recently urbanized and concentrated in metropolitan areas more rapidly than the majority population. Gross characteristics of the Mexican-American and Negro populations for the state in 1960 indicated the high dependency ratios, high unemployment and low education symbolic of poverty in urban America. Other nonwhites, by contrast, generally have social-economic and dependency status patterns more comparable with that of Anglos (other white or non-Mexican-American Caucasians).

Within each minority sharp contrasts have emerged, involving nativity and mother tongue for Mexican-Americans [Penalosa 1967], differences in duration of metropolitan residence and social-economic status differentials for Negroes [Taeuber and Taeuber 1965], and acculturation, assimilation and social-economic distinctions among the other nonwhites [Schmid and Nobbe 1965a, 1965b]. Our population portraits, however, are not so finely drawn; our data reflect rather broad differentiations among the minorities and only rough distinctions within the Mexican-American.

Our concern is with accounting for ethnic spatial shifts within Los Angeles County from 1940 to 1960 in the context of intrametropolitan aggregation and expansion. We begin by viewing such changes in a historical context which controls for both the expansion of older urban subareas and the addition of newer suburbs. Secondly, the growth and redistribution of Mexican-American, Negro, other nonwhite and other white (Anglo) population categories during the two decades are examined. Third, shifts in spatial segregation and dissimilarity among the three ethnic categories are described. Finally, we indicate how neighborhoods vary in ethnic composition within older and newer areal "cohorts," and how these changes relate to shifts in neighborhood social structure and housing. Our basic premise is that further consideration of ethnic change within American metropolitan areas should take into account the historical contexts of urban growth and the coalescence of such growth from different historical "seed communities."

MEASURING THE HISTORY OF ETHNIC POPULATION REDISTRIBUTION

Successive cross-sectional comparisons provide inadequate descriptions of intrametropolitan population changes [O. D. Duncan, Cuzzort, and B. Duncan 1961: 160–174; B. Duncan 1964]. Population aggregation and expansion in the large metropolis and in the megalopolis represent an interlacing of growth strands from different points of origin. Coalescing settlements, characteristic of developing megalopolitan areas, are particularly emergent in Los Angeles County. The county encompasses several seed communities, and has had high rates of population growth and intrametropolitan residential mobility [B. Duncan, Sabagh, and Van Arsdol 1962: 418]. Spatial variations are here magnified [Grey, Jr. 1959], a tendency due perhaps to past areal expansion coterminus with increased automobile use, as well as to the current megalopolitan character of the region.

Our initial view of ethnic population redistribution is taken from Hoover and Vernon [1962: Ch. 8] and B. Duncan, Sabagh and Van Arsdol [1962]. They reaffirmed that older subareas in intensive urban use have more restricted growth potentials than newer subareas having large tracts of undeveloped land. Thus, intrametropolitan configurations, including ethnic patterns, should reflect metropolitan history. These elements, together with the fact that the "flight to the suburbs" represents "the growth of the city" [B. Duncan, Sabagh, and Van Arsdol 1962: 428–429], are probable ingredients in ethnic population redistribution. Furthermore, if persistence is a factor in such redistribution [B. Duncan 1964], initial settlement in older urban neighborhoods should also help to explain the continued residential segregation of ethnic categories. Hoover and Vernon have further indicated that neighborhood growth often follows a cyclical pattern of subdivision and residential construction, transition to intensive and diversified land use, obsolescence of residences, thinning out of residences as commercial operations intrude, and finally some form of renewal [1962: Ch. 8].

The aforementioned perspectives suggest a study design that controls for this cycle and for ethnic population growth and persistence, as well as for the expansion of both older and newer segments of the metropolis. A technique developed by B. Duncan was originally applied to the City of Los Angeles to identify census tract grid "cohorts" by their date built up and, by this means, to determine neighborhood age [B. Duncan, Sabagh, and Van Arsdol 1962: 419–421]. An examination of census tract combina-

tions for different time points thus yielded a description of neighborhood changes over time. Grid units were classified as "built up" or "not built up" to a density of two dwelling units per acre prior to 1920, and as of a series of subsequent census dates. Gross acreage data were combined with dwelling unit counts listed in the 1940 and 1950 Census Tract Bulletins, while estimates of the 1920 and 1930 housing unit inventories were obtained from the 1940 Block Statistics Bulletins. (Errors of classification associated with this procedure are discussed in the earlier publication, p. 421.)

Our data are drawn from a comparability grid of 480 census tract combinations, encompassing all of Los Angeles County. The same description of neighborhood maturation was applied to the county as used to describe the city in the earlier study [B. Duncan, Sabagh, and Van Arsdol 1962: 419–421]. Tract combinations were also designated "built up" as of the census dates when thirty percent of their land areas were estimated to be used for industry, commerce, or transportation. This indexing of changes occurring from prior to 1920 until 1960 traces much of the historical aggregation and expansion of population within Los Angeles County (the county acquired 85 percent of its 1960 population after 1920).

It is of particular importance that the date built up criterion, when applied to the comparability grid, permits simultaneous cross-sectional and longitudinal comparisons. These comparisons make it possible to delimit a shifting base of "older" and "newer" subareas defined relative to different census dates (in this case, 1940, 1950 and 1960) in order to facilitate county wide growth comparisons for each period. In an expanding metropolis containing coalesced populations emanating from several nuclei, indexes of older and newer subareas should provide more useful descriptions of "suburbanization" than the traditional central city/noncentral city dichotomy. When making intrametropolitan comparisons of urban subpopulations over time, demographers have frequently ignored the consequences of the spread of older areas. Locating ethnic populations within a shifting grid of older and newer subareas controls for the effects of succeeding land use changes and of metropolitan aggregation and expansion in the residential separation of ethnic categories.

AGGREGATION AND EXPANSION
Patterns: 1940 to 1960

Aggregation and expansion of the Los Angeles County population from 1920 to 1960 is set out in Figure 1.* In 1960 mainland Los Angeles County encompassed 3,987 square miles, with extreme north-south and east-west axes measuring approximately eighty miles. Built up subareas were concentrated in the southern portion of the county shown in Figure 1. (The northern portion included high deserts, military bases, mountain forest and several small cities.) By 1920 the core of Los Angeles and the established outlying nuclei in Pasadena, Long Beach and Santa Monica attained a housing density of two units per gross acre. Subsequent development built up other outlying nuclei and interstitial areas, reaching southwest to the Pacific Ocean, west toward Ventura County, and east into Orange and San Bernardino Counties. (Contiguous counties contain several urban nuclei historically linked to Los Angeles County, expansion from which is responsible for some county growth, but these were excluded from consideration because of insufficient data.)

* * *

Table 1 summarizes the number, distribution, and concentration of the total population and each considered population category. These are described for all subareas of Los Angeles County from 1940 to 1960 and for older and newer subareas based on the previously described 480 census tract combinations. *"Older" and "newer" subareas are defined in relation to the dates at which observations were made.* Older sub-

areas are those which had attained a residential density of two dwelling units per gross acre or which had been developed for non-residential use for two or more decades prior to the given census date. Newer subareas did not have such a history of urbanization. Longitudinal comparisons of older and newer subareas defined in this way control for the position of subareas in the neighborhood cycle described by Hoover and Vernon. (Specific neighborhoods to which the comparisons of older and newer subareas refer as of 1940, 1950 and 1960 can be located in Figure 1 by subtracting twenty years from the year at which the observations are made. Such comparisons illustrate both the increased size of older subareas resulting from the aging of metropolitan housing stock and the shrinkage of land available for urban settlement that accompanied population expansion and coalescence. In Los Angeles County, built up subareas increased from 4.2 percent of the land area in 1940 to 15.0 percent in 1960. Like other areas with a megalopolitan character, Los Angeles County still contains large tracts of non-urban land.)

Census definitions of the ethnic categories listed in Table 1 underwent some alteration between 1940 and 1960. In 1940 and 1950, the "other white" or Anglo category was defined as white minus all reported Mexican born; in 1960 this category referred to white minus persons reported of Mexican birth *and* Spanish name. (The Spanish name Mexican-American criterion was not instituted by the Bureau of the Census until 1950, and usable 1950 tract tabulations by Spanish name are not available.) The detailed breakdown of Spanish name population in 1960 was used only to facilitate evaluation of Mexican-American changes over the two decades. The definition of "other white" (Anglo) has remained relatively stable over time, although the Mexican born population in 1960 (which include only those of Spanish name) are probably underestimated by about eight percent; no adjustments were made for this difference. Thus the Mexican born populations have unknown comparability over

---

*See *Demography,* Vol. 8, No. 4 (November 1971) for Figure 1. For technical reasons this figure not reproducible for this text.

TABLE 1. Population by Ethnic Category and Residence in Older or Newer Sub-areas, for 480 Subareas of Los Angeles County, 1940, 1950 and 1960

Item and Ethnic Category	All Subareas			Older Subareas[a]			Newer Subareas[a]		
	1940	1950	1960	1940	1950	1960	1940	1950	1960
Population (000's)									
Total	2789	4152	6036	858	1741	1906	1932	2411	4131
White	2664	3878	5452	777	1530	1492	1887	2348	3960
Spanish Name	(na)	(na)	577	(na)	(na)	248	(na)	(na)	330
Born in Mexico	59[b]	66[b]	99	28[b]	41[b]	57	31[b]	25[b]	42
Born in U.S.			459			180			280
Born elsewhere	2605[c]	3812[c]	19	749[c]	1489[c]	11	1856[c]	2323[c]	8
Other (Anglo)	(na)	(na)	4875	(na)	(na)	1244	(na)	(na)	3630
Negro	75	218	462	56	174	343	20	44	119
Other Nonwhite	50	56	122	25	37	71	25	19	52
Pct. Distribution by Subpopulation									
Total	100.0	100.0	100.0	100.0	100.0	100.0	100.0	100.0	100.0
White	95.5	93.4	90.3	90.6	87.9	78.3	97.7	97.4	95.9
Spanish Name	(na)	(na)	9.5	(na)	(na)	13.0	(na)	(na)	8.0
Born in Mexico	2.1[b]	1.6[b]	1.6	3.3[b]	2.4[b]	3.0	1.6[b]	1.0[b]	1.0
Born in U.S.			7.6			9.4			6.8
Born elsewhere	93.4[c]	91.8[c]	0.3	87.3[c]	85.5[c]	0.6	96.1[c]	96.4[c]	0.2
Other (Anglo)	(na)	(na)	80.8	(na)	(na)	65.3	(na)	(na)	87.9
Negro	2.7	5.2	7.7	6.5	10.0	18.0	1.0	1.8	2.9
Other Nonwhite	1.8	1.4	2.0	2.9	2.1	3.7	1.3	0.8	1.2
Pct. Concentration by Subarea									
Total	100.0	100.0	100.0	30.7	41.9	31.6	69.3	58.1	68.4
White	100.0	100.0	100.0	29.2	39.5	27.3	70.8	60.5	72.7
Spanish Name	(na)	(na)	100.0	(na)	(na)	42.8	(na)	(na)	57.2
Born in Mexico	100.0[b]	100.0[b]	100.0	47.2[b]	61.7[b]	57.6	52.8[b]	38.3[b]	42.4
Born in U.S.			100.0			39.1			60.9
Born elsewhere	100.0[c]	100.0[c]	100.0	28.7[c]	39.1[c]	56.2	71.3[c]	60.9[c]	43.8
Other (Anglo)	(na)	(na)	100.0	(na)	(na)	25.5	(na)	(na)	74.5
Negro	100.0	100.0	100.0	73.7	79.5	74.3	26.3	20.5	25.7
Other Nonwhite	100.0	100.0	100.0	50.4	66.8	57.7	49.6	33.2	42.3
Subareas, number	480	480	480	166	311	331	314	169	149

[a] Subareas which reached a gross residential density of two dwelling units per gross acre or had been developed for non-residential use at least 20 years prior to specified observation date (1940, 1950 or 1960) are older.

[b] All reported Mexican born.

[c] All white except reported Mexican born.

the two decades. Negroes and other nonwhites, on the other hand, were classified according to generally comparable definitions at the three census dates.

The first panel of Table 1 shows an increase in the total population of all Los Angeles County subareas from 2.8 million in 1940 to 6.0 million in 1960. The Mexican born and other nonwhites increased slowly in number during the '40's and more rapidly during the '50's. Throughout the '40's Negroes grew at a rate substantially higher than that of Mexican born and other nonwhites and showed large increments in the '50's.

Three summary measures assist in evaluating Table 1: annual growth rates by population category, a standardized annual redistribution index of populations into newer or older subareas, and the ratio of the redistribution index to the growth rate. The standardized annual redistribution index is equal to half the sum of the absolute values that represent the differences between the percentage concentrations of population defined in relation to two dates according to older and newer subareas. Here, it is expressed positively if redistribution favors newer subareas and negatively if older subareas are favored. The ratio of redistribution to growth denotes the proportion of growth which is focused on newer or older subareas. These indexes, tabulated in Table 2, are constructed from data in Table 1 and provide evidence of intrametropolitan population shifts accompanying numeric changes.

The negative standardized annual redistribution index values shown in Table 2 and values in the percentage concentration panel of Table 1 indicate that the "flight to the suburbs" (i.e., to newer subareas) during the 1940's did not keep pace with population growth in older nuclei. During that decade there occurred a net redistribution of all population categories to older subareas, probably as a result of lack of construction during World War II and early postwar construction in older subareas. Figure 1 shows extensive settlement in outlying segments of Los Angeles County as first taking

TABLE 2. Selected Summary Measures of Change in Population Size and Distribution by Ethnic Category

	Annual		
Period and Ethnic Category	Growth Rate (1)	Std. Redistr. Index (2)	Ratio (2) / (1) (3)
1940–1950			
Total	4.9	−1.1	−0.22
White			
Born in Mexico	1.1	−1.4	−0.31
Other (Anglo)	5.1	−1.3	−0.25
Negro	19.1	−0.5	−0.03
Other Nonwhite	1.0	−1.6	−1.60
1950–1960			
Total	4.8	1.1	0.23
White			
Born in Mexico	5.0	0.4	0.08
Other (Anglo)	4.0	0.8	0.20
Negro	11.2	0.5	0.04
Other Nonwhite	11.8	0.9	0.07

Note: Based on data in Table 1.

place during the 1950's. During the same decade positive standardized annual redistribution index values indicate that all minorities and other whites redistributed toward newer subareas.

Negro numerical increments and high growth rates in the 1940's were focused in older subareas. This may have retarded Negro redistribution to newer areas in the '50's, although the buildup of the other nonwhites in older subareas during the '40's was followed by a redistribution to newer areas in the '50's. Ratios of redistribution to growth for the '50's reveal that the relative thrust toward newer subareas was almost three times greater among the other white (Anglo) than for any other population category. Likewise this thrust was approximately twice as great among the Mexican born and other nonwhite as for the Negro.

One mode of reducing metropolitan residential segregation is that minorities aggregated in older subareas redistribute to newer subareas at a more rapid rate than the majority population. (An exception is redistribution of minorities from older subareas which have been invaded by non-residential functions to other older subareas.) The percentage distribution panel of Table 1 shows that Negroes increased from 2.7 percent of Los Angeles County population in 1940 to 7.7 percent in 1960; the percentage of other nonwhites fluctuated slightly around 2.0 percent; and the percentage of the Mexican born decreased. Over the course of these two decades Negroes plus other nonwhites increased to one-fifth of the population in older subareas. In addition, as seen by the percentage concentration panel of Table 1, concentration of all minorities in older subareas increased from 1940 to 1960. By the latter year, concentrations in older subareas were highest for the Negro, followed by the other nonwhite and the Mexican born.

Distribution and Concentration: 1960

Participation in metropolitan expansion from 1940 to 1960 was greater for the Mexican born and other nonwhite than for the Negro. Persons of Spanish name appear to have shared in such expansion more than other minorities. It was expected that by 1960 the Mexican born of Spanish name would show less movement to newer subareas than those born in the United States, and that the other Spanish name category (foreign born from outside Mexico) would exhibit less suburbanization than the Spanish name born in the United States. (It is to be remembered that detailed Spanish name tract tabulations were not available until the 1960 Censuses.)

These assumptions are generally confirmed by the percentage concentration panel of Table 1. Negroes and other nonwhites have not redistributed away from the older subareas left in the wake of metropolitan expansion. For the Mexican born from 1950 to 1960, changes included slight deconcentration from older subareas. It is likely that the total Spanish name population had participated in metropolitan expansion by 1960, but confirming 1950 data are lacking. Assumed 1960 "suburbanization" dif-

ferentials among native and foreign born Spanish name categories are verified in the same panel of Table 1. These values denote greater concentration in newer subareas for the native born. Moreover, ethnic placements within older and newer subareas (described in the percentage concentration panel) show that the percentages of each ethnic category are related positively to urban maturation.

SEGREGATION AND DISSIMILARITY
Measurement of the Context of Redistribution

It has been shown that ethnic population growth in Los Angeles County from 1940 to 1960 represented aggregation within newer subareas as well as expansion within older subareas. A second question concerns the degree to which spatial segregation and spatial dissimilarity of ethnic categories have accompanied metropolitan aggregation and expansion. Dissimilarity between areal distributions of any two ethnic categories was defined as half the sum of the absolute values of the differences between their respective percentage distributions, taken grid unit by grid unit. Segregation for a given category was defined as the index of dissimilarity computed against all other categories combined [Duncan and Duncan 1955].

Segregation and dissimilarity indexes were calculated for each ethnic category, measured collectively over all 480 grid units of the county and separately over the grids of older and newer subareas for 1940, 1950 and 1960. Each index is a gauge of displacement that describes the percentage of persons in a category that would have to relocate to other grid units within the scope of comparison in order to make proportionate distributions across grid units identical with that of another category (dissimilarity index), or with the remainder of the population (segregation index). A summary measurement of the *magnitude* of segregation was obtained by multiplying the segregation index values by the number of persons in the ethnic category. This gives the *number* of persons in a category who would have to move to other grid units to create proportionate distributions across grid units equivalent with that for the rest of the population.

Segregation and Settlement Maturation

Table 3 provides indexes of segregation for ethnic categories in the entire county from 1940 to 1960, as well as for older and newer subareas for the three relevant census dates. Segregation index values for Mexican born over all subareas and over newer subareas decreased during the 1940's and increased slightly in the '50's. Consistent increases in these values occurred in older subareas from 1940 to 1960: "desegregation" was confined to newer subareas in the

'40's. (Relative to other ethnic populations, the Spanish name—as defined in the tables—were stable in number; they were also confined to older subareas.) For both the Mexican and native born Spanish name populations in 1960, segregation was greater in older than in newer subareas, and likely reflected population increments in areas of older settlement. In both types of subareas, segregation was greater for the Mexican born than for the native born. The other nonwhites showed a slight increase in segregation index values over all subareas in the '40's but decreased in the '50's. Older subareas followed this pattern, but newer subareas experienced decreasing segregation throughout

TABLE 3. Indexes of the Degree and Magnitude of Residential Segregation for Each Ethnic Category, Measured Over 480 Subareas of Los Angeles County and Separately Over Older and Newer Subareas, 1940, 1950 and 1960

Item and Ethnic Category	All Subareas			Older Subareas			Newer Subareas		
	1940	1950	1960	1940	1950	1960	1940	1950	1960
Degree of Segregation[a]									
White									
Spanish Name	(na)	(na)	43.4	(na)	(na)	54.2	(na)	(na)	36.0
Born in Mexico	56.3	50.9	51.6	50.1	54.4	56.3	53.1	41.9	43.3
Born in U.S.			41.8			52.7			35.1
Born elsewhere	60.4	50.3	38.2	66.2	54.0	36.3	49.3	38.5	26.4
Other (Anglo)	(na)	(na)	58.7	(na)	(na)	68.0	(na)	(na)	43.3
Negro	80.5	79.9	82.4	83.8	79.0	78.8	69.4	72.5	78.5
Other Nonwhite	55.7	56.6	52.8	59.8	60.4	55.6	50.4	43.9	42.9
Magnitude of Segregation[b]									
White									
Spanish Name	(na)	(na)	250	(na)	(na)	134	(na)	(na)	119
Born in Mexico	33	34	51	14	22	32	16	11	18
Born in U.S.			192			95			98
Born elsewhere	1573	1917	7	496	804	4	915	894	2
Other (Anglo)	(na)	(na)	2862	(na)	(na)	846	(na)	(na)	1572
Negro	60	174	381	47	138	270	14	32	93
Other Nonwhite	28	32	64	15	22	40	13	8	22

[a] Pct. of group who would have to change subarea of residence to make their areal distribution proportional to that for all other groups combined.

[b] Number (000's) of group who would have to change subarea of residence to make their distribution proportional.

Note: See Table 1 for definitions of ethnic categories and subareas.

the '40's and '50's. For the Negro population, the spread of older subareas was associated with a small decrease in segregation over the two decades, while the same time span witnessed an increase in Negro segregation in newer subareas. Thus, the Negro population which redistributed to newer metropolitan subareas was again drawn into a web of racial segregation.

The magnitude of segregation accompanying aggregation and expansion of the Los Angeles County population is also shown in Table 3. Despite slight decreases in degree of segregation of the Mexican born and other nonwhites from 1940 to 1960, population increments led to major increases in the extent of segregation for all three ethnic categories by 1960. A comparison of the indexes of segregation magnitude shown in Table 3 with the populations in their respective ethnic categories (Table 1) suggests that in all, older, and newer subareas the magnitude of segregation experienced by each ethnic category is directly related to its size. As might be expected on the basis of their numerical increases, absolute increases in the magnitude of segregation were greatest for the Negro. Of particular importance is the intensification of Negro segregation in newer subareas. In fact, the magnitude of

Negro segregation in newer subareas in 1960 was greater than observed for all subareas and for older subareas in 1940. Metropolitan expansion has thus seen the extension of historical patterns of central core segregation of large Negro populations into newer neighborhoods.

Dissimilarity and Settlement Maturation

Table 4 furnishes dissimilarity index values among the born in Mexico, other white, Negro, and other nonwhite categories for 1940, 1950 and 1960. These values, computed for all, older and newer subareas, are here interpreted as a measure of the spatial rapprochement between ethnic categories over time. As such, they indicate changing ethnic mixes and opportunities for neighborhood assimilation. Dissimilarity index values for the Mexican born in 1940, 1950 and 1960 were greatest with respect to the Negro, followed by the other white (Anglo) and the other nonwhite. Dissimilarity for the other white generally decreased over the two decades, but increased from 1950 to 1960 with respect to the Negro. The highest total dissimilarities in 1950 and 1960 existed between the Negro and other white, followed by the Negro and the Mexican born, and the Negro and other nonwhite. For each temporal and spatial comparison, the Mexican born were more similar

TABLE 4. Indexes of Residential Dissimilarity Between Each Pair of Ethnic Categories, Measured Over 480 Subareas of Los Angeles County and Separately Over Older and Newer Subareas, 1940, 1950, and 1960

Ethnic Category	All Subareas			Older Subareas			Newer Subareas		
	1940	1950	1960	1940	1950	1960	1940	1950	1960
White, Born in Mexico vs.									
All Other White	58.2	56.3	55.4	62.8	55.2	61.8	54.1	42.1	45.0
Negro	75.7	72.0	74.2	78.0	70.8	73.0	69.9	69.9	74.2
Other Nonwhite	52.0	45.6	49.8	50.1	45.3	54.0	53.7	44.2	44.1
All Other White vs.									
Negro	81.1	76.4	83.3	84.8	72.1	81.0	69.8	73.3	78.8
Other Nonwhite	57.2	57.2	56.4	62.3	61.3	60.7	51.0	44.1	44.2
Negro vs.									
Other Nonwhite	74.1	63.2	66.2	73.9	63.6	63.8	73.2	60.6	68.5

Note: See Table 1 for definitions of ethnic categories and subareas.

to the other white than to the Negro. In general, dissimilarities between population categories residing in older subareas were less than those in newer subareas.

More detailed dissimilarity index values for the Spanish name category components with other ethnic categories in 1960 are given in Table 5. (The Anglo category here includes white all Spanish name.) The Spanish name are more similar to the Anglo than to the Negro for all comparisons. For all subareas, the Mexican and United States born Spanish name are the most alike. In both older and newer subareas the Spanish name born in Mexico are more similar to the other nonwhite than to the

TABLE 5. Indexes of Residential Dissimilarity Between Each Pair of Detailed Ethnic Categories, Measured Over 480 Subareas of Los Angeles County and Separately Over Older and Newer Subareas, 1960

| | Subareas | | |
Ethnic Category	All	Older	Newer
White, Spanish Name vs.			
Other White (Anglo)	47.1	61.0	37.9
Negro	75.2	73.0	73.2
Other Nonwhite	48.6	54.3	39.7
White, Spanish Name Born in Mexico vs.			
Spanish Name, Born in U.S.	23.0	19.0	15.8
Other White (Anglo)	59.2	69.3	47.6
Negro	74.2	73.0	74.2
Other Nonwhite	49.8	54.0	44.1
White, Spanish Name Born in U.S. vs.			
Other White (Anglo)	45.9	60.9	37.6
Negro	76.0	73.4	73.2
Other Nonwhite	50.3	55.6	39.8
Other White (Anglo) vs.			
Negro	84.4	82.7	79.5
Other Nonwhite	58.9	64.8	45.6
Negro vs.			
Other Nonwhite	66.2	63.8	68.5

Note: See Table 1 for definitions of ethnic categories and subareas.

other white. In newer subareas, however, the total Spanish name and the United States born Spanish name may be moving in the direction of the residential patterns exhibited by the other Anglos.

Population redistribution to newer subareas from 1940 to 1960 has been associated with some indication of segregation and dissimilarity decreases for the Mexican born and the other nonwhites and with increases in the magnitude of segregation for these categories and for the Negro. (In newer subareas it is possible that the residential distribution of the native born Spanish name may be approaching that of the Anglo.) It seems reasonable, then, that newer subareas may provide a settlement mode that allows for decreasing segregation and decreasing dissimilarity for other nonwhites and those of Spanish name, but not for the Negro. As neighborhoods mature and are added to the increasing inventory of older subareas, on the other hand, they rapidly take on the isolation patterns of previous older subareas, especially with respect to the Negro.

ETHNICITY AND NEIGHBORHOOD CHANGE

Segregation and/or assimilation processes have been viewed as occurring within contexts of structural patterns accompanying metropolitan growth [Hoover and Vernon 1962; Weissbourd 1964; Taeuber and Taeuber 1958]. Hoover and Vernon particularly have described metropolitan expansion in terms of developing nuclei that display varied land use. With the exception of initial construction and urban renewal, successive changes in the land use cycle imply aging of housing stock which is often accompanied by a "downgrading" of the physical and social environment [Hoover and Vernon 1962: 183–198]. Some neighborhoods, however, may be maintained as showplaces for the elite [Firey 1947]. Nevertheless, areas usually filter down—often in deteriorating condition—to different population categories or develop characteristics reflecting such categories. The Spanish name population has a history of many years of settlement in small ethnic pockets; its redistribution may have a somewhat different interpretation than that of the Negro population. It is therefore important to determine if land use maturation in older and newer metropolitan neighborhoods relates in a systematic way to ethnic and neighborhood characteristics.

Measurements were made of changes for the Mexican born, Negro, and other nonwhite minority populations and of changes in a series of characteristics describing "neighborhood" social structure for our grid of 480 Los Angeles County subareas from 1940 to 1960. (Longitudinal data were not available for the Spanish name Mexican-American category.) Neighborhood (subarea) characteristics included housing pattern, indexed by median home value, labor force participation, as measured by white-collar employment and females in the labor force indices, and the family life cycle, marked by the child-woman ratio, percent of population age 14 or younger and percent of population 65 or older. The six variables selected reflect Hoover and Vernon [1962: 146, 207–219, 223] and Gordon's [1964: 30–31] themes that assimilation reflects metropolitan growth. A detailed examination of these variables is beyond the scope of this paper; they are considered only as they relate to the three ethnic categories.

Aggregation, Piling-Up and Dispersion

We have already shown that ethnics tend to remain or redistribute within the increasing number of aging subareas in the metropolis. Depending upon their rate of growth, then, the ethnic categories can be expected to increase in aggregation within these subareas over time. Table 6 summarizes grid mean levels of ethnic aggregation over all subareas and for "areal cohorts" in the older and newer subareas from 1940 to 1960. In the remainder of this paper changes in areal cohorts are distinguished by indexing the same sets of older or newer subareas at the beginning and end of the decade.

TABLE 6. Mean Value, Index of Skewness, and Standard Deviation of Ethnic-Specific Percentage of the Total Population in Each Subarea, Measured Over 480 Subareas of Los Angeles County and Separately Over Areal Cohorts for Older and Newer Subareas, 1940, 1950 and 1960

| Ethnic Category | All Subareas | | | Older Subareas | | | | Newer Subareas | | | |
| | | | | As of 1940 | | As of 1950 | | As of 1940 | | As of 1950 | |
	1940	1950	1960	1940	1950	1950	1960	1940	1950	1950	1960
				Mean Percentage							
Born in Mexico	2.1	2.0	2.7	3.2	3.1	2.3	3.5	1.5	1.3	1.2	1.2
Negro	3.0	7.0	14.7	6.6	14.1	9.8	20.9	1.1	3.2	1.8	3.5
Other Nonwhite	2.3	1.9	3.6	3.2	3.4	2.4	4.6	1.9	1.2	1.2	1.8
Other White	92.6	89.1	78.9	87.0	79.4	85.5	71.0	95.5	94.3	95.8	93.5
				Index of Skewness							
Born in Mexico				2.6	2.3	3.0	2.4	4.3	4.6	4.0	2.8
Negro				3.2	2.1	2.7	1.3	8.1	5.3	6.4	5.0
Other Nonwhite				3.3	2.7	2.4	3.0	8.3	6.4	7.2	4.0
				Standard Deviation							
Born in Mexico				5.4	4.6	3.9	5.4	3.0	2.5	2.2	1.9
Negro				18.2	25.7	21.6	30.2	4.6	10.8	6.1	11.2
Other Nonwhite				6.3	5.2	4.4	6.8	6.3	2.8	2.8	3.5
Subareas, no.	480	480	480	166	166	311	311	314	314	169	169

Note: See Table 1 for definitions of ethnic categories and subareas.

In this way it is possible to ascertain shifts over time within sets of older or newer subareas. In addition, those subareas that obtained an age of twenty or more years over a decade are added to the previously defined older subareas (i.e., a different areal cohort is defined) and then compared with a second set of values for this cohort ten years later. Thus in Table 6, for example, there are two sets of values relevant for 1950, in the older and in the newer subareas.

From 1940 to 1960 there have been substantial absolute as well as relative increases in subarea aggregation levels for the ethnic categories in older areal cohorts. The most sizeable upward shift within older areal cohorts was for the Negro. The Mexican born show little absolute increase in aggregation within any set of older subareas, while relative shifts for the other nonwhite approximate those for the Negro from 1950 to 1960. In newer subareas, by contrast, mean levels of areal aggregation for each ethnic category remained at a low level over the two decades.

Relative to the growth of each ethnic category it was expected that these categories, besides displaying heightened levels of tract aggregation, would become less "bunched up" into a few grid units and would spread out more evenly as the number of older neighborhoods multiplied. Ethnic categories with high rates of numerical increase were thus expected to particularly reflect such a pattern. Indexes of skewness, based on the first three moments around the mean [McNemar 1962: 25–26], were used to gauge such areal changes within older and newer areal cohorts. The skewness index indicates deviations from symmetry, as well as the direction of bunching of the distribution. A zero value represents a "symmetrical" distribution, while positive values indicate the degree of concentration into a relatively few older or newer subareas. The skewness indexes on older and newer subareas are shown in Table 6. The data indicate that ethnic aggregation is approaching a symmetrical pattern over time in older areal cohorts. This trend is most pronounced for the Negro. The skewness index

values within newer subareas, on the other hand, are higher than in older subareas, and though decreasing by 1960, they had not yet approached the 1940 levels for the older subareas. Within newer areal cohorts (especially for the Negro) there is evidence of a continuous "piling up" of ethnic categories into a few neighborhoods. Likewise, standard deviations of mean areal grid levels of ethnic aggregation (shown in Table 6) indicate that ethnic categories, and again the Negro particularly, were spreading out across older subareas.

Relative Stability and Change

The restricted population redistribution of minorities described above suggests relatively constant residential succession, particularly in older areal cohorts. An ethnic category with high rates of increase (see Tables 1 and 6) should reflect increasing instability as more neighborhoods age over time and are included as older subareas. To measure ethnic stability within areal cohorts, each subarea's ethnic proportion at the beginning of a decade was correlated with a second observation at the end of that decade. These "inter-annual" correlations, thus, reflect the stability of ethnic representation.

An overview of the inter-annual correlations in Table 7 reveals three consistent patterns. First, residential composition of the three ethnic categories by subareas in each areal cohort generally showed high rank stability over time. Second, the populations of older areal cohorts, although reflecting greater stability in ethnic succession than populations of newer cohorts, decreased in stability from 1940 to 1960. Third, the Negro experienced a general movement away from stability, as well as the greatest instability within older cohorts. The Negro also exhibited the only increase in relative residential stability within the newer areal cohorts. This suggests a "locking in" of Negro residence status in newer subareas.

To determine where aggregated segments of each ethnic category change more rapidly in the areal cohorts, inter-annual regression coeffi-

TABLE 7.   Summary of Inter-Annual Correlations and Regressions for Ethnic-Specific Percentage of the Total Population in Each Subarea, Measured Over 480 Subareas of Los Angeles County and Separately Over Areal Cohorts for Older and New Subareas, 1940, 1950 and 1960

| Ethnic Category | All Subareas | | Older as of 1940: | Older as of 1950: | Newer as of 1940: | Newer as of 1950: |
	1950 on 1940	1960 on 1950	1950 on 1940	1960 on 1950	1950 on 1940	1960 on 1950
			Correlation Coefficient			
Born in Mexico	.87	.84	.89	.86	.81	.76
Negro	.86	.78	.88	.76	.82	.86
Other Nonwhite	.69	.75	.85	.80	.61	.47
Other White	.85	.77	.90	.75	.68	.77
			Regression Coefficient			
Born in Mexico	.73	1.13	.75	1.18	.67	.66
Negro	1.35	1.13	1.24	1.06	1.90	1.60
Other Nonwhite	.43	1.14	.76	1.23	.27	.59
Other White	1.14	1.08	1.15	1.00	.92	1.24

Note: See Tables 1 and 6 for definitions of ethnic categories and subareas.

cients were calculated; they are presented in Table 7. These coefficients, which are for subareas and the same variable over two points in time, serve as linear average indicators of change. A coefficient of unity suggests that ethnic neighborhood composition changed at more or less equal rates over time. Coefficients of less than one indicate that areal units which had smaller ethnic representation at time 1 increased (or decreased for a negative coefficient) more rapidly in ethnic representation over the subsequent decade than did those with originally higher ethnic proportions. Coefficients exceeding units have a reciprocal interpretation [Duncan and Duncan 1957: 137–142; Taeuber and Taeuber 1965: 175–180).

For the 1940–1950 areal cohorts, Mexican born and other nonwhites increased most rapidly in those neighborhoods where they had originally had low representation, in both older and newer segments of Los Angeles County. During the '50's a similar pattern persisted in the newer subareas, though for older cohorts, the Mexican born and other nonwhite increased more rapidly where they had already been present in large proportions at the beginning of 1950. By contrast, Negro representation in both older and newer cohorts increased more rapidly in subareas having high Negro proportions at the beginning of each decade. Unlike the other two ethnic categories, however, the Negro evinced less clustering in neighborhoods already possessing large proportions of Negro population, particularly in older sections. Some redistribution of Negro population thus occurred within older subareas. Within newer cohorts it appears that Negro representation increased in neighborhoods already relatively high in proportions of Negroes. These redistribution trends of the Negro are less evident for the other ethnic categories.

Changing Neighborhood Characteristics

The previously detailed ethnic redistribution patterns might be expected as a consequence of limited housing opportunities for ethnics in newer subareas. Population growth tends to produce a "spilling" and "leap-frogging" of ethnics into the rising number of older neighborhoods, wherever they are located. At the same time, ethnic categories remain residentially separated from the larger Anglo population. This separation may delay the assimilation process as older neighborhoods develop and maintain ethnically identifiable social structures and institutions. Such characteristics, when confined to ethnic neighborhoods, are here viewed as indexes of cultural separation.

We will now consider relationships between population and neighborhood structure. In this respect, it was anticipated that metropolitan ethnic population growth (see Tables 1 and 6) would influence the relationships between ethnic composition and neighborhood structure. Ethnic populations with a constant growth rate relative to other populations should exhibit high and continued relationships with their neighborhood (subarea) social structures. The degree and direction of such relationships can be indicated by "cross-sectional" product-moment correlations. Moreover, the strength of the relationship as expressed by cross-sectional regression coefficients was expected to be intense where ethnic growth rates were relatively constant. When an ethnic category has a dynamic growth rate, however, a different form of association with neighborhood social structure should be anticipated in addition to cross-sectional correlations with neighborhood characteristics. Due to the necessary search for restricted housing and a "spilling" of the population into additional available subareas, one can expect the rates of neighborhood increase in ethnic categories to be associated with the velocity of change in neighborhoods. (Such associations are presented later in an analysis of "deviational" change.)

Cross-sectional relationships between and among each of the three ethnic categories and the six selected neighborhood variables are summarized by product-moment correlations in Table 8.

The first of the expectations proposed above is partially supported. The Mexican born have already been shown to be the most static ethnic category. They also have the largest number of high associations with the neighborhood characteristics. These relations generally persist over time. Moreover, they occur for the older as well as newer cohorts. A continuing trend within both older and newer areal cohorts

involves substantial negative correlations between Mexican born representation and participation of grid unit populations in white-collar occupations. In addition, there are increasing negative correlations with female labor force participation among the Mexican born in the older areal cohorts. High positive grid unit correlations are found in the older cohorts of the proportion of Mexican born and the population 14 years of age or younger with the child-woman ratio. There are consistent negative grid unit relationships between the Mexican born and older populations. Finally, moderately negative correlations exist between the Mexican born and home value, a relationship largely confined to this ethnic category. These generally high and enduring cross-sectional correlations, particularly within older cohorts, may reflect influences associated with continued migration from nearby Mexico [Penalosa and McDonagh 1966; Penalosa 1967; Fogel 1966; Grebler, Newman, and Wyse 1966].

The Negro has fewer prominent cross-sectional associations with neighborhood variables. Nevertheless, as with the Mexican born, there are moderately high negative relationships with white-collar employment for subareas in older areal cohorts. The shifts in Table 8 from low to moderate or moderately high associations on certain selected variables for older subareas may reflect in-migration during the '50's of a young Negro population [de-Graaf 1962; Hamilton 1964: 284–295].

In contrast to the born in Mexico, the other nonwhite exhibit few significant cross-sectional tract patterns of association. Such absence of relationships may in part indicate the ethnic heterogeneity of this category. On the other hand, the initial increase and then decrease in negative associations of the other nonwhite with white-collar occupations over the two decades may reflect restricted social mobility until after World War II of this category which has a large composition of Japanese stock [Grodzins 1955].

The cross-sectional regression coefficients in Table 9 summarize the forms of relationship that ethnic categories have with the neighbor-

TABLE 8. Cross-Sectional Correlation Coefficients for Selected Neighborhood Characteristics on Ethnic-Specific Percentage of the Total Population in Each Subarea, Measured Over 480 Subareas of Los Angeles County and Separately Over Areal Cohorts for Older and Newer Subareas, 1940, 1950 and 1960

| | | | | Older Subareas | | | | Newer Subareas | | | |
| | All Subareas | | | As of 1940 | | As of 1950 | | As of 1940 | | As of 1950 | |
Variable[a]	1940	1950	1960	1940	1950	1950	1960	1940	1950	1950	1960
Pct. Born in Mexico **and**											
Home Val	−.28	−.35	−.35	−.29	−.23	−.33	−.34	−.28	−.37	−.36	−.33
W-C Occ	−.43	−.49	−.48	−.49	−.49	−.52	−.47	−.40	−.48	−.41	−.44
Fs in LF	−.05*	−.03*	−.12*	−.16	−.21	−.16	−.36	−.14*	−.13*	−.10*	.06*
Ch/Woman	.44	.29	.37	.67	.62	.55	.44	.44	.29	.22	.40
Age <15	.40	.28	.26	.65	.59	.53	.41	.39	.28	.15*	.22
Age 65+	−.25	−.21	−.15	−.46	−.44	−.36	−.33	−.23	−.22	−.13*	−.08*
Pct. Negro **and**											
Home Val	−.07*	−.15	−.36	−.07*	.02*	−.13*	−.35	.03*	−.15	−.10*	−.21
W-C Occ	−.35	−.49	−.55	−.53	−.62	−.56	−.59	−.20	−.36	−.26	−.28
Fs in LF	.13	.13	.23	.04*	−.06*	−.01*	−.07*	.09*	.06*	.12*	.19*
Ch/Woman	.05*	.02*	.33	.15*	.15*	.20	.45	.15	.14*	.05*	.14*
Age <15	.09*	.07*	.29	.26	.29	.28	.52	.12*	.14*	−.01*	.09*
Age 65+	−.10*	−.19	−.25	−.30	−.47	−.38	−.51	.01*	−.15	−.02*	−.06*
Pct. Other Nonwhite **and**											
Home Val	−.24	−.25	−.17	−.28	−.17*	−.22	−.12*	−.22	−.19	−.28	−.13*
W-C Occ	−.20	−.32	−.14	−.17*	−.31	−.30	−.07*	−.20	−.28	−.35	−.22
Fs in LF	−.08*	.03*	.11	−.25	−.16*	−.03*	−.04*	−.06*	−.08*	−.19*	.16*
Ch/Woman	−.13	.10*	.00*	.20	.27	.18	.00*	.14*	.20	.31	.14*
Age <15	.09*	.04*	−.05*	.15*	.23	.14*	.02*	.12*	.11*	.14*	.06*
Age 65+	−.11*	−.09*	−.02*	−.19*	−.29	−.18	−.16	−.15	−.16	−.21	−.02*
Pct. Other White **and**											
Home Val	.23	.24	.42	.21	.06	.22	.42	.25	.24	.27	.27
W-C Occ	.47	.59	.62	.61	.71	.66	.66	.37	.48	.43	.36
Fs in LF	−.05*	−.11*	−.22	.08*	.12*	.04*	.00*	.04*	−.01*	.00*	−.22
Ch/Woman	−.21	−.09*	−.37	−.36	−.29	−.31	−.51	.32	−.23	−.21*	−.22
Age <15	−.21	−.12	−.30	−.43	−.41	−.37	−.57	−.27	−.21	−.08*	−.12*
Age 65+	.18	.22	.26	.43	.57	.44	.58	.17	.21	.13*	.07*

* Not significant at .01 level; all other coefficients differ significantly from zero at the .01 level.

[a] Definition of variables: Home val, Mean of median home values for tracts aggregated into each subarea; W-C Occ, Prof., mgr., clerical, and sales workers as pct. of all employed persons reporting occupation; Fs in LF, Females emp., unemp., or in armed forces as pct. of all females age 14+; Ch/Woman, Ratio of persons aged 0–5 to females aged 15–44; Age <15 or 65+, Persons of given age as pct. of all persons.

Note: See Tables 1 and 6 for definitions of ethnic categories and subareas.

TABLE 9. Cross-Sectional Regression Coefficients for Selected Neighborhood Characteristics on Ethnic-Specific Percentage of the Total Population in Each Subarea, Measured Over 480 Subareas of Los Angeles County and Separately Over Areal Cohorts for Older and Newer Subareas, 1940, 1950 and 1960

| | All Subareas | | | Older Subareas | | | | Newer Subareas | | | |
| | | | | As of 1940 | | As of 1950 | | As of 1940 | | As of 1950 | |
Variable	1940	1950	1960	1940	1950	1950	1960	1940	1950	1950	1960
Pct. Born in Mexico and											
Home Val	−145	−459	−368	−79	−215	−384	−274	−214	−623	−716	−903
W-C Occ	−1.62	−2.46	−1.92	−1.34	−1.81	−2.38	−1.65	−2.06	−3.26	−2.97	−3.81
Fs in LF	−.11	−.07	−.20	−.22	−.36	−.29	−.48	−.36	−.67	−.27	.19
Ch/Woman	1.09	1.16	1.49	1.18	1.58	1.54	1.59	1.42	1.57	1.26	3.32
Age <15	.70	.63	.55	.84	.94	.89	.74	.86	.82	.47	1.01
Age 65+	−.24	−.30	−.24	−.41	−.55	−.45	−.44	−.21	−.32	−.18	−.18
Pct. Negro and											
Home Val	−13	−38	−66	−6	−3	−28	−52	6	−58	−70	−98
W-C Occ	−.46	−.47	−.39	−.43	−.40	−.46	−.37	−.66	−.57	−.67	−.41
Fs in LF	.10	.06	.07	.02	−.02	−.00	.02	.16	.04	.13	.11
Ch/Woman	.04	.01	.23	.08	.06	.10	.29	.32	.18	.11	.19
Age <15	.05	.03	.11	.10	.08	.09	.17	.17	.10	−.01	.07
Age 65+	−.03	−.05	−.07	−.08	−.11	−.09	−.12	.01	.05	−.01	−.02
Pct. Other Nonwhite and											
Home Val	−80	−292	−140	−66	−139	−231	−80	−78	−289	−437	−192
W-C Occ	−.48	−1.39	−.54	−.40	−.98	−1.23	−.19	−.50	−1.68	−2.04	−1.04
Fs in LF	−.11	.06	.15	−.32	−.23	−.04	−.05	−.08	−.20	−.43	.29
Ch/Woman	.20	.36	−.01	.31	.59	.44	.00	.21	.97	1.44	.63
Age <15	.10	.08	−.08	.16	.32	.21	.02	.12	.29	.36	.15
Age 65+	−.07	−.12	−.03	−.15	−.31	−.20	−.17	−.07	−.21	−.23	−.03
Pct. Other White and											
Home Val	32	55	73	15	9	41	59	59	84	150	110
W-C Occ	.48	.50	.41	.44	.43	.49	.40	.64	.65	.87	.48
Fs in LF	−.03	−.05	−.06	.03	.03	.01	.00	.04	.00	.00	−.11
Ch/Woman	−.14	−.06	−.24	−.16	−.12	−.14	−.32	−.34	−.25	−.34	−.27
Age <15	−.10	−.05	−.10	−.14	−.11	−.10	−.18	−.20	−.12	−.07	−.08
Age 65+	.05	.05	.06	.10	.12	.09	.14	.05	.06	.05	.02

Note: See Tables 1 and 6 for definitions of ethnic categories and subareas, and Table 8 for definitions of variables.

hood characteristics. These coefficients suggest important differences between the Mexican born and other ethnic categories. In Table 9 the Mexican born generally show the highest positive or negative regression values, both in the older and in the newer areal cohorts and particularly with respect to home value and white-collar occupation. Furthermore, little change occurred in these regression values over time; this is most evident with regard to the family life cycle indexes. Regression coefficients for the Mexican born here mirror the traits ordinarily ascribed to the Mexican-American and sharpen the contrast between the Mexican born and the other two ethnic categories.

Cross-sectional regression coefficients for the Negro were lower in general than comparable coefficients for the Mexican born, but higher than those for other nonwhites and increasing in the older 1950–1960 areal cohorts for family life cycle indexes. Increments of this type suggest that a rise in Negro representation leads to a younger family structure. Lastly, as might be expected from the heterogeneity of the other nonwhite population, this category is characterized by a substantial shifting in regression coefficients over all areal cohorts.

Velocities of Change

We have suggested that rapidly increasing ethnic populations tend to spill or leap-frog into the older subareas previously represented by other populations. This change should be shown by a measure of the relationship between the velocity of change in ethnic composition within areal cohorts and the velocity of change in neighborhood characteristics, particularly in the older areal cohorts.

Measurements were made by grid units of the velocity of changes in ethnic proportions and selected neighborhood characteristics in the form of "deviational change correlations." Table 10 summarizes these correlations between the three ethnic categories and each of the selected housing, labor force and family life cycle indexes [for examples of this form of analysis, see Duncan and Cuzzort 1958; Myers 1964]. The deviational change correlation is the product-moment correlation wherein the two variables are residuals off least squares inter-annual regression lines. This correlation represents the velocity of concomitant change of two variables between time 1 and time 2 after "removing" the "natural" influence of relative stability or change for each variable. (Increases or decreases in value between time 1 and time 2 are typically defined by an inter-annual linear regression equation: $Y_2{}^1 = a + bY_1$.) The deviational change correlation is the relationship between two sets of values above or below relative stability, as measured by inter-annual regression slopes. O. D. Duncan, Cuzzort and B. Duncan [1961, pp. 164–165] have shown that the deviational change correlation is a function of two inter-annual, two cross-sectional, and two lag correlations.

Table 10 indicates that rapid rates of cohort change in the Negro category are related to changes in neighborhood character. The Mexican born and other nonwhite each have only one of thirty-six deviational correlations above .30. The Negro, by comparison, has ten such coefficients exceeding this value—five of which exceed .50. Of these five, four are for subareas in older cohorts and none are for subareas in newer cohorts.

A salient pattern for the Negro exists in regard to the family life cycle indexes. Table 8 indicated high cross-sectional correlations within the older subareas in 1960 between Negro representation and a young family structure. The deviational correlations in Table 10 suggest further that subareas within the older 1950–1960 areal cohorts that rapidly changed in Negro representation also tended to experience accelerated shifts toward a young family neighborhood structure. These same subareas also had a rapidly decreasing representation of white-collar workers.

Velocities of change for the Mexican born, compared with those for the Negro, are not consistently related to velocities of change of structural variables. Velocity of change of the

TABLE 10.   Deviational Correlation Coefficients for Selected Neighborhood Characteristics on Ethnic-Specific Percentage of the Total Population in Each Subarea, Measured Over 480 Subareas of Los Angeles County and Separately Over Areal Cohorts for Older and Newer Subareas, 1940–50 and 1950–60

| Variable | All Subareas | | Older as of 1940: | Older as of 1950: | Newer as of 1940: | Newer as of 1950: |
	1940 to 1950	1950 to 1960	1940 to 1950	1950 to 1960	1940 to 1950	1950 to 1960
Pct. Born in Mexico and						
Home Val	−.10*	.06*	.05*	.02*	−.19	−.28
W-C Occ	−.23	−.18	−.20*	−.06*	−.23	−.30
Fs in LF	.00*	.14	.09*	.19	−.07*	−.01*
Ch/Woman	−.08*	.18	.16*	.08*	−.14*	.34
Age <15	−.09*	.09*	−.02*	.06*	−.08*	.07*
Age 65+	.11*	−.04*	.12*	−.09*	.06*	.07*
Pct. Negro and						
Home Val	−.04*	−.26	.10*	−.27	−.05*	−.14*
W-C Occ	−.37	−.57	−.52	−.66	−.26	−.25
Fs in LF	.12*	.23	.15*	.23	.07*	.20*
Ch/Woman	−.13	.37	−.16*	.33	−.09*	.24
Age <15	−.01*	.47	.12*	.58	−.01*	.17*
Age 65+	−.25	−.41	−.42	−.54	−.14*	−.01*
Pct. Other Nonwhite and						
Home Val	−.14	−.06*	.01*	.06*	−.10*	−.14*
W-C Occ	−.33	−.23	−.20*	−.17	−.27	−.16*
Fs in LF	.25	.19	−.01*	.22	.17	.20*
Ch/Woman	−.08*	.07*	.19*	.02*	.00*	.12*
Age <15	.00*	.08*	.24	.12*	.03*	.00*
Age 65+	−.00*	−.10*	−.14*	−.17	−.00*	.06*
Pct. Other White and						
Home Val	.06*	.27	−.12*	.27	.11*	.28
W-C Occ	.37	.59	.46	.65	.31	.34
Fs in LF	−.27	−.27	−.14*	−.26	−.27	−.19*
Ch/Woman	.22	−.40	.12*	−.34	.20	−.27
Age <15	.06*	−.47	−.12*	−.58	.04*	−.14*
Age 65+	.12*	.40	.37	.56	.02*	−.03*

* Not significant at .01 level; all other coefficients differ significantly from zero at the .01 level.

Note: See Tables 1 and 6 for definitions of ethnic categories and subareas, and Table 8 for definitions of variables.

Mexican born shows "low" positive and negative relations to changing velocities of home value, white-collar occupation and the child-woman ratio, a phenomenon evident in newer areal cohorts only. Data in Table 10 suggest that the positive and negative relationships with neighborhood structures for the areal cohorts, which has been characteristic of the Mexican born population over time (see Table 8), generally dissipate when rapid changes in neighborhood ethnic composition take place. On the other hand, subareas in the older 1950–1960 areal cohort having comparatively high rates of increase in Negro representation underwent changes similar to those that have more or less typified neighborhoods with high proportions of this ethnic category—namely, rapidly increasing young family structure and rapidly decreasing white-collar employment.

DISCUSSION

It has been suggested that ethnic populations adapt to dominant populations at different rates [Park 1950] through a process that entails separation, accommodation, acculturation, assimilation and amalgamation [Marden and Meyer 1962: 34–38]. In Los Angeles County, the dissimilarity and segregation of the Mexican born and the other nonwhite decreased slightly from 1940 to 1960—perhaps to the extent that they participated in metropolitan expansion within a relatively free housing market. Percentage increments of Negroes have occurred in neighborhoods during the later phases of the housing cycle, while areas of newer Negro settlement were developing "ghetto" characteristics by 1960.

Ethnic participation in metropolitan expansion is not necessarily associated with diminished differences between the ethnic social structures and the social structure of the majority population. Prior to 1960 the expanding Negro population maintained older segregated neighborhoods and extended segregation into newer (suburban) areas. Historical patterns of Negro residential segregation appear to have solidified in both older and newer subareas by 1960. When Negro enclaves develop in newer

areas, white policies of residential containment and rapid Negro increments suggest that additional sections of aging suburbs, as well as the "gray areas" of cities, will take on an ethnic flavor. Anglos have abandoned more than the central city; they have initiated a continued thrust toward new subareas at the beginning stages of the neighborhood-use cycle, wherever such subareas may be located within the metropolis.

While some degree of residential desegregation and assimilation has been attained by the Mexican-American and other nonwhite ethnic categories, the future of the Negro is much less certain. In an expanding metropolis with several nuclei and many possible foci of coalesced growth, it is likely that scattered Negro enclaves will develop ghetto characteristics.

Three tenable themes relevant to relations between the three ethnic categories and between these populations and the structure of urban neighborhoods become discernible. These themes have admittedly emerged from our analysis of only one metropolis; their further exploration, however, is warranted.

First, while there is a relatively consistent increase in ethnic minorities over time, both extreme spatial separation and "piling up"—once typical of ethnic categories in the urban area—are diminishing. Ethnic increments and dispersion, however, are almost exclusively restricted to the continually expanding older metropolitan neighborhoods. As such, the spatial expansion of ethnic populations is not occurring at a rate equal to the spread of the metropolis or even to the growth of older subareas. This suggests that increased de facto segregation can be expected in urban neighborhoods where there is a conversion, downgrading, or a thinning out of housing units.

Second, segregation is greater in newer neighborhoods for the Negro than for either the Mexican born or the other nonwhite categories. Although the levels of aggregation in newer neighborhoods have risen for the Negro more than for other ethnics, the Negro has experienced greater degrees of relative subarea stability over time. Negroes are also showing the greatest proportional increases in neighborhoods where they are already highly represented, a pattern not applicable to the other minority categories.

Finally, spatial segregation of ethnic populations—particularly in the expanding number of older subareas—has apparently had a dilatory effect on assimilation, reflected in unique patterns of neighborhood structure that have come to characterize different ethnic categories. Gross changes in proportions of ethnic groups residing in segregated metropolitan subareas, moreover, influence the way populations are linked to neighborhood structure. If an ethnic category is relatively static in its proportional areal representation, a unique and ongoing association with neighborhood structure exists. Increasing numbers of ethnics require additional housing in a restricted market, while housing becomes more and more available as metropolitan neighborhoods age. Older subareas open up as the Anglo population vacates housing that over time passes into obsolescence and deterioration, and is marked by general living inconveniences. Such variations in neighborhood character mirror the relationships between the velocity at which an ethnic composition alters and the rate of change in neighborhood structure.

By abandoning traditional central city-suburban intrametropolitan distinctions in favor of indexes of subarea maturity defined relative to different time points, our analysis has partially controlled for effects of the life histories of urban neighborhoods, the persistence of neighborhood patterns, and the spread of older subareas. When applied to 1960 and prior data, these analyses provide illustrative forecasts and refutations of specific trends in metropolitan areas that at first glance appeared to be emergent in the late 1960's [Birch 1970].

First, we expect that reports of the 1970 Censuses will continue to emphasize "increased suburbanization" of the metropolitan population, and will indicate that suburbanization now applies to ethnic as well as to Anglo populations. Our data concerning population concentration in older and newer subareas within Los Angeles County from 1940 to 1960 shows that even in Los Angeles suburbanization is more illusory than real. Past and current "suburban" population redistribution merely represents an extension of the real city beyond the limits of the corporate city. Second, the spreading out of ethnic populations over expanding older subareas of Los Angeles County from 1940 to 1960 may be a precursor of reported population declines in central city poverty areas in the 1960's and "rapid growth in the adjacent inner suburbs" [Birch 1970: 24]. Third, the recent redistribution of Negroes from one enclave to another [Birch 1970: 34] is forecast from Los Angeles data reflecting ethnic population redistribution across a shifting grid of older and newer subareas from 1940 to 1960. Furthermore, our Los Angeles data indicate that the bunching up of Negroes within such enclaves in newer subareas is more pronounced than in the older areas of more traditional Negro occupancy. Our mode of analysis does not lead to a sanguine view of the future of either city or suburb.

The aforementioned themes and comparisons with more traditionally derived generalizations support our contention that ethnic residential segregation is not confined to the central city but pervades the entire metropolis. Ethnic segregation is a residual phenomenon that is growing in the wake of continued metropolitan expansion. The restricted drift of ethnic spatial redistribution into the older metropolitan neighborhoods appears to impede assimilation, and additional ethnic enclaves develop as newer subareas mature. As a result, the growth processes involved in metropolitan sprawl will continue to forge successive iron rings of discrimination [Mendelson 1962] and metastasized ghettos that will effect greater spatial and structural segregation than has been anticipated from more traditional perspectives.

ACKNOWLEDGMENTS

Sections of this paper are reprinted, with revisions, from Richard Galyon Ames, Maurice D. Van Arsdol, Jr., et al., *Analysis of a Proposal for Industrial Redevelopment in Watts*, Chapter XII by

Maurice D. Van Arsdol, Jr., and Leo A. Schuerman (pp. 163–179), by permission of the University of Southern California, Los Angeles, copyright © 1967 by the University of Southern California. Other portions were presented in a paper, "Spanish Origin Populations, Mobility and Assimilation: The Los Angeles Case," by Maurice D. Van Arsdol, Jr., and Leo A. Schuerman read at the American Sociological Association Meeting, San Francisco, August 31, 1967, and in an unpublished M.A. thesis, "Assimilation in Minority Subpopulations in Los Angeles County," by Schuerman, Department of Sociology and Anthropology, University of Southern California, 1969. Various aspects of the research were supported through the University of Southern California Department of Sociology and Anthropology Population Research Laboratory; National Science Foundation Grant G9452; U.S. Public Health Service Contract PH–86–62–163–1 and 2; and by National Institute of Mental Health Training Grant MH–10243 in the Demography of Social Disorganization. Data were processed on a Honeywell 800 computer at the University of Southern California Computing Center. Linda Dickey, Rita Sabagh, Gladys Searle, Nancy Edwards, Sara Saucier, and Ann Woods provided able assistance, and Edgar W. Butler, Judith J. Friedman, Edward C. McDonagh, Joan W. Moore, Rodger R. Rice, Muriel Schad, Alma Taeuber, Herman Turk, and Carl-Gunnar Janson and the staff of the National Swedish Institute for Building Research and Planning critically evaluated the manuscript.

REFERENCES

Allport, Gordon W., 1954. *The Nature of Prejudice.* Cambridge, Massachusetts: Addison-Wesley Publishing Company.

Birch, David L., 1970. "The Economic Future of City and Suburb." CED Supplementary Paper No. 30: Committee for Economic Development. New York, New York.

Burgess, Ernest W., 1925. "The Growth of the City," in Robert E. Park, Ernest W. Burgess and Robert D. McKenzie (eds.) *The City.* Chicago: The University of Chicago Press.

Crowell, John F., 1898. *The Logical Process of Social Development.* New York: Henry Holt and Company.

deGraaf, Lawrence B., 1962. "Negro Migration to Los Angeles, 1930 to 1950." Unpublished Ph.D. dissertation, Department of History. Los Angeles: University of California at Los Angeles.

Duncan, Beverly, 1964. "Variables in Urban Morphology," in Ernest W. Burgess and Donald J. Bogue (eds.), *Contributions to Urban Sociology.* Chicago: The University of Chicago Press.

——, Georges Sabagh and Maurice D. Van Arsdol, Jr., 1962. "Patterns of City Growth." *The American Journal of Sociology,* 67: 419–421. [No. 4 in this volume.]

Duncan, Otis Dudley, and Beverly Duncan, 1955. "Residential Distribution and Occupational Stratification." *The American Journal of Sociology,* 60: 493–503. [No. 32 in this volume.]

—— and ——, 1957. *The Negro Population of Chicago.* Chicago: The University of Chicago Press.

——, and Ray P. Cuzzort, 1958. "Regional Differentiation and Socio-Economic Change," *Papers and Proceedings of the Regional Science Association*, 4: 163–177.

——, Ray P. Cuzzort, and Beverly Duncan, 1961. *Statistical Geography*. Glencoe, Illinois: The Free Press.

Firey, Walter, 1947. *Land Use in Central Boston*. Cambridge, Massachusetts: Harvard University Press.

Fogel, Walter, 1966. *Education and Income of Mexican-Americans in the Southwest*. Advance Report, Mexican-American Study Project, Division of Research, Graduate School of Business Administration, University of California at Los Angeles.

Goldstein, Sidney, 1963. "Some Economic Consequences of Suburbanization in the Copenhagen Metropolitan Area," *The American Journal of Sociology*, 68: 551–564.

Gordon, Milton M., 1964. *Assimilation in American Life*. New York: Oxford University Press.

Grebler, Leo, Philip M. Newman, and Ronald Wyse, 1966. *Mexican Immigration in the United States: The Record and Its Implications*. Advance Report, Mexican-American Study Project, Division of Research, Graduate School of Business Administration, University of California at Los Angeles.

Grey, Arthur, Jr., 1959. "Los Angeles: Urban Prototype," *Land Economics*, 35: 232–242.

Grodzins, Morton, 1955. "Making Un-Americans." *The American Journal of Sociology*, 60: 570–582.

——, 1958. *The Metropolitan Area as a Racial Problem*. Pittsburgh: University of Pittsburgh Press.

Hamilton, Horace C., 1964. "The Negro Leaves the South," *Demography*, 1: 272–295.

Hawley, Amos H., 1944. "Dispersion versus Segregation: Apropos of a Solution of Race Problems." *Papers of the Michigan Academy of Science, Art, and Letters*, 30: 674.

Hoover, Edgar M., and Raymond Vernon, 1962. *Anatomy of a Metropolis*. Garden City, New York: Doubleday and Company. First pub. 1959.

Hoyt, Homer, 1939. *The Structure and Growth of Residential Neighborhoods in American Cities*. Washington: Government Printing Office.

Lieberson, Stanley, 1963. *Ethnic Patterns in American Cities*. New York: The Free Press of Glencoe.

Marden, Charles F., and Gladys Meyer, 1962. *Minorities in American Society*. 2nd edition. New York: American Book Company.

McNemar, Quinn, 1962. *Psychological Statistics*. 3rd edition. New York: John Wiley and Sons.

Mendelson, Wallace, 1962. *Discrimination*. Englewood Cliffs, N.J.: Prentice-Hall.

Myers, George C., 1964. "Variations in Urban Population Structure," *Demography*, 1: 156–163.

Park, Robert E., 1950. *Race and Culture*. Glencoe, Ill.: The Free Press.

Penalosa, Fernando, and Edward C. McDonagh, 1966. "A Socio-Economic Class Typology of Mexican-Americans." *Sociological Inquiry*, 36: 19–30.

——, 1967. "The Changing Mexican-American in Southern California." *Sociology and Social Research*, 51: 405–416.

Schmid, Calvin F., and Charles F. Nobbe, 1965a. "Socio-Economic Differentials among Non-White Races." *American Sociological Review*, 30: 909–922.

—— and ——, 1965b. "Socio-Economic Differentials among Non-White Races in the State of Washington," *Demography*, 2: 549–566.

Schnore, Leo F., 1962. "City-Suburban Income Differentials in Metropolitan Areas." *American Sociological Review*, 27: 252–255.

——, 1963. "The Socio-Economic Status of Cities and Suburbs," *American Sociological Review*, 28: 76–85.

——, 1964. "Urban Structure and Suburban Selectivity," *Demography*, 1: 164–176.

Taeuber, Conrad, and Irene B. Taeuber, 1958. *The Changing Population of the United States.* New York: John Wiley and Sons.

Taeuber, Karl E., and Alma F. Taeuber, 1965. *Negroes in Cities.* Chicago: Aldine Publishing Company.

Weissbourd, Bernard, 1964. "Segregation, Subsidies and Megalopolis." Occasional Paper No. 1 on the City. Santa Barbara, California: Center for the Study of Democratic Institutions.

44

KARL E. TAEUBER

The Effect of Income Redistribution on Racial Residential Segregation

A number of myths hamper formulation of effective public policy to foster racial residential desegregation:

Negroes prefer to live with their own kind.
Negroes formerly sought integration, but the black power movement has changed all that.
Laws can't change attitudes.
The presence of Negroes in a white neighborhood drives down property values.
Selling or renting to the first Negro family is block-busting, an unethical means of making a fast buck.
The presence of a few Negro families in a white neighborhood is tolerable (or even desirably liberal), but if the number exceeds the tipping point (one, five, twenty-five percent?) the neighborhood inevitably and rapidly becomes all Negro.

"The Effect of Income Redistribution on Racial Residential Segregation" by Karl E. Taeuber is reprinted from *Urban Affairs Quarterly*, Volume 4, Number 1 (September 1968), pp. 5–14, by permission of the Publisher, Sage Publications, Inc.

The analysis was originally reported in an unpublished working paper, "Population Distribution and Residential Segregation in Cleveland," prepared for the United States Commission on Civil Rights as part of its study, "Racial Isolation in the Public Schools." Support for revision and rewriting was provided from funds granted to the Institute for Research on Poverty at the University of Wisconsin by the Office of Economic Opportunity, pursuant to the provisions of the Economic Opportunity Act of 1964. The conclusions are the sole responsibility of the author.

The housing market is essentially non-discriminatory; people get what they pay for.
Negroes can't afford to live in most neighborhoods.

These and many other beliefs are widespread among persons in the real estate industry and among the general public. Readers of this journal are familiar with the fallacies and half-truths of most, and there exists a substantial social science literature on some. The last couple of items in this brief list derive from the notion that poverty is a major contributory factor in racial residential segregation, and this notion, I believe, is still current even among informed students. As a test of the relevance of Negro poverty to Negro housing patterns, I shall consider the likely effects on residential segregation in Cleveland of a hypothetical program of income redistribution.

Previous analysis of Census data has demonstrated empirical inadequacies in the poverty explanation of racial residential segregation. In *Negroes in Cities*, we reported various models for a number of cities, comparing racial differentials in economic status with residential patterns of the several economic status groups. I shall clarify the approach later, but for the moment I wish to call attention to our conclusions [1]:

> According to the models, the net effect of economic factors in explaining residential segregation is slight. Their power in explaining racial residential segregation diminishes as differentials between the races in the quality of the housing they occupy, in the occupations they hold, and in the rents they pay also diminish. Economic differentials diminish, but residential segregation persists. . . . Clearly, residential segregation is a more tenacious social problem than economic discrimination. Improving the economic status of Negroes is unlikely by itself to alter prevailing patterns of racial residential segregation.

In this paper I shall report a case study of the effects of hypothetically enhancing the economic status of Negroes. In contrast to the earlier work, the entire metropolitan area is regarded as the housing market. Restriction of the previous analyses to central cities excluded from consideration much of the housing that is presumed to be beyond the economic reach of Negro families. Because of lack of comparability over time in Census income data, the previous analysis relied on such economic status indicators as occupation, housing quality, and housing price. Use of the 1960 family income data in the current analysis permits a direct test of the potential impact of income redistribution policies.

The case chosen for study is the Cleveland metropolitan area. Why Cleveland? First, a special census was conducted there in 1965 [2]. These data permit some updating of the background discussion of population trends. Unfortunately, the detailed social and economic data collected in that Census were never tabulated, and hence the basic analysis in this paper relies on 1960 Census data. Second, I wanted to avoid Chicago. As a sociologist who began his urban studies at the University of Chicago, I am sensitive to, though not especially sympathetic with, arguments about the uniqueness of Chicago. Would that Chicago, in its racial settlement pattern, were unique! The switch to Cleveland was not too difficult; rotating a Chicago map ninety degrees shifts the lake to the north instead of the east, so that one can pretend Cleveland is simply a miniature Chicago. Uyeki's recent study suggests that socioeconomic residential patterns in the two cities are quite similar [3]. A final reason for choosing Cleveland, or at least for accepting it as the locale of a case study: it's as good as any other city. All cities share the distinction of a high degree of racial residential segregation [4].

Trends in racial composition of the Cleveland metropolitan area are summarized in Table 1 (Note 8). The metropolitan area has grown steadily throughout this century, but the city has quite a different trend than the balance of the metropolitan area (hereafter referred to for convenience as the suburbs). The city was fully built up by 1930. Its population dipped during the depression, recovered during the war, but since 1950 has been in a rapid decline. The 1965 census total of 811,000 is more than 100,000 below the 1950 count. Suburban growth has more than compensated for city population loss. The greatest suburban growth *rate* was in the 1920's; thus, rapid suburbanization in Cleveland antedates the presence of a large Negro population.

TABLE 1. Population Trends in the Cleveland Metropolitan Area, 1910–1965 (Numbers in thousands)

Figure and Year	Metropolitan Area	Cleveland City	Suburbs
Total Population			
1910	661	561	100
1920	972	797	175
1930	1,243	900	343
1940	1,267	878	389
1950	1,466	915	551
1960	1,797	876	921
1965	–	811	–
Negro Population			
1910	9	8	1
1920	36	35	1
1930	75	72	3
1940	88	85	3
1950	152	148	4
1960	257	251	6
1965	–	275	–
Percent Negro			
1910	1.4	1.5	0.6
1920	3.7	4.3	0.7
1930	6.1	8.0	0.9
1940	6.9	9.6	0.8
1950	10.4	16.2	0.8
1960	14.3	28.6	0.7
1965	–	34.0	–

Note: The metropolitan area for all dates is defined as Cuyahoga and Lake counties (the 1960 Standard Metropolitan Statistical Area). "Suburbs" refers to the balance of the metropolitan area excluding Cleveland City. Data are from the respective Censuses. Metropolitan area figures are not available for 1965. Figures for Negroes in 1965 are estimated from published figures for nonwhites.

A small Negro population has resided in the city throughout its history, but by 1910 numbered only 9,000 [5]. The subsequent pattern of growth parallels that of a number of other northern cities: rapid growth rates during

the First World War and the early twenties, slow growth during the depression, and a resumption of rapid growth during the Second World War. The 1965 Census results confirm local estimates that the rate of net Negro in-migration to the city has recently slowed; but the population base is sufficient to produce a large numerical growth, even without in-migration. The percentage of Negroes among city residents has risen from 1.5 in 1910 to 10 in 1940, 29 in 1960, and 34 in 1965.

Meanwhile, out in the suburbs, the *rate* of growth of Negro population has been surprisingly parallel to the rate of growth of white population. Such high growth rates from a small population base tend to be numerically deceiving. Negro suburban population multiplied twelvefold from 1910 to 1960, from 552 to 6,455. White suburban population multiplied ninefold, to a 1960 total of 914,000. As a result, the percentage of Negroes in the suburbs has remained relatively constant: six-tenths of one percent in 1910 and seven-tenths of one percent in 1960.

The city of Cleveland houses the overwhelming majority of the metropolitan area's Negro population. This racial segregation between city and suburbs is paralleled within the city by an east-west split. Consider the percentage of city Negroes who live east of the Cuyahoga River:

1910	97.6
1920	97.8
1930	98.5
1940	99.0
1950	99.1
1960	99.8
1965	99.5

For more than half a century, Cleveland's Negroes have lived only on the east side of town. The west side has ever been, and remains still, for whites only.

The concentration of the metropolitan Negro population within one segment of the central city is a striking illustration of the degree of residential segregation. Elsewhere I have described a segregation index that serves as a summary measure of the degree of racial residential segregation in a city or other areal unit. The index is calculated from Census data showing the distribution of Negro and non-Negro households among the Census tracts of the city (or metropolitan area) [6]. If each neighborhood (Census tract) is all white or all Negro, the index will be 100. If each neighborhood is racially mixed to the same degree as every other—each with the same percentage of Negroes as the entire city—the index will be 0. The specific index value indicates the minimum percentage of the city's white households (or, alternatively, of the city's Negro households) that would have to be shifted from tracts of overrepresentation to tracts of underrepresentation to effect complete residential desegregation. A trend series of such indices for Cleveland *City* moves generally upward [7]:

1910	69
1920	72
1930	83
1940	87
1950	86
1960	85
1965	87

Metropolitan data are not available for a time series, but addition of the predominantly white suburbs to the calculation yields a 1960 metropolitan area index of 90. The 6,000 Negro suburban residents were not randomly distributed. Among the 162 suburban tracts delineated in the 1960 Census, four had more than 500 Negro residents and another eight had 100 to 500. Together, these twelve suburban tracts contained three-fourths of all Negro suburban residents. A segregation index calculated just for the suburbs is 64. Although since 1960 there has been an accelerated suburbanization of Negro families in the Cleveland area, it is obvious that suburbanization and desegregation are not synonymous [8].

My approach to the analysis of the effects of income redistribution on residential segregation begins with data from the 1960 Census,

showing for each Census tract in the metropolitan area the number of families at each income level. Consider, for example, a division of the population into high-income families (over $10,000) and low-income families (under $10,000). For each tract, the actual number of high-income families and low-income families living there is known. The Census also provides information on the income distribution of white and nonwhite families in the Cleveland metropolitan area. Of high-income families, 4.2% were Negro. Of low-income families, 15.0% were Negro.

Assume that family income is the only determinant of where a family lives, that Negroes neither choose to live in predominantly Negro areas nor are barred from living in predominantly white neighborhoods. A tract in which all of the families have high incomes would, under these conditions, be expected to have a racial composition of 4.2% Negro families. The expected racial composition of a tract containing both high- and low-income families could be readily calculated, summing the products of .042 times the number of high-income families plus .150 times the number of low-income families. Repeating this process for each Census tract, a hypothetical "expected" distribution of white and Negro families is obtained. Under these assumptions, Negro families are expected to be found in every Census tract, and the same is true of white families. In fact, the distribution of "expected Negroes" among Census tracts is very similar to that of "expected whites." The segregation index comparing expected Negroes and whites is 6.0, only trivially greater than the minimum index value of zero and dramatically below the index of 90 that compares actual Negroes and whites.

Another way of looking at these results is to compare the Census tract distribution of the expected high-income Negroes with the actual distribution of high-income Negroes. The expected cases are scattered throughout the metropolitan area, with some concentration in the suburbs. The actual cases are concentrated in the Negro sections of the city. The segregation index comparing expected high-income Negroes with actual high-income Negroes is 89. Similarly, low-income Negro families are not distributed throughout the metropolis as are white low-income families, but are concentrated in the Negro areas. The segregation index comparing expected low-income Negroes with actual low-income Negroes is 77.

The division of the population into only two income classes is arbitrary, and one might expect the use of such crude categories to distort the findings. The same analysis was repeated, this time using all eleven income classes reported by the Census. The segregation index between expected white families and expected Negro families is 5.3 instead of the 6.0 obtained with the two-fold income break. The additional income detail does not alter the results of the analysis.

These simple analyses demonstrate that poverty has little to do directly with Negro residential segregation in the Cleveland metropolitan area. They demonstrate that if income were the only factor at work in determining where white and Negro families live, there would be very little racial residential segregation. These results clearly foreshadow the subsequent conclusion that income redistribution cannot serve as a means to residential desegregation.

Income maintenance programs and other means of income redistribution currently under discussion typically seek to raise above the poverty line most family incomes below that line. To simplify assessment of the impact of such programs on housing patterns, let us divide the population into three income classes (1960 data): high-income families ($10,000 and above), middle-income families ($3,000–9,999), and poor families (below $3,000). Let us assume that poor families are enabled by the program to buy or rent housing of the type currently occupied by middle-income families. Specifically, we shall assume that all of the housing in the Cleveland metropolitan area that is occupied by poor families is vacated. It's extrinsic to the model whether it is torn down and converted to recreational and industrial

parks or left standing, boarded up, as a monument. The poor families are then redistributed among Census tracts according to the current pattern of middle-income families. Note that only incomes have been changed, not skin colors. Hence, the hypothetical residential redistribution must be done separately for white and nonwhite families: poor white families are distributed among tracts in the pattern established by middle-income white families, and poor Negro families are redistributed according to the pattern of middle-income Negro families. High-income families, white and Negro, retain their existing residential patterns.

After completion of the residential redistribution brought about by these income changes, the segregation index between white and Negro families is 91, compared to the 90 obtaining prior to the income and residential redistribution. The elimination of poverty has enabled poor whites and Negroes to live according to the slightly more segregated patterns of middle-income families. The same results could be accomplished through rent-subsidy and mortgage-assistance schemes, if they enabled poor families to occupy middle-income housing but entailed no provisions for changing the impact of skin color on residential location.

To carry the analysis one step further, assume an even more extensive income redistribution (or program of housing subsidies) that again enabled poor families to adopt the residential location patterns of middle-income families, but in addition enabled half of the middle-income families to adopt the residential location patterns of high-income families. Under this scheme, not only are poor white and Negro families enabled to live according to the segregated residential patterns of middle-income families, but some middle-income families adopt the even more segregated residential patterns of high-income families. The segregation index between white and Negro families moves up to 92.

The implications of these hypothetical models may be easily summarized. Altering income distributions without eliminating discrimination would only tend to increase segregation. Income improvements or housing subsidies enable additional white families to emulate the segregated residential patterns enjoyed by middle- and high-income whites. Such programs enable Negro families to seek improved housing, but the search must be conducted within the confines of a tightly segregated housing market.

The poverty explanation of racial residential segregation is not only a principal rationale for opposition by various parts of the real estate industry to fair-housing legislation, but also colors the approach of many ardent integrationists. At the little-remembered June 1-2, 1966, White House Conference, "To Fulfill These Rights," the *Council's Report and Recommendations to the Conference* included the following paragraphs:

Federal assistance to every local governmental unit should be conditioned on the submission of a metropolitan-wide plan providing for the desegregation of housing and promotion of communities inclusive of all races and incomes.

The principle that the emerging neighborhood must be broadly inclusive of a range of incomes and racial and ethnic groups must be a conscious and controlling policy from the inception and continue indefinitely in the management of neighborhood affairs.

These recommendations and others like them may overstate the need for explicit governmental policy to foster residential integration along economic as well as racial lines. Whatever the merits of such policies on other grounds, they do not appear to be necessary to attainment of a very substantial degree of racial integration in housing in the Cleveland metropolitan area. This may be demonstrated by another hypothetical scheme.

Allow the family income distribution of whites and Negroes to remain fixed. Hypothetically remove racial discrimination and any other race-connected factors that affect housing choice among low-income families. Assume that anti-discrimination policies are not effective among high-income families, who continue

to maintain segregated residential patterns. Specifically, then, calculate the racial composition of each tract by adding to the actual number of high-income white and Negro families the "expected" numbers of low-income white and Negro families derived from the first illustrative approach described above. This merges a high-income residentially segregated pattern with a non-segregated pattern among low-income families. The resulting white-Negro segregation index would be 10. In other words, the great bulk of the problem of racial residential segregation would be solved if the housing of middle-income and poor families were integrated, even though segregation persisted among high-income families.

The persistence of the poverty explanation of racial residential segregation is puzzling. It is not necessary to resort to elaborate statistical models to dispute it; simpler statistics might suffice. In Cleveland City in 1960, the median monthly rent reported by nonwhite households was $82, by white households, $76. The median value of nonwhite-owned houses was $13,100, of white-owned homes $13,900. Racial segregation in central city housing clearly has little relation to ability to pay. But it is not even necessary to resort to statistics. Simple observation reveals that poor whites are segregated from poor Negroes, and wealthy Negroes are segregated from wealthy whites. The ghetto exists.

Two prevalent images of metropolitan housing patterns seem to lend credence to the poverty notion, but these images also belie reality. One image is that of dilapidated central cities, filled with slum tenements and cheap housing, inhabited by poor blacks, surrounded by plush commuting suburbs, lily-white and expensive. In fact, in most metropolitan areas a substantial proportion of whites, if not a majority, still reside in the central city. Most city housing, like most suburban housing, is decent by contemporary standards, but not fancy or expensive. Large lots in rigidly zoned suburbs may be home for the majority of those who write about urban problems and may compose the image of suburbia, but for all the space they consume they house only a small number of people. In Cleveland in 1960, only one-fifth of owner-occupied housing in the suburbs was valued at $25,000 or over. If much new housing is priced beyond the reach of most Negro families, it is also beyond the reach of most white families. The older housing stock that is home to most metropolitan residents is spatially differentiated much more sharply by race than by price.

A second image is that of the traditional southern town. Whites hold regular employment and live in houses; Negroes survive on casual laboring jobs and live in shacks. In the traditional case, the occupational and income segregation between whites and Negroes is as complete as the housing segregation. It may be true in this extreme case that Negroes cannot afford the housing occupied by whites, but in such a society it is not obvious that poverty should be adduced as the underlying explanation of residential segregation. Whatever the reality of this image as applied to a traditional southern town, it cannot meaningfully be transferred to a northern metropolis or even to a growing southern city. The Negro population of Cleveland came to a city in which the housing stock was not initially structured with an accommodation to racial separation. Negroes took over housing formerly occupied by whites, in large part by outbidding them in the marketplace. Racial residential segregation came about through deliberate discrimination and related social factors. A peculiarly distorted housing market evolved, based not on the color of a man's money but the color of his skin. The poverty explanation of residential segregation and its associated images can best be understood, I believe, as efforts to cover up the more uncomfortable image of white racism.

NOTES

1. Karl E. Taeuber and Alma F. Taeuber. *Negroes in Cities: Residential Segregation and Neighborhood Change* (Chicago: Aldine, 1965), pp. 94–95.

2. United States Bureau of the Census. "Special Census of Cleveland, Ohio, April 1, 1965," *Current Population Reports*, Series p–28, No. 1390.

3. Eugene S. Uyeki. "Residential Distribution and Stratification, 1950–1960," *American Journal of Sociology*, LXIX (March 1964): 491–498.

4. Taeuber and Taeuber, op. cit., chap. 3.

5. In Census procedures the total population is split into "color"—white and nonwhite—and nonwhite is further split into "Negro" and "other nonwhite races." Except where clearly indicated, my tabulations separate Negro from non-Negro population rather than nonwhite from white. For convenience, I generally refer to non-Negroes as whites. In the Cleveland metropolitan area in 1960, there were 3,500 persons of other nonwhite races, 2,100 of whom were Japanese or Chinese. It doesn't make much difference to my analysis whether "other nonwhite races" is combined with white into a non-Negro aggregate or with Negro into a nonwhite aggregate.

6. United States Bureau of the Census, *U.S. Censuses of Population and Housing: 1960. Census Tracts, Cleveland, Ohio,* Final Report PHC (1)–28 (Washington: U.S. Government Printing Office, 1962).

7. In *Negroes in Cities*, op. cit. note 1, we reported a 1940–1960 series of indices calculated from block data. These block indices reflect the more detailed pattern of segregation by small areas, and are numerically higher than tract indices. The trends are similar.

8. "Changes in the Non-white Population," *Regional Church Planning Office Newsletter*, No. 21, Dec., 1965 (2230 Euclid Ave., Cleveland, Ohio).

45

REYNOLDS FARLEY
KARL E. TAEUBER

Population Trends and Residential Segregation since 1960

"A great tide of migration is segregating American life, as most of us live it, faster than all of our laws can desegregate it" [1]. A national concern with civil rights developed in the late 1950's in part as a response to the problems engendered by momentous demographic change, but the change itself was largely unrecognized. The 1960 census eventually produced evidence of the absolute loss of white population and gain of Negro population in many large central cities [2]. In many other cities, there was net out-migration of whites, particularly in the young adult ages, but the natural increase prevented decline in total numbers and masked the magnitude of change. Census results also documented the wider spread of Negro urbanization. As news stories were subsequently to reveal, Negro population was increasing rapidly, not only in New York and Chicago, but in Los Angeles, Syracuse, Boston, Milwaukee, and most other large cities.

The 1960 decennial census provided the most recent reliable basis for detailed assessment of population trends. No comprehensive data for localities are available for any subsequent date, and results of the 1970 census are several years in the future. Fortunately, the Bureau of the Census from time to time conducts special censuses in various cities. Some are taken at the request and expense of local areas which need current data; some are conducted to pretest census methodologies; and some are conducted under congressional mandate (for example, the Voting Rights Act of 1965). These special censuses provide the best available information about population change, migration patterns, and trends in residential segregation since 1960.

We have assembled data for all 13 cities in which a special enumeration conducted after 1960 reported a total population of at least 100,000 and a Negro population of at least 9000, and for which the 1960 and later census tract grids are reasonably comparable [3]. These cities, their populations, and their growth rates are shown in Table 1.

Reprinted by permission from *Science*, Vol. 159, pp. 953–956, 1 March 1968. Copyright 1968 by the American Association for the Advancement of Science.

TABLE 1.   Population Change and Racial Composition, 1960 to Mid-Decade. The data are taken from note [3]

City	Date of Special Census	Total Population (thousands)		Change 1960 to Later (%)		Negroes (%)	
		1960	Later	White*	Negro	1960	Later
Buffalo	4–18–66	535	481	−13.5	15.7	13.2	17.0
Providence	10– 1–65	208	187	−11.9	24.5	5.4	7.4
Rochester	10– 1–64	319	306	− 7.1	34.6	7.4	10.4
Cleveland	4– 1–65	876	811	−14.7	10.2	28.6	34.1
Des Moines†	4–28–66	209	206	− 1.5	6.3	4.9	5.3
Evansville†	10–20–66	142	143	0.4	6.2	6.6	6.9
Fort Wayne	1–24–67	155	160	0.2	39.8	7.5	10.2
Greensboro	1–25–66	120	132	8.8	13.9	25.8	26.7
Louisville†	5–14–64	391	387	− 3.0	11.7	17.9	20.2
Memphis†	3–27–67	491	497	− 6.8	14.8	37.6	42.6
Raleigh	1–25–66	94	105	12.2	12.7	23.4	23.4
Shreveport†	6–15–66	158	147	− 9.1	− 2.2	33.1	34.7
Sacramento†	10– 9–64	189	192	− 0.8	29.7	6.5	8.3

* Includes "other races."
† Areas annexed after 1960 are excluded.

POPULATION CHANGE

Seven of the 13 cities experienced a decline in total population, as much as 10 percent in Providence and Buffalo. In each city the Negro population grew more rapidly or—in the case of Shreveport—decreased less rapidly than the white population. As a consequence the percentage of Negroes rose after 1960. This occurred in the southern cities and in Sacramento as well as in the northern cities.

National sample surveys conducted by the Bureau of the Census document on an aggregate basis the prevalence of the demographic change observed in the 13 cities [4]:

In the first six years of the 1960's, the Negro population in large cities increased by more than 2 million while the white population in the same areas decreased by 1 million. The survey of March, 1966, confirms that, to an increasing extent, Negroes are living in metropolitan areas, and, within these areas, in the central cities. Between 1960 and 1966, the Negro population living in metropolitan areas increased by 21 per cent, from 12,198,000 to 14,790,000, and almost all of this increase occurred within central cities. The white population living in metropolitan areas increased by 9 per cent, from 99,688,000 to 108,983,000, and all of this metropolitan increase occurred outside central cities.

MIGRATION PATTERNS

Special census tabulations, like those from the decennial census, show the population by age, sex, and color. From these data estimates of net migration were calculated. As a first step, survival ratios from a national life table for 1962 were applied to the 1960 population of each city (specifically for age, sex, and color) to estimate its population at the special census date [5]. This estimated population was then compared to the population enumerated by the special census and the difference represented net migration. Table 2 presents the estimated net migration, by color, and the net migration per 100 original population by age and color. Except for Sacramento, at least 94 percent of the nonwhites in each city are Negroes.

TABLE 2.   Estimated Net Migration, by Color and Age, 1960 to Mid-Decade. The data are taken from Table 1 and note [5]

Color	Net Migration	Net Migration per 100 Persons in Age Group in 1960							
		Total	0–9	10–19	20–29	30–39	40–49	50–64	65+
Buffalo									
White	− 68,565	−15	−19	− 9	−26	−16	−11	−12	−13
Nonwhite	+ 574	+ 1	+ 3	0	+ 6	+ 1	− 6	− 2	− 7
Providence									
White	− 24,292	−12	−19	+ 3	−31	−17	−11	− 8	− 8
Nonwhite	+ 1,125	+ 9	+13	+23	+13	+ 2	− 1	+ 5	*
Rochester									
White	− 22,477	− 8	−12	+ 8	−19	−14	− 9	− 8	−16
Nonwhite	+ 4,210	+17	+12	+29	+23	+10	+ 3	+ 3	*
Cleveland									
White	−110,893	−18	−33	− 5	−38	−32	−19	−18	−20
Nonwhite	+ 1,878	+ 1	+ 3	+ 3	+ 4	− 5	− 2	+ 2	− 3
Des Moines									
White	− 12,973	− 7	−12	+ 6	−17	−11	− 5	− 4	− 2
Nonwhite	− 306	− 3	+ 1	− 9	− 3	− 1	− 1	− 2	*
Evansville									
White	− 6,824	− 5	− 7	− 7	− 4	− 5	− 5	− 2	− 5
Nonwhite	− 363	− 4	+ 1	−24	*	+ 1	− 2	+26	*
Fort Wayne									
White	− 9,311	− 6	−11	+ 8	−15	−10	− 7	− 5	− 6
Nonwhite	+ 1,806	+15	+16	+29	+19	+ 7	+ 3	*	*
Greensboro									
White	+ 941	+ 1	− 1	+15	0	− 2	− 5	− 6	− 4
Nonwhite	+ 954	+ 3	+ 6	+26	−24	+ 1	−14	− 1	*
Louisville									
White	− 23,030	− 7	−14	+ 3	−20	−11	− 5	− 4	− 2
Nonwhite	+ 2,483	+ 4	+ 4	+ 9	+ 5	+ 3	+ 5	+ 6	− 2
Memphis									
White	− 35,991	−12	−20	+ 4	−22	−16	−11	− 7	− 5
Nonwhite	+ 2,266	+ 1	+ 4	− 5	−10	0	− 3	+ 7	− 7
Raleigh									
White	+ 3,875	+ 5	0	+39	−27	− 2	− 4	− 6	− 5
Nonwhite	+ 1,333	+ 6	+ 5	+23	− 6	+ 3	+ 1	+ 4	*
Shreveport									
White	− 13,531	−13	−21	− 6	−23	−16	−11	− 4	− 1
Nonwhite	− 9,420	−17	−18	−26	−24	−16	−14	+ 1	−11
Sacramento†									
White	− 5,264	− 3	− 4	+ 1	−11	+ 2	− 1	− 4	− 6

* Rate not calculated because denominator is less than 1000.
† No migration rates for nonwhites were calculated for Sacramento since 40 percent of the nonwhites in this city were Orientals.

From 11 of the 13 cities there was a substantial net out-migration of whites in the post-1960 period. Cleveland had the highest rate of migration loss, 110,000 people or 18 percent of the white population, in a 5-year span. Buffalo's migration loss was 15 percent during a 6-year period, and Shreveport, Memphis, and Providence also had net out-migration of more than 10 percent in the 5- to 7-year period.

Migration losses were proportionately greatest among whites aged 20 to 29 at the start of the period. The 30- to 39-year-olds also had high migration losses, and the 0- to 9-year-olds migrated along with their parents. For eight cities there was a net migration balance into the city among whites aged 10 to 19. These results are consistent with a variety of other migration data indicating a continued attractiveness of central cities to young adults, but a marked out-movement during the family-expansion stage of the life cycle [6]. In all cities there was a net out-migration of older white population, giving no evidence of a "back-to-the-city" movement among those whose children are grown.

Migration patterns for nonwhites are diverse. Among those aged 20 to 29 in 1960, there tends to appear the pattern long thought to be typical: net out-migration from southern cities and net in-migration to northern cities. But there is no simple way to summarize the patterns among other age groups. In some northern cities with large Negro populations (Buffalo and Cleveland), net migration during the early 1960's was slight. In northern cities with smaller Negro populations, net migration was sometimes large (Rochester and Providence) and sometimes small or negative (Des Moines and Evansville). Some southern cities had a net gain of Negro population through migration (Greensboro, Memphis, Louisville, and Raleigh), but some lost (Shreveport). The early 1960's may represent a transitional period in Negro migration. As Negro migrants seek out a variety of urban destinations, the earlier pattern of movement from southern cities to a few large northern cities may no longer be a dominant feature [7].

Growth of Negro population and increases in Negro percentages are not dependent on continued in-migration of Negroes. Negro populations in most cities are youthful, with many women in the childbearing ages and many more about to enter those ages. White populations not only have a significant out-migration, but their more elderly age structures are less conducive to high rates of natural increase. For instance, in Providence in 1965 the median age of whites was 35 years, of Negroes 19 years. In Buffalo in 1966 the median age of whites was 35 years, of Negroes 21 years. In Rochester in 1965, 17 percent of the whites, but 44 percent of the Negroes, were under age 15. Differential natural increase and white out-migration from cities are sufficient for continued increases in Negro percentages regardless of the pace of Negro migration to cities.

TRENDS IN RESIDENTIAL SEGREGATION

The growing Negro populations in many cities have expanded into housing outside the previously established Negro residential areas. Inspection of census tract data reveals this type of change. Census tracts are small areas, containing on the average about 4000 persons, for which basic census data are tabulated. In Buffalo, for example, in 1960 most Negroes lived in a belt of tracts extending south and west of downtown. By 1966 this belt had grown to include several more tracts. In Cleveland tracts were added to the principally Negro areas on the east side. Almost all of Cleveland's Negroes, in both 1960 and 1965, lived east of the Cuyahoga River in a broad belt stretching from downtown to the city limits. Local estimates indicate the development of several predominantly Negro residential areas in the eastern suburbs [8]. Few Negroes lived on the other side of downtown: in 1965 the special census counted 300,000 Clevelanders west of the Cuyahoga, of whom more than 99 percent were white.

The other cities were lacking in such extensive established Negro areas in 1960, but solidly Negro residential areas have developed. In Rochester, areas southwest and immediately north of the central business district became increasingly Negro. In Providence, Negroes replaced whites in tracts in the Federal Hill area and south of downtown along the Providence River. In each of the 13 cities the development and spread of predominantly Negro residential areas can be traced.

It is also possible to use these data to calculate summary indices of the degree of residential segregation. In contrast to the detailed descriptions of Negro residential patterns obtained from maps, such indices facilitate comparisons among cities and through time.

Using city block data for a large number of U.S. cities, the Taeubers assessed trends in residential segregation from 1940–1960 [9]. In cities of all sizes and in every part of the country, Negroes and whites were found to be residentially segregated. From 1940 to 1950, the housing market was very tight. Existing segregation patterns were maintained and additional white and Negro population was housed in a highly segregated pattern. Residential segregation generally increased. During the 1950's there was an increased availability of housing. A multiple regression analysis for 69 cities relating changes in segregation to changes in other characteristics suggested that in many northern cities "the growing Negro populations, together with the demand for improved housing created by the improving economic status of Negroes, were able to counteract and in many cases to overcome the historical trend toward increasing residential segregation. In southern cities Negro population growth was slower and economic gains were less. The long-term trend toward increasing segregation slowed but was not reversed" [10].

DISSIMILARITY INDEX

The Taeubers' measure of segregation was the dissimilarity index, calculated from city block data on the number of housing units occupied by whites and by nonwhites. For assessment of post-1960 trends, we shall use the dissimilarity index calculated from census tract data on the number of Negroes and non-Negroes. The magnitude of the index depends on the

areal units from which it is calculated, and the indices shown here are not directly comparable with the Taeubers' [9]. Calculation of the index requires a percentage distribution of Negroes across all the census tracts of a city, and a similar percentage distribution of non-Negroes. The index is one-half the sum of absolute differences between the two percentage distributions. The numerical value of the index indicates the minimum percentage of Negroes (or of non-Negroes) whose census tract of residence would have to be changed to obtain an areally homogeneous distribution of the two groups. A value of 100 indicates complete segregation; of zero, no segregation.

Dissimilarity indices for the 13 cities for 1960 and the special census dates are shown in the first two columns of Table 3. The differences indicate a pattern of increasing residential segregation. Only in Fort Wayne and Sacramento did Negroes and non-Negroes become less segregated from one another during the early 1960's. There is no evidence in these data of an acceleration or even continuation of the trend toward decreasing segregation observed for northern cities from 1950–1960.

The 13 cities are not a random sample, and we cannot claim to show that residential segregation in American cities is generally increasing. Putting these results together with those for 1940–1960, there is strong evidence that the pervasive pattern of residential segregation has not been significantly breached. Whether the temporal trend for a particular city has been up, down, or fluctuating, the magnitude of the change has usually been small. Stability in segregation patterns has been maintained despite massive demographic transformation, marked advances in Negro economic welfare, urban renewal and other clearance and resettlement programs, considerable undoubling of living quarters and diminished room-crowding, high vacancy rates in many of the worst slums, and an array of federal, state, and local anti-discrimination laws and regulations.

The analysis of census data points to stability in segregation patterns, with some preponderance recently of small increases in a segregation index. How may these results be reconciled with the rapidly increasing segregation perceived by most civil rights groups and many other observers? Such observers are likely to be looking at something more than simply the patterns of housing segregation.

For example, consider the problems of de facto educational segregation faced by a city with a small but completely segregated Negro population. Negroes live in only a few areas of the city, but there are not enough Negroes to make an extensive "ghetto." One or two elementary school districts may be solidly Negro, but no high school district is solidly Negro. If the Negro population increases, and continues to be housed in a segregated manner, additional elementary school districts will become all Negro, and one or more high school districts may become all Negro. If the white population is declining (the total city population is constant or declining), the Negro percentage in the city will be increasing rapidly. Hence the magnitude of the desegregation task will increase. Yet the basic segregated residential pattern is merely persisting, not worsening. If this example is modified slightly so that the initial segregation pattern is one of great rather than complete racial segregation, we have an approximation to the actual situation in many U.S. cities. It is the increasing number and proportion of Negroes in most central cities that account for the increasing visibility of segregation-induced problems, not any change in the residential pattern.

Composite indices may be formulated which combine measures of the proportion Negro with measures of residential segregation. Because the two components are not highly correlated, the Taeubers argued against use of a composite index for comparisons between cities [9: 195]. Nevertheless, we believe there may be heuristic value to the calculation of selected composite indices. From among the many that have been proposed, two seem particularly well formulated to represent, respectively, the magnitude of the desegregation problem and magnitude of the segregation problem.

DESEGREGATION PROBLEM

By the desegregation problem, we refer to the proportion of the population that would have to be moved to effect complete residential desegregation. The index of dissimilarity gives a superficial answer to this problem. It specifies the desegregation problem on the assumption that persons of only one race are to be moved, from areas in which they are overrepresented to areas of underrepresentation. Moving persons of only one race is unrealistic in the sense that it would depopulate many areas and require substantial additional housing in others. More realistic is a series of exchanges of white and Negro households, accomplishing desegregation while maintaining existing housing stock. The minimum percentage of the total population that would be moved by such a procedure is given by

$$2q(1 - q)D$$

where q is the proportion Negro in the total population, and D is the index of dissimilarity. This measure has been called the replacement index [11].

By the segregation problem, we refer to the tendency of residential segregation to create racial homogeneity among neighborhood contacts (on the street and in stores, schools, and other neighborhood facilities). For an objective, census-based measure of this type, it is necessary to assume that contacts within an area (census tract, city block, school district) are made at random from among the resident population. For a Negro chosen at random from the city's population, the probability of residing in tract i is n_i/N, where n_i is the number of Negroes in tract i and N is the total number of Negroes in the city. The probability that another individual randomly chosen from tract i is also a Negro is $(n_i - 1) / (t_i - 1)$ where t_i is the total population in tract i. For convenience, this term may be approximated by n_i / t_i. If we take the joint probability of the two events, sum over tracts, and express the result in percentage scale, we have [12]

$$(100/N)\Sigma^n{}_i^z/t_i.$$

This index may also be interpreted as the average percentage Negro in census tracts, weighted by the number of Negroes in the tract. From the Coleman report, some evidence may be adduced for the proposition that the educational achievement of Negro pupils is less the higher the percentage of Negroes in their schools [13]. Calculating the index for schools would provide a measure of the average Negro percentage faced by Negro school children. More generally, the social-psychological consequences of residential segregation might be hypothesized to be some function of the average Negro percentage encountered by Negroes in their neighborhoods. It is in this sense that the index may be regarded as measuring the segregation problem. We designate it the Negro homogeneity index.

The dissimilarity and replacement indices are racially symmetrical. Negroes and non-Negroes are equally segregated from each other.

The Negro homogeneity index is racially specific. The average Negro percentage encountered by Negroes may differ from the average white percentage (non-Negro) encountered by whites (the white homogeneity index). The complements of these measures are also of interest: the weighted average white percentage encountered by Negroes in tracts and the weighted average Negro percentage encountered by whites in tracts.

Values of the replacement and homogeneity indices are shown in Table 3. In contrast to the dissimilarity index, there is a wide range in magnitude of these indices. This reflects the wide range in values of q (the proportion Negro) and the additional variance introduced by the squared terms appearing in each composite index. The replacement and Negro homogeneity indices are highly correlated. Both indices increased for each of the 13 cities between 1960 and the later date. For most cities, both segregation (D) and proportion Negro (q) increased, but the relative increase was small in the former

TABLE 3. Indices of residential segregation, 1960 and mid-decade. The data are taken from note [3].

| City | Dissimilarity Index | | Replacement Index | | Homogeneity Index | | | |
| | | | | | Negro | | White* | |
	1960	Later	1960	Later	1960	Later	1960	Later
Buffalo	84.5	85.1	19.4	24.0	65	74	95	95
Providence	64.2	70.3	6.6	9.6	23	30	96	94
Rochester	76.7	79.3	10.5	14.8	44	53	96	95
Cleveland	85.2	87.2	34.8	39.2	81	86	92	92
Des Moines	76.7	77.3	7.1	7.8	35	40	97	97
Evansville	76.9	80.5	9.5	10.3	54	61	97	97
Fort Wayne	79.8	79.2	11.1	14.5	38	52	95	95
Greensboro	83.8	89.1	32.1	34.9	83	88	94	96
Louisville	78.6	81.2	23.1	26.2	68	73	93	93
Memphis	79.3	83.7	37.2	40.2	79	86	88	89
Raleigh[†]	75.0	78.0	26.9	28.0	72	74	92	93
Shreveport	82.5	85.1	36.5	38.6	81	85	90	92
Sacramento	58.2	57.2	7.1	8.7	24	29	95	94

* Includes "other races."
† Indices were calculated from data for 19 tracts lying entirely within the city and 11 tracts lying across the city boundary.

compared to the latter. Trends in the composite indices are largely determined by trends in the Negro proportion.

We examined special census data for 13 cities to assess trends in population, migration, and residential segregation from 1960 to mid-decade. In these cities, the demographic trends of the 1950's are continuing. There is a net out-migration of white population, and in several cities a decline in total population. Negro population is growing rapidly, but natural increase rather than net in-migration increasingly is the principal source. The concentration of whites in the suburbs and Negroes in the central cities is continuing. Within the cities, indices of racial residential segregation generally increased. The combination of small increases in residential segregation and large increases in the Negro percentage has greatly intensified the magnitude of the problems of segregation and desegregation of neighborhoods, local institutions, and schools.

REFERENCES AND NOTES

1. Editorial, Washington *Post* (28 Dec. 1966).

2. L. F. Schnore. *The Urban Scene* (New York: Free Press, 1965), p. 255.

3. The 13 cities are listed in Table 1. Data for the later date were published as follows: U.S. Bureau of the Census, *Current Population Reports,* Ser. P–28, Nos. 1376, 1377, 1386, 1390, 1393, 1411, 1413, 1430, 1431, 1435, 1441, 1446, and 1453 (1964–1967); data for 1960: U.S. Bureau of the Census, *Censuses of Population and Housing: 1960* PHC(1) (1961), Parts 21, 28, 39, 45, 49, 57, 83, 89, 122, 124, 127, 129, and 143.

4. U.S. Bureau of the Census. *Current Population Reports,* Ser. P–20, No. 157 (1966), p. 1.

5. U.S. National Center for Health Statistics. *Vital Statistics of the United States: 1962,* II, Section 5 (1964).

6. H. S. Shryock. *Population Mobility within the United States* (Chicago: Community and Family Study Center, 1964), p. 424.

7. K. E. Taeuber and A. F. Taeuber. *American Journal of Sociology* 70: 429 (1965).

8. Regional Church Planning Office (Cleveland, Ohio), *Newsletter,* "Changes in the Non-white Population," No. 21 (1965).

9. K. E. Taeuber and A. F. Taeuber. *Negroes in Cities* (Aldine, Chicago, 1965).

10. K. E. Taeuber, *Scientific American* 213: 17 (1965).

11. D. Walker, A. L. Stinchcombe, M. J. McDill, *School Desegregation in Baltimore* (Johns Hopkins Center for the Study of Social Organization of Schools, Baltimore, 1967), p. 5.

12. W. Bell, *Social Forces* 32: 357 (1954).

13. J. S. Coleman, E. Q. Campbell, A. M. Mood, *Equality of Educational Opportunity* (Government Printing Office, Washington, D.C., 1966), p. 21.

14. Support for this study was provided by a faculty research grant from Duke University to R.F. and by the Computation Laboratories of Duke University and the University of Michigan. Taeuber's participation was facilitated by appointment as expert, U.S. Commission on Civil Rights Race and Education Project, with support from funds granted to the Institute for Research on Poverty at the University of Wisconsin by the Office of Economic Opportunity. The conclusions are the sole responsibility of the authors.

46

THEODORE G. CLEMENCE

Residential Segregation in the Mid-Sixties

Special censuses conducted by the Bureau of the Census at the request and expense of local governments provide current statistics for many large cities which are compared with corresponding data from the 1960 Census. An analysis was made of the changes in the racial composition of the cities, and of the areas within the cities (defined by census tracts) which had a high concentration of Negro population in 1960 for ten cities of 100,000 or more population at mid-decade.

As in the 1950–60 period, Negroes continue to move into the central cities of metropolitan areas while white persons continue to move out to the suburbs at a faster rate, and this results in net declines in the populations of the cities. The proportion of nonwhite persons living in areas of high Negro concentration has remained about the same or increased slightly in a majority of the cities, while in a few (such as Cleveland, Rochester, and Raleigh) this proportion has declined; that is, relatively more Negroes in these cities now live outside the ghetto neighborhoods. When the racial composition of the ghettos is examined, however, a higher proportion of the residents are now Negro when compared to 1960 in each of the ten cities.

Thus, the concentration of Negroes in ghetto areas has shown little change, but the trend of white persons moving away from the Negro neighborhoods, either to other parts of the cities or to the suburbs, has increased sharply, and this has tended to polarize the Negro and white populations within large cities.

A high degree of racial segregation is universal in American cities. Whether a city is a metropolitan center or a suburb; whether it is in the North or South; whether the Negro population is large or small in every case, white and Negro households are highly segregated from each other. Negroes are more segregated residentially

Reprinted with permission from *Demography*, Vol 4, No. 2 (1967), pp. 562–568.

than are Orientals, Mexican Americans, Puerto Ricans, or any nationality group. In fact, Negroes are by far the most residentially segregated urban minority group in recent American history. This is evident in the virtually complete exclusion of Negro residents from most new suburban developments of the past fifty years as well as in the block-by-block expansion of Negro residential areas in the central portions of many large cities.[1]

This statement, made by Karl and Alma Taeuber in their recent book, *Negroes in Cities*, is amply supported by their analysis. Much of their data was drawn from the 1960 Census. Most would agree that residential segregation remains both a fact and a problem in the mid-sixties, though it is still several years until substantiating data will be available from the 1970 Census.

Interim data are available for a few large cities from special censuses taken by the Census Bureau. Since 1960, approximately 26 million of the nation's inhabitants have been enumerated in a special census. Approximately 1,200 censuses have been conducted, of which about 100 were in cities of 50,000 or more people. Statistics for the population by age, race, and sex for census tracts are published for these cities, and these reports provide the means for comparisons with 1960.

To examine some of the current trends in the white and nonwhite populations as affected by residential segregation, ten cities have been selected for study, all of which had 100,000 or more inhabitants at mid-decade. Four of the cities are in the Northeast, the others in the South and West. The criteria for selection were that (1) census tract boundaries in the central portion of the city remained unchanged since 1960; (2) a special census was conducted in 1964, 1965, or 1966; and (3) considered as a group, the cities are geographically scattered. The censuses of Louisville and Cleveland were part of the Bureau's 1970 test program. Buffalo, Raleigh, and Rochester were included in county-wide special censuses, and Providence

was included in the 1965 census of Rhode Island taken by the Census Bureau. The other four censuses were requested by the respective cities.

TABLE 1. White and Nonwhite Population, for Ten Selected Cities, and Increase from 1960 to Special Census in 1964, 1965, or 1966

| City | Total | | |
	1960	Special Census	Change
Buffalo, 1966	532,759	481,453	−51,306
Cleveland, 1965	876,050	810,852	−65,192
Providence, 1965	207,498	187,061	−20,437
Rochester, 1964	318,611	305,739	−12,872
Louisville, 1964	390,639	389,044	− 1,595
Raleigh, 1966	93,931	105,722	11,791
Shreveport, 1966	164,372	160,535	− 3,837
Des Moines, 1966	208,982	206,739	− 2,243
Evansville, 1966	141,543	144,463	2,920
Sacramento, 1964	191,667	237,712	46,045

| City | White | | |
	1960	Special Census	Change
Buffalo, 1966	459,371	397,507	−61,864
Cleveland, 1965	622,942	531,506	−91,436
Providence, 1965	195,525	172,252	−23,273
Rochester, 1964	294,383	273,399	−20,984
Louisville, 1964	320,190	310,717	− 9,473
Raleigh, 1966	71,772	80,507	8,735
Shreveport, 1966	107,653	103,411	− 4,242
Des Moines, 1966	198,424	195,412	− 3,012
Evansville, 1966	132,154	134,466	2,312
Sacramento, 1964	167,371	202,355	34,984

| City | Nonwhite | | |
	1960	Special Census	Change
Buffalo, 1966	73,388	83,946	10,558
Cleveland, 1965	253,109	279,352	26,244
Providence, 1965	11,973	14,809	2,836
Rochester, 1964	24,228	32,340	8,112
Louisville, 1964	70,449	78,327	7,878
Raleigh, 1966	22,159	25,215	3,056
Shreveport, 1966	57,619	57,124	− 405
Des Moines, 1966	10,558	11,327	769
Evansville, 1966	9,389	9,997	608
Sacramento, 1964	12,103[a]	21,110[a]	9,007[a]

(a) Negroes only; other races excluded.

---

[1] Karl E. and Alma F. Taeuber, *Negroes in Cities* (Chicago: Aldine Publishing Company, 1965), p. 2.

TABLE 2. Average Annual Change in the White and Nonwhite Population for Ten Selected Cities, 1950–60 and 1960 to Date of Special Census (Figures rounded to nearest hundred)

City	White		Nonwhite	
	Increase, 1960 to Special Census	Increase, 1950–60	Increase, 1960 to Special Census	Increase, 1950–60
Buffalo	−10,300	− 8,300	1,800	− 3,600
Cleveland	−18,300	−14,200	5,200	10,400
Providence	− 4,700	− 4,400	600	300
Rochester	− 5,200	− 3,000	2,000	1,600
Louisville	− 2,400	900	2,000	1,300
Raleigh	1,500	2,400	500	400
Shreveport	− 700	2,300	− 100	1,400
Des Moines	− 500	2,900	100	200
Evansville	400	1,200	100	100
Sacramento	8,700	4,000	2,200[a]	800[a]

[a] Negroes only; excludes other races.

Table 1 illustrates population changes by race in the ten cities between 1960 and the year in which the special census was taken. Table 2 shows average annual changes in this decade compared to the 1950–60 decade, expressed as absolute numbers. The four cities in the northeast continue to experience the types of change evident during the decade 1950–60. White people are moving out of these cities faster than nonwhites are moving in. (Higher Negro birth rates do not account for all of the shift in percent nonwhite in the central cities.) Moreover, the decreases in the white population of these four cities have accelerated since 1960. In Buffalo and Cleveland, the nonwhite population continues to increase rapidly, but at a slower pace now than during the 1950's. In Providence and Rochester, on the other hand, nonwhites are increasing, and at an accelerated rate.

In Buffalo, whites decreased at a rate of 8,300 per year during the decade 1950–60. This rate of change has accelerated to more than 10,000 per year since 1960. Nonwhites increased by 3,600 a year during the 1950's, but only by about one-half that rate during the 1960's. The same pattern is observed in Cleveland. In Des Moines and Evansville, moreover, the nonwhite population is increasing at a slower pace than in the previous decade. In the remaining cities, the nonwhite population is increasing, and at an accelerated rate.

Gross changes do not, of course, reveal patterns of residential change within these cities; they merely point to the general concentration of nonwhites in the central cities. In the 212 Standard Metropolitan Statistical Areas as a group, from 1960 to 1965, the central cities experienced a decline of 0.6 percent in the white population and a 20.3 percent increase in nonwhites. As of 1965, four out of five metropolitan nonwhites lived in the central cities, compared to less than two out of every five white people.[2]

In order to examine these trends with reference to segregated areas within the ten cities in this comparison, census tracts were studied to reveal the rate of dispersion or concentration which had taken place within the central city since 1960. The established Negro area in each city was defined simply as those census tracts in 1960 in which more than half of the nonwhites lived. The identical area is used in presenting post-census data. Generally this is a compact area of neighboring tracts comprising

[2] United States Bureau of the Census, Current Population Reports, Series P–20, No. 151 (April 1966).

less than a dozen of the city's census tracts. In Cleveland and Louisville, however, the predominantly nonwhite areas are quite large, consisting of 37 and 21 census tracts, respectively. In Shreveport, the area is actually comprised of two noncontiguous areas of several tracts each, on opposite sides of the city. In nine of the cities, the nonwhite population is almost entirely Negro. In Sacramento, where other races comprise a substantial minority, only Negroes are included in the comparisons in these tables.

Table 3 shows the concentration of nonwhites in 1960 and in the special census year. One would expect, for example, that perhaps where whites are moving out more rapidly than nonwhites are moving in (as in Buffalo), dispersion of nonwhites would occur. Actually, the proportion of the city's nonwhites who live in the established Negro area of Buffalo has risen since 1960 from 85.8 to 88.4 percent—74,000 nonwhites living in ten of the city's 75 census tracts. This trend, in which the increasing nonwhite population of the central cities tends to concentrate in areas already predominantly nonwhite, might be termed the "polarization" of the Negro. But, this phenomenon is not true for all ten cities. In Cleveland, Rochester, Sacramento, Louisville, and Raleigh the proportion of the city's nonwhites living in established Negro areas is lower now than in 1960, and this suggests that some dispersion has taken place. When census-tract maps for these cities are examined, it becomes apparent that some of the dispersion results from a shift from the tracts of highest concentration of nonwhites to tracts with a lower initial concentration. This has occurred chiefly where slum clearance and the construction of interstate highways or office buildings have brought about a relocation of Negro families from one section to another.

A different and perhaps more direct way to see the changes in residential segregation is through examining the extent to which the nonwhite neighborhoods have become more or less racially mixed. Table 4 presents this comparison. For example, in Buffalo, most nonwhites

TABLE 3. Nonwhite Population Living in Established Negro Area, for Ten Selected Cities 1960, and Special Census Date

City and Year of Special Census	Proportion of All Nonwhites in City Living in Established Negro Area	
	1960	1964–66
Buffalo, 1966	85.8	88.4
Cleveland, 1965	80.5	65.2
Providence, 1965	73.8	76.2
Rochester, 1964	62.8	56.0
Louisville, 1964	83.2	82.2
Raleigh, 1966	82.3	75.3
Shreveport, 1966	79.3	81.6
Des Moines, 1966	74.5	77.4
Evansville, 1966	79.1	80.9
Sacramento, 1964[a]	62.6	49.6

[a] Negroes only.

in 1960 lived in an area which was almost one-half white. In 1966, the same census tracts are now nonwhite by a ratio of three-to-one. In all of the ten cities, the developments since 1960 indicate that Negro predominance has increased in the established areas or, conversely, racial segregation in housing has been maintained. One would not expect to observe this pattern if all of the city housing were equally accessible to nonwhites. The increases in the percent nonwhite in the established Negro areas are most dramatic in Buffalo, Rochester, and Louisville. Even in Des Moines and Providence, where Negroes constitute a small minority in the area where most live, the proportion of the area which is now nonwhite has increased. Many of the census tracts where Negroes are concentrated are declining in total population, and the growing concentration of Negroes in such areas reflects the movement of white families out of those tracts as well as restrictions on the housing market for Negroes.

Special censuses do not usually provide economic statistics for the population. For Cleveland, however, the publication of sample data from the 1965 test census permits a com-

TABLE 4. Percent of the Population in Established Negro Area Which is Non-white, for Ten Selected Cities, 1960 and Special Census Date

City	Percent Nonwhite		Number of Tracts in Negro Area	Number of Tracts in City (1960)
	1960	1964–66		
Buffalo	55.3	73.2	10	75
Cleveland	82.6	88.5	37	205
Providence	17.7	27.6	9	37
Rochester	55.9	71.2	8	90
Louisville	67.5	80.1	21	128
Raleigh	91.6	94.7	12	43
Shreveport	88.9	93.3	12	41
Des Moines	28.1	37.3	7	47
Evansville	51.4	59.4	4	38
Sacramento[a]	22.4	31.1	8	54

[a] Negroes only.

parison of Negro neighborhoods with the 1960 Census.[3] The report shows that nearly all Negro neighborhoods in Cleveland have suffered economic decline since 1960. This is reflected most obviously by decreases in family income when measured in constant dollars.

A more indirect indication of the impact of population change on the central cities may be observed through changes in age distribution. Buffalo is used for illustration in Table 5. Whites 25–44 years old account for almost one-half of the decrease in the city's white population; but these age groups comprise only one-fourth of the total white population. Thus, they are disproportionately represented in the movement of white people out of the city.

These white adults, together with their small children, make up the great urban stream to suburbia. Among nonwhites, on the other hand, about four-fifths of the increase in population is in the ages 5–24 years. This age group comprised only 35 percent of the nonwhites in 1960 (40 percent in 1966). White adults in their prime working years are leaving the city and being replaced by nonwhite children and by young adults who have not yet reached their most productive working years.

A review of recent special census data for ten large cities offers little assurance that patterns of residential segregation are giving way to a racially integrated urban society. On the contrary, it is evident from these observations that established Negro areas are becoming more, rather than less, racially distinct, and that the general trend is toward polarization rather than dispersion of the nonwhite population.

---

[3] United States Bureau of the Census, *Current Population Reports*, Series P–23, No. 21 (January 1967).

TABLE 5. Population of Buffalo, New York, 1960 and 1966, by Age and Color, and Increase Since 1960

Age	Total			White			Nonwhite		
	1966	1960	Increase	1966	1960	Increase	1966	1960	Increase
Number total	481,453	532,759	−51,306	397,507	459,371	−61,864	83,946	73,388	10,558
Under 5 Years	43,243	54,934	−11,691	32,250	43,463	−11,213	10,993	11,471	− 478
5–14 Years	86,846	87,773	− 927	64,787	71,844	− 7,057	22,059	15,929	6,130
15–24 Years	74,037	67,781	6,256	62,249	58,270	3,979	11,788	9,511	2,277
25–34 Years	50,270	65,965	−15,695	39,170	53,944	−14,774	11,100	12,021	− 921
35–44 Years	57,415	70,152	−12,737	45,761	59,872	−14,111	11,654	10,280	1,374
45–54 Years	60,351	66,198	− 5,847	52,467	59,247	− 6,780	7,884	6,951	933
55–64 Years	50,419	58,358	− 7,939	45,500	53,702	− 8,202	4,919	4,656	263
65–74 Years	39,398	43,270	− 3,872	36,696	41,335	− 4,639	2,702	1,935	767
75–84 Years	16,722	15,547	1,175	16,001	15,021	980	721	526	195
85 years and Over	2,752	2,781	− 29	2,626	2,673	− 47	126	108	18
Percent Total	100.0	100.0		100.0	100.0		100.0	100.0	
Under 5 Years	9.0	10.3		8.1	9.5		13.1	15.6	
5–14 Years	18.0	16.5		16.3	15.6		26.3	21.7	
15–24 Years	15.4	12.7		15.7	12.7		14.0	13.0	
25–34 Years	10.4	12.4		9.9	11.7		13.2	16.4	
35–44 Years	11.9	13.2		11.5	13.0		13.9	14.0	
45–54 Years	12.5	12.4		13.2	12.9		9.4	9.5	
55–64 Years	10.5	11.0		11.4	11.7		5.9	6.3	
65–74 Years	8.2	8.1		9.2	9.0		3.2	2.6	
75–84 Years	3.5	2.9		4.0	3.3		0.9	0.7	
85 Years and Over	0.6	0.5		0.6	0.6		0.2	0.1	

47

HAROLD M. ROSE

The Spatial Development of Black Residential Subsystems

A satisfactory housing environment has long been one of the major goals of America's black population. While some progress has been made in the attainment of that goal [10], there yet remains a sizeable differential in the proportion of housing meeting some minimal standard of quality. The question of the quality of the housing stock is exceedingly complex and has its roots in many aspects of American life. One of the many forces which impinge upon the quality and nature of black occupied housing is its location within metropolitan space; and among the several factors which dictate the location of housing stock available to the black home seeker, none would deny the importance of housing cost. Few would minimize the role played by these two forces upon emerging black residential patterns. The focus of this study is upon these factors along with others which influence black residential patterns in Boston, Denver, Indianapolis, Milwaukee, Minneapolis, San Francisco, and Seattle.

In each of the selected cities there will be an attempt to translate the changing magnitude of the black population into changes in scale of emerging residential configurations. What is being attempted here is to move one step beyond the traditional demographic projection of the changing numerical levels of the population at specified points in time to that of projecting the spatial locus of that population. Kingsley Davis has appropriately remarked:

> Yet cities almost never grow in population alone but grow also in territory. A model of city growth, if it is to approximate reality, and especially if it is to be used for prediction, must therefore be a two variable model—that is, one in which both population and area are allowed to change [4, p. 1].

Any attempt to employ this approach, and to subsequently develop a model based upon it, incorporates all of the weaknesses inherent in population projection techniques lacking spatial parameters. But if Davis is correct, this represents an important starting point in the analysis of black residential development patterns from a territorial perspective.

THE STUDY CITIES

The seven cities selected for inclusion in the present investigation are all metropolitan in character and were part of metropolitan systems containing more than a recommended threshold of 300,000 people in 1950 [11]. In the initial year, 1950, the smallest of the central cities, Denver, contained no fewer than 400,000 people and the largest, Boston, contained slightly more than 800,000. Duncan has described four of these complexes as regional metropolises, one a regional capital, one a diversified manufacturing center, and another a manufacturing center [5]. The latter three categories de-

Reprinted by permission from *Economic Geography*, Vol. 48, No. 1 (January 1972), pp. 43–65.

The writer wishes to acknowledge the support received from the National Institute of Health (NIMH 14012–01) which enabled this research project to be undertaken.

scribe Indianapolis, Boston, and Milwaukee, respectively. The regional metropolises are centers of metropolitan dominance in the upper Midwest, the western Great Plains, the Pacific Northwest, and the central Pacific coast area.

The selection of this set of metropolitan complexes was motivated principally by their being the place of residence of relatively small black populations as recently as 1950. In only a single instance, Indianapolis, did the black population exceed 50,000 people. The population of the other cities ranged from slightly more than 8,000 in Minneapolis to more than 43,000 in San Francisco. Because of their small black population size, the spatial pattern of black residential development could be readily observed.

THE DYNAMICS OF URBAN BLACK POPULATIONS

Sizeable black populations have not been among the resident population of the selected cities for an extended period of time. The phenomenon of black urbanization was not directed toward this city group prior to 1940. Only Indianapolis has long been an area of extensive black occupance, and it has been described elsewhere as a second generation ghetto center [24]. A black population lower limit of 25,000, which was employed to define ghetto centers, was not attained by any of the remaining cities prior to World War II, although Boston with more than 23,000 blacks in its population was approaching this threshold in 1940. Clearly, then, this study deals with cities in various stages of black community development, that is, if we think of community development as being a function of population size.

In 1940, both San Francisco and Seattle were the places of residence of fewer than 5,000 blacks, while Minneapolis only slightly exceeded this value. Even though the absolute size of the black population was small during this period, that population was highly clustered spatially. Thus, incipient ghettos prevailed even when the black population was smaller than that which is generally considered minimal

for the development of a functional neighborhood.

Wartime and Postwar Growth

Prior to World War II, black migration streams had been essentially directed at the set of major cities found along the Atlantic seaboard, those fringing the lower Great Lakes, and a few major river cities. But with the new opportunities associated with a sudden gearing up for war, new migration paths began to emerge. For the first time large numbers of blacks began to abandon the Southwest in favor of Pacific coast urban agglomerations. This resulted in the development of a third migration path which could be added to the already well developed courses leading out of the Southeast to the Middle West, and from the South Atlantic region to the Middle Atlantic region. The emergence of this third path added to the racial heterogeneity of Pacific coast cities, which heretofore had known only a relatively small oriental population. It was the wartime displacement of a segment of that population that permitted the initial wave of migrating blacks to secure residential accommodations without great difficulty.

The most phenomenal wartime growth of the black population in the Pacific coast cities took place in San Francisco, but with rapid rates of increase characterizing a number of others. The combination of accelerated migration rates and high fertility levels placed San Francisco and Boston well beyond the limits of the minimum population required for them to be added to the growing list of ghetto centers within the nation in 1950. Milwaukee's position, in terms of the absolute size of the black population, was similar to the position held by Boston in 1940, just below the minimum threshold.

While war-based economic development spurred rapid growth of the black population in the study cities during the decade of the forties, the major concern here is with the growth having taken place since 1950. For by 1950, the minimum critical mass had been reached that assured ghetto center status for each of the

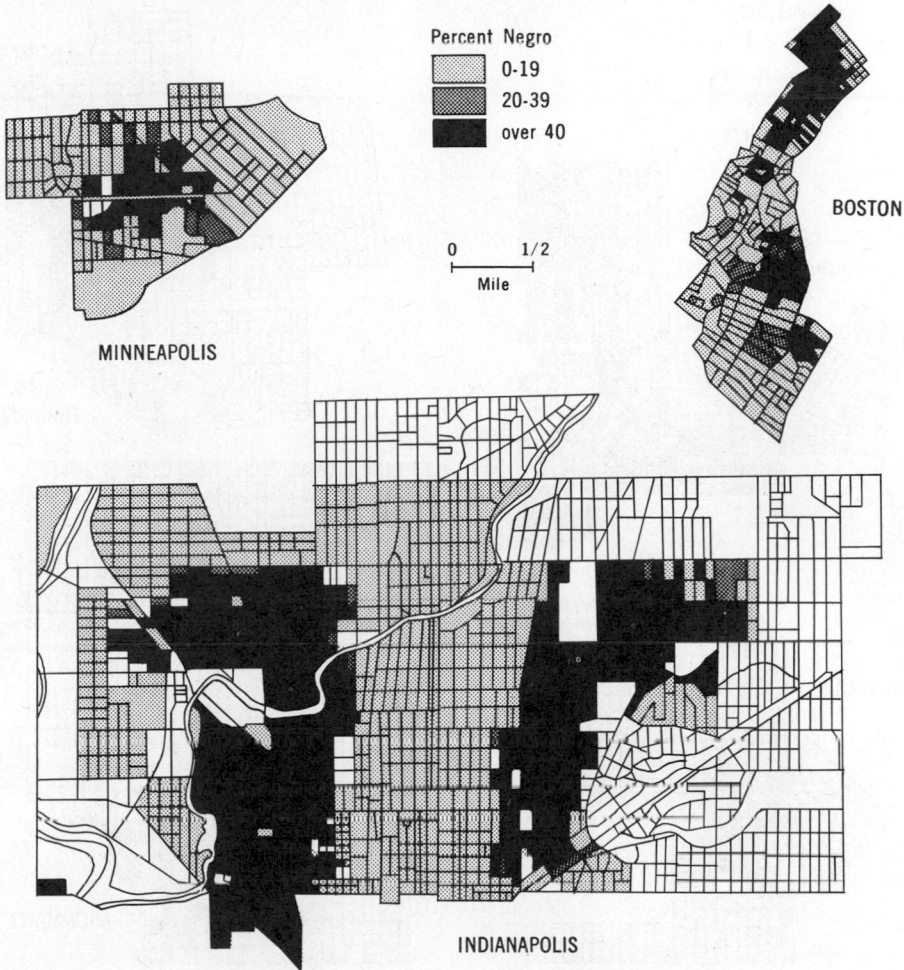

Percent Negro
0-19
20-39
over 40

0   1/2
Mile

MINNEAPOLIS

BOSTON

INDIANAPOLIS

FIGURE 1a.   Variations in Intensity of Black Occupance within Individual Ghetto
Spaces, 1950

cities within a single generation; see Figures 1a and 1b. Ten years later, in 1960, only Minneapolis among this group of cities had not surpassed the 25,000 population threshold. During the previous ten-year interval, growth rates of the black population in one or more of these cities were such that population doubling could take place within ten years. Milwaukee's black population showed an 185.5 percent increase over the period 1950 to 1960, which resulted in a net addition of more than 42,000 persons. While the rate that prevailed in Milwaukee during this interval was exceeded by only one other American city in the over 250,000 class,

Rochester, annual growth rates in excess of 5 percent per annum were common to each city in the sample group. These growth rates were typical of those prevailing in non-Southern cities. Black growth rates in large Southern cities are on the average approximately two percentage points lower per annum.

Population Growth Factors
There is some evidence of variations in the strength of the components of population growth among the sample cities. It is quite apparent that natural increase accounted for the greater percentage of black population change

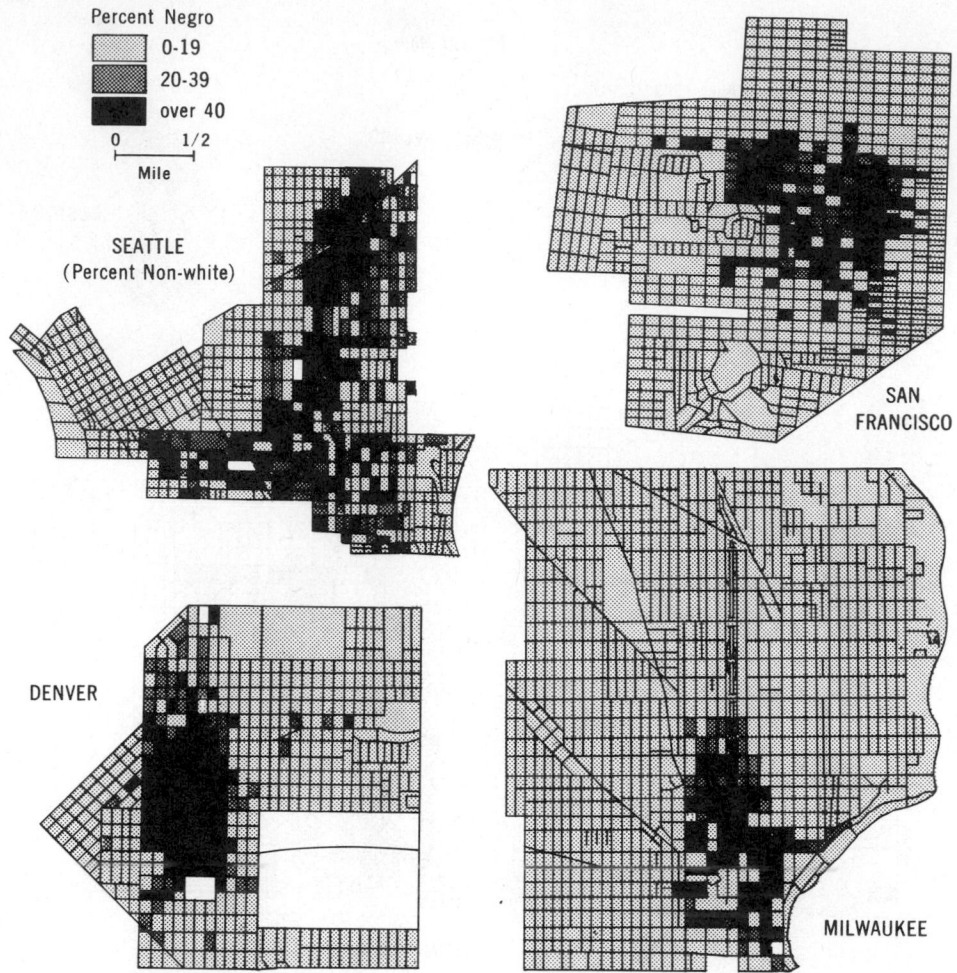

FIGURE 1b.   Variations in Intensity of Black Occupance within Individual Ghetto Spaces, 1950

in each city except Seattle, where net migration seems to have played the dominant role. Migration directly accounted for approximately one-third of the change in the magnitude of the black population in San Francisco, Denver, Milwaukee, and Minneapolis during this interval, while more than one-half of Seattle's change could be accounted for in terms of migration. Only one-fourth of the growth in Indianapolis was associated with migration, while Boston was at the low end of the spectrum with less than fifteen percent of its change being attributed to the migration component. A recent national estimate of the role of migration as a

contributor to black metropolitan growth during the period 1960–1966 was set at 34 percent [1]. It is generally conceded that there has been a slowdown in the rate of movement of blacks out of the South since 1966. Likewise, there is some limited evidence of a sudden downturn in black metropolitan fertility levels since 1966 [22]. The direct contribution of migration to total growth is generally less than that of natural increase, but natural increase is compounded by selectivity in terms of age structure and area of origin of the migrating population. It has been stated that one-half of the population in the 25 to 29 age group abandoned the

Deep South between 1950 and 1960 [30]. Irene Taeuber, in summing up the situation of black population growth during the fifties, said: "The fundamental problem of growth was not so much the extent of the migration as the level of the fertility in the local and in-migrant populations alike" [30: 124]. Thus, the indirect impact of migration on changes in the size of the black population is far reaching.

The ultimate size of the black population within these specific cities at any point in time will be governed by changes in the net volume of migration and the prevailing level of fertility. Fertility levels among the black population continue to remain higher than those of the white population in central cities, even when standardized for age. Urbanization has apparently not had the same impact in reducing fertility levels as it has among other urbanizing groups. Farley [8] has posited, as a partial explanation for the continuation of high levels of fertility among blacks, an improvement in health; that is, the proportion of subfecund elements in the

population has been reduced owing to the lessening of the impact of diseases which, in turn, led to a condition of subfecundity. One is not sure of the role of urbanization on the fertility level of different groups in a society, therefore one's expectations regarding changes in levels of fertility simply as a function of place of residence might be devoid of meaning (see Figure 2).

While it has been demonstrated that the effect of urbanization on fertility is not always apparent among first generation migrant populations, there is evidence which indicates that black women show a pronounced desire to regulate their family size. Bogue [3] in a recent study found that the ideals of reproduction among ghetto women in Chicago were lower than those of the public at large. The extent to which relatively high levels of fertility are likely to continue appears to be a function of level of educational attainment of the black population and of the continuation of past practices of ineffective family planning. This prob-

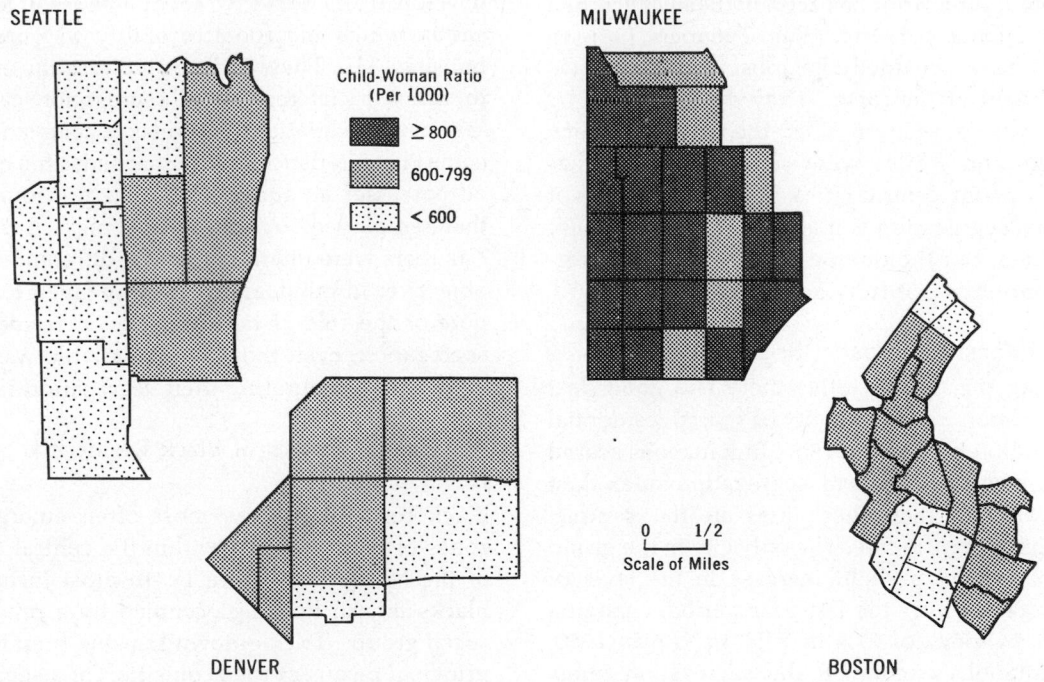

FIGURE 2. Black Fertility Levels in Selected Ghetto Areas, 1950

lem is further compounded by the number of black women that enter the reproductive ages between 1960 and 1990. Taeuber [30] indicates it will be necessary to halve the reproduction rate of black women in order to maintain an unchanging number of births. Finally, the level of fertility among black women might be partially conditioned by the effectiveness of the diffusion of black nationalist philosophies within American urban areas.

THE TERRITORIAL LOCUS OF BLACK POPULATIONS

The previous discussion of the changing magnitude of the black population residing in the sample cities has skirted the locational question of that population within the metropolitan systems. The question of residential location is a very complex one, and explanations for variations in residential location patterns are no less complex. Nevertheless, even the most casual observer is aware that black populations occupy specific zones within metropolitan areas. And, while this phenomenon has been well documented, little work has actually been concerned with spatial patterns. The Taeubers [30], to date, have provided the most comprehensive treatment of the topic. They demonstrated by way of a segregation index the extent to which blacks and whites were separated in the nation's major central cities. The universality of spatial segregation is made quite clear by these scholars, but the unique pattern of spatial segmentation is not fully addressed.

The Intensity of Spatial Segregation

Among the sample cities there is a good deal of variation in the intensity of spatial residential separation by race. In 1960, Indianapolis scored higher on the Taeubers' segregation index than did any of the other cities in the sample. Further, it represented the only city in the group to experience a slight increase in the level of segregation over the ten year period, changing from an index of 91.4 in 1950 to 91.6 in 1960. Indianapolis's score on the segregation index was closer to the Southern regional average

than to that of its region, although the variation is rather minimal. In many ways the Indianapolis pattern of racial residential segregation places it in the category of being more typically Southern than non-Southern. Among the remaining cities, each showed a slight decrease in the intensity of residential segregation. The western region was characterized by the lowest regional segregation index among all regions, and similarly the western cities in the sample demonstrated relatively low scores. San Francisco, with an index of 69.3, was among the lowest of all the cities analyzed by the Taeubers. Minneapolis's score of 79.3 in 1960 was more typically western in its level of residential segregation. Boston, Denver, and Milwaukee all had segregation indexes in the eighties, a pattern which represents the modal class of American cities.

The index employed by the Taeubers has recently come under criticism from Zelder [32, pp. 271–273]. His criticism largely revolves around the development of an index which views urban space as isomorphic. Zelder has developed an alternative set of indexes of segregation which incorporates ability to purchase housing [33]. These indexes indicate the extent to which racial residential segregation can be ascribed to variations in housing costs and income characteristics, and in that sense his method possesses an added advantage not found in that employed by the Taeubers. But the Taeubers were operating with a different set of objectives in mind, and in no way failed to take note of the role of housing cost on residential segregation, even though this variable was not included in computing their segregation index.

The Spatial Pattern of Black Residential Development

Black residential areas most often emerge in zones of older housing within the central cities of the North (see Figure 1). In most instances blacks inherit housing occupied by a previous social group. Trickle-down housing then is the principal means of the acquisition of a segment of the housing stock by black occupants. Historically, in the South housing was built specifically for black occupance and there was little evidence of racial filtering prior to the present generation; today, both forces are operating. While black residential areas are expected to emerge within a specific type of housing environment, the spatial patterning of the initial black enclaves may reflect a single locational cluster or a polynucleated pattern.[1] The specific pattern which emerges generally reflects some of the unique qualities of a specific place as well as conditions prevailing during the historical period of emergence. Further, the absence of spatial contiguity is sometimes attributed to variations in the income characteristics of segments of the black population, which result in those with minimal income being constrained to one zone and those with greater income being found in alternative locations. Likewise, it is apparent that the evolution of spatially noncontiguous entities might well reflect the impact of the locational decision which determines the location of public housing as opposed to the pattern which emerges solely in association with the operation of the private housing market.

The initial zone of black occupance is sometimes regarded as a historical accident. Schmid and McVey [26:3] in describing the evolution of one of Seattle's initial zones of black occupance, attributed the acquisition of the site which became the focus of black residential activity to just such a phenomenon. Thus, the Madison Street area, or the zone which is frequently identified as the Central area, came into existence largely as a result of the relationship which existed between a wealthy black hotel owner and several white pioneer developers of the city of Seattle; a relationship that permitted him to acquire owner-

ship of a tract of land on one of Seattle's several hills, a tract subsequently developed for black occupance. This became the zone of occupance of a group in one stage of the life cycle, while a second area of black occupance was emerging in an alternative zone that was, initially, largely the place of residence of male transients [20]. No doubt a similar situation might have occurred within any of the sample cities. It is apparent that there is a sorting out in space of persons whose housing requirements vary as a function of income and stage in the life cycle. This internal sorting out is frequently not as highly developed as in the larger community, but nevertheless exists. Therefore, if the various types of housing requirements on the part of the individual cannot be fulfilled within a single zone, alternative noncontiguous zones evolve to satisfy these needs. Nowhere does this appear to be more evident than in San Francisco.

In San Francisco, Record [22:11–12] has identified five zones of black population concentration (see Figure 3). These zones are referred to as the Fillmore, Bayview, Hunter's Point, Western Addition, and Ingleside Districts. Referring back to our definition of black enclaves, not all of these zones are spatially noncontiguous. By 1960, the Western Addition and the Fillmore districts represented a single

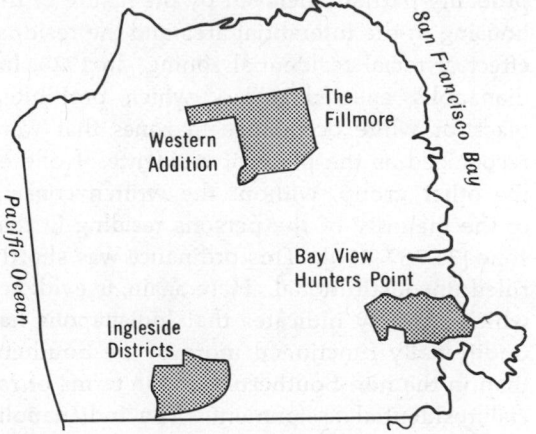

FIGURE 3. Zones of Black Population Concentration, San Francisco

---

[1] Residential enclaves here refer to either (a) that set of contiguous census tracts wherein more than 50 percent of the resident population is described as black; or, (b) if the black population does not yet constitute an entity of sufficient magnitude to form a functional neighborhood, that set of contiguous blocks wherein more than 40 percent of the household heads are identified as nonwhite.

contiguous area, even though they possessed individual territorial identities. Similarly, Hunter's Point and Bayview represented contiguous districts. Ocean View, within the Ingleside District, was a third distinct residential enclave wherein the intensity of black occupancy surpassed the requisite minimal threshold. Fillmore was the area of initial occupance, and expansion has radiated out from there. In this instance, leap frogging was necessary to satisfy the increasing demand for single family, owner-occupied structures. This resulted in the rise of the black, middle income enclave of Ocean View. It was in this area that Laurenti [13] investigated changes in housing value as a function of minority group entry. The Hunter's Point enclave grew out of the development of a temporary public housing complex to provide shelter for war workers.

In a number of cities, individual black enclaves have a tendency to fuse or fill in with an increase in the size of the black population. The rate of fusion is associated with the rate of increase in black housing demand and the distance separating the individual enclaves during the period of initial development. The process of filling-in has been recognized in Boston, Seattle, and Indianapolis. The black enclaves of Milwaukee and Denver have grown as single residential zones devoid of the filling-in process. In Indianapolis this process was probably partially delayed by the nature of the housing in the interstitial area and the residual effect of racial residential zoning. In 1926, Indianapolis enacted a law which prohibited black or white occupance in zones that were recognized as the place of residence of one or the other group, without the written consent of the majority of the persons residing in that zone [31:187–190]. This ordinance was shortly ruled unconstitutional. Here again, is evidence which strongly indicates that Indianapolis has traditionally functioned more in the Southern than in the non-Southern mode in terms of racial residential assignment. The Indianapolis ordinance was fashioned after a similar ordinance that had been legally upheld and permitted to stand in New Orleans [32].

The Economic Characteristics of Ghetto Areas

The process of cluster formation appears to be partially related to the level and extent of economic differentiation within the black population. Variations in the intensity of black occupance within individual clusters are not always apparent, depending upon the scale of analysis. This is especially true in those cities where the initial black population is small. Considering that economic characteristics of the population are unavailable at levels smaller than the census tract and that the proportion of blacks at the tract level is small, one can easily fail to detect local variations in economic status. A crude attempt has been made to coordinate tract and block indicators so as to differentiate the economic characteristics of black residential space during the formative period of development.

In each of the sample cities, an economic characterization was made of the territorial units which contained at least one of the city's black residential enclaves together with the contiguous zones representing areas of potential black residential expansion. This bounded space was then classified according to economic status: lower class areas, working class areas, and middle class areas. The selected terminology is certain to provoke criticism, given the ambiguity surrounding the employment of such terminology. Since the purpose here was to crudely test the notion that black residential enclaves are most often sited initially in the low income sector of the city, this procedure for defining poverty areas was felt to be adequate.

During the past decade, the voluminous literature on poverty has contained numerous definitions of poverty. Many writers have criticized the federal government's use of a fixed value for defining poverty. The method for identifying lower class or poverty areas in this study follows that used by Mooney [17]. A lower class area is a census tract in which the median family income level is two-thirds or less than the median family income for the city. Working class areas were identified as those whose median income ranged between 0.67 and

0.89 of the city's median; and middle class areas were represented by all of those tracts whose median family income level was greater than 0.90 of the city's median. Working class areas were thought to represent those areas above the poverty line, but just below the income level that represented the city's median. It is obvious that these arbitrarily chosen limits possess serious drawbacks, but they possess the advantage of promoting easy comparison from city to city through time.

The most intensive areas of black occupance during the early stages of development are to be found in areas of lower and working class neighborhoods. But as expansion continues, middle class zones likewise become intensively settled by segments of the black population. Of course, at the same time, the areas themselves undergo changes in their relative positions on the income scale. (Most of the neighborhoods in the sample cities dropped one level between 1950 and 1960.) Since the bulk of the black population would be largely concentrated in lower and working class neighborhoods, given variations in the demand for housing, expansion takes place within each of the neighborhood types along a continuum of variation in intensity of black occupance. That is, if neighborhoods representing each of the income classes are found along one or more of the edges of the zone of original black occupance, entry will be initiated in keeping with the nature of the housing demand.

Various writers have attempted to develop a set of descriptive terms to spatially differentiate the level of black occupance. The Taeubers, as well as other ecologists, have chosen to employ such terms as "established Negro areas" and "zones of succession and invasion" to reflect these differences. McEntire [15:34] employs a somewhat different approach to the problem. He employs the terms: "segregated" when the census tracts contain 75 percent or more nonwhite persons; "concentrated" when the level of intensity is between 50 and 74 percent; "mixed" when 10 to 49 percent is nonwhite; "dispersed" when it is 1 to 9 percent; and "exclusion" when the proportion is less than 1 percent. In the study here, the selected terminology reflects the process orientation of the Taeubers as well as the static descriptive terminology of McEntire. Neighborhoods or census tracts characterized by having 75 percent or more of their population black are termed ghetto core neighborhoods; those containing less than 75 percent, but 50 percent or more are designated ghetto fringe neighborhoods; and those with levels of black occupance between 30 and 49 percent are described as neighborhoods in transition. The areas contiguous to the zones of transition during a specific interval might be referred to as zones of temporary stability. The 30 percent value was employed as the lower limit for designating areas as transitional, since many writers have come to view it as a significant threshold value that elicits a response from white persons in the form of acceleration of outmovement. The point to be emphasized here is that, regardless of the intensity of black neighborhood occupance, at any given point in time a single neighborhood can be identified as a middle class, working class, or lower class area. Thus, it is possible for a transitional neighborhood to be lower class, or a core neighborhood to be middle class. The appropriate designation seems to be largely a function of location in the city and the economic characteristics of its previous residents.

Those who have previously concerned themselves with economic differentiation within black residential zones tend to verify the existence of an increase in the level of socioeconomic status with distance from the city center. Marston [14] has also indicated that emerging black neighborhoods are characterized by higher status than established neighborhoods, regardless of their location. This would indicate that a zone in transition is always characterized by the presence of higher class persons than core areas or fringe areas, irrespective of where they are located within the urban milieu. Among our sample cities, this was not always found to be true. In Denver in 1950 and Seattle in 1960, transitional neighborhoods which were closer to the city center were characterized as lower class and lower-to-working class, while fringe and core neighborhoods located slightly farther from the center of the city were characterized as working class areas. It does appear to be true that the transitional areas that possess the more peripheral locations are always higher status areas. Thus, transitional areas in the initial time period are generally working class or middle class areas.

Areas clearly undergo change within relatively short periods of time. Middle class neighborhoods within a period of ten years can be transformed into working class areas, and working class areas into lower class areas. These changes no doubt reflect the rate of urban spatial expansion and the availability of alternative housing choices. This phenomenon facilitates the filtering process. It appears that in the ecology of ghetto formation middle income blacks move into zones contiguous to those that might be described as core or fringe neighborhoods and thereby set middle income whites into flight. An increase in the vacancy rate permits working class blacks to gain access to such areas. Likewise, a similar phenomenon appears to characterize the transformation from working class area to lower class area.

Static analyses based on census data generally show that whites and blacks occupying ghetto fringe areas possess similar economic status, but dissimilar life cycle characteristics. This fact tends to be corroborated in all of the sample cities with the exception of Indianapolis. In Indianapolis, areas undergoing racial change most often include middle income whites and working class blacks, or working class whites and lower class blacks. Whether this reflects the lessened importance of propinquity when social status remains unthreatened or something else is not clear. What is clear, though, is that this represents an anomalous situation among the cities in the sample. Whether the changes which occur when blacks enter neighborhoods of any given description reflect responses to class differences or differences in style of living is a topic of increasing interest.

Life Style Differences Within Ghetto Space

The unwillingness of groups who possess dissimilar life styles to share social space is apparently a widespread phenomenon. Suttles [28], in describing the use and identification with space in a very small area in Chicago, used the term "ordered segmentation" to illustrate ethnic identification with territory. Territoriality, or ordered segmentation, generally escapes the attention of researchers who employ only objective data in areal analysis. This is an obvious shortcoming of attempts to specify the level of racial integration within areal units by specifying simply the proportion of the population of a given racial identity residing in an area. Molotch's [16] recent analysis of a community in the throes of racial transition points out that there is little sharing of basic institutional facilities among blacks and whites within the community. He clearly identifies the existence of ordered segmentation within this territorial realm and points out that the area might be described as racially integrated in a demographic sense, but this does not connote the existence of social interaction, and that there is to be found little evidence of an interactional type of integration which he describes as transracial solidarity [16]. Dissimilarity in life styles are associated with differences in cultural or subcultural characteristics which are held in high esteem among individual groups. Territories which are the site of groups possessing incongruent life styles frequently promote a flight reaction on the part of that group which views its value system as being threatened.

The life style of black Americans is generally described as lower class, as it is the lower income segment of the black population that has been the focus of most social science research. Life style differences within the black community do exist, as Hannerz [12] has recently demonstrated by identifying four main life styles within a single low income neighborhood in Washington, D. C. Hannerz attributes the evolution of black culture to at least three specific forces, other than poverty which is frequently employed as a principal explanatory variable. These factors are to be found in African origin, Southern background, and subjection to racism [12: 178–188].

The ghetto-specific life style which has evolved is frequently described by social scientists as pathological, as it represents a deviant case when measured against the white middle class pattern which is considered normative. This kind of an assessment leads to further problems as it ignores the validity of the evolution of distinctive patterns of behavior which are valued by their practitioners. The devaluation of unique black attributes on the part of white America has led to demands for the development of cultural nationalism and the maintenance of cultural integrity on the part of black Americans. Until there is more information available which describes the relationship between culture and the use of space, it will be difficult to specify the most satisfactory living environment for groups possessing unique life styles. There is great need for hard data on this subject. The lack of such data leads to pseudo-scientific speculation about the nature of behavior and its consequences for urban America.

A noted political scientist [2] was recently inclined to speculate about the role of culture in urban problems. A novel nomenclature was employed to distinguish variations in expected group behavior, referred to as class culture. While the concept of class and culture are not independent, neither are they synonymous, and thus combining the two concepts does not lead to clarification or order. But, in this instance, a novel definition is derived, which is based upon the extent to which individuals are present or future-oriented. Persons who are members of the lower class culture are said to be present-oriented, and thus the situation in which they find themselves is an inextricable one. This point is driven home by the following comment:

> He does not care how dirty and dilapidated his housing is either inside or out, nor does he mind the inadequacy of such public facilities as schools, parks, and libraries; indeed, where such things exist he destroys them by acts of vandalism if he can. Features that make the slums repellent to others actually please him. He finds it satisfying in several ways [2: 62].

The writer is careful to point out that while black Americans represent the largest single segment of persons possessing the lower class culture in American cities, that by and large most black Americans are not possessors of this life style. Such a disclaimer will not serve as a very convincing argument for those who will interpret this treatment as racist—a fact that the writer is aware of [2]. But, in the absence of hard data, notions of the type developed out of the class culture concept are likely to be proliferated. Thus, the only point on which there appears to be consensus at this time is that persons possessing dissimilar life styles seldom share a common social space, even when found in close physical proximity to one another. What is sorely needed at this point are more definitive works which get at the crux of the problem of the impact of culture on the use of space at the neighborhood level.

THE HOUSING MARKET

The pattern of the spatial distribution of black people in American cities largely reflects the nature of the operation of housing markets, but housing markets themselves simply mirror the value systems of the larger society. The manner in which housing is allocated in northern urban markets has generally led to complaints that the markets act as a quasi-closed system denying free access to the full spectrum of choice, as determined by one's ability to pay. Traditionally, one's choice was limited to the range of housing types found in zones which were written off as markets within which prospective white buyers would no longer consider making a purchase. Attempts to correct such practices have emanated from the office of the President of the United States in the form of an executive order and from the Congress in the form of open occupancy legislation. There are those who contend that these interventionist strategies, which are aimed at altering the practices of realtors, will not promote the anticipated results as long as preferences remain wherein persons possessing common racial characteristics choose to live near one another.

Muth [19, pp. 106–111], in an examination of a series of hypotheses attempting to explain the operation of the housing market in promoting racial residential segregation, rejected the hypothesis which puts the onus of responsibility on the real estate operator and accepted the hypothesis that customers exercised preferences. He is of the opinion that white persons have a greater aversion to residing among blacks than do other blacks; therefore, the realtors are only responding to the tastes of their customers. This is clearly in line with the notion that "real estate interests are strong supporters of the perceived public will" [23: 11]. Muth indicates that tactics designed to correct these practices will result in penalizing the real estate fraternity for simply catering to the wishes of its clientele [19: 109]. Strict economic interpretation fails to comprehend the broad range of social implications associated with such a judgment. While the customer preference hypothesis has more appeal in terms of its logic than the alternative hypotheses, the evidence which portends to verify the congruence of the tastes of the customer and those of the real estate industry might possibly be faulty, at least in some situations. Likewise, the assumption that the real estate industry is principally concerned with its customers, who happen to be white, may also be faulty. In fact, it appears that the industry is simply fearful of offending a segment of the population which they possibly perceive as their most important potential customers.

One of the principal objectives of this paper is to assess the manner in which the housing market has operated in the sample cities in promoting the evolution of black residential communities, which have come to be regarded as ghettos. It has been argued elsewhere that these communities need not bear euphemisms of this form, but for the time being, given the mechanism by which such communities come into existence, the assigned terminology still possesses merit [25]. The ultimate identification of black residential communities will have to be determined by the residents themselves.

In each city the focus is on one or two black residential clusters. The clusters were framed or bounded in such a way that the bounded zone might be able to satisfy the housing needs of an expanding black population over a ten-year interval. The bounded space was designated ghetto space, as it was assumed that it would operate as a closed system wherein all black residential demands reflecting growth of the original core population would be satisfied. These very stringent assumptions are not totally realistic as they represent a situation of strict segregation, when in fact there is evidence which indicates that approximately ten percent of black metropolitan populations reside outside of contiguous black residential clusters. Needless to say, the ghetto escape rate varies from one urban center to another, but the variance tends to be small.

In 1960, 82.9 percent of Milwaukee's black population resided in the ghetto core and fringe, or what has been locally designated the "inner core," while another 12 percent was found in a contiguous changing area [7]. Thus, 95 percent of Milwaukee's black population resided within a single bounded space. Similar patterns prevailed both in Denver, Boston, and Seattle at the same time. The distance separating individual black residential clusters in San Francisco and Minneapolis resulted in confining attention to a single ghetto space rather than the two or more which were actually present in these two cities. Thus, in both San Francisco and Minneapolis a smaller fraction of the total black population came under scrutiny than was the case in the remaining cities. A further complicating factor in analyzing housing market behavior in San Francisco and Seattle was the presence of other nonwhite groups in the population. The problem was less serious in San Francisco, as the principal oriental residential zone was noncontiguous to the black residential area under investigation.

THE GHETTO DEVELOPER MODEL

If one assumes that the customer preference hypothesis of Muth is essentially correct, then a model describing the spatial allocation of housing to segments of the black population should not be too difficult to develop. The model employed here has been described previously [25] as a ghetto developer model; it is a member of that family of models usually identified as simulation models. The ghetto developer model incorporates parameters which describe the assumed responses of whites to black occupance at the block level. The model subsequently generates individual household assignments as a function of housing cost and tenure characteristics of the universe of residential blocks within ghetto space. These operations have been described elsewhere [25] as producer and consumer components of the model, respectively. These are components which are internal to the model. The demand component, here termed the demographic vector, is external to the spatial allocation segment of the model, and utilizes data at the tract level rather than the block level. The model might be described as a mixed model, as it employs both deterministic and probabilistic components.

The housing producer or vacancy mechanism, which is here referred to as the vector of white response to black encroachment, represents a deterministic component. The response vector was developed on intuitive grounds and represents an attempt to operationalize the notion of the existence of a tipping process. In this instance, a curve was developed describing variations in the intensity of the white response as a function of the level of blacks present in a block during a previous interval (see Figure 4). Thus, instead of employing a single point to represent a critical threshold, a series of thresholds was described along a continuum.

No attempt was made to differentiate the white response on the basis of identifiable objective characteristics, as this would indicate a strength of understanding of behavior that is lacking. Therefore, the same response parameters were employed in each of the sample cities as a means of generating housing vacancies within the individual ghetto spaces. Given differences in both the objective and subjective characteristics of the resident white population located within the bounded area, a great deal of variation in actual response should be anticipated. But even if the response vector which is predicated upon assumed behavior at the household level were essentially accurate, the actual mobility patterns might be conditioned by decisions made by the public sector. Only if there were no changes in the quantity of housing existing within a given block could reasonable results be expected under the best of conditions. In older areas of the city such as these, demolitions and conversions are fairly commonplace and thereby further reduce the strength of the behavior variable in generating accurate results.

The housing assignment component of the model reflects the known propensity of blacks to seek housing within specific cost categories and possessing given tenure characteristics.

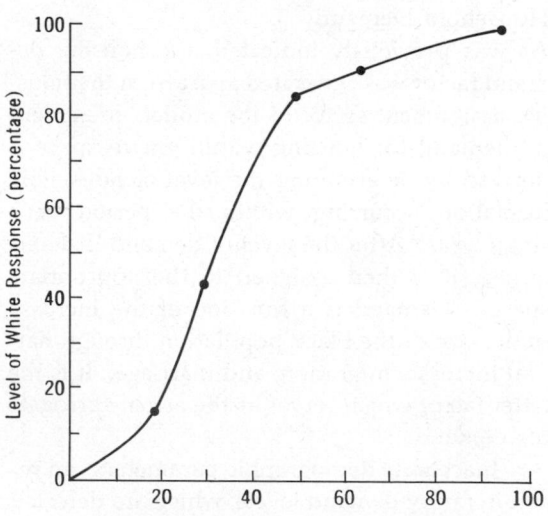

FIGURE 4.   Variations in the Intensity of White Response as a Function of Percent Black

Within the individual ghetto space of each of the sample cities, a household assignment probability surface was developed which illustrates variations in the cost of both rental and owner occupancy housing at the block level. The probability of receiving an assignment in a given block was determined first as to whether the assignee was a renter or a buyer, and second, on the basis of the known proportion of persons residing in blocks with specified housing cost characteristics at the beginning of the interval. There is a weakness in employing conditions existing at the beginning of the period to determine assignments throughout a ten-year interval, but in the absence of a sounder alternative, data for a single time interval were employed. Thus, the assignment probabilities are not influenced by dynamic changes taking place within local housing markets. An attempt was made to alter the tenure characteristic of demand over time, so as to reflect the average rate of change in demand for owner-occupied versus renter-occupied units through the ten-year interval. This was possible simply because the model was initially run post-facto.

Determining the Level of
Household Demand
As was previously indicated, the housing demand factor was generated apart from the housing assignment sector of the model. Incremental demand for housing within ghetto space is derived by determining the level of household formation occurring within the period of a single year. After the level of demand is determined, it is then assigned to the appropriate spaces. Demand is a function of the increase in the size of the black population through natural increase, migration, and marriage. It is the latter factor which serves as the actual surrogate for demand.

Inaccurate demographic parameters can result in faulty demand levels, which are detected in highly incorrect spatial patterns during any given time interval. Needless to say, even if levels of black housing demand are fairly ac-

curate, the simulated spatial patterns are sometimes characterized by a poor fit when compared with the actual pattern of residential assignment. The projections of future housing demand are characterized by the same weaknesses that characterize any attempt to specify the level of the population at some future point in time. The method chosen to specify the general level of demand, that is, the number of marriages occurring annually, might provide a more accurate index in a more stable population. The common practice among some sectors of the black population of forming nonlegal unions and the existence of a disproportionate number of female heads of households tends to increase the margin of error in the surrogate for demand. This is particularly true when one operates with a static set of marriage rates that may or may not describe the behavior of the population under investigation.

Model Results
The success of the model in predicting the incremental change in the level of housing demand on the part of the black population residing within ghetto space between 1950 and 1960 was highly variable. The error varied from less than one percent in Boston to more than 50 percent in Minneapolis. The margin of error for Indianapolis was only 2.5 percent. The margin of error for Milwaukee, Seattle, and San Francisco was 7, 10, and 15 percent, respectively, while Denver was characterized by a margin of error of approximately 35 percent. The unduly large error associated with Minneapolis occurred as a result of the elimination of a large volume of housing within ghetto space, resulting in demand being satisfied in an alternative bounded space. In the Denver case, the selected demographic parameters failed to produce realistic results. Denver represents the sole case in which the demand level was under-represented. It appears that the smallest error in demand is associated with those cities where migration played only a minor role in its contribution to total population growth.

Given the wide variation in the ability of the model to specify, within reasonable limits of accuracy, the level of black housing demand over a ten-year period, one might logically expect similar results to characterize the ability of the spatial assignment mechanism in the performance of its function. It is possible, though, for the spatial assignment mechanism to allocate the generated demand in a fashion which closely reflects the operation of the housing market, provided that the operating parameters are essentially correct. If this should occur, it is only the variations in intensity of occupance at specific time intervals that are in error rather than the basic operation of the model. But like the demand component of the model, the spatial assignment was characterized by wide rang-

ing results in its ability to predict accurately the emerging pattern of black occupance.

The success of the model in replicating the actual housing assignment process varies with the scale employed to judge the success of the operation. Since the model was calibrated on a block basis, it appears only logical to test the results at this level. The simulated results for each city show only a few instances wherein the simulated level of black occupance varies less than 20 percent from the actual level of occupance. The less than ten percent variation on a block basis occurs on a very limited scale, especially outside of ghetto core neighborhoods (see Figures 5a and 5b).

The best block level performances are to be found in changing neighborhoods in Boston

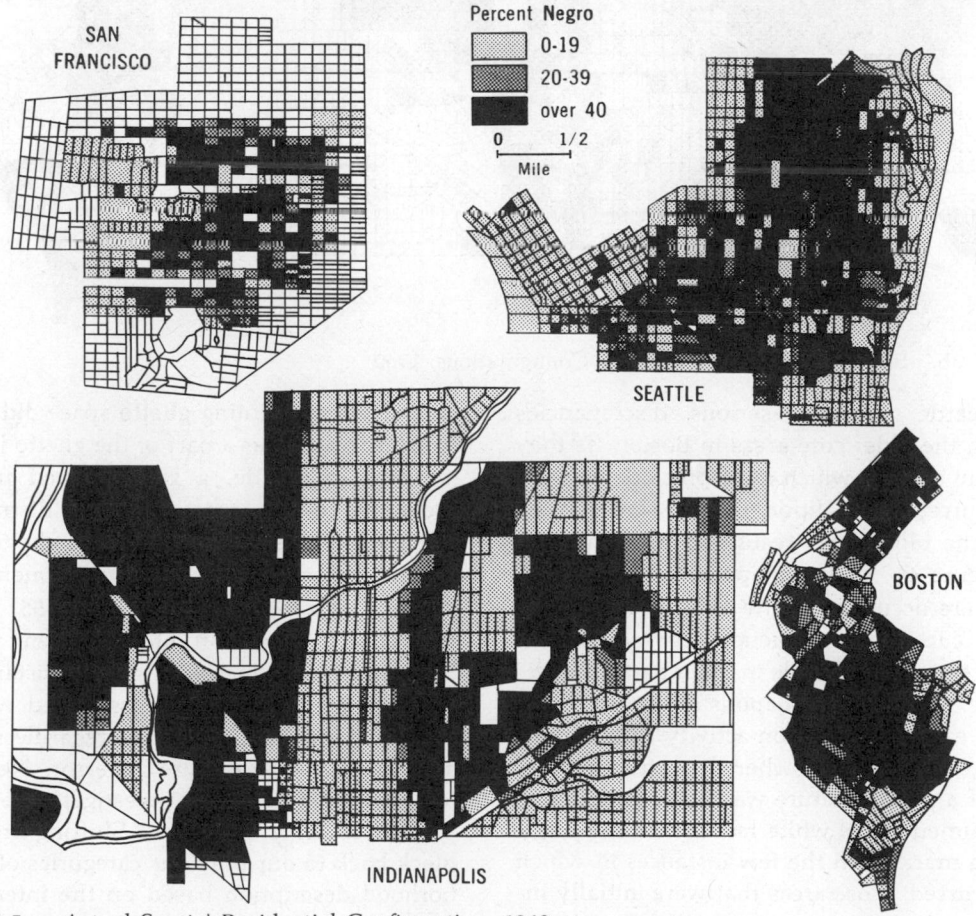

FIGURE 5a. Actual Spatial Residential Configuration, 1960

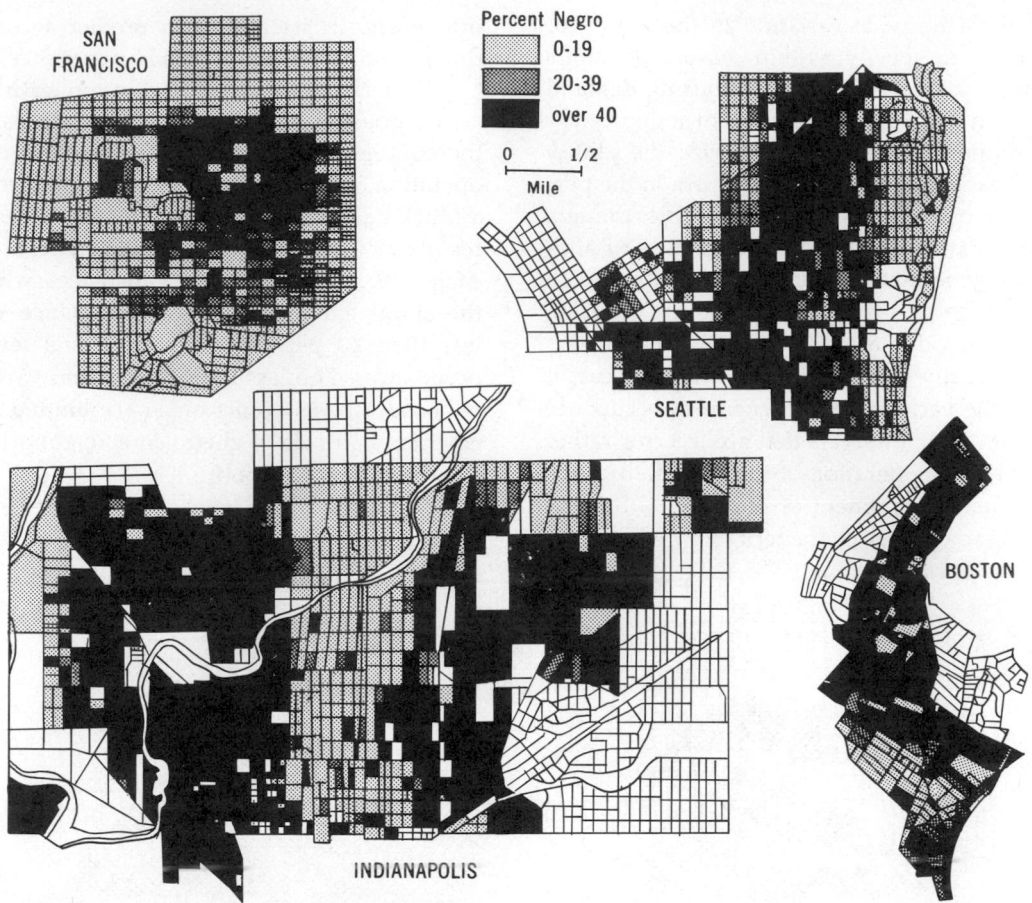

FIGURE 5b.   Simulated Spatial Residential Configurations, 1960

and Seattle. Various serious discrepancies occur in the older core areas in Boston, as they represent areas in which widespread demolition has occurred. Demolition likewise seriously affected the block level results in San Francisco (see Figure 6). In Indianapolis, while demolitions were occurring in the older core areas of black occupance, construction activity was taking place on a larger scale in other parts of ghetto space. Only in Indianapolis did construction activity exceed demolition activity within ghetto space. Elsewhere, where construction activity of a private nature was being conducted, it was aimed at the white rather than the black housing market. In the few instances in which this occurred, those areas that were initially in-

cluded as representing ghetto space did not effectively operate as a part of the ghetto housing market. In Seattle, a zone located in close proximity to the central business district was effectively voided as a segment of ghetto space by the construction of new apartment units within that zone. Morrill [18, p. 355] has remarked that expansion into apartment areas in Seattle has been met with great resistance.

The amount of error associated with the simulated outcome is serious, regardless of the scale employed to analyze the error. Nevertheless, it is instructive to investigate the spatial pattern of error variation. Shifting from the block back to our previous categories of neighborhood description based on the intensity of

NET CHANGE IN HOUSING STOCK

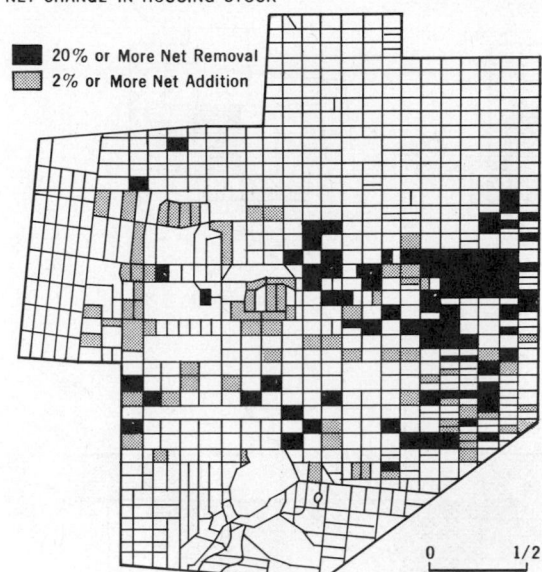

- ■ 20% or More Net Removal
- ▧ 2% or More Net Addition

0   1/2

Scale of Miles

FIGURE 6.   Demolition and Construction Activity in San Francisco Ghetto Space, 1950–1960

black occupance, one can employ as a measure of error the actual and predicted neighborhood identities. Core neighborhoods, fringe neighborhoods, transitional neighborhoods, and temporarily stable neighborhoods were the categories employed for description. The matter of predicting the specific state of a neighborhood some period of years removed from the present appears to be a more realistic way of evaluating model success than a simple accounting of total misidentifications. If the latter measure is employed, it can be shown that the greatest error in predicting future outcomes occurred in the model's treatment of San Francisco, for 80 percent of the neighborhoods were improperly identified.

The extent of the discrepancy between the actual and the simulated patterns in the San Francisco case can be partially attributed to choosing a bounded space that exceeded the necessary scale so as to satisfy the housing needs of the black population under conditions of strict segregation. Employing this same mea-

sure of absolute error in neighborhood identification, Indianapolis was characterized by the least amount of error, 30 percent (see Figure 7). Each of the other cities was found to be somewhere between these two, but generally being characterized by a slightly less than 50 percent error.

More significant than the total error are the neighborhood types that are most often incorrectly identified by the model. This tends to vary somewhat from city to city. The least serious error is universally associated with the identification of core neighborhoods, and the most serious error tends to be associated with identifying neighborhoods in transition. It is the spread of the black population into the more remote parts of ghetto space where the model most often was unable to provide accurate results. Forty percent of the error in identifying neighborhoods in San Francisco was associated with the identification of temporarily stable neighborhoods. These neighborhoods were most often identified as neighborhoods in transition. The selection of a smaller bounded space might have resulted in an improvement in the outcome.

Finally, the predicted outcomes might be assessed within the framework of an evolving zonal pattern. A series of concentric bands possessing one-quarter mile radii were drawn around the center or centers of the most intensive black concentrations occurring in each of the sample cities in the year 1950. In order to measure the extent of change in spatial spread of the black population over a ten-year interval, the actual percentage of black households found in each band was compared with the simulated percentage. In employing this technique only the gross features of spatial expansion can be detected. Nevertheless, the technique does permit one to observe indirectly the outcome of white response to black encroachment at varying distances from the location of the original cluster.

The curve describing the simulated variation in intensity of occupance with distance

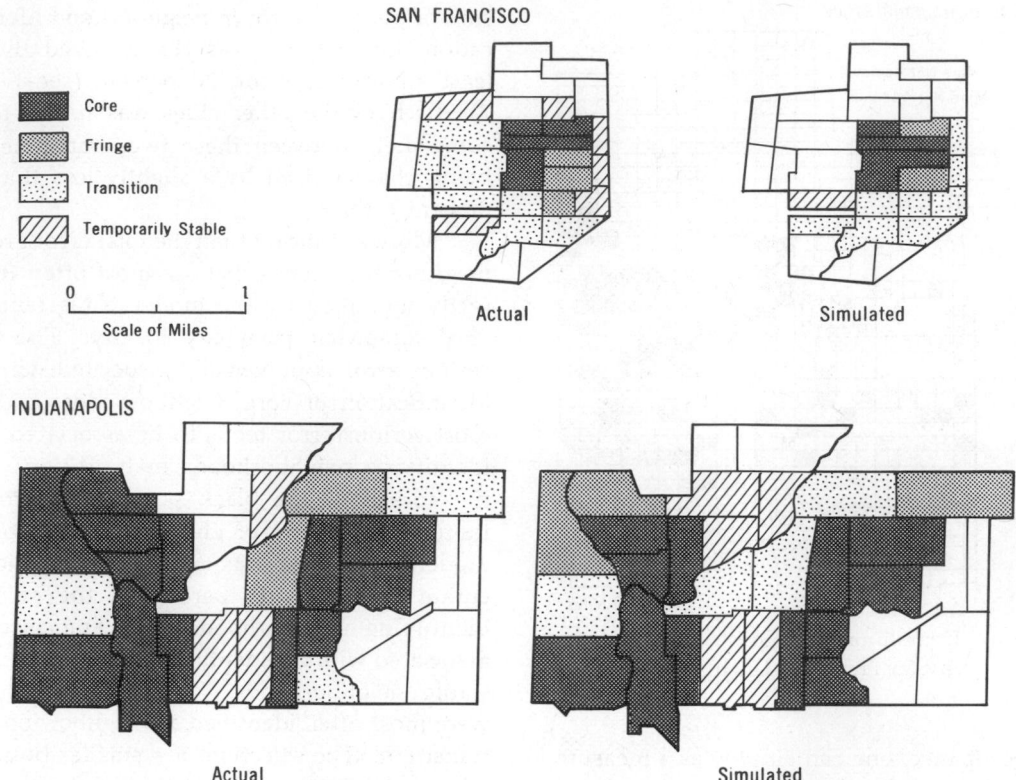

FIGURE 7. Actual and Simulated Neighborhood Types, San Francisco and Indianapolis, 1960

from an initial cluster bears the same general form as the actual curve in each of the sample cities. The most nearly congruent situation occurs in Seattle. It would appear, then, that the behavioral component of the model best describes the behavior of the residents of ghetto space in Seattle. In Milwaukee this component seriously underestimates white reaction to black neighbors. Only in San Francisco was there clear evidence of the white response mechanism failing to overpredict the proportion of whites in more than a single band. In one zone in Boston there was also evidence that the proportion of white residents had been underpredicted. But as a rule, the proportion of whites in each distance band was overpredicted. Thus, the cumulative impact of the response mechanism is to underestimate white reaction to the presence of black neighbors (see Figure 8).

Alterations in the Structure of Ghetto Space

After evaluating the workability of the model in producing simulated black residential patterns during the ten year interval 1950 to 1960, a number of changes were introduced as a means of trying to reproduce more realistic spatial patterns. One of the most obvious errors in the simulated spatial patterns was the greater dispersal of black residents within ghetto space than actually occurred. This weakness was evident in the simulated results in each city.

Before providing the model with 1960 information on population and housing characteristics used to develop future patterns, changes were made in the handling of ghetto space. During the previous ten-year interval, the total area described as ghetto space was potentially available for black occupance throughout the entire time interval. The free access to all housing within ghetto space, conditioned

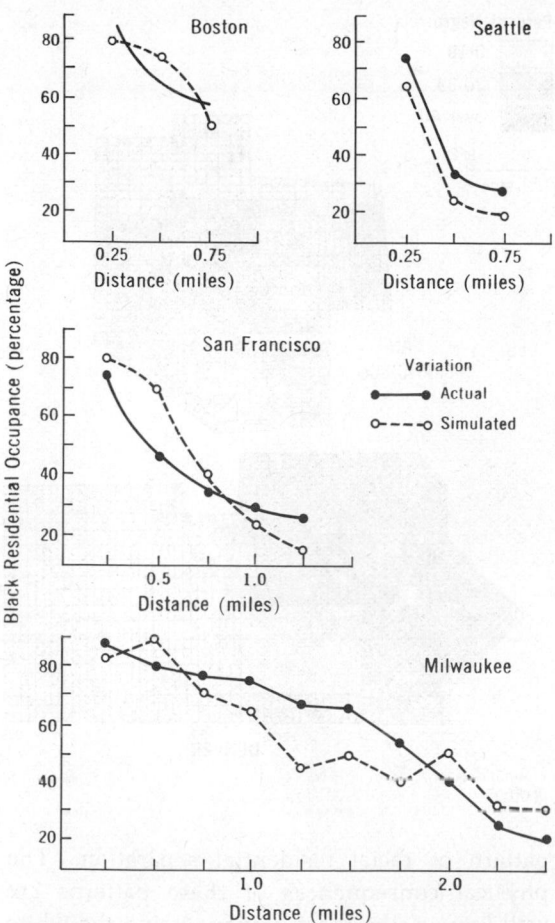

FIGURE 8. Actual and Simulated Response Curves

only by housing cost and tenure characteristics, no doubt strongly contributed to a pattern of excessive dispersion. In order to correct for this weakness, ghetto space was segmented for entry during specific time intervals. Thus, a zone enclosing those areas already heavily occupied by black residents was open to further black entry during an initial three-year period, and other zones within the bounded space were made available for entry at later times. These temporal-spatial constraints did not preclude the possibility of black households receiving an assignment in a restricted area; but because the white response vector was not operating in the quasi-restricted areas, the available vacancies would not exceed the normal vacancy rate and would thereby limit the number of potential as-

signments. Thus, the outer zones during the initial interval would still be open to white entry, a phenomenon which actually occurred.

One serious problem which arises when ghetto space is segmented strictly on the basis of distance zones is a failure to take into consideration the spatial pattern of housing costs and tenure types. If this matter is unattended, then the problem arises of being unable to match householders with units for which they have a known propensity to purchase. When this occurs, adjustments have to be made in the housing cost assignment mechanism, which then assigns persons with lower housing cost propensities to blocks which call for persons with a higher propensity. These kinds of adjustments must be made in the real world in response to the dynamics of the market. By employing static parameters, the possibility of producing changes in the wrong direction as they relate to housing cost might occur. What actually occurs in the adjustment process with regard to housing cost is unclear, but making adjustments in the structure of ghetto space has opened up another significant area for investigation.

After making these and other minor changes in the model's operation, black residential patterns were simulated for five of the original seven cities covering the period 1960 to 1970 (three of the cities are shown in Figure 9). No attempt has as yet been made to evaluate the model's success other than through casual observation. The model performed poorly in Milwaukee and Denver. Similar observations indicate that a much more realistic simulated spatial configuration characterizes the output for Boston, San Francisco, and Seattle.

SUMMARY AND CONCLUSIONS

The previous attempt to describe the spatial evolution of black residential communities by observing the pattern of development in a selected set of cities possessing small black populations during an initial period has demonstrat-

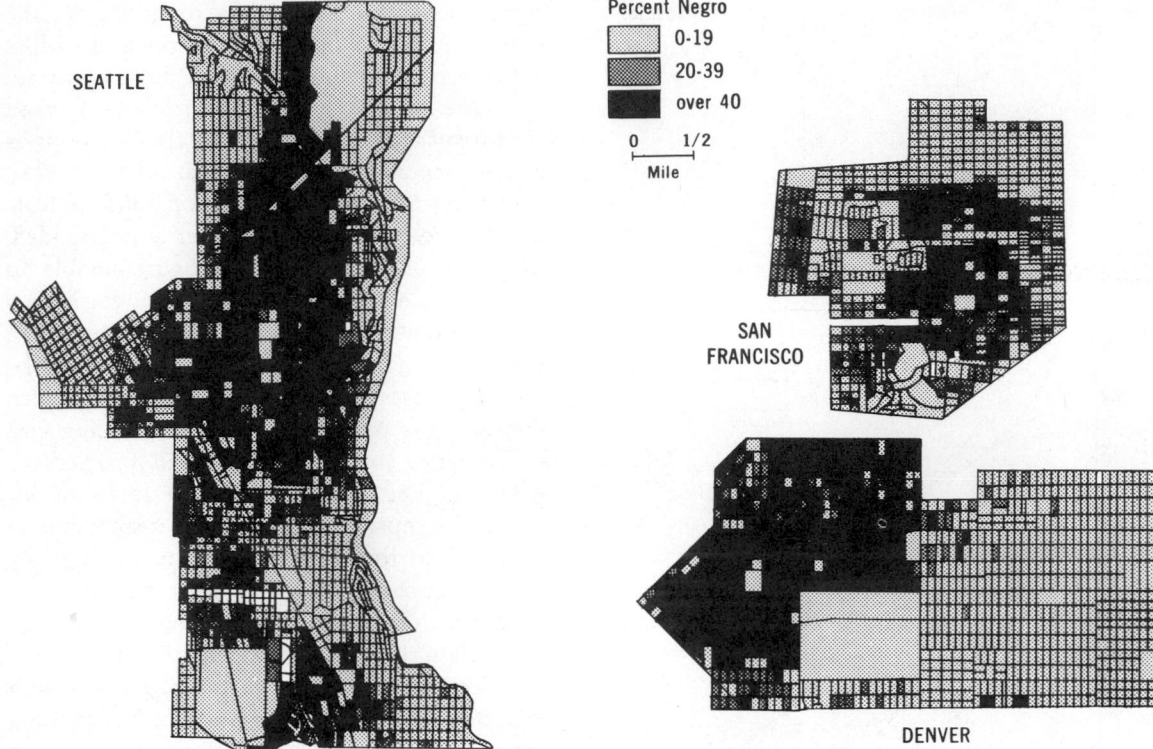

FIGURE 9.   Simulated Black Residential Configurations, 1970

ed that a basic set of forces appear to operate universally. While regional variations tend to occur in the strength of the basic forces, the end result in each instance is the emergence of residential communities which are largely populated by black residents. The principal difference tends to be the amount of time required for a community to move through the transition from white to black. Only one of the sample cities tends to deviate significantly from the others in the manner in which black residential communities tend to evolve. In this instance, Indianapolis represented the deviant case, as it tended to conform in many respects to the basic paradigm of black community development in Southern cities.

The continuation of the forces that led to the initial emergence of incipient ghettos in the sample cities and ultimately in full blown ghettos (areas in excess of 100,000 black residents) has done much to promote an intense national

pattern of racial residential separation. The physical consequences of these patterns are well known, the most obvious being the white exodus to the suburbs and the growing dominance of blacks in the central cities. The social consequences of the phenomenon are highly debatable, but nevertheless of increasing social concern. Since 1968, some weak efforts have been made to alter the spatial pattern of black residential development through the use of programs associated with recent housing legislation. The success of these attempts is difficult to evaluate at this time, but it is possible that such efforts could lead to a more polynucleated pattern of black residential development than currently exists. Furthermore, these attempts could provide black householders with a more complete range of housing choices within given cost categories. At the same time, some segments of the black population will view these as attempts to reduce the growing black political potential that emerges from residential separation.

The failure of efforts of the type mentioned above will no doubt result in the emergence of an ever larger number of super-ghettos wherein the life chances of the average black resident are depressed rather than enhanced.

While this need not be the case, there is little evidence from past experiences to indicate the contrary. If the pattern does in fact continue in an unaltered form, then black Americans are likely to be no nearer a satisfactory housing environment than they were a decade ago, or even a generation ago.

REFERENCES

1. Alonzo, W. "What Are New Towns For?" *Urban Studies*, 7 (February 1970): 42.

2. Banfield, E. C. *The Unheavenly City*. Boston: Little, Brown and Company, 1970.

3. Bogue, D. J. "Family Planning in the Negro Ghettos of Chicago," *The Milbank Memorial Fund Quarterly*, 48 (April 1970): 284–286.

4. Davis, K., and E. Langlois. *Future Demographic Growth of the San Francisco Bay Area*. Berkeley: University of California Press, 1963.

5. Duncan, O. D. et al. *Metropolis and Region*. Baltimore: Johns Hopkins Press, 1960.

6. Drake, St. Clair. "The Social and Economic Status of the Negro in the United States," *Daedalus* (Fall 1965).

7. Edwards, O. L. "Patterns of Residential Segregation within a Metropolitan Ghetto," *Demography*, 7 (May 1970). [No. 48 in this volume.]

8. Farley, R. "Fertility Among Urban Blacks," *The Milbank Memorial Fund Quarterly*, 48 (April 1970): 192–193.

9. Frieden, B. J. "Housing and National Urban Goals," in J. Q. Wilson (ed.), *The Metropolitan Enigma*. Cambridge: Harvard University Press, 1968.

10. Friedman, J., and J. Miller. "The Urban Field," *Journal of the American Institute of Planners*, 31 (November 1965).

11. Hall, E. T. *The Hidden Dimension*. New York: Doubleday, 1966.

12. Hannerz, U. *Soulside, An Inquiry into Ghetto Culture*. New York: Columbia University Press, 1969.

13. Laurenti, L. *Property Values and Race*. Berkeley: University of California Press, 1961.

14. Marston, W. G. "Socioeconomic Differentiation within Negro Areas of American Cities," *Social Forces*, 48 (December 1969).

15. McEntire, D. *Residence and Race*. Berkeley: University of California Press, 1960.

16. Molotch, H. "Racial Integration in a Transition Community," *American Sociological Review*, 34 (December 1969): 878–893.

17. Mooney, J. D. "Urban Poverty and Labor Force Participation," *The American Economic Review*, 57 (March 1967).

18. Morrill, R. L. "The Negro Ghetto: Problems and Alternatives," *The Geographical Review*, 55 (July 1965).

19. Muth, R. F. *Cities and Housing*. Chicago: University of Chicago Press, 1969.

20. Northwood, L. K., and E. A. T. Barth. *Urban Desegregation, Negro Pioneers and Their White Neighbors*. Seattle: University of Washington Press, 1965.

21. *One Year Later*. New York: Frederick Praeger, 1969.

22. Record, W. *Minority Groups and Intergroup Relations in the San Francisco Bay Area*. Berkeley: University of California Press, 1963.

23. Rose, H. M. "Social Processes in the City: Race and Urban Residential Choice." Commission on College Geography, Resource Paper No. 6, Washington, D.C.: Association of American Geographers, 1969.

24. Rose, H. M. "The Origin and Pattern of Development of Urban Black Social Areas," *The Journal of Geography*, (September 1969): 327–332.

25. Rose, H. M. "The Development of an Urban Subsystem: The Case of the Negro Ghetto," *Annals of the Association of American Geographers*, 60 (March 1970).

26. Schmid, C. F. and W. W. McVey, Jr. *Growth and Distribution of Minority Races in Seattle, Washington*. Seattle: Seattle Public Schools, 1964.

27. Schnore, L. F., and H. Sharp. "Racial Changes in Metropolitan Areas, 1950–1960," *Social Forces*, 41 (March 1963).

28. Suttles, G. D. *The Social Order of the Slum*. Chicago: University of Chicago Press, 1968.

29. Taeuber, I. B. "Change and Transition of the Black Population in the United States," *Population Index*, 34 (April-June 1968): pp. 124–145.

30. Taeuber, K. E., and A. F. Taeuber. *Negroes in Cities*. Chicago: Aldine Publishing Company, 1965.

31. Thornbrough, E. L. "Segregation in Indiana During the Klan Era of the 1920s," in A. Meier and E. Rudwick (eds.), *The Making of Black America*, Vol. 2. New York: Atheneum, 1969.

32. Zelder, R. E. "Residential Desegregation: Can Nothing be Accomplished?" *Urban Affairs Quarterly*, 5 (March 1970).

33. Zelder, R. E. "Racial Segregation in Urban Housing Markets," *Journal of Regional Science*, 10 (1970): 96–101.

48

OZZIE L. EDWARDS

Patterns of Residential Segregation Within a Metropolitan Ghetto

The residential segregation of families by income and by stage of the family life cycle within Milwaukee's black community resembles in both pattern and degree that in the white community. The greater the difference in income, the more dissimilar are the distributions by census tract. Dissimilarity is greater between younger couples without children and older couples with children than between any other pair of family types defined by husband's age and presence of children. However, segregation by income was substantially greater than by family type in 1960. The bases of selectivity of blacks in "changing" areas of the city, where the proportion black is still relatively low, and of whites in the "suburban" areas adjoining the city are similar. Families in the higher income groups and couples with children are over-represented in these areas. It would appear that given the pressures of limited housing space in the inner core of the black community, given the fact that certain amenities are not available in that area, and given the economic and social barriers which restrict the movement of blacks into the suburbs, the changing areas must function as "suburbs" for the black community.

In summarizing the findings of his study of the ecological structure of Chicago's Black Belt, E. Franklin Frazier [1937: 72] stated that "as a result of the selection and segregation incident to the expansion of population, the Negro community had assumed a definite spatial pattern." Similarly, Frazier [1937] found a spatial pattern in his study of New York's Harlem. It was his conclusion that the ghettoes of these metropolitan communities—themselves a consequence of residential segregation based on race—are the locus of residential segregation based on economic and social characteristics of their population.

In a more recent study, Duncan and Duncan [1957] found a pattern of differentiation with respect to socioeconomic status within

Chicago's black community which resembled the pattern of differentiation within the white community. In both communities high-status groups were found to be residentially segregated from low-status groups. Schnore [1965], using 1960 census materials, found patterns of social class segregation within the nonwhite communities of twenty-four cities in various regions of the United States.

This report begins with a consideration of the dissimilarity in residential distribution of groups of families which differ in income and then pursues the question of residential segregation within metropolitan ghettoes by considering the dissimilarity in residential distribution of families which differ in stage in the family life cycle. Wirth's [1938: 15] observation that "diverse population elements inhabiting a compact settlement thus tend to become segregated from one another in the degree in which their requirements and modes of life are incompatible" together with the evidence supporting the notion that there is variation in style of life as the family passes through the stages of the life cycle [see Lansing and Kish 1957; Glick 1947] leads to the expectation that families at different stages of their life cycle might be residentially segregated from each other.

Ernest R. Mowrer's [1939] study suggests that this is in fact the case. Mowrer found the distribution of families in Chicago to be such that it was possible to identify areas of the city in terms of the type of family living in that area. Census data do not permit a classification of families such as was used by Mowrer (i.e., in terms of the roles of the marital partners). However, this study is seen as a further pursuit of the line of investigation which he initiated.

As a point of particular interest, this study considers the extent to which changing areas of the central city provide for expansion of black families in the way that suburban areas provide for expansion of white families. For this reason we will be comparing (1) nonwhite families residing in the established black community with nonwhite families residing in the changing area and (2) white families residing in the central city with white families residing in the suburban area and noting similarities in these two sets of comparisons.

DATA AND METHODS

Data for this study are taken from the Milwaukee Standard Metropolitan Statistical Area Census Tract Report of the 1960 Censuses of Population and Housing [U.S. Bureau of the Census 1961]. Milwaukee was selected because its black community is, in area and in population, both adequate and manageable for the purposes of this study. Milwaukee County's 1960 black population was reported to be 63,024, 6.1 percent of the total population. Table 1 presents selected characteristics of the population of Milwaukee County for the total county and for sub-areas.

For purposes of this research, census tracts in the city of Milwaukee were classified as being part of either the Inner Core, the Changing Area, or the White Community. Those census tracts within Milwaukee County but outside of the city of Milwaukee form the Suburban Area. The twenty-one Inner Core census tracts are those in which the nonwhite population is at least 400 persons and is fifty percent or more of the total population. In 1960, the 52,229 blacks in the Inner Core constituted 82.9 percent of the black population of Milwaukee County and 72.4 percent of the total population of the Inner Core. The 21 census tracts are contiguous and form a rectangular area located approximately one mile northwest of Milwaukee's Central Business District.

The ten census tracts which we refer to as the Changing Area are those in which the nonwhite population is at least 400 persons but is less than 50 percent of the total population. Blacks in the Changing Area constitute 12.0 percent of the black population of Milwaukee County and 16.1 percent of the total population of the Changing Area. Relatively few blacks live in the census tracts which make up the White Community. Only seven of these 157 census tracts contain more than 100 blacks. By definition none has more than four hundred. The 566 blacks in the Suburban Area of Milwaukee County are less than one percent of the county's black population and only 0.2 percent of the total population of the Suburban Area. We might also note that only 53.5 percent of the nonwhite population of the White Community and 55.2 percent of the nonwhite population of the Suburban Area is black. In contrast, 94.0 percent of the nonwhite population of the Changing Area and 99.3 percent of the nonwhite population of the Inner Core is black.

Income statistics presented here are based on family income in 1959 as reported for the census tracts in these subareas of Milwaukee County. Obviously, not all of the population is found in households containing families. Table 1 indicates, for each sub-area, the proportion of the total population found in

TABLE 1.   Selected Characteristics of the Population of Milwaukee County, by Sub-Area: 1960

| | | Milwaukee City | | | | |
Subject	County, Total	Total	Inner Core	Changing Area	White Community	Suburban Area
Number of Census Tracts	258	189[a]	21[b]	10[c]	157	69
Blacks as Percent of						
Total population	6.1	8.4	72.4	16.1	0.4	0.2
Nonwhite population	94.4	95.0	99.3	94.0	53.5	55.2
Percent Distribution of Blacks	100.0	99.1	82.9	12.0	4.2	0.9
Percent in Household with Relative[d]						
Whites	90.5	89.4	85.8	81.4	90.0	93.2
Nonwhites	89.7	90.4	90.9	93.3	80.8	44.9
Percent of Families with Wife of Head[e]						
Whites	89.0	87.5	82.1	81.9	88.0	92.3
Nonwhites	75.6	75.1	73.2	77.7	94.2	125/90[f]

[a] Excludes one tract reserved for reporting data for crews of vessels.

[b] Tracts in which nonwhites number 400+ and are 50% or more of population.

[c] Tracts in which nonwhites number 400+ and are under 50% of population.

[d] Includes Head of Primary Family and "Wife," "Child under 18," and "Other Relative" of head.

[e] No. in "Wife of Head" category div. by no. of Heads of Primary Family.

[f] Discrepancy reflects error in tabulations rather than real differences in color of Heads and their wives.

households with relatives. These figures indicating the proportion of the population covered by family income statistics provide an estimate of the proportion of the population included in our subsequent discussion of the distribution of income groups. For both the nonwhite and the white populations, approximately nine-tenths of the total population is found in family groups. However, the percentages are considerably lower for whites in the Inner Core or Changing Area and for nonwhites in the White Community or Suburban Area.

Using data provided in census tract reports, it is possible to classify married couples as follows:

Younger Couple—husband under 45 and no child under age 18;

Younger Family—husband under age 45 and at least one child under age 18;

Older Family—husband age 45 or over and at least one child under age 18;

Older Couple—husband age 45 or over and no child under age 18.

This classification of married couples generally reflects the stages of the family life cycle in that the typical family begins as a younger couple, becomes a younger family with the birth of a child, becomes an older family with the passing of time, and becomes an older couple as children marry and leave home.

The above is a classification of married couples rather than of families. These terms are not synonymous in census tract reports in that the latter includes two or more related persons in a household (and all related persons in a household are regarded as one family) while the former includes only those families in which both husband and wife are present (and there may be more than one married couple in a household). As an estimate of the proportion of the total number of families included in our subsequent discussion of family types, we have indicated in Table 1, for each subarea, the proportion of primary families in which the wife of the head of household is present. The accuracy of this estimate is modified by the fact that the number of married couples is based on sample data while the number of primary families is based on a complete count. After consultation with members of the staff of the Bureau of the Census we are convinced that the excess of individuals in the "wife of head" category as compared to the "head of primary family" category which we find in the Suburban Area of Milwaukee County reflects errors rather than real differences in color of husbands and their wives.

In Milwaukee County as a whole and in each of the sub-areas except the White Community, a greater proportion of white primary family households include the wife of the head than is true for nonwhite primary family households. In the White Community the percentages are 94.2 percent for nonwhites and 88.0 percent for whites. For both whites and nonwhites, a greater proportion of the primary families in the white community include the wife of head than is true for primary families in the black communities. It should be obvious that these figures also provide us with information concerning the distribution of families headed by persons whose spouse, if any, is absent.

As a further note concerning the classification of married couples, we might note that a married couple whose youngest child is born before the husband reaches age twenty-seven will not pass through the older family stage as defined here. Glick and Parke [1965] indicate median age at birth of last child to be 31.5 and 30.0 respectively for women in the 1910–1919 and 1920–1929 birth cohorts, i.e., those who would be reaching the older family stage during the 1950's and 1960's. Age of husband would be slightly higher. The decline in age at birth of last child has significant implications with regard to the kinds of census classifications needed for future research in this area. Moreover, married couples classified here as older couples may or may not have passed through

the two previous stages of the life cycle. Census reports [U.S. Bureau of the Census 1964: Tables 2 and 3] indicate approximately one-fourth of the nonwhite ever-married women and one-fifth of the white ever-married women in the above birth cohorts remained childless.

DISTRIBUTION OF INCOME GROUPS
Within Established Communities

Previous studies of residential segregation within nonwhite communities have been concerned with residential segregation of socioeconomic groups. Our attention is directed first toward this type of segregation within Milwaukee's Inner Core. In Table 2 we have collapsed the eleven income categories used in census reports into eight for purposes of analysis and have indicated the indexes of dissimilarity for nonwhite families in these eight income categories for Milwaukee's Inner Core and for all families in these same eight income categories for the city's White Community.

We find a degree of segregation between nonwhite income groups in the Inner Core which is not a great deal less than that between income groups in the White Community. Moreover, we find a basic similarity in the pattern of segregation between income groups in these two communities. In both cases there is, with some exception, an increase in the magnitude of indexes of dissimilarity as the disparity in level of income increases. Reversals in the usual direction of change in magnitude of indexes are largely due to the limited segregation of families in the lowest income category. This may reflect the distribution of older families whose residential distribution was determined when their income was greater.

If we consider level of income to be an indicator of social status, this may be interpreted as further evidence of the positive relationship between social distance and spatial distance. [For a more detailed discussion of this relationship see Duncan and Duncan 1957 and 1955.] In an analysis of data not presented here, it was found that, for nonwhites in the Inner Core, there is also a positive relationship be-

TABLE 2.   Indexes of Dissimilarity in Residential Distribution for Families in Eight
Income Categories for Milwaukee's Inner Core and White Community:
1960
(Above diagonal, nonwhite families in Inner Core; below diagonal, all families in
White Community)

Family Income (dollars)	(1)	(2)	(3)	(4)	(5)	(6)	(7)	(8)
(1) Under 1,000		21	22	23	26	34	33	41
(2) 1,000–1,999	34		19	24	28	36	36	40
(3) 2,000–2,999	24	30		19	21	28	30	33
(4) 3,000–4,999	22	31	15		14	23	22	29
(5) 5,000–6,999	27	36	24	16		14	24	20
(6) 7,000–8,999	30	39	29	23	11		23	21
(7) 9,000–9,999	35	41	36	24	17	15		30
(8) 10,000 and Over	35	43	34	27	20	17	14	

Note: The index is one-half the sum of the absolute differences between the tract-specific percentages
in the respective income groups. See Table 1 for definition of areas.

tween social distance and spatial distance for males in eight occupational categories.

Between Established and Developing Communities

We have considered the degree of residential segregation of nonwhite income groups within the White Community. These areas may be conceived of as the established communities of the respective groups. We might conceive of the Changing Area and the Suburban Area as developing communities for the nonwhite and white populations respectively. In Table 3 we consider the relative distribution of nonwhite and white income groups between their respective established and developing communities.

If income were the only factor determining whether or not nonwhite families live in the Changing Area or white families in the Suburban Area, we would expect that changes in percentages given in Table 3 would be unidirectional. While this is generally the case, there are exceptions. Both nonwhite and white families in the lowest income category have greater representation in their respective developing areas than do those in the immediately higher income category. This may be another reflection of the distribution of older families whose residential distribution was determined when their income was greater.

While this is the only reversal in the pattern for white families, we find several other reversals in the pattern for nonwhite families. These variations are difficult to explain in the light of previous findings which indicate that it is those who, relative to other members of the minority group, are of higher social and economic status who lead the way in the invasion-succession process. [For more detailed discussion of this idea, see Taeuber and Taeuber 1965: 164–165; Duncan and Duncan 1957: 221–229; and Gibbard 1941.] It would appear that factors other than income are operating to determine the distribution of nonwhite families.

DISTRIBUTION BY LIFE CYCLE STAGE
Within Established Communities

In Table 4 we note the indexes of dissimilarity for the four types of married couples discussed earlier for nonwhites in Milwaukee's Inner Core and for all married couples in the White Community. We might again note that we are including only those families in which both husband and wife are present. The magnitude of the indexes in Table 4 indicates the limited segregation of these four family types from each other. In both cases the greatest difference in distribution (indexes of 19 and 23 for non-

TABLE 3. Percentage Distribution of Families with Given Income and Color in Milwaukee County, by Place of Residence, and Percentage Distribution of Married Couples of Given Family Type and Color in Milwaukee County, by Place of Residence: 1960

Family Characteristic	Nonwhite Families			White Families		
	Inner Core	Changing Area	Other Areas	Black Community	White Community	Suburban Area
Income (Dollars)						
Total	80.7	12.1	7.2	5.5	64.3	30.2
Under 1,000	85.6	10.5	3.9	13.3	67.2	19.5
1,000–1,999	85.0	9.4	5.6	13.0	68.4	18.6
2,000–2,999	80.1	14.5	5.4	11.1	69.6	19.3
3,000–4,999	83.3	11.9	4.8	9.6	68.6	21.8
5,000–6,999	82.0	11.0	7.0	5.1	68.1	26.8
7,000–8,999	76.8	12.9	10.3	4.4	64.7	30.9
9,000–9,999	67.7	16.9	15.4	3.4	63.6	33.0
10,000 and over	70.6	14.2	15.2	2.7	55.1	42.2
Family Type						
Total	79.7	12.2	8.1	5.1	63.7	31.2
Younger Couple	81.2	10.5	8.3	4.8	68.1	27.1
Younger Family	77.7	14.1	8.2	4.5	62.6	32.9
Older Family	74.9	12.9	12.2	4.9	60.9	34.2
Older Couple	87.1	7.5	5.4	6.1	65.0	28.9

Note: See Table 1 for definition of areas.

TABLE 4. Indexes of Dissimilarity in Residential Distribution for Four Family Types for Milwaukee's Inner Core and White Community: 1960
(Above diagonal, nonwhite families in Inner Core; below diagonal, all families in White Community)

Family type	(1)	(2)	(3)	(4)
(1) Younger Couple		15	19	16
(2) Younger Family	17		17	17
(3) Older Family	18	17		15
(4) Older Couple	18	23	14	

whites and whites respectively) is between younger couples and older families.

In view of the earlier observations concerning the relationship between social distance and spatial distance, it would seem logical that those families which differ most in life style would have most discrepant spatial distributions.

There might be the inclination to assume that those families at opposite ends of the life cycle (i.e., younger and older couples) would differ most in life style. However, previous research has indicated a curvilinear pattern of change in a number of social and economic characteristics of the family as it proceeds through the life cycle. (Lansing and Kish [1957], Table 1, for example, show that the proportion reporting debts is substantially higher for younger and older families than for either younger couples or older couples; the proportion of home owners is substantially higher for younger families than for younger couples, higher still for older families, but similar for older families and older couples. See also Glick, [1957] and [1947].) Thus, the family life cycle may be considered to be a "cycle" rather than a continuum. If these social and economic characteristics are related to social status and style of life, and if there is a positive relationship between spatial distance and social distance, then we would expect that spatial distance would reflect this curvilinear pattern of change in life style.

There is very limited variation in the magnitude of indexes of dissimilarity for nonwhites shown above the diagonal in Table 4 and only slightly more in that of those for whites shown below the diagonal. This variation is too limited to be considered sufficient empirical support for the notions advanced here. However, given this limited degree of variation in magnitude of the indexes, there is general conformity to the predicted pattern of change. This is the case both for nonwhites in the Inner Core and for the population of the White Community.

Between Established and Developing Communities

We took note earlier of the distribution of nonwhite families of different income levels between the Inner Core and Changing Area and of the distribution of white families of different income level between the White Community and the Suburban Area. Table 3, lower panel, provides information concerning distribution between these respective areas for nonwhite and white married couples who differ in terms of life cycle stage.

There is considerable difference in the proportions of these four family types found in the developing areas. Approximately fourteen percent of the nonwhite younger families in Milwaukee County reside in the Changing Area. Only 7.5 percent of the nonwhite older couples are located in this area. Those nonwhite married couples, both older and younger, who have a child under age eighteen in the home are found in the Changing Area in disproportionately large numbers.

Comparing the distributions of nonwhite family types with those of white family types, we find that nonwhite married couples make use of the Changing Area in much the same manner as white married couples make use of the Suburban Area. It would appear that given the pressures of limited housing space within the Inner Core, given the fact that certain amenities are not available in that area, and given the economic and social barriers which restrict their movement into the Suburban Area, nonwhite families resort to the Changing Area. Just as the Suburban Area is conceived of as the "breeding grounds" for the white population of the metropolitan community, so it would appear that the Changing Area serves in a similar capacity for nonwhite population of the metropolitan community.

As further evidence of this function of changing areas we might note that 7.0 percent of the nonwhite younger couples in Milwaukee County, 7.1 percent of the nonwhite younger families, 10.3 percent of the nonwhite older families, and 5.2 percent of the nonwhite older couples are located in the White Community. This does not mean that they are evenly dispersed throughout the White Community. Approximately three-fourths of the black population in the White Community is found in census tracts which are located adjacent to the Inner Core or Changing Area. These census tracts may be considered (in terms of our definition) future changing areas. It would appear that the pattern of distribution of nonwhite married couples between the developing and established communities will continue into the immediate future.

SUMMARY

In this study we have attempted to measure residential segregation within a metropolitan ghetto. We discovered that Milwaukee's Inner Core, the place of residence of a racially segregated population, is not an undifferentiated mixture of elements of the nonwhite population. Within this area, nonwhite families of different income level are segregated to a degree which is moderate in an absolute sense but approximates that of similar income groups in Milwaukee's white community. In addition, nonwhite married couples living in the Inner Core were classified according to stage in the family life cycle and segregation between family types measured. This form of residential segregation was disappointingly small in the light of previous suggestions as to the family type composition of areas of urban communities. However, residential segregation of nonwhite family types within the Inner Core approximated that of family types within the White Community.

The data of this study provide further evidence of the positive relationship between social distance and spatial distance. Segregation is greatest between those families which differ most in level of income. Although the distinctions are less pronounced, segregation between family types also reflects this positive relationship between social distance and spatial distance. Those family types which differ most in life style are most segregated from each other. Indexes of segregation for family types reflect the curvilinear pattern of change in life style as the family passes through its life cycle. These principles are applicable to the Inner Core as well as to the White Community.

Of particular interest was the function of the Changing Area as a place of residence for elements of the nonwhite population. It appears that the Changing Area serves the nonwhite population in much the same way as the Suburban Area does the white population. The Changing Area is characterized by a disproportionately large number of nonwhite families in higher income categories and nonwhite families with children as is the Suburban Area by white families of higher income and white families with children.

The patterns suggested here may be obscured somewhat by the size of the areal unit. However, they are sufficiently distinct to create general impressions and to provoke further interest. Level of income is a key factor in the distribution of urban families. The life cycle also seems to be a useful frame of reference for studying this distribution. There is particular need for further consideration of this subject as it applies to the nonwhite family.

ACKNOWLEDGMENTS
This research was supported with a Faculty Fellowship granted by the Graduate College of the University of Illinois at Chicago Circle. The author is grateful to Robert Grymes and Paul C. Glick for valuable comments.

REFERENCES

Duncan, Otis Dudley, and Beverly Duncan, 1955. "Residential Distribution and Occupational Stratification," *American Journal of Sociology*, 60: 493–503. [No. 32 in this volume.]

—— and ——, 1957. *The Negro Population of Chicago.* Chicago: University of Chicago Press.

Frazier, E. Franklin, 1937. "Negro Harlem: An ecological study," *American Journal of Sociology*, 43: 72–88.

Gibbard, Harold, 1941. "The Status Factor in Residential Succession," *American Journal of Sociology*, 46: 835–842.

Glick, Paul C., 1947. "The Family Cycle," *American Sociological Review*, 12: 164–168.

——, 1957. *American Families.* New York: Wiley.

——, and Robert Parke, Jr., 1965. "New Approaches in Studying the Life Cycle of the Family," *Demography*, 2: 187–202.

Lansing, John B., and Leslie Kish, 1957. "Family Life Cycle as an Independent Variable," *American Sociological Review*, 22: 512–516.

Mowrer, Ernest R., 1939. *Family Disorganization*. Chicago: University of Chicago Press.

Schnore, Leo F., 1965. *The Urban Scene*. New York: Free Press.

Taeuber, Karl E., and Alma F. Taeuber, 1965. *Negroes in Cities*. Chicago: Aldine.

U.S. Bureau of the Census, 1961. *U.S. Censuses of Population and Housing: 1960. Census Tracts.* Final Report PHC(1)–92. Washington: Government Printing Office.

———, 1964. *U.S. Census of Population: 1960. Subject Reports: Women by Number of Children Ever Born.* Final Report PC(2)–3A. Washington: Government Printing Office.

Wirth, Louis, 1938. "Urbanism as a Way of Life," *American Journal of Sociology*, 44: 1–24.

49

F. JAMES DAVIS

The Effects of a Freeway Displacement on Racial Housing Segregation in a Northern City

Much of the recent comment about racially segregated housing implies that Northern whites are widely agreed that nonwhites should be denied free access to urban housing.[1] In his final report to the Commission on Race and Housing, Davis McEntire states explicitly that housing discrimination is strongly institutionalized.[2] He presents supporting evidence about popular attitudes, governmental policies, and the various activities of the housing industry;

but he also notes certain counter forces.[3] This suggests conflicting values and actions, not a set, monolithic pattern. Whether less than uniform discrimination can produce the marked degree of residential segregation now so common in Northern cities is an important question for sociological theories of race relations.

Any crisis which subjects a city's racial housing pattern to marked strain provides an excellent opportunity to study the processes involved in supporting segregation, those promoting integration, and the consequences. Such a crisis occurred in St. Paul, Minnesota, from 1959 to 1961, when a clearance for freeway construction was made through the most nonwhite part of the city. This paper reports a study of the actions most of the displaced families took,

Reprinted by permission from *Phylon*, Vol. XXVI, No. 3 (Fall 1965), pp. 209–215.

[1] Charles F. Marden and Gladys Meyer, *Minorities in Human Society* (New York, 1962), pp. 310–319.

[2] Davis McEntire, *Residence and Race* (Berkeley and Los Angeles, 1960), p. 5. See Scott Greer, *The Emerging City* (New York, 1962), p. 35, for the view that residential neighborhoods reflect differential rewards in the urban division of labor.

[3] Ibid., pp. 349–350.

their experiences in the housing market and the pattern of relocation. The fact that both whites and nonwhites were displaced made it possible to test for racial differences.

THE DISPLACEMENT

By 1950 nearly three-fourths of St. Paul's rapidly increasing nonwhite population lived in the racially mixed Selby-Dale Area, just west and a little north of the central business district. About 93 percent of the nonwhites in the area were in the northeast half of it, so the south and west parts were predominantly white. There were no nonwhites in that small portion of the Selby-Dale Area south of Selby Avenue; so the remainder of the area came to be thought of as the city's "nonwhite area," and it will be so called in this paper.

The city's nonwhite population continued to grow in the 1950's, and to become more concentrated. In 1958 probably over nine-tenths of St. Paul's colored people lived in the nonwhite area.[4] Many of the previously all-white blocks in the southwest part of the area were becoming mixed, and the percentage of whites was declining throughout the area. This trend was accentuated by two redevelopment projects adjacent to (one partly within) the area which compelled most of the 186 colored families involved to seek housing in the nonwhite area. The housing shortage for nonwhites became acute before the freeway clearance.

The St. Anthony-Rondo Freeway demolition went straight west near the north boundary of the area, eliminating 433 household units, 72 percent of them nonwhite. This was about 14 percent of the city's nonwhite housing.[5] It is estimated that about three-fifths of both the

white and nonwhite families owned the condemned homes. Most of the families, with limited help from voluntary groups, entered the housing market on their own. The Housing and Redevelopment Authority lent some moral support by keeping an office in the area for over a year to make a survey of the situation, but no public agency received funds for relocation assistance.

THE INTERVIEW SAMPLE

This study became possible when the Hallie Q. Brown Community House made a list of the households in the condemned area just before demolition, and later determined the new addresses of three-fourths of the relocated households. The other one-fourth had no forwarding address in the local post office, and adequate data for comparing these with the known three-fourths were unavailable. This incomplete and possibly nonrepresentative list was the best available, so it was used for analysis of the pattern of relocation and the sampling for interviewing.

The plan was to make a random sample of half the 328 householders whose new addresses were known, and to make additional selections to replace those not interviewed. The rate of failure was rather high, so ultimately 310 sampling selections were made, using a table of random numbers. Of these, 177 (57.1 percent) were successfully interviewed.[6] The failure to interview 133 sampled householders, together with the absence of one-fourth of the new addresses on the master list, must be kept in mind in assessing this study.

The interviews were relatively non-directive, but an interview schedule was followed to ensure inclusion of certain questions. The modal interview length was one hour. About half the interviews were done by Negroes, half by whites.

---

[4] Ernest C. Cooper, "St. Paul's Urban Renewal Program as it Relates to Non-White Citizens," a report to the Sixth Urban League sponsored Urban Renewal Institute at Milwaukee, Wisconsin, May 19–20, 1958.

[5] "Report on Survey of Residents to be Displaced by St. Anthony Expressway," Housing and Redevelopment Authority of the City of St. Paul, Minnesota, May, 1958, p. 3. It appeared that 485 households would be removed, but 39 were not. This and other corrections produced our final figure of 433.

---

[6] Only 15 percent returned a mailed request for an interview appointment. Despite many telephone and door calls, some were not reached. The majority were cooperative, but some refused to be interviewed.

THE PATTERN OF RELOCATION

Hypothesis: As compared with displaced whites, a much smaller proportion of nonwhites were relocated outside the nonwhite area. Table 1 supports this hypothesis. Of the whites with known addresses in mid-1962, 90.5 percent were outside the nonwhite area, but only 15.5 percent of the nonwhites were. This large difference could not be eliminated even if the racial pattern of relocation were completely the opposite for the 105 whose new addresses were unknown. The whites were scattered rather widely over the Twin Cities and their suburbs, while most of the 36 Negro families that had succeeded in leaving the nonwhite area were located in small pockets in St. Paul. The clearance contributed to the increase in the nonwhite density in all parts of the (still mixed) nonwhite area.

INTERVIEW FINDINGS
Difficulties and Success in Moving
Out of the Area

Of the 177 nonwhite families interviewed, only 12.8 percent had left the nonwhite area. To determine how much discrimination was actually encountered,[7] one must know how many tried to leave the area, what experiences they had, and the outcome. These matters were discussed in all interviews with whites and nonwhites.

Hypothesis: As compared with displaced white families, a significantly smaller proportion of nonwhites attempted to move outside the nonwhite area. As shown in Table 2, only about one-third of the nonwhites said they attempted to leave the area, while well over two-thirds of the whites did. The racial difference is significant at far better than the desired .05 level. Most of the reasons given for not trying were in terms of satisfaction with the neighborhood, attachment to family and friends, desire

to stay close to work or institutional facilities, less expense, etc.; but ten Negroes said they feared discrimination and three implied it. Some of the ten said they should be able to spread out more, but they did not wish to jeopardize family interests by "pioneering."

Hypothesis: As compared with displaced white families, a significantly larger proportion of nonwhites had difficulty when they tried to leave the nonwhite area. This hypothesis is supported by Table 3. The three white and five of the nonwhite families specified only financial problems. But 18 nonwhites reported discriminatory experiences, mainly in getting to see a house or in completing the purchase, and half of these mentioned discrimination at two or more points in the home-buying process. Thus, almost two-fifths of the Negroes who tried to move out of the nonwhite area said they were discriminated against at least once.

One of the nine Negroes who had difficulty getting an appointment reported that the agent said his company would not sell to Negroes in that neighborhood, but the other reactions from agents and home owners were more subtle. The eight nonwhites who reported not being able to see a house after getting an appointment complained mainly that they were shown only poor quality homes when the agent discovered their race. Some were told falsely the house had been sold; others were discouraged by the quoting of a high down payment or selling price, or by having the worst features of a house pointed out.

Four Negroes (and two whites) talked about difficulty in getting a loan, but three of these indicated that they considered other matters than racial discrimination responsible. It appears that most of the pressure to keep nonwhites in the area occurred before the lending stage was reached. Six Negroes related troubles other than with the loan in completing the purchase, three specifying the negative reactions of white neighbors. Most of these difficulties involved attempts to buy outside the nonwhite area, but some concerned previously all-white blocks within it.

---

[7] The proper relating of ecological patterns to social processes is difficult. See Alvin Boskoff, *The Sociology of Urban Regions* (New York, 1962), p. 153; and James M. Beshers, *Urban Social Structure* (New York, 1962), pp. 23–26.

TABLE 1.   Race of Householders Displaced by 1959–61 St. Anthony-Rondo Freeway Clearance by Location in 1962

Race	Number Inside Nonwhite Area	Number Outside Nonwhite Area	Number In State Twin Cities Area	Number Out of State	No Information	Total
White	7	67	3	4	37	118
Nonwhite	197	36	2	9	67	311
No Information	2	1	0	0	1	4
Total	206	104	5	13	105	433

TABLE 2.   Race of Interviewees by Response to "Did You Try to Get Outside the Nonwhite Area?"

| Race | Number Making the Given Response: | | | | Total |
	Yes	No	No Reply*	Indeter-minate*	
White	25	10	1	1	37
Nonwhite	46	94	0	0	140
Total	71	104	1	1	177

Chi square equals 17.3
p is less than .001
Phi equals .35

* (Not included in computations)

TABLE 3.   Race of Interviewees Who Tried to Leave the Nonwhite Area by Response to, "Did You Have Any Difficulties in the Attempt?"

Race	Number of Yes Responses	Number of No Responses	Total
White	3	22	25
Nonwhite	23	23	46
Total	26	45	71

Chi square equals 10.14
p is less than .01
Phi equals .24

Those who said they did not have difficulty when attempting to move out of the nonwhite area gave varied explanations. Some Negroes said white real estate agents and neighbors were helpful and accepting, and some emphasized that they had experienced no discrimination of any kind. Some avoided barriers by getting help from friends, voluntary associations, or lawyers. Some did not continue their efforts to leave the area because they wished to avoid troubles.

Since the nonwhites who attempted to leave the area did not encounter a united front, it is important to know how many succeeded.

TABLE 4. Race of Interviewees Who Tried to Leave the Nonwhite Area by New Location

Race	Number Inside Nonwhite Area	Number Outside Nonwhite Area	Number In State Out of Twin Cities Area*	Total
White	0	25	0	25
Nonwhite	29	16	1	46
Total	29	41	1	71

Chi square equals 27.81
p is less than .001
Phi equals .63

* (Not included in computations)

Hypothesis: As compared with displaced white families, a significantly smaller proportion of nonwhites succeeded when they attempted to leave the nonwhite area. This hypothesis is supported by Table 4, which shows a large racial difference, all the whites, but only about two-thirds of the nonwhites being relocated outside the nonwhite area. Even so, it appears that the chances for nonwhites to move out of the area were greater than suggested by the pattern of resettlement shown in Table 1.

Satisfaction with Present Housing

Hypothesis: Relocated whites were significantly more satisfied with their new housing than relocated nonwhites were. The interviewees were asked if they were satisfied in general with their new housing, and with nine particular aspects. The responses called for rejection of the hypothesis. About four-fifths of both whites and nonwhites expressed general dissatisfaction. Three-fourths of the whites as compared with two-thirds of the nonwhites considered their present housing better than what they had prior to displacement, but the difference is not significant at the .05 level. The whites were significantly less satisfied with present access to work, but no other aspect showed a significant difference.

Residential Status

Hypothesis: The freeway clearance reduced white home ownership significantly less than it did for the displaced nonwhites. This

hypothesis was rejected. For both races, the percent of home ownership among the interviewees increased roughly from 60 to 70 percent.[8] Perhaps the Negro interviewee was correct when he said that the move was hard on many families, of both races, but that it compelled them to make an effort and that the majority now have better housing than before.

INTERPRETATION

While one-fourth of the 433 displaced families were unaccounted for, the pattern of relocation of the known three-fourths shows a very great racial difference. Thus the freeway clearance, along with the earlier redevelopment projects, increased the density of the nonwhite concentration and extended its boundaries, a trend typical of Northern cities since World War II.[9] The 177 interviews provided data that help explain the ecological result.

The pattern of the relocation suggests more discrimination than interviewed nonwhites directly encountered. Nearly two-fifths of the interviewed Negroes who attempted to move out of the nonwhite area met discrimination, half of these more than once; and fear of discrimination was one reason why only one-third made the try. But some others received

[8] For all 177 interviewees, those who changed from renter to owner status were the most satisfied; next came owner to owner, then renter to renter, with owner to renter the least.

[9] Marden and Meyer, op. cit., pp. 311–312.

assistance from white agents, friends, or new neighbors, so there were conflicting values and practices rather than a uniform system of housing discrimination. The white resistance might have been stiffer, of course, if much larger numbers of nonwhites had tried to move outward.[10] A definite effort by a nonwhite interviewee to leave the area increased the chances to over one-third, while if one reasoned from the pattern of resettlement alone he would reckon the chances at about one in eight.

The study provided a unique opportunity to study the dynamics of a racial housing pattern subjected to the strain of an imposed community crisis, and to test for racial differences in relocation experiences. A major limitation is the loss of cases, both the one-fourth displaced households not found and the over two-fifths of the sampled families not interviewed. Many characteristics of the families that might

be important were not included in the study, such as age, number of children, class level, etc. The economic level of Negroes and whites is believed to have been about the same, an assumption supported by the finding that the percentage of home ownership was about the same for the two groups before the move as well as afterwards.

With these limitations in mind, it would seem that the great racial difference in the (known) pattern of resettlement resulted from an imperfectly institutionalized system of discrimination. Direct discriminatory action does not appear sufficient to account for the increase in racial housing segregation after the freeway clearance.[11] Much of the increased concentration of nonwhites was evidently due to fear of discrimination outside of the nonwhite area, and to in-group cohesiveness in the face of potential discrimination.

---

[10] Chester Rapkin and William G. Grigsby, *The Demand For Housing in Racially Mixed Areas* (Berkeley and Los Angeles, 1960), pp. 52–72.

[11] Boskoff, op. cit., pp. 123–124, suggests that the persistence of segregated housing is due to more than discrimination.

50

W. CLARK ROOF

Residential Segregation of Blacks and Racial Inequality in Southern Cities: Toward A Causal Model

This paper examines the relation of non-white residential segregation to black-white differentials in education, occupation, and income for southern cities as of 1960. Utilizing van den Berghe's paternalistic-to-competitive theory of race relations in an indus-

---

Reprinted from *Social Problems*, Vol. 19, No. 3 (Winter 1972), pp. 393–407, by permission of the Society for the Study of Social Problems.

trializing society, a causal model is postulated and empirically examined which views the black ghetto as instrumental in institutionalizing inequalities. The 1960 census data for a sample of southern cities provide some support for conceptualizing residential segregation as an "intervening" variable, between age of city and percent non-white, on the one hand, and the status inequality measures, on the other. A discussion of the theoretical significance of the residential factor, and of the methodological complexities involved in such research, follows.

Residential segregation of blacks and whites in American cities is a subject that has attracted considerable attention in recent years. At a time when phenomenal changes in black-white relations are occurring, a number of researchers have singled out the factor of residential segregation as having particular salience for contemporary race relations. Notable among these are Taeuber and Taeuber [1965], whose work clearly delineates the persisting reality of residential segregation by color in contemporary American cities.

While the demographic aspects of residential segregation are generally understood, less is known about the consequences of this phenomenon for minority-group relations. In research on minority assimilation, Lieberson [1961] has called attention to the important results which follow for a minority, depending on whether the group is residentially segregated or dispersed. With comparative minority-group data from ten American cities, he shows that the degree of residential segregation of an immigrant group is associated with the group's assimilation into the host society. Ability to speak English, citizenship, intermarriage, and occupational composition are shown to be affected by residential distribution patterns. Lieberson's work demonstrates that ecological patterns are not only indices of existing social relations but may be potentially significant factors in accounting for other aspects of minority-group relations [see also Duncan and Lieberson 1959].

Apart from Lieberson's research, few attempts have been made to examine the importance of the residential segregation factor and to assess its significance for race relations

theory. This paper reports an exploratory investigation of how residential segregation may be conceptualized as a variable phenomenon and incorporated into an economic competition theory of minority-group relations. The proposed model applies to the American South, although with some slight modification it should be relevant for other societal settings. The objective is twofold: (1) to show that residential segregation indices are related to measures of educational, occupational, and income inequality; and (2) to suggest how the residential segregation factor may be incorporated into an empirically testable theory of minority-group relations. Since our foremost concern is with the theoretical implications of residential segregation, this paper may be viewed as an exercise in theory building and the testing of causal inferences.

RESIDENTIAL SEGREGATION, COMPETITION, AND INEQUALITY

Even though the residential segregation factor has generally not been incorporated into minority relations theory, social scientists have alluded to its importance. The causal connections are not always stated explicitly, but there are two fundamental ways in which residential segregation is conceptualized in the literature as important theoretically: (a) as a structural basis for institutional and organizational separation, and (b) as heightening the visibility of racial group differences.

Residential segregation, first of all, enables a group to evolve and to maintain separate institutional structures which, in turn, may serve as a means for institutionalizing inequalities. Myrdal [1944: 618] underscored this consequence of spatial separation when he described residential segregation as "basic in a mechanical sense" to other forms of discrimination. Likewise, Hawley [1944] notes that group isolation is essential to the preservation of group structures, and that residential segregation by color ensures the maintenance of a subordinate minority status. Theorists of this persuasion single out the structural consequences of residential segregation and the importance of these for preserving inequalities. Separate institutions, fostered under conditions of residential isolation, facilitate unequal and discriminatory school budget allocations [McEntire, 1960:89], school segregation [Rose, 1964:111], deprived learning opportunities [Commission on Race and Housing, 1958:35], reduced incentives to learn [McEntire, 1960:96], isolation from achievement values of the dominant culture [Frazier, 1940:290], and reduced opportunities for intergroup contacts [Williams, 1964:132].

A second way in which residential segregation functions is to increase minority visibility. The importance of minority visibility lies in its capacity to evoke social psychological reactions on the part of the dominant group. Kephart's [1954] finding that the greater the number of Negroes arrested in a district in Philadelphia, the greater the over-estimation by policemen of the Negro rate, suggests that visibility increases at a more rapid rate than sheer number. Minority visibility is acknowledged as important also in theories of race relations which focus upon competition. Blalock, for example, observes that minority visibility accents *perceived* minority competition [1967:102]. According to his theoretical model, the dominant group's motivation to discriminate is a function of both the *actual* and *perceived* economic threats and/or political power of the minority. To the extent that the perception factor is salient, one may say that minority visibility, rather than minority size itself, is the immediate provocation of the dominant group's sense of threat. Residential segregation by color, by virtue of its massiveness, is one of the most significant mechanisms underlying minority visibility.

The greater the residential concentration, the greater the chances that a racial minority is perceived as a visible threat.

FROM PATERNALISTIC TO COMPETITIVE RACE RELATIONS: THE AMERICAN SOUTH

In the preceding discussion, two functions of residential segregation were described. Both of these rest upon the assumption of a competitive racial order. Further elaboration of how residential segregation is linked to economic competition is possible if we examine van den Berghe's [1967:25–34] formulation of how race relations in modern industrial society have tended to shift their form from "paternalistic" to "competitive." The American South provides the setting in which to examine this transition.

In the agrarian South, race relations typically followed the master-servant model, where the division of labor was rigidly ascribed. Racial roles were generally well-defined, with the social expectations generally solidified around paternalistic norms of subservience and respect. In the agrarian order, van den Berghe notes that physical proximity is not problematic since status inequality is not threatened by close residential contact [1967:27]. The "back-yard" pattern of scattered black residences, so frequently observed among the older southern cities [Myrdal 1944:621; Demerath and Gilmore 1954:157], is reflective of this era in southern history. Older southern cities even today continue to show evidence of the ante bellum housing patterns and are much less segregated residentially than the newer cities in the region [Schnore and Evenson 1966].

The newer southern cities, particularly those that grew up after the Civil War, emerged under industrializing economic conditions. Paternalistic patterns of residential intimacy were never established in these cities as they had been in the preceding era. These younger cities are characterized today by much larger black ghettos and, according to Taeuber and Taeuber, by the highest rates of increase in residential segregation of any in the United States as of 1960 [1965:43]. If human ecologists are correct in their assertion that spatial pattern is a suggestive index of social relationships, then the evidence in these younger southern cities points toward a distinctly new and different form of black-white relations. These cities reflect a "competitive" form of race relations, characterized by fewer intimate inter-racial contacts, greater ghetto segmentation, and more intense economic competition between racial groups. Van den Berghe [1967:30], in discussing these correlates of industrialization, singles out the importance of residential segregation in the process:

> To the extent that social distance diminishes physical segregation is introduced as a second line of defense for the preservation of the dominant group's position. The amount of contact between castes declines as the society becomes increasingly compartmentalized into racially homogeneous ghettoes with their nearly self-sufficient institutional structures.

"Physical" distance replaces "social" distance as a decisive regulatory mechanism in the transition from paternalistic to competitive race relations. Spatial concentration, by ensuring greater institutional separation and minority visibility, imposes barriers to effective economic competition and thereby aids in preserving dominant group privileges.

Van den Berghe's formulation of competitive race relations draws attention to two features of the southern scene which have not always been made clear: (a) the variable and provocative nature of prejudice and (b) the significance of residential ghettoes for sustaining what Blumer [1958] calls a "sense of group position."

With respect to the first, it should be noted that theorists have often assumed a homogeneity in southern racial practices that was in fact not the case. Despite the cultural heritage of racism, southern discrimination in the post-Civil War years can also be described as increasingly provocative. C. Vann Woodward [1955] reminds us that much of the "Jim Crow"

legislation—so important symbolically to lower-status whites—took place around the turn of the century when poor whites were gaining political leverage but yet were little better off economically than blacks. Blalock's [1957] research indicates that black-white differences in education, occupation, and income vary with percent non-white in 245 southern counties. Both of these studies call attention to minority threat as an instigative factor. Van den Berghe notes the variability of southern prejudice, and, thereby, calls attention to the *dynamics*, rather than the castelike features of competitive race relations in the recent South. Viewed in this manner, minority visibility may be far more important as a precipitating factor in race relations in the industrializing South than is often thought to be the case.

Van den Berghe also links the persistence of racial cleavages in contemporary, industrial societies to the enduring phenomenon of the racial ghetto. This formulation departs from much of earlier theorizing on southern race relations which tended to assume that industrialization and urbanization in the region would result in the decline of racial prejudice and the eventual assimilation of the black community.[1] Killian and Grigg [1966] challenge the assumption that such racial changes necessarily follow. Blalock [1959], in his analysis of southern census data, finds little support for believing that urbanization prompts significant decreases in status inequalities. Matthews and Prothro [1963], likewise, find little evidence that either urbanization or industrialization is significantly associated with southern black voter registration and political participation.

Much of the literature of assimilation tends to minimize the significance of structural pluralism in race and ethnic relations, and the importance of residential patterns undergirding such

---

[1] These assumptions follow, in large part, from Myrdal and the assimilationists who tended to view ethnicity as a survival of primary, quasi-tribal loyalties. For a discussion and critique of these assumptions, see L. Paul Metzger [1971].

pluralism. The residential base of a minority, in fact, takes on added significance in a modern competitive society, both as a locus of racial-ethnic identity and as a structural basis for sustaining inter-group images in the broader society. If racial prejudice consists essentially of a "sense of group position," as Blumer [1958] says, the role of the residential factor in the collective processes of image-making may be of considerable importance in a competitive order. Since prejudice is to a large extent a product of the processes in which racial groups form images of themselves and others, residential segregation undergirds these collective processes, for it facilitates both group separation and perceived minority threat. In the absence of clearly-defined racial norms, residential structures foster competitive relations by ensuring a collective sense of group position, i.e., blacks relative to whites.

HYPOTHESES AND CAUSAL MODEL

Studies of residential segregation and its relation to black-white status differentials report inconsistent findings. Bahr and Gibbs [1967], using a very small sample of SMSA's and tract-based indices, find weak negative relationships between residential segregation scores for metropolitan areas and educational, occupational, and income inequalities. More recent research [Roof and Van Valey 1972] indicates however that moderately strong positive relationships obtain among the same variables for southern cities if the more discriminating block-based indices of residential segregation are used.[2] Such differences in findings are primarily issues of measurement and need not concern us insofar as our attention here is upon

theory construction. The major exploratory hypothesis is:

1. Residential segregation indices of blacks in southern cities are positively related to black-white inequalities in education, occupation, and income.

Drawing from the theoretical statements of van den Berghe, Blalock, and others, we can formalize two additional propositions:

2. Percent non-white is positively related to educational, occupational, and income inequalities.

3. Age of southern city is inversely related to educational, occupational, and income inequalities.

Proposition 2 is supported by previous research [Blalock 1957]. The third proposition logically follows from (a) Schnore and Evenson's [1966] finding of a negative association between age of southern city and degree of residential segregation, and (b) Proposition 1 stated above. Age of city, also, is an indirect measure of paternalistic heritage, in van den Berghe's meaning of the term.

Examining the three "independent" variables—residential segregation, percent non-white, and age of city—in relation to status inequalities is facilitated through the use of postulated causal models [see Simon 1954; Blalock 1964]. The advantages of this procedure, primarily, are that assumptions about the causal ordering of variables are made explicit; and the inferences made are subject to critical examination within the logic of those assumptions.

Based on the above reasoning, the following simple chain model is proposed in Figure 1. Given certain simplifying assumptions,[3] it

---

[2] Measurement considerations are particularly salient with respect to residential segregation indices. The interrelationships between residential segregation and educational, occupational, and income differentials vary depending on *both* the index areal unit used and the census unit used. Block scores and central city units both result in stronger relationships between residential segregation scores and the status differentials. Bahr and Gibbs' finding [1967] of a weak, negative relationship holds only where SMSA tract indices are used. Central city indices—either block or tract-based—result in stronger and positive associations [see Roof and Van Valey 1972].

[3] The following assumptions are required: (1) linear, additive relationships among variables; (2) one-way causation, i.e., each successive dependent variable is presumed to be caused by some of the previous variables but not by any which appear after it; (3) negligible measurement error; and (4) variables not included in the causal system are presumed not to be producing confounding effects which systematically distort underlying relationships among the model variables. Admittedly, there may be violations of these assumptions since "feed-back" effects are indeed likely. Yet such "feed-back" effects, even though present, are assumed to be secondary to the major direction of causal influences. For further rationale for not entering such complexities into the model, see Blalock and Blalock [1968:155-197].

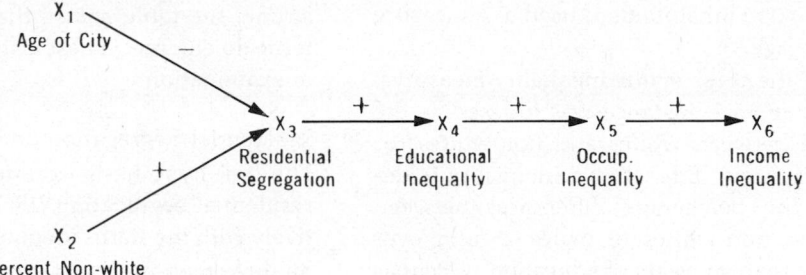

FIGURE 1. Model I

is possible to formulate a set of prediction equations based upon the postulated model. In general we may write a prediction equation for each pair of variables that are *not* linked directly by a causal arrow; usually, these predictions take the form of the absence of correlations or the disappearance of higher-order partial correlations. With Model I shown above, the following predictions are made:[4]

$$r_{12} \qquad = 0$$
$$r_{14.3} \qquad = 0$$
$$r_{15.34} \qquad = 0 \text{ (reducing to } r_{15.3} = 0)$$
$$r_{16.345} \qquad = 0 \text{ (reducing to } r_{16.3} = 0)$$
$$r_{24.3} \qquad = 0$$
$$r_{25.34} \qquad = 0 \text{ (reducing to } r_{25.3} = 0)$$
$$r_{26.345} \qquad = 0 \text{ (reducing to } r_{26.3} = 0)$$
$$r_{35.4} \qquad = 0$$
$$r_{46.5} \qquad = 0$$

Since a simple chain model is postulated, r_{36} may be stated in terms of the cross-products of the intervening variables connecting the two end variables. This gives the prediction:

$$r_{36} = r_{34}r_{45}r_{56}$$

The predictions, along with the three exploratory hypotheses, may be examined empirically, and on the basis of this examination the adequacy of the model can be judged.

---

[4] A larger number of predictions pertaining to partial correlations can be made. In a simple chain model, one may control for *any* intervening variable and still expect (if the model is correct) the partial correlation between the two end variables to disappear. For the purposes of this analysis, only those predictions which are critical to testing the fit of the model are presented.

SAMPLE AND MEASURES

A sample of 100 cities was randomly selected from a universe of all incorporated places of 50,000 or more inhabitants in the United States, having at least 1,000 non-white housing units for which block data were collected in the 1960 Census of Housing. Thirty-nine cities were southern by definition of the U. S. Census Bureau, and it is these city units on which the present analysis is carried out.

The major independent variable is the degree of black residential segregation in 1960. Taeuber and Taeuber's "index of residential segregation" (IRS), which is based upon block-specific data, was used in the operational procedure; index scores for each city were taken directly from their computations (1965, pp. 39–41). This index is computed as follows:

$$D = \frac{\Sigma |X - Y|}{2}$$

where D is the index of dissimilarity, X is the percentage of one population in a given subclass, and Y is the percentage of the other population in the same subclass. D for an urban area is computed by summing the absolute differences between X and Y for all city blocks and dividing the sum by two. The index may assume values between 0 and 100. The higher the value, the higher the degree of residential segregation.

Percent non-white was taken directly from the U. S. Census. Age of southern city was not as simple to construct. Following other researchers [Schnore 1965; Bogue and Harris 1954], the number of decades since the city reached 10,000 inhabitants is used as a measure of a city's age.[5]

With the three status inequality measures, inequality in each instance was indexed as the difference between whites and non-whites for a given city unit. Educational inequality is defined as the percentage differences between whites and non-whites of males 25 and over with more than six years of education. Occupational inequality is measured similarly by taking the percentage difference between the two groups of males fourteen years of age and over, employed in professional, managerial, clerical, and sales jobs. Income inequality is measured by the percentage differences of males 14 years of age and over with an income of $1,500 or more.[6]

Following conventional procedures, "non-white" is used interchangeably with "black." While other ethnic groups are included in "non-white," the errors resulting from this procedure using a sample of southern cities should be minimal. Also, interval measures are assumed for all variables, and Pearson correlations used as measures of association.

FINDINGS

Table 1 presents the zero-order associations among all pairs of variables. While few of the correlation coefficients can be considered

[5] U. S. Bureau of the Census, *U. S. Census of Population: 1960, Vol. I: Characteristics of the Population, Part A: "Number of Inhabitants"* (Washington, D. C.: Gov. Printing Office, 1961), Table 5 for each state.

[6] Ibid., Tables 77 and 78 for each state.

strong, the table shows that the expected patterns do emerge. These patterns require specific examination.

Residential Segregation and Inequality

The first hypothesis examined is: the index of residential segregation (IRS) should vary positively with the status inequality measures. Using all three measures of status inequalities—educational, occupational, and income—the data support this conclusion. All three relationships are positive and are statistically significant at the .05 level. In order to minimize the possibility of making a spurious inference, partial correlation analysis was used as a means of statistically controlling for other, possibly confounding, variables. Table 2 shows the relationships of IRS and the three inequality measures while controlling for the effects due to percent non-white, city size, and age of city. As customary, the partials are somewhat weaker than the zero-order coefficients. Controlling for these additional variables produces noticeable effects in the case of income inequality. The relationship between IRS and income inequality weakens, with the controls introduced singularly or jointly, to a point below the .05 level of statistical significance. This result is not too surprising, however, given the ordering of the variables. Income inequality is farthest removed in the sequence of variables from IRS and would, most likely, be less related to it than the other two inequality measures. Judged on the basis of what happens to the relationships between IRS and both educational and occupational in-

TABLE 1.   Zero-Order Correlation Coefficients for 39 Southern Cities

Variable	1	2	3	4	5	6	7
(1) Age of City		.061	.566*	−.231	−.542*	−.205	−.344*
(2) Percent Non-white			−.079	.279	.174	.146	.178
(3) City Size				−.186	−.581*	−.272	−.462*
(4) IRS					.367*	.415*	.293*
(5) Educational Inequality						.504*	.637*
(6) Occupational Inequality							.370*
(7) Income Inequality							

* Statistically significant at .05 level.

TABLE 2. Correlation Coefficients for IRS by Educational, Occupational, and Income Inequality Controlling for Percent Non-White, City Size, and Age of City

(N = 39)

| IRS by | Total | Partial Correlations | | | |
		Percent Non-White Controlled	City Size Controlled	Age of City Controlled	Percent Non-White, City Size, and Age of City Controlled
Educational Inequality	.367*	.336*	.341*	.300*	.282*
Occupational Inequality	.415*	.404*	.389*	.392*	.379*
Income Inequality	.293*	.261	.254	.248	.236

Note: Dependent Variable is IRS.
* Statistical significance at .05 level.

equalities, our conclusion is that the hypothesized relationship is not substantially altered by controlling for percent non-white, city size, or age of city.

Percent Non-White, Age of City, and Residential Segregation

Percent non-white is shown to be positively related with IRS as well as with the educational, occupational, and income inequality measures. These relationships are generally weak, however, the strongest association being with IRS.

Age of city, as expected, is inversely associated with IRS and the inequality measures. The older the southern city, the less the residential segregation by color and the black-white status differentials. Though the association between age of city and residential segregation falls below the .05 level of statistical significance,[7] yet two of the correlations between age of city and the inequality measures are moderately strong.

Since age of city as used here is at best only an indirect measure of paternalistic heritage, the possibility that its relationship to IRS is spurious deserves further examination. Quite clearly, age of city is bound up with city size (r = .566); and from a theoretical point of view it may seem somewhat more "sociological" to utilize the latter as the explanatory variable. Findings reported in Table 3 raise some question about such procedure however. Partial correlations are shown which indicate the association between IRS and each of the three independent variables—percent non-white, city size, and age of city—while controlling simultaneously for the other two. When age of city and percent non-white are controlled, the partial correlation between city size and residential segregation is reduced from −.186 to a modest −.091. By contrast, the second-order partials involving percent non-white and age of city as independent variables are substantially increased from .279 to .315 and from −.231 to −.345, respectively. [8] These findings indicate,

---

[7] It should be noted that with an N of this size (N = 39), a test for statistical significance at the .05 level is quite rigorous.

[8] Similar results are reported by Schnore and Evenson [1966]. Compared to the findings of Table 3, their partial correlations are .031, .223, and −.371, respectively, using identical control variables.

TABLE 3.   Summary of Partial Correlation Analysis: IRS, City Size, Percent Non-White, and Age of City for 39 Southern Cities

Independent Variable	Controlled Variables	Partial Correlation
City Size	Percent Non-White and Age	.091
Percent Non-White	City Size and Age	.315*
Age	Percent Non-White and City Size	−.345*

Note: Dependent Variable is IRS.
* Statistical significance at .05 level.

at the very least, that variation in IRS attributable to age of city is *not* accounted for by city size. Moreover, the data suggest that the age of a city is a rather potent factor in affecting its current (1960) level of residential segregation regardless of size or non-white percentage.

Causal Predictions

Given this initial support for the hypotheses, next we examine the prediction equations. The prediction equations and their degrees of fit for the simple chain model (see Figure 1) are shown in Table 4. City size as a variable was not brought into the model since, as already shown, age of city and percent non-white are much more strongly related to IRS when simultaneous controls are introduced.

TABLE 4.   Predictions and Degrees of Fit for Model I

Predictions (Expected)	Degrees of Fit (Actual)
1: r_{12} = 0	.031
2: $r_{14.3}$ = 0	−.693
3: $r_{15.3}$ = 0	−.223
4: $r_{15.34}$ = 0	.008
5: $r_{16.3}$ = 0	−.443
6: $r_{16.345}$ = 0	.000
7: $r_{24.3}$ = 0	.060
8: $r_{25.3}$ = 0	.034
9: $r_{25.34}$ = 0	.005
10: $r_{26.3}$ = 0	.104
11: $r_{26.345}$ = 0	.045
12: $r_{35.4}$ = 0	.286
13: $r_{46.5}$ = 0	.558
14: r_{36} = $r_{34}r_{45}r_{56}$ = .068	.293

As Table 4 shows, about half of the predictions made either do not hold or are quite poor. Such results are not too surprising given the fact that Model I was purposely simple as a first-approximation of the data patterns. What is more important to note is which of the predictions seem to hold and which do not. First of all, the expected relationship between age of city and educational inequality "intervening" through IRS is definitely *not* supported. Rather than vanishing, the partial correlation is greater than the zero-order coefficients. This discrepancy indicates quite clearly that the chain model over-simplifies the actual relationships among the variables. In fact, most of the predictions involving age of city as an independent variable and IRS as a control variable are unsatisfactory. Better predictions are obtained in this set only when multiple controls are introduced (e.g., Predictions 4 and 6).

Neither is there support for the chain model linkages connecting IRS and the three inequality measures. The pivotal linkage predicted was between IRS and educational inequality. Controlling for the latter, the model predicted that the partial correlation between IRS and occupational inequality should disappear; however, $r_{35.4}$ = .286. Likewise, the partial correlation between educational inequality and income inequality, controlling for occupational inequality, takes on the value of .558 when it is expected to disappear. Finally, the poor fit of the chain linkage model is apparent in Prediction 14. We would expect, if the model indeed approximated reality, the correlation between the two end variables should be about equal to the product of the intervening intercorrelations, i.e., $r_{36} = r_{34}r_{45}r_{56}$. The actual correlation for r_{36} is .293 whereas the model calculation is .068.

Notice those predictions, however, that are reasonably good: (1) percent non-white and age of city are unrelated (Prediction 1), and (2) the set involving percent non-white as an independent variable (Predictions 7 through 11). Predictions in the latter set are reasonably good, perhaps because percent non-white is weakly related to most of the variables included in the study. On the other hand, the consistency of results for the set as a whole should not be overlooked. In every instance but one, the partial correlation reduces to zero or within a margin easily attributable to measurement error distortion. These results provide support, then, for conceptualizing IRS as an "intervening" variable in the model, between percent non-white and the inequality measures. In the case of Prediction 10, which is not so good, the reason why is also understandable. Prediction 10 involves the end variables in the sequence, where it has already been shown that a chain model conceptualization over-simplifies the relationships among the intervening variables.

DISCUSSION AND RE-FORMULATION OF MODEL

As shown above, the data provide some support for the causal model. While the findings are by no means conclusive, there is enough support to suggest that the residential segregation hypothesis is plausible. At the very least, it seems worthy of further examination.

Following the logic of causal model construction, one approach in examining such a hypothesis is to modify the model in ways that are theoretically meaningful and will yield somewhat better empirical predictions. In doing so, it makes sense to introduce modifications where the largest discrepancies occur between actual and predicted values and, where possible, among variables operating near the beginning of the causal sequence [see Blalock 1964:80]. Both criteria point to the need for

modifying the model with respect to the relationship between a southern city's age and educational inequality. Not only do $r_{14.3}$, $r_{15.3}$, and $r_{16.3}$ involve a variable taken as independent in the causal sequence, but these relationships differ considerably from the predicted value of zero. The data suggest adding an arrow between X_1 and X_4, i.e., the influence attributable to a city's age upon educational inequality being both direct and indirect (through the intervening variable of residential segregation). From a theoretical point of view, this possibility is quite consistent with the argument advanced in this paper. Among the younger, more industrialized cities of the South where competitive race relations are more keenly felt, educational institutions play a critical role in preparing whites to take advantage of competitive opportunities. By 1960, certainly, anything like comparable educational opportunity for blacks did not exist.

A second major discrepancy in Model I concerns the chain linkages among the inequality measures. On the basis of the empirical results, it appears that an arrow is needed directly linking residential segregation and occupational inequality, i.e., between X_3 and X_5. Segregated ghetto life results very likely in motivational and, perhaps, discriminatory consequences apart from those directly affecting educational opportunities. Stunted incentives and aspirations, isolation from dominant group opportunities for achievement, the evolution of distinctive subcultural and counter-cultural norms—all are examples of how occupational values may be aggravated by ghetto life. Moreover, perceived minority threat due to residential concentration may be a factor evoking dominant group members to intensify occupational discrimination, thereby restricting even those blacks with competitive skills to inferior positions. One final point should be made about how educational inequality is measured: using "years" of schooling ignores the serious issue of quality of education. These considerations point to the inescapable fact that southern blacks with educational levels com-

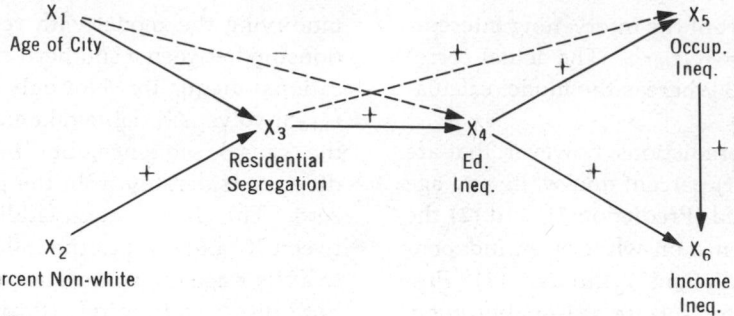

FIGURE 2. Model II

parable to whites are not as prepared to take full competitive advantage of their education.

In constructing a more satisfactory model the following modifications are introduced: (a) an arrow drawn between X_1 and X_4; (b) an arrow drawn between X_3 and X_5; and (c) an arrow drawn between X_4 and X_6. The latter, involving a direct linkage between educational inequality and income inequality, is suggested due to the poor fit in Prediction 14. These modifications are shown in Model II as dotted lines.

Table 5 presents the predictions and degrees of fit for Model II. As is apparent from a comparison with Table 4, this set of predictions is much more satisfactory. By linking directly age of city with educational inequality, we are able to discard a number of previously unsatisfactory partials; the predictions which now evolve are reasonably good. For example, the relationship between age of city and occupational inequality, controlling for both IRS and educational inequality, reduces to near zero (.008). Similarly, $r_{16.45}$ and $r_{16.34}$ reduce almost to zero (−.063 and −.002, respectively).

By linking directly residential segregation and occupational inequality, a much better fit is obtained for the set of predictions involving percent non-white. The partial $r_{26.3}$ (Prediction 8) is least satisfactory. One could reason that an arrow linking percent non-white directly with income inequality, if inserted, would improve the prediction. This has not been done because of the relatively good predictions when

TABLE 5. Predictions and Degrees of Fit for Model II

	Predictions (Expected)	Degrees of Fit (Actual)
1: r_{12} = 0		.031
2: $r_{15.34}$ = 0		.008
3: $r_{16.34}$ = 0		−.002
4: $r_{16.45}$ = 0		−.063
5: $r_{16.345}$ = 0		.000
6: $r_{25.3}$ = 0		.034
7: $r_{25.34}$ = 0		.005
8: $r_{25.3}$ = 0		.104
9: $r_{26.4}$ = 0		.078
10: $r_{26.34}$ = 0		.067
11: $r_{26.345}$ = 0		.045
12: $r_{36.45}$ = 0		.033

either X_4, or X_3, and X_4 together, are controlled. Given that the sample is small and the magnitude of measurement error unknown, it is quite possible that extraneous factors may be operative here. Since the major discrepancy in Model I ($r_{46.5}$ = .558 instead of Zero) is removed in Model II, there is still less reason to modify the ordering of variables any further. Model II predictions as a whole are a reasonably good fit, especially if allowances are made for the distortive effects of measurement error and sampling variation.

CONCLUSION

The purpose of this paper was to examine how residential segregation as a variable may be incorporated into an economic competitive model of race relations in the American South. Age of southern city and percent non-white were suggested as determinants of level of residential segregation, which, together with the status inequality measures, provided the variables for testing a causal ordering of their interrelationships.

While the data do not support the simple chain model, considerable support was found for the modified, more complex, system of relationships. It appears that level of residential segregation is important not only for its direct effects on educational inequality but because of its direct and indirect effects upon occupational inequality as well. Moreover, as the fit of the causal predictions suggests, there is support for conceptualizing residential segregation as an intervening variable, between percent non-white and age of city on the one hand, and the three status inequality measures on the other.

Specifically, these findings raise the question as to whether it is the minority percentage itself or the *dispersion* of the minority population that is salient insofar as motivations to discriminate are concerned. Aside from implications for public policy, the inferences pertaining to residential segregation, if valid, are pertinent to race relations theory. If indeed the dispersion factor is pre-eminent, then greater attention to a minority's visibility is called for in competition theories of race relations. More research is needed to examine, particularly, the empirical interrelation between minority size and group dispersion. The possibility of interaction effects between these two variables should be examined. Perhaps, a joint-effects model (high percent non-white and high level of residential concentration) would better predict differentials in educational, occupation, and income than the additive model here.

Also, the findings demonstrate the crucial importance of the residential ghetto, with respect both to its structural and perceptual consequences. Whatever conclusions are reached in subsequent research on the motivational factors underlying discrimination, the implications of ghetto segmentation and its functions in a modern, industrial society have only begun to be examined. Van den Berghe's assertion that racial cleavages evolving out of ghetto segmentation "constitute one of the major sources of strain and disequilibrium in such systems" [1967:30] is likely to be borne out, and promises to be a theoretically significant point of departure for subsequent research. Further analyses of residential segregation will likely uncover the need for more complex models of causal influence. One-way causation as assumed in the present research is an obvious simplification of social reality; what is needed is exploration into two-way causation, using perhaps a "feedback" model where some allowance is made for the effects of a subordinate minority status upon residential segregation itself. A more refined model of this kind promises to link together into a single, testable theory (a) the structural and motivational factors underlying discrimination in a competitive order, and (b) the so-called "vicious cycle" effects which, once set in motion, operate as a continuous series of reciprocal stimuli and responses.

Whatever refinements may come, methodologically and theoretically, the fact that residential segregation scores, age of city, and percent non-white are related as they are to status inequalities suggests that sociologists should proceed with caution in inferring that modernization brings about vast improvements in race relations. Current efforts at implementing school desegregation through busing in the South may, if continued long enough, modify the effects of ghetto life in the direction of less inequality. However, the ghetto is an enduring phenomenon, its importance in contemporary race relations will not soon disappear. If the findings of this study are at all valid, it appears that ghetto structures are in fact firmly implicated in a system of competitive race relations, and that the latter warrants less optimism about the elimination of racism in American life than many are prone to expect.

REFERENCES

Bahr, Howard M., and Jack P. Gibbs, 1967. "Racial Differentiation in American Metropolitan Areas," *Social Forces,* 45 (June): 521–532.

Blalock, Hubert M., 1957. "Per Cent Non-White and Discrimination in the South," *American Sociological Review,* 22(December): 677–682.

———, 1959. "Urbanization and Discrimination," *Social Problems,* 7(Fall): 146–152.

———, 1964. *Causal Inferences in Nonexperimental Research.* Chapel Hill: University of North Carolina Press.

———, 1967. *Toward a Theory of Minority-Group Relations.* New York: John Wiley and Sons, Inc.

Blalock, Hubert M., and Ann B. Blalock, 1968. *Methodology in Social Research.* New York: McGraw-Hill.

Blumer, Herbert, 1958. "Race Prejudice as a Sense of Group Position," *Pacific Sociological Review,* 1(Spring): 3–7.

Bogue, Donald O., and Dorothy L. Harris, 1954. *Comparative Population and Urban Research via Multiple Regression and Covariance Analysis.* Oxford, Ohio: Scripps Foundation for Research in Population Problems.

Commission on Race and Housing, 1958. *Where Shall We Live?* Berkeley: University of California Press.

Demerath, N. J., and Harlan W. Gilmore, 1954. "The Ecology of Southern Cities," in Rupert B. Vance and N. J. Demerath (eds.), *The Urban South.* Chapel Hill: University of North Carolina Press, pp. 135–165.

Duncan, Otis D., and Stanley Lieberson, 1959. "Ethnic Segregation and Assimilation," *American Journal of Sociology,* 4(January): 364–374.

Frazier, E. Franklin, 1940. *Negro Youth at the Crossways.* Washington, D.C.: American Council on Education.

Hawley, Amos H., 1944. "Dispersion Versus Segregation: Apropos of a Solution of Race Problem," *Papers of the Michigan Academy of Science, Arts, and Letters,* 30: 667–674.

Kephart, William M., 1954. "Negro Visibility," *American Sociological Review,* 19(August): 462–467.

Killian, Lewis M., and Charles Grigg, 1966. "Race Relations in an Urbanized South," *Journal of Social Issues* 22(January): 20–29.

Lieberson, Stanley, 1961. "The Impact of Residential Segregation on Ethnic Assimilation," *Social Forces,* 40(October): 52–57. [No. 40 in this volume.]

Matthews, Donald R., and James W. Prothro, 1963. "Social and Economic Factors and Negro Voter Registration in the South," *American Political Science Review* 57(March): 24–44.

McEntire, Davis, 1960. *Residence and Race.* Berkeley: University of California Press.

Metzger, L. Paul, 1971. "American Sociology and Black Assimilation," *American Journal of Sociology,* 76(January): 627–647.

Myrdal, Gunnar, 1944. *An American Dilemma.* New York: Harper and Row.

Roof, W. Clark, and Thomas L. Van Valey, 1972. "Residential Segregation and Social Differentiation in American Urban Areas," *Social Forces,* forthcoming.

Rose, Peter I., 1964. *They and We.* New York: Random House.

Schnore, Leo P., 1965. *The Urban Scene: Human Ecology and Demography.* New York: Free Press.

Schnore, Leo F., and Philip C. Evenson, 1966. "Segregation in Southern Cities," *American Journal of Sociology,* 72(July): 58–67.

Simon, Herbert A., 1954. "Spurious Correlation: A Causal Interpretation," *Journal of the American Statistical Association,* 49(September): 467–479.

Taeuber, Karl E., and Alma F. Taeuber, 1965. *Negroes in Cities,* Chicago: Aldine Publishing Company.

van den Berghe, Pierre, 1967. *Race and Racism: A Comparative Perspective.* New York: John Wiley and Sons, Inc.

Williams, Robin M. 1964. *Strangers Next Door.* Englewood Cliffs: Prentice Hall, Inc.

Woodward, C. Vann, 1955. *The Strange Career of Jim Crow.* New York: Oxford University Press.

1 2 3 4 5 6 7 8 9 10